MILESTONES

Real Life, Real Development

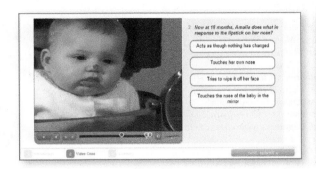 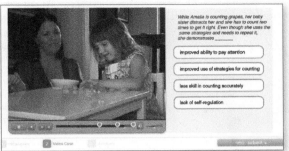

Available only through McGraw-Hill CONNECT, *Milestones* is an assessable video-based program that tracks a diverse group of infants and children through major milestones of physical, cognitive, social, and emotional development from infancy through adolescence.

Milestones **of Child Development:** By watching one child over time or comparing various children, *Milestones* provides a unique, experiential learning environment that can only be achieved by watching real human development as it happens.

Milestones **Transitions:** Students meet a series of people, from teenagers to individuals in late adulthood, to hear testimonials and perspectives on experiences and changes that occur throughout the life-span. Through a series of interviews, students are given the opportunity to think critically while exploring the differences in attitudes on everything from body image to changes in emotion, sexuality, cognitive processes, and death and dying.

Milestones provides the opportunity for students to:

* hone their observational skills

* engage with real children developing over time

* identify concepts and apply theories to real childr

* answer comprehension and application-level questions

FROM BIRTH TO ADOLESCENCE
CANADIAN EDITION

Director of Product Management: *Rhondda McNabb*
Senior Product Manager: *Marcia Siekowski*
Marketing Manager: *Margaret Janzen*
Senior Product Developer: *Jennifer Cressman*
Product Developer: *Catherine Gillespie-Lopes*
Supervising Editor: *Cathy Biribauer*
Senior Product Team Associate: *Marina Seguin*
Learning Solutions Consultant: *Meghan Hillyard*
Photo/Permission Researcher: *Derek Capitaine, www.mrmassociates.ca*
Copy Editor: *Mike Kelly*
Proofreader: *Dawn Hunter*
Plant Production Coordinator: *Scott Morrison*
Manufacturing Production Coordinator: *Lena Keating*
Cover and Inside Design: *Jennifer Stimson Design*
Composition: *ArtPlus Limited*
Cover Photo: © *Todd Wright/Getty Images*
Printer: *Webcom*

CHILD
Canadian Edition

Statistics Canada information is used with the permission of Statistics Canada. Users are forbidden to copy this material and/or redisseminate the data, in an original or modified form, for commercial purposes, without the expressed permission of Statistics Canada. Information on the availability of the wide range of data from Statistics Canada can be obtained from Statistics Canada's Regional Offices, its Website at www.statcan.gc.ca and its toll-free access number 1-800-263-1136.

The Internet addresses listed in the text were accurate at the time of publication. The inclusion of a website does not indicate an endorsement by the authors or McGraw-Hill Ryerson, and McGraw-Hill Ryerson does not guarantee the accuracy of information presented at these sites.

ISBN-13: 978-1-25-901454-3
ISBN-10: 1-25-901454-1

3 4 5 6 7 8 9 WEB 1 9 8 7 6

Printed and bound in Canada

Care has been taken to trace ownership of copyright material contained in this text; however, the publisher will welcome any information that enables it to rectify any reference or credit for subsequent editions.

Library and Archives Canada Cataloguing in Publication Data

Martorell, Gabriela, author
        CHILD : from birth to adolescence / Gabriela Martorell,
Richard Kruk. -- Canadian edition.

Includes bibliographical references and index.
ISBN 978-1-25901454-3 (pbk.)

        1. Child development. 2. Child psychology.
I. Kruk, Richard, 1960-, author II. Title.

HQ767.9.M37 2014   305.231   C2013-903928-7

MEET THE AUTHORS

GABRIELLA MARTORELL

Gabriela Alicia Martorell obtained her bachelor's degree in psychology from the University of California, Davis, followed by her Ph.D. in developmental and evolutionary psychology from the University of California, Santa Barbara. Since that time, she has served a number of learning institutions including Portland State University, Norfolk State University, and her current full-time position at Virginia Wesleyan College. Gabriela has taught graduate and undergraduate courses in lifespan human development, infant development, child development, adolescent development, adulthood and aging, cultural issues in psychology, evolutionary psychology, developmental psychopathology, and a Capstone practicum in early childhood education. She is committed to teaching, mentoring, and advising. She is currently conducting research on attachment processes in immigrant Latino adolescents, which is funded by the Virginia Foundation for Independent Colleges, and is co-investigator for a National Science Foundation grant focused on student retention and success in science, technology, engineering, and math.

RICHARD KRUK

Richard Kruk teaches school psychology in the Department of Psychology at the University of Manitoba. He has taught college, undergraduate, and graduate students in Quebec, Ontario, Manitoba, and Saskatchewan. He received his master's and Ph.D. from the Ontario Institute for Studies in Education of the University of Toronto, where he focused on reading difficulty, perceptual development, and applied linguistics. He continued his research training in an SSHRC-sponsored post-doctoral fellowship in Australia, examining the relationships between perceptual development and cognitive skills in reading difficulty. He has published articles in such professional journals as *Canadian Journal of Behavioural Science*, *Journal of Experimental Child Psychology*, *Journal of Learning Disabilities*, and *Journal of Research in Reading*; written book chapters on reading processes; and co-edited, with Dale Willows and Evelyne Corcos, *Visual Processes in Reading and Reading Disabilities*, published by Lawrence Erlbaum Associates. Most of his published work has dealt with his major research focus, perceptual and neurological factors related to reading skill development and to difficulties in learning to read.

BRIEF CONTENTS

Chapters

1 INTRODUCTION TO CHILD DEVELOPMENT 2

2 CONCEPTION, HEREDITY, AND ENVIRONMENT 32

3 PREGNANCY AND PRENATAL DEVELOPMENT 54

4 BIRTH AND THE NEWBORN BABY 72

5 PHYSICAL DEVELOPMENT AND HEALTH, BIRTH TO AGE 3 96

6 COGNITIVE DEVELOPMENT, BIRTH TO AGE 3 118

7 PSYCHOSOCIAL DEVELOPMENT, BIRTH TO AGE 3 142

8 PHYSICAL DEVELOPMENT AND HEALTH IN EARLY CHILDHOOD 162

9 COGNITIVE DEVELOPMENT IN EARLY CHILDHOOD 180

10 PSYCHOSOCIAL DEVELOPMENT IN EARLY CHILDHOOD 200

11 PHYSICAL DEVELOPMENT AND HEALTH IN MIDDLE CHILDHOOD 222

12 COGNITIVE DEVELOPMENT IN MIDDLE CHILDHOOD 240

13 PSYCHOSOCIAL DEVELOPMENT IN MIDDLE CHILDHOOD 264

14 PHYSICAL DEVELOPMENT AND HEALTH IN ADOLESCENCE 284

15 COGNITIVE DEVELOPMENT IN ADOLESCENCE 304

16 PSYCHOSOCIAL DEVELOPMENT IN ADOLESCENCE 322

Glossary GL-1
References RE-1
Credits CR-1
Name Index NI-1
Subject Index SI-1

CONTENTS

Deirche
Mallehe
2017

CHAPTER 1 INTRODUCTION TO CHILD DEVELOPMENT 2

The Study of Child Development 4
Periods of Development 4
Domains of Development 6

Influences on Development 6
Heredity, Environment, and Maturation 6
Contexts of Development 6
Normative and Non-Normative Influences 11
Timing of Influences: Critical or Sensitive
Periods 12

Issues in Development 12
Is Development Based More on Nature or
Nurture? 12
Is Development Active or Passive? 13
Is Development Continuous or
Discontinuous? 13
An Emerging Consensus 14

Theories of Child Development 14
Perspective 1: Psychoanalytic 15
Perspective 2: Learning 17
Perspective 3: Cognitive 19
Perspective 4: Contextual 21
Perspective 5: Evolutionary/Sociobiological
Perspectives 22

Research Methods 23
Forms of Data Collection 23
Basic Research Designs 24
Developmental Research Designs 26
Ethics of Research 27

CHAPTER 2 CONCEPTION, HEREDITY, AND ENVIRONMENT 32

Conception and Infertility 34
Fertilization 34
Infertility 34
Assisted Reproductive Technologies 35
Adoption 37

Mechanisms of Heredity 37
The Genetic Code 37
Sex Determination 38
Patterns of Genetic Transmission 39
Epigenesis: Environmental Influence on Gene
Expression 40

Genetic and Chromosomal Abnormalities 41
Dominant or Recessive Inheritance of
Defects 43
Sex-Linked Inheritance of Defects 43
Chromosomal Abnormalities 44
Genetic Counselling and Testing 45

Studying the Influence of Heredity and Environment 46
Measuring Heritability 46
How Heredity and Environment Work
Together 47

Characteristics Influenced by Heredity and Environment 49
Physical and Physiological Traits 49
Intelligence 50
Temperament and Personality 50
Psychopathology 51

CHAPTER 3 PREGNANCY AND PRENATAL DEVELOPMENT 54

Stages of Prenatal Development 56
Principles of Growth 56
The Germinal Stage 56
The Embryonic Stage 58
The Fetal Stage 59

Influences on Prenatal Development 61
Maternal Factors 61
Paternal Factors 69

Monitoring Prenatal Development 69

CHAPTER 4 BIRTH AND THE NEWBORN BABY 72

How Childbirth Has Changed 74

The Birth Process 76
Stages of Childbirth 76
Labour and Delivery Options 76

The Newborn Baby 79
Size and Appearance 79
Reflexes and Their Development 80
Body Systems 81
Medical and Behavioural Assessment 82

Birth Complications and Their Aftermath 84
Low Birth Weight 84
Postmaturity 86
Stillbirth 86
Infant Mortality 87

Newborns and Parents 90
Childbirth and Bonding 90
The Mother-Infant Bond 91
The Father's Role 92
How Parenthood Affects Marital
    Satisfaction 92

CHAPTER 5 PHYSICAL DEVELOPMENT AND HEALTH, BIRTH TO AGE 3 96

Early Growth and Physical Development 98
Principles of Early Growth and Physical
    Development 98
Physical Growth 98
Nutrition 99

The Developing Brain 101
Building the Brain 101
Brain Plasticity 102

Early Sensory Capacities 104
Touch and Pain 104
Smell and Taste 105
Hearing 105
Sight 105

Motor Development 106
Milestones 106
Motor Development and Perception 108
Theories of Motor Development 108

Health 110
Immunizations 110
States of Arousal and Activity Levels in Infancy
    and Toddlerhood 111
Child Maltreatment 112

CHAPTER 6 COGNITIVE DEVELOPMENT, BIRTH TO AGE 3 118

Behaviourist Approach: Basic Mechanics of Learning 120
Classical Conditioning 120
Operant Conditioning 120

Psychometric Approach: Developmental and Intelligence Testing 121
Testing Infants and Toddlers 121
Assessing the Impact of the Home
    Environment 122
Early Intervention 122

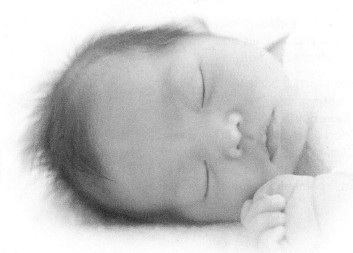

Piagetian Approach: The Sensorimotor Stage 124
  Sensorimotor Substages 124
  Object Concept 126
  Evaluating Piaget's Sensorimotor Stage 126

Information-Processing Approach: Perceptions and Representations 127
  Habituation 127
  Visual Processing Abilities 128
  Information Processing as a Predictor of Intelligence 128
  Information Processing and the Development of Piagetian Abilities 128

Cognitive Neuroscience Approach: The Brain's Cognitive Structures 130

Social-Contextual Approach: Learning from Caregivers 131

Language Development 132
  Sequence of Early Language Development 133
  Characteristics of Early Speech 135
  Influences on Language Development 135
  Preparing for Literacy 138

CHAPTER 7 PSYCHOSOCIAL DEVELOPMENT, BIRTH TO AGE 3 142

Emotions and Temperament 144
  Emotions 144
  Early Emotional Responses 145
  Temperament 146

Attachment 149
  Developing Trust 149
  Developing Attachments 149
  Mutual Regulation 152

The Developing Self 153
  The Emerging Sense of Self 153
  Developing Autonomy 154
  Socialization 155
  Gender 156

Relationships with Other Children 158
  Siblings 158
  Peers 159

CHAPTER 8 PHYSICAL DEVELOPMENT AND HEALTH IN EARLY CHILDHOOD 162

Physical Growth 164
  Height and Weight 164
  The Brain 164

Sleep 165
  Sleep Disturbances 166
  Bed-Wetting and Toilet Training 166

Motor Development 167
  Gross Motor Skills and Fine Motor Skills 167
  Handedness 168

Health and Safety 169
  Obesity 169
  Undernutrition 170
  Food Allergies 171
  Oral Health 172
  Accidental Injuries and Deaths 172
  Environmental Influences on Health 174

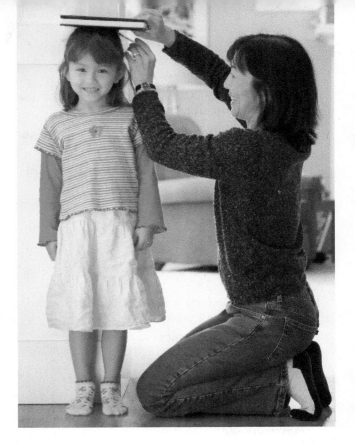

CHAPTER 9 COGNITIVE DEVELOPMENT IN EARLY CHILDHOOD 180

Piagetian Approach: The Preoperational Child 182
Advances of Preoperational Thought 182
Limits of Preoperational Thought 184
Theory of Mind 185

Information-Processing Approach: Memory Development 188
Basic Processes and Capacities 188
Memory in Childhood 189

Psychometric Approaches to Intelligence 190
Traditional Psychometric Measures 190
Influences on Measured Intelligence 190

Vygotskian Approach to Measurement and Teaching 191

Language Development 192
Areas of Language Development 192
Delayed Language Development 194
Preparation for Literacy 194

Early Childhood Education 195
Types of Preschools 195
Kindergarten 197

CHAPTER 10 PSYCHOSOCIAL DEVELOPMENT IN EARLY CHILDHOOD 200

The Developing Self 202
The Self-Concept and Self-Definition 202
Self-Esteem 203
Understanding and Regulating Emotions 203
Erikson: Initiative versus Guilt 204

Gender 205
Gender Differences 205
Perspectives on Gender Development 206

Play 211
Cognitive Levels of Play 211
The Social Dimension of Play 211
How Gender Influences Play 212
How Culture Influences Play 212

Parenting 213
Forms of Discipline 213
Parenting Styles 214

Prosocial and Aggressive Behaviour 217
Prosocial Behaviour 217
Aggressive Behaviour 218

CHAPTER 11 PHYSICAL DEVELOPMENT AND HEALTH IN MIDDLE CHILDHOOD 222

Physical Development 224
Height and Weight 224
Tooth Development and Dental Care 224
Brain Development 224

Nutrition and Sleep 226
Nutritional Needs 226
Sleep Patterns and Problems 227

Motor Development and Physical Play 228
Recess 228
Organized Sports 229

Health and Safety 229
Overweight 229
Chronic Medical Conditions 231
Factors in Children's Health 232
Accidental Injuries 232

Mental Health 234
   Disruptive Conduct Disorders 234
   School Phobia and Other Anxiety
     Disorders 234
   Childhood Depression 235
   Treatment Techniques 236

CHAPTER 12 COGNITIVE DEVELOPMENT IN MIDDLE CHILDHOOD 240

Piagetian Approach: The Concrete Operational Child 242
   Spatial Relationships 242
   Categorization 242
   Inductive and Deductive Reasoning 243
   Conservation 243
   Number and Mathematics 244
   Moral Reasoning 244

Information-Processing Approach: Attention, Memory, and Planning 245
   Influences on the Development of Executive
     Function 245
   Selective Attention 246
   Working Memory 246
   Metamemory 246
   Information Processing and Piagetian Tasks 246

Psychometric Approach: Assessment of Intelligence 247
   Measuring Intelligence 247
   The IQ Controversy 247
   Is There More Than One Intelligence? 248
   Influences on Intelligence 249

Language and Literacy 250
   Vocabulary, Grammar, and Syntax 250
   Pragmatics 251
   Literacy 251

The Child in School 252
   Social and Home Influences on Academic
     Achievement 252
   Classroom and School System Influences on
     Academic Achievement 253
   Educating Children with Special Needs 255

CHAPTER 13 PSYCHOSOCIAL DEVELOPMENT IN MIDDLE CHILDHOOD 264

The Developing Self 266
   Self-Concept Development: Representational
     Systems 266
   Self-Esteem 266
   Emotional Growth 267

The Child in the Family 268
   Family Atmosphere 268
   Family Structure 270
   Sibling Relationships 276

The Child in the Peer Group 276
   Positive and Negative Effects of Peer
     Relations 276
   Gender Differences in Peer-Group
     Relationships 277
   Popularity 277
   Friendship 278
   Aggression and Bullying 278

CHAPTER 14 PHYSICAL DEVELOPMENT AND HEALTH IN ADOLESCENCE 284

Adolescence 286
Adolescence as a Social Construction 286
A Time of Opportunities and Risks 286

Puberty 287
How Puberty Begins: Hormonal Changes 287
Timing, Signs, and Sequence of Puberty and Sexual Maturity 288
Implications of Early and Late Maturation 291

The Brain 291
The Frontal Cortex 291
Environmental Influences 292

Physical and Mental Health 292
Physical Activity 292
Sleep Needs and Problems 293
Nutrition and Eating Disorders 294
Self-Injurious Behaviour 296
Drug Use 296
Depression 299
Death 300

CHAPTER 15 COGNITIVE DEVELOPMENT IN ADOLESCENCE 304

Cognitive Development 306
Piaget's Stage of Formal Operations 306
Immature Characteristics of Adolescent Thought 308
Language Development 309
Changes in Information Processing in Adolescence 309

Moral Development 310
Kohlberg's Theory of Moral Reasoning 311
Gilligan's Theory: An Ethic of Care 313

Educational and Vocational Issues 314
Influences on School Achievement 314
Dropping Out of High School 318
Preparing for Higher Education or Vocations 318

CHAPTER 16 PSYCHOSOCIAL DEVELOPMENT IN ADOLESCENCE 322

The Search for Identity 324
Erikson: Identity versus Identity Confusion 324
Marcia: Identity Status—Crisis and Commitment 324
Gender Differences in Identity Formation 325
Ethnic Factors in Identity Formation 325
Prosocial Behaviour and Volunteer Activity 326

Sexuality 327
Sexual Orientation and Identity 327
Sexual Behaviour 328
Sexually Transmitted Infections (STIs) 330
Teenage Pregnancy and Child-Bearing 331

Relationships with Family and Peers 332
Is Adolescent Rebellion a Myth? 332
Adolescents and Parents 332
Adolescents and Siblings 335
Peers and Friends 335

Antisocial Behaviour and Juvenile Delinquency 337
Biological Influences 337
Family Influences 338
Environmental Influences 338
Preventing and Treating Delinquency 339

Emerging Adulthood 339

GLOSSARY GL-1
REFERENCES RE-1
CREDITS CR-1
NAME INDEX NI-1
SUBJECT INDEX SI-1

MEET *CHILD* with McGraw Hill Education **connect**®

Scholarly content combined with critical thinking and real-life applications. *CHILD* is designed to visually and intellectually engage students with the biological, psychological, and social forces that influence child and adolescent development. In addition to thorough scholarship, *CHILD* prompts students to apply critical thinking skills and to apply course concepts to everyday life.

CHILD is a contemporary resource that stems from research on student study habits, learning behaviours, and reader expectations. McGraw-Hill conducted in-depth surveys and focus groups with students to understand what makes their reading and learning experiences more engaging, memorable, and enjoyable. We observed students and faculty in classes. We then interviewed instructors to identify their biggest challenges and find out how a completely different way to deliver content could help to overcome those challenges. Students want visually appealing course materials with interactive pedagogy, an integrated approach, and relevant content geared to different learning styles. Faculty told us they want a way to engage their students without compromising academic quality.

Portable, multimodal, and visual, *CHILD* offers a dynamic learning experience designed for today's students.

WHATS INSIDE?

AS YOU READ

LO1 Summarize how conception occurs and describe alternative paths to parenthood.
LO2 Explain how traits are passed down across generations.
LO3 Describe how abnormalities are transmitted in the genes and the options prospective parents have for testing for them.
LO4 Describe how researchers determine the relative influence of genes and environments, and how these variables interact with each other.
LO5 Summarize how genes affect physical, intellectual, and personality development, as well as psychopathologies.

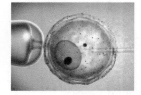  

« Learning objectives, listed in the *As You Read* section of each chapter, help students preview chapter content and study effectively.

A brief review of each learning objective is provided in each chapter's *Summary* section. »

Did you know?

Every person has unique fingerprints—even identical twins. While the basic whorls, loops, and ridges of the fingertips of identical twins are similar in their broad patterns, they are not exact copies.

ʌ
ʌ

Did You Know? boxes introduce short, interesting facts relevant to the chapter's topics to further engage students.

SUMMARY — CHAPTER 2 CONCEPTION, HEREDITY, AND ENVIRONMENT

LO1

Summarize how conception occurs and describe alternative paths to parenthood.

- Fertilization, the union of an ovum and a sperm, results in the formation of a one-celled zygote, which then duplicates itself by cell division.
- Early beliefs about conception reflected incorrect beliefs about nature and about male and female anatomy.
- The most common cause of infertility in men is a low sperm count; the most common cause in women is blockage of the fallopian tubes. Infertile couples now have several options for assisted reproduction, but these techniques may involve thorny ethical and practical issues.
- Dizygotic (fraternal) twins have different genetic makeups and may be of different sexes; monozygotic (identical) twins have the same genetic makeup but may differ in some respects.
- Adoption is an alternative for couples who cannot conceive. While there is a higher incidence of special needs, most adopted children are healthy and fare well on most indices of social and emotional well-being.

LO2

Explain how traits are passed down across generations.

- The basic functional units of heredity are the genes, which are made of deoxyribonucleic acid (DNA). DNA carries the set of biochemical instructions, or genetic code, that governs bodily functions and determines inherited characteristics. Each gene seems to be located by function in a definite position on a particular chromosome. The complete sequence of genes in the human body is the human genome.

Continued

Perspectives on Diversity

THE RESIDENTIAL SCHOOL EXPERIENCE OF ABORIGINAL CHILDREN

The importance of looking at the life course in its social and historical context is exemplified by the experience of Aboriginal youth in Canada from the 1920s to the 1970s. Before that time, Aboriginal communities gave children the freedom to explore their environment and to develop independence, without the use of corporal punishment (Johnson & Cremo, 1995). Aboriginal languages and traditional spirituality and customs flourished. The established European majority saw the typical child-rearing practice of Aboriginal communities as permissive and neglectful. Drawing upon public opinion and an emphasis on assimilation to the majority culture, the federal government in the 1920s followed a policy of removing Aboriginal children from their families and placing them in government-sponsored residential schools (Sinclair, Phillips, & Bala, 1991), typically run by church missionaries (Miller, 1996). The era of residential schools, which ended in the 1970s, exacted a huge toll in human suffering among members of Aboriginal communities. The residential school authorities did not permit the children to use their heritage languages, and as a consequence of their experiences, the children lost touch with their cultures and traditional ways (Grant, 1996). In some cases, evidence emerged of physical, psychological, and sexual abuse, along with human rights violations. The impact of this experience on the cohort of Aboriginal youth from the early 1920s to the 1970s involved feelings of inferiority, apathy, unwillingness to work, confusion over values, and anti-religious attitudes (Grant, 1996). Today, the effects of the residential school era are beginning to be addressed. Part of this process involves recognizing the practice as a form of cultural genocide (Miller, 1996), and emphasizing healing and renewing of language and cultural traditions for future generations of Aboriginal people by promoting distinct Aboriginal peoples' educational programs. Government initiatives,

such as the Statement of Reconciliation, a formal apology by the Canadian prime minister in 2008 to the people who experienced abuse; an Aboriginal Healing Foundation for community-based healing projects; and a truth and reconciliation process as a form of restorative justice, are beginning to facilitate the process. This healing is beginning to be seen in increasing numbers of Aboriginal people celebrating the diversity of their cultures through annual celebrations and gatherings, both in individual communities and nationally. Aboriginal groups are emerging as a political force, changing the social and cultural landscape through the Assembly of First Nations, Aboriginal educational institutions, and popular cultural outlets such as the Aboriginal Peoples Television Network.

As the history of the residential school cohort of Aboriginal youth has emerged, their life experiences—as documented by interviews with former students and school and government officials, archival data, and photographs—give researchers a window into the processes of development and their links with socio-historical change. The longer-term effects of the residential school era are being documented particularly with children of survivors and changes in the roles of elders and Aboriginal education.

«

Perspectives on Diversity boxes emphasize connections, or the lack of connections, across different groups.

Ask Yourself

13. A theory is
    a. an observation of something.
    b. a proven fact.
    c. a description or explanation of an observed phenomena.
    d. a statistical relationship between two variables.

14. If I believe that you are experiencing anxiety as an adult because your mother was rigid and stingy in her breastfeeding practices with you, I am probably a _____ theorist.

15. When my dog gets into the garbage can, I yell at him and tell him he is a bad dog. This is an example of _____ and is drawn from the _____ theoretical approach.
    a. adaptation; cognitive
    b. punishment; behaviourist
    c. gratification of an urge; psychoanalytic
    d. cross-species comparison; ethological

16. Three-year-old Ava has never seen a zebra before. On a visit to the zoo, she points to a zebra and says, "horse!" Ava has just engaged in
    a. the ZPD.
    b. accommodation.
    c. equilibrium.
    d. assimilation.

17. Bronfenbrenner would call the societal changes that were the result of the women's movement part of the
    a. microsystem.
    b. mesosystem.
    c. exosystem.
    d. macrosystem.
    e. chronosystem.

18. An evolutionary psychologist would be most interested in studying which of the following?
    a. What is the relationship between television viewing and body image?
    b. How does your early relationship with your opposite sex parent impact later romantic relationships?
    c. How do physical attractiveness and amount of resources impact a man's versus a woman's likelihood of dating a person?
    d. How does neighbourhood composition influence child development?

What Do You Do? >>

boxes provide students with short descriptions of professions that are related to child development, and point them to Canadian web-based resources to learn more about those professions, as well as what they need to do to obtain education and training for them.

WHAT DO YOU **DO**?

Developmental Psychologist

Developmental psychologists focus on lifespan or developmental issues from conception through death, often specializing in a specific stage of the lifespan. A developmental psychologist might work in a hospital or private practice, at a home for adolescents, or at a clinic for the elderly. Developmental psychologists might also research and teach at a university or work for the government or a private corporation. For example, a developmental psychologist interested in infants might work for an early intervention program or at a toy company advising on the next developmentally appropriate "must have" toy. Alternatively, a developmental psychologist interested in emerging adulthood might work and teach at a university while also conducting research on university students' risky behaviours. Or a developmental psychologist might research ways to improve seniors' lives, such as increasing the time for a crosswalk signal to accommodate the elderly or implementing an exercise program for seniors. A master's degree or doctoral degree is required to become a developmental psychologist. To learn more about what a developmental psychologist does, visit www.cpa.ca.

---

^
^

Self-test questions, distributed throughout each chapter in the *Ask Yourself* sections, are effective aids for students to monitor their understanding of the material they are reading, and to help them engage with content that might be particularly challenging to them. Answers are provided at the end of each chapter.

Child development is full of controversial issues. The questions posed in *Where Do You Stand?* boxes are designed to foster reflection and critical thinking about current debates about child development, care, and policy. >>

WHERE DO **YOU** STAND?

Would you want to know if you had a gene predisposing you to lung cancer? To Alzheimer's disease? Would you want your child to be tested for these genes?

INTRODUCTION
TO CHILD DEVELOPMENT

WHAT'S TO COME

The Study of Child Development

Influences on Development

Issues in Development

Theories of Child Development

Research Methods

In 1877, a young father sat gazing at his newborn son and, pen in hand, took careful notes on his child's behaviours. "During the first seven days various reflex actions, namely sneezing, hiccupping, yawning, stretching, and of course sucking and screaming, were well performed by my infant," the proud new father wrote. "On the seventh day, I touched the naked sole of his foot with a bit of paper, and he jerked it away, curling at the same time his toes, like a much older child when tickled. The perfection of these reflex movements shows that the extreme imperfection of the voluntary ones is not due to the state of the muscles or of the coordinating centres, but to that of the seat of the will."

The young Charles Darwin who theorized about his son's motor capacities was one of the first members of the field of child development. Although modern-day researchers are more likely to use electrodes to view the pattern of brain activation in a baby, show them computerized scenarios of imaginary events, or analyze microexpressions on a videotape, they share with Darwin an interest in the changes that occur in childhood, changes that emerge with extraordinary speed and organization. In this chapter, we outline the basics of the field. We discuss how development is conceptualized, some of the major influences on development, and recurrent issues in the field. Finally, we address the major theoretical perspectives and touch on how scientific data are collected.

AS YOU READ

LO1 Describe how development is conceptualized.
LO2 Summarize how individual differences, contexts, and the timing of influences affect development.
LO3 Summarize the recurrent philosophical issues of and points of consensus in the study of development.
LO4 Describe the major theoretical approaches.
LO5 Discuss the primary means of data collection and methodologies used in developmental research.

The Study of Child Development

The field of **child development** focuses on the scientific study of systematic processes of change and stability in human children. Developmental scientists look at ways in which children change from conception through adolescence, as well as at characteristics that remain fairly stable. The study of child development is part of the broader study of human development, which covers the entire human lifespan from conception to death. The study of child development is organized around periods and domains of development.

PERIODS OF DEVELOPMENT

Division of the lifespan into periods of development is a **social construction**: an idea that is generally accepted to be real by a particular culture or society. In *CHILD*, we follow a social construction about human development as a sequence of five periods, generally accepted in Western industrial societies. After examining the crucial changes that occur in the first period, before birth, we trace physical, cognitive, and psychosocial development through infancy and toddlerhood, early childhood, middle childhood, and adolescence (Table 1.1).

child development The scientific study of systematic processes of change and stability in human children.

social construction Concept about what is real based on societally shared perceptions or assumptions.

Development is a complex web of influences, and understanding the multiple influences requires multiple perspectives. Just as a fly caught on one thread of a web sends reverberations across the entire structure, development in one area sends ripples through all other areas of development. For example, a child with frequent ear infections may develop language more slowly than a child without this physical problem, and the failure to develop language may lead to feelings of frustration because of the difficulty in communicating with others. Thus, students of child development draw collaboratively from a wide range of disciplines, including psychology, psychiatry, sociology, anthropology, biology, genetics, family science, education, history, and medicine. *CHILD* includes findings from research in all these fields.

WHAT DO YOU DO?

Early Childhood Educator

Early childhood educators (ECEs) support children's early development in the classroom, focusing on infants, toddlers, and children up to age 6. These educators plan children's environments that encourage exploration and learning, lead developmentally appropriate activities, and guide their students. There are a variety of early childhood education approaches, but all emphasize the importance of developmentally appropriate strategies with which to engage their students. ECEs work in both public and private early childhood education and care (ECEC) settings, including schools that offer preschool education. All provinces typically require all ECEs or a percentage (about two-thirds) at ECEC settings to have a university degree or a college diploma. If you plan to teach in an ECEC setting that takes a particular approach—for example, Montessori—you may need to receive training in that particular approach. To learn more about becoming an ECE, visit www.childcarecanada.org, www.ccsc-cssge.ca/ece-post-secondary-information/ecec-programs, or provincial or territorial organizations like http://collegeofece.on.ca.

TABLE 1.1 Five Periods of Child Development

Age Period	Physical Developments	Cognitive Developments	Psychosocial Developments
Prenatal Period (conception to birth)	▪ Conception occurs by normal fertilization or other means. The genetic endowment interacts with environmental influences from the start. ▪ Basic body structures and organs form; brain growth spurt begins. Physical growth is the most rapid in the lifespan. ▪ Vulnerability to environmental influences is great.	▪ Abilities to learn and remember and to respond to sensory stimuli are developing.	▪ Fetus responds to mother's voice and develops a preference for it.
Infancy and Toddlerhood (birth to age 3)	▪ All senses and body systems operate at birth to varying degrees. The brain grows in complexity and influence. ▪ Physical growth and development of motor skills are rapid.	▪ Ability to learn and ability to remember are present, even in the early weeks. ▪ Use of symbols and ability to solve problems develop by end of 2nd year. ▪ Comprehension and use of language develop rapidly.	▪ Attachment to parents and others forms. ▪ Self-awareness develops. ▪ Shift from dependence to autonomy begins. ▪ Interest in other children increases.
Early Childhood (ages 3 to 6)	▪ Growth is steady; appearance becomes more slender and proportions more adultlike. ▪ Appetite diminishes, and sleep problems are common. ▪ Handedness appears; fine and gross motor skills and strength improve.	▪ Thinking is somewhat egocentric, but understanding of other people's perspectives grows. ▪ Cognitive immaturity results in some illogical ideas about the world. ▪ Memory and language improve. ▪ Intelligence becomes more predictable. ▪ Kindergarten experience is common.	▪ Self-concept and understanding of emotions become more complex; self-esteem is global. ▪ Independence, initiative, and self-control increase. ▪ Gender identity develops. ▪ Play becomes more imaginative, more elaborate, and usually more social. ▪ Altruism, aggression, and fearfulness are common. ▪ Family is still the focus of social life, but other children become more important.
Middle Childhood (ages 6 to 11)	▪ Growth slows. ▪ Strength and athletic skills improve. ▪ Respiratory illnesses are common, but health is generally better than at any other time in lifespan.	▪ Egocentrism diminishes. Children begin to think logically but concretely. ▪ Memory and language skills increase. ▪ Cognitive gains permit children to benefit from formal schooling. Some children show special educational needs and strengths.	▪ Self-concept becomes more complex, affecting self-esteem. ▪ Coregulation reflects gradual shift in control from parents to child. ▪ Peers assume greater importance.
Adolescence (ages 11 to about 20)	▪ Physical growth and other changes are rapid and profound. ▪ Reproductive maturity occurs. ▪ Major health risks arise from behavioural issues, such as eating disorders and drug abuse.	▪ Ability to think abstractly and use scientific reasoning develops. ▪ Immature thinking persists in some attitudes and behaviours. ▪ Education focuses on preparation for college or vocation.	▪ Search for identity, including sexual identity, becomes central. ▪ Relationships with parents are generally good. ▪ Peer group may exert a positive or negative influence.

DOMAINS OF DEVELOPMENT

Developmental scientists generally study three broad domains, or areas, of the self—physical, cognitive, and psychosocial—in the different periods of development. Growth of the body and brain, sensory capacities, motor skills, and health are parts of biological or **physical development**. Learning, attention, memory, language, thinking, reasoning, and creativity make up **cognitive development**. Emotions, personality, and social relationships are aspects of **psychosocial development**. How and what behaviours are studied may reflect a researcher's stand on basic issues in the field. *CHILD* is organized so that each domain is considered within each period.

Influences on Development

"I feel sure, from what I have seen with my own infants, that the period of development of the several faculties will be found to differ considerably in different infants," wrote Darwin. What he was referring to are now known as **individual differences**, differences among children in characteristics, influences, or developmental outcomes. Children differ in a range of areas—from gender to body build to energy level to personality. How they develop can be impacted by heredity, environment, and maturation; the contexts of their lives; and normative and nonnormative influences. Also a factor is the timing of these variables.

HEREDITY, ENVIRONMENT, AND MATURATION

Scientists have found ways to measure the contributions of heredity, or nature, and environment, or nurture, to the development of specific traits within a population. For example, even though intelligence is strongly affected by heredity, environmental factors such as parental stimulation, education, and peer influences also affect it. Contemporary theorists and researchers are increasingly interested in explaining how nature and nurture work together rather than arguing about which factor is more important.

---

physical development Growth of body and brain, including biological and physiological patterns of change in sensory capacities, motor skills, and health.

cognitive development Pattern of change in mental abilities, such as learning, attention, memory, language, thinking, reasoning, and creativity.

psychosocial development Pattern of change in emotions, personality, and social relationships.

individual differences Differences among children in characteristics, influences, or developmental outcomes.

maturation Unfolding of a universal, natural sequence of physical and behavioural changes.

Many typical changes of infancy and early childhood, such as the emergence of the abilities to walk and talk, are tied to **maturation** of the body and brain—the unfolding of a universal, natural sequence of physical changes and behaviour patterns. These maturational processes, which are seen most clearly in the early years, act in concert with the influences of heredity and environment. As children grow into adolescents and then into adults, individual differences in innate personal characteristics (heredity) and life experience (environment) play an increasing role as children adapt to the internal and external conditions in which they find themselves.

CONTEXTS OF DEVELOPMENT

In Victorian England, fathers were generally remote figures and did not typically take part in child caregiving activities. However, Charles Darwin was different. By all accounts, he was a loving and involved father. As described by his daughter, he was "the most delightful play-fellow, and the most perfect sympathizer." Modern-day fathers in Canada show a wide range of involvement, with some fathers completely absent from family life, some closely involved with caregiving, and some taking on the role of stay-at-home parent (Bolté, Devault, St-Denis, & Gaudet, 2001; Daly, 2004; Paquette, Bolté, Turcotte, Dubeau, & Bouchard, 2000).

For a child, the immediate context typically is the family, and the family, in turn, is subject to the wider and ever-changing influences of neighbourhood, community, and society. How might the family experiences of Darwin's children have shaped them? And how would the wider societal norms interact with their immediate family environment?

Charles Darwin with his oldest son, William, in 1842.

Family

What type of family did you grow up in? If you lived with two parents, you were part of a **nuclear family**. The nuclear family is a household unit generally consisting of one or two parents and their children, whether biological, adopted, or stepchildren. Historically, the two-parent nuclear family has been the most common family unit in Canada and other Western societies. However, the structure of the modern family is becoming increasingly diverse. We now see families of single or divorced parents, households may include a stepparent and stepsiblings or a parent's live-in partner, and there are increasing numbers of unmarried parents and gay and lesbian households with children (Lipman, Offord, Dooley, & Boyle, 2002; Pew Social Trends, 2010; Statistics Canada, 2007, 2012b).

In many societies in Asia, Africa, and Latin America, the **extended family**—a multigenerational kinship network of grandparents, aunts, uncles, cousins, and more distant relatives—is the traditional family form (Johnson et al., 2003). Today, the extended-family household is becoming slightly less typical in some developing countries because of industrialization and migration to urban centres (Kinsella & Phillips, 2005). Extended families often spread through all regions of Canada, with family members moving for work or education. However, among many Canadian ethnic groups, particularly Aboriginal Canadians—including First Nations, Inuit, and Métis—the extended family and community members are integral parts of children's experiences (Gerlach, 2008; Ward, 1998). Grandparents traditionally assumed a major role in raising children in Aboriginal communities, and

despite the practices of the mainstream culture that undermined this strength of Aboriginal families (see the Perspectives on Diversity box), the traditional roles are beginning to return (Gerlach, 2008; Parler, 2001).

Culture, Ethnicity, and Race

Culture, race, and ethnicity can influence development. **Culture** refers to a society's or group's total way of life, including customs, traditions, laws, knowledge, beliefs, values, language, and physical products, from tools to artworks—all the behaviours and attitudes that are learned, shared, and transmitted among members of a social group. Culture is constantly changing, often through contact with other cultures. Today, computers and telecommunications enhance cultural contact among adults and children alike; email and social networking sites offer almost immediate communication across the globe.

Canada is a nation of many ethnic groups. An **ethnic group** consists of people united by a distinctive culture, ancestry, religion, language, or national origin, all of which contribute to a sense of shared identity and shared attitudes, beliefs, and values. Within large societies, ethnic groups may also be characterized by minority status. Ethnic minorities are those ethnic groups that have different national or cultural traditions from the majority of the population, and they are often affected by prejudice and discrimination. By 2031, because of rising immigration and high birthrates among immigrant families, ethnic minorities in Canada—roughly one-third of the population in 2006—are expected to grow to about half of the population, while the proportion of visible minorities—people other than Aboriginal Canadians and descendants of European immigrants—is also expected to increase (Statistics Canada, 2010; see also Figure 1.1). Geographic dispersion and adaptation to local conditions, together with a steady rise in interracial marriages—about 4 percent of Canadian marriages in 2006 (Milan, Maheux, & Chui, 2010)—have produced a wide variety of physical and cultural characteristics within populations (Smedley & Smedley, 2005).

There is also diversity within ethnic groups. Québécois, Franco-Ontarians, Franco-Manitobans, and Acadians—all French Canadians—have different histories and cultures and socio-economic status. Similarly, African-Canadian descendants of immigrants from the United States differ

---

nuclear family Two-generational household unit consisting of one or two parents and their biological children, adopted children, or stepchildren.

extended family Multigenerational kinship network of parents, children, and other relatives, sometimes living together in an extended-family household.

culture A society's or group's total way of life, including customs, traditions, beliefs, values, language, and physical products—all learned behaviours passed on from adults to children.

ethnic group A group united by ancestry, race, religion, language, or national origin that contributes to a sense of shared identity.

Canada's Cultural Mosaic

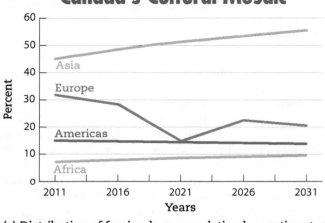

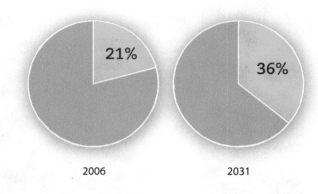

(a) Distribution of foreign-born population by continent of origin   (b) Ages 14 and under

FIGURE 1.1 (a) According to Statistics Canada, the proportion of the Canadian population made up of foreign-born people will increase to about 28 percent of the population by 2031, the highest proportion of foreign-born people since Confederation. (b) The proportion of Canadians ages 14 and under belonging to a visible minority group will continue to increase.

Source: Statistics Canada. 2010. *Study: Projections of the diversity of the Canadian population, 2006 to 2031.* Cat. no. 91-551-X. Ottawa, ON. (a) Figure 2, p. 17; (b) Figure 9, p. 24.

from those of Caribbean ancestry. Asian-Canadians, too, come from a variety of countries with distinct cultures and linguistic groups. Aboriginal peoples constitute the original inhabitants of Canada and are made up of many linguistic and ethnic groups: First Nations, Inuit, and Métis populations represent a diverse group of over one and a half million people in Canada. With 11 language groups and 58 dialects across 596 bands, living in 2,284 reserves and in small and large urban centres, there is a large amount of cultural and linguistic diversity, along with differences in values both between and within Aboriginal communities (Kirmayer, Brass, & Tait, 2000; Statistics Canada, 2008).

Ethnic and cultural patterns affect child development by their influence on the composition of a household, its economic and social resources, the way its members act toward one another, the foods they eat, the games children play, the way they learn, how well they do in school, the occupations adults engage in, and the way family members think about and perceive the world. In time, however, immigrants tend to learn one or both official languages, customs, and attitudes needed to get along in the dominant culture, although many make an effort to preserve some of their unique cultural practices and values (Johnson et al., 2003). According to the National Longitudinal Survey of Children and Youth (NLSCY), an ongoing study that began in 1994, tracking 35,000 children from all regions of Canada every two years from birth, children of immigrant families do as well as or better than Canadian-born children in reading, writing, and mathematics achievement by the end of elementary school (Worswick, 2001).

All humans belong to the same taxonomic classification—that of *Homo sapiens.* However, there are salient differences in outward appearance among people from different geographical regions—note, for instance, the different skin colour of people from northern European countries and

from Africa. These salient differences have led people to speak of individuals as being of different races. However, there is no clear scientific consensus on the definition of race, and it is impossible to measure reliably (Bonham, Warshauer-Baker, & Collins, 2005; Sternberg, Grigorenko, & Kidd, 2005). Human genetic variation occurs along a broad continuum, and 90 percent of such variation occurs *within* rather than *among* socially defined races (Ossorio & Duster, 2005). In other words, the differences between two people on the opposite ends of a distribution within one race are larger than the differences between two people of different races. Nevertheless, race as a social category clearly remains a factor in research because it makes a difference in "how individuals are treated, where they live, their employment opportunities, the quality of their health care, and whether [they] can fully participate" in their society (Smedley & Smedley, 2005, p. 23). This chapter's Perspectives on Diversity explores a difficult but important part of the history of Aboriginal groups in Canada.

Socio-Economic Status and Neighbourhood

A family's **socio-economic status (SES)** is based on family income and the educational and occupational levels of the adults in the household. Throughout *CHILD*, we examine many studies that relate SES to developmental processes, such as mothers' verbal interactions with their children, and to developmental outcomes, such as health and cognitive performance. SES affects these processes and outcomes indirectly, through the kinds of homes and neighbourhoods people live in and the quality of nutrition,

---

socio-economic status (SES) Combination of economic and social factors, including income, education, and occupation, that describe an individual or a family.

Perspectives on Diversity

THE RESIDENTIAL SCHOOL EXPERIENCE OF ABORIGINAL CHILDREN

The importance of looking at the life course in its social and historical context is exemplified by the experience of Aboriginal youth in Canada from the 1920s to the 1970s. Before that time, Aboriginal communities gave children the freedom to explore their environment and to develop independence, without the use of corporal punishment (Johnson & Cremo, 1995). Aboriginal languages and traditional spirituality and customs flourished. The established European majority saw the typical child-rearing practice of Aboriginal communities as permissive and neglectful. Drawing upon public opinion and an emphasis on assimilation to the majority culture, the federal government in the 1920s followed a policy of removing Aboriginal children from their families and placing them in government-sponsored residential schools (Sinclair, Phillips, & Bala, 1991), typically run by church missionaries (Miller, 1996). The era of residential schools, which ended in the 1970s, exacted a huge toll in human suffering among members of Aboriginal communities. The residential school authorities did not permit the children to use their heritage languages, and as a consequence of their experiences, the children lost touch with their cultures and traditional ways (Grant, 1996). In some cases, evidence emerged of physical, psychological, and sexual abuse, along with human rights violations. The impact of this experience on the cohort of Aboriginal youth from the early 1920s to the 1970s involved feelings of inferiority, apathy, unwillingness to work, confusion over values, and anti-religious attitudes (Grant, 1996). Today, the effects of the residential school era are beginning to be addressed. Part of this process involves recognizing the practice as a form of cultural genocide (Miller, 1996), and emphasizing healing and renewing of language and cultural traditions for future generations of Aboriginal people by promoting distinct Aboriginal peoples' educational programs. Government initiatives,

such as the Statement of Reconciliation, a formal apology by the Canadian prime minister in 2008 to the people who experienced abuse; an Aboriginal Healing Foundation for community-based healing projects; and a truth and reconciliation process as a form of restorative justice, are beginning to facilitate the process. This healing is beginning to be seen in increasing numbers of Aboriginal people celebrating the diversity of their cultures through annual celebrations and gatherings, both in individual communities and nationally. Aboriginal groups are emerging as a political force, changing the social and cultural landscape through the Assembly of First Nations, Aboriginal educational institutions, and popular cultural outlets such as the Aboriginal Peoples Television Network.

As the history of the residential school cohort of Aboriginal youth has emerged, their life experiences—as documented by interviews with former students and school and government officials, archival data, and photographs—give researchers a window into the processes of development and their links with socio-historical change. The longer-term effects of the residential school era are being documented particularly with children of survivors and changes in the roles of elders and Aboriginal education.

medical care, and schooling available to them (Friendly & Prentice, 2009; McCain, Mustard, & McCuaig, 2011).

Child poverty in Canada has decreased since the 1990s (Figure 1.2). In Canada, the proportion has dropped from a high of 18 percent in 1996 to 9 percent in 2007. Children living with single parents or stepparents, or with non-parental caregivers such as grandparents, and those with less educated parents are especially likely to be poor (Children in North America Project, 2008; Statistics Canada, 2011a). About one in eight Canadian children ages 12 years

or younger experiences a severe period of poverty, defined as four or more consecutive years of family income below the low-income cut-off, an indicator of straightened circumstances, reflecting families spending 20 percent more of their after-tax income than the average family does for food, shelter, and clothing (Canadian Council on Social Development, 2001; Statistics Canada, 2012a).

Poverty is stressful and can damage the physical, cognitive, and psychosocial well-being of children and families (see Table 1.2). Poor children are more likely

Child Poverty Rates—Canada: 1998–2007

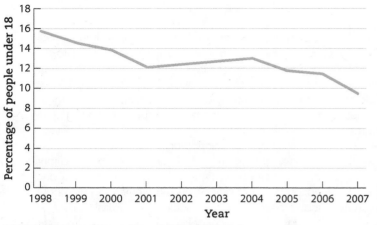

(a) Percentage of Canadian children living in poverty

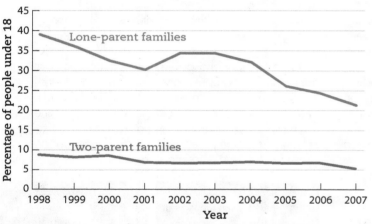

(b) Percentage of Canadian children living in lone- and two-parent families who live in poverty

FIGURE 1.2 (a) According to Statistics Canada, the percentage of Canadian children living in poverty continues to decrease. (b) The percentages of Canadian children in lone-parent and two-parent families who live in poverty are each decreasing, though the percentage for lone-parent families is still much higher than for two-parent families.

Source: Statistics Canada. (2009b). *Income in Canada 2007.* Catalogue no.75-202-X. Ottawa, ON.

than other children to go hungry; to have frequent illnesses; to lack access to health care; to experience accidents, violence, and family conflict; and to show emotional or behavioural problems. Their cognitive potential and school performance suffer as well (Children in North America Project, 2008; Statistics Canada, 2009a; Wadsworth & Santiago, 2008). The harm done by poverty is often indirect, through its impact on parents' emotional state and parenting practices and on the home environment they create (see Chapter 10). Threats to well-being multiply if, as often happens, several **risk factors** —conditions that increase the likelihood of a negative outcome—are present.

The composition of a neighbourhood affects the way children develop. Living in a neighbourhood with large numbers of people who are poor has been demonstrated to impact physical health and well-being, as well as school readiness (Cushon, Vu, Janzen, & Muhajarine, 2011). According the NLSCY study, although coming from a disadvantaged neighbourhood can contribute to emotional and behavioural problems in childhood, the most powerful factor that predicts future behavioural problems is family socioeconomic status (Boyle & Lipman, 1998; Caro, 2010; Racine & Boyle, 2002; Willms, 2002; Xue, Leventhal, Brooks-Gunn, & Earls, 2005). Positive development can occur despite serious risk factors, however (Kim-Cohen, Moffitt, Caspi, & Taylor, 2004). Consider television star Oprah Winfrey, singer and songwriter Shania Twain, and singer Justin Bieber, all of whom grew up in poverty.

The Historical Context

At one time, developmental scientists paid little attention to historical context—the time in which people live. Then, as the early longitudinal studies

risk factors Conditions that increase the likelihood of a negative developmental outcome.

TABLE 1.2 Higher Risk for Low-Income Children	
Outcome	Low-Income Children's Higher Risk Relative to More Affluent Children
Mental Health	
Emotional Problems	1.3 times more likely
Behavioural Problems	1.3 times more likely
Family Environment	
Single Parent	5.5 times more likely
Ineffective Parenting	1.04 times more likely
Parental Depression	1.8 times more likely
Family Dysfunction	1.3 times more likely

Source: Adapted from Beiser M, Hou F, Hyman I, Tousignant M. (2002). Poverty, family process, and the mental health of immigrant children in Canada. *American Journal of Public Health* 92(2):220–7. p. 222.

Despite experiencing developmental risks early in life, Justin Bieber became one of Canada's international music stars.

of childhood extended into the adult years, investigators began to focus on how certain experiences, tied to time and place, affect the course of people's lives. For example, because of the recent economic recession, longer lifespans, and immigration from countries where multi-generational families are common, there has been a substantial increase in multi-generational families in Canada (Bascaramurty, 2012; Loney, 2011; Statistics Canada, 2012b). This shift in family structure affects the influences to which children are exposed.

Children in the mid-1800s often worked from an early age, with kinship networks giving secure social bases where few social institutions existed (Parr, 1982). As Canada developed as an industrial nation in the late 1800s and early 1900s, new perspectives focused on children's health, access to quality education, and victims of abuse and neglect, who were cared for in homes rather than large institutions (Sutherland, 2000). Canada today is a more culturally diverse country; children are brought up in substantially different ways from those of past generations as ideas, customs, and practices have evolved (Sutherland, 2000). Children are no longer regarded as family property, as was the case in Canada's colonial period, or as dependent on the protection of the state, as during the first half of the twentieth century. Today, children are recognized as having inherent rights, in the 1982 *Canadian Charter of Rights and Freedoms* and in Canada's adoption of the UN Convention on the Rights of the Child (Howe, 1995). However, Canada has not yet recognized the right of children to protection from poverty (Howe, 1995). Although

Canada is a wealthy country, one in ten children—almost 640,000 children—still lives in poverty. The situation is worse among recent immigrant and Aboriginal families, where about one in every three children grows up in poverty (First Call: BC Child and Youth Advocacy Coalition, 2011). Today, as we discuss in the next section, historical context is an important part of the study of development.

NORMATIVE AND NON-NORMATIVE INFLUENCES

To understand similarities and differences in development, we need to look at **normative** influences, biological or environmental events that affect many or most people in a society in similar ways, and at **non-normative** influences, events that touch only certain individuals (Baltes & Smith, 2004).

Normative age-graded influences are highly similar for people in a particular age group, such as starting school at age 5. The timing of biological events is fairly predictable within a normal range. For example, children do not experience puberty at age 3 or menopause at 12.

Normative history-graded influences are significant events (such as the new Internet applications of social media and music, film, and ebook downloading; Hurricane Katrina; or the Japan tsunami) that shape the behaviour and attitudes of a **historical generation**, a group of people who experience the event at a formative time in their lives. For example, the generations that came of age during the Depression and World War II tend to show a strong sense of social interdependence and trust that has declined among more recent generations (Rogler, 2002).

A historical generation is not the same as an age **cohort**, a group of people born at about the same time that experiences similar influences. A historical generation may contain more than one cohort, but not all cohorts are part of historical generations unless they experience major, shaping historical events at a formative point in their lives (Rogler, 2002).

Non-normative influences are unusual events that have a major impact on individual lives because they disturb the expected sequence of the life cycle. They are either typical events that happen at an atypical time of life, such as the death of a parent when a child is young, or atypical events, such as surviving a plane crash.

Taken together, the three types of influences—normative age-graded, normative history-graded, and non-normative—contribute to the complexity of human development as well as to the challenges people experience in trying to build their lives.

normative Characteristic of an event that occurs in a similar way for most people in a group.

non-normative Characteristic of an unusual event that happens to a particular person or a typical event that happens at an unusual time of life.

historical generation A group of people strongly influenced by a major historical event during their formative period.

cohort A group of people born at about the same time.

TIMING OF INFLUENCES: CRITICAL OR SENSITIVE PERIODS

Konrad Lorenz (1957), an Austrian zoologist, got new-born ducklings to follow him as they would a mother duck. Lorenz showed that newly hatched ducklings will instinctively follow the first moving object they see. This phenomenon is called **imprinting**, and Lorenz believed that it is automatic and irreversible. Usually, this instinctive bond is with the mother; but if the natural course of events is disturbed, other attachments, like the one to Lorenz—or none at all—can form. Imprinting, said Lorenz, is the result of a predisposition toward learning, the readiness of an organism's nervous system to acquire certain information during a brief critical period in early life.

A **critical period** is a specific time when a given event, or its absence, has a specific impact on development. If a necessary event does not occur during a critical period of maturation, normal development will not occur, and the resulting abnormal patterns are generally irreversible (Kuhl, Conboy, Padden, Nelson, & Pruitt, 2005).

Do human children experience critical periods, as ducklings do? One example of a critical period occurs during gestation. If a woman receives X-rays, takes certain drugs, or contracts certain diseases at certain times during pregnancy, the fetus may show specific ill effects, depending on the nature of the shock and on its timing. For example, exposure to rubella measles during the time in which the heart is forming will damage heart structure. The same effects do not happen after the heart has already been formed. Many environmental influences may affect development irreversibly after pregnancy as well. If a muscle problem interfering with the ability to focus both eyes on the same object is not corrected within a critical period early in childhood, depth perception probably will not develop (Bushnell & Boudreau, 1993).

However, the concept of critical periods in humans is controversial. Because many aspects of development, even in the biological/neurological domain, have been found to show **plasticity**, or modifiability of performance, it may be more useful to think about **sensitive periods**, when a developing person is especially responsive to certain kinds of experiences (Bruer, 2001).

Did you know?

The most critical time for a pregnancy is in the first trimester. The reason for this is that this is when the major structures of the body are forming. Therefore, any adverse substances encountered during this time can profoundly affect the developing fetus. However, many women do not realize at first that they are pregnant. Luckily, nature has provided us with a safety clause: the lack of a shared blood supply for approximately two weeks after conception diminishes the likelihood of exposure.

Ask Yourself

4. Nine-month-old Sally is an active and smiley baby, while her playmate John is quiet and shy. The variations in their behaviour are known as
   a. emotional variants.
   b. social emotions.
   c. individual differences.
   d. maturation.

5. Which of the following could best be described as a maturational process?
   a. learning to read
   b. getting a tooth
   c. understanding that another person is sad
   d. knowing how to roller skate

6. Important environmental influences include
   a. ethnicity.
   b. home environment.
   c. neighbourhood.
   d. culture.
   e. all of these.

7. An example of a normative influence is _____; an example of a non-normative influence is _____.

8. While generally people learn to read in childhood, illiterate adults can learn to read later in life. However, most programs to promote literacy in adults have low success rates. Does this mean that childhood is a critical or sensitive period for learning how to read? Why or why not?

Issues in Development

What drives development? Is nature more important than nurture, or vice versa? Is development active or passive? Continuous or discontinuous? Out of the debate over these issues, different explanations, or models, of development have emerged.

IS DEVELOPMENT BASED MORE ON NATURE OR NURTURE?

Some influences on development originate primarily with **heredity** (nature), inborn traits or characteristics inherited

imprinting Instinctive form of learning in which, during a critical period in early development, a young animal forms an attachment to the first moving object it sees, usually the mother.

critical period Specific time when a given event or its absence has a profound and specific impact on development.

plasticity Modifiability of performance.

sensitive periods Times in development when a given event or its absence usually has a strong effect on development.

heredity Inborn characteristics inherited from the biological parents.

from a child's biological parents. Other influences come largely from the inner and outer **environment** (nurture), the world outside the self, beginning in the womb, and the learning that comes from experience. Which of these factors—heredity or environment—has more impact on development? Most researchers today agree that nature and nurture always work together. For example, while tall parents pass on "tall genes" to their children, and thus tend to have tall children, it is also the case that nutritional status in childhood will affect eventual height.

IS DEVELOPMENT ACTIVE OR PASSIVE?

Some models of development see development as passive. In this view, people are like machines that react to environmental input (Pepper, 1961). A machine is the sum of its parts. To understand it, we can break it down into its smallest components and then reassemble it. Fill a car with gas, turn the ignition key, press the accelerator, and the vehicle will move. In this view, human behaviour is much the same: it results from the operation of biological parts in response to external or internal stimuli. If we know enough about how the human "machine" is put together and about the forces acting on it, we can predict what the person will do. Rather than being active and internally driven, development is reactive and externally driven.

Others models see children as active, growing organisms that set their own development in motion. They initiate events; they do not just react. Thus, the driving force for change is internal. Environmental influences do not cause development, though they can speed or slow it. Because human behaviour is viewed as an organic whole, it cannot be predicted by breaking it down into simple responses to environmental stimulation.

IS DEVELOPMENT CONTINUOUS OR DISCONTINUOUS?

Development can be viewed as *continuous*—that is, gradual and incremental—or *discontinuous*—that is, abrupt or uneven. Some theorists see development as continuous, like walking or crawling up a ramp (Figure 1.3a). This is a **quantitative change**, a change in number or amount, such as in height, weight, size of vocabulary, or frequency of communication. A baby who can say three words at 12 months and then 20 words at 15 months experiences a quantitative change.

Other theorists emphasize **qualitative change**, changes in kind, structure, or organization.

Qualitative change is discontinuous; it is marked by the emergence of new phenomena that cannot be predicted easily on the basis of earlier functioning. The change from a nonverbal child to one who understands words and can communicate verbally is a qualitative change.

These theorists see development as occurring in a series of distinct stages, like stair steps (Figure 1.3b). At each stage, children cope with different types of problems and develop different abilities. Each stage builds on the previous one and prepares the way for the next.

All stage theories imply qualitative change. So, whenever you read or hear about a stage approach to development—whether from Freud or Piaget or Kohlberg—one of the things they are arguing is that development at each stage is fundamentally different from development at other points.

---

environment Totality of non-hereditary, or experiential, influences on development.

quantitative change Change in number or amount, such as in height, weight, or size of vocabulary.

qualitative change Change in kind, structure, or organization, such as the change from nonverbal to verbal communication.

The Nature of Change

FIGURE 1.3 A major difference among developmental theories is (a) whether it proceeds continuously, as learning theories and information processing theories propose, or (b) whether development occurs in distinct stages, as Freud, Erikson, and Piaget maintained.

(a) Continuity

(b) Stage theory (Discontinuity)

AN EMERGING CONSENSUS

While there are many different viewpoints in the study of child development, as the study of children has matured, broad agreement has emerged on several fundamental points concerning child development:

1. *All domains of development are interrelated.* Development in each of the different domains—physical, cognitive, and psychosocial—affects the others in a series of complex interactions.

2. *Normal development includes a wide range of individual differences.* Each child, from the start, is unlike anyone else in the world. Some of the influences on individual development are inborn; others come from experience. Most often, these influences work together.

3. *Influences are bidirectional.* Children affect the environment around them as much as the environment shapes them.

4. *Historical and cultural contexts strongly influence development.* Each child develops within a specific environment, bounded by time and place.

5. *Early experience is important, but children can be remarkably resilient.* A traumatic incident or a severely deprived childhood may well have grave emotional consequences, but the effects of painful experience, such as growing up in poverty or the death of a parent, often can be overcome.

6. *Development in childhood affects development throughout the lifespan.* As long as people live, they have the potential to change in both positive and negative directions.

Now that you have had a brief introduction to the field of child development and its basic concepts, we can look more closely at the issues developmental scientists think about and how they do their work. In the following section, we discuss some influential theories of how development takes place and the methods that investigators commonly use to study it.

Theories of Child Development

When Ahmed graduated from high school with honours in math and science, his father, an award-winning engineer, beamed. "The apple doesn't fall far from the tree," he said. Statements like this are informal, or intuitive, theories about why children develop as they do. Fundamentally, these are no different from the theories that scientists develop. Like laypeople's informal theories, scientific theories are not dry, abstract, or esoteric. They deal with the substance of real life and they are an attempt to explain the world around us.

A scientific **theory** is a set of logically related concepts or statements that seek to describe and explain development and to predict what kinds of behaviour might occur under certain conditions. Theories organize and explain data, the information gathered by research. Throughout *CHILD*, different aspects of development are explored through different theories. The major theories used in child development fall under five perspectives:

---

theory Coherent set of logically related concepts that seeks to organize, explain, and predict data.

psychoanalytic, learning, cognitive, contextual, and evolutionary/sociobiological (Table 1.3).

PERSPECTIVE 1: PSYCHOANALYTIC

While most commonly associated with the work of Sigmund Freud, the term *psychoanalytic perspective* is actually a broader umbrella that incorporates an array of related perspectives, generally focused on the lasting effects of childhood experiences and unconscious drives and motivations. In the following section, we describe the two approaches most relevant to the study of child development: the psychosexual and psychosocial perspectives popularized by Sigmund Freud and Erik Erikson.

Sigmund Freud: Psychosexual Development

Sigmund Freud (1953, 1964a, 1964b), a Viennese physician, originated the **psychoanalytic perspective**. He believed that development was shaped by unconscious, universal biological drives. He proposed three hypothetical parts of the personality: the id, the ego, and the superego. Newborns are governed by the id, which operates under the pleasure principle—the drive to seek immediate satisfaction of needs and desires. When gratification is delayed, as it is when infants have to wait to be fed, they begin to see themselves as separate from the outside world. The ego, which represents reason, develops gradually during the first year or so of life and operates under the reality principle. The ego's aim is to find realistic ways to gratify the id that are acceptable to the superego, which develops at about age 5 or 6. The superego includes the conscience and incorporates socially approved "shoulds" and "should nots" into the child's own value system. The superego is highly demanding; if its standards are not met, a child may feel guilty and anxious. The ego mediates between the impulses of the id and the demands of the superego.

Freud proposed that development is shaped by an unvarying sequence of five stages of **psychosexual development** (Table 1.4), in which sensual pleasure shifts from one body zone to another. At each stage, the behaviour that is the chief source of gratification (or frustration) changes. According to Freud, if children receive too little or too much gratification in any of these stages, they are at risk of fixation—an arrest in development that can show up in adult personality. For example, babies whose needs are not met during the oral stage, when feeding is the main source of sensual pleasure, may grow up to become nail-biters or smokers.

> ### "Anatomy is destiny."
> ### –Sigmund Freud

Freud's theory made historic contributions and inspired a whole generation of followers, some of whom took psychoanalytic theory in new directions. Many of Freud's ideas, however, now are widely considered obsolete, because they cannot be scientifically tested or have not been supported in research. Several of his central themes have nonetheless stood the test of time. Freud made us aware of the importance of unconscious thoughts, feelings, and motivations; the role of childhood experiences in forming personality; the ambivalence of emotional responses, especially responses to parents; the role of mental representations of the self and others in

WHAT DO YOU DO?

Developmental Psychologist

Developmental psychologists focus on lifespan or developmental issues from conception through death, often specializing in a specific stage of the lifespan. A developmental psychologist might work in a hospital or private practice, at a home for adolescents, or at a clinic for the elderly. Developmental psychologists might also research and teach at a university or work for the government or a private corporation. For example, a developmental psychologist interested in infants might work for an early intervention program or at a toy company advising on the next developmentally appropriate "must have" toy. Alternatively, a developmental psychologist interested in emerging adulthood might work and teach at a university while also conducting research on university students' risky behaviours. Or a developmental psychologist might research ways to improve seniors' lives, such as increasing the time for a crosswalk signal to accommodate the elderly or implementing an exercise program for seniors. A master's degree or doctoral degree is required to become a developmental psychologist. To learn more about what a developmental psychologist does, visit www.cpa.ca.

psychoanalytic perspective View of human development as being shaped by unconscious forces.

psychosexual development In Freudian theory, an unvarying sequence of stages of personality development during infancy, childhood, and adolescence, in which gratification shifts from the mouth to the anus and then to the genitals.

TABLE 1.3 Five Perspectives on Human Development

Perspective	Important Theories	Basic Propositions
Psychoanalytic	Freud's psychosexual theory Erikson's psychosocial theory	■ Behaviour is controlled by powerful unconscious urges. ■ Personality is influenced by society and develops through a series of crises.
Learning	Behaviourism, or traditional learning theory (Pavlov, Skinner, Watson)	■ People are responders; the environment controls behaviour.
	Social learning (social cognitive) theory (Bandura)	■ Children learn in a social context by observing and imitating models. ■ Children are active contributors to learning.
Cognitive	Piaget's cognitive-stage theory	■ Qualitative changes in thought occur between infancy and adolescence. ■ Children are active initiators of development.
	Vygotsky's socio-cultural theory	■ Social interaction is central to cognitive development.
	Information-processing theory	■ Human beings are processors of symbols.
Contextual	Bronfenbrenner's bioecological theory	■ Development occurs through interaction between a developing person and five surrounding, interlocking contextual systems of influences, from microsystem to chronosystem.
Evolutionary/ Sociobiological	Bowlby's attachment theory	■ Human beings have the adaptive mechanisms to survive; critical or sensitive periods are stressed; evolutionary and biological bases for behaviour and predisposition toward learning are important.

the establishment of intimate relationships; and the path of normal development from an immature, dependent state to a mature, interdependent one. In all these ways, Freud left an indelible mark on psychoanalysis and developmental psychology (Westen, 1998).

Erik Erikson: Psychosocial Development

Erik Erikson (1902–1994) modified and extended Freudian theory by emphasizing the influence of society on the developing personality. He is notable in that he was one of the first theorists to emphasize the lifespan perspective.

Erikson's (1950) theory of **psychosocial development** covers eight stages across the lifespan (see Table 1.4). Each stage involves what Erikson originally called a "crisis" in personality—a major psychosocial theme that is particularly important at that time.

Each stage requires the balancing of a positive trait and a corresponding negative one. The critical theme of infancy, for example, is basic trust versus basic mistrust. People need to trust the world and the people in it, but they also need to learn some mistrust to protect themselves from danger. Successful

psychosocial development   In Erikson's eight-stage theory, the socially and culturally influenced process of development of the ego, or self.

> "Children love and want to be loved and they very much prefer the joy of accomplishment to the triumph of hateful failure."
> –Erik Erikson

resolution of one crisis produces a "virtue" or personal strength like hope that puts the child in a particularly good position to address the next crisis, a process that occurs iteratively across the lifespan.

WHAT DO YOU DO?

Child Clinical Psychologist

Child clinical psychologists work directly with children of all ages to help identify and manage mental and behavioural disorders and to overcome traumatic events. For example, parents might be referred to a child clinical psychologist if their toddler was having developmental delays, or if they were divorcing and wanted to provide additional support for their children. A child clinical psychologist might also conduct research or work together with social workers. Child clinical psychologists typically work out of hospitals, private practices, or schools. Becoming a child clinical psychologist typically requires a doctoral degree, which includes an internship. To learn more about what a child clinical psychologist does, visit www.cpa.ca.

Technique Used	Stage-Oriented	Causal Emphasis	Active or Reactive Individual
Clinical observation	Yes	Innate factors modified by experience	Reactive
Clinical observation	Yes	Interaction of innate and experiential factors	Active
Rigorous scientific (experimental) procedures	No	Experience	Reactive
Rigorous scientific (experimental) procedures	No	Experience modified by innate factors	Active and reactive
Flexible interviews; meticulous observation	Yes	Interaction of innate and experiential factors	Active
Cross-cultural research; observation of child interacting with more competent person	No	Experience	Active
Laboratory research; technological monitoring of physiologic responses	No	Interaction of innate and experiential factors	Active
Naturalistic observation and analysis	No	Interaction of innate and experiential factors	Active
Naturalistic and laboratory observation	No	Interaction of innate and experiential factors	Active and reactive (theorists vary)

Erikson's theory is important because of its emphasis on social and cultural influences, on the positive strengths inherent in development, and on development beyond adolescence.

PERSPECTIVE 2: LEARNING

The predominant orientation within the field of psychology in the 1950s was the **learning perspective**. This theoretical approach was an attempt to make psychology an objective science, and as such, the focus was on observable behaviours that could be quantified. Two of the major subtheories were behaviourism and the social learning approach.

Learning Theory 1: Behaviourism

Behaviourism is an approach within psychology that is centred on the observation of behaviours and the belief in the strong influence of the environment. Behaviourists hold that human beings at all ages learn about the world by reacting to aspects of their environment that they find pleasing, painful, or threatening, and that these processes govern learning in all areas of development in the same way. Behavioural research focuses on associative learning, in which a mental link is formed between two events. Two kinds of associative learning are classical conditioning and operant conditioning.

CLASSICAL CONDITIONING   Ivan Pavlov (1849–1936) was a Russian physiologist who was studying the role of saliva in dogs' digestive processes. Pavlov's dogs were presented with meat powder in order to get them to salivate. Pavlov noticed that his dogs began to salivate when they heard clicking noises produced by the device that distributed the meat powder and, later as he tested out his ideas, a bell. This occurred before the meat powder was even presented. This accidental breakthrough was the foundation for the discovery of **classical conditioning**, a type of learning in which a response (salivation) to a stimulus (a bell) is elicited after repeated association with a stimulus that normally elicits the response (food).

American behaviourist John B. Watson (1878–1958) applied stimulus-response theories to children, claiming that he could mould any infant in any way he chose. In one of the earliest and most famous demonstrations of classical conditioning in human beings, he taught an 11-month-old baby known as "Little Albert" to fear a furry white rat (Watson & Rayner, 1920).

In this study, Albert was exposed to a loud noise when he started to stroke the rat. The noise frightened him, and he began to cry. After repeated pairings of the rat with the loud noise, Albert whimpered with fear when he saw the rat. Moreover, Albert also started showing fear responses to white rabbits and cats, and the beards of elderly men. Although the study would be considered highly unethical

learning perspective   View of human development that holds that changes in behaviour result from experience.

behaviourism   Learning theory that emphasizes the predictable role of environment in causing observable behaviour.

classical conditioning   Learning based on association of a stimulus that does not ordinarily elicit a particular response with another stimulus that does elicit the response.

TABLE 1.4 Developmental Stages According to Freud, Erikson, and Piaget

Psychosexual Stages (Freud)	Psychosocial Stages (Erikson)	Cognitive Stages (Piaget)
Oral *(birth to 12–18 months)*. Baby's chief source of pleasure involves mouth-oriented activities (sucking and feeding).	**Basic trust versus mistrust** *(birth to 12–18 months)*. Baby develops sense of whether world is a good and safe place. Virtue: hope.	**Sensorimotor** *(birth to 2 years)*. Infant gradually becomes able to organize activities in relation to the environment through sensory and motor activity.
Anal *(12–18 months to 3 years)*. Child derives sensual gratification from withholding and expelling feces. Zone of gratification is anal region, and toilet training is important activity.	**Autonomy versus shame and doubt** *(12–18 months to 3 years)*. Child develops a balance of independence and self-sufficiency over shame and doubt. Virtue: will.	**Preoperational** *(2 to 7 years)*. Child develops a representational system and uses symbols to represent people, places, and events. Language and imaginative play are important manifestations of this stage. Thinking is still not logical.
Phallic *(3 to 6 years)*. Child becomes attached to parent of the other sex and later identifies with same-sex parent. Superego develops. Zone of gratification shifts to genital region.	**Initiative versus guilt** *(3 to 6 years)*. Child develops initiative when trying out new activities and is not overwhelmed by guilt. Virtue: purpose.	
Latency *(6 years to puberty)*. Time of relative calm between more turbulent states.	**Industry versus inferiority** *(6 years to puberty)*. Child must learn skills of the culture or face feelings of incompetence. Virtue: skill.	**Concrete operations** *(7 to 11 years)*. Child can solve problems logically if they are focused on the here and now but cannot think abstractly.
Genital *(puberty through adulthood)*. Re-emergence of sexual impulses of phallic stage, channelled into mature adult sexuality.	**Identity versus identity confusion** *(puberty to young adulthood)*. Adolescent must determine sense of self ("Who am I?") or experience confusion about roles. Virtue: fidelity.	**Formal operations** *(11 years through adulthood)*. Person can think abstractly, deal with hypothetical situations, and think about possibilities.
	Intimacy versus isolation *(young adulthood)*. Person seeks to make commitments to others; if unsuccessful, may suffer from isolation and self-absorption. Virtue: love.	
	Generativity versus stagnation *(middle adulthood)*. Mature adult is concerned with establishing and guiding the next generation or else feels personal impoverishment. Virtue: care.	
	Integrity versus despair *(late adulthood)*. Elderly person achieves acceptance of own life, allowing acceptance of death, or else despairs over inability to relive life. Virtue: wisdom.	

Note: All ages are approximate.

> *"Give me a dozen healthy infants, well-formed, and my own specified world to bring them up in and I'll guarantee to take any one at random and train him to become any type of specialist I might select—doctor, lawyer, artist, merchant-chief and yes, even beggar-man and thief, regardless of his talents, penchants, tendencies, abilities, vocations, and race of his ancestors."*
> —John Watson

today, it did demonstrate that a baby could be conditioned to fear something he or she had not been afraid of before.

OPERANT CONDITIONING Angel lies in his crib. When he starts to babble ("ma-ma-ma"), his mother smiles and repeats the syllables. Angel learns that his behaviour (babbling) can produce a desirable consequence (loving attention from a parent), and so he learns to keep babbling to attract his mother's attention. An unintentional (or originally accidental) behaviour (babbling) becomes an operant behaviour, increasing in frequency because it elicits something pleasurable (parental attention) from the environment.

This type of learning is called **operant conditioning**. The individual learns from the consequences of "operating"

operant conditioning Learning based on association of behaviour with its consequences.

on the environment. Unlike classical conditioning, operant conditioning involves voluntary behaviour, such as Angel's babbling, and involves the consequences of behaviour.

American psychologist B. F. Skinner (1904–1990), who formulated the principles of operant conditioning, found that an organism will tend to repeat a response that has been reinforced by desirable consequences and will suppress a response that has been punished. Thus, **reinforcement** is the process by which a behaviour is strengthened, increasing the likelihood that the behaviour will be repeated. In Angel's case, his mother's attention reinforces his babbling. **Punishment** is the process by which a behaviour is weakened, decreasing the likelihood of repetition. If Angel's mother frowned when he babbled, he would be less likely to babble again. While Skinnerian psychology is good at describing learned associations such as this, it is limited in application because it does not adequately address individual differences, cultural and social influences, or other aspects of human development that can be attributed to a combination of factors.

Learning Theory 2: Social Learning (Social Cognitive) Theory

Canadian-born psychologist Albert Bandura (b. 1925) developed many of the principles of **social learning theory** in which behaviours are learned by observation. Whereas behaviourists see the environment as the chief impetus for development, Bandura (1977, 1989) suggests that the impetus for development is bidirectional. Bandura called this concept **reciprocal determinism**—the child acts on the world as the world acts on the child.

Classic social learning theory maintains that people learn appropriate social behaviour chiefly by observing and imitating models—that is, by watching other people and learning both about what potential behaviours might be, as well as learning about the likely consequences of such behaviours. This process is called **observational learning**, or modelling. Observational learning can occur even if a person does not imitate the observed behaviour.

Bandura's (1989) updated version of social learning theory is social cognitive theory. The change of name reflects a greater emphasis on cognitive processes as central to development. Cognitive processes are at work as people observe models, learn "chunks" of behaviour, and mentally put the chunks together into complex, new behaviour patterns. Rita, for example, imitates the toes-out walk of her dance teacher but models her dance steps after those of Carmen, a slightly more advanced student. Even so, she develops her own style of dancing by putting her observations together into a new pattern. As children experience success in areas of functioning, they also begin to develop a sense of **self-efficacy**, or confidence in their abilities.

PERSPECTIVE 3: COGNITIVE

Where behaviourists were reluctant to study the inner workings of the mind, believing that events that were not directly observable could not be viewed through a scientific lens, cognitive psychologists argued that this **cognitive perspective** is exactly what should be illuminated by research. In the following section, we discuss Piaget's cognitive theory, Vygotsky's socio-cultural theory, and the information-processing approach to cognition.

Jean Piaget's Cognitive-Stage Theory

Our understanding of how children think owes a great deal to the work of Swiss theoretician Jean Piaget (1896–1980). Piaget, a biologist and philosopher by training, viewed development as the product of children's active efforts to understand and act on their world.

Piaget suggested that cognitive development is initially based on motor activities such as reflexes. By rooting for a nipple, feeling a pebble, or exploring the boundaries of a room, young children first learn how to control and refine their movements, and then learn how to explore their world with their bodies. In this way, they develop a more accurate understanding of their surroundings and greater competence in dealing with them. This cognitive growth occurs through three interrelated processes: organization, adaptation, and equilibration.

> *"Coping with the demands of everyday life would be exceedingly trying if one could arrive at solutions to problems only by actually performing possible options and suffering the consequences."*
> –Albert Bandura

reinforcement In operant conditioning, a process that increases the likelihood that a behaviour will be repeated.

punishment In operant conditioning, a process that decreases the likelihood that a behaviour will be repeated.

social learning theory Theory that behaviours also are learned by observing and imitating models. Also called *social cognitive theory*.

reciprocal determinism Bandura's term for bidirectional forces that affect development.

observational learning Learning through watching the behaviour of others.

self-efficacy Sense of one's capability to master challenges and achieve goals.

cognitive perspective Perspective that looks at the development of mental processes such as thinking.

Organization is the tendency to create categories, such as birds, by observing the characteristics that individual members of a category, such as sparrows and cardinals, have in common. According to Piaget, people create increasingly complex cognitive structures called **schemes**, or ways of organizing information about the world. These schemes can be either motor or mental in nature. Take sucking, for example. A newborn infant has a simple scheme for sucking but soon develops varied schemes for how to suck at the breast, a bottle, or a thumb. The infant may have to open her mouth wider, or turn her head to the side, or suck with varying strength.

Adaptation is Piaget's term for how children handle new information in light of what they already know. Adaptation occurs through two complementary processes: (1) **assimilation**, taking in new information and incorporating it into existing cognitive structures; and (2) **accommodation**, adjusting one's cognitive structures to fit the new information.

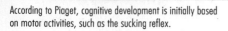

According to Piaget, cognitive development is initially based on motor activities, such as the sucking reflex.

Equilibration—a constant striving for a stable balance—motivates the shift from assimilation to accommodation. For example, a child knows what birds are and sees a plane for the first time. The child labels the plane a "bird" (assimilation). Over time, the child notes differences between planes and birds, which makes her somewhat uneasy (disequilibrium) and motivates her to change her understanding (accommodation) and provide a new label for the plane. She then is at equilibrium. Throughout life, the quest for equilibrium is the driving force behind cognitive growth.

Piaget's **cognitive-stage theory** described cognitive development as occurring in four qualitative stages (listed in Table 1.4 and discussed in detail in later chapters). At each stage, a child's mind develops a new way of operating. From infancy through adolescence, mental operations evolve from learning based on simple sensory and motor activity to logical, abstract thought. An implication of this view is that children's minds are not just miniature adult minds. Children think, fundamentally, in a different manner than adults do.

While Piaget was profoundly influential in the field and provided a series of rough but useful benchmarks of development, he underestimated the abilities of infants and young children. Some contemporary psychologists question his distinct stages, pointing to evidence that cognitive development is more gradual and continuous (Courage & Howe, 2002). Others have pointed out that children's cognitive processes seem closely tied to specific content (what they are thinking about), as well as to the context of a problem and the kinds of information and thought a culture considers important (Case & Okamoto, 1996). We explore further critiques of Piaget's work in the chapters that follow.

Lev Vygotsky's Socio-Cultural Theory

Russian psychologist Lev Semenovich Vygotsky (1896–1934) focused on the social and cultural processes that guide children's cognitive development. Vygotsky's **socio-cultural theory** saw cognitive growth as a collaborative process. Children, said Vygotsky, learn through social interaction and shared activities. Rather than believing in universal aspects of development, Vygotsky believed that there are as many ways to develop as there are different cultures and different experiences.

> *"Through others, we become ourselves."*
> *–Lev Vygotsky*

> *"The principal goal of education in the schools should be creating men and women who are capable of doing new things, not simply repeating what other generations have done."*
> *–Jean Piaget*

organization Piaget's term for the creation of categories or systems of knowledge.

schemes Piaget's term for organized patterns of thought and behaviour used in particular situations.

adaptation Piaget's term for adjustment to new information about the environment.

assimilation Piaget's term for incorporation of new information into an existing cognitive structure.

accommodation Piaget's term for changes in a cognitive structure to include new information.

equilibration Piaget's term for the tendency to seek a stable balance among cognitive elements; achieved through a balance between assimilation and accommodation.

cognitive-stage theory Piaget's theory that children's cognitive development advances in a series of four stages involving qualitatively distinct types of mental operations.

socio-cultural theory Vygotsky's theory of how contextual factors affect children's development.

Vygotsky has been credited with drawing attention not to just what a person knows at any one particular time but also to what they could know with help. Do you agree with this perspective? And does this mean then that traditional intelligence tests, which assess knowledge already learned, are measuring the wrong thing?

According to Vygotsky, adults or more advanced peers must help direct and organize a child's learning. This guidance is most effective in helping children cross the **zone of proximal development (ZPD)**, the imaginary psychological space between what children can do on their own and what they could achieve with assistance from another person. Over time, as a child's abilities increase, responsibility for directing and monitoring learning gradually shifts from the adult to the child— much as when an adult teaches a child to float, the adult first supports the child in the water and then lets go gradually as the child's body relaxes into a horizontal position. This temporary support that parents, teachers, or others give a child is known as **scaffolding**.

Vygotsky's theory has important implications for education and for cognitive testing. Tests that focus on a child's potential for learning provide a valuable alternative to standard intelligence tests that assess what the child has already learned, and many children may benefit from the sort of expert guidance Vygotsky prescribes.

The Information-Processing Approach

The **information-processing approach** seeks to explain cognitive development by analyzing the processes involved in making sense of incoming information and performing tasks effectively. The information-processing approach is not a single theory but is best viewed as a framework that undergirds a wide range of theories and research.

The most common model for this theory is that of a computer. There are certain inputs (such as sensory impressions) and certain outputs (such as behaviours). Information-processing theorists are interested in what happens in the middle. How does the brain use sensations and perceptions, say, of an unfamiliar word, to recognize that word again? Why does the same input sometimes result in different outputs? How do people gather, store, retrieve, and use information?

Information-processing theorists view development as continuous. They note age-related increases in the speed, complexity, and efficiency of mental processing and in the amount and variety of material that can be stored in memory.

The information-processing approach has taught us a great deal about the mechanics of how the mind works.

It has also demonstrated that we *can* access cognitive processes, even though they are internal.

PERSPECTIVE 4: CONTEXTUAL

According to the **contextual perspective**, development can be understood only in its social context. Contextualists see the individual not as a separate entity interacting with the environment but as an inseparable part of it. Vygotsky's socio-cultural theory, which we discussed as part of the cognitive perspective, also can be classified as contextual.

American psychologist Urie Bronfenbrenner's (1917–2005) **bioecological theory** (1979, 1986, 1994; Bronfenbrenner & Morris, 1998) identifies five levels of environmental influence, ranging from very intimate to very broad: microsystem, mesosystem, exosystem, macrosystem, and chronosystem (Figure 1.4).

According to Bronfenbrenner, a person is not merely an outcome of development but a shaper of it. People affect their own development through their biological and psychological characteristics, talents and skills, disabilities, and temperament.

By looking at systems that affect individuals in and beyond the family, this bioecological approach helps us to see the variety of influences on development. The contextual perspective also reminds us that findings about the development of children in one culture or one group within a culture (such as white, middle-class Canadians) may not apply equally to children in other societies or cultural groups.

> *"Development, it turns out, occurs through this process of progressively more complex exchange between a child and somebody else—especially somebody who's crazy about that child."*
> *–Urie Bronfenbrenner*

zone of proximal development (ZPD) Vygotsky's term for the difference between what a child can do alone and what the child can do with help.

scaffolding Temporary support to help a child master a task.

information-processing approach Approach to the study of cognitive development by observing and analyzing the mental processes involved in perceiving and handling information.

contextual perspective View of child development that sees the individual as inseparable from the social context.

bioecological theory Bronfenbrenner's approach to understanding processes and contexts of child development that identifies five levels of environmental influence.

Bronfenbrenner's Bioecological Theory

FIGURE 1.4 Concentric circles show five levels of environmental influence on the individual, from the most intimate environment (the microsystem) to the broadest (the chronosystem)—all within the perpendicular dimension of time.

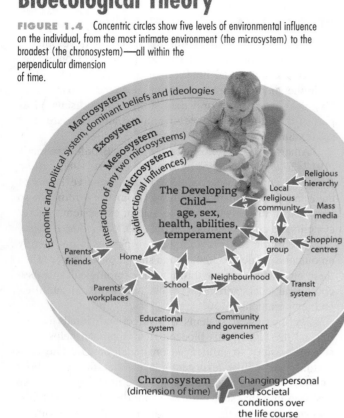

Macrosystem
Economic and political system, dominant beliefs and ideologies
Exosystem
Mesosystem
(interaction of any two microsystems)
Microsystem
(bidirectional influences)

The Developing Child— age, sex, health, abilities, temperament

Religious hierarchy
Local religious community
Mass media
Parents' friends
Home
Peer group
Shopping centres
Parents' workplaces
School
Neighbourhood
Transit system
Educational system
Community and government agencies

Chronosystem (dimension of time)
Changing personal and societal conditions over the life course

Source: Kopp, Claire B./Krakow, Joanne B., *The Child: Development in Social Context*, 1st, © 1982. Printed and Electronically reproduced by permission of Pearson Education, Inc., Upper Saddle River, New Jersey. This figure was adapted from Urie Bronfenbrenner, *The Ecology of Human Development: Experiments by Nature and Design.* Reprinted by permission of Harvard University Press.

PERSPECTIVE 5: EVOLUTIONARY/ SOCIOBIOLOGICAL PERSPECTIVES

The **evolutionary/sociobiological perspective** originally proposed by E. O. Wilson (1975) focuses on evolutionary and biological bases of behaviour. Influenced by Darwin's theory of evolution, it draws on findings of anthropology, ecology, genetics, ethology, and evolutionary psychology

> *"In the distant future I see open fields for more important researches. Psychology will be based on a new foundation, that of the necessary acquirement of each mental power and capacity by gradation."*
> *—Charles Darwin*

to explain the adaptive, or survival, value of behaviour for an individual or species.

According to Darwin, species have developed through natural selection. Individuals with heritable traits that are well adapted to those environments survive and reproduce at higher rates than individuals less well adapted to their environments. Thus, through differential reproduction success (that is, "survival of the fittest"), individuals with more adaptive characteristics pass on more of their traits to future generations. In this way, "fit" characteristics are selected and are passed on, while others die out. Over vast spans of time, this results in the development of new species.

Traits can be physical, behavioural, and psychological in nature. *Evolved mechanisms* are behaviours that developed to solve adaptive problems. For example, aversion to certain foods during the first trimester of pregnancy, when the fetus is most vulnerable, may originally have evolved to protect the fetus from toxic substances (Flaxman & Sherman, 2008). Such evolved mechanisms may survive even though they no longer serve a useful purpose or they may evolve further in response to changing environmental conditions. Although most evolved mechanisms are tailored to a specific problem, others, such as human intelligence, are viewed as having evolved to help people face a wide range of problems (MacDonald, 1998).

Ethology is the study of the distinctive adaptive behaviours of animal species. Ethologists suggest that for each species, certain innate behaviours, such as squirrels' burying of nuts in the fall, spiders' spinning of webs, and human infants' attachment to their caregivers, have evolved to increase the odds of survival. By observing animals (and humans), usually in their natural surroundings and often comparing across different species, ethologists seek to identify which behaviours are universal and which are specific to a particular species or are modified by culture.

Evolutionary psychology applies Darwinian principles to human behaviour. Just as we have a heart that evolved to pump blood and lungs that evolved to exchange gasses, we also have parts of our brains that evolved to solve particular adaptive problems. So, for example, our brains are designed by natural selection to view certain faces as attractive, to strive for dominance, and to find babies cute. While certainly the environment has an effect on us as well, these inborn perceptions and motivations help us make decisions about our behaviours that, over time, generally result in greater survival or reproduction.

evolutionary/sociobiological perspective View of human development that focuses on evolutionary and biological bases of social behaviour.

ethology Study of distinctive adaptive behaviours of species of animals that have evolved to increase survival of the species.

evolutionary psychology Application of Darwinian principles of natural selection and survival of the fittest to human psychology.

13. A theory is
   a. an observation of something.
   b. a proven fact.
   c. a description or explanation of an observed phenomena.
   d. a statistical relationship between two variables.

14. If I believe that you are experiencing anxiety as an adult because your mother was rigid and stingy in her breastfeeding practices with you, I am probably a _____ theorist.

15. When my dog gets into the garbage can, I yell at him and tell him he is a bad dog. This is an example of _____ and is drawn from the _____ theoretical approach.

   a. adaptation; cognitive
   b. punishment; behaviourist
   c. gratification of an urge; psychoanalytic
   d. cross-species comparison; ethological

16. Three-year-old Ava has never seen a zebra before. On a visit to the zoo, she points to a zebra and says, "horse!" Ava has just engaged in
   a. the ZPD.
   b. accommodation.
   c. equilibrium.
   d. assimilation.

17. Bronfenbrenner would call the societal changes that were the result of the women's movement part of the
   a. microsystem.
   b. mesosystem.
   c. exosystem.
   d. macrosystem.
   e. chronosystem.

18. An evolutionary psychologist would be most interested in studying which of the following?

   a. What is the relationship between television viewing and body image?
   b. How does your early relationship with your opposite sex parent impact later romantic relationships?
   c. How do physical attractiveness and amount of resources impact a man's versus a woman's likelihood of dating a person?
   d. How does neighbourhood composition influence child development?

In naturalistic observation, a researcher might collect data by observing real-world events, such as a teacher interacting with schoolchildren.

Evolutionary psychology is one of the most controversial perspectives within the field of psychology. Do you think evolution can explain animal behaviour? Can it explain human psychology? Is there a qualitative difference between the two?

Research Methods

Theories help frame our thinking—they tell us what is important, where to look for it, and how to study it. Theories generate **hypotheses**, or educated guesses that can be tested by further research. Sometimes, research supports a hypothesis and the theory on which it was based. At other times, scientists must modify their theories to account for unexpected data. This process is known as the *scientific method* (Figure 1.5). In the following section, we review some of the major ways in which researchers collect such data and design their experiments.

FORMS OF DATA COLLECTION

The three forms of data collection most frequently used by development researchers are self-reports, including diaries, visual techniques, interviews, and questionnaires; naturalistic and laboratory observation; and performance measures.

Self-Reports

A self-report involves asking people for information. In studying young children, parental self-reports—diaries, journals, interviews, or questionnaires—are commonly used, often together with other methods, such as videotaping or recording.

hypotheses Possible explanations for phenomena, used to predict the outcome of research.

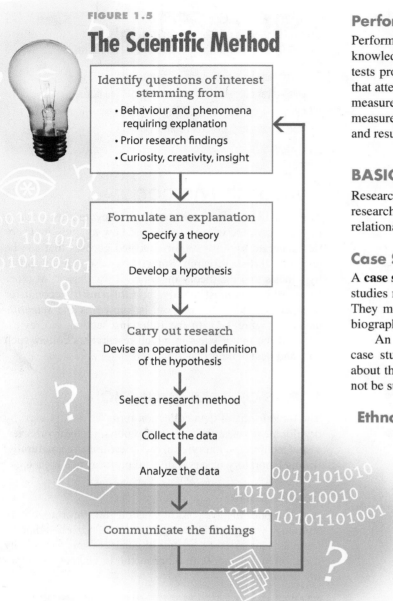

FIGURE 1.5

The Scientific Method

Identify questions of interest stemming from
- Behaviour and phenomena requiring explanation
- Prior research findings
- Curiosity, creativity, insight

↓

Formulate an explanation

Specify a theory

↓

Develop a hypothesis

↓

Carry out research

Devise an operational definition of the hypothesis

↓

Select a research method

↓

Collect the data

↓

Analyze the data

↓

Communicate the findings

Source: From p. 28 in Feldman, *Essentials of Understanding Psychology*, 8th Ed. Copyright © 2009 by The McGraw-Hill Companies, Inc. Reprinted by permission.

Self-report measures can be meaningful and useful only if they are both valid (that is, the tests measure the abilities they claim to measure) and reliable (that is, the results are reasonably consistent from one time to another). Additionally, any characteristics to be measured must be carefully operationalized—that is, defined solely in terms of the operations or procedures used to produce or measure a phenomenon.

Naturalistic and Laboratory Observation

Observation can take two forms: naturalistic observation and laboratory observation. In **naturalistic observation**, researchers look at or video-record children in real-life settings. In **laboratory observation**, researchers observe and record behaviour in a controlled situation.

Performance Measures

Performance measures are tasks that reflect abilities, skills, knowledge, competencies, or physical responses. These tests provide objectively measurable information in a way that attempts to avoid subjective distortions. However, such measures have limitations, as they are difficult to use to measure attitudes or other non-behavioural phenomena, and results may be affected by extraneous factors.

BASIC RESEARCH DESIGNS

Research designs used most frequently by development researchers include case studies, ethnographic studies, correlational studies, and experiments.

Case Studies

A **case study** is a study of a single case or individual. Case studies may include careful observation and interpretation. They may use behavioural or physiological measures and biographical, autobiographical, or documentary materials.

An advantage of case studies is flexibility. However, case studies do have shortcomings. We can learn much about the development of a single child; however, we cannot be sure the information applies to children in general.

Ethnographic Studies

An **ethnographic study** is like a case study of a culture. An ethnography seeks to describe the pattern of relationships, customs, beliefs, technology, arts, and traditions that make up a society's way of life. It uses a combination of methods, including informal, unstructured interviewing and participant observation. **Participant observation** is a form of naturalistic observation in which researchers live or participate in the societies or smaller groups they observe, as anthropologists often do for long periods of time. Because of ethnographer's close involvement with a culture, findings are especially open to observer bias.

Correlational Studies

A **correlational study** is an attempt to find a correlation, or statistical association, between two or more variables.

---

naturalistic observation Research method in which behaviour is studied in natural settings without intervention or manipulation.

laboratory observation Research method in which all participants are observed under the same controlled conditions.

case study A study of a single subject, such as an individual or a family.

ethnographic study In-depth study of a culture, which uses a variety of methods, including participant observation.

participant observation Research method in which the observer lives with the people or participates in the activity being observed.

correlational study Research design intended to discover whether a statistical relationship between variables exists.

People often have everyday hypotheses about how human psychology works, but it is important to verify them through research. Experimental design has shown that rewards—at least with respect to eating your vegetables—work.

Correlations are expressed in terms of direction (positive or negative) and magnitude (how strong they are). Two variables that are related positively increase or decrease together. For example, the more texting someone engages in while driving, the more likely that person is to get into a car crash. Two variables have a negative, or inverse, correlation if as one increases, the other decreases. Studies show a negative correlation between the amount of time students spend on Facebook and the grades they receive. The more time they are on Facebook, the lower their grades are (Kirschner & Karpinski, 2010).

Correlations are reported as numbers ranging from +1.0 (a perfect positive relationship) to −1.0 (a perfect negative relationship). The closer a correlation comes to +1.0 or −1.0, the stronger the relationship, either positive or negative. A correlation of 0 means that the variables have no relationship (Figure 1.6).

Although strong correlations suggest possible cause-and-effect relationships, these are merely hypotheses and need to be examined and tested very critically. Correlation does not equal causation. It is possible that the causation goes the other way or that a third variable explains the relationship.

Correlational Outcomes

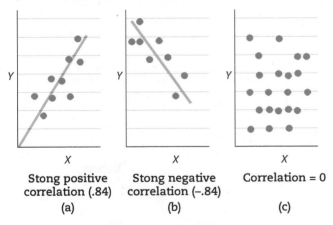

Stong positive correlation (.84)
(a)

Stong negative correlation (−.84)
(b)

Correlation = 0
(c)

FIGURE 1.6 Correlational studies may find positive or negative correlations or no correlation. In a positive, or direct, correlation (a), data plotted on a graph cluster around a line showing that one variable (*X*) increases as the other variable (*Y*) increases. In a negative, or inverse, correlation (b), one variable (*X*) increases as the other variable (*Y*) decreases. No correlation, or a zero correlation (c), exists when increases and decreases in two variables show no consistent relationship (that is, data plotted on a graph show no pattern).

Source: From Fig. 2.4, p. 41 in *A Child's World,* 12th Ed., 2011, by Diane E. Papalia, Sally Wendkos Olds, Ruth Duskin Feldman. Copyright © 2011 by The McGraw-Hill Companies, Inc. Reprinted by permission.

Experiments

While correlational studies are a valuable tool, their inability to establish causal relationships limits their use. Thus, psychologists often use experimental design. The only way to show with certainty that one variable causes another is through experimentation.

GROUPS AND VARIABLES An experiment is a controlled procedure, which allows stronger causal statements to be made. A common way to conduct an experiment is to randomly divide participants into two kinds of groups. An **experimental group** consists of people who are to be exposed to the experimental manipulation or treatment—the phenomenon the researcher wants to study. A **control group** consists of people who are similar to the experimental group but do not receive the treatment or may receive a different treatment. You can think of them as the "status quo"—what would happen if the variable of interest were not there.

For example, in one recent study, researchers were interested in whether giving rewards to children to eat their vegetables is an effective strategy. In their study, roughly 400 4- to 6-year-olds were divided into two experimental groups and one control group. One group was rewarded with a sticker for eating their least favourite vegetable, one group was rewarded with verbal praise, and the control group was given no reward for eating

experimental group In an experiment, the group receiving the treatment under study.

control group In an experiment, a comparison group of people similar to those in the experimental group who do not receive the treatment under study.

their vegetables. The results? After two weeks, the sticker group liked vegetables as much (or as little!) as the control group; however, the sticker group was more likely to eat more vegetables later even in the absence of a reward. The researchers concluded that rewards resulted in increased consumption of vegetables (Cooke et al., 2011).

In this experiment, the type of reward was the independent variable (the conditions were a sticker, verbal praise, or no reward) and the amount of vegetables children ate at the conclusion of the study was the dependent variable. An **independent variable** is something the researcher directly manipulates in order to see if it has an effect on another variable. A **dependent variable** is the end measure that tells researchers if their hypotheses were supported.

LABORATORY, FIELD, AND NATURAL EXPERIMENTS In a laboratory experiment, the participants are brought to a laboratory, where they experience conditions manipulated by the experimenter. This allows researchers to establish cause-and-effect relationships and permits replication. However, not all experiments can be readily done in the laboratory. Sometimes, researchers conduct field experiments, controlled studies conducted in an everyday setting, such as home or school.

When, for practical or ethical reasons, it is impossible to conduct a true experiment, a natural experiment may provide a way of studying certain events. A natural experiment, also called a quasi-experiment, compares people who have been accidentally "assigned" to separate groups by circumstances of life—one group of children who were exposed, say, to famine and another group who were not. A natural experiment, despite its name, is actually a correlational study because controlled manipulation of variables and random assignment to treatment groups are not possible.

DEVELOPMENTAL RESEARCH DESIGNS

The primary task of developmental researchers is to study change over time. But just as there are different theoretical perspectives, there are also different ways of

addressing the nuts and bolts of how this will be done. The two most common research strategies used to study child development are cross-sectional and longitudinal studies (Figure 1.7). Because each of these designs has drawbacks, researchers also have devised sequential designs.

In a **cross-sectional study**, children of different ages are assessed at one time. In one cross-sectional study, researchers presented 3- to 11-year-old children with scenarios depicting a story in which one character copied the ideas of another for a project in art class. At 3 to 4 years of age, children did not judge the copier negatively; however, by about 5 years of age, children judged copiers more negatively. These findings suggest a relatively sophisticated view about intellectual property—that ideas can be stolen (Olson & Shaw, 2010). However, we cannot draw such a conclusion with certainty. We don't know whether the 5-year-olds' awareness of mental activity when they were 3 years old was the same as that of the

independent variable In an experiment, the set of conditions over which the experimenter has direct control.

dependent variable In an experiment, the outcome that the experimenter measures that may or may not change as a result of changes in the independent variable.

cross-sectional study Study designed to assess age-related differences, in which people of different ages are assessed on one occasion.

A Sequential Design

FIGURE 1.7 Two successive cross-sectional groups of 2-, 4-, 6-, and 8-year-olds are tested in 2008 and 2010. Also, a longitudinal study of a group of children first measured in 2008, when they were 2 years old, is followed by a similar longitudinal study of another group of children who were 2 years old in 2010.

Source: From Fig. 2.7, p. 50 in A Child's World, 12th Ed., by Diane E. Papalia, Sally Wendkos Olds, Ruth Duskin Feldman. Copyright © 2011 by The McGraw-Hill Companies, Inc. Reprinted by permission.

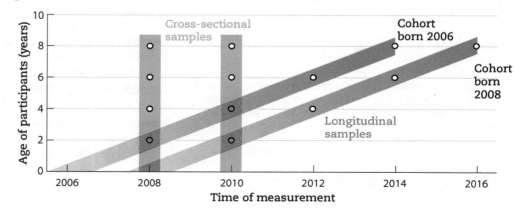

TABLE 1.5 Cross-Sectional, Longitudinal, and Sequential Research

Type of Study	Procedure	Advantages	Disadvantages
Cross-sectional	Data are collected on people of different ages at the same time.	Can show similarities and differences among age groups; is speedy and economical; presents no problem of attrition or repeated testing.	Cannot establish age effects; masks individual differences; can be confounded by cohort effects.
Longitudinal	Data are collected on same person or persons over a period of time.	Can show age-related change or continuity; avoids confounding age with cohort effects.	Is time-consuming and expensive; presents problems of attrition, bias in sample, and effects of repeated testing; results may be valid only for cohort tested or sample studied.
Sequential	Data are collected on successive cross-sectional or longitudinal samples.	Can avoid drawbacks of both cross-sectional and longitudinal designs.	Requires large amount of time and effort and analysis of very complex data.

current 3-year-olds in the study. The only way to see whether change occurs with age is to conduct a longitudinal study of a particular person or group.

In a **longitudinal study**, researchers study the same person or group of people more than once, sometimes years apart. For example, in one study, researchers were interested in whether Internet usage was associated with loneliness and what the patterns over time were. The researchers found that people who were initially lonely and spent more and more time on the Web over the course of a year reported becoming more and more lonely and having lower life satisfaction at the conclusion of the study (Stepanikova, Nie, & He, 2010).

The National Longitudinal Survey of Children and Youth (NLSCY), as another example, has shown that a child's family socio-economic status (SES) has a large influence on later school achievement (Ryan & Adams, 1998). However, the presence of protective factors, such as having close affectionate relationships or authoritative parenting, can reduce the likelihood that a child will develop difficult behaviours (Jenkins & Keating, 1999; Miller, Jenkins, & Keating, 2002).

Both cross-sectional and longitudinal designs have strengths and weaknesses (Table 1.5). The **sequential study** is a complex strategy designed to overcome the drawbacks of longitudinal and cross-sectional research. In this technique, researchers study people of different ages (like cross-sectional) over time (like longitudinal). A combination of cross-sectional and longitudinal sequences (as shown in Figure 1.7) can provide a more complete picture of development than would be possible with either alone.

ETHICS OF RESEARCH

Institutional review boards at colleges, universities, and other institutions that receive federal funding must review proposed research from an ethical standpoint. Guidelines

of the Canadian Psychological Association (2000) cover such issues as informed consent, avoidance of deception, protection of participants from harm and loss of dignity, guarantees of privacy and confidentiality, the right to decline or withdraw from an experiment at any time, and the responsibility of investigators to correct any undesirable effects, such as anxiety or shame.

Three Canadian government research funding bodies—the Social Sciences and Humanities Research Council of Canada (SSHRC), the Natural Sciences and Engineering Research Council of Canada (NSERC), and the Canadian Institutes of Health Research (CIHR)—have developed the *Tri-Council Policy Statement: Ethical Conduct for Research Involving Humans*, a policy on ethical conduct for research involving humans (Adair, 2001; CIHR, NSERC, & SSHRC, 2010), which has been adopted by universities across Canada. The policy is based on principles of ethics that include, in addition to those listed above, protection of vulnerable persons. Information about this policy is available online at www.nserc.ca.

Right to Informed Consent

Informed consent exists when participants voluntarily agree to be in a study, are competent to give consent, are aware of the risks as well as the potential benefits, and are not being exploited. The National Commission for the Protection of Human Subjects of Biomedical and Behavioral Research (1978) recommends that children ages 7 or over be asked to give their consent to take part in research and that any children's objections should be overruled only if the research promises direct benefit to the child.

---

longitudinal study Study designed to assess changes in a sample over time.

sequential study Study design that combines cross-sectional and longitudinal designs.

Avoidance of Deception

Ethical guidelines call for withholding information only when it is essential to the study; and even then investigators should avoid methods that could cause pain, anxiety, or harm. Participants should be debriefed afterward to let them know the true nature of the study and why deception was necessary and to make sure they have not suffered as a result.

Right to Privacy and Confidentiality

Research participants need to know that their information will be kept private and that their responses are confidential. However, there are cases in which researchers are obligated to breach confidentiality—such as when an investigator discovers signs of abuse. Thus, researchers need to inform participants of their legal responsibility to report abuse or neglect or any other illegal activity of which they become aware, and confidentiality must be guarded otherwise.

Research with Children

Researchers in child development must consider children's developmental needs (CIHR et al., 2010; Thompson, 1990), as well as rights of participants, which include informed consent (from parents, and verbal agreement to participate from children). Even research that seems to involve minimal risk may be too risky for a particular child or at a particular level of development. Age-appropriate standards for the treatment of children in research need to be developed; for example, infants' and very young children's ability to cope with the stress of the research situation may hinge on the presence of a parent or trusted caregiver, a familiar setting and procedure, and familiar objects.

Research with Diverse Populations

Developmental researchers working in most locations in Canada inevitably work with children who are new immigrants to the country and individuals who are members of ethnic minorities. In making decisions about the methods and materials they use, researchers must be sensitive to their participants' characteristics to ensure that the dignity of those individuals are protected, over and above the protections set in place for members of the majority culture. In Canada and elsewhere, Aboriginal peoples have distinctive perspectives embodied in their cultures and histories. The *Tri-Council Policy Statement* recognizes that Aboriginal peoples' heritage, customs, and community interests must be safeguarded. Researchers must recognize historical reasons why some Aboriginal participants might feel apprehensive in taking part in research. In conducting research with Aboriginal children, researchers must work in respectful ways that ensure that research results do not promote inaccurate or insensitive interpretations that have in the past contributed to the stigmatization of Aboriginal communities. For example, treating Aboriginal groups simply as sources of data could have negative repercussions for the well-being of the community, if the data were used inappropriately. Language differences and differences in values should be recognized and respected, and care must be taken to interpret the meaning of those differences appropriately in how they influence the results of research (CIHR et al., 2010).

Ask Yourself

19. A study in which a researcher collects questionnaire data on exercise and health is probably a _____ study, while a study in which a researcher interviews people about why they do or do not exercise is probably a _____ study.

20. I believe that taking vitamins leads to increases in energy. So I design a study in which my experimental group gets a vitamin and my control group gets a placebo. Then I assess both groups on how energetic they feel. What is my independent variable?

    a. the vitamin
    b. the placebo
    c. the dose (that is, the vitamin or the placebo)
    d. levels of energy

21. Susan takes a photo of her daughter every year on her birthday. Which developmental research design is this most similar to?

    a. cross-sectional
    b. longitudinal
    c. sequential
    d. correlational

22. If I am conducting research with a young child who becomes scared and screams, "no, no, no!" while I am trying to conduct data, and I back off and decide not to continue with the experiment, I am illustrating concern with the principle of _____.

SUMMARY

INTRODUCTION TO CHILD DEVELOPMENT

LO1

Describe how development is conceptualized.

- Child development is the scientific study of processes of change and stability.
- The concept of periods of development is a social construction. In this book, child development is divided into five periods: the prenatal period, infancy and toddlerhood, early childhood, middle childhood, and adolescence. In each period, children have characteristic developmental needs and tasks.
- The three major domains, or aspects, of development are physical, cognitive, and psychosocial. Each affects the others.

LO2

Summarize how individual differences, contexts, and the timing of influences affect development.

- Influences on development come from both heredity and environment. Many typical changes during childhood are related to maturation. Individual differences increase with age.
- In some societies, the nuclear family predominates; in others, the extended family. Socio-economic status (SES) affects developmental processes and outcomes through the quality of home and neighbourhood environments, nutrition, medical care, supervision, and schooling. Multiple risk factors increase the likelihood of poor outcomes. Important environmental influences stem from ethnicity, culture, and historical context. In large, multiethnic societies, immigrant groups often acculturate to the majority culture while preserving aspects of their own.
- Influences may be normative (age-graded or history-graded) or non-normative.
- There is strong evidence of critical periods for certain kinds of early development.

LO3

Summarize the recurrent philosophical issues of and points of consensus in the study of development.

- Developmental scientists study the relative importance of heredity, the environment, and especially the interaction between the two as influences on development.
- Developmental scientists study developmental change as internally driven, or as passive responses to stimuli in the environment.
- Developmental scientists study developmental change, both quantitative and qualitative, as well as stability of personality and behaviour.
- Consensus has emerged on several important points: (1) the interrelationship of domains of development, (2) the existence of a wide range of individual differences, (3) the bidirectionality of influence, (4) the importance of history and culture, (5) children's potential for resilience, and (6) the continuity of development throughout life.

LO4

Describe the major theoretical approaches.

- A theory is used to explain data and generate hypotheses that can be tested by research.
- Developmental theories differ on three basic issues: the relative importance of heredity and environment, the active or passive character of development, and the existence of stages of development.
- The psychoanalytic perspective sees development as motivated by unconscious emotional drives or conflicts. Leading examples are Freud's and Erikson's theories.
- The learning perspective views development as a result of learning based on experience. Leading examples are Watson's and Skinner's behaviourism and Bandura's social learning theory.
- The cognitive perspective is concerned with thought processes. Leading examples are Piaget's cognitive-stage theory, the information-processing approach, and Vygotsky's socio-cultural approach that spans cognitive and contextual perspectives.
- The contextual perspective focuses on interaction between the individual and the social context. Leading examples are Bronfenbrenner's and Vygotsky's theories.
- The evolutionary/sociobiological perspective, represented by Wilson, describes adaptive behaviours that promote group survival.

LO5

Discuss the primary means of data collection and methodologies used in developmental research.

- To arrive at sound conclusions, researchers use the scientific method.
- Three forms of data collection are self-reports (diaries, journals, interviews, and questionnaires), naturalistic and laboratory observation, and performance measures.
- Four basic designs used in developmental research are the case study, ethnographic study, correlational study, and experiment. Only experiments can firmly establish causal relationships. Cross-cultural research can indicate whether certain aspects of development are universal or culturally influenced. Experiments must be rigorously controlled in order to be valid and replicable. Random assignment of participants can ensure validity. Laboratory experiments are easiest to control and replicate, but findings of field experiments may be more generalizable beyond the study situation. Natural experiments may be useful in situations in which true experiments would be impractical or unethical.
- The two most common designs used to study age-related development are longitudinal and cross-sectional. Cross-sectional studies compare age groups; longitudinal studies describe continuity or change in the same participants. The sequential study is intended to overcome the weaknesses of the other two designs.
- Ethical issues in research on child development involve the rights of participants to informed consent and avoidance of deception, protection from harm and loss of dignity, and guarantees of privacy and confidentiality.

ANSWERS TO Ask Yourself

connect **LEARNSMART** **SMARTBOOK**

For more information on the resources available from McGraw-Hill Ryerson, go to **www.mcgrawhill.ca/he/solutions**.

CONCEPTION, HEREDITY, AND ENVIRONMENT

WHAT'S TO COME

Conception and Infertility

Mechanisms of Heredity

Genetic and Chromosomal Abnormalities

Studying the Influence of Heredity and Environment

Characteristics Influenced by Heredity and Environment

Before Tania and Paul were married, they talked about having children one day but agreed to wait until they were financially and emotionally secure as a couple before starting a family. After three years of marriage, they decided they were ready for parenthood. Tania carefully watched the calendar, counting the days after each menstrual period to take advantage of her "fertile window." When after two months Tania had not yet become pregnant, she wondered what possibly might have gone wrong. What she and Paul didn't realize is that although a woman is usually fertile between the 6th and 21st days of the menstrual cycle, the timing of the fertile window can be highly unpredictable (Wilcox, Dunson, & Baird, 2000). This means that although conception is far more likely at certain times, she may be able to conceive at any time during the month. Concurrently, while conception is more likely during certain parts of the month, it may not always occur during that time. Indeed, the average woman takes about six months to conceive.

We begin this chapter by examining how a life is conceived. We consider the mechanisms and patterns of heredity—the inherited factors that affect development—and how genetic counselling can help couples make the decision whether to become parents. Finally, we look at how heredity and environment work together and how their effects on development can be understood.

AS YOU READ

LO1 Summarize how conception occurs and describe alternative paths to parenthood.
LO2 Explain how traits are passed down across generations.
LO3 Describe how abnormalities are transmitted in the genes and the options prospective parents have for testing for them.
LO4 Describe how researchers determine the relative influence of genes and environments, and how these variables interact with each other.
LO5 Summarize how genes affect physical, intellectual, and personality development, as well as psychopathologies.

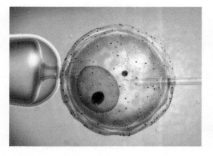

Conception and Infertility

The arrival of a new family member effects an enormous change in the lives of caregivers. It involves sleepless nights and harried days, dirty diapers and stained onesies, and for most parents, an all-encompassing love for the squalling squirming creature now in their care. In the following section, we address the means by which this addition to the family is brought about. For some families, conception occurs easily; for others, artificial reproductive technologies are needed. For still other parents, the arrival of a child occurs via adoption. For all families, however, this is the beginning of a new relationship filled with a multitude of both stressors and joys.

FERTILIZATION

Fertilization, or conception, is the process by which sperm and ovum—the male and female gametes, or sex cells—combine to create a single cell called a **zygote**, which then duplicates itself again and again by cell division to produce all the cells that make up a baby. At birth, a female is believed to have about 2 million immature ova in her two ovaries, each ovum in its own small sac, or follicle. In a sexually mature woman, ovulation occurs about once every 28 days until menopause. After being expelled from the ovary, the ovum is swept along through one of the fallopian tubes by tiny hair cells, called cilia, toward the uterus, or womb.

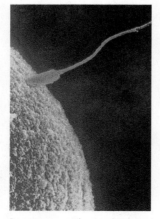
Conception occurs when a male's sperm cell penetrates a female's egg cell.

Sperm are produced in the testicles (testes), or reproductive glands, of a mature male at a rate of several hundred million a day and are ejaculated in the semen at sexual climax. Deposited in the vagina, they try to swim through the cervix (the opening of the uterus) and into the fallopian tubes, but only a tiny fraction make it that far. As we will see, which sperm meets which ovum has tremendous implications for the new person.

Fertilization typically occurs while the ovum is passing through the fallopian tube. If fertilization does not occur, the ovum and any sperm cells in the woman's body die. The sperm are absorbed by the woman's white blood cells, and the ovum passes through the uterus and exits through the vagina.

INFERTILITY

Tania and Paul tried to get pregnant for one long, dispiriting year before seeking assistance from a fertility doctor. At the year mark, they joined the estimated 12 to 16 percent of Canadian couples ages 15 to 44 years who experience **infertility** (Bushnik, Cook, Yuzpe, Tough, & Collins, 2012). After a variety of tests, it was determined that Tania's eggs were of low quality. While her chances of having a baby with her own eggs and her husband's sperm were still relatively good, pregnancy was by no means assured, even with the advances of modern medicine available to prospective parents nowadays.

The most common cause of infertility in men is a low sperm count or insufficiently motile sperm. A sperm count that is lower than 60 million to 200 million per ejaculation makes conception unlikely. Some cases of male infertility

fertilization Union of sperm and ovum to produce a zygote; also called *conception*.

zygote One-celled organism resulting from fertilization.

infertility Inability to conceive after 12 months of trying.

Perspectives on Diversity

FOLK BELIEFS ABOUT CONCEPTION AND FERTILITY

Folk beliefs regarding the origin of new life have been common throughout history. The belief that children came from wells, springs, or rocks was common in north and central Europe as recently as the early 1900s. Conception was believed to be influenced by cosmic forces. A baby conceived under a new moon would be a boy; during the moon's last quarter, a girl (Gélis, 1991). Even today, beliefs about spiritual influences on conception persist in many traditional societies. Among the Warlpiri people of Australia, a baby conceived in a place associated with a particular spirit is believed to have been given life by that spirit (DeLoache & Gottlieb, 2000). Even in modern Western countries such as Canada, beliefs about how personality might be shaped by the time of year in which children are born persist—as the

astrology sections in many newspapers and magazines attest.

Likewise, infertility is far from a new concern. To enhance fertility, ancient doctors advised men to eat fennel and women to drink the saliva of lambs and wear necklaces of earthworms. It was recommended that, after intercourse, a woman lie flat with her legs crossed and avoid becoming angry (Fontanel & d'Harcourt, 1997, p. 10).

The prevalence of folk beliefs about all aspects of pregnancy speaks to the great wonder of how we become who we are. Even now, despite our ability to see the baby in the womb with ultrasound technology and to test for disorders in fetuses via prenatal genetic testing, the specifics of how the unique mix of genes a baby receives results in a completely new individual remains a delightful mystery.

---

seem to have a genetic basis. For example, some men appear to have gene mutations that affect the quality and quantity of sperm they produce (Krausz, 2010). Men's fertility is less affected by age than women's, but it declines significantly by the late 30s (Dunson, Colombo, & Baird, 2002).

In a woman, common causes of infertility include the failure to produce eggs, or ova, or to produce normal ova; mucus in the cervix, which prevents sperm from penetrating it; or a disease of the uterine lining, which prevents implantation of the fertilized ovum. A major cause of declining fertility in women after age 30 is deterioration in the quality of ova (Broekmans, Soules, & Fauser, 2009). However, the most common cause is blockage of the fallopian tubes, preventing ova from reaching the uterus, sometimes as a consequence of scar tissue from sexually transmitted diseases (Rhoton-Vlasak, 2000).

ASSISTED REPRODUCTIVE TECHNOLOGIES

Unless there is a known cause for failure to conceive, the chances of conception after 18 months to two years are high (Dunson, 2002). For couples struggling with infertility, science today offers several alternative ways to parenthood. **Assisted reproductive technology (ART)**, or conception through artificial means (International Committee for Monitoring Assisted Reproductive Technologies

[ICMART], 2006), provides couples who are having difficulty conceiving naturally a means by which to augment their fertility. Since it was first tested in 1978, more than 3 million children worldwide have been conceived through ART (ICMART, 2006) including 3,500 per year in Canada (Canadian Fertility and Andrology Society [CFAS], 2011; Infertility Awareness Association of Canada, 2009).

The simplest form of ART is *artificial insemination*. This procedure involves the injection of sperm into a woman's vagina, cervix, or uterus and can be used to facilitate conception if a man has a low sperm count. If the man is infertile, a couple may choose artificial insemination by a donor.

In another common method, *in vitro fertilization* (IVF), a woman first receives fertility drugs to stimulate the production of multiple ova. Then the ova are surgically

---

assisted reproductive technology (ART) Methods used to achieve conception through artificial means.

WHAT DO YOU DO?

Fertility Specialist

Fertility specialists diagnose, counsel, and treat women who are having difficulty becoming pregnant and delivering a child. Based on the diagnosis, a fertility specialist might prescribe a fertility medication or conduct in vitro fertilization. Fertility specialists are medical doctors who work out of a hospital, a clinic, or a private practice. As medical doctors, they must complete medical school and a residency, as well as pass board certification.

removed, fertilized in a laboratory dish, and implanted in the woman's uterus. These implanted ova are less likely to become established in the womb and more likely to result in miscarriage. In an attempt to increase the odds of success, it is common to transplant multiple ova, but this procedure also increases the likelihood of multiple, usually premature births. In 2006, nearly half (48 percent) of infants born through ART were twins or higher multiples (Saswati et al., 2009). Births of multiples carry increased risks, both for the children and the mother.

In vitro fertilization—sperm being introduced into an egg.

Typically, multiple births are the product of the mother's body releasing two ova that are then fertilized by separate sperm. The resulting children are dizygotic (two-egg), or fraternal, twins, and are no more alike in hereditary makeup than any other siblings, and may be the same or different sexes. Monozygotic (single-egg), or identical, twins form as a result of a single fertilized ovum splitting in two. These twins have the same hereditary makeup and are the same sex, but—in part because of epigenetic influences—they can differ in some respects, including physical characteristics and temperament. The incidence of multiples births in Canada has grown rapidly (Fell & Joseph, 2012; Millar, Wadhera, & Nimrod, 1992), in part because of delayed child-bearing, but mainly because of the increased use of fertility drugs and the use of IVF (Hoyert, Mathews, Menacker, Strobino, & Guyer, 2006; Martin et al., 2005).

IVF also addresses severe male infertility. A single sperm can be injected into the ovum—a technique called intracytoplasmic sperm injection (ICSI). This procedure is now used in the majority of IVF cycles (Van Voorhis, 2007). Singleton infants conceived through IVF or ICSI are two to four times more likely than naturally conceived infants to have certain types of heart defects, cleft lip, and gastrointestinal defects, although the incidence of such defects is still quite small (Reefhuis et al., 2008).

A woman who is producing poor-quality ova or who has had her ovaries removed may try ovum transfer. In this procedure, a donor egg provided by a fertile younger woman is fertilized in the laboratory and implanted in the prospective mother's uterus. IVF using donor eggs tends to be highly successful (Van Voorhis, 2007). Alternatively, the ovum can be fertilized in the donor's body by artificial insemination. The embryo is retrieved from the donor and inserted into the recipient's uterus.

Although success rates have improved (Duenwald, 2003), only 34 percent of women who attempted assisted reproduction in 2010 had live births (CFAS, 2011). The likelihood of success with IVF using a mother's own ova drops precipitously as a woman advances in age—from 43 percent for women under 35 years, to 12 percent for women 40 or over (CFAS, 2011; Shanner & Nisker, 2001; Van Voorhis, 2007).

Assisted reproduction can result in a tangled web of legal, ethical, and psychological dilemmas (ISLAT Working Group, 1998; Schwartz, 2003). Should the children know about their parentage? Should genetic tests be performed on prospective donors and surrogates? When IVF results in multiple fertilized ova, should some be discarded so as to improve the chances of health for the survivors? Should there be limits on how many embryos can be implanted in a woman?

The desire for IVF is greater than its availability in Canada. Because individuals pay for the procedure, it is not an option for many Canadians and can create a financial burden for others (Canadian Reproduction and Andrology Society, 2009). Recently, some jurisdictions in Canada have started to offer funding for the procedure (Walker & Edmonds, 2010). Science has outpaced our legal system, and there are serious questions about ethics and legal oversight that have not yet been addressed. In particular, many people have called for legislation to limit the number of embryos fertility clinics can implant.

The issues multiply when a *surrogate mother* is involved (Schwartz, 2003). The surrogate, a fertile woman, is impregnated by the prospective father, usually by artificial insemination. She agrees to carry the baby to term and give it to the father and his partner. But who is the "real" parent—the surrogate or the woman whose baby she bears? What if a surrogate wants to keep the baby, as has happened in a few highly publicized cases? Surrogate motherhood is strictly regulated in Canada. In 2004, the Canadian government passed the *Assisted Human Reproductive Act*, placing strict conditions on the practice, including a ban on payment to the surrogate mother (Department of Justice Canada, 2004). This

Sarah Jessica Parker and Matthew Broderick's twin daughters were born via a surrogate.

act was developed in response to recommendations by the Royal Commission on New Reproductive Technologies (1993), which called for legislation on reproductive and genetic technologies, not only for surrogacy but also for sex selection, buying and selling of ova and sperm, human embryo cloning, and the use of human stem cells for research (Bernier & Gregoire, 2004).

ADOPTION

While a desire to adopt children is not contingent upon not being able to bear biological children, it is certainly an option for those faced with infertility. In the event that a woman cannot conceive on her own, and she is either unwilling or unable to conceive with the use of ART, adoption is an alternative option. In Canada, adoptions may either be national or international. Although there are no nationally based statistics on the number of adopted children in Canada, about 2,000 are adopted internationally each year, and about the same number are adopted each year from provincial child welfare agencies across Canada (Adoption Council of Canada, 2010). Since the mid-1970s, the percentage of never-married women who adopt out their children has declined from approximately 9 percent to under 1 percent of live births (Jones, 2008), in part because of society's increasing acceptance of unwed mothers. While the incidence of

children with special needs is higher in adopted samples (39 percent) than in the general population (19 percent), most adopted children are healthy and fare well on most indices of social and emotional well-being (Vandivere, Malm, & Radel, 2009).

Mechanisms of Heredity

The science of genetics is the study of heredity, the inborn factors from the biological parents that affect development. When the ovum and sperm unite, they endow the baby-to-be with a genetic makeup that influences a wide range of characteristics, from colour of hair to health, intellect, and personality.

THE GENETIC CODE

The "stuff" of heredity is a chemical called **deoxyribonucleic acid (DNA)**. The double-helix structure of DNA resembles a long, spiralling ladder whose steps are made of pairs of chemical units called *bases* (Figure 2.1). **Chromosomes** are coils of DNA that consist of smaller segments called **genes** and are found in every cell in the human body. Each gene has a specific location on its chromosome and contains thousands of bases. The sequence of bases in a gene tells the cell how to make the proteins that enable it to carry out its specific functions. The complete sequence of genes in the human body constitutes the **human genome**.

Every cell in the normal human body except the sex cells (sperm and ova) has 23 pairs of chromosomes—46 chromosomes in all. Through a type of cell division called *meiosis*, each sex cell ends up with only 23 chromosomes.

deoxyribonucleic acid (DNA) Chemical that carries inherited instructions for the development of all cellular forms of life.

chromosomes Coils of DNA that consist of genes.

genes Small segments of DNA located in definite positions on particular chromosomes; functional units of heredity.

human genome The complete sequence of genes in the human body.

Ask Yourself

1. In conception, the moment when genes are combined and a new individual is formed is
   a. when the fertilized egg implants in the uterus.
   b. when the sperm breaks through the egg and fuses with it.
   c. during meiosis when the pairs of chromosomes are halved and gametes are produced.
   d. when the one-celled zygote starts replicating itself.

2. The most common cause of infertility in men is _____, and the most common cause of infertility in women is _____.

3. In vitro fertilization involves
   a. injecting sperm directly into a woman's vagina, cervix, or uterus.
   b. injecting a woman with a variety of hormones in order to stimulate egg production.
   c. the removal and fertilization of a woman's eggs, and the subsequent implantation back into the woman's uterus.
   d. b and c.
   e. all of these.

4. Name two facts about adoption in Canada.

DNA: The genetic code

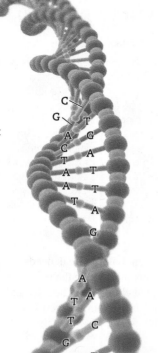

FIGURE 2.1 DNA is the genetic material in all living cells. It consists of four chemical units, called bases. These bases are the letters of the DNA alphabet. A (adenine) pairs with T (thymine) and C (cytosine) pairs with G (guanine). There are 3 billion base pairs in human DNA.

Source: From Fig. 3.1, p. 64 in *A Child's World*, 12th Ed., 2011, by Diane E. Papalia, Sally Wendkos Olds, Ruth Duskin Feldman. Copyright © 2011 by The McGraw-Hill Companies, Inc. Reprinted by permission.

Thus, when sperm and ovum fuse at conception, they produce a zygote with 46 chromosomes, 23 from the father and 23 from the mother (Figure 2.2).

At the moment of conception, the single-celled zygote receives all the biological information needed to guide its development into a unique individual. Through a process known as *mitosis*, the DNA replicates itself so that each newly formed cell is a genetic copy with the same hereditary information. As the cells divide, they differentiate, specializing in a variety of complex bodily functions that enable the child to grow and develop.

SEX DETERMINATION

In many villages in Nepal, it is common for a man whose wife has borne no male babies to take a second wife. In some societies, a woman's failure to produce sons is justification for divorce. In Muslim villages in central Turkey, a traditional belief is that the foods a woman eats influence the sex of her baby—red meat and tomato sauce making it more likely she will have a boy; white foods such as chicken and rice, a girl (Delaney, 2000). The irony in these customs and beliefs is that it is the father's sperm that genetically determines a child's sex.

Twenty-two of our 23 pairs of chromosomes are **autosomes**, chromosomes that aren't related to sexual expression. The 23rd pair are **sex chromosomes**—one from the father and one from the mother—which govern

Did you know?

The Greek philosopher Aristotle believed that baby girls result from disturbances in "normal" male development. This is particularly notable as embryos are female by default until genetic triggers switch on.

the baby's sex. Females have two X chromosomes (XX) and males have one of each type (XY). Each ovum carries only one X chromosome, but the sperm cell carries either an X or a Y; thus it is the father who determines sex.

Initially, the embryo's rudimentary reproductive system appears almost identical in males and in females. Surprisingly, sexual differentiation is not automatic. About six to eight weeks after conception, male embryos normally

---

autosomes In humans, the 22 pairs of chromosomes not related to sexual expression.

sex chromosomes Pair of chromosomes that determines sex; XY in the normal human male, XX in the normal human female.

Hereditary Composition of the Zygote

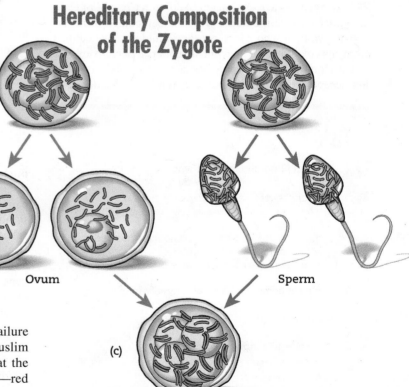

FIGURE 2.2 (a) Body cells of women and men contain 23 pairs of chromosomes, which carry the genes, the basic units of inheritance. (b) Each sex cell (ovum and sperm) has only 23 single chromosomes because of meiosis, a special kind of cell division in which the total number of chromosomes is halved. (c) At fertilization, the 23 chromosomes from the sperm join the 23 from the ovum so that the zygote receives 46 chromosomes, or 23 pairs.

Source: From Fig. 3.2, p. 66 in *Human Development*, 10th Ed., 2007, by Diane E. Papalia, Sally Wendkos Olds, and Ruth Duskin Feldman. Copyright © 2007 by The McGraw-Hill Companies, Inc. Reprinted by permission.

start producing the male hormone testosterone, which results in the development of male sexual organs. Research with mice has found that hormones must first signal the SRY gene, which then triggers formation of the testes. Without this signalling, male sexual development will not occur, and the embryo will develop genitals that appear female (Ahmed & Hughes, 2002). The developing female reproductive system also depends on a signalling gene known as WNT-4, which suppresses development of male sexual organs, permitting development of female sexual organs. However, a variant form of this gene that has reduced suppressive effects can "masculinize" a genetically female fetus (Biason-Lauber, Konrad, Navratil, & Schoenle, 2004; Hughes, 2004; Vainio, Heikkiia, Kispert, Chin, & McMahon, 1999).

PATTERNS OF GENETIC TRANSMISSION

During the 1860s, Gregor Mendel, an Austrian monk, laid the foundation for our understanding of patterns of inheritance. By cross-breeding strains of pea with each other, Mendel discovered two fundamental principles of genetics. First, he realized that traits could be either dominant or recessive. *Dominant traits* are always expressed, while *recessive traits* are expressed only if both copies of the gene are recessive. Second, he realized that traits are passed down independently of each other. For example, the colour of your hair and your height are both hereditable traits that are not linked.

While Mendel's groundbreaking insights were the beginning of the study of genetics, we now know that the genetic picture in humans is far more complex than Mendel ever imagined. Moreover, who we are is not just a product of our genetic code but also depends on the interaction of that code with the environment. In the following section, we discuss dominant and recessive transmission, as well as the transmission of multifactorial traits. Last, we discuss how epigenetic processes can alter the expression of the underlying genetic code.

Dominant and Recessive Inheritance

Genes that can produce alternative expressions of a characteristic, such as the presence or absence of dimples, are called **alleles**. Alleles are the different versions of a particular gene. Every person receives one maternal and one paternal allele for any given trait. When both alleles are the same, the person is **homozygous** for the characteristic; when they are different, the person is **heterozygous**. In **dominant inheritance**, when an offspring receives at least one dominant allele for a trait, it will be expressed. **Recessive inheritance**, or the expression of

What is the recessive gene expressed in this family?

a recessive trait, occurs only when a person receives two recessive alleles, one from each parent.

Let's take the presence of dimples as an example. Dimples are a dominant trait, so you will have dimples if you receive at least one copy (D) from either parent. If you inherited one allele for dimples from each parent (Figure 2.3), you are homozygous for this trait and have one or more dimples. If you receive one copy of the dimple allele (D) and one copy of an allele for lack of dimples (d), you are heterozygous. In both cases, your expressed characteristic is that you have dimples. The only situation in which you would not have dimples is if you received two recessive copies (d), one from each parent.

Traits may also be affected by **mutations**, permanent alterations in genetic material. Mutations generally result from copying errors and are usually harmful.

Multifactorial Transmission

Relatively few traits are determined via a single dominant-recessive gene pair. Most traits result from **polygenic inheritance**, the interaction of many genes. For example, skin colour is the result of three or more sets of genes on three different chromosomes. These genes work together to produce different amounts of brown pigment, resulting in hundreds of shades of skin colour. Complex traits are produced by a combination of genetic and environmental factors. This phenomenon is known as **multifactorial transmission**. Some

alleles Two or more alternative forms of a gene that can occupy the same position on paired chromosomes and affect the same trait.

homozygous Possessing two identical alleles for a trait.

heterozygous Possessing differing alleles for a trait.

dominant inheritance Pattern of inheritance in which, when a child receives different alleles, only the dominant one is expressed.

recessive inheritance Pattern of inheritance in which a child receives identical recessive alleles, resulting in expression of a non-dominant trait.

mutations Permanent alterations in genes or chromosomes that usually produce harmful characteristics but provide the raw material of evolution.

polygenic inheritance Pattern of inheritance in which multiple genes at different sites on chromosomes affect a complex trait.

multifactorial transmission Combination of genetic and environmental factors to produce certain complex traits.

Dominant and Recessive Inheritance

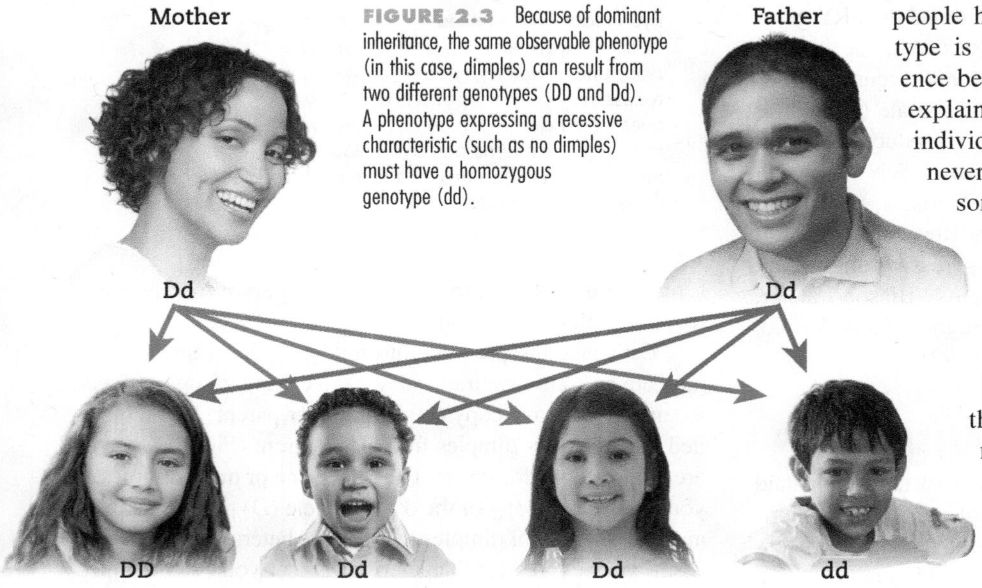

Mother

FIGURE 2.3 Because of dominant inheritance, the same observable phenotype (in this case, dimples) can result from two different genotypes (DD and Dd). A phenotype expressing a recessive characteristic (such as no dimples) must have a homozygous genotype (dd).

Father

Dd

Dd

DD   Dd   Dd   dd

Source: From Fig. 3.4, p. 67 in *A Child's World*, 12th Ed., 2011, by Diane E. Papalia, Sally Wendkos Olds, Ruth Duskin Feldman. Copyright © 2011 by The McGraw-Hill Companies, Inc. Reprinted by permission.

physical characteristics, including height and weight, and most psychological characteristics, such as intelligence and musical ability, are products of this process.

EPIGENESIS: ENVIRONMENTAL INFLUENCE ON GENE EXPRESSION

Who you are is a product of your genes and of the environmental influences you are exposed to. Your **genotype** is what is coded in your genes—the recipe for making you. It may be expressed in varying ways. What is expressed— who you actually are—is your *phenotype*. For example, if you have dimples, that trait is part of your *phenotype*, the observable characteristics through which your *genotype*, or underlying genetic makeup, is expressed. Except

for monozygotic twins (identical twins who started out as a single fertilized ovum), no two people have the same genotype. The phenotype is the genotype in action. The difference between genotype and phenotype helps explain why a clone (a genetic copy of an individual), or even an identical twin, can never be an exact duplicate of another person. The environment has an effect, and thus, phenotypic differences emerge even between genetically identical twins.

Mounting evidence suggests that gene expression is controlled by reversible chemical reactions that turn genes on or off as they are needed but that do not change the underlying genetic code. This phenomenon is called **epigenesis**. Epigenesis works via chemical molecules, or *tags*, attached to a gene that affect the way a cell "reads" the gene's DNA (Figure 2.4). Because every cell in the body inherits the same DNA sequence, the function of the chemical tags is to differentiate various types of body cells, such as brain cells, skin cells, and liver cells—somewhat like sticking sticky notes in your textbook to tell you where to look for information. These tags work by "switching" particular genes on or off during embryonic formation. Having mapped the human genome, scientists are joining forces internationally to decode the epigenome (Mayo Foundation for Medical Education and Research, 2009).

Epigenetic changes can occur throughout life in response to environmental factors such as nutrition, sleep habits, stress, and physical affection. Sometimes errors arise, which may lead to birth defects or disease

genotype Genetic makeup of a person, containing both expressed and unexpressed characteristics.

phenotype Observable characteristics of a person.

epigenesis Mechanism that turns genes on or off and determines functions of body cells.

Despite having identical genes, the epigenome of twins diverges over time because of different environmental influences, leading to different expression of those genes.

Did you know?

Cells are especially susceptible to epigenetic modification during critical periods such as puberty and pregnancy. And epigenetic changes may be heritable. Therefore, it's very important for women to practise good health and nutritional practices during their reproductive years to protect the health of future children and grandchildren. For example, the granddaughters of women who experienced famine while in the womb lived shorter lives on average (Pembrey et al., 2006).

FIGURE 2.4 Epigenesis

1. The human body has trillions of cells, each one with a nucleus, its command centre. The nucleus of each cell contains chromosomes. Within the chromosomes, long double-helix stands of DNA are made up of specific segments of genetic code, known as genes. DNA is tightly coiled around histones that work as support structures for genes. Genes contain the codes for cells to produce the various proteins that organisms need to function.

2. Experiences leave a chemical "signature", or epigenetic mark, that sits atop the genes, which determines whether and how the genes are expressed—or switched on or off. Collectively, those signatures are called epigenome.

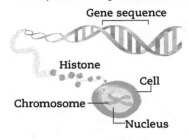

Gene sequence
Histone
Chromosome
Cell
Nucleus

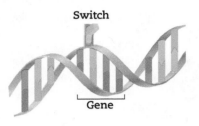

Switch
Gene

3. All cell types—muscle celles, nerve cells, liver cells, etc.—contain the exact same DNA. Epigenetic marks silence certain gene sequences and activate others so that nascent cells can differentiate.

4. Stressors like abuse or poor nutrition can activate epigenetic marks, modifying histones or adding methyl groups to DNA strands. These changes can turn genes on or off and may affect what gets passed down to the next generation.

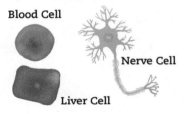

Blood Cell
Nerve Cell
Liver Cell

Source: McCain, M.N., Mustard, J.F., & McCuaig, K. (2011). Early Years Study 3: Making Decisions, Taking Action. Toronto: Margaret & Wallace McCain Family Foundation. Figure 2.1. p. 29.

(Gosden & Feinberg, 2007). Epigenetic changes may also contribute to such common ailments as cancer, diabetes, and heart disease; for instance, Canadian-led researchers found that childhood resistance to conventional treatments for a type of brain cancer disappears by adulthood because of epigenetic changes in DNA regulation (Schwartzentruber et al., 2012). In addition, epigenetic changes may explain why one monozygotic twin is susceptible to a disease such as alcoholism whereas the other twin is not, and why some twins get the same disease but at different ages (Fraga et al., 2005; Wong, Gottesman, & Petronis, 2005).

Genetic and Chromosomal Abnormalities

After two failed IVF attempts, Tania and Paul were finally pregnant. Early ultrasound tests indicated that, luckily, only one embryo had implanted and Tania was pregnant with a singleton. At 20 weeks pregnant, Tania went to her obstetrician for a mid-pregnancy anatomy scan. Now she would find out the sex of her baby and be screened for soft markers of disorders. Soft markers are physical abnormalities that can be seen on an ultrasound that indicate an increased risk of having a baby with a

genetic disorder. By looking for various soft markers—shorter legs, a thicker nuchal fold (skin on the back of the neck), and heart abnormalities—Tania's doctor could give her an idea of whether her baby was likely to have certain genetic or developmental disorders.

Most birth disorders are fairly rare, affecting only about 3 percent of live births (Health Canada, 2002; Waknine, 2006). Nevertheless, they are the leading cause of infant death in Canada, accounting for 21.7 percent of all deaths in the first year in 2008 (Statistics Canada, 2011b). The most common birth disorders in Canada are cleft lip and cleft palate, followed by Down syndrome, a chromosomal disorder that we will discuss later in this chapter, and neural tube defects (Health Canada, 2002; Public Health Agency of Canada, 2008). Other serious malformations involve the eye, the face, the mouth, or the circulatory, digestive, or musculoskeletal systems (Health Canada, 2002; Centers for Disease Control and Prevention [CDC], 2006b).

Not all genetic or chromosomal abnormalities are apparent at birth. Table 2.1 lists some of the disorders caused by genetic and chromosomal abnormalities. Tay-Sachs, a

Ask Yourself

5. Which is the best analogy for what genes do?
   a. a set of on/off buttons on a switchboard
   b. a large balloon that fills and deflates on a cycle
   c. a set of instructions for making a person
   d. a chalkboard upon which experiences write

6. Humans have _____ pairs of chromosomes. Of those, _____ are autosomes and _____ is/are sex chromosomes. Males are _____ and females are _____.

7. Under what condition would a recessive trait be displayed?
   a. when both genes in a pair are dominant
   b. when the first gene in a pair is recessive and the second is dominant
   c. when the first gene in a pair is dominant and the second is recessive
   d. when both genes in a pair are recessive

8. Skin cells and stomach cells are expressed differently from each other because
   a. they code for different genes.
   b. of epigenetic tags instructing some genes to turn on and some to turn off.
   c. they differentiate over time as they adapt to their local environment.
   d. This is untrue; they are expressed in an identical way regardless of location.

TABLE 2.1 Some Birth Defects

Problem	Characteristics of Condition	Who Is at Risk	What Can Be Done
Alpha-1 antitrypsin deficiency	Enzyme deficiency that can lead to cirrhosis of the liver in early infancy and emphysema and degenerative lung disease in middle age.	1 in 1,000 white births	No treatment.
Alpha thalassemia	Severe anemia that reduces ability of the blood to carry oxygen; nearly all affected infants are stillborn or die soon after birth.	Primarily families of Malaysian, African, and Southeast Asian descent	Frequent blood transfusions.
Beta thalassemia (Cooley's anemia)	Severe anemia resulting in weakness, fatigue, and frequent illness; usually fatal in adolescence or young adulthood.	Primarily families of Mediterranean descent	Frequent blood transfusions.
Cystic fibrosis	Overproduction of mucus, which collects in the lungs and digestive tract; children do not grow normally and usually do not live beyond age 30; the most common inherited *lethal* defect among white people.	1 in 2,000 white births	Daily physical therapy to loosen mucus; antibiotics for lung infections; enzymes to improve digestion; gene therapy (in experimental stage).
Duchenne muscular dystrophy	Fatal disease usually found in males, marked by muscle weakness; minor mental retardation is common; respiratory failure and death usually occur in young adulthood.	1 in 3,000 to 5,000 male births	No treatment.
Hemophilia	Excessive bleeding, usually found in males; in its most severe form, can lead to crippling arthritis in adulthood.	1 in 10,000 families with a history of hemophilia	Frequent transfusions of blood with clotting factors.
Neural-tube defects Anencephaly	Absence of brain tissues; infants are stillborn or die soon after birth.	1 in 1,000	No treatment.
Spina bifida	Incompletely closed spinal canal, resulting in muscle weakness or paralysis and loss of bladder and bowel control; often accompanied by hydrocephalus, an accumulation of spinal fluid in the brain, which can lead to mental retardation.	1 in 1,000	Surgery to close spinal canal prevents further injury; shunt placed in brain drains excess fluid and prevents mental retardation.
Phenylketonuria (PKU)	Metabolic disorder resulting in mental retardation.	1 in 15,000	Special diet begun in first few weeks of life can prevent mental retardation.
Polycystic kidney disease	*Infantile form:* enlarged kidneys, leading to respiratory problems and congestive heart failure. *Adult form:* kidney pain, kidney stones, and hypertension resulting in chronic kidney failure.	1 in 1,000	Kidney transplants.
Sickle-cell anemia	Deformed, fragile red blood cells that can clog the blood vessels, depriving the body of oxygen; symptoms include severe pain, stunted growth, frequent infections, leg ulcers, gallstones, susceptibility to pneumonia, and stroke.	1 in 500 children of African descent	Painkillers, transfusions for anemia and to prevent stroke, antibiotics for infections.
Tay-Sachs disease	Degenerative disease of the brain and nerve cells, resulting in death before age 5.	Historically found mainly in eastern European Jews	No treatment.

Source: Adapted from AAP Committee on Genetics (1996); NIH Consensus Development Panel (2001); Tisdale (1988, pp. 68–69).

Sex-Linked Inheritance

FIGURE 2.5 In the most common form, the female sex chromosome of an unaffected mother carries one recessive abnormal gene and one dominant normal one (X). The father has one normal male X and Y chromosome complement.

Source: From p. 72 in *Human Development,* 10th Ed., 2007, by Diane E. Papalia, Sally Wendkos Olds, and Ruth Duskin Feldman. Copyright © 2007 by The McGraw-Hill Companies, Inc. Reprinted by permission.

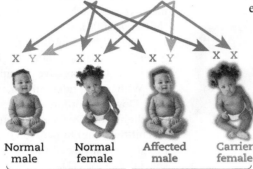

Carrier mother   Normal father

X X   X Y

X Y   X X   X Y   X X

Normal male   Normal female   Affected male   Carrier female

Possible hereditary results

The odds for each *male* child are 50/50:
1. 50% risk of inheriting the abnormal X and the disorder
2. 50% chance of inheriting normal X and Y chromosomes

The odds for each *female* child are 50/50:
1. 50% chance of inheriting one abnormal X, to be a carrier like mother
2. 50% chance of inheriting no abnormal genes

fatal degenerative disease of the central nervous system most common in Jews of eastern European ancestry, and sickle-cell anemia, a blood disorder more common among people of African descent, do not generally appear until at least 6 months of age. Likewise, cystic fibrosis, a condition most common in people of northern European descent in which excess mucus accumulates in the lungs and digestive tract, may not appear until age 4. Some diseases show an even later onset, such as glaucoma, a disease in which fluid pressure builds up in the eyes, and Huntington's disease, a progressive degeneration of the nervous system, which do not typically appear before middle age.

It is in genetic defects and diseases that we see most clearly the operation of dominant and recessive transmission, and also of a variation, sex-linked inheritance, discussed in a subsequent section.

DOMINANT OR RECESSIVE INHERITANCE OF DEFECTS

Most of the time, normal genes are dominant over those carrying abnormal traits, but sometimes the gene for an abnormal trait is dominant. When this is the case, even one copy of the "bad" gene will result in a child expressing the disorder. Among the 1,800 disorders known to be transmitted by dominant inheritance are achondroplasia (a type of dwarfism) and Huntington's disease. Although they can be quite serious, defects transmitted by dominant

inheritance are less likely to be lethal at an early age than those transmitted by recessive inheritance. This is because if a dominant gene is lethal at an early age, then affected children would be likely to die before reproducing. Therefore, that gene would soon disappear from the population.

Recessive defects are expressed only if the child is homozygous for that gene; in other words, a child must inherit a copy of the recessive gene from each parent to be affected. Because recessive genes are not expressed if the parent is heterozygous for that trait, both parents may be carriers without realizing it. In this case, any child they had would have a 25 percent chance of getting both of the recessive copies and thus expressing the trait. Defects transmitted by recessive genes tend to be lethal at an earlier age, in contrast to those transmitted by dominant genes, as they can be passed down to the next generation by carriers. Tay-Sachs disease, for example, occurs only if both parents are carriers of the defective gene; children with this degenerative condition typically die by age 4 or 5.

Some traits are only partly dominant or partly recessive. In **incomplete dominance**, a trait is not fully expressed. For example, people with one sickle-cell allele and one normal allele do not have sickle-cell anemia but do show some manifestations of the condition, such as shortness of breath at high altitudes.

SEX-LINKED INHERITANCE OF DEFECTS

Certain recessive disorders are linked to genes on the sex chromosomes—**sex-linked inheritance**—and affect male and female children differently (Figure 2.5). In humans, the Y chromosome is smaller and carries fewer genes than the X chromosome. Remember that males are XY and females are XX. One consequence of this is that females receive two copies of any gene carried on the X chromosome, whereas males receive only one. Therefore, males are more likely to be affected by any trait carried on the X chromosome because they have only one chance to get it right.

When a mother is a carrier of a sex-linked disorder—in other words, when she is heterozygous for an allele carried on the sex chromosomes—she has a 50 percent chance of passing that gene on to her children. If a particular child is a male, then that child has a 50 percent chance of getting the faulty gene and having the disorder because there is no backup copy. If that child is a female, then even if she

incomplete dominance Pattern of inheritance in which a child receives two different alleles, resulting in partial expression of a trait.

sex-linked inheritance Pattern of inheritance in which certain characteristics carried on the X chromosome inherited from the mother are transmitted differently to her male and female offspring.

gets a copy of the faulty gene from her mother, she will receive another allele from her father. Red-green colour blindness is one of these sex-linked conditions. Another is hemophilia, a disorder in which blood does not clot when it should.

Occasionally, a female does inherit a sex-linked condition. For example, if her father has hemophilia and her mother happens to be a carrier for the disorder, the daughter has a 50 percent chance of receiving the abnormal X chromosome from each parent and having the disease.

Did you know?

Ever wonder why calico cats are almost always female? It's because the gene for coat colour is carried on the X chromosome. If a female gets one orange copy and one black copy, then through a process called X-inactivation, one or another of the genes is turned off in a random fashion. Thus, the calico's randomly mottled orange and black fur!

CHROMOSOMAL ABNORMALITIES

Chromosomal abnormalities typically occur because of errors in cell division. For example, Klinefelter syndrome, found only in males, is caused by an extra female sex chromosome (shown by the pattern XXY). While some boys born with Klinefelter may not show any symptoms, others may have impaired fertility, have problems with language or reading, and are often tall, with long legs and a short trunk. Klinefelter occurs in approximately one out of 650 males (Bojesen, Juul, & Hojbjerg Gravholt, 2003). Turner syndrome results from a missing sex chromosome (XO) and is found only in females. Girls with Turner syndrome tend to have a webbed neck, low-set ears, and short stature, and are usually infertile (National Institute of Child Health and Human Development [NICHD], 2013). Estimates are that Turner syndrome occurs in one out of every 2,000 live births (Donaldson, Gault, Tan, & Dunger, 2006). In yet another variation, Triple X syndrome results from an extra X chromosome. Also known as trisomy X, it is associated with delayed language and motor development and affects approximately one in 1,000 females (National Library of Medicine, n.d.). The likelihood of genetic errors may increase in offspring of women age 35 or older (University of Virginia Health System, 2004).

The most common genetic disorder in children is **Down syndrome** (Davis, 2008). Down syndrome is responsible for about 40 percent of cases of moderate-to-severe mental retardation (Pennington, Moon, Edgin, Stedron, & Nadel, 2003) as defined by performance on an intelligence test. The condition is also called trisomy-21 because it is characterized in more than 90 percent of cases by an extra 21st chromosome. The most obvious

Down syndrome Chromosomal disorder characterized by moderate-to-severe mental retardation and by such physical signs as a downward-sloping skin fold at the inner corners of the eyes.

physical characteristic associated with Down syndrome is a downward-sloping skin fold at the inner corners of the eyes. Children with Down syndrome also tend to have slowed growth, poor muscle tone, congenital heart defects, thick hands, ear infections and early hearing loss, and impaired communication, language, memory, and motor skills (Davis, 2008).

About 1 in every 800 Canadian babies born alive has Down syndrome (Public Health Agency of Canada, 2008). Although the risk of having a child with Down syndrome rises with age (Society for Neuroscience, 2008), because of the higher birthrates of younger women, there are actually more young mothers with children with Down syndrome (NICHD, 2008). In 95 percent of cases, the extra chromosome seems to come from the mother's ovum; in the other 5 percent, from the father's sperm (Antonarakis & Down Syndrome Collaborative Group, 1991).

With early intervention, the prognosis for children with Down syndrome is brighter than was once thought. Children with Down syndrome, like other children with disabilities, tend to benefit cognitively, socially, and emotionally when placed in regular classrooms rather than in special schools (Davis, 2008) and when provided with regular, intensive therapies designed to help them achieve important skills. As adults, many live in small group homes and support themselves; they tend to do well in structured job situations. More than 70 percent of people with Down syndrome live into their 60s, but they are at

A young girl with Down syndrome.

elevated risk of early death from various causes, including leukemia, cancer, Alzheimer's disease, and cardiovascular disease (Bittles, Bower, Hussain, & Glasson, 2006; Hayes & Batshaw, 1993; Hill et al., 2003).

Did you know?

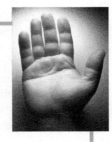

Rather than having the three familiar branching lines on their palm, children with Down syndrome are more likely to have one horizontal line across their palms, a characteristic known as the single transverse palmar crease. This trait sometimes occurs in the general population, but is more likely in Down syndrome.

GENETIC COUNSELLING AND TESTING

Tania's anatomy scan showed two soft markers for Down syndrome, and she was told that her risk for having an affected child was thus 1/23. Tania and Paul had a decision to make. They could opt to live with those risks and proceed with the pregnancy with no further intervention, or they could schedule an *amniocentesis*—a genetic test that would give a definitive answer but put Tania at a small risk of miscarriage. Tania and Paul weren't sure what to do.

Genetic counselling can help prospective parents like Paul and Tania assess their risk of bearing children with genetic or chromosomal defects. People who have already had a child with a genetic defect, who have a family history of hereditary illness, who suffer from conditions known or suspected to be inherited, or who come from ethnic groups at higher-than-average risk of passing on genes for certain diseases can get information about their likelihood of producing affected children. A genetic counsellor tries to help clients understand the mathematical risk of a particular condition, explains its implications, and presents information about alternative courses of action. Screening for disorders can either happen before pregnancy—when parents can be screened for the presence of recessive genetic disorders—or after conception—via genetic assessments such as chorionic villi sampling (CVS) and amniocentesis. Both of these tests involve extracting fetal cells from the uterus, growing them in a laboratory, and doing genetic tests on them; however, CVS is generally done at 11- to 12-weeks gestation, while amniocentesis occurs during the 16th week of pregnancy.

Geneticists have made great contributions to the prevention of birth defects. For example, since so many Jewish couples have been tested for genes that carry Tay-Sachs, a fatal disease involving degeneration of mental and physical abilities,

WHERE DO **YOU** STAND?

Pregnant women over the age of 35 years are routinely advised to have genetic testing. Of those women who opt for genetic testing, approximately 90 percent who receive a diagnosis of Down syndrome terminate the pregnancy (Mansfield, Hopfer, & Marteau, 1999). As a consequence, the number of children with Down syndrome in is declining. Is this a positive or a negative development for society?

far fewer Jewish babies have been born with the disease (Kolata, 2003). Similarly, screening and counselling of women of child-bearing age from Mediterranean countries, where beta thalassemia (severe anemia that is generally fatal in adolescence or young adulthood) is common, have resulted in a decline in births of affected babies and greater knowledge of the risks of being a carrier (Cao, Rosatelli, Monni, & Galanello, 2002).

It is recommended that Canadians undergoing genetic testing be made aware of potential consequences and limitations. These include discrimination, negative family impact, and loss of some types of services like life insurance, especially for those likely to have genetically based late-onset diseases (Jamieson, 2001). A major concern is genetic determinism, the misconception that a person with a gene for a disease is bound to get the disease. This can lead to the creation of a new stigmatized group: the "not-yet-ill" (Jamieson, 2001). All genetic testing can tell us is the likelihood that a person will get a disease. Most diseases involve a complex combination of genes or depend in part on lifestyle or other environmental factors (Clayton,

genetic counselling Clinical service that advises prospective parents of their probable risk of having children with hereditary defects.

WHAT DO YOU **DO?**

Genetic Counsellor

Geneticists are experts in the area of genes and heredity. For example, genetic counsellors work with prospective or soon-to-be parents to consult on genetically based disorders that might occur in their child. They often work with patients to create a genetic family tree, determine if testing is needed, help interpret results from testing, and counsel patients as they make decisions related to findings. For example, a couple who are both of eastern European descent might consult a genetic counsellor regarding risk of Tay-Sachs disease. Or a couple with one child with a particular disorder that research has shown to have a genetic basis might consult a genetic counsellor before trying to become pregnant again. A master's degree and certification exam are required to become a genetic counsellor. Graduate programs are very competitive. Visit www.cagc-accg.ca for more information about genetic counsellors.

2003; Rutter, 2002). An additional issue is the prevention of sex selection through termination of the pregnancy; recent recommendations by Canadian health authorities are to avoid disclosing the sex of the fetus until after gestational age, the minimum age of viability, has been reached (Thiele & Leier, 2010).

Ask Yourself

9. Consider a trait coded for by a recessive gene. Which of the following people will express the trait?
   a. a woman who is heterozygous for a recessive trait
   b. a man who is heterozygous for a recessive trait
   c. a woman who is a homozygous for a dominant trait
   d. a man who is homozygous for the recessive trait

10. Sex-linked traits
    a. are usually passed from father to son.
    b. are never manifested in females.
    c. can be carried by females who do not display them.
    d. are carried by dominant genes.

11. A chromosomal disorder characterized by moderate-to-severe mental retardation and a downward sloping skin fold at the inner corners of the eyes is called
    a. cystic fibrosis.
    b. Tay-Sachs disease.
    c. Down syndrome.
    d. sickle-cell anemia.

12. Which of the following is the best description of what is done in an amniocentesis or chorionic villi sampling test?
    a. Parents are assessed to find out if they carry any recessive genes that might lead to a disorder prior to becoming pregnant.
    b. Parents are asked to meet with a genetic counsellor and are told about different genetic disorders.
    c. Pregnant mothers are given blood tests to determine hormone levels in their blood.
    d. Fetal cells are extracted from the pregnant mother and tested in a lab.

Studying the Influence of Heredity and Environment

How much of who we are is due to heredity and how much is due to environment? Although certain rare physical disorders are virtually 100 percent inherited, phenotypes for more complex normal traits, such as those having to do with health, intelligence, and personality, are subject to a complex array of hereditary and environmental forces. Here we explore how scientists study the influences of heredity and environment and how these two forces work together.

MEASURING HERITABILITY

Heritability is a statistical estimate of how much heredity contributes to variations in a specific trait at a certain time within a given population. Heritability does not refer to the relative influence of heredity and environment in a particular individual. It merely indicates the statistical extent to which genes contribute to a trait among a group of people.

Heritability is expressed as a proportion ranging from 0.0 to 1.0; the higher the number, the greater the heritability of a trait. A heritability estimate of 1.0 indicates that genes are 100 percent responsible for variances in the trait within the population. For example, the heritability of eye colour approaches 1.0; whether your eyes are blue or brown is not driven by environment. Because heritability cannot be measured directly, researchers rely chiefly on three types of correlational methods: family, adoption, and twin studies.

These studies are all based on the assumption that if we know, on average, how many genes people share by virtue of knowing their genetic relationship, then we can measure how similar they are on traits (that is, their *concordance rate*) and work backward to determine the relative environmental influences. For example, immediate family members are more genetically similar than more distant relatives, adopted children are genetically more like their biological families than their adoptive families, and monozygotic twins are more genetically similar than *dizygotic twins* (fraternal twins formed from two fertilized ova). Thus, if heredity has a large influence on a particular trait, siblings should be more alike than cousins with regard to that trait, adopted children should be more like their biological parents than their adoptive parents, and monozygotic twins should be more alike than dizygotic twins. By the same token, if the environment exerts a large influence on a trait, persons who live together should be more similar with regard to that trait than persons who do not live together, regardless of how closely related they are.

In *family studies*, researchers measure the degree to which biological relatives share certain traits and determine whether the closeness of the familial relationship is associated with the degree of similarity. In other words, the more closely two people are related, the more likely it is that they will be similar on a trait if that trait is indeed genetically influenced. Therefore, researchers use concordance rates on traits to infer genetic influences. Generally, concordance rate is defined as the probability that both twins in a pair will share a trait.

Adoption studies look at similarities between adopted children and their adoptive families and also between adopted children and their biological families. When adopted children are more like their biological parents and siblings in a particular trait (say, obesity),

---

heritability Statistical estimate of the contribution of heredity to individual differences in a specific trait within a given population at a particular time.

we see the influence of heredity. When they resemble their adoptive families more, we see the influence of environment.

Twin studies compare pairs of monozygotic twins with same-sex dizygotic twins. Monozygotic twins are twice as genetically similar, on average, as dizygotic twins. When monozygotic twins are more alike, or more **concordant**, on a trait than dizygotic twins, we see the likely effects of heredity. As an extension of this, twins raised in either their biological family or an adoptive family can be studied.

HOW HEREDITY AND ENVIRONMENT WORK TOGETHER

In actuality, as noted before, the effects of genetic influences, especially on behavioural traits, are rarely inevitable. Even in a trait strongly influenced by heredity, the environment can have substantial impact (Rutter, 2002). In fact, environmental interventions sometimes can overcome genetically determined conditions. For example, a special diet begun soon after birth often can prevent mental retardation in children with the genetic disease phenylketonuria (PKU), a metabolic disorder (Widaman, 2009).

From conception on, a combination of constitutional (biological and psychological), social, economic, and cultural factors help shape development. The more advantageous these circumstances and the experiences to which they give rise, the greater is the likelihood of optimum development. Here we consider several ways in which inheritance and experience work together.

Reaction Range and Canalization

Many characteristics vary, within limits, under differing hereditary or environmental conditions. The concepts of reaction range and canalization can help us visualize how this happens.

Reaction range is the conventional term for a range of potential expressions of a hereditary trait. Body size, for example, depends largely on biological processes,

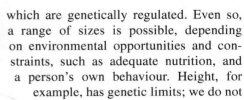

Even if well fed in childhood, two different people may reach different heights, reflecting the influence of their genes.

which are genetically regulated. Even so, a range of sizes is possible, depending on environmental opportunities and constraints, such as adequate nutrition, and a person's own behaviour. Height, for example, has genetic limits; we do not see people who are only a foot tall or any who are 10 feet tall, regardless of how well fed they were as children.

Heredity can influence whether a reaction range is wide or narrow. In other words, the genotype places limits on the range of possible phenotypes. For example, a child born with a defect producing mild cognitive limitations is more able to respond to a favourable environment than a child born with more severe limitations. The child with a mild impairment has a wider range of reaction.

Some traits have an extremely narrow range of reaction. The metaphor of **canalization** illustrates how heredity restricts the range of development for some traits. After a heavy storm, the rainwater that has fallen on a pavement has to go somewhere. If the street has potholes, the water will fill them. If deep canals have been dug along the edges of the street, the water will flow into the canals. Some human characteristics, such as eye colour, are so strongly programmed by genes that they are said to be highly *canalized*; there is little opportunity for variance in their expression. The canal is too deep for the water to slosh over.

Highly canalized traits require an extreme change in environment to alter their course. For example, normal babies follow a predictable sequence of motor development: crawling, walking, and running, in that order, at certain approximate ages. And this process occurs in a wide range of cultures with a wide range of experiences.

Genotype–Environment Interaction

Genotype–environment interaction usually refers to the effects of similar environmental conditions on genetically

concordant Term describing the tendency of twins to share the same trait or disorder.

reaction range Potential variability, depending on environmental conditions, in the expression of a hereditary trait.

canalization Limitation on variance of expression of certain inherited characteristics.

genotype–environment interaction Effect of the interaction between genes and the environment on phenotypic variation.

different individuals, and a discussion of these interactions is a way to conceptualize and talk about the different ways nature and nurture interact. To take a familiar example, many children are exposed to pollen and dust, but those with a genetic predisposition are more likely to develop allergic reactions. Interactions can work the other way as well: genetically similar children often develop differently depending on their home environments (Collins, Maccoby, Steinberg, Hetherington, & Bornstein, 2000). A child born with a difficult temperament may develop adjustment problems in one family and thrive in another, depending largely on how parents respond to the child. Thus it is the interaction of hereditary and environmental factors, not just one or the other, that produces certain outcomes. In reality, there are multiple ways in which individual differences—driven by genetics—and the environment interact to produce outcomes.

Genotype–Environment Correlation

The environment often reflects or reinforces genetic differences. This tendency is called **genotype–environment correlation**, and it works in three ways to strengthen the phenotypic expression of a genotypic tendency (Bergeman & Plomin, 1989; Scarr, 1992; Scarr & McCartney, 1983):

- *Active correlations:* Children actively select experiences that are consistent with their genetic tendencies. A shy child is more likely than an outgoing child to spend time in solitary pursuits. An adolescent with a talent for music probably will seek out musical friends, take music classes, and go to concerts if such opportunities are available. This tendency to seek out environments compatible with one's genotype is called *niche-picking*; it helps explain why identical twins reared apart tend to be quite similar. Children are always involved in creating the environment they inhabit, but their ability to find niches for themselves increases with age and independence.

- *Passive correlations:* You not only inherit genes from your parents but also inherit environments. For example, a musical parent is likely to create a home environment in which music is heard regularly, to give a child music lessons, and to take the child to musical events. If the child inherited the parent's musical talent, the child's musicality will reflect a combination of genetic and environmental influences. This type of correlation is called passive because the child does not control it. Passive correlations are most applicable to young children, whose parents have a great deal of control over their early experiences. Additionally, passive correlations function only when a child is living with a biologically related parent.

- *Reactive, or evocative, correlations:* Children with differing genetic makeups evoke different responses from adults. If a child shows interest and ability in music, parents who are not musically inclined may react by making a special effort to provide that child with musical experiences. This response, in turn, strengthens the child's genetic inclination toward music.

What Makes Siblings So Different?

You might assume that siblings, as they share approximately 50 percent of their genes, might be very similar to each other. However, siblings can differ greatly in intellect and especially in personality, and these differences increase with age (Plomin, 1989; Plomin & Daniels, 2011). One reason may be genetic differences, which lead children to need different kinds of stimulation or to respond differently to a similar home environment, and thus develop along increasingly divergent

genotype–environment correlation   Tendency of certain genetic and environmental influences to reinforce each other; may be active, passive, or reactive (evocative).

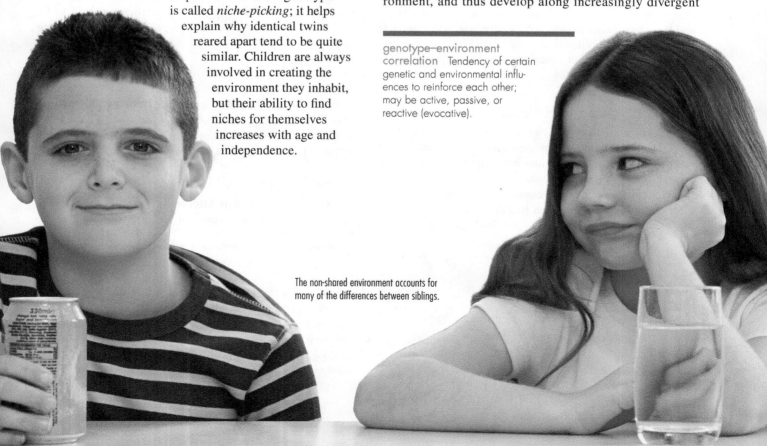

The non-shared environment accounts for many of the differences between siblings.

paths. For example, twin studies have identified that how family conflict is experienced is driven in part by genetic differences between siblings (Horwitz et al., 2010).

In addition, there are what have been called **non-shared environmental effects**. These non-shared environmental effects result from the unique environment in which each child in a family grows up. Children in a family have a shared environment—the home they live in, the people in it, and the activities a family jointly engages in—but they also, even if they are twins, have experiences that are not shared by their brothers and sisters. Parents and siblings may treat each child differently; a firstborn gets undivided attention, but later-born children must compete for it. Certain events, such as illnesses and accidents, and experiences outside the home affect one child and not another. Indeed, some researchers have concluded that although heredity accounts for most of the similarities between siblings, the non-shared environment accounts for most of the differences (Plomin, 2004). However, other researchers point to the more moderate conclusion that non-shared environmental effects do not greatly outweigh shared ones; rather, there seems to be a balance between the two (Rutter, 2002).

Ask Yourself

13. If we find that identical twins are more concordant on a trait than fraternal twins, we can deduce that the trait is strongly influenced by _____.

14. Jiro is born to very athletic parents, who provide him with genes for athleticism. They also provide him with an environment rich in opportunity to engage in athletic activities. Because of his genes, he is uniquely well suited to take advantage of the environment his parents provide. Which of the following best describes the interaction of heredity and environment?

   a. active genotypen–environment correlations
   b. passive genotype–environment correlations
   c. evocative genotype–environment correlations
   d. niche-picking

Characteristics Influenced by Heredity and Environment

A full four years after first starting to try to become pregnant, Tania and Paul finally had a baby girl. Even from the first day at the hospital, their daughter behaved and acted differently from the other children in the nursery, with distinct likes and dislikes and patterns of behaviours. Although it would take years for her abilities and tendencies to emerge fully, many of the tiny baby's characteristics were already in place. While developmentalists have studied heredity–environment interactions in great detail, it is unlikely that the true complexity of this dynamic relationship will ever be known. Nonetheless, some general truths have emerged in the areas of physical and physiological traits, intelligence, personality, and psychopathology.

PHYSICAL AND PHYSIOLOGICAL TRAITS

Not only do monozygotic twins generally look alike, but they also are more concordant than dizygotic twins in their risk for medical disorders such as high blood pressure, heart disease, stroke, rheumatoid arthritis, peptic ulcers, and epilepsy (Brass, Isaacsohn, Merikangas, & Robinette, 1992; Plomin, Owen, & McGuffin, 1994). Lifespan, too, seems to be influenced by genes (Hjelmborg et al., 2006).

Another characteristic with a genetic basis is weight. **Obesity** is measured by *body mass index*, or *BMI* (comparison of weight to height). A child who is at or above the 95th percentile of BMI for his or her age and sex is considered obese. Studies suggest that 40 to 70 percent of the risk is genetic (Chen et al., 2004) and that more than 430 genes or chromosome regions are associated with obesity (Nirmala, Reddy, & Reddy, 2008; Snyder et al., 2004).

The risk of obesity is two to three times higher for a child with a family history of obesity (Nirmala et al., 2008). However, this increased risk is not solely genetic. Childhood obesity is an important issue in Canada; the proportion of obese and overweight Canadian children has increased in the last generation, from 15 to 26 percent over the past 30 years (Tremblay et al., 2010). The prevalence of overweight is linked to lower activity levels and to family income (Tremblay & Willms, 2000). Children from lower-income families are more likely to be overweight than children from higher-income families (Statistics Canada, 2002), possibly because of the quality of food available to low-income families, as well as the higher stress levels in poorer families that could be linked to increases in appetites and overeating (Phipps, Burton, Osberg, & Lethbridge, 2006).

non-shared environmental effects The unique environment in which each child grows up, consisting of distinctive influences or influences that affect one child differently from another.

obesity Extreme overweight in relation to age, sex, height, and body type.

The kind and amount of food eaten in a particular home or in a particular social or ethnic group, and the amount of exercise that is encouraged, can increase or decrease the likelihood that a child will become overweight. The rise in the prevalence of obesity in Western countries seems to stem from the interaction of supersized portions, inadequate exercise, and a genetic predisposition with overeating (Arner, 2000).

INTELLIGENCE

Heredity exerts a strong influence on general intelligence, as measured by intelligence tests, and a moderate effect on specific abilities such as memory, verbal ability, and spatial ability (Plomin & Spinath, 2004). While there are suggestions that specific genes might contribute to intelligence (Posthuma & de Gues, 2006), intelligence is influenced by the effects of large numbers of genes working together.

Indirect evidence of the role of heredity in intelligence comes from adoption and twin studies. Adopted children's scores on standardized intelligence tests are consistently closer to the scores of their biological mothers than to those of their adoptive parents and siblings, and monozygotic twins are more alike in intelligence than dizygotic twins (Petrill et al., 2004; Plomin & DeFries, 1999).

Intelligence also depends in part on brain size and structure, which are under strong genetic control (Toga & Thompson, 2005). Experience counts too; an enriched or impoverished environment can substantially affect the development and expression of innate ability (Ceci & Gilstrap, 2000).

TEMPERAMENT AND PERSONALITY

Temperament is a characteristic way of responding to the environment that is apparent from early infancy and is a precursor to personality. It appears to be largely inborn and is often consistent over the years (Thomas & Chess, 1984). Siblings tend to be similar in temperament (Saudino, Wertz, Gagne, & Chawla, 2004). An observational study of 294 twin pairs (about half of them monozygotic and half dizygotic) found significant genetic influences on behaviour regulation, activity, sociability, and emotionality (Gagne & Saudino, 2010; Schmitz, Saudino, Plomin, Fulker, & DeFries, 1996).

Scientists have identified genes directly linked with specific aspects of personality, such as a trait called *neuroticism*, which may contribute to depression and anxiety (Lesch et al., 1996). Heritability of personality traits appears to be between 40 and 50 percent, and there is little evidence of shared environmental influence (Bouchard, 2004).

---

temperament Characteristic disposition, or style of approaching and reacting to situations.

Genetic differences and non-shared environments account for many of the differences between siblings in physical traits and physiology, intelligence, temperament and personality, and psychopathologies.

Ask Yourself

15. Although Roberto's adoptive parents are short in stature, he is growing to be tall like his biological mother. What might we conclude about Roberto's height?
    a. It is influenced primarily by environment.
    b. It is influenced primarily by heredity.
    c. It was not influenced by nutrition.
    d. It is primarily a result of independent segregation.

16. Which of the following statements supports the assertion that genes influence intelligence?
    a. Siblings are rarely similar in intelligence.
    b. Monozygotic twins are more similar in intelligence then dizygotic twins.
    c. Genetic influences on intelligence seem to decrease with age.
    d. Adoptive children are more similar in intelligence to their adoptive parents than to their biological parents.

17. What are two temperament traits in which genetic influences have been identified?

18. Which of the following statements is evidence that schizophrenia is not entirely due to genetics?
    a. Infants born in rural areas are at greater risk.
    b. Advanced paternal age is a risk factor.
    c. Siblings who have a close family member with schizophrenia are at higher risk.
    d. Not all monozygotic twins are concordant for schizophrenia.

PSYCHOPATHOLOGY

There is evidence for a strong hereditary influence on such mental disorders as schizophrenia, autism, alcoholism, and depression. All tend to run in families and to show greater concordance between monozygotic twins than between dizygotic twins. However, heredity alone does not produce such disorders; an inherited tendency can be triggered by environmental factors.

Schizophrenia can be viewed as an example of heredity-environment interaction. *Schizophrenia* is a neurological disorder that affects about 1 percent of the Canadian population (Public Health Agency of Canada, 2012). It is characterized by loss of contact with reality; hallucinations and delusions; loss of coherent, logical thought; and inappropriate emotionality. Estimates of heritability for this disorder are as high as 80 to 85 percent (McGuffin, Owen, & Farmer, 1995; Picker, 2005). However, monozygotic twins are not always concordant for schizophrenia, perhaps because of epigenesis (Fraga et al., 2005). Researchers also have looked at possible non-genetic influences, such as minor brain damage in fetal life (Picker, 2005); exposure to influenza or the mother's loss of a close relative in the first trimester of pregnancy (Khashan et al., 2008); or maternal rubella or respiratory infections in the second and third trimesters. Infants born in urban areas or in late winter or early spring appear to be at increased risk, as are those whose mothers experienced obstetric complications or who were poor or severely deprived as a result of war or famine (Picker, 2005). Advanced paternal age is also a risk factor for schizophrenia (Byrne, Agerbo, Ewald, Eaton, & Mortensen, 2003).

In this chapter, we saw how heredity and environment interact to make children what they are. A child's first environment is within the uterus, which we discuss in Chapter 3.

SUMMARY

CHAPTER **2** CONCEPTION, HEREDITY, AND ENVIRONMENT

LO1

Summarize how conception occurs and describe alternative paths to parenthood.

- Fertilization, the union of an ovum and a sperm, results in the formation of a one-celled zygote, which then duplicates itself by cell division.
- Early beliefs about conception reflected incorrect beliefs about nature and about male and female anatomy.
- The most common cause of infertility in men is a low sperm count; the most common cause in women is blockage of the fallopian tubes. Infertile couples now have several options for assisted reproduction, but these techniques may involve thorny ethical and practical issues.
- Dizygotic (fraternal) twins have different genetic makeups and may be of different sexes; monozygotic (identical) twins have the same genetic makeup but may differ in some respects.
- Adoption is an alternative for couples who cannot conceive. While there is a higher incidence of special needs, most adopted children are healthy and fare well on most indices of social and emotional well-being.

LO2

Explain how traits are passed down across generations.

- The basic functional units of heredity are the genes, which are made of deoxyribonucleic acid (DNA). DNA carries the set of biochemical instructions, or genetic code, that governs bodily functions and determines inherited characteristics. Each gene seems to be located by function in a definite position on a particular chromosome. The complete sequence of genes in the human body is the human genome.

Continued

LO2

Explain how traits are passed down across generations.

Continued

- At conception, each normal human being receives 23 chromosomes from the mother and 23 from the father. These form 23 pairs of chromosomes—22 pairs of autosomes and one pair of sex chromosomes. A child who receives an X chromosome from each parent will be a female. If the child receives a Y chromosome from the father, a male will be conceived.

- The simplest patterns of genetic transmission are dominant and recessive inheritance. When a pair of alleles are the same, a person is homozygous for the trait; when they are different, the person is heterozygous.

- Most normal human characteristics are the result of multifactorial transmission. Except for monozygotic twins, each child inherits a unique genotype. Dominant inheritance and multifactorial transmission explain why a person's phenotype (the observable characteristics of the underlying genetic makeup) does not always express the underlying genotype.

- Epigenesis is the process by which the environment has an influence on how the genotype is manifested in the phenotype.

LO3

Describe how abnormalities are transmitted in the genes and the options prospective parents have for testing for them.

- Birth disorders and diseases may result from simple dominant, recessive, or sex-linked inheritance; or from mutations. Chromosomal abnormalities also can cause birth disorders.

- Through genetic counselling, prospective parents can receive information about the mathematical odds of bearing children with certain disorders.

- Genetic testing involves risks as well as benefits.

LO4

Describe how researchers determine the relative influence of genes and environments, and how these variables interact with each other.

- Research in behavioural genetics is based on the assumption that the relative influences of heredity and environment can be measured statistically. If heredity is an important influence on a trait, genetically closer persons will be more similar in that trait. Family studies, adoption studies, and studies of twins enable researchers to measure the heritability of specific traits.

- The concepts of reaction range, canalization, genotype–environment interaction, genotype–environment correlation, and niche-picking describe ways in which heredity and environment work together.

- Siblings tend to be more different than alike in intelligence and personality. According to behaviour genetics research, heredity accounts for most of the similarities, and non-shared environmental effects account for most of the differences. Critics claim that this research, for methodological reasons, minimizes the role of the shared family environment; there seems to be a balance in influences of shared and non-shared environments.

LO5

Summarize how genes affect physical, intellectual, and personality development, as well as psycho-pathologies.

- Obesity, longevity, intelligence, and temperament are influenced by both heredity and environment. The relative influences of heredity and environment may vary across the lifespan.
- Schizophrenia is a psychopathological disorder influenced by both heredity and environment.

ANSWERS TO Ask Yourself

Answers: 1–b; 2–The most common cause of infertility in men is production of too few sperm, and the most common cause of infertility in women is blockage of the fallopian tubes; 3–d; 4–The major trend in Canadian adoption is a decline in the number of never-married women who adopt out their babies; although the incidence of children with special needs is higher in adopted samples than in the general population, most adopted children are healthy; 5–c; 6–Humans have 23 pairs of chromosomes. Of those, 22 are autosomes and one is/are sex chromosomes. Males are XY and females are XX; 7–d; 8–b; 9–d; 10–c; 11–c; 12–d; 13–genes; 14–b; 15–b; 16–b; 17–b; 18–d

---

connect LEARNSMART SMARTBOOK

For more information on the resources available from McGraw-Hill Ryerson, go to **www.mcgrawhill.ca/he/solutions**.

PREGNANCY AND PRENATAL DEVELOPMENT

WHAT'S TO COME

Stages of Prenatal Development

Influences on Prenatal Development

Monitoring Prenatal Development

Fetal alcohol syndrome (FAS) and fetal alcohol effects (FAS/E) are clusters of abnormalities shown by children whose mothers drank during pregnancy, and they are leading causes of mental retardation. But in the late 1970s, when Jan Lutke adopted the first of her eight adopted children diagnosed with FAS/E, the facts about FAS were not widely publicized or scientifically investigated, though the syndrome had been observed for centuries.

The child, a girl named Karen, was diagnosed at age 3 with FAS. She was removed from her birth mother soon after she was born and was placed in a succession of family and foster-care homes for the first three years of her life. Her disruptive behaviour and hyperactivity made it difficult for caregivers to cope, and she was ultimately placed in a resource facility before being adopted by Lutke.

Seventeen years later, as Lutke relates in "Works in Progress: The Meaning of Success for Individuals with FAS/E" (Lutke, 2000), Karen is typical of many young Canadian adults with FAS. She is a self-assured young woman, she works as a dog-groomer, and she gives public talks on FAS. Despite her successes, she has had to overcome the challenges of a lower-than-average IQ, immature social and emotional functioning, and susceptibility to persistently repeating specific behaviours. Throughout her life, in particular during her adolescence, a key factor in her successful development was unobtrusive supervision by peer mentors, older unaffected siblings, adult friends, and social services staff. This supervision worked to protect her from poor decisions that could have led to dangerous situations. With an emphasis on her strengths, Karen has acquired the skills needed for active and independent living, while at the same time developing techniques for overcoming the challenges of potentially difficult behaviour, particularly that associated with persistent repetition of behaviours.

Fetal alcohol syndrome was identified during the 1970s, while Karen was growing up. Once alcohol enters a fetus's bloodstream, it remains there in high concentrations for long periods of time, causing brain damage and harming other body organs. There is no cure. As one medical expert wrote, "for the fetus the hangover may last a lifetime" (Enloe, 1980, p. 15).

AS YOU READ

LO1 Describe the three stages of prenatal development.
LO2 List the different substances or parental characteristics that can negatively impact prenatal development and summarize their effects.
LO3 Summarize prenatal monitoring options for expectant parents.

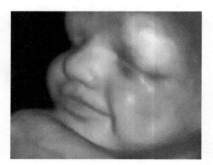

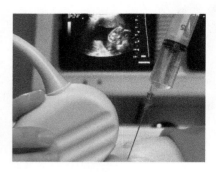

Stages of Prenatal Development

Ethan and Sophia had decided to try to become pregnant. One Tuesday morning, Sophia woke up feeling no different than she had on any other day. However, deep inside her body within her fallopian tubes, a tiny sperm had broken through her egg's defences and conception had occurred. While Sophia did not know it at the time, the tiny fertilized egg had begun a nine-month gestation journey after which, if all went well, a newborn child would be delivered into her arms.

PRINCIPLES OF GROWTH

The prenatal period of development, between conception and birth, is called **gestation**. The normal range of gestation is between 37 and 41 weeks (Martin et al., 2009). Prenatal development takes place in three stages: germinal, embryonic, and fetal. During these stages, the fertilized ovum, or *zygote*, grows into an embryo and then a fetus. (Table 3.1 summarizes the stages of prenatal development.)

Both before and after birth, development proceeds according to two fundamental principles: growth and motor development occur from the top down and from the centre of the body outward. The **cephalocaudal principle**, from Latin, meaning "head to tail," dictates that development proceeds from the head to the lower part of the trunk. An embryo's head, brain, and eyes develop earliest and are disproportionately large until the other parts catch up.

Did you know?

Women are born with a finite number of eggs. Men, however, produce new sperm throughout their lifespan.

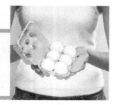

Did you know?

Pregnancy tests detect the presence of *human chorionic gonadotropin*, a hormone that is produced only by fetuses. Thus, there are no false positives for pregnancy tests, because detection of the naturally occurring hormone always means a conception has occurred regardless of whether the pregnancy is ultimately viable.

At two months of gestation, the embryo's head is half the length of the body. By the time of birth, the head is only one-fourth the length of the body but is still disproportionately large. According to the **proximodistal** principle, from Latin, "near to far," development proceeds from parts near the centre of the body to outer ones. The embryo's head and trunk develop before the limbs, and the arms and legs before the fingers and toes.

THE GERMINAL STAGE

The **germinal stage** includes the first two weeks of development after fertilization. During this time, the zygote divides, becomes more complex, and is implanted in the wall of the uterus (Figure 3.1).

---

gestation The prenatal period of development, between conception and birth.

cephalocaudal principle Principle that development proceeds in a head-to-tail direction; that is, upper parts of the body develop before lower parts of the trunk.

proximodistal principle Principle that development proceeds from within to without; that is, parts of the body near the centre develop before the extremities.

germinal stage First two weeks of prenatal development, characterized by rapid cell division, increasing complexity and differentiation, and implantation in the wall of the uterus.

TABLE 3.1 Milestones in Prenatal Development

Age	Accomplishments
3 weeks	Nervous system begins to form
4 weeks	Heart begins to beat
5 weeks	Head continues rapid growth
8 weeks	Almost all body parts are differentiated
12 weeks	Possible to visually determine baby's sex Growth of head slows Formation of red blood cells by liver slows
14 weeks	Begins to coordinate limb movement
16 weeks	Ultrasound shows clearly defined bone structure
20 weeks	Possible to hear heartbeat with stethoscope Baby covered by fine downy hair called lanugo
21 weeks	Rapid eye movement commences Substantial weight gain
24 weeks	Fingernails can be seen
28 weeks	Eyes open and close Lungs capable of breathing
32 weeks	Skin pink and smooth Chubby appearance
38 weeks	Nervous system can carry out some integrative functions Reacts to light Usually assumes upside-down position as birth approaches

Sources: Leifer (2003); Moore & Persaud (2003); Olds, London & Ladewig (1996). Reprinted with permission from p. 67 in *LifeSmart*, 2011, by Lisa Fiore. Copyright © 2011 by The McGraw-Hill Companies, Inc. Reprinted by permission.

Within 36 hours after fertilization, the zygote enters a period of rapid cell division and duplication, or *mitosis*. Some 72 hours after fertilization, it has divided into 16 to 32 cells; 24 hours later, it has 64 cells.

While the fertilized ovum is dividing, it is also making its way down the fallopian tube to the uterus, a journey of three or four days. Its form changes into a *blastocyst*, a fluid-filled sphere that floats freely in the uterus until the sixth day after fertilization, when it begins to implant itself in the uterine wall. Only about 10 to 20 percent of fertilized ova complete the task of implantation and continue to develop.

Early Development of a Human Embryo

FIGURE 3.1 Early development of a human embryo. This simplified diagram shows the progress of the ovum as it leaves the ovary, is fertilized in the fallopian tube, and then divides while travelling to the lining of the uterus. Now a blastocyst, it is implanted in the uterus, where it will grow larger and more complex until it is ready to be born.

Source: From Fig. 4.1, p. 89 in *A Child's World*, 12th Ed., 2011, by Diane E. Papalia, Sally Wendkos Olds, Ruth Duskin Feldman. Copyright © 2011 by The McGraw-Hill Companies, Inc. Reprinted by permission.

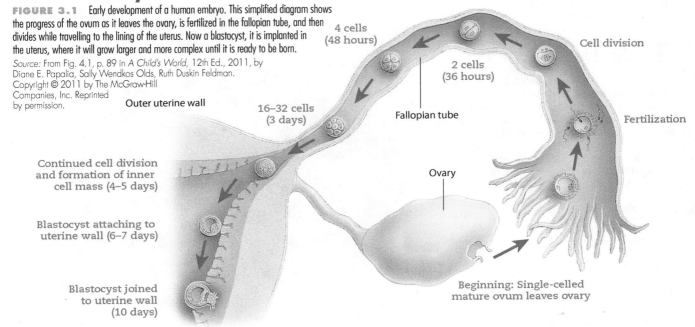

4 cells (48 hours)

Cell division

2 cells (36 hours)

Fallopian tube

Fertilization

Outer uterine wall

16–32 cells (3 days)

Continued cell division and formation of inner cell mass (4–5 days)

Ovary

Blastocyst attaching to uterine wall (6–7 days)

Blastocyst joined to uterine wall (10 days)

Beginning: Single-celled mature ovum leaves ovary

Before implantation, as cell differentiation begins, some cells around the edge of the blastocyst cluster on one side to form the *embryonic disk*, a thickened cell mass from which the embryo begins to develop. This mass is already differentiating into two layers. The upper layer, the *ectoderm*, will become the outer layer of skin, nails, hair, teeth, sensory organs, and nervous system, including the brain and spinal cord. The lower layer, the *endoderm*, will become the digestive system, liver, pancreas, salivary glands, and respiratory system. Later a middle layer, the *mesoderm*, will develop and differentiate into the inner layer of skin, muscles, skeleton, and excretory and circulatory systems.

Other parts of the blastocyst begin to develop into organs that will nurture and protect the embryo (Figure 3.2). The *amniotic sac* is a fluid-filled membrane that encases the developing embryo, giving it room to move. The *placenta*, which contains both maternal and embryonic tissue, develops in the uterus to allow oxygen, nourishment, and wastes to pass between mother and embryo. It is connected to the embryo by the *umbilical cord*. Nutrients from the mother pass from her blood to the embryonic blood vessels and are then carried, via the umbilical cord, to the embryo. In turn, embryonic blood vessels in the umbilical cord carry embryonic wastes to the placenta, where they can be eliminated by maternal blood vessels. The placenta also helps to combat internal infection, gives the unborn child immunity to various diseases, and produces the hormones that support pregnancy. In short, it is a complex life-support system for the developing child.

THE EMBRYONIC STAGE

Sophia woke up one morning with sore breasts. Oddly, her much-loved morning coffee did not smell good, and in fact the smell of it made her feel slightly nauseated. Some hours later, she realized these might be early signs of pregnancy; a pregnancy test later that day indicated that a conception had indeed occurred. Sophia had entered the embryonic stage, when most women first realize they are pregnant.

Did you know?

Most miscarriages occur early in the pregnancy, before a heartbeat can be heard. Women often agonize over their choices and the things they did or did not do when they lose a pregnancy. However, most early miscarriages—by some estimates, as much as 70 percent—are due to chromosomal abnormalities; these pregnancies were never viable. Miscarriage later in pregnancy, however, can be the result of smoking, drinking alcohol, or drug use.

During the **embryonic stage**, from about two to eight weeks, the organs and major body systems—respiratory, digestive, and nervous—develop rapidly. Because the major organ systems and overall body structure are in the process of forming, the embryo is most vulnerable during this time (Figure 3.3). Defects that occur at this point in the pregnancy are likely to be more serious than those that occur later.

The most severely defective embryos usually do not survive beyond the first *trimester*, or three-month period, of pregnancy. As many as one in four recognized pregnancies ends in a **spontaneous abortion**, commonly called a *miscarriage*, which is the expulsion from the uterus of an embryo or a fetus that is unable to survive outside the womb. The actual figure may be as high as one in two because many spontaneous abortions take place before the woman realizes she is pregnant. About three out of four miscarriages occur during the first trimester (Regan & Rai, 2000). The rate of miscarriages varies little across cultures.

embryonic stage   Second stage of prenatal development (two to eight weeks), characterized by rapid growth and development of major body systems and organs.

spontaneous abortion   Natural expulsion from the uterus of an embryo that cannot survive outside the womb; also called *miscarriage.*

The Developing Embryo

FIGURE 3.2   The developing embryo (approximately six weeks gestational age). Throughout its development, the embryo is enclosed and cushioned by the expandable, fluid-filled amniotic cavity. The umbilical cord develops to contain the embryonic blood vessels that carry blood to and from the placenta. Diffusion across the chorionic villi removes wastes from the embryonic blood and adds nutrients and oxygen without the commingling of maternal and embryonic blood.

Source: From p. 88 in *Human Development*, 10th Ed., 2007, by Diane E. Papalia, Sally Wendkos Olds, and Ruth Duskin Feldman. Copyright © 2007 by The McGraw-Hill Companies, Inc. Reprinted by permission.

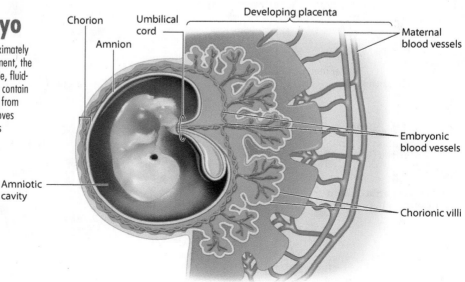

Chorion
Umbilical cord
Amnion
Developing placenta
Maternal blood vessels
Embryonic blood vessels
Amniotic cavity
Chorionic villi

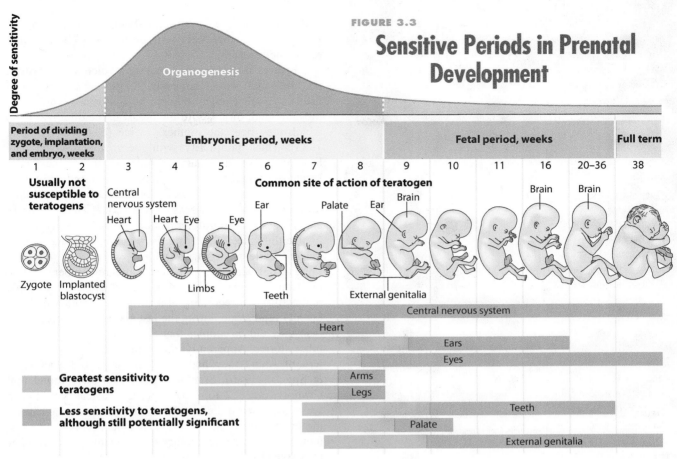

FIGURE 3.3

Sensitive Periods in Prenatal Development

Source: From Fig 3.8, p. 72 in *LifeSmart*, 2011, by Lisa Fiore. Copyright © 2011 by The McGraw-Hill Companies, Inc. Reprinted by permission.

Males are more likely than females to be spontaneously aborted or to be *stillborn*, dead at or after the 20th week following conception. Thus, although about 125 males are conceived for every 100 females, only about 105 boys are born for every 100 girls. Males' greater vulnerability continues after birth: More of them die early in life, and at every age they are more susceptible to many disorders. As a result, among Canadian adults over age 65, there are only 80 males for every 100 females (Urquijo & Milan, 2011).

THE FETAL STAGE

Sophia and Ethan had visited their obstetrician at seven weeks gestation and heard for the first time the tiny, rapid heartbeat of their developing baby. Once that milestone has been passed, the chances of miscarriage drop dramatically. Sophia and Ethan knew now that their chances of having a healthy baby born in approximately seven months' time were high. They had entered the fetal period of development.

The appearance of the first bone cells at about eight weeks signals the beginning of the **fetal stage**, the final stage of gestation. During this period, the fetus grows rapidly to about 20 times its previous length, organs and body systems become more complex, and the fetus puts on a layer of fat in preparation for birth. Right up to that moment, "finishing touches" such as fingernails, toenails, and eyelids continue to develop.

Fetuses are not passive passengers in their mothers' wombs. They breathe, kick, turn, flex their bodies, do somersaults, squint, swallow, make fists, hiccup, and suck their thumbs. The flexible membranes of the uterine walls and amniotic sac, which surround the protective buffer of amniotic fluid, permit and stimulate limited movement; however, after approximately 16 to 25 weeks of gestation, the movements are strong enough to be detected by expectant mothers. Fetal movement is positively related to later well-being and developmental outcomes (Mesbah et al., 2011). Fetuses also can feel pain, but it is unlikely that they do so before the third trimester (Lee, Ralston, Drey, Partridge, & Rosen, 2005; Lowery et al., 2007).

Scientists can observe fetal movement through **ultrasound**, high-frequency sound waves that allow them to detect the outline of the fetus. Other instruments can monitor heart rate, changes in activity level, states of sleep and wakefulness, and cardiac reactivity.

The movements and activity level of fetuses show marked individual differences, and their heart rates vary in regularity and speed. There also are differences

fetal stage Final stage of prenatal development (from eight weeks to birth), characterized by increased differentiation of body parts and greatly enlarged body size.

ultrasound Prenatal medical procedure using high-frequency sound waves to detect the outline of a fetus and its movements, used to determine whether a pregnancy is progressing normally.

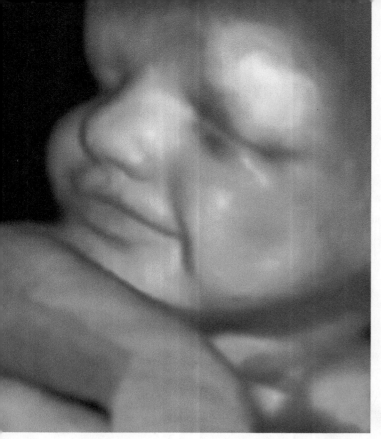

3D ultrasound uses stacked sound wave reflections to produce a computer-aided three-dimensional image of the developing fetus.

that early exposure to different flavours in the amniotic fluid may influence later taste preferences (Beauchamp & Mennella, 2009).

Fetuses respond to the mother's voice and heartbeat and the vibrations of her body, suggesting that they can hear and feel. Hungry infants, no matter on which side they are held, turn toward the breast in the direction from which they hear the mother's voice (Noirot & Algeria, 1983). Thus, familiarity with the mother's voice may have an evolutionary survival function: to help newborns locate the source of food. Responses to sound and vibration seem to begin at 26 weeks of gestation, rise, and then level off at about 32 weeks (Kisilevsky & Haines, 2010), and fetuses nearing full term show the basic ability to recognize the voice of their mothers and of their native language (Kisilevsky et al., 2009)

Fetuses also seem to learn and remember. In one experiment, 3-day-old infants sucked more on a nipple that activated a recording of a story their mother had frequently read aloud during the last six weeks of pregnancy than they did on nipples that activated recordings of two other stories. Apparently, the infants recognized the pattern of sound they had heard in the womb (DeCasper & Spence, 1986). Similar experiments have found that newborns aged 2 to 4 days prefer musical and speech sequences heard before birth. They also prefer their mother's voice to those of other women, female voices to male voices, and their mother's native language to another language (Kisilevsky et al., 2003).

between males and females. Male fetuses, regardless of size, are more active and tend to move more vigorously than female fetuses throughout gestation (Almli, Ball, & Wheeler, 2001). Thus, infant boys' tendency to be more active than girls may be at least partly inborn (DiPietro et al., 2002).

Beginning during the eighth week of gestation, an estimated 250,000 immature *neurons*—nerve cells—are produced every minute. The number of neurons increases most rapidly between the 25th week of gestation and the first few months after birth. Originally, the neurons are simply cell bodies with a nucleus, or centre, composed of deoxyribonucleic acid (DNA), which contains the cell's genetic programming. As the brain grows, these rudimentary cells migrate to various parts of the brain (Bystron, Rakic, Molnar, & Blakemore, 2006). Most of the neurons in the higher areas of the brain are in place by 20 weeks of gestation, and the structure becomes fairly well defined during the next 12 weeks.

From about the 12th week of gestation, the fetus swallows and inhales some of the amniotic fluid in which it floats. Mature taste cells appear at about 14 weeks of gestation. The olfactory system, which controls the sense of smell, also is well developed before birth (Savage, Fisher, & Birch, 2007). The amniotic fluid contains substances that cross the placenta from the mother's bloodstream and enter the fetus's bloodstream. There are indications

Ask Yourself

1. Because of the proximodistal principle, we would expect that an embryo's
   a. head would develop before the arms.
   b. arms would develop before the legs.
   c. arms would develop before the fingers.
   d. feet would develop before the heart.

2. The zygote implants in the uterine wall during
   a. the germinal stage of development.
   b. the embryonic stage of development.
   c. the fetal stage of development.
   d. the germinal or embryonic stage; it varies for each zygote.

3. During the fetal stage of development, the developing child
   a. is unable to perceive any sensory stimulation.
   b. can perceive some limited sensory information and appears to be able to use it to learn from it.
   c. can perceive sensory information at nearly adult levels.
   d. this information is not known because it is impossible to test for it.

Influences on Prenatal Development

Generally, when we think of environmental influences, we consider those influences that occur once we are born. However, it is important to remember that on the day of their birth, infants have already been exposed to nine months of environmental influences and, moreover, that this exposure has occurred during a period of rapid growth and vulnerability. A healthy pregnancy with proper nutrition and prenatal care can promote development and put the newborn on an optimal path. However, exposure to harmful substances or suboptimal nutrition and care can result in a baby being born vulnerable and at risk. Here, we consider the primary source of early environmental influences—the mother. We also consider the influences of paternal factors in a pregnancy, which, while less pivotal in development, can nonetheless impact the developing child.

MATERNAL FACTORS

In traditional societies, pregnancy is recognized as a dangerous time for both a woman and her unborn baby. Among the Beng people of West Africa's Ivory Coast, for example, a woman who has "taken a belly" is warned to stay away from corpses, lest her baby be born diseased; not to offend someone who might curse her pregnancy; and not to eat certain foods, such as puréed yams, lest her labour be difficult (Gottlieb, 2000). Some of these folk beliefs may have a basis in fact. The prenatal environment is the mother's body, and virtually everything that affects her well-being, from her diet to her moods, may alter her unborn child's environment and influence its growth and health.

Alcohol, bacteria from spoiled food, and even the hormones produced by a highly stressed pregnant mother's body can all have negative effects on a developing fetus. They are examples of **teratogens**, environmental agents, such as a virus, a drug, or radiation, that can interfere with normal prenatal development. Teratogens have their most damaging effects on systems and organs that are developing during that time (refer back to Figure 3.3). In other words, there are sensitive periods of development during which exposure to teratogens will cause maximal harm, when systems and organs are developing (**organogenesis**).

Not all environmental hazards are equally risky for all fetuses. Sometimes, vulnerability may depend on a gene either in the fetus or in the mother. For example, fetuses with a particular variant of a growth gene, called *transforming growth factor alpha*, have greater risk than other fetuses of developing a cleft palate if the mother smokes while pregnant (Zeiger, Beaty, & Liang, 2005). The timing of exposure (refer back to Figure 3.3), dose, duration, and interaction with other teratogenic factors also may make a difference.

Nutrition and Maternal Weight

Pregnant women typically need 300 to 500 additional calories a day, including extra protein. Women of normal weight and body build who gain about 7 to 18 kg are less likely to have birth complications or to bear babies whose weight at birth is dangerously low or overly high. Yet about one in three mothers gains more or less than the recommended amounts (Martin et al., 2009). If a woman does not gain enough, her baby is likely to suffer growth retardation in the womb, to be born prematurely, to experience distress during labour and delivery, or to die at or near birth. Interestingly, some research indicates that not eating enough calories during pregnancy might put children at risk for later obesity, perhaps by setting their metabolism to burn fewer calories (Caballero, 2006). A woman who gains too much weight risks having a large baby (Lowell & Miller, 2010) that needs to be delivered by induced labour or surgically by Caesarean section (Martin et al., 2009). Additionally, very large babies are more likely to become overweight or obese later in life (Hillier et al., 2008; Schack-Nielsen, Michaelsen, Gamborg, Mortensen, & Sørensen, 2010).

Women who are overweight or obese before becoming pregnant or in the early months of pregnancy tend to have longer deliveries, to need more health care services (Chu et al., 2008), and to bear infants with birth defects (Stothard, Tennant, Bell, & Rankin, 2009). Obesity also

---

teratogen Environmental agent, such as a virus, a drug, or radiation, that can interfere with normal prenatal development and cause developmental abnormalities.

organogenesis Process of development of emerging body systems and organs.

WHAT DO YOU **DO**?

Nutritionist

The importance of good nutrition is a lifelong process, and establishing good habits and providing a balanced diet in infancy and toddlerhood is important. To this aim, parents sometimes seek the assistance of a nutritionist. A nutritionist working with infants and toddlers might advise on nutrition for a child who has allergies or is either overweight or underweight. Other jobs include working at a hospital or school to develop menus for foods served to young children. University programs typically involve courses in biology, nutrition, food science, physiology, psychology, and statistics. To learn more about the field of nutrition, visit www.cns-scn.ca and www.dietitians.ca.

increases the risk of other complications of pregnancy, including miscarriage, difficulty inducing labour, and a greater likelihood of Caesarean delivery (Brousseau, 2006; Chu et al., 2008).

What an expectant mother eats is also important. For example, newborns whose mothers ate fish high in DHA, an omega-3 fatty acid found in certain fish, such as Atlantic salmon and tuna, showed more mature sleep patterns, a sign of advanced brain development, than infants whose mothers' blood had lower levels of DHA (Cheruku, Montgomery-Downs, Farkas, Thoman, & Lammi-Keefe, 2002), and also were more attentive at 12 and 18 months of age (Colombo et al., 2004).

Folic acid, or folate, a B vitamin found in leafy vegetables and in fortified cereals and breads, is a critical part of a pregnant woman's diet. Inadequate levels of folic acid leave babies at risk of developing a neurological defect such as *anencephaly*, a condition in which the brain is formed incompletely or improperly, or *spina bifida*, a condition in which the baby's spinal cord is not properly enclosed. Canadian women of child-bearing age are urged to take daily multivitamins and folic acid, and to eat plenty of fresh fruits and vegetables even before becoming pregnant, as damage from folic acid deficiency can occur during the early weeks of gestation (Kaczorowski & Lee, 2009; Miller, Liu, Wen, & Walker, 2011; Mills & England, 2001; Van Allen, McCourt, & Lee, 2002). If all women took 5 mg of folic acid each day before pregnancy and during the first trimester, an estimated 85 percent of neurological defects could be prevented (Wald, 2004).

Malnutrition

Prenatal malnutrition may have long-range effects. In rural Gambia, in western Africa, people born during the *hungry season*, when foods from the previous harvest are depleted, are 10 times as likely to die in early adulthood as people born during other parts of the year (Moore et al., 1997). In a study done in the United Kingdom, children whose mothers had had low vitamin D levels late in pregnancy showed low bone-mineral content at age 9, potentially increasing their risk of osteoporosis in later life (Javaid et al., 2006).

It is important to identify malnutrition early in pregnancy so that it can be treated. Malnourished women who take dietary supplements while pregnant tend to have bigger, healthier, more active, and more visually alert infants (Brown, 1987; Vuori et al., 1979). And women with low zinc levels who

Did you know?

For many years it was a mystery why China had the highest incidence of anencephaly and spina bifida. The reason? Traditionally, Chinese couples marry in January or February and try to conceive as soon as possible. Thus, their pregnancies often begin in the winter, when rural women have little access to fresh fruits and vegetables, important sources of folic acid. Programs to give folic acid supplements to pregnant mothers have drastically reduced the incidence of these birth defects in China (Berry et al., 1999). Closer to home, when folate became a mandatory ingredient in Canadian cereal products in 1998, the incidence of neural tube defects decreased by up to 50 percent (De Wals et al., 2007; Persad, Van den Hoff, Dubé, & Zimmer, 2002).

take daily zinc supplements are less likely to have babies with low birth weight and small head circumference (Hess & King, 2009). In a large-scale randomized study of low-income households in 347 Mexican communities, infants whose mothers took nutrient-fortified dietary supplements while pregnant or lactating tended to grow more rapidly and were less likely to be anemic (Rivera, Sotres-Alvarez, Habicht, Shamah, & Villalpando, 2004). In northern regions of Canada, fresh fruits and vegetables may not be readily available or reasonably priced; restricted access to healthful foods and potential food insecurity for pregnant women in remote regions could also be risk factors for the developing fetus (Chan et al., 2006; Ledrou & Gervais, 2005; Willows, 2011; Willows, Iserhoff, Napash, Leclerc, & Verrall, 2005; Willows, Veugelers, Raine, & Kuhle, 2009; Young et al., 2002).

Physical Activity and Strenuous Work

Among the Ifaluk people of the Western Caroline Islands, women are advised to refrain from harvesting crops during the first seven months of pregnancy, when the developing fetus is thought to be weak, but to resume manual labour during the last two months to encourage a speedy delivery (Le, 2000). Actually, moderate exercise at any time during pregnancy does not seem to endanger the fetuses of healthy women. Regular exercise prevents constipation and improves respiration, circulation, muscle tone, and skin elasticity, all of which contribute to a more comfortable pregnancy and an easier, safer delivery (Committee on Obstetric Practice, 2002). However, strenuous working conditions, occupational fatigue, and long working hours may be associated with a greater risk of premature birth (Bell, Zimmerman, & Diehr, 2008).

What an expectant mother eats is important to the healthy development of her unborn child.

Moderate, regular exercise is beneficial for pregnant women and does not seem to endanger the fetus.

The Society of Obstetricians and Gynaecologists of Canada (2000) recommends that women in low-risk pregnancies be guided by their own abilities and stamina. The safest course seems to be for pregnant women to exercise moderately, not pushing themselves and not raising their heart rate above about 150 beats per minute, and, as with any exercise, to taper off at the end of each session rather than stop abruptly (Charlesworth, Foulds, Burr, & Bredin, 2011; Davies, Wolfe, Mottola, & MacKinnon, 2003).

Maternal Illnesses

Both prospective parents should try to avoid all infections, including common colds and flu. If the mother does contract an infection, she should have it treated promptly. Among the diseases that can cause serious problems for her offspring are AIDS, rubella, toxoplasmosis, and diabetes.

Acquired immune deficiency syndrome (AIDS) is a disease caused by the human immunodeficiency virus (HIV), which undermines functioning of the immune system. An infected mother can pass the virus to the fetus's bloodstream through the placenta during pregnancy, labour, or delivery or, after birth, through breast milk. The biggest risk factor for HIV transmission is a mother who is unaware she has HIV. In Canada, new pediatric AIDS cases and the proportion of perinatal infections from HIV-positive mothers have declined steadily since the mid-1980s because of routine testing and treatment of pregnant women and newborn babies and because of advances in the prevention, detection, and treatment of HIV infection in infants (Public Health Agency of Canada, 2009). The risk of transmission also can be reduced by choosing Caesarean delivery, especially when an infected woman has not been treated for HIV,

and by promoting alternatives to breast-feeding among high-risk women (CDC, 2006a).

Rubella (German measles), if contracted by a woman before her 11th week of pregnancy, is almost certain to cause deafness and heart defects in her baby. Chances of catching rubella during pregnancy have been greatly reduced in Canada since the late 1960s, when a vaccine was developed that is now routinely administered to infants and children (Canadian Institute of Child Health [CICH], 2000; Public Health Agency of Canada, 2006). Recent efforts in less developed countries to provide rubella vaccinations have resulted in a decrease of reported rubella cases of over 80 percent from 2000 to 2009 (Reef, Strebel, Dabbagh, Gacic-Dobo, & Cochi, 2011).

An infection called *toxoplasmosis*, caused by a parasite harboured in the bodies of cattle, sheep, and pigs and in the intestinal tracts of cats, typically produces either no symptoms or symptoms like those of the common cold. In an expectant woman, however, especially in the second and third trimesters of pregnancy, it can cause fetal brain damage, severely impaired eyesight or blindness, seizures, miscarriage, stillbirth, or death of the baby. If the baby survives, there may be later problems, including eye infections, hearing loss, and learning disabilities. Treatment with antiparasitic drugs during the first year of life can reduce brain and eye damage (McLeod et al., 2006). To avoid infection, expectant mothers should not eat raw or very rare meat, should peel or thoroughly wash raw fruits and vegetables, and should not dig in a garden where cat feces may be buried. Women who have a cat can have it checked for the disease and should have someone else empty the litter box (March of Dimes Foundation, 2002).

To avoid toxoplasmosis infection, expectant mothers should have someone else empty the cat's litter box.

Offspring of mothers with diabetes are three to four times as likely as offspring of other women to develop a wide range of birth defects (Correa et al., 2008). Research on mice suggests why: High blood glucose levels, typical in diabetics, deprive an embryo of oxygen, with resultant cell damage, during the first eight weeks of pregnancy when its organs are forming. Women with diabetes need to be sure their blood glucose levels are under control before becoming pregnant (Li, Chase, Jung, Smith, & Loeken, 2005).

Maternal Anxiety and Stress

Some tension and worry during pregnancy are normal and do not necessarily increase risks of birth complications (Littleton, Breitkopf, & Berenson, 2006). Moderate maternal anxiety may even spur organization of the developing brain. In a series of studies, 2-year-olds whose mothers had shown moderate anxiety midway through pregnancy scored higher on measures of motor and mental development than did age-mates whose mothers had not shown anxiety during pregnancy (DiPietro, Novak, Costigan, Atella, & Reusing, 2006).

Unusual maternal stress during pregnancy may have harmful effects on the unborn child (Dingfelder, 2004; Huizink, Mulder, & Buitelaar, 2004). In one study, pregnant women whose partners or children died or were hospitalized for cancer or heart attacks were at elevated risk of giving birth to children with malformations, such as cleft lip, cleft palate, and heart malformations (Hansen, Lou, & Olsen, 2000). Even stress before conception may have injurious long-term effects. Prenatal anxiety in mothers has been associated with higher distress to novel experiences, difficulty being soothed, less positive emotion, and lower attention spans in infants (Coplan, O'Niel, & Arbeau, 2005). In another experimental study, when female rats were subjected to ongoing, unpredictable stressors, such as 24-hour isolation, food and water deprivation, constant light, crowding, and electric shocks, for seven days before being mated, their adult offspring engaged in less social interaction than the offspring of a control group, and the female offspring of the stressed mothers were more fearful. These findings suggest that a child born to a woman who has suffered physical, emotional, or sexual abuse may bear permanent scars (Shachar-Dadon, Schulkin, & Leshem, 2009).

Maternal Age

The average age of new mothers has increased over the past several decades, in part because of concerns about financial stability (Milan, 2011; Tough, Benzies, Fraser-Lee, & Newburn-Cook, 2007). In 2008, the average age of first-time mothers in Canada was 28.1 years, compared to 23.5 years in the mid-1960s (Milan, 2011), with most births occurring when women are in their late 20s and early 30s. In 2008, almost half of all births in Canada were to women 30 years of age and over, double the rate for this age group in 1981. Birthrates of Canadian women in their 30s and 40s are at their highest levels since the 1960s. The number of births to women in their early 40s more than doubled between 1991 and 2008, as has the number of births to women in their late 40s (Milan, 2011).

Although most risks to the baby's health are not much greater than for babies born to younger mothers, the chance of miscarriage or stillbirth rises with maternal age, reaching 90 percent for women age 45 or older (Heffner, 2004). Women over 30 to 35 years of age are more likely to experience complications and are at higher risk of premature delivery. Their babies are more likely to show retarded fetal growth, birth defects, and chromosomal abnormalities, such as Down syndrome. However, because of widespread screening among older expectant

Tina Fey, a successful comedian and writer, had her two daughters at ages 35 and 41.

mothers, fewer malformed infants are born nowadays (Heffner, 2004).

Adolescents also tend to have premature or underweight babies (Fraser, Brockert, & Ward, 1995; Martin et al., 2007). These newborns are at heightened risk of death in the first month, disabilities, or health problems. Teenage pregnancy is discussed further in Chapter 16.

Outside Environmental Hazards

Air pollution, chemicals, radiation, and other hazards of modern life can affect prenatal development. For example, pregnant women who regularly breathe air that contains high levels of fine combustion-related particles, such as smoke and gas fumes, are more likely to bear infants who are premature or undersized (Parker, Woodruff, Basu, & Schoendorf, 2005) or have chromosomal abnormalities (Bocskay et al., 2005). Exposure to high concentrations of disinfection by-products is associated with low birth weight and slowed fetal growth (Hinckley, Bachand, & Reif, 2005).

Fetal exposure to low levels of environmental toxins, such as lead, mercury, and dioxin, as well as nicotine and ethanol, may help explain the sharp rise in asthma, allergies, and autoimmune disorders such as lupus in children (Dietert, 2005).

TABLE 3.2 Effects of Prenatal Exposure to Substances

Drug	Effects on Fetus	Effects on Newborn	Long-Term Effects
Tobacco	Miscarriage Premature labour Low birth weight Restricted growth Separation of placenta	Increased mortality Sudden infant death syndrome (SIDS)	Childhood asthma Behaviour and cognitive problems Attention deficit hyperactivity disorder (ADHD)
Alcohol	Miscarriage Premature birth	Fetal alcohol spectrum disorders (FASD) Neurological disorders Small head circumference	Behaviour and cognitive problems Retarded growth Motor impairments
Marijuana	Inconsistent effects	Neurobehavioural effects: ■ Poor self-quieting ■ Increased tremors, startles ■ Changing sleep patterns	Disturbed sleep Behaviour problems Depression, anxiety
Heroin	Premature labour Low birth weight Restricted growth	Increased mortality	Behaviour problems Physical, social, and learning difficulties
Methadone		Withdrawal symptoms Strabismus	
Cocaine	Miscarriage Premature labour Restricted growth Separation of placenta	Genital, urinary tract anomalies Smaller length, head circumference Neurological impairment	Expressive language delays
Amphetamines	Fetal death Restricted growth	Central nervous system anomalies Cardiovascular anomalies Oral clefts, limb defects Neurobehavioural effects: ■ Decreased arousal ■ Increased stress ■ Poor quality of movement	Behaviour problems
Hallucinogens (e.g., LSD)		Cardiovascular anomalies Kidney defects	

Sources: Carter et al. (2005); Wong, S., et al. (2011). Substance use in pregnancy. *International Journal of Gynecology & Obstetrics*, 114(2), 190–202.

Drug Intake

How do specific drugs taken during pregnancy affect the developing child? Let's look first at medical drugs; then at alcohol, nicotine, and caffeine; and finally at the illegal drugs marijuana, cocaine, and methamphetamine (Table 3.2).

MEDICAL DRUGS It was once thought that the placenta protected the fetus against drugs the mother took during pregnancy—until the early 1960s, when a tranquilizer and anti-nausea drug called thalidomide was banned after it was found to have caused stunted or missing limbs, severe facial deformities, and defective organs in some 12,000 babies worldwide, with about 120 survivors living in Canada today. The thalidomide disaster sensitized medical professionals and the public to the potential dangers of taking drugs while pregnant, and since then, doctors and pregnant women alike have exercised great care in the use of medication during pregnancy. Today, nearly 30 drugs have been found to be teratogenic in clinically recommended doses (Koren, Pastuszak, & Ito, 1998).

Among the prescription drugs that may be harmful when taken during pregnancy are the antibiotic tetracycline; certain barbiturates, opiates, and other central nervous system depressants; several hormones, including diethylstilbestrol (DES) and androgens; certain anticancer drugs, such as methotrexate; Accutane, a drug often prescribed for severe acne (Koren, Pastuszak, & Ito, 1998); drugs used to treat epilepsy (FDA, 2011);

Did you know?

While animal research has its place in medical testing, it also has limitations. Thalidomide was tested on animals before being prescribed for pregnant woman and indicated no ill effects. However, in humans, it quickly became clear that thalidomide was closely linked to major birth defects.

and several antipsychotic drugs (Einarson & Boskovic, 2009). Angiotensin-converting enzyme (ACE) inhibitors and non-steroidal anti-inflammatory drugs (NSAIDs), such as naproxen and ibuprofen, have been linked to birth defects when taken any time from the first trimester on (Cooper et al., 2006; Ofori, Oraichi, Blais, Rey, & Berard, 2006).

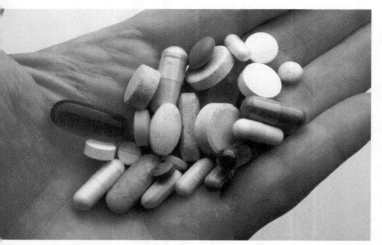

Any medications taken during pregnancy should be cleared with an obstetrician.

The AAP Committee on Drugs (2001) recommends that no medication be prescribed for a pregnant or breast-feeding woman unless it is essential for her health or her child's. When practical and consistent with controlling her symptoms, a woman should be withdrawn from psychiatric medication prior to conception. Infants whose mothers take antidepressants, such as Prozac, during pregnancy can show signs of disrupted neurobehavioural activity, such as a tendency to startle easily and a decreased tendency to form a regular sleep cycle (Zeskind & Stephens, 2004), and are at increased risk of transient, but in rare cases severe, respiratory failure if the antidepressant is used in the third trimester (Chambers et al., 2006; Jefferies & Canadian Paediatric Society [CPS], Fetus and Newborn Committee, 2011); careful monitoring of the newborn in the first days after birth is recommended (Jefferies & CPS, 2011). Certain drugs used to manage severe psychiatric disorders, such as lithium, may have serious potential effects on the fetus, including withdrawal symptoms at birth (AAP Committee on Drugs, 2000). If medication is necessary, the most effective drug with the fewest side effects should be selected. Pregnant women should not take over-the-counter drugs without consulting a doctor.

Research has shown that most psychiatric drugs administered to a lactating woman can be found in her breast milk. The concentration tends to be low, and therefore, there is little likelihood of an effect on the infant. Thus, there appears to be no concrete evidence at the present time for recommending that a woman requiring psychiatric medication avoid breast-feeding. However, it must be emphasized that if a mother chooses to breast-feed while on medication, the baby should be observed for signs of drug effects (AAP Committee on Drugs,

2001). The Motherisk program at Toronto's Hospital for Sick Children reports that most prescription drugs do not pose a risk to the breast-fed infant; the major exceptions being medications for cancer therapy and anticonvulsants (Moretti, Lee, & Ito, 2000). Drugs of abuse, like alcohol, cocaine, and amphetamines, should be avoided as they have been found to pass through to breast milk.

ALCOHOL Like Karen Lutke, whose story opened this chapter, about one infant in 750 suffers from fetal alcohol syndrome (FAS), a combination of slow prenatal and postnatal growth, facial and bodily malformations, and disorders of the central nervous system. Over 100 FAS-affected infants are born in Canada each year (Willms, 2002a). FAS and other less severe alcohol-related conditions—including fetal alcohol effects (FAS/E), partial fetal alcohol spectrum disorder (pFASD), alcohol-related neurodevelopmental disorder (ARND), and alcohol-related birth defects (ARBD)—are examples of **fetal alcohol spectrum disorders (FASD)** (Carson et al., 2010), and are estimated to occur in nearly one in every 100 births (Sokol, Delaney-Black, & Nordstrom, 2003). Problems related to the central nervous system in infancy, can include poor sucking response, brain-wave abnormalities, and sleep disturbances (Carter et al., 2005; Sokol et al., 2003), and, throughout childhood, slow information processing, poor social judgment, short attention span, restlessness, irritability, hyperactivity, learning disabilities, retarded growth, and motor impairments (Sood et al., 2001; Willms, 2002a). Prebirth exposure to alcohol seems to affect a portion of the corpus callosum, which coordinates signals between the two hemispheres of the brain. In macaques (and presumably in humans as well), the affected portion, toward the front of the head, is involved in initiating voluntary movement and other higher-order processing (Miller, Astley, & Clarren, 1999).

The more the mother drinks, the greater are the effects. An estimated 5.8 percent of Canadian women have reported consuming some alcohol during pregnancy (Thanh, 2010). Furthermore, more than half of women of child-bearing age who do not use birth control (and could become pregnant) report alcohol use (Tsai & Floyd, 2004). Research with rats shows that even a single drinking binge of four hours or more can do tremendous damage to the developing brain (Ikonomidou et al., 2000). Moderate or heavy drinking during pregnancy seems to disturb an infant's neurological and behavioural functioning, and this may affect early social interaction with the mother, which is vital to emotional development (Connor & Mcintyre, 2002; Hannigan & Armant, 2000; Nugent, Lester, Greene, Wieczorek-Deering, & O'Mahony, 1996). Heavy drinkers who continue to drink after becoming pregnant are likely to have babies with smaller skulls and brains than babies of

fetal alcohol spectrum disorders (FASD) Combination of mental, motor, and developmental abnormalities affecting the offspring of some women who drink heavily during pregnancy.

non-drinking women or expectant mothers who stop drinking (Handmaker et al., 2006).

Recent studies of the relationship between genetics and environment indicate that fetuses with a certain variant of the ADH1B gene can be more vulnerable to the effects of alcohol exposure than those without that specific variant (Jaffee & Price, 2007; Reynolds et al., 2011; Warren & Li, 2005). The gene variant can influence how alcohol is metabolized in the fetus, producing potentially toxic materials that can lead to negative physiological and behavioural outcomes (Jaffee & Price, 2007).

FASD-related problems can include, in infancy, reduced responsiveness to stimuli, slow reaction time, and reduced visual acuity (sharpness of vision) (Carter et al., 2005), and, throughout childhood, short attention span, distractibility, restlessness, hyperactivity, learning disabilities, memory deficits, and mood disorders (Sokol et al., 2003), as well as aggressiveness and problem behaviour (Sood et al., 2001). Some FASD problems recede after birth, but others, such as retardation, behavioural and learning problems, and hyperactivity, tend to persist. Enriching these children's education or general environment does not always seem to enhance their cognitive development (Kerns, Don, Mateer, & Streissguth, 1997), but recent interventions targeted at cognitive skills in children with FASD are showing promise (Paley & O'Connor, 2011). Children with FASD may be less likely to develop behavioural and mental health problems if they are diagnosed early and are reared in stable, nurturing environments (Streissguth et al., 2004).

Approximately 25 percent of Canadian women report smoking during pregnancy (Greaves et al., 2011; Human Resources Development Canada, 1996).

Did you know?

The harmful effects of first- and second-hand smoke are well documented, but less is known about the effects of third-hand smoke, left-over residual tobacco smoke contamination after cigarettes have been extinguished. The same "cocktail" of toxic chemicals settle on all surfaces in homes, such as furniture, curtains, flooring—places easily accessible to young infants. Recent surveys have found a growing awareness of the dangers of third-hand smoke, and with this awareness a growing acceptance of the need to restrict smoking in enclosed spaces that children inhabit, including cars and homes (Winickoff et al., 2009).

Because there is no known safe level of drinking during pregnancy, it is best to avoid alcohol from the time a woman begins thinking about becoming pregnant until she stops breast-feeding (Carson et al., 2010; Sokol et al., 2003). Breast-feeding mothers should avoid alcoholic beverages because alcohol has been shown to become concentrated in breast milk, and its use can inhibit milk production.

NICOTINE About a quarter of Canadian women report smoking during pregnancy (Greaves et al., 2011; Human Resources Development Canada, 1996), with 84 percent of smokers continuing throughout pregnancy and 90 percent doing so during the first trimester (CICH, 2000; Willms, 2002a). Maternal smoking has been identified as the single most important factor in low birth weight in developed countries (DiFranza, Aligne, & Weitzman, 2004). Women who smoke during pregnancy are more than one-and-a-half times as likely as non-smokers to bear low-birth-weight (less than 2.5 kg at birth) babies. Even light smoking, fewer than five cigarettes a day, is associated with a greater risk of low birth weight (Martin et al., 2007).

Tobacco use during pregnancy also brings increased risks of miscarriage, growth retardation, stillbirth, small head circumference, and sudden infant death; in early infancy, risks include hyperkinetic disorder (excessive movement) and long-term respiratory, neurological, cognitive, and behavioural problems (AAP Committee on Substance Abuse, 2001; Hoyert et al., 2006; Martin et al., 2007; Pendlebury et al., 2008). Second-hand smoke has similar effects and has been linked with low birth weight, infant respiratory infections, sudden infant death, and cancer in childhood and adulthood (Ji et al., 1997; Kharrazi et al., 2004).

CAFFEINE Can the caffeine a pregnant woman consumes in coffee, tea, cola, or chocolate cause trouble for her fetus? For the most part, research results have been mixed. It does seem clear that caffeine is not a teratogen for human babies (Christian & Brent, 2001). A controlled study of 1,205 new mothers and their babies showed no effect of reported caffeine use on low birth weight, premature birth, or retarded fetal growth (Santos, Victora, Huttly, & Carvalhal, 1998). But in a controlled study of 1,063 pregnant women, those who consumed at least two cups of regular coffee or five cans of caffeinated soda daily had twice the risk of miscarriage as those who consumed no caffeine (Weng, Odouli, & Li, 2008).

MARIJUANA, COCAINE, AND METHAMPHETAMINE Studies of marijuana use by pregnant women are sparse and the results are inconsistent. However, some evidence suggests that heavy marijuana use can lead to birth defects, low birth weight, withdrawal-like symptoms (excessive crying and tremors) at birth, and increased risk of attention disorders and learning problems later in life (March of Dimes Birth Defects Foundation, 2004b). Research using functional magnetic resonance imaging (fMRI) shows that young adults who were exposed to marijuana prenatally, compared with those who were not exposed, experienced different patterns of neural activation when carrying out tasks requiring inhibitory behaviours (Smith, Fried, Hogan, & Cameron, 2004).

Cocaine use during pregnancy has been associated with spontaneous abortion, delayed growth, premature labour, low birth weight, small head size, birth defects,

impaired neurological development, and mild cognitive deficits into preadolescence (Bennett, Bendersky, & Lewis, 2008; March of Dimes Birth Defects Foundation, 2004a; Shankaran et al., 2004). In some studies, cocaine-exposed newborns show acute withdrawal symptoms

Perspectives on Diversity

DISPARITIES IN PRENATAL CARE

In developing countries, one in four pregnant women does not receive prenatal care, and more than four out of ten give birth without a skilled attendant. These facts may help explain why almost 40 percent of deaths of children under age 5 occur during the first four weeks of life from complications of birth (UNICEF, 2007).

In Canada, prenatal care is widespread, but despite universal health insurance, socio-economic status affects the quality of prenatal care provided to pregnant women (Canadian Perinatal Surveillance System, 2000; Willms, 2002a). As an indicator of different effectiveness of prenatal care, low-income groups experience over 150 percent the infant mortality rate of higher-income groups. However, the disparity in infant mortality rates between income groups and between regions in Canada is decreasing (Dzakpasu, Joseph, Kramer, & Allen, 2000).

There is also ethnic disparity in fetal and postbirth mortality. The chances of perinatal death (death between 20 weeks gestation and one week after birth) remain at least two times as high for Aboriginal as for non-Aboriginal groups (Public Health Agency of Canada, 2008).

Even as usage of prenatal care has increased, rates of low birth weight and premature birth have worsened (Kogan et al., 1998). Why?

One answer is the increasing number of multiple births, which require especially close prenatal attention. Twin pregnancies often end, for precautionary reasons, in early births, either induced or by Caesarean delivery. Intensive prenatal care may allow early detection of problems requiring immediate delivery, as, for example, when one or both fetuses are not thriving. This may explain why a Canadian study of twin births between 1986 and 1997 found parallel upward trends in use of prenatal care and rates of preterm birth—along with a decline in mortality of twin infants (Joseph et al. 2001).

Another possible explanation for these parallel trends is that the benefits of prenatal care are not evenly distributed, particularly in northern and remote communities. Merely increasing the quantity of prenatal care does not address the content of care (Misra & Guyer, 1998). Most prenatal care programs in Canada focus on screening for major complications and are not designed to attack the causes of low birth weight.

and sleep disturbances (O'Brien & Jeffery, 2002). Other studies, however, have found no specific connection between prenatal cocaine exposure and physical, motor, cognitive, emotional, or behavioural deficits that could not also be attributed to other risk factors, such as low birth weight; exposure to tobacco, alcohol, or marijuana; or a poor home environment (Messinger et al., 2004; Singer et al., 2004). Many of the effects associated with prenatal cocaine exposure may be due to indirect effects such as these rather than stemming directly from the drug itself.

Methamphetamine use among pregnant women is an increasing concern in Canada (Hutson, 2006). In a U.S. study of 1,618 infants, 84 were found to have been exposed to methamphetamine. The methamphetamine-exposed infants were more likely to have low birth weight and to be small for their gestational age than the remainder of the sample. This finding suggests that prenatal methamphetamine exposure is associated with restricted fetal growth (Smith et al., 2006).

Early treatment for alcohol, nicotine, and other substance abuse can greatly improve health outcomes. Among 2,073 women enrolled in an early prenatal care program, risks of stillbirth, preterm delivery, low birth weight, and placental separation from the uterus were no higher than for a control group of 46,553 women with no evidence of substance abuse, whereas risks for 156 untreated substance abusers were dramatically higher (Goler, Armstrong, Taillac, & Osejo, 2008).

PATERNAL FACTORS

Sophia was careful during her pregnancy to make sure to eat healthy, and she diligently avoided alcohol and her favourite sushi restaurant in order to ensure a healthy pregnancy. Did Ethan need to do the same thing? What is the father's role in early environmental influences?

While the woman's exposure to teratogens has a larger effect, men's exposure to deleterious substances can still exert an effect on a pregnancy. A man's exposure to lead, marijuana or tobacco smoke, large amounts of alcohol or radiation, DES, pesticides, or high ozone levels may result in abnormal or poor quality sperm (Sokol et al., 2006). For example, offspring of male workers at a British nuclear processing plant were at elevated risk of being born dead (Parker, Pearce, Dickinson, Aitkin, & Craft, 1999). Babies whose fathers had high lead exposure tended to have low birth weight and slowed fetal growth (Chen & Wang, 2006). In addition, men who smoke are more likely to transmit genetic abnormalities to their offspring (AAP Committee on Substance Abuse, 2001).

Older fathers may be a significant source of birth defects because of damaged or deteriorated sperm. Birthrates for fathers ages 30 to 49 have risen significantly since 1980 (Martin et al., 2009). Advancing paternal age is associated with increases in the risk of several rare conditions, including dwarfism (Wyrobek et al., 2006).

Advanced age of the father also may be a factor in a disproportionate number of cases of schizophrenia (Byrne et al., 2003; Malaspina et al., 2001), bipolar disorder (Frans et al., 2008), and autism and related disorders (Reichenberg et al., 2006; Tsuchiya et al., 2008).

Ask Yourself

4. The developing child is most sensitive to teratogens during the embryonic stage of development because
   a. it has not yet implanted and thus does not have an umbilical cord.
   b. the fetus becomes more active during this time and thus metabolizes substances more quickly.
   c. the major organ systems and body structures are forming during this time.
   d. this is not true; the developing child is most sensitive to teratogens during the fetal stage of development.

5. List three maternal factors that can negatively impact a pregnancy.

6. One's age during a pregnancy is a risk factor
   a. only for mothers.
   b. only for fathers.
   c. for neither parent.
   d. for both parents, although for mothers to a greater degree.
   e. for both parents, although for fathers to a greater degree.

Monitoring Prenatal Development

Sophia's pregnancy was proceeding in a textbook fashion from the outside, but Sophia and Ethan, because of the development of modern prenatal assessment tools now available to expectant parents, could opt to do any one of a number of different tests to assess the health of their baby. Because Sophia was under 35 years of age and had no obvious risk factors, their doctor suggested they use ultrasound and blood tests to receive a risk assessment of their baby's health. Happily, the baby appeared to be healthy and thriving, and so the young parents opted against further genetic testing.

Not long ago, almost the only decision parents had to make about their babies before birth was the decision to conceive. Most of what happened in the intervening months was beyond their control. Now scientists have developed an array of tools to assess an unborn baby's progress and well-being.

Progress is being made in the use of non-invasive procedures, such as ultrasound and blood tests, to detect chromosomal abnormalities. Screening is most effective when begun during the first trimester (Simpson, 2005). In one study, a combination of three non-invasive tests conducted at 11 weeks of gestation predicted the presence of Down syndrome with 87 percent accuracy. When the 11-week tests were followed by further non-invasive testing early in the second trimester, accuracy reached 96 percent (Malone et al., 2005).

Other assessment techniques include *amniocentesis*, a procedure in which a sample of amniotic fluid is withdrawn for analysis, and *chorionic villus sampling*, in which tissue from the membrane surrounding the fetus is removed and analyzed. Both procedures provide definitive evidence of a genetic issue, can be used earlier in pregnancy, and have been shown to carry only a slightly higher miscarriage risk than non-invasive techniques (Caughey, Hopkins, & Norton, 2006; Eddleman et al., 2006). *Embryoscopy*, the insertion of a tiny viewing scope into the mother's uterus through the abdominal wall for a direct look at the embryo, can

help diagnose non-chromosomal disorders, and *umbilical cord sampling* allows direct access to fetal DNA in the blood vessels of the umbilical cord for diagnosis.

Screening for defects and diseases is only one reason for the importance of early prenatal care. Early, high-quality prenatal care, which includes educational, social, and nutritional services, can help prevent maternal or infant death and other birth complications. It can provide first-time mothers with information about pregnancy, childbirth, and infant care. Poor women who get prenatal care benefit by being put in touch with other needed services, and they are more likely to get medical care for their infants after birth (Shiono & Behrman, 1995).

Good prenatal care can give every child the best possible chance for entering the world in good condition to meet the challenges of life outside the womb—challenges we discuss in the next chapter.

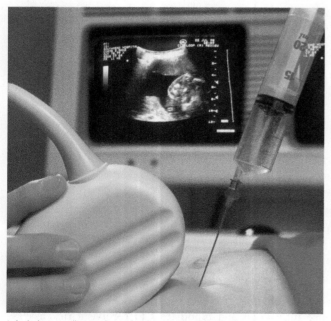

In both chorionic villus sampling and amniocentesis, an ultrasound machine can be used to guide the procedure.

Ask Yourself

7. Which of the following tests assess the genetic risk for the child?
   a. maternal blood tests
   b. chorionic villus sampling
   c. embryoscopy
   d. amniocentesis
   e. b and d

LO1

Describe the three stages of prenatal development.

- Prenatal development occurs in three stages of gestation: the germinal, embryonic, and fetal stages.
- Growth and development both before and after birth follow the cephalocaudal principle (head to tail) and the proximodistal principle (centre outward).
- As many as one-half of all conceptions end in spontaneous abortion, usually in the first trimester of pregnancy.
- As fetuses grow, they move less but more vigorously. Swallowing amniotic fluid, which contains substances from the mother's body, stimulates taste and smell. Fetuses seem able to hear, exercise sensory discrimination, learn, and remember.

LO2

List the different substances or parental characteristics that can negatively impact prenatal development and summarize their effects.

- The developing organism can be greatly affected by its prenatal environment. The likelihood of a birth defect may depend on the timing and intensity of an environmental event and its interaction with genetic factors.
- Important environmental influences involving the mother include nutrition, physical activity, smoking, intake of alcohol or other drugs, transmission of maternal illnesses or infections, maternal age, and external environmental hazards, such as chemicals and radiation. External influences may also affect the father's sperm.

LO3

Summarize prenatal monitoring options for expectant parents.

- Ultrasound, amniocentesis, chorionic villus sampling, embryoscopy, umbilical cord sampling, and maternal blood tests can be used to determine whether an unborn baby is developing normally.
- Early, high-quality prenatal care is essential for healthy development. It can lead to detection of defects and disorders and, especially if begun early and targeted to the needs of at-risk women, may help reduce maternal and infant death, low birth weight, and other birth complications.

ANSWERS TO Ask Yourself

Answers: 1–c; 2–a; 3–b; 4–c; 5–Among the maternal factors that can impact a pregnancy are exposure to teratogens, nutrition and weight, physical activity and strenuous work, drug intake, illness, stress, age, and environmental hazards; 6–d; 7–e

connect **LEARNSMART** **SMARTBOOK**

For more information on the resources available from McGraw-Hill Ryerson, go to **www.mcgrawhill.ca/he/solutions**.

BIRTH AND
THE NEWBORN BABY

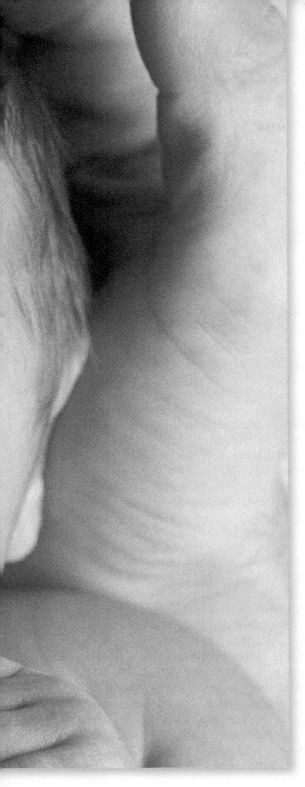

WHAT'S TO COME

How Childbirth Has Changed

The Birth Process

The Newborn Baby

Birth Complications and Their Aftermath

Newborns and Parents

Emily rested her hand on her swollen belly and sighed. After eight months of pregnancy she was tired of swollen feet, heartburn, and feeling out of breath. She looked forward to meeting her new son and felt a mix of excitement and apprehension when she thought about what was to come. What was labour like? Would it hurt a lot? What would it be like to have a newborn? Would she know what to do?

In this chapter, we describe the first steps in the journey of life outside the womb. We describe how babies come into the world, what newborn babies look like, and how their body systems work. We discuss techniques used to assess newborn health and the different ways in which birth complications can affect development. We also consider how the birth of a baby affects the people most vital to the infant's well-being: the parents.

LO1   Describe what traditional and modern childbirth look like.
LO2   Summarize the stages of childbirth and common medical interventions.
LO3   Describe a newborn's appearance and characteristics and how health is assessed.
LO4   Summarize the causes and consequences of low birth weight, postmaturity, and infant mortality.
LO5   Describe the importance of bonding and how the birth of a newborn affects the marital relationship.

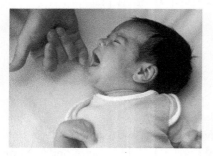
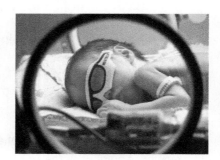

How Childbirth Has Changed

Customs surrounding childbirth reflect the beliefs, values, and resources of a culture. The reproductive role is a source of social status among First Nations peoples, and women who raise families successfully are influential in their communities, with the wisdom of elderly women recognized in the esteem in which grandmothers were held (Carroll & Benoit, 2001). In Yucatan, a Mayan woman gives birth in the hammock in which she sleeps every night; both the father-to-be and a midwife are expected to be present (Jordan, 1993). By contrast, among the Ngoni in East Africa, men are excluded from the birth (Gardiner & Kosmitzki, 2005). While cultural differences abound, differences can also be seen across time within many countries, as childbirth and labour became increasingly medicalized and moved from the home to hospital settings.

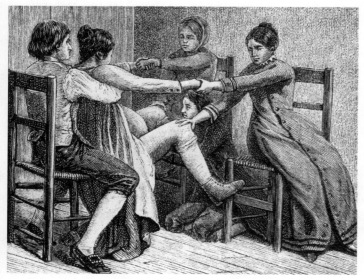

An example of nineteenth-century childbirth practice in Canada and Europe.

Childbirth in earlier times was "a struggle with death" (Fontanel & d'Harcourt, 1997) for both mother and baby. In seventeenth- and eighteenth-century France, a woman had a one in ten chance of dying while or shortly after giving birth. Thousands of babies were stillborn, and one out of four who were born alive died during their first year. At the end of the nineteenth century in England and Wales, an expectant mother was almost 50 times as likely to die in childbirth as is a woman giving birth today (Saunders, 1997).

At this time, childbirth in Europe and in Canada followed somewhat similar patterns. The woman, surrounded by female relatives and neighbours, sat up in her bed or perhaps in the stable, modestly draped in a sheet; if she wished she might stand, walk around, or squat over a birth stool. Cracks in the walls, doors, and windows were stuffed with cloth to keep out chills and evil spirits. Neither the prospective father nor doctors were anywhere to be seen, although midwives without formal training were often present. Salves made of fat of viper, gall of eel, powdered hoof of donkey, tongue of chameleon, or skin of snake or hare might be rubbed on the prospective mother's abdomen to ease her pain or hasten her labour.

After the turn of the twentieth century in Europe and Canada, childbirth began to be professionalized, at least in urban settings. The growing use of maternity hospitals led to somewhat safer, more antiseptic conditions for childbirth. Hospital deliveries reduced mortality for women, and the new field of obstetrics grew. In 1926, the first year that national statistics were taken, 18 percent of Canadian deliveries took place in hospitals; by 1960, the rate was 95 percent, and the rate is now about 99 percent (Statistics Canada, 2012c). A growing number of deliveries are now attended by midwives, usually certified nurse-midwives (Martin et al., 2006).

About 96 percent of births are attended by physicians and 4 percent by midwives. Midwives provide care during pregnancy, labour, and the postpartum period, and also offer assistance in breast-feeding and other primary care services to women. Most midwives are registered nurses with special training in midwifery, and some have been trained by apprenticeship; they are certified by health authorities—a significant shift from earlier decades in which midwives had no legal status in Canada (Benoit & Carroll, 2005).

In many provinces, such as British Columbia, Aboriginal midwifery, which incorporates traditional Aboriginal practices and contemporary techniques and tools, is becoming recognized and supported by mainstream health authorities (Carroll & Benoit, 2001). New training programs for Aboriginal midwifery combine traditional and mainstream approaches. Most Aboriginal midwives work in birthing clinics located in northern regions (Benoit & Carroll, 2005).

In many traditional cultures, and increasingly in developed countries as well, child-bearing women are attended by a *doula*, an experienced mentor, coach, and helper who furnishes emotional support and information and stays at a woman's bedside throughout labour. A doula does not actively participate in the delivery but supports the mother throughout the process. In 14 randomized, controlled studies, women attended by doulas had shorter labour, less anesthesia, and fewer Caesarean deliveries than mothers who had not had doulas (Hodnett, Gates, Hofmeyr, & Sakala, 2005). Doulas (who often take special training) attend about 1 percent of births; they are, however, gaining wider acceptance (Eftekhary, Klein, & Xu, 2010; Gilbert, 1998).

The dramatic reductions in risks surrounding pregnancy and childbirth in the industrialized world are largely due to the availability of universally accessible prenatal health care, antibiotics, blood transfusions, safe anesthesia, improved hygiene, and drugs for inducing labour when necessary. In addition, improvements in prenatal assessment and care make it far more likely that a baby will be born healthy. Mortality rates for both mothers and children have decreased dramatically. For example, in 1890s, infant mortality—deaths from all causes in the first year of life—was 145 deaths per 1,000 live births; by 2005, this number had decreased to approximately 5 deaths per 1,000 live births (Chief Public Health Officer of Canada, 2009).

Still, childbirth is not risk-free for women or babies. Obese women, those with difficult medical histories, those who had previous Caesarean deliveries, and those who had several children are at elevated risk of hemorrhage and other dangerous complications (Chazotte, quoted in Bernstein, 2003).

The medicalization of childbirth has had social and emotional costs, costs that some modern women are rejecting. About a third of Canadian women prefer birthing centres rather than hospitals, while 80 percent are willing to be cared for by a nurse or midwife after birth (Wen et al., 1999); however, attitudes toward home birth are

Birth with the support of a doula.

mixed (Tyson, 1991). A small but growing percentage of women in economically developed countries are reviving the intimate experience of home birth. Some studies suggest that planned home births with speedy transfer to a hospital available in case of need can be as safe as hospital births for low-risk deliveries attended by skilled, certified midwives or nurse-midwives (American College of Nurse-Midwives, 2005). In fact, home births attended by registered midwives are associated with lower need for obstetric intervention (Janssen et al., 2009). Although the Society of Obstetricians and Gynaecologists of Canada does not take a strong stand on the practice (Society of Obstetricians and Gynaecologists of Canada, 2003), there are varying attitudes from medical practitioners (Klein et al., 2009, 2011).

WHAT DO YOU **DO**?

Doula

A certified doula supports women emotionally during labour and childbirth. A doula helps the mother create a birth plan and supports the mother and her partner during labour and delivery. After the baby's birth, a postpartum doula helps the family adjust to the new baby, does light housekeeping and cooking, and supports the mother during her recovery. Becoming a doula requires certification that involves educational activities that vary from attending workshops to enrolling in childbirth education series. To learn more about being a doula, go to www.doulacare.ca.

For example, the American College of Obstetricians and Gynecologists (ACOG, 2011) and the American Medical Association (AMA, 2008), although respecting the right of mothers to make informed choices about home birth, oppose home births, maintaining that complications can arise suddenly, even in low-risk pregnancies, and hospitals or accredited birthing centres are best equipped to respond to such emergencies.

In response to these social trends, hospitals are finding ways to "humanize" childbirth; family-centred approaches, with warm, comforting, one-room, quiet, home-like environments for labour, birth, and recovery experienced with family members, have been adopted by hospitals (Health Canada, 2000) and overwhelmingly accepted by families (Janssen, Klein, Harris, Soolsma, & Seymour, 2000). Families feel more welcome and better prepared for childbirth, and birthing mothers and their families are more active in deciding how birthing takes place (Roudebush, Kaufman, Johnson, Abraham, & Clayton, 2006). The woman may receive local anesthesia if she wants and needs it, but she can see and consciously participate in the birth process and can hold her newborn on her belly immediately afterward. Rooming-in policies allow a baby to stay in the mother's room much or all of the time.

Ask Yourself

1. Women in the industrialized world who give birth today have benefited from a dramatic reduction in risks surrounding pregnancy and childbirth, because of
   a. use of antibiotics.
   b. use of anesthesia.
   c. implementation of prenatal care.
   d. all of these.

The Birth Process

Emily woke up with some strange sensations in her belly. She had felt the baby, her first, moving all through her second and third trimesters, but this felt different. Her due date was still two weeks off. Could she be feeling the birth contractions she had heard and read so much about? Was she in labour?

Labour is an apt term for the process of giving birth. Chiefly because of the size of the fetal head, birth is hard work for both mother and baby. From an evolutionary perspective, the advantage of an enlarged head that can contain a brain capable of advanced thought outweighs the difficulty of passing through the birth canal (Bjorklund & Pellegrini, 2000).

Labour is brought on by a series of uterine, cervical, and other changes, called **parturition**, that begin about two weeks before delivery. While the definitive trigger for the advent of labour is unclear, it is likely to be due at least in part to hormones released by the placenta and fetus

Did you know?

Only 5 percent of women give birth on their expected due dates. Most pregnant women deliver at some point between 37 and 42 weeks.

(Mendelson, 2009). The uterine contractions that expel the fetus begin—typically, about 266 days after conception—as tightenings of the uterus. A woman may have felt false contractions (known as Braxton-Hicks contractions) at times during the final months of pregnancy. These contractions may help tone the uterine muscles and promote the flow of blood to the placenta, but they are mild and irregular and do not result in any of the cervical changes required for birth to take place. In comparison, real labour contractions are more frequent, rhythmic, and painful, and they increase in frequency and intensity.

STAGES OF CHILDBIRTH

Labour takes place in three overlapping stages (Figure 4.1). The first stage, dilation of the cervix, is the longest, typically lasting 12 to 14 hours for a woman having her first child. In subsequent births, the first stage tends to be shorter. During this stage, regular and increasingly frequent uterine contractions—15 to 20 minutes apart at first—cause the cervix to shorten and dilate, or widen, in preparation for delivery. Toward the end of the first stage, contractions occur every two to five minutes. This stage lasts until the cervix is fully open (10 cm, or about 4 inches) so that the baby can descend into the birth canal.

The second stage, descent and emergence of the baby, typically lasts up to an hour or two. It begins when the baby's head begins to move through the cervix into the vaginal canal, and it ends when the baby emerges completely from the mother's body. Mothers often feel a strong urge to push at this time. If this stage lasts longer than two hours, signalling that the baby may need help, a doctor may grasp the baby's head with forceps or, more often, use vacuum extraction with a suction cup to pull it out of the mother's body. At the end of this stage, the baby is born but is still attached to the placenta in the mother's body by the umbilical cord, which must be clamped and cut.

The third stage, expulsion of the placenta, lasts between 10 minutes and an hour. During this stage, the placenta and the remainder of the umbilical cord are expelled from the mother.

LABOUR AND DELIVERY OPTIONS

With the development of varied methods to manage difficult labour and deliveries have come a wealth of options—medical and non-medical—for women to take

parturition Process of uterine, cervical, and other changes, usually lasting about two weeks preceding childbirth.

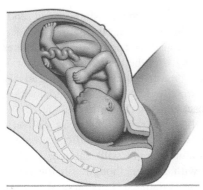

Stage one: Baby positions itself

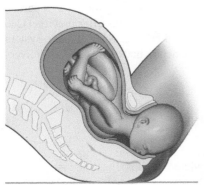

Stage two: Baby begins to emerge

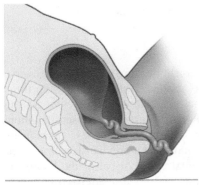

Stage three: Placenta is expelled

FIGURE 4.1

The Stages of Birth

Source: From Fig 4.1, p. 82 in *LifeSmart*, 2011, by Lisa Fiore. Copyright © 2011 by The McGraw-Hill Companies, Inc. Reprinted by permission.

advantage of during the birthing process. In the following sections, we discuss the use of fetal monitors, as well as birthing options for expectant women.

Electronic Fetal Monitoring

Electronic fetal monitoring can be used to track the fetus's heartbeat during labour and can help detect any serious problems. In 2007, the procedure was used in 74 percent of Canadian hospitals (Levitt et al., 2011). While electronic fetal monitoring can provide valuable information in high-risk deliveries, it can have major drawbacks if used routinely in low-risk pregnancies. It is costly; it restricts the mother's movements during labour; and most important, it has an extremely high false-positive rate, suggesting that fetuses are in trouble when they are not. Such warnings may prompt doctors

to deliver by the riskier Caesarean method rather than the vaginal one (Banta & Thacker, 2001; Dzakpasu & Chalmers, 2005).

Vaginal versus Caesarean Delivery

The usual method of childbirth is vaginal delivery. Alternatively, **Caesarean delivery** can be used to surgically remove the baby from the uterus through an incision in the mother's abdomen. For pregnancies complicated by factors such as unusual fetal position or large head size, a Caesarean delivery can be life-saving (Armson, 2007).

The operation is commonly performed when labour progresses too slowly, when the fetus seems to be in trouble, or when the mother is bleeding vaginally. A Caesarean is often needed when the fetus is in the breech position (feet or buttocks first) or in the transverse position (lying crosswise in the uterus) or when the head is too big to pass through the mother's pelvis. Additionally, when labour is induced, as is common in women whose pregnancy progresses past 40 weeks, a Caesarean delivery is more likely to occur (Wilson, Effken & Butler, 2010).

Caesarean birth rates in Canada are among the highest in the world. In 2009, 27 percent of Canadian births occurred this way, as compared with only 5 percent in the late 1960s (Canadian Institute for Health Information, 2010; Canadian Perinatal Surveillance System, 2000; Guyer

electronic fetal monitoring Mechanical monitoring of fetal heartbeat during labour and delivery.

Caesarean delivery Delivery of a baby by surgical removal from the uterus.

et al., 1999). Strategies are being considered to reduce the potential complications of the procedure for the mother and newborn (Betran et al., 2007). The increase in Caesarean rates can be attributed to many factors. One factor is a rising proportion of older first-time mothers, who tend to have multiple births, and of very premature infants (Martin et al., 2009); another factor is the rise in obesity among expectant mothers (Public Health Agency of Canada, 2008). Physicians' fear of malpractice suits and women's preferences also may play a part in the choice of Caesarean deliveries (Ecker & Frigoletto, 2007; Martin et al., 2009).

Caesarean deliveries carry risks of serious complications for the mother, such as bleeding, infection, damage to pelvic organs, post-operative pain, and heightened risks of problems in future pregnancies (Ecker & Frigoletto, 2007). They also deprive the baby of important benefits of normal birth such as the surge of hormones that clears the lungs of

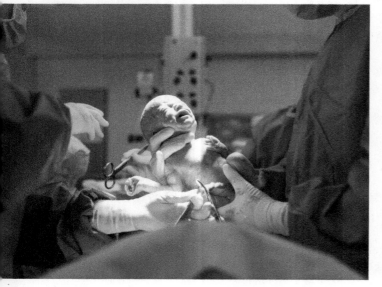

Baby born via Caesarean delivery.

excess fluid, mobilizes stored fuel to nourish cells, and sends blood to the heart and brain. In making the baby more alert and ready to interact with another person, these hormones also may promote bonding with the mother (Lagercrantz & Slotkin, 1986). Further, breast-feeding is often negatively impacted in mothers who undergo Caesarean deliveries, which may further impact bonding (Zanardo et al., 2010).

Once a woman has had one Caesarean delivery, many physicians warn that a vaginal birth after Caesarean (VBAC) should be attempted only with caution. VBACs have been associated with greater, though still low, risks of uterine rupture and brain damage (Landon et al., 2004), as well as infant death (Smith, Pell, Cameron, & Dobbie, 2002). Perhaps these considerations figure in the 8 percent increase since 1994 in Caesarean births after previous Caesarean delivery (Canadian Perinatal Surveillance System, 2000). Today, if a woman has had a Caesarean delivery,

chances are about 80 percent that any subsequent deliveries will be by Caesarean (Canadian Institute for Health Information, 2007; Martin et al., 2009; Public Health Agency of Canada, 2008). However, a growing consensus among medical practitioners is that a trial of labour is a reasonable option for women who have had a previous Caesarean section involving a horizontal cut at or below the bikini line (Society of Obstetricians and Gynaecologists of Canada, 2005).

Medicated versus Non-Medicated Delivery

Emily had attended a childbirth preparation class offered by her hospital. In the class, various options for childbirth were presented to the prospective parents, and Emily puzzled over what she wanted to experience for her own labour and delivery. Should she focus on learning pain management techniques and attempt a medication-free birth? Should she request an epidural? How might these different choices impact both her and her new baby?

For centuries, pain was considered an unavoidable part of giving birth. Then, in the mid-nineteenth century, sedation with ether or chloroform became common practice as more births took place in hospitals (Fontanel & d'Harcourt, 1997).

Because of growing concerns that the use of drugs that might pose risks for babies, and a desire to enable

Winnipegger Chantal Kreviazuk reportedly chose to give birth to her third son, Salvador, in hospital without pain medication.

both parents to participate fully in a natural, empowering experience, several alternative methods of **natural, or prepared, childbirth** were developed during the twentieth century. The most common model of natural childbirth is the *Lamaze method*, introduced by the French obstetrician Fernand Lamaze in the late 1950s. The woman is trained to pant or breathe rapidly in sync with the increasing intensity of her contractions and to concentrate on other sensations to ease the perception of pain. She learns to relax her muscles as a conditioned response to the voice of her coach (usually the prospective father, a friend, or a midwife), who attends classes with her, takes part in the delivery, and helps with the exercises.

Today, improvements in medicated delivery have led many mothers to choose pain relief. General anesthesia, which renders the woman completely unconscious and greatly increases the risks to mother and baby, is rarely used, even in Caesarean births (Eltzschig, Lieberman, & Camann, 2003). Most women—approximately 55 percent—use a regional anesthesia known as an *epidural block*, though the rate in some provinces, such as Manitoba and British Columbia, are substantially lower, hovering at about 35 percent (Canadian Institute for Health Information, 2012). During an epidural, an anesthetic is injected into a space in the spinal cord between the vertebrae in the lumbar (lower) region, which blocks the nerve pathways that would carry the sensation of pain to the brain. Epidurals given early can shorten labour with no added risk of needing Caesarean delivery (Wong et al.,

2005) and allow the woman to see and participate in the birth process. However, these drugs do pass through the placenta to the fetal blood supply and tissues and thus there are some relatively minor risks associated with their use.

Ask Yourself

2. What are the three stages of the birth process?

3. List two options for pain management during delivery.

The Newborn Baby

Emily cuddled her newborn—after 11 hours of labour, she had given birth to a healthy 7-pound baby boy. While he seemed so helpless in many ways—kicking his legs and tightly curled fists at random and peering around with his murky grey eyes—in other ways he seemed to know exactly what to do. He nursed vigorously, cried when he was hungry or needed changing, and calmed when held by an adult. Emily was exhausted from caring for her new baby, but was overjoyed at her new role in life and falling every day more in love with her new son.

The **neonatal period**, the first four weeks of life, is a time of transition from the uterus, where a fetus is supported entirely by the mother to an independent existence. What are the physical characteristics of newborn babies, and how are they equipped for this crucial transition?

SIZE AND APPEARANCE

An average newborn, or **neonate**, in Canada is about 50 cm (20 inches) long and weighs about 3.5 kg (7 pounds). At birth, the vast majority of full-term babies weigh between 2.5 and 5 kg (5 and 10 pounds) and are between 45 and 55 cm (18 and 22 inches) long. Boys tend to be slightly longer and heavier than girls, and a firstborn child is likely to weigh less at birth than later-born children. When the baby is born, the mother produces a special high-protein type of milk called *colostrum*. Colostrum provides babies with important immunological substances and has laxative effects that help babies begin to eliminate toxins. However, colostrum contains less fat and calories than breast milk. Thus, in their first few days, neonates lose as much as 10 percent of their body

WHERE DO **YOU** STAND?

If you or your partner were expecting a baby, and the pregnancy seemed to be going smoothly, would you prefer (a) a hospital, birth centre, or home birth; (b) attendance by a physician or midwife; and (c) medicated or non-medicated delivery? Why?

natural, or prepared, childbirth   Method of childbirth that seeks to reduce or eliminate the use of drugs, enable both parents to participate fully, and control perceptions of pain.

neonatal period   First four weeks of life, a time of transition from intrauterine dependency to independent existence.

neonate   Newborn baby, up to four weeks old.

weight. Babies begin to gain weight by about the fifth day, when the mother's milk comes in, and are generally back to birth weight by the 10th to the 14th day.

New babies have distinctive features, including a large head, red skin, various temporary skin conditions or blotches, permanent birthmarks, and a receding chin, which makes it easier to nurse. Additionally, there are **fontanels**—soft spots on the head covered with a tough membrane—where an infant's skull bones are not yet fused.

Many newborns have a pinkish cast; their skin is so thin that it barely covers the capillaries through which blood flows. However, a baby's skin colour can vary greatly, depending on the baby's age, racial/ethnic origin, health status, temperature, the environment, and whether the baby is crying. During the first few days, some neonates are very hairy because some of the **lanugo**, a fuzzy prenatal hair on the shoulders, back, forehead, and cheeks, has

not yet fallen off. Almost all new babies are covered with **vernix caseosa** ("cheesy varnish"), a white, oily, cheese-like substance that is formed in the womb by secretions from the fetal oil glands and protects against infection. This coating is absorbed into the skin after birth.

REFLEXES AND THEIR DEVELOPMENT

If you were to release an infant in a swimming pool, the baby will hold his or her breath, divert any ingested water into the stomach, and show movements of the arms and legs that are coordinated and strong enough to propel the baby a metre through the water. This is known as the diving reflex, and while it is one of the more puzzling behaviours that babies come equipped with, it occurs in all neurologically normal babies (Table 4.1).

Reflex behaviours, or *reflexes*, are automatic, innate responses to stimulation. Reflex behaviours are controlled by the lower brain centres that govern other involuntary processes, such as breathing and heart rate. Both the presence of reflexes and the disappearance of unneeded reflexes on schedule are signs of neurological development and organization, and are markers of good health. Many reflex behaviours diminish over time, and indeed, their continued persistence after they should have disappeared can be evidence of neurological problems. Brain development during the first three years is described in detail in Chapter 5.

Infants are born with a set of newborn reflexes. Primitive reflexes, like the rooting reflex (where a baby turns his head towards a soft touch on the cheek and begins to search for a nipple), the sucking reflex, and the Moro reflex (a response to being startled or beginning to fall) are clearly related to needs for survival and protection. Others are holdovers from our adaptive past, as when

fontanels Soft spots on the head of the young infant.

lanugo Fuzzy prenatal body hair, which drops off within a few days after birth.

vernix caseosa Oily substance on a neonate's skin that protects against infection.

reflex behaviours Automatic, innate responses to stimulation; also called *reflexes*.

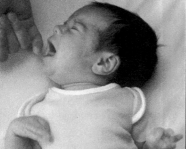

The rooting reflex.

The sucking reflex.

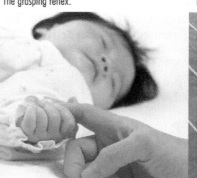

The grasping reflex.

The Moro reflex.

TABLE 4.1 Early Human Reflexes

Reflex	Stimulation	Baby's Behaviour	Typical Age of Appearance	Typical Age of Disappearance
Moro	Baby is dropped or hears loud noise.	Extends legs, arms, and fingers; arches back; draws back head.	7th month of gestation	3 months
Palmar (Darwinian/grasping)	Palm of baby's hand is stroked.	Makes strong fist, can be raised to standing position if both fists are closed around a stick.	7th month of gestation	4 months
Tonic neck	Baby is laid down on back.	Turns head to one side, assumes "fencer" position, extends arms and legs on preferred side, flexes opposite limbs.	7th month of gestation	5 months
Babkin	Both of baby's palms are stroked at once.	Mouth opens, eyes close, neck flexes, head tilts forward.	Birth	3 months
Babinski	Sole of baby's foot is stroked.	Toes fan out, foot twists in.	Birth	4 months
Rooting	Baby's cheek or lower lip is stroked with finger or nipple.	Head turns, mouth opens, sucking movements begin.	Birth	9 months
Walking	Baby is held under arms, with bare feet touching flat surface.	Makes steplike motions that look like well-coordinated walking.	1 month	4 months
Swimming	Baby is put into water face down.	Makes well-coordinated swimming movements.	1 month	4 months

babies grasp whatever is placed into their palm much as baby monkeys cling to their mother's fur. Still others do not appear to have a clear function. For example, when a baby's head is turned to one side, one arm extends and one bends back, as if the baby were getting ready to fire an arrow from a bow. The origins of this tonic neck reflex are unclear.

As the higher brain centres become active during the first two to four months, babies begin to show postural reflexes—reactions to changes in position or balance. For example, infants who are tilted downward extend their arms in the parachute reflex, an instinctive attempt to break a fall. Locomotor reflexes, such as the walking reflex, resemble voluntary movements that do not appear until months after these reflexes have disappeared.

Most of the early reflexes disappear during the first six months to one year. Reflexes that continue to serve protective functions, such as blinking, yawning, coughing, gagging, sneezing, and shivering, remain.

BODY SYSTEMS

Before birth, blood circulation, respiration, nourishment, elimination of waste, and temperature regulation are accomplished through the mother's body. After birth, all of the baby's systems and functions must operate on their own

(Table 4.2). Most of this transition occurs during the first four to six hours after delivery (Ferber & Makhoul, 2004).

The fetus and mother have separate circulatory systems and separate heartbeats; the fetus's blood is cleansed through the umbilical cord, which carries "used" blood to the placenta and returns a fresh supply. A neonate's heartbeat at first is fast and irregular, and blood pressure does not stabilize until about the 10th day of life.

The fetus gets oxygen and carries away carbon dioxide through the umbilical cord. Once birth occurs, a newborn must start breathing for itself. Most babies start to breathe as soon as they are exposed to air. If breathing has not begun within about five minutes, the baby may suffer permanent brain injury from anoxia, lack of oxygen, or

TABLE 4.2 A Comparison of Prenatal and Postnatal Life

Characteristic	Prenatal Life	Postnatal Life
Environment	Amniotic fluid	Air
Temperature	Relatively constant	Fluctuates with atmosphere
Stimulation	Minimal	All senses stimulated by various stimuli
Nutrition	Dependent on mother's blood	Dependent on external food and functioning of digestive system
Oxygen supply	Passed from maternal bloodstream via placenta	Passed from neonate's lungs to pulmonary blood vessels
Metabolic elimination	Passed into maternal bloodstream via placenta	Discharged by skin, kidneys, lungs, and gastrointestinal tract

hypoxia, a reduced oxygen supply. **Anoxia** or hypoxia may occur during delivery as a result of repeated compression of the placenta and umbilical cord with each contraction, or after the birth occurs, if the baby has difficulty taking in sufficient amounts of air. Babies have only one-tenth the lung capacity of adults and are susceptible to respiratory problems, which can cause permanent brain damage and lead to mental retardation (cognitive impairment), behaviour problems, or even death.

Many babies are born alert and ready to begin feeding. Full-term babies have a strong sucking reflex to take in milk and their own gastrointestinal secretions to digest it. Babies must also eliminate toxins from their bodies independently. During the first few days, infants secrete **meconium**, a stringy, greenish-black waste matter formed in the fetal intestinal tract. Additionally, babies begin to urinate on a regular basis, and the volume of urine is proportionate to food intake.

The layers of fat that develop during the last two months of fetal life enable healthy full-term infants to keep their body temperature constant after birth despite changes in air temperature. Newborn babies also maintain body temperature by increasing their activity when air temperature drops. These early fat deposits also provide babies with a reserve of energy until their mother's milk comes in.

Three or four days after birth, about half of all babies, and a larger proportion of babies born prematurely, develop **neonatal jaundice**: their skin and eyeballs look yellow. This kind of jaundice is caused by the immaturity of the

liver and failure to filter out bilirubin, a by-product resulting from the breakdown of red blood cells. Usually it is not serious, does not need treatment, and has no long-term effects. However, severe jaundice that is not monitored and treated promptly can result in brain damage.

MEDICAL AND BEHAVIOURAL ASSESSMENT

Although the great majority of births result in normal, healthy babies, some do not. The first few minutes, days, and weeks after birth are crucial for development. It is important to know as soon as possible whether a baby has any problem that needs special care.

The Apgar Scale

One minute after delivery, and then again five minutes after birth, most babies are assessed by using the **Apgar scale** (Figure 4.2). Its name helps us remember its five subtests: appearance (colour), pulse (heart rate), grimace (reflex irritability), activity (muscle tone), and respiration (breathing). The newborn is rated 0, 1, or 2 on each measure, for a maximum score of 10. A five-minute score of 7 to 10—achieved by about 98 percent of babies born in Canada—indicates that the baby is in good to excellent condition (Burstyn, Kapur, & Cherry, 2010; Martin et al., 2009). A score of 5 to 7 at one minute may mean the baby needs help to establish breathing, and the test should be repeated every five minutes up to 20 minutes (AAP Committee on Fetus and Newborn & American College of Obstetricians and Gynecologists [ACOG] Committee on Obstetric Practice, 2006).

A score below 5 may reflect a variety of problems and is rare. For example, the heart or respiratory system may not be working at peak levels. In this event, a mask may be placed over the newborn's face to pump oxygen directly into the lungs; or, if breathing still does not start, a tube can be placed

anoxia Lack of oxygen, which may cause brain damage.

meconium Fetal waste matter, excreted during the first few days after birth.

neonatal jaundice Condition in many newborn babies caused by immaturity of the liver and evidenced by a yellowish appearance; can cause brain damage if not treated promptly.

Apgar scale Standard measurement of a newborn's condition; it assesses appearance, pulse, grimace, activity, and respiration.

FIGURE 4.2

The Apgar Scale

Score	0	1	2
Heart rate	Absent	Slow—fewer than 100 beats per minute	Fast—100–140 beats per minute
Respiratory rate	No breathing for more than one minute	Irregular and slow	Good breathing with normal crying
Muscle tone	Limp and flaccid	Weak, inactive, but some flexion of extremities	Strong, active motion
Body colour	Blue and pale	Body pink, but extremities blue	Entire body pink
Reflex irritability	No response	Grimace	Coughing, sneezing, and crying

Source: Adapted from "A Proposal for A New Method of Evaluation of a Newborn Infant" by Virginia A. Apgar in *Anesthesia and Analgesia*, Volume 21, pp. 260–267, 1975.

in the windpipe. Additionally, medications and fluids may be administered through the blood vessels in the umbilical cord to strengthen the heartbeat. If resuscitation is successful, bringing the baby's score to 5 or more, long-term damage is unlikely. Scores of 0 to 3 at 10, 15, and 20 minutes after birth are increasingly associated with cerebral palsy (muscular impairment from brain damage caused prenatally or during birth) or other neurological problems (AAP Committee on Fetus and Newborn & ACOG Committee on Obstetric Practice, 2006). Prematurity, low birth weight, trauma, infection, birth defects, medication given to the mother, and other conditions may affect the scores (AAP Committee on Fetus and Newborn & ACOG Committee on Obstetric Practice, 2006; Jefferies & Canadian Paediatric Society [CPS], Fetus and Newborn Committee, 2011).

The Brazelton Scale

The **Brazelton Neonatal Behavioral Assessment Scale (NBAS)** is used to assess neonates' responsiveness to their environment, to identify strengths and vulnerabilities in neurological functioning, and to predict future development. The test is suitable for infants up to 2 months old and assesses motor organization as shown by such behaviours as activity level and the ability to bring a hand to the mouth; reflexes; state changes, such as irritability, excitability, and ability to quiet down after being upset; attention and interactive capacities, as shown by general alertness and response to visual and auditory stimuli; and indications of central nervous system instability, such as tremors and changes in skin colour (Brazelton, 1973, 1984; Brazelton & Nugent, 1995, 2011). The NBAS takes about 30 minutes, and scores are based on a baby's best performance. It is most commonly used in research applications, although it is useful as an educational tool for parents and in interventions.

Neonatal Screening for Medical Conditions

As we mentioned in Chapter 2, children who inherit the enzyme disorder phenylketonuria, or PKU, will become cognitively impaired unless they are fed a special diet beginning in the first three to six weeks of life (National Institutes of Health [NIH] & National Institute of Child Health & Human Development [NICHD], 2010). Screening tests administered soon after birth often can discover this and other correctable defects, and in the case of PKU, environmental intervention can prevent the manifestation of the disease. Generally, blood is collected via a heelstick from newborn babies at the hospital and used to screen for this and other conditions.

Routine screening of all newborn babies for such rare conditions as PKU (1 case in 15,000 births), congenital hypothyroidism (1 in 3,600 to 5,000), and other, even rarer,

Brazelton Neonatal Behavioral Assessment Scale (NBAS) Neurological and behavioural test to measure a neonate's responses to the environment.

Did you know?

Giving babies a sweet liquid to suck on during painful procedures such as a heel stick significantly reduces their pain response.

disorders is expensive. Yet the cost of testing thousands of newborns to detect one case of a rare disease may be less than the cost of caring for one cognitively impaired person for a lifetime. Now, with more sophisticated blood tests, a single blood specimen can be screened for 20 or more disorders, which has prompted many developed countries to expand their mandatory screening programs (Howell, 2006). All provinces require routine screening for PKU and congenital hypothyroidism, though they vary on other screening tests (Canadian PKU and Allied Disorders Inc., 2012; Hanley, 2005; Society of Obstetricians and Gynaecologists of Canada, 1998).

Ask Yourself

4. Describe what a newborn baby looks like.

5. The reason that reflexes are a good way to assess a newborn's health is because
   a. they should develop rapidly following birth.
   b. they are a marker of neurological organization.
   c. they don't require any learning.
   d. This is incorrect; reflexes have little to do with newborn health.

6. Neurological health can be gauged by
   a. the presence of reflexes when they are supposed to be there.
   b. the absence of reflexes by the age of 6 months.
   c. the disappearance of reflexes on schedule.
   d. both a and c.

7. Rooting is an example of a _____ reflex, and the walking reflex is an example of a _____ reflex.

8. A few days after birth, a baby develops a yellowish tinge to the skin and the eyeballs. These symptoms indicate _____, which is due to immaturity of the _____.
   a. anoxia; liver
   b. anoxia; kidneys
   c. neonatal jaundice; liver
   d. neonatal jaundice; kidneys

9. What screening test assesses a baby's health at one and five minutes after birth has occurred?
   a. Brazelton Neonatal Behavioral Assessment Scale
   b. heel stick and blood draw
   c. Apgar scale
   d. amniocentesis

Birth Complications and Their Aftermath

Emily was fortunate: She had good prenatal care and a healthy pregnancy, and her newborn son was born without complications. As in Emily's case, the great majority of births result in normal, healthy babies; some, sadly, do not. Some infants are born prematurely or very small, some remain in the womb too long, and some are born dead or die soon after birth. Let's look at these potential complications of birth and how they can be avoided or treated to maximize the chances of favourable outcomes.

LOW BIRTH WEIGHT

Low-birth-weight babies weigh less than 2,500 grams (5½ pounds) at birth, and represent 6.1 percent of Canadian births—the lowest rate in all G-7 countries (Canadian Institute for Health Information, 2012; Statistics Canada, 2010b); about 0.4 percent are extremely low birth weight (less than 1,000 grams; Joseph et al., 2012). Low-birth-weight babies may be either preterm (born early) or small-for-date (born small by comparison to other babies of the same age), or both (Figure 4.3). About two out of three low-birth-weight infants are **preterm (premature)**, born before completing the 37th week of pregnancy (Martin et al., 2009, 2005). Proportions of preterm births increase in cases of multiple births (57 percent of twins, and 96 percent of higher-order multiples) (Fiore, 2003; Public Health Agency of Canada, 2008). **Small-for-date (small-for-gestational-age) infants**, who may or may not be preterm, weigh less than 90 percent of babies born at the same age. Their small size is generally a result of inadequate prenatal nutrition, which slows fetal growth.

Factors increasing the likelihood that a woman will have an underweight baby include the following:

- *Demographic and socio-economic factors:* These may include being under age 17 or over 40; poor, unmarried, or undereducated; and being born in certain regions, such as Alberta and Nunavut (Luo et al., 2010; Ohlsson & Shah, 2008; Statistics Canada, 2010b; Thompson, Goodman, Chang, & Stukel, 2005; Willms, 2002a).

- *Medical factors predating the pregnancy:* Factors may include having no children or more than four children, being short or thin, having had previous low-birth-weight infants or multiple miscarriages, having had low birth weight oneself, or having genital or urinary abnormalities or chronic hypertension.

- *Prenatal behavioural and environmental factors:* Such factors may be poor nutrition, inadequate prenatal care, smoking, use of alcohol or other drugs, or exposure to stress, high altitude, or toxic substances

- *Medical conditions:* These may include vaginal bleeding, infections, high or low blood pressure, anemia, too little weight gain, and having last given birth less than 12 months or more than five years before (Arias, MacDorman, Strobino, & Guyer, 2003; DeFranco, Stamilio, Boslaugh, Gross, & Muglia, 2007; O'Leary, Nassar, Kurinczuk, & Bower, 2009; Zhu, Rolfs, Nangle, & Horan, 1999).

An estimated 15 percent of all infants worldwide are born with low birth weight, and the percentages are far greater in less economically developed countries (UNICEF, 2008b; Table 4.3). Low birth weight in developing regions stems primarily from the mother's poor health and nutrition. In a double-blind study of 8,468 pregnant women in Tanzania, daily multivitamin supplements reduced the incidence of low birth weight (Fawzi et al., 2007). In the industrialized world, smoking during pregnancy is the leading factor in low birth weight (UNICEF & WHO, 2004).

Low-birth-weight and preterm births have increased in the past four decades, primarily because of delayed child-bearing,

Birth Complications, Canada, 2008

FIGURE 4.3 Percentages of live births that were (a) preterm (less than 37 weeks) or postterm (42 weeks or more) and (b) low birth weight (less than 2,500 grams). Low-birth-weight babies can be preterm or small-for-date or both. Note that, as the graphs show, the vast majority of births in Canada involve both healthy gestation periods and healthy birth weight.

Source: Statistics Canada. Table 102-4516—Live births and fetal deaths (stillbirths), by place of birth (hospital and non-hospital), Canada, provinces and territories, annual, CANSIM (database).

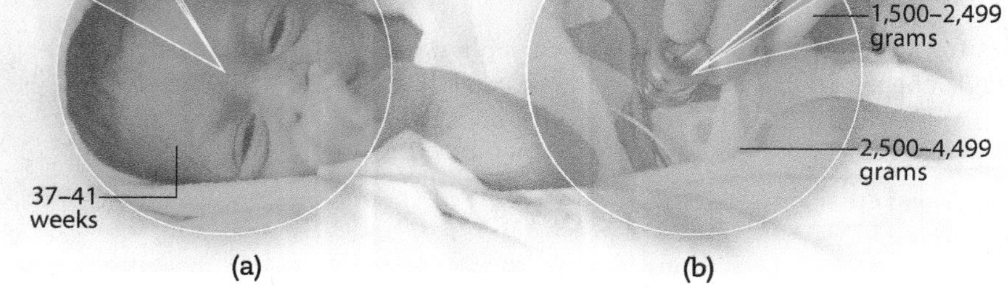

42 weeks or more
27 weeks or less
28–36 weeks
37–41 weeks
(a)

Less than 500 grams
4,500 grams or more
500–1,499 grams
1,500–2,499 grams
2,500–4,499 grams
(b)

low-birth-weight babies Infants who weigh less than 2,500 grams (5 pounds) at birth because of prematurity or being small-for-date.

preterm (premature) infants Infants born before completing the 37th week of gestation.

small-for-date (small-for-gestational-age) infants Infants whose birth weight is less than that of 90 percent of babies of the same gestational age as a result of slow fetal growth.

TABLE 4.3 Percentage of Low-Birth-Weight Infants by Selected United Nations Regions, 1999–2006	
	% Low-Birth-Weight Infants
WORLD	15
Industrialized countries	7
Developing countries	16
Least developed countries	17
AFRICA	
Eastern and Southern Africa	14
Sub-Saharan Africa	14
Western and Central Africa	14
Northern Africa and Middle East	16
ASIA	
Eastern Asia and Pacific	6
South Asia	29
EASTERN EUROPE (CEE/CTS)	6
LATIN AMERICA AND CARIBBEAN	9

*Data refer to the most recent year available during 1999–2006.
Source: UNICEF (2008b).

multiple births, use of fertility drugs, and induced and Caesarean deliveries (Canadian Institute for Health Information, 2007; Martin et al., 2009).

Congenital malformations (i.e., birth defects) are the most common cause of death in infancy (Kung, Hoyert, Xu & Murphy, 2007); however, birth weight and length of gestation are among the two most important predictors of an infant's survival and health (Mathews & MacDorman, 2008). Together they constitute the second leading cause of death in infancy in Canada and the leading cause during the neonatal period (Kung, Hoyert, Xu & Murphy, 2008; Statistics Canada, 2012d). Preterm birth is involved in nearly half of neurological birth defects, such as cerebral palsy, and more than one-third of infant deaths. Worldwide, low birth weight is an underlying factor in 60 to 80 percent of neonatal deaths (UNICEF, 2008b).

Canada has been more successful than most other countries in saving low-birth-weight babies, but the rate of such births remains higher than in some European nations, though not as high as in the United States (CICH, 2000; UNICEF & WHO, 2004). Preventing preterm births would greatly increase the number of babies who survive the first year of life, but such measures as enhanced prenatal care, nutritional interventions, home monitoring of uterine activity, and administration of drugs, bed rest, and hydration for women who go into labour early have failed to stem the tide (Goldenberg & Rouse, 1998; Lockwood, 2002).

Immediate Treatment and Outcomes

The most pressing fear regarding very small babies is that they will die in infancy. Because their immune systems are not fully developed, they are especially vulnerable to infection, which has been linked to slowed growth and developmental delays (Stoll et al., 2004). Moreover, their status sometimes requires a variety of aggressive interventions such as intramuscular injections, intubation, or the insertion of a chest or feeding tube. Invasive procedures such as these increase the chances of infection. Also, these infants' nervous systems may be too immature for them to perform functions basic to survival, such as sucking, so they may need to be fed intravenously (through the veins). Because they do not have enough fat to insulate them and to generate heat, it is hard for them to stay warm.

A low-birth-weight or at-risk preterm baby is placed in an *incubator*, an antiseptic, temperature-controlled crib, and fed through tubes. To counteract the sensory impoverishment of life in an incubator, hospital workers and parents are encouraged to give these small babies special handling. Gentle massage seems to foster growth, weight gain, motor activity, alertness, and behavioural organization (Field, Diego, & Hernandez-Reif, 2007), and can shorten the hospital stay (Field, Hernandez-Reif, & Freedman, 2004). **Kangaroo care**, a method of skin-to-skin contact in which a newborn is laid face down between the mother's breasts for an hour or so at a time after birth, seems to reduce stress on the central nervous

kangaroo care Method of skin-to-skin contact between newborn and mother to reduce stress on the central nervous system and help with self-regulation of sleep and activity.

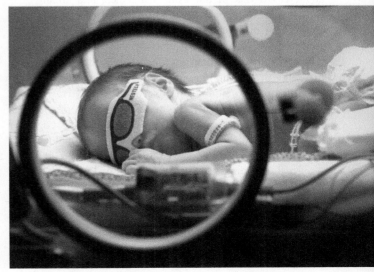

An incubator provides a safe environment for premature and low-birth-weight babies.

system and help with self-regulation of sleep and activity (Ferber & Makhoul, 2004).

Respiratory distress syndrome, also called hyaline membrane disease, is common in preterm babies who lack an adequate amount of *surfactant*, an essential lung-coating substance that keeps air sacs from collapsing. These babies may breathe irregularly or stop breathing altogether. Since 1994, administering surfactant to high-risk preterm newborns has dramatically increased survival rates (Stoelhorst et al., 2005), as well as the neurological and developmental status of these children at 18 to 22 months (Vohr, Wright, Poole, & McDonald for the NICHD Neonatal Research Network Follow-up Study, 2005). However, survival rates of preterm newborns increase dramatically with even one additional week of gestation. According to one Canadian study of births in 30 health centres, the percentage of preterm infants in 2011 who survived increased from 27 percent at less than 23 weeks gestation, to 42 percent at 23 weeks, 54 percent at 24 weeks, and 78 percent at 25 weeks (Canadian Neonatal Network, 2012). In addition, the proportion of extreme preterm newborns without neurological impairment increases with increased gestational age (Jefferies, Kirpalani, & Canadian Paediatric Society [CPS], Fetus and Newborn Committee, 2012).

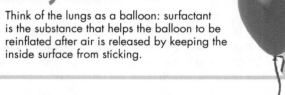

Did you know?

Think of the lungs as a balloon: surfactant is the substance that helps the balloon to be reinflated after air is released by keeping the inside surface from sticking.

Long-Term Outcomes and Protective Factors

Even if low-birth-weight babies survive the dangerous early days, their trials may not be over. For example, both preterm and small-for-date infants are at increased risk of adult-onset diabetes, and small-for-date infants appear to be at increased risk of cardiovascular disease (Hofman et al., 2004; Sperling, 2004). Additionally, preterm birth is associated with a heightened risk of death throughout childhood, diminished reproductive rates in adulthood, and, for women, increased risk of bearing preterm infants themselves (Swamy, Ostbye, & Skjaerven, 2008). Generally, the shorter the period of gestation, the greater the likelihood of cerebral palsy, cognitive impairment, autistic disorders, and low educational and job-related income levels (Moster, Lie, & Markestad, 2008).

In longitudinal studies of extremely low-birth-weight infants (about 500 to 1,000 grams at birth) and infants born before 26 weeks of gestation, the survivors tend to be smaller than full-term children and are more likely to have neurological, sensory, cognitive, educational, and behavioural problems (Anderson, Doyle & the Victorian Infant Collaborative Study Group, 2003; Samara, Marlow, & Wolke for the EPICure Study Group, 2008). Cognitive

deficits, especially in memory and information processing speed, have been noted among very-low-birth-weight babies (those weighing less than 1,500 grams at birth) by age 5 or 6 months, continuing throughout childhood (Rose & Feldman, 2000; Rose, Feldman, & Jankowski, 2001) and persisting into adulthood (Fearon et al., 2004; Greene, 2002; Hack et al., 2002; Hardy, Kuh, Langenberg, & Wadsworth, 2003). Very-low-birth-weight children and adolescents also tend to have more behavioural and mental health problems than those born at normal weight (Hack et al., 2004).

Nevertheless, environmental factors can make a difference. In a prospective longitudinal study of 166 extremely low-birth-weight babies in Canada, a significant majority overcame earlier difficulties to become functioning, independent young adults with high school diplomas and jobs. The children were predominantly white and from two-parent families, about half of them of high socio-economic status (SES) (Saigal et al., 2006). And, in a U.S. longitudinal study of 296 infants who weighed, on average, just over 1,000 grams at birth, most showed intelligence in the normal range by age 8 despite early predictions of cognitive impairment. Children in two-parent families, those whose mothers were highly educated, those who had not suffered significant brain damage, and those who did not need special services such as occupational or speech therapy did best (Ment et al., 2003). These studies show that babies are highly resilient, and a high-quality postnatal environment can do much to moderate the potential effects of being born small.

POSTMATURITY

Less than 1.0 percent of pregnant women in Canada (0.5 percent in 2009) have not gone into labour after 42 or more weeks' gestation (Joseph et al., 2007; Statistics Canada, 2011c). At that point, a baby is considered **postmature**. Postmature babies tend to be long and thin as they continue to grow in the womb but the placenta becomes less efficient as the pregnancy progresses, resulting in a decrease in the levels of nutrients and oxygen that are available to the baby. The baby's greater size also complicates labour; the mother has to deliver a baby the size of a normal 1-month-old.

Because postmature fetuses are at risk of brain damage or even death, doctors sometimes induce labour or perform Caesarean deliveries. The increasing use of both of these techniques probably explains a decline in postterm births in recent years (Martin et al., 2006).

STILLBIRTH

Stillbirth, the sudden death of a fetus at or after the 20th week of gestation, is a tragic union of opposites—birth and death. Sometimes fetal death is diagnosed prenatally;

postmature A fetus not yet born as of 42 weeks' gestation.
stillbirth Death of a fetus at or after the 20th week of gestation.

in other cases, the baby's death is discovered during labour or delivery. Worldwide, about 3.2 million fetuses are stillborn annually (Lawn et al., 2010). In Canada, the incidence of stillbirth has remained steady for the past decade, but is well below the rate during the first half of the twentieth century. The reduction in stillbirths may be due to electronic fetal monitoring, ultrasound, measures to identify fetuses at risk for restricted growth, and even corrective prenatal surgery in the womb (Goldenberg, Kirby, & Culhane, 2004). Still, the number of reported stillbirths—2,734, or 7.13 for every 100,000 live births plus fetal deaths in 2009 (Statistics Canada, 2011d)—is nearly greater than the total of all infant deaths.

What causes stillbirth? Although the cause of stillbirth is often not clear, many stillborn fetuses are small-for-date, indicating malnourishment in the womb (Surkan, Stephansson, Dickman, & Cnattingius, 2004). Boys are more likely to be stillborn than girls, and twins and higher multiples are more likely to be stillborn than singletons (MacDorman & Kirmeyer, 2009).

INFANT MORTALITY

Great strides have been made in protecting the lives of new babies, but these advances are not evenly distributed. Worldwide, 47 infants die during their first year for every 1,000 live births—about 6 million infant deaths. Nearly 60 percent of these deaths occur during the first month, one-half of these in the first 24 hours. The vast majority of these early deaths are in developing countries, especially in South Asia and West and Central Africa (UNICEF, 2008b; Table 4.4).

Eighty-six percent of all neonatal deaths are the result of severe infections, including sepsis or pneumonia, tetanus, and diarrhea (36 percent); preterm delivery (27 percent); and asphyxia (difficulty breathing) at birth (23 percent) (UNICEF, 2008b). Many of these deaths are preventable, resulting from a combination of poverty, poor maternal health and nutrition, infection, and inadequate medical care (Lawn et al., 2005; UNICEF, 2008b). Community-based postnatal care for mothers and babies in the first few days after birth might save many of these lives.

In Canada, the **infant mortality rate**—the proportion of babies who die within the first year— is the lowest ever. In 1995, there were seven deaths in the first year for every 1,000 live male births and six for every 1,000 live

TABLE 4.4 Neonatal Mortality Rate

Regions	Neonatal mortality rate (deaths per 1,000 live births)		Decline (percent)	Number of neonatal deaths (thousands)	
	1990	2010	1990–2010	1990	2010
Developed regions	7	4	43	106	53
Developing regions	36	25	31	4,319	3,019
Nothern Africa	29	13	55	107	46
Sub-Saharan Africa	43	35	19	969	1,123
Latin America and the Caribbean	23	11	52	265	117
Caucasus and Central Asia	30	21	30	58	34
Eastern Asia	23	11	52	589	189
Excluding China	12	9	25	14	8
Southern Asia	48	32	33	1,875	1,256
Excluding India	48	33	31	576	381
Southeast Asia	28	15	46	335	169
Western Asia	28	16	43	116	79
Oceania	26	21	19	5	5
World	32	23	28	4,425	3,072

Source: UNICEF, State of the World's Children, 2009, Figure 1-4. Reprinted by permission of UNICEF.

female births, compared with 15 per 1,000 for males and 12 per 1,000 for females in 1975 (Canadian Institute of Child Health [CICH], 2000). By 2009, the infant mortality rate dropped to 4.9 deaths for every 1,000 live births (Statistics Canada, 2012c). The overall infant mortality rate in Aboriginal communities has been about twice the Canadian national annual average (Chalmers & Wen, 2004; Smylie, Fell, Ohlsson, & the Joint Working Group on First Nations, Indian, Inuit, and Métis Infant Mortality of the Canadian Perinatal Surveillance System, 2010). Two-thirds of infant deaths take place during the neonatal period (Hoyert, Heron, Murphy, & Kung, 2006; Kochanek & Smith, 2004; Kochanek, Murphy, Anderson, & Scott, 2004). Most likely to die in infancy are babies whose mothers were teenagers, did not finish high school, were unmarried, smoked during pregnancy, had no prenatal care, or had multiple births; and those who were born preterm or of low birth weight (Mathews, Curtin, & MacDorman, 2000). Canadian initiatives, such as the *Community Action Programme for Children* and the *Canada Prenatal Nutrition Program*, aim to reduce the discrepancies in infant mortality across Aboriginal and other groups in Canada (Judge, 2009).

Birth defects are the leading cause of infant deaths in Canada, followed by disorders related to prematurity or low birth weight; maternal complications of pregnancy; complications of the placenta, umbilical cord, and

infant mortality rate Proportion of babies born alive who die within the first year.

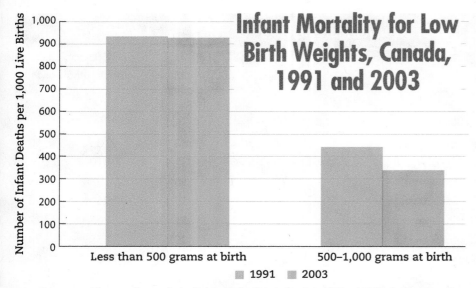

Infant Mortality for Low Birth Weights, Canada, 1991 and 2003

■ 1991   □ 2003

FIGURE 4.4 Infant mortality rates for low-birth-weight live births in Canada in 1991 and 2003, showing improved rates that reflect better infant care at low birth weights. However, the rate for extremely low birth weights remains high.

Source: Public Health Agency of Canada, Canadian Perinatal Health Report, 2008. p. 221. Cat. No. HP10-12/2008E. Reproduced by permission of the Minister of Health, 2012.

membranes; and sudden infant death syndrome (SIDS) (Statistics Canada, 2012c). As outlined above, the proportion of preterm and low-birth-weight births has increased steadily since the mid-1980s. In 2009, almost 20 percent of all deaths in infancy were of preterm babies, and more than half were of very preterm infants (less than 28 weeks gestation) (Statistics Canada, 2012c). Despite the increase in low-birth-weight infants over the past several decades, the mortality rate of low-birth-weight infants is decreasing. However, for extremely low birth weights (below 500 grams), the infant mortality rate remains high (Public Health Agency of Canada, 2008; Figure 4.4).

Infant Mortality Rates in Industrialized Countries, 2003

Hong Kong 2.3; Singapore 2.7; Japan 3.0; Finland 3.1; Sweden 3.1; Norway 3.4; Czech Republic 3.9; Spain 3.9; Greece 4.0; Portugal 4.1; Germany 4.2; Switzerland 4.3; France 4.4*; Denmark 4.4; Austria 4.5; Italy 4.6; Australia 4.8; Netherlands 4.8; Israel 4.9*; New Zealand 4.9; Korea 5.0*; Ireland 5.1; United Kingdom 5.3*; Canada 5.3; Cuba 6.3*; United States 6.9

*Provisional data

FIGURE 4.5 In recent years, most nations, including Canada, have shown dramatic improvement in infant mortality rates.

Sources: Hamilton et al. (2007); Statistics Canada (2007d); United Nations Demographic Yearbook (2003).

The continuing improvement in infant mortality rates during the 1990s, even at a time when more babies are born perilously small, has been due in part to effective treatment for respiratory distress and to prevention of sudden infant death syndrome (SIDS) (discussed below), as well as to medical advances in keeping very small babies alive and treating sick newborns. Still, in 2009, 1,872 Canadian infants died during their first year. Despite dramatic improvements in recent years, the mortality rate for Canadian babies, especially Aboriginal infants, has lagged behind that of many other industrialized countries (see Figure 4.5). The higher survival rates of infants in Canada and other industrialized countries may be attributable to free and accessible prenatal and postnatal health care, and better public education regarding infant care (Gardiner, Mutter, & Kosmitzki, 1998; Public Health Agency of Canada, 2011).

Racial/Ethnic Disparities in Infant Mortality

Although infant mortality has declined for all ethnic groups since 1980, largely as a result of improvements in treatment and care of low-birth-weight newborns, disparities have increased—perhaps because such measures have disproportionately benefited some groups more than others (Alexander, Tompkins, Allen, & Hulsey, 2000; CICH, 2000; Smylie et al., 2010). Children living in low-income neighbourhoods, for example, are less likely to experience preventative care, despite the universal health care system in Canada (Guttmann, Shipman, Lam, Goodman, & Stukel, 2010).

Infant mortality in Aboriginal communities has been estimated to be about twice the national average (Health Canada, 2011a; Luo et al., 2004), and the rate among Inuit communities is estimated to be three times as high (Smylie et al, 2010; Luo, Senecal, et al., 2010). Rates of birth defects, particularly heart anomalies, are higher among Inuit newborns (Arbour et al., 2004; Sheppard & Hetherington, 2012). Perinatal period conditions (those occurring in the months immediately before and immediately after birth, such as low birth weight, short length of gestation, and birth trauma) are the greatest cause of death in Aboriginal infants, accounting for 36 percent of total deaths, followed by birth defects (25 percent) and other

INFANT CARE:
A CROSS-CULTURAL VIEW

Infant care practices vary greatly around the world and across Canada. In some societies, infants have multiple caregivers. Among the Efe people of central Africa, for example, infants typically receive care from five or more people per hour (Tronick, Morelli, & Ivey, 1992). Among the Gusii in western Kenya, where infant mortality is high, parents keep their infants close to them, respond quickly when they cry, and feed them on demand (LeVine, 1994). The same is true of Aka foragers in central Africa who live in small groups marked by sharing, cooperation, and concern about danger. However, Ngandu farmers in the same region, who tend to live farther apart and to stay in one place for long periods of time, are more likely to leave their infants alone (Hewlett, Lamb, Shannon, Leyendecker, & Schölmerich, 1998).

Infant care practices vary among the many cultural groups across Canada. How recently immigrants have arrived in Canada can influence how parents choose to make use of community supports for prenatal and infant care (Edwards & Boivin, 1997). The diversity of Aboriginal groups in Canada contributes to unique approaches to infant care, particularly in the context of challenges faced by families in many communities (Native Women's Association of Canada, n.d.). For example, low-income Aboriginal parents in general tend to be less verbal and use praise less frequently than parents from other backgrounds; however, the quality of how they interact with their children is no different from low-income parents from other groups in Canada (Letourneau, Hungler, & Fisher, 2005).

We need to remember that patterns of interaction we take for granted may be culture-based. Moreover, from the very first day, the ways in which babies' needs and desires are managed begins the lifelong process of socialization.

anomalies, including SIDS (12 percent) (Health Canada, 2011a). There is a higher prevalence of high birth weight in Aboriginal compared with non-Aboriginal babies in Canada, and this might be an influence in the higher rates of diabetes in Aboriginal communities (Harder, Rodekamp, Schellong, Dudenhausen, & Plagermann, 2007; Health Canada, 2011a).

Disparities in access to and quality of health care for minority children, in both rural and urban areas (Flores, Olson, & Tomany-Korman, 2005; Luo, Wilkins, Heaman, et al., 2010; Simonet et al., 2010; Wassimi et al., 2010), may help account for differences in mortality, but other factors also may play a part. Social factors like poverty, food insecurity, and inadequate housing; higher prevalence of medical conditions in infancy, like congenital anomalies, respiratory conditions, and SIDS; as well as behavioural factors involving obesity, smoking, and alcohol consumption during pregnancy can play important roles in explaining the higher mortality rates of Aboriginal infants (Luo, Wilkins, Hart, et al., 2010; Smylie et al., 2010).

WHERE DO **YOU** STAND?

Medicine has gotten better at keeping very small preterm babies alive. However, these infants often suffer from developmental consequences such as mental retardation or cerebral palsy. Is it always best to try and help a baby survive, no matter how small?

Because causes and risk factors for infant mortality vary among ethnic groups, efforts to further reduce infant deaths need to focus on factors specific to each ethnic group (Hesso & Fuentes, 2005). Reductions in public funding to programs designed to address specific health needs for those groups might be adding to the risks (Smylie et al., 2010; Webster, 2012).

Sudden Infant Death Syndrome

Sudden infant death syndrome (SIDS), sometimes called crib death, is the sudden and unexplained death of an infant under age 1. In 2009, 114 Canadian babies died as a result of SIDS (Statistics Canada, 2012d), making SIDS one of the top five causes of infant death in Canada, accounting for 6 percent of infant deaths. It peaks between 2 and 4 months of age and is common among low SES babies, Aboriginal babies, boy babies, those born preterm, and those whose mothers are young and received late or no prenatal care (Public Health Agency of Canada, 2011).

SIDS most likely results from a combination of factors. An underlying biological defect may make some infants vulnerable during a critical period to certain contributing or triggering experiences, such as prenatal exposure to smoke—an identified risk factor (AAP Task Force on Sudden Infant Death Syndrome, 2005). The underlying defect may be a delay in maturation of the neural network

sudden infant death syndrome (SIDS) Sudden and unexplained death of an apparently healthy infant.

that is responsible for arousal from sleep in the presence of life-threatening conditions (AAP Task Force on Sudden Infant Death Syndrome, 2005), a disturbance in the brain mechanism that regulates breathing (Tryba, Peña, & Ramirez, 2006), or a genetic factor (Opdal & Rognum, 2004). Such factors may prevent some babies from waking or turning their heads when they breathe stale air containing carbon dioxide trapped under their blankets (AAP Task Force, 2000; Canadian Foundation for the Study of Infant Deaths, the Canadian Institute of Child Health, the Canadian Paediatric Society, and Health Canada, 1999, reaffirmed 2000). In support of this, sleeping with a fan, which circulates the air, has been associated with a 72 percent reduction in SIDS risk (Coleman-Phox, Odouli, & De-Kun, 2008).

Doctors recommend that infants not sleep on soft surfaces, such as pillows or quilts, or under loose covers, which may increase the risk of overheating or breathing exhaled waste products (AAP Task Force on Sudden Infant Death Syndrome, 2005). The risk of SIDS is increased 20-fold when infants sleep in adult beds, sofas, or chairs, or on other surfaces not designed for infants (Scheers, Rutherford, & Kemp, 2003). Studies associate use of pacifiers with lower risk of SIDS (Mitchell, Blair, & L'Hoir, 2006). Research strongly supports a relationship between SIDS and sleeping on the stomach. Following recommendations that healthy babies be laid on their backs to sleep, SIDS rates in Canada declined by 50 percent between 1999 and 2004 (Public Health Agency of Canada, 2011).

Injuries

Unintentional injuries are among the leading causes of death in infancy in Canada (Anderson & Smith, 2005; Statistics Canada, 2012d). In a three-year study of injury deaths of infants, based on Canadian national data collected between 1994 and 1997, the greatest cause of injury death was surgery, accounting for 11 deaths per 100,000, followed by falls, at 9 per 100,000 deaths (CICH, 2000). Among the rest, the leading causes of death were from intentional injuries (we discuss child abuse and related fatalities below), medical misadventure, being struck, and drug side effects. In Aboriginal communities, 7 percent of infant deaths between 1989 and 1993 resulted from injury (CICH, 2000). Many accidental injuries occur at home. In a study of 990 infants brought to emergency rooms in Kingston, Ontario, by far the most injuries were caused by falls (61.1 percent), followed by ingesting harmful substances (6.6 percent), and then by burns (5.7 percent) (Pickett, Streight, Simpson, & Brison, 2003).

These statistics speak to the importance of baby-proofing the home environment, as many accidents are avoidable.

Newborns and Parents

Emily and her husband were thrilled with their new baby, but with that joy came unanticipated challenges. Their baby, as is typical for newborns, woke every few hours wanting to feed, needed constant care, and seemed to spend

every early evening crying without any identifiable reason the frantic parents could find for distress. Emily and her husband found themselves irritable and overtired, and stressed by both their new baby and the unending stream of advice given to the new parents.

Childbirth is a major transition, not only for the baby but also for the parents. Suddenly, almost all their time and energy, it seems, is focused on this newcomer in their lives. Parents, and perhaps siblings, are getting acquainted with this newcomer and developing emotional bonds. Especially with a first birth, a newborn brings insistent demands that challenge the parents' ability to cope—and may affect their marital relationship.

CHILDBIRTH AND BONDING

How and when does the **caregiver-infant bond**—the close, caring connection between caregiver and newborn—develop? Some researchers studying this topic have followed the ethological approach (introduced in Chapter 1), which considers behaviour in human beings, as in animals, to be biologically influenced and emphasizes critical or sensitive periods for the development of certain behaviours.

Charles Darwin (1872) suggested that we are prewired by natural selection to want to care for infants. We find them cute, not because there is anything objectively cute about them but because our minds see them that way. We find their cries unpleasant and rush to help them because

caregiver-infant bond   Mother's and father's feeling of close, caring connection with the newborn.

those parents who took good care of their newborns were the parents who passed their genes on to us. In other words, we are biologically prepared by evolution to engage in the parenting relationship. From an evolutionary perspective, parental bonding is a mechanism to ensure that the parents invest the tremendous energy and resources needed to enable a helpless infant to survive and reproduce.

A study using magnetic brain imaging suggests a neurological basis for parental bonding. Adults' brains showed an almost immediate surge of activity in response to the faces of unfamiliar infants, but not to the equally attractive faces of unfamiliar adults, in an area of the frontal cortex involved in processing feelings of reward and pleasure (Kringelbach et al., 2008).

Fathers, like mothers, form close bonds with their babies. This may even be influenced at a biological level; there are indications that involved fathers show decreases in testosterone levels over the course of a pregnancy, suggesting their bodies' physiology is helping to prepare them for engagement in parenting behaviours (Gettler, McDade, Feranil, & Kuzawa, 2011; Gray, Yang, & Pope Jr., 2006). Fathers who are present at the birth of a child often see the event as a "peak emotional experience" (May & Perrin, 1985) or as the best thing that has happened to them (Longworth & Kingdon, 2010), but a man can become emotionally committed to his newborn whether or not he attended the birth (Palkovitz, 1985). This relationship, however, is

Fathers, just like mothers, form close bonds with their babies.

often impacted by the quality of the relationship between the mother and father (Fagan, Palkovitz, Roy, & Farrie, 2009).

THE MOTHER-INFANT BOND

For many years, psychology theorists thought babies bonded to their parents because parents provided food, which babies naturally enjoyed. Over time, babies would start to associate their parents with the provision of food and would then become attached to them. A series of pioneering experiments with monkeys by Harry Harlow and his colleagues established that more than feeding is involved in the mother-infant bond. In these experiments, rhesus monkeys were separated from their mothers and raised in a laboratory. The infant monkeys were put into cages with two kinds of surrogate "mothers": a plain cylindrical wire-mesh form with an attached bottle for nursing or a form covered with terry cloth that provided no food. The essential question being asked was "to which mother would the baby monkeys become attached?" If earlier theorists were right, then the babies should have become attached to the wire "mother" because she provided food. However, what actually happened was that the monkeys became attached to the soft terry-cloth "mother." When the monkeys were allowed to spend time with either kind of "mother," they all spent more time— indeed the majority of their time—clinging to and cuddling with the cloth surrogates.

It is hardly surprising that a dummy mother would not provide the same kinds of stimulation and opportunities for positive development as a live mother. These studies show that feeding is not the most important thing babies get from their mothers. Mothering includes the comfort of close bodily contact and, at least in monkeys, the satisfaction of an innate need to cling.

When given the choice, infant rhesus monkeys spend more time clinging to a warm, soft terry-cloth mother even if the alternative, a wire surrogate mother, provides the food.

THE FATHER'S ROLE

In Canada, fathers' involvement in caregiving and play has greatly increased since 1970 as more mothers have begun to work outside the home, as concepts of fathering have changed (Cabrera, Tamis-LeMonda, Bradley, Hofferth, & Lamb, 2000; Marshall, 2006, 2008; Wood & Repetti, 2004), and as publicly funded parental leave has become universally available to new working parents. A father's frequent and positive involvement with his child, from infancy on, is directly related to the child's well-being and physical, cognitive, and social development (Allen & Daly, 2007; Cabrera et al., 2000; Shannon, Tamis-LeMonda, London, & Cabrera, 2002).

The fathering role has different meanings in different cultures, and recent immigrant fathers can experience very different perspectives on their roles. A series of interviews of recent immigrant fathers to Canada and Israel showed that many experienced a loss of authority in the household related to not understanding the majority language and systems in the new country, but they felt that the immigration experience was positive for their children's futures. Overall, the findings showed that immigrant fathers integrated fathering roles from their countries of origin with the parenting values and approaches of the new country (Roer-Strier, Strier, Este, Shimoni, & Clarke, 2005).

The fathering role may be taken or shared by someone other than the biological father, such as the mother's brother, as in Botswana, where young mothers remain with their childhood family until their partners are in their 40s, or a grandfather, as in Vietnam (Engle & Breaux, 1998; Richardson, 1995; Townsend, 1997). In some societies, fathers are more involved in their young children's lives—economically, emotionally, and in time spent—than in other cultures, and this may change over historical time periods as well (Engle & Breaux, 1998).

In China, fathers tend to be stern and aloof, and their children respect and fear them. Men rarely hold infants. Fathers interact more with toddlers but perform child care duties only if the mother is absent. However, urbanization and maternal employment are changing these attitudes. Fathers—especially college- and university-educated fathers—now seek more intimate relationships with children, especially sons (Engle & Breaux, 1998). Alternatively, among the Aka people of central Africa, fathers are as nurturing and emotionally supportive as mothers. In fact, "Aka fathers provide more direct infant care than fathers in any other known society" (Hewlett, 1992, p. 169).

HOW PARENTHOOD AFFECTS MARITAL SATISFACTION

Marital satisfaction typically declines during the child-raising years. An analysis of 146 studies including nearly 48,000 men and women found that parents report lower marital satisfaction than non-parents do, and the more

children, the less satisfied parents are with their marriage. The difference is most striking among mothers of infants; 38 percent report high marital satisfaction compared with 62 percent of childless wives, probably because of the restriction on mothers' freedom and the need to adjust to a new role (Twenge, Campbell, & Foster, 2003). Two prospective longitudinal studies had similar findings: Young couples who had babies reported a small but steady decline in marital satisfaction, whereas couples who remained childless did not (Schulz, Cowan, & Cowan, 2006; Shapiro & Gottman, 2003).

Ask Yourself

14. According to ethologists, the reason parents love their babies is because
    a. they are prewired to engage in attachment relationships by natural selection.
    b. they are worried at how people would respond if they did not love our babies.
    c. they learned from their culture that that is what parents are supposed to do.
    d. they imprint on their babies.

15. According to research with young primates, what is the most important thing mothers provide?
    a. protection against aggressive others
    b. physical contact and warmth
    c. food
    d. water

16. From infancy on, a father's frequent and positive involvement with his child is directly related to
    a. level of educational achievement.
    b. the child's social, cognitive, and physical development.
    c. marital satisfaction.
    d. the child's ability to self-regulate.

17. Marital satisfaction typically _____ during the child-raising years.
    a. increases
    b. decreases
    c. increases, then decreases
    d. decreases, then increases

What accounts for the typical decline in satisfaction? New parents are likely to experience multiple stressors, which may affect their health and state of mind. They may feel isolated and lose sight of the fact that other parents are going through similar problems. The division of household tasks between the man and the woman can become an issue; for example, if a woman who was previously working outside the home now stays home, the burden of housework and child care falls mostly on her (Cowan & Cowan, 2000; Schulz et al., 2006). Something as simple as a baby's crying, which keeps the parents up at night, can lessen marital satisfaction during the first year of parenthood (Meijer & van den Wittenboer, 2007). Time stress is another factor that increases in parenthood, especially in dual-earner families (Marshall, 2006). Despite the pressures on marital satisfaction, feelings of community belonging seem to act as a buffer for stresses related to parenting in Canada (Muhammad & Gagnon, 2009).

The birth of a baby, as momentous an achievement as it is, marks the start of a challenging but rewarding journey. In the next chapter, we start our examination of the rapidly growing understanding of the physical developments of infancy and toddlerhood, mindful of the fact that physical, cognitive, and psychosocial development are always intertwined.

SUMMARY

CHAPTER **4** BIRTH AND THE NEWBORN BABY

LO1

Describe what traditional and modern childbirth look like.

- In Canada, the United States, and Europe, childbirth before the twentieth century took place in a manner much like that in some developing countries today. Birth was a female ritual, which occurred at home and was attended by a midwife. Pain relief was minimal, and risks for mother and baby were high.
- The development of the science of obstetrics professionalized childbirth. Births took place in hospitals, attended by physicians. Medical advances dramatically improved safety.
- Today, some women again are choosing the "demedicalized" experience of home birth, but with the resources of medical science close at hand. Delivery at home or in birth centres attended by midwives can be relatively safe alternatives to physician-attended hospital delivery for women with normal, low-risk pregnancies. The presence of a doula can provide physical benefits, as well as emotional support.

LO2

Summarize the stages of childbirth and common medical interventions.

- Labour normally begins after a preparatory period of parturition.
- Birth consists of three stages: (1) dilation of the cervix; (2) descent and emergence of the baby; (3) expulsion of the umbilical cord and the placenta.
- Electronic fetal monitoring is widely used (and may be overused) during labour and delivery. It is intended to detect signs of fetal distress, especially in high-risk births.
- The rate of Caesarean births in Canada is at a record high. Twenty-seven percent of births in Canada are by Caesarean delivery—an unnecessarily high rate, according to critics.
- Natural or prepared childbirth can minimize the need for pain-killing drugs and maximize parents' active involvement. Modern epidurals can give effective pain relief with smaller doses of medication than in the past.

Describe a
newborn's
appearance and
characteristics
and how health
is assessed.

- The neonatal period is a time of transition from intrauterine to extrauterine life. During the first few days, the neonate loses weight and then regains it; the lanugo (prenatal hair) falls off and the protective coating of vernix caseosa dries up. The fontanels (soft spots) in the skull close within the first 18 months.

- At birth, the circulatory, respiratory, gastrointestinal, and temperature regulation systems become independent of the mother's. If a newborn cannot start breathing within about five minutes, brain injury may occur.

- Newborns have a strong sucking reflex.

- Newborns secrete meconium from the intestinal tract. They are commonly subject to neonatal jaundice, because of immaturity of the liver.

- At one minute and five minutes after birth, a neonate's Apgar score can indicate how well he or she is adjusting to extrauterine life. The Brazelton Neonatal Behavioral Assessment Scale can assess responses to the environment and predict future development.

- Neonatal screening is done for certain rare conditions, such as PKU and congenital hypothyroidism.

Summarize
the causes and
consequences of
low birth weight,
postmaturity,
and infant
mortality.

- Complications of childbirth include postmature birth, prematurity, low birth weight, and stillbirth.
- A small minority of infants suffer lasting effects of birth trauma.
- Low-birth-weight babies may be either preterm (premature) or small-for-gestational age. Low birth weight is a major factor in infant mortality and can cause long-term physical and cognitive problems. Very-low-birth-weight babies have a less promising prognosis than those who weigh more.
- Postmature births have decreased with the increase in induced and Caesarean deliveries.
- A supportive postnatal environment and other protective factors can often improve the outcome for babies suffering from birth complications.
- Stillbirth has been substantially reduced in Canada but still accounts for half of perinatal deaths in the developing world.
- Although infant mortality has diminished, it is still disturbingly high for Aboriginal babies. Perinatal conditions and birth defects are the leading causes of death in the first year.
- Sudden infant death syndrome (SIDS) is a leading cause of death in infants in Canada. Major risk factors are exposure to smoke and, prenatally, to caffeine, and sleeping in the prone position.

Describe the importance of bonding and how the birth of a newborn affects the marital relationship.

- Researchers following the ethological approach have suggested that there is a critical period for the formation of the mother-infant bond. However, research has not confirmed this hypothesis. Fathers typically bond with their babies whether or not they are present at the birth.

- Infants have strong needs for maternal closeness and warmth as well as physical care.

- Parents' responsiveness to babies' states and activity levels is an important bidirectional influence on development.

- Fatherhood is a social construction. Fathering roles can differ in various cultures.

- Child-raising practices and caregiving roles vary around the world.

- Lower marital satisfaction seems to be associated with the stresses of caring for newborns.

ANSWERS TO Ask Yourself

Answers: 1-d; 2—First stage: dilation of the cervix; second stage: descent and emergence of the infant; third stage: expulsion of the placenta; 3—Lamaze method, epidural block; 4—Healthy full-term infants are on average 50 cm (20 inches) long and weigh about 3.5 kg (7 pounds). They have a large head, various skin conditions, a receding chin, and often a misshapen head. They are covered with lanugo (soft downy hair) and vernix caseosa (a cheese-like substance). They may also have swollen breast tissue and genitals; 5—b; 6—d; 7—primitive, locomotor; 8—c; 9—c; 10—c; 11—b; 12—c; 13—Higher rates of birth defects, especially among Inuit babies; higher rates of perinatal conditions such as low birth weight, birth trauma, and short gestation durations; less access to and lower quality of health care in remote communities; social factors such as poverty, food insecurity, and inadequate housing; higher prevalence of medical conditions in infancy, such as congenital anomalies, respiratory conditions, and SIDS; maternal behavioural factors involving obesity, smoking, and alcohol consumption during pregnancy; 14-a; 15-b; 16-b; 17-b

PHYSICAL DEVELOPMENT
AND HEALTH, BIRTH TO

WHAT'S TO COME

Early Growth and Physical Development

The Developing Brain

Early Sensory Capabilities

Motor Development

Health

When William was born, he was 45 cm (19½ inches) long and weighed 3.5 kg (7 pounds). He slept for most of the day and night, but only for short periods of time. He cried when he needed to be fed or changed or soothed, and until he started smiling at about 2 months, this was the primary way in which he communicated with his parents. Over the next 12 months, William grew nearly 25 cm (10 inches) and gained 7 kg (15 pounds). Most remarkable, however, were the changes in his ability to get around by himself and his increasing ability to have a "conversation" with his mom and dad. Although he was not walking by himself when he turned 1, as long as he was holding on to another person or object, he could stand or cruise around the room or, when motivated, crawl, with astonishing speed. Using gestures, such as outstretched arms to show that he wanted to be picked up, and a small vocabulary of one-word utterances ("no" was his favourite word), 1-year-old William could make his needs and desires quite clear. To his parents' relief, he now slept through the night and took two short naps during the day. William was a typically developing infant, who at 12 months was on the verge of toddlerhood.

Infancy begins at birth and ends when a child begins walking and stringing words together—two events that usually take place between 12 and 18 months of age. Toddlerhood lasts from about 18 to 36 months, a period when children become more verbal, independent, and able to move about. As we study how newborns become infants and toddlers and later grow into children and adolescents, we see how each of the three aspects of development is bound up with the others. Although we focus on the physical development of infants and toddlers in this chapter, on their cognitive development in Chapter 6, and on their psychosocial development in Chapter 7, we will see many examples of how these aspects of development intertwine. All areas of development are interrelated, and development proceeds in a complex, reciprocal fashion.

In this chapter, we examine typical growth patterns of body and brain, and we see how a nourishing environment can stimulate both. We explore how sensory perception goes hand in hand with an infant's growing motor skills and shapes the astoundingly rapid development of the brain. We study how young infants become busy, active toddlers. And we discuss threats to an infant's life and health, including abuse and neglect, and ways to prevent them.

AGE 3

AS YOU READ

LO1   Describe early patterns of growth and appropriate nutrition for young children.
LO2   Outline brain development in infants and explain the importance of early experiences.
LO3   Summarize the early sensory capacities of young infants.
LO4   List the major motor milestones and summarize the major theories of motor development
        and the impact of culture.
LO5   Review major health and safety issues for infants and toddlers.

Early Growth and Physical Development

The first three years are a time of explosive growth and development. Never again will a person grow so quickly or change so rapidly. Despite its rapidity, however, the developing body grows in an orderly and patterned way. And, for growth to be optimal, good nutrition and healthy eating habits are important. In the following section, we discuss these processes.

PRINCIPLES OF EARLY GROWTH AND PHYSICAL DEVELOPMENT

An infant's head is gigantic compared with the rest of the body. If you had the same body proportions as an infant, your head would approach the size of a watermelon. This characteristic highlights the cephalocaudal and proximodistal principles of early growth and physical development. According to the *cephalocaudal principle*, growth occurs from top down. Thus, a newborn baby's head is disproportionately large. At 1 year, the brain is 70 percent of its adult weight, but the rest of the body is only 10 to 20 percent of its adult weight. The head becomes proportionately smaller as the child grows in height and the lower parts of the body develop (Figure 5.1). Sensory and motor development follow the same principle; infants see objects before they can control their torso, and they learn to use the upper parts of the body before the lower parts.

According to the *proximodistal principle*, growth and motor development proceed from the centre of the body outward. For example, babies first develop the ability to use their upper arms and upper legs, then the forearms and forelegs, then hands and feet, and finally fingers and toes.

PHYSICAL GROWTH

Growth is faster in the first few months of life than it ever will be again. Babies continue to grow amazingly fast during the first two years, tapering off after the third. Boys and girls show similar patterns of growth; however, boys are generally a bit heavier and taller than girls (McDowell, Fryar, Ogden, & Flegal, 2008). At 5 months, the average baby boy's birth weight has doubled to 7 kg, and by 1 year, it has nearly tripled to 10 kg. This rapid growth rate slows during the second and third years; a boy typically gains about 2 kg (4½ pounds) by his second birthday and 1.5 kg (3 pounds) by his third, when he tips the scales at about 14 kg (31 pounds). A boy's height typically increases by 25 cm (10 inches) during the first year (making the typical 1-year-old boy about 75 cm [30 inches] tall), by almost 13 cm (5 inches) during the second year (so that the average 2-year-old boy is approaching 90 cm [35 inches] tall), and by a little more than 8 cm (3 inches) during the third year to top 95 cm (37 inches). Girls follow a parallel pattern but are slightly smaller; at 3, the average girl weighs 500 g (1 pound) less and is 1 cm (just under a half-inch) shorter than the average boy (Kuczmarski et al., 2000.) As a baby grows into a toddler, its body shape and proportions change too. A 3-year-old typically is slender compared with a chubby, potbellied 1-year-old.

Teething usually begins around 3 or 4 months, when infants begin grabbing almost everything in sight to put into their mouths, but the first tooth may not actually arrive until sometime between 5 and 9 months of age, or even later. By the first birthday, babies generally have six to eight teeth; by age 2½, they have a mouthful of 20.

The genes that an infant inherits have a strong influence on whether the child will be tall or short, thin or stocky, or somewhere in between. This genetic influence interacts with environmental influences, such as nutrition and living conditions, to determine characteristics.

FIGURE 5.1

Changes in Proportions of the Human Body

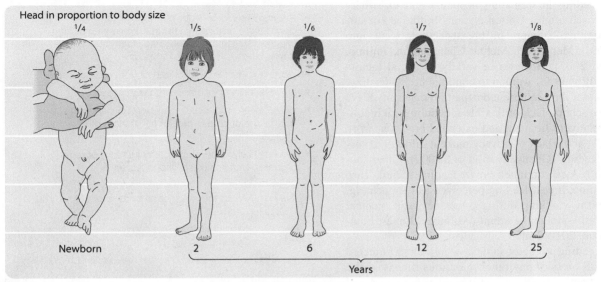

Head in proportion to body size

| 1/4 | 1/5 | 1/6 | 1/7 | 1/8 |

| Newborn | 2 | 6 | 12 | 25 |

Years

Source: From Fig. 6.1 in *Children*, 9th Ed., by John W. Santrock. © 2007 The McGraw-Hill Companies, Inc. Reprinted with permission.

NUTRITION

Like most babies, William was an avid eater from the beginning. Whether breast-feeding or taking a bottle from his dad, he seemed happiest while eating. Cereals and other solid foods were gradually introduced before his first birthday, and William happily adjusted to this new experience. As he matured into toddlerhood, he became pickier, gobbling down his favourite foods with gusto and throwing others—like broccoli and green peppers—onto the ground in disgust.

The importance of good nutrition for infants and toddlers cannot be overstated. Normal growth and brain development requires the proper mix of vitamins, minerals, calories, and high-quality protein sources. Failure to secure these essential substances can have effects lasting far past the early years in areas as diverse as cognitive development, physical health, work capacity, and earning power (Habicht & Martorell, 2010). Babies who eat well in the first year are smarter, stronger, healthier, and better suited to life's challenges. Given this, how and what should babies be fed?

Breast-Feeding

Through most of human history, all babies were breast-fed. With the advent of dependable refrigeration, pasteurization, and sterilization in the first decade of the twentieth century, manufacturers began to develop formulas to modify and enrich cow's milk for infant consumption. During the next half-century, formula feeding became the norm in Canada and some other industrialized countries. By 1971, only 25 percent of Canadian mothers even tried to nurse (Ryan, 1997). Since the 1970s, recognition of the benefits of breast milk has brought about a reversal of this trend. By about 2009, 87.5 percent of new mothers in Canada

reported breast-feeding, and about 54 percent were still breast-feeding after six months (Statistics Canada, 2011e), following Health Canada (2011b) guidelines, and 16 percent for more than a year. Many supplement breast milk with formula and other foods (Canadian Perinatal Surveillance System, 2000; Ryan, 2000), but about a quarter of Canadian mothers reported breast-feeding exclusively (no other liquids or solid foods) for six months or longer (Statistics Canada, 2011e). In addition, Health Canada (2011b) recommends daily vitamin D supplements for all infants to prevent bone diseases such as rickets.

Nutritionally speaking, breast-feeding is almost always best for infants (Table 5.1). Breast-feeding should begin immediately after birth and should continue for at least one year. Economically, breast-feeding can have significant benefits to the family, in reduced food costs, and to the community, in reduced health care

The Canadian Paediatric Society advocates breast-feeding for at least the first six months of a child's life, and then combined with other foods for the next year and a half.

costs resulting from lowered incidence of childhood illness (Bartick & Reinhold, 2010; Breastfeeding Committee for Canada, n.d.).

Breast-feeding in Canadian hospitals and elsewhere greatly increased after a United Nations initiative encouraging institutional support of breast-feeding went into effect in 1991 (Merewood, Mehta, Chamberlain, Philipp, & Bauchner, 2005). However, a variety of social factors can make it difficult for women to continue breast-feeding. Such factors as a short or absent postpartum maternity leave from work or school, lack of flexible scheduling, an inability to take relatively frequent and extended breaks at work to pump milk, and a lack of privacy make it difficult to sustain breast-feeding (Guendelman et al., 2009). Other factors that can reduce continued breast-feeding include ease of bottle-feeding, breast-feeding perceived as unappealing, Caesarean birth, smoking during pregnancy, and medical conditions in the mother or infant (Al-Sahab, Lanes, Feldman, & Tamim, 2010; Millar & Maclean, 2005).

Breast-feeding is inadvisable if a mother is infected with the AIDS virus or any other infectious illness, if she has untreated active tuberculosis, if she has been exposed to radiation, or if she is taking any drug that would not be safe for the baby (Canadian Paediatric Society, 2006; Health Canada, 2011b). The risk of transmitting HIV infection to an infant continues as long as an infected mother breast-feeds (Breastfeeding and HIV International Transmission Study Group, 2004; World Health Organization, 2008a, 2009), although this risk can be reduced via the use of retroviral medications for the infected mother, and zidovudine and/or nevirapine during the first 14 weeks of life (Kumwenda et al., 2008; World Health Organization, 2010).

Did you know?

In 2010, Facebook came under fire for removing photos of breast-feeding mothers from their profiles. Facebook classified the photos as "indecent" and even deactivated the accounts of some repeat offenders. What do you think? Are such photos indecent?

Overweight in Infancy

Obesity, defined as having a weight for height in the 95th percentile, has increased in infancy as in all age groups. In 2004, the prevalence of overweight in Canadian children ages 2 to 5 was 15 percent and the obesity rate was 6 percent (Shields, 2005), and higher rates have been found among Canadian Aboriginal children (Anderson et al., 2010). Having an obese parent is highly predictive of future problems (AAP Committee on Nutrition, 2003). Thus, a young child who has an obese parent—or especially two obese parents—may be a candidate for preventive efforts.

How do babies become obese? Can babies be overfed? Pediatric experts recommend that iron-enriched solid

TABLE 5.1 Benefits of Breast-Feeding

Breast-fed babies . . .
- Are less likely to contract infectious illnesses such as diarrhea; respiratory infections; otitis media (an infection of the middle ear); and staphylococcal, bacterial, and urinary tract infections.
- Have a lower risk of SIDS and of postneonatal death.
- Have less risk of inflammatory bowel disease.
- Have better visual acuity, neurological development, and long-term cardiovascular health, including cholesterol levels.
- Are less likely to develop obesity, asthma, eczema, diabetes, lymphoma, childhood leukemia, and Hodgkin's disease.
- Are less likely to show language and motor delays.
- Score slightly higher on cognitive tests at school age and into young adulthood, but cognitive benefits have been questioned.
- Have fewer cavities and are less likely to need braces.

Breast-feeding mothers . . .
- Enjoy quicker recovery from childbirth with less risk of postpartum bleeding.
- Are more likely to return to their prepregnancy weight and less likely to develop long-term obesity.
- Have reduced risk of anemia and decreased risk of repeat pregnancy while breast-feeding.
- Report feeling more confident and less anxious.
- Are less likely to develop osteoporosis or ovarian and premenopausal breast cancer.

Sources: AAP Section on Breastfeeding (2005); Black, Morris, & Bryce (2003); Chen & Rogan (2004); Dee, Li, Lee, & Grummer-Strawn (2007); Kramer et al. (2008); Lanting, Fidler, Huisman, Touwen, & Boersma (1994); Mortensen, Michaelson, Sanders, & Reinisch (2002); Ogbuanu, Karmaus, Arshad, Kurukulaaratchy, & Ewart (2009); Owen, Whincup, Odoki, Gilg, & Cook (2002); Singhal, Cole, Fewtrell, & Lucas (2004); Soliday (2007); United States Breastfeeding Committee (2002).

foods—usually beginning with cereal—be introduced gradually between ages 6 and 12 months (AAP Section on Breastfeeding, 2005; Health Canada, 2011b). Unfortunately, many parents do not follow these guidelines. According to random telephone interviews with parents and caregivers of more than 3,000 U.S. infants and toddlers, 29 percent of infants are given solid food before 4 months, 17 percent drink juice before 6 months, and 20 percent drink cow's milk before 12 months. By 7 to 24 months, the median food intake is 20 to 30 percent above normal daily requirements (Fox, Pac, Devaney, & Jankowski, 2004). Thirty percent of 19- to 24-month-old children eat no fruit, and french fries are the most commonly consumed vegetable in this age group. Sixty percent eat baked desserts, 20 percent eat candy, and 44 percent drink sweetened beverages on a daily basis (American Heart Association [AHA] et al., 2006).

Another contributing factor is sedentary behaviour, particularly in boys (Tremblay & Rinaldi, 2010). Canada was the first country to develop guidelines for young children's sedentary behaviour. The Canadian Society for Exercise Physiology recommends minimizing sedentary activity (sitting in a stroller or high chair) to one hour per session for infants and toddlers, and limiting screen time (such as computer, electronic games, and television) to one hour a day for children ages 2 to 4, with no screen time prior to those ages to prevent adverse effects on body development (Tremblay et al., 2012).

While infants and toddlers in Canada may eat too much, in many low-income communities around the world, malnutrition in early life is widespread. Malnutrition, discussed in Chapter 8, is implicated in more than half of deaths of children globally, and many children are irreversibly damaged by age 2 from malnutrition (World Bank, 2006).

Ask Yourself

1. The reason that babies learn how to use their arms before using their legs has to do with the _____, while the reason that babies learn how to use their arms before grasping objects has to do with the _____.

2. What are the recommended foods for babies according to the ages listed below?
   a. 6 months of age and younger
   b. 6–12 months of age

The Developing Brain

Holding a newborn has been compared to "holding a three-pound bag of corn" (Wingert & Underwood, 1997). But underneath the flailing limbs, the fuzzy eyesight, and the wailing cries of newborn infants, the brain is already starting to change and grow with amazing speed as it takes in

environmental information and starts to make sense of the new world. How does this happen? How does a baby move from uncontrolled movements and reflexes to deliberate actions? Are these emerging skills reflected in the structure of the brain?

BUILDING THE BRAIN

The brain's growth occurs in fits and starts called *brain growth spurts*. Beginning about 3 weeks after conception, the brain gradually develops from a long hollow tube into a spherical mass of cells (Figure 5.2). By birth, the spinal cord and brain stem, the part of the brain responsible for basic bodily functions such as breathing, heart rate, body temperature, and the sleep-wake cycle, are nearly complete. The brain at birth is only about one-fourth to one-third of its eventual adult volume (Toga, Thompson, & Sowell, 2006). The cerebellum, the part of the brain that maintains balance and motor coordination, grows fastest during the first year of life (Knickmeyer, et al., 2008). By age 3, the typical child's brain will weigh about 1.5 kg (3½ pounds), nearly 90 percent of its eventual adult weight (Gabbard, 1996).

The cerebrum, which resembles a giant wrinkled walnut, is the largest part of the brain and is divided into right and left halves, or hemispheres, each with specialized functions. The left hemisphere is the centre of language and logical thinking. The right hemisphere processes visual and spatial information, enabling us to read maps or draw. Joining the two hemispheres is a tough band of tissue called the corpus callosum. If you were looking at a side view of one-half of the human brain, the corpus callosum would resemble the cross-section of a mushroom cap. The corpus callosum is like a giant switchboard of fibres connecting the hemispheres and allowing them to share information and coordinate commands. It grows dramatically during childhood, reaching adult size by about age 10.

Brain Development during Gestation

FIGURE 5.2 Fetal nervous system development begins at about 3 weeks. At 1 month, major regions of the brain appear: the forebrain, midbrain, and hindbrain. As the brain grows, the front part expands to form the cerebrum, the seat of conscious brain activity. The cerebellum grows most rapidly during the 1st year of life.

Source: Adapted from Cowan W. Maxwell, "The Development of the Brain," *Scientific American*, v241, n3, pp. 113–133, September 1979.

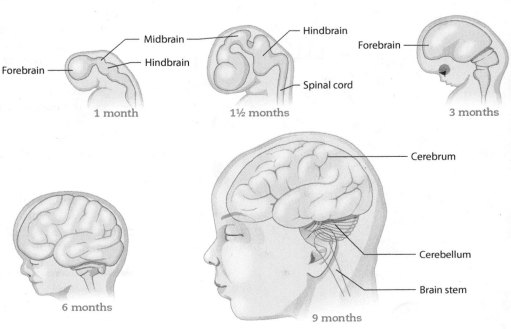

Each cerebral hemisphere has four lobes, or sections: the occipital, parietal, temporal, and frontal lobes, which control different functions (Figure 5.3) and develop at different rates. The regions of the cerebral cortex that govern vision, hearing, and other sensory information grow rapidly in the first few months after birth and are mature by 6 months of age, but the areas of the frontal cortex responsible for abstract thought, mental associations, remembering, and deliberate motor responses grow little during this period and remain immature through adolescence (Gilmore et al., 2007). The growth of the brain is a lifelong process fundamental to physical, cognitive, and emotional development.

BRAIN PLASTICITY

Although the brain's early development is in large part genetically directed, its structure is continually modified by environmental experiences. The technical term for this is **plasticity**. Because of this plasticity, early experiences can have lasting effects on the capacity of the brain to learn and store information (Society for Neuroscience, 2008); good-quality early care and intervention can have significant benefits at this stage (McCain & Mustard, 1999; McCain et al., 2011).

The brain is like a car—it needs gas, brake fluid, oil, coolant, and other substances in order to perform at peak efficiency. When a brain is malnourished, it cannot form new connections or add appropriate amounts of myelin to the axons of nerve cells because it lacks the required substances for these projects. Additionally, exposure to

hazardous drugs, environmental toxins, or maternal stress can threaten the developing brain. For example, early abuse or sensory impoverishment can delay neural development or negatively affect brain structure (Glaser, 2000). The lack of enriching experiences may inhibit the normal process of **cell death** and the streamlining of neural connections (Figure 5.4), resulting in smaller head size and reduced brain activity (C. A. Nelson, 2008).

If certain neural connections are not made early in life, these brain circuits may shut down forever (Society for Neuroscience, 2008). For example, children with a "lazy eye" who are not treated when young will forever lose the ability to process visual input through the affected eye, even if their muscle control is later corrected.

But just as negative experiences can affect the brain adversely, positive experiences or an enriched environment can spur brain development and even make up for past deprivation (Figure 5.5) (Black, 1998; Society for Neuroscience, 2008). Animals raised in toy-filled cages sprout more axons, dendrites, and synapses than animals raised in bare cages (Society for Neuroscience, 2008). Such findings have sparked successful efforts to stimulate the brain development of premature infants (Als et al., 2004) and children with Down syndrome, and to help victims of brain damage recover function.

Ethical constraints prevent controlled experiments on the effects of profound environmental deprivation on human infants and young children. However, the thousands of orphaned or abandoned children who had spent virtually their entire lives in overcrowded Romanian orphanages offered a natural experiment (Beckett et al., 2006). The Bucharest Early Intervention Project (BEIP) has studied these children—one group abandoned at birth and placed in institutions; a second group abandoned at birth and placed in institutions but then randomly assigned to

FIGURE 5.3

The Human Brain

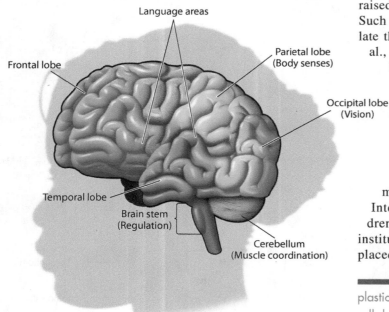

Language areas

Frontal lobe

Parietal lobe (Body senses)

Occipital lobe (Vision)

Temporal lobe

Brain stem (Regulation)

Cerebellum (Muscle coordination)

plasticity   Modifiability of the brain through experience.

cell death   In brain development, normal elimination of excess cells to achieve more efficient functioning.

TIME

Wiring the Brain: Development of Neural Connections before and after Birth

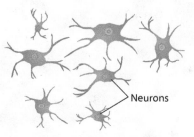

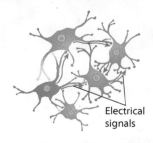

1. An embryo's brain produces many more neurons, or nerve cells, than it needs, then eliminates the excess.

3. Spontaneous bursts of electrical activity strengthen some of these connections, while others (the connections that are not reinforced by activity) atrophy.

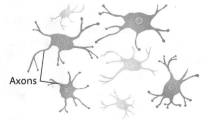

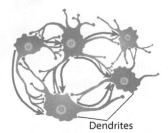

2. The surviving neurons spin out axons, the long-distance transmission lines of the nervous system. At their ends, the axons spin out multiple branches that temporarily connect with many targets.

4. After birth, the brain experiences a second growth spurt, as the axons (which send signals) and dendrites (which receive them) explode with new connections. Electrical activity, triggered by a flood of sensory experiences, fine-tunes the brain's circuitry—determining which connections will be retained and which will be pruned.

Source: Nash, J.M. (1997) From "Fertile lands," *Time*, 149(5), Feb 3, 1997, p49–56. Figure p. 51. © 1997. Time Inc. All rights reserved. Reprinted from TIME Magazine and published with permission of Time Inc. Reproduction in any manner in any language in whole or in part without written permission is prohibited.

foster care; and a comparison group living with their biological parents. Findings so far suggest that long-term institutional care in severely deprived settings has a

Growth of Neural Connections during the First Two Years of Life

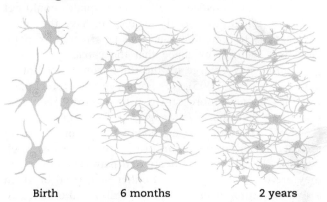

| Birth | 6 months | 2 years |

FIGURE 5.5   The rapid increase in the brain's density and weight is due largely to the formation of dendrites, extensions of nerve cell bodies, and the synapses that link them. This mushrooming communications network sprouts in response to environmental stimulation and makes possible impressive growth in every domain of development.

Source: Adapted from The Postnatal Development of the Cerebral Cortex, Vol. 1, 1939, Vol. 3, 1947, and Vol. 4, 1951, by Conel, J. LeRoy. Copyright © 1939–1967 by Harvard University Press.

profound negative effect on many areas of development, including physical growth, cognitive development, and social-emotional functioning, but that foster care can help prevent problems in many of these areas. Age of adoption, length of previous institutionalization, and the specific features of the institutional experience were key factors in the children's prospects for improvement (C. A. Nelson, 2008). This suggests that high-quality foster care may moderate the adverse effects of early institutionalization (Moulson, Fox, Zeanah, & Nelson, 2009).

Canadian families adopted many of these children, who at the time of adoption showed delayed motor, language, or psychosocial development. Three years later, when compared with children left behind in the Romanian institutions, they showed remarkable progress. Even when compared with Canadian children reared in their own homes from birth, about one-third had no serious problems and were doing well—in a few cases, better than the average home-raised child. Another third—generally those who had been in institutions the longest—still had serious developmental problems. The rest were moving toward average performance and behaviour (Ames, 1997; Morison, Ames, & Chisholm, 1995).

However, another study suggests that age of adoption makes a difference. Among 111 Romanian children adopted in England before age 2, those adopted before 6 months of age had largely caught up physically and had made a complete cognitive recovery by age 4, compared with a control group of English adopted children. However, 85 percent of the English adoptees were more cognitively advanced than the average Romanian child adopted after 6 months of age (Rutter & the English and Romanian Adoptees [ERA] Study Team, 1998). A further study of Romanian children adopted by Canadians showed that those who spent eight months or more in Romanian orphanages scored lower in cognitive development than Romanian children who spent less than four months in orphanages before being adopted by Canadians. However, the early adoptees scored lower than Canadian-born control children, indicating that prenatal and perinatal environments, genetic factors, and the experience of adoption can influence cognitive development (Morison & Ellwood, 2000). It may take very early environmental stimulation to overcome the effects of extreme deprivation.

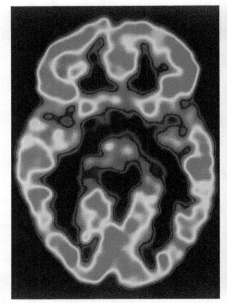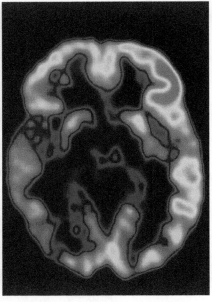

Extreme environmental deprivation in infancy can affect the structure of the brain, resulting in cognitive and emotional problems. A PET scan of a normal child's brain (left) shows regions of high (red) and low (blue and black) activity. A PET scan of the brain of a Romanian orphan institutionalized after birth (right) shows little activity.

Ask Yourself

3. In general, the areas of the brain responsible for sensation and perception _____, while areas of the brain specialized for higher cognitive functions _____.
   a. develop slowly over a number of years; are absent at birth
   b. develop rapidly in the first few months after birth; remain immature through adolescence
   c. develop prenatally; develop rapidly in the first few months after birth
   d. develop slowly over a number of years; develop prenatally

4. What kind of environmental experiences are likely to have a negative effect on early brain development?

Early Sensory Capacities

The regions of the developing brain that control sensory information grow rapidly during the first few months of life, enabling newborn infants to make fairly good sense of what they touch, see, smell, taste, and hear (Gilmore et al., 2007). It does not take long, for example, for newborns to recognize the smell of their mother's breast milk on a pad or to learn the sound of her voice.

TOUCH AND PAIN

Anytime you have comforted a crying baby by cuddling her or tickled a drowsy child to wake him up, you have made use of what is perhaps the most important sense in infancy: touch. Touch is the first sense to develop, and for the first several months it is the most mature sensory system. By 32 weeks of gestation, all body parts are sensitive to touch, and this sensitivity increases during the first five days of life (Field, 2010; Haith, 1986). When a newborn's cheek is stroked near the mouth, the baby responds by trying to find a nipple, a reflex that is probably an evolved survival mechanism (Rakison, 2005).

In the past, physicians performing surgery, such as circumcision, on newborn babies often used no anesthesia because of a mistaken belief that neonates could not feel pain, felt it only briefly, or did not have the memory capacity to remember, and thus be affected by, pain. However, there is evidence that the capacity for pain perception may emerge by the third trimester of pregnancy (Lee et al., 2005). Newborns can and do feel pain, and they become more sensitive to it during their first few days. Anesthesia is dangerous for young infants, however, so alternative methods of pain management are used for minor procedures (e.g., circumcision) when possible. Infants show a decreased pain response when they are held or cuddled, and either breast-fed or given a sweet solution to suck on (Campbell-Yeo, Fernades, & Johnston, 2011).

The Canadian Paediatric Society maintains that prolonged or severe pain can do long-term harm to newborns, that pain relief is essential, and that pain prevention should be practised in health care facilities (Barrington, Batton, Finley, Wallman, & Canadian

Paediatric Society, Fetus and Newborn Committee, 2007). Although hospitals in Canada routinely use anesthetic during major surgery for infants, they have used anesthetic less frequently in minor surgery and in easing postoperative and disease-related pain (Fernandez & Rees, 1994).

SMELL AND TASTE

The senses of smell and taste also begin to develop in the womb, and some taste preferences may be largely innate. Newborns prefer sweet tastes to sour, bitter, or salty ones (Haith, 1986). These are probably survival mechanisms; breast milk is very sweet (Ventura & Mennella, 2011) and poisons are often bitter (Beauchamp & Mennella, 2009).

Taste preferences developed in infancy may last into early childhood. In one study, 4- and 5-year-olds who, as infants, had been fed different types of formula had differing food preferences (Mennella & Beauchamp, 2002). Exposure to the flavours of healthy foods through breastfeeding may improve acceptance of healthy foods after weaning and later in life (AHA et al., 2006).

Did you know?

It is developmentally typical for children to become picky eaters in the toddler years—and up to 78 percent of the variance in pickiness is genetic. Reluctance to trying new foods has more to do with genes than with parenting practices, indicating that different children can respond to the same environment differently. The other 22 percent of the variance is the part you can affect by exposing children to varied flavours (Cook, Haworth, & Wardle, 2007).

HEARING

Hearing, too, is functional before birth. It is likely that by the time a baby is born, she has been listening to her mother's muffled voice—and the rumbles in her stomach as she digests food—for months. From an evolutionary perspective, early recognition of voices and language heard in the womb may in part lay the foundation for the relationship with the mother, which is critical to early survival (Rakison, 2005).

Auditory discrimination develops rapidly after birth. Even 3-day-old infants can tell new speech sounds from those they have heard before (L. R. Brody, Zelazo, & Chaika, 1984), and infants as young as 2 days old are able to recognize a word they heard up to a day earlier (Swain, Zelazo, & Clifton, 1993). At 1 month, babies can distinguish sounds as close as *ba* and *pa* (Eimas, Siqueland, Jusczyk, & Vigorito, 1971), even when they are pronounced by different people.

Because hearing is a key to language development, and hearing impairments are the most common cause of speech delays, hearing impairments should be identified as early as possible. Hearing loss occurs in 1 to 3 of 1,000 infants (Gaffney, Gamble, Costa, Holstrum, & Boyle, 2003). Although there is support for universally testing hearing in newborns (Hyde & Riko, 2000), only Ontario and British Columbia have fully implemented such programs, and other provinces have partial programs, mainly focusing on infants in neonatal intensive care units (Patel, Feldman, & Canadian Paediatric Society, Community Paediatrics Committee, 2011). Such programs conduct hearing screening by 1 month, final diagnosis by 3 months, and intervention by the 6th month (Patel et al., 2011).

SIGHT

What does a baby see when in his or her parents' arms? Vision is the least developed sense at birth. From an evolutionary developmental perspective, the other senses are more directly related to a newborn's survival. Visual perception and the ability to use visual information—identifying caregivers, finding food, and avoiding dangers—become more important as infants become more alert and active (Rakison, 2005).

The eyes of newborns are smaller than those of adults, the retinal structures are incomplete, and the optic nerve is underdeveloped. A neonate's eyes focus best from about a foot away—just about the typical distance from the face of a person holding a newborn. This is probably not an accident; this focusing distance may have evolved to promote mother-infant bonding.

Newborns blink at bright lights. Their peripheral vision is very narrow; it more than doubles between 2 and 10 weeks of age (Tronick, 1972). The ability to follow a moving target also develops rapidly in the first months, as does colour perception (Haith, 1986).

Visual acuity at birth is approximately 20/400 but improves rapidly, reaching the 20/20 level by about 8 months (Kellman & Arterberry, 1998). Binocular vision—the use of both eyes to focus, enabling perception of depth and distance—usually does not develop until 4 or 5 months (Bushnell & Boudreau, 1993).

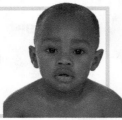
Early screening is essential to detect any problems that interfere with vision. Infants should be examined by 3 months of age for any signs of eye disease, and at 6 to 12 months for visual fixation preference, ocular alignment, and any signs of eye disease again. Formal vision screening, including visual acuity, should begin by age 3 (Amit & Canadian Paediatric Society, Community Paediatrics Committee, 2009). Doctor's offices have modified eye charts for toddlers specifically for this purpose; in place of letters are shapes such as stars, hearts, and circles, which are easily recognized by most toddlers.

Ask Yourself

5. At birth, the most mature sensory system is
   _____.

6. Babies whose mothers consume garlic while pregnant seem to like the smell of garlic more than those babies whose mothers did not consume garlic while pregnant. This suggests that
   a. liking garlic is an innate preference.
   b. babies learn to like certain flavours or smells prenatally.
   c. babies learn to like certain flavours or smells postnatally.
   d. babies must be taught to like garlic.

7. It is important to identify hearing impairments early in life because
   a. if they are not identified by 6 months of age, the neural pathways for auditory information will disappear.
   b. being able to respond to parents is heavily dependent upon hearing.
   c. hearing is key to language development.
   d. hearing impairments can lead to failure to thrive.

8. What are three differences between an infant's and an adult's eyes?

Motor Development

While William flailed and thrashed around in his crib when first born and was floppy and uncoordinated when held, his parents noticed a continual and rapid increase in his ability to control his body's movements. By about 4 months, he was rolling over and could no longer be left unattended on his changing table without risking a fall. By 6 months, he was sitting up by himself, although he had a tendency to topple over when reaching for a toy and needed help to reach a sitting position. And just after his first birthday, William took his first, halting, unaided steps. William was a typically developing baby, showing the same patterned timeline of development marking humans worldwide.

MILESTONES

Motor development is marked by a series of milestones that develop systematically (Figure 5.6). Babies are driven to develop these skills and need nothing more than room to move and freedom to see what they can do.

Early assessment and screening measures, like the *Bayley Scales of Infant and Toddler Development—III* (Bayley, 2005), *Denver Developmental Screening Test II* (Frankenburg, Dodds, Archer, Shapiro, & Bresnick, 1990), *Gesell Developmental Schedules* (Knobloch, Stevens, & Malone, 1980), and the Canadian **Nipissing District Developmental Screen** (NDDSIPA, 2000) are used to chart progress in infants and toddlers in a variety of areas, including **gross motor skills** involving the use of large muscle groups, such as rolling over and catching a ball, and **fine motor skills** requiring precise coordination of small muscles, such as grasping a rattle and copying a circle. Generally, gross motor development occurs before fine motor development. Tests like the *Denver*, though, have been criticized largely because of low sensitivity in identifying at-risk children and weaknesses in standardization and norms (Dahinten & Ford, 2004; Feightner, 1994; Lee & Harris, 2005), which may not reflect the diversity of Canada's population. It is important to remember that normality covers a wide range, but that loss of already acquired skills is a major cause for concern (Canadian Paediatric Society & Sacks, 2009).

The pace of motor development responds to certain cultural factors. In Uganda, for example, babies generally walk at 10 months, as compared with 14 months in Canada and France (Gardiner & Kozmitzki, 2005; Grenier & Leduc, 2008). Asian babies tend to develop these skills more slowly. Such differences may be related in part to ethnic differences in temperament or may reflect a culture's child-rearing practices (Gardiner & Kozmitzki, 2005). Normal development need not follow the same timetable to reach the same destination, and there are many paths leading to proficiency in motor movements. Key milestones in the first three years of life relate to head control, hand control, and locomotion.

Nipissing District Developmental Screen Screening test given to children from infancy to 6 years to determine whether they are developing normally.

gross motor skills Physical skills that involve the large muscles.

fine motor skills Physical skills that involve the small muscles and eye-hand coordination.

FIGURE 5.6

Milestones in Gross Motor Development

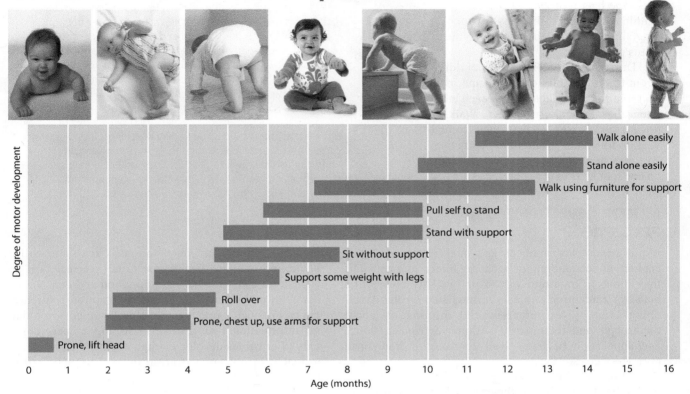

Degree of motor development | Age (months)

- Walk alone easily
- Stand alone easily
- Walk using furniture for support
- Pull self to stand
- Stand with support
- Sit without support
- Support some weight with legs
- Roll over
- Prone, chest up, use arms for support
- Prone, lift head

0 1 2 3 4 5 6 7 8 9 10 11 12 13 14 15 16

Age (months)

Source: From "The Denver Development Screening Test" by W.K. Frankenburg and J.B. Dodds in *Journal of Pediatrics,* 71, August 1967, pp. 181–191. Copyright © 1967, Elsevier. Reprinted with permission.

Developing Motor Control

At birth, most infants can turn their heads from side to side while lying on their backs and can lift their heads enough to turn them while lying chest down. By 4 months of age, almost all infants can keep their heads erect while being held or supported in a sitting position.

At about 3 months, most infants can grasp an object of moderate size, such as a rattle, but have trouble holding a small object. By 11 months of age, their hands become coordinated enough to pick up a tiny object, such as a pea, using the pincer grasp, and by 15 months, most can build a tower of two cubes. A few months after the third birthday, the average toddler can copy a circle fairly well.

The average baby begins to roll over deliberately after 3 months—first from front to back and then from back to front—can sit without support by 6 months, and can assume a sitting position without help by about 8 months. Although not technically a milestone, crawling emerges between 6 and 10 months. This achievement of self-locomotion has striking cognitive and psychosocial benefits (Karasik, Tamis-LeMonda, & Adolph, 2011).

Crawling infants become more sensitive to where objects are, how big they are, whether they can be moved, and how they look. Crawling helps babies learn to better judge distances and perceive depth. Some babies move directly from sitting to walking, sometimes scooting on their bottoms in place of crawling.

By holding onto a helping hand or a piece of furniture, the average baby can stand at a little past 7 months and can stand well alone at about 11 months. At this point, the baby is ready to learn how to walk. Babies

WHAT DO YOU **DO?**

Occupational Therapist

Occupational therapists help individuals with mental, physical, or developmental disabilities improve their ability to perform everyday tasks at home and in working environments. Such activities may consist of computer usage, dressing, eating, or cooking. For example, an occupational therapist might help a toddler with a developmental disorder use utensils or manipulate toys. They work in a range of settings, including hospitals, rehabilitation clinics, private practices, schools, and mental health facilities. A master's degree or higher is required in most provinces. To learn more about becoming an occupational therapist, visit www.caot.ca.

often practise standing and walking more than six hours a day, on and off, and may take enough steps to cover the length of 29 football fields! Within a few weeks, the baby is walking fairly well and thus achieves the status of toddler.

During the second year, children begin to climb stairs one at a time, putting one foot after another on each step; later, they will alternate feet. Walking down stairs comes later. In their second year, toddlers also begin to run and jump. By age 3, most children can balance briefly on one foot and begin to hop.

MOTOR DEVELOPMENT AND PERCEPTION

Motor experience sharpens and modifies infants' perceptual understanding of what is likely to happen if they move in a certain way. This two-way connection between perception and action, mediated by the developing brain, gives infants useful information about themselves and their world (Adolph & Eppler, 2002) and appears to be fairly well coordinated from birth (von Hofsten, 2004).

Infants begin reaching for objects at about 4 to 5 months; by 5 months, they can adapt their reach to moving or spinning objects (Wentworth, Benson, & Haith, 2000). While infants most frequently use vision to help them reach, infants in this age group can also use other sensory cues to reach for an object. They can locate an unseen rattle by its sound, and they can reach for a glowing object in the dark, even though they cannot see their hands (McCall & Clifton, 1999). They even can reach for an object based only on their memory of its location (McCarty, Clifton, Ashmead, Lee, & Goubet, 2001). Slightly older infants, at 5 to 7 months, can grasp a moving, fluorescent object in the dark—a feat that requires awareness of the object's path and speed, so as to anticipate the likely point of contact (Robin, Berthier, & Clifton, 1996).

Depth perception, the ability to perceive objects and surfaces in three dimensions, depends on cues that affect the image of an object on the retina of the eye where the sensory receptor cells are located. These cues involve both binocular coordination and motor control (Bushnell & Boudreau, 1993). Kinetic cues are produced by movement of the object or the observer, or both. To find out whether an object is moving, a baby might hold his or her head still for a moment, an ability that is well established by about 3 months.

Between 5 and 7 months of age, babies respond to such cues as relative size and differences in texture and shading. These cues depend on **haptic perception**, the ability to acquire information by handling objects rather than just looking at them. Putting objects in the mouth—common in infants—is also a way to collect haptic information. The tongue's multiple receptors are capable of fine-grained discrimination and can provide a wealth of information. Haptic perception centred on the mouth occurs immediately after birth; however, haptic information that involves grasping objects comes only after babies develop enough eye-hand coordination to reach for objects and grasp them (Bushnell & Boudreau, 1993).

THEORIES OF MOTOR DEVELOPMENT

Developmental psychologists are interested not just in documenting the sequence and timing of events, but also in understanding the underlying processes. Given the complexity of motor development, it is not surprising that a variety of theoretical perspectives have been proposed as explanatory frameworks. Here, we focus on two of the most important approaches: the ecological theory of perception and the dynamic systems approach.

Ecological Theory of Perception

In a classic experiment by Richard Walk and Eleanor Gibson (1961), 6-month-old babies were placed on a Plexiglas tabletop laid over a checkerboard pattern that created the illusion of a vertical drop in the centre of the table—a **visual cliff**. Would the infants perceive this illusion of depth? The babies did see a difference between the "ledge" and the "drop." They crawled freely on the "ledge" but avoided the "drop," even when they saw their mothers beckoning from the far side of the table.

depth perception Ability to perceive objects and surfaces in three dimensions.

haptic perception Ability to acquire information about properties of objects, such as size, weight, and texture, by handling them.

visual cliff Apparatus designed to give an illusion of depth and used to assess depth perception in infants.

Putting objects in the mouth is a great way for babies to collect haptic information.

According to Gibson's theory, locomotion does not develop in functionally related stages. Instead, "each problem space has its own . . . learning curve" (Adolph, 2008, p. 214). Babies who learn how far they can reach for a toy across a gap while in a sitting position must acquire this knowledge anew when they begin to crawl. Likewise, when crawling babies who have mastered slopes begin to walk, they have to learn to cope with slopes all over again (Adolph & Eppler, 2002).

Dynamic Systems Theory

The typical sequence of motor development was traditionally thought to be genetically programmed—a largely automatic, preordained series of steps directed by the maturing brain. Today, many developmental scientists consider this view too simplistic. Instead, according to Esther Thelen's **dynamic systems theory (DST)** (1995; Smith & Thelen, 2003), motor development is a continuous process of interaction between baby and environment.

According to Eleanor Gibson's and James J. Gibson's **ecological theory of perception** (E. J. Gibson, 1969; J. J. Gibson, 1979; Gibson & Pick, 2000), babies continually gauge their abilities and the surroundings in which they move and adapt their movements accordingly, devising new strategies as needed. This process of "learning to learn" (Adolph, 2008, p. 214) involves visual and manual exploration, testing of alternatives, and flexible problem-solving. In visual cliff experiments, infants who have been crawling for some time are more likely than new crawlers to avoid the cliff. Likewise, when faced with a downward slope, infants who have just begun to crawl or walk seem unaware of the limits of their abilities and plunge recklessly down. In time, however, their judgment becomes more accurate and their explorations more discerning as they practise their new skills and learn from experience how far they can push their limits without losing their balance (Adolph, 2008).

Thelen pointed to the walking reflex: stepping movements a neonate makes when held upright with the feet touching a surface. This behaviour usually disappears by the fourth month. These movements do not appear again until late in the first year. The usual explanation is the re-emergence is a new—and deliberate—skill masterminded by the developing brain. But, as Thelen observed, a newborn's stepping involves the same kinds of movements the neonate makes while lying down and kicking. Why would stepping stop, whereas kicking continues? She proposed the answer might be that babies' legs become thicker and heavier during the early months but the muscles are not yet strong enough to carry the increased weight (Thelen, 1995). In fact, when infants who had stopped stepping were held in warm water, which helps support their legs, stepping reappeared.

Thelen argued that there is not a single, simple cause—such as maturation—that sufficiently explains motor development. Infant and environment form an interconnected, continually changing system, which includes such variables as the infant's motivation and muscular strength, and the environmental affordances that are available. Ultimately, a solution emerges as the baby explores various combinations of

The visual cliff.

ecological theory of perception Theory developed by Eleanor and James Gibson that describes developing motor and perceptual abilities as interdependent parts of a functional system that guides behaviour in varying contexts.

dynamic systems theory (DST) Thelen's theory that holds that motor development is a dynamic process of active coordination of multiple systems within the infant in relation to the environment.

movements and selects and assembles those that most efficiently contribute to that end. Furthermore, the solution must be flexible, subject to modification in changing circumstances. The maturing brain is only one part of it.

According to Thelen's dynamic systems theory, typical babies develop the same skills in the same order because they are built approximately the same way and have similar physical challenges and needs. Thus, they eventually discover that walking is more efficient than crawling in most situations. However, this discovery arises from each particular baby's physical characteristics and experience in a particular context, which explains why some babies learn to walk earlier than others.

Ask Yourself

9. What motor skills are developing at the following ages?
   a. 0–3 months
   b. 3–6 months
   c. 6–12 months
   d. 12–24 months
   e. 24–36 months

10. The best way to describe the way perception and motor development are related to each other is
    a. perception leads to advances in motor development.
    b. motor development leads to changes in perceptual abilities.
    c. perception and motor development do not influence each other.
    d. perception and motor development mutually influence each other.

11. Which would be the best analogy of a developing child's development according to the ecological theory of perception?
    a. a person carefully following instructions in a manual
    b. a magician waving a wand to cast a spell
    c. a scientist exploring the world
    d. a gambler rolling dice multiple times

Health

William was born to parents with the resources to provide him with good nutrition, enriching experiences, and quality health care. Perhaps most importantly, his parents were also loving and kind, and able to help him establish trust in others and confidence in his own fledgling abilities. William lived in a sunny world filled with toys and affection. He was lucky—many babies do not grow up in these circumstances and face numerous physical and emotional risks in early childhood. What are the risks faced by such children?

IMMUNIZATIONS

Such once-familiar and sometimes fatal childhood illnesses as measles, pertussis (whooping cough), and polio are now largely preventable, thanks to the development of vaccines. Unfortunately, many children still are not adequately protected.

Worldwide, more than 78 percent of children now receive routine vaccinations during their first year (UNICEF, 2007). Still, during 2002, 2.5 million vaccine-preventable deaths occurred among children under 5 years old, nearly 2 million of them in Africa and Southeast Asia.

Since the development of the Canadian Immunization Guide (Health Canada, 1998a), vaccination rates have jumped and the prevalence of vaccine-preventable illnesses has dropped sharply. By 1997, immunization rates for 19- to 35-month-olds had reached 87 percent. Still, many children lack one or more of the required shots, and there is substantial variation in coverage (National Advisory Committee on Immunization [NACI], 2006).

Some parents hesitate to immunize their children because of speculation that vaccines may cause autism disorders, but the preponderance of evidence suggests no reason for this concern (Hornig et al., 2008) and the original research on vaccines and autism has been widely discredited by the scientific community. However, many parents continue to worry about vaccines and fail to immunize their children. With nearly 8 percent of children who are eligible for vaccination left unprotected against measles, recent outbreaks of the disease have occurred in certain communities (Darling, Kolasa, & Wooten, 2008). Moreover, this puts pregnant women and young infants in danger of contracting the diseases.

Another parental worry is that infants receive too many vaccines for their immune system to handle safely. Actually, the opposite is true. Multiple vaccines fortify the immune system against a variety of bacteria and viruses, and reduce related infections (Offit et al., 2002). A single day at a children's museum exposes children to a far greater immune system load than a regular course of vaccines.

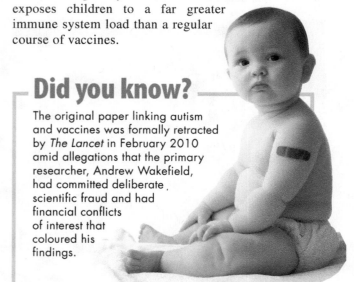

Did you know?

The original paper linking autism and vaccines was formally retracted by *The Lancet* in February 2010 amid allegations that the primary researcher, Andrew Wakefield, had committed deliberate scientific fraud and had financial conflicts of interest that coloured his findings.

WHERE DO **YOU** STAND?

Vaccines work only if a high enough proportion of the population is inoculated. Parents who opt not to vaccinate their children are thus relying on herd immunity—on the fact that others *are* vaccinating. Is this ethical?

STATES OF AROUSAL AND ACTIVITY LEVELS IN INFANCY AND TODDLERHOOD

Babies have an internal clock that regulates their daily cycles of eating, sleeping, and elimination, and perhaps even their moods. These periodic cycles of wakefulness, sleep, and activity, which govern an infant's **state of arousal**, or degree of alertness (Table 5.2), seem to be inborn and highly individual. Changes in state are coordinated by multiple areas of the brain and are accompanied by changes in the functioning of virtually all body systems (Ingersoll & Thoman, 1999; Scher, Epstein, & Tirosh, 2004). The establishment of "stable and distinct" states of arousal is associated with newborn health and positive outcomes because they are a marker of neurological organization.

Most new babies sleep about 75 percent of the time—up to 18 hours a day—but wake up every three to four hours, day and night, for feeding (Ferber & Makhoul, 2004). Newborns' sleep alternates between quiet (regular) and active (irregular) sleep. Active sleep appears to be the equivalent of rapid eye movement (REM) sleep, which in adults is associated with dreaming. Active sleep appears rhythmically in cycles of about one hour and accounts for up to 50 percent of a newborn's total sleep time. The amount of REM sleep declines to less than 30 percent of daily sleep time by age 3 and continues to decrease steadily throughout life (Hoban, 2004).

Beginning in the first month, nighttime sleep periods gradually lengthen and babies grow more wakeful in the daytime. By 6 months, an infant typically sleeps for six hours straight at night, but brief nighttime waking is normal even during late infancy and toddlerhood. A 2-year-old typically sleeps about 13 hours a day, including naps (Hoban, 2004).

Babies' sleep schedules vary across cultures. Among the Micronesian Truk, babies and children have no regular sleep schedules; they fall asleep whenever they feel tired. Mothers in rural Kenya allow their babies to nurse as they please, and their 4-month-olds continue to sleep only four hours at a stretch (Broude, 1995). In many predominantly Asian countries, bedtimes are later and total sleep time is shorter than in predominately Caucasian countries (Mindell, Sadeh, Wiegand, How, & Goh, 2010). In Canada,

TABLE 5.2 States of Arousal in Infancy

State	Eyes	Breathing	Movements	Responsiveness
Regular sleep	Closed; no eye movements	Regular and slow	None, except for sudden, generalized startles	Cannot be aroused by mild stimuli.
Irregular sleep	Closed; occasional rapid eye movements	Irregular	Muscles twitch, but no major movements	Sounds or light bring smiles or grimaces in sleep.
Drowsiness	Open or closed	Irregular	Somewhat active	May smile, startle, suck, or have erections in response to stimuli.
Alert inactivity	Open	Even	Quiet; may move head, or limbs, and trunk while looking around	An interesting environment (with people, things to watch); may initiate or maintain this state.
Waking activity	Open	Irregular	Much activity	External stimuli (such as hunger, cold, pain, being restrained, or being laid down) bring about more activity, perhaps starting with soft whimpering and gentle movements and turning into a rhythmic crescendo of crying or kicking, or perhaps beginning and enduring as uncoordinated thrashing and spasmodic screeching.

Sources: Adapted from Prechtl & Beintema (1964); Wolff (1969).

Perspectives on Diversity

SLEEP CUSTOMS

In many cultures, co-sleeping with young infants is expected. For example, Gusii infants in Kenya fall asleep in someone's arms or on a caregiver's back. In many societies, infants sleep in the same room with their mothers for the first few years of life and frequently in the same bed, making it easier to nurse at night (Broude, 1995). Mayan mothers sleep with children until the birth of a new baby, and even express shock at the idea that anyone would let a baby sleep in a room all alone (Morelli, Rogoff, Oppenheim & Goldsmith, 1992). Globally, differences in co-sleeping have been found for parents of children from birth to 36 months, with 65 percent of Asian parents reporting co-sleeping, compared with 12 percent of European and North American parents (Mindell, Sadeh, Wiegand, How, & Goh, 2010).

Although parents in Canada are likely to have their child sleep in the same room but not in the same bed, co-sleeping has become more popular in recent years. About 18 percent of Canadian and U.S. infants at 4 weeks of age sleep with a parent, while this number drops to 15 percent by 36 months (Sadeh, Mindell, Luedtke, & Wiegand, 2009).

Some researchers have argued that co-sleeping is a safe and desirable choice (Goldberg & Keller, 2007). The physical closeness of mother and baby tends to facilitate breast-feeding, touching, and maternal responsiveness (Ball, 2009).

However, under certain conditions, bed sharing can increase the risk of sudden infant death syndrome or suffocation. The risk seems to be particularly high when the infant is under 11 weeks, when more than one person co-sleeps with the baby, or when a bed sharer has been smoking, drinking alcohol, or is overtired (AAP Task Force on Sudden Infant Death Syndrome, 2005).

Sources: Ball, H. L. (2009). Bed-sharing and co-sleeping: Research overview. NCT New Digest, 48, 22-27; Goldberg, W. A. & Keller, M. A. (2007). Co-sleeping during infancy and early childhood: Key findings and future directions. Infant and Child Development, 16, 457–469; Hauck, F. R., Signore, C., Fein, S. B., & Raju, T.N.K. (2008). Infant sleeping arrangements and practices during the first year of life. Pediatrics, 122, S113–S120. DOI: 10.1542/peds.2008-1315o)

parents often time the evening feeding to encourage night-time sleep; many spend a great deal of energy trying, often unsuccessfully, to change babies' states, mostly by soothing a fussy infant to sleep.

CHILD MALTREATMENT

Although most parents are loving and nurturing, some cannot or will not take proper care of their children, and some deliberately harm them. Maltreatment can take several specific forms (Public Health Agency of Canada, 2010a):

- Physical abuse, injury to the body through punching, beating, kicking, or burning

- Neglect, failure to meet a child's basic needs, such as food, clothing, medical care, protection, and supervision

- Sexual abuse, any sexual activity involving a child and an older person

- Emotional maltreatment, including rejection, terrorization, isolation, exploitation, degradation, ridicule, or failure to provide emotional support, love, and affection

- Exposure to intimate partner violence

Child-welfare service workers across Canada investigated 235,842 cases of alleged maltreatment of children in 2008, and 85,440 were substantiated, a rate of about 14.9 substantiated investigations per 1,000 children (Public Health Agency of Canada, 2010a). About one-third (34 percent) of the children identified as maltreated were primarily exposed to violence and neglect of intimate partners, 34 percent involved neglect, 20 percent were physically abused, 9 percent were exposed to emotional maltreatment, and 3 percent were sexually abused. An estimated 8 percent of substantiated cases involved physical harm (3 percent of cases involved harm severe enough to require treatment), but there were no documented fatalities. Referrals to child-welfare agencies came primarily from schools (24 percent), police (22 percent), and custodial or non-custodial parents (11 percent).

Maltreatment in Infancy and Toddlerhood

Children are abused and neglected at all ages, but the highest rates of victimization from maltreatment are for the youngest children. In 2008, although overall 39 investigations were conducted per 1,000 children, the rate was 52 per 1,000 for infants, and 43 per 1,000 for children 1 to 3 years. The rate drops to 34 per 1,000 for children 12 to 15 years. There were significant concerns associated with child functioning in 46 percent of substantiated cases, the most common of which were academic difficulties, depression/anxiety/withdrawal, aggression, and attachment concerns (Public Health Agency of Canada, 2010a).

Theo Fleury, a successful hockey player, overcame early sexual abuse.

Some infants die of **non-organic failure to thrive**, slowed or arrested physical growth with no known medical cause accompanied by poor developmental and emotional functioning. Symptoms may include lack of appropriate weight gain, irritability, excessive sleepiness and fatigue, avoidance of eye contact, lack of smiling or vocalizing, and delayed motor development. Failure to thrive can result from a combination of inadequate nutrition, difficulties in breast-feeding, improper formula preparation or feeding techniques, and disturbed interactions with parents. Poverty is the greatest single risk factor for failure to thrive worldwide. Infants whose mother or primary caregiver is depressed, abuses alcohol or other substances, is under severe stress, or does not show warmth or affection toward the baby also are at heightened risk (Block, Krebs, the Committee on Child Abuse and Neglect, & the Committee on Nutrition, 2005; Lucile Packard Children's Hospital at Stanford, 2009).

Head trauma was reported in 325 substantiated cases of maltreatment in 2008 (Public Health Agency of Canada, 2010a). It can result from a baby being shaken, dropped, or thrown. **Shaken baby syndrome** is found mainly in children under 2 years old, most often in infants. The baby's weak neck muscles and heavy head result in the brain bouncing back and forth inside the skull during a shaking episode, with damage even more likely if the baby is thrown into bed or against a wall. This can cause bruising, bleeding, and swelling, and can lead to permanent and severe brain damage, paralysis, and even death (AAP, 2000; National Institute of Neurological Disorders and Stroke [NINDS], 2006). Often, victims are difficult to identify or

not provided with medical care (Ward & Bennett, 2003). A 10-year review of 364 cases of shaken baby syndrome in 11 Canadian centres found that 40 percent of victims had no sign of external injury, and 19 percent died. Of the surviving children, 78 percent had continuing health or developmental impairment when discharged from hospital (King, MacKay, Sirnick, & the Canadian Shaken Baby Study Group, 2003). In another study, only 45 percent of cases investigated for shaken baby syndrome were thought to require medical attention (Trocmé, MacMillan, Fallon, & DeMarco, 2003).

Contributing Factors

In nearly 80 percent of cases of maltreatment, the perpetrator is the child's parent, usually the mother (USDHHS, Administration on Children, Youth and Families, 2008). Maltreatment by parents is a symptom of extreme disturbance in child-rearing, usually aggravated by other family problems, such as poverty, lack of education, alcoholism, depression, or antisocial behaviour. The main risk factors associated with the primary caregiver in substantiated cases of child maltreatment in Canada include having been a victim of domestic abuse, having few social supports, experiencing mental health issues, abusing alcohol or drugs and being the perpetrator of domestic violence (Public Health Agency of Canada, 2010a). Abuse may begin when a parent who is already anxious, depressed, or hostile tries to control a child physically but loses self-control and shakes or beats the child. Parents who abuse children tend to have marital problems and to fight physically. Their households are often disorganized, and they experience more stressful events than other families.

Characteristics of the household environment are related to the likelihood a child will be physically abused (Jaffee et al., 2004). Household risks in substantiated cases of maltreatment include poverty (parents relying on social assistance, employment insurance, or other benefits such as public housing), household transience (at least one move in the past 12 months), and the presence of at least one household hazard (such as accessible weapons, drugs, drug production and trafficking, and other home injury or health hazards) (Public Health Agency of Canada, 2010a).

Abuse and neglect reflect the interplay of multiple layers of contributing factors, and in addition to family characteristics there are also cultural factors that impact the likelihood of maltreatment. Two cultural factors associated with child abuse are societal violence and physical punishment of children. For example, more frequent use of corporal punishment is related to higher rates of violence in societies (Lansford & Dodge, 2008). In Canada, 12 of the

---

non-organic failure to thrive In infancy, lack of appropriate growth for no known medical cause, accompanied by poor developmental and emotional functioning.

shaken baby syndrome Form of maltreatment in which shaking an infant or a toddler can cause brain damage, paralysis, or death.

13 provinces and territories prohibit physical punishment in child care settings, and 10 prohibit the practice in schools. Although these restrictions have reduced the incidence of corporal punishment by teachers and child care providers (Durrant, Trocmé, Fallon, Milne, & Black, 2009), the prohibitions do not go far enough to protect children from maltreatment since the majority of child maltreatment cases involve physical punishment by parents that fits within guidelines of what the Canadian Criminal Code would consider a permissible and reasonable use of force by parents (Durrant et al., 2009). According to one study, more than 90 percent of parents of 3- and 4-year-olds—and about 50 percent of parents of 12-year-olds—report using physical punishment at home (Straus, 2010).

Helping Families in Trouble

Preventing maltreatment before it occurs is an effective and fiscally sound policy. Some prevention activities, such as public service announcements, are aimed at raising awareness among the general population. Others, such as parenting classes for single teen mothers, are targeted to high-risk families or to families where abuse or neglect has already occurred (Child Welfare Information Gateway, 2008b).

If maltreatment is suspected, child welfare service agencies, organized at the provincial and territorial levels, investigate claims and determine what steps, if any, need to be taken. Agency staff may try to help the family resolve their problems or arrange for alternative care for children who cannot safely remain at home. Services for children who have been abused and for their parents include shelters, education in parenting skills, and therapy and supervision.

New structures for child welfare services among Aboriginal communities are becoming established to ensure the needs of Aboriginal children are appropriately met. Many services are now delivered by fully mandated Aboriginal child welfare agencies, or Aboriginal organizations that work collaboratively with mainstream child welfare agencies (Public Health Agency of Canada, 2010a). Although children from Aboriginal backgrounds are over-represented in out-of-home (foster) care in Canada, the complexities of family risks experienced by many Aboriginal children may help explain some of the discrepancy (Gough, Trocmé, Brown, Knoke, & Blackstock, 2005).

When authorities remove children from their homes, the usual alternative is foster care. Foster care removes a child from immediate danger, but it can occasionally be a source of stress and potential risk, given the shortages in numbers of foster homes and limited training for foster parents (CBC, 2012; Matheson, 2010). Often a child's basic health and educational needs are not met (David and Lucile Packard Foundation, 2004; National Research Council [NRC], 1993b). Calls for better recruitment, training, and retention of foster parents, as well

Did you know?

Prison inmates, both male and female, are more likely to have been abused as children than non-incarcerated adults (Carlson & Shafer, 2010).

as recognition of the importance of cultural sensitivity, may ameliorate some of the issues that have been identified for foster care (Brown, 2010; Matheson, 2010; Twigg, 2010).

Long-Term Effects of Maltreatment

Without help, maltreated children often grow up with serious problems and may continue the cycle of maltreatment when they have children of their own. An estimated one-third of adults who were abused and neglected in childhood victimize their own children (National Clearinghouse on Child Abuse and Neglect Information [NCCANI], 2004).

Childhood abuse or neglect can delay or alter brain development and undermine emotion regulation. Long-term effects of maltreatment include poor physical, mental, and emotional health; impaired brain development; cognitive, language, and academic difficulties; memory problems; emotional instability; problems in attachment and social relationships; and attentional and behavioural problems (American Academy of Pediatrics et al., 2008; Twardosz, 2010). As adolescents, children who have been abused or neglected are at heightened risk of poor academic achievement, delinquency, pregnancy, alcohol and drug use, and suicide (NCCANI, 2004). As adults, they tend to be in poor health and to develop illnesses, such as stroke, cancer, and heart disease, as a function of adverse life events, risky health behaviours, and emotional problems (Chartier, Walker, & Naimark, 2009; Min, Minnes, Kim, & Singer, 2013). Adults who were maltreated early in life tend to be anxious or depressed; those who were older when maltreated are more likely to show aggression and to engage in substance abuse (Kaplow & Widom, 2007).

WHERE DO **YOU** STAND?

One of the assumptions held by child welfare service agencies and policy-makers is that it is always best to keep children with their parents when their safety can be assured. Do you agree with this policy?

The consequences of sexual abuse vary with age. Sexually abused children tend to show disturbed behaviour, to have low self-esteem, to be depressed, anxious, or unhappy (Putnam, 2002; Swanston, Tebbutt, O'Toole, & Oates, 1997), and to develop certain eating disorders (Smolak & Murnen, 2002), and they may become sexually active at an early age (Noll, Trickett, & Putnam, 2003). Adults who were sexually abused as children tend to be anxious, depressed, angry, or hostile; to mistrust people; to feel isolated and stigmatized; to be sexually maladjusted; and to abuse alcohol or drugs (Dube, Huhman, & Heitzler, 2003; Fergusson, Boden, & Horwood, 2008; USDHHS, 1999a). One study found that adults who were victims of severe childhood sexual abuse were more likely to engage in violence in their relationships (Friesen, Woodward, Horwood, & Fergusson, 2010).

Many maltreated children show remarkable resilience. Optimism, self-esteem, intelligence, creativity, humour, and independence are protective factors, as is the social support of a caring adult (NCCANI, 2004). In later chapters, we further discuss factors that promote healthy development in difficult contexts.

Fortunately, most babies survive and grow up healthy and well cared for. Their physical development forms the underpinning for cognitive and psychosocial developments that enable infants and toddlers to become more at home in their world, as we will see in Chapters 6 and 7.

Ask Yourself

12. Evidence suggests that the link between autism and vaccines
    a. does not exist.
    b. is very strong.
    c. exists, but only for the measles vaccine.
    d. exists, but only for boys.

13. What are states of arousal?
    a. how excited or angry a baby becomes in response to environmental stimulation
    b. the sleep cycles of a newborn
    c. times where the baby is awake or drowsy
    d. periodic cycles of wakefulness, sleep, and activity

14. Name three contributing factors to child maltreatment.

SUMMARY CHAPTER 5 PHYSICAL DEVELOPMENT AND HEALTH, BIRTH TO AGE 3

LO1

Describe early patterns of growth and appropriate nutrition for young children.

- Normal physical growth and sensory and motor development proceed according to the cephalocaudal and proximodistal principles.

- A child's body grows most dramatically during the first year of life; growth proceeds at a rapid but diminishing rate throughout the first three years.

- Historic shifts in feeding practices reflected efforts to improve infant survival and health.

- Breast-feeding offers many health advantages and sensory and cognitive benefits. However, the quality of the relationship between parents and infant may be more important than the feeding method.

- Babies should not start solid foods and fruit juices until 6 months of age.

- Overweight and obesity in infancy is becoming a significant issue; sedentary behaviour can contribute to overweight.

LO2

Outline brain development in infants and explain the importance of early experiences.

- The brain grows most rapidly during the months before and immediately after birth as neurons migrate to their assigned locations, form synaptic connections, and undergo integration and differentiation. Cell death and myelination improve the efficiency of the nervous system.
- Especially during the early period of rapid growth, environmental experience can influence brain development positively or negatively.

LO3

Summarize the early sensory capacities of young infants.

- Sensory capacities, present from birth and even in the womb, develop rapidly in the first months of life. Very young infants can discriminate between stimuli.
- Touch seems to be the first sense to develop and mature. Newborns are sensitive to pain. Smell, taste, and hearing also begin to develop in the uterus.
- Vision is the least developed sense at birth but sharpens within the first six months.

LO4

List the major motor milestones and summarize the major theories of motor development and the impact of culture.

- Motor skills develop in a certain sequence, which may depend largely on maturation but also on context, experience, and motivation. Simple skills combine into increasingly complex systems. Early screening tests assess gross and fine motor skills.
- Depth perception is present at a very early age and is related to motor development.
- Environmental factors, including cultural practices, may affect the pace of early motor development.
- According to Gibson's ecological theory of perception, sensory perception and motor activity are coordinated from birth, helping infants figure out how to navigate in their environment.
- Thelen's dynamic systems theory holds that infants develop motor skills, not by maturation alone, but by active coordination of multiple systems of action within a changing environment.

LO5

Review major health and safety issues for infants and toddlers.

- Vaccine-preventable diseases have declined as rates of immunization have improved, but many preschoolers are not fully protected.
- A newborn's state of arousal is governed by periodic cycles of wakefulness, sleep, and activity, which seem to be inborn.
- Sleep takes up the major, but diminishing, amount of a neonate's time.
- Forms of maltreatment are physical abuse, neglect, sexual abuse, and emotional maltreatment.
- Characteristics of the abuser or neglecter, the victim, the family, the community, and the larger culture all contribute to child abuse and neglect.
- Maltreatment can interfere with physical, cognitive, emotional, and social development, and its effects can continue into adulthood. Still, many maltreated children show remarkable resilience.
- Preventing or stopping maltreatment may require multi-faceted, coordinated community efforts.

ANSWERS TO **Ask Yourself**

Answers: 1—cephalocaudal; proximodistal; 2—(a) breast milk; (b) iron-enriched solid foods to supplement breast milk; 3—b; 4—exposure to hazardous drugs, environmental toxins, maternal stress, malnutrition, early abuse, and sensory impoverishment; 5—touch; 6—b; 7—c; 8—Newborn eyes are smaller than adults', their retinal structure is incomplete, and the optic nerve is underdeveloped; 9—0—3 months: lift head, keep chest up, grasp an object of moderate size, begin to roll over deliberately; 3—6 months: sit without support, support some weight with legs, begin reaching for objects; 6—12 months: pick up a tiny object, such as a pea, using the pincer grasp; grasp a moving fluorescent object in the dark; assume a sitting position without help; crawling emerges; pull self to stand; stand well alone; walk using furniture for support; 12—24 months: can build a tower of two cubes, walk alone easily, begin to climb stairs one at a time, begin to run and jump; 24—36 months: can copy a circle fairly well, can balance briefly on one foot and begin to hop; 10—d; 11—c; 12—a; 13—d; 14—Contributing factors to maltreatment include family variables (large, single-parent, high stress, disorganized, critical, uncommunicative, parent having been a victim of domestic abuse, having few social supports, experiencing mental health issues, abusing alcohol or drugs, and being the perpetrator of domestic violence); household characteristics; household transience involving at least one move in the past 12 months; the presence of at least one household hazard, such as accessible weapons or drugs; drug production and trafficking; and cultural values (high levels of societal violence, physical punishment of children seen as appropriate).

CHAPTER 6

COGNITIVE
DEVELOPMENT, BIRTH

WHAT'S TO COME

Behaviourist Approach: Basic Mechanics of Learning

Psychometric Approach: Developmental and Intelligence Testing

Piagetian Approach: The Sensorimotor Stage

Information-Processing Approach: Perceptions and Representations

Cognitive Neuroscience Approach: The Brain's Cognitive Structures

Social-Contextual Approach: Learning from Caregivers

Language Development

When Ava was born, the most obvious sign of her development over time was her rapid increase in size and the development of motor skills. However, even bigger changes were occurring in her mind. As an infant, she focused her wide eyes thoughtfully on objects that she found interesting or clumsily pulled toys toward her mouth to explore them. As she began to crawl and then walk, her world grew with her. She used her hands and eyes and ears to learn more about the world around her, shaking and throwing toys, pointing at objects that interested her, saying her first word, and tracing her fingers over magazines as if they were iPad touchscreens. In the space of three years, she went from a helpless infant to a busy toddler, full of questions and comments about the expanding world around her. In this chapter, we will be studying cognitive development—the series of achievements that supported Ava's newfound abilities.

As in any area, multiple perspectives exist to help us in our quest for understanding. By covering each of six fundamental approaches to the study of cognition, we will illustrate how multiple perspectives provide a more complete understanding of development. Then, we will move to a fundamental achievement of the first three years made possible by increases in cognition—language—and discuss some of the influences on language development, its typical progression, and how to prepare children for later literacy.

TO AGE 3

AS YOU READ

LO1   Explain operant and classical conditioning.
LO2   Describe how to assess toddlers' intelligence and summarize relevant early experiences.
LO3   Discuss changes in cognition in early childhood and evaluate Piaget's theoretical approach for this area.
LO4   Summarize how data on intelligence is collected within the information-processing approach and evaluate its value as a predictor of other advances.
LO5   Summarize how the physical structure of the brain is related to cognitive development.
LO6   Identify some early social and contextual influences on development.
LO7   Summarize the sequence of early language development, identify the relevant influences, and discuss the relationship to literacy.

Behaviourist Approach: Basic Mechanics of Learning

As one of the two major approaches of learning theory, behaviourism, or the **behaviourist approach**, is interested in how we learn—how behaviour changes in response to experience. Babies are born with the ability to learn from what they see, hear, smell, taste, and touch. This ability then develops as part of the child's cognitive development. Two important processes behaviourists study to understand how we learn are classical conditioning and operant conditioning.

CLASSICAL CONDITIONING

Eager to capture Ava's memorable moments on film, her father took pictures of the infant smiling, crawling, and showing off her other achievements. Whenever the flash went off, Ava blinked. One evening when Ava was 11 months old, she saw her father hold the camera up to his eye—and she blinked before the flash. She had learned to associate the camera with the bright light so that the sight of the camera alone activated her blinking reflex.

Ava's blinking is an example of **classical conditioning**, in which a person learns to make a reflex or involuntary response (in this case, blinking) to a stimulus (the camera) that originally did not provoke the response. Classical conditioning enables infants to anticipate an event before it happens by forming associations between stimuli (such as the camera and the flash) that regularly occur together. Classically conditioned learning becomes extinct, or fades, if it is not reinforced by repeated association. Thus, if Ava frequently saw the camera without the flash, she would eventually stop blinking.

OPERANT CONDITIONING

In contrast, in **operant conditioning** the learner operates, or acts, on the environment. The infant learns to make a certain response to an environmental stimulus (e.g., babbling at the sight of parents) in order to produce a particular effect (e.g., smiles). Operant conditioning can involve either reinforcements, which increase behaviours, or punishments, which decrease behaviours. Conditioning can also be positive (adding a stimulus to the environment) or negative (removing a stimulus from the environment). For example, praising a child for sharing is an example of positive reinforcement, as the addition of a positive stimulus (praise) should lead to the repetition of the behaviour (sharing). By contrast, the seat belt buzzer's sudden cessation as soon as the seat belt is fastened is negative reinforcement, as the removal of the irritating stimulus (the buzzer) leads to a greater likelihood of the target behaviour (buckling the seat belt).

We can use conditioning in research to ask babies questions about what they know. In a series of experiments by Carolyn Rovee-Collier and her associates (1999), infants were operantly conditioned to kick in order to activate a mobile attached to one ankle by a ribbon. Babies 2 to 6 months old, when shown the same mobile days or weeks later, repeated the kicking even though their ankle was no longer attached to the mobile.

behaviourist approach   Approach to the study of behavioural development that is concerned with the basic mechanics of learning.

classical conditioning   Learning based on associating a stimulus that does not ordinarily elicit a particular response with another stimulus that does elicit the response.

operant conditioning   Learning based on reinforcement and punishment.

Conditioning allowed researchers to ask the infants if they remembered the mobiles. The infants' responses showed that the mobiles triggered a memory of their initial experience with them and illustrated that babies have recognition memory.

Ask Yourself

1. Which of the following is an example of classical conditioning?
   a. Clara smiles more after her mother gives her attention for doing so.
   b. John is less likely to hit his brother after being punished by his parents for hitting.
   c. Maria does not like how cucumbers taste.
   d. Michael learns that the sound of the front door being opened means his mother is getting home from work.

2. In operant conditioning, a _____ results in a greater chance of a behaviour being performed, while a _____ results in a decrease in the chance a behaviour will be performed.

3. Describe one way in which operant conditioning has been used to demonstrate babies' memory abilities.

Psychometric Approach: Developmental and Intelligence Testing

The **psychometric approach** to child development measures quantitative differences in abilities that make up intelligences by using tests that indicate or predict these abilities. Although there is no clear scientific consensus on a definition of intelligence, most professionals agree that **intelligent behaviour** is goal-oriented and adaptive. Intelligence enables people to acquire, remember, and use knowledge, to understand concepts and relationships, and to solve everyday problems.

The most well-known approach to intelligence is the psychometric one. The goals of psychometric testing are to measure the factors that are thought to make up intelligence, such as comprehension and reasoning, and to then predict future performance, such as school achievement. **IQ (intelligence quotient) tests** consist of questions or tasks that are supposed to show how much of the measured abilities a person has, by comparing that person's performance with standardized norms. Using the psychometric approach, three areas of interest related to cognitive development during ages 0 to 3 are intelligence testing, assessing the impact of the home environment, and early intervention.

Babies 2 to 6 months old who learn that kicking activates a mobile remember this skill even if the mobile is removed for up to two weeks. When the mobile is returned, the baby starts kicking as soon as he sees it.

TESTING INFANTS AND TODDLERS

It is difficult to measure infants' intelligence. Babies cannot tell us what they know and how they think, so the most obvious way to gauge their intelligence is by assessing what they can do. But if they do not grasp a rattle, it is hard to tell whether they do not know how, do not feel like doing it, do not realize what is expected of them, or have simply lost interest. However, it is possible to test their developmental functioning. Developmental tests compare a baby's performance on tasks with established age-graded norms.

The **Bayley Scales of Infant and Toddler Development** (see Chapter 5) is a widely used developmental test designed to assess children from 1 month to 3½ years. Scores on the Bayley-III (Bayley, 2005) indicate a child's strengths and weaknesses in each of five developmental areas: cognitive, language, motor, social-emotional, and adaptive behaviour. Separate scores, called **developmental quotients (DQs)**, are calculated for each scale. DQs are most useful for early detection of emotional

psychometric approach Approach to the study of cognitive development that seeks to measure the quantity of intelligence a person possesses.

intelligent behaviour Behaviour that is goal-oriented and adaptive to circumstances and conditions of life.

IQ (intelligence quotient) tests Psychometric tests that seek to measure intelligence by comparing a test-taker's performance with standardized norms.

Bayley Scales of Infant and Toddler Development Standardized test of infants' and toddlers' mental and motor development.

developmental quotient (DQ) Standardized score calculated for each area measured by the Bayley Scales.

disturbances and sensory, neurological, and environmental deficits and in helping parents and professionals plan for a child's needs.

ASSESSING THE IMPACT OF THE HOME ENVIRONMENT

We know that intelligence is influenced by both inheritance and experience. Given this, what characteristics of the early home environment might influence intelligence and cognitive development?

Using the **Home Observation for Measurement of the Environment (HOME)** (Bradley, 1989), trained observers interview the primary caregiver and rate on a yes-or-no checklist the intellectual stimulation and support observed in a child's home. The version for infants and toddlers (Table 6.1) lasts about one hour. HOME scores are significantly correlated with measures of cognitive development (Totsika & Sylva, 2004).

Factors that have been identified as important include parental responsiveness, the number of books in the home, the presence of playthings that encourage the development of concepts, and parents' involvement in children's play. These factors have been consistently associated with kindergarten achievement scores, language competence, and motor and social development (Bradley, Corwyn, Burchinal, McAdoo, & Coll, 2001). Keep in mind that

HOME items are correlations and not necessarily causal. Therefore, all we can say is that these factors are associated with high intelligence and achievement. Intelligent, well-educated parents may be more likely to provide a positive, stimulating home environment.

EARLY INTERVENTION

Early intervention is a systematic process of planning and providing therapeutic and educational services for families

Home Observation for Measurement of the Environment (HOME) Instrument designed to measure the influence of the home environment on children's cognitive growth.

early intervention Systematic process of providing services to help families meet young children's developmental needs.

TABLE 6.1 The Infant-Toddler HOME Inventory (ages 0 to 3)

Name of Subscale	Description	Example Item
Emotional and verbal responsivity of the primary caregiver (items 1–11)	The communicative and affective interactions between the caregiver and the child	Mother spontaneously vocalizes to the child at least twice during visit. Mother caresses or kisses child at least once during visit.
Avoidance of restriction and punishment (items 12–19)	How the adult disciplines the child	Primary caregiver (PC) does not shout at child during visit. PC does not express overt annoyance with or hostility toward the child.
Organization of the physical and temporal environment (items 20–25)	How the child's time is organized outside the family house; what the child's personal space looks like	When PC is away, care is provided by one of three regular substitutes. The child's play environment appears safe and free of hazards.
Provision of appropriate play materials (items 26–34)	Presence of several types of toys available to the child and appropriate for his/her age	Child has one or more large-muscle activity toys or pieces of equipment. Provides equipment appropriate to age, such as infant seat, infant rocker, playpen.
Parental involvement with the child (items 35–40)	How the adult interacts physically with the child	PC tends to keep child within visual range and look at him/her often. PC talks to child while doing her work.
Opportunities for variety in daily stimulation (items 41–45)	The way the child's daily routine is designed to incorporate social meetings with people other than the mother	Father provides some caregiving every day. Family visits or child receives visits from relatives approximately once a month.

Source: Totsika & Sylva (2004).

that need help in meeting infants', toddlers', and preschool children's developmental needs.

In Ontario, the *Early Years Report*, which makes public policy recommendations about early years support for children, demonstrates how intervention in the first three years can influence developmental gains more than at any other time in the lifespan (McCain & Mustard, 1999). Building on this, the Ontario government has introduced early child and family centres (Ontario Early Years Centres) as a start in providing early support to young children (Ministry of Children and Youth Services, 2010; Pascal, 2009).

One common location for early support lies in early child education and care. In 2002–03, 54 percent of Canadian children were experiencing some form of non-parental child care (up from 42 percent in 1994–95), 28 percent of whom were in child care centres (Bushnick, 2006). This kind of care outside of the home can have beneficial effects in promoting the kinds of skills, like vocabulary, that children need to succeed in school (Dahinten & Wilms, 2002). By the time they arrive in Grade 1, they are more ready to learn, and they are more likely to complete high school than was the case in the past (Ministry of Children and Youth Services, 2005). Nevertheless, as illustrated in Figure 6.1, more public support is needed for programs devoted to learning, behaviour problems, and health for children in the early years to ensure healthy development when brain growth is most rapid.

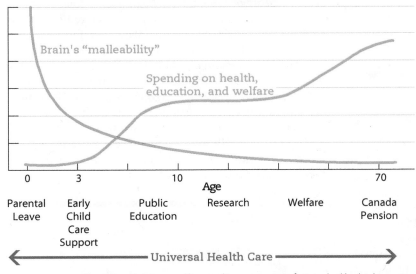

The Mismatch between Opportunity and Investment

FIGURE 6.1 The relationship between public expenditures on programs fostering healthy development throughout the life cycle and public expenditures aimed at the critical years of rapid brain development.

Source: Adapted from "The Mismatch Between Opportunity and Investment" from *How Nurture Becomes Nature: The Influence of Social Structures on Brain Development* by B. Perry, 2002. http://www.ChildTrauma.org.

In addition to child care, early intervention programs for children at high risk of not reaching their full potential have been found to be effective in supporting healthy development. One of the first home-based intervention programs in Canada was started in British Columbia in the 1970s and subsequently spread throughout Canada (Mitchell, Brynelsen, & Holm, 1988). More recently, the Community Action Plan for Children (CAPC) is a federal government initiative to provide diverse community-based early intervention programs in communities across the country. These programs are designed to support children living in low-income families; experiencing developmental delays and social, emotional, or behavioural problems; or living with teenage parents; or who have been victims of abuse and neglect. Of particular concern are Aboriginal children, children who are recent immigrants or refugees, those with a lone parent, and those who live in remote communities. Recent evaluations show that CAPC programs can have positive outcomes for children's healthy growth in motor skills, social competence, language and cognitive development, and school readiness (Public Health Agency of Canada, 2010b). Similar efforts in the U.S., such as Project CARE and the Abecedarian Program, have been successful in promoting healthy early development in children as well.

The strongest support for the effectiveness of early intervention programs is from data from Project CARE (Wasik, Ramey, Bryant, & Sparling, 1990) and the Abecedarian (ABC) Project (Campbell, Ramey, Pungello, Sparling, & Miller-Johnson, 2002; Ramey & Campbell, 1991). In each project, from age 6 weeks through age 5, an experimental group was enrolled in Partners for Learning, a full-day, year-round early childhood education program at a university child development centre.

Control groups received pediatric and social work services, formula, and home visits, as the experimental groups did, but were not enrolled in Partners for Learning (Ramey & Ramey, 2003).

In both projects, the children who received the early intervention showed a widening advantage over the control groups in developmental test scores between 12 and 18 months. By age 3, the average IQ of the Abecedarian experimental group was 101 and that of the CARE experimental group 105, as compared with only 84 and 93 for the control groups (Ramey & Ramey, 1998).

These findings show that early educational intervention can help offset environmental risks and provide significant benefits. The most effective early interventions are those that (1) start early and continue throughout the preschool years; (2) are time-intensive; (3) are centre-based, not just parental training; (4) take a comprehensive approach; and (5) are tailored to individual needs. As occurred in Project CARE and the ABC Project, initial gains tend to diminish without sufficient ongoing environmental support (Brooks-Gunn, 2003).

Ask Yourself

4. What are the five developmental areas assessed by the Bayley Scales of Infant and Toddler Development?

5. List four factors in the home that have been identified as being important for intelligence.

6. What is the best way to characterize the findings of studies on intervention programs?
   a. Intervention programs result in few, if any, gains in intelligence.
   b. Intervention programs show no immediate effects, although they often show later benefits.
   c. Intervention programs show strong initial gains that fade without ongoing environmental support.
   d. Intervention programs result in strong and long-lasting gains in intelligence.

Piagetian Approach: The Sensorimotor Stage

The **Piagetian approach** to cognitive development looks at changes, or stages, in the quality of cognitive functioning. It is concerned with how the mind structures its activities and adapts to the environment. The first of Piaget's four stages of cognitive development is the sensorimotor stage. During this stage, from birth to approximately age 2, infants learn about themselves and their world through their developing sensory and motor activity as they change from creatures who respond primarily through reflexes and random behaviour into goal-oriented toddlers.

Early educational intervention can help offset environmental risks and provide significant benefits to young children.

SENSORIMOTOR SUBSTAGES

The **sensorimotor stage** consists of six substages (Table 6.2). During the first five substages, babies learn to coordinate input from their senses and organize their activities in relation to their environment. During the sixth substage, they progress from trial-and-error learning to the use of symbols and concepts to solve problems.

Much of this early cognitive growth comes about through **circular reactions**, in which an infant learns to reproduce pleasurable or interesting events originally discovered by chance. The original chance behaviour eventually becomes consolidated into a new scheme.

In the *first substage* (birth to about 1 month), neonates practise reflex behaviours. For example, they might practise sucking even when they are not eating. In the *second substage* (about 1 to 4 months), babies learn to repeat a pleasant bodily sensation first achieved by chance (say, sucking their thumbs, as shown in Figure 6.2a). Piaget called this a *primary circular reaction*.

The *third substage* (about 4 to 8 months) coincides with a new interest in manipulating objects and learning about their properties. Babies engage in *secondary circular reactions*: pleasurable intentional actions that have results beyond the infant's own body. For example, a baby this age will repeatedly shake a rattle to hear its noise or (as shown in Figure 6.2b) coo when a friendly face appears, so that it stays longer.

Piagetian approach   Approach to the study of cognitive development that describes qualitative stages in cognitive functioning.

sensorimotor stage   In Piaget's theory, first stage in cognitive development, during which infants learn through senses and motor activity.

circular reactions   Piaget's term for processes by which an infant learns to reproduce desired occurrences originally discovered by chance.

TABLE 6.2 Six Substages of Piaget's Sensorimotor Stage of Cognitive Development*

Substages	Ages	Description	Behaviour
1. Use of reflexes	Birth to 1 month	Infants exercise their inborn reflexes and gain some control over them. They do not coordinate information from their senses. They do not grasp an object they are looking at.	Dorri begins sucking when her mother's breast is in her mouth.
2. Primary circular reactions	1 to 4 months	Infants repeat pleasurable behaviours that first occur by chance (such as thumb sucking). Activities focus on the infant's body rather than the effects of the behaviour on the environment. Infants make first acquired adaptations; that is, they suck different objects differently. They begin to coordinate sensory information and grasp objects.	When given a bottle, Dylan, who is usually breast-fed, is able to adjust his sucking to the rubber nipple.
3. Secondary circular reactions	4 to 8 months	Infants become more interested in the environment; they repeat actions that bring interesting results (such as shaking a rattle) and prolong interesting experiences. Actions are intentional but not initially goal directed.	Alejandro pushes pieces of dry cereal over the edge of his highchair tray one at a time and watches each piece as it falls to the floor.
4. Coordination of secondary schemes	8 to 12 months	Behaviour is more deliberate and purposeful (intentional) as infants coordinate previously learned schemes (organized patterns of behaviour, such as looking at and grasping a rattle) and use previously learned behaviours to attain their goals (such as crawling across the room to get a desired toy). They can anticipate events.	Anica pushes the button on her musical nursery rhyme book, and "Twinkle, Twinkle, Little Star" plays. She pushes this button over and over again, choosing it instead of the buttons for the other songs.
5. Tertiary circular reactions	12 to 18 months	Toddlers show curiosity and experimentation; they purposefully vary their actions to see results (for example, by shaking different rattles to hear their sounds). They actively explore their world to determine what is novel about an object, an event, or a situation. They try out new activities and use trial and error in solving problems.	When Bjorn's big sister holds his favourite board book up to his crib bars, he reaches for it. His first efforts to bring the book into his crib fail because the book is too wide. Soon, Bjorn turns the book sideways and hugs it, delighted with his success.
6. Mental combinations	18 to 24 months	Because toddlers can mentally represent events, they are no longer confined to trial and error to solve problems. Symbolic thought enables toddlers to begin to think about events and anticipate their consequences without always resorting to action. Toddlers begin to demonstrate insight. They can use symbols, such as gestures and words, and can pretend.	Jenny plays with her shape box, searching carefully for the right hole for each shape before trying—and succeeding.

*Infants show enormous cognitive growth during Piaget's sensorimotor stage, as they learn about the world through their senses and their motor activities. Note their progress in problem solving and the coordination of sensory information. All ages are approximate.

By the time infants reach the *fourth substage—coordination of secondary schemes* (about 8 to 12 months)—they have built on the few schemes they were born with. They have learned to generalize from past experience to solve new problems. They will crawl to get something they want, grab it, or push away a barrier to it. They try out, modify, and coordinate previous schemes to find one that works. This substage marks the development of complex, goal-directed behaviour.

In the *fifth substage* (about 12 to 18 months), babies begin to experiment with new behaviour to see what will happen. They now engage in *tertiary circular reactions*, varying an action to test out the result. For example, a toddler may squeeze a rubber duck that squeaked when stepped on, to see whether it will squeak again (as shown in Figure 6.2c). By trial and error, they try out behaviours until they find the best way to attain a goal.

The *sixth substage—mental combinations* (about 18 months to 2 years)—is a transition into the preoperational stage of early childhood. **Representational ability**—the ability to mentally represent objects and actions in memory, largely through symbols such as words, numbers, and mental pictures—frees toddlers from immediate experience. They can pretend, and their representational ability affects the sophistication of their pretending (Bornstein, Haynes, O'Reilly, & Painter, 1996). They can think about

representational ability Piaget's term for capacity to store mental images or symbols of objects and events.

FIGURE 6.2

Primary, Secondary, and Tertiary Circular Reactions

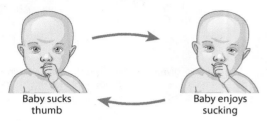

Baby sucks thumb — Baby enjoys sucking

(a) Primary circular reaction: Action and response both involve infant's own body (1 to 4 months).

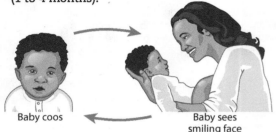

Baby coos — Baby sees smiling face

(b) Secondary circular reaction: Action gets a response from another person or object, leading to baby's repeating original action (4 to 8 months).

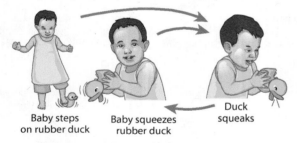

Baby steps on rubber duck — Baby squeezes rubber duck — Duck squeaks

(c) Tertiary circular reaction: Action gets one pleasing result, leading baby to perform similar actions to get similar results (12 to 18 months).

Source: From "Object permanence in young infants: Further evidence," by R. Baillargeon and J. DeVos in *Child Development*, Vol. 62, 1991, pp. 1227–1246. Copyright © 1991 by the Society for Research in Child Development, Inc. Reprinted with permission.

actions before taking them. They no longer have to go through laborious trial and error to solve problems.

OBJECT CONCEPT

Piaget, in his close observations of children, noted that infants under the age of about 8 months act as if an object no longer exists once it is out of their line of sight. This led to his theorizing about the *object concept*—the understanding that objects have independent existence, characteristics, and locations in space.

object permanence   Piaget's term for the understanding that a person or an object still exists when out of sight.

One aspect of the object concept is **object permanence**, the realization that something continues to exist when out of sight. At first, infants appear to have no such concept. If you hide an interesting toy, babies will not show any sign that they understand it still exists. However, by the age of 18 to 24 months, almost all babies understand that objects have independent existences and will reliably search for hidden objects. According to Piaget, object permanence develops gradually during the sensorimotor stage as children develop the ability to symbolically represent objects.

There are a number of other explanations for the development of the object concept. For example, some research suggests that babies may fail to search for hidden objects because they cannot yet carry out complex sequences of actions, such as lifting the cover of a box before grasping the object. This explanation suggests that infants know it is there, but they cannot coordinate a motor response to demonstrate their knowledge (Bojczyk & Corbetta, 2004).

EVALUATING PIAGET'S SENSORIMOTOR STAGE

According to Piaget, the journey from reflex behaviour to the beginnings of thought is a long, slow one, and it is not until the last half of the second year that children make the breakthrough to conceptual thought. More recent research using simplified tasks and modern tools suggests that certain limitations Piaget saw in infants' early cognitive abilities, such as object permanence, may instead have reflected immature linguistic and motor skills. The answers that Piaget received were as much a function of the ways in which he asked the questions as they were a reflection of the actual abilities of young children.

In terms of describing what children do under certain circumstances and the basic progression of skills, Piaget was correct. However, in some ways infants and toddlers are more cognitively competent than Piaget imagined. It is true, as Piaget observed, that immature forms of cognition precede more mature forms. However, he may have been

WHERE DO YOU STAND?

On the basis of observations by Piaget and the research they inspired, what factors would you consider in designing or purchasing a toy or book for an infant or a toddler? How accurate are the age recommendations for toys for toddlers?

mistaken in his emphasis on motor experience as the primary engine of cognitive growth. Infants' perceptions are far ahead of their motor abilities, and today's methods enable researchers to make observations and inferences about those perceptions. The relationship between perception and cognition is a major area of investigation, and we discuss it in the next section.

Ask Yourself

7. Baby Gus kicks his legs over and over again and seems to enjoy repeating the action. Piaget would say this is an example of
   a. a primary circular reaction.
   b. a secondary circular reaction.
   c. a tertiary circular reaction.
   d. object permanence.

8. Infants under the age of 6 months do not generally cry in response to separation from their mothers; however, by 1 year of age, they strongly protest maternal separation and are not easily calmed by strangers. How might this be related to object permanence?

9. In general, many abilities Piaget researched develop earlier than he thought they did. Why did he underestimate infants' abilities?
   a. He did not use brain imaging techniques.
   b. He relied on immature linguistic and motor skills to assess cognitive development.
   c. He did not use careful research methodology and design.
   d. He did not conduct longitudinal work.

Information-Processing Approach: Perceptions and Representations

The **information-processing approach** focuses on perception, learning, memory, and problem solving. It aims to discover how children process information from the time they encounter it until they use it. Information-processing researchers analyze the separate parts of a complex task to figure out what abilities are necessary for each part of the task and at what age these abilities develop, often by using children's attentional processes to infer what they know. Key aspects of information processing related to the 0–3 age range include habituation, visual processing abilities, information processing as a predictor of intelligence, and information processing in the development of Piagetian abilities.

HABITUATION

At about 6 weeks, Stefan lies peacefully in his crib near a window, sucking a pacifier. It is a cloudy day, but suddenly

information-processing approach Approach to the study of cognitive development by observing and analyzing processes involved in perceiving and handling information.

habituation Type of learning in which familiarity with a stimulus reduces, slows, or stops a response.

dishabituation Increase in responsiveness after presentation of a new stimulus.

the sun breaks through and an angular shaft of light appears on the end of the crib. Stefan stops sucking for a few moments, staring intently at the pattern of light and shade. Then he looks away and starts sucking again. The analysis of this simple behaviour underlies a vast body of research in infant development.

Much information-processing research with infants is based on **habituation**, in which repeated exposure to a stimulus, such as the shaft of light, reduces attention to that stimulus. In other words, familiarity breeds boredom. Researchers study habituation in newborns by repeatedly presenting a stimulus, usually a sound or visual pattern, and then monitoring such responses as heart rate, sucking, eye movements, and brain activity. A baby who has been sucking typically stops or sucks less vigorously when the stimulus is first presented and pays attention to the new stimulus—somewhat like how an adult might stop talking for an instant when he or she notices something interesting going on. However, after a while, the stimulus loses its novelty and no longer causes the baby to suck less. Resumption of vigorous sucking shows that the infant has habituated to the stimulus. A new sight or sound, however, will capture the baby's attention and the baby will again stop or reduce sucking. This response to a new stimulus is called **dishabituation**.

Researchers gauge the efficiency of infants' information processing by measuring how quickly babies habituate, how quickly they reorient to new stimuli, and how much time they spend looking at the new and the old. Liking to look at new things and quickly habituating to them correlates with later signs of cognitive development. In fact, as we will see, speed of habituation and other information-processing abilities show promise as predictors of intelligence (Fagan, Holland, & Wheeler, 2007).

Did you know?

Habituation is a general property of our nervous systems. Have you ever worn an uncomfortable shoe? You may have noticed that your feet hurt more when you stand after sitting for a while than they do while walking around. That's because when you walk around, you habituate to the pain. When you sit down and then stand again, you feel the pain in its full intensity anew because you have become dishabituated.

VISUAL PROCESSING ABILITIES

Researchers assume that the more time a baby spends looking at something, the more that baby must like it—an assumption that has been used to develop the **visual preference** paradigm. Researchers merely present two stimuli and look to see which one babies look at more. In this way, they have determined that babies less than 2 days old prefer curved lines to straight lines, complex patterns to simple patterns, three-dimensional objects to two-dimensional objects, and moving objects to stationary objects. Newborns also prefer pictures of faces or face-like configurations to pictures of other things. Last, infants tend to prefer new sights to familiar ones (Rakison, 2005; Turati, Simion, Milani, & Umilta, 2002), a tendency known as *novelty preference.*

We can examine **visual recognition memory** using a similar method. Babies like to look at new things. If we show a baby two stimuli side by side and the baby looks longer at a novel stimuli than a familiar one, then we can assume the baby recognized the familiar stimulus. In other words, because the novel stimulus is new, it is more interesting and thus warrants a better look.

Contrary to Piaget's view, these studies suggest that babies are able to represent objects in memory, even before achieving object permanence. Additionally, there are individual differences in efficiency of information processing. When shown two sights at the same time, infants who quickly shift attention from one to another tend to have better recognition memory and stronger novelty preference than infants who take longer looks at each sight (Jankowski, Rose, & Feldman, 2001). Speed of processing is also developmental—it increases rapidly during the first three years of life (Rose, Jankowski, & Feldman, 2002; Zelazo, Kearsley, & Stack, 1995).

Vision is particularly important in the development of joint attention, a fundamental capacity. **Joint attention**, also known as shared attention, involves understanding that you and I are both looking at the same thing. It is key to understanding social interactions, language acquisition, and the understanding of others' intentions and mental states. Joint attention develops between 10 and 12 months, when babies follow an adults' gaze by looking in the same direction. Moreover, babies who engage in early joint attention activities, and who spontaneously point at objects as well, have better vocabularies at 18 months and two years (Brooks & Meltzoff, 2005, 2008). Responding effectively to joint attention situations in infancy can be an indicator of healthy self-regulation abilities (like being able to delay gratification when asked to wait for a snack), social competence, and executive functions—reflecting emerging social and cognitive abilities—in children (Vaughan Van Hecke et al., 2012).

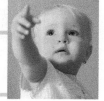

Did you know?

Pointing helps regulate joint attention and does not need to be taught.

Did you know?

Of all primates, humans have the largest amount of sclera—the white part of the eye. Theorists have speculated this is so that we can more easily engage in joint attention activities. The large sclera allows us to more easily see where others around us are looking.

INFORMATION PROCESSING AS A PREDICTOR OF INTELLIGENCE

There is a weak correlation between infants' scores on developmental tasks such as the Bayley Scales and their later IQ, with the exception of scores for habituation, attention-recovery, and visual-recognition memory abilities. In many longitudinal studies, scores during the first six months to one year of life were moderately useful in predicting childhood IQ (Colombo, 1993; McCall & Carriger, 1993). Why is this the case? These measurements are thought to indicate attentiveness and processing speed, as well as the tendency to form expectations on the basis of experience. Thus, it seems likely that children who from the start are efficient at taking in and interpreting sensory information later score well on intelligence tests. However, other items—for example, motor skills—do not seem to relate well to later IQ.

INFORMATION PROCESSING AND THE DEVELOPMENT OF PIAGETIAN ABILITIES

As we discussed earlier in this chapter, evidence suggests that several of the cognitive abilities Piaget identified as developing toward the end of the sensorimotor stage seem to arise much earlier. Research based on infants' visual processing has given developmental scientists a window into the timing of such cognitive developments as categorization, causality, object permanence, and number, all of which depend on formation of mental representations.

Categorization

Dividing the world into meaningful categories is vital to thinking about objects or concepts and their relationships. It is the foundation of language, reasoning, problem solving, and memory; without it, the world would seem chaotic and meaningless (Rakison, 2005).

According to Piaget, the ability to classify, or group things into categories, does not appear until the sixth sensorimotor substage, around 18 months. Yet by looking longer at items in a new category, even 3-month-olds seem to know, for example,

visual preference Tendency of infants to spend more time looking at one sight than another.

visual recognition memory Ability to distinguish a familiar visual stimulus from an unfamiliar stimulus when shown both at the same time.

joint attention Involves understanding that you and I have a shared focus of attention.

violation-of-expectations   Research method in which dishabituation to a stimulus that conflicts with experience is taken as evidence
that an infant recognizes the new stimulus as surprising.

Infants can categorize objects on the basis of perceptual features, such as shape, colour,
and pattern.

that a dog is not a cat (French, Mareschal, Mermillod, &
Quinn, 2004; Quinn, Eimas, & Rosenkrantz, 1993).

Infants at first seem to categorize on the basis of perceptual features, such as shape, colour, and pattern, but by 12
to 14 months, their categories become conceptual, based on
real-world knowledge, particularly of function
(Mandler, 2007). As time goes on, broad concepts become more specific. For example, while
7-month-olds can categorize vehicles and furniture, 2-year-olds recognize particular categories,
such as "car" and "airplane," within the overall
category of "vehicles" (Mandler, 2007).

Causality

Causality involves understanding that one event
causes another. Piaget maintained that this understanding develops slowly during the first year of
life. At about 4 to 6 months, as infants become
able to grasp objects, they begin to recognize
that they can act on their environment. However,
according to Piaget, infants do not yet know that
causes must come before effects; and not until
close to 1 year do they realize that forces outside
of themselves can make things happen.

Current research suggests that an understanding of causality does not emerge until at
least the second half of the first year (Saxe &
Carey, 2006). Infants 6½ months old have shown
by habituation and dishabituation that they
seem to see a difference between events that are
the immediate cause of other events (such as a
brick striking a second brick and pushing it) and

events that occur with no apparent cause (such as a brick
moving away from another brick without having been struck
by it) (Leslie, 1984, 1995). Researchers have attributed the
growth of causal understanding to a gradual improvement in
information-processing skills. As infants accumulate more
information about how objects behave, they are better able
to understand (Cohen, Chaput, & Cashon, 2002; Cohen,
Rundell, Spellman, & Cashon, 1999).

Object Permanence

Violation-of-expectations research begins with a famil-
iarization phase, in which infants see an event or a series
of events happen normally. After the infant is habituated to
this procedure, the event is changed in a way that violates
(conflicts with) normal expectations. An infant's tendency
to look longer at the changed event is interpreted as evidence that the infant recognizes it as surprising.

Using the violation-of-expectations method, Renée
Baillargeon (Baillargeon & DeVos, 1991; Hespos &
Baillargeon, 2008) found evidence of object permanence in
infants as young as 3½ months. The babies watched as a tall
carrot moved behind a screen of the same height but failed to
appear in a large notch in the upper part of the screen before
reappearing again on the other side. The infants showed surprise by looking longer at this "impossible event" than at a "possible event" involving a short carrot, as shown in Figure 6.3.

Violation-of-Expectations Research

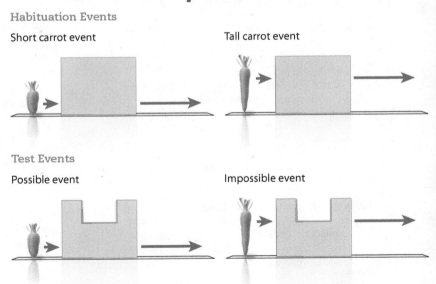

FIGURE 6.3   How early do infants show object permanence? In this violation-of-expectations experiment,
3½-month-olds watched a short carrot and then a tall carrot slide along a track, disappear behind a screen, and
then reappear. After they became accustomed to seeing these events, the opaque screen was replaced by a screen
with a large notch at the top. The short carrot did not appear in the notch when passing behind the screen; the
tall carrot, which should have appeared in the notch, also did not. The babies looked longer at the tall, than at the
short, carrot event, suggesting that they were surprised that the tall carrot did not reappear in the notch.
Source: Baillargeon & DeVos (1991).

Because they remembered the carrot existed (they could not have been surprised otherwise), this illustrates object permanence.

These findings are controversial. The fact that an infant looks longer at one scene than at another may show only that the infant can see a difference between the two, and the longer look at an unexpected event may simply reflect temporary uncertainty about it. It's also possible that an infant, in becoming accustomed to the habituation event, develops the expectations that are then violated by the surprising event and did not have such knowledge or expectations before (Kagan, 2008; Munakata, 2001). However, defenders of violation-of-expectations research insist that a conceptual interpretation is still the best account for the findings (Baillargeon, 1999; Hespos & Baillargeon, 2008; Spelke, 1998).

Ask Yourself

10. Habituation is most like which of the following states?
    a. interest
    b. fear
    c. affection
    d. boredom

11. If a baby looks longer at a picture of a face than a square, what do researchers take this as evidence of?
    a. Babies don't like squares.
    b. Babies cannot tell the difference between faces and squares.
    c. Babies like faces better than squares.
    d. Babies like squares better than faces.

12. Speed of habituation seems to be related to later intelligence. Why might this be?
    a. Easily bored babies are always eager to learn new things.
    b. Rapid habituation indicates a child who can quickly process information.
    c. Speed of habituation is related to learning words more quickly, and verbal abilities are then related to intelligence.
    d. This is untrue; rapid habituation actually indicates rushed and shallow processing, which then leads to less learning over time.

13. In general, research conducted using babies' visual responses to stimuli suggests that they develop an understanding of concepts such as categorization, causality, object permanence, and a primitive understanding of number _____ than Piaget thought they did.
    a. earlier
    b. later
    c. at about the same time
    d. The research has not show a consistent pattern across different areas of knowledge.

Number

Some violation-of-expectations research suggests that an understanding of number may begin long before Piaget's sixth substage, when he claimed children first begin to use symbols. Karen Wynn (1992) tested whether 5-month-old babies can add and subtract small numbers of objects. The infants watched as Mickey Mouse dolls were placed behind a screen, and a doll was either added or taken away. The screen then was lifted to reveal either the expected number or a different number of dolls. Babies looked longer at surprising "wrong" answers than at expected "right" ones, suggesting that they had mentally computed the right answers. A follow-up to this study found that in addition to looking longer at incorrect solutions, infants aged 6 to 9 months also had brain activity that supported violation-of-expectations (Berger, Tzur, & Posner, 2006)

Cognitive Neuroscience Approach: The Brain's Cognitive Structures

The **cognitive neuroscience approach** examines the hardware of the central nervous system. It seeks to identify what brain structures are involved in specific areas of cognition. Brain research bears out Piaget's assumption that neurological maturation is a major factor in cognitive development. Brain growth spurts coincide with changes in cognitive behaviour similar to those Piaget described (Fischer, 2008; Fischer & Rose, 1995).

Some researchers have used brain scans to determine which brain structures affect which cognitive functions and to chart developmental changes. Brain scans provide physical evidence of the location of two separate long-term memory systems—implicit and explicit (Vargha-Khadem et al., 1997). **Implicit memory**, also called *procedural memory*, which develops early in infancy, refers to remembering that occurs without effort or even conscious awareness; it pertains to habits and skills, such as knowing how to throw a ball. **Explicit memory**, also called *declarative memory*, is conscious or intentional recollection, usually of facts, names, events, or other things that can be stated or declared.

In early infancy, when the structures responsible for memory storage are not fully formed, memories are relatively fleeting. This infantile amnesia is tied to brain development. The maturing of the *hippocampus*, a structure

cognitive neuroscience approach Approach to the study of cognitive development that links brain processes with cognitive ones.

implicit memory Unconscious recall, generally of habits and skills; sometimes called *procedural memory*.

explicit memory Intentional and conscious memory, generally of facts, names, and events; sometimes called *declarative memory*.

deep in the temporal lobes, along with the development of cortical structures coordinated by the hippocampal formation, make longer-lasting memories possible (Bauer, 2002).

The *prefrontal cortex* is believed to control many aspects of cognition. This part of the brain develops more slowly than most others (Diamond, 2000, 2002; M. H. Johnson, 1998). During the second half of the first year, the prefrontal cortex and associated circuitry develop the capacity for *working memory*—short-term storage of information the brain is actively processing, or working on. It is in working memory that mental representations are prepared for, or recalled from, storage.

Although memory systems continue to develop beyond infancy, the early emergence of the brain's memory structures underlines the importance of environmental stimulation from the first months of life. Social-contextual theorists and researchers pay particular attention to the impact of environmental influences.

Guided participation, like this boy helping his father stir batter in the kitchen, can help children learn the skills, knowledge, and values important in their culture.

Ask Yourself

14. Knowing how to tie a shoelace is an example of _____ memory, while knowing what the word "dog" means is an example of _____ memory.

15. The key role of the hippocampus is to _____, while the major function of the prefrontal cortex includes _____.

Social-Contextual Approach: Learning from Caregivers

The **social-contextual approach** examines the effects of environmental aspects on the learning process. Researchers influenced by Vygotsky's socio-cultural theory study how the cultural context affects early social interactions that may promote cognitive competence, sometimes through the process of guided participation. **Guided participation** refers to interactions with adults that help structure children's activities and bridge the gap between a child's understanding and an adult's. It often occurs in shared play and in ordinary, everyday activities in which children learn informally the skills, knowledge, and values important in their culture much as an apprentice would.

In one cross-cultural study (Göncü, Mistry, & Mosier, 2000; Rogoff, Mistry, Göncü, & Mosier, 1993), researchers visited the homes of fourteen 1- to 2-year-olds in each of four different cultures. The investigators

interviewed caregivers about their child-rearing practices and watched them help the toddlers learn to dress themselves and play with unfamiliar toys. Cultural differences affected the types of guided participation the researchers observed. In a Guatemalan town and an Indian village, the children customarily played alone or with older siblings while the mother worked nearby. After initial demonstration and instruction, mostly nonverbal, in, for example, how to tie shoes, the children took over, while the caregiver remained available to help. In the U.S., toddlers, who had full-time caregivers, interacted with adults in the context of play rather than work or social worlds. Caregivers motivated children's learning with praise and excitement. Turkish families, who were in transition from a rural to an urban way of life, showed a pattern somewhere between.

The cultural context, then, influences the way caregivers contribute to cognitive development. However, despite the different means by which caregivers teach their children valuable life skills, all children learn the things they need to learn to be effective members of society. Through the combined influences of experience and growth in behavioural, cognitive, and neural capacities, children become equipped to make huge strides in their skills during the first three years. We focus on one of these in the next section: language.

social-contextual approach Approach to the study of cognitive development that focuses on environmental influences, particularly parents and other caregivers.

guided participation Participation of an adult in a child's activity in a manner that helps to structure the activity and to bring the child's understanding of it closer to that of the adult.

16. Which is the best way to characterize what social contextual theorists believe?

a. The best way for children to learn is in formal educational settings.

b. While different cultures use different techniques, all children learn the things they need to learn to be effective members of their culture.

c. The most important contextual variable is the extended family system.

d. Despite cultural differences, most human traits can be characterized as universals that do not vary across cultures.

17. From the social-contextual perspective, why is guided participation important to child development?

How do we acquire language?

Language Development

When Ava was a small baby, far before she ever spoke her first word, she was already communicating a great deal to her parents. Through smiles, crying, laughing, facial expressions, and sounds of pleasure and pain, she let her parents know exactly how she was feeling. However, when she said her first word—"ba"—uttered in response to the birds outside her window, she had crossed a threshold of profound importance. Language is a communication system based on words and grammar, and is inextricably intertwined with cognition. A certain level of cognitive development is necessary for language, and once language develops, it promotes cognitive development. Once children know words, they can use them to represent objects and actions. They can reflect on people, places, and things, and they can communicate their needs, feelings, and ideas in order to exert control over their lives.

Is linguistic ability learned or inborn? In the 1950s, a debate raged between two schools of thought: one led by B. F. Skinner, the foremost proponent of learning theory, and the other by the linguist Noam Chomsky.

Skinner (1957) maintained that language learning, like all learning, is based on experience. There is nothing innate about language per se; rather, language is learned in the same way that all things are learned—through environmental influences. According to learning theory, children learn language through operant conditioning. At first, babies utter sounds at random. By chance, some of these sounds may approximate speech (e.g., "da"), and parents generally reinforce these vocalizations with smiles, attention, and praise. Gradually, by selectively reinforcing closer and closer approximations to adult speech (e.g., "dada"), parents shape the emerging language abilities of children. Additionally, as children develop, they begin to imitate words as well, which their parents also reinforce. Over time, these processes result in the emergence of speech. Although the child can participate actively via imitation, this is predominantly a passive view of language development.

Chomsky's view is called **nativism**. Nativism emphasizes the active role of the learner. Chomsky (1957, 1972, 1995) proposed that the human brain has an innate capacity for acquiring language; babies learn to talk as naturally as they learn to walk. It is part of our species heritage. He suggested that an inborn **language acquisition device (LAD)** programs children's brains to analyze the language they hear and to figure out its rules. Nativists point out that almost all children master their native language in the same age-related sequence without formal teaching, that our brains appear to be specialized for language (Gannon, Holloway, Broadfield, & Braun, 1998), that newborns appear to have "perceptual mechanisms that are tuned to the properties of speech" (Eimas, 1985, p. 49) as well as to the existence of sensitive periods in support of their position.

Most developmental scientists today believe that language acquisition, like most other aspects of development, depends on an intertwining of nature and nurture. Children probably have an inborn capacity to acquire language, which may be activated or constrained by experience.

Now let's look first at the typical sequence of language development (Table 6.3). Next we will note some special characteristics of early speech and then examine competing explanations of how infants acquire language.

---

nativism Theory that human beings have an inborn capacity for language acquisition.

language acquisition device (LAD) In Chomsky's terminology, an inborn mechanism that enables children to infer linguistic rules from the language they hear.

SEQUENCE OF EARLY LANGUAGE DEVELOPMENT

Before babies can use words, they make their needs and feelings known through sounds that progress from crying to cooing and babbling, then to accidental imitation, and finally to deliberate imitation. These sounds are known as **prelinguistic speech**. These achievements go hand in hand with calibration of babies' perceptual system with their native language. Babies are then ready to begin to engage in language, an ability that is expressed via both their use of gestures and their first words and sentences.

Early Vocalization

Crying is a newborn's first means of communication and has great adaptive value. Different pitches, patterns, and intensities signal hunger, sleepiness, or anger (Lester & Boukydis, 1985). Adults find crying aversive for a reason—it motivates them to find the source of the problem and fix it.

Between 6 weeks and 3 months, babies start cooing when they are happy—squealing, gurgling, and making vowel sounds like "ahhh." At about 3 to 6 months, babies begin to play with speech sounds, matching the sounds they hear from people around them.

Babbling—repeating consonant-vowel strings, such as "ma-ma-ma-ma"—occurs between ages 6 and 10 months. Babbling is not real language because it does not hold meaning for the baby, but it becomes more word-like over time.

Imitation is a key to early language development. At about 9 to 10 months, infants deliberately imitate sounds without understanding them. Once they have a repertoire of sounds, they string them together in patterns that sound like language but seem to have no meaning. Once infants become familiar with the sounds of words and phrases, they begin to attach meanings to them (Fernald, Perfors, & Marchman, 2006).

Did you know?

Infants have distinct cries for hunger and pain, and the higher the need for assistance, the higher the frequency of the cry (Dessureau, Kurowski, & Thompson, 1998).

TABLE 6.3 Language Milestones from Birth to 3 Years

Age in Months	Development
Birth	Can perceive speech, cry, make some response to sound.
1½ to 3	Coos and laughs.
3	Plays with speech sounds.
5 to 6	Recognizes frequently heard sound patterns.
6 to 7	Recognizes all phonemes of native language.
6 to 10	Babbles in strings of consonants and vowels.
9	Uses gestures to communicate and plays gesture games.
9 to 10	Intentionally imitates sounds.
9 to 12	Uses a few social gestures.
10 to 12	No longer can discriminate sounds not in own language.
10 to 14	Says first word (usually a label for something).
10 to 18	Says single words.
12 to 13	Understands symbolic function of naming; passive vocabulary grows.
13	Uses more elaborate gestures.
14	Uses symbolic gesturing.
16 to 24	Learns many new words, expanding expressive vocabulary rapidly, going from about 50 words to as many as 400; uses verbs and adjectives.
18 to 24	Says first sentence (2 words).
20	Uses fewer gestures; names more things.
20 to 22	Has comprehension spurt.
24	Uses many two-word phrases; no longer babbles; wants to talk.
30	Learns new words almost every day; speaks in combinations of three or more words; understands very well; makes grammatical mistakes.
36	Says up to 1,000 words, 80 percent intelligible; makes some mistakes in syntax.

Sources: Bates, O'Connell, & Shore (1987); Capute, Shapiro, & Palmer (1987); Kuhl (2004); Lalonde & Werker (1995); Lenneberg (1969); Newman (2005).

Perceiving Language Sounds and Structure

Imitation of language sounds requires the ability to perceive subtle differences between sounds. Infants' brains seem to be preset to discriminate basic linguistic units, perceive linguistic patterns, and categorize them as similar or different (Kuhl, 2004).

Every language has its own system of sounds, or *phonemes*, that are used in the production of speech. At first, infants can discriminate the sounds of any language. However, starting as early as 6 months for vowels and by 10 months for consonants, babies lose their sensitivity to sounds that are not part of the language or languages they usually hear spoken. This may be in

prelinguistic speech Forerunner of linguistic speech; utterance of sounds that are not words, including crying, cooing, babbling, and accidental and deliberate imitation of sounds without understanding their meaning.

the service of rapid language learning. Early experience modifies the neural structure of the brain, facilitating the detection of word patterns in the native language while suppressing attention to non-native patterns that would slow native language learning. In one study, toddlers who, at 7½ months, had shown better neural discrimination of native phonemes were more advanced in word production and sentence complexity at 24 months and at 30 months than toddlers who, at 7½ months, had been better able to discriminate phonetic contrasts in other non-native languages (Kuhl & Rivera-Gaxiola, 2008).

Between 6 and 12 months, babies also begin to become aware of the phonological rules of their language—how sounds are arranged in speech. In one series of experiments, 7-month-olds listened longer to "sentences" containing sound combinations not typically found in their native language than to those that had more typical sound combinations. This finding suggests that infants may have a mechanism for discerning abstract rules of sentence structure (Marcus, Vijayan, Rao, & Vishton, 1999; Saffran, Pollak, Seibel, & Shkolnik, 2007).

Long before infants can connect sounds to meanings, they learn to recognize sound patterns they hear frequently, such as their name. Infants 5 months old listen longer to their name than to other names (Newman, 2005). Six-month-olds look longer at a video of their mothers when they hear the word "mommy" and of their fathers when they hear "daddy" (Tincoff & Jusczyk, 1999), and they look longer at videos of adult hands and feet when they hear the words "hand" and "feet" (Tincoff & Jusczyk, 2011).

Gestures

Before babies can speak, they point (Liszkowski, Carpenter, & Tomasello, 2008). At 11 months, Maika pointed to

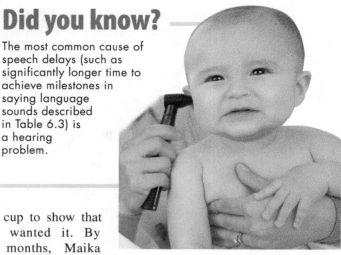

her cup to show that she wanted it. By 12 months, Maika learned some conventional social gestures: waving bye-bye and nodding her head to mean yes. By about 13 months, she used more elaborate representational gestures; for example, she would hold an empty cup to her mouth to show that she wanted a drink or hold up her arms to show that she wanted to be picked up.

Symbolic gestures, such as blowing to mean hot or sniffing to mean flower, often emerge around the same time as babies say their first words, and they function much like words. By using them, babies show an understanding that symbols can refer to specific objects, events, desires, and conditions. Gestures usually appear before children have a vocabulary of 25 words and drop out when children learn the word for the idea they were gesturing and can say it instead (Lock, Young, Service, & Chandler, 1990).

Learning gestures seems to help babies learn to talk. Early gestures are a good predictor of later vocabulary size (Goldin-Meadow, 2007). In one study, parents' use of gestures predicted their child's use of gestures at 14 months, which in turn predicted the size of the child's vocabulary at 42 months (Rowe, Özçaliskan, & Goldin-Meadow, 2008).

First Words

The average baby says a first word sometime between 10 and 14 months, initiating **linguistic speech**—verbal expression that conveys meaning. At first, an infant's total verbal repertoire is likely to be "mama" or "dada." Or it may be a simple syllable that has more than one meaning depending on the context in which the child utters it. "Da" may mean "I want that," "I want to go out," or "Where's Daddy?" A word like this, which expresses a complete thought, is called a **holophrase**.

Addition of new words to the expressive (spoken) vocabulary is slow at first. Then, sometime between 16 and 24 months, a "naming explosion" often occurs (Ganger & Brent, 2004). Within a few months, many

Symbolic gestures often emerge around the same time that babies say their first words and can help them learn to talk.

linguistic speech   Verbal expression designed to convey meaning.

holophrase   Single word that conveys a complete thought.

toddlers progress from saying about 50 words to saying several hundred (Courage & Howe, 2002).

Passive (receptive, or understood) vocabulary continues to grow as verbal comprehension gradually becomes faster and more accurate and efficient (Fernald et al., 2006). By 18 months, three out of four children can understand 150 words and can say 50 of them (Kuhl, 2004). Early language learning is related to later cognitive development. In a longitudinal study, children's speed of recognition of spoken words and vocabulary size at 25 months predicted linguistic and cognitive skills, including the efficiency of working memory, at 8 years (Marchman & Fernald, 2008).

Nouns seem to be the easiest type of word for most children to learn. In cross-cultural studies, it did not matter whether a family's native language was Spanish, Dutch, French, Hebrew, Italian, Korean, or English; in all these languages, parents reported that their 20-month-old children knew more nouns than any other class of words (Bornstein & Cote, 2004). At 24 months, children quickly recognize names of familiar objects in the absence of visual cues (Swingley & Fernald, 2002).

First Sentences

The next linguistic breakthrough comes when a toddler puts two words together to express one idea ("Dolly fall"). Generally, children do this between 18 and 24 months, but this age range varies greatly. Although prelinguistic speech is fairly closely tied to chronological age, linguistic speech is not. Most children who begin talking fairly late catch up eventually.

A child's first sentences typically deal with everyday events, things, people, or activities (Rice, 1989). Children often use **telegraphic speech**, consisting of only a few essential words. So when Rita says, "Damma deep," she means "Grandma is sweeping the floor." Children's use of telegraphic speech and the form it takes vary, depending on the language being learned (Slobin, 1983). Word order generally conforms to what a child hears; Rita does not say, "Deep Damma," when she sees her grandmother pushing a broom. In other words, children illustrate their implicit understanding of the structure of their language with the word order they use.

By about 3 years, children become increasingly aware of the communicative purpose of speech and of

whether their words are being understood (Dunham, Dunham, & O'Keefe, 2000; Shwe & Markman, 1997), a sign of growing sensitivity to the mental lives of others. Additionally, their speech is fluent, longer, and more complex.

CHARACTERISTICS OF EARLY SPEECH

Early speech has a character all its own—no matter what language a child is speaking (Slobin, 1970, 1990). As we have seen, children simplify. They use telegraphic speech to say just enough to get their meaning across ("No drink milk!").

Children understand grammatical relationships they cannot yet express. At first, Nina may understand that a dog is chasing a cat, but she cannot string together enough words to express the complete action. Her sentence comes out as "Puppy chase" rather than "Puppy chase kitty."

Children underextend word meanings. In other words, they use a word to refer to too small of a category. Calling your dog "doggy" but no other dogs by that term is an example. Children also overextend word meanings and use a word for too large of a category. Calling all men with grey hair "Grandpa" would be an example of this. As children develop a larger vocabulary and get feedback from adults on the appropriateness of what they say, they commit these common language errors less.

Children also overregularize rules. They apply them rigidly, without exception—as when 21-month-old Delilah, looking out the window, explained "Daddy goed to the store." They learn the rule, but need time to learn the exceptions to those rules.

INFLUENCES ON LANGUAGE DEVELOPMENT

What determines how quickly and how well children learn to understand and use language? Research has focused on influences both within and outside the child.

Did you know?

Just like hearing babies, deaf babies of deaf parents imitate the sign language they see their parents using—they even "hand-babble"!

telegraphic speech Early form of sentence use consisting of only a few essential words.

Perspectives on Diversity

INVENTING SIGN LANGUAGE

There are hundreds of different languages across the world. But this diversity reflects a deep universal commonality—we are made for language. It is part of our species heritage.

Even when we have only the bits and pieces of language, we are adept at developing it. Consider the following example. In Nicaragua prior to the fall of the Sandinista government, deaf children were raised by their hearing parents who generally could not speak sign language. As a result, these children were raised in linguistic isolation and never truly learned language. Although they would use a variety of signs with their families, there was no syntax or grammatical complexity—they spoke in a pidgin of sorts. In the 1980s, after the fall of the Sandinista government, the first schools for the deaf were established. At this point, deaf Nicaraguan schoolchildren spontaneously developed a true sign language, which, as adapted by successive cohorts of deaf children, has evolved from simple gestures into words and sentences that follow linguistic rules (Senghas, Kita, & Özyürek, 2004). The children, without assistance from adults, without rewards or encouragement, without anything but their own desire to communicate and their own innate machinery, created a brand new language out of their shared experience.

All sign languages, including American Sign Language, probably came into existence through a similar process. Thus the development of new sign languages offers a unique opportunity to glimpse language in its infant stages and watch it grow. Watching the development of new languages such as this suggests a recipe for human language. All you need is rudimentary communication symbols and a group of interacting children. Nature will do the rest.

Brain Development

The tremendous brain growth during the early years is closely linked with language development. A newborn's cries are controlled by the brain stem and pons, the most primitive parts of the brain and the earliest to develop. Repetitive babbling may emerge with the maturation of parts of the motor cortex, which control movements of the face and larynx. A brain imaging study points to a link between the brain's phonetic perception and motor systems as early as 6 months (Imada et al., 2006). The development of language actively affects brain networks, committing them to the recognition of native language sounds (Kuhl et al., 2005).

Brain scans confirm the sequence of vocabulary development outlined earlier in this chapter. In about 98 percent of people, the left hemisphere is dominant for language (Knecht et al., 2000). And in toddlers with large vocabularies, brain activation tends to focus on the left temporal and parietal lobes, whereas in toddlers with smaller vocabularies, brain activation is more scattered (Kuhl & Rivera-Gaxiola, 2008). Cortical regions associated with language continue to develop until at least the late preschool years or beyond—some, even until adulthood.

Social Interaction: The Role of Parents and Caregivers

Language is a social act. It takes not only the necessary biological machinery and cognitive capacity but also interaction with a live communicative partner. Children who grow up without normal social contact and children who are exposed to language only through television will not develop normal language. For example, babies who are exposed to Mandarin via interaction with a native speaker will retain Mandarin syllables not used in English, but those exposed via television or audio-only tutors will not (Kuhl & Rivera-Gaxiola, 2008).

Parents or other caregivers play an important role at each stage of language development. They do so both by providing

Did you know?

When children are first learning language, they use the correct grammatical form—Daddy went to the store, I drew the picture, the plane flew. The later overregularization of these phrases—Daddy goed to the store, I drawed the picture, the plane flied—looks like backsliding, but actually illustrates progress. Children have internalized the rule, and rather than merely parroting back the correct form they have heard previously, they are now changing verb forms on the fly according to the rules of grammar. Because English is full of irregular verbs, however, babies get the verbs that "break the rule" wrong.

opportunities and motivation for communicative experience and by providing models of language use (Hoff, 2006). The age of parents or caregivers, the way they interact with and talk with an infant, the child's birth order, child care experience, and, later, schooling, peers, and television exposure all affect the pace and course of language acquisition.

At the babbling stage, adults help an infant advance toward true speech by repeating the sounds the baby makes. The baby soon joins in the game and repeats the sounds back. Parents' imitation of babies' sounds affects the amount of infant vocalization (Goldstein, King, & West, 2003) and the pace of language learning (Hardy-Brown & Plomin, 1985; Schmitt, Simpson, & Friend, 2011). It also helps babies experience the social aspect of speech, the sense that a conversation consists of alternating or taking turns (Kuhl, 2004), an idea most babies seem to grasp at about age 7½ to 8 months.

Caregivers may help babies understand spoken words by, for example, pointing to a doll and saying, "Please give me Kermit," encouraging the infant to follow the caregiver's gaze (Kuhl, 2004). In one longitudinal study, mothers' responsiveness to 9-month-olds' and, even more so, to 13-month-olds' vocalization and play predicted the timing of language milestones, such as first spoken words and sentences (Tamis-LeMonda, Bornstein, & Baumwell, 2001).

A strong relationship exists between the frequency of specific words in mothers' speech and the order in which children learn these words (Brent & Siskind, 2001; Huttenlocher, Haight, Bryk, Seltzer, & Lyons, 1991) as well as between mothers' talkativeness and the size of toddlers' vocabularies (Huttenlocher, 1998; Schmitt et. al., 2011). When babies begin to talk, parents or caregivers can boost vocabulary development by repeating their first words and pronouncing them correctly. Mothers with higher socio-economic status tend to use richer vocabularies and longer utterances, and their 2-year-olds have spoken vocabularies up to eight times as large as those of low-SES children (Hoff, 2003; Ramey & Ramey, 2003). However, parental sensitivity and responsiveness may count even more than the number of words a mother uses. In a yearlong study of 290 low-income families of 2-year-olds, both parents' sensitivity, positive regard for the child, and the cognitive stimulation they provided during play predicted the child's receptive vocabulary and cognitive development at ages 2 and 3 (Tamis-LeMonda, Shannon, Cabrera, & Lamb, 2004).

In households where two languages are spoken, babies achieve similar milestones in each language on the same schedule as children who hear only one language (Petitto et al., 2001; Petitto & Kovelman, 2003), and develop phonological skills in the dominant language at the same rate as monolingual children (MacLeod, Laukys, & Rvachew, 2011). Bilingual children often use elements of both languages at first, sometimes in the same utterance— a phenomenon called **code mixing**. However, code mixing does not cause them to confuse the two languages

(Petitto et al., 2001; Petitto & Kovelman, 2003). A naturalistic observation in Montreal (Genesee, Nicoladis, & Paradis, 1995) suggests that children as young as 2 years old in dual-language households differentiate between the two languages, using French, for example, with a predominantly French-speaking father and English with a predominantly English-speaking mother. This ability to shift from one language to another is called **code switching**.

The persistence of additional language proficiency depends on the degree to which children continue to use it in meaningful contexts. Among Inuktitut speakers in eastern Canada, the language has a strong chance of long-term survival. Over 90 percent of Inuit children are bilingual in both Inuktitut and English. They learn Inuktitut from birth, regardless of degree of exposure to English at home, and they attain strong command of the language by age 4. However, children's Inuktitut language skills can became weaker as they make greater use of English over time through more intense exposure to English from media and schooling (Allen, 2007).

Use of Child-Directed Speech

If, when you talk to an infant or a toddler, you speak slowly in a high-pitched voice with exaggerated ups and downs, simplify your speech, exaggerate vowel sounds, and use short words and sentences and much repetition, you are using **child-directed speech (CDS)**, sometimes called *parentese* or *motherese*. Most adults and even children do it naturally. Such "baby talk" has been documented in many cultures. In one cross-cultural observational study, mothers in the United States, Russia, and Sweden were audiotaped speaking to their 2- to 5-month-old infants. Whether the mothers were speaking English, Russian, or Swedish, they

code mixing Use of elements of two languages, sometimes in the same utterance, by young children in households where both languages are spoken.

code switching Process of changing one's speech to match the situation, as in people who are bilingual.

child-directed speech (CDS) Form of speech often used in talking to babies or toddlers; includes slow, simplified speech, a high-pitched tone, exaggerated vowel sounds, short words and sentences, and much repetition; also called *parentese*.

produced more exaggerated vowel sounds when talking to the infants than when talking to other adults (Kuhl et al., 1997).

Some investigators challenge the value of CDS, contending that babies speak sooner and better if they are exposed to more complex adult speech (Oshima-Takane, Goodz, & Derevensky, 1996). However, most researchers believe that CDS helps infants learn their native language or at least pick it up faster by exaggerating and directing attention to the distinguishing features of speech sounds (Kuhl et al., 2005). Infants themselves—practically from birth—prefer to hear simplified speech (Kuhl & Rivera-Gaxiola, 2008).

In line with this idea, 2-day-old infants of both English-speaking and Japanese-speaking parents pre-fer infant-directed to adult-directed singing (Masataka, 1999). In fact, a McMaster University team found that by 6 months of age infants were able to distinguish between and alter their behaviour in response to lullabies and songs intended for play. This shows that parents may use singing to communicate with and regulate their children's internal states between sleep-oriented and play-oriented emotions (Rock, Trainor, & Addison, 1999).

Language-related preferences can develop even before birth. Newborns whose mothers used English only during pregnancy, preferred English language sounds over Tagalog language sounds, whereas those whose mothers spoke both languages during pregnancy showed equal preferences for the two languages. These preferences help direct newborns' attention to the languages perceived before birth, ensuring further language learning in each (Byers-Heinlein, Burns, & Werker, 2010).

PREPARING FOR LITERACY

Most babies love to be read to. The frequency with which caregivers read to them can influence how well children speak and eventually how well and how soon they develop literacy—the ability to read and write. In a study of 2,581 low-income families, about half of the mothers reported reading daily to their preschool children between 14 months and 3 years. Children who had been read to daily had better cognitive and language skills at age 3 and better reading comprehension at age 7 than did their peers (Raikes et al., 2006; Sénéchel & LeFevre, 2002).

The way parents or caregivers read to children makes a difference. Adults tend to have one of three styles of reading to children: the describer, the comprehender, and a performance-oriented style. A *describer* focuses on describing what is going on in the pictures and invites the child to do so as well ("What are the Mom and Dad having for breakfast?"). A *comprehender* encourages the child to look more deeply at the meaning of a story and to make inferences and predictions ("What do you think the lion will do now?"). A *performance-oriented* reader reads the story straight through, introducing the main themes beforehand and asking questions afterward. An adult's read-aloud style is best tailored to the needs and skills of the child. In one study, the describer style resulted in the greatest overall benefits for vocabulary and print skills, but the performance-oriented style was more beneficial for children who started out with large vocabularies (Reese & Cox, 1999).

How often caregivers read to children can influence how well children speak and how soon they learn to read.

18. Which of the following is the correct order of acquisition?
    a. babble, coo, cry, telegraphic speech
    b. telegraphic speech, babble, coo, cry
    c. cry, coo, babble, telegraphic speech
    d. cry, babble, coo, telegraphic speech

19. Why is it significant that Cora says "want juice" instead of "juice want"?
    a. It shows that Cora understands pragmatics.
    b. It illustrates Cora's knowledge of syntactic rules.
    c. It shows semantic knowledge.
    d. It is telegraphic speech.

20. What are two ways in which parents often promote language development?

21. Provide a sentence that might be said by each of these three types of readers while reading a story to a young child.
    a. Describer
    b. Comprehender
    c. Performer

SUMMARY CHAPTER 6 COGNITIVE DEVELOPMENT, BIRTH TO AGE 3

LO1
Explain operant and classical conditioning.

- Two simple types of learning that behaviourists study are classical conditioning and operant conditioning.
- Rovee-Collier's research suggests that infants' memory processes are much like those of adults, but their memories fade quickly without periodic reminders.

LO2
Describe how to assess toddlers' intelligence and summarize relevant early experiences.

- Psychometric tests measure factors presumed to make up intelligence.
- Developmental tests, such as the Bayley Scales of Infant and Toddler Development, can indicate current functioning but are generally poor predictors of later intelligence.
- Socio-economic status, parenting practices, and the home environment may affect measured intelligence.
- If the home environment does not provide the necessary conditions that pave the way for cognitive competence, early intervention may be needed.

LO3

Discuss changes in cognition in early childhood and evaluate Piaget's theoretical approach for this area.

- During Piaget's sensorimotor stage, infants' schemes become more elaborate. They progress from primary to secondary to tertiary circular reactions and finally to the development of representational ability, which makes possible pretending and problem solving.
- Object permanence develops gradually throughout the sensorimotor stage.
- Research suggests that a number of abilities develop earlier than Piaget described. For example, he may have underestimated young infants' grasp of object permanence.

LO4

Summarize how data on intelligence is collected within the information-processing approach and evaluate its value as a predictor of other advances.

- Information-processing researchers measure mental processes through habituation and other signs of visual and perceptual abilities. Contrary to Piaget, such research suggests that representational ability is present virtually from birth.
- Indicators of the efficiency of infants' information processing, such as speed of habituation, tend to predict later intelligence.
- Such information-processing research techniques as habituation, novelty preference, and the violation-of-expectations method have yielded evidence that infants as young as 3½ to 5 months may have a rudimentary grasp of such Piagetian abilities as categorization, causality, object permanence, and a sense of number.

LO5

Summarize how the physical structure of the brain is related to cognitive development.

- Explicit memory and implicit memory are located in different brain structures.
- Working memory emerges between 6 and 12 months.
- Neurological developments help explain the emergence of Piagetian skills and memory abilities.

LO6

Identify some early social and contextual influences on development.

- Social interactions with adults contribute to cognitive competence through shared activities that help children learn skills, knowledge, and values important in their culture.

Summarize the sequence of early language development, identify the relevant influences, and discuss the relationship to literacy.

- The acquisition of language is an important aspect of cognitive development.

- Prelinguistic speech includes crying, cooing, babbling, and imitating language sounds. By 6 months, babies have learned the basic sounds of their language and have begun to link sound with meaning. Perception of categories of sounds in the native language may commit the neural circuitry to further learning in that language only.

- Before they say their first word, babies use gestures.

- The first word typically comes sometime between 10 and 14 months, initiating linguistic speech. A "naming explosion" typically occurs sometime between 16 and 24 months of age.

- The first brief sentences generally come between 18 and 24 months. By age 3, syntax and communicative abilities are fairly well developed.

- Early speech is characterized by simplification, underextending and overextending word meanings, and overregularizing rules.

- Two classic theoretical views about how children acquire language are learning theory and nativism. Today, most developmentalists hold that an inborn capacity to learn language may be activated or constrained by experience.

- Influences on language development include brain maturation and social interaction.

- Family characteristics, such as socio-economic status, adult language use, and maternal responsiveness, affect a child's vocabulary development.

- Children who hear two languages at home generally learn both at the same rate as children who hear only one language (phonological aspects of the dominant language are learned at the same rate as monolingual children), and they can use each language in appropriate circumstances.

- Child-directed speech (CDS) seems to have cognitive, emotional, and social benefits, and infants show a preference for it. However, some researchers dispute its value. The preference for language seems to originate before birth.

- Reading aloud to a child from an early age helps pave the way for literacy.

ANSWERS TO Ask Yourself

Answers: 1-d; 2-reinforcer, punisher; 3-Babies who have been operantly conditioned to kick in order to activate a mobile will repeat the action when shown the mobile days or weeks later, demonstrating that they recognize the mobile and remember their earlier training; 4-cognitive, language, motor, social-emotional, and adaptive behaviour; 5-Factors that have been related to high HOME scores include parental responsiveness (both emotional and verbal), avoidance of restriction and punishment, organization of the physical and temporal environment, presence of appropriate playthings (including books and toys), parental involvement, and opportunities for variety in daily stimulation; 6-c; 7-a; 8-Object permanence involves the realization that an object or person continues to exist when out of sight. By 1 year of age, babies cry in response to separation from their mothers, because they understand she still exists even if she is not present; 9-b; 10-d; 11-c; 12-b; 13-a; 14-implicit, explicit; 15-make longer-lasting memories possible; working memory storage; 16-b; 17-The adult's participation helps to structure the activity and to bring the child's understanding of it closer to that of the adult; 18-c; 19-b; 20-The ways in which parents can support language development include repeating the sounds a baby makes, pointing to labelled objects, using a rich vocabulary and longer utterances, being sensitive and responsive, and using child-directed speech; 21-An example of a describer-style sentence might be, "What are the Mom and Dad having for breakfast?" An example of the comprehender-style sentence might be, "What do you think the lion will do now?" An example of the performance-oriented reader might involve reading the story straight through and later asking questions.

PSYCHOSOCIAL DEVELOPMENT, BIRTH

WHAT'S TO COME

Emotions and Temperament

Attachment

Relationships with Other Children

Peers

Paola was a difficult baby from the start. She cried vigorously at diaper changes or if she was cold or hungry, and once she got older, she strongly protested being held by anyone but her mother. But her parents' gentle handling built her confidence over time, and although at 18 months she would still check in visually with her parents before picking up a new toy or taking a potential risk, Paola would happily toddle around a new playground as long as they stayed nearby. At 3 years of age, although she was frightened the first day she was dropped off at preschool, the trust she felt in her parents led her to expect other people to be good to her too, and she was able to haltingly establish new relationships with other children. All of these related developments—occurring during the fundamental first three years of life—can be viewed as existing under the umbrella of psychosocial development and are the topic of this chapter.

In this chapter, we examine the role of attachment in development. We discuss early emotional development, individual differences and early experiences that impact the formation of this foundational system. We then examine how peer relationships, including those with siblings, impact development.

TO AGE 3

AS YOU READ

LO1 Describe the development of and major changes in the expression of emotions and temperament in early childhood.

LO2 Discuss the causes and consequences of the development of attachment.

LO3 Explain how the developing sense of self and the emergence of autonomy impact socialization and the development of moral behaviours.

LO4 Discuss how siblings and peers affect the psychosocial development of young children.

Emotions and Temperament

Newborn Zev was a happy baby. He cried little, slept on a relatively consistent schedule, and spent much of his time calmly watching the world with his large brown eyes. Friends and family commented on his ease, asking his parents how they managed to mould his behaviour in this way. "We didn't," his parents answered. "He just seemed to be born like that."

Although babies share common patterns of development, each, from the start, shows a relatively consistent and predictable way of responding to the environment. Each baby has his or her own unique temperament. One baby may usually be cheerful; another, easily upset. One toddler plays happily with other children; another prefers to play alone. Such characteristic ways of feeling, thinking, and acting affect the way children respond to others and adapt to their world. From infancy on, temperament is intertwined with social relationships (Table 7.1). This combination is called *psychosocial development*.

EMOTIONS

Emotions are subjective reactions to experience that are associated with physiological and behavioural changes. Fear, for example, is accompanied by a faster heartbeat. People differ in how often and how strongly they feel a particular emotion, in the kinds of events that may

emotions Subjective reactions to experience that are associated with physiological and behavioural changes.

TABLE 7.1 Highlights of Infants' and Toddlers' Psychosocial Development, Birth to 36 Months

Approximate Age, Months	Characteristics
0–3	Infants are open to stimulation. They begin to show interest and curiosity, and they smile readily at people.
3–6	Infants can anticipate what is about to happen and experience disappointment when it does not. They show this by becoming angry or acting warily. They smile, coo, and laugh often. This is a time of social awakening and early reciprocal exchanges between the baby and the caregiver.
6–9	Infants play "social games" and try to get responses from people. They "talk" to, touch, and cajole other babies to get them to respond. They express more differentiated emotions, showing joy, fear, anger, and surprise.
9–12	Infants are intensely preoccupied with their principal caregiver, may become afraid of strangers, and act subdued in new situations. By 1 year, they communicate emotions more clearly, showing moods, ambivalence, and gradations of feeling.
12–18	Toddlers explore their environment, using the people they are most attached to as a secure base. As they master the environment, they become more confident and more eager to assert themselves.
18–36	Toddlers sometimes become anxious because they now realize how much they are separating from their caregiver. They work out their awareness of their limitations in fantasy and in play and by identifying with adults.

Source: Adapted from Sroufe (1997).

produce it, in the physical manifestations they show, and in how they act as a result.

Emotional development follows a relatively standard developmental timeline, beginning in early infancy. It is an orderly process; complex emotions unfold from simpler ones (Lewis, 1997; Figure 7.1). Emotions also become increasingly social and include the self-conscious emotions, altruism and empathy. Last, emotions then prompt young children into engaging in shared intentionality and collaborative activity.

EARLY EMOTIONAL RESPONSES

Early emotional responses include crying, smiling and laughing, self-conscious emotions, altruistic helping and empathy, and shared intentionality and collaborative activity.

Crying

Newborns plainly show when they are unhappy. They let out piercing cries, flail their arms and legs, and stiffen their bodies. Adults find the sound of crying unpleasant, and therein lies its function. Crying is the primary way in which infants communicate their needs and is considered to be an "honest" signal of need.

Infants cannot be spoiled by picking them up when they cry, and indeed, repeatedly not soothing infants when they are upset may interfere with an infant's developing ability to regulate his or her emotional state (R. A. Thompson, 1991). The most developmentally sound approach to crying may be to prevent distress.

Smiling and Laughing

The earliest faint smiles occur spontaneously soon after birth, apparently as a result of subcortical nervous system activity. Through 1 month of age, smiles are often elicited by high-pitched tones when an infant is drowsy or in REM sleep. During the second month, as visual recognition

develops, babies smile more at visual stimuli, such as faces they know (Sroufe, 1997).

Social smiling, when newborn infants gaze at their parents and smile at them, develops in the second month of life. Laughter is a smile-linked vocalization that becomes more common between 4 and 12 months when it may signify the most intense positive emotion (Salkind, 2005).

As babies grow older, they become more actively engaged in mirthful exchanges. A 6-month-old may giggle in response to the mother appearing with a towel over her face; a 10-month-old may laughingly try to put the towel back on her face when it falls off. This change reflects cognitive development. By laughing at the unexpected, babies show that they know what to expect. By turning the tables, they show awareness that they can make things happen. By 12 to 15 months, infants are intentionally communicating to the partner about objects.

Anticipatory smiling—in which infants smile at an object and then gaze at an adult while continuing to smile—rises sharply between 8 and 10 months and seems

Differentiation of Emotions

FIGURE 7.1 The primary, or basic, emotions emerge during the first 6 months or so; the self-conscious emotions develop around 18 to 24 months, as a result of the emergence of self-awareness (consciousness of self) together with accumulation of knowledge about societal standards and norms.

*Note: There are two kinds of embarrassment. The earlier kind does not involve evaluation of behaviour and may simply be a response to being singled out as the object of attention. The second kind, elusive embarrassment, which emerges during the third year, is a mild form of shame.

Source: From "The self in self-conscious emotions," by M. Lewis in S.G. Snodgrass and R.L. Thompson (eds.), "The Self across psychology: Self-recognition, self-awareness, and the self-concept," 1997, Annals of the New York Academy of Sciences, Vol. 818, Fig. 1, p. 120. Reprinted by permission obtained via RightsLink.

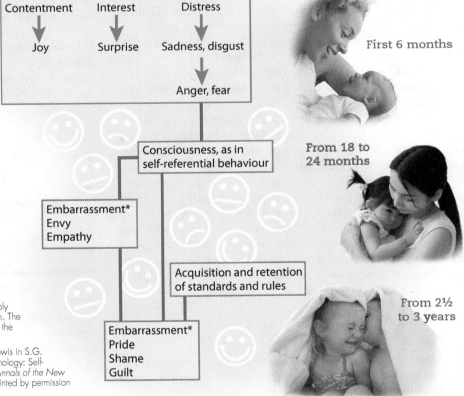

Contentment → Joy

Interest → Surprise

Distress → Sadness, disgust → Anger, fear

Consciousness, as in self-referential behaviour

Embarrassment*
Envy
Empathy

Acquisition and retention of standards and rules

Embarrassment*
Pride
Shame
Guilt

First 6 months

From 18 to 24 months

From 2½ to 3 years

to be among the first types of communication in which the infant refers to an object or experience.

Self-Conscious Emotions

Self-conscious emotions, such as embarrassment, envy, and shame, arise only after children have developed self-awareness at about the age of 3. **Self-awareness** involves the cognitive understanding that they have a recognizable identity, separate and different from the rest of their world. Children must understand that others might have opinions about the wrongness or rightness of their behaviour different from their own before they can understand and feel these social emotions (Lewis, 1998).

Guilt and shame are distinct emotions, even though both may be responses to wrongdoing. Children who fail to live up to behavioural standards may feel guilty, that is, regret their behaviour, but they do not necessarily feel a lack of self-worth, as when they feel ashamed. Their focus is on a bad act, not a bad self (Eisenberg, 2000).

Altruistic Helping and Empathy

A guest of 18-month-old Alex's father—a person Alex had never seen before—dropped his pen on the floor, and it rolled under a cabinet, where the guest couldn't quite reach it. Alex, being small enough, crawled under the cabinet, retrieved the pen, and gave it to the guest. By acting out of concern for a stranger with no expectation of reward, Alex showed **altruistic behaviour** (Warneken & Tomasello, 2006).

The roots of altruism can be seen in early empathic reactions in infancy. For example, 2- to 3-month-olds react to others' emotional expressions (Tomasello, 2007). Six-month-olds value someone on the basis of that person's treatment of others. In one series of experiments (Hamlin, Wynn, & Bloom, 2007), 6- and 10-month-old infants saw a wooden character ("the climber") repeatedly attempt to climb a hill. Sometimes the climber was either assisted by a "helper," who pushed up from behind, or pushed down by a "hinderer." When given the choice, infants overwhelmingly reached for the helper.

Altruistic behaviour seems to come naturally to toddlers. Well before the second birthday, children often help others, share belongings and food, and offer comfort (Zahn-Waxler, Radke-Yarrow, Wagner, & Chapman, 1992). Empathy seems to play a role as well; in situations in which they perceive a person needs help, 18-month-olds tend to spontaneously offer it. Such behaviour emerges during the second year, increases with age (Eisenberg, 2000), and can be promoted in children experiencing social and emotional difficulties, in classroom-based programs such as Roots of Empathy (Gordon & Green, 2008; Gordon & Letchford, 2009).

Shared Intentionality and Collaborative Activity

The motivation to help and share, and the ability to understand the intentions of others, together contribute to an important development between 9 and 12 months of age,

By helping his mother water the garden, this boy displays altruistic behaviour.

collaboration with caregivers in joint activities, such as a child holding and handing over a pair of socks and a caregiver dressing the child.

Collaborative activities increase during the second year of life as toddlers become more adept at communication. At 12 months, Alex points at a ball to show that he wants to play a game of rolling it back and forth with his father. When the ball rolls under a chair, he points to let his father know where it is. The vocabulary explosion that frequently occurs during the second year enables more complex and flexible collaborative communication (Tomasello, 2007).

TEMPERAMENT

Temperament is a person's characteristic, biologically based way of approaching and reacting to people and situations (Thomas & Chess, 1977). One toddler may happily run toward a large dog, eager to pet it; another may shrink back in fear. Also, temperament may affect not only the way children approach and react to the outside world but also the way they regulate their mental, emotional, and

self-conscious emotions Emotions, such as embarrassment, empathy, and envy, that depend on self-awareness.

self-awareness Realization that one's existence and functioning are separate from those of other people and things.

altruistic behaviour Activity intended to help another person with no expectation of reward.

temperament Characteristic disposition or style of approaching and reacting to situations.

TABLE 7.2 Categories of Temperment

Easy Child	Difficult Child	Slow-to-Warm-Up Child
Has moods of mild to moderate intensity, usually positive.	Displays intense and frequently negative moods; cries often and loudly; also laughs loudly.	Has mildly intense reactions, both positive and negative.
Responds well to novelty and change. Quickly develops regular sleep and feeding schedules.	Responds poorly to novelty and change. Sleeps and eats irregularly.	Responds slowly to novelty and change. Sleeps and eats more regularly than the difficult child, less regularly than the easy child.
Takes to new foods easily.	Accepts new foods slowly.	Shows mildly negative initial response to new stimuli (a first encounter with a new person, place, or situation).
Smiles at strangers.	Is suspicious of strangers.	
Adapts easily to new situations	Adapts slowly to new situations.	
Accepts most frustrations with little fuss.	Reacts to frustration with tantrums.	
Adapts quickly to new routines and rules of new games.	Adjusts slowly to new routines.	Gradually develops liking for new stimuli after repeated, unpressured exposures.

Source: Adapted from A. Thomas & S. Chess, Genesis and Evolution of Behavioral Disorders: From Infancy to Early Adult Life. *American Journal of Psychiatry,* 141(1) 1984, pp. 1–9. Copyright © 1984 by the American Psychiatric Association. Reproduced with permission

behavioural functioning (Rothbart, Ahadi, & Evans, 2000). Individual differences in temperament form the core of the developing personality.

Temperament Patterns

To better appreciate how temperament affects behaviour, let's look at three children. Sarita was a cheerful, calm baby who ate, slept, and eliminated at regular times. She greeted each day and most people with a smile, and the only sign that she was awake during the night was the tinkle of the musical toy in her crib. When Caroline, the second child, woke up, she would open her mouth to cry before she even opened her eyes. She slept little; she laughed and cried loudly; and she had to be convinced that new people and new experiences were not threatening before she would have anything to do with them. The last child, Ariana, was mild in her responses. She did not like most new situations, but if allowed to proceed at her own slow pace, she would eventually become interested and involved.

Sarita, Caroline, and Ariana exemplify the three main types of temperament found by the New York Longitudinal Study (NYLS). In this pioneering study, researchers followed 133 infants into adulthood. The researchers collected data from parents and used it to place most of the children in the study into one of three categories (Table 7.2).

- Forty percent were **easy children** like Sarita: generally happy, rhythmic in biological functioning, and accepting of new experiences.

- Ten percent were what the researchers called **difficult children** like Caroline: more irritable and harder to please, irregular in biological rhythms, and more intense in expressing emotion.

- Fifteen percent were **slow-to-warm-up children** like Ariana: mild but slow to adapt to new people and situations (Thomas & Chess, 1977, 1984).

While Thomas and Chess' research captured broad temperament trends, many children (including 35 percent of the NYLS sample) do not fit neatly into any of these three categories.

How you do think Sarita, Caroline, and Ariana would respond to this dog?

easy children Children with a generally happy temperament, regular biological rhythms, and a readiness to accept new experiences.

difficult children Children with irritable temperament, irregular biological rhythms, and intense emotional responses.

slow-to-warm-up children Children whose temperament is generally mild but who are hesitant about accepting new experiences.

Stability of Temperament

Newborn babies show different patterns of sleeping, fussing, and activity, and these differences tend to persist to some degree (Korner, 1996). Studies have found strong links between infant temperament and childhood personality at age 7 (Rothbart, Ahadi, Hershey, & Fisher, 2001), and between temperament at age 3 and aspects of personality at ages 18 and 21 (Caspi, 2000). Temperament, measured between ages 9 and 12 years, is associated with happiness; extraverted children tend to be happier, while neurotic children tend to be less happy (Holder & Klassen, 2009).

That does not mean, however, that temperament is fully formed at birth. Temperament develops as various emotions and self-regulatory capacities appear (Rothbart et al., 2000) and can change in response to parental treatment and other life experiences (Kagan & Snidman, 2004). Temperament may also be affected by culturally influenced child-raising practices. Infants in Malaysia tend to be less adaptable, more wary, and more responsive to stimuli than U.S. babies. This may be because Malay parents do not often expose young children to situations that require adaptability, and they encourage infants to be acutely aware of sensations, such as the need for a diaper change (Banks, 1989).

Goodness of Fit

According to the NYLS, the key to healthy adjustment is **goodness of fit**, the match between a child's temperament and the environmental demands. A shy child will do better with gentle handling, a bold one with more stimulation. Children differ, and their ideal environments differ as well. We can think of goodness of fit as a descriptor of the child-caregiver relationship, or of the fit between the child and the wider social context.

Children also differ in their susceptibility to environmental influences. For example, infants with difficult temperaments may be more susceptible to the quality of parenting than infants with easy or slow-to-warm-up temperaments and may need more emotional support and respect for their autonomy (Stright, Gallagher, & Kelley, 2008).

Biological Basis of Temperament

Temperament has a biological basis. In longitudinal research with about 500 children starting in infancy, Jerome Kagan and his colleagues studied an aspect of temperament called behavioural inhibition, which has to do with how cautiously the child approaches unfamiliar objects and situations. Behavioural inhibition is believed to be associated with certain biological characteristics.

When presented at 4 months with a series of new stimuli, about 20 percent of the infants became extremely excited, pumping their legs and arms and eventually getting so aroused that they started crying. This group of infants was called inhibited. About 40 percent of infants showed interest in the new stimuli, but were calm and evidenced low levels of motor

---

goodness of fit Appropriateness of environmental demands and constraints to a child's temperament.

Infants identified at 4 months as highly behaviourally inhibited are generally noisy and active in response to a new stimulus, but at 2 years of age tend to be shy and withdrawn. The difference in response can be attributed to children's increasing ability to regulate themselves behaviourally. A child scared by an unfamiliar stimulus at 4 months can do nothing but squirm in its presence. A child of 2 years, faced with the same event, can retreat to safety.

activity; they were labelled uninhibited. The researchers suggested that inhibited children may be born with an unusually excitable amygdala, a part of the brain that detects and reacts to unfamiliar events and is involved in emotional reactions (Kagan & Snidman, 2004). In other words, such children were "set" to respond to stimuli in a more extreme fashion than others, so new stimuli were unpleasantly arousing.

Infants identified as inhibited or uninhibited seemed to maintain these patterns during childhood (Kagan & Snidman, 2004). However, experience can moderate or accentuate early tendencies. When mothers responded neutrally to infants who were behaviourally inhibited, the inhibition tended to remain stable or increase, suggesting that caregivers' sensitivity may affect the neural systems that underlie reactions to stress and novelty (Fox, Hane, & Pine, 2007). Other environmental influences, such as birth order, race/ethnicity,

Ask Yourself

1. What is the earliest form of communication that babies use?
   a. smiles, to show they are happy
   b. eye gaze, to get a parent's attention
   c. cries, to show they are unhappy
   d. None of these; babies cannot easily communicate in infancy.

2. The self-conscious emotions (e.g., embarrassment, empathy, and envy) require self-awareness. Why is self-awareness required?

3. When guests show up at her parents' dinner party, Esme hides behind her father's legs and avoids contact with the guests. However, a half-hour later, she sits on a guest's lap and chatters happily away. With respect to temperament, Esme is likely to be
   a. easy.
   b. difficult.
   c. slow to warm up.
   d. high in behavioural inhibition.

The attachment bond is one of the oldest mammalian characteristics.

culture, relationships with teachers and peers, and unpredictable events, also can reinforce or soften a child's original temperament bias (Kagan & Snidman, 2004). Influences can operate on a cross-national scale as well. Chinese children, more than Canadian children, experience shyness as a culturally acceptable characteristic (Rubin et al., 2006). However, Chinese children see unsociability in children as a characteristic that is less under the child's control, while Canadian children see it as more intentional, indicating differences in what unsociability implies for children between the two countries (Coplan, Zheng, Weeks, & Chen, 2012).

Attachment

How does a dependent newborn, with a limited emotional repertoire and pressing physical needs, become a child with complex feelings and the abilities to understand and control them? Much of this development revolves around issues regarding relationships with caregivers, especially in the development of trust, attachments, and mutual regulation.

DEVELOPING TRUST

Human babies are dependent on others for food, for protection, and for their very lives for a far longer period than the young of most other mammals. For example, baby rats are with their mothers for only about a month, and many baby mammals stay with their mothers only for the duration of the breeding season. How do human infants—with their need for extended maternal care—come to trust that their needs will be met? According to Erikson (1950), early experiences are the key.

The first of Erikson's eight stages in psychosocial development (refer to Table 1.4) is **basic trust versus basic mistrust**. This stage begins in infancy and continues until about 18 months. In these early months, babies need to develop a balance between trust, which lets them form intimate relationships, and mistrust, which enables them to protect themselves. If trust predominates, as it should, children develop the virtue of hope: the belief that they can fulfill their needs and obtain their desires (Erikson, 1982). If mistrust predominates, children will view the world as unfriendly and unpredictable and will have trouble forming quality relationships.

The critical element in developing trust is sensitive, responsive, consistent caregiving. Erikson saw the feeding situation as the setting for establishing the right mix of trust and mistrust. Can the baby count on being fed when hungry, and can the baby therefore trust the mother as a representative of the world (Erikson, 1950, p. 247)?

DEVELOPING ATTACHMENTS

A young gosling follows his mother, waddling quickly to catch up when he falls too far behind. A kitten purrs with pleasure, kneading her mother's stomach as she nurses. A baby rhesus monkey clings to his mother's soft fur with tiny hands. And in a dark room late at night, a newborn infant snuggles close to her mother and is soothed by her calm voice and warm body. All of these processes illustrate one of the oldest mammalian characteristics—the attachment bond.

Attachment is a reciprocal and enduring emotional tie between an infant and a caregiver, each of whom

basic trust versus basic mistrust   Erikson's first stage in psychosocial development, in which infants develop a sense of the reliability of people and objects.

attachment   Reciprocal, enduring tie between two people—especially between infant and caregiver—each of whom contributes to the quality of the relationship.

contributes to the quality of the relationship. From an evolutionary point of view, attachments have profound adaptive value for babies, ensuring that their psychosocial as well as physical needs will be met (MacDonald, 1998).

Attachment Patterns

The study of attachment owes much to the ethologist John Bowlby (1951), a pioneer in the study of bonding. From his knowledge of animal studies and from observations of disturbed children in a London psychoanalytic clinic, Bowlby became convinced of the importance of the mother-baby bond. Mary Ainsworth (1967), a student of Bowlby's in the early 1950s, went on to study attachment in African babies in Uganda through naturalistic observation in their homes. Ainsworth later developed the **Strange Situation**, a now-classic laboratory-based technique designed to assess attachment patterns between a 10- to 24-month-old infant and an adult. The Strange Situation consists of a sequence of eight short episodes of gradually increasing stress designed to trigger the emergence of attachment-related behaviours. During that time, the mother twice leaves the baby in an unfamiliar room. Upon her return, the mother gives comfort if the baby seems to need it (Ainsworth, Blehar, Waters, & Wall, 1978). Of particular concern is the baby's response each time the mother returns.

When Ainsworth and her colleagues observed 1-year-olds in the Strange Situation and at home, they found three main patterns of attachment. These are **secure attachment**, the most common category, into which about 60 to 75 percent of low-risk North American babies fall, and two forms of insecure attachment: **avoidant attachment** (15 to 25 percent) and **ambivalent, or resistant, attachment** (10 to 15 percent) (Vondra & Barnett, 1999). Security of attachment to father and mother is usually quite similar (Fox, Kimmerly, & Schafer, 1991).

Babies with secure attachment might cry or protest when a caregiver leaves but are able to obtain the comfort they need quickly and effectively upon her return, and they calm easily upon contact. If they do not become upset at separations, they nonetheless illustrate their preference for the mother over strangers when she re-enters the room, often greeting her with smiles and vocalizations. Babies with avoidant attachment are outwardly

WHERE DO **YOU** STAND?

The Strange Situation is designed to be a stressful experience for the baby. Is such research warranted? Is it ethical to deliberately subject young children to stress? How do we decide what is and what is not acceptable in research?

unaffected by a caregiver leaving or returning. They show little emotion either positively or negatively to the mother's return. Babies with ambivalent (resistant) attachment become anxious even before a caregiver leaves and become increasingly upset when he or she departs. Upon the caregiver's return, resistant babies demonstrate their distress and anger by seeking contact while at the same time resisting it by kicking or squirming. These three attachment patterns are universal in all cultures in which they have been studied—cultures as different as those in Africa, China, and Israel—though the percentage of infants in each category varies (van IJzendoorn & Sagi, 1999).

Other research (Main & Solomon, 1986) identified a fourth pattern, **disorganized-disoriented attachment**, which is the least secure. Babies with the disorganized pattern seem to lack a cohesive strategy to deal with the stress of the Strange Situation. Instead, they show contradictory, repetitive, or misdirected behaviours. They may greet the mother brightly when she returns but then turn away or approach without looking at her, freeze during a moment of stress, or show repetitive self-stimulatory movements. They often seem confused and afraid (Carlson, 1998).

Disorganized attachment is thought to occur in at least 10 percent of low-risk infants but in much higher proportions in certain at-risk populations, such as babies with mothers who are insensitive, intrusive, or abusive; who are fearful; or who have suffered unresolved loss or have unresolved feelings about their childhood attachment to their own parents. Disorganized attachment is a reliable

---

Strange Situation Laboratory technique used to study infant attachment.

secure attachment Pattern in which an infant is quickly and effectively able to find comfort from a caregiver when faced with a stressful situation.

avoidant attachment Pattern in which an infant rarely cries when separated from the primary caregiver and avoids contact on his or her return.

ambivalent, or resistant, attachment Pattern in which an infant becomes anxious before the primary caregiver leaves, is extremely upset during his or her absence, and both seeks and resists contact on his or her return.

disorganized-disoriented attachment Pattern in which an infant, after separation from the primary caregiver, shows contradictory behaviours on his or her return.

Did you know?

In the Strange Situation, what the baby does when the mother is gone—and thus not available—is not diagnostic. The crucial behaviours emerge upon the mother's return. This makes sense because in order to assess attachment, we need to see how the baby uses the mother for comfort when under stress, something that is impossible if the mother is not there.

predictor of later behavioural and adjustment problems (Bernier & Meins, 2008; Carlson, 1998).

How Attachment Is Established

On the basis of a baby's interactions with the mother, proposed Bowlby, the baby builds an internal **working model** of what can be expected from her. A working model is a set of expectations the baby has about how the mother is likely to respond in interactions, and is similar to Erikson's concept of basic trust. The various patterns of emotional attachment represent different cognitive representations that result in different expectations. As long as the mother continues to act the same way, the model holds up. If her behaviour changes—not just once or twice, but consistently—the baby may revise the model, and security of attachment may change.

Securely attached babies have learned to trust not only their caregivers but also their own ability to get what they need. Mothers of securely attached infants and toddlers tend to be sensitive and responsive (Braungart-Rieker, Garwood, Powers, & Wang, 2001), and according to Bowlby, have cultivated what he called a "secure base." This secure base allows children to explore their environment more effectively, as they know they can rely on their caregivers to quickly come to the rescue if needed. Equally important are mutual interaction, stimulation, a positive attitude, warmth and acceptance, and emotional support (De Wolff & van IJzendoorn, 1997; Lundy, 2003).

The Role of Temperament in Attachment

How much influence does temperament exert on attachment and in what ways? Neurological or physiological conditions may underlie temperament differences in attachment. For example, variability in heart rate is associated with irritability, and heart rate seems to vary more in insecurely attached infants (Izard, Porges, Simons, Haynes, & Cohen, 1991).

However, attachment is a relational process—child temperament and parenting interact. In one study of 6- to 12-month-olds and their families, both a mother's sensitivity and her baby's temperament influenced attachment patterns (Seifer, Schiller, Sameroff, Resnick, & Riordan, 1996). A baby's temperament may have not only a direct impact on attachment but also an indirect impact through its effect on the parents. In a series of studies in the Netherlands (Van den Boom, 1994), 15-day-old infants classified as irritable were much more likely than non-irritable infants to be avoidantly attached at 1 year unless their mothers had received instruction on how to soothe their babies. Thus, irritability on an infant's part may prevent the development

working model   A set of expectations the baby has about how the mother is likely to respond in interactions.

stranger anxiety   Wariness of strange people and places, shown by some infants from age 6 to 12 months.

separation anxiety   Distress shown by someone, typically an infant, when a familiar caregiver leaves.

A working model is a set of expectations a baby has about how the mother is likely to respond in interactions, like this baby raising her hands in anticipation of a hug from mom.

of secure attachment, but not if the mother has the skills to cope with the baby's temperament (Rothbart et al., 2000). Goodness of fit between parent and child may well be a key to understanding security of attachment.

Stranger and Separation Anxiety

Alex was always a friendly baby, smiling at strangers and going to them, continuing to coo happily as long as someone—anyone—was around. Now, at 8 months, he prefers to stay in his mother's arms when a new person approaches and clings to his parents when they try to leave him with a babysitter. Alex is experiencing two types of anxiety typically seen in infants: **stranger anxiety**, wariness of a person he does not know, and **separation anxiety**, distress when a familiar caregiver leaves him.

Babies rarely react negatively to strangers before age 6 months, commonly do so by 8 or 9 months, and do so more and more throughout the rest of the first year (Sroufe, 1997). This change may reflect cognitive development. Alex's stranger anxiety involves memory for faces, the ability to compare the stranger's appearance with his mother's, and perhaps the recollection of situations in which he has been left with a stranger (Lewis, 1997; Sroufe, 1997).

Long-Term Effects of Attachment

As attachment theory proposes, security of attachment seems to affect emotional, social, and cognitive competence (van IJzendoorn & Sagi, 1999). The more secure a child's attachment to a nurturing adult, the easier it seems to be for the child to develop good relationships with others.

Securely attached toddlers tend to have more positive interactions with peers, their friendly overtures are more likely to be accepted (Fagot, 1997), and they have an easier time adapting to child care (Ahnert, Gunnar, Lamb, & Barthel, 2004). Insecurely attached toddlers tend to show more fear, distress, and anger, whereas securely attached children are more joyful (Kochanska, 2001), and related ways of thinking and feeling can persist into adulthood (Simard, Moss, & Pascuzzo, 2011).

Between ages 3 and 5, securely attached children are likely to be more curious, competent, empathic, resilient, and self-confident; to get along better with other children; and to form closer friendships than children who were insecurely attached as infants (J. L. Jacobson & Wille, 1986; Youngblade & Belsky, 1992). They interact more positively with parents, preschool teachers, and peers, and are better able to resolve conflicts (Elicker, Englund, & Sroufe, 1992). They tend to have a more positive self-image (Verschueren, Marcoen, & Schoefs, 1996). Their advantages continue. In a Canadian laboratory observation, attachment patterns and the emotional quality of 6-year-olds' interactions with their mothers predicted the strength of the children's communicative skills, cognitive engagement, and mastery motivation at age 8 (Moss & St-Laurent, 2001).

Insecurely attached children, in contrast, sometimes have inhibitions and negative emotions in toddlerhood, hostility toward other children at age 5, and dependency during the school years (Calkins & Fox, 1992; Kochanska, 2001; Lyons-Ruth, Alpern, & Repacholi, 1993; Sroufe, Carlson, & Shulman, 1993). Those with disorganized attachment tend to have behaviour problems at all levels of schooling and psychiatric disorders at age 17 (Carlson, 1998).

Transmission of Attachment Patterns

The *Adult Attachment Interview (AAI)* (George, Kaplan, & Main, 1985; Main, 1995) asks adults to recall and interpret feelings and experiences related to their childhood attachments. Studies using the AAI have found that the way adults recall early experiences with parents or caregivers is related to their emotional well-being and may influence the way they respond to their own children (Adam, Gunnar, & Tanaka, 2004). A mother who recalls being securely attached to her mother or who has effectively dealt with memories of insecure attachment is better at recognizing her baby's attachment behaviours, responding encouragingly, and helping the baby form a secure attachment to her (Bretherton, 1990). Mothers who are preoccupied with their past attachment relationships tend to show anger and intrusiveness in interactions with their children. Depressed mothers who dismiss memories of their past attachments tend to be cold and unresponsive to their children (Adam et al., 2004).

Fortunately, the cycle of insecure attachment can be broken. Interventions that focus on maternal sensitivity—teaching mothers to more accurately "read" their babies' emotional signals—are effective in affecting the security of infants (Klein-Velderman, Bakermans-Kranenburg, Juffer, & van IJzendoorn, 2006).

MUTUAL REGULATION

At 1 month, Alex gazed attentively at his mother's face. At 2 months, when his mother smiled at him and rubbed his tummy, he smiled back. By the third month, Alex smiled first, inviting his mother to play (Lavelli & Fogel, 2005).

Infants have a strong drive to interact with others; they want and need to communicate with us. The ability of both infant and caregiver to respond appropriately and sensitively to each other's mental and emotional states is known as **mutual regulation**. Infants take an active part in mutual regulation by sending behavioural signals, like Alex's smile, that influence the way caregivers behave toward them (Lundy, 2003). Healthy interaction occurs when a caregiver reads a baby's signals accurately and responds appropriately. When a baby's goals are met, the baby is joyful or at least interested (Tronick, 1989). If a caregiver ignores an invitation to play or insists on playing when the baby has signalled "I don't feel like it," the baby may feel frustrated or sad. Normally, interaction moves back and forth between well-regulated and poorly regulated states, and babies learn from these shifts how to send signals and what to do when their initial signals are not effective. Even very young infants can perceive emotions expressed by others and can adjust their own behaviour accordingly (Legerstee & Varghese, 2001; Montague & Walker-Andrews, 2001). Researchers have developed a means of investigating this process—the still-face paradigm—and have also studied social referencing, where toddlers use interaction partners deliberately to make sense of ambiguous situations.

Measuring Mutual Regulation

Mutual regulation in 2- to 9-month-old infants is measured using the **still-face paradigm** (Tronick, Als, Adamson, Wise, & Brazelton, 1978). In the still-face episode, the mother suddenly becomes stony-faced, silent, and unresponsive after

mutual regulation Process by which infant and caregiver communicate emotional states to each other and respond appropriately.

still-face paradigm Research procedure used to measure mutual regulation in infants 2 to 9 months old.

first interacting normally with the baby. During the still-face episode, infants tend to stop smiling and looking at the mother. They may make faces, sounds, or gestures or may touch themselves, their clothing, or a chair, apparently to comfort themselves or to relieve the emotional stress created by the mother's unexpected behaviour (Weinberg & Tronick, 1996). In essence, they become dysregulated.

How do infants react after the still-face procedure? Most babies show sad or angry facial expressions, "pick-me-up" gestures, distancing, and indications of stress, as well as an increased tendency to fuss and cry, suggesting that the negative feelings stirred by a breakdown in mutual regulation were not readily eased (Weinberg & Tronick, 1996).

The still-face reaction seems to be similar in Eastern and Western cultures and in interactions with both fathers and mothers. In cross-cultural experiments, both Chinese and Canadian infants responded similarly to mothers and fathers—and also to strangers—in comparison with control groups that did not experience the still-face episode (Kisilevsky et al., 1998).

Social Referencing

Alex and his mother are visiting a new daycare for the first time. Alex's mother places him on the ground and he looks around, taking in the toys, laughing children, and bright colours. Still unsure, he turns back toward his mother, makes eye contact, and notes her warm smile. Comforted by this, he begins to explore his environment.

When babies look at their caregivers upon encountering an ambiguous, confusing, or unfamiliar situation they are engaging in **social referencing**, seeking out emotional information to guide behaviour (Hertenstein & Campos, 2004). For example, when exposed to jiggling or vibrating toys, both 12- and 18-month-olds moved closer to or farther from the toys depending on the experimenters' expressed emotional reactions ("Yecch!" or "Nice!") (Moses, Baldwin, Rosicky, & Tidball, 2001). Social referencing may play a role in such key developments of toddlerhood as the rise of self-conscious emotions (embarrassment and pride), the development of a sense of self, and the processes of socialization and internalization.

The Developing Self

About halfway between their first and second birthdays, babies become toddlers. This transformation can be seen in such physical and cognitive skills as walking and talking, and also in the ways children express their personalities and interact with others. A toddler becomes a more active, intentional partner in interactions and sometimes initiates them. This helps toddlers gain communicative skills and social competence and motivate compliance with a parent's wishes (Harrist & Waugh, 2002).

Three key areas of psychosocial development for toddlers are the emerging sense of self; the growth of autonomy, or self-determination; and socialization, or internalization of behavioural standards.

THE EMERGING SENSE OF SELF

The **self-concept** is our image of ourselves—our total picture of our abilities and traits. It describes what we know and feel about ourselves and guides our actions (Harter, 1998).

Ask Yourself

4. Erikson argued that the first stage of psychosocial development involved developing a sense of trust. The following parental characteristics most important for this are
   a. being biological (as opposed to adoptive) parents.
   b. being a mother (as opposed to a father).
   c. being of higher socio-economic status.
   d. being sensitive, responsive, and consistent in caregiving.

5. The Strange Situation is used to assess attachment by exposing the baby to gradually increasing levels of stress and thereby triggering attachment behaviours. Describe two events in the real world in which babies would be expected to show similar attachment behaviours.

6. April cries loudly when her mother leaves the room during the Strange Situation, but quiets immediately upon her return, snuggling in close to her mother. John cries loudly when his mother leaves the room, but upon her return, continues to cry in an angry fashion for some time. April is likely to have a(n) _____ attachment style while John is likely to have a(n) _____ attachment style.
   a. secure; resistant
   b. resistant; secure
   c. resistant; avoidant
   d. avoidant; secure
   e. avoidant; resistant

7. Name two variables that influence the development of attachment in infants.

8. Eight-month-old Gus cries loudly when carried by people he does not know well. Gus is showing
   a. separation anxiety.
   b. stranger anxiety.
   c. temperament.
   d. social referencing.

9. Generally, babies respond to the still-face paradigm with
   a. flat emotional affect.
   b. emotional distress.
   c. increased physical activity.
   d. increased vocalization.

---

social referencing Understanding an ambiguous situation by seeking out another person's perception of it.

self-concept Sense of self; descriptive and evaluative mental picture of one's abilities and traits.

When does the self-concept develop? By at least 3 months, infants pay attention to their mirror image (Courage & Howe, 2002). Four- to 9-month-olds show more interest in images of others than of themselves (Rochat & Striano, 2002). This early perceptual discrimination may be the foundation of the conceptual self-concept that develops in the middle of the second year.

Between 4 and 10 months, when infants learn to reach, grasp, and make things happen, they experience a sense of *personal agency*, the realization that they can control external events. At about this time, infants develop *self-coherence*, the sense of being a physical whole with boundaries separate from the rest of their world (Harter, 1998). These developments occur in interaction with caregivers in games such as peekaboo, in which the infant becomes increasingly aware of the difference between self and others ("I see you!").

The emergence of self-recognition ("the idea of the me")—a conscious knowledge of the self as a distinct, identifiable being (Lewis, 2003)—builds on this dawning perceptual discrimination between self and others. Self-recognition can be tested by studying whether infants recognize themselves in a mirror (Lewis & Carmody, 2008). In a classic line of research, investigators dabbed rouge on the noses of 6- to 24-month-olds and sat them in front of a mirror. Three-fourths of 18-month-olds and all 24-month-olds touched their red noses more often than before, whereas babies younger than 15 months never did. This behaviour suggests that these toddlers had self-awareness. They knew they did not normally have red noses and recognized the image in the mirror as their own (Lewis & Brooks, 1974).

Pretend play, which typically begins during the last half of the second year, is an early indication of the ability to understand others' mental states as well as the child's own (Lewis & Carmody, 2008). A third measure or sign of self-recognition is the use of first-person pronouns, such as *me* and *mine*, usually at 20 to 24 months (Lewis & Carmody, 2008). Between 19 and 30 months, children's rapid language development enables them to think and talk about the self and to incorporate parents' verbal descriptions ("You're so smart!" "What a big boy!") into their emerging self-image (Stipek, Gralinski, & Kopp, 1990).

Brain maturation underlies the development of self-representation. Magnetic resonance imaging (MRI) scans of 15- to 30-month-olds showed that signal intensities in a specific brain region, the left temporo-parietal junction, were strongest in children,

A girl showing clear signs of self-recognition.

regardless of age, who recognized their image in a mirror, engaged in pretend play with others, and used personal pronouns (Lewis & Carmody, 2008).

DEVELOPING AUTONOMY

As children mature, they are driven to seek independence from the very adults to whom they are attached. "I do it!" is the byword as toddlers use their developing muscles and minds to try to do everything on their own—not only to walk but also to feed and dress themselves and to explore their world.

Erikson (1950) identified the period from about 18 months to 3 years as the second stage in psychosocial development, **autonomy versus shame and doubt**. Having come through infancy with a sense of basic trust in the world and an awakening self-awareness, toddlers begin to substitute their own judgment for their caregivers'. The virtue, or strength, that emerges during this stage is will. As children are better able to make their wishes understood, they become more powerful and independent. Since unlimited freedom is neither safe nor healthy, said Erikson, shame and doubt have a necessary place. Toddlers need adults to set appropriate limits, and shame and doubt help them recognize the need for those limits.

In Canada, the "terrible twos" are a normal sign of the drive for autonomy—from this perspective, this period is better described as the "terrific twos"! This drive typically shows itself in the form of negativism, the tendency to shout "No!" just for the sake of resisting authority. Almost all Canadian children show negativism to some degree; it usually

autonomy versus shame and doubt Erikson's second stage in psychosocial development, in which children achieve a balance between self-determination and control by others.

Did you know?

Chimpanzees and dolphins also pass the self-recognition task and will twist and turn to view a stripe of paint on their body in a mirror.

Perspectives on Diversity

STRUGGLES WITH TODDLERS

Are the "terrible twos" a normal phase in child development? Although many Western parents and psychologists think so, this transition does not appear to be universal.

One arena in which issues of autonomy and control appear in Western cultures is in sibling conflicts over toys. To explore these issues, a cross-cultural study compared 16 Mayan families in San Pedro, Guatemala, with 16 middle-class European-American families in Salt Lake City, Utah (Mosier & Rogoff, 2003). All of the families had toddlers and older siblings. The researchers handed the mother a series of attractive objects and, in the presence of the older sibling, asked the mother to help the toddler operate them.

The older siblings in Salt Lake City often tried to take and play with the objects. However, the older San Pedro children would offer to help their younger siblings work the objects, or the two children would play with them together. When there was a conflict over possession of the objects, San Pedro mothers favoured the toddlers and gave them the toy. In contrast, in more than one-third of the interactions

in Salt Lake City, the mothers tried to treat both children equally, negotiating with them or suggesting that they take turns or share.

What explains these cultural contrasts? A clue emerged when the mothers were asked at what age children can be held responsible for their actions. Most of the Salt Lake City mothers maintained that their toddlers already understood the consequences of touching prohibited objects. Yet all but one of the San Pedro mothers placed the age of understanding social consequences of actions much later—between 2 and 3 years. The Salt Lake City mothers regarded their toddlers as capable of intentional misbehaviour and punished their toddlers for it; most San Pedro mothers did not.

The researchers suggest that the terrible twos may be a phase specific to societies that place individual freedom before the needs of the group. Research such as this suggests that in societies that place higher value on group needs, freedom of choice does still exist, but it goes hand in hand with interdependence, responsibility, and expectations of cooperation.

begins before age 2, tends to peak at about 3½ to 4, and declines by age 6. This "battle of wills" is a healthy part of growing up, showing children's growing awareness that their own goals can be different from those of their caregivers

Sometimes a source of conflict, autonomy, and will, like that which leads you to brush your own teeth, comes from a combination of awareness of your own goals, supportive parenting, and learning self-control.

(Baillargeon, Sward, Keenan, & Cao, 2011). Caregivers who view children's expressions of self-will as a normal, healthy striving for independence—not as stubbornness— can help them learn self-control, contribute to their sense of competence, and avoid excessive conflict.

With supportive parenting, the terrible twos can be relatively conflict-free (Lipscomb et al., 2011), and benefits can persist into middle childhood (Davidov & Grusec, 2006). In some developing countries, the transition from infancy to early childhood is relatively smooth and harmonious, as we discuss in the Perspectives on Diversity box.

SOCIALIZATION

Moral development, the process by which children grow to understand what is right or wrong, is a complex ongoing process that encompasses cognitive, emotional, and environmental influences. Moral development is based upon the internalization of parental beliefs, a process known as socialization.

Socialization is the process by which children develop habits, skills, values, and motives that make them responsible, productive members of society. Compliance with

socialization Development of habits, skills, values, and motives shared by responsible, productive members of a society.

parental expectations can be seen as a first step toward compliance with societal standards; however, the ultimate goal is the **internalization** of these standards. Children who are successfully socialized no longer merely obey rules or commands to get rewards or avoid punishment; they have made society's standards their own (Grusec & Goodnow, 1994; Kochanska, Tjebkes, & Forman, 1998). Areas of socialization that are developing during the toddler years include self-regulation and conscience. Successful socialization is impacted by both internal and external factors (Almas, Grusec, & Tackett, 2011; Awong, Grusec, & Sorensen, 2008).

Developing Self-Regulation

Alex, age 2, is about to poke his finger into an electric outlet. In his child-proofed apartment, the sockets are covered, but not here in his grandmother's home. When Alex hears his father shout, "No!" the toddler pulls his arm back. The next time he goes near an outlet, he starts to point his finger, hesitates, and then says "No." He has stopped himself from doing something he remembers he is not supposed to do. He is beginning to show **self-regulation**: control of his behaviour to conform to a caregiver's demands or expectations, even when the caregiver is not present.

Before they can control their behaviour, children may need to be able to regulate their attentional processes and to modulate negative emotions (Eisenberg, 2000). Attentional regulation enables children to develop willpower and cope with frustration (Sethi, Mischel, Aber, Shoda, & Rodriguez, 2000).

The growth of self-regulation parallels the development of the self-conscious and evaluative emotions, such as empathy, shame, and guilt (Lewis, 1998). It requires the ability to wait for gratification. It is correlated with measures of conscience development, such as resisting temptation and making amends for wrongdoing (Eisenberg, 2000). In most children, the full development of self-regulation takes at least three years (Kopp, 1982).

Developing Conscience

Conscience includes both emotional discomfort about doing something wrong and the ability to refrain from doing it. Conscience depends on a willingness to do the right thing because a child believes it is right, not, as in self-regulation, just because someone else said so.

Grazyna Kochanska (1993, 1995, 1997a, 1997b) and her colleagues have looked for the origins of conscience. Researchers videotaped 103 children, aged 26 to 41 months, and their mothers playing together with toys. After a free-play period, a mother would give her child 15 minutes to put away the toys, a task that required ignoring a special shelf with other, unusually attractive toys, such as a bubble gum machine, a walkie-talkie, and a music box.

Children were judged to show **committed compliance** if they willingly followed the orders to clean up and not to touch the special toys without reminders or lapses. Children showed **situational compliance** if they needed prompting (Kochanska & Aksan, 1995). Committed compliance is related to internalization of parental values and rules (Kochanska, Coy, & Murray, 2001) and tends to increase with age, whereas situational compliance decreases (Kochanska et al., 1998). Mothers of committed compliers tend to rely on gentle guidance rather than force, threats, or other forms of negative control (Eisenberg, 2000; Kochanska, Aksan, Knaack, & Rhines, 2004).

Factors in the Success of Socialization

The way parents go about socializing a child, together with a child's temperament and the quality of the parent-child relationship, may help predict how hard or easy socialization will be. Factors in the success of socialization include security of attachment, observational learning from parents' behaviour, and the mutual responsiveness of parent and child (Kochanska et al., 2004). However, not all children respond to socialization in the same way. For example, a temperamentally fearful toddler may respond better to gentle reminders than to strong admonitions, whereas a bolder toddler may require more assertive parenting (Kochanska, Aksan, & Joy, 2007).

Secure attachment and a warm, mutually responsive parent-child relationship seem to foster committed compliance and conscience development. Children with mutually responsive relationships with their mothers at age 2 tended to show moral emotions such as guilt and empathy, moral conduct in the face of strong temptation, and more advanced moral cognition in the early school years (Kochanska, 2002). Constructive conflict that involves negotiation, reasoning, and resolution can help children develop moral understanding by enabling them to see another point of view. In one observational study, 2½-year-olds whose mothers gave clear explanations for their requests, compromised, discussed emotions, or bargained with the child were better able to resist temptation at age 3 than children whose mothers had threatened, teased, insisted, or given in (Laible & Thompson, 2002).

GENDER

Being male or female affects how people look, how they move their bodies, and how they work, play, and dress. It influences what they think about themselves and what

internalization During socialization, process by which children accept societal standards of conduct as their own.

self-regulation A person's independent control of behaviour to conform to understood social expectations.

conscience Internal standards of behaviour, which usually control one's conduct and produce emotional discomfort when violated.

committed compliance Kochanska's term for wholehearted obedience of a parent's orders without reminders or lapses.

situational compliance Kochanska's term for obedience of a parent's orders only in the presence of signs of ongoing parental control.

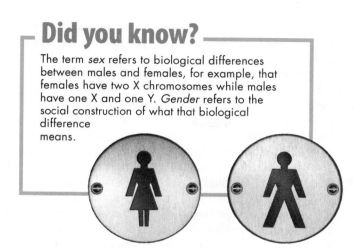

others think of them. All these characteristics—and more—are included in the word **gender**: what it means to be male or female.

The following discussion focuses primarily on gender differences, a controversial area in the field of psychology. Most of the differences are small; indeed, the controversy would not exist if the differences were large and obvious. However, it is important to note prior to moving on to this discussion that while there are small differences, overall males and females are more alike than different (Hyde, 2005).

Sex and Gender Differences in Infants and Toddlers

Measurable differences between baby boys and baby girls are few. Boys are a bit longer and heavier and may be slightly stronger and more active, but are physically more vulnerable from conception on. Girls are less reactive to stress and more likely to survive infancy (Davis & Emory, 1995; Keenan & Shaw, 1997). Boys' brains at birth are about 10 percent larger than girls' brains, a difference that continues into adulthood (Gilmore et al., 2007). Despite these differences, they achieve the motor milestones of infancy at about the same times.

One of the earliest *behavioural* differences between boys and girls, appearing between ages 1 and 2, is a preference for toys, play activities, and playmates of the same sex. For example, in one study, 18-month-old boys preferred to play with toy cars, while the girls preferred to play with dolls (Serbin, Poulin-Dubois, Colburne, Sen, & Eichstedt, 2001). Toddlers, and to a lesser extent babies, prefer to play with others of the same sex (Campbell, Shirley, Heywood, & Crook, 2000), perhaps because boys as young as 17 months tend to play more aggressively than girls (Baillargeon et al., 2007).

Infants begin to perceive differences between males and females long before their behaviour is gender-differentiated

and even before they can talk. Habituation studies have found that 6-month-olds respond differently to male and female voices. By 9 to 12 months, infants can tell the difference between male and female faces, apparently on the basis of hair and clothing. From about 24 to 36 months, infants begin to associate gender-typical toys, such as dolls, with a face of the correct gender, although boys lag a bit behind girls in this regard (Martin, Ruble, & Szkrybalo, 2002).

How Parents Shape Gender Differences

Parents begin to influence boys' and girls' personalities very early. Fathers, especially, promote **gender-typing**, the process by which children learn behaviour that their culture considers appropriate for each sex (Bronstein, 1988). Fathers treat boys and girls more differently than mothers do, even during the first year (Doucet, 2009; M. E. Snow, Jacklin, & Maccoby, 1983). During the second year, fathers talk more and spend more time with sons than with daughters (Lamb, 1981). Mothers talk more, and more supportively, to daughters than to sons (Leaper, Anderson, & Sanders, 1998), and girls at this age tend to be more talkative than boys (Leaper & Smith, 2004). Fathers of toddlers play more roughly with sons and show more sensitivity to daughters (Kelley, Smith, Green, Berndt, & Rogers, 1998), and parents often react differently to aggressive behaviours in boys and girls (Martin & Ross, 2005).

However, a highly physical style of play, characteristic of many fathers in Canada, is not typical of fathers in all cultures. Swedish and German fathers usually do not play with their babies this way (Lamb, Frodi, Frodi, & Hwang, 1982). African Aka fathers (Hewlett, 1987) and those in New Delhi, India, also tend to play gently with small children (Roopnarine, Hooper, Ahmeduzzaman, & Pollack, 1993). Such cross-cultural variations suggest that rough play may not be entirely a biologically based gender difference but is strongly culturally influenced.

Preference for toys is one of the earliest behavioural differences between boy and girls.

---

gender   Significance of being male or female.

gender-typing   Socialization process by which children, at an early age, learn appropriate gender roles.

10. Two-year-old Billy reaches up to touch his new haircut after looking at himself in the mirror. Billy is exhibiting
    a. self-coherence.
    b. self-regulation.
    c. internalization.
    d. self-awareness.

11. Committed compliance involves _____ while situational compliance involves _____.

12. Shy babies can become overwhelmed with harsh parenting techniques, while very bold babies may need a firmer hand. The match between child temperament and parenting techniques can be considered as an issue of
    a. receptive cooperation.
    b. mutual synchrony.
    c. goodness of fit.
    d. gender.

13. Name two factors that impact successful socialization.

14. What is one of the earliest behavioural differences between boys and girls?

15. Gender-typing can be defined as
    a. a genetic test to determine sex.
    b. highly characteristic play styles.
    c. adult sex roles of a culture.
    d. the process by which children learn the appropriate behaviours for their sex.

Relationships with Other Children

Although parents exert a major influence on children's lives, relationships with other children—both in the home and out of it—are important too. These relationships shape and mould us over time, and become increasingly important with age.

SIBLINGS

If you have brothers or sisters, your relationships with them are likely to be the longest-lasting you will ever have. They share your roots; they knew you when you were young; they accepted or rejected the same parental values; and they probably deal with you more candidly than almost anyone else you know.

Sibling relationships begin with the birth of a new baby in a household and continue to develop, both positively and negatively, throughout childhood. Sibling relationships play a distinct role in socialization, different from the role of relationships with parents or peers (Vandell, 2000). Lessons and skills learned from interactions with siblings—such as conflict and cooperation—carry over to relationships outside the home (Brody, 1998).

Children react in various ways to the arrival of a sibling. To bid for the mother's attention, some suck their thumbs, wet their pants, or use baby talk. Some suggest taking the baby back to the hospital or flushing it down the toilet. Some take pride in being the "big ones," who can dress themselves and help care for the baby. Much of the variation in children's adjustment to a new baby may have to do with such factors as the older child's age, the quality of his or her relationship with the mother, and the family atmosphere.

As babies begin to move around and become more assertive, they inevitably come into conflict with siblings—at least in Western culture. Sibling conflict increases dramatically after the younger child reaches age 18 months (Vandell & Bailey, 1992). During the next few months, younger siblings begin to participate more fully in family interactions. As they do, they become more aware of others' intentions and feelings. They begin to recognize what kind of behaviour will upset or annoy an older brother or sister and what behaviour is considered naughty or good (Dunn & Munn, 1985; Perlman, Garfinkel, & Turrell, 2007).

As this cognitive and social understanding grows, sibling conflict tends to become more constructive, and the younger sibling participates in attempts to reconcile. Constructive conflict helps children recognize each other's needs, wishes, and point of view, and it helps them learn how to fight, disagree, and compromise within the context of a safe, stable relationship (Vandell & Bailey, 1992).

Sibling relationships play a distinct role in socialization, with lessons and skills learned that carry over to relationships outside the home.

PEERS

Infants and, even more so, toddlers show interest in people outside the home, particularly people their own size. During the first few months, they look, smile, and coo at other babies. From about 6 to 12 months, they increasingly smile at, touch, and babble to them (Hay, Pedersen, & Nash, 1982). From about 1½ years to almost 3, children show growing interest in and increased understanding of what other children do (Eckerman, Davis, & Didow, 1989).

Games such as follow-the-leader help toddlers connect with other children and pave the way for more-complex games during the preschool years (Eckerman et al., 1989). Imitation of each other's actions leads to more frequent verbal communication ("You go in playhouse" or "Look at me"), which helps peers coordinate joint activity (Eckerman & Didow, 1996). Cooperative activity develops

during the second and third years as social understanding grows (Brownell, Ramani, & Zerwas, 2006). Conflict too can have a purpose, helping children learn how to negotiate and resolve disputes (Caplan, Vespo, Pedersen, & Hay, 1991), and children learn to apply culture-based expectations in these situations (French et al., 2011).

Sociability is also influenced by experience; babies who spend time with other babies, as in child care, become sociable earlier than those who spend all their time at home alone. They also engage in increasingly complex play with peers. However, this depends on the quality of caregiving and the security of the child's attachment (Howes, 1997a, 1997b).

Ask Yourself

16. Name three factors that impact how children respond to the birth of a new sibling.

17. Conflict within peer relationships
    a. is rare in preschool children.
    b. can be useful for learning skills such as the resolution of disputes.
    c. drops sharply once children attain language.
    d. increases sharply once children attain language.

SUMMARY

CHAPTER 7 — PHYSIOSOCIAL DEVELOPMENT, BIRTH TO AGE 3

LO 1

Describe the development of and major changes in the expression of emotions and temperament in early childhood.

- Crying, smiling, and laughing are early signs of emotion. Other indicators include facial expressions, motor activity, body language, and physiological changes.
- The repertoire of basic emotions seems to be universal, but there are cultural variations in their expression.
- Complex emotions seem to develop from earlier, simpler ones. Self-conscious and evaluative emotions arise after the development of self-awareness.
- Separate but interacting regions of the brain may be responsible for various emotional states.

Continued

LO1

Describe the development of and major changes in the expression of emotions and temperament in early childhood.

Continued

- Many children seem to fall into three categories of temperament: *easy, difficult,* and *slow-to-warm-up.* Temperamental patterns appear to be largely inborn and to have a biological basis. They are generally stable but can be modified by experience.
- Goodness of fit between a child's temperament and environmental demands aids adjustment.
- Cross-cultural differences in temperament may reflect child-raising practices.

LO2

Discuss the causes and consequences of the development of attachment.

- According to Erikson, infants in the first 18 months experience the first crisis in personality development, basic trust versus basic mistrust. Sensitive, responsive, consistent caregiving is the key to successful resolution of this crisis.
- Research based on the Strange Situation has found four patterns of attachment: secure, avoidant, ambivalent (resistant), and disorganized-disoriented.
- Attachment patterns may depend on a baby's temperament, as well as on the quality of parenting, and may have long-term implications for development. A parent's memories of childhood attachment can influence his or her own child's attachment.
- Separation anxiety and stranger anxiety may arise during the second half of the first year and appear to be related to temperament and circumstances.
- Mutual regulation enables babies to play an active part in regulating their emotional states.
- Social referencing has been observed by 12 months and may play a role in key psychosocial developments of toddlerhood.

LO3

Explain how the developing sense of self and the emergence of autonomy impact socialization and the development of moral behaviours.

- Self-concept develops by the middle of the second year and depends on perceptual self-discrimination.
- Erikson's second stage concerns autonomy versus shame and doubt. Negativism is a normal manifestation of the shift from external control to self-control.
- Socialization, which rests on internalization of societally approved standards, begins with the development of self-regulation.
- A precursor of conscience is committed compliance to a caregiver's demands; toddlers who show committed compliance tend to internalize adult rules more readily than those who show situational compliance.
- Parenting practices, a child's temperament, and the quality of the parent-child relationship may affect the ease and success of socialization.
- Although significant gender differences typically do not appear until after infancy, parents—particularly fathers—begin gender-typing boys and girls almost from birth.

LO4

Discuss how siblings and peers affect the psychosocial development of young children.

- A child's adjustment to a new baby may depend on the child's age, the quality of her or his relationship with the mother, and the family atmosphere.
- Sibling relationships play a distinct role in socialization; what children learn from relations with siblings carries over to relationships outside the home.
- Between 1½ and 3 years of age, children tend to show more interest in other children and increasing understanding of how to deal with them.

ANSWERS TO Ask Yourself

Answers: 1–c; 2–Self-awareness involves the cognitive understanding that one has a recognizable identity, separate and different from the rest of their world. This is required for the self-conscious emotions because children must understand that others might have opinions about the wrongness or rightness of their behaviour different from their own before they can understand and feel these social emotions; 3–c; 4–d; 5–Any situation in which an infant is separated and then reunited with parents would be expected to elicit attachment-related behaviours. For example, you might expect similar processes at daycare drop-offs and pick-ups, or when parents leave a child with an alternative caregiver such as a babysitter or nanny; 6–a; 7–Among the variables that influence attachment are parenting practices (such as how sensitive or responsive the parent is) and infant temperament; 8–b; 9–b; 10–d; 11–Committed compliance involves willingly following orders given by parents without reminders or lapses, while situation compliance involves following orders given by parents with prompting; 12–c; 13–Factors that impact successful socialization include how parents socialize a child, child temperament, the quality of the parent–child relationship, security of attachment, observational learning from parents' behaviour, and the mutual responsiveness of parent and child; 14–One of the earliest behavioural differences between boys and girls is a preference for toys, play activities, and playmates of the same sex; 15–d; 16–Among the factors that impact how a child responds to the birth of a new sibling are the older child's age, the quality of his or her relationship with the mother, and the family atmosphere; 17–b

connect | **LEARNSMART** | **SMARTBOOK**

For more information on the resources available from McGraw-Hill Ryerson, go to **www.mcgrawhill.ca/he/solutions**.

PHYSICAL DEVELOPMENT AND HEALTH IN

WHAT'S TO COME

Physical Growth

Sleep

Motor Development

Health and Safety

It was Eva's first day of kindergarten. As her father drove her to school, he reflected on how much she had changed in just a few short years. At 2, Eva had been a chunky baby with round cheeks and brown curls, enthusiastically toddling around her rapidly expanding world. Now at 5 years old, Eva had lost her baby belly, and her limbs had lengthened. She could hop on either foot, walk backwards, and use utensils with ease. She chattered away and asked questions about everything around her, and she had strong preferences about foods, clothes, and toys.

In this chapter, we will discuss physical development during the years from ages 3 to 6. In early childhood, children's body proportions change and they get taller and slimmer. They need less sleep and are more likely to develop sleep problems. They improve in running, hopping, skipping, jumping, and throwing balls. They also become better at tying shoelaces (in bows instead of knots), drawing with crayons (on paper rather than on walls), and pouring cereal (into the bowl, not onto the floor); they also begin to show a preference for using either the right or left hand. They also, as a group, encounter a range of health and safety risks from obesity to allergies to those with environmental bases.

EARLY CHILDHOOD

AS YOU READ

LO1   Describe the physical changes in young children's height, weight, and brain structure.

LO2   Summarize common sleep problems and disturbances in early childhood.

LO3   Summarize the continued development of fine and gross motor skills and discuss the influences on handedness.

LO4   Describe the common health risks of early childhood and describe how environmental influences can impact health.

Physical Growth

In early childhood, children slim down and shoot up. They need less sleep and are more likely to develop sleep problems. They improve in running, hopping, skipping, jumping, and throwing balls. They also become better at tying shoelaces (in bows instead of knots), drawing with crayons (on paper rather than on walls), and pouring cereal (into the bowl, not onto the floor); they also begin to show a preference for using either the right or left hand.

HEIGHT AND WEIGHT

Children grow rapidly between ages 3 and 6 but less quickly than during infancy and toddlerhood. At about age 3, children begin to take on the slender, athletic appearance of childhood. As abdominal muscles develop, the toddler potbelly tightens. The trunk, arms, and legs grow longer. The head is still relatively large, but the other parts of the body continue to catch up as proportions

steadily become more adultlike. Both boys and girls typically grow 5 to 8 cm (2 to 3 inches) a year during early childhood and gain about 2 to 3 kg (4 to 6 pounds) annually (Table 8.1). Boys' slight edge in height and weight continues until the growth spurt of puberty, which generally starts a few years earlier in girls and thus for a short while gives them a growth advantage.

Muscular and skeletal growth progresses, making children stronger. Cartilage turns to bone at a faster rate than before, and bones become harder, giving the child a firmer shape and protecting the internal organs. The increased capacities of the respiratory and circulatory systems build physical stamina and, along with the developing immune system, keep children healthier.

THE BRAIN

By the age of 3, the brain is approximately 90 percent of adult weight (Gabbard, 1996). The density of synapses in the prefrontal cortex peaks at age 4 (Lenroot & Giedd, 2006). Myelination of pathways for hearing is also complete around that age (Benes, Turtle, Khan, & Farol, 1994). By age 6, the brain has attained about 95 percent of its peak volume. However, wide individual differences exist. Two healthy, normally functioning children of the same age could have as much as a 50 percent difference in brain volume (Lenroot & Giedd, 2006).

From ages 3 to 6, the most rapid brain growth occurs in the frontal areas that regulate planning and organizing actions (P. M. Thompson et al., 2000). During early childhood, a gradual change occurs in the corpus callosum, a thick band of nerve fibres that links the left and right hemispheres. Progressive myelination of fibres in the corpus callosum permits more rapid transmission of information and better integration between hemispheres (Toga et al., 2006). This development, which continues until age 15, improves such functions as coordination of the senses, memory

	Height (cm)		Weight (kg)	
Age	Boys	Girls	Boys	Girls
3	96.0	95.0	14.5	14.0
4	103.0	103.0	16.5	16.0
5	110.0	109.5	18.5	18.0
6	116.0	115.0	20.5	20.0

TABLE 8.1 Physical Growth, Ages 3 to 6 (50th percentile*)

*Fifty percent of children in each category are above this height or weight level and 50 percent are below it.

Source: Based on the World Health Organization (WHO) Child Growth Standards (2006) and adapted for Canada by Dieticians of Canada, Canadian Paediatric Society, the College of Family Physicians of Canada and Community Health Nurses of Canada. (c) Dieticians of Canada, 2010.

processes, attention and arousal, and speech and hearing (Lenroot & Giedd, 2006). Given that frontal areas of the brain are still developing, it is not surprising that children's behaviours are not as easily self-regulated and inhibited as they are in later years.

Ask Yourself

1. Between the ages of 3 to 6 years, children's growth
   a. speeds up relative to growth in infancy and toddlerhood.
   b. continues, but slows relative to growth in infancy and toddlerhood.
   c. slows down dramatically until puberty.
   d. may slow down or speed up, depending on the individual child.

2. Name three bodily changes that occur in early childhood.

3. The most rapid brain growth from ages 3 to 6 is in
   a. the corpus callosum.
   b. the brain stem.
   c. motor areas of the brain.
   d. the frontal lobes.

Sleep

"Just one more drink of water," begged Eva, and 20 minutes later, "I need to go potty." Finally, Eva fell asleep at 10 p.m., occasionally mumbling in her sleep. Late at night, her parents woke to screaming. Her father ran into the bedroom to find Eva sitting up, bleary-eyed and confused. After a pat on the back, she settled back down. The next morning, she did not remember waking. Eva's sleep patterns are typical of young school-aged children, as we will see in the following section.

Sleep patterns change throughout the growing-up years (Iglowstein, Jenni, Molinari, & Largo, 2003; Figure 8.1), and early childhood has its own distinct rhythms. By age 5, most children average about 11 hours of sleep at night and give up daytime naps (Hoban, 2004).

Bedtime may bring on a form of separation anxiety, and the child may do all she or he can to avoid it. About a third of parents or caregivers report that their preschool child stalls at bedtime and that it takes 15 minutes or more for the child to fall asleep, and about 60 percent of children wake up at least once each night (National Sleep Foundation, 2004; Petit, Touchette, Tremblay, Boivin, & Montplaisir, 2007). Regular, consistent sleep routines can help minimize these problems. Children are likely to want a light left on and to sleep with a favourite toy or blanket. Such transitional objects, used repeatedly as bedtime companions, help a child shift from the dependence of infancy to the independence of later childhood. Young children who have become accustomed to going to sleep while feeding or rocking, however, may find it hard to fall asleep on their own (Hoban, 2004). Moreover, some children, even once they do get to sleep, show sleep disturbances that make it difficult for them to stay asleep; poor sleep quality has been associated with behavioural difficulties at home and in child care settings, and with less harmonious parent-child interactions (Bordeleau, Bernier, & Carrier, 2012; Hall, Scher, Zaidman-Zait, Espezel, & Warnock, 2011). Additional strategies for helping children go to sleep include establishing a regular, unrushed bedtime routine with about 20 minutes of quiet activities like story reading, bath time, avoiding scary or loud television shows or active play before bedtime, not feeding or rocking a child at bedtime, staying calm and not yielding to requests for "just one more story" or a drink of water, rewarding good bedtime behaviour, putting a child to sleep a little later, and helping a child to learn to relax, substituting pleasant thoughts for frightening ones (HealthlinkBC, 2011).

Sleep Requirements in Childhood

FIGURE 8.1 Unlike infants, who sleep about as long day and night, preschoolers get all or almost all their sleep in one long nighttime period. The number of hours of sleep steadily decreases throughout childhood, but individual children may need more or fewer hours than shown here.

Sources: Adapted from Galland, Taylor, Elder, & Herbison (2012); Mindell & Owens (2010); Sadeh, Mindell, Luedtke, & Wiegand (2009).

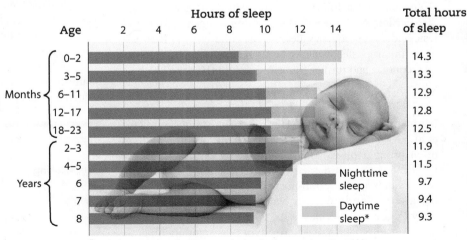

Age		Total hours of sleep
Months	0–2	14.3
	3–5	13.3
	6–11	12.9
	12–17	12.8
	18–23	12.5
Years	2–3	11.9
	4–5	11.5
	6	9.7
	7	9.4
	8	9.3

Nighttime sleep
Daytime sleep*

*Divided into typical number of naps per day. Length of naps may be quite variable.

SLEEP DISTURBANCES

About one in ten parents or caregivers of preschoolers say that their child has a sleep problem (National Sleep Foundation, 2004). Sleep disturbances may be caused by accidental activation of the brain's motor control system (Hobson & Silvestri, 1999) or by incomplete arousal from a deep sleep (Hoban, 2004), or may be triggered by disordered breathing or restless leg movements (Guilleminault, Palombini, Pelayo, & Chervin, 2003). These disturbances tend to run in families (Hoban, 2004), are often associated with separation anxiety (Petit et al., 2007), and may predict anxiety and depression in toddlers (Jansen et al., 2011). In most cases, they are only occasional and usually are outgrown. Some sleep issues may be the result of ineffective parenting practices that exacerbate rather than ease the problem. For example, allowing young children to nap in the daytime in order to catch up on sleep can result in difficulty getting to sleep later that evening. Persistent sleep problems may indicate an emotional, physiological, or neurological condition that needs to be examined. Possible sleep disturbances include night terrors, walking and talking while asleep, and nightmares.

Night Terrors

A child who experiences a **night terror** appears to awaken abruptly early in the night from a deep sleep in a state of agitation. The child may scream and sit up in bed, breathing rapidly and staring or thrashing about. Yet he is not really awake. He quiets down quickly, and the next morning remembers nothing about the episode. Night terrors generally peak between 2½ and 4 years of age and decline thereafter, and some researchers believe them to be related to anxiety (Petit et al., 2007). Prevalence estimates of night terrors vary widely, ranging from approximately 6 (Laberge, Tremblay, Vitaro, & Montplaisir, 2000) to almost 40 (Petit et al., 2007) percent of children.

Sleep Walking and Talking

Walking and talking during sleep are fairly common in early and middle childhood. Estimates are that approximately 9 percent of children between the ages of 3 and 10 years sleepwalk, and a full 37 percent sleeptalk (Laberge et al., 2000). **Sleepwalking** and **sleeptalking** are generally harmless, and their frequency declines as children age. It is best not to interrupt sleepwalking or night terrors, as interruptions may confuse and further frighten the child (Hoban, 2004).

Nightmares

Nightmares are common during early childhood (Petit et al., 2007). They usually occur toward morning and are often brought on by staying up too late, eating a heavy meal close to bedtime, or overexcitement—for example, from watching an action-packed television program, seeing a terrifying movie, or hearing a frightening bedtime story (Vgontzas & Kales, 1999). An occasional bad dream is no cause for alarm, but frequent or persistent nightmares, especially those that make a child fearful or anxious during waking hours, may signal excessive stress (Hoban, 2004). A Canadian intervention for persistent nightmares (one or more times per week for at least six months) involves image rehearsal therapy. Children are instructed to change the content of their most recent nightmare, and to visualize and rehearse the new version while relaxed. This intervention reduced nightmare frequency in the short and long term in children (St.-Onge, Mercier, & De Koninck, 2009).

Did you know?

Sleeping less than 12 hours a day as an infant is associated with an increased risk of being overweight in preschool and childhood (Taveras, Rifas-Shiman, Oken, Gunderson, & Gillman, 2008).

BED-WETTING AND TOILET TRAINING

Most children stay dry, day and night, by age 3 to 5 years, but **enuresis**—repeated, involuntary urination at night by children old enough to be expected to have bladder control—is not unusual. About 10 to 15 percent of 5-year-olds, more commonly boys, wet the bed regularly, often while sleeping deeply. More than half outgrow bed-wetting by age 8 without special help (Community Paediatrics Committee, Canadian Paediatric Society, 2005).

Children of preschool age normally recognize the sensation of a full bladder while asleep and awaken to empty it. Children who wet the bed do not yet have this awareness. Enuresis runs in families, suggesting that genetics may play a role. The discovery of the approximate site of a gene linked to enuresis (Eiberg, 1995; von Gontard, Heron, & Joinson 2011) points to heredity as a major factor, possibly in combination with slow motor maturation (von Gontard, Schmelzer, Seifen, & Pukrop, 2001), sleep apnea (Umlauf & Chasens, 2003), allergies, or poor behavioural control (Goleman, 1995). About 75 percent of bed-wetters have a close relative who also wets the bed, and identical twins are more concordant for the condition than fraternal twins (American Psychiatric Association, 1994).

Children and their parents need to be reassured that enuresis is common and not serious. Treatment is most effective if delayed until the child is able to understand and

---

night terror Abrupt awakening from a deep sleep in a state of agitation.

sleepwalking Walking around and sometimes performing other functions while asleep.

sleeptalking Talking while asleep.

nightmares A bad dream, sometimes brought on by staying up too late, eating a heavy meal close to bedtime, or overexcitement.

enuresis Repeated urination in clothing or in bed.

adhere to instruction, and often includes either enuresis alarms that wake the child when he or she begins to urinate, or medications. The child is not to blame and should not be punished. Generally, parents need not do anything unless children themselves are distressed by bed-wetting. Enuresis that persists beyond age 8 to 10 may be related to poor self-concept or other psychological problems (Canadian Paediatric Society, 2012a; Community Paedriatics Committee, Canadian Paediatric Society, 2005).

Although there is very little evidence to favour any one method for toilet training, the Canadian Paediatric Society recommends starting by 18 months, but only if the child shows interest. Children learn when physiologically (with bowel and bladder control, have basic gross motor skills) and emotionally ready. A positive and consistent approach, involving praise and child-oriented guidance is generally effective (Kiddoo, 2012).

Ask Yourself

4. Which of the following is abnormal in young children and cause for medical or behavioural intervention?
   a. attempts to delay bedtime
   b. enuresis
   c. night terrors
   d. nightmares
   e. All of these are normal.

5. Enuresis runs in families, and identical twins are more likely to be concordant for this behaviour than fraternal twins. This suggests that
   a. parents are probably responsible for it because of poor parenting practices.
   b. punishment is an appropriate means by which to address bed-wetting.
   c. there are likely to be genetic factors that contribute to enuresis.
   d. bed alarms are likely to be ineffective.

Motor Development

Children ages 3 to 6 make great advances in motor skills—both *gross motor skills*, which involve the large muscles, such as running and jumping (Table 8.2), and *fine motor skills*, manipulative skills involving eye-hand and small-muscle coordination, such as buttoning and drawing. They also begin to show a preference for using either the right or left hand.

GROSS MOTOR SKILLS AND FINE MOTOR SKILLS

At 3, Eva could walk a straight line and jump a short distance. At 4, she could hop a few steps on one foot. At 5, she could jump nearly 1 m (3 feet) and hop for 5 m (16 feet), and was learning to roller-skate.

Motor skills do not develop in isolation. The skills that emerge in early childhood build on the achievements of infancy and toddlerhood. Development of the sensory and motor areas of the cerebral cortex permits better coordination between what children want to do and what they can do. Their bones and muscles are stronger, and their lung capacity is greater, making it possible to run, jump, and climb farther, faster, and better.

At about age 2½, children begin to jump with both feet, a skill they have not been able to master before this time. Hopping is hard to master until about 4. Going upstairs is easier than going down; by 3½, most children comfortably alternate feet going up, but not until about 5 do they easily descend that way. Skipping is challenging; although some 4-year-olds can skip, most children cannot do it until age 6 (Corbin, 1973). Of course, children vary in adeptness, depending on their genetic endowment and their opportunities to learn and practise motor skills.

The gross motor skills developed during early childhood are the basis for sports, dancing, and other activities that begin during middle childhood and may continue for a lifetime. However, children under 6 are rarely ready to take part in any organized sport. If the demands of the sport exceed the child's physical and motor capabilities, it

TABLE 8.2 Gross Motor Skills in Early Childhood

3-Year-Olds	4-Year-Olds	5-Year-Olds
▪ Cannot turn or stop suddenly effectively or quickly	▪ Have more effective control of stopping, starting, and turning	▪ Can start, turn, and stop effectively in games
▪ Can jump a distance of 38 to 61 cm (15 to 24 inches)	▪ Can jump a distance of 61 to 84 cm (24 to 33 inches)	▪ Can make a running jump of 71 to 91 cm (28 to 36 inches)
▪ Can ascend a stairway alternating feet, unaided	▪ Can descend a long stairway alternating feet, if supported	▪ Can descend a long stairway alternating feet, unaided
▪ Can hop, using largely an irregular series of jumps with some variations added	▪ Can hop four to six steps on one foot	▪ Can easily hop a distance of about 5 m (16 feet)

Source: Corbin (1973).

Four-year-olds show more flexibility than before in how they grip objects, which lets them learn complex skills like tying shoes.

can result in feelings of frustration on the part of the child (AAP Committee on Sports Medicine and Fitness & Committee on School Health, 2001).

Young children develop best physically when they can be active at an appropriate maturational level in unstructured free-play, for about three hours a day (Healthy Active Living and Sports Medicine Committee, Canadian Paediatric Society, 2012). Parents and teachers can help by offering young children the opportunity to climb and jump on safe, properly sized equipment, by providing balls and other toys small enough to be grasped easily and soft enough not to be harmful, and by offering gentle coaching when a child seems to need help.

Gains in fine motor skills, such as tying shoelaces and cutting with scissors, allow young children to take more responsibility for their personal care. At 3, Eva can pour milk into her cereal bowl, eat with silverware, and use the toilet alone. She can also draw a circle and a rudimentary person—without arms. At 4, she can dress herself with help. She can cut along a line, draw a fairly complete person, make designs and crude letters, and fold paper into a double triangle. At 5, Eva can dress herself without much help, copy a square or triangle, and draw a more elaborate person than before.

How voluntary grasping and object manipulation emerges in children is a good example of how fine motor skills develop. Children gain more control over muscles in the fingers and learn what objects of different shapes (like pegs and blocks) demand. Developing independent finger motions, from a rudimentary grasp, to a "scissor" grasp, to a pincer grasp, depends on gaining independent control over the muscles in each finger, and learning the movements and amount of power

needed to hold and manipulate objects of different shapes and weights. This takes time, as the ability to rotate small objects between fingers doesn't emerge until after the third year. Two-year-olds typically have rigid grips, while 4-year-olds show more flexibility in how they grip objects. Young children show more variety of gripping patterns for simple objects, like pegs, compared with complex objects, like blocks (Geerts, Einspieler, Dibiasi, Garzarolli, & Bos, 2003).

HANDEDNESS

Handedness, the preference for using one hand over the other, is usually evident by about age 3. Handedness is not always clear-cut; not everybody prefers one hand for every task. Boys are more likely to be left-handed than are girls. For every 100 left-handed girls, there are 123 left-handed boys (Papadatou-Pastou, Martin, Munafo, & Jones, 2008).

Did you know?

If you are right-handed but break your right hand as a child, you are likely to learn how to use your left hand well, and may even stay left-handed after your break heals.

Is handedness genetic or environmental? That question has been controversial. Some researchers argue that, given that such factors as low birth weight and difficult deliveries are related to increased likelihood of left-handedness, the environment must be more important (Bailey & McKeever, 2004). As further evidence of environmental effects, the percentage of left-handed children has risen as schools no longer force all children to use their right hands for writing (Annett, 2002; Searleman & Porac, 2003). Other researchers argue that handedness is more influenced by either a single gene (Klar, 1996) or by a variety of genes working together (Medland et al., 2009). It is likely that both viewpoints hold some truth to them.

Did you know?

Handedness does not necessarily indicate how language functions are lateralized between brain hemispheres, despite popular myths that language in left-handed people resides in the right and not left hemisphere. Language in most children is lateralized to the left hemisphere, despite handedness (Szaflarski et al., 2012). Even with motor movements, hemispheric dominance follows the same pattern for left- and right-handers, though left-handers are more likely to show a balance (symmetry) between left and right hemisphere control (Vingerhoets et al., 2012).

Ask Yourself

6. An example of a gross motor skill is _____ and an example of a fine motor skill is _____.

7. Being left-handed is more common in
   a. boys.
   b. girls.
   c. neither boys nor girls.

Health and Safety

A few weeks before starting kindergarten, Eva's mother took her to the doctor for her annual healthy child check-up and required vaccinations for starting school. While some parents in Canada worry about potential negative effects of vaccines, Eva's mother knew that the benefits outweigh the low risk of complications. As the doctor immunized Eva against the major diseases of childhood, Eva's mother remembered her grandfather's shrivelled leg, the result of a bout with polio in his childhood. Because of widespread immunization, Eva would probably not have to worry about preventable diseases such as polio, rubella, and mumps. In the developing world, however, many preventable diseases still take a large toll.

In Canada, advances in public health have made many of the previously common childhood illnesses, accidents, and deaths rare. However, children nonetheless continue to face risks to optimal development. Some children eat too much food and may become overweight or obese, while others suffer the effects of malnourishment. Some children need to be careful not to consume foods to which they are allergic. Oral health is also an issue; not all children practise good habits or have access to dentists. And while deaths in childhood are relatively few compared with deaths in adulthood, and most are caused by injury rather than illness (Heron et al., 2009; Statistics Canada, 2011f), some children, like some Aboriginal children, live in risky environments that increase the chances of accidents (Banerji & Canadian Paediatric Society, First Nations, Inuit and Métis Health Committee, 2012; Oliver, Peters, & Kohen, 2012).

OBESITY

Obesity is a serious problem among Canadian preschoolers. Obesity rates have tripled among Canadian children in the last 25 years; obesity affects one in four Canadian children (Canadian Paediatric Society, 2012b; Tucker, Irwin, Bouck, & Pollet, 2006) and is related to both ethnicity and family income. Aboriginal children, children living in remote northern communities without regular access to nutritious foods, as well as those from families lower on the socio-economic ladder, are more likely to be obese (Anderson et al., 2010; Majid & Grier, 2010; Skelton, Cook, Auinger, Klein, & Barlow, 2009; Willows, Johnson, & Ball, 2007).

Worldwide, an estimated 22 million children under age 5 are obese (Belizzi, 2002). As junk food spreads through the developing world, as many as 20 to 25 percent of 4-year-olds in some countries, such as Egypt, Morocco, and Zambia, are overweight or obese—a larger proportion than are malnourished.

A tendency toward obesity can be hereditary, but the main factors driving the obesity epidemic are environmental (AAP, 2004; Canadian Paediatric Society, 2012b). As growth slows, preschoolers need fewer calories in proportion to their weight than they did before. A key to preventing obesity may be to make sure older preschoolers are served appropriate portions (Rolls, Engell, & Birch, 2000; Table 8.3). Children 1 or 2 years old who are at risk of being overweight or obese may be given reduced-fat milk instead of whole milk; after age 2, they can drink fat-free milk (Daniels, Greer, & the Committee on Nutrition, 2008). Too little physical activity is an important factor in obesity as well; Canadian health guidelines recommend limiting screen time to less than one hour a day for children 2 to 4 years of age (Lipnowski, LeBlank, & Canadian Paediatric Society, Healthy Active Living and Sports Medicine Committee, 2012; Tremblay et al., 2012). The average Canadian child watches about 14 hours of television per week (Canadian Paediatric Society, 2003) and spends 8.6 hours per day in sedentary behaviour (Colley et al., 2011). The risk of increased prevalence of overweight and obesity is very real; each additional hour of TV-watching above two hours a day increases the likelihood of obesity at age 30 by 7 percent (Viner & Cole, 2005). Having a TV set in a child's bedroom further increases the risk (Dennison, Erb, & Jenkins, 2002), as does eating while watching TV, combining sedentary behaviour with poor food choices (Liang, Kuhle, & Veugelers, 2009).

What children eat is as important as how much they eat. To avoid obesity and prevent cardiac problems, young children should get only about 30 percent of their total calories from fat, and no more than one-third of fat calories should come from saturated fat. Young people of all ages, particularly in low-income families, eat too much fat and sugar and too few servings of fruits, vegetables, grains, and dairy products (Garriguet, 2006). Although well-planned vegetarian diets are healthy, most children should eat lean meat and dairy foods that provide protein, iron, and calcium. Milk and other dairy products should be skim or low fat (AAP Committee on Nutrition, 2006; Health Canada, 2011c).

Prevention of overweight and obesity in the early years, when excessive weight gain usually begins, is critical; the long-term success of treatment, especially when it is delayed, is limited (AAP Committee on Nutrition, 2003; Quattrin, Liu, Shaw, Shine, & Chiang, 2005). Overweight children, especially those who have overweight parents, tend to become obese adults (AAP Committee on Nutrition, 2003). Early childhood is a good time to

TABLE 8.3 Encouraging Healthy Eating Habits

- Parents, not children, should choose mealtimes.

- If the child is not overweight, allow him or her to decide how much to eat. Don't pressure the child to clean the plate.

- Serve portions appropriate to the child's size and age.

- Serve simple, easily identifiable foods. Preschoolers often balk at mixed dishes such as casseroles.

- Serve finger foods as often as possible.

- Introduce only one new food at a time, along with familiar food the child likes. Offer small servings of new or disliked foods; give second helpings if wanted.

- After a reasonable time, remove the food and do not serve more until the next meal. A healthy child will not suffer from missing a meal, and children need to learn that certain times are appropriate for eating.

- Give the child a choice of foods containing similar nutrients: rye or whole wheat bread, a peach or an apple, yogourt or milk.

- Serve nonfat or lowfat dairy products as sources of calcium and protein.

- Encourage a child to help prepare food; a child can help make sandwiches or mix and spoon out cookie dough.

- Limit snacking while watching television. Discourage nutrient-poor foods such as salty snacks, fried foods, ice cream, cookies, and sweetened beverages, and instead suggest nutritious snack foods, such as fruits and raw vegetables.

- Turn childish delights to advantage. Serve food in appealing dishes; dress it up with garnishes or little toys; make a party out of a meal.

- Don't fight rituals in which a child eats foods one at a time, in a certain order.

- Have regular family meals. Make mealtimes pleasant with conversation on interesting topics, keeping talk about eating itself to a minimum.

Sources: American Heart Association et al. (2006); Health Canada (2011c); Rolls, Engell, & Birch (2000); Williams & Caliendo (1984).

treat obesity, when a child's diet is still subject to parental influence or control (Quattrin et al., 2005), and to reduce risks to healthy development. Even at age 5, overweight is associated with behavioural problems (Datar & Sturm, 2004) and low reading and math scores (Datar, Sturm, & Magnabosco, 2004).

UNDERNUTRITION

Worldwide, undernutrition is an underlying cause in more than half of all deaths before age 5 (Bryce, Boschi-Pinto, Shibuya, Black, & the WHO Child Health Epidemiology Reference Group, 2005). South Asia has the highest level of undernutrition; 42 percent of young children in South Asia are moderately or severely underweight as compared with 28 percent in sub-Saharan Africa, 7 percent in Latin America and the Caribbean, and 25 percent of young children worldwide (UNICEF, 2008a). Even in Canada, 11 percent of families with at least one child under age 6 lived in food-insecure households in 2008, and the proportion rises for lone-parent, recent immigrant, and Aboriginal families, as well as in families with three or more children (Health Canada, 2012). Food-bank use in Canada is on the increase. Thirty-eight percent of food bank users in Canada are children under 18 years of age, yet they make up only a quarter of the population (Food Banks Canada, 2011; Wilson & Steinman, 2000; Wilson & Tsoa, 2001). In 2004, about 317,000 food bank users were children, up from 166,000 Canadian children in 1989

(Canadian Press, 2004). Food insecurity—inconsistent access to adequate, safe, and nutritionally sound food—is becoming a fact of life for many Canadian children. As family income deteriorates, food insecurity increases dramatically; increases in number of siblings, parental job loss, and health problems contribute to the likelihood of childhood hunger (Che & Chen, 2001; Tarasuk & Eakin, 2003). Children who experience the physical and psychological stresses of food insecurity often do poorly in school, experience attention problems, and are at risk of developing psychosocial functioning problems (Doherty, 1997).

Because undernourished children usually live in extremely deprived circumstances, the specific effects of malnutrition are hard to determine. However, taken together, these deprivations may negatively affect not only growth and physical well-being but also cognitive and psychosocial development. In an analysis of data on a nationally representative U.S. sample of 3,286 children ages 6 to 11, those whose families had insufficient food were more likely to do poorly on arithmetic tests, to have repeated a grade, to have seen a psychologist, and to have had difficulty getting along with other children (Alaimo, Olson, & Frongillo, 2001). Moreover, cognitive effects of malnutrition may be long-lasting. Among 1,559 children born on the island of Mauritius (off the African continent) in a single year, those who were undernourished at age 3 had poorer verbal and spatial abilities, reading skills, scholastic ability, and neuropsychological performance

Perspectives on Diversity

SURVIVING THE FIRST FIVE YEARS OF LIFE

In Canada, we have grown accustomed to children's health. While our children may suffer the long-term effects of obesity or exposure to environmental toxins, a child's death is a rare event in the lives of most families. But this is not true across the world. In many countries, surviving through childhood is not guaranteed, and the death of a young child is shockingly common. A difficult birth, an unclean bottle, an insect bite—events that in developed countries can be handled relatively easily—can kill a young child in countries without adequate medical care.

The chances of a child's living to his or her fifth birthday have doubled during the past four decades, but the prospects for survival depend on where the child lives. Canada's infant mortality rate is approximately 4.9 infants per 1,000 live births. Most of those deaths occur in preterm or low-birth-weight babies (Mathews & McDorman, 2010). Between ages 1 and 4 years, the mortality rate in Canada drops to about 0.2 deaths per 1,000 children (Statistics Canada, 2011f). Worldwide, almost 9 million children a year under the age of 5 die (UNICEF, 2009). The four major causes of death, accounting for over half of deaths in children younger than age 5, are communicable diseases: pneumonia, diarrhea, malaria, and neonatal sepsis.

Ninety percent of childhood deaths occur during the first five years, and fully 98 percent of child deaths occur in poor, rural regions of developing countries (UNICEF, 2009). With the exception of China, India, Pakistan, and Nepal, boys are more likely to die than girls, and the poor in all countries are at greater risk (WHO, 2003).

More than 60 countries have reduced their mortality rate for children under age 5 by 50 percent (UNICEF, 2007). In general, the most improvement has occurred in industrialized nations and in those developing countries where child mortality was already relatively low (WHO, 2003).

In some African countries, HIV/AIDS is responsible for as many as 60 percent of child deaths. Fourteen African countries saw more young children die in 2002 than in 1990. On the other hand, eight countries in the region, among them Gabon, Gambia, and Ghana, have reduced child mortality by more than 50 percent since 1970 (WHO, 2003).

In Latin America, the most dramatic reductions in child mortality have taken place in Chile, Costa Rica, and Cuba, where child deaths have dropped more than 80 percent since 1970. In contrast, Haitian children still die at a rate of 133 per 1,000 (WHO, 2003).

than their peers at age 11 (Liu, Raine, Venables, Dalais, & Mednick, 2003).

Some studies suggest that some of the effects of malnutrition can be lessened with improved diet (Engle et al., 2007; Lewit & Kerrebrock, 1997). In one study, Mauritanian children 3 to 5 years old who received a variety of services, including nutritional supplements, had lower rates of antisocial behaviour and mental health problems than a control group. The effects were greatest among those who had been undernourished to begin with (Raine, Mellingen, Liu, Venables, & Mednick, 2003). In another longitudinal study, children who were supplemented early in childhood performed better than control group children in adolescence on a variety of cognitive tasks (Pollit, Gorman, Engle, Rivera, & Martorell, 1995) and in tests of physical work capacity (Martorell, 1995).

Early education may help counter the effects of undernourishment. A longitudinal study (Grantham-McGregor, Powell, Walker, Chang, & Fletcher, 1994; Walker, Grantham-McGregor, Powell, & Chang, 2000) followed two groups of Jamaican infants and toddlers who came from extremely poor, often unstable homes and who had been hospitalized for severe undernourishment.

Health care paraprofessionals played with an experimental group in the hospital and, after discharge, visited them at home every week for three years, showing the mothers how to make toys and encouraging them to interact with their children. Three years after the program stopped, the experimental group's IQs were well above those of a control group who had received only standard medical care, though not as high as those of a third, well-nourished group. Furthermore, the IQs of the experimental group remained higher than those of the control group as much as 14 years after leaving the hospital.

FOOD ALLERGIES

A food allergy is an abnormal immune-system response to a specific food. Reactions can range from tingling in the mouth and hives to more serious, life-threatening reactions such as shortness of breath and even death. Ninety percent of food allergies can be attributed to nine foods: milk, eggs, peanuts, tree nuts, fish, soy, shellfish, sesame seeds, and wheat (Health Canada, 2003; Sampson, 2004). The prevalence of allergies depends on the type of food (Figure 8.2). Food allergies are more prevalent in children than adults, and most children

FIGURE 8.2

Canadian Childhood Rates of Food Allergy, in Percentages, for Each of Health Canada's Priority Allergens

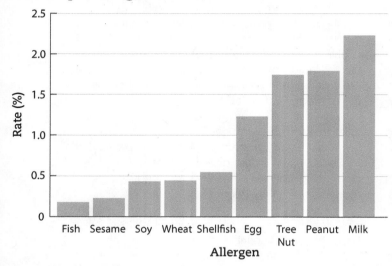

Sources: Adapted from Health Canada. (2003). Paper on the allergen control activities within the Canadian Food Inspection Agency. Ottawa, ON: Author. Cat. No. H39-649/2002E-IN. Reproduced by permission of the Minister of Public Works and Government Services Canada 2013; Soller, L., et al. (2012). Overall prevalence of self-reported food allergy in Canada. *Journal of Allergy and Clinical Immunology, 130* (4), 986–988.

will outgrow their allergies (Branum & Lukas, 2008). About seven out of every 100 children in Canada suffer from some type of food allergy (Soller et al., 2012). This challenge is particularly notable in schools, given that many schools lack appropriate procedures for preventing exposure as well as for care and treatment in the event of an allergic reaction (Young, Munoz-Furlong, & Sicherer, 2009).

Research on children under age 18 has demonstrated an increase in the prevalence of food allergies over the past 10 years (Branum & Lukas, 2008); however, rates seem to be stabilizing in Canada (Ben-Shoshan et al., 2009, 2010). Changes in diet, how foods are processed, and decreased vitamin D based on less exposure to the sun have all been suggested as contributors to the increase in allergy rates. Another theory—that society is too clean and that children's immune systems are less mature because they are not exposed to enough dirt and germs—has also been explored. The link between eczema and food allergies has also led some researchers to theorize that sensitization to allergens develops through skin exposure (Lack, 2008). Although possible explanations abound, not enough evidence exists to pinpoint a cause.

ORAL HEALTH

Poor oral health and untreated oral disease can impact quality of life. Oral health is an

dental caries   Tooth decay, a cavity.

important component of overall health, and it starts in childhood. In early childhood, two common areas of oral health of concern to parents are thumb-sucking and tooth decay. By age 3, all the primary (baby) teeth are in place, and the permanent teeth, which will begin to appear at about age 6, are developing. Thus, parents usually can safely ignore the common habit of thumb-sucking in children under age 4. If children stop sucking thumbs or fingers by that age, their permanent teeth are not likely to be affected (ADA, 2007).

Use of fluoride and improved dental care have dramatically reduced the incidence of tooth decay since the 1970s, but disadvantaged children still have more untreated **dental caries**—or cavities—than other children (Bloom, Cohen, Vickerie, & Wondimu, 2003). Tooth decay in early childhood often stems from overconsumption of sweetened milk and juices in infancy together with a lack of regular dental care. Some of the worst effects have been found in children who take bottles to bed with them, and bathe their teeth in sugar over the course of an afternoon or evening (Canadian Dental Association, 2012). Though decay in primary teeth has declined overall from the early 1970s, there has been a slight reverse in this trend since the mid-1990s (Centers for Disease Control and Prevention, 2007b). The Canadian Paediatric Society recommends that parents use fluoride supplements for children 6 months of age and older in areas that do not fluoridate the water supply, but also to limit the amount of toothpaste used in order to avoid fluorosis, a pitting and staining of the teeth, particularly in the first six months (Canadian Paediatric Society, 2012c).

ACCIDENTAL INJURIES AND DEATHS

While Eva was generally a compliant child, one day when her mother was in the other room, she stood on the back of the couch dancing and jumping, and then fell to the floor.

WHAT DO YOU DO?

Dentist

Dentists care for teeth and the mouth. The Canadian Academy of Pediatric Dentistry recommends that children start visiting the dentist when the first teeth appear. With young children, dentists will check to ensure that teeth are coming in as expected and there are no cavities or problems. One reason for early visits to the dentist is to get children comfortable with the experience. Most dental students complete a non-specific undergraduate degree that focuses on biology, science, and anatomy, and write the Canadian Dental Aptitude Test, before pursuing a four-year dental program. Dentists work in shared or private practices. To learn more about dentistry, visit www.capd-acdp.org and www.rcdc.ca.

Car seats can significantly reduce the risk of injury in a car accident.

Eva landed on her arm, and the impact of the fall broke a bone in her upper arm.

Young children are naturally venturesome and often are unaware of danger. Although most cuts, bumps, and scrapes are "kissed away" and quickly forgotten, some accidental injuries result in lasting damage or death. Indeed, accidents (unintentional injuries), especially motor vehicle collisions, drowning, and suffocation, are the leading causes of death after infancy and throughout childhood and adolescence in Canada (Public Health Agency of Canada, 2009b). Worldwide, more than 800,000 children die each year from burns, drowning, car crashes, falls, poisonings, and other accidents (WHO, 2008). Injuries from falls, such as those associated with bicycle accidents, trampoline mishaps, and consumer items, such as wheeled shoes, are the major cause of hospitalizations related to injury for young children (Public Health Agency of Canada, 2009b; Public Health Agency of Canada, Health Surveillance and Epidemiology Division, 2006, 2004–2006).

All provinces and territories in Canada require young children to ride in specially designed car seats or to wear seat belts. New recommendations suggest that 4-year-olds should use forward-facing car seats with a harness until they reach the top weight or height limit for their seat. After that time, belt-positioning booster seats should be used until children are big enough to fit a seat belt properly, with the lap belt across their thighs and the shoulder belt snug against the shoulder and chest. Airbags are designed to protect adults, not children. They have been shown to increase the risk of fatal injury to children under age 13 who are riding in the front seat. Car safety requirements and campaigns to keep children in the back seats of cars have reduced the number of child and adolescent deaths in motor vehicle crashes by over 4 percent each year from 1990 to 2005 (Public Health Agency of Canada, 2009b). Hospitalization for injury from motor vehicle traffic accidents and other road injuries become more common in childhood. In 2005–06, over 29,000 children and youth aged 19 years and younger were hospitalized as a result of a traffic accident, a 40 percent drop from 10 years prior (Public Health Agency of Canada, 2009b).

The cost to the health care system of unintentional injury can be staggering, and injuries caused by falls account for over half of the costs of caring for accidents (Cloutier & Albert, 2001). Prevention is the key way of reducing the costs of injuries, including using bicycle helmets, child safety seats, road safety improvements, smoke alarms, and poison control services (Cloutier & Albert, 2001; Table 8.4).

Most deaths from injuries, especially among preschoolers, occur in the home—from fires, drowning in bathtubs, suffocation, poisoning, or falls (Nagaraja et al., 2005). Everyday medications, such as Aspirin, acetaminophen, cold and cough preparations, and even vitamins, can be dangerous to inquisitive young children (Health Canada, 1998b). Because these substances are so commonplace, parents do not often perceive them as highly dangerous (Health Canada, 1998b). Safe storage could prevent many poisonings (Litovitz et al., 1999; Shannon, 2000). Parents modelling safety behaviours and teaching older siblings (who can increase the risk of injury when supervising their younger siblings) to practise safety

Did you know?

Hollywood is wrong—drowning children don't call for help, noisily splashing and kicking in the water. Rather, they are silent and glassy-eyed, and any time their mouth comes up above the surface of the water, they are busy breathing, not calling for help.

TABLE 8.4 Reducing Accident Risks for Children

Activity	Precautions
Bicycling	Properly fitting bicycle helmets reduce risk of head injury by 85 percent and brain injury by 88 percent. Children under 10 should not ride bicycles on roads.
Skateboarding and rollerblading	Children should wear helmets and protective padding on knees, elbows, and wrists.
Using fireworks	Families should not purchase fireworks for home use.
Lawn mowing	Children under 12 should not operate walk-behind mowers; those under 14 should not operate ride-on mowers; small children should not be close to a moving mower.
Swimming	Swimming pools should not be installed in backyards of homes with children under 5; pools already in place need a high fence all around, with gates having high, out-of-reach, self-closing latches. Adults need to watch children very closely near pools, lakes, and other bodies of water.
Playing on a playground	A safe surface under swings, slides, and other equipment can be sand 25 cm (10 inches) deep, wood chips 30 cm (12 inches) deep, or rubber outdoor mats; separate areas should be maintained for active play and quiet play, and for older and younger children.
Using firearms	Guns should be kept unloaded and locked up, with bullets locked in a separate place; children should not have access to keys; adults should talk with children about the risks of gun injury; firearms should not be kept in homes where children or youth live.
Eating	To prevent choking, young children should not eat hard candies, nuts, grapes, and hot dogs (unless sliced lengthwise, then across); food should be cut into small pieces; children should not eat while talking, running, jumping, or lying down.
Ingesting toxic substances	Only drugs and toxic household products with safety caps should be used; toxic products should be stored out of children's reach in a locked box. Suspected poisoning should be reported immediately to the nearest poison control centre.
Riding in motor vehicles	Young children should sit in approved car seats in the back seat. Adults should observe traffic laws and avoid aggressive drivers.

Sources: Adapted in part from American Academy of Pediatrics Committee on Injury and Poison Prevention (1995, 2000); Canadian Paediatric Society (2012d); Rivara (1999); Safe Kids Canada (2012); Shannon (2000).

behaviours can also help prevent injuries in young children (Morrongiello, Schell, & Schmidt, 2010).

Canadian laws requiring childproof caps on medicine bottles and other dangerous household products, regulation of product safety, car seats for young children, mandatory helmets for bicycle riders, and safe storage of firearms and medicines have improved child safety. Making playgrounds safer would be another valuable measure. Table 8.4 summarizes suggestions for reducing accident risks in various settings.

ENVIRONMENTAL INFLUENCES ON HEALTH

Why do some children have more illnesses or injuries than others? Genetic heritage contributes; some children seem predisposed

Did you know?

A skull and crossbones—the traditional symbol for poison—makes a poor warning for young children, who are more likely to interpret it within the context of pirates and buried treasure.

toward some medical conditions. However, environmental factors, including socio-economic status, race and ethnicity, homelessness, and exposure to pollutants, play major roles.

Socio-Economic Status

Eight percent of Canadian children and youth 18 years or younger lived in poverty in 2011, down from 15 percent in 1991 (Canadian Council on Social Development, The Annie E. Casey Foundation, & Red por los Derechos de la Infancia en México, 2008; Family Service Toronto, 2011; Statistics Canada, 2012e). The lower a family's socio-economic status (SES), the greater a child's risk of illness, injury, and death (Chen, Matthews, & Boyce, 2002). Low income can be a risk to healthy child development (Phipps & Lethbridge, 2006), either directly through less enriched home environments or indirectly through increased parental stress and depression, which can reduce parents' capacity to provide supportive and consistent parenting, and increase the risk of hostile parenting (Family Service Toronto, 2011; Lipman, Boyle, Dooley, & Offord, 1998; Ryan & Adams, 1998). The prevalence of low-income families in urban neighbourhoods has been linked to poor developmental outcomes in children. For example, entire neighbourhoods of Vancouver have been shown to include higher proportions of children experiencing higher risks of developing multiple problems in physical health, social competence, emotional maturity, and communication skills (Hertzman, 2002).

Although no official definition of "poverty" exists in Canada, a commonly used "poverty line" measure is Statistics Canada's low-income cut-off (LICO), which is an income level required for basic needs, adjusted for family size and size of the community in which a family resides (Statistics Canada, 2012f). A higher income is typically needed to meet the needs of larger families living in larger urban centres, compared with rural communities. Although social assistance, such as the Canada Child Tax Benefit, the Universal Child Care Benefit, and the Child Disability Benefit, is provided to families in need across Canada, it does not always provide families with adequate means to meet their needs. For example, the level of assistance available to a lone-parent family with one child ranges from a low of 50 percent of LICO in Alberta to a high of 69 percent of LICO in Newfoundland and Labrador (Canadian Institute of Child Health, 2000). With rising costs of food and housing, many families struggle to make ends meet each month. Nevertheless, social assistance programs in Canada have helped many more families avoid poverty (Family Service Toronto, 2011).

The *Canada Health Act* is designed to ensure universal access to medically necessary health services for all Canadians. However, despite the principles of the act, accessibility to health services is not necessarily consistent in all regions. Canadians in remote and northern areas are concerned about limited health services in their communities (Kulig & Williams, 2012). In response, health initiatives have been introduced for people living in remote areas, designed to improve capacity, service delivery, and access to health care in rural and remote areas (Kulig & Williams, 2012).

In addition to the concerns of people living in remote and northern communities, equality of access is not always guaranteed in urban communities. For example, although residents of Winnipeg's poorest neighbourhoods were more likely to see family doctors than were residents of middle- and upper-income neighbourhoods, people in the poor neighbourhoods were less likely to be referred to specialists. In Ontario, people living in lower- and middle-income neighbourhoods were less likely to receive cardiac surgery and more likely to die after being hospitalized with a heart attack, in comparison to residents of wealthier areas (Canadian Institute for Health Information, 2000).

Race/Ethnicity

Access to quality health care is a particular problem among Aboriginal and recent immigrant children, especially those who are poor or near poor (Flores, Olson, & Tomany-Korman, 2005; Statistics Canada, 2008a, 2009c). Language and cultural barriers and the need for more culturally sensitive care providers may help explain some of these disparities (Flores et al., 2002). Even Asian immigrant children, who tend to be in better health than non-immigrant European-background children, are less likely to access and use health care, perhaps because of similar barriers (NCHS, 2005; Yu, Huang, & Singh, 2004).

About 34 percent of recent immigrant children live in poverty at some time during their early years in Canada but seem resilient to emotional and behavioural problems experienced by many non-immigrant Canadian children who live in poverty (Beiser, Hou, Hyman, & Tousignant, 2002; Canadian Council on Social Development et al., 2008), likely because adjusting to a new country involves temporary low income (Beiser, Hou, Hyman, & Tousignant, 1998; Smith & Jackson, 2002). Over 40 percent of Aboriginal children live in low-income families, as do 43 percent of visible minorities (Canadian Council on Social Development et al., 2008; Canadian Institute for Child Health, 2000; Statistics Canada, 2008b). Although children with lone parents are also more likely to be in low-income families, the developmental outcomes for these children are typically no different from those of other children in low-income families (Chao & Willms, 2002; Lipman et al., 1998; Willms, 2002a).

Homelessness and Poor Housing

Homelessness results from complex circumstances that force people to choose between food, shelter, and other basic needs (National Coalition for the Homeless, 2009). Since the 1980s, as affordable rental housing has become scarce and poverty has spread, homelessness has increased dramatically in Canada. On a typical day, over 3,600 children (usually accompanied by single mothers) are admitted to homeless shelters in Canada (Burczycka & Cotter, 2011). Many homeless families are headed by single mothers in their 20s (Buckner, Bassuk, Weinreb, & Brooks, 1999; Park, Metraux, & Culhane, 2010). Often, these families are fleeing domestic violence (Burczycka & Cotter, 2011; National Coalition for the Homeless, 2009). About one-third of Canada's homeless population are between 16 and 24 years of age (Laird, 2007).

Many homeless children spend their crucial early years in unstable, insecure, and often unsanitary environments. They and their parents may be cut off from a supportive community, family ties, and institutional resources, as well as from ready access to medical care and schooling. These children suffer more health problems than children from low-SES families who have homes, including diarrhea, respiratory, skin, and eye and ear infections, asthma, and other chronic diseases, and face barriers to accessing health care (Hwang et al., 2010). Homeless children also tend to suffer severe depression and anxiety, and to have neurological and visual deficits, developmental delays, behaviour problems, and learning difficulties. As many as half do not go to school; if they do, they tend to have problems, partly because they miss a lot of it and have no place to do homework. They tend to do poorly on standardized reading and math tests, even when their cognitive functioning is normal, and they are more likely to repeat a grade or be placed in special classes than are children with homes (Children's Defense Fund [CDF], 2004; Weinreb et al., 2002). In large cities that have safe housing for poor and homeless families in stable, lower-poverty neighbourhoods, the children's behaviour and school performance improved greatly (CDF, 2004).

Children in Aboriginal families, in particular, live in inadequate housing (Durbin, 2009; Statistics Canada, 2008b) and face higher rates of respiratory problems and other infectious diseases, as a function of inadequate housing and crowded living conditions (Clark, Riben, & Nowgesic, 2002). Typically, less affluent neighbourhoods that have declining median incomes and increases in low-income families, single-parent families, and proportion of income spent on rent were associated with higher numbers of developmental risks. Part of the problem has to do with the lower availability of social supports such as child-care facilities and neighbourhood recreation centres in less affluent neighbourhoods.

To combat homelessness, a number of communities and community development groups, such as Habitat for Humanity, are building low-income housing units and reclaiming neighbourhoods with the help of federal, provincial, local, foundation, and private financing (Laird, 2007). In addition, the Government of Canada's Homelessness Partnership Strategy is designed to help eradicate homelessness in Canada (Human Resources Development Canada, 2013).

Exposure to Smoking, Air Pollution, Pesticides, and Lead

Smoking is bad for everyone; however, children, with their still-developing lungs and faster rate of respiration, are

Second-hand smoke is responsible for hundreds of thousands of illnesses in Canadian children every year.

particularly sensitive to the damaging effects of exposure (Constant et al, 2011). Parental smoking is a preventable cause of childhood illness and death. The potential damage caused by exposure to tobacco smoke is greatest during the early years of life (DiFranza et al., 2004). Children exposed to parental smoke are at increased risk of respiratory infections such as bronchitis and pneumonia, ear problems, worsened asthma, and slowed lung growth (Figure 8.3).

Although there has been a decline in the prevalence of smoking among Canadians over 15 years of age over the past decade—from 25 percent in 1999 to 17 percent in 2010 (Health Canada, 2011e)—15 percent of Canadian children are exposed to second-hand smoke at home (Physicians for a Smoke-Free Canada, 2010). About 10.5 percent of Canadian mothers report having smoked during pregnancy, with almost 7 percent smoking daily (Al-Sahab, Saqib, Hauser, & Tamim, 2010). This pre-natal exposure could have detrimental long-term effects on children after birth, with higher likelihood of behavioural

Impact per Year of Second-Hand Smoke and Parents' Smoking: Percentage of Medical Conditions and Number of Canadian Children Affected

FIGURE 8.3 Additionally, 13 to 20 children die from infection in lower respiratory areas, 15 from tobacco-related fires, and 180 to 270 from sudden infant death syndrome (SIDS).

Source: Physicians for a Smoke-Free Canada, 1999. Second hand smoke & children's health. Ottawa, ON: Author.

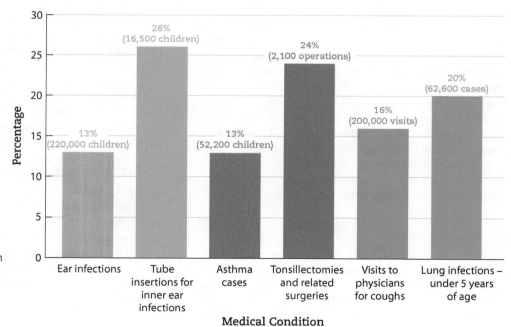

and cognitive problems in children of mothers who smoked during pregnancy (Connor & McIntyre, 2002). Second-hand smoke is responsible for over 400,000 illnesses in Canadian children every year (Physicians for a Smoke-Free Canada, 1999). Second-hand smoke contains hundreds of *carcinogens*, or cancer-causing chemicals, and can lead to premature death (Office on Smoking and Health, Centers for Disease Control and Prevention, 2006). In an effort to reduce children's exposure to second-hand smoke, the Canadian government in 2010 passed legislation making it illegal to smoke in a car carrying children younger than 16 years as passengers.

Air pollution is associated with increased risks of death and of chronic respiratory disease. Environmental contaminants also may play a role in certain childhood cancers, neurological disorders, attention deficit hyperactivity disorder, and mental retardation (Woodruff et al., 2004).

Children are more vulnerable than adults to chronic pesticide damage (Goldman et al., 2004). There is some, though not definitive, evidence that low-dose pesticide exposure may affect the developing brain (Weiss, Amler, & Amler, 2004). Pesticide exposure is greater in children in agricultural and inner-city families (Dilworth-Bart & Moore, 2006). Almost half of all reported pesticide poisonings in Canada—over 2,500 per year—occur in children younger than age 6 (Boyd, 2007).

Children can get elevated concentrations of lead from lead-contaminated food or water, from airborne industrial wastes, from putting contaminated fingers in their mouths, or from inhaling dust or playing with paint chips in homes or schools where there is lead-based paint. Lead poisoning can seriously interfere with cognitive development and can lead to neurological and behavioural problems (Health Canada, 2007a). Very high levels of blood lead concentration may cause headaches, abdominal pain, loss of appetite, agitation, or lethargy, and eventually vomiting, stupor, and convulsions (AAP Committee on Environmental Health, 2005; Health Canada, 2007a).

Ask Yourself

8. List two variables related to risk of overweight or obesity in children.

9. Which of the following is not a likely outcome of undernourishment in children?
   a. They do poorly on arithmetic tests.
   b. They repeat a grade.
   c. They are very shy.
   d. They have difficulty getting along with other children.

Ask Yourself

10. Which of the following is theorized to be a contributing variable to food allergies?
    a. age
    b. changes in the modern diet
    c. "too clean" environments
    d. all of these

11. Which of the following children is likely to have the worst oral health?
    a. a 3-year-old who sucks her thumb frequently
    b. a 2-year old who takes a bottle of juice to bed nightly
    c. a 5-year-old who brushes daily but does not floss
    d. a 4-year-old who receives fluoride through his water supply

12. When riding in a car, young children
    a. need to use a seat belt, but no other precautions are necessary.
    b. should use a car or booster seat.
    c. should not sit in the front seat.
    d. Both b and c are correct.

13. Name three reasons that children of lower socio-economic status might have worse health than those of higher socio-economic status.

14. Homeless families are more likely to be from _____ areas and to be headed by _____.
    a. rural; two parents
    b. rural; single mothers
    c. urban; two parents
    d. urban; single mothers

15. Damage from tobacco exposure is _____ during the early years of life.
    a. worse
    b. unlikely to result in long-lasting damage
    c. rare
    d. illegal

16. With respect to lead poisoning, prevention is particularly important because
    a. it is the ethically right thing to do.
    b. treatment following exposure may not be very effective.
    c. it is difficult to identify children with lead poisoning.
    d. This is incorrect; it is more cost-effective to intervene following exposure than to prevent exposure.

SUMMARY

LO1

Describe the physical changes in young children's height, weight, and brain structure.

- Physical growth increases during the years from ages 3 to 6 but more slowly than during infancy and toddlerhood. Boys are on average slightly taller, heavier, and more muscular than girls. Internal body systems are maturing, and all primary teeth are present.
- Preschool children generally eat less for their weight than before—and need less—but the prevalence of obesity has increased.
- Tooth decay has decreased since the 1970s but remains a problem among disadvantaged children.
- Thumb-sucking can safely be ignored unless it continues beyond age 4, when permanent teeth begin to develop.
- By the age of 3, the brain is approximately 90 percent of adult weight, and from ages 3 to 6, the most rapid brain growth occurs in the frontal areas that regulate planning and organizing actions.

LO2

Summarize common sleep problems and disturbances in early childhood.

- Sleep patterns change during early childhood, as throughout life. Poor sleep quality is associated with behavioural difficulties and less harmonious parent-child interactions.
- It is normal for preschool children to develop bedtime rituals that delay going to sleep. Prolonged bedtime struggles or persistent sleep terrors or nightmares may indicate emotional disturbances that need attention.
- Bed-wetting is common and is usually outgrown without special help.

LO3

Summarize the continued development of fine and gross motor skills and discuss the influences on handedness.

- Children progress rapidly in gross and fine motor skills and eye-hand coordination, developing more complex systems of action.
- Handedness is usually evident by age 3, likely influenced by a combination of genetic and environmental factors.

- Although major contagious illnesses are rare today in industrialized countries as a result of widespread immunization, preventable disease continues to be a major problem in the non-industrialized world.

- Minor illnesses, such as colds and other respiratory illnesses, are common during early childhood and help build immunity to disease.

- Obesity is a serious problem among Canadian preschoolers, with obesity rates rising threefold over the past 25 years.

- About 7 out of every 100 children in Canada have some type of food allergy.

- Accidents, most commonly motor vehicle injuries, are the leading cause of death in childhood in Canada. Most fatal non-vehicular accidents occur at home.

- Environmental factors such as exposure to smoking, poverty, and homelessness increase the risks of illness or injury. Lead poisoning can have serious physical, cognitive, and behavioural effects.

ANSWERS TO Ask Yourself

Answers: 1–b; 2–Among the bodily changes that occur are the proportions of the body become more adult-like; the abdominal muscles develop and the stomach tightens; and the trunk, arms, and legs grow longer; 3–d; 4–e; 5–c; 6–An example of a gross motor skill is any movement that uses the large muscles of the body, and an example of a fine motor skill is any movement that requires eye-hand and small-muscle coordination; 7–a; 8–Among the variables related to risk of overweight/obesity in children are genes, poor portion control in preschool, too little physical activity, and watching television; 9–c; 10–d; 11–b; 12–d; 13–Among the reasons children from low socio-economic status might have worse health than those of higher socio-economic status are their greater risk of illness, injury, and death; their higher likelihood of having chronic conditions and activity limitations; and their higher likelihood of having unmet medical and dental needs; 14–b; 15–a; 16–b

connect LEARNSMART SMARTBOOK™

For more information on the resources available from McGraw-Hill Ryerson, go to **www.mcgrawhill.ca/he/solutions**.

CHAPTER

9

COGNITIVE
DEVELOPMENT

Piagetian Approach: The Preoperational Child

Information-Processing Approach: Memory Development

Psychometric Approaches to Intelligence

Vygotskian Approach to Measurement and Teaching

Language Development

Early Childhood Education

WHAT'S TO COME

A young researcher sat across from 6-year-old Schi. "What is memory?" he asked him, pen in hand ready to take notes on the child's response. Schi glanced up at the scientist, "When you remember something," he stated simply. "But how do you remember?" the researcher pressed. "Well," the little boy answered, "It suddenly comes into the mind. When you've been told something, it comes into your mind, then it goes out and then it comes back . . . into the sky."

While most people would smile at such flights of fancy and move on, the young researcher interviewing Schi was none other than Jean Piaget. Piaget would use Schi's interviews, as well as those of other children of varying ages, to help him develop his theories of cognitive development. Through Piaget's brilliant musings and careful analysis of children's behaviour, the seeds of both the cognitive revolution and developmental psychology as a field were planted. Piaget was one among a number of researchers who have advanced our knowledge of children's cognition. While he focused on children's logical errors, others have focused on their information processing capacities, how to measure their intelligence, what social factors help them learn, their use of language, and last, how all these factors can be used to design and implement quality early childhood education.

In this chapter, we examine Piaget's theoretical approach of cognitive development in early childhood. We will see how children's thinking advances after toddlerhood and in what ways it remains immature. We also touch on Vygotsky, a contemporary of Piaget's, as well as on the modern extensions of their early work. We examine the beginnings of autobiographical memory, and we compare psychometric intelligence tests with assessments based on Vygotsky's theories. We look at children's increasing fluency with language and how this impacts other domains of development. Finally, we look at the widening world of preschool and kindergarten.

IN EARLY CHILDHOOD

AS YOU READ

LO1   Summarize the advances and immature aspects of a young child's thinking processes.
LO2   Discuss the changes in memory capabilities and how they impact recall, recognition, and childhood memory.
LO3   Describe how intelligence is measured, and summarize influences on how intelligence is measured and how this informs teaching practices.
LO4   Understand measurement and teaching methods based on Vygotsky's theory.
LO5   Summarize the typical sequence of language development and describe how language delays, preparation for literacy, and exposure to media sources impact these processes.
LO6   Discuss the impact of early childhood education and intervention programs on development.

Piagetian Approach: The Preoperational Child

Jean Piaget called early childhood the **preoperational stage** of cognitive development because children of this age are not ready to engage in logical mental operations. This period is characterized by a great expansion in the use of symbolic thought, or representational ability, which first emerges near the end of the sensorimotor stage, and is most notably illustrated by the growth of language abilities. In this section, we look at advances and immature aspects of preoperational thought, as well as the development of theory of mind.

ADVANCES OF PREOPERATIONAL THOUGHT

As children's cognitive development proceeds, they begin to think in fundamentally different ways. Young children are grounded in the concrete here-and-now, according to Piaget, and the fundamental achievements in cognitive ability stem from advances in symbolic thought. These advances are accompanied by a growing understanding of objects in space, causality, identities and categorization, and number, an understanding that was previously impossible.

The Symbolic Function

"I want ice cream!" announces Lila, age 4, trudging indoors from the hot, dusty backyard. She has not seen anything that triggered this desire—no open freezer door, no television commercial. She no longer needs a sensory cue to think about something; she can remember ice cream and she purposefully seeks it out. This is an illustration of the **symbolic function**, the ability to use symbols or mental representations. For example, language is a symbolic representational system. The word "key" is a symbol for the object that we use to open doors. Without symbols, people could not communicate verbally, make change, read maps, or treasure photos of distant loved ones.

Preschool children show the symbolic function through deferred imitation, pretend play, and language. **Deferred imitation**, which becomes more common after 18 months, is based on having kept a mental representation of an observed action—as when 3-year-old Bart scolds his little sister, using the same words he heard his father say to the delivery boy who was late bringing the pizza. In **pretend play**, also called *fantasy play*, *dramatic play*, or *imaginary play*, children may make an object, such as a doll, represent, or symbolize, something else, such as a person. Language is also symbolic; words stand for objects and concepts in our world.

Objects in Space

Another area tied to the development of symbolic abilities involves representations of the world. It is not until at least age 3 that most children reliably grasp the relationships between pictures, maps, or scale models and the larger or smaller objects or spaces they represent. Older preschoolers can use simple maps, and they can transfer the spatial understanding gained from working with models to maps

---

preoperational stage   In Piaget's theory, the second major stage of cognitive development, in which children become more sophisticated in their use of symbolic thought but are not yet able to use logic.

symbolic function   Piaget's term for the ability to use mental representations (words, numbers, or images) to which a child has attached meaning.

deferred imitation   Piaget's term for reproduction of an observed behaviour after the passage of time by calling up a stored symbol of it.

pretend play   Play involving imaginary people or situations; also called *fantasy play*, *dramatic play*, or *imaginary play*.

and vice versa (Sharon & DeLoache, 2003). For example, when shown on a map where a toy is hidden in a room, they can then be taken to that room and effectively find the toy.

Causality

Piaget maintained that preoperational children cannot yet reason logically about cause and effect. Instead, he said, they reason by **transduction**. They mentally link two events close in time, whether or not there is logically a causal relationship. For example, Luis may think that his "bad" thoughts or behaviour caused his own or his sister's illness or his parents' divorce.

Yet, in naturalistic observations of 2½ - to 5-year-olds' everyday conversations with their parents, the children do show flexible causal reasoning. Types of explanations range from physical ("The scissors have to be clean so that I can cut better") to social–conventional ("I have to stop now because you said to") (Hickling & Wellman, 2001).

Identities and Categorization

Categorization, or classification, requires a child to identify similarities and differences between classes of objects. By age 4, many children can classify by two criteria, such as colour and shape. Children use this ability to order many aspects of their lives, categorizing people as "good" or "bad," "nice" or "mean," and so forth.

One type of categorization is the ability to distinguish living from non-living things. The tendency to attribute life to objects that are not alive is called **animism**. Younger children are likely to behave as if they believe that cars, toys, or clouds are alive. However, when 3- and 4-year-olds are questioned about something more familiar to them— differences between objects such as a rock and a person—

transduction In Piaget's terminology, a preoperational child's tendency to mentally link particular experiences, whether or not there is logically a causal relationship.

animism Tendency to attribute life to objects that are not alive.

the children showed they understood that people are alive and rocks are not (Jipson & Gelman, 2007).

Number

Research suggests that infants as young as 4½ months seem to know that if one doll is added to another doll, there should be two dolls, not just one. Other research has found that *ordinality*—the concept of comparing quantities (more or less, bigger or smaller)—seems to begin at around 9 to 11 months (Brannon, 2002).

When asked to count six items, children younger than 3½ years tend to recite the number-names (one through six) but not to say how many total items there are (six). It is not until age 3½ or older that most children consistently apply the *cardinality* principle in counting (Sarnecka & Carey, 2007). However, there is some evidence that children as young as 2½ use cardinality in practical situations, such as checking to make sure which plate has more cookies on it (Gelman, 2006).

By age 4, most children can say that one tree is bigger than another or that one cup holds more juice than another. If they have one cookie and then get another cookie, they know they have more cookies than they had before. By age 5, most children can count to 20 or more and know the relative sizes of the numbers 1 through 10 (Siegler, 1998).

By the time they enter elementary school, most children have developed basic "number sense" (Jordan, Kaplan, Oláh, & Locunia, 2006). This basic level of number skills (Table 9.1) includes counting, number knowledge (ordinality), number transformations (simple addition and subtraction), estimation ("Is this group of dots more or less than 5?"), and recognition of number patterns (2 plus 2 equals 4, and so does 3 plus 1).

Socio-economic status (SES) and preschool experience affect how rapidly children advance in math. By age 4, children from middle-income families have markedly better number skills than children from lower-income families, and their initial advantage tends to continue. Children whose preschool teachers do a lot of "math talk," such as asking children to help count days on a calendar, tend to make greater gains than children whose teachers do not use this technique (Klibanoff, Levine, Huttenlocher, Vasilyeva, & Hedges, 2006). Finally, playing number board games with children enhances their numerical knowledge, especially if they are from low-SES backgrounds (Ramani & Siegler, 2008).

TABLE 9.1 Key Elements of Number Sense in Young Children

Area	Components
Counting	■ Grasping one-to-one correspondence ■ Knowing stable order and cardinality principles ■ Knowing the count sequence
Number knowledge	■ Discriminating and coordinating quantities ■ Making numerical magnitude comparisons
Number transformation	■ Simple addition and subtraction ■ Calculating in story problems and non-verbal contexts ■ Calculating "in the head"
Estimation	■ Approximating or estimating set sizes ■ Using reference points
Number patterns	■ Copying number patterns ■ Extending number patterns ■ Discerning numerical relationships

Source: Adapted from Jordan et al. (2006).

LIMITS OF PREOPERATIONAL THOUGHT

According to Piaget, one of the main characteristics of pre-operational thought is **centration**, the tendency to focus on one aspect of a situation and neglect others, such as noting the height of a glass of juice, but not the width. This is an immature area of preoperational thought for children ages 3 to 5. Piaget argued that preschoolers come to illogical conclusions because they cannot **decentre**—focus on more than one aspect of a situation at one time. Two forms of centration are egocentrism and conservation.

Egocentrism

Egocentrism, as a form of centration, is the inability to distinguish between the child's own and another person's point of view. According to Piaget, young children centre so much on their own point of view that they cannot take in another's. Egocentrism may help explain why young children sometimes have trouble separating reality from what goes on inside their heads and why they may show confusion about what causes what. When Emily believes that her "bad thoughts" have made her brother sick or that she caused her parents' marital troubles, she is thinking egocentrically.

To study egocentrism, Piaget designed the *three-mountains task* (Figure 9.1). A child sits facing a table that holds three large mounds. A doll is placed on a chair at the opposite side of the table. The investigator asks the child how the mountains would look from the vantage point of the doll. Piaget found that young children usually described the mountains from their own perspective and could not take a point of view different from their own (Piaget & Inhelder, 1967).

However, when children are asked to take the view of others in a more simple and familiar way, their performance

improves. In one study, a child was given instructions to select one object from a set of objects by an experimenter who could see only some of the objects. The researchers found that children as young as 3 were able to take the experimenter's perspective. For example, two of the objects were rubber ducks, one small and one large. In one condition, the experimenter could see only one of the rubber ducks. When the child heard the instructions to retrieve the rubber duck, the child more often selected the rubber duck that the experimenter could see even though the child could see both rubber ducks (Nilsen & Graham, 2009).

Why were these children able to take another person's point of view when those doing the mountain task were not? Most children do not look at mountains and do not think about what other people might see when looking at them, but most preschoolers know something about hiding. Thus, young children may show egocentrism primarily in situations beyond their immediate experience.

Conservation

A classic example of centration is the failure to understand **conservation**, the fact that two things that are equal remain so if their appearance is altered, so long as nothing is added or taken away. In Piaget's classic conservation-of-liquid task, a child is shown two identical clear glasses, each short and wide and each holding the same amount of water. The child is then asked, "Is the amount of water in the two glasses the same?" When he or she agrees, the researcher pours the water in one glass into a third glass, a tall, thin one. Then the child is asked, "Do both glasses contain the same amount of water? Or does one contain more? Why?" In early childhood—even after watching the water being poured out of one of the short, fat glasses into a tall, thin glass, or even after pouring it themselves—children will say that either the taller glass or the wider one contains more water. When asked why, they tend to say that the glass is taller, or the glass is wider, taking into account only one of the relevant dimensions. They centre on only one aspect and use that to answer the question. Table 9.2 shows how various dimensions of conservation have been tested.

The ability to conserve is also limited by **irreversibility**, the failure to understand that an operation or action can be undone. Once Justin can imagine restoring the original

Piaget's Three-Mountains Task

FIGURE 9.1 A preoperational child is unable to describe the mountains from the doll's point of view—an indication of egocentrism, according to Piaget.

Source: Adapted from Figure 10.1, p. 270 in Diane E. Papalia, Sally Wendkos Olds, and Ruth Duskin Feldman, *A Child's World: Infancy Through Adolescence*, 10th Ed. Copyright © 2006 by The McGraw-Hill Companies, Inc. Reprinted with permission.

centration   In Piaget's theory, tendency of preoperational children to focus on one aspect of a situation and neglect others.

decentre   In Piaget's terminology, to think simultaneously about several aspects of a situation.

egocentrism   Piaget's term for the inability to consider that another person's point of view can be different from one's own; a characteristic of young children's thought.

conservation   Piaget's term for awareness that two objects that are equal according to a certain measure remain equal in the face of perceptual alteration as long as nothing has been added to or taken away from either object.

irreversibility   Piaget's term for a preoperational child's failure to understand that an operation can go in two or more directions.

TABLE 9.2 Tests of Various Kinds of Conservation

Conservation Task	Show Child (and Have Child Acknowledge) That Both Items Are Equal	Perform Transformation	Ask Child	Preoperational Child Usually Answers
Number	Two equal, parallel rows of candies	Space the candies in one row farther apart.	"Are there the same number of candies in each row, or does one row now have more?"	"The longer one has more."
Length	Two parallel sticks of the same length	Move one stick to the right.	"Are both sticks the same size, or is one longer?"	"The one on the right (or left) is longer."
Liquid	Two identical glasses holding equal amounts of liquid	Pour liquid from one glass into a taller, narrower glass.	"Do both glasses have the same amount of liquid, or does one have more?"	"The taller one has more."
Matter (mass)	Two balls of clay of the same size	Roll one ball into a sausage shape.	"Do both pieces have the same amount of clay, or does one have more?"	"The sausage has more."
Weight	Two balls of clay of the same weight	Roll one ball into a sausage shape.	"Do both weigh the same, or does one weigh more?"	"The sausage weighs more."
Area	Two toy rabbits, two pieces of cardboard (representing grassy fields), with blocks or toys (representing barns on the fields); same number of "barns" on each board	Rearrange the blocks on one piece of board.	"Does each rabbit have the same amount of grass to eat, or does one have more?"	"The one with the blocks close together has more to eat."
Volume	Two glasses of water with two equal-sized balls of clay in them	Roll one ball into a sausage shape.	"If we put the sausage back in the glass, will the water be the same height in each glass, or will one be higher?"	"The water in the glass with the sausage will be higher."

state of the water by pouring it back into the other glass, he will realize that the amount of water in both glasses must be the same.

THEORY OF MIND

Amalia, age 4, hates brussels sprouts, but when her father asks for them to be passed at the dinner table, she picks up the bowl and places it in her father's hands. She does this because she now understands that her father might like brussels sprouts, even though she herself finds them highly suspect. In understanding this, Amalia is illustrating the emergence of theory of mind.

Theory of mind is the understanding that others have their own thoughts, beliefs, desires, and intentions. Having a theory of mind allows us to understand and predict the behaviour of others and makes the social world understandable. Different people may have different theories of mind, depending upon social experiences. Theory of mind includes knowledge of thinking about mental states, false beliefs, and distinguishing between fantasy and reality. How theory of mind develops has several influences.

theory of mind Awareness and understanding of mental processes of others.

Conservation-of-liquid task.

Knowledge about Thinking and Mental States

Between ages 3 and 5, children come to understand that thinking goes on inside the mind; that it can deal with either real or imaginary things; that someone can be thinking of one thing while doing or looking at something else; that a person whose eyes and ears are covered can think about objects; and that thinking is different from seeing, talking, touching, and knowing (Flavell, 2000).

However, preschoolers generally believe that mental activity starts and stops. Not until middle childhood do children know that the mind is continuously active (Flavell, 2000). Three-year-olds, for example, tend to believe they can dream about anything they wish. Five-year-olds show a more adult-like understanding, recognizing that physical experiences, emotions, knowledge, and thoughts can affect the content of dreams.

Theory of mind accompanies the decline of egocentrism and the development of empathy, and underlies a wide range of social achievements. By the age of 4, children can understand that people have differing beliefs about the world—true or mistaken—and that these beliefs affect their actions.

False Beliefs

A researcher shows 3-year-old Madeline a cookie box and asks what is in it. "Cookies," she says. But when Madeline opens the box, she finds crayons, not cookies. "What will a child who hasn't opened the box think is in it?" the researcher asks. "Crayons," says Madeline, not understanding that another child would be fooled by the box just as she was (Flavell, 2000).

The understanding that people can hold false beliefs requires the understanding that people hold mental representations of reality that can sometimes be wrong. Three-year-olds, like Madeline, appear to lack such an understanding

(Flavell, 2000). An analysis of 178 studies in various countries, using a number of variations on false-belief tasks, found this consistent developmental pattern (Wellman & Cross, 2001).

Three-year-olds' failure to recognize false beliefs may stem in part from egocentric thinking. At that age, children tend to believe that everyone else knows what they know and believes what they do (Lillard & Curenton, 1999). Four-year-olds, by contrast, understand that people who see or hear different versions of the same event may come away with different beliefs. Not until about age 6, however, do children realize that two people who see or hear the same thing may interpret it differently (Pillow & Henrichon, 1996).

Distinguishing between Fantasy and Reality

Sometime between 18 months and 3 years, children learn to distinguish between real and imagined events. Three-year-olds know the difference between a real dog and a dog in a dream, and between something invisible, such as air, and something imaginary. They can pretend and can tell when someone else is pretending (Flavell, 2000). By age 3—in some cases, by age 2—they know that pretence is intentional; they can tell the difference between trying to do something and pretending to do the same thing (Rakoczy, Tomasello, & Striano, 2004).

Children often engage in magical thinking as a way to explain events that do not seem to have an obvious realistic explanation (usually because children lack knowledge about them) or simply to indulge in the pleasures of pretending, as with the belief in imaginary companions. Magical thinking in children age 3 and older does not seem to stem from confusion between fantasy and reality, and it tends to decline near the end of the preschool period (Woolley, Phelps, Davis, & Mandell, 1999). Moreover, there are indications that imaginary play may offer developmental benefits. In one study, children who had imaginary companions used richer and more elaborate narrative structure than children without imaginary companions when asked to recount a personal story (Trionfi & Reese, 2009).

All in all, then, the research on various theory-of-mind topics suggests that young children may have a clearer picture of reality than Piaget believed.

Influences on Individual Differences in Theory-of-Mind Development

Some children develop theory-of-mind abilities earlier than others. In part, this development reflects brain maturation and general improvements in cognition. What other influences explain individual differences?

Infant social attention has been closely linked to theory-of-mind development (Wellman & Liu, 2004). In one study, 45 children were evaluated as infants and then again as 4-year-olds. Measures of infant social attention significantly predicted later theory of mind, demonstrating strong support for continuity in social cognition (Wellman, Lopez-Duran, LaBounty, & Hamilton, 2008).

Difficulties in social interaction associated with Turner's syndrome, and typical delays in understanding of false beliefs in children with autism, support a strong genetic influence on social cognition since both of these disorders have genetic origins. Brain imaging shows increased activity in the left frontal lobe (a brain region in which autistic persons show abnormalities) during theory-of-mind tasks (Sabbagh & Taylor, 2000). A study of 119 same-sex 3-year-old twins found a heritability of 67 percent in understanding of false beliefs and deception (Hughes & Cutting, 1999).

WHAT DO YOU **DO?**

Pediatric Neurologist

Pediatric neurologists specialize in the young mind. In addition to treating head or brain injuries, seizures, and tumours, pediatric neurologists also see patients who have sleep problems, delayed speech, problems with motor skills, or other developmental issues that parents might be concerned about. Pediatric neurologists must complete medical school, a pediatric residency, and a neurological residency, as well as receive board certification. Pediatric neurologists typically practise in hospitals or in group or private practices. To learn more about pediatric neurology, visit www.childneurologysociety.org or www.cnsfederation.org (and click on CACN, for the Canadian Association of Child Neurology).

Did you know?

In 2011, more than 17 percent of Canadians were bilingual in English and French. English was the first language of 58 percent of Canadians, and French was the first language of 22 percent of Canadians. Twenty percent reported a first language other than French or English (Statistics Canada, 2012g).

Bilingual children, who speak and hear more than one language at home, do somewhat better than children with only one language on certain theory-of-mind tasks (Bialystok & Senman, 2004; Goetz, 2003). Bilingual children know that an object or idea can be represented linguistically in more than one way, and this knowledge may help them see that different people may have different perspectives. Bilingual children also recognize the need to match their language to that of their partner, and this may make them more aware of others' mental states. Finally, bilingual children tend to have better attentional control, and this may enable them to focus on what is true or real rather than on what only seems to be so (Bialystok & Senman, 2004; Goetz, 2003).

Social competence and language development are related to an understanding of mental states, and thus theory of mind (Cassidy, Werner, Rourke, Zubernis, & Balaraman, 2003). Children whose teachers and peers rate them high on social skills are better able to recognize false beliefs, to distinguish between real and feigned emotion, and to take another person's point of view. These children also tend to have strong language skills (Cassidy et al., 2003). The kind of talk a young child hears at home may also affect the child's understanding of mental states. A mother's reference to others' thoughts and knowledge is a consistent predictor of a child's later mental state language, and empathy usually arises earlier in children whose families talk a lot about feelings and causality (Dunn 2006).

Ask Yourself

1. Name three immature aspects of cognition in early childhood.

2. One of the reasons that children typically fail to conserve is because
   a. they have difficulty focusing on one aspect (e.g., height or width) of a substance at a time.
   b. they have difficulty understanding that if they were to go backwards in time, the original shape or size of the substance would be the same as it was originally.
   c. they focus on transformations rather than end-states.
   d. children's ability to hold material in short-term memory for extended periods of time is poor.

3. Which of the following behaviours requires theory of mind?
   a. smiling at someone after they have smiled at you
   b. hitting another child for taking your toy
   c. getting scared when you see your sister's skinned knee
   d. lying to your mom about eating cookies before dinner

Did you know?

Conservation requires children to hold two aspects—say, height and width—in mind at once. Likewise, understanding false beliefs also requires children to hold two things—what the person thinks and what is actually true—in mind at once.

Information-Processing Approach: Memory Development

When recalling events, young children tend to focus on exact details of an event, while simultaneously failing to notice important aspects of a situation, such as when and where an event occurred. However, as they improve in attention and in the speed and efficiency with which they process information, their memories also improve, and they begin to form long-lasting memories more focused on the "gist" of what happened. In the following sections, we summarize key changes that occur from 3 to 6 years of age in these processes.

BASIC PROCESSES AND CAPACITIES

Information-processing theorists think of memory as a filing system that has three steps: encoding, storage, and retrieval. **Encoding**, processes by which information is prepared for long-term storage and later retrieval, is like putting information in a folder to be filed in memory; it attaches a "code" or "label" to the information so that it

will be easier to find when needed. Events are encoded along with information about the context in which they are encountered. **Storage**, the retention of information for future use, is putting the folder away in the filing cabinet. **Retrieval**, the processes by which information is accessed from memory storage, occurs when the information is needed; the child then searches for the file and takes it out. Difficulties in any of these processes can impact memory.

The way the brain stores information is believed to be universal, though the efficiency of the system varies from one person to another (Siegler, 1998). Information-processing models depict the brain as containing three storehouses: sensory memory, working memory, and long-term memory.

Sensory memory is a temporary storehouse for incoming sensory information that decays rapidly. Sensory memory shows little change from infancy on (Siegler, 1998). However, without processing (encoding), sensory memories fade quickly.

Memory Systems

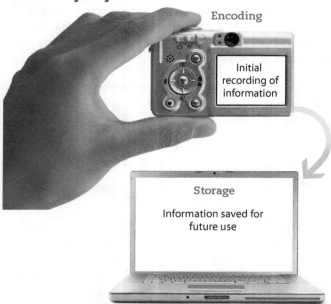

Encoding

Initial recording of information

Storage

Information saved for future use

FIGURE 9.2

Memory is like a filing system with three steps: encoding, storage, and retrieval.

Source: Adapted from Feldman, *Psychology and Your Life,* 2nd Ed., p. 207.

Retrieval

Recovery of stored information

Did you know?

Have you ever had the experience of talking to someone, not hearing them, saying, "What?" and then by the time the word leaves your mouth, you heard them? That's your sensory memory at play.

Information being encoded or retrieved is kept in **working memory**, a short-term storehouse for information a person is actively working on, trying to understand, remember, or think about. Brain imaging studies have found that working memory is located partly in the prefrontal cortex, the large portion of the frontal lobe directly behind the forehead (Nelson et al., 2000).

The efficiency of working memory is limited by its capacity. As children get older, their working memory capacity increases (Zelazo, Müller, Frye, & Marcovitch, 2003).

The growth of working memory may permit the development of **executive function**, conscious control of thoughts, emotions, and actions to accomplish goals. Executive function enables children to plan and carry out mental activity in the service of meeting a goal, and is often useful when children need to focus their attention on something or override an inappropriate response. For example, despite being eager for a turn, a child might wait in line for a slide, knowing that

---

encoding   Process by which information is prepared for long-term storage and later retrieval.

storage   Retention of information in memory for future use.

retrieval   Process by which information is accessed or recalled from memory storage.

sensory memory   Initial, brief, temporary storage of sensory information.

working memory   Short-term storage of information being actively processed.

executive function   Conscious control of thoughts, emotions, and actions to accomplish goals or solve problems.

Did you know?

Working memory can be conceptualized as a juggler keeping many objects in the air at once. What you are thinking about right at the moment—what is in your mind at that time—is the collection of objects in the air. Just as with juggling, there are a limited number of items that can be worked on in working memory at once, and when you want to add something new, something already there must be "dropped" from working memory.

The central executive plays a key role in processing information and achieving goals, like matching the cards in a game of concentration.

to cut the line would result in disciplinary action from the teacher. Executive function probably emerges around the end of an infant's first year and develops in spurts with age. Changes in executive function between ages 2 and 5 enable children to make up and use complex rules for solving problems (Zelazo et al., 2003). Good executive functioning predicts (but doesn't necessarily cause) good achievement in elementary school and reasoning abilities in adolescence (Bull, Espy, & Wiebe, 2008; Richland & Burchinal, 2013; Willoughby, Kupersmidt, & Voegler-Lee, 2012).

According to a widely used model, a **central executive** controls processing operations in working memory (Baddeley, 2001). The central executive orders information encoded for transfer to **long-term memory**, a storehouse of virtually unlimited capacity that holds information for long periods of time. The central executive also retrieves information from long-term memory for further processing.

Once material is placed in memory, it must be retrieved in order to be used. **Recognition** and recall are types of retrieval. Recognition is the ability to identify something encountered before, for example, to pick out a missing mitten from a lost-and-found box. **Recall** is the ability to reproduce knowledge from memory, for example, to describe the mitten to someone. Preschool children, like those in all age groups, do better on recognition than on recall, but both abilities improve with age. The more familiar children are with an item, the better they can recall it. However, young children often fail to use strategies for remembering—even strategies they already know—unless reminded (Schwenck, Bjorklund, & Schneider, 2009).

central executive   In Baddeley's model, the element of working memory that controls the processing of information.

long-term memory   Storage of virtually unlimited capacity that holds information for long periods.

recognition   Ability to identify a previously encountered stimulus.

recall   Ability to reproduce material from memory.

procedural memory   Memories of habitual and familiar routines to guide behaviour.

episodic memory   Long-term memory of specific experiences or events, linked to time and place.

autobiographical memory   A type of episodic memory of distinctive experiences that form a person's life history.

MEMORY IN CHILDHOOD

Three types of memory that serve different functions emerge during childhood: procedural, episodic, and autobiographical (Bauer, 2006; Bauer, Larkina, & Deocampo, 2010; Schneider, 2010).

Procedural memory produces representations of familiar, repeated actions involving habits and skills, such as riding a bicycle or tying shoelaces, and emerges in an early form in infancy (Lloyd & Newcombe, 2009). It helps a child to act in habitual ways without awareness (Bauer, 2006; Schneider, 2010).

Episodic memory refers to awareness of having experienced a particular event that occurred at a specific time and place, like a particularly fun day at the park on a sunny day. Given a young child's limited memory capacity, episodic memories are temporary. Unless they recur several times, they last for a few weeks or months and then fade. Talking about events with parents often helps children remember them on a more long-term basis, presumably by providing verbal labels for aspects of an event and giving it an orderly, comprehensible structure (Nelson & Fivush, 2004).

Autobiographical memory, a type of episodic memory, refers to memories of distinctive experiences that form a person's life history. Not everything in episodic memory becomes part of autobiographical memory—only those memories that have a special, personal meaning to the child (Fivush & Nelson, 2004). Autobiographical memory generally emerges between ages 3 and 4 (Nelson, 2005).

A suggested explanation for the relatively slow arrival of autobiographical memory is that children cannot store in memory events pertaining to their own lives until they develop a concept of self (Nelson & Fivush, 2004). Also critical is the emergence of language, which enables children to share memories and organize them into personal narratives (Nelson, 2005).

Psychometric Approaches to Intelligence

One factor that may affect the strength of early cognitive skills such as memory capacity and language is intelligence. Intelligence is traditionally measured through psychometric tests; however, the accuracy of these may be influenced by environmental factors.

TRADITIONAL PSYCHOMETRIC MEASURES

The two most commonly used individual intelligence tests for preschoolers are the Stanford-Binet Intelligence Scale and the Wechsler Preschool and Primary Scale of Intelligence.

The **Stanford-Binet Intelligence Scale** is used for children ages 2 and up and takes 45 to 60 minutes to complete. The child is asked to define words, string beads, build with blocks, identify the missing parts of a picture, trace mazes, and show an understanding of numbers. The child's score is supposed to measure fluid reasoning (the ability to solve abstract or novel problems), knowledge, quantitative reasoning, visual-spatial processing, and working memory. The fifth edition of the test includes non-verbal methods of testing all five of these dimensions of cognition and permits comparisons of verbal and non-verbal performance. In addition to providing a full-scale IQ, the Stanford-Binet yields separate measures of verbal

Stanford-Binet Intelligence Scale Individual intelligence test for ages 2 and up, used to measure knowledge, quantitative reasoning, visual-spatial processing, and working memory.

Wechsler Preschool and Primary Scale of Intelligence, Fourth Edition (WPPSI-IV) Individual intelligence test for children ages 2½ to 7 that yields verbal and performance scores, as well as a combined score.

and non-verbal IQ, plus composite scores spanning the five cognitive dimensions.

The **Wechsler Preschool and Primary Scale of Intelligence, Fourth Edition (WPPSI-IV)** is an individual test taking 30 to 60 minutes. It has separate levels for ages 2½ to 4 and ages 4 to 7 and yields separate verbal and performance scores, as well as a combined score. The most current version includes subtests designed to measure both verbal and non-verbal fluid reasoning, receptive versus expressive vocabulary, and processing speed.

Although American IQ tests, like the Stanford-Binet and the WPPSI–IV, are used in Canada, their use for Canadian children may not be appropriate. The test norms used to compare individual children's performance do not reflect the makeup of the Canadian population (French, French, & Rutherford, 1999), and the tests could be biased against some ethnic groups in Canada. This bias, which results in systematic differences in scores in groups for which the tests were not originally developed, can occur when test items are not well translated (for children with different first languages), when items can mean different things to children from different cultural groups, when the content of questions is not familiar to or is inappropriate for cultural minority children, and when cultural minorities are not included in the standardization groups for the tests (Van de Vijver & Tanzer, 2004).

New Canadians and Aboriginal children could obtain lower scores than they would have achieved if the tests were appropriate to their language backgrounds, cultural experiences, and upbringing (Dolan, 1999; Riddell, 2007; Saklofske & Schwean, 1995). To address some of these issues, the WPPSI-IV has been restandardized on samples of children representing the population of preschool-age children in Canada, and validated for special populations, such as children with intellectual disabilities, developmental delays, language disorders, and autistic disorders.

INFLUENCES ON MEASURED INTELLIGENCE

A common misconception is that IQ scores represent a fixed quantity of inborn intelligence. In reality, an IQ score is simply a measure of how well a child can do certain tasks at a certain time in comparison with others of the same age. This can be used to identify gifted children, as well as children who need extra assistance. Thus, children who might benefit from special attention can be provided with appropriate programming. Additionally, most tests have been in use for some time and as such are standardized, normed, and reliable. Moreover, they do indeed help predict academic achievement. However, there are also negatives to IQ testing. Most notably, they may track children inappropriately, and while many people interpret them to mean innate ability, in reality, IQ tests are more reflective of experiences. Indeed, test scores of children in many industrialized countries have risen steadily since testing began, forcing test developers to raise standardized norms (Flynn, 1984, 1987). This trend was thought to reflect better nutrition in early childhood, exposure to educational television and preschools, better-educated parents, smaller families in which each child receives more attention, and a wide variety of mentally demanding games, as well as changes in the tests themselves.

The degree to which family environment influences a child's intelligence is difficult to determine. Twin and adoption studies suggest that family life has its strongest influence in early childhood, and this influence diminishes greatly by adolescence (Bouchard & McGue, 2003) when children's exposure to different experiences is more self-driven. However, these studies have been done largely with white, middle-class samples; their results may not apply to low-income and non-white families (Neisser et al., 1996).

The correlation between socio-economic status and IQ is well documented (Strenze, 2007). Family income is associated with cognitive development and achievement in the preschool years and beyond. Family economic circumstances can exert a powerful influence, not so much in themselves as in the way they affect other factors, such as health, stress, parenting practices, and the atmosphere in the home (NICHD Early Child Care Research Network, 2005a; Ryan & Adams, 1998; Willms, 2002a).

But SES is only one of several important risk and protective factors for healthy cognitive development in children. According to the National Longitudinal Survey of Children and Youth, a variety of family- and neighbourhood-based factors, such as positive parent-child interactions, bedtime reading, and participation in sports, are related to Canadian children's

"readiness to learn." When they begin school, children experiencing these protective factors tend to have better vocabulary, communication skills, number knowledge, and copying and symbol use abilities (Bushnik & Garner, 2008; Thomas, 2006), beneficial to early school learning.

Vygotskian Approach to Measurement and Teaching

Tests of cognitive potential, based on Vygotsky's theories, allow more information about intelligence than do traditional measures. According to Vygotsky, children learn by internalizing the results of interactions with adults. This interactive learning is most effective in helping children cross the **zone of proximal development (ZPD)**, the imaginary psychological space between what they are already able to do by themselves and what they could do with help (refer to Chapter 1). The ZPD can be assessed by dynamic tests that provide a better measure of children's intellectual potential than do traditional psychometric tests. Examiners help the child when necessary by asking questions, giving examples or demonstrations, and offering feedback, making the test itself a learning situation.

Tests based on Vygotsky's approach emphasize potential rather than present achievement. These tests contain items up to two years above a child's current level of competence. The items a child can answer with help determine the ZPD, or potential level of development. Vygotsky (1956) gives an example of two children, each with a mental age of 7 years (based on ability to do various cognitive tasks). With the help of leading questions, examples, and demonstrations, Natasha can easily solve problems geared to a mental age of 9, two years beyond her mental age; however, Ivan, with the same kind of help, can do tasks at only a 7½-year-old level. If we measure these children by what they can do on their own (as traditional IQ tests do), their intelligence seems

Ask Yourself

7. Name two commonly used intelligence tests for children.

8. What is the best definition of an IQ score?
   a. a description of a fixed quantity of inborn intelligence
   b. a relatively direct measure of exposure to educational programming, preschools, and formative experiences
   c. a measure of how well a child can do certain tasks at a certain time in comparison to others of the same age
   d. a measure of genetic potential

9. The influence of the family environment
   a. increases in influence with age.
   b. decreases in influence with age.
   c. exerts a steady influence across age.
   d. has no effect at any age.

Did you know?

Vygotsky argued that pretend play was an ideal situation for learning. The "rules" of pretend play require children to stretch their abilities and to work at the higher end of their zone of proximal development. For example, if two girls are playing Sleeping Beauty, then one must lie still until woken. Lying still requires self-regulation and inhibition of impulses. The rules of the game provide the scaffolding that helps the child achieve this.

zone of proximal development (ZPD) Vygotsky's term for the difference between what a child can do alone and what the child can do with help.

about the same, but if we measure them by their immediate potential development (their ZPD), they are quite different.

The ZPD, in combination with the related concept of **scaffolding**, also can help parents and teachers efficiently guide children's cognitive progress. The less able a child is to do a task, the more scaffolding, or support, an adult must give. As the child can do more and more, the adult helps less and less. When the child can do the job alone, the adult takes away the scaffold that is no longer needed. Essentially, learning is most effective when it is aimed at the ZPD.

In one study, 3- and 4-year-olds were asked to give their parents directions for finding a hidden mouse in a dollhouse. The parents gave the children feedback when their directions needed clarifying. The parents proved to be highly sensitive to the children's scaffolding needs; they gave more directive prompts to 3-year-olds, whose directions tended to be less clear than those of 4-year-olds. The parents used fewer directive prompts as the children gained experience in giving clear directions (Plumert & Nichols-Whitehead, 1996).

Thus, Vygotsky's concept of the ZPD is useful not just from a measurement perspective but also from a teaching one. Pre-kindergarten children who receive scaffolding are better able to regulate their own learning when they get to kindergarten (Neitzel & Stright, 2003). In a longitudinal study of 289 families with infants, the skills that children developed during interactions with their mothers at 2 and 3½ enabled them, at 4½, to regulate goal-directed problem solving, to show independence in cognitive and social skills, and to initiate social interactions (Landry, Smith, Swank, & Miller-Loncar, 2000).

Ask Yourself

10. Which of the following is an example of working in a child's zone of proximal development?
    a. doing a child's homework for him or her
    b. giving hints to a child so that he or she can complete his or her homework with assistance
    c. encouraging a child to expend more effort to finish his or her homework
    d. hiring a tutor to help a child struggling with homework

11. Give two examples of how the ZPD can be assessed by dynamic testing.

Language Development

Preschoolers are full of questions: "How many sleeps until tomorrow?" "Who filled the river with water?" "Do babies have muscles?" "Do smells come from inside my nose?" Young children's growing facility with language helps them express their unique view of the world. The child who, at 3, describes how Daddy "hatches" wood (chops with a hatchet) or asks Mommy to "piece" her food (cut it into little pieces) may, by age 5, tell her mother, "Don't be ridiculous!" or proudly point to her toys and say, "See how I organized everything?" In this section, we will discuss some of the major changes in language development. We will also address delayed language, as well as the contribution language makes to pre-literacy.

AREAS OF LANGUAGE DEVELOPMENT

During the early childhood years, key language development occurs in the areas of vocabulary, grammar and syntax, and pragmatics and social speech.

Vocabulary

At age 3, the average child knows and can use 900 to 1,000 words. By age 6, a child typically has an *expressive* (speaking) vocabulary of 2,600 words and understands more than 20,000. With the help of formal schooling, a child's *passive*, or *receptive*, vocabulary—words she or he can understand—will quadruple to 80,000 words by the time the child enters high school (Owens, 1996).

This rapid expansion of vocabulary may occur through **fast mapping**, which allows a child to pick up the approximate meaning of a new word after hearing it only once or twice in conversation. From the context, children seem to form a quick hypothesis about the meaning of the word, which then is refined with further exposure and usage.

Grammar and Syntax

The ways children combine syllables into words, and words into sentences, grow increasingly sophisticated during early childhood. At age 3, children typically begin to use plurals, possessives, and past tense, and they know the difference between I, you, and we. They can ask and answer what and where questions. However, their sentences are generally short, simple, and declarative ("Kitty wants milk").

Between ages 4 and 5, children's sentences average four to five words and may be declarative ("I'm very tired."), negative ("I'm not hungry"), interrogative ("Why can't I go outside?"), or imperative ("Catch the ball!"). Four-year-olds use complex, multi-clause sentences ("I'm eating because I'm hungry") more frequently if their parents often use such sentences (Huttenlocher, Vasilyeva, Cymerman, & Levine, 2002). Children this age also tend to string sentences together in long run-on stories ("... And then ... And then ...").

scaffolding Temporary support to help a child master a task.

fast mapping Process by which a child absorbs the meaning of a new word after hearing it once or twice in conversation.

Perspectives on Diversity

PATHS TO LEARNING

In Canada and other Western nations, the primary way in which children learn the skills they need in order to be productive adult members of society is via formal education. In other words, they attend school. However, Vygotsky's theory of socio-cultural development, which implies that there are as many paths to effective development as there are potential interactions between "teachers" and "learners," suggests that there might be alternative ways that children could learn about their world. For example, parents interviewed in three First Nations communities in Ontario stressed the importance of play as an appropriate way of learning in early childhood, and had positive attitudes toward play-oriented daycare centres, which they saw as consistent with their cultural values (Gillis, 1992). Family-based learning programs can effectively complement formal education as they address diverse needs, like those of Aboriginal communities (Timmons, Walton, O'Keefe, & Wagner, 2008).

This idea has been studied by Barbara Rogoff (2003), who has conducted extensive cross-cultural research focused on the different ways in which cultural communities affect the development of children. In her work, she has found that non-industrialized cultures, rather than send children away to learn in a classroom, are more likely to involve children in everyday activities and experiences, which then transmit valuable cultural information and practical skills. For example, a young Mayan child might accompany her mother to the market, and while playing at her mother's feet, hear her mother negotiate and set a price for an item she is selling, thereby learning about currency conversions and mathematics. The child may be viewed as an apprentice of sorts, who acquires vital cultural knowledge through the practices and routine activities of daily life.

What Rogoff's research demonstrates is that, while in Western cultures formal educational practices may be effective for the transmission of information, it does not have to be this way. Other cultures have varying, and equally valid, ways of teaching their children what they need to know

---

By ages 5 to 7, children's speech has become quite adult-like. They speak in longer and more complicated sentences. They use more conjunctions ("and," "but"), prepositions ("by," "of"), and articles ("a," "the"), and can handle all parts of speech.

Still, although school-age children speak fluently, comprehensibly, and fairly grammatically, they have yet to master many fine points of language, with grammar emerging in a piecemeal fashion—some aspects emerging early, others emerging later on. For example, they rarely use and have difficulty understanding the passive voice ("I was dressed by Grandpa"), conditional sentences ("If I were big, I could drive the bus"), or the auxiliary verb *have* ("I have seen that lady before"), and they often have trouble identifying what is referred to in ambiguous sentences ("The spotted cow tickled the pig with a curly tail") (C. S. Chomsky, 1969; Ibbotson, Theakston, Lieven, & Tomasello, 2011; Theakston, 2012; Tomasello, 2000a, 2000b). These abilities emerge once they have had opportunities to listen to and use them in meaningful conversations (Tomasello, 2000a, 2000b). Children often make errors because they have not yet learned exceptions to rules. Saying "holded" instead of "held" or "eated" instead of "ate" is a normal sign of linguistic progress. When young children discover a rule, such as adding -*ed* to a verb for past tense, they tend to overgeneralize—to use it even with words that do not conform to the rule. Eventually, they notice that -*ed* is not always used to form the past tense of a verb.

Pragmatics and Social Speech

When Clara was 3 years old, she would ask for a cookie by demanding "Cookie now!" However, as she got older, she realized that saying "Momma, can I have a cookie please?" was far more effective.

As children learn vocabulary, grammar, and syntax, they become more competent in **pragmatics**, the social context of language, and **social speech**, language intended to be understood by a listener. These include knowing how to ask for things, how to tell a story or joke, how to begin and continue a conversation, and how to adjust comments to the listener's perspective (M. L. Rice, 1982).

With improved pronunciation and grammar, it becomes easier for others to understand what children say. Most 3-year-olds are quite talkative, and they pay attention to the effect of their speech on others. If people cannot understand them, they try to explain themselves more clearly.

Most 5-year-olds can adapt what they say to what the listener knows. They can use words to resolve disputes, and they use more polite language and fewer direct commands in talking to adults than to other children. Almost half of 5-year-olds can stick to a conversational topic for about a dozen turns—if they are comfortable with their partner and if the topic is one they know and care about (Owens, 1996).

---

pragmatics Practical knowledge needed to use language for communicative purposes.

social speech Speech intended to be understood by a listener.

Not all speech is directed toward others. **Private speech**, talking aloud to oneself with no intent to communicate with others, is normal and common in childhood. Theorists have disagreed on the precise nature of private speech. Piaget saw it as a sign of cognitive immaturity whereas Vygotsky saw it as mediating learning and problem-solving. Research generally supports Vygotsky as to the functions of private speech.

Like Piaget, Vygotsky (1962/1934) believed that private speech helps young children integrate language with thought. However, Vygotsky did not look upon private speech as egocentric. He saw it as a special form of communication: conversation with the self. As such, he said, it serves a very important function in the transition between early social speech (often experienced in the form of adult commands) and inner speech (thinking in words)—a transition toward the internalization of socially derived control of behaviour ("Now I have to put the pictures somewhere to dry").

The most sociable children and those who engage in the most social speech tend to use the most private speech as well, apparently supporting Vygotsky's view that private speech is stimulated by social experience. There also is evidence for the role of private speech in self-regulation (Berk & Garvin, 1984). Private speech tends to increase when children are trying to perform difficult tasks, especially without adult supervision (Berk, 1992).

DELAYED LANGUAGE DEVELOPMENT

Although for most children, language proceeds normally, a minority of children show delays in their language acquisition. The fact that Albert Einstein did not start to speak until he was between 2 and 3 years old (Isaacson, 2007) may encourage parents of other children whose speech develops later than usual. About 5 to 11 percent of preschool children show speech and language delays (Carscadden et al., 2010; U.S. Preventive Services Task Force, 2006).

Hearing problems, head and facial abnormalities, premature birth, family history, socio-economic factors, and some developmental delays can all be associated with speech and language delays (Dale et al., 1998; U.S. Preventive Services Task Force, 2006). Heredity seems to play a major role (Spinath, Price, Dale, & Plomin, 2004), and boys are more likely than girls to be late talkers (U.S. Preventive Services Task Force, 2006).

private speech Talking aloud to oneself with no intent to communicate with others.

emergent literacy Preschoolers' development of skills, knowledge, and attitudes that underlie reading and writing.

Many children who speak late, especially those whose comprehension is normal, eventually catch up. One of the largest studies to date on language emergence determined that 80 percent of children with language delays at age 2 catch up with their peers by age 7 (Rice, Taylor, & Zubrick, 2008). However, some 40 to 60 percent of children with early language delays, if left untreated, may experience far-reaching cognitive, social, and emotional consequences (U.S. Preventive Services Task Force, 2006).

PREPARATION FOR LITERACY

What is the link between language and literacy? While for all normally developing children, language is as natural as learning how to grasp a rattle or to walk, literacy is not something we are designed by natural selection to do. Rather, reading borrows from a variety of systems—vision, audition, memory, language, motor skills, and more. It is a testament to our flexibility and intelligence as a species that most children readily learn to read; however, it is neither easy nor natural, and by the time a child learns to read his or her first word, many skills have already been mastered. **Emergent literacy** refers to the development of these skills. Language is necessary for literacy, but it is by no means enough.

Pre-reading skills can be divided into two types: (1) oral language skills, such as vocabulary, syntax, narrative structure, and the understanding that language is used to communicate; and (2) specific phonological skills (linking letters with sounds) that help in decoding the printed word. Each of these types of skills seems to have its own independent effect (NICHD Early Child Care Research Network, 2005b). In a two-year longitudinal study of 90 British schoolchildren, the development of word recognition appeared critically dependent on phonological skills, whereas oral language skills such as vocabulary and grammatical skills were more important predictors of reading comprehension (Muter, Hulme, Snowling, & Stevenson, 2004).

Social interaction promotes emergent literacy. Children are more likely to become good readers and writers if, during the preschool years, parents provide conversational challenges the children are ready for—if they use a rich vocabulary and centre dinner-table conversation on the day's activities, on

Although not easy or natural like language, most children readily learn to read.

mutually remembered past events, or on questions about why people do things and how things work (Reese, 1995).

As children learn the skills they will need to translate the written word into speech, they also learn that writing can express ideas, thoughts, and feelings. Preschool children often pretend to write through drawings or scribbles (Levin & Bus, 2003; Whitehurst & Lonigan, 2001). Later, they begin using letters, numbers, and letter-like shapes to represent words, syllables, or phonemes. Often, their spelling is so inventive that they cannot read it themselves (Whitehurst & Lonigan, 2001).

Reading to children is one of the most effective paths to literacy. Between 55 (in low-income families) and 67 percent (in high-income families) of Canadian children age 5 years are read to daily by a family member (Thomas, 2006). Children who are read to from an early age learn that reading and writing in English move from left to right and from top to bottom and that words are separated by spaces. They also are motivated to learn to read (Whitehurst & Lonigan, 2001).

Ask Yourself

12. When young children say things such as, "Daddy goed to the store," this should be viewed as
    a. a normal developmental occurrence.
    b. a sign that a speech problem or delay is likely.
    c. a sign that a cognitive development problem or delay is likely.
    d. a sign of a specific language impairment.

13. Name three things that can contribute to speech delays.

14. One of the most effective pre-literacy activities for children is
    a. letter/sound flashcards.
    b. reading to them.
    c. exposure to television and other media sources.
    d. exposure to music.

Early Childhood Education

Going to preschool around age 3 is an important step that widens a child's physical, cognitive, and social environment. The transition to kindergarten, the beginning of "real school," at age 5 is another momentous step. Preschool enrollments have increased over the past 20 years as more Canadian mothers entered the workforce (Friendly & Prentice, 2009). By 2010, 21.8 percent of Canadian children between 0 and 5 years of age were enrolled in full- or part-time regulated centre-based early child education and care (Human Resources and Skills Development Canada, 2012). However, quality and access in early childhood education and care (ECEC) settings are limited in Canada (Friendly & Prentice, 2009; UNICEF, 2008c).

TYPES OF PRESCHOOLS

Preschools vary greatly in their goals and curriculums. In some countries, such as China, preschools provide academic preparation for schooling. In contrast, many preschools in Canada have followed progressive, child-centred philosophies stressing social and emotional growth in line with young children's developmental needs. Two of the most influential programs, Montessori and Reggio Emilia, were founded on similar child-centred philosophical premises.

Montessori and Reggio Emilia Methods

The Montessori method, introduced by Maria Montessori in 1907, is based on the belief that children's natural intelligence involves rational, spiritual, and empirical aspects (Edwards, 2003). Montessori stresses the importance of children learning independently at their own pace in multi-age classrooms as they work with developmentally appropriate materials and self-chosen tasks. Teachers serve as guides, and older children help younger ones (Montessori, 1995). An evaluation of Montessori education in an inner-city sample in Milwaukee found that 5-year-old Montessori students were better prepared for elementary school in reading and math than children who attended other types of preschools (Lillard & Else-Quest, 2006). Close adherence to Montessori principles and methods in Montessori schools appears to have better outcomes than mixed and conventional preschool approaches (Lillard, 2012).

The Reggio Emilia approach, named for the town in Italy in which the movement first started in the 1940s, is a less formal model than Montessori. Children are highly valued, capable, and given the opportunity to explore what they desire. Teachers follow children's interests and support them in exploring and investigating ideas and feelings through words, movement, dramatic play, and music. Learning is purposeful but less defined than with the Montessori curriculum. Teachers ask questions that draw out children's ideas and then create flexible plans to explore these ideas with the children. Classrooms are carefully constructed to offer complexity, beauty, organization, and a sense of well-being (Edwards, 2002).

Project Head Start

Since the 1960s, large-scale programs in the United States have been developed to help children in low-income families and neighbourhoods compensate for what they have missed and to prepare them for school. The best known of these preschool intervention programs is Project Head Start, a U.S. federally funded program launched in 1965 to enhance cognitive skills, improve physical health, and foster self-confidence and social skills.

Head Start is effective in improving school readiness, and teacher and program quality continue to improve (Administration for Children and Families [ACF], 2006; Aikens, Kopack Klein, Tarullo, & West, 2013; USDHHS, 2003b). Children who attend Head Start show better cognitive and language skills and do better in school than children who do not attend (USDHHS, 2003a). Furthermore, their skills continue to progress in kindergarten, with gains being closely related to parental involvement (ACF, 2006).

Long-term, Head Start benefits lessen with time, but they nonetheless outweigh the costs (Ludwig & Phillips, 2007; Puma et al., 2012). Low-income children from Head Start and other programs are less likely to be placed in special education or to repeat a grade, are more likely to finish high school than those who did not attend such programs (Deming, 2009), and are less likely to become juvenile delinquents or to become pregnant in their teens (Schweinhart, 2007). Outcomes are best with earlier and longer-lasting intervention through high-quality, centre-based programs (Brooks-Gunn, 2003; Zigler & Styfco, 2001).

Aboriginal Head Start

The Aboriginal Head Start Program (AHS) is an intervention started in 1995 to meet the social and cultural needs of First Nations, Métis, and Inuit children living in urban and northern communities and on reserves across Canada. Funded by Health Canada under the Aboriginal Head Start Initiative, over 130 programs in eight provinces and three northern territories involve about 10 percent of Aboriginal children from 2½ to 5 years, with the aim of preparing children for elementary school and building understanding and pride in their traditional cultures and languages (Ball, 2008; Dunning, 2000; Health Canada, 2001; Statistics Canada, 2004). The programs are operated as high-quality child care centres, emphasizing social and cognitive skill development, and include cultural elements with formal involvement of the family and Aboriginal community to promote the retention and growth of Aboriginal cultures and languages. The family and community are integral parts of the AHS; parents work as aides in the classroom, curriculum planners, kitchen helpers, and custodians, among other roles.

All aspects of the children's experiences, including curriculum activities and materials, daily snacks, parent education, and resources, are designed to reflect their traditional culture whenever possible. The key is to develop a connection between Aboriginal language and culture and the educational experiences of the children. Community elders, who are active daily in the AHS centres, maintain a special role in promoting language and culture. Programs such as the Waabinong Head Start Family Resource Centre in Sault Ste. Marie (Dunning, 2000) and the Tungasuvvingat Inuit Head Start in Ottawa (Reynolds, 1998) are examples of positive school environments that give parents opportunities to be involved in the decision-making of their children's education, and help children become exposed to their own cultural heritage. For many of the parents, this experience is the first contact with their own language and culture, given their past in mainstream and residential school systems. Often, parents are beginning to learn their language alongside their children. The AHS programs offer a unique opportunity for Aboriginal youth to develop self-awareness and pride in their own backgrounds. Recent evaluations of AHS show benefits, including cognitive development, school readiness, social skills, and cultural knowledge in children, as well as in positive family relations (Benzies, Tough, Edwards, Mychasiuk, & Donnelly, 2011; Public Health Agency of Canada, 2012b).

Universal Early Learning and Care

The correlation between good-quality early childhood education and future academic success has been closely investigated. Studies have indicated that the gaps in academic achievement between low-SES and middle-SES students can be documented before children enter school (McCain, Mustard, & Shanker, 2007). These findings have prompted interest in—and debate over—the development of **universal early childhood education and care**, a national system for early education and child care (Friendly & Prentice, 2009). The goal of programs such as this is to improve school readiness and educational success by (1) providing access to high-quality child care and developmentally appropriate preschool, (2) building parent involvement, and (3) providing support services for parents that enhance family functioning. Preliminary findings from one such program have indicated enhanced academic skills through second grade by children who have attended preschool (Henrich, Ginicola, Finn-Stevenson, & Zigler, 2006); however, because these programs are relatively new, little long-term data are available. Critics argue that the cost is too high for an as-yet-unproven intervention and protest the tax increases to fund them. While Quebec has instituted low-cost universal ECEC, the availability of such programs remains spotty across Canada (Friendly & Prentice, 2009), and may not show expected benefits across SES groups if program quality is low (e.g., Lefebvre, Merrigan, & Verstraete, 2008).

Advocates of compensatory early childhood development programs say that the results point to a need for earlier and longer-lasting intervention (Brooks-Gunn, 2003; Kruk, Prentice, & Moen, 2013; Reynolds & Temple, 1998; Zigler & Styfco, 1993, 1994). Many economically disadvantaged children need more time and a continuous, predictable learning environment to fully absorb the benefits; the transition to formal schooling is a sensitive or critical period, when children need extra support and stability (McCain et al., 2007; Reynolds & Temple, 1998). The *Early Years Study-2* outlines how benefits of high-quality early childhood development programs can come about, particularly for at-risk preschoolers, but more government support is needed to promote development in the first six years (McCain et al., 2007). In response to the first *Early Years Study*'s recommendations (McCain & Mustard, 1999), the Ontario government has funded community-based Ontario Early Years Centres to provide parents with support and resources to ensure that all children in Ontario have access to enriched environments that support healthy growth (Ministry of Community, Family and Children's Services, 2002).

---

universal early childhood education and care A national system for early child education and care that makes access to preschool similar to kindergarten.

Experience in good-quality early learning and care can give children lasting positive benefits for academic achievement.

KINDERGARTEN

Originally a year of transition between the relative freedom of home or preschool and the structure of grade school, kindergarten in Canada has become more like Grade 1. Children spend less time on self-chosen activities and more time on worksheets and preparing to read. A successful transition to kindergarten lays the foundation for future academic achievement (Schulting, Malone, & Dodge, 2005).

Although some provinces do not require kindergarten, most 5-year-olds in Canada attend either half- or full-day kindergarten in public schools, with an increasing number of provinces offering full-day kindergarten in recognition of research indicating the importance of children's experiences in the early years as a foundation for lifelong learning and success in school and beyond—as summarized in the *Early Years Study* reports in Ontario (McCain & Mustard, 1999; McCain et al., 2007, 2011). Do children learn more in full-day kindergarten? Initially, they do, but a U.S.-based comparison showed that the full-day advantage can soon fade out (Votruba-Drzal, Li-Grining, & Maldonado-Carreno, 2008). However, lasting benefits might depend on many factors, such as the quality of full-day kindergarten, especially if it involves play-based programs that support children's learning and promote positive relations with schools (Government of Ontario, 2010/2011), and the characteristics of the children. A longitudinal comparison of full-day and half-day kindergarten children in a francophone school division in Ontario found better long-term language, reading, and math development in children in full-day kindergarten, though no differences were found in social-emotional and motor skill development (Maltais, Herry, Emond, & Mougeot, 2011).

In general, full-day compared with half-day kindergarten benefits children's academic and social skill development, giving children more opportunities to explore language and other topics, and spend individual time with their teachers (Ackerman, Barnett, & Robin, 2005; Baskett, Bryant, White, & Rhoads, 2005; DeCesare, 2004; Elicker & Mathur, 1997).

Children in full-day kindergarten are more likely to experience academic successes in later grades, have more positive attitudes and behaviours in school (Clark & Kirk, 2000; Cryan, Sheehan, Wiechel, & Bandy-Hedden, 1992), and achieve better reading by Grade 4 (Phillips, Norris, & Mason, 1996).

Findings highlight the importance of the preparation a child receives before kindergarten. The resources with which children come to kindergarten—pre-literacy skills and the richness of a home literacy environment—predict reading achievement in Grade 1, and these individual differences tend to persist or increase throughout the first four years of school (Denton, West, & Walston, 2003; Rathbun, West, & Germino-Hausken, 2004). Emotional and social adjustment affect readiness for kindergarten and strongly predict school success. More important than knowing the alphabet or being able to count to 20 are the abilities to sit still, follow directions, wait one's turn, and regulate one's own learning (Blair, 2002; Brooks-Gunn, 2003; McCain et al., 2007). The quality of the neighbourhood can also influence readiness for school (Bertrand, 2007). The Early Development Index is a screening tool developed in Canada that can be administered by kindergarten teachers to measure readiness for education. Classroom results across a community can reflect the degree to which early development efforts are successful in getting children ready for school (Janus, 2007; Janus & Offord, 2007).

Because cut-off birth dates for kindergarten entrance vary among the provinces, children enter kindergarten at ages ranging from 4 to 6. As academic and emotional pressures mount, some parents choose to hold their child back for a year in the belief that the child will then be more ready for kindergarten. Results are mixed about the benefits of this practice (see Chapter 12).

Ask Yourself

15. With respect to early education programs, "child-centred" refers to
    a. children being allowed to make up most rules for their classrooms.
    b. classrooms in which children are allowed to direct their own learning experiences.
    c. classrooms in which children of different ages are schooled together.
    d. avoiding the use of traditional preschools and teaching children at home.

16. Name three characteristics of effective compensatory preschool programs.

17. In addition to academic preparation, another variable that appears to predict success in kindergarten is
    a. gender.
    b. whether children are "younger" or "older" kindergarteners.
    c. emotional and social adjustment.
    d. whether children have older siblings at home.

LO1

Summarize the advances and immature aspects of a young child's thinking processes.

- Children in the preoperational stage show several important advances, as well as some immature aspects of thought.
- The symbolic function enables children to reflect upon people, objects, and events that are not physically present. It is shown in deferred imitation, pretend play, and language.
- Early symbolic development helps preoperational children make more accurate judgments of spatial relationships. They can link cause and effect, categorize living and non-living things, and understand principles of counting.
- Centration keeps preoperational children from understanding principles of conservation. Their logic also is limited by irreversibility and a focus on states rather than transformations.
- Preoperational children appear to be less egocentric than Piaget thought.
- The theory of mind, which develops markedly between the ages of 3 and 5, includes awareness of a child's own thought processes, social cognition, understanding that people can hold false beliefs, ability to distinguish appearance from reality, and ability to distinguish fantasy from reality. Hereditary and environmental influences affect individual differences in theory-of-mind development.

LO2

Discuss the changes in memory capabilities and how they impact recall, recognition, and childhood memory.

- Information-processing models describe three steps in memory: encoding, storage, and retrieval.
- Although sensory memory shows little change with age, the capacity of working memory increases greatly. The central executive controls the flow of information to and from long-term memory.
- At all ages, recognition is better than recall, but both increase during early childhood.
- Procedural memory is a form of memory about habitual actions that emerges in early infancy. Early episodic memory is only temporary. Autobiographical memory begins at about age 3 or 4 and may be related to early self-recognition ability and language development.
- The way adults talk with children about events influences memory formation.

LO3

Describe how intelligence is measured, and summarize influences on how intelligence is measured and how this informs teaching practices.

- The two most commonly used psychometric intelligence tests for young children are the Stanford-Binet Intelligence Scale and the Wechsler Preschool and Primary Scale of Intelligence, Fourth Edition (WPPSI–IV).
- Intelligence test scores may be influenced by social and emotional functioning, as well as by parent–child interaction and socio-economic factors.

LO4

Understand measurement and teaching methods based on Vygotsky's theory.

- Newer tests based on Vygotsky's concept of the zone of proximal development (ZPD) indicate immediate potential for achievement. Such tests, when combined with scaffolding, can help parents and teachers guide children's progress.
- Providing children with scaffolding at an early age can help children later to regulate goal-directed problem solving, to show independence in cognitive and social skills, and to initiate social interactions.

LO5

Summarize the typical sequence of language development and describe how language delays, preparation for literacy, and exposure to media sources impact these processes.

- During early childhood, vocabulary increases greatly, and grammar and syntax become fairly sophisticated. Children become more competent in pragmatics and social speech.
- Private speech is normal and common; it may aid in the shift to self-regulation.
- Causes of delayed language development are unclear. If untreated, it may have serious cognitive, social, and emotional consequences.
- Interaction with adults can promote emergent literacy.

LO6

Discuss the impact of early childhood education and intervention programs on development.

- Goals of preschool education vary in different cultures. Most early childhood education programs in Canada take a child-centred approach.
- Compensatory preschool programs have had positive outcomes. Programs that extend into the primary grades have better long-term results.
- Adjustment to kindergarten may depend on interaction among the child's characteristics and those of the home, school, and neighbourhood environments.
- Many children today attend full-day kindergarten. Success in kindergarten depends in part on emotional and social adjustment and pre-kindergarten preparation.

ANSWERS TO Ask Yourself

Answers: 1—Three immature aspects of cognition in early childhood include egocentrism, centration, and irreversibility; 2–b; 3–d; 4–b; 5–recall; 6–c; 7—Two commonly used intelligence tests for children are the Stanford-Binet Intelligence Scale and the Wechsler Preschool and Primary Scale of Intelligence, Fourth Edition (WPSSIV); 8–c; 9–b; 10–b; 11—Examples of how the ZPD can be assessed by dynamic testing include measuring potential ability by asking children to solve problems geared to older children, to find out how much they can achieve with the help of leading questions, examples, and demonstration from adults; and measuring the amount of scaffolding needed for a child to achieve a goal; 12–a; 13—Among the factors that can contribute to speech delays are hearing problems, head and facial abnormalities, premature birth, family history, socio-economic factors, and developmental delays; 14–b; 15–b; 16—Among the variables associated with effective compensatory preschool programs are early and long-lasting intervention, high parental participation, well-trained teachers, low staff-to-child ratios, longer school days and weeks, and extensive services; 17–c.

Mc Graw Hill Education connect · **Mc Graw Hill Education LEARNSMART** · **Mc Graw Hill Education SMARTBOOK**

For more information on the resources available from McGraw-Hill Ryerson, go to **www.mcgrawhill.ca/he/solutions**.

PSYCHOSOCIAL
DEVELOPMENT

WHAT'S TO COME

The Developing Self

Gender

Play

Parenting

Prosocial and Aggressive Behaviour

Five-year-old twins Derek and Sophie have been raised in the same family with the same parents and attend the same daycare. Sophie is both more outgoing and more aggressive than Derek, and she frequently gets into arguments with her playmates. Derek is quieter but plays much more actively than Sophie, tumbling around with the other boys and spending much of his free time running and jumping. Derek and Sophie's parents have noted that while Sophie needs a relatively firm hand, Derek responds much more quickly to appeals to empathy and to discussions about the ways in which his actions affect others. Why are these two children so different? Are their differences due to gender? To the different ways in which their parents handle them? To innate differences in their temperament and personality? What influences who they are?

The years from ages 3 to 6 are pivotal ones in children's psychosocial development. A child's emotional development and sense of self are rooted in the experiences of those years. In this chapter, we discuss the developing self, and how sense of male or female identity arises and how it affects behaviour. We explore play and why it is so vitally important for children. Finally, we consider the influence of what parents do and why children engage in both prosocial and aggressive behaviour.

IN EARLY CHILDHOOD

AS YOU READ

LO1 Describe changes in the understanding of and feelings about the self, and discuss how this impacts emotional development.
LO2 Summarize and contrast the different theories of gender development.
LO3 Discuss the influences on play in early childhood.
LO4 Summarize different forms of parental discipline and parenting styles.
LO5 Discuss the development of and influences on prosocial and antisocial behaviour.

The Developing Self

"Who in the world am I? Ah, that's the great puzzle," said Alice in Wonderland, after her size had abruptly changed—again. Solving Alice's "puzzle" is a lifelong process of getting to know one's self. Our comprehension of the self is informed by self-concept, self-esteem, and our ability to understand and regulate emotions.

THE SELF-CONCEPT AND SELF-DEFINITION

The **self-concept** is our total picture of our abilities and traits that determines how we feel about ourselves—who we think we are. It is a cognitive construction (Harter, 1996) that includes representations of the self. It also has a social aspect that incorporates children's growing understanding of how others see them. For example, a child who is chronically rejected by other children might form a self-concept of herself as unlikable. During the early childhood years, the self-concept develops through changes in self-definition and is impacted by culture.

Changes in Self-Definition

Children develop a sense of self-awareness in toddlerhood, which develops along with gains in cognitive abilities. Children's **self-definition**—the way they describe themselves—typically changes between about ages 5 and 7, reflecting this development. At age 4, Jason says,

> My name is Jason and I live in a big house with my mother and father and sister, Lisa. I have a kitty that's orange and a television set in my own room. . . . I like pizza and I have a nice teacher. I can count up to 100, want to hear me? I love my dog, Skipper. I can climb to the top of the jungle gym, I'm not scared! Just happy. You can't be

happy and scared, no way! I have brown hair, and I go to preschool. I'm really strong. I can lift this chair, watch me! (Harter, 1996, p. 208)

The way Jason describes himself is typical of Canadian children his age. He talks mostly about concrete, observable behaviours; external characteristics, such as physical features; preferences; possessions; and members of his household. He mentions a particular skill (climbing) rather than general abilities (being athletic). His self-descriptions are unrealistically positive. Not until around age 7 will he describe himself in terms of generalized traits, such as popular, smart, or dumb; recognize that he can have conflicting emotions; and be self-critical while holding a positive overall self-concept. And it will take until later in middle childhood for Jason's self-descriptions to become more balanced and realistic ("I'm good at hockey but bad at arithmetic.").

Cultural Differences in Self-Definition

Culture helps shape the understanding of the self. For example, one major cultural dimension—that of individualism versus collectivism—impacts the understanding of the self in relation to others. In primarily individualistic cultures like Canada, individuals are seen in general as separate from one another, and independence and self-reliance are highly valued. In collectivistic cultures, such as India and China, individuals are seen in general as fundamentally interrelated, and group harmony and cohesiveness take precedence over individual concerns (Oyserman, Coon, & Kemmelmeir, 2002). In a country as diverse as Canada, many groups in which a more collectivist approach is emphasized—such as children in Aboriginal communities—can experience different degrees of connection

---

self-concept Sense of self; descriptive and evaluative mental picture of one's abilities and traits.

self-definition Cluster of characteristics used to describe oneself.

between the sense of self and their cultural values. A strong sense of identification with cultural values, either with their own culture or with the mainstream culture, is related to healthy development in Aboriginal children and youth (Fryberg et al., 2013).

Parents transmit, often through everyday conversations, cultural ideas and beliefs about how to define the self. For example, Chinese parents tend to encourage *interdependent* aspects of the self, such as compliance with authority, appropriate conduct, humility, and a sense of belonging to the community. European parents tend to encourage *independent* aspects of the self: individuality, self-expression, and self-esteem. A comparative study of 180 European-American and Chinese preschoolers, kindergartners, and second graders (Wang, 2004) found that children absorb such differing cultural styles of self-definition as early as age 3 or 4, and these differences increase with age.

SELF-ESTEEM

Self-esteem is the evaluative part of the self-concept, the judgment children make about their overall self-worth. Self-esteem is based on children's growing cognitive ability to describe and define themselves.

Developmental Changes in Self-Esteem

Before about 5 to 7 years of age, young children's self-esteem is not necessarily based on reality. They tend to overrate their abilities (Harter, 2006). For example, despite coming in last in a race, 4-year-old Mateo might still believe himself to be the best and fastest runner. Moreover, like the overall self-concept, self-esteem in early childhood tends to be all-or-none: "I am good" or "I am bad." Not until middle childhood does it become more realistic, as personal evaluations of competence based on internalization of parental and societal standards begin to shape and maintain self-worth (Harter, 1998).

Contingent Self-Esteem

Children whose self-esteem is contingent on success tend to become demoralized when they fail. Often, these children attribute failure to their personality deficiencies, which they believe they are unable to change. About one-third to one-half of preschoolers, kindergartners, and first graders show elements of this "helpless" pattern, sometimes referred to as "learned helplessness" (Dweck & Grant, 2008). Rather than trying new strategies in the face of failure, they repeat unsuccessful ones or just give up. For example, a child who was unable to complete a puzzle, rather than persevering, might instead throw down the pieces in frustration, saying, "I'm no good at puzzles."

Children with non-contingent self-esteem, in contrast, tend to attribute failure or disappointment to factors outside themselves or to the need to try harder. For example, when faced with the same puzzle, such a child might assume the

Did you know?

Dweck and Grant's research (2008) implies that praise in childhood should focus on effort, not ability. An explanation for failure of "I didn't try hard enough" suggests that if you tried harder, you could succeed. If, by contrast, you assume that success is due to your ability and you fail, the implication is that you aren't able to do it, so why bother trying?

puzzle was for older children or might continue to try to put it together despite having initial difficulty. If initially unsuccessful or rejected, these children persevere, trying new strategies until they find one that works (Pomerantz & Saxon, 2001).

UNDERSTANDING AND REGULATING EMOTIONS

"I hate you!" Maya, age 5, shouts to her mother. "You're a mean mommy!" Angry because her mother sent her to her room for pinching her baby brother, Maya cannot imagine ever loving her mother again. "Aren't you ashamed of yourself for making the baby cry?" her father asks Maya a little later. Maya nods, but only because she knows what response he wants. In truth, she feels a jumble of emotions—not the least of which is feeling sorry for herself.

The ability to understand and regulate, or control, one's feelings is one of the key advances of early childhood (Dennis, 2006). Children who can understand their emotions are better able to control the way they show them and to be sensitive to how others feel (Garner and Estep, 2001). Emotional self-regulation helps children guide their behaviour (Eisenberg, Fabes, & Spinrad, 2006), helps children adjust their responses to meet societal expectations, and contributes to their ability to get along with others (Denham et al., 2003).

Preschoolers can talk about their feelings and often can discern the feelings of others, and they understand that emotions are connected with experiences and desires (Saarni, Campos, Camras, & Witherington, 2006). They understand that someone who gets what he wants will be happy, and someone who does not get what she wants will be sad (Lagattuta, 2005).

Did you know?

Emotion regulation includes both minimizing certain emotions (e.g., not having a temper tantrum when you don't get your way) and maximizing others (e.g., acting happy when you receive a gift you don't really like).

self-esteem   Judgment a person makes about his or her self-worth.

Did you know?

Poor childhood self-control, even at the age of 3 years, is related to a host of negative adult outcomes, including credit issues, health problems, and criminal offences (Moffitt et al., 2011).

Emotional understanding becomes more complex with age. In one study, 32 largely middle-class 4- through 8-year-olds and 32 adults were asked to tell, for example, how a young boy would feel if his ball rolled into the street and he either retrieved it, and by doing so broke the rule of not going into the street, or refrained from retrieving it. The results revealed a "5-to-7 shift" in emotional understanding much like that found for self-concept development. The 4- and 5-year-olds tended to believe that the boy would be happy if he got the ball—even though he would be breaking a rule—and unhappy if he didn't. The older children, like the adults, were more inclined to believe that obedience to a rule would make the boy feel good and disobedience would make him feel bad (Lagattuta, 2005). Part of understanding emotions involves developing a grasp of what conflicting emotions and social emotions mean.

Understanding Conflicting Emotions

One reason for young children's confusion about their feelings is that they do not understand that they can experience contrary emotional reactions at the same time. For example, a child might have difficulty identifying that she is both excited about and scared of starting a new school. Individual differences in understanding conflicting emotions are evident by age 3. In one study, 3-year-olds who could identify whether a face looked happy or sad and who could tell how a puppet felt when enacting a situation involving basic emotions of happiness, sadness, anger, or fear were less likely to show aggressive or antisocial behaviours in social situations in kindergarten (Denham et al., 2003). Most children acquire a more sophisticated understanding of conflicting emotions during middle childhood (Harter, 1996; see Chapter 13).

Understanding Social Emotions

Social emotions are emotions that involve a comparison of oneself or one's actions to social standards. These emotions are directed toward the self and include guilt, shame, and pride. They typically develop by the end of the third year, after children gain self-awareness and accept the standards of behaviour their parents have set. However, even children a few years older often lack the cognitive sophistication to recognize these emotions and what brings them on (Pons, Harris, & de Rosnay, 2004).

social emotions Emotions directed at the self that involve a comparison of oneself or one's actions to social standards.

initiative versus guilt Erikson's third crisis in psychosocial development, in which children balance the urge to pursue goals with moral reservations that may prevent carrying them out.

In one study (Harter, 1993), 4- to 8-year-olds were told two stories. In the first story, a child takes a few coins from a jar after being told not to do so; in the second story, a child performs a difficult gymnastic feat—a flip on the bars. Each story was presented in two versions: one in which a parent sees the child doing the act and another in which no one sees the child. The children were asked how they and the parent would feel in each circumstance.

Again, the answers revealed a gradual progression in understanding of feelings about the self, reflecting the 5-to-7 shift (Harter, 1996). At ages 4 to 5, children did not say that either they or their parents would feel pride or shame. Instead, they used such terms as "worried" or "scared" (for the money jar incident) and "excited" or "happy" (about the gymnastic accomplishment). At ages 5 to 6, children said their parents would be ashamed or proud of them but did not acknowledge feeling these emotions themselves. At ages 6 to 7, children said they would feel ashamed or proud, but only if they were observed. Not until age 7 or 8 did children say that they would feel ashamed or proud of themselves even if no one saw them.

ERIKSON: INITIATIVE VERSUS GUILT

The need to deal with conflicting feelings about the self is at the heart of the third crisis of personality development identified by Erik Erikson (1950): **initiative versus guilt**. The conflict arises from the growing sense of purpose, which lets a child plan and carry out activities, and the growing pangs of conscience the child may have about such plans.

Preschool children can do—and want to do—more and more. At the same time, they are learning that some of the things they want to do meet social approval, while others do not. How do they reconcile their desire to do with their desire for approval? This conflict marks a split between two parts of the personality: the part that remains a child, full of exuberance and a desire to try new things and test new powers, and the part that is becoming an adult, constantly

Did you know?

Guilt, shame, and pride are known as the social emotions because they help regulate social interactions and are involved with moral development. If you feel ashamed after getting caught doing something that others think is bad, that might keep you from doing that thing again.

examining the propriety of motives and actions. Children who learn how to regulate these opposing drives develop the "virtue" of purpose, the courage to envision and pursue goals without being unduly inhibited by guilt or fear of punishment (Erikson, 1982).

If this crisis is not resolved adequately, said Erikson, a child may turn into an adult who is constantly striving for success or showing off, or who is inhibited and not spontaneous or self-righteous and intolerant, or who suffers from impotence or psychosomatic illness. With ample opportunities to do things on their own—but under guidance and consistent limits—children can attain a healthy balance between the tendency to overdo competition and achievement and the tendency to be repressed and guilt-ridden.

Most young children tend to dress in clothes that are stereotypical for their gender.

Ask Yourself

1. At age 5, Emma is most likely to describe herself as
   a. a really nice person.
   b. good at school, but not good at gym class.
   c. a really good runner with brown hair.
   d. usually quiet, but sometimes loud.

2. Children with a "helpless" pattern of self-esteem tend to attribute failure to _____, and are _____ likely to persevere at difficult tasks.
   a. personal characteristics; more
   b. personal characteristics; less
   c. effort; more
   d. effort; less

3. Name three changes in emotions in early childhood.

Gender

Five-year-old twins Derek and Sophie argued about what game to play. "I want to play Batman," Derek insisted, "And you can be the Joker and I will come get you." "No," Sophie replied, "I will be the fairy princess and you will be my brave knight." "I don't play princess games," Derek replied, "because I am a boy."

Gender identity, awareness of one's femaleness or maleness and all it implies, is an important aspect of the developing self-concept. How different are young boys and girls? What causes those differences? How do children develop gender identity, and how does it affect their attitudes and behaviour?

GENDER DIFFERENCES

Gender differences are psychological or behavioural differences between males and females. As we discussed in Chapter 8, measurable differences between younger boys and girls are few. Although some gender differences

become more pronounced after age 3, boys and girls on average remain more alike than different. Extensive evidence from many studies supports this gender-similarities hypothesis. Fully 78 percent of gender differences are small to negligible, and some differences, such as in self-esteem, change with age (Hyde, 2005).

Physically, among the larger gender differences are boys' higher activity level; superior motor performance, especially after puberty; and moderately greater propensity for physical aggression (Hyde, 2005).

Research involving children ages 2½ to 8 has consistently identified striking differences in playtime preferences and styles, with boys engaging in higher levels of rough-and-tumble play such as wrestling with and chasing each other. Sex-typed preferences increase between toddlerhood and middle childhood and the degree of sex-typed behaviour exhibited early in life is a strong indicator of later gender-based behaviour (Golombok et al., 2008).

Cognitive gender differences are few and small (Spelke, 2005). Overall, intelligence test scores show no gender differences (Keenan & Shaw, 1997). However, there are small differences in specific abilities. Girls tend to perform better on tests of verbal fluency, mathematical computation, and memory for locations of objects. Boys tend to perform better in verbal analogies, mathematical word problems, and memory for spatial configurations. In most studies, these differences do not emerge until elementary school or later (Spelke, 2005). Also, boys' mathematical

gender identity Awareness, developed in early childhood, that one is male or female.

Did you know?

Biologically based gender differences are a controversial area of research precisely because they are small in magnitude. If they were large, there would be no reason to argue their existence.

abilities vary more than girls', with more boys at both the highest and lowest ends of the ability range (Halpern et al., 2007.)

We need to remember, of course, that gender differences are valid for large groups of boys and girls but not necessarily for individuals. By knowing a child's sex, we cannot predict whether that particular boy or girl will be faster, stronger, smarter, more obedient, or more assertive than another child.

PERSPECTIVES ON GENDER DEVELOPMENT

What accounts for gender differences, and why do some of them emerge as children grow older? Some explanations centre on the differing experiences and social expectations that boys and girls meet almost from birth. These experiences and expectations concern three related aspects of gender identity: gender roles, gender-typing, and gender stereotypes.

Gender roles are the behaviours, interests, attitudes, skills, and personality traits that a culture considers appropriate

for males or females. Historically, in most cultures, women have been expected to devote most of their time to caring for the household and children, and men have been providers and protectors. Women have been expected to be compliant and nurturant; men, to be active, aggressive, and competitive. Today, gender roles in Western cultures have become more diverse and more flexible.

Gender-typing, involving the acquisition of a gender role, takes place early in childhood (Iervolino, Hines, Golombok, Rust, & Plomin, 2005).

Gender stereotypes are overgeneralizations about male or female behaviour. For example, "All females are passive and dependent; all males are aggressive and independent." They appear to some degree in children as young as 2 or 3, increase during the preschool years, and reach a peak at age 5 (Campbell, Shirley, & Candy, 2004).

How do children acquire gender roles, and why do they adopt gender stereotypes? Five theoretical perspectives—biological, evolutionary developmental, psychoanalytic, cognitive, and social learning (Table 10.1)—contribute to our understanding of gender development, though none

gender roles Behaviours, interests, attitudes, skills, and traits that a culture considers appropriate for each sex; differ for males and females.

gender-typing Socialization process whereby children, at an early age, learn appropriate gender roles.

gender stereotypes Preconceived generalizations about male or female role behaviour.

TABLE 10.1 Five Perspectives on Gender Development

Theories	Major Theorists	Key Processes	Basic Beliefs
Biological Approach		Genetic, neurological, and hormonal activity	Many or most behavioural differences between the sexes can be traced to biological differences.
Evolutionary Developmental Approach	Charles Darwin	Natural sexual selection	Children develop gender roles in preparation for adult mating and reproductive behaviour.
Psychoanalytic Approach Psychosexual theory	Sigmund Freud	Resolution of unconscious emotional conflict	Gender identity occurs when child identifies with same-sex parent.
Cognitive Approach Cognitive-developmental theory	Lawrence Kohlberg	Self-categorization	Once a child learns she is a girl or he is a boy, child sorts information about behaviour by gender and acts accordingly.
Gender-schema theory	Sandra Bem Carol Lynn Martin Charles F. Halverson	Self-categorization based on processing of cultural information	Child organizes information about what is considered appropriate for a boy or a girl on the basis of what a particular culture dictates and behaves accordingly. Child sorts by gender because the culture dictates that gender is an important schema.
Social Learning Approach Social cognitive theory	Albert Bandura	Observation of models, reinforcement	Child mentally combines observations of multiple models and creates own behavioural variations.

fully explains why boys and girls differ in some respects but not in others.

Biological Approach

The existence of similar gender roles in many cultures suggests that some gender differences may be biologically based. Investigators are uncovering evidence of genetic, hormonal, and neurological explanations for gender differences.

Scientists have identified more than 50 genes that may explain differences in anatomy and function between the brains of male and female mice. It is likely that similar genetic differences exist in humans, suggesting that sexual identity may be hardwired into the brain early in development, prior to differentiation of sex organs (Dewing, Shi, Horvath, & Vilain, 2003).

Hormones in the bloodstream during pregnancy affect the developing brain. The male hormone testosterone is related to aggressiveness in animals, but the relationship in humans is less clear (Simpson, 2001). However, an analysis of fetal testosterone levels has shown a link between higher testosterone levels and male-typical play in boys (Auyeng et al., 2009). Estrogens—female hormones—seem to have less influence on boys' gender-typed behaviour (van de Beek, van Goozen, Buitelaar, & Cohen-Kettenis, 2009).

Perhaps the most dramatic examples of the influence of biology are found in infants born with ambiguous genitalia. John Money and his colleagues (Money, Hampson, & Hampson, 1955) developed guidelines for infants born with such disorders, recommending that the child be assigned as early as possible to the "best guess" as to what gender that child will be. However, this is controversial, as in multiple studies boys born genetically male but without normal penises who were gender assigned and raised as females overwhelmingly rejected that identity, and, as adults, lived and identified as male (Reiner, 2000; Reiner & Gearhart, 2004). Studies such as these suggest that gender identity cannot be assigned and is rooted in biology.

Evolutionary Developmental Approach

The evolutionary developmental approach sees gendered behaviour as biologically influenced. From this controversial perspective, children's gender roles are a consequence of the evolved mating and child-rearing strategies of adult males and females.

According to Darwin's (1871) **theory of sexual selection**, the selection of sexual partners is a response to the differing reproductive pressures that early men and women confronted in the struggle for survival (Wood & Eagly, 2002). In humans, females must contribute far more to the raising of children because of the constraints placed upon them by pregnancy and nursing. Males, however, may contribute as little as a few teaspoonfuls of sperm. Because a woman invests more resources in pregnancy and can bear only a limited number of children, each child's survival is of utmost importance to her. Thus, she looks for a mate who will remain with her and support

their offspring as this increases the likelihood of survival of the child (Wood & Eagly, 2002).

According to evolutionary theory, male competitiveness and aggressiveness and female nurturance develop during childhood as preparation for these adult roles. Boys play at fighting; girls play at parenting. Males value physical prowess because it enables them to compete for mates and for control of resources and social status, which women value. Women, by contrast, are the primary caregivers. Thus, young girls tend to be more nurturant and better able than young boys to control and inhibit their emotions and to refrain from impulsive behaviour (Bjorklund & Pellegrini, 2000).

Critics of evolutionary theory suggest that society and culture are as important as biology in determining gender roles. However, evolutionary theorists counter that the development of gender roles is a dynamic process, and that the culture that influences us is itself a product of our own evolved minds.

Psychoanalytic Approach

"Dad, where will you live when I grow up and marry Mommy?" asks Juan, age 4. From the psychoanalytic perspective, Juan's question is part of his acquisition of gender identity. That process, according to Freud, is one of **identification**, the adoption of characteristics, beliefs, attitudes, values, and behaviours of the parent of the same sex. Freud considered identification an important personality development of early childhood.

According to Freud, identification will occur for Juan when he represses or gives up the wish to possess the parent of the other sex (his mother) and identifies with the parent of the same sex (his father). But although this explanation for gender development has been influential, it has been difficult to test and has little research support (Maccoby, 2000). The majority of developmental psychologists today favour other explanations.

---

theory of sexual selection Darwinian theory, which holds that selection of sexual partners is influenced by the differing reproductive pressures that early men and women confronted in the evolutionary past.

identification In Freudian theory, process by which a young child adopts characteristics, beliefs, attitudes, values, and behaviours of the parent of the same sex.

Cognitive Approaches

Sarah figures out that she is a girl because people call her a girl. As she continues to observe and think about her world, she concludes that she will always be a girl. She comes to understand gender by actively thinking about and constructing her own gender-typing. This is the heart of cognitive-developmental theories of gender development. Included in the cognitive approach to understanding gender are cognitive-developmental theory (advanced by Kohlberg) and gender-schema theory.

KOHLBERG'S COGNITIVE-DEVELOPMENTAL THEORY   In Kohlberg's (1966) theory, gender knowledge ("I am a boy.") precedes gendered behaviour ("I like to do boy things."). Children actively search for cues about gender in their social world. As children come to realize which gender they belong to, they adopt behaviours they perceive as consistent with being male or female (Martin & Ruble, 2004).

The acquisition of gender roles, said Kohlberg, hinges on **gender constancy**, more recently called *sex-category constancy*—a child's realization that his or her sex will always be the same. Once children achieve this realization, they are motivated to adopt behaviours appropriate to their sex. Gender constancy seems to develop in three stages: gender identity, gender stability, and gender consistency (Martin et al., 2002). *Gender identity*, awareness of one's own gender and that of others, typically occurs between ages 2 and 3. *Gender stability* comes when children realize that gender does not change. However, children at this stage may base judgments about gender on superficial appearances, clothing or hairstyle, and stereotyped behaviours. Sometime between ages 3 and 7, or even later—comes *gender consistency*, the realization that a girl remains a girl even if she has a short haircut and plays with trucks. Once children realize that their behaviour or dress will not affect their sex, they may become less rigid in their adherence to gender norms (Martin et al., 2002).

Some researchers challenge Kohlberg's view that gender-typing depends on gender constancy. For example, long before children attain the final stage of gender constancy, they show gender-typed preferences (Martin & Ruble, 2004). Gender preferences in toys and playmates appear as early as 12 to 24 months, prior to any real understanding of what it means to be a boy or a girl.

GENDER-SCHEMA THEORY   Four-year-old Brandon has watched from his window as a new boy his age moves next door. When he finally is allowed to go visit the new family, he eagerly brings two of his favourite toy trucks, assuming that the new boy will like the same toys he likes. How does he reach this conclusion?

gender constancy   Awareness that one will always be male or female; also called *sex-category constancy*.

gender-schema theory   Theory that children socialize themselves in their gender roles by developing a mentally organized network of information about what it means to be male or female in a particular culture.

An explanation can be found in **gender-schema theory**. Once children know what sex they are, they develop a concept of what it means to be male or female in their culture. Children then match their behaviour to their culture's view of what boys and girls are "supposed" to be and do.

A major issue with both gender-schema theory and Kohlberg's theory is that gender-stereotyping does not always become stronger with increased gender knowledge; in fact, the opposite is often true (Bandura & Bussey, 2004). Around ages 4 to 6, when children are constructing their gender schemas, they tend to notice and remember only information consistent with these schemas. In fact, they tend to misremember information that challenges gender stereotypes, such as photos of a girl sawing wood or a boy cooking, and to insist that the genders in the photos were the other way around.

By ages 5 and 6, children develop a repertoire of rigid stereotypes about gender that they apply to themselves and others. A boy will pay more attention to what he considers boys' toys and a girl to girls' toys. Then, around age 7 or 8, schemas become more complex as children begin to take in and integrate contradictory information, such as the fact that many girls have short hair. This results in greater flexibility in their views about gender roles (Martin & Ruble, 2004; Trautner et al., 2005).

Cognitive approaches to gender development have made an important contribution by exploring how children think about gender and what they know about it at various ages. However, these approaches may not fully explain the link between knowledge and conduct. There is disagreement about precisely what mechanism prompts children to act out gender roles and why some children become more strongly gender-typed than others (Bussey & Bandura, 1999; Martin & Ruble, 2004). Some investigators point to socialization.

Social Learning Approach

Five-year-old Sophie loves Disney movies and is particularly enamoured of *Cinderella*. Her parents walk into the kitchen one day to find her on her hands and knees, scrubbing the floor as she sings about a nightingale at the top of her lungs—just as Cinderella does in the film. They smile and laugh at Sophie, and

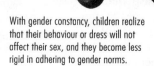

With gender constancy, children realize that their behaviour or dress will not affect their sex, and they become less rigid in adhering to gender norms.

she basks in their approval. What do social interactions such as these do to children's understanding of gender?

According to Walter Mischel (1966), a traditional social learning theorist, children acquire gender roles by imitating models and being rewarded for gender-appropriate behaviour—in other words, by responding to environmental stimuli. Typically, one model is a parent, often of the same sex, but children also pattern their behaviour after other adults, peers, or even characters in books or media. Behavioural feedback, together with direct teaching by parents and other adults, reinforces gender-typing. A boy who models his behaviour after his father is commended for acting "like a boy." A girl gets compliments on a pretty dress or hairstyle. In this model, gendered behaviour precedes gender knowledge ("I am rewarded for doing boy things, so I must be a boy.").

Since the 1970s, however, studies have cast doubt on the power of same-sex modelling alone to account for gender differences. As cognitive explanations have come to the fore, traditional social learning theory has required updates. Albert Bandura's (1986; Bussey & Bandura, 1999) **social cognitive theory**, an expansion of social learning theory, incorporates some cognitive elements in an attempt to address these issues.

According to social cognitive theory, observation enables children to learn much about gender-typed behaviours before performing them. Children are active participants, and they mentally combine observations of multiple models and generate their own behavioural variations. Additionally, children create their environments through their choice of playmates and activities. However, critics say that social cognitive theory does not explain how children differentiate between boys and girls before they have a concept of gender, or what initially motivates children to acquire gender knowledge, or how gender norms become internalized—questions that other cognitive theories attempt to answer (Martin et al., 2002).

Socialization plays a central role and begins in infancy, long before a child has a conscious understanding of gender. Gradually, as children begin to regulate their activities,

social cognitive theory Albert Bandura's expansion of social learning theory; holds that children learn gender roles through socialization.

standards of behaviour become internalized. A child no longer needs praise, rebukes, or a model's presence to act in socially appropriate ways. Children feel good about themselves when they live up to their internal standards and feel bad when they do not. A substantial part of the shift from socially guided control to self-regulation of gender-related behaviour may take place between ages 3 and 4 (Bussey & Bandura, 1992; Bussey, 2011). Families, peers, and culture all influence gender development.

FAMILY INFLUENCES   When former Louisiana governor Kathleen Blanco's 4-year-old grandson David was asked what he wanted to be when he grew up, he was not sure. He shrugged off all his mother's suggestions—firefighter, soldier, policeman, airplane pilot. Finally, she asked whether he'd like to be governor. "Mom," he replied, "I'm a boy!" (Associated Press, 2004). David's response illustrates how strong family influences may be.

Boys tend to be more strongly gender-socialized concerning play preferences than girls. Parents, especially fathers, generally show more discomfort if a boy plays with a doll than if a girl plays with a truck (Ruble, Martin, & Berenbaum, 2006). Girls have more freedom to violate their gender roles, such as wearing boys' clothes or playing like a boy (Fagot, Rogers, & Leinbach, 2000).

How do family members influence gender socialization? In egalitarian households, the father's role seems especially important (Deutsch, Servis, & Payne, 2001). In an observational study of 4-year-olds in British and Hungarian cities, boys and girls whose fathers did more housework and child care were less aware of gender stereotypes and engaged in less gender-typed play than peers in more gender-typical families (Turner & Gervai, 1995). In an analysis of 43 different studies, Tenenbaum and Leaper (2002) found that parents who adhered to traditional gender schemas were more likely to have children with gender-typed ideas about themselves and other individuals when compared with parents who had non-traditional gendered schemas. Siblings also influence gender development. Second-borns tend to become more like their older siblings in attitudes, personality, and leisure activities, whereas first-borns are more influenced by their parents and less by their younger siblings (McHale, Updegraff, Helms-Erikson, & Crouter, 2001). Young children with an

Did you know?

The nicknames given to non-gender-conforming children echo the research finding that adults are generally more tolerant of non-conforming girls than boys. Girls who are "tomboys" are not generally seen in a negative light; however, boys who are "sissies" are often subject to teasing and reprimands.

Having an older sibling of the same sex is associated with more gender-typed play than is having an older sibling of the other sex.

Social cognitive theory predicts that children who watch a lot of television will become more gender-typed by imitating the models they see on the screen. Dramatic supporting evidence emerged from a natural experiment in several western Canadian towns, one of which, dubbed "Notel" to protect the anonymity of the participants, obtained access to television transmission for the first time in 1973. Children who had had relatively unstereotyped attitudes in Notel showed marked increases in traditional views two years later (Kimball, 1986). In another study, children who watched a series of non-traditional episodes, such as a father and son cooking together, had less stereotyped views than children who had not seen the series (Johnston & Ettema, 1982).

Children's books, especially illustrated ones, have long been a source of gender stereotypes. An analysis of 200 top-selling and award-winning children's books uncovered nearly twice as many male as female main characters and strong gender-stereotyping. Female main characters nurtured more, were portrayed in indoor settings, and appeared to have no paid occupations (Hamilton, Anderson, Broaddus, & Young, 2006). Fathers were largely absent, and when they appeared, they were shown as withdrawn and ineffectual (Anderson & Hamilton, 2005).

Major strengths of the socialization approach include the breadth of processes it addresses. But this very complexity makes it difficult to establish clear causal connections between the way children are raised and the way they think and act. Just what aspects of the home environment and the peer culture promote gender-typing? Do parents and peers treat boys and girls differently because they are different or because the culture says they should be different? Further research may help us see how socializing agents mesh with children's biological tendencies and cognitive understandings with regard to gender-related attitudes and behaviour.

older sibling of the same sex tend to be more gender-typed than those whose older sibling is of the other sex (Iervolino et al., 2005).

PEER INFLUENCES   Anna, at age 5, insisted on dressing in a new way. She wanted to wear leggings with a skirt over them and boots—indoors and out. When her mother asked her why, Anna replied, "Because Katie dresses like this—and Katie's the king of the girls!"

Even in early childhood, the peer group is a major influence on gender-typing. By age 3, preschoolers generally play in sex-segregated groups that reinforce gender-typed behaviour, and the influence of the peer group increases with age (Martin et al., 2002). Children who play in same-sex groups tend to be more gender-typed than children who do not (Maccoby, 2002). Peer groups show more disapproval of boys who act like girls than of girls who are tomboys (Ruble & Martin, 1998). Indeed, play choices at this age may be more strongly influenced by peers and the media than by the models children see at home (Martin & Fabes, 2001). Generally, however, peer and parental attitudes reinforce each other (Bussey & Bandura, 1999).

CULTURAL INFLUENCES   In Western countries, television is a major format for the transmission of cultural attitudes toward gender. Although women on television are now more likely to be working outside the home and men are sometimes shown caring for children or cooking, for the most part, life as portrayed on television continues to be more stereotyped than life in the real world (Ruble & Martin, 1998), as are televised commercials for children's toys (Kahlenberg & Hein, 2010).

Ask Yourself

4. Cognitive gender differences between girls and boys
   a. are large.
   b. are small.
   c. are large in mathematics and small in language.
   d. do not exist.

5. Dr. Smith believes that hormones are the most important variable in explaining gender differences, while Dr. Frank believes exposure to violent models is more important. Dr. Smith is likely to believe the _____ approach to gender development, while Dr. Frank is more likely to be a proponent of the _____ approach.
   a. cognitive; psychoanalytic
   b. evolutionary; cognitive
   c. social learning; evolutionary
   d. biological; social learning

It seems likely that none of the theories we have discussed has the full answer to how gender identity and gender-typing develop. Today "it is widely acknowledged that . . . cognitive, environmental, and biological factors are all important" (Martin et al., 2002, p. 904).

Play

Carmen, age 3, pretends that the pieces of cereal floating in her bowl are "fishies" swimming in the milk, and she "fishes," spoonful by spoonful. After breakfast, she puts on her mother's hat, picks up a briefcase, and is a "mommy" going to work. She rides her tricycle through the puddles, comes in for an imaginary telephone conversation, turns a wooden block into a truck and says, "Vroom, vroom!" Carmen's day is one round of play after another.

It would be a mistake to dismiss Carmen's activities as "just fun." Play has important current and long-term functions (Smith, 2005b). Play contributes to all domains of development. Through play, children stimulate the senses, exercise their muscles, coordinate sight with movement, gain mastery over their bodies, make decisions, and acquire new skills. As they sort blocks of different shapes, count how many they can pile on each other, or announce that "my tower is bigger than yours," they lay the foundation for mathematical concepts. As they cooperate to build sandcastles or tunnels on the beach, they learn skills of negotiation and conflict resolution.

Researchers categorize children's play in varying ways. Two common classification systems include cognitive complexity and the social dimension of play. Research has also uncovered gender and cultural influences on play.

COGNITIVE LEVELS OF PLAY

Jane, at 1 year of age, happily banged a spoon on a pot while sitting on the kitchen floor. Courtney, at 3, talked for a doll, using a deeper voice than her own. Miguel, at 4, wore a kitchen towel as a cape and "flew" around as Batman. These children were engaged in various types of play and, as is typical, showed increasing cognitive complexity with age.

Four levels of play have been identified by Smilansky (1968): functional play, constructive play, dramatic play, and formal games with rules. Although there is a general developmental progression to the types of play, this is not a stage theory.

The simplest level, which begins during infancy, is **functional play**, sometimes called *locomotor play*. It consists of repeated practice of large muscular movements, such as rolling a ball (Bjorklund & Pellegrini, 2002).

The second level, **constructive play**, also called *object play*, is the use of objects or materials to make something, such as a house of blocks or a crayon drawing (Bjorklund & Pellegrini, 2002).

The third level, which Smilansky called **dramatic play** (also called *pretend play*, *fantasy play*, or *imaginative play*) involves make-believe objects, actions, or roles; it rests on the symbolic function, which emerges during the last part of the second year (Piaget, 1962). Although functional play and constructive play precede dramatic play in Smilanksy's hierarchy, these three types of play often occur at the same ages (Smith, 2005a).

Dramatic play peaks during the preschool years, increasing in frequency and complexity (Bjorklund & Pellegrini, 2002; Smith, 2005a), and then declines as school-age children become more involved in **formal games with rules**—organized games with known procedures and penalties, such as hopscotch and marbles. However, many children continue to engage in pretending well beyond the elementary school years.

THE SOCIAL DIMENSION OF PLAY

In a classic study done in the 1920s, Mildred B. Parten (1932) identified six types of play ranging from the least to the most social (Table 10.2). She found that as children get older, their play tends to become more social—that is, more interactive and more cooperative. At first, children play alone, then alongside other children, and finally together. Today, however, many researchers view Parten's characterization of children's play development as too simplistic, as children of all ages engage in all of Parten's categories of play (Rubin, Bukowski, & Parker, 1998).

Parten apparently regarded non-social play as less mature than social play. While solitary play can sometimes be a sign of shyness, anxiety, fearfulness, or social rejection (Coplan, Prakash, O'Neil, & Armer, 2004; Henderson, Marshall, Fox, & Rubin, 2004; Spinrad et al., 2004), it is more likely that some children just prefer to play by themselves. For instance, in one study of 567 kindergartners, almost two out of three children who played alone were rated as socially and cognitively competent (Harrist, Zain, Bates, Dodge, & Pettit, 1997).

One kind of play that becomes more social during the preschool years is dramatic play (K. H. Rubin et al., 1998). Children typically engage in more dramatic play when playing with someone else than when playing alone (Bjorklund & Pellegrini, 2002). As dramatic play becomes more collaborative, story lines become more complex and innovative, offering rich opportunities to practise interpersonal and language skills and to explore social conventions and roles.

---

functional play Lowest cognitive level of play, involving repetitive muscular movements; also called *locomotor play*.

constructive play Second cognitive level of play, involving use of objects or materials to make something; also called *object play*.

dramatic play Play involving imaginary people or situations; also called *fantasy play*, *pretend play*, or *imaginative play*.

formal games with rules Organized games with known procedures and penalties.

TABLE 10.2 Parten's Categories of Social and Non-social Play

Category	Description
Unoccupied behaviour	The child does not seem to be playing but watches anything of momentary interest.
Onlooker behaviour	The child spends most of the time watching other children play. The onlooker talks to them, asking questions or making suggestions, but does not enter into the play. The onlooker is definitely observing particular groups of children rather than anything that happens to be exciting.
Solitary independent play	The child plays alone with toys that are different from those used by nearby children and makes no effort to get close to them.
Parallel play	The child plays independently but among the other children, playing with toys like those used by the other children but not necessarily playing with them in the same way. Playing beside rather than with the others, the parallel player does not try to influence the other children's play.
Associative play	The child plays with other children. They talk about their play, borrow and lend toys, follow one another, and try to control who may play in the group. All the children play similarly if not identically; there is no division of labour and no organization around any goal. Each child acts as she or he wishes and is interested more in being with the other children than in the activity itself.
Cooperative or organized supplementary play	The child plays in a group organized for some goal—to make something, play a formal game, or dramatize a situation. One or two children control who belongs to the group and direct activities. By a division of labour, children take on different roles and supplement each other's efforts.

Source: Adapted from Parten, "Social Participation Among Preschool Children," *Journal of Abnormal and Social Psychology,* 1932, Vol. 27, Issue 3 (October), pp. 243–269

HOW GENDER INFLUENCES PLAY

As we have mentioned, sex segregation is common among preschoolers and becomes more prevalent in middle childhood. This tendency seems to be universal across cultures (Smith, 2005a). By 3 years of age, girls are much more likely to play with dolls and tea sets whereas boys prefer toy guns and trucks (Dunn & Hughes, 2001). Girls tend to select other girls as playmates, and boys prefer other boys (Martin & Fabes, 2001), a phenomenon known as **gender segregation**. Boys' tendency to be more active and physically aggressive as compared with girls' more nurturing play styles are likely contributors to gender segregation.

Girls engage in more dramatic play than boys. Boys' pretend play often involves danger or discord and competitive, dominant roles, as in mock battles. Girls' pretend stories generally focus on social relationships and nurturing, domestic roles, as in playing house (Martin, Fabes, & Hamish, 2011; Pellegrini & Archer, 2005; Smith, 2005a). However, boys' play is more strongly gender-stereotyped than girls' (Bjorklund & Pellegrini, 2002). Thus, in mixed-sex groups, play tends to revolve around traditionally masculine activities (Fabes, Martin, & Hamish, 2003). See Table 10.3 for a summary of gender differences in play styles.

gender segregation The tendency of children to select same-sex playmates.

HOW CULTURE INFLUENCES PLAY

Cultural values affect the play environments adults set up for children, and these environments in turn affect the frequency of specific forms of play across cultures (Bodrova & Leong, 2005; Roopnarine, 2011). One observational study compared middle-class Korean-American and Anglo-American preschool children (Farver, Kim, & Lee, 1995). The Anglo-American preschools encouraged independent thinking and active involvement in learning by letting children select from a wide range of activities. The Korean-American preschool emphasized developing academic skills and completing tasks, and children were allowed to talk and play only during outdoor recess.

TABLE 10.3 Early Childhood Play Styles

	Boys	Girls
Toys	Toy guns	Dolls
	Trucks and cars	Tea sets
	Trains	Domestic toys
Playmates	Large groups of other boys	Small groups of other girls
	Friendships founded on shared activities and interests	Friendships founded on emotional and physical closeness
Activities	Rough-and-tumble	Conversational
	Physically aggressive	Nurturing
Conflict Resolution	Physical force	Compromise
Communication Style	Talk to give information and commands	Talk to strengthen relationships

Source: Golomobok et al. (2008).

Not surprisingly, the Anglo-American children engaged in more social play, whereas the Korean-Americans engaged in more unoccupied or parallel play. At the same time, Korean-American children played more cooperatively, often offering toys to other children—very likely a reflection of their culture's emphasis on group harmony. Anglo-American children were more aggressive and often responded negatively to other children's suggestions, reflecting the competitiveness of American culture.

Culture can influence how children deal with conflict in play situations. Canadian and Chinese children, observed when playing freely in four-child groups, showed different patterns of resolving conflicts over limited toy availability. Canadian children emphasized rules and norms around sharing, whereas Chinese children were more assertive in their bids to obtain the toy, showed more spontaneous giving, and gave more positive reactions to bids by other children to share. All children relied on *cultural scripts*—problem-solving strategies that are consistent with cultural norms—learned early in life for sharing and avoiding conflict, involving cooperating and deferring to group leaders for Chinese children, and sharing and turn-taking for Canadian children (D. C. French et al. 2011).

Parenting

As children increasingly become their own persons, their upbringing can be a complex challenge. Parents must deal with small people who have minds and wills of their own but who still have a lot to learn about what kinds of behaviour work well in society. Two areas that impact child development are forms of discipline and parenting styles.

FORMS OF DISCIPLINE

The word **discipline** means instruction or training. In the field of child development, *discipline* refers to methods of moulding character and teaching self-control and acceptable behaviour. It can be a powerful tool for socialization with the goal of developing self-discipline. What forms of discipline work best? Researchers have looked at a wide range of techniques, including reinforcement and punishment, inductive reasoning, power assertion, and withdrawal of love.

Reinforcement and Punishment

"You're such a wonderful helper, Nick! Thank you so much for putting away your toys." Nick's mother smiles warmly at her son as he plops his dump truck into the toy box. Her words and actions provide gentle discipline for her son and teach him that putting away his toys is a positive behaviour that should be repeated.

Parents sometimes punish children to stop undesirable behaviour, but children usually learn more from being reinforced for good behaviour. External reinforcements may be tangible (treats, more playtime) or intangible (a smile, a word of praise, a hug). Whatever the reinforcement, the child must see it as rewarding and must receive it fairly consistently and immediately after showing the desired behaviour. Eventually, the behaviour should provide an internal reinforcement: a sense of pleasure or accomplishment.

Still, at times punishment, such as isolation or denial of privileges, is necessary. Children cannot be permitted to run out into traffic or hit another child. Sometimes a child is wilfully defiant. In such situations, punishment—if consistent,

discipline Methods of moulding children's character and teaching them to exercise self-control and engage in acceptable behaviour.

immediate, and clearly tied to the offence—may be effective. It is most effective when accompanied by a short, simple explanation (AAP Committee on Psychosocial Aspects of Child and Family Health, 1998). However, the Canadian Medical Association recommends against corporal punishment, such as disciplinary spanking, and promotes alternatives such as positive parenting, a time out, and away-from-the-moment reasoning (Fletcher, 2012).

Corporal punishment is a form of coercive parenting in which physical force is used in an attempt to correct or control the child's behaviour. The goal is to cause the child to experience pain, but not physical harm or injury. Corporal punishment can include spanking, hitting, slapping, pinching, shaking, and other physical acts. It is popularly believed to be more effective than other remedies and to be harmless if done in moderation (McLoyd & Smith, 2002), but a growing body of evidence points to serious negative consequences (Gershoff, 2002; Straus & Stewart, 1999). Children who are punished harshly and frequently may have trouble interpreting other people's actions and words; they may attribute hostile intentions where none exist (Weiss, Dodge, Bates, & Pettit, 1992); they may later act aggressively (Gershoff, 2002); or they may become frightened when their parents lose control and may eventually try to avoid a punitive parent, undermining the parent's ability to influence behaviour (Grusec & Goodnow, 1994). Unlike child abuse, which bears little relation to the child's personality or behaviour, corporal punishment is more frequently used with children who are aggressive and hard to manage (Jaffe et al., 2004).

Inductive Reasoning, Power Assertion, and Withdrawal of Love

When Sara took candy from a store, her father did not lecture her on honesty, spank her, or tell her what a bad girl she had been. Instead, he explained how the owner of the store would be harmed by her failure to pay for the candy, asked her how she thought the store owner might feel, and then took her back to the store to return the candy.

Inductive reasoning techniques include setting limits, demonstrating logical consequences of an action, explaining, discussing, negotiating, and getting ideas from the child about what is fair. Inductive reasoning tends to arouse empathy for the victim of wrongdoing as well as guilt on the part of the wrongdoer (Kochanska, Gross, Lin & Nichols, 2002). Inductive reasoning techniques are usually the most effective method of getting children to accept parental standards (Kerr, Lopez, Olson, & Sameroff, 2004).

Two other broad categories of discipline are power assertion and temporary withdrawal of love. **Power assertion** is intended to stop or discourage undesirable behaviour through physical or verbal enforcement of parental control; it includes demands, threats, withdrawal of privileges, spanking, and other types of punishment. **Withdrawal of love** may include ignoring, isolating, or showing dislike for a child. Neither of these is as effective

corporal punishment Use of physical force with the intention of causing pain but not injury so as to correct or control behaviour.

inductive reasoning techniques Disciplinary techniques designed to induce desirable behaviour by appealing to a child's sense of reason and fairness.

power assertion Disciplinary strategy designed to discourage undesirable behaviour through physical or verbal enforcement of parental control.

withdrawal of love Disciplinary strategy that involves ignoring, isolating, or showing dislike for a child.

as inductive reasoning in most circumstances, and both may be harmful (Baumrind, Larzelere, & Owens, 2010).

The effectiveness of parental discipline may hinge on how well the child understands and accepts the parent's message, both cognitively and emotionally. For the child to accept the message, the parents need to be fair and accurate as well as clear and consistent about their expectations. They need to fit the discipline to the child's temperament and cognitive and emotional level. A child may be more motivated to accept the message if the parents are normally warm and responsive and if they arouse the child's empathy for someone the child has harmed (Kerr et al., 2004). How well children accept a disciplinary method also may depend on whether the type of discipline used is accepted in the family's culture (Lansford et al., 2005).

One point on which many experts agree is that a child interprets and responds to discipline in the context of an ongoing relationship with a parent. Some researchers, therefore, look beyond specific parental practices to overall styles, or patterns, of parenting.

PARENTING STYLES

Why does Stacy hit and bite the nearest person when she cannot finish a jigsaw puzzle? What makes David sit and sulk when he cannot finish the puzzle, even though his teacher offers to help him? Why does Consuela work on the puzzle for 20 minutes and then shrug and try another? Why are children so different in their responses to the same situation? Temperament is

Although parents sometimes punish children to stop unwanted behaviour, children learn more by being reinforced for good behaviour.

Perspectives on Diversity

CROSS-CULTURAL DIFFERENCES IN CORPORAL PUNISHMENT

"Spare the rod and spoil the child" may sound old-fashioned, but corporal punishment still exists in Canada. Some form of corporal punishment is widely used on Canadian toddlers. In interviews, 70 to 90 percent of Canadian parents report spanking their children, and one-third of those report doing so at least once a week (Durrant, Broberg, & Rose-Krasnor, 1999). While over half of Canadians report being spanked, and almost two-thirds believe that spanking should be a legal option for parents, non-parents and those who experienced abuse in childhood are less likely to approve of corporal punishment (Bell & Romano, 2012; Gagné, Tourigny, Joly, & Pouliot-Lapointe, 2007). Canadian mothers are more likely than Swedish mothers to spank their children, and the likelihood of spanking is higher if mothers have a positive attitude toward spanking and believe that their children's behaviours are changeable (Durrant et al., 1999). In fact, 80 percent of respondents in a retrospective study of non-abused adults in Ontario reported having experienced some form of corporal punishment as children (MacMillan et al., 1999).

Legal sanction of corporal punishment is not the case everywhere, however. Corporal punishment is banned in many countries, including Austria, Bulgaria, Croatia, Cyprus, Denmark, Finland, Germany, Hungary, Iceland, Israel, Latvia, Norway, Romania,

Sweden, and Ukraine. Canada's "spanking law," Section 43 of the Criminal Code, has strict limits set by the Supreme Court of Canada. The court ruled out corporal punishment in schools and also forbade its use with infants or teenagers in any setting. But the court stopped short of ruling out its use by parents of young children (Repeal 43 Committee, n.d.). The United Nations Convention on the Rights of Children opposes all forms of physical violence against children.

Many people still believe that spanking instills respect for authority, motivates good behaviour, and is a necessary part of parenting (Kazdin & Benjet, 2003). However, some professionals view any corporal punishment as verging on child abuse (Straus, 1994). Other professionals find no harm in corporal punishment in moderation when prudently administered by loving parents (Baumrind, Larzelere, & Cowan, 2002). Still others argue the effect depends on cultural norms for behaviour (Lansford et al., 2005; McLoyd & Smith, 2002). Canadian authorities on corporal punishment, such as the Canadian Medical Association, call it an outmoded form of discipline that shows no evidence of effectiveness for developmental health and that it is a risk for negative developmental outcomes; they recommend that it not be practised (Durrant & Enrom, 2012; Fletcher, 2012).

---

a major factor, of course, but some research suggests that styles of parenting affect children's competence in dealing with their world. Researchers have identified four primary parenting styles.

Diana Baumrind and the Effectiveness of Authoritative Parenting

In pioneering research, Diana Baumrind (Baumrind & Black, 1967) measured how children were functioning, identified three parenting styles—authoritarian, permissive, and authoritative parenting—and described typical behaviour patterns of children raised according to each. Baumrind's work and the large body of research it inspired have established associations between each parenting style and child behaviours (Baumrind, 1989; Darling & Steinberg, 1993; Pettit, Bates, & Dodge, 1997).

Authoritarian parenting emphasizes control and unquestioning obedience. Authoritarian parents try to make children conform rigidly to a set standard of conduct and punish them for violating it, often using power-assertive techniques. They are more detached and less warm than

other parents. Their children tend to be more discontented, withdrawn, and distrustful.

Permissive parenting makes few demands and allows children to monitor their own activities as much as possible. Permissive parents are warm, non-controlling, and undemanding or even indulgent. Their preschool children tend to be immature—the least self-controlled and the least exploratory.

Authoritative parenting respects children's independent decisions, interests, opinions, and personalities. Authoritative parents are loving and accepting but also demand good behaviour and are firm in maintaining standards. They impose limited, judicious punishment when necessary, within the context of a warm, supportive relationship. They

---

authoritarian parenting Parenting style emphasizing control and obedience.

permissive parenting Parenting style emphasizing self-expression and self-regulation.

authoritative parenting Parenting style blending warmth and respect for a child's individuality with an effort to instill social values.

favour inductive discipline, explaining the reasoning behind their stand and encouraging verbal negotiation and give-and-take. Their children typically feel secure in knowing both that they are loved and what is expected of them. These preschoolers tend to be the most self-reliant, self-controlled, self-assertive, exploratory, and content.

Eleanor Maccoby and John Martin (1983) added a fourth parenting style—**neglectful, or uninvolved, parenting**—to describe parents who focus on their own needs rather than on those of the child. Neglectful parenting has been linked with a variety of behavioural disorders in childhood and adolescence (Steinberg, Eisengart, & Cauffman, 2006).

Why does authoritative parenting tend to enhance children's social competence? It may be because by making clear, consistent rules, authoritative parents let children know what is expected of them and give them a standard of behaviour by which to judge themselves, and thus develop competence in making decisions and expressing their own perspectives in positive ways. In authoritarian homes, children are so strictly controlled that often they cannot make independent choices about their behaviour; in permissive homes, children receive so little guidance that they may be uncertain and anxious about whether they are doing the right thing.

Support and Criticism of Baumrind's Model

In research based on Baumrind's work, the superiority of authoritative parenting has repeatedly been supported (Dishion et al., 2008; Rinaldi & Howe, 2012). Still, Baumrind's model has provoked controversy because it seems to suggest that there is one "right" way to raise children. Also, because Baumrind's findings are correlational, they merely establish associations between each parenting style and a particular set of child behaviours and don't rule out the possibility that children's behaviours can influence parenting styles. They do not show that different styles of child-rearing cause children to be more or less competent. In addition, Baumrind did not consider innate factors, such as temperament, that might have affected children's competence and exerted an influence on the parents. Children may elicit parenting styles based on their own behaviour; an easy child might, for example, elicit authoritarian parenting.

Cultural Differences in Parenting Styles

Baumrind's categories reflect the dominant North American view of child development, may not apply to other cultures or socio-economic groups, and can be modified by the influences of the immediate social environment. For example, a cross-cultural comparison of factors influencing parenting styles of mainland Chinese,

Chinese-Canadian, and European-Canadian mothers showed that higher parental stress, traditional parenting beliefs, and lower social support were linked to authoritarian parenting. Location also had an influence: Canadian-based mothers were more likely to use authoritative parenting than mainland Chinese mothers. However, for all three groups, more authoritative parenting was seen when stress levels were low, when traditional parenting beliefs were low, and when mothers were more individualist in their orientations (Su & Hynie, 2011).

The traditional Aboriginal parenting style in Canada is much like Baumrind's permissive style (Neckoway, Brownlee, & Castellan, 2007). However, as is the case with the preferred parenting style in families of Asian background, there is no detrimental influence on Aboriginal children's development (Johnson & Cremo, 1995). Among Canadian immigrant groups, there are differences in parenting style, which may reflect differences in social values in the countries of origin. Egyptian Canadians, for example, were found to score higher on measures of authoritarianism and collectivism than were Anglo-Canadians (Rudy & Grusec, 2001). The best predictor of authoritarian parenting style in Egyptian-Canadian parents was high levels of collectivism, in comparison to individualism, whereas in Anglo-Canadians the best predictor of authoritarian parenting was a combination of collectivism and lack of warmth (Rudy & Grusec, 2001). It may be misleading, then, to consider parenting styles without looking at the goals parents are trying to achieve and the constraints their life circumstances present.

Positive Parenting

In general, Canadian parents adopt a positive parenting style, characterized by offering support and encouragement to children (Landy & Tam, 1996). Positive parenting approaches

---

neglectful, or uninvolved, parenting Parenting style in which parents focus on their own needs rather than those of children.

are associated with good developmental outcomes in social development and helping behaviour (Chao & Willms, 2002). However, children are particularly vulnerable to poor developmental outcomes if their family situations contain more than several risk factors, including family dysfunction, low social support, being in a single-parent family, having a teenage parent, and living in poverty (Willms, 2002a). The impact of these factors on child development is typically diminished by positive parenting practices (Landy & Tam, 1996).

In fact, positive parenting can be a protective factor in the presence of some psychological conditions, such as ADHD; children with ADHD show better functional abilities when parents follow a positive parenting style (Healey, Flory, Miller, & Halperin, 2011). Although outcomes involving reduction of parental stress, family functioning, and child behaviour are mixed, parenting programs that promote this style, such as the Triple P (Positive Parenting Program), have been effective in improving parents' feelings of competence in dealing with children's behavioural difficulties (McConnell, Breitkreuz, & Savage, 2011), and are perceived as being consistent with cultural values and having an impact on promoting styles of parenting that support healthy development in children in Aboriginal families (Houlding, Schmidt, Stern, Jamieson, & Borg, 2012).

Did you know?

The match between a child's and parents' traits can be viewed as a passive genotype-environment association. And it can be either beneficial or harmful. For example, prosocial parents provide their children with (presumably) prosocial genes, as well as an environment that cultivates prosocial behaviour. Similarly, antisocial parents may provide their children with both antisocial genes and environments as well.

both prosocial—voluntary behaviour to help others—and aggressive behaviours. How do such behaviours emerge?

PROSOCIAL BEHAVIOUR

Altruism—helping another person with no expectation of reward—is at the heart of **prosocial behaviour**. Even before their second birthday, children often help others, share belongings and food, and offer comfort (Dunfield, Kuhlmeier, O'Connell, & Kelley, 2011; Warneken, 2013; Warneken & Tomasello, 2009). Research has revealed three preferences: a preference to share with close relations, reciprocity (a preference to share with people who have shared with you), and indirect reciprocity (a preference to share with people who share with others). These preferences are present and functional in children as young as 3½ years of age (Olson & Spelke, 2008).

Is there a prosocial personality or disposition? A longitudinal study that followed 32 children ages 4 and 5 suggests that there is and that it emerges early and remains somewhat consistent throughout life. Preschoolers who were sympathetic and spontaneously shared with classmates tended to show prosocial understanding and empathic behaviour as much as 17 years later (Coplan et al., 2004).

There are also interactions between genes and environments. Parents of prosocial children typically are prosocial themselves. They point out models of prosocial behaviour and steer children toward stories, films, and television programs that depict cooperation, sharing, and empathy and encourage sympathy, generosity, and helpfulness (Singer & Singer, 1998). And if their children have a natural tendency to be prosocial, parents who show affection and follow positive (inductive) disciplinary strategies tend to magnify those natural tendencies (Knafo & Plomin, 2006). Media, peers, and teachers also can model and reinforce prosocial behaviour (Wilson, 2008).

Cultures vary in the degree to which they foster prosocial behaviour. Traditional cultures in which people live

Prosocial and Aggressive Behaviour

Derek, at 3½, responded to two preschool classmates' complaints that they did not have enough modelling clay, his favourite plaything, by giving them half of his. However, a few days later when his twin sister had a toy he wanted, he hit her on the head in order to take the toy from her. Derek, like most children, is displaying

altruism *Motivation to help others without expectation of reward; may involve self-denial or self-sacrifice.*

prosocial behaviour *Any voluntary behaviour intended to help others.*

in extended family groups and share work seem to foster prosocial values more than cultures that stress individual achievement (Eisenberg & Fabes, 1998).

AGGRESSIVE BEHAVIOUR

When Noah roughly snatches a ball away from Jake, he is interested only in getting the ball, not in hurting or dominating Jake. This is **instrumental aggression**, or aggression used as an instrument to reach a goal—the most common type of aggression in early childhood. Between ages 2½ and 5, children commonly struggle over toys and control of space. Instrumental aggression surfaces mostly during social play; children who fight the most also tend to be the most sociable and competent.

As children develop more self-control and become better able to express themselves verbally, they typically shift from showing aggression physically to doing it with words (Tremblay et al., 2004). However, individual differences remain. In a longitudinal study of 383 preschoolers, 11 percent of the girls and 9 percent of the boys showed high levels of aggression between ages 2 and 5. Boys and girls who were inattentive at age 2, and girls who showed poor emotion regulation at that age, tended to have conduct problems at age 5 (Hill, Degan, Calkins, & Keane, 2006). Children who, as preschoolers, often engage in violent fantasy play may, at age 6, be prone to violent displays of anger (Dunn & Hughes, 2001). The preschool period, though, is a critical period when most children learn alternatives to aggressive behaviour (Broidy et al., 2003; Tremblay, 2008).

Gender Differences in Aggression

Aggression is an exception to the generalization that boys and girls are more similar than different (Hyde, 2005). In all cultures studied, as among most mammals, boys are more physically aggressive than girls. This gender difference is apparent by age 2 (Baillargeon et al., 2007), though the emotional toll on aggressive girls in self-concept and behavioural difficulties is similar to that experienced by aggressive boys (Pepler & Sedighdeilami, 1998).

However, girls may be more aggressive than they seem (Putallaz & Bierman, 2004). Whereas boys engage in more **overt (direct) aggression**—physical or verbal aggression openly directed at its target—girls, especially as they grow older, are more likely to engage in **relational (indirect or social) aggression**. This more subtle kind of aggression consists of damaging or interfering with relationships, reputation, or psychological well-being, often through teasing, manipulation, ostracism, or bids for control. It may include spreading rumours,

instrumental aggression Aggressive behaviour used as a means of achieving a goal.

overt (direct) aggression Aggression that is openly directed at its target.

relational (indirect or social) aggression Aggression aimed at damaging or interfering with another person's relationships, reputation, or psychological well-being; can be overt or covert.

name-calling, put-downs, or excluding someone from a group. Among preschoolers, it tends to be direct and face-to-face ("You can't come to my party if you don't give me that toy.") (Brendgen et al., 2005). These patterns are consistent in Canada and across countries (Lansford et al., 2012; Lussier, Corrado, & Tzoumakis, 2012).

Influences on Aggression

Why are some children more aggressive than others? Temperament plays a part. Children who are intensely emotional and low in self-control tend to express anger aggressively (Rubin, Burgess, Dwyer, & Hastings, 2003), and physical aggression has been estimated to be 50 to 60 percent heritable (Brendgen et al., 2005).

Parental behaviours also influence aggressiveness. In several longitudinal studies, insecure attachment and lack of maternal warmth and affection in infancy predicted aggressiveness in early childhood (Coie & Dodge, 1998; Rubin, Burgess, & Hastings, 2002). Manipulative behaviours, such as withdrawal of love and making a child feel guilty or ashamed, may foster social aggression (Brendgen et al., 2005).

Aggressiveness may also be influenced by a combination of a stressful and unstimulating home atmosphere, harsh discipline, lack of maternal warmth and social support, family dysfunction, exposure to aggressive adults and neighbourhood violence, poverty, and transient peer groups, which prevent stable friendships (Dodge, Pettit, & Bates, 1994; Grusec & Goodnow, 1994; Kohen, Oliver, & Pierre, 2009; Olson et al., 2011;

WHAT DO YOU DO?

Behavioural Specialist

Behavioural specialists analyze student behaviour to determine the cause of unwanted behaviours and create plans for changing them. For example, a behavioural specialist might help parents develop strategies for a child with an autism spectrum disorder who is showing aggression toward other children or who is very late in potty training. Behavioural specialists work within school systems, hospitals and group practices, and in private practice. Behavioural specialists typically have a master's degree in applied behavioural analysis and have been certified by the Behavior Analyst Certification Board. Visit www.bacb.com to learn more.

Romano, Tremblay, Boulerice, & Swisher, 2005). In a study of 431 Head Start participants in a U.S. inner-city neighbourhood, parents reported that more than half had witnessed gang activity, drug trafficking, police pursuits and arrests, or people carrying weapons, and some of the children and families had been victimized themselves. These children showed symptoms of distress at home and aggressive behaviour at school (Farver, Xu, Eppe, Fernandez, & Schwartz, 2005).

Electronic media, including television, movies, and video games, have enormous power for modelling either prosocial behaviour or aggression. In Chapter 13, we discuss the influence of media violence on aggressive behaviour.

Ask Yourself

13. What is a prosocial behaviour?

14. Overall, boys engage in _____ levels of aggression than girls, although girls tend to engage in more _____ aggression.
   a. higher; relational
   b. lower; relational
   c. higher; instrumental
   d. lower; instrumental

SUMMARY

_{CHAPTER} **10** **PSYCHOSOCIAL DEVELOPMENT IN EARLY CHILDHOOD**

LO1

Describe changes in the understanding of and feelings about the self, and discuss how this impacts emotional development.

- The self-concept undergoes major change in early childhood.
- Culture affects self-definition.
- Self-esteem in early childhood tends to be global and unrealistic, reflecting adult approval.
- Understanding of emotions directed toward the self and of simultaneous emotions develops gradually.

LO2

Summarize and contrast the different theories of gender development.

- Gender identity is an important aspect of the developing self-concept.
- The main gender difference in early childhood is boys' greater aggressiveness. Girls tend to be more empathic and prosocial and less prone to problem behaviour. Some cognitive differences appear early.
- Children learn gender roles at an early age through gender-typing. Gender stereotypes peak during the preschool years.
- Five major perspectives on gender development are the biological, evolutionary developmental, psychoanalytic, cognitive, and social-learning approaches.
- Evidence suggests that some gender differences may be biologically based.
- In Freudian theory, a child identifies with the same-sex parent after giving up the wish to possess the other parent.
- Evolutionary developmental theory sees children's gender roles as preparation for adult mating behaviour.

Continued

LO2

Summarize and contrast the different theories of gender development.

Continued

- Traditional social-learning theory attributed the learning of gender roles to imitation of models and reinforcement. The expanded social-cognitive theory credits cognitive elements as well.
- Cognitive-developmental theory maintains that gender identity develops from thinking about one's gender. Gender constancy enhances the acquisition of gender roles. Gender-schema theory holds that children categorize gender-related information by observing what males and females do in their culture.
- Children also learn gender roles through socialization. Parents, peers, the media, and culture influence gender-typing.

LO3

Discuss the influences on play in early childhood.

- Play has physical, cognitive, and psychosocial benefits, and may have had evolutionary functions.
- Changes in the types of play children engage in reflect cognitive and social development.
- According to Smilansky, children progress cognitively from functional play to constructive play to dramatic play and then to formal games with rules. Dramatic play becomes increasingly common during early childhood and helps children develop social and cognitive skills. Rough-and-tumble play also begins during early childhood.
- According to Parten, play becomes more social during early childhood. However, later research has found that non-social play is not necessarily immature.
- Children prefer to play with (and play more socially with) others of their sex.
- Cognitive and social aspects of play are influenced by the culturally approved environments adults create for children.

LO4

Summarize different forms of parental discipline and parenting styles.

- Discipline can be a powerful tool for socialization.
- Both positive reinforcement and prudently administered punishment can be appropriate tools of discipline within the context of a positive parent–child relationship.
- Inductive reasoning techniques, power assertion, and withdrawal of love can each be effective in certain situations. Inductive reasoning is generally the most effective and power assertion the least effective in promoting internalization of parental standards. Spanking and other forms of corporal punishment can have negative consequences.
- Baumrind identified three child-rearing styles: authoritarian, permissive, and authoritative. A fourth style, neglectful or uninvolved, was identified later. Authoritative parents tend to raise more competent children. However, Baumrind's findings may not apply to some cultures or socio-economic groups.
- Canadian parents typically adopt a positive parenting style, characterized by offering support and encouragement to children.

LO5

Discuss the development of and influences on prosocial and antisocial behaviour.

- The roots of altruism and prosocial behaviour appear early. This may be an inborn disposition, which can be cultivated by parental modelling and encouragement.
- Instrumental aggression—first physical, then verbal—is most common in early childhood.
- Most children become less aggressive after age 6 or 7, but the proportion of hostile aggression increases. Boys tend to practise overt aggression, whereas girls engage in relational or social aggression.

ANSWERS TO Ask Yourself

Answers: 1–c; 2–b; 3–In early childhood, children get better at regulating emotions, understanding emotions, and at understanding emotions directed at the self; 4–b; 5–d; 6–Through play, children stimulate the senses, exercise their muscles, coordinate sight with movement, gain mastery over their bodies, make decisions, acquire new cognitive skills, learn to cooperate, and learn about conflict resolution; 7–a; 8–b; 9–c; 10–Children's play styles across different cultures look slightly different because play is influenced both by the play environments that are provided to children and by cultural values (e.g., cooperation or competition); 11–e; 12–a; 13–Prosocial behaviour is defined as voluntary activity intended to benefit another; 14–a

connect LEARNSMART SMARTBOOK

For more information on the resources available from McGraw-Hill Ryerson, go to **www.mcgrawhill.ca/he/solutions**.

PHYSICAL DEVELOPMENT AND HEALTH

WHAT'S TO COME

Physical Development

Nutrition and Sleep

Motor Development and Physical Play

Health and Safety

Mental Health

Alex ran as fast as he could through the playground, laughing as his friends tried and failed to catch him. His wide gap-toothed grin flashed back at them as he looked back in glee. Alex's legs were sturdy and sure as he jumped from the playground on to the soccer field by its side, although his skinned knees and a purple bruise on his arm showed he was not always so lucky. Alex was doing what children love most—playing. By dinner, Alex would be famished, and by night, his physical exertions would sink him into a heavy sleep.

In this chapter, we focus on physical development and health in middle childhood. We explore normal growth and brain development, and the factors that promote it, including proper nutrition, adequate sleep, and good health. In addition, we focus on when health is not ideal, and on some of the factors that can put children at risk for obesity, accidental injury, or emotional disturbances.

IN MIDDLE CHILDHOOD

AS YOU READ

LO1   Describe how school-age children's bodies and brains grow.
LO2   Summarize nutritional needs and sleep patterns in middle childhood.
LO3   Describe what play looks like in middle childhood.
LO4   List the principle health and safety concerns of middle childhood.
LO5   Describe some common mental health problems of childhood and how children respond to the stresses of modern life.

Physical Development

If we were to walk by a typical elementary school during recess, we would see a virtual explosion of children of all shapes and sizes. Tall ones, short ones, husky ones, and skinny ones would be bursting out of the school doors into the open air, running and jumping, tumbling and scrambling in the grass. We would see them throwing and catching balls, twisting and hanging on the monkey bars, and pumping their legs vigorously on the swings. We would see that school-age children look very different from children a few years younger.

HEIGHT AND WEIGHT

Growth during middle childhood slows considerably. Still, although day-by-day changes may not be obvious, they add up to a startling difference between 6-year-olds, who are still small children, and 11-year-olds, many of whom are now beginning to resemble adults.

Children grow about 5 to 7 cm (2 to 3 inches) and gain about 2 to 4 kg (4½ to 9 pounds) each year between ages 6 and 11 (Dieticians of Canada, 2012a; McDowell, Fryar, et al., 2008; Figure 11.1). Girls retain somewhat more fatty tissue than boys, a characteristic that will persist through adulthood. The recommended weights for the average 10-year-old are 31 kg (68 pounds) for boys and 32 kg (71 pounds) for girls (Dieticians of Canada, 2010).

TOOTH DEVELOPMENT AND DENTAL CARE

Middle childhood ushers in the excitement of the Tooth Fairy. Primary teeth begin to fall out at about age 6 and are replaced by permanent teeth at a rate of about four teeth per year for the next five years.

The number of Canadian children aged 6 to 11 with untreated cavities in their permanent teeth dropped from 74 percent in the 1970s to 25 percent in 2009 (Health Canada, 2010a). Improvements cut across ethnic and socio-economic lines, although Aboriginal children and those living in families with lower incomes and lower parental education have more decay (Health Canada, 2010a; Lawrence et al., 2009; Schroth, Harrison, & Moffatt, 2009).

Improvement in children's dental health is also attributed to use of adhesive sealants on the rough, chewing surfaces (Rethman, 2000). Dental sealants in children's teeth have increased from the early 1970s to the point where up to 32 percent of children aged 6 to 11 have dental sealants (Health Canada, 2010a). Access to proper dental care is important for young children. Untreated oral disease may lead to problems in eating, speaking, and sleeping (Health Canada, 2010a; Schroth et al., 2009).

BRAIN DEVELOPMENT

Changes in the brain's structure and functioning support the cognitive advances of middle childhood. Maturation and learning in middle childhood and beyond depend on fine-tuning the brain's connections, along with more efficient selection of the regions of the brain appropriate for particular tasks. Together, these changes increase the speed and efficiency of brain processes and enhance the ability to filter out irrelevant information (Amso & Casey, 2006).

Did you know?

Although most children grow normally, some do not. The little people who played the Munchkins in *The Wizard of Oz* had a hormone deficiency. Nowadays, we see few people with this condition, as synthetic growth hormone is given to them as children so that they can attain near normal height.

Growth Chart for Boys and Girls, Ages 5–12

FIGURE 11.1 During middle childhood, growth slows and boys and girls gain height and weight at approximately equivalent rates.

Source: Based on the World Health Organization (WHO) Child Growth Standards (2006) and adapted for Canada by Dieticians of Canada, Canadian Paediatric Society, the College of Family Physicians of Canada and Community Health Nurses of Canada. (c) Dieticians of Canada, 2010.

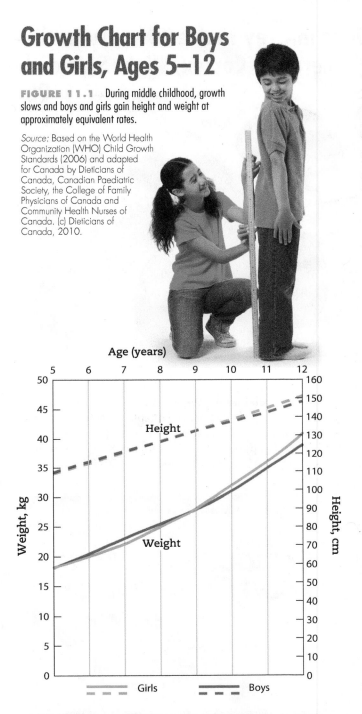

One important maturational change, identified with the use of brain imaging techniques, is a loss in the density of *grey matter*—closely packed neuronal bodies—in certain regions of the cerebral cortex (Figure 11.2). This process reflects pruning of unused dendrites. The volume of grey matter in the cortex forms an inverted "U," peaking at different times in different lobes. Grey matter in the parietal lobes, which deal with spatial understanding, reaches its maximum volume, on average, at about age 10 in girls and 11½ in boys. In the frontal lobes, which handle higher-order functions such as thinking, and which may be involved with differences in IQ (Toga & Thompson, 2005), grey matter peaks at age 11 in girls and age 12 in boys. In the temporal lobes, which help with language, grey matter peaks at about age 16 in both girls and boys. Beneath the cortex, grey matter volume in the caudate—a part of the basal ganglia, which are involved in control of movement and muscle tone and in mediating higher cognitive functions, attention, and emotional states—peaks at age 7½ in girls and age 10 in boys (Lenroot & Giedd, 2006).

This loss in density of grey matter is balanced by a steady increase in *white matter*—axons or nerve fibres that transmit information between neurons to distant regions of the brain. These connections thicken and myelinate, beginning with the frontal lobes and moving toward the rear of the brain. Between ages 6 and 13, striking growth takes place in connections between the temporal and parietal lobes. White matter growth may not begin to drop off until well into adulthood (Kuhn, 2006; Lenroot & Giedd, 2006; NIMH, 2001).

Another way neuroscientists measure brain development is by changes in the thickness of the cortex. Researchers have observed cortical thickening between ages 5 and 11 in regions of the temporal and frontal lobes. At the same time, thinning occurs in the rear portion of the frontal and parietal cortex in the brain's left hemisphere. This change correlates with improved performance on the vocabulary portion of an intelligence test (Toga et al., 2006).

WHERE DO **YOU** STAND?

In many municipalities in Canada, drinking water is fluoridated as a matter of public health. Many argue that small doses of fluoride help to strengthen tooth enamel and thus promote dental health. However, others argue that levels of fluoride in water supplies are too variable, that the correct dosage depends on weight and nutritional status, and that high doses of fluoride could potentially have adverse effects on health. What's your view?

Ask Yourself

1. Between the ages of 6 and 11 years, the typical child will grow
   a. 0.1 to 2 cm a year.
   b. 5 to 7 cm a year.
   c. 10 to 12 cm a year.
   d. 10 to 12 cm a year, but only if given synthetic growth hormone.

2. Name two ways in which children's dental health has been promoted.

3. With respect to brain development, the grey matter _____ and the white matter _____ in volume over childhood.

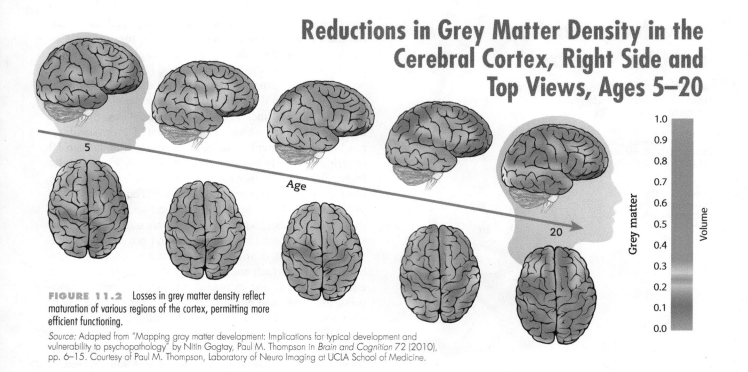

Reductions in Grey Matter Density in the Cerebral Cortex, Right Side and Top Views, Ages 5–20

FIGURE 11.2 Losses in grey matter density reflect maturation of various regions of the cortex, permitting more efficient functioning.

Source: Adapted from "Mapping gray matter development: Implications for typical development and vulnerability to psychopathology" by Nitin Gogtay, Paul M. Thompson in *Brain and Cognition* 72 (2010), pp. 6–15. Courtesy of Paul M. Thompson, Laboratory of Neuro Imaging at UCLA School of Medicine.

Nutrition and Sleep

Emily refuses to eat any vegetables and subsists mostly on pasta and fruit. Nathan learned to read and since that time has stayed up late at night with a flashlight under the covers every night, reading until he falls asleep. Sarah loves fruits and vegetables and falls asleep promptly at eight. How do different patterns of eating and sleep affect these children?

NUTRITIONAL NEEDS

Schoolchildren need, on average, 2,400 calories every day—more for older children and less for younger ones (Canada's Food Guide to Healthy Eating, 2007). Nutritionists recommend a varied diet including plenty of grains, fruits, and vegetables, which are high in natural nutrients (Dieticians of Canada, 2012b; Health Canada, 2011c). To avoid overweight and prevent cardiac problems, children's diets should have no more than 30 percent as fat and 10 percent as saturated fat (CPS and Health Canada, 1994/2001). Studies have found no negative effects on height, weight, body mass, or neurological development from a moderately low-fat diet at this age (Rask-Nissilä et al., 2000).

As children grow older, pressures and opportunities for unhealthy eating increase. Most Canadian children's diets do not meet Health Canada recommendations. Children report eating snack foods at least once a week, with older children doing worse in their eating patterns than younger children (Garriguet, 2009; Pabayo, Spence, Casey, & Storey, 2012). Although school cafeterias and vending machines have offered unhealthy foods (Leo, 2007; National Center for Education Statistics [NCES],

2006), provincial ministries of education are developing guidelines on foods that are acceptable for sale in schools (B.C. Ministry of Education and Ministry of Healthy Living and Sport, 2010; Healthy Child Manitoba, n.d.; Ontario Ministry of Education, 2010). Children

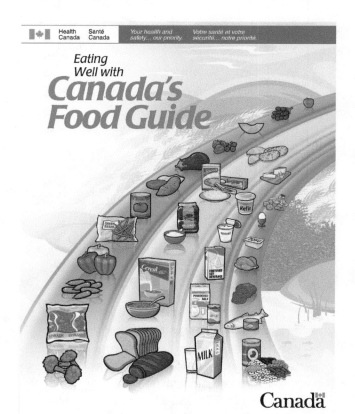

To encourage healthy eating, Canada's food guide encourages a varied diet including plenty of grains, fruits, and vegetables.

frequently eat out, often at fast food restaurants. The media strongly influence children's food choices, and not for the better. For example, commercials that focus on fast food restaurants and the enticing toys they often offer children are common during children's programming hours. Socio-economic status (SES) can be a factor as well because healthy, fresh food is often more expensive than highly processed, high-calorie food with low nutrient content. Because of the difficulties in transporting healthy food to northern regions, diet in remote communities often consists of convenience foods that are less nutritious than fresh fruit and vegetables that are readily available in less remote centres (Canadian Institute of Child Health, 2000).

Nutrition education in schools can be helpful when combined with parental education and changes in school lunch menus. Changes in food labelling, taxes on unhealthy foods, restrictions on foods provided by government-supported school lunch programs, regulation of food advertising directed toward children, and requirements for restaurants to list nutrition information on their menus are among proposed legislative recommendations (American Heart Association et al., 2006).

SLEEP PATTERNS AND PROBLEMS

Sleep needs decline from about 11 hours a day at age 5 to a little more than 10 hours at age 9 and about 9 hours at age 13. Even so, many Canadian children get less sleep than they need. Sleep problems, such as resistance to going to bed, insomnia, and daytime sleepiness, are common during these years, in part because many children, as they grow older, are allowed to set their own bedtimes (Hoban, 2004). Nighttime access to electronic entertainment devices is associated with shortened sleep duration in children (Chahal, Fung, Kuhle, & Veugelers, 2012).

Prevalence of school-age children with sleeping problems ranges from 11 to 40 percent (Hoedlmoser, Kloesch, Wiater, & Schabus, 2010; National Sleep Foundation, 2004; Quach, Hiscock, Ukoumunne & Wake, 2011). Up to 40 percent of children regularly stall about going to bed, and 29 percent have difficulty getting up in the morning. In one study, teachers noted that at least 10 percent of kindergarten through fourth-grade students struggled to stay awake in class (Owens, Spirito, McGuinn, & Nobile, 2000). There are also indications that older children report more morning drowsiness and are more likely to fall asleep during the day (Sadeh, Raviv, & Gruber, 2000).

About one out of every five children under 18 snores. Persistent snoring, at least three times per week, may indicate a child has sleep-disordered breathing (SDB), a condition that has been linked to behavioural and learning difficulties (Halbower et al., 2006). Obstructive sleep apnea (OSA), a severe form of SDB, affects one in 20 children and is associated with significant deficits in IQ, memory, and verbal fluency (Halbower et al., 2006). Many children with SDB may undergo the surgical removal of their adenoids and tonsils—a treatment that has been found to improve neurobehavioural deficits and improve quality of life (Chervin et al., 2006). Children who are not candidates for surgery may benefit from continuous positive airway pressure (CPAP) therapy in which an electronic device keeps airways open via air pressure delivered through a nasal mask (Lamberg, 2007).

Ask Yourself

4. Which of the following is the best description of a healthy diet in middle childhood?
   a. a high-protein, high-fat diet
   b. a low-protein diet rich in complex carbohydrates
   c. a varied diet that includes plenty of grains, fruits, vegetables, and complex carbohydrates
   d. None of these; what a healthy diet is depends upon the individual child's nutritional needs.

5. With respect to sleep, most children
   a. get adequate sleep.
   b. get less sleep than they need.
   c. get more sleep than they need.
   d. get less sleep than they need on weekdays and adequate amounts on weekends.

Motor Development and Physical Play

During the middle years, children's motor abilities continue to improve (see Table 11.1). Children keep getting stronger, faster, and better coordinated—and they derive great pleasure from testing their bodies and learning new skills.

As motor skills improve in middle childhood, play becomes an important context for health, both physical and psychological. In Canada, there has been a trend toward more sedentary activities for elementary school-age children (Barnes, Colley, & Tremblay, 2012; Juster, Ono, & Stafford, 2004). At the same time, many children participate in organized sports. How do these physical activities—or their lack—shape development?

Using playground equipment is a great way for children to stay active, but less than half of Canadian children are active enough to ensure healthy growth. Unstructured outdoor physical activity has added benefits, by promoting children's developing personal autonomy and combatting sedentary indoor play.

RECESS

The games schoolchildren play at recess tend to be informal and spontaneously organized. Boys play more physically active games (Rose & Rudolph, 2006), whereas girls favour games that include verbal expression or counting aloud, such as hopscotch and jump rope (Pellegrini, Kato, Blatchford & Baines, 2002). Such recess-time activities promote growth in agility and social competence and foster adjustment to school (Pellegrini et al., 2002), and perhaps more surprisingly, are also related to cognitive performance (Pellegrini & Bohn, 2005) and positive classroom behaviour (Barros, Silver, & Stein, 2009).

About 10 percent of schoolchildren's free play in the early grades consists of **rough-and-tumble play**, vigorous play that involves wrestling, kicking, tumbling, grappling, and chasing, often accompanied by laughing and screaming (Bjorklund & Pellegrini, 2002). This kind of play may look like fighting but is done playfully among friends (Smith, 2005a). Rough-and-tumble play peaks in middle childhood and then drops to about 5 percent at age 11 (Bjorklund & Pellegrini, 2002).

Rough-and-tumble play appears to be universal in humans, as well as in most mammals (Bjorklund & Pellegrini, 2002). Moreover, boys around the world participate in rough-and-tumble play more than girls do, which may be one reason for the sex segregation found during play (Smith, 2005a). Seemingly universal, rough-and-tumble play has been reported in such diverse places as India, Mexico, Okinawa, the Kalahari in Africa, the Philippines, Great Britain, the United States, and Canada, as well as among most mammals (Bjorklund & Pellegrini, 2002; Humphreys & Smith, 1984). From an evolutionary standpoint, rough-and-tumble play has important adaptive benefits: It hones skeletal and muscle development, offers safe practice for hunting and fighting skills, and channels aggression and competition. By age 11, it often becomes a way to establish dominance within the peer group (Bjorklund & Pellegrini, 2000, 2002; Smith, 2005b).

TABLE 11.1	Motor Development in Middle Childhood
Age	Selected Behaviours
6	Girls are superior in movement accuracy; boys are superior in forceful, less complex acts. Skipping is possible. Can throw with proper weight shift and step.
7	One-footed balancing without looking becomes possible. Can walk 5-cm-wide balance beams. Can hop and jump accurately into small squares. Can execute accurate jumping-jack exercise.
8	Have 5.4-kg pressure on grip strength. Number of games participated in by both sexes is greatest at this age. Can engage in alternate rhythmic hopping in a 2-2, 2-3, or 3-3 pattern. Girls can throw a small ball 12 m.
9	Boys can run 5 m per second. Boys can throw a small ball 21 m.
10	Can judge and intercept pathways of small balls thrown from a distance. Girls can run 5 m per second.
11	Standing broad jump of 1.5 m is possible for boys; 15 cm less for girls.

Source: Papalia, D. E., Olds, S. W., Feldman, R.D., & Kruk, R. (2008). *A Child's World: Infancy Through Adolescence* (2nd Canadian ed.). McGraw-Hill Ryerson.

rough-and-tumble play Vigorous play involving wrestling, hitting, and chasing, often accompanied by laughing and screaming.

ORGANIZED SPORTS

When children begin playing games with rules, some join organized, adult-led sports. About 60 percent of Canadian families participate in common physical activities at least once a week, (Eggertson, 2007), with 47 percent of 5- to 10-year-olds reporting participating in supervised sports at least once a month; soccer, swimming, and basketball are the top three sports (Clark, 2008). Activity in unsupervised sports is much higher, with over 80 percent of children taking part at least once a month (Offord, Lipman, & Duku, 1998). Girls tend to spend less time than boys on sports, but the gap is narrowing (Clark, 2008; Juster et al., 2004).

Although it is well established that exercise promotes health and fitness, less than half of Canadian children are active enough to ensure healthy growth (Craig, Cameron, Russell, & Beaulieu, 2001), and the number drops to less than 20 percent for 9- to 12-year-olds (Ahamed et al., 2007). On average, Canadian children spend about 17 hours a week in physical activity, with bicycling, swimming, and using playground equipment as the top three physical activities (Craig et al., 2001). However, only 7 percent of Canadian children meet the level recommended by the Canadian Physical Activity Guidelines of at least 60 minutes a day of moderate-to-vigorous physical activity (Barnes et al., 2012; Colley et al., 2011). Aboriginal people tend to be more physically active than non-Aboriginal people in Canada (Bryan, Tremblay, Pérez, Ardern, & Katzmarzyk, 2006; Findlay, 2011).

There are developmental changes in what types of organized sports are most effective. Children aged 6 to 9 years need more-flexible rules, shorter instruction time, and more free time for practice than older children. At this age, girls and boys are about equal in weight, height, endurance, and motor skill development. Older children are better able to process instruction and learn team strategies.

Besides improving motor skills, regular physical activity has immediate and long-term health benefits: weight control, lower blood pressure, improved cardiorespiratory functioning, and enhanced self-esteem and well-being. Active children tend to become active adults. Inactive children who spend many hours watching television tend to be overweight. They are likely to get too little exercise and eat too many fattening snacks.

In addition to the importance of regular physical activity in structured environments, it is becoming increasingly clear that unstructured outdoor physical activity is an important part of children's developing personal autonomy. Unstructured outdoor play is a way of combatting passive technology-based indoor play that can increase sedentary behaviour, as well as increasing children's engagement with natural environments, and is promoted by organizations such as Canada's Child and Nature Alliance (Public Health Agency of Canada, 2011b).

Ask Yourself

6. What are two benefits conferred by recess-time play?

7. In general, boys spend _____ time playing sports than girls.

Health and Safety

Middle childhood is a relatively safe period in the lifespan, and in the modern world most children enjoy good health. However, while the death rate in the middle childhood years is the lowest in the lifespan, the increasingly sedentary nature of modern life allied with the easy availability of high-calorie food has resulted in an epidemic of overweight and obesity in Canada. Moreover, some children suffer from chronic medical conditions, accidental injuries, or emotional disturbances.

OVERWEIGHT

Overweight, a body mass index between the 85 and 95 percentile, and obesity, a body mass index over the 95 percentile, in children has become a major health issue worldwide. The prevalence of children who are overweight or obese has more than doubled in the past 25 years. Nearly 50 percent of the children in North and South America, 39 percent in Europe, and 20 percent in China are likely to be overweight (Wang & Lobstein, 2006).

In Canada, about 13 percent of children between the ages of 5 and 11 are obese, and another 20 percent are overweight (Roberts, Shields, de Groh, Aziz, & Gilbert, 2012). Boys are more likely to be overweight than girls (Ogden et al., 2006). Although the number of overweight children has increased in all ethnic groups (Center for Weight and Health, 2001), it is most prevalent among Aboriginal children

WHAT DO YOU DO?

Public/Community Health Nurse

Public or community health nurses work in a variety of community settings, including schools. The nurse communicates with teachers, parents, and doctors about student health; administers medications students need during the day; advises on supports needed for students with chronic illnesses; monitors students with chronic illnesses; helps prevent the spread of contagious illnesses; and assesses and cares for students who become sick during the school day. Public/community health nurses typically have registered nurse (RN) certification. To learn more about public/community health nursing, visit www.chnc.ca.

in Canada, with over 40 percent reported as overweight or obese (Shields, 2006; Willows, 2005; Willows et al., 2007, Willows, Hanley, & Delormier, 2012).

Causes of Overweight

What are the causes of overweight in children? Overweight can be the result of an inherited tendency aggravated by too little exercise and too much of the wrong kinds of food (AAP Committee on Nutrition, 2003).

Children are more likely to be overweight if they have overweight parents or other relatives. Poor nutrition, encouraged by media advertising and the wide availability of snack foods and beverages, also contribute (Council on Sports Medicine and Fitness and Council on School Health, 2006). Eating out is another culprit; children who eat outside the home consume an estimated 200 more calories a day than when the same foods are eaten at home (French, Story, & Jeffery, 2001).

Inactivity is a major factor in the sharp rise in overweight children. Activity levels decrease significantly as children get older, from an average level of approximately 180 minutes of activity per day for 9-year-olds to 40 minutes per day for 15-year-olds (Nader, Bradley, Houts, McRitchie, & O'Brien, 2008). Typical Canadian children are sedentary about 8.5 hours per day (Colley et al., 2011). Television viewing appears to be an important variable. Children who watch TV five hours a day are 4.6 times as likely to be overweight as those who watch no more than two hours daily (Institute of Medicine of the National Academies, 2005); eating meals while watching TV is associated with higher sedentary behaviour and poorer food choices in Canadian children (Liang, Kuhle, & Veugelers, 2009). Preadolescent girls, children with disabilities, children who live in public housing, and children in unsafe neighbourhoods where facilities for outdoor exercise are lacking are most likely to be

The prevalence of children who are overweight or obese has more than doubled in the past 25 years. Having access to neighbourhood facilities for outdoor exercise can be a solution to the problem.

sedentary (Council on Sports Medicine and Fitness and Council on School Health, 2006). Children who have recently immigrated to Canada are less likely to participate in sports than native-born children (Clark, 2008).

SES and the availability of nutritious foods can also have an impact. Consuming energy-dense snack foods and beverages can contribute to the high rates of obesity; among Aboriginal children living in remote northern areas, low-income families may not be able to afford or have access to a nutritional diet that includes fresh fruit and vegetables (Downs et al., 2009; Willows et al., 2012). Early life events, such as having a mother who is obese, or not being breast-fed, and social and historical factors that are related to food insecurity, can contribute to the higher rates in Aboriginal communities (Willows et al., 2012). In addition, parents in higher-SES families tend to encourage healthy eating and physical activity in children (Simen-Kapeu & Veugelers, 2010).

Impact of Overweight

The adverse health effects of overweight for children are similar to those faced by adults and include behaviour problems, depression, and low self-esteem (AAP Committee on Nutrition, 2003; Datar & Sturm, 2004), as well as high blood pressure, high cholesterol, and high insulin levels (NCHS, 2004). Childhood diabetes is one of the prime results of rising obesity rates (Perrin, Finkle, & Benjamin, 2007). Overweight children tend to become obese adults, at risk for high blood pressure, heart disease, orthopedic problems, and diabetes. Indeed, childhood overweight may be a stronger predictor of some diseases than adult overweight (Li et al., 2004). It is clear that overweight and obesity is a serious concern in Canada.

Prevention and Treatment of Overweight

Healthy attitudes about food and appropriate activity levels are the best ways to prevent and treat childhood obesity. Prevention of weight gain is easier, less costly, and more effective than treating overweight (Council on Sports Medicine and Fitness and Council on School Health, 2006).

Effective programs should include efforts of parents, schools, physicians, communities, and the larger culture (Krishnamoorthy, Hart, & Jelalian, 2006; Luttikhuis et al., 2009). Schools that serve healthy foods and offer nutrition education have reduced the number of overweight children in their classrooms by 50 percent (Foster et al., 2008). The Canadian Paediatric Society suggests that children need at least 60 minutes of moderate-to-vigorous physical activity (MVPA) per day (Healthy Active Living and Sports Medicine Committee Canadian Paediatric Society, 2012). The average school, however, conducts only 85 to 98 minutes per week of physical education classes (NCES, 2006). Less time in front of television and computers, and changes in food labelling and advertising would also help (American Psychiatric Association, 2004).

Parents can encourage healthy habits by making exercise a family activity and by limiting television

(Tremblay et al., 2011). Parents should watch children's eating and activity patterns and address excessive weight gain before a child becomes severely overweight (AAP Committee on Nutrition, 2003).

CHRONIC MEDICAL CONDITIONS

Illness in middle childhood tends to be brief. **Acute medical conditions**—occasional, short-term conditions, such as infections and warts—are common. Six or seven bouts a year with colds, flu, or viruses are typical as germs pass among children at school or at play (Behrman, 1992).

In Canada, about 3.8 percent of boys and 2.2 percent of girls between 5 and 14 years of age have a **chronic medical condition**: long-lasting or recurrent physical, developmental, behavioural, or emotional conditions requiring special health services (Statistics Canada, 2007b). Often, they experience multiple conditions. The most prevalent chronic medical conditions for this age group include asthma, diabetes, hypertension, and stuttering (Kogan, Newacheck, Honberg, & Strickland, 2005).

Asthma

Asthma is a chronic, allergy-based respiratory disease characterized by sudden attacks of coughing, wheezing, and difficulty in breathing. Its incidence is increasing worldwide (Asher et al., 2006) and its prevalence in Canada is increasing, but the severity of the illness is diminishing (Garner & Kohen, 2008). Over 13 percent of Canadian children up to age 10 have been diagnosed with asthma at some time. It is more likely to be diagnosed in boys than in girls, and in children living in households where at least one parent smokes (McDaniel, Paxson, & Waldfogel, 2006). Although childhood asthma affects children equally across SES groups, children living in western Canada and the Prairie provinces experience asthma less frequently than children living in the Atlantic provinces (Garner & Kohen, 2008).

The causes of the asthma increase are uncertain, but a genetic predisposition is likely to be involved (Eder, Ege, & von Mutius, 2006; Ober et al., 2008). Some researchers also point to environmental factors such as tightly insulated houses that intensify exposure to indoor air pollutants and allergens such as tobacco smoke, moulds, and cockroach droppings. Allergies to household pets also

---

acute medical conditions Occasional illnesses that last a short time.

chronic medical conditions Long-lasting or recurrent physical, developmental, behavioural, and/or emotional conditions that require special health services.

asthma A chronic respiratory disease characterized by sudden attacks of coughing, wheezing, and difficulty in breathing.

diabetes One of the most common diseases of childhood, characterized by high levels of glucose in the blood as a result of defective insulin production, ineffective insulin action, or both.

hypertension High blood pressure.

Did you know?

The best way to avoid a cold? Wash your hands and wash them often! And note that hand sanitizers are not effective when hands are visibly dirty (Health Canada, 2010b).

have been suggested as risk factors (Bollinger, 2003; Etzel, 2003). However, findings regarding these proposed causes, except for smoke exposure, are inconclusive.

Diabetes

Diabetes is one of the most common diseases in school-age children. Over 5,200 children in Canada younger than 10 years have diabetes (Public Health Agency of Canada, 2011c). Diabetes is characterized by high levels of glucose in the blood as a result of deficient insulin production, ineffective insulin action, or both. Type 1 diabetes is the result of an insulin deficiency that occurs when insulin-producing cells in the pancreas are destroyed. Type 1 diabetes accounts for 5 to 10 percent of all diabetes cases and for almost all diabetes in children under 10 years of age. Symptoms include thirst and urination, hunger, weight loss, blurred vision, and fatigue. Treatment includes insulin administration, nutrition management, and physical activity (National Diabetes Education Program, 2008).

Type 2 diabetes is characterized by insulin resistance and used to be found mainly in overweight and older adults. With the increase in childhood obesity, more and more children are being diagnosed with this form of diabetes. Each year, about 3,000 children and adolescents to age 19 are diagnosed with type 1 or 2 diabetes, and statistics show increased incidence of the disease among non-Inuit Aboriginal populations, likely because of lifestyle and environmental changes over the past 50 years (Public Health Agency of Canada, 2011c). Symptoms of type 2 diabetes are similar to type 1 diabetes (Zylke & DeAngelis, 2007). Treatment with nutrition management and increased physical activity can be effective, although glucose-lowering medication or insulin may be needed for resistant cases.

Childhood Hypertension

Hypertension, or high blood pressure, is relatively rare in Canadian children—0.8 percent, based on the Canadian Health Measures Survey of 2,079 individuals between the ages of 6 and 19 years. However, obese boys between 12 and 19 years have higher average blood pressure (Paradis, Tremblay, Janssen, Chiolero, & Bushnik, 2010). Higher blood pressure has been found among Canadian adolescents with lower fitness levels (Flouris, Canham, Faught, & Klentrou, 2007). In the U.S., however, it has been termed an "evolving epidemic" of cardiovascular risk, especially among ethnic minorities (Sorof, Lai, Turner, Poffenbarger, & Portman, 2004, p. 481) with reports of 4.5 percent prevalence of hypertension, with overweight the major contributing factor (Sorof et al., 2004). Discrepancies in prevalence rates might be related to differences in how blood pressure is measured across studies.

Weight reduction through dietary modification and regular physical activity is the primary treatment for overweight-related hypertension. If blood pressure does not come down, drug treatment can be considered. However, care must be taken in prescribing such drugs, as their long-term effects on children are unknown—as are the long-term consequences of untreated hypertension in children (National High Blood Pressure Education Program Working Group on High Blood Pressure in Children and Adolescents, 2004).

Stuttering

Stuttering is involuntary audible or silent repetition or prolongation of sounds or syllables. It usually begins between ages 2 and 5 (Büchel & Sommer, 2004). By Grade 5, it is four times more common in boys than in girls. Five percent of children stutter for a period of six months or more, but three-quarters of these recover by late childhood, leaving about 1 percent with a long-term problem (Stuttering Foundation, 2006).

Stuttering is now widely regarded as a neurological condition. The more common type, persistent developmental stuttering (PDS), is especially noticeable at the beginning of a word or phrase or in long, complex sentences. It seems likely that two factors are at work in PDS. The basic cause may be a structural or functional disorder of the central nervous system. This may then be reinforced by parental reactions to the stuttering, which may make the child nervous or anxious about speaking (Büchel & Sommer, 2004). Additionally, there are suggestions that there is a genetic component (Kang et al., 2010). There is no known cure for stuttering, but speech therapy can help a child talk more easily and fluently (Canadian Stuttering Foundation, 2013; Stuttering Foundation, 2006).

Did you know?

The actor Bruce Willis treated his stuttering by joining a drama club, which forced him to speak before an audience (Büchel & Sommer, 2004).

FACTORS IN CHILDREN'S HEALTH

Social disadvantage plays an important part in children's health, even with the benefits of universal health care. Poor children and those living with a single parent or parents with low educational status are more likely than other

children to be in fair or poor health, to have chronic conditions or health-related limitations on activities, to miss school because of illness or injury, to be hospitalized, to have unmet medical and dental needs, and to experience delayed medical care (Bauman, Silver, & Stein, 2006; Bloom et al., 2003; Chen, 2012; Flores et al., 2002).

Why does economic disadvantage result in these findings? Parents with higher socio-economic and educational status tend to know more about good health habits. Families that tend to have higher incomes typically have more wholesome diets than families of a lower socio-economic status (Patrick & Nicklas, 2005). They can also more readily afford their children's participation in organized sports teams. Children in low-income and minority families are more likely than other children to have no usual place of health care, or to go to clinics or hospital emergency rooms rather than doctors' offices (Bloom et al., 2003). Some individuals maintain good health despite persisting adversities of low income; resilient attitudes and ability to cope with stress might help reduce physiological reactions that can be harmful to long-term health (Chen, 2012).

ACCIDENTAL INJURIES

As in early childhood, accidental injuries are the leading cause of death among school-age Canadian children (Public Health Agency of Canada, 2010c). In 2004, nearly 950,000 children under the age of 18 worldwide died of an injury, with the majority resulting from traffic accidents (as vehicle occupants or pedestrians), drowning, or burns (WHO, 2008). Between 2000 and 2005, almost 129,000 Canadian children under 15 years of age were hospitalized because of unintentional injuries, and 1,775 died (Figure 11.3). Children's injury rates are higher in lower-SES families (Brownell et al. 2010).

Encouraging or requiring the use of safety devices has been shown to lower injury rates. Child seats, seat belts, and bicycle helmets have significantly lowered the number of injuries in the road environment, and smoke alarms and hot water temperature regulations have reduced the number of burns (WHO, 2008).

stuttering Involuntary, frequent repetition or prolongation of sounds or syllables.

Perspectives on Diversity

HOW CULTURAL ATTITUDES AFFECT HEALTH CARE

One morning, Buddi Kumar Rai, a university-educated resident of Badel, a remote hill village in Nepal, carried his 2½-year-old daughter, Kusum, to the shaman, the local medicine man. Kusum's little face was sober, her golden complexion pale, and her almond-shaped eyes droopy from the upper-respiratory infection she had been suffering with the past week. Two days before, Kusum had been in her father's arms when he had slipped and fallen backward. Neither was hurt, but Kusum had screamed in fright. Now the shaman told Buddi that Kusum's illness was due to that fright. He prescribed incantations and put a mark on the child's forehead to drive away the evil spirit that had entered her body when she had her scare.

Adherence to ancient beliefs about illness is common in many parts of the non-industrialized world, but it is not limited to them. Many cultures see illness and disability as punishment inflicted on someone who has transgressed in this or a previous life or is paying for an ancestor's sin. Another belief, common in Latin America and Southeast Asia, is that an imbalance of elements in the body causes illness, and the patient has to re-establish equilibrium. Arab Americans tend to attribute disease to such causes as the evil eye, grief and loss, exposure to drafts, and eating the wrong combinations of foods.

How do we address this diversity in perspectives? Medical professionals need to explain clearly, in the family's language, what course of treatment they recommend, why they favour it, and what they expect to happen. Such concern can help prevent incidents like one that occurred when an Asian mother became hysterical as an American nurse took her baby to get a urine sample. Three children had been taken from this mother in Cambodia. None had returned.

Sources: Al-Oballi Kridli (2002); Groce & Zola (1993); Olds (2002).

FIGURE 11.3

Unintentional Injury Hospitalizations and Deaths, under Age 15

a) Leading causes of unintentional injury hospitalizations* in Canada for 2000/01 to 2005/06, both sexes, ages 0–14 years

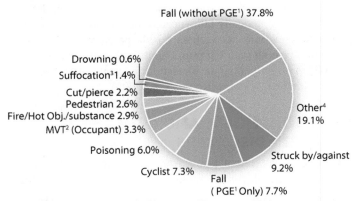

Fall (without PGE[1]) 37.8%
Drowning 0.6%
Suffocation[3] 1.4%
Cut/pierce 2.2%
Pedestrian 2.6%
Fire/Hot Obj./substance 2.9%
MVT[2] (Occupant) 3.3%
Poisoning 6.0%
Cyclist 7.3%
Fall (PGE[1] Only) 7.7%
Struck by/against 9.2%
Other[4] 19.1%

[1]Playground equipment
[2]Motor vehicle traffic
[3]Includes strangulation and choking on objects/food
[4]Includes other and unspecified unintentional injuries (e.g., other transport, dog bites, exposure to excessive cold)
*Injury and Child Maltreatment Section analysis of hospitalization data from the Canadian Institute for Health Information.

b) Leading causes of unintentional injury deaths* in Canada for 2000–2005, both sexes, ages 0–14 years

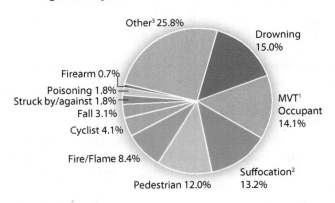

Other[3] 25.8%
Firearm 0.7%
Poisoning 1.8%
Struck by/against 1.8%
Fall 3.1%
Cyclist 4.1%
Fire/Flame 8.4%
Pedestrian 12.0%
Drowning 15.0%
MVT[1] Occupant 14.1%
Suffocation[2] 13.2%

[1]Motor vehicle traffic
[2]Includes strangulation and choking on objects/food
[3]Includes other and unspecified unintentional injuries (e.g., other transport, dog bites, exposure to excessive cold)
*Injury and Child Maltreatment Section analysis of mortality data from the Statistics Canada.

Source: Public Health Agency of Canada, 2010. Adapted with permission from the Minister of Health, 2013.

FIRST AID

One reason for some accidents is children's immaturity, both cognitive (preventing them from being aware of some dangers) and emotional (leading them to take dangerous risks). The major cognitive and emotional changes that take place in middle childhood are described in the next two chapters.

Ask Yourself

8. Which of the following children is most likely to be overweight?

   a. a European-Canadian girl
   b. an Asian-Canadian boy
   c. an Aboriginal-Canadian boy
   d. an African-Canadian girl

9. Which of the following medical conditions has increased in middle childhood over the past few decades?

   a. asthma
   b. diabetes
   c. hypertension
   d. all of these

10. Name two ways to explain the relationship between being poor and not having adequate health care.

11. What is the leading cause of death in school-aged children?

    a. diabetes
    b. cancer
    c. accidents
    d. asthma

Mental Health

After her parents divorced, 8-year-old Emma started acting differently. She refused to go to her gymnastics class, which she had previously loved, her grades dropped, and she complained of stomach aches and headaches on a regular basis. She was also irritable and seemed to have difficulty staying asleep at night. Her concerned mother took her to a therapist, and Emma was diagnosed with depression.

While many people believe that young children cannot suffer from depression, in reality, children can suffer from a variety of disruptive conduct disorders, anxiety disorders, and depression. Such childhood mental and behavioural conditions are described in the most current version of the *Diagnostic and Statistical Manual of Mental Disorders*-5 (American Psychiatric Association, 2013).

DISRUPTIVE CONDUCT DISORDERS

Temper tantrums and defiant, argumentative, hostile, or deliberately annoying behaviours are typically outgrown by middle childhood. When such a pattern of behaviour persists after age 8, children, usually boys, may be diagnosed with **oppositional defiant disorder (ODD)**, a pattern of excessive defiance, disobedience, and hostility toward adult authority figures lasting at least six months. Children with ODD constantly fight, argue, lose their temper, snatch things, blame others, are angry and resentful, have few friends, are in constant trouble in school, and test the limits of adults' patience (American Psychiatric Association, 2013; National Library of Medicine, 2004).

Some children with ODD also develop **conduct disorder (CD)**, a persistent, repetitive pattern of aggressive, antisocial acts, such as truancy, setting fires, habitual lying, fighting, bullying, theft, vandalism, assaults, and drug and alcohol use (National Library of Medicine, 2003). An estimated 4.2 percent of children under age 18 in Canada are diagnosed with clinical levels of externalizing behaviour or conduct problems (Waddell, McEwan, Shepherd, Offord, & Hua, 2005). Some children progress from conduct disorder to criminal violence—mugging, rape, and break-ins—and by age 17 may be frequent, serious offenders (Broidy et al., 2003). Between 25 and 50 percent of these highly antisocial children become antisocial adults (USDHHS, 1999b).

What determines whether a particular child with antisocial tendencies will become severely and chronically antisocial? Neurobiological deficits, such as weak stress-regulating mechanisms, may fail to warn children to restrain themselves from dangerous or risky behaviour. Such deficits may be genetically influenced or may be brought on by adverse environments such as hostile parenting or family conflict, or both (van Goozen, Fairchild, Snoek, & Harold, 2007). Also influential are stressful life events and association with deviant peers (Roosa et al., 2005).

SCHOOL PHOBIA AND OTHER ANXIETY DISORDERS

Children with **school phobia** have an unrealistic fear of going to school. Some children have realistic reasons to

oppositional-defiant disorder (ODD) Pattern of behaviour, persisting into middle childhood, marked by negativity, excessive defiance, disobedience, and hostility toward adult authority figures lasting at least six months.

conduct disorder (CD) Repetitive, persistent pattern of aggressive, antisocial behaviour violating societal norms or the rights of others.

school phobia Unrealistic fear of going to school.

separation anxiety disorder Condition involving excessive, prolonged anxiety concerning separation from home or from people to whom a person is attached.

social phobia Extreme fear and/or avoidance of social situations; also called *social anxiety*.

generalized anxiety disorder Anxiety not focused on any single target.

obsessive-compulsive disorder (OCD) Anxiety aroused by repetitive, intrusive thoughts, images, or impulses, often leading to compulsive ritual behaviours.

childhood depression Mood disorder characterized by such symptoms as a prolonged sense of friendlessness, inability to have fun or concentrate, fatigue, extreme activity or apathy, feelings of worthlessness, weight change, physical complaints, and thoughts of death or suicide.

---

fear going to school: a sarcastic teacher, overly demanding work, or a bully in the schoolyard. In such cases, the environment may need changing, not the child. However, true school phobia may be more closely related to either separation anxiety disorder or social phobia. Anxiety disorders affect about 6.4 percent of Canadian children and adolescents (Waddell et al., 2005).

Although **separation anxiety** is normal in infancy, when it persists in older children, it is cause for concern. Separation anxiety disorder involves excessive anxiety for at least four weeks concerning separation from home or from attachment figures. It affects some 4 percent of children and young adolescents. These children often come from close-knit, caring families. They may develop the disorder spontaneously or after a stressful event, such as the death of a pet, an illness, or a move to a new school (American Psychiatric Association, 2000; Harvard Medical School, 2004).

Sometimes, school phobia may be a form of **social phobia**, *or social anxiety*: extreme fear and/or avoidance of social situations, such as speaking in class or meeting an acquaintance on the street. Social phobia affects about 5 percent of children. It runs in families, so there is likely a genetic component. Often, these phobias are triggered by traumatic experiences, such as a child's mind going blank after being called on in class or writing on the chalkboard (Rao et al., 2007). Social anxiety tends to increase with age, whereas separation anxiety decreases (Costello, Compton, Keeler, & Angold, 2003).

Some children have **generalized anxiety disorder**, which is not focused on any specific aspect of their lives. These children worry about everything: school grades, storms, earthquakes, hurting themselves on the playground, or the amount of gas in the tank. They tend to be self-conscious, self-doubting, and excessively concerned with meeting the expectations of others. They seek approval and need constant reassurance, but their worry seems independent of performance or of how they are regarded by others (Harvard Medical School, 2004).

Far less common is **obsessive-compulsive disorder (OCD)**. Those with this disorder may be obsessed by repetitive, intrusive thoughts, images, or impulses that often involve irrational fears, or may show compulsive behaviours, such as constant hand-washing, or both (Harvard Medical School, 2004).

Anxiety disorders tend to run in families (Harvard Medical School, 2004) and are twice as common among girls as among boys. Anxiety may be neurologically based or may stem from early experiences. For example, parents who reward an anxious child with attention to the anxiety may unwittingly perpetuate it through operant conditioning (Harvard Medical School, 2004).

CHILDHOOD DEPRESSION

Childhood depression is a disorder of mood that goes beyond normal, temporary sadness. Depression is estimated to occur in 3.5 percent of Canadian children and adolescents (Waddell et al., 2005) and is more common in girls by age 13 (Hankin & Abramson, 2001). Symptoms include inability to have fun or concentrate, fatigue, extreme activity or apathy, crying, sleep problems, weight change, physical complaints, feelings of worthlessness, a prolonged sense of friendlessness, or frequent thoughts about death or suicide. Childhood depression may signal the beginning of a recurrent problem that is likely to persist into adulthood (Katz, Conway, Hammen, Brennan, & Najman, 2011).

Childhood depression may be an indicator of the start of a problem that is likely to persist into adulthood.

The exact causes of childhood depression are unknown, but depressed children tend to come from families with high levels of parental depression, anxiety, substance abuse, or antisocial behaviour. The atmosphere in such families may increase children's risk of depression (Franic, Middeldorp, Dolan, Ligthart, & Boomsma, 2010). It is also likely that a genetic component is at play, given the existence of gene variants that increase the risk of depression (Caspi et al., 2003; Young et al., 2007).

Children as young as 5 or 6 can report depressed moods and feelings that forecast later trouble, from academic problems to major depression and ideas of suicide (Ialongo, Edelsohn, & Kellam, 2001). Depression often emerges during the transition to middle school and may be related to the stress of adjusting to adolescence and higher expectations (Stroud et al., 2009), weak self-efficacy beliefs, and lack of personal investment in academic success (Rudolph, Lambert, Clark, & Kurlakowsky, 2001). Depression becomes more prevalent during adolescence (Costello et al., 2003).

Developmental trends differ among Aboriginal children (Beiser, Sack, Manson, Redshirt, & Dion, 1998): in Grade 2, non-Aboriginal children report higher levels of depression compared with Aboriginal children, and this difference gradually decreases until Grade 4, when it disappears. However, there is a higher rate of depression among Aboriginal adolescents (Sack, Beiser, Baker-Brown, & Redshirt, 1994).

Play therapy, such as this child playing freely with a therapist, has proven effective with a variety of emotional, cognitive, and social problems, especially when parents or other close family members are part of the process.

TREATMENT TECHNIQUES

Psychological treatment for emotional disturbances can take several forms and must be calibrated to the developmental level of the child involved. When children have limited verbal and conceptual skills or have suffered emotional trauma, **art therapy** can help them describe what is troubling them without the need to put their feelings into words (Hanney & Kozlowska, 2002). Likewise, in **play therapy**, a child plays freely while a therapist occasionally comments, asks questions, or makes suggestions. Play therapy has proven effective with a variety of emotional, cognitive, and social problems, especially when consultation with parents or other close family members is part of the process (Bratton & Ray, 2002).

For older children, alternative methods may be more effective. In **individual psychotherapy**, a therapist sees a child one-on-one, to help the child gain insights into his or her personality and relationships and to interpret feelings and behaviour. Such treatment may be helpful at a time of stress, such as the death of a parent or parental divorce. In **family therapy**, the therapist sees the family together, observes how members interact, and points out both growth-producing and growth-inhibiting, or destructive, patterns of family functioning. **Behaviour therapy**, or *behaviour modification*, is a form of therapy that uses principles of learning theory to eliminate undesirable behaviours or to develop desirable ones. **Cognitive behavioural therapy**, which seeks to change negative thoughts through gradual exposure, modelling, rewards, or positive self-talk has proven the most effective treatment for anxiety disorders in children and adolescents (Harvard Medical School, 2004).

The use of **drug therapy**—antidepressants, stimulants, tranquilizers, and antipsychotic medications—to treat childhood emotional disorders is controversial. Between 1997 and 2002, there was an increase in prescriptions of antidepressants (from about 0.7 to 1.6 percent of children) and stimulants (from about 2.0 to 2.6 percent)

art therapy Therapeutic approach that allows a person to express troubled feelings without words, using a variety of art materials and media.

play therapy Therapeutic approach that uses play to help a child cope with emotional distress.

individual psychotherapy Psychological treatment in which a therapist sees a troubled person one-on-one.

family therapy Psychological treatment in which a therapist sees the whole family together to analyze patterns of family functioning.

behaviour therapy Therapy that uses principles of learning theory to eliminate undesirable behaviours; also called *behaviour modification*.

cognitive behaviour therapy Therapy that seeks to change negative thoughts through gradual exposure, modelling, rewards, or positive self-talk.

drug therapy Administration of drugs to treat emotional disorders.

for Canadian children (Mitchell et al., 2008). Sufficient research on the effectiveness and safety of many of these drugs, especially for children, is lacking (Murray, de Vries, & Wong, 2004), and in the case of antidepressants, prescriptions are often made despite lack of sufficient evidence for appropriateness for use with children (Tournier et al., 2010).

The use of selective serotonin reuptake inhibitors (SSRIs) to treat obsessive-compulsive, depressive, and anxiety disorders increased rapidly in the 1990s (Leslie, Newman, Chesney, & Perrin, 2005) but has since slipped by about 20 percent (Daly, 2005). Some studies show moderate risks of suicidal thought and behaviour for children and adolescents taking antidepressants, whereas others show no significant added risk (Hammad, Laughren, & Racoosin, 2006; Simon, Savarino, Operskalski, & Wang, 2006) or lessened risk (Simon, 2006). An analysis of 27 randomized, placebo-controlled studies found that the benefits of antidepressant use for children and adolescents outweigh the risks (Bridge et al., 2007).

Ask Yourself

12. Name three variables that contribute to childhood depression.

13. Extreme fear and avoidance of social situations is known as
    a. generalized anxiety disorder.
    b. social phobia.
    c. school phobia.
    d. obsessive-compulsive disorder.

14. Describe six psychological therapies for childhood emotional disturbances.

SUMMARY

CHAPTER **11** PHYSICAL DEVELOPMENT AND HEALTH IN MIDDLE CHILDHOOD

LO1

Describe how school-age children's bodies and brains grow.

- Physical development is less rapid in middle childhood than in earlier years. Wide differences in height and weight exist.
- Children with retarded growth because of growth-hormone deficiency may be given synthetic growth hormone.
- The permanent teeth arrive in middle childhood. Dental health has improved, in part because of the use of sealants on chewing surfaces.
- Brain growth continues during childhood with a gradual increase in white matter and decrease in grey matter. The corpus callosum connecting the two hemispheres becomes progressively myelinated.

LO2

Summarize nutritional needs and sleep patterns in middle childhood.

- Proper nutrition is essential for normal growth and health.
- Malnutrition can affect all aspects of development.
- Most children do not get enough sleep and may have sleep problems.

LO3

Describe what play looks like in middle childhood.

- Because of improved motor development, boys and girls in middle childhood can engage in a wide range of motor activities.
- About 10 percent of schoolchildren's play, especially among boys, is rough-and-tumble play.
- Many children, mostly boys, go on to organized, competitive sports.
- Informal, spontaneous play helps develop physical and social skills. Boys' games are more physical and girls games more verbal. However, less than half of Canadian children are active enough to ensure healthy growth.

LO4

List the principle health and safety concerns of middle childhood.

- Middle childhood is a relatively healthy period; most children are immunized against major illnesses, and the death rate is the lowest in the lifespan. However, many children, especially girls, do not meet fitness standards.
- Overweight, which is increasingly common among Canadian children, is influenced by genetic and environmental factors and can be prevented more easily than it can be treated.
- Respiratory infections and other acute medical conditions are common. Chronic conditions such as asthma are most prevalent among poor children.
- Children's understanding of health and illness is related to their cognitive level. Cultural beliefs affect expectations of health care.
- Stuttering is fairly common but usually not permanent.
- Accidents are the leading cause of death in middle childhood. Use of helmets and other protective devices and educating children, parents, and coaches about safe equipment and practices during play and sports can greatly reduce injuries.

LO5

Describe some common mental health problems of childhood and how children respond to the stresses of modern life.

- Common emotional and behavioural disorders among school-age children include disruptive behavioural disorders, anxiety disorders, and childhood depression.
- Treatment techniques include art therapy, play therapy, individual psychotherapy, family therapy, behaviour therapy, cognitive behaviour therapy, and drug therapy. Often therapies are used in combination.

ANSWERS TO Ask Yourself

connect LEARNSMART SMARTBOOK

For more information on the resources available from McGraw-Hill Ryerson, go to **www.mcgrawhill.ca/he/solutions**.

COGNITIVE
DEVELOPMENT

WHAT'S TO COME

Piagetian Approach: The Concrete Operational Child

Information-Processing Approach: Attention, Memory, and Planning

Psychometric Approach: Assessment of Intelligence

Language and Literacy

The Child in School

"What will my new teacher be like?" 6-year-old Amira wonders as she walks up the steps to her school, shrugging her small shoulders into her new flowered backpack and pushing her short bob behind her ears. "Will the work be hard? Will the other kids like me? What games will we play at recess?" Amira stops at the front entrance, takes a deep breath, and steps inside. "I hope I like real school," she says softly.

Just like Amira, most children approach Grade 1 with a mixture of eagerness and anxiety. The first day of "regular" school is a milestone, a sign of the developmental advances that make this new status possible. In this chapter, we examine cognitive advances during the first five or six years of formal schooling, from about age 6 to 11. Entry into Piaget's stage of concrete operations enables children to think logically and to make more mature moral judgments. As children improve in memory and problem solving, intelligence tests become more accurate in predicting school performance. The abilities to read and write open the door to a wider world. We discuss all these changes, and we look at controversies over IQ testing, bilingual education, homework, and mathematics instruction. Finally, we examine influences on school achievement and how schools try to meet special educational needs.

IN MIDDLE CHILDHOOD

AS YOU READ

LO1   Summarize the cognitive advances in Piagetian abilities in middle childhood.
LO2   Summarize the changes in information-processing skills in middle childhood.
LO3   Explain what IQ is, how it is measured, and what influences it.
LO4   Summarize the changes in language in middle childhood and how literacy can be promoted.
LO5   Describe influences on academic achievement and how children with special needs are educated.

Piagetian Approach: The Concrete Operational Child

At about age 7, according to Piaget, children enter the stage of concrete operations and begin to use mental operations to solve concrete (actual) problems. Children now can think logically because they can take multiple aspects of a situation into account. However, their thinking is still limited to real situations in the here and now.

Children in the stage of concrete operations can perform many tasks at a much higher level than they could in the preoperational stage (Table 12.1). They have a better understanding of spatial concepts, causality, categorization, inductive and deductive reasoning, conservation, and number. In the following section, we address the cognitive advances typical of this age.

TABLE 12.1 Advances in Selected Cognitive Abilities during Middle Childhood

Ability	Example
Spatial thinking	Danielle can use a map or model to help her search for a hidden object and can give someone else directions for finding the object. She can find her way to and from school, can estimate distances, and can judge how long it will take her to go from one place to another.
Categorization	Elena can sort objects into categories, such as shape, colour, or both. She knows that a subclass (roses) has fewer members than the class of which it is a part (flowers).
Seriation and transitive inference	Catherine can arrange a group of sticks in order, from the shortest to the longest, and can insert an intermediate-size stick into the proper place. She knows that if one stick is longer than a second stick, and the second stick is longer than a third, then the first stick is longer than the third.
Inductive and deductive reasoning	Dominic can solve both inductive and deductive problems and knows that inductive conclusions (based on particular premises) are less certain than deductive ones (based on general premises).
Conservation	Felipe, at age 7, knows that if a clay ball is rolled into a sausage, it still contains the same amount of clay (conservation of substance). At age 9, he knows that the ball and the sausage weigh the same. Not until early adolescence will he understand that they displace the same amount of liquid if dropped in a glass of water.
Number and mathematics	Kevin can count in his head, can add by counting up from the smaller number, and can do simple story problems.

Source: From Table 13.1, p. 336 in Diane E. Papalia, Sally Wendkos Olds, and Ruth Duskin Feldman, *A Child's World: Infancy through Adolescence*, 10th Ed. Copyright © 2006 by The McGraw-Hill Companies, Inc. Reprinted with permission.

SPATIAL RELATIONSHIPS

Children in the stage of concrete operations can better understand spatial relationships than those in the preoperational stage, which is tied to their increasing sophistication with symbolic thinking. They have a clearer idea of how far it is from one place to another and how long it will take to get there, and they can more easily remember the route and the landmarks along the way. Experience plays a role in this development. For example, a child who walks to school becomes more familiar with the neighbourhood than one who takes the bus each day.

CATEGORIZATION

Categorization includes such relatively sophisticated abilities as seriation, transitive inference, and class inclusion, all of which improve gradually between early and middle childhood. Children show that they understand **seriation** when they can arrange objects in a series according to one or more dimensions, such as length (shortest to longest) or colour (lightest to darkest). By 7 or 8, children can grasp the relationships among a group of sticks on sight and arrange them in order of size (Piaget, 1952).

Transitive inference is the ability to infer a relationship between two objects from the relationship between each of them and a third object. For example, if A > B, and B > C, then A > C. Catherine is shown three sticks: a yellow one, a green one, and a blue one. She is shown that the yellow stick is longer than the green one, and the green one is longer than the blue one. Without physically comparing the yellow and blue sticks, she immediately says that the yellow one is longer than the blue one (Piaget & Inhelder, 1967).

Class inclusion is the ability to see the relationship between a whole and its parts. Piaget (1964) showed preoperational children a bunch of 10 flowers—7 roses and 3 carnations—and asked whether there were more roses or more flowers. The children tended to say there were more roses because they were comparing the roses with the carnations rather than with the whole bunch. Not until age 7 or 8, and sometimes not even then, do children consistently reason that roses are a subclass of flowers and that, therefore, there cannot be more roses than flowers (Flavell, Miller, & Miller, 2002).

INDUCTIVE AND DEDUCTIVE REASONING

According to Piaget, children in the stage of concrete operations use only **inductive reasoning**. Starting with observations about particular members of a class of people, animals, objects, or events, they are able to draw general conclusions about the class as a whole. "My dog barks. So does Terry's dog and Melissa's dog. So it looks as if all dogs bark."

During a visit to the zoo, Asher, who loves dinosaurs, asks his mom, "Is that rhinoceros a kind of dinosaur?" "No," his mother responds, "rhinoceroses are warm-blooded, and dinosaurs are cold-blooded." Later, in the reptile house, Asher's mother points out that snakes also are cold-blooded. "Oh," says Asher, "so they are dinosaurs too, right?" Asher has just engaged in deductive reasoning. **Deductive reasoning** starts with a general statement or premise about a class and applies it to particular members of the class. If the premise is true of the whole class and the reasoning is sound, then the conclusion must be true. While

Class inclusion lets a child see how a single row can never hold more blocks than the whole set.

seriation Ability to order items along a dimension.

transitive inference Understanding the relationship between two objects by knowing the relationship of each to a third object.

class inclusion Understanding the relationship between a whole and its parts.

inductive reasoning Type of logical reasoning that moves from particular observations about members of a class to a general conclusion about that class.

deductive reasoning Type of logical reasoning that moves from a general premise about a class to a conclusion about a particular member or members of the class.

Piaget did not believe that children could use deductive reasoning to solve abstract logic problems, research shows that children can do so with simple logic problems by using concrete objects as early as second grade (Markovits & Thompson, 2008; Pillow, 2002). However, hypothetical-deductive reasoning, involving reasoning with abstract possibilities and generating best guesses or hypotheses to systematically solve problems, does not emerge until adolescence, according to Piaget (see Chapter 15).

CONSERVATION

If one of two identical clay balls is rolled or kneaded into a different shape—say, a long, thin snake—Stacy, who is in the preoperational stage, is deceived by appearances. She says the long, thin roll contains more clay because it looks longer. Felipe, who is in the stage of concrete operations, will say that the ball and the snake still contain the same amount of clay.

Felipe, unlike Stacy, understands the principle of identity: He knows the clay is still the same clay even though it has a different shape. He also understands the principle of reversibility: He knows he can change the snake back into a ball. And he can decentre: He can focus on both length and width. He recognizes that although the ball is shorter than the snake, it is also thicker.

Typically, children can solve problems involving conservation of substance, like this one, by about age 7 or 8. However, in tasks involving conservation of weight—in which they are asked, for example, whether the ball and the snake weigh the same—children typically do not give correct answers until about age 9 or 10. In tasks involving conservation of volume—in which children must judge whether the snake and the ball displace an equal amount of liquid when placed in a glass of water—correct answers are rare before age 12.

Piaget's term for this inconsistency in the development of different types of conservation is **horizontal décalage**. Children's thinking at this stage is so concrete, so closely tied to a particular situation, that they cannot readily transfer what they have learned about one type of conservation to another type, even though the underlying principles are the same.

NUMBER AND MATHEMATICS

By age 6 or 7, many children can count in their heads. They also learn to count on: to add 5 and 3, they start counting at 5 and then go on to 6, 7, and 8. It may take two or three more years for them to perform a comparable operation for subtraction. Children at this stage also become more adept at solving simple story problems, such as "Pedro went to the store with $5 and spent $2 on candy. How much did he have left?" When the original amount is unknown ("Pedro went to the store, spent $2 and had $3 left. How much did he start out with?"), few children can solve such problems before age 8 or 9 (Resnick, 1989).

Some intuitive understanding of fractions seems to exist by age 4, as children show when they distribute portions of pizza (Mix, Levine, & Huttenlocher, 1999) or separate a box of chocolates (Singer-Freeman & Goswami, 2001). However, young children tend not to think about the quantity a fraction represents; instead, they focus on the numerals that make it up. Thus, they may say that ½ plus ⅓ equals ²⁄₅, or think that ½ is smaller than ¼ (Geary, 2006).

The ability to estimate progresses with age. When asked to place 24 numbers along a line from 0 to 100, almost all kindergartners exaggerate the distances between low numbers and minimize the distances between high numbers, although they improve with age (Siegler & Opfer, 2003). Besides improving in *number line estimation*, school-age children also improve in three other types of estimation: *computational estimation*, such as estimating the sum in an addition problem; *numerosity estimation*, such as estimating the number of candies in a jar; and *measurement estimation*, such as estimating the length of a line (Booth & Siegler, 2006).

horizontal décalage   Piaget's term for an inability to transfer learning about one type of conservation to other types, which causes a child to master different types of conservation tasks at different ages.

MORAL REASONING

Piaget proposed that moral reasoning develops in three stages (Piaget & Inhelder, 1969). The first stage (approximately ages 2 to 7, corresponding with the preoperational stage) is based on rigid obedience to authority. Because young children are egocentric, they cannot imagine more than one way of looking at a moral issue. They believe that rules cannot be bent or changed, that behaviour is either right or wrong, and that any offence deserves punishment, regardless of intent.

The second stage (ages 7 to 11, corresponding with the concrete operations stage) is characterized by increasing flexibility. As children interact with more people and come into contact with a wider range of viewpoints, they begin to discard the idea that there is a single, absolute standard of right and wrong and to develop their own sense of justice based on fairness or equal treatment for all. Because they can consider more than one aspect of a situation, they can make more subtle moral judgments, such as taking into consideration the intent behind behaviour.

Around age 11 or 12, when children may become capable of formal reasoning (see Chapter 15), the third stage of moral development arrives. The belief that everyone should be treated alike gives way to the ideal of equity, of taking specific circumstances into account. Thus, a child of this age might say that a 2-year-old who spilled ink on a tablecloth should be held to a less demanding moral standard than a 10-year-old who did the same thing.

Current perspectives are challenging the traditional view that children pass through universal stages of moral development. Sensitivity to the context and domain of moral issues can emerge in children as young as 6 years of age. In a study of 72 Canadian children, Helwig and Jasiobedzka (2001) found that, using simple tasks that did not require responses to open-ended questions, 6-year-old children were as capable as 8- and 10-year-old children in evaluating fairness of just and unjust laws, and reasoning about the consequences of violating socially unjust laws. In fact, children as young as 3 years are capable of understanding the nature of psychological harm in making moral judgments, though they tend to focus on the outcome of the act rather than the intention of the act, which older children tend to do (Helwig, Zelazo, & Wilson, 2001).

Information-Processing Approach: Attention, Memory, and Planning

As children move through the school years, they make steady progress in their abilities to regulate and sustain attention, process and retain information, and plan and monitor their own behaviour. All of these interrelated developments are central to executive function, the conscious control of thoughts, emotions, and actions to accomplish goals or solve problems. School-age children also understand more about how memory works, and this knowledge enables them to plan and use strategies, or deliberate techniques, to help them remember.

INFLUENCES ON THE DEVELOPMENT OF EXECUTIVE FUNCTION

The gradual development of **executive function** from infancy through adolescence is the result of developmental changes in brain structure. The prefrontal cortex, the region that enables planning, judgment, and decision-making shows significant development during this period (Lamm, Zelazo, & Lewis, 2006) (Figure 12.1). As unneeded synapses are pruned away and pathways become myelinated, processing speed—usually measured by reaction time—improves dramatically (Camarata & Woodcock, 2006).

executive function Conscious control of thoughts, emotions, and actions to accomplish goals or solve problems.

Faster, more efficient processing increases the amount of information children can keep in working memory, enabling complex thinking and goal-directed planning (Luna, Garver, Urban, Lazar, & Sweeney, 2004).

The home environment also contributes to the development of executive skills. In a longitudinal study of 700 children from infancy on, the quality of the family environment, especially between ages 4½ and 6—including such factors as available resources, cognitive stimulation, and maternal sensitivity—predicted attentional and memory performance in first grade (NICHD Early Child Care Research Network, 2005c). The home environment can also influence how children's reasoning abilities develop. Children from higher socio-economic status (SES) families tend to show better logical thinking abilities, likely related to more openness to alternatives and stronger divergent (creative) thinking in those children (Markovits & Brunet, 2012).

In general, younger children, about age 6, have an easier time making "if-then" conclusions about what is

Major Structures of the Brain

FIGURE 12.1 Primary divisions of the brain and major motor, sensory, and associated cortices.

Source: From Fig. 7.3, p. 157 in Fiore, *LifeSmart*, 1st Ed. Copyright © 2011 by The McGraw-Hill Companies, Inc. Reprinted by permission.

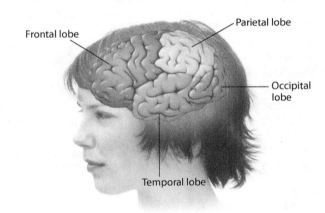

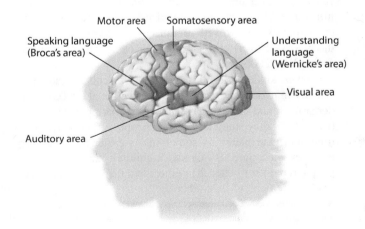

true when there is only one possible outcome for a problem ("*If all things with six sides are cubes, and this thing has six sides, then this thing is a cube*"; the answer here is true), than conclusions about problems that involve considering counter-examples, where there is more than one possible outcome ("*If throwing rocks can break windows, and this window is broken, then a rock broke this window*"; the answer here is false because other things can break windows). This ability emerges by the age of 9 (Markovits & Thompson, 2008).

SELECTIVE ATTENTION

School-age children can concentrate longer than younger children and can focus on the information they need and want while screening out irrelevant information (Harnishfeger & Pope, 1996). For example, they can summon up from memory the appropriate meaning of a word and suppress other meanings that do not fit the context, and they can focus on the teacher rather than on a classmate making faces at them. This growth in *selective attention*—the ability to deliberately direct one's attention and shut out distractions—may hinge on the executive skill of *inhibitory control*, the voluntary suppression of unwanted responses (Luna et al., 2004). The increasing capacity for selective attention is believed to be due to neurological maturation (Booth et al., 2003).

WORKING MEMORY

The efficiency of working memory increases greatly in middle childhood, a development that stems from improvements in processing speed and storage capacity (Bayliss, Jarrod, Baddeley, Gunn, & Leigh, 2005). Because working memory is necessary to store information while other material is being mentally manipulated, the capacity of a child's working memory can directly affect his or her academic success (Alloway, 2006). Children with low working memory struggle with structured learning activities and have difficulty following lengthy instructions (Gathercole & Alloway, 2008). Estimates are that as many as 10 percent of school-aged children suffer from low working memory (Alloway, Gathercole, Kirkwood, & Elliot, 2009).

METAMEMORY

Between ages 5 and 7, the brain's frontal lobes undergo significant development and reorganization. These changes may make possible improved **metamemory**, knowledge about the processes of memory (Chua, Schacter, Rand-Giovanetti, & Sperling, 2006).

From kindergarten through Grade 5, children advance steadily in understanding memory (Flavell et al., 2002). Kindergartners and Grade 1 students know that people remember better if they study longer, that people forget things with time, and that relearning something is easier than learning it for the first time. By Grade 3, children know that some people remember better than others and that some things are easier to remember than others.

---

metamemory Understanding of processes of memory.

Did you know?

The reason preoperational children do poorly on Piagetian tasks can be related to their information-processing skills. For example, perhaps these children fail the conservation task because their poor working memory leads them to forget that two differently shaped pieces of clay were originally the same size.

INFORMATION PROCESSING AND PIAGETIAN TASKS

Improvements in information processing may help explain the advances Piaget described. For example, 9-year-olds may be better able than 5-year-olds to find their way to and from school because they can scan a scene, take in its important features, and remember objects in context, in the order in which the children encountered them (Allen & Ondracek, 1995).

Improvements in memory may contribute to the mastery of conservation tasks. Young children's working memory is so limited that, even if they are able to master the concept of conservation, they may not be able to remember all the relevant information (Chen & Siegler, 2000; Siegler & Richards, 1982). They may forget that two differently shaped pieces of clay were originally identical. Gains in short-term memory may contribute to the ability to solve problems like this in middle childhood.

Ask Yourself

6. Name two influences on the development of executive functioning in middle childhood.

7. Selective attention relies on both the ability to _____ as well as _____.
   a. select which stimuli you are interested in; change your selection rapidly if your needs change
   b. deliberately direct attention to target stimuli; inhibit attention to distractions
   c. be able to use inductive reasoning; be able to use deductive reasoning
   d. All of these statements are true.

8. What two abilities underlie the improvements in working memory in middle childhood?

9. If you are able to realize that you are better at recognizing the correct answer on a multiple-choice exam than you are at writing down the answer without cues, you are engaging in
   a. selective attention.
   b. deductive reasoning.
   c. inference activities.
   d. metamemory.

Robbie Case (1985, 1992), a neo-Piagetian theorist, suggested that as a child's application of a concept or scheme becomes more automatic, it frees space in working memory to deal with new information. This may help explain horizontal décalage: Children may need to become comfortable enough with one kind of conservation to use it without conscious thought before they can extend and adapt that scheme to other kinds of conservation.

Psychometric Approach: Assessment of Intelligence

The colloquial phrase "I know it when I see it" can be used to describe a large variety of somewhat subjective concepts, but it is particularly apt in the description of intelligence. Most of us feel we intuitively know what intelligence is, but, as psychologists have found, the process of objectively defining what it is proves to be a challenge. In the following section, we discuss how intelligence has been measured, what its relationship is to IQ, and whether or not intelligence should be viewed in a broader fashion. Last, we focus in on some of the important influences on intelligence.

MEASURING INTELLIGENCE

While there are a variety of ways to assess intelligence, the most widely used individual test is the **Wechsler Intelligence Scale for Children (WISC-IV)**. This test for ages 6 through 16 measures verbal and performance abilities, yielding separate scores for each as well as a total score. The separate subtest scores pinpoint a child's strengths and help diagnose specific problems. For example, if a child does well on verbal tests, such as general information and basic arithmetic operations, but poorly on performance tests, such as doing a puzzle or drawing the missing part of a picture, the child may be slow in perceptual or motor development. A child who does well on performance tests but poorly on verbal tests may have a language problem.

Some other diagnostic and predictive tools are based on neurological research and information-processing theory. The second edition of the **Kaufman Assessment Battery for Children (K-ABC-II)** (Kaufman & Kaufman, 2003), an individual test for ages 3 to 18, is designed to evaluate cognitive abilities in children with diverse needs, such as autism, hearing impairments, and language disorders, and from varying cultural and linguistic backgrounds. It has subtests designed to minimize verbal instructions and responses, as well as items with limited cultural content.

Most intelligence tests used in Canada are produced in the United States. As with tests aimed at younger children (see Chapter 9), this can be a problem because many items may not be appropriate measures of intelligence of Canadian children (for example,

Wechsler Intelligence Scale for Children (WISC-IV) Individual intelligence test for schoolchildren that yields verbal and performance scores as well as a combined score.

Kaufman Assessment Battery for Children (K-ABC-II) Nontraditional individual intelligence test designed to provide fair assessments of minority children and children with disabilities.

dynamic tests Tests based on Vygotsky's theory that emphasize potential rather than past learning.

using imperial measures instead of metric for arithmetic problems, or items requiring knowledge of U.S. culture and history, rather than Canadian). In addition, developers of American tests use American representative samples of children as the basis for the norms against which individual children's scores are compared. The characteristics of the U.S. samples are different enough from the Canadian population to raise concerns about the appropriateness of using American norms for Canadian children. Canadian children score differently from American children (Weiss, Saklofske, Prifitera, Chen, & Hildebrand, 1999); for example, Aboriginal children might be at a disadvantage on tests that rely heavily on verbal abilities (Baydala et al., 2009; Mushquash & Bova, 2007; Scaldwell, Frame, & Cookson, 1985). Canadian norms have been developed for the WISC-IV (Bremner, McTaggart, Saklofske, & Janzen, 2011; Saklofske, Zhu, Coalson, Raiford, & Weiss, 2010; Saklofske, Zhu, Raiford, Weiss, & Coalson, 2008; Wechsler, 2004), as have ways of using the test that are appropriate for Canadian children (Saklofske, Caravan, & Schwartz, 2000; Wechsler, 2004; Weiss et al., 1999).

Dynamic tests based on Vygotsky's theories emphasize potential rather than present achievement. Dynamic tests contain items up to two years above a child's current level of competence. Examiners help the child when necessary by asking leading questions, giving examples or demonstrations, and offering feedback; thus, the test itself is a learning situation. The difference between the items a child can answer alone and the items the child can answer with help is the child's zone of proximal development (ZPD).

THE IQ CONTROVERSY

The use of psychometric intelligence tests such as the Wechsler is controversial. On the positive side, because IQ tests have been standardized and widely used, there is extensive information about their norms, validity, and reliability. Also, scores on IQ tests can be used as predictors. IQ tests taken during middle childhood are fairly good predictors of school achievement, and IQ at age 11 has even been found to predict length of life, functional independence later in life, and the presence or absence of dementia (Starr, Deary, Lemmon, & Whalley, 2000; Whalley & Deary, 2001).

On the other hand, critics claim that the tests underestimate the intelligence of children who, for one reason or another, do not do well on standardized tests (Sternberg, 2004). For example, because the tests are timed, they equate intelligence with speed and penalize a child who works slowly and deliberately.

A more fundamental criticism is that IQ tests do not directly measure native ability; instead, they infer intelligence on the basis of what children already know. It is virtually impossible to design a test that requires no prior knowledge. Further, the tests are validated against measures of achievement, such as school performance, which are affected by such factors as schooling and culture (Sternberg, 2005).

IS THERE MORE THAN ONE INTELLIGENCE?

A serious criticism of IQ tests is that they focus almost entirely on abilities used in school. They do not cover other important aspects of intelligent behaviour, such as common sense, social skills, creative insight, and self-knowledge. Yet these abilities, in which some children with modest academic skills excel, may become equally or more important in later life and may even be considered separate forms of intelligence. Two of the chief advocates of this position are Howard Gardner and Robert Sternberg.

Gardner's Theory of Multiple Intelligences

Is a child who is good at analyzing paragraphs and making analogies more intelligent than one who can play a challenging violin solo or organize a closet or pitch a curveball at the right time? The answer is no, according to Gardner's (1993) **theory of multiple intelligences**.

Gardner identified eight independent types of intelligence. According to Gardner, conventional intelligence tests tap only three "intelligences": linguistic, logical-mathematical, and, to some extent, spatial. The other five,

which are not reflected in IQ scores, are musical, bodily-kinesthetic, interpersonal, intrapersonal, and naturalistic.

High intelligence in one area does not necessarily accompany high intelligence in any of the others. A person may be extremely gifted in art (spatial), precision of movement (bodily-kinesthetic), social relations (interpersonal), or self-understanding (intrapersonal). Thus, basketball player Jeremy Lin, painter Frida Kahlo, and cellist Yo Yo Ma could be viewed as equally intelligent, each in a different area.

Sternberg's Triarchic Theory of Intelligence

Sternberg's (1985, 2004) *triarchic theory of intelligence* identifies three elements, or aspects, of intelligence: componential, experiential, and contextual (Figure 12.2).

- The **componential element** is the analytic aspect of intelligence, and it encompasses information-processing skills. It tells people how to solve problems, how to monitor solutions, and how to evaluate the results. This is what is commonly tested in conventional IQ tests.

- The **experiential element** is insightful or creative; it determines how people approach novel or familiar tasks. It allows people to compare new information with what they already know and to come up with new ways of putting facts together—in other words, to think originally. A creative-verbal test might ask children to solve deductive reasoning problems that start with factually false premises (such as, "Money falls off trees.").

- The **contextual element** is practical; it determines how people deal with their environment. It is the ability to size up a situation and decide what to do: adapt to it, change it, or get out of it. A test of practical-quantitative intelligence might be to solve an everyday math problem having to do with buying tickets to a ball game or following a recipe for making cookies.

theory of multiple intelligences   Gardner's theory that there are eight distinct forms of intelligence.

componential element   Sternberg's term for the analytic aspect of intelligence.

experiential element   Sternberg's term for the insightful aspect of intelligence.

contextual element   Sternberg's term for the practical aspect of intelligence.

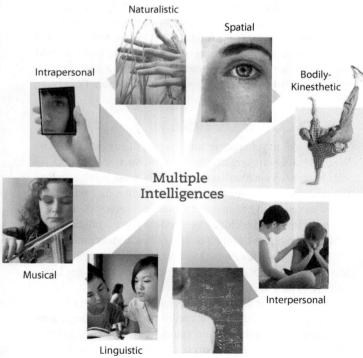

Naturalistic
Spatial
Intrapersonal
Bodily-Kinesthetic
Multiple Intelligences
Musical
Interpersonal
Linguistic
Logical-Mathematical

Gardner's eight types of intelligence.

Sternberg's Triarchic Theory

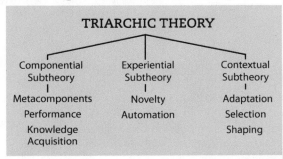

FIGURE 12.2 Sternberg argued that to truly assess intelligence, componential, experiential, and contextual elements all needed to be considered.

Source: Reprinted with permission of Greg Kearsley, *Theory into Practice.*

According to Sternberg, everyone has these three kinds of abilities to a greater or lesser extent, and you cannot really measure intelligence without taking all three into account. The failure of conventional tests to measure experiential (insightful or creative) and contextual (practical) intelligence, says Sternberg, may explain why conventional tests are less useful in predicting success in the outside world.

INFLUENCES ON INTELLIGENCE

Both heredity and environment influence intelligence. Keeping in mind the controversy over whether IQ tests actually measure intelligence and whether intelligence is one or many things, let's look more closely at these influences.

Genes and Brain Development

Brain imaging research shows a moderate correlation between brain size or amount of grey matter and general intelligence (Gray & Thompson, 2004). One study found that the amount of grey matter in the frontal cortex is largely inherited, varies widely among individuals, and is linked with differences in IQ (Thompson et al., 2001). However, there are suggestions that the key is not the amount of grey matter a child has at a certain age, but rather the pattern of development of the prefrontal cortex, the seat of executive function and higher-level thinking. In children of average IQ, the prefrontal cortex peaks in thickness by age 8, and then gradually thins as unneeded connections are pruned. In the most intelligent 7-year-olds, the cortex does not peak in thickness until age 11 or 12. The prolonged thickening of the prefrontal cortex may represent an extended critical period for developing high-level thinking circuits (Shaw et al., 2006; see Chapter 11).

Influences of Race/Ethnicity on IQ

Average test scores vary among racial/ethnic groups, inspiring claims that the tests are unfair to minorities. Although there is a great deal of individual diversity, Aboriginal children tend to score lower than non-Aboriginal children on standardized measures of IQ, particularly on

tests involving verbal intelligence (Beiser & Gotowiec, 2000). On the other hand, Inuit children in Arctic Quebec have been found to score higher than U.S. norms on a non-verbal intelligence test (the Raven's Coloured Progressive Matrices, measuring analytic intelligence), and similar to their non-Inuit counterparts in southern Quebec (Wright, Taylor, & Ruggiero, 1996). In the United States, African Americans on average have historically scored about 15 points lower than white children, although these gaps have narrowed in recent years—as much as four to seven IQ points (Dickens & Flynn, 2006). Conventional tests may not be sensitive to hidden abilities in some groups, such as Aboriginal children; the abilities of "invisible under-achievers" may be identified by using dynamic intelligence measures that focus on responsiveness to educational interventions (Chaffey, Halliwell, & McCluskey, 2006).

What accounts for these racial/ethnic differences in IQ? Some writers have argued for a substantial genetic factor (Rushton & Jensen, 2005). But although there is strong evidence of a genetic influence on individual differences in intelligence, there is no direct evidence that differences among ethnic, cultural, or racial groups are hereditary (Gray & Thompson, 2004; Sternberg et al., 2005). Instead, many studies attribute ethnic differences in IQ largely to inequalities in environment (Nisbett, 2005; Rouse, Brooks-Gunn, & McLanahan, 2005)—income, nutrition, living conditions, health, parenting practices, early child care, intellectual stimulation, schooling, culture, or other circumstances such as the effects of oppression and discrimination. For example, when IQ scores, showing differences between groups of Aboriginal and non-Aboriginal children, were adjusted on measures of prenatal maternal health, English-language skills, socio-economic status, and parental attitudes toward school and cultural separation, the IQ score differences were virtually eliminated (Beiser & Gotowiec, 2000).

The strength of genetic influence itself appears to vary with socio-economic status. In a longitudinal study of 319 pairs of twins followed from birth, the genetic influence on IQ scores at age 7 among children from impoverished families was close to zero and the influence of environment was strong, whereas among children in affluent families the opposite was true. In other words, high SES strengthens genetic influence, whereas low SES tends to override it (Turkheimer, Haley, Waldron, D'Onofrio, & Gottesman, 2003).

Culture can also have an effect. For example, although Asian Americans outperform European-American students on a number of academic indices, it does not appear that genetic factors can account for this advantage (Sue & Okazaki, 2009). Generally, Asian-American children's strong scholastic achievement seems to be best explained by their culture's emphasis on obedience and respect for elders, the supreme importance that Asian-American parents place on education as a route to upward mobility, and the devotion of Asian-American students to homework and study (Sue & Okazaki, 2009). In the Perspectives on Diversity section, we focus more closely on culture and its influences.

CULTURE AND IQ

Some critics of IQ tests attribute ethnic differences in IQ to cultural bias: a tendency to include questions that use vocabulary or tasks that are more familiar to some cultural groups than others (Sternberg, 1985, 1987). These critics argue that intelligence tests are built around the dominant thinking style and language of white people of European ancestry, putting minority children at a disadvantage (Matsumoto & Juang, 2008). Thus, test developers have tried to design **culture-free tests**—tests with no culture-linked content—by posing tasks that do not require language, such as tracing mazes, putting the right shapes in the right holes, and completing pictures; but they have been unable to eliminate all cultural influences.

Robert Sternberg (2004) maintains that intelligence and culture are inextricably linked. Behaviour seen as intelligent in one culture may be viewed as foolish in another. For example, when given a sorting task, North Americans would be likely to place a robin under the category of birds, whereas the Kpelle people in North Africa would consider it more intelligent to place the robin in the functional category of flying things (Cole, 1998). Thus, a test of intelligence developed in one culture may not be equally valid in another. Furthermore, the schooling offered in a culture may prepare a child to do well in certain tasks and not in others, and the competencies taught and tested in school are not necessarily the same as the practical skills needed to succeed in everyday life (Sternberg, 2004, 2005).

Sternberg (2004) defines successful intelligence as the skills and knowledge needed for success within a particular social and cultural context. The mental processes that underlie intelligence may be the same across cultures, says Sternberg, but their products may be different—and so should the means of assessing performance. Sternberg proposes **culture-relevant tests** that take into account the adaptive tasks that confront children in particular cultures.

Ask Yourself

10. If you are most interested in what children could know with help, rather than what they actually know at any point in time, then you are probably most interested in
    a. the WISC-III.
    b. the K-ABC-II.
    c. dynamic testing.
    d. the influence of schooling on IQ.

11. What are two positive aspects and two negative aspects of IQ tests?

12. List Gardner's eight kinds of intelligence.

13. The reason that race and ethnicity are related to performance on IQ tests is because
    a. there is a genetic factor for intelligence that varies between people of different races.
    b. minority children have traditionally scored lower on IQ tests than Caucasian children.
    c. race and ethnicity are related to socio-economic status, which in turn affects IQ test scores.
    d. This is untrue; the gap in scores has disappeared in recent years.

culture-free tests   Intelligence tests that, if it were possible to design, would have no culturally linked content.

culture-relevant tests   Intelligence tests that take into account the adaptive tasks children face in their culture.

Language and Literacy

Language abilities continue to grow during middle childhood. School-age children become better at understanding and interpreting oral and written communication and making themselves understood. These tasks are challenging for children who are not native-language speakers. Areas of particular importance during this age stage are vocabulary, grammar, and syntax; pragmatics; and literacy.

VOCABULARY, GRAMMAR, AND SYNTAX

As vocabulary grows during the school years, children use increasingly precise verbs. They learn that a word like *run* can have more than one meaning, and they can tell from the context which meaning is intended. Similes and metaphors become increasingly common (Owens, 1996). Although grammar is quite complex by age 6, children during the early school years rarely use the passive voice (as in "The sidewalk is being shovelled."). Older children use more subordinate clauses ("The boy who delivers the newspapers rang the doorbell."). Still, some constructions, such as clauses beginning with *however* and *although*, do not become common until early adolescence (Owens, 1996). Children's understanding of rules of syntax (how words are organized into phrases and sentences) becomes more sophisticated with age (C. S. Chomsky, 1969). Sentence structure continues to become more elaborate.

PRAGMATICS

The major area of linguistic growth during the school years is in **pragmatics**: the social context of language. For example, there is a pragmatic difference between a child asking "Can I have the last cookie?" and "You don't want that last cookie, do you?" Pragmatics has to do with the characteristics of the speaker and listener, the context of the utterance, the inferred intent of the speaker, and the understanding of the "rules" that govern conversation.

Good conversationalists probe by asking questions before introducing a topic with which the other person may not be familiar. They quickly recognize a breakdown in communication and do something to repair it. There are wide individual differences in such skills; some 7-year-olds are better conversationalists than some adults (Anderson, Clark, & Mullin, 1994). There are also gender differences; boys tend to use more controlling statements and utter more negative interactions, while girls phrase their remarks in a more tentative, conciliatory manner (Leman, Ahmed, & Ozarow, 2005).

LITERACY

Literacy—the ability to read and write—is vital to success in the modern world. Moreover, literacy allows children access to the ideas and imagination of people in faraway lands and long-ago times. Once children can translate the

pragmatics Practical knowledge needed to use language for communicative purposes.

decoding Process of phonetic analysis by which a printed word is converted to spoken form before retrieval from long-term memory.

phonetic (code emphasis) approach Approach to teaching reading that emphasizes decoding unfamiliar words.

whole-language approach Approach to teaching reading that emphasizes visual retrieval and use of contextual clues.

marks on a page into patterns of sound and meaning, they can develop increasingly sophisticated strategies to understand what they read. They also learn that they can use written words to express ideas, thoughts, and feelings.

Reading and Writing

Children can identify a printed word in two contrasting ways. The first is through phonetics or decoding. **Decoding** involves matching the printed alphabet to the spoken sound and, after sounding it out, retrieving the word from long-term memory. This method is known as **phonetic (code emphasis) approach**. The second method is the **whole-language approach**, in which the child simply looks at the word and then retrieves it, based on clues from surrounding text.

The whole-language approach to reading instruction is based on the belief that children can learn to read and write naturally, just like they learn to speak. The central claim of the approach, however, is fundamentally flawed, in that we are adapted for language, but not for reading. Research has found little support for its efficacy and supports the view that phonemic awareness and early phonics training are keys to reading proficiency for most children (Jeynes & Littell, 2000; National Reading Panel, 2000).

Many experts recommend a blend of the best of both approaches (National Reading Panel, 2000; Simner, 1998). Children who can summon both visually based and phonetic strategies, using visual retrieval for

New technologies can offer powerful supports for children learning to read.

familiar words and phonetic decoding for unfamiliar words, become better, more versatile readers (Siegler, 2000).

The acquisition of writing skills goes hand in hand with the development of reading. Older preschoolers begin using letters, numbers, and letter-like shapes as symbols to represent words or parts of words—syllables or phonemes. Often, their spelling is quite inventive (Ouellette & Sénéchal, 2008)—so much so that they may not be able to read it themselves.

Did you know?

While children in many classrooms are discouraged from discussing their work with other children, research based on Vygotsky's theory suggests that such policies are misguided. In one study, fourth graders working in pairs wrote stories with more solutions to problems, more explanations and goals, and fewer errors in syntax and word use than did children working alone (Daiute, Hartup, Sholl, & Zajac, 1993).

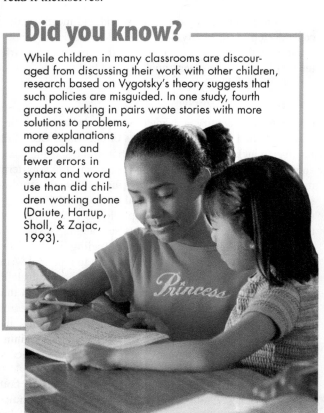

Ask Yourself

14. Which of the following become more common in middle childhood?
    a. metaphors and similes
    b. language errors
    c. sentences in active voice
    d. verbs

15. Which of the following sentences illustrates pragmatic knowledge?
    a. I like to eat cookies.
    b. Go away.
    c. I'll wait until she's off the phone before asking for a cookie because she's more likely to say yes that way.
    d. I think butterflies and flowers look kind of the same.

16. Briefly summarize recommendations for promoting literacy in young children.

The Child in School

The earliest school experiences are critical in setting the stage for future success or failure. Even today, with most Canadian children attending kindergarten, children often approach the start of Grade 1 with a mixture of eagerness and anxiety.

SOCIAL AND HOME INFLUENCES ON ACADEMIC ACHIEVEMENT

As Bronfenbrenner's bioecological theory would predict, in addition to children's own characteristics, each level of the context of their lives influences how well they do in school—from the immediate family to what goes on in the classroom to the messages children receive from peers and from the larger culture (such as "It's not cool to be smart."). In the following sections, we address the social and home influences on school achievement, including self-efficacy beliefs, gender, parenting practices, socio-economic status, and peer acceptance.

Self-Efficacy Beliefs

Students who are high in self-efficacy—who believe that they can master schoolwork and regulate their own learning—are more likely to succeed than students who do not believe in their own abilities (Caprara et al., 2008). Self-regulated learners set challenging goals and use appropriate strategies to achieve them. They try hard, persist despite difficulties, and seek help when necessary. Students who do not believe in their ability to succeed tend to become frustrated and depressed—feelings that make success more elusive.

Gender

Girls tend to do better in school than boys: They receive higher marks, on average, in every subject (Halpern et al., 2007); are less likely to repeat grades; have fewer school problems; outperform boys in national reading and writing assessments (Freeman, 2004); and tend to do better than

Did you know?

Redshirting—postponing kindergarten entrance for age-eligible children born late in the year to give them an extra year of development—has risen sharply in the last 40 years (Deming & Dynarski, 2008). While some research suggests this could lead to higher levels of academic achievement (Datar, 2004; DeCicca & Smith, 2011; West, Denton, & Germino-Hausken, 2000), other research suggests that delayed entry is associated with long-term decreases in motivation, engagement, and performance (Martin, 2009).

boys on timed tests (Camarata & Woodcock, 2006). On the other hand, boys do significantly better than girls on science and math tests that are not closely related to material taught in school, and tend to show an advantage on spatial tasks (Levine, Vasilyeva, Lourenco, Newcombe, & Huttenlocher, 2005). Gender differences tend to become more prominent in high school. A combination of several factors—early experience, biological differences, and cultural expectations—may help explain these differences (Halpern et al., 2007).

Parenting Practices

Parents of achieving children create an environment for learning. They provide a place to study and to keep books and supplies; they set times for meals, sleep, and homework; they monitor how much television their children watch and what their children do after school; and they show interest in their children's lives by talking with them about school and being involved in school activities. Children whose parents are involved in their schools do better in school (Hill & Taylor, 2004). Children who are securely attached to parents also tend to have higher scores in school than children who are insecurely attached (Moss & St.-Laurent, 2001).

Socio-Economic Status

Socio-economic status can be a powerful factor in educational achievement—not in and of itself, but through its influence on such factors as family atmosphere, choice of neighbourhood, and parenting practices (Evans, 2004; Rouse et al., 2005). In a nationally representative longitudinal study of over 22,000 children that began in 1994 (the National Longitudinal Survey of Children and Youth), achievement gaps between advantaged and disadvantaged students were identified from ages 7 to 11 years, and widened from age 11 to 15 years (Caro, McDonald, & Willms, 2009). Summer vacation contributes to these gaps because of differences in the summer learning experiences that children have. This contributes heavily toward differences in high school achievement and completion and college and university attendance of low-income students (Alexander, Entwisle, & Olson, 2007).

Peer Acceptance

Children who are liked and accepted by peers tend to do better in school. Among 248 fourth graders, those whose teachers reported that they were not liked by peers had poorer academic self-concepts and more symptoms of anxiety or depression in fifth grade and lower reading and math grades in sixth grade. Early teacher identification of children who exhibit social problems could lead to interventions that would improve such children's academic as well as emotional and social outcomes (Flook, Repetti, & Ullman, 2005).

Did you know?

Not all low-SES homes involve low levels of intellectual stimulation, and indeed, low-income children whose home environment was cognitively stimulating at age 8 showed higher intrinsic motivation for academic learning at ages 9, 10, and 13 than children who had similar economic circumstances but lived in less stimulating homes (Gottfried, Fleming, & Gottfried, 1998).

CLASSROOM AND SCHOOL SYSTEM INFLUENCES ON ACADEMIC ACHIEVEMENT

While variables unique to each child impact how well that child does in school, there are wider systems variables that also impact academic achievement. In the following section, we address some of these variables. First, we discuss the impact of educational reforms in Canadian provinces. Then we address the impact of class size, alternative educational models, and the use of computers in the classroom.

Educational Reform

Educational reform involves large-scale changes to how schools operate in entire school systems to help students learn more effectively. If successful, they can support improved learning, but there are risks; if not successful, they can waste limited resources for education, and potentially risk educational outcomes in children. Despite the challenges, there are reasons to believe that educational reform can be beneficial if handled well.

In Canada, education is a provincial government responsibility. Across the country, several province-wide approaches to educational reform have been introduced—such as the Kindergarten to Senior 4 Education Agenda for

WHAT DO YOU DO?

Elementary Teacher

Elementary teachers are responsible for the education of students in their classrooms. They teach children with a range of abilities and needs. While each province has its own curriculum, it is up to the classroom teacher to determine how to implement it in his or her classroom to meet provincial standards. The typical educational path for a classroom teacher is to receive a bachelor's degree from a teacher education program and then obtain a provincial teacher's certificate. To learn more about becoming an elementary teacher, visit www.ctf-fce.ca.

Student Success in Manitoba, gradual reform of the provincial curriculum in Quebec, and the Student Success/Learning to 18 strategy in Ontario (Canadian Council on Learning, 2009a)—to improve student outcomes by taking on a more consultative approach with teachers. The focus among Canadian provinces is to build on strengths, rather than punish schools for underperforming, and to support lower-performing schools with the resources and expertise they need to become successful. A picture is emerging that shows that these more inclusive and supportive approaches to educational reform are linked to better student outcomes, given Canada's successes in increased graduation rates, high achievement by immigrant children, and recent high rankings on international comparisons of educational achievement such as the Program for International Student Assessment [PISA] (Hargreaves & Shirley, 2011; Organisation for Economic Co-operation and Development [OECD], 2011; Santos, 2012).

Class Size

Most educators consider small class size a key factor in achievement, especially in the early grades, though findings on this point are mixed (Schneider, 2002). A longitudinal study found lasting academic benefits for students randomly assigned to classes of about 15 students in kindergarten through third grade (Finn, Gerber, & Boyd-Zaharias, 2005). However, in most schools, small classes are larger than that, though class sizes have been dropping (Canadian Council on Learning, 2005a). In classroom observations of 890 first graders, classes with 25 students or fewer tended to be more social and interactive (with a bit more disruptive behaviour), and to enable higher quality instruction and emotional support than those with more than 25 students. Students in these classes tended to score higher on standardized achievements tests and beginning reading skills (NICHD Early Childhood Research Network, 2004b).

Alternative Educational Models

In 2009, Canada ranked sixth out of 70 countries in reading literacy, eighth out of 70 in scientific literacy, and tenth out of 70 in mathematic literacy (OECD, 2010). Despite

WHERE DO YOU STAND?

Many schools practise social promotion, where children are sent on to the next grade despite not meeting academic standards. Arguments for social promotion are that it can prevent decreased self-esteem and dropping out of school. Arguments against social promotion are that it sets up children for academic failure, communicates that you don't have to work hard to pass a course, and forces teachers to work with under-prepared students. The data on which approach is most effective are unclear. What's your view?

French immersion An educational program that uses French as the language of instruction to English-speaking students as a way to promote fluency in French.

these positive outcomes, many Canadian children struggle with the demands of school, for many reasons: Recent immigrants who are not familiar with the language of instruction; Aboriginal children; children from low-income families; students experiencing social, emotional, behavioural, or cognitive difficulties, or psychological conditions like ADHD and autism spectrum disorder may need supports to succeed in school. How to properly educate children is a contentious issue with no easy answers, and some parents and educators have considered alternative educational models for at-risk children. A variety of different models are currently in use for public education, including support for inclusive education, alternative programs for at-risk students, theme-focused schools, charter schooling (in Alberta), and home-schooling.

Many educators say the only real solution to children who struggle in school is to identify at-risk students early and intervene before they fail (Bronner, 1999). Recent changes in provincial legislation on inclusion provide for appropriate education in the most supportive environment for all children, including those experiencing challenges in schools: alternative programs, smaller classes, remedial instruction, counselling, and crisis intervention (Council of Ministers of Education, Canada, 2008). Summer school may be effective as an early intervention. In one study, kindergartners and first graders who attended summer instruction in reading and writing over three summers at an average attendance rate outscored their non-participating peers in achievement tests (Borman & Dowling, 2006).

Canada is an officially bilingual (French and English), multicultural nation, which celebrates its ethnic diversity as a cultural mosaic. Educating students to ensure proficiency in both official languages is encouraged in schools. Outside of Quebec, over 50 percent of public school students in Canada are enrolled in either French immersion or regular French-language programs (Canadian Council on Social Development, 2001; Canadian Parents for French, 2013).

Canadian families have up to seven publicly funded options for children's education—English, French, French immersion, separate (publicly funded Catholic schools in Ontario, Saskatchewan, and Alberta) English, separate French, separate immersion, and publicly funded charter schools in Alberta—as well as semi–publicly funded independent schools (typically religious schools) and private schools (Janosz, Bisset, Pagani, & Levin, 2011). Children of French-speaking parents, or parents who attended school in French, are guaranteed access to French-language education. The same right holds for children of English-speaking parents, for access to school in English.

Many parents, recognizing the importance of fluency in both of Canada's official languages, choose to enroll their children in **French immersion** programs. One of Canada's educational success stories, French immersion began in Montreal in the 1960s (Lambert & Tucker, 1972) and has spread across the country since, with over 350,000 children enrolled (Canadian Parents for French, 2012, 2013). The program uses French as the language of instruction to English-speaking students as a way to promote fluency in French. Many studies have shown that French immersion is an effective way of teaching French-language skills to children. What is its effect on English-language skills? Research on French immersion has shown no negative effects on native language proficiency and academic achievement (Genesee, 1991), and longitudinal studies have demonstrated that, relative to those of non-immersion children, first-language skills seem to be enhanced by Grade 3 when basic proficiency in French is attained (Swain & Lapkin, 1991). These benefits continue through to at least Grade 6, even when French immersion students are compared with students in enriched English programs (Turnbull, Hart, & Lapkin, 2003). Children who are at-risk of reading difficulties do as well in literacy learning in French immersion as in English programs (Kruk & Reynolds, 2012; Genesee, 2007), if the same supports are offered as in English programs (Fortune & Menke, 2010). There are no public English immersion programs in Quebec (McMullen & Brockington, 2011).

Home-schooling is another educational option. An estimated 60,000 children are home-schooled in Canada (Ontario Federation of Teaching Parents, n.d.). Interviews with 23 Canadian home-schooling families showed a wide diversity of educational and SES backgrounds; the main reasons for choosing home-schooling include negative perceptions of school environments (e.g., overcrowding, lack of individualized attention) and curriculum, and desires to ensure high-quality education for their children (Arai, 2000).

Computer and Internet Use

Access to the Internet in public schools has skyrocketed. A 2004 survey of 6,700 schools across Canada showed that 99 percent of schools have computers (with one computer for every five students, half located in classrooms and the rest in computer labs), and 97 percent are connected to the Internet. Computers are used for a variety of educational purposes (Plante & Beattie, 2004). Word processing is the most common use (with 78 percent of students having access), followed by Internet access (34 percent) and special needs or remedial programs to provide individualized programming (29 percent); one out of ten students participates in online courses. Although computers are in schools, finding effective ways to incorporate computers with learning experiences is a challenge, as is keeping up with new technology. Girls and boys spend about the same amount of time on computer and Internet use (Day, Janus, & Davis, 2005; DeBell & Chapman, 2006).

Computer literacy offers new possibilities for individualized instruction, global communication, and early training in independent research skills. However, this tool poses dangers. Foremost is the risk of exposure to harmful or

Computer use in schools has skyrocketed as a way to keep kids engaged with their learning.

inappropriate material while using school or other computers. Also, students need to learn to critically evaluate information they find in cyberspace and to separate facts from opinion and advertising.

Children are engaged with a wide variety of technology-based tools and resources at home and school, to learn, play, and communicate, including sending text messages to friends and family with smart phones, electronic tablets, Internet-based virtual worlds, social media, and game console–based interactive environments, among others. The range of ways that children engage with one another and with technology is rapidly expanding, and how children engage with these resources depends very much on how technology is used in the home (Stephen, Stevenson, & Adley, 2013). Time spent in front of screens can have negative influences, particularly in creating barriers to physical activity and in potential dangers related to exposure to inappropriate material. (New provincial and federal legislation is designed to protect against such dangers; see www.cyberbullying.ca.) However, there are also cognitive benefits in technology, providing additional options to children to develop literacy and social skills. Children are very much engaged by interactive media, with patterns of interpersonal involvement that they establish face-to-face often being re-created in virtual worlds like Club Penguin (Marsh, 2011). Web-based interactive tools, such as the Canadian-developed ABRACADABRA web-based literacy system (Savage et al., 2013), are effective ways of promoting literacy and addressing reading difficulties in children.

EDUCATING CHILDREN WITH SPECIAL NEEDS

Public schools do a tremendous job educating children of varying abilities from all sorts of families and cultural backgrounds. They must educate children who have special needs: immigrant children for whom the school's language of instruction is different from their own, Aboriginal children, children with learning difficulties, and those who are gifted, talented, or creative.

Second- (Alternative-) Language Learning

In 2006, 20 percent of Canadian children younger than 15 years were recent immigrants (Statistics Canada, 2008), and about 20 percent of all Canadians report speaking a language other than English or French at home, most commonly Punjabi, Cantonese, other Chinese languages, and Spanish, with the most rapid growth, between 2006 and 2011, in the Philippine-based language Tagalog, Mandarin, Arabic, and Hindi (Statistics Canada, 2012g, 2012h). With rising immigration, schools are under pressure to meet the special needs of immigrant children, with the aim of helping preserve students' cultural identity, while encouraging success in school. Although immigrant students generally do well, there are sizable numbers (such as refugees and children from low-income families) who experience particular difficulties in succeeding in school (Canadian Council on Learning, 2008; Gunderson, D'Silva, & Odo, 2012; McAndrew et al., 2009; Toohey & Derwing, 2008).

What kinds of supports do immigrant children need to adjust well and succeed in school? Some researchers emphasize the importance of providing instruction that supports children's understanding of academic concepts and basic skills (Adesope, Lavin, Thompson, & Ungerleider, 2011), while others advocate providing opportunities for first-language use in clarifying concepts (such as using Internet resources in the first language). Other ways include giving chances to activate background knowledge through the first language in assignments and activities, showing that their cultural and language identities are valued by encouraging their use in classroom tasks and instruction, and encouraging a sense of awareness and control over language by engaging them in comparing and contrasting their languages (Cummins, Mirza, & Stille, 2012).

There are different ways of teaching English language learners (ELLs). Some schools use an **English immersion approach**, sometimes called ESL, or English as a second (or alternative) language, in which language-minority children are immersed in English from the beginning, in special classes. Other schools have adopted programs of **bilingual education**, in which children are taught in two languages, first learning in their native language with others who speak it and then switching to regular classes in English when they become more proficient in it.

Advocates of early English immersion claim that the sooner children are exposed to English and the more time they spend speaking it, the better they learn it. Proponents of bilingual programs claim that children progress faster academically in their native language, and do well on English-proficiency tests (Crawford, 2007; Padilla et al., 1991). These programs can encourage children to become bilingual (fluent in two languages) and to feel pride in their cultural identity. Heritage Language Programs provide language and culture classes as a way for children to maintain and improve their native language abilities, and by doing so demonstrate that children's native languages and backgrounds are valued (Jean & Geva, 2012). When a child's first language is used and valued in schools, learning of an additional, or second, language and academic achievement can be enhanced (Cummins et al., 2012; Swain & Lapkin, 1991).

Needs of Aboriginal Children

Although the proportion of Aboriginal students attending band-operated schools has risen (Frideres, 1998), more has to be done to improve the academic achievement and self-image of Aboriginal children. The most appropriate measures of success in learning for Aboriginal students involve more than indicators of acquisition of knowledge, but also include community involvement and social well-being (Canadian Council on Learning, 2009b). Aboriginal children attend a variety of types of schools. In 2006, about 60 percent (or 120,000) of Aboriginal students living on-reserve attended schools operated by Aboriginal communities, and the rest, living off-reserve, attended provincial/territorial public schools (Council of Ministers of Education, Canada, 2008). The percentage of Aboriginal children completing elementary school rose from 63 to 76 percent between 1981 and 1991. During this same time, the percentage completing high school rose from 29 to 43 percent (Frideres, 1998), and by 2006, the completion rate was 60 percent (Canadian Council on Learning, 2009b). However, on-reserve, this number drops to 39 percent, while off-reserve completion rates are over 62 percent. Inuit students have a 40 percent completion rate, while 75 percent of Métis students complete high school.

The gaps between Aboriginal and non-Aboriginal completion rates are narrowing. However, self-perceived competence in the classroom is low, and it contributes to difficulties that Aboriginal children experience when they attend majority-culture schools (Beiser, Sack, Manson, Redshirt, & Dion, 1998). Efforts to close achievement gaps and to address the unique cultural and spiritual needs of Aboriginal children are also increasing, with programs such as Aboriginal Head Start; the inclusion of Aboriginal cultural knowledge, content, and perspectives; and the use of Aboriginal languages in public schools (Beach, Friendly, Ferns, Prabhu, & Forer, 2009; Burnaby, 1996/2007; Canadian Institute of Child Health, 2000; Kanu, 2005; Manitoba Education and Youth, 2003). These efforts can have effects beyond learning success; promoting the use of Aboriginal

---

English immersion approach Approach to teaching English as a second language in which instruction is presented only in English.

bilingual education System of teaching non-English-speaking children in their native language while they learn English and later switching to all-English instruction.

languages may have significant psychosocial benefits (Hallett, Chandler, & Lalonde, 2007).

Educating Children with Disabilities

In 2006, 4.5 percent of children (174,810) in Canada between age 5 and 14 years experienced a disability, based on information gathered from the Canadian Participation and Activity Limitation Survey (Miller, Mâsse, Shen, Schiariti, & Roxborough, 2013). As of 2001, about 38 percent of children with disabilities receive special education services. Of all children experiencing a disability, 55 percent were in regular classrooms, 25 percent had a combination of regular and special education classes, 7 percent were in special education classes in mainstream schools, 6 percent were not in regular schools, 3 percent were not attending school, 1 percent were receiving tutoring at home provided by public schools, and for 3 percent, information was not provided by parents (Uppal, Kohen, & Khan, 2007). Commonly diagnosed disabilities for school-age children include intellectual disabilities, learning disabilities, language disabilities, and behavioural difficulties. Often referred to as neurodevelopmental disorders and disabilities, these make up about three-quarters of all disabilities in children between 5 and 14 years (Miller et al., 2013).

In Canada, provincial and territorial laws and policies on appropriate education for children with disabilities ensure that services with individual education plans, involving parents, are provided for each child. Children are educated in the least restrictive environment appropriate to their needs, which means, whenever possible, the regular, or inclusive, classroom.

INTELLECTUAL DISABILITY **Intellectual disability** refers to cognitive functioning significantly below the average. It is indicated by an IQ of 70 or less, coupled with a deficiency in age-appropriate adaptive behaviour, such as communication, social skills, and self-care, appearing before age 18 (Kanaya, Scullin, & Ceci, 2003). Intellectual disability is sometimes referred to as cognitive disability or mental retardation. An estimated 1.0 to 1.4 percent of Canadian children between age 5 and 14 have an intellectual disability (Crawford, 2008; Statistics Canada, 2007c).

Most children with an intellectual disability can benefit from schooling. Intervention programs have helped many of those with mild or moderate disabilities and those considered borderline (with IQs ranging from 70 up to about 85) to hold jobs, live in the community, and function in society. Those with profound disabilities need constant care and supervision, usually in institutions. For some, day-care centres, hostels for intellectually disabled adults, and homemaking services for caregivers can be less costly and more humane alternatives.

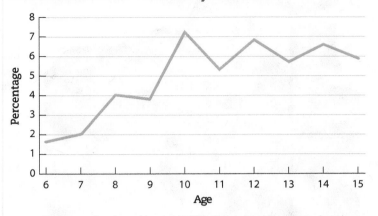

Percentage of Children with Learning Disabilities in Canada, 2007

FIGURE 12.3 Prevalence of learning disabilities in Canadian children change depending on the age of children, with a low of less than 2 percent at age 6 to a high of over 7 percent at age 10.

Source: Learning Disabilities Association of Canada. (2007). Putting a Canadian Face on Learning Disabilities (PACFOLD): What does it mean to have learning disabilities in Canada? Ottawa, ON: Author.

OVERVIEW OF LEARNING DISABILITIES **Learning disabilities (LDs)** interfere with specific aspects of school achievement, such as listening, speaking, reading, writing, or mathematics, resulting in performance substantially lower than would be expected given a child's age, intelligence, and amount of schooling (American Psychiatric Association, 1994). Children with LDs tend to be less task-oriented and more easily distracted than other children; they are less well organized as learners and less likely to use memory strategies. They often have near-average to higher-than-average intelligence and normal vision and hearing, but they seem to have trouble processing sensory information. A large number of children—about 121,000, or 3.2 percent of the Canadian school population between age 5 and 14—have been diagnosed with LDs (Statistics Canada, 2007b; Figure 12.3). Often, learning disabilities co-occur with other conditions in children.

DYSLEXIA Nelson Rockefeller, former vice president of the United States, had so much trouble reading that he ad-libbed speeches instead of using a script. Rockefeller was just one of many people who struggle with **dyslexia**, a language-processing disorder in which reading is substantially below the level predicted by IQ or age. Other famous persons reportedly having dyslexia include actors Tom Cruise, Whoopi Goldberg, Keanu Reeves, and Cher; baseball Hall-of-Famer Nolan Ryan;

intellectual disability Significantly subnormal cognitive functioning; also referred to as *cognitive disability* or *mental retardation*.

learning disabilities (LDs) Disorders that interfere with specific aspects of learning and school achievement.

dyslexia Developmental disorder in which reading achievement is substantially lower than predicted by IQ or age.

attention deficit hyperactivity disorder (ADHD) Syndrome characterized by persistent inattention and distractibility, impulsivity, low tolerance for frustration, and inappropriate overactivity.

ATTENTION DEFICIT HYPERACTIVITY DISORDER **Attention deficit hyperactivity disorder (ADHD)** is a chronic condition usually marked by persistent inattention, distractibility, impulsivity, low tolerance for frustration, and a great deal of activity at the wrong time and in the wrong place, such as the classroom (Woodruff et al., 2004). Some children with ADHD are inattentive but not hyperactive; others show the reverse pattern (USDHHS, 1999b). Among well-known people who reportedly have had ADHD are John Lennon, Robin Williams, and Jim Carey.

One of the most commonly diagnosed conditions causing behavioural problems in school-age children, ADHD is more common in boys than in girls. A recent study of medical records of over 900,000 children in British Columbia revealed that about 6.6 percent of boys and 2.2 percent of girls have received a diagnosis of ADHD (Morrow et al., 2012). Curiously, children born in December of each year, the cut-off month for school entry, were more likely to be diagnosed than children born in January (December children are the youngest, and January children are the oldest in each grade, indicating possible danger of overdiagnosis of younger children in each grade). The rate of ADHD diagnosis has increased in Canada. Based on results from the National Longitudinal Survey of Children and Youth, the increase—from 1.7 in 2000 to 2.6 percent in 2006—happened in school-age rather than in preschool children, and at a more rapid rate in school-age girls than in school-age boys (Brault & Lacourse, 2012). Still, boys were diagnosed at over twice the rate of girls.

Because hyperactivity and inattention appear to some degree in all children, some practitioners question whether ADHD is actually a distinct neurological or psychological disorder (Bjorklund & Pellegrini, 2002; Furman, 2005). Some research suggests that it

Many children with dyslexia can be taught to read through systematic phonological training.

television host Jay Leno; and filmmaker Steven Spielberg. Dyslexia is the most commonly diagnosed of a large number of learning disabilities.

About four out of five children with LDs have been identified as having dyslexia. Dyslexia is generally considered to be a chronic, persistent medical condition that tends to run in families (Shaywitz, 1998, 2003). It hinders the development of oral and written language skills and may cause problems with reading, writing, spelling, grammar, and understanding speech (National Center for Learning Disabilities, 2004). Reading disability is more frequent in boys than in girls (Rutter et al., 2004).

Brain imaging studies have found that dyslexia is due to a neurological defect that disrupts recognition of speech sounds (Shaywitz, Mody, & Shaywitz, 2006). Several identified genes contribute to this disruption (Kere et al., 2005; Meng et al., 2005). Many children—and even adults—with dyslexia can be taught to read through systematic phonological training, but the process does not become automatic, as it does with most readers (Eden et al., 2004; Shaywitz, 1998, 2003).

WHAT DO YOU DO?

Educational Assistant

An educational assistant (EA), paraprofessional, or teacher aide works as an assistant to the classroom teacher to provide instructional support. Typically, EAs work with specific children who have special needs. For example, as part of a student's individual education plan (IEP), she may be assigned an EA to work with her for certain tasks or for the entire day. Requirements for the EA role vary by province, but they generally include an associate degree and/or passage of a provincial test. EAs may require special education or English language learner (ELL) background/experience in some cases. To learn more about becoming an EA, visit www.eamb.ca or other provincial EA associations.

Did you know?

People are sometimes puzzled by why a stimulant such as Ritalin can lead to improved attentional processes. The reason is that children with ADHD can be thought of as having sluggish frontal lobes. The Ritalin "wakes up" those areas and helps them function more effectively.

may be underdiagnosed (Rowland et al., 2002), but physicians warn that it may be overdiagnosed, resulting in unnecessary overmedication of children whose parents or teachers do not know how to control them (Elliott, 2000).

Similar to LD, ADHD diagnosis rates vary greatly by gender, ethnicity, geographic area, and other contextual factors. Boys are more likely than girls to have each of the diagnoses (Brault & Lacourse, 2012; Morrow et al., 2012; Pastor & Reuben, 2008). Some of the diagnoses may be environmentally driven and related to the demands or characteristics of the school involved.

Imaging studies reveal that certain regions in the brains of children with ADHD—most notably, areas in the frontal cortex—show delays in development. These frontal regions enable a person to set goals, focus attention, monitor progress, and inhibit negative impulses—all functions that are often disturbed in children with ADHD. The motor cortex is the only area that matures faster than normal, and this mismatch may account for the restlessness and fidgeting characteristic of the disorder (Shaw, Krause, Liang, & Bennett, 2007).

ADHD is often managed with drugs, sometimes combined with behavioural therapy, counselling, training in social skills, and special classroom placement. Ritalin, a stimulant, is a commonly prescribed drug and is generally very effective. However, Ritalin may be related to slower growth in height and weight (MTA Cooperative Group, 2004), and long-term effects of Ritalin are unclear (Wolraich et al., 2005).

Gifted Children

Giftedness is hard to define and identify. Educators disagree on who qualifies as gifted, on what basis, and on what kinds of educational programs these children need. Another source of confusion is that creativity and artistic talent are sometimes viewed as aspects or types of giftedness and sometimes as independent of it.

IDENTIFYING GIFTED CHILDREN The traditional criterion of giftedness is high general intelligence (IQ of 130 or above) as well as high intellectual, creative, artistic, or leadership capacity or ability in specific academic fields. Gifted children need special educational services and

activities in order to fully develop those capabilities. Many school districts now use multiple criteria for admission to programs for the gifted, including achievement test scores, grades, classroom performance, creative production, parent and teacher nominations, and student interviews. An estimated 2 to 5 percent of the student population is considered gifted (National Association for Gifted Children, n.d.; Winzer, 2008).

CAUSES OF GIFTEDNESS Psychologists who study the lives of extraordinary achievers find that high levels of performance require strong intrinsic motivation and years of rigorous training (Gottfried, Cook, Gottfried, & Morris, 2005). However, motivation and training will not produce giftedness unless a child is endowed with unusual ability (Winner, 2000). Conversely, children with innate gifts are unlikely to show exceptional achievement without motivation and hard work (Achter & Lubinski, 2003).

Gifted children tend to grow up in enriched family environments with much intellectual or artistic stimulation. Their parents recognize and often devote themselves to nurturing the children's gifts but also give their children an unusual degree of independence. Parents of gifted children typically have high expectations and are hard workers and high achievers themselves. But although parenting can enhance the development of gifts, it cannot create them (Winner, 2000).

Brain research suggests that the brains of gifted children are wired somewhat differently. For example, children with mathematical, musical, and artistic gifts tend to have unusual activity in the right hemisphere while doing tasks normally done by the left. They are also more likely to be left-handed (Winner, 2000).

DEFINING AND MEASURING CREATIVITY One definition of creativity is the ability to see things in a new light—to produce something never seen before or to discern problems others fail to recognize and find new and unusual solutions. High creativity and high academic intelligence (IQ) do not necessarily go hand in hand. Classic research found only modest correlations (Anastasi & Schaefer, 1971; Getzels & Jackson, 1962, 1963).

J. P. Guilford (1986) distinguished two kinds of thinking: convergent and divergent. **Convergent thinking**—the kind that IQ tests measure—seeks a single correct answer; **divergent thinking** comes up with a wide array of fresh possibilities. Tests of creativity call for divergent thinking. The Torrance Tests of Creative Thinking (Torrance & Ball, 1984), among the most widely known tests of creativity, include such tasks as listing unusual

---

convergent thinking Thinking aimed at finding the one right answer to a problem.

divergent thinking Thinking that produces a variety of fresh, diverse possibilities.

Divergent thinking helps us come up with new ways of seeing the world.

placement in fast-paced classes, or advanced courses. Other options include ability grouping within the classroom, which has been found to help children academically and not harm them socially (Winner, 2000); dual enrollment, such as when a Grade 8 student takes algebra at a nearby high school; and enrollment in magnet schools and specialized schools for the gifted.

Moderate acceleration does not seem to harm social adjustment, at least in the long run (Winner, 1997). A 30-year study of 3,937 young people who took advanced placement (AP) courses in high school found that they were more satisfied with their school experience and ultimately achieved more than equally gifted young people who did not take AP courses (Bleske-Rechek, Lubinski, & Benbow, 2004).

uses for a paper clip, completing a figure, and writing down what a sound brings to mind.

EDUCATING GIFTED CHILDREN Programs for gifted children generally stress either enrichment or acceleration. **Enrichment** deepens knowledge and skills through extra classroom activities, research projects, field trips, or expert coaching. **Acceleration**, sometimes recommended for highly gifted children, speeds up their education through early school entrance, grade skipping,

enrichment Approach to educating the gifted that broadens and deepens knowledge and skills through extra activities, projects, field trips, or mentoring.

acceleration Approach to educating the gifted that moves them through the curriculum at an unusually rapid pace.

Ask Yourself

17. Which of the following is NOT positively associated with academic achievement?
   a. being high in self-efficacy
   b. being a boy rather than a girl
   c. being of high socio-economic status
   d. being liked by peers

18. If Bob has difficulty focusing in class, frequently interrupts his teacher, and has problems completing his schoolwork, he is likely to be diagnosed
   a. as mentally retarded.
   b. with ADHD.
   c. as gifted.
   d. as uneducable.

SUMMARY

LO1

Summarize the cognitive advances in Piagetian abilities in middle childhood.

- A child from about age 7 to age 12 is in the stage of concrete operations. Children are less egocentric than before and are more proficient at tasks requiring logical reasoning, such as spatial thinking, understanding of causality, categorization, inductive and deductive reasoning, conservation, and working with numbers. However, their reasoning is largely limited to the here and now.
- According to Piaget, moral development is linked with cognitive maturation and occurs in three stages in which children move from strict obedience to authority toward more autonomous judgments based first on fairness and later on equity.

LO2

Summarize the changes in information-processing skills in middle childhood.

- Executive function—including attentional, memory, and planning skills—improves during middle childhood as a result of pruning of neurons in the prefrontal cortex.
- Processing speed, inhibitory control, selective attention, working memory capacity, and metamemory are specific skills that improve during the school years.
- Gains in information processing may help explain the advances Piaget described.

LO3

Explain what IQ is, how it is measured, and what influences it.

- The intelligence of school-age children is assessed by group or individual tests. Although intended as aptitude tests, they are validated against measures of achievement.
- IQ tests, such as the WISC-IV, are fairly good predictors of school success but may be unfair to some children.
- Differences in IQ among ethnic groups appear to result to a considerable degree from socio-economic and other environmental differences. Schooling seems to increase measured intelligence.
- Attempts to devise culture-free tests have been unsuccessful.
- IQ tests tap only three of the "intelligences" in Howard Gardner's theory of multiple intelligences. According to Robert Sternberg's triarchic theory, IQ tests mainly measure the componential element of intelligence, not the experiential and contextual elements.
- New directions in intelligence testing include the Kaufman Assessment Battery for Children (K-ABC-II) and dynamic tests based on Vygotsky's theory.

LO4

Summarize the changes in language in middle childhood and how literacy can be promoted.

- Use of vocabulary, grammar, and syntax become increasingly sophisticated, but the major area of linguistic growth is in pragmatics.
- Despite the popularity of whole-language programs, early phonics training is a key to reading proficiency.

LO5

Describe influences on academic achievement and how children with special needs are educated.

- Children's self-efficacy beliefs affect school achievement.
- Parents influence children's learning by becoming involved in their schooling, motivating them to achieve, and transmitting attitudes about learning.
- Socio-economic status can influence parental beliefs and practices, which, in turn, influence achievement.
- The school environment and class size affect learning.
- Innovative programs for Aboriginal education aim to address disparities in academic achievement.
- Methods of second-language education are controversial. Issues include speed and facility with English, long-term achievement in academic subjects, and pride in cultural identity.
- French immersion, a Canadian innovation, is effective in teaching French in English-language communities, while at the same time not adversely affecting English-language proficiency or academic achievement.
- Three frequent sources of learning problems are intellectual disability, learning disabilities (LDs), and attention-deficit/hyperactivity disorder (ADHD). Dyslexia is the most common learning disability.
- In Canada, all children with disabilities are entitled to a free, appropriate education. However, because there is no national legislation, the specific provisions for educating children with disabilities vary from province to province. In general, children must be educated in the least restrictive environment possible, often in the regular classroom.
- An IQ of 130 or higher is a common standard for identifying gifted children. Broader definitions include creativity, artistic talent, and other attributes and rely on multiple criteria for identification.
- Creativity and IQ are not closely linked. Tests of creativity seek to measure divergent thinking.
- Special educational programs for gifted, creative, and talented children stress enrichment or acceleration.

ANSWERS TO Ask Yourself

Mc Graw Hill Education connect **Mc Graw Hill Education** LEARNSMART **Mc Graw Hill Education** SMARTBOOK

For more information on the resources available from McGraw-Hill Ryerson, go to **www.mcgrawhill.ca/he/solutions**.

PSYCHOSOCIAL
DEVELOPMENT

The Developing Self

The Child in the Family

The Child in the Peer Group

WHAT'S TO COME

"I'm in Grade 3," Emily says, "I live with my mom and brother, and my dad lives in another house. I like to play with my friends. I'm good at swimming and I like cats and I am funny and silly. I think I am helpful but my mom says that is a lie."

Eight-year-old Emily is typical of girls her age. In this chapter, we trace the rich and varied emotional and social lives of school-age children such as Emily. We see how children develop a more realistic concept of themselves and achieve more competence, self-reliance, and emotional control. Through being with peers, they make discoveries about their own attitudes, values, and skills. Still, the family remains a vital influence. Children's lives are affected, not only by the way parents approach child-rearing but also by whether and how they are employed, by the family's economic circumstances, and by its structure or composition.

IN MIDDLE CHILDHOOD

AS YOU READ
LO1 Summarize the changes in self-esteem, self-concept, and emotional understanding and regulation.
LO2 Describe the influences of the family atmosphere, the family structure, and siblings on psychosocial development.
LO3 Summarize the positive and negative effects of peers, and the typical relationships with peers found in middle childhood.

The Developing Self

The cognitive growth that takes place during middle childhood enables children to develop more complex concepts of themselves and to grow in emotional understanding and control. In the following section, we address the development of self-concept and self-esteem, and then focus on emotional growth and prosocial behaviour.

SELF-CONCEPT DEVELOPMENT: REPRESENTATIONAL SYSTEMS

"At school, I'm really good at some things. I really like math and science and I get the best scores on tests of all the other kids," says 8-year-old Emily. "I got A's in them on my last report card and was really proud of myself.

With the formation of representational systems, children have more realistic, balanced, and inclusive self-concepts that bring together different aspects of themselves.

But I'm not so good at social studies and English, and sometimes I feel bad when I see how good the other kids are doing. I still like myself as a person though, because I don't really care that much about social studies and English."

Around age 7 or 8, children reach a new stage of self-concept development introduced in Chapter 10. At this time, judgments about the self become more conscious, realistic, balanced, and comprehensive as children form **representational systems**: broad, inclusive self-concepts that integrate various aspects of the self (Harter, 1998).

We see these changes in Emily's self-description. She has outgrown her earlier all-or-nothing, black-or-white self-definition. Now she recognizes that she can be "really good" in certain subjects and "not so good" in others. She can verbalize her self-concept better, and she can weigh different aspects of it. She can compare her real self with her ideal self and can judge how well she measures up to social standards in comparison with others. All of these changes contribute to the development of self-esteem, her assessment of her global self-worth.

SELF-ESTEEM

Middle childhood is the time when children must learn skills valued in their society. Arapesh boys in New Guinea learn to make bows and arrows and to lay traps for rats; Arapesh girls learn to plant, weed, and harvest. Inuit children in northern regions of Canada learn to hunt and fish. Children in industrialized countries learn to read, write, do math, and use computers.

According to Erikson (1982), a major determinant of self-esteem is children's view of their capacity for productive work. Erikson's fourth stage of psychosocial

representational systems Broad, inclusive self-concepts that integrate various aspects of the self.

development focuses on **industry versus inferiority**. The virtue that follows successful resolution of this stage is competence, a view of the self as able to master skills and complete tasks. If children feel inadequate compared with their peers, they may retreat to the protective embrace of the family. If, on the other hand, they become too industrious, they may neglect social relationships and turn into workaholics in adulthood.

Parents strongly influence a child's beliefs about competence. In a large-scale longitudinal study of middle-class U.S. children, parents' beliefs about their children's competence in reading, math, music, and sports were strongly associated with the children's beliefs, and these influences persisted into adolescence (Fredricks & Eccles, 2002; Simpkins, Fredricks, & Eccles, 2012).

EMOTIONAL GROWTH

As children grow older, they are more aware of their own and other people's feelings. They can better regulate or control their emotions and can respond to others' emotional distress (Saarni et al., 2006).

By age 7 or 8, children typically are aware of feeling shame and pride, and they have a clearer idea of the difference between guilt and shame (Olthof, Schouten, Kuiper, Stegge, & Jennekens-Schinkel, 2000). These emotions affect their opinion of themselves (Harter, 1996). Children also understand their conflicting emotions. As Emily says, "I think boys are pretty yucky and I don't like most of them. My brother is okay though but he can be annoying sometimes. I love him but he does things that make me mad. But I don't yell at him because if I do, he cries and then I feel guilty."

By middle childhood, children are aware of their culture's rules for acceptable emotional expression (Cole, Bruschi, & Tamang, 2002). Children learn what makes them angry, fearful, or sad and how other people react to displays of these emotions, and they learn to behave accordingly. When parents respond to displays of negative emotions with disapproval or punishment, emotions such as anger and fear may become more intense and may impair children's social adjustment (Fabes, Leonard, Kupanoff, & Martin, 2001). As children approach early

adolescence, parental intolerance of negative emotion may heighten parent-child conflict (Eisenberg et al., 1999; Fabes et al., 2001).

Emotional self-regulation involves effortful (voluntary) control of emotions, attention, and behaviour. Effortful control may be temperamentally based but generally increases with age. Children with high effortful control can stifle the impulse to show negative emotion at inappropriate times. Children low in effortful control tend to become visibly angry or frustrated when interrupted or prevented from doing something they want to do, and this predicts later behaviour problems (Eisenberg et al., 2004).

Children tend to become more empathic and more inclined to prosocial behaviour in middle childhood. Prosocial children tend to act appropriately in social situations, to be relatively free from negative emotion, and to cope with problems constructively (Eisenberg, Fabes, & Murphy, 1996). Parents who acknowledge children's feelings of distress and help them focus on solving the root problem foster empathy, prosocial development, and social skills (Bryant, 1987; Eisenberg et al., 1996).

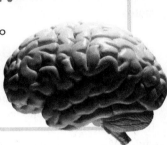

Ask Yourself

1. What are two changes that occur in a child's self-concept in middle childhood?

2. Which of Erikson's stages is relevant to the development of self-esteem in middle childhood?
   a. trust vs. mistrust
   b. industry vs. inferiority
   c. identity vs. identity confusion
   d. generativity vs. stagnation

3. Which of the following traits is related to the ability to effectively regulate emotions?
   a. anxiety
   b. empathy
   c. effortful control
   d. aggression

---

industry versus inferiority Erikson's fourth crisis of psychosocial development, in which children must learn the productive skills their culture requires or else face feelings of inferiority.

The Child in the Family

School-age children spend more of their free time away from home than when they were younger, visiting and socializing with peers, and as children approach adolescence, parents report spending less time in leisure activities with children (Canadian Fitness and Lifestyle Research Institute, 2011). Children also spend more time at school and on their studies and less time at family meals than 20 or so years ago (Juster et al., 2004). Still, home and the people who live there remain an important part of most children's lives. To understand the child in the family, we need to look at the family environment—its atmosphere and structure—and examine it within the context of the modern world.

FAMILY ATMOSPHERE

Contributing to the family environment is the family atmosphere. The family atmosphere can be described as the ways in which members interact with each other and the outside world, including the interpersonal dynamics as well as such factors as socio-economic level and work status. Key influences on the family atmosphere are parenting during this age, specifically how parents respond to emerging control of behaviour; whether or not they work in or outside the home; and the family's economic status.

Parenting: Emerging Control of Behaviour

One of the major influences on the family atmosphere is how parents and children navigate the changing balance of power as children become older, more independent, and desirous of autonomy. During the course of childhood, control of behaviour gradually shifts from parent to child. Middle childhood brings a transitional stage of **co-regulation**, in which parent and child share power. Parents exercise oversight, but children enjoy moment-to-moment self-regulation (Maccoby, 1984, 1992). With regard to problems among peers, for example, parents now rely less on direct intervention and more on discussion with their child (Parke & Buriel, 1998). Children are more apt to follow their parents' wishes when they recognize that the parents are fair and are concerned about the child's welfare and that they may "know better" because of experience. It helps if parents try to acknowledge children's maturing judgment and take strong stands only on important issues (Maccoby, 1984, 1992).

The shift to co-regulation affects the way parents handle discipline (Kochanska, Aksan, Prisco, & Adams, 2008). Parents of school-age children are more likely to use inductive techniques. Inductive techniques involve explaining why a behaviour is wrong and focusing on

the effects of that behaviour on others. For example, 8-year-old Emily's father might point out: "Hitting John hurts him and makes him feel bad." In other situations, Emily's parents may appeal to her self-esteem ("What happened to the helpful girl who was here yesterday?") or moral values ("A big girl like you shouldn't sit on the train and let an old person stand."). Above all, Emily's parents let her know that she must bear the consequences of her behaviour ("No wonder you missed the school bus today—you stayed up too late last night! Now you'll have to walk to school."). How parents handle discipline and decision-making can be influenced by cultural factors; for example, children in Aboriginal families—including those with developmental disabilities—are often involved in family decision-making because they are regarded as independent persons who are free in exploring their environments (Gerlach, 2008; Neckoway, Brownlee, & Castellan, 2007).

The way parents and children resolve conflicts may be more important than the specific outcomes. If family conflict is constructive, it can help children see the need for rules and standards. They also learn what kinds of issues are worth arguing about and what strategies can be effective (Eisenberg, 1996). However, parents who are negative or coercive in their approach to resolving family issues are at higher risk of having children who as adolescents are more likely to engage in problem behaviours and have adjustment problems (Low, Snyder, & Shortt, 2011). Witnessing family conflict, particularly violence in the household (about 8 percent of Canadian children between ages 4 and 7 have been reported to witness physical aggression in the home), can also have long-term negative consequences on children's behavioural development (Moss, 2004).

Did you know?

Asking kids to promise to tell the truth makes them more likely to do so (Evans & Lee, 2010).

Employed Mothers

Most studies of the impact of parents' work on children's well-being have focused on employed mothers. From 1976 to 2009, the labour force participation rate of Canadian mothers of children under age 16 rose from 39 percent to 73 percent (Ferrao, 2009), with most previously employed mothers returning to work within a year of childbirth (Zhang, 2008). Despite the increase in working mothers, not all parents in two-parent households work full-time for the full year; in 2005, 32 percent of two-parent families had both parents working full-time, up from 15 percent in 1980 (LaRochelle-Côté, Gougeon, & Pinard, 2009). Nevertheless, many children have never known a time when their mothers were not working for pay.

co-regulation *Transitional stage in the control of behaviour in which parents exercise general supervision and children exercise moment-to-moment self-regulation.*

In general, the more satisfied a mother is with her employment status, the more effective she is likely to be as a parent (Parke, 2004). However, the impact of a mother's work depends on many other factors, including the child's age, sex, temperament, and personality; whether the mother works full- or part-time; why she is working; whether she has a supportive or unsupportive partner, or none; the family's socio-economic status (SES); and the kind of care the child receives before and/or after school (Parke & Buriel, 1998). While it is difficult to pin down the effect of maternal employment, given the multiplicity of influences, longitudinal research indicates that overall, children from dual-earner families do well, and they may even in some ways show an advantage (Gottfried & Gottfried, 2008).

How children are cared for may be more important than whether the mother works for pay (Crouter, MacDermid, McHale, & Perry-Jenkins, 1990; Jacobson & Crockett, 2000). Some children of employed mothers, especially younger children, are supervised by relatives. Many children receive several types of out-of-school care (Canadian Child Care Federation, 2006; Carver & Iruka, 2006). Like good child care for preschoolers, good after-school programs have relatively low enrollment, low child-staff ratios, and well-educated staff. Children, especially boys, in organized after-school programs with flexible programming and a positive emotional climate tend to adjust better and do better in school (Mahoney, Lord, & Carryl, 2005). Initiatives, like the Toronto First Duty Program, can benefit kindergarten children and their families by integrating in-school and out-of-school programs (Corter, Janmohamed, & Pelletier, 2012). Recent full-day early learning kindergarten programs in Ontario have also shown positive benefits, lasting to at least Grade 2 (Pelletier, 2012a, 2012b).

About 9 percent of school-age children and 23 percent of early adolescents are reported to be in self-care as "latch-key kids," regularly caring for themselves at home without adult supervision (Hofferth & Jankuniene, 2000; NICHD Early Childhood Research Network,

WHAT DO YOU DO?

After-School Program Director

An after-school director manages after-school programs for children. During after-school programs, children may participate in formal or informal activities and do homework. After-school program directors are typically responsible for managing all aspects of the program, including hiring and managing staff. Requirements vary by position, but typically directors have a degree in child development or education, as well as experience working directly with children. After-school programs are in schools, in organizations like the YMCA, and in independent organizations and institutions. To learn more about becoming an after-school program director, visit www.naaweb.org and www.childcarecanada.org.

Did you know?

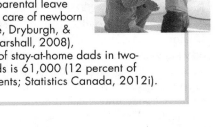

While the numbers have risen, out of the roughly 4.3 million fathers of children younger than 18 in Canada, approximately one in five take parental leave from work to take care of newborn children (Beaupré, Dryburgh, & Wendt, 2010; Marshall, 2008), and the number of stay-at-home dads in two-parent households is 61,000 (12 percent of stay-at-home parents; Statistics Canada, 2012i).

2004a). This arrangement is advisable only for older children who are mature, responsible, and resourceful and know how to get help in an emergency—and even then, only if a parent stays in touch by telephone (Canada Safety Council, 2009).

Poverty and Economic Stress

In Canada in 2010, 979,000 children, or 14.5 percent of children under age 18, lived in poverty (below the low-income cut-off measure)—about the same as in 1989 (Campaign 2000, 2012; Fleury, 2008). However, the economic recession drew the proportion of children living in poverty up, a trend that has continued along with the economic challenges Canada and other countries have faced—current estimates show a child poverty rate of 15.1 percent in Canada, ranking seventh of 17 developed nations (Conference Board of Canada, 2013).

Some groups of children in Canada are more likely to experience poverty than the average (Figure 13.1). Children living with single mothers are over four times as likely to be poor as children living with married couples (Baker, 2010; Gornick & Jäntti, 2012), and the rate is about one in three for children in Aboriginal, immigrant, and visible minority groups (Campaign 2000, 2012; Canadian Council on Social Development, 2006; Fleury, 2008). Persistent poverty—living for at least a year below the low-income cut-off—affected 25.5 percent of Canadian children between 1999 and 2003, with 18.4 percent experiencing poverty for more than a year (Canadian Council on Social Development, 2006).

Poor children are more likely than other children to have emotional or behavioural problems (Wadsworth et al., 2008) and lower cognitive potential and school performance (Najman et al., 2009). Poverty can harm children's development through its impact on parents' emotional state and parenting practices, and on the home environment they create (Evans, 2004; NICHD Early Child Care Research Network, 2005a).

Vonnie McLoyd's (1998; Mistry, Vandewater, Huston, & McLoyd, 2002) analysis of the effects of poverty suggests that parents who live in poverty are likely to become anxious, depressed, and irritable, and thus may become less affectionate with and less responsive to their children. They may discipline inconsistently, harshly, and arbitrarily. The children also tend to become depressed, to have trouble getting along with peers, to lack self-confidence, to develop behavioural and academic problems, and to engage in antisocial acts.

Fortunately, this pattern is not inevitable. Effective parenting can buffer children from the effects of low SES. Family interventions that reduce family conflict and anger and increase cohesion and warmth are especially beneficial (Repetti, Taylor, & Seeman, 2002). It appears as if material hardship—insufficient food, unstable housing, and inadequate medical care—often leads to parental stress. This, in turn, affects how much time, money, and energy parents invest in their children's development and the way parents treat their children; and these factors, in turn, predict children's cognitive skills and social and emotional competence. Families that, despite poverty, manage to make ends meet do not show this pattern (Gershoff, Aber, Raver, & Lennon, 2007).

Parents who can turn to relatives or to community resources for emotional support, help with child care, and child-rearing information often can parent their children more effectively. A four-year longitudinal study of 152 single mother–headed African-American families in Georgia found a pattern opposite to the one McLoyd described. Mothers who, despite economic stress, were emotionally healthy and had relatively high self-esteem tended to have academically and socially competent children who reinforced the mothers' positive parenting; this, in turn, supported the children's continued academic success and socially desirable behaviour (Brody, Kim, Murry, & Brown, 2004).

Aboriginal children living in poverty face particular challenges in being overrepresented in child welfare caseloads involving neglect and in having caregivers who struggle with substance abuse (Blackstock, Trocmé, & Bennett, 2004). To address this problem, researchers point to the need to develop alternative ways of supporting Aboriginal children, families, and communities, and to increase the sensitivity of social welfare agencies, both on and off reserve, to address stresses related to poverty, unemployment, substandard housing, loss of parenting knowledge related to the history of residential schools, and a lack of culturally sensitive services, among other issues (Blackstock et al., 2004; Fallon et al., 2013; Stokes & Schmidt, 2011).

FAMILY STRUCTURE

Family structure in Canada has changed dramatically in recent decades. In earlier generations, the vast majority of children grew up in traditional families, with two biological parents or two parents who had adopted one or more children in infancy. In 2011, 63.6 percent of the almost 5.6 million children 14 and under in Canada lived with two married biological, adoptive, or stepparents. That

FIGURE 13.1

Poverty Rates for Children 0–14 Years in Canada, Selected Population Groups, 1996–2006

Source: Adapted from Family Service Toronto. "Campaign 2000: End Child and Family Poverty in Canada." Chart 7, p. 11. www.campaign2000.ca

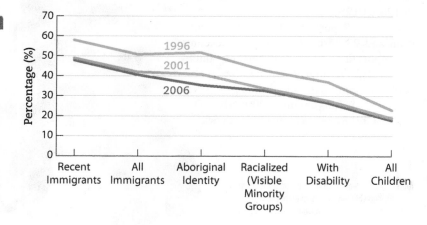

percentage represents a dramatic decline over the past two decades (Canadian Council on Social Development, 2006; Statistics Canada, 2012j, 2012k). During this period, there has been an increase in common-law families with children (7.3 percent of all families, 16.3 percent of children 14 and under), as well as a growing number of other non-traditional families, including lone-parent families (Statistics Canada, 2012j). Among two-parent families, new structures, in addition to common-law families, including blended families (resulting from divorce and remarriage), gay and lesbian families, and grandparent-headed families, are becoming more common (Statistics Canada, 2012j). How do these various family structures affect children?

Other things being equal, children tend to do better in families with two continuously married parents than in cohabiting, divorced, lone-parent, or stepfamilies, or when the child is born outside of marriage (S. L. Brown, 2004). The distinction is even stronger for children growing up with two happily married parents. These children tend to experience a higher standard of living, more effective parenting, more cooperative co-parenting, closer relationships with both parents (especially fathers), and fewer stressful events (Amato, 2005). However, the parents' relationship, the quality of their parenting, and their ability to create a favourable family atmosphere may affect children's adjustment more than their marital status does (Amato, 2005; Bray & Hetherington, 1993; Bronstein, Clauson, Stoll, & Abrams, 1993; D. A. Dawson, 1991).

Family instability may be more harmful to children than the particular type of family they live in. In a study of a nationally representative sample of 5- to 14-year-olds, children who experienced several family transitions, such as moving homes, changing schools, and divorcing parents, were more likely to have behaviour problems and to engage in delinquent behaviour than children in stable families (Fomby & Cherlin, 2007).

Divorced Parents

Divorce is the end of a marriage, and the event can be a significant stressor for children and parents, even though it may be the best choice for a family. Divorce can have negative psychological influences on children. The divorce rate in Canada is currently 2.1 per 1,000 people, with about 40 percent of marriages projected to end in divorce before the 30th anniversary. This rate, which is among the higher rates in the world, has been relatively stable for the past 20 years (Ambert, 2009; Human Resources and Skills Development Canada, 2013; Statistics Canada, 2011i). About the same number of common-law couples separate annually. The frequency of common-law dissolutions is about the same as marriages. Approximately four in ten divorces or separations involve a dependent child (Beaupré & Cloutier, 2007).

ADJUSTING TO DIVORCE   When Emily was 6 years old, her parents divorced. In the year following the divorce, Emily was sometimes anxious and upset, and she missed her father as she was no longer able to see him on a daily basis. She wondered if her parents got divorced because of something that she did. She was also sad that she and her mother and brother had to move away from their old neighbourhood, although she was able to keep attending the same school. However, in about a year's time, Emily adjusted to her new reality and seemed to return to her previous sunny self. What factors might account for Emily's adjustment? What might the long-term effects be?

Divorce is stressful for children. First, there is the stress of marital conflict and then of parental separation and the departure of one parent, usually the father. Children may not fully understand what is happening. Divorce is, of course, stressful for the parents as well and may negatively affect their parenting. The family's standard of living is likely to drop, and if a parent moves away, a child's relationship with the non-custodial parent may suffer (Kelly & Emery, 2003). A divorced parent's remarriage can increase the stress on children, renewing feelings of loss (Ahrons & Tanner, 2003; Amato, 2003).

Children's emotional or behavioural problems may reflect the level of parental conflict before the divorce (Amato, 2005). In a longitudinal study of almost 11,000 Canadian children, those whose parents later divorced showed more anxiety, depression, or antisocial behaviour than those whose parents stayed married (Strohschein, 2005). If pre-divorce parental discord is chronic, overt, or destructive, children may be as well or better off after a divorce (Amato, 2005).

A child's adjustment to divorce may depend in part on the child's age or maturity, gender, and psychosocial adjustment before the divorce. Younger children tend to be more anxious about divorce, to have less realistic perceptions of what caused it, and to be more likely to blame themselves. However, they may adapt more quickly than older children,

Divorce is stressful for children. How well they adjust depends on many factors, including the child's age and gender, support from the custodial parent, less parental conflict, and close contact with the non-resident parent.

who better understand what is going on. School-age children are sensitive to parental pressures and loyalty conflicts and, like younger children, may fear abandonment and rejection. Boys find it harder to adjust than girls do and are more susceptible to social and conduct problems (Amato, 2005).

CUSTODY, VISITATION, AND CO-PARENTING   Children do better after divorce if the custodial parent is warm, supportive, and authoritative, monitors the child's activities, and holds age-appropriate expectations; if parental conflict subsides; and if the non-resident parent maintains close contact and involvement (Ahrons & Tanner, 2003; Kelly & Emery, 2003).

In most divorce cases, the mother gets custody, though paternal custody is a growing trend. Children living with divorced mothers adjust better when the father pays child support, which may be a barometer of the tie between father and child and also of cooperation between the ex-spouses (Kelly & Emery, 2003). Many children of divorce say that losing contact with a father is one of the most painful results of divorce (Fabricius, 2003). However, frequency of contact with the father is not as important as the quality of the father-child relationship and the level of parental conflict.

Emily was lucky in that her parents established a cordial co-parenting relationship and were able to successfully negotiate conflict, making her adjustment to divorce less painful than it might have been. In a sample of 354 divorced families, *cooperative parenting*—active consultation between a mother and a non-resident father on parenting decisions—led to more frequent contact between father and child, and this, in turn, led to better father-child relationships and more responsive fathering (Sobolewski & King, 2005). Unfortunately, cooperative parenting is not the norm (Amato, 2005). Parent education programs that teach separated or divorced couples how to prevent or deal with conflict, keep lines of communication open, develop an effective co-parenting relationship, and help children adjust to divorce have been introduced in many courts with measurable success (Wolchik et al., 2002). *Joint custody*—custody shared by both parents—can be advantageous if the parents can cooperate. An analysis of 33 studies found that children or parents with joint custody were as well-adjusted as children in non-divorced families (Bauserman, 2002). It is likely, though, that couples who choose joint custody are those that have less conflict.

LONG-TERM EFFECTS OF DIVORCE   As Emily did, most children of divorce adjust reasonably well. Children with divorced parents tend to have lower academic achievement and more problems with social relationships, but most do not suffer long-term negative outcomes (Lansford, 2009). However, the timing of the divorce often affects the outcome. Children who experience their parents' divorce during elementary school are more likely to develop internalizing or externalizing problems, whereas children whose parents divorce later are more likely to suffer a drop in grades (Lansford et al., 2006). Other research has also shown an age effect: Children who experience parental divorce before age 16 tend to have emotional and educational problems, to initiate sexual activity early, and to be at risk for depression and suicidal thoughts (D'Onofrio et al., 2006). In adolescence, parental divorce increases the risk of antisocial behaviour and difficulties with authority figures (Amato, 2005; Kelly & Emery, 2003).

The anxiety connected with parental divorce may surface as children enter adulthood and try to form intimate relationships of their own (Amato, 2003). Having experienced their parents' divorce, some young adults are afraid of making commitments that might end in disappointment (Glenn & Marquardt, 2001). According to some research, 25 percent of children of divorce reach adulthood with serious social, emotional, or psychological problems, compared with 10 percent of children whose parents stay together (Hetherington & Kelly, 2002). As adults, the children of divorce tend to have lower SES, poorer psychological well-being, and a greater chance of having a birth outside marriage. Their marriages tend to be less satisfying and are more likely to end in divorce (Amato, 2005). However, much depends on how young people resolve and interpret the experience of parental divorce. Some are able to learn from that negative example and to form functional relationships themselves (Shulman, Scharf, Lumer, & Maurer, 2001).

Lone-Parent Families

Lone-parent families result from divorce or separation, unwed parenthood, or death, and the proportions of these have changed over the past 50 years (Figure 13.2). Currently, approximately 19.3 percent of dependent children age 14 and under live with a single parent, and of these 80 percent were female-headed and 20 percent were male-headed (Statistics Canada, 2012j, 2012k).

WHAT DO YOU DO?

Forensic Psychologist

A forensic psychologist works in the field of criminal justice. In relation to cases involving children, forensic psychologists may be involved in custody disputes, investigating suspected child abuse and assessing parental visitation risk. Forensic psychologists typically have doctoral degrees and then must receive certification. Forensic psychologists typically work within the court system, in prisons, and in private practice. To learn more about becoming a forensic psychologist, go to www.abfp.com and http://cpa.ca (click About CPA, CPA Sections, Criminal Justice Psychology).

FIGURE 13.2

Living Arrangements of Children in Lone-Parent Families, 1961–2011

Source: Statistics Canada, Census in Brief: Fifty Years of Families in Canada: 1961-2011. Figure 2, p. 3. Cat. No.: 98-312-X2011003. Reprinted by the Minister responsible for Statistics Canada. (c) Ministry of Industry, 2013.

- ■ Never married
- ■ Divorced or separated
- ■ Widowed

Although children are far more likely to live with a single mother than with a single father, the number of father-only families has grown, apparently largely because of the increase in paternal custody after divorce (Statistics Canada, 2012j). In addition, 0.5 percent of Canadian children live with their grandparents.

Children in lone-parent families do fairly well overall but tend to lag socially and educationally behind peers in two-parent families. This is true both of children born out of wedlock and of those whose parents are divorced. What explains these findings? Children living with a single parent are exposed to many stressful experiences; most notably they tend to be economically disadvantaged. Because their parent is struggling to maintain the household, these children often receive poorer parenting than children living with two parents. Moreover, losing contact with a parent or observing conflict and hostility between parents can produce emotional insecurity (Lugaila, 2003). However, negative outcomes for children in lone-parent families are far from inevitable. The child's age and level of development, the family's financial circumstances, whether there are frequent moves, and the non-resident parent's involvement make a difference (Amato, 2005; Seltzer, 2000).

A father's frequent and positive involvement with his child, from infancy on, is directly related to the child's well-being and physical, cognitive, and social development (Cabrera et al., 2000; Shannon et al., 2002). The factors that are positively related to the degree of father's involvement with his child include lower age of the child, higher father's educational level, higher maternal involvement with the child, and lower domestic discord (Flouri & Buchanan, 2003). Increased work responsibilities can reduce time spent with children (Beaupré, Dryburgh, & Wendt, 2010). In 2011, 15.9 percent of families with children younger than

15 years had no father (Statistics Canada, 2012b). Fortunately, more fathers are actively involved with their children than in previous generations (Doucet, 2006; Eggebeen & Knoester, 2001), and few fathers living with or without their children report that work responsibilities interfere with their ability to be involved with their children (Beaupré et al., 2011).

Cohabiting Families

Cohabiting families in Canada are similar in many ways to married families, with developmental outcomes in research studies showing quite a bit of diversity. Often, parents have been more disadvantaged in cohabiting than in married families, and so developmental outcomes in many U.S. studies have been negative for cohabiting compared with married families (Thomson & McLanahan, 2012). The difference in outcomes is due largely to differences in economic resources, parental well-being, and parenting effectiveness, rather than family structure per se (S. L. Brown, 2004). Longitudinal comparisons of behavioural outcomes in Canadian children living in stable married and stable common-law families showed no developmental differences, after controlling for SES and family processes. Surprisingly, the dissolution of common-law couples did not seem to have the same negative consequences on children as divorce of married couples (Wu, Hou, & Schimmele, 2008). Similar results have been found for school engagement, but not on self-perceptions of achievement (Wu, Costigan, Hou, Kampen, & Schimmele, 2010).

In Canada, cohabiting, or common-law, families are becoming more commonplace (making up 7.3 percent of all families in 2011), with 16.3 percent of children 14 years of age and under in 2011 living in cohabiting families; the proportion is larger in Quebec (about 38 percent of children) than in the other provinces (Statistics Canada, 2012j). Growing acceptance of cohabitation, increased numbers of stable long-term cohabiting families, and societal norms around marriage breakup might explain part of the discrepancies in findings. Across family structures, high levels of emotional support and connection with parents are key factors behind fostering healthy behavioural and academic growth in children.

Stepfamilies

Most divorced parents eventually remarry or enter into new common-law relationships (cohabitation), and many lone mothers marry men who were not the father of their children (Amato, 2005; Juby, Marcil-Gratto, & Le Bourdais, with Huot, 2006), thus forming stepfamilies or complex stepfamilies (or blended families). Some 12.6 percent of Canadian families are stepfamilies, with 7.4 percent simple stepfamilies (involving children of one member of the new couple), and 5.2 percent complex stepfamilies (involving children from previous relationships, and a new child from the new relationship) (Statistics Canada, 2013a).

Adjusting to a new stepparent may be stressful. A child's loyalties to an absent or dead parent may interfere with forming ties to a stepparent (Amato, 2005). Many stepchildren maintain ties with their non-custodial parents. Non-custodial mothers tend to keep in touch more than do non-custodial fathers and offer more social support (Gunnoe & Hetherington, 2004).

Some studies have found that boys—who often have more trouble than girls in adjusting to divorce and living with a single mother—benefit from a stepfather. A girl, though, may find the new man in the house a threat to her independence and to her close relationship with her mother (Bray & Hetherington, 1993; Hetherington, 1987; Hetherington, Bridges, & Insabella, 1998; Hetherington, Stanley-Hagan, & Anderson, 1989; Hines, 1997). In a

Did you know?

Over 6,000 Canadian families with children have a gay or lesbian head of household (Statistics Canada, 2013b). Perhaps reflecting this trend, the popular ABC sitcom *Modern Family* includes a characteristically modern family—gay couple Cameron and Mitchell adopt Lily, a Vietnamese girl.

longitudinal study of a nationally representative sample of U.S. adults, mothers who remarried or formed new cohabiting relationships tended to use gentler discipline than mothers who remained single, and their children reported better relationships with them. However, supervision was greater in stable single-mother families (Thomson, Mosley, Hanson, & McLanahan, 2001).

Gay or Lesbian Parents

About 9 percent of the approximately 64,575 same-sex couples in Canada are raising children (Statistics Canada, 2013b). Of those, more are raised by female couples (about 80 percent of same-sex couples with children) than by male couples (Statistics Canada, 2013b). Some are raising children born of previous heterosexual relationships. Others conceive by artificial means, become foster parents, or adopt children (Pawelski et al., 2006). Since July 2005, same-sex marriages have been legal in Canada, and as a result, 42 percent of same-sex couples with children are now married.

A considerable body of research has examined the development of children of gays and lesbians, including physical and emotional health, intelligence, adjustment, sense of self, moral judgment, and social and sexual functioning, and has indicated no special concerns (American Psychiatric Association, 2004). There is no consistent difference between homosexual and heterosexual parents in emotional health or parenting skills and attitudes; where there are differences, they tend to favour gay parents (Meezan & Rauch, 2005; Pawelski et al., 2006; Wainright, Russell, & Patterson, 2004). Gay or lesbian parents usually have positive relationships with their children, and the children are no more likely than children raised by heterosexual parents to have emotional, social, academic, or psychological problems (American Psychiatric Association, 2004; Gartrell, Deck, Rodas, Peyser, & Banks, 2005; Meezan & Rauch, 2005; Wainright et al., 2004). Furthermore, the sexual orientations of children of gays and lesbians follow the same patterns as children of heterosexuals (Meezan & Rauch, 2005; Pawelski et al., 2006; Wainright et al., 2004).

Children of same-sex parents usually have positive relationships and do as well as children of heterosexual parents in emotional, social, and academic development.

GRANDPARENTING

Grandparenting is a role most parents look forward to—one where the joys of having children can be experienced without the accompanying responsibilities of parenthood. In Canada, grandparents often feel the licence to shower their grandchildren with affection and gifts. There is generally a feeling that one need not worry about spoiling a child within the context of the grandparenting role. However, the changing demographics of the modern world are altering that expected relationship, not just in Canada, but worldwide.

In Canada, an increasing number of grandparents are serving as "parents by default" for children whose parents are unable to care for them—often as a result of teenage pregnancy, substance abuse, illness, divorce, or early death (Allen, Blieszner, & Roberto, 2000; Milan & Hamm, 2003). In 2001, about 3.3 percent of children lived with grandparents, though 0.4 percent lived in *skip-generation families*, in which the parents were not present. By 2011, 4.8 percent of children lived in a household with grandparents, and 0.5 percent were skip-generation families (Statistics Canada, 2012j). More than 17 percent of skip-generation households

are headed by Aboriginal grandparents (Fuller-Thomson, 2005).

In many societies, such as those in Latin America and Asia, extended-family households predominate, and resident grandparents play an integral role in the family. One reason in developing countries is rural parents' migration to urban areas to find work. The AIDS epidemic, in sub-Saharan Africa, has also pushed grandparents into the parenting role. The disease has left many orphans whose grandparents must step into the parents' place. As such, skip-generation families exist in all regions of the world—not just in Canada—including Afro-Caribbean countries in particular (Kinsella & Velkoff, 2001).

Most grandparents who take on the responsibility to raise their grandchildren do it because they love the children and do not want them placed in a stranger's foster home. However, the age difference can become a barrier, and both generations may feel cheated out of their traditional roles (Crowley, 1993; Larsen, 1990–1991). Also, aging grandparents may lack the stamina to keep up with an active child.

Such findings about gay and lesbian parenting have social policy implications for legal decisions on custody and visitation disputes, foster care, and adoptions. In Canada, there are no legal restrictions on adoption by same-sex couples, including partners in same-sex couples adopting the other partner's child.

Adoptive Families

Adoption is found in all cultures throughout history. It is not only for infertile people; single people, older people, gay and lesbian couples, and people who already have biological children have become adoptive parents. An estimated 60 percent of legal adoptions are by stepparents or relatives, usually grandparents (Kreider, 2003). Grandparents care for about 0.5 percent of Canadian children under 15 years; 0.3 percent are cared for by other family members; and

0.5 percent of children are in foster care (Statistics Canada, 2012j).

Adoption is regulated provincially. Each year, about 2,000 children are adopted from the child welfare system in Canada, children who are removed from their birth families and placed into foster care. About 2,000 children a year are international adoptions, and another 500 to 600 children are private adoptions (Adoption Council of Canada, 2010).

Adopting a child carries special challenges: integrating the adopted child into the family, explaining the adoption to the child, helping the child develop a healthy sense of self, and perhaps eventually helping the child find and contact the biological parents. With respect to positive outcomes, adoptive children in two-parent families do as well as biological children in two-parent families (Hamilton, Cheng, & Powell, 2007), and there are few significant differences in adjustment between adopted and non-adopted children in families that are good at communicating with one another (Rueter & Koerner, 2009). Cognitively, adoption is usually beneficial. An analysis of 62 studies of a total of 17,767 adopted children found that they scored higher on IQ tests and performed better in school than siblings or peers who remained in the birth family or in institutional care. Their IQ scores

WHERE DO YOU STAND?

Although it's legal in Canada, gay marriage is still a contentious issue. Do you support gay marriage? Why or why not?

also equalled those of their adoptive siblings and non-adopted peers, but their school performance and language abilities tended to lag (van IJzendoorn & Juffer, 2005; van IJzendoorn, Juffer, & Poelhuis, 2005).

A large proportion of international adoptions are transracial, most often involving white parents adopting children from Asian countries (Baxter & Canadian Paediatric Society, Community Paediatrics Committee, 2006). Does international adoption entail special problems? Aside from the possibility of malnourishment or other serious medical conditions in children from developing countries (Bosch et al., 2003), a number of studies find no significant problems with the children's psychological adjustment, school adjustment and performance, or observed behaviour at home or in the way they cope with being adopted (Levy-Shiff, Zoran, & Shulman, 1997; Sharma, McGue, & Benson, 1996a). However, not all international adoptions proceed so smoothly, especially when the children have had substandard care or are older at the time of adoption. For example, children adopted after a year of age are more likely to show disturbances in their attachment patterns (van IJzendoorn & Bakersman-Kranenburg, 2009) than children adopted before their first birthday, and some adopted children with early deprivation histories show cognitive deficits relative to those from less disadvantaged circumstances (Odenstad et al., 2008).

SIBLING RELATIONSHIPS

"Give it back!" Emily screamed at her brother John, "It's mine." "No fair," whined 6-year-old John back, "It was supposed to be for sharing and so you have to share." Their mother stepped into the room and sighed. "Patch it up, guys, or we won't go to the park later," she warned. "Emily, you're older. You should know better." Though Emily and John scowled at each other for a few minutes, within a short while they were once again playing together happily.

Siblings influence each other, not only directly, through their own interactions (Howe, Aquan-Asee, Bukowski, Lehoux, & Rinaldi, 2001), but also indirectly through their impact on each other's relationship with the parents. Parents' experience with an older sibling influences their expectations and treatment of a younger one (Brody, 2004). Conversely, behaviour patterns a child establishes with parents tend to "spill over" into the child's behaviour with siblings. In a study of 101 English families, when the parent-child relationship was warm and affectionate, siblings tended to have positive relationships as well. When the parent-child relationship was conflictual, sibling conflict was more likely (Pike, Coldwell, & Dunn, 2005).

Sibling relations can be a laboratory for conflict resolution. Siblings are motivated to make up after quarrels because they know they will see each other every day. They learn that expressing anger does not end a relationship. Children are more apt to squabble with same-sex

siblings, and two brothers quarrel more than any other combination (Cicirelli, 1976, 1995).

Ask Yourself

4. Which of the following variables affects the impact of maternal employment on children's well-being?
   a. how satisfied the mother is
   b. the child's temperament
   c. how well the child is monitored and kept track of
   d. all of these

5. When all other factors are held equal, what type of family structure seems to be the best for children?

6. Which of the following is an indirect sibling influence?
   a. A child's parents are warm and loving toward her, so she tends to treat her sister the same way.
   b. A child's parents are happy that he is a boy.
   c. Two siblings are punished for fighting with each other.
   d. Siblings from large families receive less one-on-one time with parents.

The Child in the Peer Group

Emily was glad that her parents' divorce did not mean she had to change schools. Although she had a number of friends and was well liked by most of her peers, she was by nature a bit shy, and the thought of navigating a new social world filled her with dread. Luckily, she and her best friend were able to continue to play together and even ended up in the same classroom that year.

In middle childhood, the peer group comes into its own. Groups form naturally among children who live near one another or go to school together and often consist of children of the same racial or ethnic origin and similar socio-economic status. Children who play together are usually close in age and of the same sex (Hartup, 1992; Pellegrini et al., 2002).

How does the peer group influence children? What determines their acceptance by peers and their ability to make friends?

POSITIVE AND NEGATIVE EFFECTS OF PEER RELATIONS

As children begin to move away from parental influence, the peer group opens new perspectives and frees them to make independent judgments. Children develop skills needed for sociability and intimacy, and they gain a sense of belonging. They are motivated to achieve, and they attain a sense of identity. The peer group helps children learn how to get along in society—how to adjust their needs and desires to those of others, when to yield, and when to stand firm. Moreover, the peer group offers emotional security. It is reassuring for children to find out that they are not alone in harbouring thoughts that might offend an adult.

On the negative side, peer groups may reinforce **prejudice**: unfavourable attitudes toward "outsiders," especially members of certain racial or ethnic groups. Prejudice and discrimination can lead to depression and conduct problems in those who see themselves as targets of discrimination (Brody et al., 2006). The peer group can also foster antisocial tendencies. Preadolescent children are especially susceptible to pressure to conform. It is usually in the company of peers that some children shoplift and begin to use drugs (Dishion & Tipsord, 2011).

GENDER DIFFERENCES IN PEER-GROUP RELATIONSHIPS

Boys' and girls' peer groups engage in different types of activities. Groups of boys more consistently pursue gender-typed activities. They play in large groups with well-defined leadership hierarchies and engage in more competitive and rough-and-tumble play. Girls have more intimate conversations characterized by prosocial interactions and shared confidences (Rose & Rudolph, 2006). Also, girls are more

prejudice Unfavourable attitude toward members of certain groups outside one's own, especially racial or ethnic groups.

likely than boys to engage in cross-gender activities, such as team sports (McHale, Kim, Whiteman, & Crouter, 2004).

Why do children segregate themselves by sex and engage in such different activities? One of the most clearly identified reasons is because of boys' higher activity levels and more vigorous play (Pellegrini & Archer, 2005; Rosenkranz, Welk, Hastmann, & Dzewaltowski, 2011; Trost, Rozencranz, & Dzewaltowski, 2008). However, it appears that socialization influences are also at play. Even very active girls tend to end up in same-sex groups (Pellegrini et al., 2007). Same-sex peer groups help children learn gender-appropriate behaviours and incorporate gender roles into their self-concept.

POPULARITY

Popularity becomes more important in middle childhood. Schoolchildren whose peers like them are likely to be well adjusted as adolescents. Those who have trouble getting along with peers are more likely to develop psychological problems, drop out of school, or become delinquent (Dishion & Tipsord, 2011; Hartup, 1992; Newcomb, Bukowski, & Pattee, 1993). Peer rejection also has consequences for academics; it has been linked to lower levels of classroom participation (Ladd, Herald-Brown, & Reiser, 2008).

Researchers measure popularity by asking children to identify peers they like most and least, and use the responses to construct a tally for each child of their positive and negative nominations. These sociometric studies have identified five peer status groups: popular, youngsters who receive many positive nominations; rejected, those who receive many negative nominations; neglected, those who receive few nominations of either kind; controversial, those who receive many positive and many negative nominations; and average, those who do not receive an unusual number of nominations of either kind.

Popular children typically have good cognitive abilities, are high achievers, are good at solving social problems, help other children, and are assertive without being disruptive or aggressive. Their superior social skills make others enjoy being with them (Cillessen & Mayeux, 2004; LaFontana & Cillessen, 2002).

Children can be unpopular, either rejected or neglected, for many reasons. Some unpopular children are aggressive; others are hyperactive, inattentive, or withdrawn (Dodge, Coie, Pettit, & Price, 1990; LaFontanta & Cillessen, 2002; Pope, Bierman, & Mumma, 1991). Still others act silly and immature or anxious and uncertain. Unpopular children are often insensitive to other children's feelings and do not adapt well to new situations (Bierman, Smoot, & Aumiller, 1993). Some unpopular children expect not

FIGURE 13.3

Measured Popularity: Five Peer Status Groups

to be liked, and this becomes a self-fulfilling prophecy (Rabiner & Coie, 1989).

Cultural differences can also have an influence on popularity. In a cross-cultural comparison of children in China and Canada, in Grades 2 and 4, sociable and cooperative children were popular and aggressive children were rejected in both countries. However, shy, sensitive children were well liked in China, but not in Canada (Chen, Rubin, & Li, 1995; Chen, Rubin, & Sun, 1992). This seems to reflect culturally based perceptions of sensitivity and shyness—reflecting good behaviour in China and lack of self-confidence in Canada. Social change can temper perceptions, though. A more recent study comparing cohorts of children across 1990 to 2002, a decade of social change in China, showed that in comparison with a 1990 cohort, shy children in China in 2002 tended to be rejected by their peers (Chen, Cen, Li, & He, 2005). These findings suggest that the social acceptability of shy children is closely related to cultural norms. In the society that China has become, social assertiveness and initiative may be more highly appreciated and encouraged than in the past, and shyness and sensitivity may lead to social difficulties for children.

FRIENDSHIP

Children may spend much of their free time in groups, but only as individuals do they form friendships. Popularity is the peer group's opinion of a child, but friendship is a two-way street.

Children look for friends who are like them in age, sex, and interests. The strongest friendships involve equal commitment and mutual give-and-take. Though children tend to choose friends with similar ethnic backgrounds, a recent study of 509 fourth graders showed that cross-racial/ethnic friendships were associated with positive developmental outcomes (Kawabata & Crick, 2008).

Unpopular children can make friends, but they tend to have fewer friends than popular children and demonstrate a preference for younger friends, other unpopular children, or children in a different class or a different school (Deptula & Cohen, 2004; Hartup, 1996).

Why are friends important? Children learn to communicate and cooperate with their friends.

Did you know?

By age 6, children show preferences based on physical appearance. Pictures of children who squint were less likely to be selected by children 6 and over to be invited to birthday parties than twin pictures without a squint; younger children showed no such preference (Mojon-Azzi, Kunz, & Mojon, 2011).

instrumental aggression Aggressive behaviour used as a means of achieving a goal.

hostile aggression Aggressive behaviour intended to hurt another person.

They help each other weather stressful situations, such as starting at a new school or adjusting to parents' divorce. The inevitable quarrels help children learn to resolve conflicts (Hartup, 1996; Hartup & Stevens, 1999; Newcomb & Bagwell, 1995). Friendship seems to help children feel good about themselves, though it's also likely that children who feel good about themselves have an easier time making friends.

Children's concepts of friendship and the ways they act with their friends change with age, reflecting cognitive and emotional growth. Preschool friends play together, but friendship among school-age children is deeper, more reciprocal, and more stable. Children cannot be or have true friends until they achieve the cognitive maturity to consider other people's views and needs as well as their own (Dodge, Coie, & Lynam, 2006).

School-age children distinguish among "best friends," "good friends," and "casual friends" on the basis of intimacy and time spent together (Hartup & Stevens, 1999). Children this age typically have three to five "best" friends (Hartup & Stevens, 1999). School-age girls seem to care less about having many friends than about having a few close friends they can rely on. Boys have more friendships, but they tend to be less intimate and affectionate (Furman & Buhrmester, 1985; Hartup & Stevens, 1999).

AGGRESSION AND BULLYING

Aggression declines and changes in form during the early school years. After age 6 or 7, most children become less aggressive as they grow less egocentric, more empathic, more cooperative, and better able to communicate. They can now put themselves in someone else's place, can understand another person's motives, and can find positive ways of asserting themselves. **Instrumental aggression**, aggression aimed at achieving an objective, the hallmark of the preschool period, becomes much less common. However, as aggression declines overall, **hostile aggression**—action intended to hurt another person—proportionately increases (Dodge, Coie, & Lynam, 2006), often taking verbal rather than physical form (Pellegrini & Archer, 2005). Boys continue to engage in more direct aggression, and girls are increasingly more likely to engage in social or indirect aggression, although a recent meta-analysis found negligible gender differences, calling into question the common portrayal of indirect aggression as a predominantly female form of aggression (Card, Stucky, Sawalani, & Little, 2008).

Aggressive children often egg each other on to antisocial acts.

group of 905 urban fifth through ninth graders, physical aggression became less disapproved of as children moved into adolescence, and relational aggression was increasingly reinforced by high status among peers (Cillessen & Mayeux, 2004).

Adults can help children curb aggression by teaching them how to recognize when they are getting angry and how to control their anger. In a New York City school study, children exposed to a conflict resolution curriculum that involved discussions and group role-playing showed less hostile attribution bias, less aggression, fewer behaviour problems, and more effective responses to social situations than children who did not participate in the program (Aber et al., 2003). Canada is ranked 26th out of 35 countries on measures of bullying (Craig & Harel, 2004). The PREVNet (Promoting Relationships and Eliminating Violence Network) initiative is a national strategy that aims to provide children's caregivers with resources to combat bullying in the schools (Craig & Pepler, 2007; Pepler & Craig, 2011; www.prevnet.ca).

A small minority of children do not learn to control physical aggression (Coie & Dodge, 1998) and seem to process social information with a **hostile attribution bias**, immediately assuming other children are acting with hostile intent. These children, usually boys, tend to strike out quickly in retaliation or self-defence and are also likely to have social and psychological problems. While it is clear that they are poor at reading and interpreting social cues, it is not clear whether aggression causes these problems or is a response to them, or both (Crick & Grotpeter, 1995).

Since people often do become hostile toward someone who acts aggressively toward them, a hostile bias may set in motion a cycle of aggression (de Castro, Veerman, Koops, Bosch, & Monshouwer, 2002). Hostile attribution biases become more common between ages 6 and 12 (Aber, Brown, & Jones, 2003). Moreover, highly aggressive children often egg each other on to antisocial acts. Thus, school-age boys who are physically aggressive may become juvenile delinquents in adolescence (Broidy et al., 2003). Being a boy, having a reactive temperament, parental separation, early onset of motherhood, and controlling parenting have all been shown to contribute to physical aggression in 6- to 12-year-olds (Joussemet et al., 2008). Rejected children and those exposed to harsh parenting also tend to have a hostile attribution bias (de Castro et al., 2002).

Although aggressors tend to be personally disliked, physically aggressive boys and some relationally aggressive girls, those who, for example, talk behind another girl's back or exclude her socially, are perceived as among the most popular in the classroom (Cillessen & Mayeux, 2004; Rodkin, Farmer, Pearl, & Van Acker, 2000). In a study of peer-rejected fourth graders, aggressive boys tended to gain in social status by the end of fifth grade, suggesting that behaviour shunned by younger children may be seen as cool or glamorous by preadolescents (Sandstrom & Coie, 1999). In a longitudinal study of a multiethnic

Influence of Media on Aggression

"Please please please, Mom," Emily begged, "I really want to see it! It's only PG and all my friends saw it!"

As television, movies, video games, cellphones, and computers take on larger roles in children's daily lives, it is critical to understand the impact mass media has on children's behaviour. Children spend more time on entertainment media than on any other activity besides school and sleeping. The AAP Committee on Public Education (2001) recommends that parents limit children's media exposure to one to two hours a day; however, on average, children spend about four hours a day in front of a television or computer screen (Anderson, Berkowitz, et al., 2003).

Violence is prevalent in media that children see. About 6 out of 10 television programs portray violence, usually glamourized, glorified, or trivialized (Gosselin, Paquette, & DeGuise, 1997; Yokota & Thompson, 2000). Music videos disproportionately feature violence against women and minorities. In a recent study of U.S. children, 40 movies that were rated R for violence were seen by a median of 12.5 percent of an estimated 22 million children ages 10 to 14. The most popular movie, *Scary Movie*, was seen by over 10 million children (Worth et al., 2008).

Because of the significant amount of time that children spend interacting with media, the images they see can become primary role models and sources of information

hostile attribution bias   Tendency for individuals to perceive others as trying to hurt them and to strike out in retaliation or self-defence.

In 2012's *The Hunger Games*, teenagers are pitted against each other in publicly televised fights to the death.

bullying Aggression deliberately and persistently directed against a particular target, or victim, typically one who is weak, vulnerable, and defenceless.

cyberbullying Posting negative comments or derogatory photos of the victim on a website.

about how people behave. Evidence from research conducted over the past 50 years on exposure to violence on TV, movies, and video games supports a causal relationship between media violence and violent behaviour on the viewer's part (Huesmann, 2007).

How does media violence lead to long-term aggressiveness? Longitudinal studies have demonstrated that children's exposure to violent media increases their risk for long-term effects based on observational learning, desensitization, and enactive learning that occur automatically in human children (Huesmann, 2007). Media provide visceral thrills without showing the human cost and lead children to view aggression as acceptable. Children who see characters use violence to achieve their goals are likely to conclude that force is an effective way to resolve conflicts. Negative reactions to violent scenes have been shown to decline in intensity with repeated exposure (Huesmann & Kirwil, 2007). The more realistically violence is portrayed, the more likely it is to be accepted (AAP Committee on Public Education, 2001; Anderson, Berkowitz, et al., 2003). And children who are aggressive to start with fare worse. Highly aggressive children are more strongly affected by media violence than are less aggressive children (Anderson, Berkowitz, et al., 2003).

Research on effects of video games and the Internet suggest that long-term increases in violent behaviour could be even greater for video games than for TV and movies. Players of violent games are active participants who receive positive reinforcement for violent actions (Huesmann, 2007). In experimental studies, young video game players have shown decreases in prosocial behaviour and increases in aggressive thoughts and violent retaliation to provocation (C. Anderson, 2000). A study of Canadian youth in Grades 6 to 10 showed that computer and video games were the screen-time uses that were most associated with aggressive behaviour (Janssen, Boyce, & Pickett, 2012), independent of TV use.

How can parents regulate how their children make use of new media? Although electronic blocking devices are useful in filtering out unwanted programming, they can create a false sense of security in parents who might believe that all violent programs are being eliminated. As a result, the Canadian Paediatric Society (CPS) encourages parents to monitor their children's television viewing (CPS, 2003). The best approach is to encourage healthy uses of new technologies and to talk often with children about appropriate use of technology, to build trust and skills should inappropriate content be encountered (Tynes, 2007). Parents need to be aware of online trends and new technologies, to be attentive to the websites and online applications their children use, to offer preventative education, and to keep lines of communication open to ensure that clear discussions of the what and why of removing connections to inappropriate content or people are important (Padilla-Walker, Coyne, Fraser, Dyer, & Yorgason, 2012; Rosen, Cheever, & Carrier, 2008; Tynes, 2007; Whittle, Hamilton-Giachritsis, Beech, & Collings, 2013).

Bullies and Victims

Aggression becomes bullying when it is deliberately, persistently directed against a particular target: a victim. **Bullying** can be physical (hitting, punching, kicking, or damaging or taking of personal belongings), verbal (name-calling or threatening), or relational or emotional (isolating and gossiping, often behind the victim's back) (Berger, 2007; Veenstra et al., 2005). Male bullies tend to use overt, physical aggression; female bullies may use relational aggression (Boulton, 1995; Nansel et al., 2001). **Cyberbullying**—posting negative comments or derogatory photos of the victim on a website—has become increasingly common (Berger, 2007). The increase in use of cellphones, text messaging, email, and chat rooms has opened new venues for bullies that provide access to victims without the protection of family and community (Huesmann, 2007). Cyberbullying has been identified in Canadian children as early as Grade 6, with an overall 22 percent of children and adolescents reporting having been victims of cyberbullying. It is more prevalent among girls and tends to decline in high school (Wade & Beran, 2011).

Did you know?

A recent study showed that being ignored or rejected online results in self-esteem drops in 8- and 9-year-old children, just as in real life (Abrams, Weick, Thomas, Colbe, & Franklin, 2011).

Bullying may reflect a genetic tendency toward aggressiveness combined with environmental influences, such as coercive parents and antisocial friends (Berger, 2007). Most bullies are boys who tend to victimize other boys; female bullies tend to target other girls (Berger, 2007; Pellegrini & Long, 2002; Veenstra et al., 2005).

Over the years between 1994 and 2006 in Canada, there was a decrease in reports of persistent or chronic bullying in boys (from about 18 to 12 percent) and in girls (from about 9 to 6 percent). However, occasional bullying rose for girls (from 28 to 34 percent) but stayed the same for boys (Molcho et al., 2009; Pepler & Craig, 2011). Bullying is a problem in other industrialized countries as well (Hara, 2002; Kanetsuna & Smith, 2002; Ruiz & Tanaka, 2001), but Canada rates poorly in international comparisons of prevalence of bullying (Craig et al., 2009). In a survey of 50,000 children in 34 European countries, almost one-third of the children said they were bullies, victims, or both (Currie et al., 2004). School bullying has been associated with incidents of student suicide and suicidal thoughts and behaviour in Canada and internationally (Kim, Koh, & Leventhal, 2005; Pepler, German, Craig, & Yamada, 2011; Rios-Ellis, Bellamy, & Shoji, 2000).

Unlike the pattern for bullying, the likelihood of being bullied decreases steadily. As children get older, most of them may learn how to discourage bullying, leaving a smaller pool of available victims (Pellegrini & Long, 2002). Most victims are small, passive, weak, and submissive and may blame themselves for being bullied. Other victims are provocative; they goad their attackers, and they may even attack other children themselves (Berger, 2007; Veenstra et al., 2005).

Risk factors for victimization seem to be similar across cultures (Schwartz, Chang, & Farver, 2001). Victims do not fit in. They tend to be anxious, depressed, cautious, quiet, and submissive; to cry easily; or to be argumentative and provocative (Veenstra et al., 2005). They have few friends and may live in harsh, punitive family environments (Nansel et al., 2001; Schwartz, Dodge, Pettit, Bates, & Conduct Problems Prevention Research Group, 2000). In a study of 5,749 Canadian children, those who were overweight were most likely to become either victims or bullies (Janssen, Craig, Boyce, & Pickett, 2004).

Bullying, especially emotional bullying, is harmful to both bullies and victims—and can even be fatal (Berger, 2007). Bullies are at increased risk of delinquency, crime, or alcohol abuse. In the wave of school shootings since 1994, the perpetrators often had been victims

Nova Scotia teen Rehtaeh Parsons attempted to commit suicide in April 2013, after an alleged gang rape and repeated bullying. Parsons was taken off life support four days after her suicide attempt.

of bullying (Anderson, Kaufman, et al., 2001). Victims of chronic bullying tend to develop behaviour problems. They may become more aggressive themselves or may become depressed (Veenstra et al., 2005). Furthermore, frequent bullying affects the school atmosphere, leading to widespread underachievement, alienation from school, stomach aches and headaches, reluctance to go to school, and frequent absences (Berger, 2007). School authorities and provincial ministries have enacted policies and laws to combat bullying, such as the Ontario's *Safe Schools Act*.

Programs to disseminate information about effective strategies for prevention and intervention, like PREVNet, can be effective in translating what we know about effective bullying prevention programs to practitioners. Programs like Roots of Empathy (Santos, Chartier, Whalen, Chateau, & Boyd, 2011), WITS (Walk Away, Ignore, Talk It Out, and Seek Help; Leadbeater & Sukhawathanakul, 2011) for early elementary grades, and Steps to Respect, a program for third to sixth graders, involve multiple components, aiming to (1) increase staff awareness and responsiveness to bullying, (2) teach students social and emotional skills, and (3) foster socially responsible beliefs to reduce peer victimization and bullying. A randomized controlled study of 1,023 third to sixth graders in Steps to Respect found a reduction in playground bullying and argumentative behaviour and an increase in harmonious interactions among children who participated in the program, as well as less bystander incitement to bullying (Frey et al., 2005). However, analysis of research done on a broad variety of these types of intervention programs has indicated that while the programs may enhance students' social competence and self-esteem, the impact on actual bullying behaviour is minimal (Merrell, Gueldner, Ross, & Isava, 2008). A larger-scale analysis of evaluations of school-based anti-bullying programs has shown that some programs can be effective in reducing bullying. The

Did you know?

Children seem to treat obesity as if it is contagious, perhaps leading to easier stigmatization of overweight kids (Klaczynski, 2008).

more effective programs were school-wide (involving the entire school community), were intensive, involved parents, included clear sanctions and behavioural intervention for bullying behaviour, and had improved playground supervision (Pepler, Craig, O'Connell, Atlas, & Charach, 2004; Ttofi & Farrington, 2011).

Ask Yourself

7. Name two positive and two negative effects of peer relations.

8. What is the most clearly identified gender difference between boys' and girls' play groups?
   a. loyalty
   b. activity level
   c. tendency to cooperate
   d. inclusion of all group members in joint activities

9. When a sociometric study is conducted at his school, Mark gets a large number of negative nominations and almost no positive nominations. This suggests that Mark is a(n) _____ child.

10. Children generally look for friends that
    a. are like them in age, sex, and interests.
    b. can help them climb socially.
    c. their parents approve of.
    d. are unique from them.

11. Children who have a hostile attributional bias
    a. tend to have a low IQ.
    b. are usually girls.
    c. chronically misinterpret social cues.
    d. are usually bullied.

SUMMARY

CHAPTER **13** PSYCHOSOCIAL DEVELOPMENT IN MIDDLE CHILDHOOD

LO1

Summarize the changes in self-esteem, self-concept, and emotional understanding and regulation.

- The self-concept becomes more realistic during middle childhood, when children form representational systems.
- According to Erikson, the chief source of self-esteem is children's view of their competence. This "virtue" develops through resolution of the crisis of industry versus inferiority.
- School-age children have internalized shame and pride and can better understand and control negative emotions.
- Empathy and prosocial behaviour increase.
- Emotional growth is affected by parents' reactions to displays of negative emotions.

LO2

Describe the influences of the family atmosphere, the family structure, and siblings on psychosocial development.

- School-age children spend less time with parents and are less close to them than before, but relationships with parents continue to be important. Culture influences family relationships and roles.
- The family environment has two major components: family atmosphere and family structure. Family atmosphere includes both emotional tone and economic well-being.
- Development of co-regulation may affect the way a family handles conflicts and discipline.
- The impact of a mother's employment depends on many factors concerning the child, the mother's work, and her feelings about it; whether she has a supportive partner; the family's socio-economic status; and the kind of care the child receives.
- Parents living in persistent poverty may have trouble providing effective discipline and monitoring and emotional support.

Continued

LO2

Describe the influences of the family atmosphere, the family structure, and siblings on psychosocial development.

Continued

- Many children today grow up in non-traditional family structures. Children tend to do better in traditional two-parent families than in divorced families, lone-parent families, and stepfamilies. The structure of the family, however, is less important than its effects on family atmosphere.
- The amount of conflict in a marriage and the likelihood of its continuing after divorce may influence whether children are better off if the parents stay together.
- Children living with only one parent are at heightened risk of behavioural and academic problems, in part related to socio-economic status.
- Boys tend to have more trouble than girls in adjusting to divorce and lone-parent living but tend to adjust better to the mother's remarriage.
- Studies have found positive outcomes in children living with gay or lesbian parents.
- Adopted children are generally well adjusted, though they face special challenges.
- Siblings learn about conflict resolution from their relationships with each other. Relationships with parents affect sibling relationships.

LO3

Summarize the positive and negative effects of peers, and the typical relationships with peers found in middle childhood.

- The peer group becomes more important in middle childhood. Peer groups generally consist of children who are similar in age, sex, ethnicity, and socio-economic status and who live near one another or go to school together.
- The peer group helps children develop social skills, allows them to test and adopt values independent of parents, gives them a sense of belonging, and helps develop the self-concept. It also may encourage conformity and prejudice.
- Popularity influences self-esteem and future adjustment. Popular children tend to have good cognitive abilities and social skills. Behaviours that affect popularity may be derived from family relationships and cultural values.
- Intimacy and stability of friendships increase during middle childhood. Boys tend to have more friends, whereas girls have closer friends.
- During middle childhood, aggression typically declines. Relational aggression becomes more common than overt aggression. Also, instrumental aggression generally gives way to hostile aggression, often with a hostile bias. Highly aggressive children tend to be unpopular, but this may change as children move into adolescence.
- Aggressiveness promoted by exposure to televised and other media violence can extend into adult life. Parents need to keep lines of communication open to ensure healthy use of new information technology.
- Middle childhood is a prime time for bullying; patterns may be established in kindergarten. Victims tend to be weak and submissive or argumentative and provocative and to have low self-esteem.

ANSWERS TO Ask Yourself

Answers: 1—Changes that occur in children's self-concepts include their becoming more comprehensive, realistic, and balanced; 2—b; 3—c; 4—d; 5—When all other factors are held equal, children tend to do best in families with two continuously married parents, regardless of whether they are adoptive or gay parents; 6—a; 7—Positive influences include the development of skills needed for sociability and intimacy, a sense of belonging, a sense of identity, learning to get along with others, and emotional security. Negative influences include the reinforcement of prejudice and the fostering of antisocial tendencies; 8—b; 9—rejected; 10—a; 11—c

connect **LEARNSMART** **SMARTBOOK**

For more information on the resources available from McGraw-Hill Ryerson, go to **www.mcgrawhill.ca/he/solutions**.

PHYSICAL DEVELOPMENT AND HEALTH IN

WHAT'S TO COME

Adolescence

Puberty

The Brain

Physical and Mental Health

"It was so embarrassing," Sara wrote in her diary. "I went shopping with Mom today for my first bra, and she kept picking up bras and just basically shouting—'Do you like this one? What about this one?'—and she just would not stop. She drives me nuts. It's like she goes out of her way to embarrass me. We finally found one and brought it home and I put it on and it just feels weird." Sara, stopped, chewing thoughtfully on the tip of her pen. "It's just all so weird," she finally wrote. Sara, like all typical girls, had hit puberty, and embarked upon life's next chapter: adolescence.

In this chapter, we address the physical transformations of adolescence and how they affect young people's feelings. We consider the impact of early or late maturation. We discuss health issues associated with this time of life, and we address a variety of risks, including eating disorders, depression, and mortality.

ADOLESCENCE

AS YOU READ

LO1 Define adolescence.
LO2 Summarize the physical changes of adolescence and their psychological impact.
LO3 Describe brain development in adolescence and how it impacts behaviour.
LO4 Summarize common health problems and risks of adolescence.

Adolescence

In most modern societies, the passage from childhood to adulthood is marked not by a single event, but by a long period known as **adolescence**—a developmental transition that involves physical, cognitive, emotional, and social changes and takes varying forms in different social, cultural, and economic settings (Larson & Wilson, 2004). In *CHILD*, we define adolescence as encompassing the years between 11 and 20.

ADOLESCENCE AS A SOCIAL CONSTRUCTION

Adolescence is a social construction. In preindustrial societies, children entered the adult world when they matured physically or when they began a vocational apprenticeship. Not until the twentieth century was adolescence defined as a separate stage of life in the Western world. Today, adolescence is global concept, though it may take different forms in different cultures. In most parts of the world, entry into adulthood takes longer and is less clearcut than in the past. Puberty begins earlier than it used to, and entrance into a vocation occurs later, often requiring longer periods of education or vocational training to prepare for adult responsibilities. Marriage with its attendant responsibilities typically comes later as well (Larson & Wilson, 2004).

A TIME OF OPPORTUNITIES AND RISKS

Adolescence offers opportunities for growth, not only in physical dimensions but also in cognitive and social

competence, autonomy, self-esteem, and intimacy. Young people who have supportive connections with parents, school, and community tend to develop in a positive, healthful way (Canadian Institute for Health Information [CIHI], 2005; Youngblade et al., 2007). However, Canadian adolescents today face hazards to their physical and mental well-being, including high death rates from accidents, homicide, and suicide (Eaton et al., 2008; Public Health Agency of Canada, 2008b; Statistics Canada, 2011h).

Risky behaviours may reflect immaturity of the adolescent brain, but surveys of high school students reveal encouraging trends. Since the 1990s, students have become less likely to use alcohol or tobacco, to ride in a car without wearing a seat belt or to ride with a driver who has been drinking, to carry weapons, to have sexual intercourse or to have it without condoms, or to attempt suicide (Centers for Disease Control and Prevention [CDC], 2006c; Eaton et al., 2008; Freeman et al., 2011; Paglia & Adlaf, 2003). Avoidance of such risky behaviours increases the chances that young people will come through the adolescent years in good physical and mental health.

adolescence Developmental transition between childhood and adulthood entailing major physical, cognitive, and psychosocial changes.

Ask Yourself

1. Adolescence is best thought of as
   a. a biological stage.
   b. a social construction.
   c. the first stage of adulthood.
   d. a universal stage of development.

2. Name two possible opportunities for growth and two risks of adolescence.

THE GLOBALIZATION OF ADOLESCENCE

Young people today live in a global neighbour-hood, a web of interconnections and interdependencies. Goods, information, electronic images, songs, entertainment, and fads sweep almost instantaneously around the planet. Western youth dance to Latin rhythms, and Arabic girls draw their images of romance from Indian cinema. Maori youth in New Zealand listen to African-American rap music to symbolize their separation from adult society. Adolescence is no longer solely a Western phenomenon. Globalization and modernization have set in motion societal changes the world over.

Globalization of adolescence does *not* mean that adolescence is the same the world over. The strong hand of culture shapes its meaning differently in different societies. In Canada, adolescents are spending less time with their parents than before and confide in them less, but most continue to be emotionally connected with their parents (Doyle & Moretti, 2000). In India, adolescents may wear Western clothing and use computers, but they maintain strong family ties, and their life decisions often are influenced by traditional Hindu values. In Western countries, teenage girls strive to be as thin as possible. In Niger and other African countries, obesity is considered beautiful.

In many non-Western countries, adolescent boys and girls seem to live in two separate worlds. In parts of the Middle East, Latin America, Africa, and Asia, puberty brings more restrictions on girls, whose virginity must be protected to uphold family status and ensure girls' marriageability. Boys, on the other hand, gain more freedom and mobility, and their sexual exploits are tolerated by parents and admired by peers.

Additionally, puberty heightens preparation for gender roles, which, for girls in most parts of the world, means preparation for domesticity. In Laos, a girl may spend 2½ hours a day husking, washing, and steaming rice. In Istanbul, a girl must learn the proper way to serve tea when a suitor comes to call. In some cultures, girls are expected to spend most of their time helping at home.

This traditional pattern is changing in some parts of the developing world, as women's employment and self-reliance become financial necessities. During the past quarter-century, the advent of public education has enabled more girls to go to school, breaking down some of the taboos and restrictions on feminine activities. Better-educated girls tend to marry later and have fewer children, enabling them to seek skilled employment in the new technological society.

Cultural change is complex; it can be both liberating and challenging. Today's adolescents are charting a new course, not always certain where it will lead.

Puberty

An important physical change in adolescence is the onset of **puberty**, the process that leads to sexual maturity, or fertility—the ability to reproduce. Puberty involves dramatic biological changes. In the following section, we discuss the hormonal changes that mark the beginning of puberty, and then focus on the changes that occur during that period. Lastly, we discuss the psychological effects of early and late maturation.

HOW PUBERTY BEGINS: HORMONAL CHANGES

Sara got her first bra when outward signs of puberty—breast development, in her case—became apparent. However, these changes were part of a long, complex process of maturation that begins even before birth.

Puberty results from the production of various hormones. An increase in gonadotropin-releasing hormone (GnRH) in the hypothalamus leads to a rise in two key reproductive hormones: follicle-stimulating hormone (FSH) and luteinizing hormone (LH). In girls, increased levels of FSH leads to the onset of menstruation. In boys, LH initiates the secretion of testosterone and androstenedione (Buck Louis et al., 2008). Puberty is marked by two stages: (1) the activation of the adrenal glands and (2) the maturing of the sex organs a few years later.

The first stage of puberty occurs between ages 6 and 8. During this stage, the adrenal glands located above the kidneys secrete gradually increasing levels of androgens, principally dehydroepiandrosterone (DHEA) (Susman & Rogol, 2004). By age 10, levels of DHEA are 10 times

puberty Process by which a person attains sexual maturity and the ability to reproduce.

what they were between ages 1 and 4. DHEA influences the growth of pubic, axillary (underarm), and facial hair. It also contributes to faster body growth, oilier skin, and the development of body odour.

The maturing of the sex organs triggers a second burst of DHEA production, which then rises to adult levels (Herdt & McClintock, 2000). In this second stage, a girl's ovaries increase their output of estrogen, which stimulates growth of female genitals and development of breasts and pubic and underarm hair. In boys, the testes increase the manufacture of androgens, particularly testosterone, which stimulate growth of male genitals, muscle mass, and body hair. Boys and girls have both types of hormones, but girls have higher levels of estrogen, and boys have higher levels of androgens. In girls, testosterone influences growth of the clitoris as well as of the bones and of pubic and axillary hair (Figure 14.1).

The precise time when this rush of hormonal activity begins seems to depend on reaching a critical amount of body fat necessary for successful reproduction, at least in girls. Thus, girls with a higher percentage of body fat in early childhood and those who experience unusual weight gain between ages 5 and 9 tend to show earlier pubertal development (Davison, Susman, & Birch, 2003; Lee et al., 2007). Studies suggest that an accumulation of leptin, a hormone associated with obesity, may be the link between body fat and earlier puberty (Kaplowitz, 2008).

Regulation of Human Puberty Onset and Progression

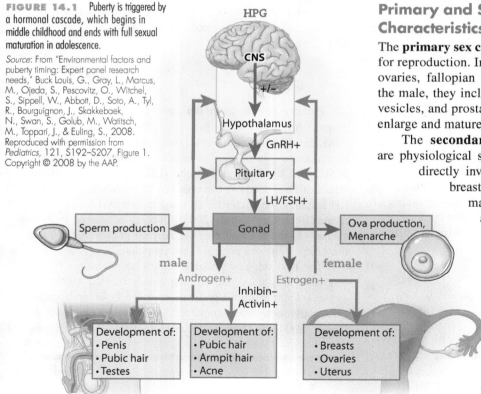

Increased levels of leptin may signal the pituitary and sex glands to increase their secretion of hormones (Susman & Rogol, 2004).

TIMING, SIGNS, AND SEQUENCE OF PUBERTY AND SEXUAL MATURITY

Changes that herald puberty typically begin at age 8 in girls and age 9 in boys (Susman & Rogol, 2004), but a wide range of ages exists for various changes (Figure 14.2). Recently, pediatrician and national longitudinal survey reports have indicated a significant number of girls with breast budding before age 8, and earlier and quicker progress through puberty for girls than for boys, with girls being over six times as likely as boys to have entered puberty by the age of 13 (Arim, Shapka, Dahinten, & Willms, 2007; Slyper, 2006). The pubertal process typically takes about three to four years for both sexes. Canadian boys and girls in families with low socio-economic status (SES), as well as those living with a stepfather, generally enter puberty earlier than others (Arim et al., 2007).

Primary and Secondary Sex Characteristics

The **primary sex characteristics** are the organs necessary for reproduction. In the female, the sex organs include the ovaries, fallopian tubes, uterus, clitoris, and vagina. In the male, they include the testes, penis, scrotum, seminal vesicles, and prostate gland. During puberty, these organs enlarge and mature.

The **secondary sex characteristics** (Table 14.1) are physiological signs of sexual maturation that do not directly involve the sex organs, for example, the breasts of females and the broad shoulders of males. Other secondary sex characteristics are changes in the voice and skin texture, muscular development, and the growth of pubic, facial, axillary, and body hair.

primary sex characteristics Organs directly related to reproduction, which enlarge and mature during adolescence.

secondary sex characteristics Physiological signs of sexual maturation (such as breast development and growth of body hair) that do not involve the sex organs.

FIGURE 14.2

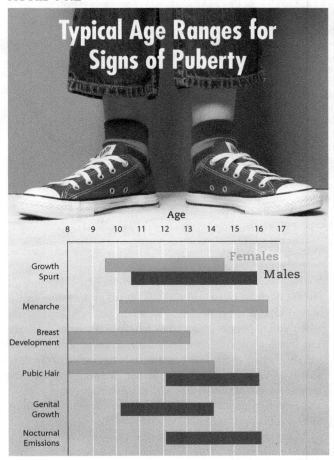

Source: From Fig. 11.4, p. 305 in *Human Development Across the Lifespan*, 7th Ed. By John Dacey, John Travers, and Lisa Fiore. Copyright © 2009 The McGraw-Hill Companies, Inc. Reprinted with permission.

Signs of Puberty

The first external signs of puberty typically are breast tissue and pubic hair in girls and enlargement of the testes in boys (Susman & Rogol, 2004). A girl's nipples enlarge and protrude; the areolae, the pigmented areas surrounding the nipples, enlarge; and the breasts assume first a conical and then a rounded shape.

Pubic hair, at first straight and silky, eventually becomes coarse, dark, and curly. It appears in different patterns in males and females. Adolescent boys are usually happy to see hair on the face and chest, but girls are usually dismayed at the appearance of even a slight amount of hair on the face or around the nipples, though this is normal.

The voice deepens, especially in boys, partly in response to the growth of the larynx and partly in response to the production of male hormones. The skin becomes coarser and oilier. Increased activity of the sebaceous glands may give rise to pimples and blackheads. Acne is more common in boys and seems related to increased amounts of testosterone.

adolescent growth spurt Sharp increase in height and weight that precedes sexual maturity.

TABLE 14.1 Secondary Sex Characteristics

Girls	Boys
Breasts	Pubic hair
Pubic hair	Axillary (underarm) hair
Axillary (underarm) hair	Muscular development
Changes in voice	Facial hair
Changes in skin	Changes in voice
Increased width and depth of pelvis	Changes in skin
Muscular development	Broadening of shoulders

The Adolescent Growth Spurt

The **adolescent growth spurt** generally begins in girls between ages 9½ and 14½, on average at about 10, and in boys, between 10½ and 16, on average at 12 or 13 (Figure 14.3). It typically lasts about two years; soon after it ends, the young person reaches sexual maturity, generally defined as the age at which an organism can reproduce. Both growth hormone and the sex hormones, androgens and estrogen, contribute to this normal pubertal growth (Susman & Rogol, 2004).

Because girls' growth spurt usually occurs two years earlier than that of boys, girls between ages 11 and 13 tend to be taller, heavier, and stronger than boys the same age. After their growth spurt, boys are again larger, as before. Girls usually reach full height at age 15 and boys by age 17. Boys and girls grow differently, not only in rate of growth but also

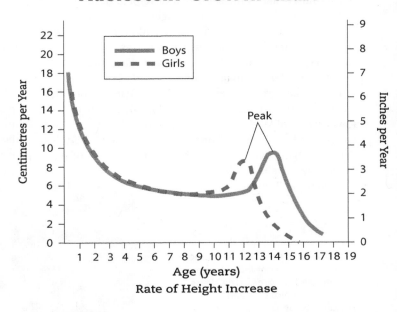

FIGURE 14.3 The adolescent growth spurt begins slightly earlier in girls than in boys and typically lasts about two years.

Source: Reprinted by permission from "Rate of Height Increase," p. 44, Introduction to Coaching Theory, written and edited by Peter J.L. Thompson. Copyright © International Amateur Athletic Federation, 1991.

Chapter 14 *Physical Development and Health in Adolescence* • **289** in form and shape. A boy becomes larger overall: his shoulders wider, his legs longer relative to his trunk, and his forearms longer relative to his upper arms and his height. A girl's pelvis widens to make child-bearing easier, and layers of fat accumulate under her skin, giving her a more rounded appearance. Fat accumulates twice as rapidly in girls as in boys (Susman & Rogol, 2004).

Because each of these changes follows its own timetable, parts of the body may be out of proportion for a while. The result is the familiar teenage gawkiness that accompanies unbalanced, accelerated growth.

The striking physical changes of puberty have psychological ramifications. Most young teenagers are more concerned about their appearance than about any other aspect of themselves, and some do not like what they see in the mirror. As we discuss in a subsequent section, these attitudes can lead to eating problems.

Signs of Sexual Maturity

The maturation of the reproductive organs brings the beginning of menstruation in girls and the production of sperm in boys. The principal sign of sexual maturity in boys is the production of sperm. The first ejaculation, or **spermarche**, occurs at an average age of 13. A boy may wake up to find a wet spot or a dried, hardened spot on the sheets—the result of a *nocturnal emission*, an involuntary ejaculation of semen (commonly referred to as a wet dream).

The principal sign of sexual maturity in girls is *menstruation*, a monthly shedding of tissue from the lining of the womb. Girl's first menstruation, called **menarche**, occurs fairly late in the sequence of female development; its normal timing can vary from ages 10 to 16½ (refer to Figure 14.2). On average, girls in Canadian provinces with smaller foreign-born populations, such as Quebec, New Brunswick, and Prince Edward Island, have higher rates of early menarche than provinces with larger foreign-born populations, such as Ontario and British Columbia. Canadian girls in higher-income families tend to have lower rates of early menarche, possibly because lower stress and lower rates of obesity experienced by adolescents in higher-income families can delay onset of menarche—see below (Al-Sahab, Ardern, Hamadeh, & Tamim, 2010).

Influences on Timing of Puberty

On the basis of historical sources, developmental scientists have found a drop in the ages when puberty begins and when young people reach adult height and sexual maturity. The trend, which also involves increases in adult height and weight, began about 100 years ago. It has occurred in such places as Canada, the United States, Western Europe, and Japan (Anderson, Dallal, & Must, 2003; Arim et al., 2007), and better evidence exists for girls than for boys (Euling, Selevan, Pescovitz, & Skakkebaek, 2008).

One proposed explanation for this secular trend is a higher standard of living. Children who are healthier, better nourished, and better cared for might be expected to mature earlier and grow bigger (Slyper, 2006). Thus, the average age of sexual maturity is earlier in developed countries than in developing countries. Because of the role of body fat in triggering puberty, a contributing factor in Canada and the United States during the last part of the twentieth century may be the increase in obesity among young girls (Lee et al., 2007).

A combination of genetic, physical, emotional, and contextual influences may affect the timing of menarche. Twin studies have documented the heritability of age of menarche (Mendle et al., 2006). Other research has found that the age of a girl's first menstruation tends to be similar to that of her mother if nutrition and standard of living remain stable from one generation to the next (Susman & Rogol, 2004). In several studies, family conflict was associated with early menarche, whereas parental warmth, harmonious family relationships, and paternal involvement in child-rearing were related to later menarche (Belsky et al., 2007; Mendle et al., 2006). On the other hand, family disruption and residential separation from the father (Tither & Ellis, 2008), as well as child maltreatment (Mendle, Leve, Van Ryzin, Natsuaki, & Ge, 2011), have been associated with earlier menarche.

spermarche A boy's first ejaculation.

menarche A girl's first menstruation.

How might family relationships affect pubertal development? While some researchers have suggested that pheromones—odorous chemicals that attract mates—from unrelated males may be responsible (Ellis & Garber, 2000), it is more likely that the association is mediated via stress. In other words, stress is what triggers the early puberty. Girls raised in homes with high levels of stress, regardless of the source of stress, tend to reach menarche earlier (Mendle et al., 2011).

IMPLICATIONS OF EARLY AND LATE MATURATION

The onset of puberty can vary by as many as five years among normal boys and girls (Golub et al., 2008). Early maturation increases the likelihood of accelerated skeletal maturation and psychosocial difficulties and has been linked to adult health issues, including reproductive tract cancers, obesity, type 2 diabetes, and cardiovascular disease (Golub et al., 2008). Other effects of early and late maturation vary in boys and girls, and the timing of maturation tends to influence adolescent mental health and health-related behaviours in adulthood (Susman & Rogol, 2004).

Research on early maturing boys has had mixed results. Some studies found that most boys who mature early seem to be better adjusted than late maturing boys (Graber, Brooks-Gunn, & Warren, 2006). Other studies have found early maturing boys to be more anxious or aggressive, more worried about being liked, more cautious, more reliant on others, and more bound by rules and routines (Ge, Conger, & Elder, 2001b). Additionally, early maturing boys may be at greater risk for substance use and delinquent behaviour (Westling, Andrews, Hampson, & Peterson, 2008). Early maturing boys demonstrate a higher incidence of conduct and behavioural disorders during adolescence (Golub et al., 2008). Late maturing boys, however, have been found to feel more inadequate, self-conscious, rejected, and dominated; to be more dependent, aggressive, insecure, or depressed; to have more conflict with parents and more trouble in school; and to have poorer social and coping skills and higher risk for aggression problems (Graber, Lewinsohn, Seeley, & Brooks-Gunn, 1997; Sontag, Graber, & Clemans, 2011).

Girls are generally happier if their timing is about the same as that of their peers. Early maturing girls are at increased risk of anxiety and depression; disruptive behaviour; eating disorders; early smoking, drinking, and substance abuse; precocious sexual activity; early pregnancy; and attempted suicide (Deardorff, Gonzales, Christopher, Roosa, & Millsap, 2005; Dick, Rose, Kaprio, & Viken, 2000; Golub et al., 2008; Graber et al., 1997; Japel, Tremblay, McDuff, & Willms, 2002; Susman & Rogol, 2004). They have difficulty coping with rejection and tend to use fewer problem-solving skills than their peers (Sontag, Graber, Brooks-Gunn, & Warren, 2008). However, this is less true of girls with no history of behaviour problems

(Susman & Rogol, 2004). Among both boys and girls, early maturers tend to be vulnerable to risky behaviour and the influence of deviant peers (Orr & Ingersoll, 1995; Susman & Rogol, 2004).

It is hard to generalize about the psychological effects of pubertal timing because they depend on how the adolescent and other people in his or her world interpret the accompanying changes. Contextual factors such as ethnicity, school, and neighbourhood can make a difference. For example, early maturing girls are more likely to show problem behaviour in mixed-gender schools than in all-girl schools and in disadvantaged urban communities than in rural or middle-class urban communities (Dick et al., 2000; Ge, Brody, Conger, Simons, & Murry, 2002).

Ask Yourself

3. What are the two stages of puberty?

4. What are secondary sexual characteristics?
   a. male sexual characteristics
   b. female sexual characteristics
   c. sexual organs necessary for reproduction
   d. physiological signs of sexual maturation that do not directly involve the sex organs

5. Overall, early maturation is
   a. strongly associated with positive outcomes for both girls and boys.
   b. strongly associated with positive outcomes for girls, and risks for boys.
   c. strongly associated with positive outcomes for boys, and risks for girls.
   d. associated with risks for both boys and girls.

The Brain

"I got in huge trouble today," Sara wrote, "I'm grounded for pretty much forever. Siobhan asked me to cut class with her and even though I knew I would get in trouble, I did it anyway. I don't know *what* I was thinking."

Not long ago, most scientists believed that the brain was fully mature by puberty. Now imaging studies reveal that the adolescent brain is still a work in progress. Dramatic changes in brain structures involved in emotions, judgment, organization of behaviour, and self-control take place between puberty and young adulthood.

THE FRONTAL CORTEX

Adolescents process information differently than adults do. To understand the immaturity of the adolescent brain, we need to look at changes in the structure and composition of the frontal cortex. First, a steady

Did you know?

Canada's *Youth Criminal Justice Act* was created in April 2003 to treat young offenders (aged 12 to 17 years) differently from adults, recognizing that youth are still maturing and should be held to a different standard of responsibility than adults. When appropriate, authorities do not involve courts, using procedures to promote healthy development while also responding appropriately to crime. These procedures include involving the individual repairing harm done, allowing victims to participate in decisions, making consequences appropriate to the seriousness of the offence, and encouraging the involvement of families, victims, and other members of the community. This has reduced the percentage of youth offenders formally charged from 63 percent in 1999 to 42 percent in 2010 (Department of Justice, 2013).

ENVIRONMENTAL INFLUENCES

Cognitive stimulation in adolescence makes a critical difference in the brain's development. The process is bidirectional: A young person's activities and experiences determine which neuronal connections will be retained and strengthened, and this in turn supports further cognitive growth in those areas (Kuhn, 2006). "Adolescents who 'exercise' their brains by learning to order their thoughts, understand abstract concepts, and control their impulses are laying the neural foundations that will serve them for the rest of their lives" (ACT for Youth, 2002, p. 1). Alternatively, adolescent drug use can have particularly devastating effects depending on how drugs interact with the growing brain.

increase in white matter, nerve fibres that connect distant portions of the brain, permits faster transmission of information. In adolescence, this process continues in the frontal lobes (ACT for Youth Upstate Center of Excellence, 2002; Blakemore & Choudhury, 2006; Kuhn, 2006; National Institute of Mental Health [NIMH], 2001). Additionally, there is a major spurt in the production of grey matter in the frontal lobes (Blakemore & Choudhury, 2006; Kuhn, 2006). Second, the pruning of unused dendritic connections during childhood results in a reduction in the density of grey matter, or nerve cells, increasing the brain's efficiency. This process begins in the rear portions of the brain and moves forward. Thus, by mid- to late adolescence, young people have fewer but stronger, smoother, and more effective neuronal connections, making cognitive processing more efficient (Kuhn, 2006). However, this process takes time, and for the most part, it has not yet reached the frontal lobes by adolescence. Underdevelopment of frontal cortical systems associated with motivation, impulsivity, and addiction may help explain why adolescents tend to seek thrills and novelty and why many of them find it hard to focus on long-term goals (Bjork et al., 2004; Chambers, Taylor, & Potenza, 2003).

Ask Yourself

6. In adolescence, there is continued development of
   a. the frontal lobes.
   b. the temporal lobes.
   c. the grey matter of the brain.
   d. the white matter of the brain, but only in girls.

Physical and Mental Health

"I really like playing soccer," Sara wrote in her diary, "but I don't know if I want to play it anymore. But I'm afraid that if I stop I might get fat. But I *hate* getting up early on Saturday—I'm always *so* sleepy in the morning now. I don't know. I guess I'll see if any of my friends are doing it too."

Some of the lifestyle patterns that Sara sets down now will have effects many years later. Many health problems are preventable, stemming from lifestyle or poverty. Health concerns related to adolescence include physical fitness, sleep needs, eating disorders, drug abuse, depression, and causes of death in adolescence.

PHYSICAL ACTIVITY

Exercise, or lack of it, affects both physical and mental health. The benefits of regular exercise include improved strength and endurance, healthier bones and muscles, weight control, and reduced anxiety and stress, as well as increased self-esteem, school grades, and well-being. Exercise also decreases the likelihood that an adolescent will participate in risky behaviour. Even moderate physical activity has health benefits if done regularly for at least 30 minutes almost every day. A sedentary lifestyle may result in increased risk of obesity and type 2 diabetes, both growing problems among adolescents. It also can lead to increased likelihood of heart disease and cancer in adulthood (Canadian Paediatric Society, Advisory Committee on Healthy Active Living for Children and Youth, 2002; Carnethon, Gulati, & Greenland, 2005; Centers for Disease Control and Prevention, 2000a; National Center for Health Statistics [NCHS], 2004; Nelson & Gordon-Larsen, 2006).

Unfortunately, only a third of Canadian youth are active enough for optimal health and development

292 • CHILD

(Canadian Paediatric Society, 2002), and only about 7 percent engage in the recommended minimum of 60 minutes of vigorous physical activity a day (Barnes et al., 2012; Canadian Society for Exercise Physiology, 2011a, 2011b; Colley et al., 2011; Tremblay et al., 2011b); the proportion of young people who are inactive increases throughout the high school years (Freeman et al., 2011). Adolescents show a steep drop in physical activity upon entering puberty, shifting from an average of 26 and 20 percent of boys and girls, respectively, having at least one hour per day of vigorous physical activity in Grade 6 to 19 and 11 percent by Grade 10 (Freeman et al., 2011). Canadian adolescents exercise less frequently and are less involved in organized sport than in past years, but rank about in the middle in comparison with adolescents in other industrialized countries (CDC, 2000a; Clark, 2008; Hickman, Roberts, & de Matos, 2000; King, Boyce, & King, 1999). Adolescents from more affluent families tend to have healthier diets and to be more physically active (Hanson & Chen, 2007), and Aboriginal-background adolescents tend to be more physically active than non-Aboriginal adolescents (Findlay, 2011).

SLEEP NEEDS AND PROBLEMS

Sleep deprivation among adolescents has been called an epidemic (Hansen, Janssen, Schiff, Zee, & Dubocovich, 2005). A study by the National Sleep Foundation (2006) found that almost half of adolescents in the U.S. get less than eight hours of sleep on school nights and over half report being sleepy during the day. An average of 40 percent of adolescents, mostly boys, in a study of 28 industrialized countries reported morning sleepiness at least once a week, and 22 percent said they are sleepy most days (Scheidt, Overpeck, Whatt, & Aszmann, 2000). About 25 percent of Canadian adolescents report having trouble getting to sleep more than once a week, and girls tend to have more difficulties in falling asleep than boys (King et al., 1999). Among Canadians aged 15 to 24 years, 12 percent of females and 9 percent of males report experiencing insomnia (Tjepkema, 2005).

There are many benefits to regular exercise, including improved strength and endurance, reduced anxiety and stress, and increased self-esteem, school grades, and well-being.

WHAT DO YOU DO?

Physical Education Teacher

Physical education teachers instruct students on caring for their bodies and physical health and guide them through exercise classes. At the elementary level, physical education teachers focus on developing students' skills and teamwork abilities. At the secondary level, physical education teachers typically offer defined programs to appeal to student interests, including both team and individual sports. Programs may include physical activities such as dance, yoga, and Pilates. Often, physical education teachers also serve as sport team coaches. To become a physical education teacher, you typically need a bachelor's degree in health and physical education. Certification varies by province. To learn more about becoming a physical education teacher, visit www.phecanada.ca.

As they get older, children generally go to sleep later and sleep less on school days. The average adolescent who slept more than 10 hours at night at age 9 sleeps less than eight hours at age 16 (Eaton et al., 2008; Hoban, 2004). Actually, adolescents need as much or more sleep than when they were younger (Hoban, 2004; Iglowstein et al., 2003). Sleeping in on weekends does not make up for the loss of sleep on school nights (Hoban, 2004; Sadeh et al., 2000). A pattern of late bedtimes and oversleeping in the mornings can contribute to insomnia, a problem that often begins in late childhood or adolescence (Hoban, 2004).

Sleep deprivation can sap motivation and cause irritability, and concentration and school performance can suffer. Sleepiness also can be deadly for adolescent drivers. Studies have found that young people aged 16 to 29 are most likely to be involved in crashes caused by the driver falling asleep (Millman, Working Group on Sleepiness in Adolescents/ Young Adults, & AAP Committee on Adolescents, 2005). A study of sleep patterns of adolescents in Ontario found that trouble sleeping was associated with attention problems, anxiety and depression, and withdrawal (Coulombe, Reid, Boyle, & Racine, 2011).

Why do adolescents stay up late? They may need to do homework, want to talk to or text friends or surf the Web, or simply wish to act grown up. While that is true, sleep experts now recognize that biological changes are also behind adolescents' sleep problems. The timing of secretion of the hormone melatonin is a gauge of when the brain is ready for sleep. After puberty, this secretion takes place later at night (Hagenauer, Perryman, Lee, & Carskadon,

Sleep deprivation among adolescents is reaching epidemic proportions.

2009). But adolescents still need just as much sleep as before; so when they go to bed later than younger children, they need to get up later as well. Yet most secondary schools start earlier than elementary schools. Their schedules are out of sync with students' biological rhythms (Hoban, 2004). Teenagers tend to be least alert and most stressed early in the morning and more alert in the afternoon (Hansen et al., 2005). Starting school later, or at least offering difficult courses later in the day, would help improve students' concentration.

Did you know?

Lying down is more restful, but laying your head down on your desk to sleep—providing your teacher lets you get away with it—still provides benefits to mental functioning (Zhao, Zhang, Fu, Tang, & Zhao, 2010).

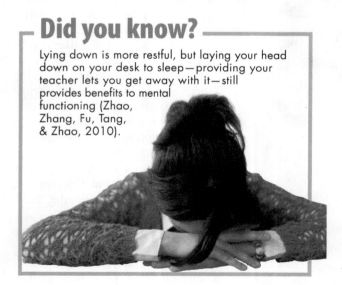

NUTRITION AND EATING DISORDERS

Good nutrition is important to support the rapid growth of adolescence and to establish healthy eating habits that will last through adulthood. Unfortunately, Canadian adolescents eat fewer fruits and vegetables—less than 50 percent eat one or more servings a day—and consume more foods

that are high in cholesterol, fat, and calories and low in nutrients than is recommended for healthy growth (Canadian Institute of Child Health [CICH], 2000; Freeman et al., 2011; King et al., 1999).

Worldwide, poor nutrition is most frequent in economically depressed or isolated populations but also may result from concern with body image and weight control (Vereecken & Maes, 2000). Eating disorders, including obesity, are most prevalent in industrialized societies, where food is abundant and attractiveness is equated with slimness; but these disorders appear to be increasing in non-Western countries as well (Makino, Tsuboi, & Dennerstein, 2004).

Obesity

Obesity among Canadian adolescents has tripled to 9 percent over the past 25 years, and overweight has more than doubled to 29 percent (Shields, 2005). Rates of overweight and obesity are similar to those of U.S. adolescents, although adolescent girls in Canada are less likely than their U.S. counterparts to be overweight or obese. Among older Canadian adolescents, obesity is more prevalent in those from middle-income families, compared with lower- and higher-income families (Shields, 2005). Aboriginal youth have a higher obesity/overweight rate than non-Aboriginal Canadians, whereas youth of Asian origin tend to have lower rates (Shields, 2005).

Although overweight teenagers in Canada tend to experience the same rate of chronic health conditions as their peers, they are more likely to perceive their health as poorer, engage in sedentary behaviour, and eat a less healthful diet (Shields, 2005). They have difficulty attending school, performing household chores, or engaging in strenuous activity or personal care (Shields, 2005; Swallen, Reither, Haas, & Meier, 2005). They are more likely to report emotional problems, and less likely to report high levels of emotional well-being (Freeman et al., 2011). They are at heightened risk of high cholesterol, hypertension, and diabetes (NCHS, 2005), which can be difficult to treat in adolescence, as changes in hormone levels can impact insulin needs (Public Health Agency of Canada, 2011c). They tend to become obese adults, subject to a variety of physical, social, and psychological risks (Patton et al., 2011).

Genetic and other factors, such as faulty regulation of metabolism and, at least in girls, depressive symptoms and having obese parents, can increase the likelihood of teenage obesity (Morrison et al., 2005; Stice, Presnell, Shaw, & Rohde, 2005). However, a study of 878 California 11- to 15-year-olds revealed that lack of exercise was the main risk factor for overweight in boys and girls (Patrick et al., 2004).

By Grade 10, about 20 percent of Canadian girls and 9 percent of boys report doing something to reduce weight, and these rates increase for overweight and obese adolescents (Freeman et al., 2011). Weight-loss

programs that use behavioural modification techniques to help adolescents make changes in diet and exercise have had some success. For many preadolescents and adolescents, however, dieting may be counterproductive. In a prospective three-year study of 8,203 girls and 6,769 boys aged 9 to 14, those who dieted gained more weight than those who did not diet (A. E. Field et al., 2003).

Body Image and Eating Disorders

Sometimes, a determination not to become overweight can result in problems more serious than overweight itself. Concern with body image may lead to obsessive efforts at weight control (Davison & Birch, 2001; Vereecken & Maes, 2000). This pattern is more common among girls than among boys.

Because of girls' normal increase in body fat during puberty, many girls become unhappy about their appearance, reflecting the cultural emphasis on women's physical attributes (Susman & Rogol, 2004). Girls' dissatisfaction with their bodies increases over the course of early to mid-adolescence, whereas boys, who are becoming more muscular, become more satisfied with their bodies (Bearman, Martinez, & Stice, 2006). By age 15, more than half the girls sampled in 16 countries were dieting or thought they should be (Vereecken & Maes, 2000). In Canada, only two-thirds of adolescents with healthy weights report feeling that their bodies are the right size; overall, 39 percent of Grade 10 girls report feeling their bodies are too fat, compared with 28 percent of boys (Freeman et al., 2011).

According to a large prospective cohort study, parental attitudes and media images play a greater part than peer influences in encouraging weight concerns. Girls who try to look like the unrealistically thin models they see in the media tend to develop excessive concern about weight and may develop eating disorders (Striegel-Moore & Bulik, 2007). In addition, both girls and boys who believe that thinness is important to their parents, especially to their fathers, tend to become constant dieters (A. E. Field et al., 2001). However, the idea that eating disorders are the result of cultural pressure to be thin is too simplistic; biological factors, including genetic factors, play an equally important role (Striegel-Moore & Bulik, 2007).

Excessive concern with weight control and body image may be a sign of anorexia nervosa or bulimia nervosa, both of which involve abnormal patterns of food intake. These chronic disorders occur worldwide, mostly in adolescent girls and young women.

ANOREXIA NERVOSA   An estimated 0.3 to 0.9 percent of adolescent girls and young women and a smaller but growing percentage of boys and men in Western countries have **anorexia nervosa** (Hoek, 2007; Hudson, Hiripi, Pope, & Kessler, 2007). People with anorexia have a distorted body image and, though typically severely underweight, think they are too fat. They are often good students but may be withdrawn or depressed and may engage in repetitive, perfectionist behaviour. They are extremely afraid of losing self-control and becoming overweight (AAP Committee on Adolescence, 2003; Martínez-González et al., 2003; Wilson, Grilo, & Vitousek, 2007). Early warning signs include determined, secret dieting; dissatisfaction after losing weight; setting new, lower weight goals after reaching an initial desired weight; excessive exercising; and interruption of regular menstruation.

Anorexia is, paradoxically, both deliberate and involuntary: An affected person deliberately refuses food needed for sustenance, yet cannot stop doing so even when rewarded or punished. These behaviour patterns have been traced back to medieval times and seem to have existed in all parts of the world. Thus, anorexia may be in part a reaction to societal pressure to be slender, but this does not seem to be the only factor or even a necessary one (Keel & Klump, 2003; Striegel-Moore & Bulik, 2007).

BULIMIA NERVOSA   **Bulimia nervosa** is an eating disorder that affects about 1 to 2 percent of international populations (Hudson et al., 2007; Wilson et al., 2007). A person with bulimia regularly goes on huge, short-lived eating binges (two hours or less) and then may try to purge the high caloric intake through self-induced vomiting, strict dieting or fasting, excessively vigorous exercise, or laxatives, enemas, or diuretics. These episodes occur at least once a week for at least three months (American Psychiatric Association, 2013). People with bulimia are usually within normal weight ranges, but they are obsessed with their weight and shape. They tend to have low self-esteem and may become overwhelmed with shame, self-contempt, and depression (Wilson et al., 2007; Wolfe, Hannon-Engel, & Mitchell, 2012).

There is some overlap between anorexia and bulimia; some people with anorexia have bulimic episodes, and some people with bulimia lose large amounts of weight ("Eating Disorders—Part I," 1997). Unlike anorexia, there is little evidence of bulimia either

anorexia nervosa   Eating disorder characterized by self-starvation and extreme weight loss.

bulimia nervosa   Eating disorder in which a person regularly eats huge quantities of food and then purges the body by laxatives, induced vomiting, fasting, or excessive exercise.

Katharine McPhee, a 2006 *American Idol* runner-up who is currently working as an actress and singer, struggled with bulimia.

historically or in cultures not subject to Western influence (Keel & Klump, 2003).

TREATMENT AND OUTCOMES OF EATING DISORDERS The immediate goal of treatment for anorexia is to get patients to eat and gain weight—goals that are often difficult to achieve given the strength of patients' beliefs about their bodies. One widely used treatment, recommended by the Canadian Paediatric Society, is a type of family therapy in which parents take control of their child's eating patterns. When the child begins to comply with parental directives, she (or he) may be given more age-appropriate autonomy (Findlay, Pinzon, Taddeo, Katzman, & Canadian Paediatric Society, Adolescent Health Committee, 2010). Cognitive behavioural therapy, which seeks to change a distorted body image and rewards eating with such privileges as being allowed to get out of bed and leave the room, may be part of the treatment (Wilson et al., 2007). Patients who show signs of severe malnutrition, are resistant to treatment, or do not make progress on an outpatient basis may be admitted to a hospital, where they can be given 24-hour nursing. Once their weight is stabilized, patients may enter less intensive daytime care (McCallum & Bruton, 2003).

Bulimia, too, is best treated with cognitive behavioural therapy (Wilson et al., 2007). Patients keep daily diaries of their eating patterns and are taught ways to avoid the temptation to binge. Individual, group, or family psychotherapy can help both anorexia and bulimia patients, usually after initial behaviour therapy has brought symptoms under control. Because these patients are at risk for depression and suicide, antidepressant drugs are often combined with psychotherapy (McCallum & Bruton, 2003), but evidence of their long-term effectiveness on either anorexia or bulimia is lacking (Wilson et al., 2007).

Mortality rates among those affected with anorexia nervosa have been estimated at about 10 percent of cases. Among the surviving anorexia patients, less than one-half make a full recovery and only one-third actually improve; 20 percent remain chronically ill (Steinhausen, 2002). It should also be noted that up to one-third of patients drop out of treatment before achieving an appropriate weight (McCallum & Bruton, 2003). Recovery rates from bulimia are a bit better and average 30 to 50 percent after cognitive behavioural therapy (Wilson et al., 2007).

SELF-INJURIOUS BEHAVIOUR

Non-suicidal self-harm, or self-injurious behaviour, is the intentional infliction of damage to one's own body without the intention to commit suicide. It is more common in adolescence than in adulthood; about 14 to 20 percent of Canadian adolescents report having experienced some form of self-injurious behaviour (Heath, Ross, Toste, Charlebois, & Nedecheva, 2009; Nixon, Cloutier, & Jansson, 2008). Self-injurious behaviours lie outside of accepted social norms (such as ear-piercing and tattooing) and include deliberate cutting, self-scratching, burning, and hitting, with cutting being the most prevalent form (Nixon et al., 2008). There are a variety of reasons why young people engage in this behaviour, mainly centring on coping with severe negative emotions (to reduce stress) and self-derogation—being highly critical or angry with oneself (as a form of self-punishment). Other reasons include social factors, such as modelling or social contagion (having a friend or family member who self-injured) and talking about self-injury with friends (Heath et al., 2009; Jarvi, Jackson, Swenson, & Crawford, 2013; Klonsky & Muehlenkamp, 2007), and having other health symptoms such as depression and attention problems (Nixon et al., 2008). Thinking about and attempting suicide are more likely among people who repeatedly self-injure (Whitlock et al., 2013). Of the individuals who self-injure, about half seek out professional help (Nixon et al., 2008). Effective interventions for self-injury focus on identifying, in a nonjudgmental way, the core issues that lead to the behaviour, and include learning skills for emotional regulation, behavioural therapies, and problem-solving techniques (Klonsky & Muehlenkamp, 2007).

DRUG USE

Although the great majority of adolescents do not abuse drugs, a significant minority do. **Substance abuse** is the harmful use of alcohol or other drugs. It can lead to **substance dependence**, or addiction, which may be physiological, psychological, or both and is likely to continue into adulthood.

substance abuse Repeated, harmful use of a substance, usually alcohol or other drugs.

substance dependence Addiction (physical or psychological, or both) to a harmful substance.

Trends in Drug Use

About 25 percent of Canadian adolescents have tried illicit drugs by the time they leave high school. An upsurge in drug use during the mid- to late 1990s accompanied a lessening of perceptions of its dangers and a softening of peer disapproval. However, that trend has begun to reverse (Table 14.2). Student use of drugs, especially central nervous stimulants like methamphetamine and cocaine, as well as LSD, ecstasy, psychoactive drugs, and marijuana has shown a gradual decline.

These findings come from the latest in a series of semi-annual surveys of adolescents, starting in 1977, of 9,288 students from Grades 7 to 12 in 181 schools across Ontario, by the Centre for Addiction and Mental Health [CAMH] (Paglia-Boak, Adlaf, & Mann, 2011). These surveys probably underestimate adolescent drug use because they are based on self-reports and do not reach high school dropouts, who are more likely to use drugs. Continued progress in eliminating drug abuse is slow because new drugs are continually introduced or rediscovered by a new generation, and young people do not necessarily generalize the adverse consequences of one drug to another (Johnston, O'Malley, Bachman, & Schulenberg, 2008). Current trends identified in the CAMH study have been found across the country (Freeman et al., 2011).

Alcohol, marijuana, and tobacco use among Canadian teenagers has followed a trend roughly parallel to that of harder drug use, with a dramatic rise during most of the 1990s followed by a smaller, gradual decline (Paglia-Boak et al., 2011; Freeman et al., 2011).

Alcohol

Alcohol is a potent, mind-altering drug with major effects on physical, emotional, and social well-being. Its use is a serious problem in many countries (Gabhainn & François, 2000). In 2011, 26 percent of Canadian Grade 8 students, 60 percent of students in Grade 10, and 78 percent of Grade 12 students said they had consumed alcohol at least once during the past year (Paglia-Boak et al., 2011). About 4 percent of high school seniors reported drinking three or more times a week, and 40 percent admitted to binge drinking—consuming five or more drinks on one occasion—in the four weeks prior to the survey (Paglia-Boak et al., 2011). A recent MRI-based study has revealed that binge drinking in teenagers may affect thinking and memory by damaging sensitive white matter in the brain (McQueeny et al., 2009). Binge drinkers are more likely than other students to report poor school performance and to engage in other risky behaviours (Miller, Naimi, Brewer, & Jones, 2007). In 2011, over 24 percent of high school students reported riding in the past year in a car driven by a person who had been drinking, 16 percent when the driver had taken drugs, and about 7 percent of Ontario students with driver's licences reported driving within an hour of drinking two or more drinks; although still high, these proportions have dropped significantly over the past decade (Paglia-Boak et al., 2011).

Adolescents are more vulnerable than adults to both immediate and long-term negative effects of alcohol on learning and memory (White, 2001). In one study, 15- and 16-year-old alcohol abusers who stopped drinking showed cognitive impairments weeks later in comparison with non-abusing peers (Brown, Tapert, Granholm, & Delis, 2000).

Marijuana

Despite the decline in marijuana use since 1999, it is still by far the most widely used illicit drug in Canada. In 2011, about 6 percent of students in Grade 8, 26 percent of Grade 10 students, and 36 percent of Grade 12 students admitted to having used it in the past year (Paglia-Boak et al., 2011).

TABLE 14.2 Substance Abuse Trends, 1999–2011 (percent using at least once in past year)

	1999	2001	2003	2005	2007	2009	2011	Changes from 1999 to 2011
Tobacco	28.4	23.1	19.2	14.4	11.9	11.7	8.7	Drop of 19.7%
Alcohol	66.0	63.9	66.2	62.0	61.2	58.2	54.9	Drop of 11.1%
Marijuana	28.0	28.6	29.6	26.5	25.6	25.6	22.0	Drop of 6%
Inhalants (glue or solvents)	8.9	7.2	7.0	6.0	6.4	6.0	5.6	Drop of 3.3%
Methamphetamine	5.1	4.1	4.4	2.7	1.8	1.6	1.0	Drop of 4.1%

Source: Paglia-Boak et al. (2011). © by The McGraw-Hill Companies, Inc. Reprinted by permission.

Marijuana smoke typically contains more than 400 carcinogens, and its potency has doubled in the past 25 years (National Institute on Drug Abuse [NIDA], 2008). Heavy use can damage the brain, heart, lungs, and immune system and cause nutritional deficiencies, respiratory infections, and other physical problems. It may lessen motivation, worsen depression, interfere with daily activities, and cause family problems. Marijuana use also can impede memory, thinking speed, learning, and school performance. It can lessen perception, alertness, attention span, judgment, and the motor skills needed to drive a vehicle and thus can contribute to traffic accidents (Messinis, Krypianidou, Maletaki, & Papathanasopoulos, 2006; Office of National Drug Control Policy, 2008; Substance Abuse and Mental Health Services Administration [SAMHSA], 2006).

Tobacco

Adolescent tobacco use is a less widespread problem in Canada than in the past. Smoking rates have declined by more than one-half among Canadian Grade 8 to Grade 12 students since the mid-1990s. Still, about 3 percent of Grade 8s, 10 percent of Grade 10s, and 14 percent of Grade 12s report smoking during the past year (Paglia-Boak et al., 2011). A randomized, controlled trial found nicotine replacement therapy plus behavioural skills training to be effective in helping adolescents stop smoking (Killen et al., 2004).

Government initiatives to educate young smokers about the health hazards of smoking—including legislated changes to health warnings on cigarette packages, restrictions on where smoking is permitted in public spaces, and an increase in government taxes on cigarette purchases—may be contributing to the continued decline in smoking among youth.

Did you know?

Urea, a chemical compound found in urine, is used to add flavour to cigarettes.

Onset of Drug Use

Substance use often begins when children enter middle school, where they become more vulnerable to peer pressure. Early adolescents may start using cigarettes, beer, and inhalants and, as they get older, move on to marijuana or harder drugs (Fergusson, Boden, & Harwood, 2006; Freeman et al., 2011). The earlier young people start using a drug, the more frequently they are

likely to use it and the greater their tendency to abuse it (Wong et al., 2006).

The average age for starting to drink is 12 to 14, and some children start earlier (Freeman et al., 2011). Young people who begin drinking early tend to have behaviour problems or to have siblings who are alcohol dependent (Kuperman et al., 2005). Those who start drinking before age 15 are more than five times as likely to become alcohol dependent or alcohol abusers as those who do not start drinking until age 21 or later (SAMHSA, 2004).

Smoking often begins in the early teenage years as a sign of toughness, rebelliousness, and passage from childhood to adulthood. This desired image enables a young initiate to tolerate the initial distaste for the first few puffs, after which the effects of nicotine begin to take over to sustain the habit. Within a year or two after starting to smoke, these young people inhale the same amount of nicotine as adults and experience the same cravings and withdrawal effects if they try to quit. Young adolescents attracted to smoking often come from homes, schools, and neighbourhoods where smoking is common. They also tend to be overweight, to have low self-esteem, and not to be succeeding at school (Jarvis, 2004).

Adolescents exposed to alcohol and drugs before the age of 15 demonstrate an increased risk for substance disorders (Hingson, Heeren, & Winter, 2006), risky sexual behaviour (Stueve & O'Donnell, 2005), low educational attainment (King, Meehan, Trim, & Chassin, 2006), and emotional and behavioural problems (Freeman et al., 2011; Paglia-Boak et al., 2011). Peer influence on both smoking and drinking has been documented extensively (Cleveland & Wiebe, 2003). As with hard drugs, the influence of older siblings and their friends increases the likelihood of tobacco and alcohol use (Rende, Slomkowski, Lloyd-Richardson, & Niaura, 2005). Additionally, having an alcoholic parent significantly increased the risk of early alcohol use and later alcohol problems (Wong et al., 2006). The omnipresence of substance use in the media is another important influence. Movies that depict smoking increase early initiation of smoking (Charlesworth & Glantz, 2005).

Aboriginal youth are particularly susceptible to using inhalants, fumes, or vapours given off by common, low-cost products such as gasoline, solvents, and adhesive glue that have intoxicating and psychoactive effects (Dell et al., 2011; Weir, 2001). Average age of first use is about 9.7 years, and it has a high rate of relapse after treatment—almost 75 percent (Coleman, Charles, & Collins, 2001). Long-term effects of chronic use of inhalants are difficult to track, given that their use is often combined with other drugs, but clinical case studies show evidence of psychosis and permanent cognitive impairment, requiring long-term hospitalization (Byrne, Kirby, Zibin, & Ensminger, 1991). Addressing this problem will require a complex combination of approaches, including dealing with the roots of the problem, such as chronic poverty and isolation (Weir, 2001), and developing therapies that are based on elements of Aboriginal culture, such as storytelling, to educate youth to prevent the onset of inhalant use and to promote health and community involvement (Dell et al., 2011).

DEPRESSION

The prevalence of depression increases during adolescence, as shown in Figure 14.4. An average of nearly 8 percent of young people in Canada aged 15 to 18 have experienced at least one episode of major depression, and almost 16 percent have experienced suicidality—thinking about or attempting suicide (Cheung & Dewa, 2006). Depression in young people does not necessarily appear as sadness but as irritability, boredom, or inability to experience pleasure. One reason it needs to be taken seriously is the danger of suicide (Brent & Birmaher, 2002).

Adolescent girls, especially early maturing girls, are more subject to depression than adolescent boys (Brent & Birmaher, 2002; National Survey on Drug Use and Health [NSDUH], 2005). This gender difference (4.3 percent of males and 11.1 percent of females in Canada, with a similar difference in suicidality; Cheung & Dewa, 2006) may be related to biological changes connected with puberty; studies show a correlation between advancing puberty status and depressive symptoms (Susman & Rogol, 2004). Other possible factors are the way girls are socialized (Birmaher et al., 1996) and their greater vulnerability to stress in social relationships (Ge, Conger, & Elder, 2001a).

In addition to female gender, risk factors for depression include anxiety, fear of social contact, stressful life events, chronic illnesses such as diabetes or epilepsy, parent-child conflict, abuse or neglect, alcohol and drug use, sexual activity, and having a parent with a history of depression. Alcohol and drug use and sexual activity are more likely to lead to depression in girls than in boys (Hallfors, Waller, Bauer, Ford, & Halpern, 2005; NSDUH, 2005; Waller et al., 2006).

Depressed adolescents who do not respond to outpatient treatment or who have substance dependence or psychosis or seem suicidal may need to be hospitalized. More commonly, medications are used. Selective serotonin reuptake inhibitors (SSRIs) are the only type of antidepressant medication currently approved for children and adolescents. However, as with the use of SSRIs for children, there is concern about the safety of these medications for adolescents. Not all SSRIs are effective, and a few have been associated with a slight increase in the risk of suicidality (Williams, O'Connor, Eder, & Whitlock, 2009). Health warnings have reduced the frequency of use of SSRIs associated with risk to adolescents in Canada (Tournier et al., 2010).

The only other treatment option is psychotherapy. An analysis of all available studies found modest short-term effectiveness of psychotherapy, cognitive or non-cognitive, with effects lasting no more than one year (Weisz, McCarty, & Valeri, 2006). In view of the greater effectiveness of antidepressant medicine, especially fluoxetine, the Society for Adolescent Medicine supports its use for adolescents when clinically warranted and closely monitored, despite the risk (Lock, Walker, Rickert, & Katzman, 2005).

Depression Rates for 12- to 17-Year-Olds

FIGURE 14.4 Rates of depression typically go up with increasing age during adolescence.

Sources: NSUDH, 2008. From Fig. 15.3, p. 412 in Papalia A Child's World, 12th Ed. Copyright © 2011 by The McGraw-Hill Companies, Inc. Reprinted with permission; Vasiliadis, H.-M., Lesage, A., Adair, C., Wang, P. S., & Kessler, R. C. (2007). "Do Canada and the United States differ in prevalence of depression and utilization of services?", Psychiatric Services, 58, 63–71.

DEATH

Death this early in life is always tragic and usually accidental but not always so. In Canada, the majority of deaths among adolescents resulted from motor vehicle crashes, other unintentional injuries, suicide, cancer, and homicide, with the remainder of deaths stemming from other medical causes such as diseases of the heart and congenital malformations. Violent death is a relatively frequent occurrence for adolescents. For instance, in people 15 to 24 years of age, suicide is the second-leading cause of death, and homicide is the fourth-leading cause, after cancer. For people aged 25 to 34, homicide drops to the fifth-leading cause, and after the age of 35 years, it does not appear in the top ten (Public Health Agency of Canada, 2008b). The frequency of violent deaths in this age group reflects adolescents' inexperience and immaturity, which often lead to risk-taking and carelessness.

Deaths from Motor Accidents

Motor vehicle collisions are the leading cause of death among Canadian teenagers, accounting for up to 35 percent of all deaths in adolescence. The risk of collision is greater among 16- to 19-year-olds than for any other age group and especially so among 16- and 17-year-olds who have recently started to drive (Emery, Mayhew, & Simpson, 2008; Mayhew, Singhal, Simpson, Beirness, 2004; Miniño, Anderson, Fingerhut, Boudreault, & Warner, 2006; National Center for Injury Prevention and Control [NCIPC], 2004). Collisions are more likely to be fatal when teenage passengers are in the vehicle, probably because adolescents tend to drive more recklessly in the presence of peers (Chen, Baker, Braver, & Li, 2000). In Canada, of all people who die in alcohol-related

Dan Savage, pictured here with his long-term partner, created the *It Gets Better* project.

traffic accidents, 11 percent are between the ages of 15 and 19, and 21 percent are between the ages of 20 and 24. Although 95 percent of Canadian drivers use seat belts, the number of adolescents who use seat belts decreases as the number of adolescent passengers increase (Transport Canada, 2011; Transport Injury Research Foundation, 2011). From 2004 to 2008, over one-third of traffic fatalities involved drivers or passengers who were unbuckled (Transport Canada, 2011).

Firearm-Related Deaths

Firearm-related deaths of 15- to 19-year-olds, including suicide, homicide, and accidental deaths, comprise about one-third of all injury deaths. About 80 percent of firearm-related deaths among Canadian adolescents are suicides. Firearm-related deaths among youth are three times as prevalent in the U.S. as in Canada (Frappier, Leonard, Sacks, & Canadian Paediatric Society, Adolescent Health Committee, 2005), likely because of stricter gun control laws in Canada that restrict access to firearms (Snider, Ovens, Drummond, & Kapur, 2009). Males are more likely to die from firearm injuries than females (Frappier et al., 2005). The presence of a firearm in the home is associated with a higher likelihood of suicide in youth, likely related to adolescents' impulsivity, sensitivity to peer pressure, and substance abuse. The Canadian Paediatric Society recommends that firearms not be present in homes where adolescents and children live (Frappier et al., 2005).

Suicide

"We found out Dan—the guy in my fourth period homeroom—shot and killed himself last weekend," wrote Sara. "It's so sad. It's terrible really. I knew he was weird and quiet and everything, but to kill yourself? That's so awful. I can't imagine what he was going through. I feel sad now that I never really paid him any attention."

Suicide is the second-leading cause of death among Canadian 15- to 19-year-olds (Chief Public Health Officer, 2011; Public Health Agency of Canada, 2008). The teenage suicide rate fell by an average of 1 percent per year between 1980 and 2008 (Skinner & McFaull, 2012). However, the suicide rate drop occurred with males; an increase occurred among female youth, with suffocation as a preferred method of suicide for both males and females. Nevertheless, males outnumber females in number of suicides, with 12.2 male and 5.2 female deaths per 100,000 (Skinner & McFaull, 2012).

Although suicide occurs in all ethnic groups, Aboriginal boys in Canada have the highest rates, although rates vary among communities (Chief Public Health Officer, 2011; Kral, 2012). Aboriginal communities that experience high degrees of community control tend to have lower youth suicide rates than communities with lower degrees of control (Chandler & Lalonde, 1998, 2008). Gay, lesbian, and bisexual youths, who have high rates of depression, also have unusually high rates of suicide and attempted suicide (AAP Committee on Adolescence, 2000; NCHS, 2009; Remafedi, French, Story, Resnick, & Blum, 1998; Wells, 2009).

Young people who consider or attempt suicide tend to have histories of emotional illness. They are likely to be either perpetrators or victims of violence and to have school problems, academic or behavioural. Many have suffered from maltreatment in childhood and have severe problems with relationships. They tend to think poorly of themselves, to feel hopeless, and to have poor impulse control and low tolerance for frustration and stress. They also tend to have attempted suicide before or to have friends or family members who did so (Borowsky, Ireland, & Resnick, 2001; Brent & Mann, 2006; Chief Public Health Officer, 2011; Johnson et al., 2002). Alcohol plays a part in half of all teenage suicides (AAP Committee on Adolescence, 2000).

Ask Yourself

7. Name three benefits associated with exercise.

8. Why have some psychologists suggested that classes for adolescents should start later in the morning?

9. Which of the following is a key difference between anorexia and bulimia?
   a. In anorexia, there is an unhealthy preoccupation with food; in bulimia, there is not.
   b. Anorexia is more common in girls, while bulimia is more common in boys.
   c. Anorexia is associated with a low weight, while girls with bulimia are more likely to be of typical weight.
   d. Anorexia is common in industrialized countries, while bulimia is common in non-industrialized countries.

10. Adolescents who use drugs or alcohol are at higher risk if they
   a. are girls.
   b. are boys.
   c. start using at an early age.
   d. are honest with their parents about their usage.

11. Name three factors associated with elevated risk for depression.

12. What is the leading cause of death in adolescence?
   a. motor fatalities
   b. firearm-related deaths
   c. suicide
   d. drug overdose

LO1

Define adolescence.

- Adolescence is the transition from childhood to adulthood. Neither its beginning nor its end is clearly marked in industrialized societies; it lasts about a decade, between ages 11 or 12 and the late teens or early twenties.
- In some non-Western cultures, coming of age is signified by special rites.
- Adolescence is full of opportunities for physical, cognitive, and psychosocial growth, but also full of risks to healthy development. Risky behaviour patterns, such as drinking alcohol, drug abuse, sexual and gang activity, and use of weapons, tend to be established early in adolescence. About four out of five young people experience no major problems.

LO2

Summarize the physical changes of adolescence and their psychological impact.

- Puberty is triggered by hormonal changes, which may affect moods and behaviour. Puberty takes about four years, typically begins earlier in girls than in boys, and ends when a person can reproduce.
- Primary sex characteristics (the reproductive organs) enlarge and mature during puberty. Secondary sex characteristics (signs of sexual maturation that do not involve the sex organs) also appear.
- During puberty, both boys and girls undergo an adolescent growth spurt. A secular trend toward earlier attainment of adult height and sexual maturity began about 100 years ago, probably because of improvements in living standards.
- The principal signs of sexual maturity are production of sperm (for males) and menstruation (for females). Spermarche typically occurs at age 13. Menarche occurs, on average, between the ages of 10½ and 16.
- Teenagers, especially girls, tend to be sensitive about their physical appearance. Girls who mature early tend to adjust less easily than early maturing boys.

LO3

Describe brain development in adolescence and how it impacts behaviour.

- The adolescent brain is not yet fully mature. Adolescents tend to make less accurate, less reasoned judgments.
- A wave of overproduction of grey matter, especially in the frontal lobes, is followed by pruning of excess dendrites. Continuing myelination of the frontal lobes facilitates maturation of cognitive processing.
- Underdevelopment of frontal cortical systems connected with motivation, impulsivity, and addiction may help explain adolescents' tendency toward risk taking.
- Because of their developing brains, adolescents are particularly vulnerable to effects of alcohol and addictive drugs.

- For the most part, the adolescent years are relatively healthy. Health problems are often associated with poverty or a risk-taking lifestyle.

- Many adolescents, especially girls, do not engage in regular vigorous physical activity.

- Many adolescents do not get enough sleep because the high school schedule is out of sync with their natural body rhythms.

- Three common eating disorders in adolescence are obesity, anorexia nervosa, and bulimia nervosa. All can have serious long-term effects. Anorexia and bulimia affect mostly girls. Outcomes for bulimia tend to be better than for anorexia.

- Self-injurious behaviour is common among adolescents, is related to emotional and social factors, and is a risk factor for suicidal thoughts and attempts.

- Adolescent substance abuse and dependence have lessened in recent years; still, drug use often begins as children move into middle school.

- Marijuana, alcohol, and tobacco are the most popular drugs with adolescents. All involve serious risks. Abuse of inhalants is a particular problem among Aboriginal youth in Canada.

- Leading causes of death among adolescents include motor vehicle accidents and suicide.

ANSWERS TO Ask Yourself

Answers: 1–b; 2–Among the opportunities for growth in adolescence are physical growth, cognitive and social competence, autonomy, self-esteem, and intimacy. Risks include accidents, homicide, suicide, drug or alcohol use, vehicle accidents, and risky sexual behaviour; 3–The stages of puberty are (1) the activation of the adrenal glands and (2) the maturing of the sex organs; 4–d; 5–d; 6–a; 7–The benefits of regular exercise include improved strength and endurance, healthier bones and muscles, weight control, reduced anxiety and stress, increased self-esteem, higher school grades, higher well-being, and a decrease in risky behaviours; 8–Psychologists have suggested schooling for adolescents start later because teens secrete melatonin (a hormone associated with sleep) later than children, making it likely they will stay up later than younger children. But they still need as much sleep as younger children and are often groggy and sleepy in the early morning. Starting school later would be in sync with their biological rhythm and help improve their concentration; 9–c; 10–c; 11–Among the risk factors for depression are being female, having high anxiety or fear of social contact, stressful life events, chronic illnesses, parent-child conflict, abuse or neglect, alcohol and drug use, sexual activity, and having a parent with a history of depression; 12–a

connect LEARNSMART SMARTBOOK

For more information on the resources available from McGraw-Hill Ryerson, go to **www.mcgrawhill.ca/he/solutions**.

COGNITIVE
DEVELOPMENT IN

Cognitive Development

Moral Development

Educational and Vocational Issues

WHAT'S TO COME

Adam is 15 years old. Sometimes he feels that his parents just don't understand the world today—they are so old-fashioned. They think Adam is obsessed with his phone, and they worry about video games and cable television. Adam is beginning to question some of his parents' moral beliefs that he accepted as a child and struggles to reconcile his views with theirs. "I'm not sure what I think or feel really, or even what I want to do when I get older," he says. "I'm still figuring it out. I don't even know if I really want to go to college or university." Like most 15-year-olds, Adam is on the cusp of adulthood. How he navigates these next few years will have profound consequences for his life's trajectory.

In this chapter, we examine the Piagetian stage of formal operations that allows Adam to think about different systems of knowledge. We look at adolescents' growth in information processing, including memory, knowledge, and reasoning, and in vocabulary and other linguistic skills. We note some immature aspects of adolescents' thought process, and we examine adolescents' moral development. Finally, we explore practical aspects of cognitive growth—issues of school and vocational choice.

ADOLESCENCE

AS YOU READ

LO1   Summarize how adolescents' thinking and use of language differ from that of younger children.

LO2   Describe the relationship between cognitive abilities and moral judgments.

LO3   Summarize the influences on adolescents' school achievement, educational planning, and vocational development.

Cognitive Development

Adolescents not only look different from younger children, they also think and talk differently. Their speed of information processing and language abilities continue to increase, though not as dramatically as in middle childhood. However, at the same time they show increases in abilities, they nonetheless retain immature aspects of thought that are characteristically adolescent in nature. And these changes are reflected in the physical structure of the brain. In this section, we address these changes and discuss their impact.

PIAGET'S STAGE OF FORMAL OPERATIONS

Adolescents enter what Piaget called the highest level of cognitive development—**formal operations**—when they develop the capacity for abstract thought. This development, usually around age 11, gives them a new, more flexible way to manipulate information. No longer limited to

In formal operations, adolescents can now use symbols to represent other symbols, like using letters to stand for unknown numerals.

the here and now, they can understand historical time and extraterrestrial space. They can use symbols for other symbols, for example, letting the letter *X* stand for an unknown numeral, and thus can learn algebra and calculus. They can better appreciate metaphor ("All the world's a stage") and allegory (*Life of Pi* as a story about a different but parallel set of events) and thus can find richer meanings in literature. They can think in terms of what might be, not just what is. They can imagine possibilities and can form and test hypotheses ("What if I keep the oven temperature the same, but increase the cooking time—will the cake turn out better?"). People in the stage of formal operations can integrate what they have learned in the past with the challenges of the present and make plans for the future.

Hypothetical-Deductive Reasoning

To appreciate the difference formal reasoning makes, let us follow the progress of a typical child in dealing with a classic Piagetian problem, the pendulum problem (adapted from Ginsburg & Opper, 1979). Adam is shown the pendulum, an object hanging from a string. He is then shown how he can change any of four factors: the length of the string, the weight of the object, the height from which the object is released, and the amount of force he uses to push the object. He is asked to figure out which factor or combination of factors determines how fast the pendulum swings. (Figure 15.1 depicts this and other Piagetian tasks for assessing the achievement of formal operations.)

When Adam first sees the pendulum, he is not yet 7 years old and is in the preoperational stage. Unable to formulate a plan for attacking the problem, he tries one thing after another in a hit-or-miss manner. First, he puts a light weight on a long string and pushes it; then he tries swinging a heavy weight on a short string; then he removes

formal operations In Piaget's theory, final stage of cognitive development, characterized by the ability to think abstractly.

Formal Operations Reasoning Tasks

FIGURE 15.1 (a) Pendulum. The pendulum's string can be shortened or lengthened, and weights of varying sizes can be attached to it. The student must determine what variables affect the speed of the pendulum's swing. (b) Motion in a horizontal plane. A spring device launches balls of varying sizes that roll in a horizontal plane. The student must predict their stopping points. (c) Balance beam. A balance scale comes with weights of varying sizes that can be hung at different points along the crossbar. The student must determine what factors affect whether the scale will balance. (d) Shadows. A board containing a row of peg holes is attached perpendicular to the base of a screen. A light source and rings of varying diameters can be placed in the holes, at varying distances from the screen. The student must produce two shadows of the same size, using different-sized rings.

Source: From Small, *Cognitive Development*, 1st Ed. Copyright © 1990 Wadsworth, a part of Cengage Learning, Inc. Reproduced by permission. www.cengage.com/permissions.

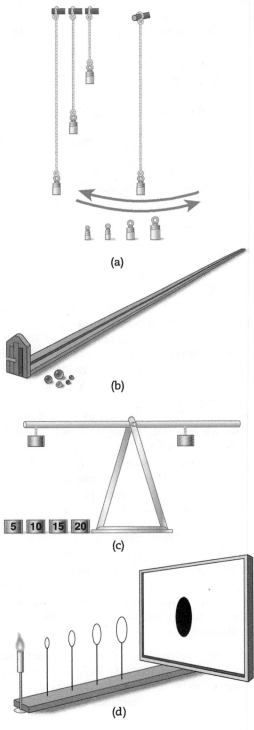

(a)

(b)

(c)

(d)

the weight entirely. Not only is his method random, but he also cannot understand or report what has happened.

Adam next encounters the pendulum at age 10, when he is in the stage of concrete operations. This time, he discovers that varying the length of the string and the weight of the object affects the speed of the swing. However, because he varies both factors at the same time, he cannot tell which is critical or whether both are.

Adam is confronted with the pendulum for a third time at age 15, and this time he goes at the problem systematically. He designs an experiment to test all the possible hypotheses, varying one factor at a time—first, the length of the string; next, the weight of the object; then, the height from which it is released; and finally, the amount of force used—each time holding the other three factors constant. In this way, he is able to determine that only one factor—the length of the string—determines how fast the pendulum swings.

Adam's solution to the pendulum problem shows that he has arrived at the stage of formal operations. He is now capable of **hypothetical-deductive reasoning**: He can develop a hypothesis and design an experiment to test it. He considers all the relationships he can imagine and tests them systematically, one by one, to eliminate the false and arrive at the true.

What brings about the shift to formal reasoning? Piaget attributed it chiefly to a combination of brain maturation and expanding environmental opportunities. Both are essential: Even if young people's neurological development has advanced enough to permit formal reasoning, they can attain it only with appropriate environmental stimulation.

Evaluating Piaget's Theory

Although adolescents tend to think more abstractly than younger children, there is debate about the precise age at which this advance occurs (Eccles, Wigfield, & Byrnes, 2003). Piaget's writings provide many examples of children displaying aspects of scientific thinking well before adolescence. At the same time, Piaget seems to have overestimated some older children's abilities. Many late adolescents and adults—perhaps one-third to one-half—seem incapable of abstract thought as Piaget defined it (Gardiner & Kozmitzki, 2005), and even those who are capable of abstract thinking do not always use it.

Piaget, in most of his early writings, paid little attention to individual differences, to variations in the same child's performance on different kinds of tasks, or to social and cultural influences. However, neo-Piagetian research suggests that children's cognitive processes are closely tied to specific content, what a child is thinking about, as well as to the context of a problem and the kinds of information and thought a culture considers important (Kuhn, 2006).

hypothetical-deductive reasoning Ability, believed by Piaget to accompany the stage of formal operations, to develop, consider, and test hypotheses.

CULTURE AND COGNITION

When Piaget first developed his theories, it was assumed that his stages of cognitive development represented universal aspects of human development, and that all people in all cultures went through the same processes as those in Western countries. However, as research in different cultures began to be carried out, it became clear that this original conception was simplistic and that culture profoundly affects the path that development takes.

For example, when adolescents in Rwanda were tested on the pendulum task, none were able to solve it (Gardiner & Kozmitzki, 2005). In Nigeria (Hollos & Richards, 1993); Papua, New Guinea; and New South Wales, Australia (Philp & Kelly, 1974), schoolchildren and teens showed some formal operational abilities. On the other hand, Chinese children in Hong Kong, who had been to British schools, did at least as well if not better than U.S. and European children. Apparently, formal reasoning is a learned ability that is not equally necessary or equally valued in all cultures, and the experiences children have shape their developing abilities.

Does this mean, then, that adults in cultures other than Western ones function at lower levels of cognitive complexity? Even Piaget (1972) eventually realized this was not the case. Rather, adults learn to reason in the ways that their culture demands and while doing culturally relevant activities. For example, when African men from the Côte d'Ivoire play a board game in which opponents capture seeds from each other, they use a mix of sophisticated cognitive strategies, including complex rules, offensive and defensive moves, and abstract calculations (Retschitzki, 1989).

That Piaget had to change his theories does not make them bad theories; rather, this is how science works. Piaget was instrumental in developing the field of cognitive and developmental psychology we know today and stimulated a wide variety of important research. However, his original theories require modification in light of what we now know.

Source: Based on Gardiner & Kozmitzki (2005).

Furthermore, Piaget's theory does not adequately consider such cognitive advances as gains in information-processing capacity, accumulation of knowledge and expertise in specific fields, and the role of *metacognition*, the awareness and monitoring of one's own mental processes and strategies (Flavell et al., 2002). This ability to "think about what one is thinking about" and, thus, to manage one's mental processes—in other words, enhanced executive function—may be the chief advance of adolescent thought, the result of changes occurring in the adolescent brain (Kuhn, 2006).

IMMATURE CHARACTERISTICS OF ADOLESCENT THOUGHT

Adam believes that parents who test positive for drug use should have their children removed permanently from their homes. "But where would those kids go?" asks his friend Maria, "I mean, yeah, their parents are bad, but are there better places for them to go? What about if their parents agree to go into treatment?" Adam stops—he had not considered these issues. As we will see, Adam's focus on the big picture while neglecting the details of how it would play out in reality is typical of adolescents his age. We have seen how children develop from egocentric beings to persons capable of solving abstract problems and imagining ideal societies. Yet in some ways, adolescents'

thinking seems strangely immature. According to psychologist David Elkind (2001), such behaviour stems from adolescents' inexperienced ventures into formal operational thought. This new way of thinking, which fundamentally transforms the way they look at themselves and their world, is as unfamiliar to them as their reshaped bodies, and they sometimes feel just as awkward in its use. As they try out their new powers, they may sometimes stumble, like an infant learning to walk.

So, for example, in addition to their idealism, they are often rude to adults, they have trouble making up their minds about what to wear each day, and they tend to act as if the whole world revolves around them.

Their immaturity of thinking, Elkind suggests, manifests itself in at least six characteristic ways:

1. *Idealism and criticalness:* As adolescents envision an ideal world, they realize how far the real world, for which they hold adults responsible, falls short. They become ultra-conscious of hypocrisy. Convinced that they know better than adults how to run the world, they frequently find fault with their parents and other authority figures.

2. *Argumentativeness:* Adolescents are constantly looking for opportunities to try out their reasoning abilities. They often become argumentative as they build a case for, say, staying out past their curfew.

As they try out their new powers of formal operational thought, teens may sometimes stumble, like an infant learning to walk.

3. *Indecisiveness:* Adolescents can keep many alternatives in mind at the same time, yet may lack effective strategies for choosing among them. They may struggle with simple decisions like whether they should go to the mall with a friend or work on a school assignment.

4. *Apparent hypocrisy:* Young adolescents often do not recognize the difference between expressing an ideal, such as conserving energy, and making the sacrifices necessary to live up to it, such as driving less often.

5. *Self-consciousness:* Adolescents can think about thinking—their own and other people's. However, in their preoccupation with their own mental state, adolescents often assume that everyone else is thinking about the same thing they are thinking about: themselves. Elkind refers to this as the **imaginary audience**, a conceptualized "observer" who is as concerned with a young person's thoughts and behaviour as he or she is. The certainty, for example, that everyone is staring at a small blemish all day long is one example of this. The imaginary audience fantasy is especially strong in the early teens but persists to a lesser degree into adult life.

6. *Specialness and invulnerability:* Elkind uses the term **personal fable** to describe a belief by adolescents that they are special, that their experience is unique, and that they are not subject to the rules that govern the rest of the world. This belief might encourage adolescents to believe they can drive fast and recklessly and not get into an accident. According to Elkind, this form of egocentrism underlies much risky, self-destructive behaviour. Like the imaginary audience, the personal fable continues into adulthood.

imaginary audience Elkind's term for an observer who exists only in an adolescent's mind and who is as concerned with the adolescent's thoughts and actions as the adolescent is.

personal fable Elkind's term for the conviction that one is special, unique, and not subject to the rules that govern the rest of the world.

LANGUAGE DEVELOPMENT

Children's use of language reflects their level of cognitive development. School-age children are quite proficient in use of language, but adolescence brings further refinements. Vocabulary continues to grow as reading matter becomes more adult. By ages 16 to 18, the average young person knows approximately 80,000 words (Owens, 1996).

With the advent of abstract thought, adolescents can define and discuss such abstractions as love, justice, and freedom. They more frequently use such terms as *however, otherwise, anyway, therefore, really,* and *probably* to express logical relationships. They become more conscious of words as symbols that can have multiple meanings, and they take pleasure in using irony, puns, and metaphors (Duthie, Nippold, Billow, & Mansfield, 2008; Katz, Blasko, & Kazmerski, 2004).

Adolescents also become more skilled in *social perspective-taking,* the ability to tailor their speech to another person's knowledge level and point of view. This ability is essential for persuasion and even for polite conversation.

Vocabulary may differ by gender, ethnicity, age, geographical region, neighbourhood, and type of school (Eckert, 2003) and varies from one clique to another. "Hipsters" and "jocks" engage in different kinds of activities, which form the main subjects of their conversation. This talk, in turn, cements bonds within the clique. Teenage slang is part of the process of developing an independent identity separate from parents and the adult world, and is likely to emerge in any culture where teenagerhood is a social category.

Did you know?

Thirty-eight percent of teens admit to using text shortcuts such as "LOL" in their school work, and 25 percent have used emoticons (Lenhart, Arafeh, Smith, & Macgill, 2008).

CHANGES IN INFORMATION PROCESSING IN ADOLESCENCE

Changes in the way adolescents process information reflect the maturation of the brain's frontal lobes and may help explain the cognitive advances Piaget described. Which neural connections wither and which become strengthened is highly responsive to experience. Thus, progress in cognitive processing varies greatly among individual adolescents (Kuhn, 2006).

Researchers have identified two broad categories of measurable change in information processing: *structural change* and *functional change* (Eccles et al., 2003). Let's look at each.

Structural Change

Structural changes in adolescence may include growth of information-processing capacity and an increase in the amount of knowledge stored in long-term memory. The capacity of working memory, which enlarges rapidly in middle childhood, may continue to increase during adolescence. The expansion of working memory enables older adolescents to deal with complex problems or decisions involving multiple pieces of information.

Information stored in long-term memory can be declarative, procedural, or conceptual.

- **Declarative knowledge** ("knowing that . . .") consists of all the factual knowledge a person has acquired (for example, knowing that 2 + 2 = 4 and that John A. Macdonald was the first Canadian prime minister).

- **Procedural knowledge** ("knowing how to . . .") consists of all the skills a person has acquired, such as being able to use a computer and drive a car.

- **Conceptual knowledge** ("knowing why") is an understanding of, for example, why an algebraic equation remains true if the same amount is added or subtracted from both sides.

Functional Change

Processes for obtaining, handling, and retaining information are functional aspects of cognition. Among these are learning, remembering, and reasoning, all of which improve during adolescence.

Among the most important functional changes are a continued increase in processing speed (Kuhn, 2006) and further development of executive function, which includes such skills as selective attention, decision making, inhibitory control of impulsive responses, and management of working memory. These skills seem to develop at varying rates (Blakemore & Choudbury,

---

declarative knowledge Acquired factual knowledge stored in long-term memory.

procedural knowledge Acquired skills stored in long-term memory.

conceptual knowledge Acquired interpretive understandings stored in long-term memory.

2006; Kuhn, 2006). Although each process appears to mature independently, each seems to aid in the development of the others (Luna et al., 2004).

However, improvements in information processing skills do not necessarily carry over to real life, where behaviour depends in part on motivation and emotion regulation. Many older adolescents make poorer real-world decisions than younger adolescents do. As we discussed in Chapter 14, adolescents' rash judgments may be related to immature brain development, which may permit feelings to override reason.

Ask Yourself

1. A research participant is given a balance beam with weights of various sizes that can be hung at different points on the crossbar, and then asked to figure out what factors affect whether the scale will balance. A person in the formal operations stage of development would be most likely to
   a. attack the problem in a hit-or-miss fashion, randomly varying the size of the weight and the hanging position.
   b. understand that both the size of the weight and the hanging position matter, but not vary them in a systematic way.
   c. start with one size weight, and then go through the hanging positions, and then take one hanging position and vary all the weights.
   d. It is impossible to answer this question without knowing the age of the participant.

2. Name the six immature aspects of adolescent thought.

3. What are two of the changes in adolescent language?

4. John is better able to concentrate on his teacher while ignoring the class clown. This is due to _____ in information processing.
   a. structural change
   b. declarative memory
   c. procedural knowledge
   d. functional change

Moral Development

Adam's parents talked him into working at a homeless shelter on Thanksgiving one year, and although he complained about it at the time, the experience was pivotal for him. Over the holiday season, he thought about how fortunate he was. He thought a great deal about what his life might have been like had he been born into a different family, and about whether it was fair that some had so much and some so little. Eventually, as his New Year's resolution, he decided to volunteer at a homeless shelter once a week. Adam, as with many people his age, was showing gains in his moral development.

As children grow older and attain higher cognitive levels, they become capable of more complex reasoning about moral issues. Their tendencies toward altruism and empathy increase as well. Adolescents are better able than younger children to take another person's perspective, to solve social problems, to deal with interpersonal relationships, and to see themselves as social beings. All of these tendencies foster moral development.

Lawrence Kohlberg's theory of moral reasoning, Carol Gilligan's influential work on moral development in women and girls, and research on prosocial behaviour in adolescence all provide insight into adolescents' moral development.

KOHLBERG'S THEORY OF MORAL REASONING

A woman is near death from cancer. A druggist has discovered a drug that doctors believe might save her. The druggist is charging $2,000 for a small dose—10 times what the drug costs him to make. The sick woman's husband, Heinz, borrows from everyone he knows but can scrape together only $1,000. He begs the druggist to sell him the drug for $1,000 or let him pay the rest later. The druggist refuses, saying, "I discovered the drug and I'm going to make money from it." Heinz, desperate, breaks into the man's store and steals the drug. Should Heinz have done that? Why or why not? (Kohlberg, 1969).

Heinz's problem is the most famous example of Lawrence Kohlberg's approach to studying moral development. Starting in the 1950s, Kohlberg and his colleagues posed hypothetical dilemmas like this one to 75 boys aged 10, 13, and 16 and continued to question them periodically for more than 30 years. By asking respondents how they arrived at their answers, Kohlberg, like Piaget, concluded that the way people look at moral issues reflects cognitive development.

Kohlberg's Levels and Stages

On the basis of thought processes shown by responses to his dilemmas, Kohlberg (1969) described three levels of moral reasoning and their substages (Table 15.1):

- Level I: **Preconventional morality**. People act under external controls. They obey rules to avoid punishment or reap rewards, or act out of self-interest. This level is typical of children ages 4 to 10.

- Level II: **Conventional morality (or morality of conventional role conformity)**. People have internalized the standards of authority figures. They are concerned about being "good," pleasing others, and maintaining the social order. This level is typically reached after age 10; many people never move beyond it, even in adulthood.

- Level III: **Postconventional morality (or morality of autonomous moral principles)**. People recognize conflicts between moral standards and make judgments on the basis of principles of right, fairness, and justice. People generally do not reach this level of moral reasoning until at least early adolescence, or more commonly in young adulthood, if ever.

In Kohlberg's theory, it is the reasoning underlying a person's response to a moral dilemma, not the answer itself, which indicates the stage of moral development. Two people who give opposite answers may be at the same stage if their reasoning is based on similar factors. For example, a young person at the conventional stage of morality might argue that Heinz should steal the drug, because it is the husband's responsibility to try and save his wife's life. Alternatively, another person might argue that although Heinz might be tempted to steal the drug, he should not, because it's always wrong to steal. Despite arriving at different answers both young people would be classified as being at the conventional stage of moral development because their reasoning focuses on social concern and conscience.

Some adolescents and even some adults remain at Kohlberg's level I. Like young children, they seek to avoid punishment or to satisfy their needs. Most adolescents and most adults seem to be at level II, usually in stage 3. They conform to social conventions, support the status quo, and do the "right" thing to please others or to obey the law. Stage 4 reasoning, upholding social norms, is less common but increases from early adolescence into adulthood. Often, adolescents show periods of apparent disequilibrium when advancing from one level to another (Eisenberg & Morris, 2004).

Kohlberg added a transitional level between levels II and III, when people no longer feel bound by society's moral standards but have not yet reasoned out their own principles of justice. Instead, they base their moral decisions on personal feelings. Before people can develop a fully principled (level III) morality, he said, they must recognize the relativity of moral standards. Many young people question their earlier moral views when they enter high school, college or university, or the world of work and encounter people whose values, culture, and ethnic background are different from their own. Still, few people reach a level where they can choose among differing moral standards. In fact, at one point, Kohlberg questioned the validity of stage 6, morality based on universal

preconventional morality   First level of Kohlberg's theory of moral reasoning in which control is external and rules are obeyed in order to gain rewards or avoid punishment or out of self-interest.

conventional morality (or morality of conventional role conformity)   Second level in Kohlberg's theory of moral reasoning in which standards of authority figures are internalized.

postconventional morality (or morality of autonomous moral principles)   Third level in Kohlberg's theory of moral reasoning in which people follow internally held moral principles and can decide among conflicting moral standards.

TABLE 15.1 Kohlberg's Six Stages of Moral Reasoning

Levels	Stages of Reasoning	Typical Answers to Heinz's Dilema
Level I: Preconventional morality (ages 4 to 10)	Stage 1: Orientation toward punishment and obedience. "What will happen to me?" Children obey rules to avoid punishment. They ignore the motives of an act and focus on its physical form (such as the size of a lie) or its consequences (such as the amount of physical damage). "He did a lot of damage and stole a very expensive drug."	Pro: "He should steal the drug. It isn't really bad to take it. It isn't as if he hadn't asked to pay for it first. The drug he'd take is worth only $200; he's not really taking a $2,000 drug." Con: "He shouldn't steal the drug. It's a big crime. He didn't get permission; he used force and broke and entered."
	Stage 2: Instrumental purpose and exchange. "You scratch my back, I'll scratch yours." Children conform to rules out of self-interest and consideration for what others can do for them. They look at an act in terms of the human needs it meets and differentiate this value from the act's physical form and consequences	Pro: "It's all right to steal the drug, because his wife needs it and he wants her to live. It isn't that he wants to steal, but that's what he has to do to save her." Con: "He shouldn't steal it. The druggist isn't wrong or bad; he just wants to make a profit. That's what you're in business for—to make money."
Level II: Conventional morality (ages 10 to 13 or beyond)	Stage 3: Maintaining mutual relations, approval of others, the golden rule. "Am I a good boy or girl?" Children want to please and help others, can judge the intentions of others, develop ideas of what a good person is, and take circumstances into account.	Pro: "He should steal the drug. He is only doing something that is natural for a good husband to do. You can't blame him for doing something out of love for his wife." Con: "He shouldn't steal. If his wife dies, he can't be blamed. It isn't because he's heartless or that he doesn't love her enough. The druggist is the selfish or heartless one."
	Stage 4: Social concern and conscience. "What if everybody did it?" People are concerned with doing their duty, showing respect for higher authority, and maintaining the social order. They consider an act always wrong, regardless of motive or circumstances, if it violates a rule and harms others.	Pro: "He should steal it. If he did nothing, he'd be letting his wife die. It's his responsibility if she dies. He has to take it with the idea of paying the druggist." Con: "It is a natural thing for Heinz to want to save his wife, but it's still always wrong to steal."
Level III: Postconventional morality (early adolescence, or not until young adulthood, or never)	Stage 5: Morality of contract, of individual rights, and of democratically accepted law. People think in rational terms, valuing the will of the majority and the welfare of society. They generally see these values as best supported by adherence to the law. While they recognize that there are times when human need and the law conflict, they believe it is better for society in the long run if they obey the law.	Pro: "The law wasn't set up for these circumstances. Taking the drug in this situation isn't really right, but it's justified." Con: "You can't completely blame someone for stealing, but extreme circumstances don't really justify taking the law into your own hands. You can't have people stealing whenever they are desperate. The end may be good, but the ends don't justify the means."
	Stage 6: Morality of universal ethical principles. People do what they as individuals think is right, regardless of legal restrictions or the opinions of others. They act in accordance with internalized standards, knowing that they would condemn themselves if they did not.	Pro: "This is a situation that forces him to choose between stealing and letting his wife die. In a situation where the choice must be made, it is morally right to steal. He has to act in terms of the principle of preserving and respecting life." Con: "Heinz is faced with the decision of whether to consider the other people who need the drug just as badly as his wife. Heinz ought to act not according to his feelings for his wife, but considering the value of all the lives involved."

Source: L. Kohlberg, "Stage and Sequence: The cognitive-development approach to socialization," in *Handbook of Socialiation Theory and Research* by David A. Goslin. Rand McNally, 1969.

ethical principles, because so few people seem to attain it. Later, he proposed a seventh, "cosmic" stage, in which people consider the effect of their actions not only on other people but on the universe as a whole (Kohlberg, 1981; Kohlberg & Ryncarz, 1990).

Evaluating Kohlberg's Theory

Kohlberg inaugurated a profound shift in the way we look at moral development. Initial research supported Kohlberg's theory. The American boys whom Kohlberg and his colleagues followed through adulthood progressed through Kohlberg's stages in sequence, and none skipped a stage. Their moral judgments correlated positively with age, education, IQ, and socio-economic status (SES) (Colby, Kohlberg, Gibbs, & Lieberman, 1983). More recent research, however, has cast doubt on the delineation of some of Kohlberg's stages (Eisenberg & Morris, 2004). Additionally, while Kohlberg paid little attention to these influences, both parents and peers also influence moral development (Eisenberg & Morris, 2004).

One of the problems with Kohlberg's approach is that people who have achieved a high level of cognitive development do not necessarily reach a comparably high level of moral development. A certain level of cognitive development is necessary but not sufficient for a comparable level of moral development. Thus, other processes besides cognition must be at work. Some investigators suggest that moral activity is motivated not only by abstract considerations of justice but also by such emotions as empathy, guilt, distress, and the internalization of prosocial norms (Eisenberg & Morris, 2004; Gibbs, 1995). It also has been argued that Kohlberg's stages 5 and 6 cannot fairly be called the most mature stages of moral development because they restrict maturity to a select group of people given to philosophical reflection and to people who hold a particular view about the value of moral relativism.

Furthermore, there is not always a clear relationship between moral reasoning and moral behaviour. People at postconventional levels of reasoning do not necessarily act more morally than those at lower levels. Other factors, such as specific situations, conceptions of virtue, and concern for others, contribute to moral behaviour (Fischer & Pruyne, 2003). Generally speaking, however, adolescents who are more advanced in moral reasoning do tend to be more moral in their behaviour as well as better adjusted and higher in social competence, whereas antisocial adolescents tend to use less mature moral reasoning (Eisenberg & Morris, 2004).

Last, Kohlberg's system does not seem to represent moral reasoning in non-Western cultures as accurately as in the Western culture in which it was originally developed (Eisenberg & Morris, 2004). Older people in non-Western countries

do tend to score at higher stages than younger people. However, they rarely score above stage 4 (Shweder et al., 2006), suggesting that some aspects of Kohlberg's model may not fit the cultural values of these societies. Differences in moral attitudes between Western and non-Western youth have been identified in the virtual world. Comparisons of Chinese and U.S. 12-year-olds showed that although Chinese youth valued moral character more than U.S. youth, Chinese youth were more accepting than U.S. youth of morally questionable online behaviour like cyberbullying and "stealing" online information. Perhaps the Internet provides an opportunity for expressing autonomy that is not as available in the real world of youth in China compared with the U.S. (Jackson et al., 2008).

GILLIGAN'S THEORY: AN ETHIC OF CARE

On the basis of research on women, Carol Gilligan (1982) asserted that Kohlberg's theory is oriented toward values more important to men than to women. Gilligan claimed that women see morality not so much in terms of justice and fairness as in responsibility to show caring and avoid harm. They focus on not turning away from others rather than on not treating others unfairly (Eisenberg & Morris, 2004).

Research has not found much support for Gilligan's claim of a male bias in Kohlberg's stages (Brabeck & Shore, 2003; Jaffee & Hyde, 2000), and she has since modified her position. However, research has found small gender differences in moral reasoning among adolescents (Eisenberg

& Morris, 2004; Jaffee & Hyde, 2000). For example, early adolescent girls tend to emphasize care-related concerns more than boys do, or self-chosen moral dilemmas related to their own experience (Garmon, Basinger, Gregg, & Gibbs, 1996; Jaffee & Hyde, 2000). This may be because girls generally mature earlier and have more intimate social relationships (Skoe & Diessner, 1994).

Educational and Vocational Issues

School is a central organizing experience in most adolescents' lives. It offers opportunities to learn information, master new skills, and sharpen old skills; to participate in sports, the arts, and other activities; to explore vocational choices; and to be with friends. It widens intellectual and social horizons. Some adolescents, however, experience school not as an opportunity but as one more hindrance on the road to adulthood. What factors might impact adolescents' trajectory?

In the following section, we focus on the influences on school achievement and then take a look at young people who drop out of school. Then, we'll consider planning for higher education and vocations.

INFLUENCES ON SCHOOL ACHIEVEMENT

Canadian adolescents, on average, do well on international assessments of academic skills (Organisation for Economic Co-operation and Development [OECD], 2010, 2011). As in the elementary grades, such factors as parenting practices, socio-economic status, and the quality of the home environment influence the course of school achievement in adolescence. Other factors include gender, ethnicity, peer influence, quality of schooling, and students' belief in themselves.

Student Motivation and Self-Efficacy

In Western countries, including Canada, educational practices are based on the assumption that students can be motivated to learn. Educators emphasize the value of intrinsic motivation—the student's desire to learn for the sake of learning (Larson & Wilson, 2004). Unfortunately, many Canadian students are not self-motivated, and motivation often declines as they enter high school (Eccles, 2004; Larson & Wilson, 2004; Legault, Green-Demers, & Pelletier, (2006). Low motivation could contribute to lack of engagement in school and ultimately dropping out (Archambault, Janosz, Fallu, & Pagani, 2009).

Students high in self-efficacy—who believe that they can master tasks and regulate their learning—are likely to do well in school. In a longitudinal study of 140 eighth graders, students' self-discipline was twice as important as IQ in accounting for their grades and achievement test scores and for selection into a competitive high school program at the end of the year (Duckworth & Seligman, 2005).

Students' self-discipline and self-efficacy can be more important than IQ in accounting for their grades and achievement in school.

In many cultures, education is based not on personal motivation but on such factors as duty (India), submission to authority (Islamic countries), and participation in the family and community (sub-Saharan Africa). In the countries of East Asia, students are expected to learn in order to meet family and societal expectations. Learning is expected to require intense effort, and students who fail or fall behind feel obligated to try again. This may help explain why, in international comparisons in science and math, East Asian students substantially surpass students in most other countries (OECD, 2011).

In developing countries, issues of motivation pale in the light of social and economic barriers to education: inadequate or absent schools and educational resources, the need for child labour to support the family, barriers to schooling for girls or cultural subgroups, and early marriage (Larson & Wilson, 2004). Thus, as we discuss factors in educational success, which are drawn largely from studies in the United States, Canada, and other Western countries, we need to remember that they do not apply to all cultures. Factors found to influence academic achievement include gender, technology, parenting, ethnicity, peers, SES and family characteristics, and the school.

Gender

On an international test of adolescents in 43 industrialized countries, girls in all countries were better readers than boys, while boys were ahead in mathematical literacy in about half of the countries (OECD, 2004). Overall, beginning in adolescence, girls do better on verbal tasks that involve writing and language usage; boys do better in activities that involve visual and spatial functions helpful in math and science.

What causes these gender differences? The answers are complex. Research points to interacting biological and environmental explanations (Halpern et al., 2007; Hyde & Mertz, 2009).

Biologically, as we described in Chapter 11, male and female brains grow differently, and they become even more different with age. Girls have more grey matter, neuronal cell bodies and nearby connections, and boys have more connective white matter (myelin) and cerebrospinal fluid, which cushion the longer paths of nerve impulses. These greater connective advantages have been linked with visual and spatial performance, which help in math and science. In addition, girls' brains are more evenly balanced across hemispheres than boys' brains, permitting a wider range of cognitive abilities, whereas boys' brains may be more specialized. Boys' brains seem to be optimized for activity within each hemisphere, whereas girls' brains seem optimized for activity across hemispheres, permitting them to integrate verbal and analytic (left-brain) tasks with spatial and holistic (right-brain) tasks (Halpern et al., 2007).

Social and cultural forces that influence gender differences include the following (Halpern et al., 2007):

Did you know?

Middle schoolers prefer to do their homework with their friends; high schoolers prefer to do it alone (Kacker, Shumow, Schmidt, & Grzetich, 2011).

- *Home influences:* Across cultures, parents' educational level correlates with their children's math achievement. Except for highly gifted sons and daughters, the amount of parental involvement in children's education affects math performance. Parents' gender attitudes and expectations also have an effect.

- *School influences:* Subtle differences in the way teachers treat boys and girls, especially in math and science classes, have been documented.

- *Neighbourhood influences:* Boys benefit more from enriched neighbourhoods and are hurt more by deprived neighbourhoods.

- *Gender influences:* Women's and men's roles in society help shape girls' and boys' choices of courses and occupations.

- *Cultural influences:* Cross-cultural studies show that the size of gender differences in math performance varies among nations and becomes greater by the end of secondary school. These differences correlate with the degree of gender equality in the society. Countries with greater gender equality demonstrate less variance in math scores between boys and girls (Hyde & Mertz, 2009).

All in all, science continues to search for answers to the perplexing question of why boys' and girls' academic abilities differ. As changes in attitudes and perceptions open opportunities, these differences seem to be shrinking. The rate of Canadian doctoral degrees in the sciences and math awarded to women is strong evidence: In 1994, only 6 percent of PhDs in mathematics and computer science and 4 percent of PhDs in engineering and architecture were granted to women. By 2009, the rates had risen to 25 and 22 percent, respectively (Statistics Canada, 2011i).

Technology

The expansion of technology and the major role it plays in children's lives has affected learning. Research has indicated that while critical thinking and analysis skills have declined as a result of the increased use of computers and video games, visual skills have improved. Students are spending more time multitasking with visual media and less time reading for pleasure (Greenfield, 2009). Reading develops vocabulary, imagination, and induction, skills that are critical to solving more complex problems. Multitasking can prevent a deeper understanding of information. In one study, students who were given access to the Internet during class did not process what was presented as well and performed more poorly than students without access (Greenfield, 2009).

Parenting Practices, Ethnicity, and Peer Influence

Family and school experiences are subject to a phenomenon referred to as spillover, wherein experiences in different contexts influence each other (Grzywacz, Almeida, & McDonald, 2002). Stress at home has been shown to predict problems with attendance and learning and, conversely, problems with attendance and learning contribute to family stress (Flook & Fuligni, 2008).

In Western cultures, the benefits of authoritative parenting continue to affect school achievement during adolescence (Baumrind, 1991; Deslandes, Potvin, & Leclerc, 1999). Authoritative parents urge adolescents to look at both sides of issues, welcome their participation in family decisions, and admit that children sometimes know more than parents. These parents strike a balance between making demands and being responsive. Their children receive praise and privileges for good grades; poor grades bring encouragement to try harder and offers of help. Authoritarian parents, in contrast, tell adolescents not to argue with or question adults. Good grades bring admonitions to do even better; poor grades may be punished by reduced allowances or grounding. Permissive parents seem indifferent to grades, make no rules about watching television, do not attend school functions, and neither help with nor check their children's homework. These parents may not be neglectful or uncaring; they may, in fact, be nurturant. They may simply believe that teenagers should be responsible for their own lives.

What accounts for the academic success of authoritatively raised adolescents? Authoritative parents' greater involvement in schooling may be a factor, as well as their encouragement of positive attitudes toward work. Additionally, parents influence how children frame their schooling. Examination of 50 studies involving over 50,000 students revealed that parents who emphasize the value of education, connect academic performance to future goals, and discuss learning strategies have a significant impact on student academic achievement (Hill & Tyson, 2009).

Among some ethnic groups, parenting styles may be less important than peer influence on motivation. In one study, Latino and African-American adolescents did less well in school than European-American students, apparently because of the lack of peer support for academic achievement (Steinberg, Dornbusch, & Brown, 1992). On the other hand, Asian-American students, whose parents are sometimes described as authoritarian, get high grades and score better than European-American students on math achievement tests, apparently because both parents and peers prize achievement (C. Chen & Stevenson, 1995). Peer influence may help explain the downward trend in academic motivation and achievement that begins for many students in early adolescence. In one study, students whose peer group included high achievers showed less decline in achievement and enjoyment of school, whereas those who associated with low achievers showed greater declines (Ryan, 2001).

Importance of SES and Related Family Characteristics

Socio-economic status is an important predictor of academic success. Parents' educational level and family income indirectly affect educational attainment based on how they influence parenting style, sibling relationships, and adolescent academic engagement (Melby, Conger, Fang, Wickrama, & Conger, 2008). According to a study of 15-year-olds' mathematical literacy in 20 relatively high-income countries, students with at least one post-secondary-educated parent performed better than students whose parents had lower educational levels (Hampden-Thompson & Johnston, 2006). A similar gap occurred between students whose parents had high occupational status (such as physicians and lawyers) and those whose parents were of middle or low occupational status (such as store clerks and unskilled labourers). In addition to family SES, the neighbourhood SES and the average SES of a classroom can have their own influences on student achievement, according to the National Longitudinal Survey of Children and Youth (NLSCY) (Frempong & Willms, 2002; Willms, 1996).

Recent Immigration

A large proportion of the school population in Canada comprises youth of diverse immigrant backgrounds—from well-to-do professional families through to refugee victims of war-ravaged countries. Being a recently arrived

New technology and the major role it plays in children's lives affects learning, including declines in critical thinking and analysis skills, and increases in visual skills.

adolescent without strong skills in the language of instruction can be especially challenging (Ngo & Schleifer, 2005). Although one of the key factors to successful transition to a new society for young people is education (Anisef & Kilbride, 2003), language and cultural differences can make it difficult for school personnel to identify students' needs. Typically, non-English-speaking newcomers take between two and five years to develop communication skills in English, and five to seven years to acquire academic language proficiency (Cummins, 2000). Without explicit language and other educational supports, students can struggle with keeping up with their English-speaking peers, and they are less likely to participate in the school culture (Rossiter & Rossiter, 2009). Dropout rates for subgroups of immigrant youth can be over 50 percent (Canadian Council on Learning, 2008; Garnett & Ungerleider, 2008; Gunderson, 2007; Watt & Roessingh, 1994, 2001). However, protective factors that can help recently arrived youth cope with the demands of unfamiliar school experiences include receiving support from family members, having parents with a strong educational background, having strong relationships with school personnel, participating in effective language-support programs at school, and allowing extra time to complete high school (Canadian Council on Learning, 2008; Derwing, DeCorby, Ichikawa, & Jamieson, 1999; Garnett & Ungerleider, 2008; MacKay & Tavares, 2005; Rossiter & Rossiter, 2009). Older-arriving learners might also have academic knowledge acquired in their first language that they could transfer to the new-language context (Roessingh & Kover, 2003; Roessingh, Kover, & Watt, 2005).

A positive school culture, with emphasis on academics and opportunities for extracurricular activities, keeps students engaged.

The School

The quality of schooling strongly influences student achievement. A good middle or high school has an orderly, safe environment, adequate material resources, a stable teaching staff, and a positive sense of community. The school culture places a strong emphasis on academics and fosters the belief that all students can learn. It also offers opportunities for extracurricular activities, which keep students engaged and prevent them from getting into trouble after school. Teachers trust, respect, and care about students and have high expectations for them, as well as confidence in their own ability to help students succeed (Eccles, 2004).

Adolescents are more satisfied with school if they are allowed to participate in making rules and feel support from teachers and other students (Samdal & Dür, 2000), and if the curriculum and instruction are meaningful and appropriately challenging and fit their interests, skill level, and needs (Eccles, 2004). In a survey of students' perceptions of their teachers, high teacher expectations were the most consistent positive predictor of students' goals and interests, and negative feedback was the most consistent negative predictor of academic performance and classroom behaviour (Wentzel, 2002).

A decline in academic motivation and achievement often begins with the transition from the intimacy and familiarity of elementary school to the larger, more pressured, and less supportive environment of middle school or junior high school (Eccles, 2004). For this reason, some school systems have tried eliminating the middle school transition by extending elementary school to Grade 8 or have consolidated some middle schools with small high schools (Gootman, 2007). Some U.S. big-city school systems, such as in New York City, Philadelphia, and Chicago, are experimenting with small schools in which students, teachers, and parents form a learning community united by a common vision of good education and often a special curricular focus, such as music or ethnic studies (Meier, 1995; Rossi, 1996). In one evaluation of a small-school initiative in Chicago, researchers found that students who attended the schools were more likely to stay in school and graduate (Barrow, Claessens, & Schanzenbach, 2010).

Did you know?

A unique educational innovation in Quebec is the CEGEP system of junior colleges that all students attend. These two-year pre-university colleges start after Grade 11, the last grade in high school in Quebec, and allow students to complete university in three years. They are designed to maximize accessibility to post-secondary education.

DROPPING OUT OF HIGH SCHOOL

In Canada, as in all other industrialized countries and in some developing countries as well, more students finish high school than ever before, and many enroll in higher education (Canadian Council on Learning, 2005; Eccles et al., 2003; OECD, 2004). In 2010, nearly 90 percent of Canadian 18- to 24-year-olds had received a high school diploma or equivalent credential. Rates vary by province; British Columbia had the highest graduation rate at 92.7 percent, and Quebec had the lowest rate at 85 percent (McMullen & Gilmore, 2010). Low-income students are four times as likely to drop out as high-income students (Laird, Lew, DeBell, & Chapman, 2006).

Aboriginal youth tend to drop out of high school more than non-Aboriginal youth, but the dropout rate has also declined in recent years (Canadian Council on Learning, 2005); see Figure 15.2. Still, the higher school-leaving rate of Aboriginal students might reflect the failings of public schools to be sensitive to Aboriginal values and needs (Rabson, 2001). The differences continue through to higher education: In 2006, 8 percent of the Aboriginal adult population (aged 25 to 64) had a university degree, compared with 23 percent of the non-Aboriginal adult population (Statistics Canada, 2008c).

Why are poor and minority adolescents more likely to drop out? One reason may be ineffective schooling: low teacher expectations or differential treatment of these students, less teacher support than at the elementary level, and the perceived irrelevance of the curriculum to culturally underrepresented groups. In schools that use ability tracking, students in low-ability or non-university tracks, where minority youth are likely to be assigned, often have inferior educational experiences. Placed with peers who are equally alienated, they tend to have feelings of incompetence and negative attitudes toward school and to engage in problem behaviours, both within and outside of school (Eccles, 2004).

Society suffers when young people do not finish school. Dropouts are more likely to be unemployed or to have low incomes, to end up on welfare, and to become involved with drugs, crime, and delinquency (Bowlby & McMullen, 2002; Rossiter & Rossiter, 2009). They also tend to be in poorer health (Laird et al., 2006; National Center for Education Statistics [NCES], 2004a).

A longitudinal study that followed 3,502 disadvantaged eighth graders into early adulthood points up the difference success in high school can make (Finn, 2006). As young adults, successful completers were most likely and non-completers least likely to obtain post-secondary education, to have jobs, and to be consistently employed.

PREPARING FOR HIGHER EDUCATION OR VOCATIONS

Adam was graduating from high school. After his work volunteering at a homeless shelter, he had realized that he wanted to work in a way that would help out the less fortunate. However, he also wanted to be able to have a career that made him decent money. Was college the best path toward this? Should he try working first and then going to college later?

In the following section, we address the development of career goals. We also look at how young people decide whether to go to college or university and, if not, how they enter the world of work. Many factors enter in, including individual ability and personality, education, socioeconomic and ethnic background, the advice of school counsellors, life experiences, and societal values.

Influences on Students' Aspirations

Self-efficacy beliefs help shape the occupational options students consider and the way they prepare for careers (Bandura, Barbaranelli, Caprara, & Pastorelli, 2001). In addition, parents' values with regard to academic achievement influence adolescents' values and occupational goals (Jodl, Michael, Malanchuk, Eccles, & Sameroff, 2001).

Despite the greater flexibility in career goals today, gender—and gender-stereotyping—may influence vocational choice (Eccles et al., 2003). Girls and boys in Canada are now equally likely to plan careers in math and science, but boys are much more likely to earn degrees and

FIGURE 15.2

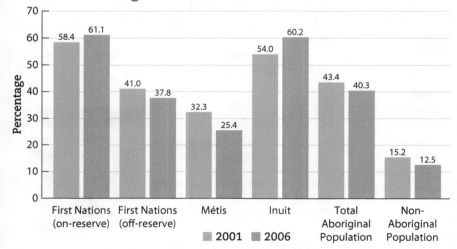

Aboriginal and Non-Aboriginal Canadians Ages 20 to 24 Who Have Not Completed High School, 2001 and 2006

Source: Statistics Canada, "Labour Force Activity (8), Aboriginal Identity (8), Highest Certificate, Diploma or Degree (14), Area of Residence (6), Age Groups (12A) and Sex (3) for the Population 15 Years and Over of Canada, Provinces and Territories, 2006 Census—20% Sample Data," Topic-based tabulation (Ottawa: March 4, 2008), Catalogue no. 97-560-X2006031. Reprinted by the Minister responsible for Statistics Canada. (c) Ministry of Industry, 2013.

diplomas in engineering, physics, and computer science (Andres & Adamuti-Trache, 2007; NCES, 2001; Statistics Canada, 2011i), whereas girls are still more likely to go into nursing, social welfare professions, and teaching (Eccles et al., 2003; Statistics Canada, 2011i). Much the same is true in other industrialized countries (OECD, 2004).

The educational system itself may act as a subtle brake on some students' vocational aspirations. The relatively narrow range of abilities valued and cultivated in many schools gives certain students the inside track. Students who can memorize and analyze tend to do well on intelligence tests that hinge on those abilities and in classrooms where teaching is geared to those abilities. Thus, as predicted by the tests, these students are achievers in a system that stresses the abilities in which they happen to excel.

Meanwhile, students whose strength is in creative or practical thinking—areas critical to success in certain fields—often do not get a chance to show what they can do. These young people may be frozen out of career paths or forced into less challenging and rewarding ones because of test scores and grades too low to put them on track to success (Sternberg, 1997). More flexible teaching and career counselling at all levels could allow more students to get the education and enter the occupations they desire and to make the contributions of which they are capable.

Conventional approaches to career counselling are sometimes inappropriate, particularly for Aboriginal youth for whom goals and values may be incompatible with those of mainstream counselling techniques (Neumann, McCormick, Amundson, & McLean, 2000). One attempt at a solution to the need for a culturally sensitive career-counselling approach is the First Nations

Career-Life Planning Model, which is designed to integrate traditional values of connection with family, community, and culture within the process of guiding an individual's career decision-making. By involving family and community members in career counselling, and offering the option of including traditional practices of prayer, a smudge ceremony, and the use of a talking stick or eagle feather, the process has been found to be effective and meaningful to the young people involved (Neumann et al., 2000).

Guiding Students Not Bound for University or College

Most industrialized countries offer guidance to non-university-or-college-bound students. Germany, for example, has an apprenticeship system in which high school students go to school part-time and spend the rest of the week in paid on-the-job training supervised by an employer-mentor.

Canada lacks coordinated policies to help non-university-or-college-bound youth make a successful transition from high school to the labour market (Eccles, 2004; Taylor, 2010). Vocational counselling is generally oriented toward university-or-college-bound youth. Whatever vocational training programs do exist tend to be less comprehensive than the German system and less closely tied to the needs of businesses and industries. Most of these young people must get training on the job or in community college courses. Many, ignorant about the job market, do not obtain the skills they need. Others take jobs beneath their abilities. Some do not find work at all (NCES, 2002).

In some communities, demonstration programs help in the school-to-work transition. The most successful ones offer instruction in basic skills, counselling, peer support, mentoring, apprenticeship, and job placement (Kash, 2008). In 1996, the federal government established the department of Human Resources and Social Development (now Human Resources and Skills Development Canada), with the aim of improving the employment prospects of Canadians by developing initiatives such as vocational training programs, in co-operation with provincial authorities.

Adolescents in the Workplace

In Canada, about 40 percent of adolescents are employed at some time during high school, mostly in service and

Part-time work can have benefits for high school students, but it can sometimes distract them from long-term educational and occupational goals.

retail jobs (Marshall, 2010; Usalcas & Bowlby, 2006). Researchers disagree over whether part-time work is beneficial to high school students, by helping them develop real-world skills and a work ethic, or detrimental, by distracting them from long-term educational and occupational goals.

Some research suggests that working students fall into two groups: those who are on an accelerated path to adulthood, and those who make a more leisurely transition, balancing schoolwork, paid jobs, and extracurricular activities (Benjamin, 2009). The "accelerators" work more than 20 hours a week during high school and spend little time on school-related leisure activities. Exposure to an adult world may lead them into alcohol and drug use, sexual activity, and delinquent behaviour. Many of these adolescents have relatively low SES; they tend to look for full-time work right after high school and not to obtain college degrees. The "balancers," in contrast, often come from more privileged backgrounds. For them, part-time work helps them to gain a sense of responsibility, independence, and self-confidence and to appreciate the value of work, but it does not deter them from their educational paths (Staff, Mortimer, & Uggen, 2004).

Ask Yourself

7. "I don't know why I even bother studying. These tests are just too hard!" says Craig. Craig is showing
   a. high self-efficacy.
   b. low self-efficacy.
   c. authoritarian parenting.
   d. transitory motivation.

8. What are two reasons that poor and minority adolescents are more likely to drop out of school?

9. Which of the following adolescents could be best described as an "accelerator"?
   a. Jenny, who did not work at all while attending high school
   b. Enzo, who worked five hours during the week and was on the track team
   c. Sara, who worked every night after school as a hostess at a local restaurant
   d. Jake, who was failing all his classes and did not have a job

SUMMARY — CHAPTER 15 COGNITIVE DEVELOPMENT IN ADOLESCENCE

LO1

Summarize how adolescents' thinking and use of language differ from that of younger children.

- People in Piaget's stage of formal operations can engage in hypothetical-deductive reasoning. They can think in terms of possibilities, deal flexibly with problems, and test hypotheses.

- Since environmental stimulation plays an important part in attaining this stage, not all people become capable of formal operations, and those who are capable do not always use it.

- Piaget's proposed stage of formal operations does not take into account such developments as accumulation of knowledge and expertise, gains in information processing capacity, and the growth of metacognition. Piaget also paid little attention to individual differences, between-task variations, and the role of the situation.

- According to Elkind, immature thought patterns can result from adolescents' inexperience with formal thinking. These thought patterns include idealism and criticalness, argumentativeness, indecisiveness, apparent hypocrisy, self-consciousness, and an assumption of specialness and invulnerability.

- Research has found both structural and functional changes in adolescent cognition, which reflect developments in the adolescent brain. Structural changes include increases in information processing capacity, in the amount of knowledge in long-term memory, and in the capacity of working memory. Functional changes include progress in learning, remembering, and reasoning.

- Vocabulary and other aspects of language development, especially those related to abstract thought, such as social perspective-taking, improve in adolescence.

LO2

Describe the relationship between cognitive abilities and moral judgments.

- According to Kohlberg, moral reasoning is based on a developing sense of justice and growing cognitive abilities. Kohlberg proposed that moral development progresses from external control to internalized societal standards to personal, principled moral codes.

- Kohlberg's theory has been criticized on several grounds, including failure to credit the roles of emotion, socialization, and parental guidance. The applicability of Kohlberg's system to women and girls and to people in non-industrialized cultures has been questioned. Research has found no significant gender differences in moral reasoning as measured by Kohlbergian methods.

- Gilligan proposed an alternative theory of moral development based on an ethic of caring, rather than justice.

LO3

Summarize the influences on adolescents' school achievement, educational planning, and vocational development.

- Academic motivation, socio-economic status, parental involvement, parenting styles, cultural and peer influences, and quality of schooling affect educational achievement. Self-efficacy beliefs and parental and peer attitudes can influence motivation to achieve.

- Although most Canadians graduate from high school, the dropout rate is higher among poor and Aboriginal students. Active engagement in studies is an important factor in keeping adolescents in school.

- Educational and vocational aspirations are influenced by several factors, including self-efficacy beliefs, parental values, and gender.

- High school graduates who do not immediately go on to college or university can benefit from vocational training.

- Part-time work seems to have both positive and negative effects on educational, social, and occupational development. The long-term effects tend to be best when working hours are limited.

ANSWERS TO Ask Yourself

Answers: 1–c; 2–The immature aspects of adolescent thought include (1) idealism and criticalness, (2) argumentativeness, (3) indecisiveness, (4) apparent hypocrisy, (5) self-consciousness, and (6) specialness and invulnerability; 3–The development of abstract thought allows for adolescents to define and discuss abstract concepts; to express logical relationships; to become conscious of words as symbols; to use irony, puns, and metaphors more effectively; and to better take the perspective of others; 4–d; 5–a; 6–showing caring and avoiding harm; 7–b; 8–Among the reasons poor or minority adolescents may drop out of school are low teacher expectations, differential treatment, less teacher support, perceived irrelevance of the curriculum, tracking to low ability or non-post-secondary tracks, being placed with alienated peers, feeling incompetent, and having negative attitudes about school; 9–c.

connect | **LEARNSMART** | **SMARTBOOK**

For more information on the resources available from McGraw-Hill Ryerson, go to **www.mcgrawhill.ca/he/solutions**.

PSYCHOSOCIAL
DEVELOPMENT IN

The Search for Identity

Sexuality

Relationships with Family and Peers

Antisocial Behaviour and Juvenile Delinquency

Emerging Adulthood

WHAT'S TO COME

John's parents were somewhat horrified when he dyed his hair bright orange and started wearing all black clothing, but they held back from making it an issue, assuming this was just a teenager's phase. John's parents knew that, as many teens do, John was likely experimenting with identity and who he wanted to be. In the next few years, his search for identity would lead beyond mere clothes and focus on the multitude of paths his future held.

In this chapter, we consider John's path through focusing on the quest for identity in adolescence. We discuss how adolescents come to terms with their sexuality, and how teenagers' burgeoning individuality expresses itself in relationships with parents, siblings, and peers. We examine sources of antisocial behaviour and ways of reducing the risks of adolescence so as to make it a time of positive growth and expanding possibilities. Finally, we look at late adolescence and the emerging adult.

ADOLESCENCE

AS YOU READ

LO1 Describe the process of identity formation, summarize how gender and ethnicity impact it, and describe how prosocial behaviour varies across adolescents.

LO2 Summarize influences on sexual orientation in adolescence, as well as common sexual behaviours and the associated risks.

LO3 Summarize the family, sibling, and peer influences on adolescent development.

LO4 Outline the causes of antisocial behaviour and what can be done to reduce the risk of juvenile delinquency.

LO5 Describe what marks the transition from adolescence to adulthood.

The Search for Identity

The search for **identity**—according to Erik Erikson, a coherent conception of the self, made up of goals, values, and beliefs to which the person is solidly committed—comes into focus during the teenage years. As Erikson (1950) emphasized, the effort to make sense of the self is part of a healthy process that builds on the achievements of earlier stages—on trust, autonomy, initiative, and industry—and lays the groundwork for coping with the challenges of adult life. Both Erikson and James Marcia provide insight into identity development in adolescence, which is also influenced by gender and ethnicity.

ERIKSON: IDENTITY VERSUS IDENTITY CONFUSION

The chief task of adolescence, said Erikson (1968), is to confront the crisis of **identity versus identity confusion** so as to become a unique adult with a coherent sense of self and a valued role in society. Identity forms as young people resolve three major issues: the choice of an occupation, the adoption of values to live by, and the development of a satisfying sexual identity.

According to Erikson (1982), the **psychosocial moratorium**, the time-out period that adolescence provides, allows young people to search for commitments to which they can be faithful. For example, going to college or university allows adolescents the time and opportunity to think about different career paths, before taking on all the responsibilities of adulthood. Adolescents who resolve the identity crisis satisfactorily develop the virtue of fidelity: sustained loyalty, faith, or a sense of belonging to a loved one or to friends and companions. Fidelity also can mean identification with a set of values, an ideology, a religion, a political movement, a creative pursuit, or an ethnic group.

Erikson saw the prime danger of this stage as identity confusion, which can greatly delay reaching psychological adulthood. According to Erikson, the identity confusion typical during this time accounts for the seemingly chaotic nature of much adolescent behaviour and for teenagers' painful self-consciousness. Cliquishness and intolerance of differences, both hallmarks of adolescence, are defences against identity confusion.

Erikson's theory describes male identity development as the norm. According to Erikson, a man is not capable of real intimacy until after he has achieved a stable identity, whereas women define themselves through marriage and motherhood, something that may have been truer when Erikson developed his theory than it is today. Thus, said Erikson, women develop identity through intimacy, not before it. As we will see, this male orientation of Erikson's theory has prompted criticism. Still, Erikson's concept of the identity crisis has inspired much valuable research.

MARCIA: IDENTITY STATUS—CRISIS AND COMMITMENT

What does the process of forming an identity look like? Are there individual differences? Erikson's perspective was extended by work in identity statuses. Marcia (1966, 2002) distinguished between four types of identity statuses

---

identity In Erikson's terminology, a coherent conception of the self made up of goals, values, and beliefs to which a person is solidly committed.

identity versus identity confusion Erikson's fifth stage of psychosocial development, in which an adolescent seeks to develop a coherent sense of self, including the role she or he is to play in society; also called *identity versus role confusion*.

psychosocial moratorium A period of time that allows young people to search for commitments to which they can be faithful.

that differ according to the presence or absence of crisis and commitment: identity achievement, foreclosure, moratorium, and identity diffusion. Crisis is a period of conscious decision-making where a young person is actively grappling with an identity issue; commitment is a personal investment in an occupation or ideology (system of beliefs). Following are sketches of the typical young person in each identity status:

- **Identity achievement** (crisis and commitment): Caterina has resolved her identity crisis. During the crisis period, she devoted much thought and some emotional struggle to major issues in her life. She has come to her own conclusions about what she believes, and expresses strong commitment about her beliefs. Her parents have encouraged her to make her own decisions; they have listened to her ideas and given their opinions without pressuring her to adopt them. Research in a number of cultures has found people in this category to be more mature and more socially competent than people in the other three (Marcia, 1993).

- **Foreclosure** (commitment without crisis): Andrea has made commitments, not as a result of exploring possible choices, but by accepting someone else's plans for her life. She is happy and self-assured, perhaps even smug and self-satisfied, and she becomes dogmatic when her opinions are questioned. She has close family ties, is obedient, and tends to follow a powerful leader, like her mother, who accepts no disagreement.

- **Moratorium** (crisis with no commitment yet): Nick is in crisis, struggling with decisions. He is lively, talkative, self-confident, and scrupulous but also anxious and fearful. He is close to his mother but resists her authority. He will probably come out of his crisis eventually with the ability to make commitments and achieve identity.

- **Identity diffusion** (no commitment, no crisis): Mark has not seriously considered options and has avoided commitments. He is unsure of himself and tends to be uncooperative. His parents do not discuss his future with him; they say it is up to him. People in this category tend to be unhappy and often lonely.

When middle-aged people look back on their lives, they most commonly trace a path from foreclosure to moratorium to identity achievement (Kroger & Haslett, 1991). However, these categories are not stages; they represent the status of identity development at a particular time, and they are likely to change in any direction as young people continue to develop.

GENDER DIFFERENCES IN IDENTITY FORMATION

Much research supports Erikson's view that, for women, identity and intimacy develop together. Rather than view this pattern as a departure from a male norm, however, some

identity achievement Identity status, described by Marcia, that is characterized by commitment to choices made following a crisis, a period spent in exploring alternatives.

foreclosure Identity status, described by Marcia, in which a person who has not spent time considering alternatives (that is, has not been in crisis) is committed to other people's plans for his or her life.

moratorium Identity status, described by Marcia, in which a person is considering alternatives (in crisis) and seems headed for commitment.

identity diffusion Identity status, described by Marcia, that is characterized by absence of commitment and lack of serious consideration of alternatives.

researchers see it as pointing to a weakness in Erikson's theory, which, they claim, is based on male-centred Western concepts of individuality, autonomy, and competitiveness. According to Carol Gilligan (1982, 1987a, 1987b; L. M. Brown & Gilligan, 1990), the female sense of self develops not so much through achieving a separate identity as through establishing relationships. Girls and women, says Gilligan, judge themselves on their handling of their responsibilities and on their ability to care for others as well as for themselves. In research on Marcia's identity statuses, however, few gender differences have appeared (Kroger, 2003).

ETHNIC FACTORS IN IDENTITY FORMATION

If you are part of the majority culture, ethnic identity formation tends not to be a primary concern. For many young people in minority groups, however, race or ethnicity is central to identity formation. Following Marcia's model,

According to Gilligan, the female sense of self develops through establishing relationships.

some research has identified four ethnic identity statuses (Phinney, 1998, 2008):

- *Diffused:* Zahra has done little or no exploration of her ethnicity and does not clearly understand the issues involved.

- *Foreclosed:* Mario has done little or no exploration of his ethnicity but has clear feelings about it. These feelings may be positive or negative, depending on the attitudes he absorbed at home.

- *Moratorium:* Cho-san has begun to explore her ethnicity but is confused about what it means to her.

- *Achieved:* Amir has explored his identity and understands and accepts his ethnicity.

Research shows evidence of the existence of these categories, with the highest proportion of adolescents falling into the moratorium status. Additionally, the proportion of people in achievement rises throughout adolescence and into adulthood, and those people who attain identity achievement are more likely to view race as central to their identity (Yip, Seaton, & Sellers, 2006).

Canada's policies on multiculturalism are designed to help ethnic groups in Canada maintain and develop their own values and cultures (Freisen, 1995), and minority rights are recognized by law. Despite this, forming an identity for adolescent immigrants and members of some ethnic groups can be difficult when the values of the ethnic group are different from those of mainstream Canadian society. Many minority youth are keenly conscious of differences between the values stressed at home and those dominant in the wider society, as they work through what being Canadian means to them (Lee & Hébert, 2006) and adapt to Canadian culture, indicated by good academic achievement and low levels of conflict with parents (Costigan, Hua, & Su, 2010; Leung, 2001). Perception of parental expectations for ethnic identity and positive parenting practice can influence the degree to which minority youth identify with their home culture (Su & Costigan, 2009). There is also quite a lot of diversity in identity formation based on whether the youth are first- or second- or later-generation immigrants, on the region and type of community where the individual lives (large urban, smaller urban, rural), and on the family circumstances before arriving in Canada (families emigrating by choice, refugee families) (Byers & Tastsoglou, 2008; Fantino & Colak, 2001; Lay & Verkuyten, 1999).

With the scale of diversity among Aboriginal cultures in Canada, it is difficult to draw general conclusions about identity formation among young Aboriginal people in Canada. However, the shared history of these groups may be related to some of the difficulties many young Aboriginal people face in identity formation. Disruption of traditional ways of life through a history of colonization, relocation to reserves, separation from families and abuse in residential schools, and efforts at assimilation have dealt a severe blow to the maintenance of strong cultural identities in many communities. More recent introduction of mass media and other economic and political changes has introduced additional challenges to the development of an Aboriginal identity for young people, who are exposed to a large variety of influences and rapid cultural changes (Kirmayer et al., 2000).

PROSOCIAL BEHAVIOUR AND VOLUNTEER ACTIVITY

Some researchers have studied prosocial, similar to care-oriented, moral reasoning as an alternative to Kohlberg's justice-based system. Prosocial moral reasoning is reasoning about moral dilemmas in which one person's needs or desires conflict with those of others in situations in which social rules or norms are unclear or non-existent. In a longitudinal study that followed children into early adulthood, prosocial reasoning based on personal reflection about consequences and on internalized values and norms increased with age, whereas reasoning based on such stereotypes as "it's nice to help" decreased from childhood into the late teens (Eisenberg & Morris, 2004).

Prosocial behaviour, too, typically increases from childhood through adolescence (Eisenberg & Morris, 2004). Girls tend to show more prosocial behaviour than boys, and this difference becomes more pronounced in adolescence (Eisenberg, Fabes, & Spinrad, 2006). Girls tend to see

Ask Yourself

1. What are the three issues in identity formation that Erikson believed needed to be resolved?

2. Nick is agonizing over his future, and is trying to decide if he should attend a community college or join the army. He is probably best described as being in Marcia's _____ stage of identity status.
   a. identity diffusion
   b. moratorium
   c. foreclosure
   d. identity achievement

3. According to Gilligan, identity is developed through intimate relationships to a greater degree in
   a. women.
   b. men.
   c. adolescents who came from difficult family circumstances.
   d. neither gender; it is equally important.

4. Ethnic identity formation is more important for adolescents
   a. as they reach adulthood.
   b. when they start working full-time.
   c. from the majority group in a culture.
   d. from minority groups in a culture.

5. Which two factors are positively related to prosocial behaviour?
   a. being male, getting older
   b. being female, getting older
   c. volunteering, being male
   d. being forced to volunteer, being younger

themselves as more empathic and prosocial than boys do, and parents of girls emphasize social responsibility more than parents of boys (Eisenberg & Morris, 2004).

About 58 percent of Canadian adolescents engage in some sort of community service or volunteer activity (Vézina & Crompton, 2012). These prosocial activities enable adolescents to become involved in adult society, to explore their potential roles as part of the community, and to link their developing sense of identity to civic involvement. Adolescent volunteers tend to have a high degree of self-understanding and commitment to others. Girls are more likely to volunteer than boys, and adolescents with high socio-economic status (SES) volunteer more than those with lower SES (Eisenberg & Morris, 2004). Students who do volunteer work outside of school tend, as adults, to be more engaged in their communities than those who do not (Eccles, 2004).

Sexuality

When John was young, he used to wonder if he was like the other kids. "I always felt different," he later said. "I just didn't know what part of me was different." It was not until adolescence, when he developed a full-blown, and secret, crush on a schoolmate that he realized that he might be gay. Afraid of being laughed at or ridiculed, he kept it to himself until his senior year of high school.

Seeing oneself as a sexual being, recognizing one's sexual orientation, coming to terms with sexual stirrings, and forming romantic or sexual attachments are all parts of achieving sexual identity. Awareness of sexuality is an important aspect of identity formation, profoundly affecting self-image and relationships.

During the twentieth century, a major change in sexual attitudes and behaviour in Canada and other industrialized countries brought more widespread acceptance of premarital sex, homosexuality, and other previously disapproved forms of sexual activity. Concordant with this increase in freedom, however, came increased risk. In the following section, we discuss important factors in sexual identity formation and sexual behaviour, as well as focus on some of the risks that today's adolescents face.

SEXUAL ORIENTATION AND IDENTITY

Although present in younger children, it is in adolescence that a person's **sexual orientation** generally becomes a pressing issue: whether that person will consistently be sexually attracted to persons of the other sex (heterosexual), of the same sex (homosexual), or of both sexes (bisexual). Although traditionally thought of as existing on a single continuum (from other-sex to same-sex orientation), research on sexual orientation shows that it is more accurate to consider sexual orientation as existing along two dimensions, one for degree of other-sex orientation, and the second for degree of

Did you know?

Same-sex activity is widespread in the animal kingdom, and found in animals as disparate as zebra finches, dolphins, and bonobos (Bailey & Zuk, 2009).

same-sex orientation (Savin-Williams & Vrangalova, 2013; Sell, 1997). Heterosexuality predominates in nearly every known culture throughout the world. The prevalence of homosexual orientation varies widely, depending on how it is defined and measured. Depending on whether it is measured by sexual, or romantic, attraction or arousal; by sexual behaviour; or by sexual identity, the rate of homosexuality in the North American population ranges from 1 to 15 percent (Savin-Williams & Ream, 2007). In 2009, about 1 percent of Canadians aged 18 years and up identified themselves as homosexual, and 1 percent as bisexual (Statistics Canada, 2011j). An accurate picture of the prevalence of LGBQT—lesbian, gay, bisexual, queer, transgendered, two-spirited (Aboriginal homosexual individuals whose gender identity embodies both male and female simultaneously; Cameron, 2005)—affects/feelings, behaviours, and identities among Canadian youth are difficult to estimate, as census questions ask respondents to indicate sexual identity only.

Origins of Sexual Orientation

Much research on sexual orientation has focused on efforts to explain homosexuality. Although it once was considered a mental illness, several decades of research have found no association between homosexual orientation and emotional or social problems—apart from those apparently caused by societal treatment of homosexuals (American Psychological Association [APA], n.d.). These findings led the psychiatric profession in 1973 to stop classifying homosexuality as a mental disorder.

Sexual orientation becomes a pressing issue in adolescence, as it was for Marc Hall, an Ontario high school student, who challenged his school's decision to prevent him from attending his end-of-year formal with his boyfriend.

---

sexual orientation Focus of consistent sexual, romantic, and affectionate interest, either heterosexual, homosexual, or bisexual.

Did you know?

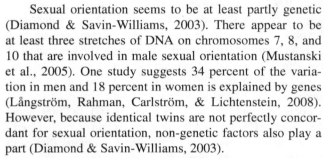

Many young people have one or more homosexual experiences as they are growing up, but isolated experiences or even occasional homosexual attractions or fantasies do not determine sexual orientation (Mosher, Chandra, & Jones, 2005).

Sexual orientation seems to be at least partly genetic (Diamond & Savin-Williams, 2003). There appear to be at least three stretches of DNA on chromosomes 7, 8, and 10 that are involved in male sexual orientation (Mustanski et al., 2005). One study suggests 34 percent of the variation in men and 18 percent in women is explained by genes (Långström, Rahman, Carlström, & Lichtenstein, 2008). However, because identical twins are not perfectly concordant for sexual orientation, non-genetic factors also play a part (Diamond & Savin-Williams, 2003).

The greater the number of older biological brothers a man has, the more likely he is to be gay. This phenomenon may be a cumulative immune-like response to the presence of successive male fetuses in the womb. If rearing or social factors influenced the fraternal birth-order effect, then the number of non-biological older brothers would predict sexual orientation, but they do not (Bogaert, 2006).

Imaging studies have found similarities in brain structure between homosexuals and heterosexuals of the other sex. Brains of gay men and straight women are symmetrical, whereas in lesbians and straight men, the right hemisphere is slightly larger. Also, in gays and lesbians, connections in the amygdala, which is involved in emotion, are typical of the other sex (Savic & Lindström, 2008). One researcher reported a difference in the size of the hypothalamus, a brain structure that governs sexual activity, in heterosexual and gay men (LeVay, 1991). In brain imaging studies on pheromones, odours that attract mates, the odour of male sweat activated the hypothalamus in gay men much as it did in heterosexual women; the analogous effect was found for lesbians and straight men exposed to female pheromones (Savic, Berglund, & Lindström, 2006). However, these differences may be an effect of homosexuality, not a cause.

Homosexual, Bisexual, and Transgendered Identity Development

Despite the increased acceptance of homosexuality in Canada, many adolescents who openly identify as gay, lesbian, or bisexual sometimes fear disclosing their sexual orientation, even to their parents (Canadian Paediatric Society, Adolescent Health Committee, 2008; Hillier, 2002). They may also find it difficult to meet potential same-sex partners. Thus, homosexuals' recognition and expression of their sexual identity are more complex than heterosexuals' (Diamond & Savin-Williams, 2003), and with no typical route to sexual identity development, some experience identity confusion (Sieving, Oliphant, & Blum, 2002). Gay, lesbian, and bisexual youth who are unable to establish peer groups that share their sexual orientation may struggle with the recognition of same-sex attractions (Bouchey & Furman, 2003).

Similarly, transgendered (or gender-variant) youth—those with gender identity different from their sex at birth—face complexities in recognition and expression of their sexual identities. They often identify outside of traditional gender notions of male and female, describing themselves as gender-fluid. Professionals who provide support to transgendered youth who are questioning or confused about identity issues can provide non-judgmental advice that focuses on normalization of feelings, consideration about options about identity formation and expression, and discussion about fears, anxiety, and ways to cope with real and potential dangers (White Holman & Goldberg, 2006).

WHERE DO YOU STAND?

Recent anti-discrimination and anti-bullying efforts by provincial governments have mandated that student support groups, such as gay-straight alliances, be permitted in all public and private schools receiving public support as a way to battle homophobic (anti-gay) attitudes. How effective do you think such efforts will be in battling homophobia?

SEXUAL BEHAVIOUR

The average age of first sexual intercourse reported by Canadian youth 15 to 19 years of age occurs between 16 and 17 years, and approximately 27 percent of boys and girls report having had intercourse by age 16 (Butler-Jones, 2011). Street-involved youth tend to begin sexual activity earlier (at 14 years) than those living in a family. The proportion of youth reporting sexual activity increases with age: in 2009, 15 percent of 15-year-olds reported having sexual intercourse at least once; by age 27, 97 percent of young people report having had sex at least once (Butler-Jones, 2011).

Early Sexual Activity and Risk Taking

Two major concerns about adolescent sexual activity are the risks of contracting sexually transmitted infections (STIs) and, for heterosexual activity, of pregnancy. Most at

Did you know?

Although earlier male initiation is the norm in most cultures, in Mali and Ghana, more women than men become sexually active at an early age (Singh, Wulf, Samara, & Cuca, 2000).

risk are young people who start sexual activity early, have multiple partners, do not use contraceptives regularly, and have inadequate information—or misinformation—about sex (Abma, Chandra, Mosher, Peterson, & Piccinino, 1997; Meade & Ickovics, 2005). Other risk factors are living in a socio-economically disadvantaged community, substance use, antisocial behaviour, and association with deviant peers. Parental monitoring can help reduce these risks (Baumer & South, 2001; Capaldi, Stoolmiller, Clark, & Owen, 2002).

Why do some adolescents become sexually active at an early age? Various factors, including early entrance into puberty, poverty, poor school performance, lack of academic and career goals, a history of sexual abuse or parental neglect, and cultural or family patterns of early sexual experience, may play a part (Klein & AAP Committee on Adolescence, 2005). The absence of a father, especially early in life, is a strong factor (Ellis et al., 2003). Teenagers who have close, warm relationships with their mothers and who perceive their mothers would disapprove are more likely to delay sexual activity. (Mcneely et al., 2002). Other reasons teenagers give for not yet having had sex are that it is against their religion or morals and that they do not want to get pregnant (Abma, Martinez, Mosher, & Dawson, 2004).

One of the most powerful influences is perception of peer group norms. Young people often feel under pressure to engage in activities they do not feel ready for. In a nationally representative survey, nearly one-third of 15- to 17-year-olds, especially boys, said they had experienced pressure to have sex (Kaiser Family Foundation, Hoff, Greene, & Davis, 2003; Table 16.1). A recent study found that as a teen's number of close friends who initiate sex grows, the likelihood that they themselves will initiate sex also rises (Ali & Dwyer, 2011). According to the Canadian Youth Sexual Health and HIV/AIDS Study, a survey of over 10,000 Canadian youth in Grades 7, 9, and 11 (Boyce, Doherty, Fortin, & MacKinnon, 2003; Boyce et al., 2006), more girls than boys reported being coerced into having sex. Twelve percent of Grade 9 girls and 17 percent of Grade 11 girls reported being pressured to have sex when they did not want it, compared with only 5 percent of boys in each grade.

Non-Intercourse Sexual Behaviour

As North American adolescents have become more aware of the risks of sexual activity, the percentage who have ever had intercourse has declined, especially among boys (Abma et al., 2004). However, non-coital forms of genital sexual activity, such as oral and anal sex and mutual masturbation, are common. In one U.S. national survey, just over half of teenage boys and girls reported having given or received oral sex, more than had had vaginal intercourse (Mosher et al., 2005). Many heterosexual teens do not define these activities as sex (Remez, 2000).

Moreover, many adolescents engage in sexual behaviour via electronic sources. For example, depending on how it is defined, 1.0 to 2.5 percent of teens between the ages of 10 to 17 have sent nude or nearly nude photos through their cellphone (Mitchell, Finkelhor, Jones, & Wolok, 2012). The proportion of teens who have done so rises with age: 8 percent of 17-year-olds have engaged in sexting, and this proportion rises to 17 percent if the teen pays for cell service themselves (Lenhart, 2009). These trends are troubling for a number of reasons. Foremost among them is that the electronic transmission of photographs of nude teens is subject to prosecution under child pornography laws. For example, in 2008–2009, it is estimated that law enforcement agencies handled 3,477 cases of youth-produced sexual images. Although some of the cases involved either the participation of an adult or were related to malicious intent or bullying, 18 percent of the "non-aggravated" youth-only cases, consisting of experimental and romantic sexual and attention seeking, resulted in arrest (Wolak, Finkelhor, & Mitchell, 2012). Moreover, arrest is not the only issue. Once released to the Internet, such photos may be available to future employers, schools, or romantic partners, and may follow a young person over time and to their detriment.

TABLE 16.1 Adolescents' Attitudes about Sexual Activity

Percentage of 15- to 17-Year-Olds Who Say They "Strongly" or "Somewhat" Agree with Each of the Following

	Male	Female	Sexually Active	Not Sexually Active
Waiting to have sex is a nice idea but nobody really does.	66%	60%	69%	59%
There is pressure to have sex by a certain age.	59%	58%	58%	59%
Once you have had sex, it is harder to say no the next time.	56%	47%	54%	50%
If you have been seeing someone for a while, it is expected that you will have sex.	50%	27%	52%	31%
Oral sex is not as big of a deal as sexual intercourse.	54%	38%	52%	42%

Source: Adapted from Kaiser Family Foundation et al., *National Survey of Adolescents and Young Adults: Sexual Health Knowledge, Attitudes and Experiences*, 2003, Table 8, p. 12, and Table 33, p. 39.

Use of Contraceptives

Sexual activity with multiple partners and unprotected sex are risky behaviours; of those who reported having sex in the previous 12 months, 37 percent of youth between 15 and 19 years reported having had more than one partner, as did 25 percent of young adults (20 to 29 years). The majority of youth—75 percent—reported having used condoms, though this number decreases as adolescents get older (Butler-Jones, 2011; Rotermann, 2008). Teens who, in their first relationship, delay intercourse, discuss contraception before having sex, or use more than one method of contraception are more likely to use contraceptives consistently throughout that relationship (Manlove, Ryan, & Franzetta, 2003; Rotermann, 2005).

The best safeguard for sexually active teens is regular use of condoms, which give some protection against STIs as well as against pregnancy. Condom use has increased in recent years, as has use of the pill and new hormonal and injectable methods of contraception or combinations of methods (Abma et al., 2004). Adolescents who start using prescription contraceptives often stop using condoms, in some cases not realizing that they leave themselves unprotected against STIs (Klein & AAP Committee on Adolescence, 2005).

Sex Education

Comprehensive sexual education, including information about the prevention of pregnancy and STIs, is critical to promoting responsible decision-making. Evidence for the positive impact of such programs is strong: Over 60 percent of programs that emphasized abstinence together with condom use realized the positive outcomes of delayed and/or reduced sexually activity and increased use of condoms or contraceptives. Further, the programs did not increase sexual activity (Kirby & Laris, 2009; Kohler, Manhart, & Lafferty, 2008).

However, some school programs promote abstinence as the only option, even though abstinence-only courses have not been shown to delay sexual activity (AAP Committee on Psychosocial Aspects of Child and Family Health and Committee on Adolescence, 2001; Kirby & Laris, 2009; Satcher, 2001). Effective programs are likely to be those that provide comprehensive information on alternatives and choices in sexuality, while addressing the underlying influences of teen pregnancy, such as low SES, low parental education, violence, and mental health difficulties (Butler-Jones, 2011; Maticka-Tyndale, 2001).

SEXUALLY TRANSMITTED INFECTIONS (STIs)

When John told his parents that he was gay, after their initial surprise and adjustment, his parents accepted his sexuality without issue. However, they were worried about sexually risky behaviour and talked to John, to his great embarrassment, about the necessity of always using condoms during sexual activity. "Just because pregnancy might not be an issue," his mother said, "doesn't mean sex carries no risk."

Sexually transmitted infections (STIs) are infections spread by sexual contact. Adolescents are disproportionately affected by STIs in Canada (The Sex Information and Education Council of Canada [SIECCAN], 2004). The chief reasons for the prevalence of STIs among teenagers include early sexual activity, which increases the likelihood of having multiple high-risk partners; failure to use condoms or to use them regularly and correctly; and, for women, a tendency to have sex with older partners (Butler-Jones, 2011; Centers for Disease Control and Prevention [CDC], 2000b; Forhan et al., 2008).

Human Papillomavirus (HPV)

The most common STI, affecting up to 29 percent of 14- to 19-year-olds, is human papillomavirus (HPV), or genital warts. There are approximately 40 types of HPV, a number of which have been identified as a leading cause of cervical cancer in women. A vaccine is available that prevents the types of HPV that cause most cases of cervical cancer and genital warts. The vaccine has been recommended by the

sexually transmitted infections (STIs) Diseases spread by sexual contact.

Canadian Paediatric Society for 9- to 13-year-old girls as well as for girls and women over age 13 who have not yet been vaccinated (Samson et al., 2007).

Chlamydia, Gonorrhea, Genital Herpes, and Trichomoniasis

The most common curable STIs are chlamydia and gonorrhea. These diseases, if undetected and untreated, can lead to severe health problems, including, in women, pelvic inflammatory disease (PID), a serious abdominal infection. Although teenagers tend to view oral sex as less risky than intercourse, pharyngeal gonorrhea can be transmitted in that way (CDC, 2004).

Genital herpes simplex is a chronic, recurring, often painful, and highly contagious disease. Its incidence has increased dramatically during the past three decades. Hepatitis B remains a prominent STI despite the availability, for more than 20 years, of a preventive vaccine. Also common among young people is trichomoniasis, a parasitic infection that may be passed along by moist towels and swimsuits (Weinstock, Berman, & Cates, 2004).

Human Immunodeficiency Virus (HIV)

The human immunodeficiency virus (HIV), which causes AIDS, is transmitted through bodily fluids, usually by sharing of intravenous drug needles or by sexual contact with an infected partner. The virus attacks the body's immune system, leaving a person vulnerable to a variety of fatal diseases. Symptoms of AIDS, which include extreme fatigue, fever, swollen lymph nodes, weight loss, diarrhea, and night sweats, may not appear until from six months to 10 or more years after initial infection.

Worldwide, of the 4.1 million new HIV infections each year, about half are in young people ages 15 to 24 (UNAIDS, 2006). Although the prevalence of AIDS among Canadian youth ages 15 to 29 is small compared with adults (approximately 11.8 percent of all cases in 2008), it is a cause for concern as many young people with undetected HIV go unreported (Public Health Agency of Canada, 2010d). As of now, AIDS is incurable, but increasingly the related infections that kill people are being stopped with antiviral therapy (Weinstock et al., 2004). Ironically, by reducing the scare factor, this advance may be responsible for giving sexually active teens less reason to take precautions when having sex. Because symptoms may not appear until a disease has progressed to the point of causing serious long-term complications, early detection is important.

TEENAGE PREGNANCY AND CHILD-BEARING

More than 28 percent of adolescent girls in Canada have been pregnant at least once before age 20. About half (48 percent) of pregnant teenagers in Canada give birth, and 52 percent choose to abort (McKay, 2012).

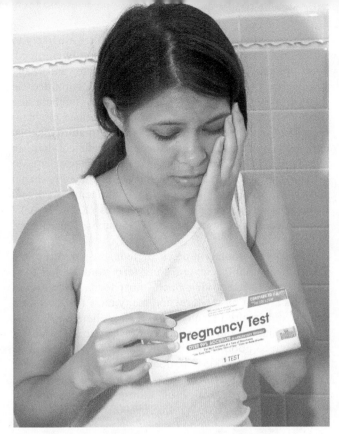

Most pregnant teenagers describe their pregnancies as unintended, though there has been a significant decline in rates of teenage pregnancy.

A substantial decline in teenage pregnancy has accompanied steady decreases in early intercourse and in sex with multiple partners and an increase in contraceptive use. Between 2001 and 2010, the teen pregnancy rate fell by 20.3 percent across Canada, though there are regional disparities—the pregnancy rate increased by over 10 percent during those years in Newfoundland, Nova Scotia, and New Brunswick, as well as in the Yukon (McKay, 2012).

More than 90 percent of pregnant teenagers describe their pregnancies as unintended, and 50 percent of teen pregnancies occur within six months of sexual initiation (Klein & AAP Committee on Adolescence, 2005). Teenage fathers tend to have limited financial resources, poor academic performance, and high dropout rates. At least one-third of teenage parents are themselves products of adolescent pregnancy (Klein & AAP Committee on Adolescence, 2005).

Teenage pregnancies often have poor outcomes. Many of the mothers are impoverished and poorly educated, and some are drug users. Many do not eat properly, do not gain enough weight, and get inadequate prenatal care or none at all. Their babies are likely to be premature or dangerously small and are at heightened risk of other birth complications; late fetal, neonatal, or infant death; health and academic problems; abuse and neglect; and developmental disabilities that may continue into adolescence (Butler-Jones, 2011; Children's Defense Fund, 2004; Klein & AAP Committee on Adolescence, 2005; Menacker, Martin, MacDorman, & Ventura, 2004).

Teenage unwed mothers and their families are likely to suffer financially. Child support laws are spottily enforced, court-ordered payments are often inadequate, and many young fathers cannot afford them (AAP Committee on Adolescence, 1999). Additionally, teenage mothers are likely to drop out of school and to have repeated pregnancies. They and their partners may lack the maturity, skills, and social support to be good parents. Their children, in turn, tend to have developmental and academic problems, to be depressed, to engage in substance abuse and early sexual activity, to engage in gang activity, to be unemployed, and to become adolescent parents themselves (Klein & AAP Committee on Adolescence, 2005; Pogarsky, Thornberry, & Lizotte, 2006).

However, poor outcomes of teenage parenting are far from inevitable. Several long-term studies find that, two decades after giving birth, most former adolescent mothers are not on welfare, and many have finished high school and secured steady jobs. Comprehensive adolescent pregnancy and home visitation programs seem to contribute to good outcomes (Klein & AAP Committee on Adolescence, 2005), as does contact with the father (Howard, Lefever, Borkowski, & Whitman, 2006) and involvement in a religious community (Carothers, Borkowski, Lefever, & Whitman, 2005).

Ask Yourself

6. What are two factors that impact sexual orientation?

7. What are four risk factors for contracting STIs and/or becoming pregnant in adolescence?

8. What is the most common STI?
   a. HIV
   b. genital herpes
   c. syphilis
   d. HPV

9. Overall, teen pregnancy has a _____ effect on outcomes.
   a. neutral
   b. negative
   c. positive
   d. variable (depending on race/ethnicity)

Relationships with Family and Peers

Age becomes a powerful bonding agent in adolescence. Adolescents spend more time with peers and less with family. However, most teenagers' fundamental values remain closer to their parents' than is generally realized (Steinberg, 2008). Even as adolescents turn to peers for role models, companionship, and intimacy, they still look to parents for a secure base from which they can try their wings.

adolescent rebellion *Pattern of emotional turmoil, characteristic of a minority of adolescents that may involve conflict with family, alienation from adult society, reckless behaviour, and rejection of adult values.*

individuation *Adolescent's struggle for autonomy and differentiation, or personal identity.*

IS ADOLESCENT REBELLION A MYTH?

The teenage years have been called a time of **adolescent rebellion**, involving emotional turmoil, conflict within the family, alienation from adult society, reckless behaviour, and rejection of adult values. But is this characterization of teens true?

Most young people feel close to and positive about their parents, share similar opinions on major issues, and value their parents' approval (J. P. Hill, 1987; Offer, Ostrov, & Howard, 1989). The vast majority of teens adapt well to their life experiences. The relatively few deeply troubled adolescents tend to come from disrupted families and, as adults, continue to have unstable family lives and to reject cultural norms (Offer, Kaiz, Ostrov, & Albert, 2002).

Still, adolescence can be a tough time for young people and their parents. Family conflict, depression, and risky behaviour are more common than during other parts of the lifespan (Arnett, 1999). Negative emotionality and mood swings are most intense during early adolescence, perhaps because of the stress connected with puberty. It may also be that some level of rebellious behaviour in the teenage years is developmentally normal (Moffitt, 1993; Steinberg, 2001). By late adolescence, emotionality tends to become more stable (Larson, Moneta, Richards, & Wilson, 2002).

ADOLESCENTS AND PARENTS

Adolescence brings special challenges. Just as adolescents feel tension between dependency on their parents and the need to break away, parents want their children to be independent yet find it hard to let go. These tensions can lead to family conflict, and parenting styles and monitoring can influence outcomes and teens' willingness to self-disclose. Also, adolescents' relationships with parents are affected by the parents' life situation—their work, as well as their marital and socio-economic status.

Individuation and Family Conflict

Individuation is an adolescent's struggle for autonomy and differentiation, or personal identity. An important aspect of individuation is carving out boundaries of control between self and parents (Nucci, Hasebe, & Lins-Dyer, 2005), and this process may entail family conflict.

Both family conflict and positive identification with parents are highest at age 13 and then diminish until age 17, when they stabilize or increase somewhat. This shift reflects increased opportunities for independent adolescent decision-making (Gutman & Eccles, 2007).

Perspectives on Diversity

CULTURE AND DISCRETIONARY TIME

One way to assess changes in adolescents' relationships with the important people in their lives is to see how they spend their discretionary time. Cultural variations in time use reflect varying cultural needs, values, and practices (Verma & Larson, 2003).

Young people in tribal or peasant societies spend most of their time producing bare necessities of life and have much less time for socializing than adolescents in technologically advanced societies (Larson & Verma, 1999). In some post-industrial societies, such as Korea and Japan, where the pressures of school work and family obligations are strong, adolescents have relatively little free time. To relieve stress, they spend their time in passive pursuits, such as watching television and "doing nothing" (Verma & Larson, 2003). In India's family-centred culture, on the other hand, middle-class urban eighth graders spend 39 percent of their waking hours with family, compared with 23 percent for U.S. eighth graders, and report being happier when with their families

than U.S. eighth graders do. For these young people, the task of adolescence is not to separate from the family but to become more integrated with it. Similar findings have been reported in Indonesia, Bangladesh, Morocco, and Argentina (Larson & Wilson, 2004). In comparison, U.S. adolescents have a good deal of discretionary time, most of which they spend with peers, increasingly of the other sex (Juster et al., 2004; Larson & Seepersad, 2003; Verma & Larson, 2003).

Ethnicity may also affect family connectedness. In some research, African-American teenagers tended to maintain more intimate family relationships and less intense peer relations than white teenagers (Giordano, Cernkovich, & DeMaris, 1993). On the other hand, those from Mexican and Chinese families, particularly immigrant families, reported a stronger sense of family obligation and assistance and spent more time on activities that carried out those obligations (Hardway & Fuligni, 2006).

Arguments most often concern control over everyday personal matters—chores, school work, dress, money, curfews, dating, and friends—rather than issues of health and safety or right and wrong (Steinberg, 2005). The emotional intensity of these conflicts—out of all proportion with the subject matter—may reflect the underlying individuation process.

Especially for girls, family relations can affect mental health. Adolescents who are given more decision-making opportunities report higher self-esteem than those who are given fewer such opportunities. In addition, negative family interactions are related to adolescent depression, whereas positive family identification is related to less depression (Gutman & Eccles, 2007). In a longitudinal study of 99 families, both individuation and family connectedness during adolescence predicted well-being in middle age (Bell & Bell, 2005).

Parenting Styles

Authoritative parents insist on important rules, norms, and values but are willing to listen, explain, and negotiate. They exercise appropriate control over a child's conduct (behavioural control) but not over the child's feelings, beliefs, and sense of self (psychological control). Authoritative parenting fosters healthy development

(Baumrind, 2005). However, psychological control, exerted through such emotionally manipulative techniques as withdrawal of love, can harm adolescents' psychosocial development and mental health. Parents who are psychologically controlling tend to be unresponsive to their children's growing need for psychological autonomy, the right to their own thoughts and feelings (Steinberg, 2005).

Teens whose parents are firm in enforcing behavioural rules have more self-discipline and fewer behaviour problems than those with more permissive parents. Those whose parents grant them psychological autonomy tend to become self-confident and competent in both the academic and social realms (Gray & Steinberg, 1999).

WHAT DO YOU DO?

Art Therapist

Art therapists use art as a part of the therapeutic process for individuals with emotional problems, disabilities, or acute or chronic health problems. Through the process of creating art, art therapists help their clients better understand their thoughts and emotions. Art therapists typically work within health and non-profit organizations, as well as in private practice. A master's degree in art therapy or a degree with an art therapy concentration is required to become an art therapist. In addition, each province has its own certification requirements. To learn more about becoming an art therapist, visit http://canadianarttherapy.org.

Problems arise when parents overstep what adolescents perceive as appropriate bounds of legitimate parental authority. The existence of a mutually agreed personal domain in which authority belongs to the adolescent has been found in various cultures and social classes from Japan to Brazil. This domain expands as parents and adolescents continually renegotiate its boundaries (Nucci et al., 2005). Nevertheless, across cultures, closeness with parents tends to be high, despite differences in perceptions of parental control—relatively low in Canada, higher in France, and highest in Italy, as found in one cross-cultural study. Across cultures, in keeping with expansion of personal domain of authority, perceptions of parental control drop as adolescents get older, with an earlier drop in Canada than in Italy (Claes et al., 2011).

Parental Monitoring and Adolescents' Self-Disclosure

Young people's growing autonomy and the shrinking areas of perceived parental authority redefine the types of behaviour adolescents are expected to disclose to parents (Smetana, Crean, & Campione-Barr, 2005). Generally, both adolescents and parents see behaviour related to health and safety, such as smoking, drinking, and drug use, as most subject to disclosure; followed by moral issues, such as lying; conventional issues, such as bad manners or swearing; and multifaceted, or borderline, issues, such as seeing an R-rated movie. Both adolescents and parents see personal issues, such as how teens spend their time and money, as least subject to disclosure. However, for each type of behaviour, parents are more inclined to expect disclosure than adolescents are to do it. This discrepancy diminishes between the 9th and 12th grades as parents modify their expectations to fit adolescents' growing maturity (Smetana, Metzger, Gettman, & Campione-Barr, 2006). Additionally, young people are more willing to disclose information about themselves when parents maintain a warm, responsive family climate in which adolescents are encouraged to speak openly and when parents provide clear expectations without being overly controlling (Soenens, Vansteenkiste, Luyckx, & Goossens, 2006)—in other words, when parenting is authoritative. Adolescents, especially girls, tend to have closer, more supportive relationships with their mothers than with their fathers, and girls confide more in their mothers (Smetana et al., 2006).

Family Structure and Family Atmosphere

Adolescents, like younger children, are sensitive to the atmosphere in the family home. In a longitudinal study of 451 adolescents and their parents, changes in marital distress or marital conflict predicted corresponding changes in adolescents' adjustment (Cui, Conger, & Lorenz, 2005). In other studies, adolescent boys and girls whose parents later divorced showed more academic, psychological, and behavioural problems before the breakup than peers whose parents did not later divorce (Sun, 2001).

Adolescents living with their continuously married parents tend to have significantly fewer behavioural problems than those in any other family structure—single-parent, cohabiting, or stepfamilies (Carlson, 2006). Adolescents in cohabiting families, like younger children, tend to have greater behavioural and emotional problems than adolescents in married families (Brown, 2004).

On the other hand, a multiethnic study of 12- and 13-year-old children of single mothers—first assessed when the children were 6 and 7 years old—found no negative effects of single parenting on school performance and no greater risk of problem behaviour. What mattered most were the mother's educational level and ability, family income, and the quality of the home environment (Ricciuti, 2004). This finding suggests that negative effects of living in a single-parent home can be offset by positive factors.

Mothers' Employment and Economic Stress

The impact of a mother's work outside the home may depend on whether there are two parents or only one in the household. Often, a single mother must work to stave off economic disaster; how her working affects her teenage children may hinge on how much time and energy she has left over to spend with them, how well she keeps track of their whereabouts, and what kind of role model she provides. Risks include alcohol and drug use and misconduct in school, especially for those adolescents who have an early history of problem behaviour. However, this is less likely to happen when parents monitor their children's activities and neighbours are actively involved (Coley, Morris, & Hernandez, 2004).

As we have discussed earlier, a major problem in many single-parent families is lack of money. In a national longitudinal study, adolescent children of low-income single mothers were negatively affected by their mother's unstable employment

Authoritative parenting, involving insisting on important rules, norms, and values, but with some flexibility, fosters healthy development.

-Many mothers, such as Quebec-based dance, film, and Cirque du Soleil costume designer Liz Vandal, seen here with her son, must juggle the demands of both a career and family life.

or being out of work for two years. The adolescents were more likely to drop out of school and to experience declines in self-esteem and mastery (Kalil & Ziol-Guest, 2005). Furthermore, family economic hardship during adolescence can affect adult well-being (Sobolewski & Amato, 2005).

ADOLESCENTS AND SIBLINGS

As adolescents spend more time with peers, they have less time and less need for the emotional gratification they used to get from the sibling bond. Adolescents are less close to siblings than to either parents or friends, are less influenced by them, and become even more distant as they move through adolescence (Cole & Kerns, 2001; Laursen, 1996). As children approach high school, their relationships with their siblings become progressively more equal, and differences in competence and independence shrink (Cole & Kerns, 2001).

Generally, sisters report more intimacy than brothers or mixed pairs. Intimacy levels between same-sex siblings remain stable; however, mixed-sex siblings tend to become less intimate over time. Sibling conflict declines across middle adolescence (Kim, McHale, Osgood, & Crouter, 2006).

Sibling relationships can have positive or negative effects, depending on context. For example, in

single-mother homes, a warm and nurturing relationship with an older sister can buffer a younger sister from engaging in substance use and risky sexual behaviour. On the other hand, having a domineering older sister may increase a younger sibling's high-risk sexual behaviour (East & Khoo, 2005), and older siblings may influence a younger one to smoke, drink, or use drugs (Pomery et al., 2005; Rende et al., 2005).

PEERS AND FRIENDS

"I came out to my parents first," John said, "I mean, I knew they would always love me. But my friends were harder. I didn't know what they would do. I was lucky. While I had one friend that dumped me after learning I was gay, for the most part, everyone was really supportive."

An important source of emotional support during the complex transition of adolescence is the peer group. The peer group is a source of affection, sympathy, understanding, and moral guidance; a place for experimentation; and a setting for achieving autonomy and independence from parents. It is a place to form intimate relationships that serve as rehearsals for adult intimacy.

In childhood, most peer interactions are one-to-one, though somewhat larger groupings begin to form in middle childhood. As children move into adolescence, cliques—structured groups of friends who do things together—become more important. In adolescence, crowds emerge. Crowd membership is a social construction, a set of labels such as the jocks, the nerds, the skaters, the stoners. All three levels of peer groupings may exist simultaneously, and some may overlap in membership, which may change over time. Both clique and crowd affiliations become looser as adolescence progresses (Brown & Klute, 2003).

The influence of peers normally peaks at ages 12 to 13 and declines during middle and late adolescence. Risk-taking is higher in the company of peers than alone, and this is especially true of younger adolescents (Gardner & Steinberg, 2005). However, attachment to peers in early adolescence is not likely to forecast real trouble (Fuligni, Eccles, Barber, & Clements, 2001).

Friendships

The intensity and importance of friendships and the amount of time spent with friends are probably greater in adolescence than at any other time in the lifespan. Friendships tend to become more reciprocal, more equal, and more stable. Those that are less satisfying become less important or are abandoned.

Greater intimacy, loyalty, and sharing with friends mark a transition toward adultlike friendships. Adolescents begin to rely more on friends than on parents for intimacy and support, and they share confidences more than younger friends do (Buhrmester & Chong, 2009). Girls' friendships tend to be more intimate than boys', with frequent sharing of confidences (Brown & Klute, 2003). Intimacy with same-sex friends increases during early to mid-adolescence, after which it typically declines as intimacy with the other sex grows (Laursen, 1996).

The increased intimacy of adolescent friendship reflects cognitive as well as emotional development (Buhrmester, 1996) and is related to psychological adjustment and social competence. Adolescents who have close, stable, supportive friendships generally have a high opinion of themselves, do well in school, are sociable, and are unlikely to be hostile, anxious, or depressed (Berndt & Perry, 1990; Hartup & Stevens, 1999). A bidirectional process seems to be at work: Good relationships foster adjustment, which in turn fosters good friendships.

Social Consequences of Online Communication

The explosion of online communication technologies such as email, text messaging, and social networking sites has changed the way many adolescents communicate. As a group, adolescents are the primary users of these technologies. They spend more time online than adults and spend a majority of their online time using the Internet to communicate. A recent study on Internet usage in over 600 adolescents found that 99 percent of the teens in the study reported using the Internet, and teens who used instant messaging experienced greater depressive symptoms than their peers who did not (van den Eijnden, Meerkerk, Vermulst, Spijkerman, & Engels, 2008).

However, as access to the Internet has increased and technology has become more sophisticated and easy to use, the effect of increased Internet use has shifted from negative to positive. Recent studies have shown that online communication can stimulate rather than reduce social connectedness (Kraut et al., 2002; Zwier, Araujo, Boukes, & Willemsen, 2011). For example, studies have found that instant messaging usage has a positive effect on relationship quality in adolescence (Valkenburg & Peter, 2009a), and social competence in adolescents who are lonely can be strengthened through using the Internet to communicate with others and experiment with their identities (Valkenburg & Peter, 2008).

The ability of online communication to enhance online self-disclosure has been identified as a primary reason for improved social connectedness and well-being. Individuals often become unusually intimate in

an online environment and feel free to express themselves (Valkenburg & Peter, 2009b). Because adolescents connect self-disclosure with quality friendships, the elevated level of self-disclosure in online environments can also be linked to friendship quality and formation (Valkenburg & Peter, 2007), which in turn elevates social connectedness and well-being.

The aspects of online communication that enhance connectedness—the level of anonymity—has made it appealing for electronic bullies. As discussed previously, bullying is a form of aggression intended to harm. Internet bullying and victimization rates have been reported by about 25 percent of middle school students (Willard, 2006).

Did you know?

Of teens who blog, 57 percent of teens claim they "never lie" on their blogs (Blinka & Smahal, 2009).

Romantic Relationships

Romantic relationships are a central part of most adolescents' social worlds. They contribute to the development of both intimacy and identity. With the onset of puberty, most heterosexual boys and girls begin to think about and interact more with members of the other sex. Typically, they move from mixed groups or group dates to one-on-one romantic relationships that involve passion and a sense of commitment (Bouchey & Furman, 2003).

Romantic relationships tend to become more intense and more intimate across adolescence. Early adolescents think primarily about how a relationship might affect their status in the peer group and pay little or no attention to attachment or support needs. Their attention to sexual needs is limited to how to engage in sexual activity and which activities to engage in (Bouchey & Furman, 2003).

In mid-adolescence, most young people have had at least one exclusive partner lasting for several months to about a year, and the effect of the choice of partner on peer status tends to become less important (Furman & Wehner, 1997). Boys appear to be less confident than girls about these early romantic relationships (Giordano, Longmore, & Manning, 2006).

By age 16, adolescents interact with and think about romantic partners more than about parents, friends, or siblings (Bouchey & Furman, 2003). Not until late adolescence or early adulthood, though, do romantic relationships begin to meet the full gamut of emotional needs that such relationships can serve and then only in relatively long-term relationships (Furman & Wehner, 1997).

Dating Violence

Dating violence is a significant problem in Canada and around the world (e.g., Connolly et al., 2010).

Did you know?

Facebook may be a good social outlet, but it harms academic performance. Students who are on Facebook while they study get 20 percent lower grades than their friends who avoid it while working (Kirscher & Karpinski, 2010).

Did you know?

Interacting with someone of the opposite gender interferes with cognitive processes, but only for males (Karremans, Verwijmeren, Pronk, & Reitsma, 2009).

The three common forms of dating violence are as follows:

Physical—when a partner is hit, pinched, shoved, or kicked

Emotional—when a partner is threatened or verbally abused

Sexual—when a partner is forced to engage in a non-consensual sex act

Statistics indicate that about 10 percent of students report having been victims of physical dating violence (Health Canada, 2007b), although the actual rate is likely higher. As many as three in 10 adolescents report being verbally or psychologically abused (Halpern, Young, Waller, Martin, & Kupper, 2003). Altogether, one in four adolescents reports verbal, physical, emotional, or sexual abuse from a dating partner each year (CDC, 2008). The overall rates of police-reported dating violence in Canada are 10 times higher for girls than for boys, but girls are disproportionately victims in cases of severe

Ask Yourself

10. Is the characterization of adolescence as a time of rebellion and alienation true?
    a. Yes, it is true for the vast majority of teens, although most outgrow it.
    b. Yes, and adolescent rebellion and alienation have increased in the last 20 years.
    c. No, only a small minority of teens rebel and become alienated.
    d. No, because in the modern world there is little to rebel against.

11. What is individuation?

12. Generally, _____ report greater levels of intimacy in adolescence.
    a. same-sex siblings
    b. cross-sex siblings
    c. siblings with more than a four-year gap in age
    d. siblings with less than a two-year-gap in age

13. "I guess I would describe myself as a jock," says John. What type of peer group is he referring to?
    a. friend
    b. clique
    c. crowd
    d. individualistic

violence (Mahony, 2010; Mulford & Giordano, 2008). Effective school-based programs aimed at preventing dating violence at the early high school level involve small-group discussion, role-playing, and explicit teaching about dating violence and prevention in classes involving healthy relationships, sexual health, and safe decision-making with dating partners (Butler-Jones, 2011; Wolfe et al., 2009).

In addition to the physical harm caused by this type of abuse, teens who are victims of dating violence are more likely to do poorly in school and to engage in risky behaviours such as drug and alcohol use. These students are also subject to eating disorders, depression, and suicide. Risk factors that may predict violence include bullying in childhood, substance abuse, conflict and/or abuse in the home, antisocial peers, and living in neighbourhoods with high crime and drug use rates (Child Trends Databank, 2010; Pepler, 2012). Unhealthy relationships can last a lifetime as victims carry patterns of violence into future relationships.

Antisocial Behaviour and Juvenile Delinquency

John had always been a "good kid," but one night, John's parents got a phone call from the police department. John, now a senior in high school, had been booked for shoplifting at a local mall. John's parents were furious, and John was embarrassed and ashamed. "We didn't raise you to be like this," they sternly told him, and took away his car, television, and cellphone privileges.

John's behaviour, while upsetting to his parents, was not out of the norm for teenagers. Many teens engage in some degree of teenage antisocial or delinquent behaviour. In this following section, we outline some of the factors that influence these behaviours.

BIOLOGICAL INFLUENCES

Antisocial behaviour tends to run in families. Analyses of many studies have concluded that genes influence 40 to 50 percent of the variation in antisocial behaviour within a population and 60 to 65 percent of the variation in aggressive antisociality (Rhee & Waldman, 2002; Tackett, Krueger, Iacono, & McGue, 2005). Genes alone, however, are not predictive of antisocial behaviour. Recent research findings suggest that both genes and environment affect the expression of antisocial behaviour (Guo, Roettger, & Cai, 2008).

Neurobiological deficits, particularly in the portions of the brain that regulate reactions to stress, may help explain why some children become antisocial adolescents. As a result of these neurological deficits, children may not receive or heed normal warning signals to restrain impulsive or reckless behaviour (van Goozen et al., 2007). Children with attention deficit hyperactivity disorder (ADHD) are at higher risk for the development of co-morbid conduct disorder (CD) and depression that contribute to antisocial behaviour (Drabick, Gadow, & Sprafkin, 2006). Also, preliminary findings of an MRI investigation of empathetic response have indicated youth with aggressive conduct disorders have atypical responses to seeing others in pain (Decety et al., 2009).

A crucial variable that must be taken into account is the age at which antisocial behaviour begins. Researchers have identified two types of antisocial behaviour: an early-onset type, beginning by age 11, which tends to lead to chronic juvenile delinquency in adolescence, and a milder, late-onset type, beginning after puberty, which tends to arise temporarily in adolescence. Late-onset adolescents tend to commit relatively minor offences (Schulenberg & Zarrett, 2006) and tend to come from families with normal family backgrounds (Collins et al., 2000).

FAMILY INFLUENCES

Authoritative parenting can help young people internalize standards that may insulate them against negative peer influences and open them to positive influences (Collins et al., 2000). Adolescents whose parents know where they are and what they are doing are less likely to engage in delinquent acts (Laird, Pettit, Bates, & Dodge, 2003) or to associate with deviant peers (Lloyd & Anthony, 2003).

Parents of children who become chronically antisocial, by contrast, may have failed to reinforce good behaviour in early childhood and may have been harsh or inconsistent—or both—in punishing misbehaviour (Coie & Dodge, 1998; Snyder, Cramer, Frank, & Patterson, 2005). When constant criticism or angry coercion characterizes parent-child interactions, the child tends to show aggressive behaviour problems (Buehler, 2006). By early adolescence, open hostility may exist between parent and child.

ENVIRONMENTAL INFLUENCES

The early negative patterns between antisocial children and their parents pave the way for negative peer influences that promote and reinforce antisocial behaviour (Collins et al., 2000). The choice of antisocial peers is affected mainly by environmental factors (Iervolino et al., 2002). Young people gravitate to others brought up like themselves who are similar in school achievement, adjustment, and prosocial or antisocial tendencies (Collins et al., 2000). Antisocial adolescents tend to have antisocial friends, and their antisocial behaviour increases when they associate with each other (Monahan, Steinberg, & Cauffman, 2009), a process sometimes referred to as "deviancy training" (Dishion & Tipsord, 2011). These problem children continue to elicit ineffective parenting, which then predicts delinquent behaviour and association with deviant peer groups (Simons, Chao, Conger, & Elder, 2001; Tolan, Gorman-Smith, & Henry, 2003).

Family economic circumstances may influence the development of antisocial behaviour. Poor children are more likely than other children to commit antisocial acts, and those whose families are continuously poor tend to become more antisocial with time. Conversely, when families rise from poverty while a child is still young, the child is no more likely to develop behaviour problems than a child whose family was never poor (Macmillan, McMorris, & Kruttschnitt, 2004).

Weak neighbourhood social organization in a disadvantaged community can influence delinquency through

The early negative patterns between antisocial children and their parents pave the way for negative peer influences that promote and reinforce antisocial behaviour: Antisocial adolescents tend to have antisocial friends, and their antisocial behaviour increases when they associate with each other.

its effects on parenting behaviour and peer deviance (Chung & Steinberg, 2006). Collective efficacy—the strength of social connections within a neighbourhood and the extent to which residents monitor or supervise each other's children—can influence outcomes in a positive direction (Odgers et al., 2009). A combination of nurturant, involved parenting and collective efficacy can discourage adolescents from association with deviant peers (Brody et al., 2001).

PREVENTING AND TREATING DELINQUENCY

Because juvenile delinquency has roots early in childhood, so should preventive efforts. To be most successful, interventions should attack the multiple factors that can lead to delinquency.

Adolescents who have taken part in certain early childhood intervention programs are less likely to get in trouble and have better educational outcomes than their equally underprivileged peers who did not have these early experiences (Reynolds, Temple, Robertson, & Mann, 2001). Effective programs are those that target high-risk urban children and last at least two years during the child's first five years of life. They influence children directly, through high-quality daycare or education, and at the same time indirectly, by offering families assistance and support geared to their needs (Loeber, Farrington, & Petechuk, 2003; Schweinhart, Barnes, & Weikart, 1993; Yoshikawa, 1994).

These programs operate on the mesosystem by affecting interactions between the home and the school and/or child care centre. The programs also go one step further to the exosystem by creating supportive parent networks and linking parents with such community services as prenatal and postnatal care and educational and vocational counselling (Loeber et al., 2003; Yoshikawa, 1994; Zigler, Taussig, & Black, 1992).

Did you know?

Programs such as teen hangouts and summer camps for behaviourally disturbed youth can be counterproductive because they bring together groups of deviant youth who tend to reinforce each other's deviancy. More effective programs integrate deviant youth into the non-deviant mainstream (Dodge, Dishion, & Lansford, 2006).

Once children reach adolescence, especially in poor, crime-ridden neighbourhoods, interventions need to focus on spotting troubled adolescents and preventing gang recruitment (Tolan et al., 2003). Successful programs boost parenting skills through better monitoring, behavioural management, and neighbourhood social support.

Fortunately, the great majority of adolescents do not become adult criminals (Kosterman, Graham, Hawkins, Catalano, & Herrenkohl, 2001), and the rate of youth crime has been dropping in Canada (Statistics Canada, 2012l). Delinquency peaks at about age 15 and then declines as most adolescents and their families come to terms with young people's need to assert independence. However, those who show disturbed behaviour can—and should—be helped. With love, guidance, and support, adolescents can avoid risks, build on their strengths, and explore their possibilities as they approach adult life.

Ask Yourself

14. If Colin began shoplifting at age 9, and by age 17 was committing armed robberies and abusing drugs, we would likely characterize Colin as being
    a. an early-onset delinquent.
    b. a temperamentally delayed delinquent.
    c. a late-onset delinquent.
    d. an imitative adopter.

15. What are four characteristics of effective early intervention programs for delinquency?

Emerging Adulthood

In industrialized societies, entrance into adulthood takes longer and follows more varied routes than in the past (Arnett, 2012). Before the mid-twentieth century, a young man just out of high school could, in short order, obtain a stable job, marry, and start a family. For a young woman, the chief route to adulthood was marriage, which occurred as soon as she could find a suitable mate. Now, the technological revolution has made higher education or specialized training increasingly essential. The gender revolution has brought more women into the workforce and broadened female roles (Furstenberg, Rumbaut, & Settersten, 2005; Fussell & Furstenberg, 2005). Today, the road to adulthood may be marked by multiple milestones—entering college or university (full- or part-time), working (full- or part-time), moving away from home, getting married, and having children—and the order and timing of these transitions varies (Schulenberg, O'Malley, Bachman, & Johnston, 2005). Thus, some developmental scientists suggest that the period from the late teens through the mid- to late 20s has become a distinct period of the life course: **emerging adulthood**—a time when young people are no longer adolescents but have not yet become

emerging adulthood Proposed transitional period between adolescence and adulthood, usually extending from the late teens through the mid-20s.

fully adult (Arnett, 2007). In the minds of many people today, the onset of adulthood is marked not so much by external criteria but rather by a sense of autonomy, self-control, and personal responsibility (Shanahan, Porfeli, & Mortimer, 2005).

There is a quite a lot of diversity in how emerging adulthood takes shape across nations and ethnic communities (Arnett, 2012). Members of visible minority groups in the U.S., for example, are more likely than those of European descent to mention criteria involving obligations to others, such as supporting one's family; recognizing role transitions, such as marriage; and complying with social norms, such as avoiding illegal drug use (Arnett, 2003). For many young people, experiences in post-secondary education offer unique opportunities for personal growth before taking on the full set of responsibilities of adulthood. A study of 97 Canadian first-year university students indicated that the majority of these emerging adults experience events that contribute to personal growth during this

period, particularly in three areas: relating to others, optimism in new opportunities and possibilities, and personal strength in overcoming adversity (Gottlieb, Sill, & Newby-Clark, 2007).

The normal developmental changes in the early years of life are obvious and dramatic signs of growth. The infant lying in the crib becomes an active, exploring toddler. The young child enters and embraces the worlds of school and society. The adolescent, with a new body and new awareness, prepares to step into adulthood.

Growth and development do not screech to a stop even then. People change in important ways throughout adulthood. They continue to shape their development, as they have been doing since birth. What occurs in a child's world is significant, but it is not the whole story. We each continue to write the story of human development for ourselves and our society for as long as we live.

Ask Yourself

16. What is the onset of adulthood marked by for most young people today?
    a. securing a stable job
    b. getting married
    c. a sense of autonomy, self-control, and personal responsibility
    d. being able to vote

LO1

Describe the process of identity formation, summarize how gender and ethnicity impact it, and describe how prosocial behaviour varies across adolescents.

- A central concern during adolescence is the search for identity, which has occupational, sexual, and values components. Erik Erikson described the psychosocial crisis of adolescence as the conflict of identity versus identity confusion. The "virtue" that should arise from this crisis is fidelity.

- James Marcia, in research based on Erikson's theory, described four identity statuses with differing combinations of crisis and commitment: identity achievement, foreclosure, moratorium, and identity diffusion.

- Ethnicity is an important part of identity. Minority adolescents seem to go through stages of ethnic identity development much like Marcia's identity statuses.

- Prosocial behaviour continues to increase during adolescence, especially among girls. Many adolescents engage in volunteer community service.

LO2

Summarize influences on sexual orientation in adolescence, as well as common sexual behaviours and the associated risks.

- Sexual orientation appears to be influenced by an interaction of biological and environmental factors and may be at least partly genetic.

- The course of homosexual identity and relationship development may vary with cohort and gender.

- Teenage sexual activity is more prevalent and more accepted than in the past, but it involves risks of pregnancy and sexually transmitted infections (STIs).

- Rates of STIs in Canada are especially high among adolescents. Adolescents at greatest risk are those who begin sexual activity early, have multiple partners, do not use contraceptives, and are ill-informed about sex.

- Teenage pregnancy and birthrates in Canada have declined. Most of these births are to unmarried mothers.

- Teenage pregnancy and child-bearing often have negative outcomes. Teenage mothers and their families tend to suffer ill health and financial hardship, and the children often suffer from ineffective parenting.

Summarize the family, sibling, and peer influences on adolescent development.

- Although relationships between adolescents and their parents are not always smooth, full-scale adolescent rebellion is unusual. For the majority of teens, adolescence is a fairly smooth transition. For the minority who seem more deeply troubled, it can predict a troubled adulthood.
- Adolescents spend an increasing amount of time with peers, but relationships with parents continue to be close and influential.
- Conflict with parents tends to be most frequent during early adolescence and most intense during middle adolescence. The intensity of minor conflicts may reflect the process of individuation.
- Authoritative parenting is associated with the most positive outcomes. Behavioural control normally diminishes across adolescence and is associated with healthy development; psychological control, which suppresses a young person's emotional autonomy, does not promote healthy development.
- Effective parental monitoring depends on adolescents' self-disclosure, which is influenced by the quality of the parent-child relationship.
- Effects of divorce, single parenting, and maternal employment on adolescents' development depend on such factors as how closely parents monitor adolescents' activity and the quality of the home environment.
- Economic stress affects relationships in lone-parent families.
- Relationships with siblings tend to become more distant during adolescence, and the balance of power between older and younger siblings becomes more equal.
- The influence of the peer group is strongest in early adolescence. Peer relationships fall into three categories: friendships, cliques, and crowds.
- Friendships, especially among girls, become more intimate and supportive in adolescence. Cliques are highly status-based; crowds are based on common features, such as ethnicity or SES.
- The explosion of online communication can enhance connectedness, but it also can introduce potential dangers.
- Romantic relationships involve several roles and develop with age and experience.
- Dating violence is a significant problem in Canada and around the world.

LO4

Outline the causes of antisocial behaviour and what can be done to reduce the risk of juvenile delinquency.

- Antisocial behaviour is associated with multiple interacting risk factors, including genes, neurological deficits, ineffective parenting, school failure, peer influence, and low socio-economic status.
- Programs that attack environmental risk factors from an early age have had success in preventing juvenile delinquency.

Describe what marks the transition from adolescence to adulthood.

- A new transitional period called emerging adulthood has developed in industrialized cultures in recent years.

- Emerging adults in various Western cultures hold similar views of what defines entrance into adulthood. The most widely accepted criteria are individualistic ones having to do with self-sufficiency and independence. However, some cultures also embrace collectivistic criteria, such as family responsibilities and conformity with social norms.

ANSWERS TO Ask Yourself

Answers: 1—The three issues were the choice of an occupation, the adoption of values to live by, and the development of a satisfying sexual identity; 2—b; 3—a; 4—d; 5—b; 6—Among the factors that impact sexual orientation are genes, having older biological brothers (for gay men), and brain structure; 7—Among the risk factors are starting sexual activity early, having multiple partners, not using contraceptives regularly, having inadequate or incorrect information about sex, living in a socio-economically disadvantaged community, substance use, antisocial behaviour, association with deviant peers, and low parental monitoring; 8—d; 9—b; 10—c; 11—Individuation is an adolescent's struggle for autonomy and differentiation, or personal identity; 12—a; 13—c; 14—a; 15—Effective programs are those that target high-risk urban children, last at least two years during the child's first five years of life, provide high-quality daycare or education, and provide family support; 16—c.

connect **LEARNSMART** **SMARTBOOK**

For more information on the resources available from McGraw-Hill Ryerson, go to **www.mcgrawhill.ca/he/solutions**.

GLOSSARY

The words in this glossary are found throughout the book and will help the student better understand the concepts.

A

acceleration Approach to educating the gifted that moves them through the curriculum at an unusually rapid pace.

accommodation Piaget's term for changes in a cognitive structure to include new information.

acquired immune deficiency syndrome (AIDS) Viral disease that undermines effective functioning of the immune system.

acute medical conditions Occasional illnesses that last a short time.

adaptation Piaget's term for adjustment to new information about the environment.

adolescence Developmental transition between childhood and adulthood entailing major physical, cognitive, and psychosocial changes.

adolescent growth spurt Sharp increase in height and weight that precedes sexual maturity.

adolescent rebellion Pattern of emotional turmoil, characteristic of a minority of adolescents that may involve conflict with family, alienation from adult society, reckless behaviour, and rejection of adult values.

alleles Two or more alternative forms of a gene that can occupy the same position on paired chromosomes and affect the same trait.

altruism Motivation to help others without expectation of reward; may involve self-denial or self-sacrifice.

altruistic behaviour Activity intended to help another person with no expectation of reward.

ambivalent, or resistant, attachment Pattern in which an infant becomes anxious before the primary caregiver leaves, is extremely upset during his or her absence, and both seeks and resists contact on his or her return.

animism Tendency to attribute life to objects that are not alive.

anorexia nervosa Eating disorder characterized by self-starvation and extreme weight loss.

anoxia Lack of oxygen, which may cause brain damage.

Apgar scale Standard measurement of a newborn's condition; it assesses appearance, pulse, grimace, activity, and respiration.

art therapy Therapeutic approach that allows a person to express troubled feelings without words, using a variety of art materials and media.

assimilation Piaget's term for incorporation of new information into an existing cognitive structure.

assisted reproductive technology (ART) Methods used to achieve conception through artificial means.

asthma A chronic respiratory disease characterized by sudden attacks of coughing, wheezing, and difficulty in breathing.

attachment Reciprocal, enduring tie between two people—especially between infant and caregiver—each of whom contributes to the quality of the relationship.

attention deficit hyperactivity disorder (ADHD) Syndrome characterized by persistent inattention and distractibility, impulsivity, low tolerance for frustration, and inappropriate overactivity.

authoritarian parenting Parenting style emphasizing control and obedience.

authoritative parenting Parenting style blending warmth and respect for a child's individuality with an effort to instill social values.

autobiographical memory A type of episodic memory of distinctive experiences that form a person's life history.

autonomy versus shame and doubt Erikson's second stage in psychosocial development, in which children achieve a balance between self-determination and control by others.

autosomes In humans, the 22 pairs of chromosomes not related to sexual expression.

avoidant attachment Pattern in which an infant rarely cries when separated from the primary caregiver and avoids contact on his or her return.

B

basic trust versus basic mistrust Erikson's first stage in psychosocial development, in which infants develop a sense of the reliability of people and objects.

Bayley Scales of Infant and Toddler Development Standardized test of infants' and toddlers' mental and motor development.

behaviour therapy Therapy that uses principles of learning theory to eliminate undesirable behaviours; also called *behaviour modification.*

behaviourism Learning theory that emphasizes the predictable role of environment in causing observable behaviour.

behaviourist approach Approach to the study of behavioural development that is concerned with the basic mechanics of learning.

bilingual education System of teaching non-English-speaking children in their native language while they learn English and later switching to all-English instruction.

bioecological theory Bronfenbrenner's approach to understanding processes and contexts of child development that identifies five levels of environmental influence.

Brazelton Neonatal Behavioral Assessment Scale (NBAS) Neurological and behavioural test to measure a neonate's responses to the environment.

bulimia nervosa Eating disorder in which a person regularly eats huge quantities of food and then purges the body by laxatives, induced vomiting, fasting, or excessive exercise.

bullying Aggression deliberately and persistently directed against a particular target, or victim, typically one who is weak, vulnerable, and defenceless.

C

Caesarean delivery Delivery of a baby by surgical removal from the uterus.

canalization Limitation on variance of expression of certain inherited characteristics.

caregiver-infant bond Mother's and father's feeling of close, caring connection with the newborn.

case study A study of a single subject, such as an individual or a family.

cell death In brain development, normal elimination of excess cells to achieve more efficient functioning.

central executive In Baddeley's model, the element of working memory that controls the processing of information.

centration In Piaget's theory, tendency of preoperational children to focus on one aspect of a situation and neglect others.

cephalocaudal principle Principle that development proceeds in a head-to-tail direction; that is, upper parts of the body develop before lower parts of the trunk.

child development The scientific study of systematic processes of change and stability in human children.

child-directed speech (CDS) Form of speech often used in talking to babies or toddlers; includes slow, simplified speech, a high-pitched tone, exaggerated vowel sounds, short words and sentences, and much repetition; also called *parentese.*

childhood depression Mood disorder characterized by such symptoms as a prolonged sense of friendlessness, inability to have fun or concentrate, fatigue, extreme activity or apathy, feelings of worthlessness, weight change, physical complaints, and thoughts of death or suicide.

chromosomes Coils of DNA that consist of genes.

chronic medical conditions Long-lasting or recurrent physical, developmental, behavioural, and/or emotional conditions that require special health services.

circular reactions Piaget's term for processes by which an infant learns to reproduce desired occurrences originally discovered by chance.

class inclusion Understanding the relationship between a whole and its parts.

classical conditioning Learning based on association of a stimulus that does not ordinarily elicit a particular response with another stimulus that does elicit the response.

code mixing Use of elements of two languages, sometimes in the same utterance, by young children in households where both languages are spoken.

code switching Process of changing one's speech to match the situation, as in people who are bilingual.

cognitive behaviour therapy Therapy that seeks to change negative thoughts through gradual exposure, modelling, rewards, or positive self-talk.

cognitive development Pattern of change in mental abilities, such as learning, attention, memory, language, thinking, reasoning, and creativity.

cognitive neuroscience approach Approach to the study of cognitive development that links brain processes with cognitive ones.

cognitive perspective Perspective that looks at the development of mental processes such as thinking.

cognitive-stage theory Piaget's theory that children's cognitive development advances in a series of four stages involving qualitatively distinct types of mental operations.

cohort A group of people born at about the same time.

committed compliance Kochanska's term for wholehearted obedience of a parent's orders without reminders or lapses.

componential element Sternberg's term for the analytic aspect of intelligence.

conceptual knowledge Acquired interpretive understandings stored in long-term memory.

concordant Term describing the tendency of twins to share the same trait or disorder.

conduct disorder (CD) Repetitive, persistent pattern of aggressive, antisocial behaviour violating societal norms or the rights of others.

conscience Internal standards of behaviour, which usually control one's conduct and produce emotional discomfort when violated.

conservation Piaget's term for awareness that two objects that are equal according to a certain measure remain equal in the face of perceptual alteration as long as nothing has been added to or taken away from either object.

constructive play Second cognitive level of play, involving use of objects or materials to make something; also called *object play*.

contextual element Sternberg's term for the practical aspect of intelligence.

contextual perspective View of child development that sees the individual as inseparable from the social context.

control group In an experiment, a comparison group of people similar to those in the experimental group who do not receive the treatment under study.

conventional morality (or morality of conventional role conformity) Second level in Kohlberg's theory of moral reasoning in which standards of authority figures are internalized.

convergent thinking Thinking aimed at finding the one right answer to a problem.

co-regulation Transitional stage in the control of behaviour in which parents exercise general supervision and children exercise moment-to-moment self-regulation.

corporal punishment Use of physical force with the intention of causing pain but not injury so as to correct or control behaviour.

correlational study Research design intended to discover whether a statistical relationship between variables exists.

critical period Specific time when a given event or its absence has a profound and specific impact on development.

cross-sectional study Study designed to assess age-related differences, in which people of different ages are assessed on one occasion.

culture A society's or group's total way of life, including customs, traditions, beliefs, values, language, and physical products—all learned behaviours passed on from adults to children.

culture-free tests Intelligence tests that, if it were possible to design, would have no culturally linked content.

culture-relevant tests Intelligence tests that take into account the adaptive tasks children face in their culture.

cyberbullying Posting negative comments or derogatory photos of the victim on a website.

D

decentre In Piaget's terminology, to think simultaneously about several aspects of a situation.

declarative knowledge Acquired factual knowledge stored in long-term memory.

decoding Process of phonetic analysis by which a printed word is converted to spoken form before retrieval from long-term memory.

deductive reasoning Type of logical reasoning that moves from a general premise about a class to a conclusion about a particular member or members of the class.

deferred imitation Piaget's term for reproduction of an observed behaviour after the passage of time by calling up a stored symbol of it.

dental caries Tooth decay, a cavity.

deoxyribonucleic acid (DNA) Chemical that carries inherited instructions for the development of all cellular forms of life.

dependent variable In an experiment, the outcome that the experimenter measures that may or may not change as a result of changes in the independent variable.

depth perception Ability to perceive objects and surfaces in three dimensions.

developmental quotient (DQ) Standardized score calculated for each area measured by the Bayley Scales.

diabetes One of the most common diseases of childhood, characterized by high levels of glucose in the blood as a result of defective insulin production, ineffective insulin action, or both.

difficult children Children with irritable temperament, irregular biological rhythms, and intense emotional responses.

discipline Methods of moulding children's character and teaching them to exercise self-control and engage in acceptable behaviour.

dishabituation Increase in responsiveness after presentation of a new stimulus.

disorganized-disoriented attachment Pattern in which an infant, after separation from the primary caregiver, shows contradictory behaviours on his or her return.

divergent thinking Thinking that produces a variety of fresh, diverse possibilities.

dominant inheritance Pattern of inheritance in which, when a child receives different alleles, only the dominant one is expressed.

Down syndrome Chromosomal disorder characterized by moderate-to-severe mental retardation and by such physical signs as a downward-sloping skin fold at the inner corners of the eyes.

dramatic play Play involving imaginary people or situations; also called *fantasy play, pretend play,* or *imaginative play.*

drug therapy Administration of drugs to treat emotional disorders.

dynamic systems theory (DST) Thelen's theory that holds that motor development is a dynamic process of active coordination of multiple systems within the infant in relation to the environment.

dynamic tests Tests based on Vygotsky's theory that emphasize potential rather than past learning.

dyslexia Developmental disorder in which reading achievement is substantially lower than predicted by IQ or age.

E

early intervention Systematic process of providing services to help families meet young children's developmental needs.

easy children Children with a generally happy temperament, regular biological rhythms, and a readiness to accept new experiences.

ecological theory of perception Theory developed by Eleanor and James Gibson that describes developing motor and perceptual abilities as interdependent parts of a functional system that guides behaviour in varying contexts.

egocentrism Piaget's term for the inability to consider that another person's point of view can be different from one's own; a characteristic of young children's thought.

electronic fetal monitoring Mechanical monitoring of fetal heartbeat during labour and delivery.

embryonic stage Second stage of prenatal development (two to eight weeks), characterized by rapid growth and development of major body systems and organs.

emergent literacy Preschoolers' development of skills, knowledge, and attitudes that underlie reading and writing.

emerging adulthood Proposed transitional period between adolescence and adulthood, usually extending from the late teens through the mid-20s.

emotions Subjective reactions to experience that are associated with physiological and behavioural changes.

encoding Process by which information is prepared for long-term storage and later retrieval.

English immersion approach Approach to teaching English as a second language in which instruction is presented only in English.

enrichment Approach to educating the gifted that broadens and deepens knowledge and skills through extra activities, projects, field trips, or mentoring.

enuresis Repeated urination in clothing or in bed.

environment Totality of non-hereditary, or experiential, influences on development.

epigenesis Mechanism that turns genes on or off and determines functions of body cells.

episodic memory Long-term memory of specific experiences or events, linked to time and place.

equilibration Piaget's term for the tendency to seek a stable balance among cognitive elements; achieved through a balance between assimilation and accommodation.

ethnic group A group united by ancestry, race, religion, language, or national origin that contributes to a sense of shared identity.

ethnographic study In-depth study of a culture, which uses a variety of methods, including participant observation.

ethology Study of distinctive adaptive behaviours of species of animals that have evolved to increase survival of the species.

evolutionary psychology Application of Darwinian principles of natural selection and survival of the fittest to human psychology.

evolutionary/sociobiological perspective View of human development that focuses on evolutionary and biological bases of social behaviour.

executive function Conscious control of thoughts, emotions, and actions to accomplish goals or solve problems.

experiential element Sternberg's term for the insightful aspect of intelligence.

experimental group In an experiment, the group receiving the treatment under study.

explicit memory Intentional and conscious memory, generally of facts, names, and events; sometimes called *declarative memory*.

extended family Multigenerational kinship network of parents, children, and other relatives, sometimes living together in an extended-family household.

F

family therapy Psychological treatment in which a therapist sees the whole family together to analyze patterns of family functioning.

fast mapping Process by which a child absorbs the meaning of a new word after hearing it once or twice in conversation.

fertilization Union of sperm and ovum to produce a zygote; also called *conception*.

fetal alcohol spectrum disorders (FASD) Combination of mental, motor, and developmental abnormalities affecting the offspring of some women who drink heavily during pregnancy.

fetal stage Final stage of prenatal development (from eight weeks to birth), characterized by increased differentiation of body parts and greatly enlarged body size.

fine motor skills Physical skills that involve the small muscles and eye-hand coordination.

fontanels Soft spots on the head of the young infant.

foreclosure Identity status, described by Marcia, in which a person who has not spent time considering alternatives (that is, has not been in crisis) is committed to other people's plans for his or her life.

formal games with rules Organized games with known procedures and penalties.

formal operations In Piaget's theory, final stage of cognitive development, characterized by the ability to think abstractly.

French immersion An educational program that uses French as the language of instruction to English-speaking students as a way to promote fluency in French.

functional play Lowest cognitive level of play, involving repetitive muscular movements; also called *locomotor play*.

G

gender Significance of being male or female.

gender constancy Awareness that one will always be male or female; also called *sex-category constancy*.

gender identity Awareness, developed in early childhood, that one is male or female.

gender roles Behaviours, interests, attitudes, skills, and traits that a culture considers appropriate for each sex; differ for males and females.

gender-schema theory Theory that children socialize themselves in their gender roles by developing a mentally organized network of information about what it means to be male or female in a particular culture.

gender segregation The tendency of children to select same-sex playmates.

gender stereotypes Preconceived generalizations about male or female role behaviour.

gender-typing Socialization process by which children, at an early age, learn appropriate gender roles.

generalized anxiety disorder Anxiety not focused on any single target.

genes Small segments of DNA located in definite positions on particular chromosomes; functional units of heredity.

genetic counselling Clinical service that advises prospective parents of their probable risk of having children with hereditary defects.

genotype Genetic makeup of a person, containing both expressed and unexpressed characteristics.

genotype–environment correlation Tendency of certain genetic and environmental influences to reinforce each other; may be active, passive, or reactive (evocative).

genotype–environment interaction Effect of the interaction between genes and the environment on phenotypic variation.

germinal stage First two weeks of prenatal development, characterized by rapid cell division, increasing complexity and differentiation, and implantation in the wall of the uterus.

gestation The prenatal period of development, between conception and birth.

goodness of fit Appropriateness of environmental demands and constraints to a child's temperament.

gross motor skills Physical skills that involve the large muscles.

guided participation Participation of an adult in a child's activity in a manner that helps to structure the activity and to bring the child's understanding of it closer to that of the adult.

H

habituation Type of learning in which familiarity with a stimulus reduces, slows, or stops a response.

handedness Preference for using a particular hand.

haptic perception Ability to acquire information about properties of objects, such as size, weight, and texture, by handling them.

heredity Inborn characteristics inherited from the biological parents.

heritability Statistical estimate of the contribution of heredity to individual differences in a specific trait within a given population at a particular time.

heterozygous Possessing differing alleles for a trait.

historical generation A group of people strongly influenced by a major historical event during their formative period.

holophrase Single word that conveys a complete thought.

Home Observation for Measurement of the Environment (HOME) Instrument designed to measure the influence of the home environment on children's cognitive growth.

homozygous Possessing two identical alleles for a trait.

horizontal décalage Piaget's term for an inability to transfer learning about one type of conservation to other types, which causes a child to master different types of conservation tasks at different ages.

hostile aggression Aggressive behaviour intended to hurt another person.

hostile attribution bias Tendency for individuals to perceive others as trying to hurt them and to strike out in retaliation or self-defence.

human genome The complete sequence of genes in the human body.

hypertension High blood pressure.

hypotheses Possible explanations for phenomena, used to predict the outcome of research.

hypothetical-deductive reasoning Ability, believed by Piaget to accompany the stage of formal operations, to develop, consider, and test hypotheses.

I

identification In Freudian theory, process by which a young child adopts characteristics, beliefs, attitudes, values, and behaviours of the parent of the same sex.

identity In Erikson's terminology, a coherent conception of the self made up of goals, values, and beliefs to which a person is solidly committed.

identity achievement Identity status, described by Marcia, that is characterized by commitment to choices made following a crisis, a period spent in exploring alternatives.

identity diffusion Identity status, described by Marcia, that is characterized by absence of commitment and lack of serious consideration of alternatives.

identity versus identity confusion Erikson's fifth stage of psychosocial development, in which an adolescent seeks to develop a coherent sense of self, including the role she or he is to play in society; also called *identity versus role confusion*.

imaginary audience Elkind's term for an observer who exists only in an adolescent's mind and who is as concerned with the adolescent's thoughts and actions as the adolescent is.

implicit memory Unconscious recall, generally of habits and skills; sometimes called *procedural memory*.

imprinting Instinctive form of learning in which, during a critical period in early development, a young animal forms an attachment to the first moving object it sees, usually the mother.

incomplete dominance Pattern of inheritance in which a child receives two different alleles, resulting in partial expression of a trait.

independent variable In an experiment, the set of conditions over which the experimenter has direct control.

individual differences Differences among children in characteristics, influences, or developmental outcomes.

individual psychotherapy Psychological treatment in which a therapist sees a troubled person one-on-one.

individuation Adolescent's struggle for autonomy and differentiation, or personal identity.

inductive reasoning Type of logical reasoning that moves from particular observations about members of a class to a general conclusion about that class.

inductive reasoning techniques Disciplinary techniques designed to induce desirable behaviour by appealing to a child's sense of reason and fairness.

industry versus inferiority Erikson's fourth crisis of psychosocial development, in which children must learn the productive skills their culture requires or else face feelings of inferiority.

infant mortality rate Proportion of babies born alive who die within the first year.

infertility Inability to conceive after 12 months of trying.

information-processing approach Approach to the study of cognitive development by observing and analyzing the mental processes involved in perceiving and handling information.

initiative versus guilt Erikson's third crisis in psychosocial development, in which children balance the urge to pursue goals with moral reservations that may prevent carrying them out.

instrumental aggression Aggressive behaviour used as a means of achieving a goal.

intellectual disability Significantly subnormal cognitive functioning; also referred to as *cognitive disability* or *mental retardation*.

intelligent behaviour Behaviour that is goal-oriented and adaptive to circumstances and conditions of life.

internalization During socialization, process by which children accept societal standards of conduct as their own.

IQ (intelligence quotient) tests Psychometric tests that seek to measure intelligence by comparing a test-taker's performance with standardized norms.

irreversibility Piaget's term for a preoperational child's failure to understand that an operation can go in two or more directions.

J

joint attention Involves understanding that you and I have a shared focus of attention.

K

kangaroo care Method of skin-to-skin contact between newborn and mother to reduce stress on the central nervous system and help with self-regulation of sleep and activity.

Kaufman Assessment Battery for Children (K-ABC-II) Non-traditional individual intelligence test designed to provide fair assessments of minority children and children with disabilities.

L

laboratory observation Research method in which all participants are observed under the same controlled conditions.

language acquisition device (LAD) In Chomsky's terminology, an inborn mechanism that enables children to infer linguistic rules from the language they hear.

lanugo Fuzzy prenatal body hair, which drops off within a few days after birth.

learning disabilities (LDs) Disorders that interfere with specific aspects of learning and school achievement.

learning perspective View of human development that holds that changes in behaviour result from experience.

linguistic speech Verbal expression designed to convey meaning.

longitudinal study Study designed to assess changes in a sample over time.

long-term memory Storage of virtually unlimited capacity that holds information for long periods.

low-birth-weight babies Infants who weigh less than 2,500 grams (5 pounds) at birth because of prematurity or being small-for-date.

M

maturation Unfolding of a universal, natural sequence of physical and behavioural changes.

meconium Fetal waste matter, excreted during the first few days after birth.

menarche A girl's first menstruation.

metamemory Understanding of processes of memory.

moratorium Identity status, described by Marcia, in which a person is considering alternatives (in crisis) and seems headed for commitment.

multifactorial transmission Combination of genetic and environmental factors to produce certain complex traits.

mutations Permanent alterations in genes or chromosomes that usually produce harmful characteristics but provide the raw material of evolution.

mutual regulation Process by which infant and caregiver communicate emotional states to each other and respond appropriately.

N

nativism Theory that human beings have an inborn capacity for language acquisition.

natural, or prepared, childbirth Method of childbirth that seeks to reduce or eliminate the use of drugs, enable both parents to participate fully, and control perceptions of pain.

naturalistic observation Research method in which behaviour is studied in natural settings without intervention or manipulation.

neglectful, or uninvolved, parenting Parenting style in which parents focus on their own needs rather than those of children.

neonatal jaundice Condition in many newborn babies caused by immaturity of the liver and evidenced by a yellowish appearance; can cause brain damage if not treated promptly.

neonatal period First four weeks of life, a time of transition from intrauterine dependency to independent existence.

neonate Newborn baby, up to four weeks old.

night terror Abrupt awakening from a deep sleep in a state of agitation.

nightmares A bad dream, sometimes brought on by staying up too late, eating a heavy meal close to bedtime, or overexcitement.

Nipissing District Developmental Screen Screening test given to children from infancy to 6 years to determine whether they are developing normally.

non-normative Characteristic of an unusual event that happens to a particular person or a typical event that happens at an unusual time of life.

non-organic failure to thrive In infancy, lack of appropriate growth for no known medical cause, accompanied by poor developmental and emotional functioning.

non-shared environmental effects The unique environment in which each child grows up, consisting of distinctive influences or influences that affect one child differently from another.

normative Characteristic of an event that occurs in a similar way for most people in a group.

nuclear family Two-generational household unit consisting of one or two parents and their biological children, adopted children, or stepchildren.

O

obesity Extreme overweight in relation to age, sex, height, and body type.

object permanence Piaget's term for the understanding that a person or an object still exists when out of sight.

observational learning Learning through watching the behaviour of others.

obsessive-compulsive disorder (OCD) Anxiety aroused by repetitive, intrusive thoughts, images, or impulses, often leading to compulsive ritual behaviours.

operant conditioning Learning based on association of behaviour with its consequences (i.e., reinforcement and punishment).

oppositional-defiant disorder (ODD) Pattern of behaviour, persisting into middle childhood, marked by negativity, excessive defiance, disobedience, and hostility toward adult authority figures lasting at least six months.

organization Piaget's term for the creation of categories or systems of knowledge.

organogenesis Process of development of emerging body systems and organs.

overt (direct) aggression Aggression that is openly directed at its target.

P

participant observation Research method in which the observer lives with the people or participates in the activity being observed.

parturition Process of uterine, cervical, and other changes, usually lasting about two weeks preceding childbirth.

permissive parenting Parenting style emphasizing self-expression and self-regulation.

personal fable Elkind's term for the conviction that one is special, unique, and not subject to the rules that govern the rest of the world.

phenotype Observable characteristics of a person.

phonetic (code emphasis) approach Approach to teaching reading that emphasizes decoding unfamiliar words.

physical development Growth of body and brain, including biological and physiological patterns of change in sensory capacities, motor skills, and health.

Piagetian approach Approach to the study of cognitive development that describes qualitative stages in cognitive functioning.

plasticity (1) Modifiability of performance. (2) Modifiability of the brain through experience.

play therapy Therapeutic approach that uses play to help a child cope with emotional distress.

polygenic inheritance Pattern of inheritance in which multiple genes at different sites on chromosomes affect a complex trait.

postconventional morality (or morality of autonomous moral principles) Third level in Kohlberg's theory of moral reasoning in which people follow internally held moral principles and can decide among conflicting moral standards.

postmature A fetus not yet born as of 42 weeks' gestation.

power assertion Disciplinary strategy designed to discourage undesirable behaviour through physical or verbal enforcement of parental control.

pragmatics Practical knowledge needed to use language for communicative purposes.

preconventional morality First level of Kohlberg's theory of moral reasoning in which control is external and rules are obeyed in order to gain rewards or avoid punishment or out of self-interest.

prejudice Unfavourable attitude toward members of certain groups outside one's own, especially racial or ethnic groups.

prelinguistic speech Forerunner of linguistic speech; utterance of sounds that are not words, including crying, cooing, babbling, and accidental and deliberate imitation of sounds without understanding their meaning.

preoperational stage In Piaget's theory, the second major stage of cognitive development, in which children become more sophisticated in their use of symbolic thought but are not yet able to use logic.

pretend play Play involving imaginary people or situations; also called *fantasy play, dramatic play,* or *imaginary play.*

preterm (premature) infants Infants born before completing the 37th week of gestation.

primary sex characteristics Organs directly related to reproduction, which enlarge and mature during adolescence.

private speech Talking aloud to oneself with no intent to communicate with others.

procedural knowledge Acquired skills stored in long-term memory.

procedural memory Memories of habitual and familiar routines to guide behaviour.

prosocial behaviour Any voluntary behaviour intended to help others.

proximodistal principle Principle that development proceeds from within to without; that is, parts of the body near the centre develop before the extremities.

psychoanalytic perspective View of human development as being shaped by unconscious forces.

psychometric approach Approach to the study of cognitive development that seeks to measure the quantity of intelligence a person possesses.

psychosexual development In Freudian theory, an unvarying sequence of stages of personality development during infancy, childhood, and adolescence, in which gratification shifts from the mouth to the anus and then to the genitals.

psychosocial development (1) In Erikson's eight-stage theory, the socially and culturally influenced process of development of the ego, or self. (2) Pattern of change in emotions, personality, and social relationships.

psychosocial moratorium A period of time that allows young people to search for commitments to which they can be faithful.

puberty Process by which a person attains sexual maturity and the ability to reproduce.

punishment In operant conditioning, a process that decreases the likelihood that a behaviour will be repeated.

 Q

qualitative change Change in kind, structure, or organization, such as the change from non-verbal to verbal communication.

quantitative change Change in number or amount, such as in height, weight, or size of vocabulary.

 R

reaction range Potential variability, depending on environmental conditions, in the expression of a hereditary trait.

recall Ability to reproduce material from memory.

recessive inheritance Pattern of inheritance in which a child receives identical recessive alleles, resulting in expression of a non-dominant trait.

reciprocal determinism Bandura's term for bidirectional forces that affect development.

recognition Ability to identify a previously encountered stimulus.

reflex behaviours Automatic, innate responses to stimulation; also called *reflexes*.

reinforcement In operant conditioning, a process that increases the likelihood that a behaviour will be repeated.

relational (indirect or social) aggression Aggression aimed at damaging or interfering with another person's relationships, reputation, or psychological well-being; can be overt or covert.

representational ability Piaget's term for capacity to store mental images or symbols of objects and events.

representational systems Broad, inclusive self-concepts that integrate various aspects of the self.

retrieval Process by which information is accessed or recalled from memory storage.

risk factors Conditions that increase the likelihood of a negative developmental outcome.

rough-and-tumble play Vigorous play involving wrestling, hitting, and chasing, often accompanied by laughing and screaming.

S

scaffolding Temporary support to help a child master a task.

schemes Piaget's term for organized patterns of thought and behaviour used in particular situations.

school phobia Unrealistic fear of going to school.

secondary sex characteristics Physiological signs of sexual maturation (such as breast development and growth of body hair) that do not involve the sex organs.

secure attachment Pattern in which an infant is quickly and effectively able to find comfort from a caregiver when faced with a stressful situation.

self-awareness Realization that one's existence and functioning are separate from those of other people and things.

self-concept Sense of self; descriptive and evaluative mental picture of one's abilities and traits.

self-conscious emotions Emotions, such as embarrassment, empathy, and envy, that depend on self-awareness.

self-definition Cluster of characteristics used to describe oneself.

self-efficacy Sense of one's capability to master challenges and achieve goals.

self-esteem Judgment a person makes about his or her self-worth.

self-regulation A person's independent control of behaviour to conform to understood social expectations.

sensitive periods Times in development when a given event or its absence usually has a strong effect on development.

sensorimotor stage In Piaget's theory, first stage in cognitive development, during which infants learn through senses and motor activity.

sensory memory Initial, brief, temporary storage of sensory information.

separation anxiety Distress shown by someone, typically an infant, when a familiar caregiver leaves.

separation anxiety disorder Condition involving excessive, prolonged anxiety concerning separation from home or from people to whom a person is attached.

sequential study Study design that combines cross-sectional and longitudinal designs.

seriation Ability to order items along a dimension.

sex chromosomes Pair of chromosomes that determines sex; XY in the normal human male, XX in the normal human female.

sex-linked inheritance Pattern of inheritance in which certain characteristics carried on the X chromosome inherited from the mother are transmitted differently to her male and female offspring.

sexual orientation Focus of consistent sexual, romantic, and affectionate interest, either heterosexual, homosexual, or bisexual.

sexually transmitted infections (STIs) Diseases spread by sexual contact.

shaken baby syndrome Form of maltreatment in which shaking an infant or a toddler can cause brain damage, paralysis, or death.

situational compliance Kochanska's term for obedience of a parent's orders only in the presence of signs of ongoing parental control.

sleeptalking Talking while asleep.

sleepwalking Walking around and sometimes performing other functions while asleep.

slow-to-warm-up children Children whose temperament is generally mild but who are hesitant about accepting new experiences.

small-for-date (small-for-gestational-age) infants Infants whose birth weight is less than that of 90 percent of babies of the same gestational age as a result of slow fetal growth.

social cognitive theory Albert Bandura's expansion of social learning theory; holds that children learn gender roles through socialization.

social construction Concept about what is real based on societally shared perceptions or assumptions.

social-contextual approach Approach to the study of cognitive development that focuses on environmental influences, particularly parents and other caregivers.

social emotions Emotions directed at the self that involve a comparison of oneself or one's actions to social standards.

social learning theory Theory that behaviours also are learned by observing and imitating models; also called *social cognitive theory*.

social phobia Extreme fear and/or avoidance of social situations; also called *social anxiety*.

social referencing Understanding an ambiguous situation by seeking out another person's perception of it.

social speech Speech intended to be understood by a listener.

socialization Development of habits, skills, values, and motives shared by responsible, productive members of a society.

socio-cultural theory Vygotsky's theory of how contextual factors affect children's development.

socio-economic status (SES) Combination of economic and social factors, including income, education, and occupation, that describe an individual or a family.

spermarche A boy's first ejaculation.

spontaneous abortion Natural expulsion from the uterus of an embryo that cannot survive outside the womb; also called *miscarriage*.

Stanford-Binet Intelligence Scale Individual intelligence test for ages 2 and up, used to measure knowledge, quantitative reasoning, visual-spatial processing, and working memory.

state of arousal Infant's physiological and behavioural status at a given moment in the periodic daily cycle of wakefulness, sleep, and activity.

stillbirth Death of a fetus at or after the 20th week of gestation.

still-face paradigm Research procedure used to measure mutual regulation in infants 2 to 9 months old.

storage Retention of information in memory for future use.

Strange Situation Laboratory technique used to study infant attachment.

stranger anxiety Wariness of strange people and places, shown by some infants from age 6 to 12 months.

stuttering Involuntary, frequent repetition or prolongation of sounds or syllables.

substance abuse Repeated, harmful use of a substance, usually alcohol or other drugs.

substance dependence Addiction (physical or psychological, or both) to a harmful substance.

sudden infant death syndrome (SIDS) Sudden and unexplained death of an apparently healthy infant.

symbolic function Piaget's term for the ability to use mental representations (words, numbers, or images) to which a child has attached meaning.

T

telegraphic speech Early form of sentence use consisting of only a few essential words.

temperament Characteristic disposition, or style of approaching and reacting to situations.

teratogen Environmental agent, such as a virus, a drug, or radiation, that can interfere with normal prenatal development and cause developmental abnormalities.

theory Coherent set of logically related concepts that seeks to organize, explain, and predict data.

theory of mind Awareness and understanding of mental processes of others.

theory of multiple intelligences Gardner's theory that there are eight distinct forms of intelligence.

theory of sexual selection Darwinian theory, which holds that selection of sexual partners is influenced by the differing reproductive pressures that early men and women confronted in the evolutionary past.

transduction In Piaget's terminology, a preoperational child's tendency to mentally link particular experiences, whether or not there is logically a causal relationship.

transitive inference Understanding the relationship between two objects by knowing the relationship of each to a third object.

U

ultrasound Prenatal medical procedure using high-frequency sound waves to detect the outline of a fetus and its movements, used to determine whether a pregnancy is progressing normally.

universal early childhood education and care A national system for early child education and care that makes access to preschool similar to kindergarten.

V

vernix caseosa Oily substance on a neonate's skin that protects against infection.

violation-of-expectations Research method in which dishabituation to a stimulus that conflicts with experience is taken as evidence that an infant recognizes the new stimulus as surprising.

visual cliff Apparatus designed to give an illusion of depth and used to assess depth perception in infants.

visual preference Tendency of infants to spend more time looking at one sight than another.

visual recognition memory Ability to distinguish a familiar visual stimulus from an unfamiliar stimulus when shown both at the same time.

W

Wechsler Intelligence Scale for Children (WISC-IV) Individual intelligence test for schoolchildren that yields verbal and performance scores, as well as a combined score.

Wechsler Preschool and Primary Scale of Intelligence, Fourth Edition (WPPSI-IV) Individual intelligence test for children ages 2½ to 7 that yields verbal and performance scores, as well as a combined score.

whole-language approach Approach to teaching reading that emphasizes visual retrieval and use of contextual clues.

withdrawal of love Disciplinary strategy that involves ignoring, isolating, or showing dislike for a child.

working memory Short-term storage of information being actively processed.

working model A set of expectations the baby has about how the mother is likely to respond in interactions.

Z

zone of proximal development (ZPD) Vygotsky's term for the difference between what a child can do alone and what the child can do with help.

zygote One-celled organism resulting from fertilization.

Aber, J. L., Brown, J. L., & Jones, S. M. (2003). Developmental trajectories toward violence in middle childhood: Course, demographic differences, and response to school-based intervention. *Developmental Psychology, 39*, 324–348.

Abma, J. C., Chandra, A., Mosher, W. D., Peterson, L., & Piccinino, L. (1997). Fertility, family planning, and women's health: New data from the 1995 National Survey of Family Growth. *Vital Health Statistics, 23*(19). Washington, DC: National Center for Health Statistics.

Abma, J. C., Martinez, G. M., Mosher, W. D., & Dawson, B. S. (2004). Teenagers in the United States: Sexual activity, contraceptive use, and childbearing, 2002. *Vital Health Statistics, 23*(24). Washington, DC: National Center for Health Statistics.

Abrams, D., Weick, M., Thomas, D., Colbe, H., & Franklin, K. (2011). On-line ostracism affects children differently from adolescents and adults. *British Journal of Developmental Psychology, 29*(1), 110–123. doi: 10.1348/026151010X494089

Achter, J. A., & Lubinski, D. (2003). Fostering exceptional development in intellectually talented populations. In W. B. Walsh (Ed.), *Counseling psychology and optimal human functioning* (pp. 279–296). Mahwah, NJ: Erlbaum.

Ackerman, D., Barnett, S., & Robin, K. (2005). *Making the most of Kindergarten: Present trends and future issues in the provision of full-day programs.* New Brunswick, NJ: National Institute for Early Education Research, Rutgers University.

ACT for Youth Upstate Center of Excellence. (2002). *Adolescent brain development. Research facts and findings* [A collaboration of Cornell University, University of Rochester, and the NYS Center for School Safety]. Retrieved March 23, 2004, from http://www.human.cornell.edu/actforyouth

Adair, J. (2001). Ethics of psychological research: New policies; continuing issues; new concerns. *Canadian Psychology, 42*, 25–37.

Adam, E. K., Gunnar, M. R., & Tanaka, A. (2004). Adult attachment, parent emotion, and observed parenting behavior: Mediator and moderator models. *Child Development*, 75, 110–122.

Adesope, O. O., Lavin, T., Thompson, T., & Ungerleider, C. (2011). Pedagogical strategies for teaching literacy to ESL immigrant students: A meta-analysis. *British Journal of Educational Psychology, 81*, 629–653. doi:10.1111/j.2044-8279.2010.02015.x

Administration for Children and Families. (2006). *FACES findings: New research on Head Start outcomes and program quality.* Washington, DC: U.S. Department of Health and Human Services.

Adolph, K. E. (2008). Learning to move. *Current Directions in Psychological Science, 17*, 213–218.

Adolph, K. E., & Eppler, M. A. (2002). Flexibility and specificity in infant motor skill acquisition. In J. Fagen & H. Hayne (Eds.), *Progress in infancy research* (Vol. 2, pp. 121–167). Mahwah, NJ: Erlbaum.

Adoption Council of Canada. (2010). *Family bonds: How the Government of Canada can support adoption.* Retrieved from http://www.adoption.ca/family-bonds

Ahamed, Y., MacDonald, H., Reed, K., Naylor, P., Liu-Ambrose, T., & McKay, H. (2007). School-based physical activity does not compromise children's academic performance. *Medicine & Science in Sports & Exercise, 39*, 371–376.

Ahmed, S. F., & Hughes, I. A. (2002). The genetics of male undermasculinization. *Clinical Endocrinology, 56*, 1–18.

Ahnert, L., Gunnar, M. R., Lamb, M. E., & Barthel, M. (2004). Transition to child care: Associations with infant-mother attachment, infant negative emotion and corticol elevation. *Child Development, 75*, 639–650.

Ahrons, C. R., & Tanner, J. L. (2003). Adult children and their fathers: Relationship changes 20 years after parental divorce. *Family Relations, 52*, 340–351.

Aikens, N., Kopack Klein, A., Tarullo, L., and West, J. (2013). *Getting ready for kindergarten: Children's progress during Head Start. FACES 2009 report.* OPRE Report 2013-21a. Washington, DC: Office of Planning, Research and Evaluation, Administration for Children and Families, U.S. Department of Health and Human Services. Retrieved from http://www.acf.hhs.gov/programs/opre/research/project/head-start-family-and-child-experiences-survey-faces-1997-2013

Ainsworth, M. D. S. (1967). *Infancy in Uganda: Infant care and the growth of love.* Baltimore: Johns Hopkins University Press.

Ainsworth, M. D. S., Blehar, M. C., Waters, E., & Wall, S. (1978). *Patterns of attachment: A psychological study of the strange situation.* Hillsdale, NJ: Erlbaum.

Alaimo, K., Olson, C. M., & Frongillo, E. A. (2001). Food insufficiency and American school-aged children's cognitive, academic, and psychosocial development. *Pediatrics, 108*, 44–53.

Alexander, G. R., Tompkins, M. E., Allen, M. C., & Hulsey, T. C. (2000). Trends and racial differences in birth weight and related survival. *Maternal and Child Health Journal, 3*, 71–79.

Alexander, K. L., Entwisle, D. R., & Olson, L. S. (2007). Lasting consequences of the summer learning gap. *American Sociological Review, 72*, 167–180.

Ali, M. M., & Dwyer, D. S. (2011). Estimating peer effects in sexual behavior among adolescents. *Journal of Adolescence, 34*(1), 183–190.

Allen, G. L., & Ondracek, P. J. (1995). Age-sensitive cognitive abilities related to children's acquisition of spatial knowledge. *Developmental Psychology, 31*, 934–945.

Allen, K. R., Blieszner, R., & Roberto, K. A. (2000). Families in the middle and later years: A review and critique of research in the 1990s. *Journal of Marriage and the Family, 62*, 911–926.

Allen, S. (2007). The future of Inuktitut in the face of majority languages: Bilingualism or language shift? *Applied Psycholinguistics, 28*, 515–536.

Allen, S., & Daly, K. (2007). *The effects of father involvement: An updated research summary of the evidence.* Guelph, ON: Centre for Families, Work & Well-Being, University of Guelph.

Alloway, T. P. (2006). How does working memory work in the classroom? *Education Research and Reviews, 1*, 134–139.

Alloway, T. P., Gathercole, S. E., Kirkwood, H., & Elliot, J. (2009). The cognitive and behavioral characteristics of children with low working memory. *Child Development, 80*(2), 606–621.

Almas, A. N., Grusec, J. E., & Tackett, J. L. (2011). Children's disclosure and secrecy: Links to maternal parenting characteristics and children's coping skills. *Social Development, 17*, 941–959. doi: 10.1111/j.1467-9507.2010.00602.x

Almli, C. R., Ball, R. H., & Wheeler, M. E. (2001). Human fetal and neonatal movement patterns: Gender differences and fetal-to-natal continuity. *Developmental Psychobiology, 38*(4), 252–273.

Al-Oballi Kridli, S. (2002). Health beliefs and practices among Arab Women. *MCN, The American Journal of Maternal/Child Nursing, 27*, 178–182.

Al-Sahab, B., Ardern, C. I., Hamadeh, M. J., & Tamim, H. (2010). Age at menarche in Canada: results from the National Longitudinal Survey of Children & Youth. *BMC Public Health, 10*, 736–743. Retrieved from http://www.biomedcentral.com/1471-2458/10/736

Al-Sahab, B., Lanes, A., Feldman, M., & Tamim, H. (2010). Prevalence and predictors of 6-month exclusive breast-feeding among Canadian women: A national survey. *BMC Pediatrics, 10*, 20. Retrieved from http://www.biomedcentral.com/1471-2431/10/20

Al-Sahab, B., Saqib, M., Hauser, G., & Tamim, H. (2010). Prevalence of smoking during pregnancy and associated risk factors among Canadian women: A national survey. *BMC Pregnancy and Childbirth, 10*, 24.

Retrieved from http://www.biomedcentral.com/1471-2393/10/24

Als, H., Duffy, F. H., McAnulty, G. B., Rivkin, M. J., Vajapeyam, S., Mulkern, R. V., et al. (2004). Early experience alters brain function and structure. *Pediatrics, 113*, 846–857.

Amato, P. R. (2003). Reconciling divergent perspectives: Judith Wallerstein, quantitative family research, and children of divorce. *Family Relations, 52*, 332–339.

Amato, P. R. (2005). The impact of family formation change on the cognitive, social, and emotional well-being of the next generation. *Future of Children, 15*, 75–96.

Ambert, A.-M. (2009). *Divorce: Facts, causes & consequences* (3rd ed.) Ottawa, ON: Vanier Institute of the Family. Retrieved from vif.redrabbit.ca/node/72

American Academy of Pediatrics. (2000). Shaken baby syndrome. Retrieved February 17, 2007, from http://aap-policy.aappublications.org/cgi/content/full/pediatrics;108/1/206

American Academy of Pediatrics. (2004, September 30). *American Academy of Pediatrics (AAP) supports Institute of Medicine's (IOM) childhood obesity recommendations* [Press release]. Elk Grove Village, IL: Author.

American Academy of Pediatrics (AAP) Committee on Adolescence. (1999). Adolescent pregnancy—current trends and issues: 1998. *Pediatrics, 103*, 516–520.

American Academy of Pediatrics (AAP) Committee on Adolescence. (2000). Suicide and suicide attempts in adolescents. *Pediatrics, 105*(4), 871–874.

American Academy of Pediatrics (AAP) Committee on Adolescence. (2003). Policy statement: Identifying and treating eating disorders. *Pediatrics, 111*, 204–211.

American Academy of Pediatrics (AAP) Committee on Drugs. (2000). Use of psychoactive medication during pregnancy and possible effects on the fetus and newborn. *Pediatrics, 105*, 880–887.

American Academy of Pediatrics (AAP) Committee on Drugs. (2001). The transfer of drugs and other chemicals into human milk. *Pediatrics, 108*(3), 776–789.

American Academy of Pediatrics (AAP) Committee on Environmental Health. (2005). Lead exposure in children: Prevention, detection, and management. *Pediatrics, 116*, 1036–1046.

American Academy of Pediatrics (AAP) Committee on Fetus and Newborn & American College of Obstetricians and Gynecologists (ACOG) Committee on Obstetric Practice. (2006). The Apgar score. *Pediatrics, 117*, 1444–1447.

American Academy of Pediatrics (AAP) Committee on Injury and Poison Prevention (1995). Skateboard injuries. *Pediatrics, 95*, 611–612.

American Academy of Pediatrics (AAP) Committee on Injury and Poison Prevention. (2000). Firearm-related injuries affecting the pediatric population. *Pediatrics, 105*(4), 888–895.

American Academy of Pediatrics (AAP) Committee on Nutrition. (2003). Prevention of pediatric overweight and obesity. *Pediatrics, 112*, 424–430.

American Academy of Pediatrics (AAP): Committee on Nutrition. (2006). Dietary recommendations for children and adolescents: A guide for practitioners. *Pediatrics, 117*(2), 544–559.

American Academy of Pediatrics (AAP) Committee on Psychosocial Aspects of Child and Family Health. (1998). Guidance for effective discipline. *Pediatrics, 101*, 723–728.

American Academy of Pediatrics (AAP) Committee on Psychosocial Aspects of Child and Family Health and Committee on Adolescence. (2001). Sexuality education for children and adolescence. *Pediatrics, 108*(2), 498–502.

American Academy of Pediatrics (AAP) Committee on Public Education. (2001). Policy statement: Children, adolescents, and television. *Pediatrics, 107*, 423–426.

American Academy of Pediatrics (AAP) Committee on Sports Medicine and Fitness and Committee on School Health. (2001). Organized sports for children and preadolescents. *Pediatrics, 107*(6) 1459–1462.

American Academy of Pediatrics (AAP) Committee on Substance Abuse. (2001). Tobacco's toll: Implications for the pediatrician. *Pediatrics, 107*, 794–798.

American Academy of Pediatrics (AAP) Section on Breastfeeding. (2005). Breastfeeding and the use of human milk. *Pediatrics, 115*, 496–506.

American Academy of Pediatrics, Stirling, J., Jr., Committee on Child Abuse and Neglect and Section on Adoption and Foster Care, American Academy of Child and Adolescent Psychiatry, Amaya-Jackson, L., National Center for Child Traumatic Stress, & Amaya-Jackson, L. (2008). Understanding the behavioral and emotional consequences of child abuse. *Pediatrics, 122*(3), 667–673. doi:10.1542/peds.2008-1885

American Academy of Pediatrics (AAP) Task Force on Infant Sleep Position and Sudden Infant Death Syndrome. (2000). Changing concepts of sudden infant death syndrome: Implications for infant sleeping environment and sleep position. *Pediatrics, 105*, 650–656.

American Academy of Pediatrics Task Force on Sudden Infant Death Syndrome. (2005). The changing concept of sudden infant death syndrome: Diagnostic coding shifts, controversies regarding sleeping environment, and new variables to consider in reducing risk. *Pediatrics, 116*, 1245–1255.

American College of Nurse-Midwives. (2005). *Position statement: Home births*. Silver Spring, MD: Author.

American Dental Association. (2007). Thumb sucking and pacifier use. *The Journal of the American Dental Association, 138*(8), 1176.

American Heart Association (AHA), Gidding, S. S., Dennison, B. A., Birch, L. L., Daniels, S. R., Gilman, M. W., et al. (2006). Dietary recommendations for children and adolescents: A guide for practitioners. *Pediatrics, 117*, 544–559.

American Medical Association House of Delegates. (2008, June). *Resolution 205: Home deliveries*. Proceedings of the American Medical Association House of Delegates, Fifteenth Annual Meeting, Chicago, IL. Retrieved from http://www.ama-assn.org/ama1/pub/upload/mm/471/205.doc

American Psychiatric Association. (1994). *Diagnostic and statistical manual of mental disorders* (4th ed.). Washington, DC: Author.

American Psychiatric Association. (2000). *Diagnostic and statistical manual of mental disorders* (4th ed., Text Revision). Washington, DC: Author.

American Psychiatric Association. (2013). *Diagnostic and statistical manual of mental disorders* (5th ed). Washington, DC.

American Psychological Association. (n.d.). *Answers to your questions about sexual orientation and homosexuality* [Brochure]. Washington, DC: Author.

American Psychological Association. (2004, July). Sexual orientation: Parents and children. Retrieved May 17, 2012, from http://www.apa.org/about/policy/parenting.aspx

Ames, E. W. (1997). *The development of Romanian orphanage children adopted to Canada: Final report* (National Welfare Grants Program, Human Resources Development, Canada). Burnaby, BC: Simon Fraser University, Psychology Department.

Amit, M., & Canadian Paediatric Society, Community Paediatrics Committee. (2009). Vision screening in infants, children and youth. *Paediatrics and Child Health, 14*, 246-248.

Amso, D., & Casey, B. J. (2006). Beyond what develops when: Neuroimaging may inform how cognition changes with development. *Current Directions in Psychological Science, 15*, 24–29.

Anastasi, A., & Schaefer, C. E. (1971). Note on concepts of creativity and intelligence. *Journal of Creative Behavior, 3*, 113–116.

Anderson, A. H., Clark, A., & Mullin, J. (1994). Interactive communication between children: Learning how to make language work in dialog. *Journal of Child Language, 21*, 439–463.

Anderson, C. (2000). *The impact of interactive violence on children*. Statement before the Senate Committee on Commerce, Science, and Transportation, 106th Congress, 1st session.

Anderson, C. A., Berkowitz, L., Donnerstein, E., Huesmann, L. R., Johnson, J. D., Linz, D., et al. (2003). The influence of media violence on youth. *Psychological Science in the Public Interest, 4*, 81–110.

Anderson, D. A., & Hamilton, M. (2005). Gender role stereotyping of parents in children's picture books: The invisible father. *Sex Roles, 52*, 145–151.

Anderson, K. D., Baxter-Jones, A. D. G., Faulkner, R. A., Muhajarine, N., Henry, C. J., & Chad, K. E. (2010). Assessment of total and central adiposity in Canadian Aboriginal children and their Caucasian peers. *International Journal of Pediatric Obesity, 5*, 342–350. doi: 10.3109/17477160903473721

Anderson, M., Kaufman, J., Simon, T. R., Barrios, L., Paulozzi, L., Ryan, G., et al. (2001). School-associated violent deaths in the United States, 1994–1999. *Journal of the American Medical Association, 286*(21), 2695–2702.

Anderson, P., Doyle, L. W., & the Victorian Infant Collaborative Study Group. (2003). *Journal of the American Medical Association, 289*, 3264–3272.

Anderson, R. N., & Smith, B. L. (2005). Deaths: Leading causes for 2002. *National Vital Statistics Reports, 53*(17). Hyattsville, MD: National Center for Health Statistics.

Anderson, S. E., Dallal, G. E., & Must, A. (2003). Relative weight and race influence average age at menarche: Results from two nationally representative surveys of U.S. girls studied 25 years apart. *Pediatrics 2003, 111*, 844–850.

Andres, L., & Adamuti-Trache, M. (2007). You've come a long way, baby? Persistent gender inequality in university enrolment and completion in Canada, 1979–2004. *Canadian Public Policy, 33*, 93–116. Retrieved from http://www.jstor.org/stable/30032515

Anisef, P., & Kilbride, K. M. (2003). Overview and implications of the research. In P. Anisef & D. M. Kilbride (Eds.), *Managing two worlds: The experiences and concerns of immigrant youth in Ontario* (pp. 235–272). Toronto, ON: Canadian Scholars' Press.

Annett, M. (2002). *Handedness and brain asymmetry: The right shift theory*. East Sussex, UK: Psychology Press.

Antonarakis, S. E., & Down Syndrome Collaborative Group. (1991). Parental origin of the extra chromosome in trisomy 21 as indicated by analysis of DNA polymorphisms. *New England Journal of Medicine, 324*, 872–876.

Arai, A. B. (2000). Reasons for home schooling in Canada. *Canadian Journal of Education, 25*, 204–217.

Arbour, L., Gilpin, C., Millor-Roy, V., Platt, R., Pekeles, G., Egeland, G. M., ... (2004). Heart defects and other malformations in the Inuit in Canada: A baseline study. *International Journal of Circumpolar Health, 63*, 251–266.

Archambault, I., Janosz, M., Fallu, J.-S., & Pagani, L. S. (2009). Student engagement and its relationship with early high school dropout. *Journal of Adolescence, 32*, 651–670. doi:10.1016/j.adolescence.2008.06.007

Arias, E., MacDorman, M. F., Strobino, D. M., & Guyer, B. (2003). Annual summary of vital statistics—2002. *Pediatrics, 112*, 1215–1230.

Arim, R. G., Shapka, J. D., Dahinten, & Willms, J. D. (2007). Patterns and correlates of pubertal development in Canadian youth: Effects of family context. *Canadian Journal of Public Health, 98*, 91–96.

Armson, B. A. (2007). Is planned cesarean childbirth a safe alternative? *Canadian Medical Association Journal, 176*, 475–476.

Arner, P. (2000). Obesity–a genetic disease of adipose tissue? *British Journal of Nutrition, 83*(1), 9–16.

Arnett, J. J. (1999). Adolescent storm and stress, reconsidered. *American Psychologist, 54*, 317–326.

Arnett, J. J. (2003). Conceptions of the transition to adulthood among emerging adults in American ethnic groups. In J. J. Arnett & N. L. Galambos (Eds.), Exploring cultural conceptions of the transition to adulthood. *New Directions for Child and Adolescent Development, 100*, 63–75.

Arnett, J. J. (2007). Emerging adulthood: What is it, and what is it good for? *Child Development Perspectives, 1*, 68–73.

Arnett, J. J. (2012). New horizons in research on emerging and young adulthood. In A. Booth, S. L. Brown, N. S. Landale, W. D. Manning, & S. M. McHale (eds.), *Early Adulthood in a Family Context* (pp. 231–244). National Symposium on Family Issues 2. New York: Springer. doi:10.1007/978-1-4614-1436-0

Arnett, J. J., & Galambos, N. L. (2003). Culture and conceptions of adulthood. In J. J. Arnett & N. L. Galambos (Eds.), Exploring cultural conceptions of the transition to adulthood. *New Directions for Child and Adolescent Development, 100*, 91–98.

Asher, M. I., Montefort, S., Björkstén, B., Lai, C. K., Strachan, D. P., Weiland, S. K., et al. (2006). Worldwide time trends in the prevalence of symptoms of asthma, allergic rhinoconjunctivitis, and eczema in childhood: ISAAC phases one and three repeat multicountry cross-sectional surveys. *Lancet, 368*(9537), 733–743.

Associated Press. (2004, November 22). "Boys have no place in politics: 4-year-old." AP Newswire.

Auyeung, B., Baron-Cohen, S., Ashwin, E., Kinckmeyer, R., Taylor, K., Hackett, G., & Hines, M. (2009). Fetal testosterone predicts sexually differentiated childhood behavior in girls and in boys. *Psychological Science, 20*, 144–148.

Awong, T., Grusec, J. E., & Sorensen, A. (2008). Respect-based control and anger as determinants of children's socio-emotional development. *Social Development, 17*, 941–959. doi: 10.1111/j.1467-9507.2008.00460.x

Baddeley, A. D. (2001). Is working memory still working? *American Psychologist, 56*, 851–864.

Bailey, L. M., & McKeever, W. F. (2004). A large-scale study of handedness and pregnancy/birth risk events: Implications for genetic theories of handedness. *Laterality, 9*, 175–188.

Bailey, N. W., & Zuk, M. (2009). Same-sex sexual behavior and evolution. *Trends in Ecology and Evolution, 24*(8), 439–446.

Baillargeon, R. (1999). Young infants' expectations about hidden objects. *Developmental Science, 2*, 115–132.

Baillargeon, R., & DeVos, J. (1991). Object permanence in young infants: Further evidence. *Child Development, 62*, 1227–1246.

Baillargeon, R. H., Sward, G. D., Keenan, K., & Cao, G. (2011). Opposition-defiance in the second year of life: A population-based cohort study. *Infancy, 16*, 418–434. doi: 10.1111/j.1532-7078.2010.00043.x

Baillargeon, R. H., Zoccolillo, M., Keenan, K., Côté, S., Pérusse, D., Wu, H.-X., et al. (2007). Gender differences in physical aggression: A prospective population-based survey of children before and after 2 years of age. *Developmental Psychology, 43*, 13–26.

Baker, M. (2010). Gendering 'Child' Poverty: Cross-National Lessons for Canada in a Deepening Recession. *International Journal of Canadian Studies/Revue internationale d'études canadiennes, 42*, 25–46. doi: 10.7202/1002170ar

Ball, J. (2008). Promoting equity and dignity for Aboriginal children in Canada. *IRPP Choices, 14*, 1–27.

Ball, H. L. (2009). Bed-sharing and co-sleeping: Research overview. *NCT New Digest, 48*, 22–27.

Baltes, P. B., & Smith, J. (2004). Lifespan psychology: From developmental contextualism to developmental biocultural co-constructivism. *Research in Human Development, 1,* 123–144.

Bandura, A. (1977). *Social learning theory.* Englewood Cliffs, NJ: Prentice Hall.

Bandura, A. (1986). *Social foundations of thought and action: A social cognitive theory.* Englewood Cliffs, NJ: Prentice Hall.

Bandura, A. (1989). Social cognitive theory. In R. Vasta (Ed.), *Annals of child development* (Vol. 6, pp. 1–60). Greenwich, CT: JAI.

Bandura, A., Barbaranelli, C., Caprara, G. V., & Pastorelli, C. (2001). Self-efficacy beliefs as shapers of children's aspirations and career trajectories. *Child Development 72*(1), 187–206.

Bandura, A., & Bussey, K. (2004). On broadening the cognitive, motivational, and socio-structural scope of theorizing about gender development and functioning: Comment on Martin, Ruble, and Szkrybalo (2002). *Psychological Bulletin, 130*(5), 691–701.

Banerji, A., & Canadian Paediatric Society, First Nations, Inuit and Métis Health Committee. (2012). Preventing unintentional injuries in Indigenous children and youth in Canada. *Paediatrics and Child Health, 17,* 393.

Banks, E. (1989). Temperament and individuality: A study of Malay children. *American Journal of Orthopsychiatry, 59,* 390–397.

Banta, D., & Thacker, S. B. (2001). Historical controversy in health technology assessment: The case of electronic fetal monitoring. *Obstetrical and Gynecological Survey, 56*(11), 707–719.

Barkley, R. A. (2002). ADHD and accident proneness. *The ADHD Report, 10*(2), 2–6. doi:10.1521/adhd.10.2.2.20561

Barnes, J. D., Colley, R. C., & Tremblay, M. S. (2012). Results from the Active Healthy Kids Canada 2011 Report Card on Physical Activity for Children and Youth. *Applied Physiology, Nutrition, and Metabolism, 37,* 793–797. doi:10.1139/H2012-033

Barrington, K. J., Batton, D. G., Finley G. A., Wallman, C., & Canadian Paediatric Society, Fetus and Newborn Committee. (2007). Prevention and management of pain in the neonate: An update. *Paediatrics and Child Health, 12,* 137–138.

Barros, R. M., Silver, E. J., & Stein, R. E. K. (2009). School recess and group classroom behavior. *Pediatrics, 123,* 431–436. doi: 10.1542/peds.2007-2825

Barrow, L., Claessens, A., & Schanzenbach, D. W. (2010). The impact of small schools in Chicago: Assessing the effectiveness of Chicago's small high school initiative. Retrieved April 11, 2012, from http://econweb.tamu.edu/common/files/workshops/ PERC%20Applied%20Microeconomics/2010_2_10_Diane_Schanzenbach.pdf

Bartick, M., & Reinhold, A. (2010). The burden of suboptimal breastfeeding in the United States: A pediatric cost analysis. *Pediatrics, 125,* 1048–1056.

Bascaramurty, D. (2012). Immigrant influx fuels uptick in multigenerational households. *Globe and Mail,* September 19. Retrieved from http://www.theglobeandmail.com/news/national/immigrant-influx-fuels-uptick-in-multigenerational-households/article4556039/

Baskett, R., Bryant, K., White, W., & Rhoads, K. (2005). Half-day to full-day Kindergarten: An analysis of educational change scores and demonstration of an educational research collaboration. *Early Child Development and Care, 175,* 419–431.

Bates, E., O'Connell, B., & Shore, C. (1987). Language and communication in infancy. In J. D. Osofsky (Ed.), *Handbook of infant development* (2nd ed., pp. 149–203). New York: Wiley.

Bauer, P. J. (2006). Event memory. In W. Damon & R. M. Lerner (Series Eds.) & D. Kuhn & R. S. Siegler (Vol. Eds.), *Handbook of child psychology: Vol 2. Cognition, perception, and language* (6th ed., pp. 373–425). Hoboken, NJ: Wiley.

Bauer, P. J., Larkina, M., & Deocampo, J. (2010). Early memory development. In U. Goswami (Ed.), *The Wiley-Blackwell Handbook of Childhood Cognitive Development, 2nd Edition* (pp. 153–179). Malden, MA: Blackwell Publishing Ltd.

Bauman, L. J., Silver, E. J., & Stein, R. E. K. (2006). Cumulative social disadvantage and child health. *Pediatrics, 117,* 1321–1328.

Baumer, E. P., & South, S. J. (2001). Community effects on youth sexual activity. *Journal of Marriage and Family, 63,* 540–554.

Baumrind, D. (1989). Rearing competent children. In W. Damon (Ed.), *Child development today and tomorrow* (pp. 349–378). San Francisco, CA: Jossey-Bass.

Baumrind, D. (1991). Parenting styles and adolescent development. In J. Brooks-Gunn, R. Lerner, & A. C. Peterson (Eds.), The encyclopedia of adolescence (pp. 746–758). New York: Garland.

Baumrind, D. (2005). Patterns of parental authority and adolescent autonomy. In J. Smetana (Ed.), *Changing boundaries of parental authority during adolescence: New directions for child and adolescent development* (No. 108, pp. 61–70). San Francisco, CA: Jossey-Bass.

Baumrind, D., & Black, A. E. (1967). Socialization practices associated with dimensions of competence in preschool boys and girls. *Child Development, 38,* 291–327.

Baumrind, D., Larzelere, R. E., & Cowan, P. A. (2002). Ordinary physical punishment: Is it harmful? Comment on Gershoff (2002). *Psychological Bulletin, 128,* 580–589.

Baumrind, D., Larzelere, R. E., & Owens, E. B. (2010). Effects of preschool parents' power assertive patterns and practices on adolescent development. *Parenting: Science and Practice, 10*(3), 157–201.

Bauserman, R. (2002). Child adjustment in joint-custody versus sole-custody arrangements: A meta-analytic review. *Journal of Family Psychology, 16,* 91–102.

Baxter, C., & Canadian Paediatric Society, Community Paediatrics Committee. (2006). Transracial adoption. *Paediatrics and Child Health, 11,* 443–447.

Baydala, L., Rasmussen, C., Birch, J., Sherman, J., Wikman, E., Charchun, J., … & Bisanz, J. (2009). Self-beliefs and behavioural development as related to academic achievement in Canadian aboriginal children. *Canadian Journal of School Psychology, 24,* 19–33. doi: 10.1177/0829573509332243

Bayley, N. (2005). *Bayley Scales of Infant Development: III.* New York: Harcourt Brace.

Bayliss, D. M., Jarrold, C., Baddeley, A. D., Gunn, D. M., & Leigh, E. (2005). Mapping the developmental constraints on working memory span performance. *Developmental Psychology, 41*(4), 579–597.

B.C. Ministry of Education and Ministry of Healthy Living and Sport. (2010). *Guidelines for food and beverage sales in BC schools.* Victoria, BC.

Beach, J., Friendly, M., Ferns, C., Prabhu, N., & Forer, B. (2009). *Early childhood care and education in Canada.* Toronto, ON: Children's Resource and Research Unit. Retrieved from http://www.childcarecanada.org

Bearman, S. K., Martinez, E., & Stice, E. (2006). The skinny on body dissatisfaction: A longitudinal study of adolescent girls and boys. *Journal of Youth and Adolescence, 35*(2), 217–229.

Beauchamp, G. K., & Mennella, J. A. (2009). Early flavor learning and its impact on later feeding behavior. *Journal of Pediatric Gastroenterology and Nutrition, 48*(1), 25–30.

Beaupré, P., & Cloutier, E. (2007). *Navigating family transitions: Evidence from the General Social Survey* (Catalogue no. 89-625-XWE2007002). Ottawa, ON: Statistics Canada. Retrieved from http://www.statcan.gc.ca/bsolc/english/bsolc?catno=89-625-X2007002

Beaupré, P., Dryburgh, H., & Wendt, M. (2010). *Making fathers "count"* (Catalogue no. 11-008). Ottawa, ON: Statistics Canada. Retrieved from http://www5.statcan.gc.ca/bsolc/olc-cel/olc-cel?catno=11-008-X201000211165&lang=eng

Beckett, C., Maughan, B., Rutter, M., Castle, J., Colvert, E., Groothues, C., et al. (2006). Do the effects of severe early deprivation on cognition persist into early adolescence? Findings from the English and Romanian adoptees study. *Child Development, 77*(3), 696–711.

Behrman, R. E. (1992). *Nelson textbook of pediatrics* (13th ed.). Philadelphia, PA: Saunders.

Beiser, M., & Gotowiec, A. (2000). Accounting for native/non-native differences in IQ scores. *Psychology in the Schools, 37*, 237–252.

Beiser, M., Hou, F., Hyman, I., & Tousignant, M. (1998). *Growing up Canadian: A study of new immigrant children.* Report No. W-98-24E. Ottawa: Applied Research Branch, Strategic Policy, Human Resources Development Canada.

Beiser, M., Hou, F., Hyman, I., & Tousignant, M. (2002). Poverty, family process, and the mental health of immigrant children in Canada. *American Journal of Public Health, 92*, 220–227.

Beiser, M., Sack, W., Manson, S. M., Redshirt, R., & Dion, R. (1998). Mental health and the academic performance of First Nations and majority-culture children. *American Journal of Orthopsychiatry, 68*, 455–467.

Belizzi, M. (2002, May). *Obesity in children— what kind of future are we creating?* Presentation at the Fifty-Fifth World Health Assembly Technical Briefing, Geneva, Switzerland.

Bell, J. F., Zimmerman, F. J., & Diehr, P. K. (2008). Maternal work and birth outcome disparities. *Maternal & Child Health Journal, 12*, 415–426.

Bell, L. G., & Bell, D. C. (2005). Family dynamics in adolescence affect midlife well-being. *Journal of Family Psychology, 19*, 198–207.

Bell, T., & Romano, E. (2012). Opinions about child corporal punishment and influencing factors. *Journal of Interpersonal Violence, 27*, 2208–2229. doi:10.1177/0886260507304550

Belsky, J., Steinberg, L. D., Houts, R. M., Friedman, S. L., DeHart, G., Cauffman, E., et al. (2007). Family rearing antecedents of pubertal timing. *Child Development, 78*(4), 1302–1321.

Benes, F. M., Turtle, M., Khan, Y., & Farol, P. (1994). Myelination of a key relay zone in the hippocampal formation occurs in the human brain during childhood, adolescence, and adulthood. *Archives of General Psychiatry, 51*, 447–484.

Benjamin, A. (2009). Double bagged or fries with that: Adolescents' perceptions of the job market in four urban Vancouver secondary schools. *The Alberta Journal of Educational Research, 55*, 143–156.

Bennett, D. S., Bendersky, M., & Lewis, M. (2008). Children's cognitive ability from 4 to 9 years old as a function of prenatal cocaine exposure, environmental risk, and maternal verbal intelligence. *Developmental Psychology, 44*, 919–928.

Benoit, C., & Carroll, D. (2005). Canadian midwifery: Blending traditional and modern practices. In C. Bates, D. Dodd, & N. Rousseau (Eds.). *On All Frontiers: Four Centuries of Canadian Nursing* (pp. 27–41). Ottawa, ON: University of Ottawa Press and Canadian Museum of Civilization.

Ben-Shoshan, M., Harrington, D. W., Soller, L., Fragapane, J., Joseph, L., St. Pierre, Y., . . . & Clarke, A. E. (2010). A population-based study on peanut, tree nut, fish, shellfish, and sesame allergy prevalence in Canada. *Journal of Allergy and Clinical Immunology, 125*, 1327–1335. doi:10.1016/j.jaci.2010.03.015

Ben-Shoshan, M., Kagan, R. S., Alizadehfar, R., Joseph, L., Turnbull, E., St. Pierre, & Clarke, A. E. (2009). Is the prevalence of peanut allergy increasing? A 5-year follow-up study in children in Montreal. *Journal of Allergy and Clinical Immunology, 123*, 783–788.

Benzies, K., Tough, S., Edwards, N., Mychasiuk, R., & Donnelly, C. (2011). Aboriginal children and their caregivers living with low income: Outcomes from a two-generation preschool program. *Journal of Child and Family Studies, 20*, 311–318. doi:10.1007/s10826-010-9394-3

Bergeman, C. S., & Plomin, R. (1989). Genotype-environment interaction. In M. Bornstein & J. Bruner (Eds.), *Interaction in human development* (pp. 157–171). Hillsdale, NJ: Erlbaum.

Berger, A., Tzur, G., & Posner, M. (2006). Infant brains detect arithmetic errors. *Proceedings of the National Academy of Sciences, 103*(33), 12649–12653.

Berger, K. S. (2007). Update on bullying at school: Science forgotten? *Developmental Review, 27*, 91–92.

Berndt, T. J., & Perry, T. B. (1990). Distinctive features and effects of early adolescent friendships. In R. Montemayor, G. R. Adams, & T. P. Gullotta (Eds.), *From childhood to adolescence: A transitional period?* (Vol. 2, pp. 269–287). Newbury Park, CA: Sage.

Bernier, A., & Meins, E. (2008). A threshold approach to understanding the origins of attachment disorganization. *Developmental Psychology, 44*, 969–982.

Bernier, L., & Gregoire, D. (2004). Reproductive and therapeutic cloning, germline therapy, and purchase of gametes and embryos: Comments on Canadian legislation governing reproductive technologies. *Journal of Medical Ethics, 30*, 527–532.

Bernstein, P. S. (2003, December 12). Achieving equity in women's and perinatal health. *Medscape Ob/Gyn & Women's Health, 8* [ePub].

Berk, L. E. (1992). Children's private speech: An overview of theory and the status of research. In R. M. Diaz & L. E. Berk (Eds.), *Private speech: From social interaction to self-regulation* (pp. 17–53). Hillsdale, NJ: Erlbaum.

Berk, L. E., & Garvin, R. A. (1984). Development of private speech among low-income Appalachian children. *Developmental Psychology, 20*, 271–286.

Berry, R. J., Li, Z., Erickson, J. D., Li, S., Moore, C. A., Wang, H., et al. (1999). Prevention of neural-tube defects with folic acid in China. *New England Journal of Medicine, 341*, 1485–1490.

Bertrand, J. (2007). Canada: Longitudinal monitoring of ECD outcomes. In M. E. Young with L. M. Richardson, *Early child development: From measurement to action. A priority for growth and equity* (pp. 129–140). Washington, DC: The World Bank.

Betran, A. P., Merialdi, M., Lauer, J. A., Bing-Shun, W., Thomas, J., Van Look, P., & Wagner, M. (2007). Rates of caesarean section: Analysis of global, regional and national estimates. *Paediatric and Perinatal Epidemiology, 21*, 98–113.

Bialystok, E., & Senman, L. (2004). Executive processes in appearance-reality tasks: The role of inhibition of attention and symbolic representation. *Child Development, 75*, 562–579.

Biason-Lauber, A., Konrad, D., Navratil, F., & Schoenle, E. J. (2004). A WNT4 mutation associated with Müllerian-duct regression and virilization in a 46, XX woman. *New England Journal of Medicine, 351*, 792–798.

Bierman, K. L., Smoot, D. L., & Aumiller, K. (1993). Characteristics of aggressive rejected, aggressive (nonrejected), and rejected (non-aggressive) boys. *Child Development, 64*, 139–151.

Birmaher, B., Ryan, N. D., Williamson, D. E., Brent, D. A., Kaufman, J., Dahl, R. E., et al. (1996). Childhood and adolescent depression: A review of the past 10 years. *Journal of the American Academy of Child, 35*, 1427–1440.

Bittles, A. H., Bower, C., Hussain, R., & Glasson, E. J. (2006). The four ages of Down syndrome. *European Journal of Public Health, 17*(2), 221–225.

Bjork, J. M., Knutson, B., Fong, G. W., Caggiano, D. M., Bennett, S. M., & Hommer, D. W. (2004). Incentive-elicited brain activities in adolescents: Similarities and differences from young adults. *Journal of Neuroscience, 24*, 1793–1802.

Bjorklund, D. F., & Pellegrini, A. D. (2000). Child development and evolutionary psychology. *Child Development, 71,* 1687–1708.

Bjorklund, D. F., & Pellegrini, A. D. (2002). *The origins of human nature: Evolutionary developmental psychology.* Washington, DC: American Psychological Association.

Black, J. E. (1998). How a child builds its brain: Some lessons from animal studies of neural plasticity. *Preventive Medicine, 27,* 168–171.

Blackstock, C., Trocmé, N., & Bennett, M. (2004). Child maltreatment investigations among Aboriginal and Non-Aboriginal families in Canada. *Violence Against Women, 10*(8), 901–916. doi: 10.1177/1077801204266312

Blair, C. (2002). School readiness: Integrating cognition and emotion in a neurobiological conceptualization of children's functioning at school entry. *American Psychologist, 57,* 111–127.

Blakemore, S., & Choudhury, S. (2006). Development of the adolescent brain: Implications for executive function and social cognition. *Journal of Child Psychology and Psychiatry, 47*(3), 296–312.

Bleske-Rechek, A, Lubinski, D., & Benbow, C. P. (2004). Meeting the educational needs of special populations. Advanced placement's role in developing exceptional human capital. *Psychological Sciences, 15,* 217–224.

Blinka, L., & Smahal, D. (2009). Fourteen is fourteen and a girl is a girl: Validating the identity of adolescent bloggers. *Cyberpsychology and Behavior, 12*(6), 735–739.

Block, R. W., Krebs, N. F., the Committee on Child Abuse and Neglect, & the Committee on Nutrition. (2005). *Pediatrics, 116*(5), 1234–1237.

Bloom, B., Cohen, R. A., Vickerie, J. L., & Wondimu, E. A. (2003). Summary health statistics for U.S. children: National Health Interview Survey, 2001. *Vital and Health Statistics, 10*(216). Hyattsville, MD: National Center for Health Statistics.

Bocskay, K. A., Tang, D., Orjuela, M. A., Liu, X., Warburton, D. P., & Perera, F. P. (2005). Chromosomal aberrations in cord blood are associated with prenatal exposure to carcinogenic polycyclic aromatic hydrocarbons. *Cancer Epidemiology Biomarkers and Prevention, 14,* 506–511.

Bodrova, E., & Leong, D. J. (2005). High quality preschool programs: What would Vygotsky say? *Early Education & Development, 16*(4), 437–446.

Bogaert, A. F. (2006). Biological versus non-biological older brothers and men's sexual orientation. *Proceedings of the National Academy of Sciences, 103,* 10771–10774.

Bojczyk, K. E., & Corbetta, D. (2004). Object retrieval in the 1st year of life: Learning effects of task exposure and box transparency. *Developmental Psychology, 40,* 54–66.

Bojesen A., Juul, S., & Hojbjerg Gravholt, C. (2003). Prenatal and postnatal prevalence of Klinefelter syndrome: A national registry study. *Journal of Clinical Endocrinology and Metabolism, 88,* 622–626.

Bollinger, M. B. (2003). Involuntary smoking and asthma severity in children: Data from the Third National Health and Nutrition Examination Survey (NHANES III). *Pediatrics, 112,* 471.

Bolté, C., Devault, A., St-Denis, M., & Gaudet, J. (2001). *On father's ground: A portrait of projects to support and promote fathering.* Groupe de Recherche et d'Action sur la Victimisation des Enfants: Montreal, QC. Retrieved from http://www.phac-aspc.gc.ca/hp-ps/dca-dea/.../father-pere/pdf/father_e.pdf

Bonham, V. L., Warshauer-Baker, E., & Collins, F. S. (2005). Race and ethnicity in the genome era. *American Psychologist, 60,* 9–15.

Booth, J. L., & Siegler, R. S. (2006). Developmental and individual differences in pure numerical estimation. *Developmental Psychology, 41,* 189–201.

Booth, J. R., Burman, D. D., Meyer, J. R., Lei, Z., Trommer, B. L., Davenport, D., . . . & Mesulam, M. M. (2003). Neural development of selective attention and response inhibition. *Neuroimage, 20,* 737–751.

Bordeleau, S., Bernier, A., & Carrier, J. (2012). Longitudinal associations between the quality of parent-child interactions and children's sleep at preschool age. *Journal of Family Psychology, 26,* 254–262. doi: 10.1037/a0027366

Borman, G. D., & Dowling, M. (2006). Longitudinal achievement effects of multiyear summer school: Evidence from the Teaching Baltimore randomized field trial. *Educational Evaluation and Policy Analysis, 28*(1), 25–48.

Bornstein, M. H. & Cote, L. R. (with Maital, S., Painter, K., Park, S. Y., Pascual, L., Pecheux, M. G., Ruel, J., et al.). (2004). Cross-linguistic analysis of vocabulary in young children: Spanish, Dutch, French, Hebrew, Italian, Korean, and American English. *Child Development, 75,* 1115–1139.

Bornstein, M. H., Haynes, O. M., O'Reilly, A. W., & Painter, K. (1996). Solitary and collaborative pretense play in early childhood: Sources of individual variation in the development of representational competence. *Child Development, 67,* 2910–2929.

Borowsky, I. A., Ireland, M., & Resnick, M. D. (2001). Adolescent suicide attempts: Risks and protectors. *Pediatrics, 107*(3), 485–493.

Bosch, J., Sullivan, S., Van Dyke, D. C., Su, H., Klockau, L., Nissen, K., et al. (2003). Promoting a healthy tomorrow here for children adopted from abroad. *Contemporary Pediatrics, 20*(2), 69–86.

Bouchard, T. J. (2004). Genetic influence on human psychological traits: A survey. *Current Directions in Psychological Science, 13,* 148–154.

Bouchard, T. J., & McGue, M. (2003). Genetic and environmental influences on human psychological differences. *Developmental Neurobiology, 54*(1), 4–45.

Bouchey, H. A., & Furman, W. (2003). Dating and romantic experiences in adolescence. In G. R. Adams & M. D. Berzonsky (Eds.), *Blackwell handbook of adolescence* (pp. 313–329). Oxford, UK: Blackwell.

Boulton, M. J. (1995). Playground behaviour and peer interaction patterns of primary school boys classified as bullies, victims and not involved. *British Journal of Educational Psychology, 65,* 165–177.

Bowlby, J. (1951). Maternal care and mental health. *Bulletin of the World Health Organization, 3,* 355–534.

Bowlby, J. W., & McMullen, K. (2002). *At a crossroads: First results for the 18- to 20-year-old cohort of the Youth in Transition Survey* (Catalogue no. 81-591-XIE). Ottawa: Human Resources Development Canada and Statistics Canada.

Boyce, W., Doherty, M., Fortin, C., & MacKinnon, D. (2003). *Canadian Youth, Sexual Health and HIV/AIDS Study: Factors influencing knowledge, attitudes, and behaviours.* Toronto, ON: Council of Ministers of Education.

Boyce, W., Doherty-Poirier, M., MacKinnon, D, Fortin, C, Saab, H, King, M., & Gallupe, O. (2006). Sexual health of Canadian youth: Findings from the Canadian Youth, Sexual Health and HIV/AIDS Study. *Canadian Journal of Human Sexuality, 15,* 59–68.

Boyd, R. (2007). *Northern exposure: Acute pesticide poisonings in Canada.* Vancouver, BC: David Suzuki Foundation.

Boyle, M. H., & Lipman, E. L. (1998). *Do places matter? A multilevel analysis of geographic variations in child behaviour in Canada* (Catalogue no. W-98-16E). Ottawa, ON: Applied Research Branch, Strategic Policy, Human Resources Development Canada.

Brabeck, M. M., & Shore, E. L. (2003). Gender differences in intellectual and moral development? The evidence refutes the claims. In J. Demick & C. Andreoletti (Eds.), *Handbook of adult development* (pp. 351–368). New York: Plenum Press.

Bradley, R. H. (1989). Home measurement of maternal responsiveness. In M. H. Bornstein (Ed.), *Maternal responsiveness: Characteristics and consequences* (pp. 63–74) [New Directions for Child Development No. 43]. San Francisco: Jossey-Bass.

Bradley, R. H., Corwyn, R. F., Burchinal, M., McAdoo, H. P., & Coll, C. G. (2001). The home environment of children in the United States: Part II: Relations with behavioral development through age thirteen. *Child Development, 72*(6), 1868–1886.

Brannon, E. M. (2002). The development of ordinal numerical knowledge in infancy. *Cognition, 83,* 223–240.

Branum, A. & Lukas, S. L. (2008). *Food allergy among U.S. children: Trends in prevalence and hospitalizations* [Data Brief No. 10]. Hyattsville, MD: National Center for Health Statistics.

Brass, L. M., Isaacsohn, J. L., Merikangas, K. R., & Robinette, C. D. (1992). A study of twins and stroke. *Stroke, 23*(2), 221–223.

Bratton, S. C., & Ray, D. (2002). Humanistic play therapy. In D. J. Cain (Ed.), *Humanistic psychotherapies: Handbook of research and practice* (pp. 369–402). Washington, DC: American Psychological Association.

Brault, M.-C., & Lacourse, É. (2012). Prevalence of prescribed attention-deficit hyperactivity disorder medications and diagnosis among Canadian preschoolers and school-age children: 1994–2007. *Canadian Journal of Psychiatry, 57,* 93–01.

Braungart-Rieker, J. M., Garwood, M. M., Powers, B. P., & Wang, X. (2001). Parental sensitivity, infant affect, and affect regulation: Predictors of later attachment. *Child Development, 72,* 252–270.

Bray, J. H., & Hetherington, E. M. (1993). Families in transition: Introduction and overview. *Journal of Family Psychology, 7,* 3–8.

Brazelton, T. B. (1973). *Neonatal Behavioral Assessment Scale.* Philadelphia, PA: Lippincott.

Brazelton, T. B. (1984). *Neonatal Behavioral Assessment Scale.* Philadelphia, PA: Lippincott.

Brazelton, T. B., & Nugent, J. K. (1995). *Neonatal Behavioral Assessment Scale* (3rd ed.). Cambridge, England: Cambridge University Press.

Brazelton, T. B., & Nugent, J. K. (2001). *Neonatal Behavioral Assessment Scale* (4th ed.). Hoboken, NJ: Wiley.

Breastfeeding and HIV International Transmission Study Group. (2004). Late postnatal transmission of HIV-1 in breastfed children: An individual patient data meta-analysis. *Journal of Infectious Diseases, 189,* 2154–2166.

Breastfeeding Committee for Canada. (n.d.). *Affordable health care begins with breastfeeding support and the use of human milk.* Retrieved from breastfeedingcanada.ca/documents/webdoc47.pdf

Bremner, D., McTaggart, B., Saklofske, D. H., & Janzen, T. (2011). WISC-IV GAI and CPI in Psychoeducational Assessment. *Canadian Journal of School Psychology, 26,* 209–219. doi:10.1177/0829573511419090

Brendgen, M., Dionne, G., Girard, A., Boivin, M., Vitaro, F., & Perusse, D. (2005). Examining genetic and environmental effects on social aggression: A study of 6-year-old twins. *Child Development, 76,* 930–946.

Brent, D. A., & Birmaher, B. (2002). Adolescent depression. *New England Journal of Medicine, 347,* 667–671.

Brent, D. A., & Mann, J. J. (2006). Familial pathways to suicidal behavior—understanding and preventing suicide among adolescents. *New England Journal of Medicine, 355,* 2719–2721.

Brent, M. R., & Siskind, J. M. (2001). The role of exposure to isolated words in early vocabulary development. *Cognition, 81,* 33–34.

Bretherton, I. (1990). Communication patterns, internal working models, and the intergenerational transmission of attachment relationships. *Infant Mental Health Journal, 11*(3), 237–252.

Bridge, J. A., Iyengar, S., Salary, C. B., Barbe, R. P., Birmaher, B., Pincus, H. A., et al. (2007). Clinical response and risk for reported suicidal ideation and suicide attempts in pediatric antidepressant treatment: A meta-analysis of randomized controlled trials. *Journal of the American Medical Association, 297,* 1683–1696.

Brody, G. H. (1998). Sibling relationship quality: Its causes and consequences. *Annual Review of Psychology, 49,* 1–24.

Brody, G. H. (2004). Siblings' direct and indirect contributions to child development. *Current Directions in Psychological Science, 13,* 124–126.

Brody, G. H., Chen, Y.-F., Murry, V. M., Ge, X., Simons, R. L., Gibbons, F. X., et al. (2006). Perceived discrimination and the adjustment of African American youths: A five-year longitudinal analysis with contextual moderation effects. *Child Development, 77*(5), 1170–1189.

Brody, G. H., Ge., X., Conger, R., Gibbons, F. X., Murry, V. M., Gerrard, M., & Simons, R. L. (2001). The influence of neighborhood disadvantage, collective socialization, and parenting on African American children's affiliation with deviant peers. *Child Development, 72*(4), 1231–1246.

Brody, G. H., Kim, S., Murry, V. M., & Brown, A. C. (2004). Protective longitudinal paths linking child competence to behavioral problems among African American siblings. *Child Development, 75,* 455–467.

Brody, L. R., Zelazo, P. R., & Chaika, H. (1984). Habituation-dishabituation to speech in the neonate. *Developmental Psychology, 20,* 114–119.

Broekmans, F. J., Soules, M. R., & Fauser, B. C. (2009). Ovarian aging: Mechanisms and clinical consequences. *Endocrine Reviews, 30*(5), 465–493.

Broidy, L. M., Tremblay, R. E., Brame, B., Fergusson, D., Horwood, J. L., Laird, R., et al. (2003). Developmental trajectories of childhood disruptive behaviors and adolescent delinquency: A six-site cross-national study. *Developmental Psychology, 39*(2), 222–245.

Bronfenbrenner, U. (1979). *The ecology of human development.* Cambridge, MA: Harvard University Press.

Bronfenbrenner, U. (1986). Ecology of the family as a context for human development: Research perspectives. *Developmental Psychology, 22,* 723–742.

Bronfenbrenner, U. (1994). Ecological models of human development. In T. Husen & T. N. Postlethwaite (Eds.), *International encyclopedia of education* (Vol. 3, 2nd ed., pp. 1643–1647). Oxford, U.K.: Pergamon Press/Elsevier Science.

Bronfenbrenner, U., & Morris, P. A. (1998). The ecology of developmental processes. In W. Damon (Series ed.) & R. Lerner (Vol. Ed.), *Handbook of child psychology: Vol. I. Theoretical models of human development* (5th ed., pp. 993–1028). New York: Wiley.

Bronner, E. (1999, January 22). Social promotion is bad; repeating a grade may be worse. *New York Times.* Retrieved from http://search.nytimes.com/search/daily/bin/fastweb?getdocPsitePsiteP13235POPwAAAPsocial%7Epromotion

Bronstein, P. (1988). Father-child interaction: Implications for gender role socialization. In P. Bronstein & C. P. Cowan (Eds.), *Fatherhood today: Men's changing role in the family* (pp. 107–124). New York: Wiley.

Bronstein, P., Clauson, J., Stoll, M. F., & Abrams, C. L. (1993). Parenting behavior and children's social, psychological, and academic adjustment in diverse family structures. *Family Relations, 42,* 268–276.

Brooks, R., & Meltzoff, A. N. (2005). The development of gaze following and its relation to language. *Developmental Science, 8,* 535–543.

Brooks, R., & Meltzoff, A. N. (2008). Infant gaze following and pointing predict accelerated vocabulary growth through two years of age: A longitudinal, growth curve modeling study. *Journal of Child Language, 35,* 207–220.

Brooks-Gunn, J. (2003). Do you believe in magic? What can we expect from early childhood intervention programs? *SRCD Social Policy Report, 17*(1), 3–14.

Broude, G. J. (1995). *Growing up: A cross-cultural encyclopedia.* Santa Barbara, CA: ABC-CLIO.

Brousseau, E. (2006, May). *The effect of maternal body mass index on efficacy of dinoprosteone vaginal insert for cervical ripening.* Paper presented at the annual meeting of the American College of Obstetricians and Gynecologists, Washington, D.C.

Brown, A. S., Tapert, S. F., Granholm, E., & Delis, D. C. (2000) Neurocognitive functioning of adolescents: Effects of protracted alcohol use. *Alcoholism: Clinical and Experimental Research, 24,* 64–171.

Brown, B. B., & Klute, C. (2003). Friendships, cliques, and crowds. In G. R. Adams & M. D. Berzonsky. (Eds.), *Blackwell handbook of adolescence* (pp. 330–348). Malden, MA: Blackwell.

Brown, J. (2010). Culture and success in foster care: Experiences of Aboriginal foster parents. *Canada's Children, 17,* 37–40.

Brown, J. L. (1987). Hunger in the U.S. *Scientific American, 256*(2), 37–41.

Brown, L. M., & Gilligan, C. (1990, April). *The psychology of women and the development of girls.* Paper presented at the Laurel-Harvard Conference on the Psychology of Women and the Education of Girls, Cleveland, OH.

Brown, S. L. (2004). Family structure and child well-being: The significance of parental cohabitation. *Journal of Marriage and Family, 66,* 351–367.

Brownell, C. A., Ramani, G. B., & Zerwas, S. (2006). Becoming a social partner with peers: Cooperation and social understanding in one- and two-year-olds. Child Development, 77, 803–821.

Brownell, M. D., Derksen, S. A., Jutte, D. P., Roos, N. P., Ekuma, O., & Yallop, L. (2010). Socio-economic inequalities in children's injury rates: Has the gradient changed over time? *Canadian Journal of Public Health, 101* (Supplement 3), s28–s33.

Bruer, J. T. (2001). A critical and sensitive period primer. In D. B. Bailey, J. T. Bruer, F. J. Symons, & J. W. Lichtman (Eds.), *Critical thinking about critical periods: A series from the National Center for Early Development and Learning* (pp. 289–292). Baltimore, MD: Paul Brooks.

Bryan, S. N., Tremblay, M. S., Pérez, C. E., Ardern, C. I., & Katzmarzyk, P. T. (2006). Physical activity and ethnicity: Evidence from the Canadian Community Health Survey. *Canadian Journal of Public Health, 97,* 271–276.

Bryant, B. K. (1987). Mental health, temperament, family, and friends: Perspectives on children's empathy and social perspective taking. In N. Eisenberg & J. Strayer (Eds.), Empathy and its development of competence in adolescence. *Child Development, 66,* 129–138.

Bryce, J., Boschi-Pinto, C., Shibuya, K., Black, R. E., & the WHO Child Health Epidemiology Reference Group. (2005). WHO estimates of the causes of death in children. *Lancet, 365,* 1147–1152.

Büchel, C., & Sommer, M. (2004). Unsolved mystery: What causes stuttering? *PLoS Biology, 2,* 0159–0163.

Buck Louis, G., Gray, L., Marcus, M., Ojeda, S., Pescovitz, O., Witchel, S., et al. (2008). Environmental factors and puberty timing: Expert panel research needs. *Pediatrics, 121,* S192–S207.

Buckner, J. C., Bassuk, E. L., Weinreb, L. F., & Brooks, M. G. (1999). Homelessness and its relation to the mental health and behavior of low-income school-age children. *Developmental Psychology, 35*(1), 246–257.

Buehler, C. (2006). Parents and peers in relation to early adolescent problem behavior. *Journal of Marriage and Family, 68,* 109–124.

Buhrmester, D. (1996). Need fulfillment, interpersonal competence, and the developmental contexts of early adolescent friendship. In W. M. Bukowski, A. F. Newcomb, & W. W. Hartup (Eds.), *The company they keep: Friendship in childhood and adolescence* (pp. 158–185). New York: Cambridge University Press.

Buhrmester, D., & Chong, C. M. (2009). Friendships in adolescence. In H. Reis & S. Sprecher (Eds.), *Encyclopedia of human relationships.* Thousand Oaks, CA: Sage.

Bull, R., Espy, K. A., & Wiebe, S. A. (2008). Short-term memory, working memory, and executive functioning in preschoolers: Longitudinal predictors of mathematical achievement at age 7 years. *Developmental Neuropsychology, 33,* 205–228. doi: 10.1080/87565640801982312

Burczycka, M., & Cotter, A. (2011). *Shelters for abused women in Canada, 2010.* Ottawa, ON: Statistics Canada. Retrieved from http://www.statcan.gc.ca/pub/85-002-x/2011001/article/11495-eng.htm

Burnaby, B. (1996/2007). Aboriginal language maintenance, development, and enhancement: A review of the literature. In G. Cantoni (ed.), *Stabilizing Indigenous Languages* (pp. 21–36). Tucson, AZ: Northern Arizona University, Center for Ecellence in Education. Retrieved from http://jan.ucc.nau.edu/~jar/SIL/

Burstyn, I., Kapur, N., & Cherry, N. M. (2010). Substance use of pregnant women and early neonatal morbidity: Where to focus intervention? *Canadian Journal of Public Health, 101,* 149–153.

Bushnell, E. W., & Boudreau, J. P. (1993). Motor development and the mind: The potential role of motor abilities as a determinant of aspects of perceptual development. *Child Development, 64,* 1005–1021.

Bushnik, T. (2006). *Child care in Canada* (Catalogue no. 89-599-MIE2006003). Ottawa, ON: Statistics Canada.

Bushnik, T., Cook, J. L., Yuzpe, A. A., Tough, S., & Collins, J. (2012). Estimating the prevalence of infertility in Canada. *Human Reproduction, 27,* 738–746.

Bushnik, T., & Garner, R. (2008). *The children of older first-time mothers in Canada: Their health and development* (Catalogue no. 89-599-M, no. 005). Ottawa, ON: Statistics Canada.

Bussey, K., & Bandura, A. (1992). Self-regulatory mechanisms governing gender development. *Child Development, 63,* 1236–1250.

Bussey, K., & Bandura, A. (1999). Social cognitive theory of gender development and differentiation. *Psychological Review, 106,* 676–713.

Butler-Jones, D. (2011). *The Chief Public Health Officer's Report on the State of Public Health in Canada, 2011: Youth and Young Adults — Life in Transition.* Ottawa, ON: Public Health Agency of Canada. Retrieved from http://www.phac-aspc.gc.ca/cphorsphc-respcacsp/2011/index-eng.php

Byers, M., & Tastsoglou, E. (2008). Negotiating ethno-cultural identity: The experience of Greek and Jewish youth in Halifax. *Canadian Ethnic Studies/Études ethniques au Canada, 40,* 5–33.

Byers-Heinlein, K., Burns, T. C., & Werker, J. F. (2010). The roots of bilingualism in newborns. *Psychological Science, 21,* 343–348.

Byrne, A., Kirby, B., Zibin, T., Ensminger, S. (1991). Psychiatric and neurological effects of chronic solvent abuse. *Canadian Journal of Psychiatry, 36,* 735–738.

Byrne, M., Agerbo, E., Ewald, H., Eaton, W. W., & Mortensen, P. B. (2003). Parental age and risk of schizophrenia. *Archives of General Psychiatry, 60,* 673–678.

Bystron, I., Rakic, P., Molnar, Z., & Blakemore, C. (2006). The first neurons of the human cerebral cortex. *Nature Neuroscience, 9*(7), 880–886.

Caballero, B. (2006). Obesity as a consequence of undernutrition. *Journal of Pediatrics, 149*(5, Suppl. 1), 97–99.

Cabrera, N. J., Tamis-LeMonda, C. S., Bradley, R. H., Hofferth, S., & Lamb, M. E. (2000). Fatherhood in the twenty-first century. *Child Development, 71,* 127–136.

Calkins, S. D., & Fox, N. A. (1992). The relations among infant temperament, security of attachment, and behavioral inhibition at twenty-four months. *Child Development, 63,* 1456–1472.

Camarata, S., & Woodcock, R. (2006). Sex differences in processing speed: Developmental effects in males and females. *Intelligence, 34*(3), 231–252.

Cameron, M. (2005). Two-spirited Aboriginal people: Continuing cultural appropriation by non-Aboriginal society. *Canadian Women Studies, 24*(2/3), 123–127.

Campaign 2000. (2012). *Needed: A federal action plan to eradicate child and family poverty in Canada. Campaign 2000 Report Card – 2012.* Toronto, ON. Retrieved from http://www.campaign2000.ca/

Campbell, A., Shirley, L., & Candy, J. (2004). A longitudinal study of gender-related cognition and behaviour. *Developmental Science, 7,* 1–9.

Campbell, A., Shirley, L., Heywood, C., & Crook, C. (2000). Infants' visual preference for sex-congruent babies, children, toys, and activities: A longitudinal study. *British Journal of Developmental Psychology, 18,* 479–498.

Campbell, F. A., Ramey, C. T., Pungello, E., Sparling, J., & Miller-Johnson, S. (2002). Early childhood education: Young adult outcomes from the Abecedarian Project. *Applied Developmental Science, 6*(1), 42–57.

Campbell-Yeo, M., Fernades, A., & Johnston, C.C. (2011). Procedural pain management for neonates using non-pharmacological strategies. Part 2: Mother-driven intervention. *Advances in Newborn Care, 11*(5), 312–318.

Canada Safety Council. (2009). Home safety: Home alone: Latchkey kids. *Safety Canada, 53*(4), 6.

Canadian Child Care Federation. (2006). *School-age child care: Policy Brief prepared for the Middle Childhood Initiative of the National Children's Alliance.* Ottawa, ON: National Children's Alliance. Retrieved from http://www.nationalchildrensalliance.com/nca/pubs/reports_topic.htm#age

Canadian Council on Learning. (2005). *Good news: Canada's high school dropout rates are falling.* Retrieved from http://www.ccl-cca.ca/CCL/Reports/LessonsInLearning.html

Canadian Council on Learning. (2005a). *Making sense of the class size debate.* Retrieved from http://www.ccl-cca.ca/CCL/Reports/LessonsInLearning.html

Canadian Council on Learning. (2008). Understanding the academic trajectories of ESL students. Retrieved from http://www.ccl-cca.ca/CCL/Reports/LessonsInLearning.html

Canadian Council on Learning. (2009a). *Changing our schools: Implementing successful educational reform.* Retrieved from http://www.ccl-cca.ca/pdfs/LessonsInLearning/01_15_09-E.pdf

Canadian Council on Learning. (2009b). *The State of Aboriginal learning in Canada: A holistic approach to measuring success.* Retrieved from http://www.ccl-cca.ca/sal2009

Canadian Council on Social Development (2001). *The progress of Canada's children.* Ottawa, ON: Author.

Canadian Council on Social Development. (2006). *The progress of Canada's children and youth, 2006.* Retrieved from http://www.ccsd.ca/pccy/2006/

Canadian Council on Social Development, The Annie E. Casey Foundation, & Red por los Derechos de la Infancia en México. (2008). *Growing up in North America: The economic well-being of children in Canada, the United States, and Mexico.* Baltimore, MD: The Annie E. Casey Foundation.

Canadian Dental Association. (2012). *Early childhood tooth decay.* Retrieved from http://www.cda-adc.ca/en/oral_health/cfyt/dental_care_children/tooth_decay.asp

Canadian Fertility and Andrology Society. (2011). *Human assisted reproduction 2011 live birth rates for Canada.* Retrieved from: http://www.cfas.ca/index.php?option=com_content&view=article&id=1129%3Alive-birth-rates-2011&catid=929%3Apress-releases&Itemid=460

Canadian Fitness and Lifestyle Research Institute. (2011). *2010 Physical Activity Monitor. Bulletin 7: Parental involvement in children's physical activity.* Canadian Fitness and Lifestyle Research Institute, Ottawa. Retrieved from http://www.cflri.ca/node/928

Canadian Foundation for the Study of Infant Deaths, the Canadian Institute of Child Health, the Canadian Paediatric Society and Health Canada. (1999, reaffirmed 2000). Reducing the risk of sudden infant death syndrome in Canada. *Paediatrics and Child Health, 4,* 223–224.

Canadian Institute for Health Information. (2000). *Health care in Canada 2000: A first annual report* (Catalogue no. 82-222-XIE). Ottawa, ON: Author.

Canadian Institute for Health Information. (2005). *Improving the health of young Canadians.* Ottawa, ON: Author.

Canadian Institute for Health Information. (2007). *Giving birth in Canada: Regional trends from 2001–2002 to 2005–2006.* Ottawa, ON: Author.

Canadian Institute for Health Information. (2010). *Health indicators 2010.* Ottawa, ON. Retrieved from http://www.phac-aspc.gc.ca/hp-ps/dca-dea/publications/fcm-smp/fcmc-smpf-05-eng.php

Canadian Institute for Health Information. (2012). *Highlights of 2010–2011 selected indicators describing the birthing process in Canada.* Ottawa, ON: Author.

Canadian Neonatal Network. (2012). *Annual report 2011.* Toronto, ON. Retrieved from http://www.canadianneonatalnetwork.org/portal/

Canadian Institute of Child Health. (2000). *The health of Canada's children* (3rd ed.). Ottawa, ON: Author.

Canadian Paediatric Society. (2002). Healthy active living for children and youth. *Paediatrics & Child Health, 7*(5), 339–345.

Canadian Paediatric Society. (2003). Impact of media use on children and youth. *Journal of Paediatrics and Child Health, 8,* 301–306.

Canadian Paediatric Society. (2006). Maternal infectious diseases, antimicrobial therapy or immunizations: Very few contraindications to breastfeeding. *Paediatrics and Child Health, 11,* 489-491.

Canadian Paediatric Society. (2012a). *Management of primary nocturnal enuresis.* Retrieved from http://www.cps.ca/en/documents/position/primary-nocturnal-enuresis

Canadian Paediatric Society. (2012b). *Paediatricians urge children and teens to get up and get moving.* Retrieved from http://www.cps.ca/en/media/release-communique/get-up-and-get-moving

Canadian Paediatric Society. (2012c). *Healthy teeth for children.* Retrieved from http://www.caringforkids.cps.ca/handouts/healthy_teeth_for_children

Canadian Paediatric Society. (2012d). *Caring for kids: Information for parents from the Canadian Paediatric Society.* Retrieved from http://www.caringforkids.cps.ca/handouts/kidssafe-index

Canadian Paediatric Society, Adolescent Health Committee. (2008). Adolescent sexual orientation. *Paediatrics and Child Health, 13*(7), 619–623.

Canadian Paediatric Society, Advisory Committee on Healthy Active Living for Children and Youth. (2002). Healthy active living for children and youth. *Paediatrics & Child Health, 7,* 339–345.

Canadian Paediatric Society, & Health Canada. (1994/2001). *Nutrition recommendations update: Dietary fat and children.* Ottawa: Canadian Paediatric Society.

Canadian Paediatric Society, & Sacks, D. (2009). *The Canadian Paediatric Society guide to caring for your child from birth to age five.* Mississauga, ON: John Wiley & Sons Canada, Ltd.

Canadian Parents for French. (2012). *The state of French-second-language education in Canada: Annual report.* Retrieved from http://www.cpf.ca

Canadian Parents for French. (2013). *National Summary Statistics FSL.* Retrieved from http://www.cpf.ca

Canadian Perinatal Surveillance System. (2000). *Canadian perinatal health report, 2000.* Ottawa, ON: Health Canada.

Canadian PKU and Allied Disorders Inc. (2012). *Newborn screening and PKU: Backgrounder.* Retrieved from http://www.healthlinkbc.ca/kb/content/medicaltest/hw41965.html

Canadian Press. (2004). *Food bank use by B.C. children up 42 percent.* Retrieved from http://www.ctv.ca/servlet/ArticleNews/story/CTVNews/100172223116_98/?hub=Canada

Canadian Psychological Association. (2000). *Canadian code of ethics for psychologists* (3rd ed.) Ottawa, ON: Author.

Canadian Reproduction and Andrology Society. (2009). *In-vitro fertilization in Canada: Cost structure analysis.* Montreal, QC: OVO Consulting.

Canadian Society for Exercise Physiology. (2011a). *Canadian physical activity guidelines for children 5–11 years.* Ottawa, ON. Retrieved from http://www.csep.ca/CMFiles/Guidelines/CSEP-InfoSheets-child-ENG.pdf

Canadian Society for Exercise Physiology. (2011b). *Canadian physical activity guidelines for youth 12–17 years.* Ottawa, ON. Retrieved from http://www.csep.ca/CMFiles/Guide lines/CSEP-InfoSheets-youth-ENG.pdf

Canadian Stuttering Foundation. (2013). *Frequently asked questions.* Retrieved from http://www.stutter.ca/whats-new/153-frequently-asked-questions

Cao, A., Rosatelli, M. C., Monni, G., & Galanello, R. (2002). Screening for thalassemia: A model of success. *Obstetrics and Gynecology Clinics of North America, 29*(2), 305–328.

Capaldi, D. M., Stoolmiller, M., Clark, S., & Owen, L. D. (2002). Heterosexual risk behaviors in at-risk young men from early adolescence to young adulthood: Prevalence, prediction, and STD contraction. *Developmental Psychology, 38,* 394–406.

Caplan, M., Vespo, J., Pedersen, J., & Hay, D. F. (1991). Conflict and its resolution in small groups of one- and two-year olds. *Child Development, 62,* 1513–1524.

Caprara, G. V., Fida, R., Vecchione, M., Del Bove, G., Vecchio, G. M., Barbaranelli, C. & Bandura, A. (2008). Longitudinal analysis of the role of perceived self-efficacy for self-regulated learning in academic continuance and achievement. *Journal of Educational Psychology, 100*(3), 525–534.

Capute, A. J., Shapiro, B. K., & Palmer, F. B. (1987). Marking the milestones of language development. *Contemporary Pediatrics, 4*(4), 24.

Card, N., Stucky, B., Sawalani, G., & Little, T., (2008) Direct and indirect aggression during childhood and adolescence: A meta-analytic review of gender differences, intercorrelations, and relations to maladjustment. *Child Development, 79*(5), 1185–1229.

Carlson, B., & Shafer, M. S. (2010). Traumatic histories and stressful life events of incarcerated parents: Childhood and adult trauma histories. *The Prison Journal, 90*(4), 475–493.

Carlson, E. A. (1998). A prospective longitudinal study of attachment disorganization/disorientation. *Child Development, 69*(4), 1107–1128.

Carlson, M. J. (2006). Family structure, father involvement, and adolescent behavioral outcomes. *Journal of Marriage and Family, 68,* 137–154.

Carnethon, M. R., Gulati, M., & Greenland, P. (2005). Prevalence and cardiovascular disease correlates of low cardiorespiratory fitness in adolescents and adults. *Journal of the American Medical Association, 294,* 2981–2988.

Caro, D. H. (2010). Socio-economic status and academic achievement trajectories from childhood to adolescence. *Canadian Journal of Education, 32,* 558–590.

Caro, D. H., McDonald, J. T., & Willms, J. D. (2009). Socio-economic status and academic achievement trajectories from childhood to adolescence. *Canadian Journal of Education, 32,* 558–590.

Carothers, S. S., Borkowski, J. G., Lefever, J. B., & Whitman, T. L. (2005). Religiosity and the socioemotional adjustment of adolescent mothers and their children. *Journal of Family Psychology, 19,* 263–275.

Carroll, D., & Benoit, C. (2001). Aboriginal midwifery in Canada: Blending traditional and modern forms. *Network Magazine, 4*(3). Retrieved from http://www.cwhn.ca/node/39589

Carscadden, J., Corsiatto, P., Ericson, L., Illchuk, R., Esopenko, C., Sterner, E., ... (2010). A pilot study to evaluate a new early screening instrument for speech and language delays. *Canadian Journal of Speech-Language Pathology and Audiology, 34,* 87–95.

Carson, G., Vitale Cox, L., Crane, J., Croteau, P., Graves, L., Kluka, S., ... & Wood, R. (2010). Alcohol use and pregnancy consensus clinical guidelines. *Journal of Obstetrics and Gynaecology Canada, 32,* S1–S32. Retrieved from http://www.phac-aspc.gc.ca/hp-ps/dca-dea/prog-ini/fasd-etcaf/index-eng.php

Carter, R. C., Jacobson, S. W., Molteno, C. D., Chiodo, L. M., Viljoen, D., & Jacobson, J. L. (2005). Effects of prenatal alcohol exposure on infant visual acuity. *The Journal of Pediatrics, 147*(4), 473–479.

Carver, P. R., & Iruka, I. U. (2006). *After-school programs and activities: 2005* (NCES 2006–076). Washington, DC: National Center for Education Statistics.

Case, R. (1985). *Intellectual development: Birth to adulthood.* Orlando, FL: Academic Press.

Case, R. (1992). Neo-Piagetian theories of child development. In R. Sternberg & C. Berg (Eds.), *Intellectual development* (pp. 161–196). New York: Cambridge University Press.

Case, R., & Okamoto, Y. (1996). The role of central conceptual structures in the development of children's thought. *Monographs of the Society for Research in Child Development, 61*(1–2) [Serial No. 246].

Caspi, A. (2000). The child is father of the man: Personality continuities from childhood to adulthood. *Journal of Personality and Social Psychology, 78,* 158–172.

Caspi, A., Sugden, K., Moffitt, T. E., Taylor, A., Craig, I. W., Harrington, H., et al. (2003). Influence of life stress on depression: Moderation by a polymorphism in the 5-HTT gene. *Science, 301,* 386–389.

Cassidy, K. W., Werner, R. S., Rourke, M., Zubernis, L. S., & Balaraman, G. (2003). The relationship between psychological understanding and positive social behaviors. *Social Development, 12,* 198–221.

Caughey, A. B., Hopkins, L. M., & Norton, M. E. (2006). Chorionic villus sampling compared with amniocentesis and the difference in the rate of pregnancy loss. *Obstetrics and Gynecology, 108,* 612–616.

CBC. (February 19, 2012). Canadian foster care in crisis, experts say. Retrieved from http://www.cbc.ca/news/canada/story/2012/02/19/foster-care-cp.html

Ceci, S. J., & Gilstrap, L. L. (2000). Determinants of intelligence: Schooling and intelligence. In A. Kazdin (Ed.), *Encyclopedia of psychology.* Washington D.C. & New York: American Psychological Association and Oxford University Press.

Center for Weight and Health. (2001). *Pediatric overweight: A review of the literature: Executive summary.* Berkeley, CA: University of California at Berkeley.

Centers for Disease Control and Prevention. (2000a). *CDC's guidelines for school and community programs: Promoting lifelong physical activity.* Retrieved May 26, 2000, from http://www.cdc.gov/nccdphp/dash/phactaag.htm

Centers for Disease Control and Prevention. (2000b). *Tracking the hidden epidemic: Trends in STDs in the U.S., 2000.* Washington, DC: Author.

Centers for Disease Control and Prevention. (2004). Gonorrhea—CDC fact sheet. Retrieved April 14, 2012, from http://www.cdc.gov/std/Gonorrhea/STDFact-gonorrhea.htm#How

Centers for Disease Control and Prevention. (2006a). Achievements in public health: Reduction in perinatal transmission of HIV infection—United States, 1985–2005. *Morbidity and Mortality Weekly Report, 55*(21), 592–597.

Centers for Disease Control and Prevention. (2006b). Improved national prevalence estimates for 18 selected major birth defects—

United States, 1999–2001. *Morbidity and Mortality Weekly Report, 54*(51 & 52), 1301–1305.

Centers for Disease Control and Prevention. (2006c). Youth risk behavior surveillance—United States, 2005. *Morbidity and Mortality Weekly Report, 55*(SS-5).

Centers for Disease Control and Prevention. (2007b). Trends in oral health status: United States, 1988–1994 and 1999–2004. *Vital Health Statistics, 11*(248).

Centers for Disease Control and Prevention. (2008). *Surveillance summaries*. Atlanta, GA: Author.

Cesario, S. K., & Hughes, L. A. (2007). Precocious puberty: A comprehensive review of the literature. *Journal of Obstetric, Gynecologic and Neonatal Nursing, 36*(3), 263–274.

Chaffey, G. W., Halliwell, G., & McCluskey, K. W. (2006). Identifying high academic potential in Canadian Aboriginal primary school children. *Gifted and Talented International, 21,* 61–70.

Chahal, H., Fung, C., Kuhle, S., & Veugelers, P. J. (2012). Availability and night-time use of electronic entertainment and communication devices are associated with short sleep duration and obesity among Canadian children. *Pediatric Obesity, 8,* 42–51. doi: 10.1111/j.2047-6310.2012.00085.x

Chalmers, B., & Wen, S. W. (2004). Perinatal Care in Canada. *BMC Women's Health, 4(Suppl 1),* S28. doi:10.1186/1472-6874-4-S1-S28. Retrieved from http://www.biomedcentral.com/1472-6874/4/S1/S28

Chambers, C. D., Hernandez-Diaz, S., Van Marter, L. J., Werler, M. M., Louik, C., Jones, K. L., & Mitchell, A. A. (2006). Selective serotonin-reuptake inhibitors and risk of persistent pulmonary hypertension of the newborn. *New England Journal of Medicine, 354,* 579–587.

Chambers, R. A., Taylor, J. R., & Potenza, M. N. (2003). Developmental neurocircuitry of motivation in adolescence: A critical period of addiction vulnerability. *American Journal of Psychiatry, 160,* 1041–1052.

Chan, H. M., Fediuk, K., Hamilton, S., Rostas, L., Caughey, A., Kuhnlein, H., . . . & Loring, E. (2006). Food security in Nunavut, Canada: Barriers and recommendations. *International Journal of Circumpolar Health, 65,* 416–431.

Chandler, M. J. & Lalonde, C. E. (1998). Cultural Continuity as a Hedge against Suicide in Canada's First Nations. *Transcultural Psychiatry, 35(2),* 191–219.

Chandler, M. J. & Lalonde, C. E. (2008). Cultural Continuity as a Protective Factor against Suicide in First Nations Youth. *Horizons, 10,* 68–72.

Chandra, A., Martin, S., Collins, R., Elliott, M., Berry, S., Kanouse, D., & Miu, A. (2008).

Does watching sex on television predict teen pregnancy? Findings from a National Longitudinal Survey of Youth. *Pediatrics, 122*(5), 1047–1054.

Chao, R. K., & Willms, J. D. (2002). The effects of parenting practices on children's outcome. In J. D. Willms (Ed.), *Vulnerable Children* (pp. 149–166). Edmonton, AB: University of Alberta Press.

Charlesworth, A., & Glantz, S. A. (2005). Smoking in the movies increases adolescent smoking: A review. *Pediatrics, 116,* 1516–1528.

Charlesworth, S., Foulds, H. J. A., Burr, J. F., & Bredin, S. S. D. (2011). Evidence-based risk assessment and recommendations for physical activity clearance: Pregnancy. *Applied Physiology, Nutrition, and Metabolism, 36,* S33–S48.

Chartier, M. J., Walker, J. R., & Naimark, B. (2009). Health risk behaviors and mental health problems as mediators of the relationship between childhood abuse and adult health. *American Journal of Public Health, 99*(5), 847–854. doi:10.2105/AJPH.2007.122408

Che, J., & Chen, J. (2001). Food insecurity in Canadian households. *Health Reports, 12,* 11–22.

Chen, C., & Stevenson, H. W. (1995). Motivation and mathematics achievement: A comparative study of Asian-American, Caucasian-American, and East Asian high school students. *Child Development, 66,* 1215–1234.

Chen, E. (2012). Protective factors for health among low-socioeconomic-status individuals. *Current Directions in Psychological Science, 21,* 189–193. doi: 10.1177/0963721412438710

Chen, E., Matthews, K. A., & Boyce, W. T. (2002). Socioeconomic differences in children's health: How and why do these relationships change with age? *Psychological Bulletin, 128,* 259–329.

Chen, L., Baker, S. B., Braver, E. R., & Li, G. (2000). Carrying passengers as a risk factor for crashes fatal to 16- and 17-year-old drivers. *Journal of the American Medical Association, 283*(12), 1578–1582.

Chen, P. C., & Wang, J. D. (2006). Parental exposure to lead and small for gestational age births. *American Journal of Industrial Medicine 49*(6), 417–422.

Chen, W., Li, S., Cook, N. R., Rosner, B. A., Srinivasan, S. R., Boerwinkle, E., & Berenson, G. S. (2004). An autosomal genome scan for loci influencing longitudinal burden of body mass index from childhood to young adulthood in white sibships. The Bogalusa Heart Study. *International Journal of Obesity, 28,* 462–469.

Chen, X., Cen, G., Li, D., & He, Y. (2005). Social functioning and adjustment in Chinese children: The imprint of historical time. *Child Development, 76,* 182-195.

Chen, X., Rubin, K. H., & Li, Z. (1995). Social functioning and adjustment in Chinese children: A longitudinal study. *Developmental Psychology, 31,* 531–539.

Chen, X., Rubin, K. H., & Sun, Y. (1992). Social reputation and peer relationships in Chinese and Canadian children: A cross-cultural study. *Child Development, 63,* 1336–1343.

Chen, Z., & Siegler, R. S. (2000). Intellectual development in childhood. In R. J. Sternberg (Ed.), *Handbook of intelligence* (pp. 92–116). Cambridge, UK: Cambridge University Press.

Cheruku, S. R., Montgomery-Downs, H. E., Farkas, S. L., Thoman, E. B., & Lammi-Keefe C. J. (2002). Higher maternal plasma docosahexaenoic acid during pregnancy is associated with more mature neonatal sleep-state patterning. *American Journal of Clinical Nutrition, 76,* 608–613.

Chervin, R. D., Ruzicka, D. L., Giordani, B. J., Weatherly, R. A., Dillon, J. E., Hodges, E. K., et al. (2006). Sleep-disordered breathing, behavior, and cognition in children before and after adenotonsillectomy. *Pediatrics, 117,* e769–e788.

Cheung, A. H., & Dewa, C. S. (2006). Canadian Community Health Survey: Major depressive disorder and suicidality in adolescents. *Health Care Policy, 2,* 76–89.

Chief Public Health Officer of Canada. (2009). *The Chief Public Health Officer's report on the state of public health in Canada, 2009: Growing up well - priorities for a healthy future.* Ottawa, ON: Her Majesty the Queen in Right of Canada. Retrieved from http://publichealth.gc.ca/CPHOreport

Chief Public Health Officer. (2011). *The Chief Public Health Officer's report on the state of public health in Canada 2011.* Ottawa, ON. Retrieved from http://www.phac-aspc.gc.ca

Child Trends (2010). Physical fighting by youth. Retrieved from http://www.childtrendsdatabank.org/?q=node/136

Child Welfare Information Gateway. (2008b). *Preventing child abuse and neglect.* Retrieved February 9, 2009, from http://www.childwelfare.gov/preventing/

Children in North America Project. (2008). *Growing up in North America: The economic well-being of children in Canada, the United States, and Mexico.* Baltimore, MD: Annie E. Casey Foundation.

Children's Defense Fund. (2004). *The state of America's children 2004.* Washington, DC: Author.

Chomsky, C. S. (1969). *The acquisition of syntax in children from five to ten.* Cambridge, MA: MIT Press.

Chomsky, N. (1957). *Syntactic structures.* The Hague, Netherlands: Mouton.

Chomsky, N. (1972). *Language and mind* (2nd ed.). New York: Harcourt Brace Jovanovich.

Chomsky, N. (1995). *The minimalist program.* Cambridge, MA: MIT Press.

Christian, M. S., & Brent, R. L. (2001). Teratogen update: Evaluation of the reproductive and developmental risks of caffeine. *Teratology, 64*(1), 51–78.

Chu, S. Y., Bachman, D. J., Callaghan, W. M., Whitlock, E. P., Dietz, P. M., Berg, C. J., et al. (2008). Association between obesity during pregnancy and increased use of health care. *New England Journal of Medicine, 358,* 1444–1453.

Chua, E. F., Schacter, D. L., Rand-Giovanetti, E., & Sperling, R.A. (2006). Understanding metamemory: Neural correlates of the cognitive process and subjective level of confidence in recognition memory. *Neuroimage, 29*(4), 1150–1160.

Chung. H. L., & Steinberg, L. (2006). Relations between neighborhood factors, parenting behaviors, peer deviance, and delinquency among serious juvenile offenders. *Developmental Psychology, 42,* 319–331.

Cicirelli, V. G. (1976). Family structure and interaction: Sibling effects on socialization. In M. F. McMillan & S. Henao (Eds.), *Child psychiatry: Treatment and research* (pp. 190–203). New York: Brunner/Mazel.

Cicirelli, V. G. (1995). *Sibling relationships across the life span.* New York: Plenum Press.

CIHR, NSERC, & SSHRC. (2010). *Tri-Council Policy Statement: Ethical conduct for research involving humans.* Ottawa, ON: Author.

Cillessen, A. H. N., & Mayeux, L. (2004). From censure to reinforcement: Developmental changes in the association between aggression and social status. *Child Development, 75,* 147–163.

Claes, M., Perchec, C., Miranda, D., Benoit, A., Bariaud, F., Lanz, M., . . . & Lacourse, É. (2011). Adolescents' perceptions of parental practices: A cross-national comparison of Canada, France, and Italy. *Journal of Adolescence 34,* 225–238. doi:10.1016/j.adolescence.2010.05.009

Clark, P., & Kirk, E. (2000). All-day Kindergarten. Review of research. *Childhood Education, 76,* 228–231.

Clark, M., Riben, P., & Nowgesic, E. (2002). The association of housing density, isolation and tuberculosis in Canadian First Nations communities. *International Journal of Epidemiology, 31,* 940–945.

Clark, W. (2008). Kids' sports. *Canadian Social Trends* (Statistics Canada Catalogue no. 11-008-X). Ottawa, ON: Statistics Canada.

Clayton, E. W. (2003). Ethical, legal, and social implications of genomic medicine. *New England Journal of Medicine, 349,* 562–569.

Cleveland, H. H., & Wiebe, R. P. (2003). The moderation of adolescent-to-peer similarity in tobacco and alcohol use by school level of substance use. *Child Development, 74,* 279–291.

Cloutier, E. & Albert, T. (2001). *Economic burden of unintentional injury in British Columbia.* Vancouver, BC: BC Injury Research and Prevention Unit.

Cohen, L. B., Chaput, H. H., & Cashon, C. H. (2002). A constructivist model of infant cognition. *Cognitive Development, 17,* 1323–1343.

Cohen, L. B., Rundell, L. J., Spellman, B. A., & Cashon, C. H. (1999). Infants' perception of causal chains. *Current Directions in Psychological Science, 10,* 412–418.

Coie, J. D., & Dodge, K. A. (1998). Aggression and antisocial behavior. In W. Damon (Series ed.) & N. Eisenberg (Vol. Ed.), *Handbook of child psychology: Vol. 3. Social, emotional, and personality development* (5th ed., pp. 780–862). New York: Wiley.

Colby, A., Kohlberg, L., Gibbs, J., & Lieberman, M. (1983). A longitudinal study of moral development. *Monographs of the Society for Research in Child Development, 48*(1–2) [Serial No. 200].

Cole, A., & Kerns, K. A. (2001). Perceptions of sibling qualities and activities of early adolescence. *Journal of Early Adolescence, 21,* 204–226.

Cole, M. (1998). *Cultural psychology: A once and future discipline.* Cambridge, MA: Belknap.

Cole, P. M., Bruschi, C. J., & Tamang, B. L. (2002). Cultural differences in children's emotional reactions to difficult situations. *Child Development, 73*(3), 983–996.

Coleman, H., Charles, G., & Collins, J. (2001). Inhalant use by Canadian Aboriginal youth. *Journal of Child & Adolescent Substance Abuse, 10*(3), 1–20.

Coleman-Phox, K., Odouli, R., & De-Kun, L. (2008). Use of a fan during sleep and the risk of sudden infant death syndrome. *Archives of Pediatric & Adolescent Medicine, 162*(10), 963–968.

Coley, R. L., Morris, J. E., & Hernandez, D. (2004). Out-of-school care and problem behavior trajectories among low-income adolescents: Individual, family, and neighborhood characteristics as added risks. *Child Development, 75,* 948–965.

Coley, R. L., Votruba-Drzal, E., & Schindler, H. S. (2009). Fathers' and mothers' parenting predicting and responding to adolescent sexual risk behaviors. *Child Development, 80,* 808–827.

Colley, R. C., Garriguet, G., Janssen, I., Craig, C. L., Clarke, J., & Tremblay, M. S. (2011). Physical activity of Canadian children and youth: Accelerometer results from the 2007 to 2009 Canadian Health Measures Survey. *Health Reports, 22*(1), 15–23 (Statistics

Canada, Catalogue no. 82-003-XPE). Retrieved from http://www.statcan.gc.ca/pub/82-003-x/2011001/article/11397-eng.pdf

Collins, W. A., Maccoby, E. E., Steinberg, L., Hetherington, E. M., & Bornstein, M. H. (2000). Contemporary research in parenting: The case for nature and nurture. *American Psychologist, 55,* 218–232.

Colombo, J. (1993). *Infant cognition: Predicting later intellectual functioning.* Thousand Oaks, CA: Sage.

Colombo, J., Kannass, K. N., Shaddy, J., Kundurthi, S., Maikranz, J. M., Anderson, C. J., et al. (2004). Maternal DHA and the development of attention in infancy and toddlerhood. *Child Development, 75,* 1254–1267.

Committee on Obstetric Practice. (2002). ACOG committee opinion: Exercise during pregnancy and the postpartum period. *International Journal of Gynaecology & Obstetrics, 77*(1), 79–81.

Community Paediatrics Committee, Canadian Paediatrics Society. (2005). Management of primary nocturnal enuresis. *Paediatrics and Child Health, 10,* 611–614.

Conference Board of Canada. (2013). *Child poverty.* Retrieved from http://www.conferenceboard.ca/hcp/details/society/child-poverty.aspx

Connolly, J., Nocentini, A., Menesini, E., Pepler, D., Craig, W., & Williams, T. S. (2010). Adolescent dating aggression in Canada and Italy: A cross-national comparison. *International Journal of Behavioral Development, 34,* 98–105. doi:10.1177/0165025409360291

Connor, S., & Mcintyre, L. (2002). The effects of smoking and drinking during pregnancy. In J. D. Willms (ed.), *Vulnerable children* (pp. 131–148). Edmonton, AB: University of Alberta Press.

Constant, C., Sampaio, I., Negreiro, F., Aguiar, P., Silva, A., Salgueiro, M., & Bandiera, T. (2011). Environmental tobacco smoke (ETS) exposure and respiratory morbidity in school-age children. *Revista Portuguesa de Pneumologia, 17,* 20–26.

Cook, L. J., Haworth, C. M., & Wardle, J. (2007). Genetic and environmental influences on children's food neophobia. *The American Journal of Clinical Nutrition, 86*(2), 428–433.

Cooper, W. O., Hernandez-Diaz, S., Arbogast, P. G., Dudley, J. A., Dyer, S., Gideon, P. S., Hall, K., & Ray, W. A. (2006). Major congenital formations after first-trimester exposure to ACE inhibitors. *New England Journal of Medicine, 354,* 2443–2451.

Coplan, R. J., O'Neil, K., & Arbeau, K. A. (2005). Maternal anxiety during and after pregnancy and infant temperament at three months of age. *Journal of Prenatal & Perinatal Psychology & Health, 19,* 199–215.

Coplan, R. J., Prakash, K., O'Neil, K., & Armer, M. (2004). Do you "want" to play? Distinguishing between conflicted-shyness and social disinterest in early childhood. *Developmental Psychology, 40,* 244–258.

Coplan, R. J., Zheng, S., Weeks, M., & Chen, X. (2012). Young children's perceptions of social withdrawal in China and Canada. *Early Child Development and Care, 182,* 591–607. Retrieved from http://dx.doi.org/10.1080/03004430.2011.566328

Corbin, C. (1973). *A textbook of motor development.* Dubuque, IA: Wm. C. Brown.

Correa, A., Gilboa, S. M., Besser, L. M., Botto, L. D., Moore, C. A., Hobbs, C. A., et al. (2008). Diabetes mellitus and birth defects. *American Journal of Obstetrics & Gynecology, 199*(237), e1–e9.

Corter, C., Janmohamed, Z., & Pelletier, J. (Eds.). (2012). *Toronto First Duty Phase 3 Report.* Toronto, ON: Atkinson Centre for Society and Child Development, OISE/University of Toronto. Retrieved from http://www.toronto.ca/firstduty/

Costello, E. J., Compton, S. N., Keeler, G., & Angold, A. (2003). Relationship between poverty and psychopathology: A natural experiment. *Journal of the American Medical Association, 290,* 2023–2029.

Costigan, C. L., Hua, J. M., & Su, T. F. (2010). Living up to expectations: The strengths and challenges experienced by Chinese Canadian students. *Canadian Journal of School Psychology, 25,* 223–245.

Coulombe, J. A., Reid, G. J., Boyle, M. H., & Racine, Y. (2011). Sleep problems, tiredness, and psychological symptoms among healthy adolescents. *Journal of Pediatric Psychology, 36,* 25–35, doi:10.1093/jpepsy/jsq028

Council of Ministers of Education, Canada. (2008). *The Development of Education Reports for Canada. Report One: The Education Systems in Canada — Facing the Challenges of the Twenty-First Century. Report Two: Inclusive Education in Canada: The Way of the Future.* Toronto, ON. Retrieved from http://www.cmec.ca

Council on Sports Medicine and Fitness and Council on School Health. (2006). Active healthy living: Prevention of childhood obesity through increased physical activity. *Pediatrics, 117,* 1834–1842.

Courage, M. L., & Howe, M. L. (2002). From infant to child: The dynamics of cognitive change in the second year of life. *Psychological Bulletin, 128,* 250–277.

Cowan, C. P., & Cowan, P. A. (2000). *When partners become parents: The big life change for couples.* Mahwah, NJ; Erlbaum.

Craig, C. L., Cameron, C., Russell, S. J., & Beaulieu, A. (2001). *Increasing physical activity: Supporting children's participation.* Ottawa, ON: Canadian Fitness and Lifestyle Research Institute.

Craig, W., Harel-Fisch, Y., Fogel-Grinvald, H., Dostaler, S., Hetland, J., Simons-Morton, B., . . . & HBSC Bullying Writing Group. (2009). A cross-national profile of bullying and victimization among adolescents in 40 countries. *International Journal of Public Health, 54 Suppl 2,* 216–224. doi:10.1007/s00038-009-5413-9

Craig, W. M., & Harel, Y. (2004). Bullying, physical fighting, and victimization. In C. Currie, C. Roberts, A. Morgan, R. Smith, W. Settertobulte, O. Samdal et al. (Eds.), *Young people's health in context: International report from the HBSC 2001/02 survey. WHO Policy Series: Health policy for children and adolescents* (pp. 133–144). Issue 4. Copenhagen, DE: WHO Regional Office For Europe.

Craig, W. M., & Pepler, D. J. (2007) Understanding bullying: From research to practice. *Canadian Psychology, 48,* 86–93. doi:10.1037/cp2007010

Crain-Thoreson, C., & Dale, P. S. (1992). Do early talkers become early readers? Linguistic precocity, preschool language, and emergent literacy. *Developmental Psychology, 28,* 421–429.

Cratty, B. J. (1986). *Perceptual and motor development in infants and children* (3rd ed.). Englewood Cliffs, NJ: Prentice-Hall.

Crawford, C. (2008). *No place like home: A report on the housing needs of people with intellectual disabilities.* Canadian Association for Community Living. Retrieved from http://www.inclusionbc.org/resources/no-place-home-report-housing-needs-people-intellectual-disabilities

Crawford, J. (2007). The decline of bilingual education: How to reverse a troubling trend? *International Multilingual Research Journal, 1*(1), 33–38.

Crick, N. R., & Grotpeter, J. K. (1995). Relational aggression, gender, and social psychological adjustment. *Child Development, 66,* 710–722.

Crouter, A. C., MacDermid, S. M., McHale, S. M., & Perry-Jenkins, M. (1990). Parental monitoring and perception of children's school performance and conduct in dual- and single-earner families. *Developmental Psychology, 26,* 649–657.

Crowley, S. L. (1993, October). Grandparents to the rescue. *AARP Bulletin,* pp. 1, 16–17.

Cryan, J.R., Sheehan, R., Wiechel, J., & Bandy-Hedden, I. (1992). Success outcomes of full-day Kindergarten: More positive behavior and increased achievement in the years after. *Early Childhood Research Quarterly, 7,* 187–203.

Cui, M., Conger, R. D., & Lorenz, F. O. (2005). Predicting change in adolescent adjustment from change in marital problems. *Developmental Psychology, 41,* 812–823.

Cummins, J. (2000). *Language, power and pedagogy: Bilingual children caught in the crossfire.* Toronto, ON: Multilingual Matters.

Cummins, J., Mirza, R., & Stille, S. (2012). English language learners in Canadian schools: Emerging directions for school-based policies. *TESL Canada Journal/Review TESL du Canada, 29,* 25–48.

Currie, C., Roberts, C., Morgan, A., Smith, R., Settertobulte, W., & Samdal, O. (Eds.). (2004). *Young people's health in context.* Geneva, Switzerland: World Health Organization.

Cushon, J. A., Vu, L. T. H., Janzen, B. L., & Muhajarine, N. (2011). Neighborhood poverty impacts children's physical health and well-being over time: Evidence from the Early Development Instrument. *Early Education and Development, 22*(2), 183–205.

Dahinten, V. S., & Ford, L. (2004). *Validation of the Nipissing District Developmental Screen for use with infants and toddlers - Working paper.* Vancouver, BC: Consortium for Health, Intervention, Learning and Development.

Dahinten, V. S., & Wilms, J. D. (2002). The effects of adolescent child-bearing on children's outcomes. In J. D. Willms (Ed.), *Vulnerable children* (pp. 229–258). Edmonton, AB: University of Alberta Press.

Daiute, C., Hartup, W. W., Sholl, W., & Zajac, R. (1993, March). *Peer collaboration and written language development: A study of friends and acquaintances.* Paper presented at the meeting of the Society for Research in Child Development, New Orleans, LA.

Dale, P. S., Simonoff, E., Bishop, D. V. M., Eley, T. C., Oliver, B., Price, T. S., et al. (1998). Genetic influence on language delay in two-year-old children. *Nature Neuroscience, 1,* 324–328.

Daly, K. (2004). *Contemporary family trends: The changing culture of parenting.* Toronto, ON: The Vanier Institute of the Family. Retrieved from http://www.vifamily.ca/library/cft/cft.html

Daly, R. (2005). Drop in youth antidepressant use prompts call for FDA monitoring. *Psychiatric News, 40*(19), 18.

Daniels, S. R., Greer, F. R., & the Committee on Nurition. (2008). Lipid screening and cardiovascular health in childhood. *Pediatrics, 122,* 198–208.

Darling, N., Kolasa, M., & Wooten, K. G. (2008). National, state, and local area vaccination coverage among children aged 19–35 Months—United States, 2007. *Morbidity & Mortality Weekly Report, 57*(35), 961–966.

Darling, N., & Steinberg, L. (1993). Parenting style as context: An integrative model. *Psychological Bulletin, 113,* 487–496.

Darwin, C. (1871). *The descent of man and selection in relation to sex.* John Murray, London.

Darwin , C. R. (1965). *The expression of emotions in man and animals.* London: John Murray. (Original work published 1872)

Datar, A. (2004). The impact of changes in kindergarten entrance age policies on children's academic achievement and the child care needs of families. Santa Monica, CA: RAND Corporation, http://www.rand.org/pubs/rgs_dissertations/RGSD177.

Datar, A., & Sturm, R. (2004). Childhood overweight and parent- and teacher-reported behavior problems. *Archives of Pediatric and Adolescent Medicine, 158,* 804–810.

Datar, A., Sturm, R., & Magnabosco, J. L. (2004). Childhood overweight and academic performance: National study of kindergartners and first-graders. *Obesity Research, 12,* 58–68.

David and Lucile Packard Foundation. (2004). Children, families, and foster care: Executive summary. *The Future of Children, 14*(1). Retrieved from http://www.futureof children.org

Davidov, M., & Grusec, J. E. (2006). Multiple pathways to compliance: Mothers' willingness to cooperate and knowledge of their children's reactions to discipline. *Journal of Family Psychology, 20,* 705–708. doi: 10.1037/0893-3200.20.4.705

Davies, G. A. L., Wolfe, L. A., Mottola, M. F., & MacKinnon, C. (2003). Joint SOGC/CSEP clinical practice guideline: Exercise in pregnancy and the postpartum period. *Canadian Journal of Applied Physiology, 28,* 329–341.

Davis, A. S. (2008). Children with Down syndrome: Implications for assessment and intervention in the school. *School Psychology Quarterly, 23,* 271–281.

Davis, M., & Emory, E. (1995). Sex differences in neonatal stress reactivity. *Child Development, 66,* 14–27.

Davison, K. K., & Birch, L. L. (2001). Weight status, parent reaction, and self concept in 5-year-old girls. *Pediatrics, 107,* 46–53.

Davison, K. K., Susman, E. J., & Birch, L. L. (2003). Percent body fat at age 5 predicts earlier pubertal development among girls at age 9. *Pediatrics, 111,* 815–821.

Dawson, D. A. (1991). Family structure and children's health and well-being. Data from the 1988 National Health Interview Survey on child health. *Journal of Marriage and the Family, 53,* 573–584.

Day, J. C., Janus, A., & Davis, J. (2005). Computer and Internet use in the United States: 2003. *Current Population Reports* (P23–208). Washington, DC: U.S. Census Bureau.

de Castro, B. O., Veerman, J. W., Koops, W., Bosch, J. D., & Monshouwer, H. J. (2002). Hostile attribution of intent and aggressive behavior: A meta-analysis. *Child Development, 73,* 916–934.

Deardorff, J., Gonzales, N. A., Christopher, S., Roosa, M. W., & Millsap, R. E. (2005). Early puberty and adolescent pregnancy: The influence of alcohol use. *Pediatrics, 116,* 1451–1456.

DeBell, M., & Chapman, C. (2006). *Computer and Internet use by students in 2003: Statistical analysis report* (NCES 2006–065). Washington, DC: National Center for Education Statistics.

DeCasper, A. J., & Spence, M. J. (1986). Prenatal maternal speech influences newborns' perceptions of speech sounds. *Infant Behavior and Development, 9,* 133–150.

DeCesare, D. (2004). Full-day Kindergarten programs improve chances of academic success. *The progress of education reform 2004: Kindergarten, 5*(4), 1–6.

Decety, J., Michalaska, K., Akitsuki, Y., & Lahey, B. (2009). Atypical empathetic responses in adolescents with aggressive conduct disorder: A functional MRI investigation. *Biological Psychology, 80,* 203–211.

DeCicca, P., & Smith, J. D. (2011). *The long-run impacts of early childhood education: Evidence from a failed policy experiment.* Working paper 17085. Cambridge, MA: National Bureau of Economic Research. Retrieved from http://www.nber.org/papers/w17085

DeFranco, E. A., Stamilio, D. M., Boslaugh, S. E., Gross, G. A., & Muglia, L. J. (2007). A short interpregnancy interval is a risk factor for preterm birth and its recurrence. *American Journal of Obstetrics and Gynecology, 197*(264), e1–e6.

Delaney, C. (2000). Making babies in a Turkish village. In J. DeLoache & A. Gottlieb (Eds.), *A world of babies: Imagined childcare guides for seven societies* (pp. 117–144). New York: Cambridge University Press.

Dell, C. A., Seguin, M., Hopkins, C., Tempier, R., Mehl-Madrona, L, Dell, D., . . . & Mosier, K. (2011). From benzos to berries: Treatment offered at an Aboriginal youth solvent abuse treatment centre relays the importance of culture. *Canadian Journal of Psychiatry, 56,* 75–83.

DeLoache, J., & Gottlieb, A. (2000). If Dr. Spock were born in Bali: Raising a world of babies. In J. DeLoache & A. Gottlieb (Eds.), *A world of babies: Imagined childcare guides for seven societies* (pp. 1–27). New York: Cambridge University Press.

Deming, D. (2009). Early childhood intervention and life-cycle skill development: Evidence from Head Start. *American Economic Journal: Applied Economics, 1*(3), 111–134.

Deming, D., & Dynarski, S. (2008). The lengthening of childhood. National Bureau of Economic Research Working Paper, http://www.nber.org/papers/w14124

Denham, S. A., Blair, K. A., DeMulder, E., Levitas, J., Sawyer, K., Auerbach-Major, S., & Queenan, P. (2003). Preschool emotional competence: Pathway to social competence? *Child Development, 74,* 238–256.

Dennis, T. (2006). Emotional self-regulation in preschoolers: The interplay of child approach reactivity, parenting, and control capacities. *Developmental Psychology, 42,* 84–97.

Dennison, B. A., Erb, T. A., & Jenkins, P. L. (2002). Television viewing and television in bedroom associated with overweight risk among low-income preschool children. *Pediatrics, 109,* 1028–1035.

Denton, K., West, J., & Walston, J. (2003). *Reading—young children's achievement and classroom experiences: Findings from The Condition of Education 2003.* Washington, DC: National Center for Education Statistics.

Department of Justice Canada. (2004). *Assisted Human Reproduction Act.* Retrieved from http://laws-lois.justice.gc.ca/eng/acts/A-13.4/

Department of Justice Canada. (2013). *The Youth Criminal Justice Act: Summary and background.* Ottawa, ON. Government of Canada. Retrieved from http://www.justice.gc.ca/eng/cj-jp/yj-jj/ycja-lsjpa/back-hist.html

Deptula, D. P., & Cohen, R. (2004). Aggressive, rejected, and delinquent children and adolescents: A comparison of their friendships. *Aggression and Violent Behavior, 9*(1), 75–104.

Derwing, T. M., DeCorby, E., Ichikawa, J., & Jamieson, K. (1999). Some factors that affect the success of ESL high school students. *Canadian Modern Language Review, 55,* 532–547.

Deslandes, R., Potvin, P., & Leclerc, D. (1999). Family characteristics as predictors of school achievement: Parental involvement as a mediator. *McGill Journal of Education, 34,* 135–153.

Dessureau, B. K., Kurowski, C. O., & Thompson, N. S. (1998). A reassessment of the role of pitch and duration in adult's responses to infant crying. *Infant Behavior and Development, 21*(2), 367–371.

De Wals, P., Tairou, F., Van Allen, M. I., Uh, S. H., Lowry, R. B., Sibbald, B., . . . & Niyonsenga, T. (2007). Reduction in neural-tube defects after folic acid fortification in Canada. *New England Journal of Medicine, 357,* 135–42.

Dewing, P., Shi, T., Horvath, S., & Vilain, E. (2003). Sexually dimorphic gene expression in mouse brain precedes gonadal differentiation. *Molecular Brain Research, 118,* 82–90.

De Wolff, M.S., & van Ijzendoorn, M.H. (1997). Sensitivity and attachment: A meta-analysis on parental antecedents of infant attachment. *Child Development, 68,* 571–591.

Diamond, A. (2000). Close interrelation of motor development and cognitive development and of the cerebellum and prefrontal cortex. *Child Development, 71*(1), 44–56.

Diamond, A. (2002). Normal development of prefrontal cortex from birth to young adulthood: Cognitive functions, anatomy, and biochemistry. In D.T. Strauss & R.T. Knight (Eds.), *Principles of frontal lobe function* (pp. 466–503). New York: Oxford University Press.

Diamond, L. M., & Savin-Williams, R. C. (2003). The intimate relationships of sexual-minority youths. In G. R. Adams & M. D. Berzonsky (Eds.), *Blackwell handbook of adolescence* (pp. 393–412). Malden, MA: Blackwell.

Dick, D. M., Rose, R. J., Kaprio, J., & Viken, R. (2000). Pubertal timing and substance use: Associations between and within families across late adolescence. *Developmental Psychology, 36,* 180–189.

Dickens, W. T., & Flynn, J. R. (2006). Black Americans reduce the racial IQ gap: Evidence from standardization samples. *Psychological Science, 17*(10), 913–920.

Dietert, R. R. (2005). *Developmental immunotoxicology (DIT): Is DIT testing necessary to ensure safety?* Proceedings of the 14th Immunotoxicology Summer School, Lyon, France, October 2005, 246–257.

Dieticians of Canada. (2010). *WHO growth charts for Canada.* Retrieved from http://www.dietitians.ca/secondary-pages/public/who-growth-charts.aspx

Dieticians of Canada. (2012a). Growth monitoring of infants and children using the 2006 World Health Organization [WHO] Child Growth Standards and 2007 WHO Growth References: Questions and answers for health professionals. *Current Issues.* Retrieved from http://www.dietitians.ca/Secondary-Pages/Public/WHO-Growth-Charts---Resources-for-Health-Professio.aspx

Dieticians of Canada. (2012b). *Dietician's views.* Retrieved from http://www.dietitians.ca

DiFranza, J. R., Aligne, C. A., & Weitzman, M. (2004). Prenatal and postnatal environmental tobacco smoke exposure and children's health. *Pediatrics, 113,* 1007–1015.

Dilworth-Bart, J. E., & Moore., C. F. (2006). Mercy mercy me: Social injustice and the prevention of environmental pollutant exposures among ethnic minority and poor children. *Child Development, 77*(2), 247–265.

Dingfelder, S. (2004). Programmed for psychopathology? Stress during pregnancy may increase children's risk for mental illness, researchers say. *Monitor on Psychology, 35*(2), 56–57.

DiPietro, J. A., Bornstein, M. H., Costigan, K. A., Pressman, E. K., Hahn, C. S., Painter, K., et al. (2002). What does fetal movement predict about behavior during the first two years of life? *Developmental Psychobiology, 40*(4), 358–371.

DiPietro, J. A., Novak, M. F. S. X., Costigan, K. A., Atella, L. D., & Reusing, S. P. (2006). Maternal psychological distress during pregnancy in relation to child development at age 2. *Child Development, 77*(3), 573–587.

Dishion, T. J., Shaw, D., Connell, A., Garnder, F., Weaver, C., & Wilson, M. (2008). The family check-up with high-risk indigent families: Preventing problem behavior by increasing parents' positive behavior support in early childhood. *Child Development, 79,* 1395–1414.

Dishion, T. J., & Tipsord, J. M. (2011). Peer contagion in child and adolescent social and emotional development. *Annual Review of Psychology, 62,* 189–214.

Dodge, K. A., Coie, J. D., & Lynam, D. (2006). Aggression and antisocial behavior in youth. In N. Eisenberg, W. Damon, & R. Lerner (Eds.), *Handbook of child psychology: Vol. 3, Social, emotional and personality development* (6th ed., pp. 719–788). Hoboken, NJ: Wiley.

Dodge, K. A., Coie, J. D., Pettit, G. S., & Price, J. M. (1990). Peer status and aggression in boys' groups: Developmental and contextual analysis. *Child Development, 61,* 1289–1309.

Dodge, K. A., Dishion, T. J., & Lansford, J. E. (2006). Deviant peer influences in intervention and public policy for youth. *Social Policy Report, 20,* 3–19.

Dodge, K. A., Pettit, G. S., & Bates, J. E. (1994). Socialization mediators of the relation between socioeconomic status and child conduct problems. *Child Development, 65,* 649–665.

Doherty, G. (1997). *Zero to six: The basics for school readiness.* Report No. R-97-8E. Ottawa: Applied Research Branch, Strategic Policy, Human Resources Development Canada.

Dolan, B. (1999). From the field: Cognitive profiles of First Nations and Caucasian children referred for psychoeducational assessment. *Canadian Journal of School Psychology, 15,* 63–71.

Donaldson, M. D. C., Gault, E. J., Tan, K. W., & Dunger, D. B. (2006). Optimising management in Turner syndrome: From infancy to adult transfer. *Archives of Disease in Childhood, 91,* 513–520.

D'Onofrio, B. M., Turkheimer, E., Emery, R. E., Slutske, W. S., Heath, A. C., Madden, P. A., & Martin, N. G. (2006). A genetically informed study of the processes underlying the association between parental marital instability and offspring adjustment. *Developmental Psychology, 42,* 486–499.

Doucet, A. (2006). *Do men mother? Fathering, care, and domestic responsibility.* Toronto, ON: University of Toronto Press.

Doucet, A. (2009). Dad and baby in the first year: Gendered responsibilities and embodiment. *The ANNALS of the American Academy of Political and Social Science, 624,* 78–98. doi:10.1177/0002716209334069

Downs, S. M., Arnold, A., Marshall, D., McCargar, L. J., Raine, K. D., & Willows, N. D. (2009). Associations among the food environment, diet quality and weight status in Cree children in Québec. *Public Health Nutrition, 12,* 1504–1511. doi:10.1017/S1368980008004515

Doyle, A. B., & Moretti, M. M. (2000). *Attachment to parents and adjustment in adolescence: Literature review and policy implications.* Ottawa, ON: Health Canada.

Drabick, D. A. G., Gadow, K. D., & Sprafkin, J. (2006). Co-occurrence of conduct disorder and depression in a clinic-based sample of boys with ADHD. *Journal of Child Psychology and Pscyhiatry, 47*(8), 766–774.

Duckworth, A., & Seligman, M. E. P. (2005). Self-discipline outdoes IQ in predicting academic performance of adolescents. *Psychological Science, 26,* 939–944.

Duenwald, M. (2003, July 15). After 25 years, new ideas in the prenatal test tube. *New York Times.* Retrieved from http://www.nytimes.com/2003/07/15/health/15IVF.html?ex

Duke, J., Huhman, M., & Heitzler, C. (2003). Physical activity levels among children aged 9–13 years—United States, 2002. *Morbidity and Mortality Weekly Report, 52,* 785–788.

Dunfield, K., Kuhlmeier, V. A., O'Connell, L., & Kelley, E. (2011). Examining the diversity of prosocial behavior: Helping, sharing, and comforting in infancy. *Infancy, 16,* 227–247 doi:10.1111/j.1532-7078.2010.00041.x

Dunham, P., Dunham, F., & O'Keefe, C. (2000). Two-year-olds' sensitivity to a parent's knowledge state: Mind reading or contextual cues? *British Journal of Developmental Psychology, 18*(4), 519–532.

Dunn, J. (2006). Moral development in early childhood and social interaction in the family. In M. Killen & J. Smetana (Eds.), *Handbook of Moral Development* (pp. 331–350). Mahwah, NJ: Erlbaum.

Dunn, J., & Hughes, C. (2001). "I got some swords and you're dead!": Violent fantasy, antisocial behavior, friendship, and moral sensibility in young children. *Child Development, 72,* 491–505.

Dunn, J., & Munn, P. (1985). Becoming a family member: Family conflict and the development of social understanding in the second year. *Child Development, 56,* 480–492.

Dunning, P. (2000). Aboriginal head start. *Education Canada, 39*(4), 38–39.

Dunson, D. (2002). *Late breaking research session. Increasing infertility with increasing age: Good news and bad news for older couples.* Paper presented at 18th Annual Meeting of the European Society of Human Reproduction and Embryology, Vienna.

Dunson, D. B., Colombo, B., & Baird, D. D. (2002). Changes with age in the level and duration of fertility in the menstrual cycle. *Human Reproduction, 17,* 1399–1403.

Durbin, A. (2009). Canada's response to the on-reserve housing crisis: A study of the Kelowna Accord. *Pimatisiwin: A Journal of Aboriginal and Indigenous Community Health, 7,* 181–200.

Durrant, J., & Ensom, R. (2012). Physical punishment of children: Lessons from 20 years of research. *Canadian Medical Association Journal, 184,* 1373–1377. doi:10.1503 / cmaj.101314

Durrant, J. E., Broberg, A. G., & Rose-Krasnor, L. (1999). Predicting mother's use of physical punishment during mother–child conflicts in Sweden and Canada. In C. C. Piotrowski & P. D. Hastings (eds.), *Conflict as a context for understanding maternal beliefs about child rearing and children's misbehaviour.* (New Directions for Child and Adolescent Development, 86). San Francisco: Jossey-Bass Publishers.

Durrant, J. E., Trocmé, N., Fallon, B., Milne, C., & Black, T. (2009). Child and adolescent maltreatment. Protection of children from physical maltreatment in Canada: An evaluation of the Supreme Court's Definition of reasonable force. *Journal of Aggression, Maltreatment & Trauma, 18,* 64–87.

Duthie, J. K., Nippold, M. A., Billow, J. L., & Mansfield, T. C. (2008). Mental imagery of concrete proverbs: A developmental study of children, adolescents, and adults. *Applied Psycholinguistics, 29*(1), 151–173.

Dweck, C. S., & Grant, H. (2008). Self theories, goals, and meaning. In J. Y. Shaw and W. L. Gardner (Eds.), *Handbook of motivation science* (pp. 405–416). New York: Guilford Press.

Dzakpasu, S., & Chalmers, B. (2005). Canadian maternity experiences survey pilot study. *Birth, 32,* 34–38.

Dzakpasu, S., Joseph, K. S., Kramer, M. S., & Allen, A. C. (2000). The Matthew Effect: Infant mortality in Canada and internationally. *Pediatrics, 106,* 1–5.

The Early College High School Initiative. (n.d.). Retrieved March 31, 2004, from http://www.earlycolleges.org

East, P. L., & Khoo, S. T. (2005). Longitudinal pathways linking family factors and sibling relationship qualities to adolescent substance use and sexual risk behaviors. *Journal of Family Psychology, 19,* 571–580.

Eating disorders—Part I. (1997, October). *The Harvard Mental Health Letter,* pp. 1–5.

Eaton, D. K., Kann, L., Kinchen, S., Shanklin, S., Ross, J., Hawkins, J., et al. (2008). Youth risk behavior surveillance—United States, 2007. *Morbidity and Mortality Weekly Report, 57*(SS-4), 1–131.

Eccles, J. S. (2004). Schools, academic motivation, and stage-environment fit. In R. M. Lerner & L. Steinberg (Eds), *Handbook of adolescent development* (2nd ed., pp. 125–153). Hoboken, NJ: Wiley.

Eccles, J. S., Wigfield, A., & Byrnes, J. (2003). Cognitive development in adolescence. In I. B. Weiner (Ed.), *Handbook of psychology: Vol. 6. Developmental psychology* (pp. 325–350). New York: Wiley.

Ecker, J. L., & Frigoletto, F. D., Jr. (2007). Cesarean delivery and the risk-benefit calculus. *New England Journal of Medicine, 356,* 885–888.

Eckerman, C. O., Davis, C. C., & Didow, S. M. (1989). Toddlers' emerging ways of achieving social coordination with a peer. *Child Development, 60,* 440–453.

Eckerman, C. O., & Didow, S. M. (1996). Nonverbal imitation and toddlers' mastery of verbal means of achieving coordinated action. *Developmental Psychology, 32,* 141–152.

Eckert, P. (2003). Language and gender in adolescence. In J. Holmes & M. Meyerhoff (Eds.), *The handbook of language and gender* (pp. 381–400). Oxford: Blackwell.

Eddleman, K. A., Malone, F. D., Sullivan, L., Dukes, K., Berkowitz, R. L., & Kharbutli, Y., et al. (2006). Pregnancy loss rates after midtrimester amniocentesis. *Obstetrics and Gynecology, 108*(5), 1067–1072.

Eden, G. F., Jones, K. M., Cappell, K., Gareau, L., Wood, F. B., Zeffiro, T. A., et al. (2004). Neural changes following remediation in adult developmental dyslexia. *Neuron, 44,* 411–422.

Eder, W., Ege, M. J., & von Mutius, E. (2006). The asthma epidemic. New England Journal of Medicine, 355, 2226–2235.

Edwards, C. P. (2002). Three approaches from Europe: Waldorf, Montessori, and Reggio Emilia. *Early Childhood Research and Practice, 4*(1), 14–38.

Edwards, C. P. (2003). "Fine designs" from Italy: Montessori education and the Reggio Emilia approach. Montesorri Life: Journal of the American Montessori Society, 15(1), 33–38.

Edwards, N. C., & Boivin, J.-F. (1997). Ethnocultural predictors of postpartum infant- care behaviours among immigrants in Canada. *Ethnicity & Health, 2,* 163–176.

Retrieved from http://dx.doi.org/10.1080/13 557858.1997.9961825

Eftekhary, S., Klein, M. C., & Xu, S. Y. (2010). The life of a Canadian doula: Successes, confusion, and conflict. *Journal of Obstetrics and Gynaecology Canada, 32,* 642–649.

Eggebeen, D. J., & Knoester, C. (2001). Does fatherhood matter for men? *Journal of Marriage and the Family, 63,* 381–429.

Eggertson, L. (2007). Physician's challenge Canada to make children, youth a priority. *Canadian Medical Association Journal, 176,* 1602–1604.

Eiberg, H. (1995). Nocturnal enuresis is linked to a specific gene. *Scandinavian Journal of Urology and Nephrology, 173*(Suppl.), 15–17.

Eimas, P. (1985). The perception of speech in early infancy. *Scientific American, 252*(1), 46–52.

Eimas, P., Siqueland, E., Jusczyk, P., & Vigorito, J. (1971). Speech perception in infants. *Science, 171,* 303–306.

Einarson, A., & Boskovic, R. (2009). Use and safety of antipsychotic drugs during pregnancy. *Journal of Psychiatric Practice, 15*(3), 183–192.

Eisenberg, A. R. (1996). The conflict talk of mothers and children: Patterns related to culture, SES, and gender of child. *Merrill-Palmer Quarterly, 42,* 438–452.

Eisenberg, N. (2000). Emotion, regulation, and moral development. *Annual Review of Psychology, 51,* 665–697.

Eisenberg, N., & Fabes, R. A. (1998). Prosocial development. In W. Damon (Series ed.), & N. Eisenberg (Vol. ed.), *Handbook of child psychology: Vol. 3. Social, emotional, and personality development* (5th ed., pp. 701–778). New York: Wiley.

Eisenberg, N., Fabes, R. A., & Murphy, B. C. (1996). Parents' reactions to children's negative emotions: Relations to children's social competence and comforting behavior. *Child Development, 67,* 2227–2247.

Eisenberg, N., Fabes, R. A., Shepard, S. A., Guthrie, I. K., Murphy, B. C., & Reiser, M. (1999). Parental reactions to children's negative emotions: Longitudinal relations to quality of children's social functioning. *Child Development, 70*(2), 513–534.

Eisenberg, N., Fabes, R. A., & Spinrad, T. L. (2006). Prosocial development. In W. Damon & R. M. Lerner (Series Eds.) & Eisenberg. N. (Vol. Ed.), *Handbook of child psychology: Vol 3. Social, emotional and personality development* (pp. 646–718). Hoboken: NJ: Wiley.

Eisenberg, N., & Morris, A. D. (2004). Moral cognitions and prosocial responding in adolescence. In R. M. Lerner & L. Steinberg (Eds.), *Handbook of adolescent psychology* (2nd ed., pp. 155–188). Hoboken, NJ: Wiley.

Eisenberg, N., Spinrad, T. L., Fabes, R. A., Reiser, M., Cumberland, A., Shepard, S. A., et al.

(2004). The relations of effortful control and impulsivity to children's resiliency and adjustment. *Child Development, 75,* 25–46.

Elicker, J., Englund, M., & Sroufe, L. A. (1992). Predicting peer competence and peer relationships in childhood from early parent-child relationships. In R. Parke & G. Ladd (Eds.), *Family peer relationships: Modes of linkage* (pp. 77–106). Hillsdale, NJ: Erlbaum.

Elicker, J., & Mathur, S. (1997). What do they do all day? Comprehensive evaluation of a full-day Kindergarten. *Early Childhood Research Quarterly, 12,* 459–480.

Elkind, D. (2001). Cognitive development. In J. V. Lerner & R. M. Lerner (Eds.), *Adolescence in America: An encyclopedia* (pp. 127–134). Santa Barbara, CA: ABC-CLIO.

Elliott, V. S. (2000, November 20). Doctors caught in middle of ADHD treatment controversy: Critics charge that medications are being both under- and overprescribed. *AMNews.* Retrieved from http://business.high beam.com/137033/article-1G1-67548190/ doctors-caught-middle-adhd-treatment-controversy

Ellis, B. J., Bates, J. E., Dodge, K. A., Fergusson, D. M., Horwood, L. J., Pettit, G. S., & Woodward, L. (2003). Does father-absence place daughters at special risk for early sexual activity and teenage pregnancy? *Child Development, 74,* 801–821.

Ellis, B. J., & Garber, J. (2000). Psychosocial antecedents of variation in girls' pubertal timing: Maternal depression, stepfather presence, and marital family stress. *Child Development, 71*(2), 485–501.

Eltzschig, H. K., Lieberman, E. S., & Camann, W. R. (2003). Regional anesthesia and analgesia for labor and delivery. *New England Journal of Medicine, 348,* 319–332.

Emery, P., Mayhew, D., & Simpson, H. (2008). *Youth and road crashes: Magnitude, characteristics and trends.* Ottawa, ON: Traffic Injury Research Foundation. Retrieved from http://www.tirf.ca.

Engle, P. L., Black, M. M., Behrman, J. R., de Mello, M. C., Gertler, P. J., Kapiriri, L., . . . & Young, M. E. (2007). Strategies to avoid the loss of developmental potential in more than 200 million children in the developing world. *The Lancet, 369*(9557), 20–26.

Engle, P. L., & Breaux, C. (1998). Fathers' involvement with children: Perspectives from developing countries. *Social Policy Report, 12*(1), 1–21.

Enloe, C. F. (1980). How alcohol affects the developing fetus. *Nutrition Today, 15*(5), 12–15.

Erikson, E. H. (1950). *The life cycle completed.* New York: Norton.

Erikson, E. H. (1968). *Identity: Youth and crisis.* New York: Norton.

Erikson, E. H. (1982). *The life cycle completed.* New York: Norton.

Etzel, R. A. (2003). How environmental exposures influence the development and exacerbation of asthma. *Pediatrics, 112*(1), 233–239.

Euling, S. Y., Selevan, S. G., Pescovitz, O. H., & Skakkebaek, N. W. (2008). Role of environmental factors in the timing of puberty. *Pediatrics, 121.* doi:10.1542.peds.2007–1813c

Evans, A. D., & Lee, K. (2010). Promising to tell the truth makes 8- to 16-year-olds more honest. *Behavioral sciences and the law.* PMID: 20878877

Evans, G. W. (2004). The environment of childhood poverty. *American Psychologist, 59,* 77–92.

Fabes, R. A., Leonard, S. A., Kupanoff, K., & Martin, C. L. (2001). Parental coping with children's negative emotions: Relations with children's emotional and social responding. *Child Development, 72*(3), 907–920.

Fabes, R. A., Martin, C. L., & Hanish, L. D. (2003, May). Young children's play qualities in same-, other-, and mixed-gender peer groups. *Child Development, 74*(3), 921–932.

Fabricius, W. V. (2003). Listening to children of divorce: New findings that diverge from Wallerstein, Lewis, and Blakeslee. *Family Relations, 52,* 385–394.

Fagan, J. F., Holland, C. R., & Wheeler, K. (2007). The prediction, from infancy, of adult IQ. *Intelligence, 35,* 225–231.

Fagan, J., Palkovitz, R., Roy, K., & Farrie, D. (2009). Pathways to paternal engagement: Longitudinal effects of risk and resilience on nonresident fathers. *Developmental Psychology, 45*(5), 1389–1405.

Fagot, B. I. (1997). Attachment, parenting, and peer interactions of toddler children. *Developmental Psychology, 33,* 489–499.

Fagot, B. I., Rogers, C. S., & Leinbach, M. D. (2000). Theories of gender socialization. In T. Eckes & H. M. Trautner (Eds.), *The developmental social psychology of gender.* Mahwah, NJ: Erlbaum.

Fallon, B., Chabot, M., Fluke, J., Blackstock, C., MacLaurin, B., & Tonmyr, L. (2013). Placement decisions and disparities among Aboriginal children: Further analysis of the Canadian incidence study of reported child abuse and neglect part A: Comparisons of the 1998 and 2003 surveys. *Child Abuse and Neglect, 37*(1), 47–60. doi:10.1016/j. chiabu.2012.10.001

Family Service Toronto. (2011). *Revisiting family security in insecure times: 2011 Report Card on Child and Family Poverty in Canada.* Toronto, ON: Author. Retrieved from http://www.campaign2000.ca

Fantino, A. M., & Colak, A. (2001). Refugee children in Canada: Searching for identity. *Child Welfare, 80,* 587–596.

Farver, J. A. M., Kim, Y. K., & Lee, Y. (1995). Cultural differences in Korean and Anglo-American preschoolers' social interaction and play behavior. *Child Development, 66,* 1088–1099.

Farver, J. A. M., Xu, Y., Eppe, S., Fernandez, A., & Schwartz, D. (2005). Community violence, family conflict, and preschoolers' socioemotional functioning. *Developmental Psychology, 41,* 160–170.

Fawzi, W. W., Msamanga, G. I., Urassa, W., Hertzmark, E., Petraro, P., Willett, W. C., & Spiegelman, D. (2007). Vitamins and perinatal outcomes among HIV-negative women in Tanzania. *New England Journal of Medicine, 356,* 1423–1431.

Fearon, P., O'Connell, P., Frangou, S., Aquino, P., Nosarti, C., Allin, M., et al. (2004). Brain volume in adult survivors of very low birth weight: A sibling-controlled study. *Pediatrics, 114,* 367–371.

Feightner, J. W. (1994). Preschool screening for developmental problems. In Canadian Task Force on the Periodic Health Examination (eds.). *Canadian Guide to Clinical Preventive Health Care* (pp. 290–296). Ottawa, ON: Health Canada.

Fell, D. B., & Joseph, K. S. (2012). Temporal trends in the frequency of twins and higher-order multiple births in Canada and the United States. *BMC Pregnancy and Childbirth, 12,* 103. Available http://www. biomedcentral.com/1471-2393/12/103

Ferber, S. G., & Makhoul, I. R. (2004). The effect of skin-to-skin contact (Kangaroo Care) shortly after birth on the neurobehavioral responses of the term newborn: A randomized, controlled trial. *Pediatrics, 113,* 858–865.

Fergusson, D. M., Boden, J. M., & Horwood, J. (2006). Cannabis use and other illicit drug use: Testing the cannabis gateway hypothesis. *Addiction, 101*(4), 556–569.

Fergusson, D. M., Boden, J. M., & Horwood, L. J. (2008). Exposure to childhood sexual and physical abuse and adjustment in early adulthood. *Child Abuse & Neglect, 32,* 607–619.

Fernald, A., Perfors, A., & Marchman, V. A. (2006). Picking up speed in understanding: Speech processing efficiency and vocabulary growth across the second year. *Developmental Psychology, 42,* 98–116.

Fernandez, C. V., & Rees, E. P. (1994). Pain management in Canadian level 3 neonatal intensive care units. *Canadian Medical Association Journal, 150,* 499–504.

Ferrao, V. (2010). *Women in Canada: A Gender-based Statistical Report. Paid Work.* Ottawa, ON: Statistics Canada. Retrieved from http://www.statcan.gc.ca/pub/89-503-x/2010001/article/11387-eng.htm#a4

Field, A. E., Austin, S. B., Taylor, C. B., Malspeis, S., Rosner, B., Rockett, H. R., et al. (2003). Relation between dieting and weight change among preadolescents and adolescents. *Pediatrics, 112*(4), 900–906.

Field, A. E., Camargo, C. A., Taylor, B., Berkey, C. S., Roberts, S. B., & Colditz, G. A. (2001). Peer, parent, and media influence on the development of weight concerns and frequent dieting among preadolescent and adolescent girls and boys. *Pediatrics, 107*(1), 54–60.

Field, T. (2010). Touch for socioemotional and physical well-being: A review. *Developmental Review, 30*(4), 367–383.

Field, T., Diego, M., & Hernandez-Reif, M. (2007). Massage therapy research. *Developmental Review, 27*, 75–89.

Field, T., Hernandez-Reif, M., & Freedman, J. (2004). Stimulation programs for preterm infants. *Social Policy Report, 18*(1), 1–19.

Findlay, L. C. (2011). Physical activity among First Nations people off reserve, Métis and Inuit. *Health Reports, 22*(1), 47–54 (Statistics Canada, Catalogue no. 82-003-XPE).

Findlay, S., Pinzon, J., Taddeo, D., Katzman, D. K., & Canadian Paediatric Society, Adolescent Health Committee. (2010). Family-based treatment of children and adolescents with anorexia nervosa: Guidelines for the community physician. *Paediatrics & Child Health, 15*, 31–35.

Finn, J. D. (2006). *The adult lives of at-risk students: The roles of attainment and engagement in high school* (NCES 2006–328). Washington, DC: U.S. Department of Education, National Center for Education Statistics.

Finn, J. D., Gerber, S. B., & Boyd-Zaharias, J. (2005). Small classes in the early grades, academic achievement, and graduating from high school. *Journal of Educational Psychology, 97*, 214–223.

Fiore, E. (2003). Multiple births and the rising rate of preterm delivery. *Contemporary Ob/ Gyn, 48*, 67–77.

First Call: BC Child and Youth Advocacy Coalition. (2011). *B.C. Campaign 2000: 2011 child poverty report card.* Vancouver, BC.

Fischer, K. W. (2008). Dynamic cycles of cognitive and brain development: Measuring growth in mind, brain, and education. In A. M. Battro, K. W. Fischer, and P. Léna (Eds.), *The educated brain* (pp. 127–150). Cambridge U.K.: Cambridge University Press.

Fischer, K. W., & Pruyne, E. (2003). Reflective thinking in adulthood. In J. Demick & C. Andreoletti (Eds.), *Handbook of adult development* (pp. 169–198). New York: Plenum Press.

Fischer, K. W., & Rose, S. P. (1995, Fall). Concurrent cycles in the dynamic development of brain and behavior. *SRCD Newsletter,* pp. 3–4, 15–16.

Fivush, R., & Nelson, K. (2004). Culture and language in the emergence of autobiographical memory. *Psychological Science, 15*, 573–577.

Flavell, J. H. (2000). Development of children's knowledge about the mental world. *International Journal of Behavioral Development, 24*(1), 15–23.

Flavell, J. H., Miller, P. H., & Miller, S. A. (2002). *Cognitive development.* Englewood Cliffs, NJ: Prentice Hall.

Flaxman, S. M., & Sherman, P. W. (2008). Morning sickness: Adaptive cause or nonadaptive consequence of embryo viability? *The American Naturalist, 172*(1), 54–62.

Fletcher, J. (2012). Positive parenting, not physical punishment. *Canadian Medical Association Journal, 184*, 1339. doi:10.1503/cmaj.121070

Fleury, D. (2008, May). Low-income children. *Perspectives on Labour and Income, 9*(5), 14–23. Retrieved from http://www.statcan.gc.ca/pub/75-001-x/2008105/pdf/10578-eng.pdf

Flook, L., & Fuligni, A. (2008). Family and school spillover in adolescents' daily lives. *Child Development, 79*(3), 776–787.

Flook, L., Repetti, R. L., & Ullman, J. B. (2005). Classroom social experiences as predictors of academic performance. *Developmental Psychology, 41*, 319–327.

Flores, G., Fuentes-Afflick, E., Barbot, O., Carter-Pokras, O., Claudio, L., Lara, M., et al. (2002). The health of Latino children: Urgent priorities, unanswered questions, and a research agenda. *Journal of the American Medical Association, 288*, 82–90.

Flores, G., Olson, L., & Tomany-Korman, S. C. (2005). Racial and ethnic disparities in early childhood health and health care. *Pediatrics, 115*, e183–e193.

Flouri, E., and Buchanan, A. (2003). What predicts fathers' involvement with their children? A prospective study of intact families. *British Journal of Developmental Psychology, 21*, 81–98.

Flouris, A. D., Canham, C. H., Faught, B., & Klentrou, P. (2007). Prevalence of cardiovascular disease risk in Ontario adolescents. *Archives of Disease in Childhood, 92*, 521–523.

Flynn, J. R. (1984). The mean IQ of Americans: Massive gains 1932 to 1978. *Psychological Bulletin, 95*, 29–51.

Flynn, J. R. (1987). Massive IQ gains in 14 nations: What IQ tests really measure. *Psychological Bulletin, 101*, 171–191.

Fomby, P., & Cherlin, A. J. (2007). Family instability and child well-being. *American Sociological Review, 72*(2), 181–204.

Fontanel, B., & d'Harcourt, C. (1997). *Babies, history, art and folklore.* New York: Abrams.

Food Banks Canada. (2011). *In brief.* Retrieved from http://www.foodbankscanada.ca/Learn-About-Hunger/About-Hunger-in-Canada.aspx

Forhan, S. E., Gottlieb, S. L., Sternberg, M. R., Xu, F., Datta, D., Berman, S., & Markowitz, L. E. (2008, March 13). *Prevalence of sexually transmitted infections and bacterial vaginosis among female adolescents in the United States: Data from the National Health and Nutritional Examination Survey (NHANES) 2003–2004.* Oral presentation at the meeting of the 2008 National STD Prevention Conference, Chicago.

Fortune, T. W., & Menke, M. R. (2010). *CARLA publication series: Struggling learners and language immersion education: Research-based, practitioner-informed responses to educators' top questions.* Minneapolis, MN: University of Minnesota, The Centre for Advanced Research on Language Acquisition.

Foster, G. D., Sherman, S., Borradaile, K. E., Grundy, K. M., Vander Veur, S. S., Nachmani, J., et al. (2008). A policy based school intervention to prevent obesity and overweight. *Pediatrics, 121*, e794–e802.

Fox, M. K., Pac, S., Devaney, B., & Jankowski, L. (2004). Feeding Infants and Toddlers Study: What foods are infants and toddlers eating? *Journal of the American Dietetic Association, 104*, 22–30.

Fox, N. A., Hane, A. A., & Pine, D. S. (2007). Plasticity for affective neurocircuitry: How the environment affects gene expression. *Current Directions in Psychological Science, 16*(1), 1–5.

Fox, N. A., Kimmerly, N. L., & Schafer, W. D. (1991). Attachment to mother/attachment to father: A meta-analysis. *Child Development, 62*, 210–225.

Fraga, M., F., Ballestar, E., Paz, M. F., Ropero, S., Setien, F., Ballestar, M. L., et al. (2005). Epigenetic differences arise during the lifetime of monozygotic twins. *Proceedings of the National Academy of Sciences, USA, 102*, 10604–10609.

Franic, S., Middledorp, C. M., Dolan, C. V., Ligthart, L., & Boomsma, D. I. (2010). Childhood and adolescent anxiety and depression: Beyond heritability. *Journal of the American Academy of Child & Adolescent Psychiatry, 49*(8), 820–829.

Frankenburg, W. K., Dodds, J., Archer, P., Shapiro, H., & Bresnick, B. (1990). The Denver II: A major revision and restandardization of the Denver Developmental Screening Test. *Pediatrics, 89*, 91–97.

Frankman, E. A., Wang L., Bunker, C. H., & Lowder, J. L. (2009). Episiotomy in the United States: Has anything changed? *American Journal of Obstetrics & Gynecology, 200*, 573.e1–573.e7. doi:10.1016/j.ajog.2008.11.022

Frans, E. M., Sandin, S., Reichenberg, A., Lichtenstein, P., Långström, N., & Hultman, C. M. (2008). Advancing paternal age and bipolar disorder. *Archives of General Psychiatry, 65,* 1034–1040.

Frappier, Y. J., Leonard, K. A., Sacks, D., & Canadian Paediatric Society, Adolescent Health Committee. (2005). Youth and firearms in Canada. *Paediatrics & Child Health, 10,* 473–477.

Fraser, A. M., Brockert, J. F., & Ward, R. H. (1995). Association of young maternal age with adverse reproductive outcomes. *New England Journal of Medicine, 332*(17), 1113–1117.

Fredricks, J. A., & Eccles, J. S. (2002). Children's competence and value beliefs from childhood through adolescence: Growth trajectories in two male-sex-typed domains. *Developmental Psychology, 38,* 519–533.

Freeman, C. (2004). *Trends in educational equity of girls & women: 2004* (NCES 2005016). Washington, DC: National Center for Education Statistics.

Freeman, J. G., King, M., & Pickett, W., with Craig, W., Elgar, F., Janssen, I., & Klinger, D. (2011). *The health of Canada's young people: A mental health focus.* Ottawa, ON: Public Health Agency of Canada.

Frempong, G., & Willms, J. D. (2002). Can school quality compensate for socioeconomic disadvantage? In J. D. Willms (Ed.), *Vulnerable Children* (pp. 277–304). Edmonton, AB: University of Alberta Press.

French, C. D., French, F., & Rutherford, P. J. (1999). Applications of the WPPSI–R with a Canadian sample. *Canadian Journal of School Psychology, 15,* 1–10.

French, D. C., Chen, X., Chung, J., Li, M., Chen, H., & Li, D. (2011). Four children and one toy: Chinese and Canadian children faced with potential conflict over a limited resource. *Child Development, 82,* 830–841. doi:10.1111/j.1467-8624.2011.01581.x

French, R. M., Mareschal, D., Mermillod, M., Quinn, P. C. (2004). The role of bottom-up processing in perceptual categorization by 3- to 4- month old infants: Simulations and data. *Journal of Experimental Psychology: General, 133*(3), 382–397.

French, S. A., Story, M., & Jeffery, R. W. (2001). Environmental influences on eating and physical activity. *Annual Review of Public Health, 22,* 309–335.

Freud, S. (1953). *A general introduction to psychoanalysis* (J. Rivière, Trans.) New York: Perma-books. (Original work published 1935)

Freud, S. (1964a). New introductory lectures on psychoanalysis. In J. Strachey (Ed. & Trans.), *The standard edition of the complete psychological works of Sigmund Freud* (Vol. 22). London: Hogarth. (Original work published 1933)

Freud, S. (1964b). An outline of psychoanalysis. In J. Strachey (Ed. & Trans.), *The standard edition of the complete psychological works of Sigmund Freud* (Vol. 23). London: Hogarth. (Original work published 1940)

Frey, K. S., Hirschstein, M. K., Snell, J. L., Edstrom, L.V.S., MacKenzie, E. P., & Broderick, C. J. (2005). Reducing playground bullying and supporting beliefs: An experimental trial of the Steps to Respect program. *Developmental Psychology, 41,* 479–491.

Frideres, J. S. (1998). *Aboriginal peoples in Canada: Contemporary conflicts.* Scarborough, ON: Prentice-Hall Allyn and Bacon Canada.

Friendly, M., & Prentice, S. (2009). *About Canada: Childcare.* Winnipeg, MB: Fernwood Publishing.

Friesen, J. W. (1995). Multicultural education as a component of formal socialization. In K. Covell (Ed.), *Readings in child development: A Canadian perspective* (pp. 172–184). Toronto: Nelson Canada.

Friesen, M. D., Woodward, L. J., Horwood, L. J., & Fergusson, D. M. (2010). Childhood exposure to sexual abuse and partner outcomes at age 30. *Psychological Medicine, 40*(4), 679–688.

Fryberg, S. A., Troop-Gordon, W., D'Arrisso, A., Flores, H., Ponizovskiy, V., Ranney, J. D., . . . & Burack, J. A. (2013). Cultural mismatch and the education of Aboriginal youths: The interplay of cultural identities and teacher ratings. *Developmental Psychology, 49,* 72–79. doi:10.1037/a0029056

Fuligni, A. J., Eccles, J. S., Barber, B. L., & Clements, P. (2001). Early adolescent peer orientation and adjustment during high school. *Developmental Psychology, 37*(1), 28–36.

Fuller-Thomson, E. (2005). Canadian First Nations grandparents raising grandchildren: A portrait in resilience. *International Journal of Aging and Human Development, 60,* 331–342.

Furman, L. (2005). What is attention-deficit hyperactivity disorder (ADHD)? *Journal of Child Neurology, 20,* 994–1003.

Furman, W., & Buhrmester, D. (1985). Children's perceptions of the personal relationships in their social networks. *Developmental Psychology, 21,* 1016–1024.

Furman, W., & Wehner, E. A. (1997). Adolescent romantic relationships: A developmental perspective. In S. Shulman & A. Collins (Eds.), Romantic relationships in adolescence: Developmental perspectives. *New Directions for Child and Adolescent Development, 78,* 21–36.

Furstenberg, Jr., F. F., Rumbaut, R. G., & Settersein, Jr., R. A. (2005). On the frontier of adulthood: Emerging themes and new directions. In R. A. Settersten Jr., F. F. Furstenberg Jr., & R. G. Rumbaut (Eds.), *On the frontier of adulthood: Theory, research,* and public policy (pp. 3–25). Chicago: University of Chicago Press.

Fussell, E., & Furstenberg, F. (2005). The transition to adulthood during the twentieth century: Race, nativity, and gender. In R. A. Settersten Jr., F. F. Furstenberg Jr., & R. G. Rumbaut (Eds.), *On the frontier of adulthood: Theory, research, and public policy* (pp. 29–75). Chicago: University of Chicago Press.

Gabbard, C. P. (1996). *Lifelong motor development* (2nd ed.). Madison, WI: Brown and Benchmark.

Gabhainn, S., & François, Y. (2000). Substance use. In C. Currie, K. Hurrelmann, W. Settertobulte, R. Smith, & J. Todd (Eds.), *Health behaviour in schoolaged children: A WHO cross-national study (HBSC) international report* (pp. 97–114) [WHO Policy Series: Healthy Policy for Children and Adolescents, Series No. 1]. Copenhagen, Denmark: World Health Organization Regional Office for Europe.

Gagne, J. R., & Saudino, K. J. (2010). Wait for it! A twin study of inhibitory control in early childhood. *Behavioral Genetics, 40*(3), 327–337.

Gagné, M.-H., Tourigny, M., Joly, J., & Pouliot-Lapointe, J. (2007). Predictors of adult attitudes toward corporal punishment of children. *Journal of Interpersonal Violence, 22,* 1285–1304. doi:10.1177/0886260507304550

Galland, B. C., Taylor, B. J., Elder, D. E., & Herbison, P. (2012). Normal sleep patterns in infants and children: A systematic review of observational studies. *Sleep Medicine Reviews, 16,* 213–222. doi:10.1016/j.smrv.2011.06.001

Ganger, J. & Brent, M. R. (2004). Reexamining the vocabulary spurt. *Developmental Psychology, 40,* 621–632.

Gannon, P. J., Holloway, R. L., Broadfield, D. C., & Braun, A. R. (1998). Asymmetry of chimpanzee planum temporale: Human-like pattern of Wernicke's brain language homlog. *Science, 279,* 22–222.

Gardiner, H. W., & Kozmitzki, C. (2005). *Lives across cultures: Cross-cultural human development.* Boston: Allyn & Bacon.

Gardiner, H. W., Mutter, J. D., & Kosmitzki, C. (1998). *Lives across cultures: Cross-cultural human development.* Boston: Allyn and Bacon.

Gardner, H. (1993). *Frames of mind: The theory of multiple intelligences.* New York: Basic. (Original work published 1983)

Gardner, M., & Steinberg, L. (2005). Peer influence on risk taking, risk preference, and risky decision making in adolescence and adulthood: An experimental study. *Developmental Psychology, 41,* 625–635.

Garmon, L. C., Basinger, K. S., Gregg, V. R., & Gibbs, J. C. (1996). Gender differences in stage and expression of moral judgment. *Merrill-Palmer Quarterly, 42*, 418–437.

Garner, P. W., & Estep, K. M. (2001). Emotional competence, emotional socialization, and young children's peer-related social competence. *Early Education & Development, 12*(1), 29–48.

Garner, R., & Kohen, D. (2008). Changes in the prevalence of asthma among Canadian children. *Health Reports, 19*(2), 1–6 (Statistics Canada, Catalogue no. 82-003).

Garnett, B., & Ungerleider, C. (2008). *An introductory look at the academic trajectories of ESL students.* Working Paper Series No. 08 – 02. Vancouver, BC: Metropolis British Columbia Centre of Excellence for Research on Immigration and Diversity. Retrieved from mbc.metropolis.net/assets/uploads/files/wp/2008/WP08-02.pdf

Garriguet, D. (2006). *Nutrition: Findings from the Canadian Community Health Survey - Overview of Canadians' eating habits 2004* (Catalogue no. 82-620-MIE). Ottawa, ON: Statistics Canada.

Garriguet, D. (2009). Diet quality in Canada. *Health Reports, 20*, 41–52.

Gartrell, N., Deck, A., Rodas, C., Peyser, H., & Banks, A. (2005). The National Lesbian Family Study: Interviews with the 10-year-old children. *American Journal of Orthopsychiatry, 75*, 518–524.

Gathercole, S. E., & Alloway, T. P. (2008). *Working memory & learning: A practical guide for teachers.* London, UK: SAGE Publications Ltd.

Ge, X., Brody, G. H., Conger, R. D., Simons, R. L., & Murry, V. (2002). Contextual amplification of pubertal transitional effect on African American children's problem behaviors. *Developmental Psychology, 38*, 42–54.

Ge, X., Conger, R. D., & Elder, G. H. (2001a). Pubertal transition, stressful life events, and the emergence of gender differences in adolescent depressive symptoms. *Developmental Psychology, 37*(3), 404–417.

Ge, X., Conger, R. D., & Elder, G. H. (2001b). The relation between puberty and psychological distress in adolescent boys. *Journal of Research on Adolescence, 11*, 49–70.

Geary, D. C. (2006). Development of mathematical understanding. In W. Damon (Ed.) & D. Kuhl & R. S. Siegler (Vol. Eds.), *Handbook of child psychology* (6th ed.): *Cognition, perception, and language*, Vol 2. (pp. 777–810). New York: John Wiley & Sons.

Geerts, W. K., Einspieler, C., Dibiasi, J., Garzarolli, B., & Bos, A. F. (2003). Development of manipulative hand movements during the second year of life. *Early Human Development, 75*, 91–103. doi:10.1016/j.earlhumdev.2003.09.006

Gélis, J. (1991). *History of childbirth: Fertility, pregnancy, and birth in early modern Europe.* Boston: Northeastern University Press.

Gelman, R. (2006). Young natural-number mathematicians. *Current Directions in Psychological Science, 15*, 193–197.

Genesee, F. (1991). Second language learning in school settings: Lessons from immersion. In A. G. Reynolds (Ed.), *Bilingualism, multiculturalism, and second language learning: The McGill conference in honour of Wallace E. Lambert* (pp. 183–201). Hillsdale, NJ: Lawrence Erlbaum Associates.

Genesee, F. (2007). French immersion and at-risk students : A review of research evidence. *Canadian Modern Language Review 63*, 655–688.

Genesee, F., Nicoladis, E., & Paradis, J. (1995). Language differentiation in early bilingual development. *Journal of Child Language, 22*, 611–631.

George, C., Kaplan, N., & Main, M. (1985). *The Berkeley Adult Attachment Interview* [Unpublished protocol]. Department of Psychology, University of California, Berkeley, CA.

Gerlach, A. (2008). "Circle of caring": A First Nations worldview of child rearing. *Canadian Journal of Occupational Therapy, 75,* 18–25.

Gershoff, E. (2002). Corporal punishment by parents and associated child behaviors and experiences: A meta-analytic and theoretical review. *Psychological Bulletin, 128,* 539–579.

Gershoff, E. T., Aber, J. L., Raver, C. C., & Lennon, M. C. (2007). Income is not enough: Incorporating material hardship into models of income associations with parenting and child development. *Child Development, 78,* 70–95.

Gettler, L. T., McDade, T. W., Feranil, A. B., & Kuzawa, C. W. (2011). Longitudinal evidence that fatherhood decreases testosterone in human males. *Proceedings of the National Academy of Sciences, 108*(39), 1–6.

Getzels, J. W., & Jackson, P. W. (1962). *Creativity and intelligence: Explorations with gifted students.* New York: Wiley.

Getzels, J. W., & Jackson, P. W. (1963). The highly intelligent and the highly creative adolescent: A summary of some research findings. In C. W. Taylor & F. Baron (Eds.), *Scientific creativity: Its recognition and development* (pp. 161–172). New York: Wiley.

Gibbs, J. C. (1995). The cognitive developmental perspective. In W. M. Kurtines & J. L. Gewirtz (Eds.), *Moral development: An introduction.* Boston: Allyn & Bacon.

Gibson, E. J. (1969). *Principles of perceptual learning and development.* New York: Appleton-Century-Crofts.

Gibson, E. J., & Pick, A. D. (2000). *An ecological approach to perceptual learning and development.* New York: Oxford University Press.

Gibson, J. J. (1979). *The ecological approach to visual perception.* Boston: Houghton Mifflin.

Gilbert, S. (1998, May 19). Benefits of assistant for childbirth go far beyond the birthing room. *New York Times,* p. F7.

Gilligan, C. (1982). *In a different voice: Psychological theory and women's development.* Cambridge, MA: Harvard University Press.

Gilligan, C. (1987a). Adolescent development reconsidered. In E. E. Irwin (Ed.), *Adolescent social behavior and health* (pp. 63–92). San Francisco: Jossey-Bass.

Gilligan, C. (1987b). Moral orientation and moral development. In E. F. Kittay & D. T. Meyers (Eds.), *Women and moral theory* (pp. 19–33). Totowa, NJ: Rowman & Littlefield.

Gillis, J. (1992). Views of Native parents about early childhood education. *Canadian Journal of Native Education, 19,* 73–81.

Gilmore, J., Lin, W., Prastawa, M. W., Looney, C. B., Vetsa, Y. S. K., Knickmeyer, R. C., et al. (2007). Regional gray matter growth, sexual dimorphism, and cerebral asymmetry in the neonatal brain. *Journal of Neuroscience, 27*(6), 1255–1260.

Ginsburg, H., & Opper, S. (1979). *Piaget's theory of intellectual development* (2nd ed.). Englewood Cliffs, NJ: Prentice Hall.

Giordano, P. C., Cernkovich, S. A., & DeMaris, A. (1993). The family and peer relations of black adolescents. *Journal of Marriage and the Family, 55,* 277–287.

Giordano, P. C., Longmore, M. A., & Manning, W. D. (2006). Gender and the meanings of adolescent romantic relationships: A focus on boys. *American Sociological Review, 71*(2), 260–287.

Glaser, D. (2000). Child abuse and neglect and the brain: A review. *Journal of Child Psychiatry, 41*(1), 97–116.

Glenn, N., & Marquardt, E. (2001). *Hooking up, hanging out, and hoping for Mr. Right: College women on dating and mating today.* New York: Institute for American Values.

Goetz, P. (2003). The effects of bilingualism on theory of mind development. *Bilingualism: Language and Cognition, 6,* 1–15.

Goldberg, W. A. & Keller, M. A. (2007). Co-sleeping during infancy and early childhood: Key findings and future directions. *Infant and Child Development, 16,* 457–469.

Goldenberg, R. L., Kirby, R., & Culhane, J. F. (2004). Stillbirth: A review. *Journal of Maternal-Fetal & Neonatal Medicine, 16*(2), 79–94.

Goldenberg, R. L., & Rouse, D. J. (1998). Prevention of premature labor. *New England Journal of Medicine, 339,* 313–320.

Goldin-Meadow, S. (2007). Pointing sets the stage for learning language—and creating language. *Child Development, 78*(3), 741–745.

Goldman, L., Falk, H., Landrigan, P. J., Balk, S. J., Reigart, J. R., & Etzel, R. A. (2004). Environmental pediatrics and its impact on government health policy. *Pediatrics, 113,* 1146–1157.

Goldstein, M., King, A., & West, M. (2003). Social interaction shapes babbling: Testing parallels between birdsong and speech. *Proceedings of the National Academy of Sciences, USA, 100,* 8030–8035.

Goleman, D. (1995, July 1). A genetic clue to bed-wetting is located: Researchers say discovery shows the problem is not emotions! *New York Times,* p. 8.

Goler, N. C., Armstrong, M. A., Taillac, C. J., & Osejo, V. M. (2008). Substance abuse treatment linked with prenatal visits improves perinatal outcomes: A new standard. *Journal of Perinatology, 28,* 597–603.

Golombok, S., Rust, J., Zervoulis, K., Croudace, T., Golding, J., & Hines, M. (2008). Developmental trajectories of sex-typed behaviors in boys and girls: A longitudinal general population study of children aged 2.5–8 years. *Child Development, 79,* 1583–1593.

Golub, M., Collman, G., Foster, P., Kimmel, C., Rajpert-De Meyts, E., Reiter, E., et al. (2008). Public health implications of altered puberty timing. *Pediatrics, 121,* S218–S230.

Göncü, A., Mistry, J., & Mosier, C. (2000). Cultural variations in the play of toddlers. *International Journal of Behavioral Development, 24*(3), 321–329.

Gootman, E. (2007, January 22). Taking middle schoolers out of the middle. *New York Times,* p. A1.

Gordon, M., & Green, J. (2008). Roots of Empathy: Changing the world, child by child. *Education Canada, 48*(2), 34–36.

Gordon, M., & Letchford, D. (2009). Program integrity, controlled growth spell success for Roots of Empathy. *Education Canada, 49*(5), 52–56.

Gornick, J. C., & Jäntti, M. (2012). Child poverty in high- and middle-income countries: Selected findings from LIS. *Child Poverty Insights.* Retrieved from https://sites.google.com/site/childpovertyinsights/

Gosden, R. G., & Feinberg, A. P. (2007). Genetics and epigenetics—nature's pen-and-pencil set. *New England Journal of Medicine, 356,* 731–733.

Gosselin, A., Paquette, G., & DeGuise, J. (1997). Violence on Canadian television and some of its cognitive effects. *Canadian Journal of Communication, 22,* 143–160.

Gottfried, A., E., Fleming, J. S., & Gottfried, A. W. (1998). Role of cognitively stimulating home environment in children's academic intrinsic motivation: A longitudinal study. *Child Development, 69,* 1448–1460.

Gottfried, A. E., & Gottfried, A. W. (2008) The upside of maternal and dual-earner employment: A focus on positive family adaptations, home environments, and child development in the Fullerton Longitudinal Study. In A. Marcus-Newhall, D. F. Halpern, & S. J. Tan (Eds.), *The changing realities of work and family: A multidisciplinary approach.* Wiley-Blackwell, Oxford, UK. doi:10.1002/9781444305272.ch2

Gottfried, A. W., Cook, C. R., Gottfried, A. E., & Morris, P. E. (2005). Educational characteristics of adolescents with gifted academic intrinsic motivation: A longitudinal investigation from school entry through early adulthood. *Gifted Child Quarterly, 49*(2), 172–186.

Gottlieb, A. (2000). Luring your child into this life: A Beng path for infant care. In J. DeLoache & A. Gottlieb (Eds.), *A world of babies: Imagined childcare guides for seven societies* (pp. 55–89). New York: Cambridge University Press.

Gottlieb, B. H., Sill, E., & Newby-Clark, I. R. (2007). Types and precipitants of growth and decline in emerging adulthood. *Journal of Adolescent Research, 22,* 132–155. doi: 10.1177/0743558406298201

Gough, P., Trocmé, N., Brown, I., Knoke, D., & Blackstock, C. (2005). *Pathways to overrepresentation of Aboriginal children in care.* CECW Information Sheet #23E. Toronto, ON, Canada: University of Toronto. Retrieved from http://www.cecw-cepb.ca/publications/424

Government of Canada. (2010, September 23). Order Adding a Toxic Substance to Schedule 1 to the Canadian Environmental Protection Act, 1999. *Canada Gazette, 144*(21). Retrieved from http://www.gazette.gc.ca/rp-pr/p2/2010/2010-10-13/html/sor-dors194-eng.html#tphp

Government of Ontario. (2010/2011). *The full-day early learning kindergarten program: Draft version.* Toronto, ON. Retrieved from http://www.edu.gov.on.ca/eng/curriculum/elementary/kindergarten_english_june3.pdf

Graber, J. A., Brooks-Gunn, J., & Warren, M. P. (2006), Pubertal effects on adjustment in girls: Moving from demonstrating effects to identifying pathways. *Journal of Youth and Adolescence, 35,* 391–401.

Graber, J. A., Lewinsohn, P. M., Seeley, J. R., & Brooks-Gunn, J. (1997). Is psychopathology associated with the timing of pubertal development? *Journal of the American Academy of Child and Adolescent Psychiatry, 36,* 1768–1776.

Grant, A. (1996). *No end of grief: Indian residential schools in Canada.* Winnipeg, MB: Pemmican Publications, Inc.

Grantham-McGregor, S., Powell, C., Walker, S., Chang, S., & Fletcher, P. (1994). The long-term follow-up of severely malnourished children who participated in an intervention program. *Child Development, 65,* 428–439.

Gray, J. R., & Thompson, P. M. (2004). Neurobiology of intelligence: Science and ethics. *Neuroscience, 5,* 471–492.

Gray, M. R., & Steinberg, L. (1999). Unpacking authoritative parenting: Reassessing a multidimensional construct. *Journal of Marriage and the Family, 61,* 574–587.

Gray, P. B., Yang, C. J., & Pope Jr., H .G. (2006). Fathers have lower salivary testosterone levels than unmarried men and married on-fathers in Beijing, China. *Proceedings of the Royal Society of Biological Sciences, 273*(1584), 333–339.

Greaves, L., Poole, N., Okoli, C. T. C., Hemsing, N., Qu, A., Bialystok, L., & O'Leary, R. (2011). *Expecting to quit: A best practices review of smoking cessation interventions for pregnant and post-partum women* (2nd ed.). Vancouver, BC: British Columbia Centre of Excellence for Women's Health.

Greene, M. F. (2002). Outcomes of very low birth weight in young adults. *New England Journal of Medicine, 346*(3), 146–148.

Greenfield, P. (2009). Technology and informal education: What is taught, what is learned. *Science, 323,* 69–71.

Grenier, D., & Leduc, D. (2008). *Well beings: A guide to health in child care,* 3rd Edition. Ottawa, ON: Canadian Paediatric Society.

Groce, N. E., & Zola, I. K. (1993). Multiculturalism, chronic illness, and disability. *Pediatrics, 91,* 1048–1055.

Grusec, J. E., & Goodnow, J. J. (1994). Impact of parental discipline methods on the child's internalization of values: A reconceptualization of current points of view. *Developmental Psychology, 30,* 4–19.

Grzywacz, J. G., Almeida, D. M., & McDonald, D. A. (2002). Work-family spillover and daily reports of work and family stress in the adult labor force. *Family Relations, 51*(1), 28–36.

Guendelman, S., Kosa, J. L., Pearl, M., Graham, S., Goodman, J., & Kharrazi, M. (2009). Juggling work and breastfeeding: Effects of maternity leave and occupational characteristics. *Pediatrics, 123,* e38–e46.

Guilford, J. P. (1986). *Creative talents: Their nature, uses and development.* Buffalo, NY: Bearly.

Guilleminault, C., Palombini, L., Pelayo, R., & Chervin, R. D. (2003). Sleeping and sleep terrors in prepubertal children: What triggers them? *Pediatrics, 111,* e17–e25.

Gunderson, L. 2007. *English only instruction and immigrant students in secondary schools: A critical examination.* Mahwah, New Jersey: Lawrence Erlbaum Associates.

Gunderson, L., D'Silva, R., & Murphy Odo, D. (2012). Immigrant students navigating Canadian schools: A longitudinal view. *TESL Canada Journal/Review TESL du Canada, 29,* 142–156.

Gunnoe, M. L., & Hetherington, E. M. (2004). Stepchildren's perceptions of noncustodial mothers and noncustodial fathers: Differences in socioemotional involvement and associations with adolescent adjustment problems. *Journal of Family Psychology, 18,* 555–563.

Guo, G., Roettger, M., & Cai, T. (2008). The integration of genetic propensities into social-control models of delinquency and violence among male youths. *American Sociological Review, 73,* 543–568.

Gutman, L. M., & Eccles, J. S. (2007). Stage-environment fit during adolescence: Trajectories of family relations and adolescent outcomes. *Developmental Psychology, 43,* 522–537.

Guttmann, A., Shipman, S. A., Lam, K., Goodman, D. C., & Stukel, T. A. (2010). Primary Care Physician Supply and Children's Health Care Use, Access, and Outcomes: Findings From Canada. *Pediatrics, 125,* 1119–1126.

Guyer, B., Hoyert, D. L., Martin, J. A., Ventura, S. J., MacDorman, M. F., & Strobino, D. M. (1999). Annual summary of vital statistics—1998. *Pediatrics, 104,* 1229–1246.

Habicht, J., & Martorell, R. (2010). The development and legacy of the INCAP Oriente studies 1969–2009. *The Journal of Nutrition, 140*(2). doi:10.3945/jn.109.114454

Hack, M., Flannery, D. J., Schluchter, M., Cartar, L., Borawski, E., & Klein, N. (2002). Outcomes in young adulthood for very low-birth-weight infants. *New England Journal of Medicine, 346*(3), 149–157.

Hack, M., Youngstrom, E. A., Cartar, L., Schluchter, M., Taylor, H. G., Flannery, D., et al. (2004). Behavioral outcomes and evidence of psychopathology among very low birth weight infants at age 20 years. *Pediatrics, 114,* 932–940.

Hagenauer, M. H., Perryman, J. I., Lee, T. M., & Carskadon, M. A. (2009). Adolescent changes in the homeostatic and circadian regulation of sleep. *Developmental Neuroscience, 31*(4), 276–284.

Haith, M. M. (1986). Sensory and perceptual processes in early infancy. *Journal of Pediatrics, 109*(1), 158–171.

Halbower, A. C., Degaonkar, M., Barker, P. B., Early, C. J., Marcus, C. L., Smith, P. L., et al. (2006) Childhood obstructive sleep apnea associates with neuropsychological deficits and neuronal brain injury. *PLoS Medicine, 3,* e301–e312.

Hall, W. A., Scher, A., Zaidman-Zait, A., Espezel, H., & Warnock, F. (2011). A community-based study of sleep and behaviour problems in 12- to 36-month-old children. *Child: Care, Health and Development, 38,* 379–389. doi:10.1111/j.1365-2214.2011.01252.x

Hallett, D., Chandler, M. J., & Lalonde, C. E. (2007). Aboriginal language knowledge and youth suicide. *Cognitive Development, 22,* 392–399. doi:10.1016/j.cogdev.2007.02.001

Hallfors, D. D. Waller, M. W., Bauer, D., Ford, C. A., & Halpern, C. T. (2005). Which comes first in adolescence—sex and drugs or depression? *American Journal of Preventive Medicine, 29,* 1163–1170.

Halpern, C., Young, M., Waller, M., Martin, S., & Kupper, L. (2003). Prevalence of partner violence in same-sex romantic and sexual relationships in a national sample of adolescents. *Journal of Adolescent Health, 35*(2), 124–131.

Halpern, D. F., Benbow, C. P., Geary, D. C., Gur, R. C., Hyde, J. S., & Gernsbacher, M. A. (2007). The science of sex differences in science and mathematics. *Psychological Science in the Public Interest, 8,* 1–51.

Hamilton, B. E., Miniño, A. M., Martin, J. A., Kochanek, K. D., Strobino, D. M., & Guyer, B. (2007). Annual summary of vital statistics, 2005. *Pediatrics, 119,* 345–360.

Hamilton, L., Cheng, S., & Powell, B. (2007). Adoptive parents, adaptive parents: Evaluating the importance of biological ties for parental involvement. *American Sociological Review, 72,* 95–116.

Hamilton, M. C., Anderson, D., Broaddus, M., & Young, K. (2006). Gender stereotyping and under-representation of female characters in 200 popular children's picture books: A 21st century update. *Sex Roles: A Journal of Research, 55,* 757–765.

Hamlin, J. K., Wynn, K., & Bloom, P. (2007). Social evaluation by preverbal infants. *Nature, 450,* 557–559.

Hammad, T. A., Laughren, T., & Racoosin, J. (2006). Suicidality in pediatric patients treated with antidepressant drugs. *Archives of General Psychiatry, 63,* 332–339.

Hampden-Thompson, G., & Johnston. J. S. (2006). *Variation in the relationship between nonschool factors and student achievement on international assessments* (NCES 2006–014). Washington, DC: U.S. Department of Education, National Center for Education Statistics.

Handmaker, N. S., Rayburn, W. F., Meng, C., Bell, J. B., Rayburn, B. B., & Rappaport, V. J. (2006). Impact of alcohol exposure after pregnancy recognition on ultrasonographic fetal growth measures. *Alcoholism: Clinical and Experimental Research, 30,* 892–898.

Hankin, B. L., & Abramson, L. Y. (2001). Development of gender differences in depression: An elaborated cognitive vulnerability-transactional stress theory. *Psychological Bulletin, 127*(6), 773–796.

Hanley, W. B. (2005). Newborn screening in Canada – Are we out of step? *Paediatrics and Child Health, 10,* 203–207.

Hanney, L., & Kozlowska, K. (2002). Healing traumatized children: Creating illustrated storybooks in family therapy. *Family Process, 41*(1), 37–65.

Hannigan, J. H., & Armant, D. R. (2000). Alcohol in pregnancy and neonatal outcome. *Seminars in Neonatology, 5,* 243–254.

Hansen, D., Lou, H. C., & Olsen, J. (2000). Serious life events and congenital malformations: A national study with complete follow-up. *Lancet, 356,* 875–880.

Hansen, M., Janssen, I., Schiff, A., Zee, P. C., & Dubocovich, M. L. (2005). The impact of school daily schedule on adolescent sleep. *Pediatrics, 115,* 1555–1561.

Hanson, M. D., & Chen, E. (2007). Socioeconomic status and health behaviors in adolescence: A review of the literature. *Journal of Behavioral Medicine, 30*(3), 263–285.

Hara, H. (2002). Justifications for bullying among Japanese school children. *Asian Journal of Social Psychology, 5,* 197–204.

Harder, T., Rodekamp, E., Schellong, K., Dudenhausen, J. W., Plagemann, A. (2007). Birth weight and subsequent risk of type 2 diabetes: A meta-analysis. *American Journal of Epidemiology, 165,* 849–857.

Hardway, C., & Fuligni, A. J. (2006). Dimensions of family connectedness among adolescents with Mexican, Chinese, and European backgrounds. *Developmental Psychology, 42,* 1246–1258.

Hardy, R., Kuh, D., Langenberg, C., &Wadsworth, M. E. (2003). Birth weight, childhood social class, and change in adult blood pressure in the 1946 British birth cohort. *Lancet, 362,* 1178–1183.

Hardy-Brown, K., & Plomin, R. (1985). Infant communicative development: Evidence from adoptive and biological families for genetic and environmental influences on rate differences. *Developmental Psychology, 21,* 378–385.

Hargreaves, A., & Shirley, D. (2011). *The far side of educational reform.* Ottawa, ON: Canadian Teachers' Federation.

Harnishfeger, K. K., & Pope, R. S. (1996). Intending to forget: The development of cognitive inhibition in directed forgetting. *Journal of Experimental Psychology, 62,* 292–315.

Harrist, A. W., & Waugh, R. M. (2002). Dyadic synchrony: Its structure and function in children's development. *Developmental Review, 22,* 555–592.

Harrist, A. W., Zain, A. F., Bates, J. E., Dodge, K. A., & Pettit, G. S. (1997). Subtypes of social withdrawal in early childhood: Sociometric status and social-cognitive differences across four years. *Child Development, 68*, 278–294.

Harter, S. (1993). Developmental changes in self-understanding across the 5 to 7 shift. In A. Sameroff & M. Haith (Eds.), *Reason and responsibility: The passage through childhood* (pp. 207–236). Chicago: University of Chicago Press.

Harter, S. (1996). Developmental changes in self-understanding across the 5 to 7 shift. In J. Sameroff & M. M. Haith (Eds.), *The five to seven year shift: The age of reason and responsibility* (pp. 207–235). Chicago: University of Chicago Press.

Harter, S. (1998). The development of self-representations. In W. Damon (Series Ed.) & N. Eisenberg (Vol. Ed.), *Handbook of child psychology: Vol. 3. Social, emotional, and personality development* (5th ed., pp. 553–617). New York: Wiley.

Harter, S. (2006). The self. In W. Damon & R. M. Lerner (Series Eds.) & N. Eisenberg (Vol. Ed.), *Handbook of child psychology: Vol 3. Social, emotional and personality development* (pp. 505–570). Hoboken, NJ: Wiley.

Hartup, W. W. (1992). Peer relations in early and middle childhood. In V. B. Van Hasselt & M. Hersen (Eds.), *Handbook of social development: A lifespan perspective* (pp. 257–281). New York: Plenum Press.

Hartup, W. W. (1996). The company they keep: Friendships and their developmental significance. *Child Development, 67*, 1–13.

Hartup, W. W., & Stevens, N. (1999). Friendships and adaptation across the life span. *Current Directions in Psychological Science, 8*, 76–79.

Harvard Medical School. (2004, December). Children's fears and anxieties. *Harvard Mental Health Letter, 21*(6), 1–3.

Hauck, F. R., Signore, C., Fein, S. B., & Raju, T. N. K. (2008). Infant sleeping arrangements and practices during the first year of life. *Pediatrics, 122*, S113–S120. doi: 10.1542/peds.2008-1315o

Hay, D. F., Pedersen, J., & Nash, A. (1982). Dyadic interaction in the first year of life. In K. H. Rubin & H. S. Ross (Eds.), *Peer relationships and social skills in children*. New York: Springer.

Hayes, A., & Batshaw, M. L. (1993). Down syndrome. *Pediatric Clinics of North America, 40*, 523–535.

Healey, D. M., Flory, J. D., Miller, C. J., & Halperin, J. M. (2011). Maternal positive parenting style is associated with better functioning in hyperactive/inattentive preschool children. *Infant and Child Development, 20*, 148–161. doi:10.1002/icd.682

Health Canada. (1998a). *Canadian immunization guide* (5th ed.). Ottawa, ON, Author.

Health Canada. (1998b). *For the safety of Canadian children and youth*. Ottawa: Author.

Health Canada. (2000). *Family-centred maternity and newborn care: National guidelines* (4th ed.). Ottawa, ON: Minister of Public Works and Government Services.

Health Canada. (2001). *Aboriginal Head Start in Urban and Northern Communities: Program and participants, 2000*. Ottawa, ON: Author.

Health Canada. (2002). *Congenital anomalies in Canada: A perinatal health report, 2002*. Ottawa, ON: Minister of Public Works and Government Services Canada.

Health Canada. (2003). *Paper on the allergen control activities within the Canadian Food Inspection Agency*. Ottawa, ON: Author. Retrieved from http://www.hc-sc.gc.ca/fn-an/securit/eval/reports-rapports/allergen_paper-evaluation_allergene-01-eng.php

Health Canada. (2007a). *Lead and health* (Catalogue number H128-1/07-496-4E). Ottawa, ON: Author.

Health Canada. (2007b). *Dating violence*. Ottawa, ON. Retrieved from http://www.childtrendsdatabank.org/pdf/66_PDF.pdf

Health Canada. (2010a). *Report on the findings of the oral health component of the Canadian Health Measures Survey 2007-2009*. Ottawa, ON: Author.

Health Canada. (2010b). *The benefits of hand washing*. Ottawa, ON. Retrieved from http://www.hc-sc.gc.ca/hl-vs/iyh-vsv/diseases-maladies/hands-mains-eng.php

Health Canada. (2011a). *A statistical profile on the health of First Nations in Canada: Vital statistics for Atlantic and Western Canada, 2001/2002*. Ottawa, ON. Retrieved from http://www.hc-sc.gc.ca/fniah-spnia/pubs/aborig-autoch/index-eng.php

Health Canada. (2011b). *Nutrition for healthy term infants: Recommendations from birth to six months - 2011 Health Canada Consultation Document*. Retrieved from http://www.hc-sc.gc.ca/fn-an/consult/infant-nourrisson/recommendations/index-eng.php

Health Canada. (2011c). *Eating well with Canada's food guide: A resource for educators and communicators*. Ottawa, ON. Retrieved from http://www.hc-sc.gc.ca/fn-an/food-guide-aliment/index-eng.php

Health Canada. (2011d). *Health Canada statement on fluoride in drinking water*. Retrieved from http://www.hc-sc.gc.ca/ahc-asc/media/ftr-ati/_2011/2011_82-eng.php

Health Canada. (2011e). *Canadian tobacco use monitoring survey (CTUMS) 2010*. Ottawa, ON: Author. Retrieved from http://www.hc-sc.gc.ca/hc-ps/tobac-tabac/research-recherche/stat/ctums-esutc_2010_graph-eng.php

Health Canada. (2012). *Household food insecurity in Canada in 2007-2008: Key statistics and graphics*. Retrieved from http://www.hc-sc.gc.ca/fn-an/surveill/nutrition/commun/insecurit/key-stats-cles-2007-2008-eng.php

HealthlinkBC. (2011). *Time for bed*. Retrieved from http://www.healthlinkbc.ca/healthfiles/pdf/hfile92e.pdf

Healthy Active Living and Sports Medicine Committee, Canadian Paediatric Society. (2012). Healthy active living: Physical activity guidelines for children and adolescents. *Paediatrics and Child Health, 17*, 209–210.

Healthy Child Manitoba. (n.d.). *Manitoba School Nutrition Handbook: Getting Started with Guidelines and Policies*. Retrieved from http://www.gov.mb.ca/healthyschools/foodinschools/resources/sngp.html#.UO361rYvH_E

Heath, N. L., Ross, S., Toste, J. R., Charlebois, A. & Nedecheva, T. (2009). Retrospective analysis of social factors and non suicidal self-injury among young adults. *Canadian Journal of Behavioral Science, 41*, 180–186.

Heffner, L. J. (2004). Advanced maternal age-how old is too old? *New England Journal of Medicine, 351*, 1927–1929.

Helwig, C. C., & Jasiobedzka, U. (2001). The relation between law and morality: Children's reasoning about socially beneficial and unjust laws. *Child Development, 72*, 1382–1393.

Helwig, C. C., Zelazo, P. D., & Wilson, M. (2001). Children's judgments of psychological harm in normal and noncanonical situations. *Child Development, 72*, 66–81.

Henderson, H. A., Marshall, P. J., Fox, N. A., & Rubin, K. H. (2004). Psychophysiological and behavioral evidence for varying forms and functions of nonsocial behavior in preschoolers. *Child Development, 75*, 251–263.

Henrich, C., Ginicola, M., Finn-Stevenson, M., & Zigler, E. (2006). *The school of the 21st century is making a difference: Findings from two evaluations* [Issue brief]. New Haven, CT: Zigler Center in Child Development and Social Policy, Yale University.

Herdt, G., & McClintock, M. (2000). The magical age of 10. *Archives of Sexual Behavior, 29*(6), 587–606.

Heron, M. P, Hoyert, D. L., Murphy, S. L., Xu, J. Q., Kochanek, K. D., & Tejada-Vera, B. (2009). Deaths: Final data for 2006. *National Vital Statistics Reports, 57*(14). Hyattsville, MD: National Center for Health Statistics.

Hertenstein, M. J., & Campos, J. J. (2004). The retention effects of an adult's emotional displays on infant behavior. *Child Development, 75*, 595–613.

Hertzman, C. (2002). *Leave no child behind! Social exclusion and child development*. Toronto: The Laidlaw Foundation.

Hespos, S. J., & Baillargeon, R. (2008). Young infants' actions reveal their developing knowledge of support variables: Converging evidence for violation-of-expectation findings. *Cognition, 107*(1), 304–316.

Hess, S. Y., & King, J. C. (2009). Effects of maternal zinc supplementation on pregnancy and lactation outcomes. *Food and Nutrition Bulletin, 30*(1), 60–78.

Hesso. N. A., & Fuentes, E. (2005). Ethnic differences in neonatal and postneonatal mortality. *Pediatrics, 115*, e44–e51.

Hetherington, E. M. (1987). Family relations six years after divorce. In K. Pasley & M. Ihinger-Tallman (Eds.), *Remarriage and stepparenting today: Research and theory* (pp. 185–205). New York: Guilford Press.

Hetherington, E. M., Bridges, M., & Insabella, G. M. (1998). What matters? What does not? Five perspectives on the association between marital transitions and children's adjustment. *American Psychologist, 53*, 167–184.

Hetherington, E. M., & Kelly, J. (2002). *For better or worse: Divorce reconsidered.* New York: Norton.

Hetherington, E. M., Stanley-Hagan, M., & Anderson, E. (1989). Marital transitions: Child's perspective. *American Psychologist, 44*, 303–312.

Hewlett, B. S. (1987). Intimate fathers: Patterns of paternal holding among Aka pygmies. In M. E. Lamb (Ed.), *The father's role: Cross-cultural perspectives* (pp. 295–330). Hillsdale, NJ: Erlbaum.

Hewlett, B. S. (1992). Husband-wife reciprocity and the father-infant relationship among Aka pygmies. In B. S. Hewlett (Ed.), *Father-child relations: Cultural and biosocial contexts* (pp. 153–176). New York: de Gruyter.

Hewlett, B. S., Lamb, M. E., Shannon, D., Leyendecker, B., & Schölmerich, A. (1998). Culture and early infancy among central African foragers and farmers. *Developmental Psychology, 34*(4), 653–661.

Hickling, A. K., & Wellman, H. M. (2001). The emergence of children's causal explanations and theories: Evidence from everyday conversations. *Developmental Psychology, 37*(5), 668–683.

Hickman, M., Roberts, C., & de Matos, M. G. (2000). Exercise and leisure time activities. In C. Currie, K. Hurrelmann, W. Settertobulte, R. Smith, & J. Todd (Eds.), *Health and health behaviour among young people: A WHO cross-national study (HBSC) international report* (pp. 73–82) [WHO Policy Series: Health Policy for Children and Adolescents, Series No. 1]. Copenhagen, Denmark: World Health Organization Regional Office for Europe.

Hill, A. L., Degan, K. A., Calkins, S. D., & Keane, S. P. (2006). Profiles of externalizing behavior problems for boys and girls across preschool: The roles of emotional regulation and inattention. *Developmental Psychology, 42*, 913–928.

Hill, D. A., Gridley, G., Cnattingius, S., Mellemkjaer, L., Linet, M., Adami, H.-O., et al. (2003). Mortality and cancer incidence among individuals with Down syndrome. *Archives of Internal Medicine, 163*, 705–711.

Hill, J. P. (1987). Research on adolescents and their families: Past and prospect. In E. E. Irwin (Ed.), *New directions in child development: Adolescent social behavior and health* (pp. 13–32). San Francisco: Jossey-Bass.

Hill, N., & Tyson, D. (2009). Parental involvement in middle school: A meta-analytical assessment of the strategies that promote achievement. *Developmental Psychology, 45*(3), 740–763.

Hill, N. E., & Taylor, L. C. (2004). Parental school involvement and children's academic achievement: Pragmatics and issues. *Current Directions in Psychological Science, 13*, 161–168.

Hillier, L. (2002). "It's a catch-22": Same-sex-attracted young people on coming out to parents. In S. S. Feldman & D. A. Rosenthal, (Eds.), Talking sexuality. *New Directions for Child and Adolescent Development, 97*, 75–91.

Hillier, T. A., Pedula, K. L., Vesco, K. K., Schmidt, M. M., Mullen, J. A., LeBlanc, E. S., & Pettitt, D. J. (2008). Excess gestational weight gain: Modifying fetal macrosomia risk associated with maternal glucose. *Obstetrics & Gynecology, 112*, 1007–1014.

Hinckley, A. F., Bachard, A. M., & Reif, J. S. (2005). Late pregnancy exposures to disinfection by-products and growth-related birth outcomes. *Environmental Health Perspectives, 113*, 1808–1813.

Hines, A. M. (1997). Divorce-related transitions, adolescent development, and the role of the parent-child relationship: A review of the literature. *Journal of Marriage and the Family, 59*, 375–388.

Hingson, R. W., Heeren., T., & Winter, M. R. (2006) Age at drinking onset and alcohol dependence: Age at onset, duration, and severity. *Archivers of Pediatrics & Adolescent Medicine, 160*, 739–746.

Hjelmborg, J., Iachine, I., Skytthe, A., Vaupel, J., McGue, M., Koskenvuo, M., et. al., (2006). Genetic influence on human lifespan and longevity. *Human Genetics 199*(3), 312–321.

Hoban, T. F. (2004). Sleep and its disorders in children. *Seminars in Neurology, 24*, 327–340.

Hobson, J. A., & Silvestri, L. (1999, February). Parasomnias. *Harvard Mental Health Letter,* pp. 3–5.

Hodnett, E. D., Gates, S., Hofmeyr, G. J., & Sakala, C. (2005). Continuous support for women during childbirth (Cochrane Review). *The Cochrane Library,* Issue 1, Oxford.

Hoedlmoser, K., Kloesch, G., Wiater, A., & Schabus, M. (2010). Self-reported sleep patterns, sleep problems, and behavioral problems among school children aged 8–11 years. *Somnologie (Berl), 14*(1), 23–31.

Hoek, H. W. (2007). Incidence, prevalence and mortality of anorexia and other eating disorders. *Current Opinion in Psychiatry, 19*(4), 389–394.

Hoff, E. (2003). The specificity of environmental influence: Socioeconomic status affects early vocabulary development via maternal speech. *Child Development, 74*, 1368–1378.

Hoff, E. (2006). How social contexts support and shape language development. *Developmental Review, 26*, 55–88.

Hofferth, S. L., & Jankuniene, Z. (2000, April 2). *Children's after-school activities.* Paper presented at biennial meeting of the Society for Research on Adolescence, Chicago, IL.

Hofman, P. L., Regan, F., Jackson, W. E., Jeferies, C., Knight, D. B., Robinson, E. M., & Cutfield, W. S. (2004). Premature birth and later insulin resistance. *New England Journal of Medicine, 351*, 2179–2186.

Holder, M. D., & Klassen, E. A. (2009). Temperament and happiness in children. *Journal of Happiness Studies, 11*, 419–439. doi:10.1007/s10902-009-9149-2

Hollos, M., & Richards, F. A. (1993). Gender-associated development of formal operations in Nigerian adolescents. *Ethos, 21*, 24–52.

Hornig, M., Briese, T., Buie, T., Bauman, M. L., Lauwer, G., Siemetzki, U., et al. (2008). Lack of association between measles virus vaccine and autism with enteropathy: A case-control study. *PloS One, 3*(9), e3140–e1371.

Horwitz, B. N., Neiderhiser, J. M., Ganiban, J. M., Spotts, E. L., Lichtenstein, P., & Reiss, D. (2010). Genetic and environmental influences on global family conflict. *Journal of Family Psychology, 24*(2), 217–220.

Houlding, C., Schmidt, F., Stern, S. B., Jamieson, J., & Borg, D. (2012). The perceived impact and acceptability of Group Triple P Positive Parenting Program for Aboriginal parents in Canada. *Children and Youth Services Review, 34*, 2287–2294. doi.org/10.1016/j.childyouth.2012.08.001

Howard, K. S., Lefever, J. B., Borkowski, J. G., & Whitman, T. L. (2006). Fathers' influence in the lives of children with adolescent mothers. *Journal of Family Psychology, 20*, 468–476.

Howe, N., Aquan-Assee, J., Bukowski, W. M., Lehoux, P. M., & Rinaldi, C. M. (2001). Siblings as confidants: Emotional understanding, relationship warmth, and sibling self-disclosure. *Social Development, 10,* 439–454.

Howe, R. B. (1995). Evolving policy on children's rights in Canada. In K. Covell (Ed.), *Readings in child development* (pp. 3–27). Toronto: Nelson.

Howell, R. R. (2006). We need expanded newborn screening. *Pediatrics, 117,* 1800–1805.

Howes, C. (1997a). Children's experiences in center-based child care as a function of teacher background and adult:child ratio. *Merrill-Palmer Quarterly, 43,* 404-425.

Howes, C. (1997b). Teacher-sensitivity, children's attachment and play with peers. *Early Education and Development, 8,* 41–49.

Hoyert, D. L., Heron, M. P., Murphy, S. L., & Kung, H. C. (2006). Deaths: Final data for 2003. *National Vital Statistics Reports, 54*(13). Hyattsville, MD: National Center for Health Statistics.

Hoyert, D. L., Mathews, T. J., Menacker, F., Strobino, D. M., & Guyer, B. (2006). Annual summary of vital statistics: 2004. *Pediatrics, 117,* 168–183.

Hudson, J. I., Hiripi, E., Pope, H. G., & Kessler, R. C. (2007). The prevalence and correlates of eating disorders in the National Comorbidity Survey Replication. *Biological Psychiatry, 61,* 348–358. doi:10.1016/j.biopsych.2006.03.040

Huesmann, L. R., & Kirwil, L. (2007). Why observing violence increases the risk of violent behavior in the observer. In D. Flannery, A. Vazinsyi, & I. Waldman (Eds.), *The Cambridge handbook of violent behavior and aggression* (pp. 545–570). Cambridge, U.K.: University Press.

Huesmann, R. (2007). The impact of electronic media violence: Scientific theory and research. *Journal of Adolescent Health, 41,* S6–S13.

Hughes, C., and Cutting, A. L. (1999). Nature, nurture, and individual differences in early understanding of mind. *Psychological Science, 10,* 429–432.

Hughes, I. A. (2004). Female development – All by default? *New England Journal of Medicine, 351,* 748–750.

Huizink, A. C., Mulder, E. J. H., & Buitelaar, J. K. (2004). Prenatal stress and risk for psychopathology: Specific effects or induction of general susceptibility? *Psychological Bulletin 130,* 80–114.

Human Resources and Skills Development Canada. (2012). *Public investments in early childhood education and care in Canada 2010.* Gatineau, QC.

Human Resources and Skills Development Canada. (2013). *Funding: Homelessness projects.* Ottawa, ON: Author. Retrieved from http://www.rhdcc-hrsdc.gc.ca/eng/communities/homelessness/funding/index.shtml

Human Resources and Skills Development Canada. (2013). *Indicators of well-being in Canada: Family life – divorce.* Ottawa, ON. Retrieved from http://www4.hrsdc.gc.ca/.3ndic.1t.4r@-eng.jsp?iid=76#foottext_1

Human Resources Development Canada. (1996). *Growing up in Canada. National longitudinal survey of children and youth.* Ottawa, ON: HRDC.

Humphreys, A. P., & Smith, P. K. (1984). Rough-and-tumble play in preschool, playground. In P. Smith (Ed.), *Play in animals and humans* (pp. 241–270). Oxford: Blackwell.

Hutson, J. (2006). A prenatal perspective on the cost of substance abuse in Canada. *Journal of FAS International, 4*(e9), 1–4.

Huttenlocher, J. (1998). Language input and language growth. *Preventive Medicine, 27,* 195–199.

Huttenlocher, J., Haight, W., Bryk, A., Seltzer, M., & Lyons, T. (1991). Early vocabulary growth: Relation to language input and gender. *Developmental Psychology, 27,* 236–248.

Huttenlocher, J., Vasilyeva, M., Cymerman, E., & Levine, S. (2002). Language input and child syntax. *Cognitive Psychology, 45,* 337–374.

Hwang, S. W., Ueng, J. J. M., Chiu, S., Kiss, A., Tolomiczenko, G., Cowan, L., Levinson, W., & Redelmeier, D. A. (2010). Universal health insurance and health care access for homeless persons. *American Journal of Public Health, 100,* 1454–1461.

Hyde, J., & Mertz, J. (2009). Gender, culture, and mathematics performance. *Proceedings of the National Academy of Sciences, 106*(8), 801–807.

Hyde, J. S. (2005). The gender similarity hypothesis. *American Psychologist, 60,* 581–592. doi:10.1037/0003-066X.60.6.581

Hyde, M. L., & Riko, K. (2000). Design and evaluation issues in Universal Newborn Hearing Screening Programs. *Journal of Speech Language Pathology and Audiology, 24,* 102–118.

Ialongo, N. S., Edelsohn, G., & Kellam, S. G. (2001). A further look at the prognostic power of young children's reports of depressed mood and feelings. *Child Development, 72,* 736–747.

Ibbotson, P., Theakston, A., Lieven, E., & Tomasello, M. (2011). The role of pronoun frames in early comprehension of transitive constructions in English. *Language Learning and Development, 7,* 24–39. doi: 10.1080/15475441003732914

Iervolino, A. C., Hines, M., Golombok, S. E., Rust, J., & Plomin, R. (2005). Genetic and environmental influences on sex-types behavior during the preschool years. *Child Development, 76,* 826–840.

Iervolino, A. C., Pike, A., Manke, B., Reiss, D., Hetherington, E. M., & Plomin, R. (2002). Genetic and environmental influences in adolescent peer socialization: Evidence from two genetically sensitive designs. *Child Development, 73*(1), 162–174.

Iglowstein, I., Jenni, O. G., Molinari, L., & Largo, R. H. (2003). Sleep duration from infancy to adolescence: Reference values and generational trends. *Pediatrics, 111,* 302–307.

Ikonomidou, C., Bittigau, P. Ishimaru, M. J., Wozniak, D. F., Koch, C., Genz, K., . . . & Olney, J. W. (2000). Ethanol-induced apoptotic neurodegeneration and fetal alcohol syndrome. *Science, 287,* 1056–1060.

Imada, T., Zhang, Y., Cheour, M., Taulu, S., Ahonen, A., & Kuhl, P. (2006). Infant speech perception activates Broca's area: A developmental magnetoencephalography study. *NeuroReport, 17,* 957–962.

Infertility Awareness Association of Canada. (2009). *A follow up on IVF Children.* Retrieved from http://www.iaac.ca/en/library/medical/ivf

Ingersoll, E. W., & Thoman, E. B. (1999). Sleep/wake states of preterm infants: Stability, developmental change, diurnal variation, and relation with care giving activity. *Child Development, 70,* 1–10.

Institute of Medicine (U.S.). Committee on Prevention of Obesity in Chldren and Youth. (2005). *Preventing childhood obesity: Health in the balance.* J. P. Koplan, C. T. Liverman, & V. I. Kraak (eds.). Washington, DC: National Academies Press.

International Committee for Monitoring Assisted Reproductive Technologies. (2006, June). *2002 World report on ART.* Report released at meeting of the European Society of Human Reproduction and Embryology, Prague.

Isaacson, W. (2007). *Einstein: His life and universe.* New York: Simon & Schuster.

ISLAT Working Group. (1998). ART into science: Regulation of fertility techniques. *Science, 281,* 651–652.

Izard, C. E., Porges, S. W., Simons, R. F., Haynes, O. M., & Cohen, B. (1991). Infant cardiac activity: Developmental changes and relations with attachment. *Developmental Psychology, 27,* 432–439.

Jackson, L. A., Zhao, Y., Qui, W., Kolenic, A., Fitzerald, H. E., Harold, R., & Von Eye, A. (2008). Cultural differences in morality in the real and virtual worlds: A comparison of Chinese and U.S. youth. *CyberPsychology & Behavior, 11,* 279–286. doi:10.1089/cpb.2007.0098

Jacobson, J. L., & Wille, D. E. (1986). The influence of attachment pattern on developmental changes in peer interaction from the toddler to the preschool period. *Child Development, 57,* 338–347.

Jacobson, K. C., & Crockett, L. J. (2000). Parental monitoring and adolescent adjustment: An ecological perspective. *Journal of Research on Adolescence, 10*(1), 65–97.

Jaffee, S., & Hyde, J. S. (2000). Gender differences in moral orientation: A meta-analysis. *Psychological Bulletin, 126,* 703–726.

Jaffee, S. R., Caspi, A., Moffitt, T. E., Polo-Tomas, M., Price, T. S., & Taylor, A. (2004). The limits of child effects: Evidence for genetically mediated child effects on corporal punishment but not on physical maltreatment. *Developmental Psychology, 40,* 1047–1058.

Jaffee, S. R., & Price, T. S. (2007). Gene–environment correlations: a review of the evidence and implications for prevention of mental illness. *Molecular Psychiatry, 12,* 432–442.

Jamieson, C. E. (2001). Genetic testing for late onset diseases: Current research practices and analysis of policy development. *Health Policy Working Paper Series* (Working Paper 01-02). Ottawa, ON: Health Canada.

Jankowski, J. J., Rose, S. A., & Feldman, J. F. (2001). Modifying the distribution of attention in infants. *Child Development, 72,* 339–351.

Janosz, M., Bisset, S. L., Pagani, L. S., & Levin, B. (2011). Educational systems and school dropout in Canada. In S. Lamb, A. Markussen, R. Teese,, N. Sandberg, & J. Polesel, J. (Eds.), *School dropout and completion: International comparative studies in theory and policy* (pp. 295–320). Dordrecht: Springer. doi: 10.1007/978-90-481-9763-7_1

Jansen, P. W., Saridjan, N. S., Hofman, A., Jaddoe, V. W. V., Verhulst, F. C., & Tiemeier, H. (2011). Does disturbed sleeping precede symptoms of anxiety or depression in toddlers? The Generation R Study. *Psychosomatic Medicine, 73,* 242–249. doi:10.1097/PSY.0b013e31820a4abb

Janson, J. (2010). 65% of Internet users have paid for online content. Pew Research Center. Retrieved from http://www.pewinternet.org/~/media//Files/Reports/2010/PIP-Paying-for-Online-Content_final.pdf

Janssen, I., Boyce, W. F., & Pickett, W. (2012). Screen time and physical violence in 10 to 16-year-old Canadian youth. *International Journal of Public Health, 57,* 325–331. doi:10.1007/s00038-010-0221-9

Janssen, I., Craig, W. M., Boyce, W. F., & Pickett, W. (2004). Associations between overweight and obesity with bullying behaviors in school-aged children. *Pediatrics, 113,* 1187–1194.

Janssen, P. A., Klein, M. C., Harris, S.J., Soolsma, J., & Seymour, L. C. (2000). Single room maternity care and client satisfaction. *Birth, 27,* 235–243.

Janssen, P. A., Saxell, L., Page, L. A., Klein, M. C., Liston, R. M., & Lee, S. K. (2009). Outcomes of planned home birth with registered midwife versus planned hospital birth with midwife or physician. *Canadian Medical Association Journal, 181,* 377–383.

Janssen, S., Murre, J., & Meeter, M. (2007). Reminiscence bump in memory for public events. *European Journal of Cognitive Psychology, 20*(4), 738–764. doi: 10.1080/09541440701554409

Janus, M. (2007). The Early Development Instrument: A tool for monitoring children's development and readiness for school. In M. E. Young with L. M. Richardson, *Early child development: From measurement to action. A priority for growth and equity* (pp. 141–155). Washington, DC: The World Bank.

Janus, M., and D. Offord. (2007). Development and psychometric properties of the Early Development Instrument (EDI): A measure of children's school readiness. *Canadian Journal of Behavioral Science, 39,* 1–22. doi:10.1037/cjbs2007001

Japel, C., Tremblay, R, McDuff, P., & Willms, J. D. (2002). Pre-adolescent girls and the onset of puberty. In J. D. Willms (ed.), *Vulnerable Children* (pp. 305–316). Edmonton, AB: The University of Alberta Press.

Jarvi, S., Jackson, B., Swenson, L., & Crawford, H. (2013). The impact of social contagion on non-suicidal self-injury: A review of the literature. *Archives of Suicide Research, 17,* 1–19. doi: 10.1080/13811118.2013.748404

Jarvis, M. J. (2004). Why people smoke. In J. Britton (Ed.), *ABC of smoking cessation* (pp. 4–6). Malden, MA: Blackwell.

Javaid, M. K., Crozier, S. R., Harvey, N. C., Gale, C. R., Dennison, E. M., Boucher, B. J., et al. (2006). Maternal vitamin D status during pregnancy and childhood bone mass at age 9 years: A longitudinal study. *Lancet, 367*(9504), 36–43.

Jean, M., & Geva, E. (2012). Through the eyes and from the mouths of young heritage-language learners: How children feel and think about their two languages. *TESL Canada Journal/Review TESL du Canada, 29,* 49–80.

Jefferies, A. L., & Canadian Paediatric Society (CPS), Fetus and Newborn Committee. (2011). *Selective serotonin reuptake inhibitors in pregnancy and infant outcomes.* Retrieved from http://www.cps.ca/en/documents/position/SSRI-infant-outcomes.

Jefferies, A. L., Kirpalani, H. M., & Canadian Paediatric Society (CPS), Fetus and Newborn Committee. (2012). *Counselling and management for anticipated extremely preterm birth.* Retrieved from http://www.cps.ca/en

Jenkins, J., & Keating, D. (1999). *Risk and resilience in six- and ten-year-old children.*

Ottawa, ON: Human Resources Development Canada, Applied Research Branch.

Jeynes, W. H., & Littell, S. W. (2000). A meta-analysis of studies examining the effect of whole language instruction on the literacy of low-SES students. *Elementary School Journal, 101*(1), 21–33.

Ji, B. T., Shu, X. O., Linet, M. S., Zheng, W., Wacholder, S., Gao, Y. T., . . . & Jin, F. (1997). Paternal cigarette smoking and the risk of childhood cancer among offspring of nonsmoking mothers. *Journal of the National Cancer Institute, 89*(3), 238–44.

Jipson, J. L., & Gelman, S. A. (2007). Robots and rodents: Children's inferences about living and nonliving kinds. *Child Development, 78*(6), 1675–1688.

Jodl, K. M., Michael, A., Malanchuk, O., Eccles, J. S., & Sameroff, A. (2001). Parents' roles in shaping early adolescents' occupational aspirations. *Child Development 72*(4), 1247–1265.

Johnson, D. J., Jaeger, E., Randolph, S. M., Cauce, A. M., Ward, J., & National Institute of Child Health and Human Development Early Child Care Research Network (2003). Studying the effects of early child care experiences on the development of children of color in the United States: Toward a more inclusive research agenda. *Child Development, 74,* 1227–1244.

Johnson, J. G., Cohen, P., Gould, M. S., Kasen, S., Brown, J., & Brook, J. S. (2002). Childhood adversities, interpersonal difficulties, and risk for suicide attempts during late adolescence and early adulthood. *Archives of General Psychiatry, 59,* 741–749.

Johnson, M. H. (1998). The neural basis of cognitive development. In D. Kuhn & R. S. Siegler (Eds.), *Handbook of child psychology: Vol. 2. Cognition, perception, and language* (5th ed., pp. 1–49). New York: Wiley.

Johnson, N., & Cremo, E. (1995). Socialization and the Native family. In K. Covell (Ed.), *Readings in child development: A Canadian perspective* (pp. 159–171). Toronto: Nelson.

Johnston, J., & Ettema, J. S. (1982). *Positive images: Breaking stereotypes with children's television.* Newbury Park, CA: Sage.

Johnston, L. D., O'Malley, P. M., Bachman, J. G., & Schulenberg, J. E. (2008). *Monitoring the future national results on adolescent drug use: Overview of key findings, 2007* (NIH No. 08-6418). Bethesda, MD: National Institute on Drug Abuse.

Jones, J. (2008). Adoption experiences of women and men and demand for children to adopt by women 18–44 years of age in the United States, 2002. National Center for Health Statistics. *Vital Health Statistics 23*(27).

Jordan, B. (1993). *Birth in four cultures: A cross-cultural investigation of childbirth in Yucatan, Holland, Sweden, and the United States* (4th ed.). Prospect Heights, IL: Waveland Press. (Original work published 1978)

Jordan, N. C., Kaplan, D., Olah, L. N., & Locunia, M. N. (2006). Number sense growth in kindergarten: A longitudinal investigation of children at risk for mathematics difficulties. *Child Development, 77,* 153–175.

Joseph, K. S., Huang, L., Liu, S., Ananth, C. V., Allen, A. C., Sauve, R., & Kramer, M.S. (2007). Reconciling the high rates of preterm and postterm birth in the United States. *Obstetrics & Gynecology, 109,* 813–822.

Joseph, K. S., Liu, S., Rouleau, J., Lisonkova, S., Hutcheon, J. A., Sauve, R., ... & Fetal and Infant Health Study Group of the Canadian Perinatal Surveillance System. (2012). Influence of definition based versus pragmatic birth registration on international comparisons of perinatal and infant mortality: population based retrospective study. *British Medical Journal, 344,* e746. doi: 10.1136/bmj.e746

Joseph, K. S., Marcoux, S., Ohlsson, A., Liu, S., Allen, A. C., Kramer, M. S., & Wen, S. W. (2001). Changes in stillbirth and infant mortality associated with increases in preterm birth among twins. *Pediatrics, 108,* 1055–1061.

Joussemet, M., Vitaro, F., Barker, E., Cote, S., Nagin, D., Zoccolillo, M., & Tremblay, R. (2008). Controlling parenting and physical aggression during elementary school. *Child Development, 79*(2), 411–425.

Juby, H., Marcil-Gratto, N., & Le Bourdais, C., with Huot, P.-M. (2006). A step further in family life: The emergence of the blended family. In A. Bélanger, Y. Carrière, & S. Gilbert (Dir.), *Report on the Demographic Situation in Canada 2000* (pp. 169–203, Catalogue no. 91-209-XIE). Ottawa, ON: Statistics Canada. Retrieved from http://www.statcan.ca

Judge, K. (2009). Inequalities in infant mortality: Patterns, trends, policy responses and emerging issues in Canada, Chile, Sweden and the United Kingdom. *Health Sociology Review, 18,* 12–24.

Juster, F. T., Ono. H., & Stafford, F. P. (2004). *Changing times of American youth: 1981– 2003* [Child Development Supplement]. Ann Arbor, MI: University of Michigan Institute for Social Research.

Kackar, H., Shumow, L., Schmidt, J., & Grzetich, J. (2011). Age and gender differences in adolescents' homework experiences. *Journal of Applied Developmental Psychology.* doi: 10.1016/j.appdev.2010.12.005

Kaczorowski, J., & Lee, L. (2009). Folic acid supplementation. In Public Health Agency of Canada. *What mothers say: The Canadian maternity experiences survey of the Canadian Perinatal Surveillance System* (pp. 57–62). Ottawa, ON: Public Health Agency of Canada.

Kagan, J. (2008). In defense of qualitative changes in development. *Child Development, 79,* 1606–1624.

Kagan, J., & Snidman, N. (2004). *The long shadow of temperament.* Cambridge, MA: Belknap.

Kahlenberg, S. G., & Hein, M. M. (2010). Progression on Nickelodeon? Gender-role stereotypes in toy commercials. *Sex Roles, 62,* 830–847. doi:10.1007/s11199-009-9653-1

Kahlenberg S. M., & Wrangham, R. W. (2010). Sex differences in chimpanzees' use of sticks as play objects resemble those of children. *Current Biology, 20,* R1067–R1068.

Kaiser Family Foundation, Hoff, T., Greene, L., & Davis, J. (2003). *National survey of adolescents and young adults: Sexual health knowledge, attitudes and experiences.* Menlo Park, CA: Henry J. Kaiser Foundation.

Kalil, A., & Ziol-Guest, K. M. (2005). Single mothers' employment dynamics and adolescent well-being. *Child Development, 76,* 196–211.

Kanaya, T., Scullin, M. H., & Ceci, S. J. (2003). The Flynn effect and U.S. policies: The impact of rising IQ scores on American society via mental retardation diagnoses. *American Psychologist, 58,* 778–790.

Kanetsuna, T., & Smith, P. K. (2002). Pupil insight into bullying and coping with bullying: A bi-national study in Japan and England. *Journal of School Violence, 1,* 5–29.

Kang, C., Riazuddin, S., Mundorff, J., Krasnewich, D., Friedman, P., Mullikin, J. C., & Drayna, D. (2010). Mutations in the lysosomal enzyme-targeting pathway and persistent stuttering. *New England Journal of Medicine, 362,* 677–685.

Kanu, Y. (2005). Teachers' perceptions of the integration of Aboriginal culture into the high school curriculum. *Alberta Journal of Educational Research, 51,* 50–68.

Kaplow, J. B., & Widom, C. S. (2007). Age of onset of child maltreatment predicts long-term mental health outcomes. *Journal of Abnormal Psychology, 116,* 176–187.

Kaplowitz, P. B. (2008). The link between body fat and the timing of puberty. *Pediatrics, 121*(2, Suppl. 3), S208–S217.

Karasik, L. B., Tamis-LeMonda, C. S., & Adolph, K. E. (2011). Transition from crawling to walking and infants' actions with objects and people. *Child Development, 82*(4), 1199–1209.

Karremans, J., Verwijmeren, T., Pronk, T., & Reitsma, M. (2009). Interacting with women can impair men's cognitive functioning. *Journal of Experimental Social Psychology, 45*(4), 1041–1044. doi: 10.1016/j.jesp.2009.05.004

Kash, K. M. (2008). School-to-work programs effectiveness. *Online Journal of Workforce Education and Development, 3*(4). Retrieved April 9, 2012, from http://opensiuc.lib.siu.edu/cgi/viewcontent.cgi?article=1060&context=ojwed

Katz, A. N., Blasko, D. G., & Kazmerski, V. A. (2004). Saying what you don't mean: Social influences on sarcastic language processing. *Current Directions in Psychological Science, 13,* 186–189.

Katz, S. J., Conway, C. C., Hammen, C. L., Brennan, P. A., & Najman, J. M. (2011). Childhood social withdrawal, interpersonal impairment, and young adult depression: A mediational model. *Journal of Abnormal Child Psychology, 39*(8), 1227–1238.

Kaufman, A. S., & Kaufman, N. L. (2003). *Kaufman Assessment Battery for Children* (2nd ed.). Circle Pines, MN: American Guidance Service.

Kawabata, Y., & Crick, N. (2008). The roles of cross-racial/ethnic friendships in social adjustment. *Developmental Psychology, 44*(4), 1177–1183.

Kazdin, A. E., & Benjet, C. (2003). Spanking children: Evidence and issues. *Current Directions in Psychological Science, 12,* 99–103.

Keel, P. K., & Klump, K. L. (2003). Are eating disorders culture-bound syndromes? Implications for conceptualizing their etiology. *Psychological Bulletin, 129,* 747–769.

Keenan, K., & Shaw, D. (1997). Developmental and social influences on young girls' early problem behavior. *Psychological Bulletin, 121*(1), 95–113.

Kelley, M. L., Smith, T. S., Green, A. P., Berndt, A. E., & Rogers, M. C. (1998). Importance of fathers' parenting to African-American toddler's social and cognitive development. *Infant Behavior & Development, 21,* 733–744.

Kellman, P. J., & Arterberry, M. E. (1998). *The cradle of knowledge: Development of perception in infancy.* Cambridge, MA: MIT Press.

Kelly, J. B., & Emery, R. E. (2003). Children's adjustment following divorce: Risk and resiliency perspectives. *Family Relations, 52,* 352–362.

Kere, J., Hannula-Jouppi, K., Kaminen-Ahola, N., Taipale, M., Eklund, R., Nopola-Hemmi, J., & Kaariainen, H. (2005, October). *Identification of the dyslexia susceptibility gene for DYX5 on chromosone 3.* Paper presented at the American Society of Human Genetics meeting, Salt Lake City, UT.

Kerns, K. A., Don, A., Mateer, C. A., & Streissguth, A. P. (1997). Cognitive deficits in nonretarded adults with fetal alcohol syndrome. *Journal of Learning Disabilities, 30,* 685–693.

Kerr, D. C. R., Lopez, N. L., Olson, S. L., & Sameroff, A. J. (2004). Parental discipline and externalizing behavior problems in early childhood: The roles of moral regulation and child gender. *Journal of Abnormal Child Psychology, 32*(4), 369–383.

Kharrazi, M., DeLorenze, G. N., Kaufman, F. L., Eskenazi, B., Bernert Jr., J. T., Graham, S., Pearl, M., & Pirkle, J. (2004). Environmental tobacco smoke and pregnancy outcome. *Epidemiology, 15*(6), 660–670.

Khashan, A. S., Abel, K. M., McNamee, R., Pedersen, M. G., Webb, R. T., Baker, P. N., Kenny, L. C., & Mortensen, P. B. (2008). Higher risk of offspring schizophrenia following antenatal maternal exposure to severe adverse life events. *Archives of General Psychiatry, 65*, 146–152.

Kiddoo, D. A. (2012). Toilet training children: when to start and how to train. *Canadian Medical Association Journal, 184*, 511–512. doi:10.1503/cmaj.110830

Killen, J. D., Robinson, T. N., Ammerman, S., Hayward, C., Rogers, J., Stone, C., ... & Schatzberg, A. F. (2004). Randomized clinical trial of the efficacy of bupropion combined with nicotine patch in the treatment of adolescent smokers. *Journal of Consulting and Clinical Psychology, 72*, 729–735.

Kim, J., McHale, S. M., Osgood, D. W., & Crouter, A. C. (2006). Longitudinal course and family correlates of sibling relationships from childhood through adolescence. *Child Development, 77*, 1746–1761.

Kim, Y, S., Koh, Y.-J., & Leventhal, B. (2005). School bullying and suicidal risk in Korean middle school students. *Pediatrics, 115*, 357–363.

Kimball, M. M. (1986). Television and sex-role attitudes. In T. M. Williams (Ed.), *The impact of television: A natural experiment in three communities* (pp. 265–301). Orlando, FL: Academic Press.

Kim-Cohen, J., Moffitt, T. E., Caspi, A., & Taylor, A. (2004). Genetic and environmental processes in young children's resilience and vulnerability to socioeconomic deprivation. *Child Development, 75*, 651–668.

King, A. J. C., Boyce, W. F., & King, M. A. (1999). *Trends in the health of Canadian youth.* Ottawa: Health Canada.

King, K. M., Meehan, B. T., Trim, R. S., & Chassin, L. (2006). Market or mediator? The effects of adolescent substance use on young adult educational attainment. *Addiction, 101*, 1730–1740.

King, W. J., MacKay, M., Sirnick, A., & the Canadian Shaken Baby Study Group. (2003). Shaken baby syndrome in Canada: clinical characteristics and outcomes of hospital cases. *Canadian Medical Association Journal, 168*, 155–159.

Kins, E., & Beyers, W. (2010). Failure to launch, failure to achieve criteria for adulthood? *Journal of Adolescent Research, 25*(5), 1–35. doi:10.1177/0743558410371126

Kinsella, K., & Phillips, P. (2005). Global aging: The challenges of success. *Population Bulletin, No. 1*. Washington, DC: Population Reference Bureau.

Kinsella, K., & Velkoff, V. A. (2001). *An aging world: 2001* [U.S. Census Bureau, Series P95/01–1]. Washington, DC: U.S. Government Printing Office.

Kirby, D., & Laris, B. (2009). Effective curriculum-based sex and STD/HIV education programs for adolescents. *Child Development Perspectives, 3*, 21–29.

Kirmayer, L. J., Brass, G. M., & Tait, C. L. (2000). The mental health of Aboriginal peoples: Transformations of identity and community. *Canadian Journal of Psychiatry, 45*, 607–616.

Kirschner, P. A., & Karpinski, A. C. (2010). Facebook® and academic performance. *Computers in Human Behavior* (0747–5632), *26*(6), 1237–1245.

Kisilevsky, B. S., & Haines, S. M. J. (2010). Exploring the relationship between fetal heart rate and cognition. *Infant and Child Development, 19*, 60–75.

Kisilevsky, B. S., Hains, S. M. J, Brown, C. A., Lee, C. T., Cowper-thwaite, B., Stutzman, S. S., ... & Wang, Z. (2009). Fetal sensitivity to properties of maternal speech and language. *Infant Behavior and Development, 32*, 59–71.

Kisilevsky, B. S., Hains, S. M., Lee, K., Muir, D.W., Xu, F., Fu, G., et al. (1998). The still-face effect in Chinese and Canadian 3- to 6-month-old infants. *Developmental Psychology, 34*, 629–639.

Kisilevsky, B. S., Hains, S. M. J., Lee, K., Xie, X., Huang, H., Ye, H. H., Zhang, K., & Wang, Z. (2003). Effects of experience on fetal voice recognition. *Psychological Science, 14*(3), 220–224.

Klaczynski, P. (2008). There's something about obesity: Culture, contagion, rationality, and children's responses to "drinks" created by obese children. *Journal of Experimental Child Psychology, 99*, 58–74.

Klar, A. J. S. (1996). A single locus, RGHT, specifies preference for hand utilization in humans. *Cold Spring Harbor Symposia on Quantitative Biology 61*, 59–65. Cold Spring Harbor, NY: Cold Spring Harbor Laboratory Press.

Klein, J. D., & the American Academy of Pediatrics Committee on Adolescence. (2005). Adolescent pregnancy: Current trends and issues. *Pediatrics, 116*, 281–286.

Klein, M. C., Liston, R., Fraser, W. D., Baradaran, N. Hearps, S. J. C., Tomkinson, J., ... & The Maternity Care Research Group. (2011). Attitudes of the new generation of Canadian obstetricians: How do they differ from their predecessors? *Birth, 38*, 129–139.

Klein, M. C., Kaczorowski, J., Hall, W. A., et al. (2009). The attitudes of Canadian maternity care practitioners towards labour and birth: Many differences but important similarities. *Journal of Obstetrics and Gynaecology Canada, 31*, 827–840.

Klein-Velderman, M., Bakermans-Kranenburg, M. J., Juffer, F., & van IJzendoorn, M. H. (2006). Effects of attachment-based interventions on maternal sensitivity and infant attachment: Differential susceptibility of highly reactive infants. *Journal of Family Psychology, 20*, 266–274.

Klibanoff, R. S., Levine, S. C., Huttenlocher, J., Vasilyeva, M., & Hedges, L. V. (2006). Preschool children's mathematical knowledge: The effect of teacher "math talk." *Developmental Psychology, 42*, 59–69.

Klonsky, E. D., & Muehlenkamp, J. J. (2007). Self-injury: a research review for the practitioner. *Journal of Clinical Psychology, 63*(11), 1045–1056. doi:10.1002/jclp.20412

Knafo, A., & Plomin, R. (2006). Parental discipline and affection and children's prosocial behavior: Genetic and environmental links. *Journal of Personality and Social Psychology, 90*, 147–164.

Knecht, S., Dräger, B., Deppe, M., Bobe, L., Lohmann, H., Floel, A., ... & Henningsen, H., (2000). Handedness and hemispheric language dominance in healthy humans. *Brain: A Journal of Neurology, 123*(12), 2512–2518.

Knickmeyer, R. C., Gouttard, S., Kang, C, Evans, D., Wilber, K., Smith, J. K., ... & Gilmore, J. H. (2008). A structural MRI study of human brain development from birth to 2 years. *The Journal of Neuroscience, 28*(47), 12176–12182.

Knobloch, H., Stevens, F., & Malone, A. F. (1980). *Manual of developmental diagnosis: The administration and interpretation of the revised Gesell and Amatruda developmental and neurologic examination.* New York: Harper & Row.

Kochanek, K. D., Murphy, S. L., Anderson, R. N., & Scott, C. (2004). Deaths: Final data for 2002. *National Vital Statistics Reports, 53*(5). Hyattsville, MD: National Center for Health Statistics.

Kochanek, K. D., & Smith, B. L. (2004). Deaths: Preliminary data for 2002. *National Vital Statistics Reports, 52*(13). Hyattsville, MD: National Center for Health Statistics.

Kochanska, G. (1993). Toward a synthesis of parental socialization and child temperament in early development of conscience. *Child Development, 64*, 325–437.

Kochanska, G. (1995). Children's temperament, mothers' discipline, and security of attachment: Multiple pathways to emerging internalization. *Child Development, 66*, 597–615.

Kochanska, G. (1997a). Multiple pathways to conscience for children with different temperaments: From toddlerhood to age 5. *Developmental Psychology, 33*, 228–240.

Kochanska, G. (1997b). Mutually responsive orientation between mothers and their young children: Implications for early socialization. *Child Development, 68*, 94–112.

Kochanska, G. (2001). Emotional development in children with different attachment histories: The first three years. *Child Development, 72*, 474–490.

Kochanska, G. (2002). Mutually responsive orientation between mothers and their young children: A context for the early development of conscience. *Current Directions in Psychological Science, 11*, 191–195.

Kochanska, G., & Aksan, N. (1995). Mother-child positive affect, the quality of child compliance to requests and prohibitions, and maternal control as correlates of early internalization. *Child Development, 66*, 236–254.

Kochanska, G., Aksan, N., & Joy, M. E. (2007). Children's fearfulness as a moderator of parenting in early socialization: Two longitudinal studies. *Developmental Psychology, 43*, 222–237.

Kochanska, G., Aksan, N., Knaack, A., & Rhines, H. M. (2004). Maternal parenting and children's conscience: Early security as moderator. *Child Development, 75*, 1229–1242.

Kochanska, G., Askan, N., Prisco, T. R., & Adams, E. E. (2008). Mother-child and father-child mutually responsive orientation in the first two years and children's outcomes at preschool age: Mechanisms of influence. *Child Development, 79*, 30–44.

Kochanska, G., Coy, K. C., & Murray, K. T. (2001). The development of self-regulation in the first four years of life. *Child Development, 72*(4), 1091–1111.

Kochanska, G., Gross, J. N., Lin, M. H., & Nichols, K. E. (2002). Guilt in young children: Development, determinants, and relations with a broader system of standards. *Child Development, 73*(2), 461–482.

Kochanska, G., Tjebkes, T. L., & Forman, D. R. (1998). Children's emerging regulation of conduct: Restraint, compliance, and internalization from infancy to the second year. *Child Development, 69*(5), 1378–1389.

Kogan, M. D., Martin, J. A., Alexander, G. R., Kotelchuck, M., Ventura, S. J., & Frigoletto, F. D. (1998). The changing pattern of prenatal care utilization in the United States, 1981–1995, using different prenatal care indices. *Journal of the American Medical Association, 279*, 1623–1628.

Kogan, M. D., Newacheck, P. W., Honberg, L., & Strickland, B. (2005). Association between underinsurance and access to care among children with special health care needs in the United States. *Pediatrics, 116*, 1162–1169.

Kohen, D., Oliver, L., & Pierre, F. (2009). Examining the effects of schools and neighbourhoods on the outcomes of Kindergarten children in Canada. *International Journal of Speech-Language Pathology, 11*, 404–418. doi:10.1080/17549500903085919

Kohlberg, L. (1966). A cognitive developmental analysis of children's sex role concepts and attitudes. In E. E. Maccoby (Ed.), *The development of sex differences*. Stanford, CA: Stanford University Press.

Kohlberg, L. (1969). Stage and sequence: The cognitive-developmental approach to socialization. In D. A. Goslin (Ed.), *Handbook of socialization theory and research* (pp. 347–480). Chicago: Rand McNally.

Kohlberg, L. (1981). *Essays on moral development*. San Francisco: Harper & Row.

Kohlberg, L., & Ryncarz, R. A. (1990). Beyond justice reasoning: Moral development and consideration of a seventh stage. In C. N. Alexander & E. J. Langer (Eds.), *Higher stages of human development* (pp. 191–207). New York: Oxford University Press.

Kolata, G. (2003, February 18). Using genetic tests, Ashkenazi Jews vanquish a disease. *New York Times,* pp. D1, D6.

Koren, G., Pastuszak, A., & Ito, S. (1998). Drugs in pregnancy. *New England Journal of Medicine, 338*, 1128–1137.

Korner, A. (1996). Reliable individual differences in preterm infants' excitation management. *Child Development, 67*, 1793–1805.

Kosterman, R., Graham, J. W., Hawkins, J. D., Catalano, R. F., & Herrenkohl, T. I. (2001). Childhood risk factors for persistence of violence in the transition to adulthood: A social development perspective. *Violence & Victims. Special Issue: Developmental Perspectives on Violence and Victimization, 16*(4), 355–369.

Kral, M. J. (2012). Postcolonial suicide among Inuit in Arctic Canada. *Culture, Medicine, and Psychiatry, 36*, 306–325.

Krausz, C. (2010). Genetic testing of male infertility. In D. T. Carrell & C. M. Peterson (Eds.), *Reproductive Endocrinology and Infertility* (pp. 431–444). New York: Springer.

Kraut, R., Kiesler, S., Boneva, B., Cummings, J., Helgeson, V., & Crawford, A. (2002). Internet paradox revisited. *Journal of Social Issues, 58*, 49–74.

Kreider, R. M. (2003). Adopted children and stepchildren: 2000. *Census 2000 Special Reports*. Washington, DC: U.S. Bureau of the Census.

Kringelbach, M. L., Lehtonen, A., Squire, S., Harvey, A. G., Craske, M. G., Holliday, I. E., et al. (2008). A specific and rapid neural signature for parental instinct. *PLoS ONE, 3*(2), e1664–e1673.

Krishnamoorthy, J. S., Hart, C., & Jelalian, E. (2006). The epidemic of childhood obesity: Review of research and implications for public policy. *Society for Research in Child Development (SRCD) Social Policy Report, 20*(2).

Kroger, J. (2003). Identity development during adolescence. In G. R. Adams & M. D. Berzonsky. (Eds.), *Blackwell handbook of adolescence* (pp. 205–226). Malden, MA: Blackwell.

Kroger, J., & Haslett, S. J. (1991). A comparison of ego identity status transition pathways and change rates across five identity domains. *International Journal of Aging and Human Development, 32*, 303–330.

Kruk, R. S., Prentice, S., & Moen, K. B. (2013). Early childhood education and care (ECEC) and reading acquisition in at-risk readers: Does quantity matter? *Canadian Journal of Behavioural Science/Revue canadienne des sciences du comportement. 45*, 49–63. doi:10.1037/a0022706

Kruk. R. S., & Reynolds, K. A. A. (2012). French Immersion experience and reading skill development in at-risk readers. *Journal of Child Language, 39*, 580–610. doi:10.1017/S0305000911000201

Kuczmarski, R. J., Ogden, C. L., Grummer-Strawn, L. M., Flegal, K. M., Guo, S. S., Wei, R., Mei, Z., ... (2000). *CDC growth charts: United States. Advance Data, No. 314*. Centers for Disease Control and Prevention, U.S. Department of Health and Human Services.

Kuhl, P., & Rivera-Gaxiola, M. (2008). Neural substrates of language acquisition. *Annual Review of Neuroscience, 31*, 511–534.

Kuhl, P. K. (2004). Early language acquisition: Cracking the speech code. *Nature Reviews Neuroscience, 5*, 831–843.

Kuhl, P. K., Andruski, J. E., Chistovich, I. A., Chistovich, L. A., Kozhevnikova, E. V., Ryskina, V. L., et al. (1997). Cross-language analysis of phonetic units in language addressed to infants. *Science, 277*, 684–686.

Kuhl, P. K., Conboy, B. T., Padden, D., Nelson, T., & Pruitt, J. (2005). Early speech perception and later language development: Implications for the "critical period." *Language Learning and Development, 1*, 237–264.

Kulig, J. C., & Williams, A. M., (2012). *Health in rural Canada*. Vancouver, BC: UBC Press.

Kuhn, D. (2006). Do cognitive changes accompany developments in the adolescent brain? *Perspectives on Psychological Science, 1*, 59–67.

Kumwenda, N. I., Hoover, D. R., Mofenson, L. M., Thigpen, M. C., Kafulafula, G., Li, Q., et al. (2008). Extended antiretroviral prophylaxis to reduce breast-milk HIV-1 transmission. *New England Journal of Medicine, 359*, 119–129.

Kung, H. C., Hoyert, D. L., Xu, J. Q., Murphy, S. L. (2007). E-stat deaths: Preliminary data for 2005 health E-stats. Hyattsville, MD: US Department of Health and Human Services, CDC. Available at http://www.cdc.gov/nchs/products/pubs/pubd/hestats/prelimdeaths05/prelimdeaths05.htm

Kung, H. C., Hoyert, D. L., Xu, J., & Murphy, S. L. (2008). Deaths: Final data for 2005. *National Vital Statistics Reports, 56*(10). Hyattsville, MD: National Center for Health Statistics.

Kuperman, S., Chan, G., Kramer, J. R., Bierut, L., Buckholz, K. K., Fox, L., et al. (2005). Relationship of age of first drink to child behavioral problems and family psychopathology. *Alcoholism: Clinical and Experimental Research, 29*(10), 1869–1876.

Kuxhaus, D. (1997, November 1). Sniffing mother came out of fog, took back her life. *Winnipeg Free Press*, A12.

Laberge, L., Tremblay, R. E., Vitaro, F., & Montplaisir, J. (2000). Development of parasomnias from childhood to early adolescence. *Pediatrics, 106*, 67–74.

Lack, G. (2008). Epidemiological risks for food allergy. *Journal of Allergy and Clinical Immunology, 121*(6), 1331–1336.

Ladd, G., Herald-Brown, S., & Reiser, M. (2008). Does chronic classroom peer rejection predict the development of children's classroom participation during the grade school years? *Child Development, 79*(4), 1001–1015.

LaFontana, K. M., & Cillessen, A. H. N. (2002). Children's perceptions of popular and unpopular peers: A multi-method assessment. *Developmental Psychology, 38*(5), 635–647.

Lagattuta, K. H. (2005). When you shouldn't do what you want to do: Young children's understanding of desires, rules, and emotions. *Child Development, 76*, 713–733.

Lagercrantz, H., & Slotkin, T. A. (1986). The "stress" of being born. *Scientific American, 254*(4), 100–107.

Laible, D. J., & Thompson, R. A. (2002). Mother-child conflict in the toddler years: Lessons in emotion, morality, and relationships. *Child Development, 73*, 1187–1203.

Laird, G. (2007). *Shelter. Homelessness in a growth economy: Canada's 21st century paradox.* Calgary, AB: Sheldon Chumir Foundation for Ethics in Leadership. Retrieved from http://www.chumirethics-foundation.ca/files/pdf/SHELTER.pdf

Laird, J., Lew, S., DeBell, M., & Chapman, C. (2006). *Dropout rates in the United States: 2002 and 2003* (NCES 2006–062). Washington, DC: U.S. Department of Education, National Center for Education Statistics.

Laird, R. D., Pettit, G. S., Bates, J. E., & Dodge, K. A. (2003). Parents' monitoring relevant knowledge and adolescents' delinquent behavior: Evidence of correlated developmental changes and reciprocal influences. *Child Development, 74*, 752–768.

Lalonde, C. E., & Werker, J. F. (1995). Cognitive influences on cross-language speech perception in infancy. *Infant Behavior and Development, 18*, 459–475.

Lamb, M. E. (1981). The development of father-infant relationships. In M. E. Lamb (Ed.), *The role of the father in child development* (2nd ed., pp. 459–488). New York: Wiley.

Lamb, M. E., Frodi, A. M., Frodi, M., & Hwang, C. P. (1982). Characteristics of maternal and paternal behavior in traditional and nontraditional Swedish families. *International Journal of Behavior Development, 5*, 131–151.

Lamberg, A. (2007). Sleep-disordered breathing may spur behavioral learning problems in children. *Journal of the American Medical Association, 297*, 2681–2683.

Lambert, W. E., & Tucker, G. R. (1972). *The bilingual education of children: The St. Lambert experiment.* Rowley, MA: Newbury House.

Lamm, C., Zelazo, P. D., & Lewis, M. D. (2006). Neural correlates of cognitive control in childhood and adolescence: Disentangling the contributions of age and executive function. *Neuropsychologia, 44*, 2139–2148.

Landon, M. B., Hauth, J. C. Leveno, K. J., Spong, C. Y., Leindecker, S., Varner, M. W., et al. (2004). Maternal and perinatal outcomes associated with trial of labor after prior cesarean delivery. *New England Journal of Medicine, 351*, 2581–2589.

Landry, S. H., Smith, K. E., Swank, P. R., & Miller-Loncar, C. L. (2000). Early maternal and child influences on children's later independent cognitive and social functioning. *Child Development, 71*, 358–375.

Landy, S., & Tam, K. K. (1996). Yes, parenting does make a difference to the development of children in Canada. In Human Resources Development Canada & Statistics Canada, *Growing up in Canada. National Longitudinal Survey of Children and Youth.* Ottawa, ON.

Långström, N., Rahman, Q., Carlström, E., & Lichtenstein, P. (2008). Genetic and environmental effects on same-sex sexual behavior: A population study of twins in Sweden. *Archives of Sexual Behavior* (ePub).

Lansford, J. (2009). Parental divorce and children's adjustment. *Perspectives on Psychological Science, 4*(2), 140–152.

Lansford, J. E., Chang, L., Dodge, K. A., Malone, P. S., Oburu, P., Palmérus, K., et al. (2005). Physical discipline and children's adjustment: Cultural normativeness as a moderator. *Child Development, 76*, 1234–1246.

Lansford, J. E., & Dodge, K. A. (2008). Cultural norms for adult corporal punishment of children and societal rates of endorsement and use of violence. *Parenting: Science & Practice, 8*(3), 257–270.

Lansford, J. E., Malone, P. S., Castellino, D. R., Dodge, K. A., Pettit, G. S., & Bates, J. E. (2006). Trajectories of internalizing, externalizing, and grades for children who have and have not experienced their parents' divorce or separation. *Journal of Family Psychology, 20*, 292–301.

Lansford, J. E., Skinner, A. T., Sorbring, E., Di Giunta, L., Deater-Deckard, K, Dodge, K. A., ... & Chang, L. (2012). Boys' and girls' relational and physical aggression in nine countries. *Aggressive Behavior, 38*, 298–308. doi:10.1002/ab.21433

LaRochelle-Côté, S., Gougeon, P., & Pinard, D. (2009). Changes in parental work time and earnings. *Perspectives on Labour and Income, 10*, 5–16 (Catalogue no. 75-001-X). Ottawa, ON: Statistics Canada. Retrieved from http://www5.statcan.gc.ca/bsolc/olc-cel/olc-cel?catno=75-001-X&chropg=1&lang=eng

Larsen, D. (1990, December–1991, January). Unplanned parenthood. *Modern Maturity*, pp. 32–36.

Larson, R., & Seepersad, S. (2003). Adolescents' leisure time in the United States: Partying, sports, and the American experiment. In S. Verma & R. Larson (Eds.), Examining adolescent leisure time across cultures: Developmental opportunities and risks. *New Directions for Child and Adolescent Development, 99*, 53–64.

Larson, R., & Wilson, S. (2004). Adolescents across place and time: Globalization and the changing pathways to adulthood. In R. M. Lerner & L. Steinberg (Eds.), *Handbook of adolescent psychology* (2nd ed., pp. 299–331). Hoboken, NJ: Wiley.

Larson, R. W., Moneta, G., Richards, M. H., & Wilson, S. (2002). Continuity, stability, and change in daily emotional experience across adolescence. *Child Development, 73*, 1151–1165.

Larson, R. W., & Verma, S. (1999). How children and adolescents spend time across the world: Work, play, and developmental opportunities. *Psychological Bulletin, 125*, 701–736.

Laursen, B. (1996). Closeness and conflict in adolescent peer relationships: Interdependence with friends and romantic partners. In W. M. Bukowski, A. F. Newcomb, & W. W. Hartup (Eds.), *The company they keep: Friendship in childhood and adolescence* (pp. 186–210). New York: Cambridge University Press.

Lavelli, M. & Fogel, A. (2005). Developmental changes in the relationship between the infant's attention and emotion during early face-to-face communication: The 2-month transition. *Developmental Psychology, 41*, 265–280.

Lawn, J. E., Cousens, S., & Zupan, J., for the Lancet Neonatal Survival Steering Team. (2005). 4 million neonatal deaths: When? Where? Why? *The Lancet, 365*, 891–900.

Lawn, J. E., Gravett, M. G., Nunes, T. M., Rubens, C. E., Stanton, C., & the GAPPS Review Group. (2010). Global report on preterm birth and stillbirth (1 of 7): Definitions, description of the burden and opportunities to improve data. *BMC Pregnancy and Childbirth, 10*(Suppl. 1), S1.

Lawrence, H. P., Binguis, D., Douglas, J., McKeown, L., Switzer, B., Figueiredo, R., & Reade, M. (2009). Oral health inequalities between young Aboriginal and non-Aboriginal children living in Ontario, Canada. *Community Dentistry and Oral Epidemiology, 37,* 495–508. doi: 10.1111/j.1600-0528.2009.00497.x

Lay, C., & Verkuyten, M. (1999). Ethnic identity and its relation to personal self-esteem: A comparison of Canadian-born and foreign-born Chinese adolescents. *Journal of Social Psychology, 139,* 288–299.

Le, H. N. (2000). Never leave your little one alone: Raising an Ifaluk child. In J. S. DeLoache & A. Gottlieb (Eds.), *A world of babies: Imagined childcare guides for seven societies* (pp. 199–201). Cambridge, UK: Cambridge University Press.

Leadbeater, B., & Sukhawathanakul, P. (2011). Multicomponent programs for reducing peer victimization in early elementary school: a longitudinal evaluation of the WITS Primary Program. *Journal of Community Psychology, 39*(5), 606–620. doi: 10.1002/jcop.20447

Leaper, C., Anderson, K. J., & Sanders, P. (1998). Moderators of gender effects on parents' talk to their children: A meta-analysis. *Developmental Psychology, 34*(1), 3–27.

Leaper, C., & Smith, T. E. (2004). A meta-analytic review of gender variations in children's language use: Talkativeness, affiliative speech, and assertive speech. *Developmental Psychology, 40,* 993–1027.

Learning Disabilities Association of Canada. (2007). *Putting a Canadian Face on Learning Disabilities (PACFOLD): What does it mean to have learning disabilities in Canada?* Ottawa, ON: Author. Retrieved from http://www.pacfold.ca/profiles/national.shtml

Ledrou, I., & Gervais, J. (2005). Food insecurity. *Health Reports, 16*(3), 47–51 (Statistics Canada catalogue 82-003).

Lee, J. M., Appugliese, D., Kaciroti, N., Corwyn, R. F., Bradley, R., & Lumeng, J. C. (2007). Weight status in young girls and the onset of puberty. *Pediatrics, 119,* E624–E630.

Lee, J. W., & Hébert, Y. M. (2006). The meaning of being Canadian: A comparison between youth of immigrant and non-immigrant origins. *Canadian Journal of Education, 29,* 497–520.

Lee, L. S., & Harris, S. R. (2005). Psychometric properties and standardization sample of four screening tests for infants and young children: A review. *Pediatric Physical Therapy, 17,* 140–147.

Lee, S. J., Ralston, H. J. P., Drey, E. A., Partridge, J. C., & Rosen, M. A. (2005). Fetal pain: A systematic multidisciplinary review of the evidence. *Journal of the American Medical Association, 294,* 947–954.

Lefebvre, P., Merrigan, P., & Verstraete, M. (2008). *Childcare policy and cognitive outcomes of children: Results from a large scale quasi-experiment on universal child-care in Canada.* Working Paper 08-23. Montreal, QC: Inter-university Centre on Risk, Economic Policies and Employment (CIRPEE).

Legault, L., Green-Demers, I., & Pelletier, L. (2006). Why do high school students lack motivation in the classroom? Toward an understanding of academic amotivation and the role of social support. *Journal of Educational Psychology, 98,* 567–582. doi: 10.1037/0022-0663.98.3.567

Legerstee, M., & Varghese, J. (2001). The role of maternal affect mirroring on social expectancies in three-month-old infants. *Child Development, 72,* 1301–1313.

Leman, P. J., Ahmed, S., & Ozarow, L. (2005). Gender, gender relations, and the social dynamics of children's conversations. *Developmental Psychology, 41,* 64–74.

Lenhart, A. (2009). Teens and sexting. Pew Research Centers. Retrieved from http://pewresearch.org/pubs/1440/teens-sexting-text-messages

Lenhart, A., Arafeh, S., Smith, A., & Macgill, A. (2008, April 24). Writing, technology and teens. Pew Internet & American Life Project, Washington, DC.

Lenneberg, E. H. (1969). On explaining language. *Science, 164*(3880), 635–643.

Lenroot, R. K., & Giedd, J. N. (2006). Brain development in children and adolescents: Insights from anatomical magnetic resonance imaging. *Neuroscience and Biobehavioral Reviews, 30*(6), 718–729.

Leo, A. (2007). *Are schools making the grade? School nutrition policies across Canada.* Ottawa, ON: Centre for Science in the Public Interest. Retrieved from http://www.cspinet.org/canada/pdf/makingthegrade_1007.pdf

Lesch, K. P., Bengel, D., Heils, A., Sabol, S. Z., Greenberg, B. D., Petri, S., et al. (1996). Association of anxiety-related traits with a polymorphism in the serotonin transporter gene regulatory region. *Science, 274,* 1527–1531.

Leslie, A. M. (1984). Spatiotemporal continuity and the perception of causality in infants. *Perception, 13,* 287–305.

Leslie, A. M. (1995). A theory of agency. In D. Sperber, D. Premack, and A. J. Premack, (Eds.), *Causal Cognition.* Oxford: Clarendon Press, 121–149.

Leslie, L. K., Newman, T. B., Chesney, J., & Perrin, J. M. (2005). The Food and Drug Administration's deliberations on antidepressant use in pediatric patients. *Pediatrics, 116,* 195–204.

Lester, B. M., & Boukydis, C. F. Z. (1985). *Infant crying: Theoretical and research perspectives.* New York: Plenum Press.

Letourneau, N. L., Hungler, K. L., & Fisher, K. (2005). Low-income Canadian Aboriginal and non-Aboriginal parent–child interactions. *Child: Care, Health & Development, 31,* 545–554.

Leung, C. (2001). The sociocultural and psychological adaptation of Chinese migrant adolescents in Australia and Canada. *International Journal of Psychology, 36,* 8–19.

LeVay, S. (1991). A difference in hypothalamic structure between heterosexual and homosexual men. *Science, 253,* 1034–1037.

Levin, I., & Bus, A. G. (2003). How is emergent writing based on drawing? Analyses of children's products and their sorting by children and mothers. *Developmental Psychology, 39*(5), 891–905.

LeVine, R. A. (1994). *Child care and culture: Lessons from Africa.* Cambridge, England: Cambridge University Press.

Levine, S. C., Vasilyeva, M., Lourenco, S. E., Newcombe, N. S., & Huttenlocher, J. (2005). Socioeconomic status modifies the sex differences in spatial skills. *Psychological Science, 16,* 841–845.

Levitt, C., Hanvey, L., Bartholomew, S., Kaczorowski, J., Chalmers, B., Heaman, M., & Li, X. (2011). Use of routine interventions in labour and birth in Canadian hospitals: comparing results of the 1993 and 2007 Canadian hospital maternity policies and practices surveys. *Journal of Obstetrics and Gynaecology Canada, 33,* 1208–1217.

Levy-Shiff, R., Zoran, N., & Shulman, S. (1997). International and domestic adoption: Child, parents, and family adjustment. *International Journal of Behavioral Development, 20,* 109–129.

Lewis, M. (1997). The self in self-conscious emotions. In S. G. Snodgrass & R. L. Thompson (Eds.), *The self across psychology: Self-recognition, self-awareness, and the self-concept* (Vol. 818, pp. 119–142). New York: Annals of the New York Academy of Sciences.

Lewis, M. (1998). Emotional competence and development. In D. Pushkar, W. Bukowski, A. E. Schwartzman, D. M. Stack, & D. R. White (Eds.), *Improving competence across the lifespan* (pp. 27–36). New York: Plenum Press.

Lewis, M. (2003). The emergence of consciousness and its role in human development. *Annals of the New York Academy of Sciences, 1001,* 104–133.

Lewis, M., & Brooks, J. (1974). Self, other, and fear: Infants' reaction to people. In H. Lewis & L. Rosenblum (Eds.), *The origins of fear: The origins of behavior* (Vol. 2, pp. 195–228). New York: Wiley.

Lewis, M., & Carmody, D. P. (2008). Self-representation and brain development. *Developmental Psychology, 44,* 1329–1334.

Lewit, E., & Kerrebrock, N. (1997). Population-based growth stunting. *The Future of Children, 7*(2), 149–156.

Li, R., Chase, M., Jung, S., Smith, P. J. S., Loeken, M. R. (2005). Hypoxic stress in diabetic pregnancy contributes to impaired embryo gene expression and defective development by inducing oxidative stress. *American Journal of Physiology: Endocrinology and Metabolism, 289,* 591–599.

Li, X., Li, S., Ulusoy, E., Chen, W., Srinivasan, S. R., & Berenson, G. S. (2004). Childhood adiposity as a predictor of cardiac mass in adulthood. *Circulation, 110,* 3488–3492.

Liang, T., Kuhle, S., & Veugelers, P. J. (2009). Nutrition and body weights of Canadian children watching television and eating while watching television. *Public Health Nutrition, 12,* 2457–2463. doi:10.1017/S1368980009005564

Lickona, T. (Ed.). (1976). *Moral development and behavior.* New York: Holt.

Lillard, A., & Curenton, S. (1999). Do young children understand what others feel, want, and know? *Young Children, 54*(5), 52–57.

Lillard, A., & Else-Quest, N. (2006). The early years: Evaluating Montessori education. *Science, 313,* 1893–1894.

Lillard, A. S. (2012). Preschool children's development in classic Montessori, supplemented Montessori, and conventional programs. *Journal of School Psychology, 50,* 379–401. doi:10.1016/j.jsp.2012.01.001

Liou, Y. M., Liou, T., & Chang, L. (2010). Obesity among adolescents: Sedentary leisure time and sleeping as determinants. *Journal of Advanced Nursing, 66*(6), 1246–1256.

Lipman, E. L., Boyle, M. H., Dooley, M. D., & Offord, D. R. (1998). *Children and lone-mother families: An investigation of factors influencing child well-being.* Report No. W-98-11E. Ottawa: Applied Research Branch, Strategic Policy, Human Resources Development Canada.

Lipman, E. L., Offord, D. R., Dooley, M. D., & Boyle, M. H. (2002). Children's outcomes in differing types of single-parent families. In J. D. Willms (Ed.), *Vulnerable Children: Findings from Canada's National Longitudinal Survey of Children and Youth* (pp. 229–242). Edmonton, AB: The University of Alberta Press.

Lipnowski, S., LeBlank, C. M. A., & Canadian Paediatric Society Healthy Active Living and Sports Medicine Committee. (2012). Physical activity guidelines for children and adolescents. *Paediatrics and Child Health, 17,* 209–210. Retrived from http://www.cps.ca/en/documents/position/physical-activity-guidelines.

Lipscomb, S. T., Leve, L. D., Harold, G. T., Neiderhiser, J. M., Shaw, D. S., Ge, X., & Reiss, D. (2011). Trajectories of parenting and child negative emotionality during infancy and toddlerhood: A longitudinal analysis. *Child Development, 82,* 1661–1675. doi:10.1111/j.1467-8624.2011.01639.x

Liszkowski, U., Carpenter, M., & Tomasello, M. (2008). Twelve-month-olds communicate helpfully and appropriately for knowledgeable and ignorant partners. *Cognition, 108,* 732–739.

Litovitz, T. L., Klein-Schwartz, W., Caravati, E. M., Youniss, J., Crouch, B., & Lee, S. (1999). Annual report of the American Association of Poison Control Centers Toxic Exposure Surveillance System. *American Journal of Emergency Medicine, 17,* 435–487.

Littleton, H., Breitkopf, C., & Berenson, A. (2006, August 13). *Correlates of anxiety symptoms during pregnancy and association with perinatal outcomes: A meta-analysis.* Presentation at the 114th annual convention of the American Psychological Association, New Orleans, LA.

Liu, J., Raine, A., Venables, P. H., Dalais, C., & Mednick, S. A. (2003). Malnutrition at age 3 years and lower cognitive ability at age 11 years. *Archives of Pediatric and Adolescent Medicine, 157,* 593–600.

Lloyd, J. J., & Anthony, J. C. (2003). Hanging out with the wrong crowd: How much difference can parents make in an urban environment? *Journal of Urban Health, 80,* 383–399.

Lloyd, M., & Newcombe, N. S. (2009). Implicit memory in childhood: reassessing developmental invariance. In M. L. Courage & N. Cowan (Eds.), *The development of memory in infancy and childhood* (pp. 93–113). Hove, UK: Psychology Press.

Lock, A., Young, A., Service, V., & Chandler, P. (1990). Some observations on the origin of the pointing gesture. In V. Volterra & C. J. Erting (Eds.), *From gesture to language in hearing and deaf children* (pp. 42–55). New York: Springer.

Lock, J., Walker, L. R., Rickert, V. I., & Katzman, D. K. (2005). Suicidality in adolescents being treated with antidepressant medications and the black box label: Position paper of the Society for Adolescent Medicine. *Journal of Adolescent Health, 36,* 92–93.

Lockwood, C. J. (2002). Predicting premature delivery—no easy task. *New England Journal of Medicine, 346,* 282–284.

Loeber, R., Farrington, D. P., & Petechuck, D. (2003). Child delinquency: Early intervention and prevention. *Report: Office of Juvenile Justice and Delinquency Prevention.* Washington, DC: Author.

Loney, S. (2011, January 20). The multi-generational home makes a comeback. *Globe and Mail.* Retrieved from http://www.theglobeandmail.com/life/relationships/the-multi-generational-home-makes-a-comeback/article570274/

Longworth, H. L., & Kingdon, C. K. (2010). Fathers in the birth room: What are they expecting and experiencing? A phenomenological study. *Midwifery, 27*(5), 588–594.

Low, S., Snyder, J., & Shortt, J. W. (2011). The drift towards problem behavior during the transition to adolescence: The Contributions of youth disclosure, parenting and older siblings. *Journal of Research on Adolescence, 22*(1), 65–79.

Lowell, H., & Miller, D. C. (2010). Weight gain during pregnancy: Adherence to Health Canada's guidelines. *Health Reports, 21* (Catalogue no. 82-003-XPE). Ottawa, ON: Statistics Canada.

Lowery, C. L., Hardman, M. P., Manning, N., Clancy, B., Hall, R. W., & Anand, K. J. S. (2007). Neurodevelopmental changes in fetal pain. *Seminars in Perinatology, 31,* 275–282.

Lucile Packard Children's Hospital at Stanford. (2009). *Failure to thrive.* Retrieved February 9, 2009, from http://www.lpch.org/DiseaseHealthInfo/Health/Library/growth/thrive.html

Ludwig, J., & Phillips, D. (2007). The benefits and costs of head start. *Social Policy Report, 21,* 3–20.

Lugaila, T. A. (2003). A child's day: 2000 (Selected indicators of child well-being). *Current Population Reports* (P70–89). Washington, DC: U.S. Census Bureau.

Luna, B., Garver, K. E., Urban, T. A., Lazar, N. A., & Sweeney, J. A. (2004). Maturation of cognitive processes from late childhood to adulthood. *Child Development, 75,* 1357–1372.

Lundy, B. L. (2003). Father- and mother-infant face-to-face interactions: Differences in mind-related comments and infant attachment? *Infant Behavior & Development, 26,* 200–212.

Luo, Z.-C., Senécal, S., Simonet, F., Guimond, É., Penney, C., & Wilkins, R. (2010). Birth outcomes in the Inuit-inhabited areas of Canada. *Canadian Medical Association Journal, 182,* 235–242.

Luo Z.-C., Wilkins, R., Heaman, M., Martens, P., Smylie, J. Hart, L., . . . & Fraser, W. D. (2010). Neighbourhood socioeconomic characteristics, birth outcomes and infant mortality among First Nations and non-First Nations in Manitoba, Canada. *The Open Women's Health Journal, 4,* 55–61.

Luo Z.-C., Wilkins, R., Heaman, M., Martens, P., Smylie, J. Hart, L., . . . & Fraser, W. D. (2010). Birth outcomes and infant mortality by the degree of rural isolation among First Nations and non-First Nations in Manitoba, Canada. *The Journal of Rural Health, 26,* 175–181.

Luo Z.-C., Wilkins, R., Platt, R. W., Kramer, M. S ., for the Fetal and Infant Health Study Group of the Canadian Perinatal Surveillance System. (2004). Risks of adverse pregnancy outcomes among Inuit and North American Indian women in Quebec, 1985-97. *Paediatric and Perinatal Epidemiology, 18,* 40–50.

Lussier, P., Corrado, R., & Tzoumakis, S. (2012). Gender differences in physical aggression and associated developmental correlates in a sample of Canadian preschoolers.

Behavioral Sciences and the Law, 30, 643–671. doi:10.1002/bsl.2035

Lutke, J. (2000). Works in progress: The meaning of success for individuals with FAS/E. In J. Kleinfeld (Ed.), *Fantastic Antone Grows Up* (pp. 19–43). Fairbanks, AK: University of Alaska Press.

Luttikhuis, H. O., Baur, L., Jansen, H., Shrewsbury, V. A., O'Malley, C., Stolk, R. P., & Summerbell, C. D. (2009). Interventions for treating obesity in children. *Cochrane Database of Systematic Reviews, 3,* 1–57. doi: 10.1002/14651858.CD001872.pub2

Lyons-Ruth, K., Alpern, L., & Repacholi, B. (1993). Disorganized infant attachment classification and maternal psychosocial problems as predictors of hostile-aggressive behavior in the preschool classroom. *Child Development, 64,* 572–585.

Maccoby, E. E. (1984). Middle childhood in the context of the family. In W. A. Collins (Ed.), *Development during middle childhood* (pp. 184–239). Washington, DC: National Academy.

Maccoby, E. E. (1992). The role of parents in the socialization of children: An historical overview. *Developmental Psychology, 28,* 1006–1017.

Maccoby, E. E. (2000). Perspectives on gender development. *International Journal of Behavioral Development, 24*(4), 398–406.

Maccoby, E. E., & Martin, J. A. (1983). Socialization in the context of the family: Parent-child interaction. In P. H. Mussen (Series Ed.) & E. M. Hetherington (Vol. Ed.), *Handbook of child psychology: Vol. 4. Socialization, personality, and social development* (pp. 1–101). New York: Wiley.

MacDonald, K. (1998). Evolution and development. In A. Campbell & S. Muncer (Eds.), *Social development* (pp. 21–49). London: UCL Press.

MacDorman, M. F., & Kirmeyer, S. (2009). Fetal and perinatal mortality, United States, 2005. *National Vital Statistics Reports, 57*(8). Hyattsville, MD: National Center for Health Statistics.

MacKay, T., & Tavares, T. (2005). *Building hope: Appropriate programming for adolescent and young adult newcomers of war-affected backgrounds and Manitoba Schools.* Winnipeg: Manitoba Education, Citizenship and Youth. Retrieved from http://www.edu. gov.mb.ca/k12/cur/eal/building_hope.pdf

MacLeod, A. A. N, Laukys, K., & Rvachew, S. (2011). The impact of bilingual language learning on whole-word complexity and segmental accuracy among children aged 18 and 36 months. *International Journal of Speech-Language Pathology, 13,* 490–499.

MacMillan, H. M., Boyle, M. H., Wong, M. Y.-Y., Duku, E. K., Fleming, J. E., & Walsh, C. A. (1999). Slapping and spanking in childhood and its association with lifetime prevalence of psychiatric disorders in a general population sample. *Canadian Medical Association Journal, 161,* 805–809.

Macmillan, R., McMorris, B. J., & Kruttschnitt, C. (2004). Linked lives: Stability and change in maternal circumstances and trajectories of antisocial behavior in children. *Child Development, 75,* 205–220.

Mahoney, J. L., Lord, H., & Carryl, E. (2005). An ecological analysis of after-school program participation and the development of academic performance and motivational attributes for disadvantaged children. *Child Development, 76*(4), 811–825.

Mahony, T. H. (2010). Police-reported dating violence in Canada, 2008. *Juristat, 30*(2) (Statistics Canada Catalogue no. 85-002- x).

Main, M. (1995). Recent studies in attachment: Overview, with selected implications for clinical work. In S. Goldberg, R. Muir, & J. Kerr (Eds.), *Attachment theory: Social, developmental, and clinical perspectives* (pp. 407–470). Hillsdale, NJ: Analytic Press.

Main, M., & Solomon, J. (1986). Discovery of an insecure, disorganized/disoriented attachment pattern: Procedures, findings, and implications for the classification of behavior. In M.Yogman & T. B. Brazelton (Eds.), *Affective development in infancy* (pp. 95–124). Norwood, NJ: Ablex.

Majid, K., & Grier, S. (2010). The Food Mail Program: "When Figs Fly"— Dispatching access and affordability to healthy food. *Social Marketing Quarterly, 16,* 78–95. doi: 10.1080/15245004.2010.503009

Makino, M., Tsuboi, K., & Dennerstein, L. (2004). Prevalence of eating disorders: A comparison of Western and non-Western countries. *Medscape General Medicine, 6*(3). Retrieved September 27, 2004, from http://www.medscape.com/ viewarticle/487413

Malaspina, D., Harlap, S., Fennig, S., Heiman, D., Nahon, D., Feldman, D., & Susser, E. S. (2001). Advancing paternal age and the risk of schizophrenia. *Archives of General Psychiatry, 58,* 361–371.

Malone, F. D., Canick, J. A., Ball, R. H., Nyberg, D. A., Comstock, C. H., Bukowski, R., et al. (2005). First-trimester or second-trimester screening, or both, for Down's syndrome. *New England Journal of Medicine, 353,* 2001–2011.

Maltais, C., Herry, Y., Emond, I., & Mougeot, C. (2011). Synthèse d'une étude longitudinale portant sur les effets d'un programme de maternelle 4 ans à temps plein. *International Journal of Early Childhood, 43,* 67–85. doi:10.1007/s13158-010-0023-5

Mandler, J. M. (2007). On the origins of the conceptual system. *American Psychologist, 62,* 741–751.

Manitoba Education and Youth. (2003). *Integrating Aboriginal perspectives into curricula: A resource for curriculum developers, teachers, and administrators.* Winnipeg, MB. Retrieved from http://www.edu.gov.mb.ca/ k12/docs/policy/abpersp/ab_persp.pdf

Manlove, J., Ryan, S., & Franzetta, K. (2003). Patterns of contraceptive use within teenagers' first sexual relationships. *Perspectives on Sexual and Reproductive Health, 35,* 246–255.

Mansfield, C., Hopfer, S., & Marteau, T. M. (1999). Termination rates after prenatal diagnosis of Down syndrome, spina bifida, anencephaly, and Turner and Klinefelter syndromes: A systematic literature review. *Prenatal Diagnosis, 19*(9), 808–812.

March of Dimes Birth Defects Foundation. (2004a). *Cocaine use during pregnancy* [Fact sheet]. Retrieved October 29, 2004, from http://www.marchofdimes.com/ professionals/681_1169.asp

March of Dimes Birth Defects Foundation. (2004b). *Marijuana: What you need to know.* Retrieved October 29, 2004, from http://www. marchofdimes.com/pnhec/159_4427.asp

March of Dimes Foundation. (2002). *Toxoplasmosis* [Fact sheet]. Wilkes-Barre, PA: Author.

Marchman, V. A., & Fernald, A. (2008). Speed of word recognition and vocabulary knowledge in infancy predict cognitive and language outcomes in later childhood. *Developmental Science, 11,* F9–16.

Marcia, J. (2002). Identity and psychosocial development in adulthood. *Identity: An International Journal of Theory and Research, 2,* 7–28.

Marcia, J. E. (1966). Development and validation of ego identity status. *Journal of Personality and Social Psychology, 3*(5), 551–558.

Marcia, J. E. (1993). The relational roots of identity. In J. Kroger (Ed.), *Discussions on ego identity* (pp. 101–120). Hillsdale, NJ: Erlbaum.

Marcus, G. F., Vijayan, S., Rao, S. B., & Vishton, P. M. (1999). Rule learning by seven-month-old infants. *Science, 283,* 77–80.

Markovits, H., & Brunet, M.-L. (2012). Priming divergent thinking promotes logical reasoning in 6- to 8-year olds: But more for high than low SES students. *Journal of Cognitive Psychology, 24*(8), 991–1001. doi:10.1080/20445911.2012.729034

Markovits, H., & Thompson, V. (2008). Different developmental patterns of simple deductive and probabilistic inferential reasoning. *Memory & Cognition, 36*(6), 1066–1078. doi:10.3758/MC.36.6.1066

Marsh, J. (2011). Young children's literacy practices in a virtual world: Establishing an online interaction order. *Reading Research Quarterly, 46,* 101–118. dx.doi. org/10.1598/RRQ.46

Marshall, K. (2006). Converging gender roles. *Perspectives on Labour and Income, 7,* 5–17 (Statistics Canada Catalogue no. 75-001-XIE).

Marshall, K. (2008). Fathers' use of paid parental leave. *Perspectives on Labour and Income, 9,* 5–14 (Catalogue no. 75-001-X). Ottawa, ON: Statistics Canada. Retrieved from http://www5.statcan.gc.ca/bsolc/olc-cel/olc-cel?catno=75-001-X&chropg=1&lang=eng

Marshall, K. (2010). Employment patterns of postsecondary students. *Perspectives on Labour and Income, 11*(9), 5–17 (Statistics Canada Catalogue no. 75-001-X). Retrieved from http://www.statcan.gc.ca/pub/75-001-x/2010109/article/11341-eng.htm

Martin, A. J. (2009, February). Age appropriateness and motivation, engagement, and performance in high school: Effects of age within cohort, grade retention, and delayed school entry. *Journal of Educational Psychology, 101*(1), 101–114. doi:10.1037/a0013100

Martin, C. L., & Fabes, R. A. (2001). The stability and consequences of young children's same-sex peer interactions. *Developmental Psychology, 37*(3), 431–446.

Martin, C. L., Fabes, R. A., & Hamish, L. D. (2011). Gender and temperament in young children's social interactions. In A. D. Pellegrini (ed.), *The Oxford Handbook of the Development of Play* (pp. 214–230). Oxford, UK: Oxford University Press.

Martin, C. L., & Ruble, D. (2004). Children's search for gender cues: Cognitive perspectives on gender development. *Current Directions in Psychological Science, 13,* 67–70.

Martin, C. L., Ruble, D. N., & Szkrybalo, J. (2002). Cognitive theories of early gender development. *Psychological Bulletin, 128,* 903–933.

Martin, J. A., Hamilton, B. E., Sutton, P. D., Ventura, S. J., Menacker, F., & Kirmeyer, S. (2006). Births: Final data for 2004. *National Vital Statistics Reports, 55*(1). Hyattsville, MD: National Center for Health Statistics.

Martin, J. A., Hamilton, B. E., Sutton, P. D., Ventura, S. J., Menacker, F., Kirmeyer, S., & Mathews, T. J. (2009). Births: Final data for 2006. *National Vital Statistics Reports, 57*(7). Hyattsville, MD: National Center for Health Statistics.

Martin, J. A., Hamilton, B. E., Sutton, P. D., Ventura, S. J., Menacker, F., Kirmeyer, S., & Munson, M. (2007). Births: Final data for 2005. *National Vital Statistics Reports, 56*(6). Hyattsville, MD: National Center for Health Statistics.

Martin, J. A., Hamilton, B. E., Sutton, P. D., Ventura, S. J., Menacker, F., & Munson, M. L. (2005). Births: Final data for 2003. *National Vital Statistics Reports, 54*(2). Hyattsville, MD: National Center for Health Statistics.

Martin, J. L., & Ross, H. S. (2005). Sibling aggression: Sex differences and parents' reactions. *International Journal of Behavioral Development, 29,* 129–138. doi: 10.1080/01650250444000469

Martínez-González, M. A., Gual, P., Lahortiga, F., Alonso, Y., de Irala-Estévez, J., & Cervera, S. (2003). Parental factors, mass media influences, and the onset of eating disorders in a prospective population-based cohort. *Pediatrics, 111,* 315–320.

Martorell, R. (1995). Promoting healthy growth: Rationale and benefits. In Anderson, P. et al., *Child growth and nutrition in developing countries.* London: Cornell University Press.

Masataka, N. (1999). Preference for infant-directed singing in 2-day-old hearing infants of deaf parents. *Developmental Psychology, 35,* 1001–1005.

Matheson, I. (2010). Recruitment of foster families: Lessons from international research. *Canada's Children, 17,* 11–18.

Mathews, T. J., Curtin, S. C., & MacDorman, M. F. (2000). Infant mortality statistics from the 1998 period linked birth/infant death data set. *National Vital Statistics Reports, 48*(12). Hyattsville, MD: National Center for Health Statistics.

Mathews, T. J., & MacDorman, M. F. (2008). Infant mortality statistics from the 2005 period linked birth/infant death data set. *National Vital Statistics Report, 57*(2), 1–32.

Mathews, T. J., & MacDorman, M. F. (2010). Infant mortality statistics from the 2006 period linked birth/death data set. *National Vital Statistics Report, 58* (17), 1–31.

Maticka-Tyndale, E. (2001). Sexual health and Canadian youth: How do we measure up? *The Canadian Journal of Human Sexuality, 10,* 1–16.

Matsumoto, D., & Juang, L., (2008). *Culture and psychology* (4th ed.). Belmont, CA: Wadsworth.

May, K. A., & Perrin, S. P. (1985). Prelude: Pregnancy and birth. In S. M. H. Hanson & F. W. Bozett (Eds.), *Dimensions of fatherhood* (pp. 64–91). Beverly Hills, CA: Sage.

Mayhew, D. R., Singhal, D., Simpson, H. M., Beirness, D. J. (2004). *Deaths and injuries to young Canadians from road crashes.* Ottawa, ON: Traffic Injury Research Foundation. Retrieved from http://www.tirf.ca.

Mayo Foundation for Medical Education and Research. (2009, January). Beyond the human genome: Meet the epigenome. *Mayo Clinic Health Letter, 27*(1), pp. 4–5.

McAndrew, M., Ait-Said, R., Ledent, J., Murdoch, J., Anisef, P., Brown, R., …, & Garnet, B. (2009). *Educational pathways and academic performance of youth of immigrant origin: Comparing Montreal, Toronto and Vancouver.* Ottawa, ON: Canadian Council on Learning/Citizenship and Immigration Canada. Retrieved from http://www.ccl-cca.ca/pdfs/OtherReports/CIC-CCL-Final12aout2009EN.pdf

McCain, M., & Mustard, J. F. (1999). *The early years: Reversing the real brain drain.* Toronto, ON: Ontario Children's Secretariat.

McCain, M. N., Mustard, J. F., & McCuaig, K. (2011). *Early years study 3: Making decisions, taking action.* Toronto, ON: Margaret & Wallace McCain Family Foundation. Retrieved from http://earlyyearsstudy.ca/.

McCain, M. N., Mustard, J. F., & Shanker, S. (2007). *The early years study 2: Putting science into action.* Toronto, ON: Council for Early Child Development.

McCall, D. D. & Clifton, R. K. (1999). Infants' means-end search for hidden objects in the absence of visual feedback. *Infant Behavior and Development, 22*(2), 179–195.

McCall, R. B., & Carriger, M. S. (1993). A meta-analysis of infant habituation and recognition memory performance as predictors of later IQ. *Child Development, 64,* 57–79.

McCallum, K. E., & Bruton, J. R. (2003). The continuum of care in the treatment of eating disorders. *Primary Psychiatry, 10*(6), 48–54.

McCarty, M. E., Clifton, R. K., Ashmead, D. H., Lee, P., & Goubet, N. (2001). How infants use vision for grasping objects. *Child Development, 72,* 973–987.

McConnell, D., Breitkreuz, R., & Savage, A. (2011). Independent evaluation of the Triple P Positive Parenting Program in family support service settings, *Child and Family Social Work, 17,* 43–54. doi:10.1111/j.1365-2206.2011.00771.x

McDaniel, M., Paxson, C., & Waldfogel, J. (2006). Racial disparities in childhood asthma in the United States: Evidence from the National Health Interview Survey, 1997 to 2003. *Pediatrics, 117,* 868–877.

McDowell, M., Fryar, C., Odgen, C., & Flegal, K. (2008). Anthropometric reference data for children and adults: United States, 2003–2006. *National health statistics report* (No. 10). Hyattsville, MD: National Center for Health Statistics.

McGuffin, P., Owen, M. J., & Farmer, A. E. (1995). Genetic basis of schizophrenia. *Lancet, 346,* 678–682.

McHale, S. M., Kim, J., Whiteman, S., & Crouter, A. C. (2004). Links between sex-typed time use in middle childhood and gender development in early adolescence. *Developmental Psychology, 40,* 868–881.

McHale, S. M., Updegraff, K. A., Helms-Erikson, H., & Crouter, A. C. (2001). Sibling influences on gender development in middle childhood and early adolescence: A longitudinal study. *Developmental Psychology, 37,* 115–125.

McKay, A. (2012). Trends in Canadian national and provincial/territorial teen pregnancy rates: 2001–2010. *The Canadian Journal of Human Sexuality, 21,* 161–175.

McLeod, R., Boyer, K,, Karrison, T., Kasza, K., Swisher, C., Roizen, N., et al. (2006). Outcome of treatment for congenital toxoplasmosis, 1981–2004: The national collaborative Chicago-based, congenital toxoplasmosis study. *Clinical Infectious Diseases: An Official Publication of the Infectious Diseases Society of America, 42*(10), 1383–1394.

McLoyd, V. C. (1998). Socioeconomic disadvantage and child development. *American Psychologist, 53,* 185–204.

McLoyd, V. C., & Smith, J. (2002). Physical discipline and behavior problems in African American, European American, and Hispanic children: Emotional support as a moderator. *Journal of Marriage and Family, 64,* 40–53.

McMullen, K., & Brockington, R. (2011). Public school indicators for Canada, the provinces and territories, 2000/2001 to 2008/2009. Ottawa, ON: Statistics Canada. *Education Matters, 8*(1). Retrieved from http://www.statcan.gc.ca/pub/81-004-x/2011001/article/11433-eng.htm

McMullen, K., & Gilmore, J. (2010). *A Note on High School Graduation and School Attendance, by Age and Province, 2009/2010.* Ottawa, ON: Statistics Canada. Retrieved from http://www.statcan.gc.ca/pub/81-004-x/2010004/article/11360-eng.htm

Mcneely, C., Shew, M. L., Beuhring, T., Sieving, R., Miller, B. C., & Blum, R. W. M. (2002). Mothers' influence on the timing of first sex among 14- and 15-year-olds. *Journal of Adolescent Health, 31*(3), 256–265.

McQueeny, T., Schweinsburg, B. C., Schweinsburg, A. D., Jacobus, J., Bava, S., Frank, L. R, & Tapert, S. F. (2009). Altered white matter integrity in adolescent binge drinkers. *Alcoholism: Clinical and Experimental Research, 33*(7), 1278–1285.

Meade, C. S., & Ickovics, J. R. (2005). Systematic review of sexual risk among pregnant and mothering teens in the USA: Pregnancy as an opportunity for integrated prevention of STD and repeat pregnancy. *Social Science & Medicine, 60*(4), 661–678.

Meezan, W., & Rauch, J. (2005). Gay marriage, same-sex parenting, and America's children. *Future of Children, 15,* 97–115.

Meier, D. (1995). *The power of their ideas.* Boston, MA: Beacon.

Meijer, A. M., & van den Wittenboer, G. L. H. (2007). Contributions of infants' sleep and crying to marital relationship of first-time parent couples in the 1st year after childbirth. *Journal of Family Psychology, 21,* 49–57.

Melby, J., Conger, R, Fang, S., Wickrama, K., & Conger, K. (2008). Adolescent family experiences and educational attainment during early adulthood. *Developmental Psychology, 44*(6), 1519–1536.

Menacker, F., Martin, J. A., MacDorman, M. F., & Ventura, S. J. (2004). Births to 10–14 year-old mothers, 1990–2002: Trends and health outcomes. *National Vital Statistics Reports, 53*(7). Hyattsville, MD: National Center for Health Statistics.

Mendelson, C. R. (2009). Minireview: Fetal-maternal hormonal signaling in pregnancy and labor. *Molecular Endocrinology, 23,* 947–954.

Mendle, J., Leve, L. D., Van Ryzin, M., Natsuaki, M. N., & Ge, X. (2011). Associations between early life stress, child maltreatment and pubertal development among girls in foster care. *Journal of Research in Adolescence, 21*(4), 871–880.

Mendle, J., Turkheimer, E., D'Onofrio, B. M., Lynch, S. K., Emery, R. E., Slutske, W. S., & Martin, N. G. (2006). Family structure and age at menarche: A children-of-twins approach. *Developmental Psychology, 42,* 533–542.

Meng, H., Smith, S. D., Hager, K., Held, M., Liu, J., Olson, R. K., et al. (2005, October). *A deletion in DCDC2 on 6p22 is associated with reading disability.* Paper presented at the American Society of Human Genetics meeting, Salt Lake City, UT.

Mennella, J. A., & Beauchamp, G. K. (2002). Flavor experiences during formula feeding are related to preferences during childhood. *Early Human Development, 68,* 71–82.

Ment, L. R., Vohr, B., Allan, W., Katz, K. H., Schneider, K. C., Westerveld, M., et al. (2003). Changes in cognitive function over time in very low-birth-weight infants. *Journal of the American Medical Association, 289,* 705–711.

Merewood, A., Mehta, S. D., Chamberlain, L. B., Philipp, B. L., & Bauchner, H. (2005). Breastfeeding rates in US baby-friendly hospitals: Results of a national survey. *Pediatrics, 116,* 628–634.

Merrell, K., Gueldner, B., Ross, S., & Isava, D. (2008). How effective are school bullying intervention programs? A meta-analysis of intervention research. *School Psychology Quarterly, 23*(1), 26–42.

Mesbah, M., Khlif, M. S., East, C., Smeathers, J., Colditz, P., & Boashash, B. (2011). Accelerometer-based fetal movement detection. Conference Proceedings of the Annual International Conference of the IEEE Engineering in Medicine and Biology Society, 7877–7880.

Messinger, D. S., Bauer, C. R., Das, A., Seifer, R., Lester, B. M., Lagasse, L. L., et al. (2004). The maternal lifestyle study: Cognitive, motor, and behavioral outcomes of cocaine-exposed and opiate-exposed infants through three years of age. *Pediatrics, 113,* 1677–1685.

Messinis, L., Krypianidou, A., Maletaki, S., & Papathanasopoulos, P. (2006). Neuropsychological deficits in long-term cannabis users. *Neurology, 66,* 737–739.

Milan, A. (2011). *Fertility: Overview, 2008* (Catalogue no. 91-209-X). Ottawa, ON: Statistics Canada.

Milan, A., & Hamm, B. (2003). Across the generations: Grandparents and grandchildren. *Canadian Social Trends, 71,* 2–7. Retrieved from http://www5.statcan.gc.ca/bsolc/olc-cel/olc-cel?catno=11-008-X20030036619&lang=eng

Milan, A., Maheux, H., & Chui, T. (2010). *Canadian social trends: A portrait of couples in mixed unions.* Ottawa, ON: Statistics Canada.

Millar, W. J., & Maclean, H. (2005). Breastfeeding practices. *Health Reports, 16,* 23–31 (Statistics Canada Catalogue no. 82-003).

Millar, W. J., Wadhera, S., & Nimrod, C. (1992). Multiple births: Trends and patterns in Canada, 1974–1990. *Health Reports, 4*(3): 223–250.

Miller, A. R., Mâsse, L. C., Shen, J., Schiariti, V., & Roxborough, L. (2013). Diagnostic status, functional status and complexity among Canadian children with neurodevelopmental disorders and disabilities: A population-based study. *Disability & Rehabilitation, 35,* 468–478. doi:10.3109/09638288.2012 .699580

Miller, E. C., Liu, N., Wen, S. W., & Walker, M. (2011). Why do Canadian women fail to achieve optimal pre-conceptional folic acid supplementation? An observational study. *Journal of Obstetrics and Gynaecology Canada, 33,* 1116–1123.

Miller, F., Jenkins, J., & Keating, D. (2002). Parenting and children's behaviour problems. In J. D. Willms (Ed.), *Vulnerable Children: Findings from Canada's National Longitudinal Survey of Children and Youth* (pp. 167–182). Edmonton, AB: The University of Alberta Press.

Miller, J. R. (1996). *Shingwauk's vision: A history of Native residential schools.* Toronto, ON: University of Toronto Press.

Miller, J. W., Naimi, T. S., Brewer, R. D., & Jones, S. E. (2007). Binge drinking and associated health risk behaviors among high school students. *Pediatrics, 119,* 76–85.

Miller, M. W., Astley, S. J., & Clarren, S. K. (1999). Number of axons in the corpus callosum of the mature Macaca Nemestrina: Increases caused by prenatal exposure to ethanol. *Journal of Comparative Neurology, 412,* 123–131.

Millman, R. P., Working Group on Sleepiness in Adolescents/Young Adults, & AAP Committee on Adolescents. (2005). Excessive sleepiness in adolescents and young adults: Causes, consequences, and treatment strategies. *Pediatrics, 115,* 1774–1786.

Mills, J. L., & England, L. (2001). Food fortification to prevent neural tube defects: Is it working? *Journal of the American Medical Association, 285,* 3022–3033.

Min, M. O., Minnes, S., Kim, H., & Singer, L. T. (2013). Pathways linking childhood maltreatment and adult physical health. *Child Abuse & Neglect, 37,* 361–373. Retrieved from http://dx.doi.org/10.1016/j.chiabu.2012.09.008

Mindell, J. A., & Owens, J. A. (2010). *A clinical guide to pediatric sleep: Diagnosis and management of sleep problems* (2nd Ed.). Philadelphia, PA: Wolters Kluwer Health.

Mindell, J. A., Sadeh, A., Wiegand, B., How, T. H., & Goh, D. Y. T. (2010). Cross-cultural differences in infant and toddler sleep. *Sleep Medicine, 11,* 274–289.

Miniño, A. M., Anderson, R. N., Fingerhut, L. A., Boudreault, M. A., & Warner, M. (2006). Deaths: Injuries, 2002. *National Vital Statistics Reports, 54*(10). Hyattsville MD: National Center for Health Statistics.

Ministry of Children and Youth Services. (2005). *Best start: Ontario's plan for early learning and child care.* Toronto, ON.

Ministry of Children and Youth Services. (2010). *Backgrounder: Ontario's Best Start Plan.* Toronto, ON. Retrieved from http://www.children.gov.on.ca/htdocs/English/news/backgrounders/07052007.aspx

Ministry of Community, Family and Children's Services. (2002). *Early years challenge fund.* Toronto, ON: Queen's Printer for Ontario.

Mischel, W. (1966). A social learning view of sex differences in behavior. In E. Maccoby (Ed.), *The development of sex differences* (pp. 57–81). Stanford, CA: Stanford University Press.

Misra, D. P., & Guyer, B. (1998). Benefits and limitations of prenatal care: From counting visits to measuring content. *Journal of the American Medical Association, 279,* 1661–1662.

Mistry, R. S., Vandewater, E. A., Huston, A. C., & McLoyd, V. (2002). Economic well-being and children's social adjustment: The role of family process in an ethnically diverse low income sample. *Child Development, 73,* 935–951.

Mitchell, B., Carleton, B., Smith, A., Prosser, R., Brownell, M., & Kozyrskyj, A. (2008). Trends in psychostimulant and antidepressant use by children in 2 Canadian provinces. *The Canadian Journal of Psychiatry, 53,* 152–159.

Mitchell, D., Brynelsen, D., & Holm, M. (1988). Evaluating the process of early intervention programmes. *Irish Journal of Psychology, 9,* 235–248.

Mitchell, E. A., Blair, P. S., & L'Hoir, M. P. (2006). Should pacifiers be recommended to prevent sudden infant death syndrome? *Pediatrics, 117,* 1755–1758.

Mitchell, K. J., Finkelhor, D., Jones, L. M., & Wolak, J. (2012). Prevalence and characteristics of youth sexting: A national study. *Pediatrics, 129*(1), 13–20.

Mix, K. S., Levine, S. C., & Huttenlocher, J. (1999). Early fraction calculation ability. *Developmental Psychology, 35,* 164–174.

Moffitt, T., Arseneault, L., Belsky, D., Dickson, N., Hancox, R., Harrington, H. L., et al. (2011). A gradient of childhood self-control predicts health, wealth, and public safety. *Proceedings of the National Academy of Sciences.* doi:10.1073/pnas.1010076108

Moffitt, T. E. (1993). Adolescent-limited and life-course persistent antisocial behavior: A developmental taxonomy. *Psychological Review, 100,* 674–701.

Mojon-Azzi, S. M., Kunz, A., & Mojon, D. S. (2011). Strabismus and discrimination in children: Are children with strabismus invited to fewer birthday parties? *British Journal of Opthamology, 95,* 473–476.

Mojza, E., Sonnentag, S., & Bornemann, C. (2011). Volunteer work as a valuable leisure-time activity: A day-level study on volunteer work, nonwork experiences, and well-being at work. *Journal of Occupational and Organizational Psychology, 84*(1), 123–152. doi: 10.1348/096317910X485737

Molcho, M., Craig, W., Due, P., Pickett, W., Harel-Fisch, Y., Overpeck, M., & the HBSC Bullying Writing Group. (2009). Cross-national time trends in bullying behaviour 1994–2006: Findings from Europe and North America. *International Journal of Public Health, 54,* S225–S234. doi:10.1007/s00038-009-5414-8

Monahan, K. C., Steinberg, L., & Cauffman, E. (2009). Affiliation with antisocial peers, susceptibility to peer influence, and antisocial behavior during the transition to adulthood. *Developmental Psychology, 45*(6), 1520–1530.

Money, J., Hampson, J. G., & Hampson, J. L. (1955). Hermaphroditism: Recommendations concerning assignment of sex, change of sex and psychologic management. *Bulletin of the Johns Hopkins Hospital, 97*(4), 284–300.

Montague, D. P. F., & Walker-Andrews, A. S. (2001). Peekaboo: A new look at infants' perception of emotion expressions. *Developmental Psychology, 37,* 826–838.

Montessori, M. (with Chattin-McNichogls, J.). (1995). *The absorbent mind.* New York: Holt.

Moore, S. E., Cole, T. J., Poskitt, E. M. E., Sonko, B. J., Whitehead, R. G., McGregor, I. A., & Prentice, A. M. (1997). Season of birth predicts mortality in rural Gambia. *Nature, 388,* 434.

Morelli, G. A., Rogoff, B., Oppenheim, D., & Goldsmith, D. (1992). Cultural variation in infants' sleeping arrangements: Questions of independence. *Developmental Psychology, 28,* 604–613.

Moretti, M. E., Lee, A., Ito, S. (2000). Which drugs are contraindicated during breastfeeding? Practice guidelines. *Canadian Family Physician, 46,* 1753–1757.

Morison, S. J., Ames, E. W., & Chisholm, K. (1995). The development of children adopted from Romanian orphanages. *Merrill-Palmer Quarterly Journal of Developmental Psychology, 41,* 411–430.

Morison, S. J., & Ellwood, A.-L. (2000). Resiliency in the aftermath of deprivation: A second look at the development of Romanian orphanage children. *Merrill-Palmer Quarterly, 46,* 717–737.

Morrison, J. A., Friedman, L. A., Harlan, W. R., Harlan, L. C., Barton, B. A., Schreiber, G. B., & Klein, D. J. (2005). Development of the metabolic syndrome in black and white adolescent girls. *Pediatrics, 116,* 1178–1182.

Morrongiello, B. A., Schell, S. L., & Schmidt, S. (2010). "Please keep an eye on your younger sister": Sibling supervision and young children's risk of unintentional injury. *Injury Prevention, 16,* 398–402. doi:10.1136/ip.2010.026377

Morrow, R. L., Garland, E. J., Wright, J. M., Maclure, M., Taylor, S., & Dormuth, C. R. (2012). Influence of relative age on diagnosis and treatment of attention-deficit/hyperactivity disorder in children. *Canadian Medical Association Journal, 184,* 755–762. doi:10.1503/cmaj .111619

Moses, L. J., Baldwin, D. A., Rosicky, J. G., & Tidball, G. (2001). Evidence for referential understanding in the emotions domain at twelve and eighteen months. *Child Development, 72,* 718–735.

Mosher, W. D., Chandra, A., & Jones, J. (2005). *Sexual behavior and selected health measures: Men and women 15–44 years of age, United States, 2002* [Advance data from vital and health statistics; No. 362]. Hyattsville, MD: Centers for Disease Control and Prevention, National Center for Health Statistics.

Mosier, C. E., & Rogoff, B. (2003). Privileged treatment of toddlers: Cultural aspects of individual choice and responsibility. *Developmental Psychology, 39,* 1047–1060.

Moss, E., & St-Laurent, D. (2001). Attachment at school age and academic performance. *Developmental Psychology, 37,* 863–874.

Moss, K. (2004). Kids witnessing family violence. *Canadian Social Trends, 73,* 12–16. (Statistics Canada Catalogue no. 11-008). Retrieved from http://www5.statcan.gc.ca/bsolc/olc-cel/olc-cel?catno=11-008-X&chropg=1&lang=eng#issue2004001

Moster, D., Lie, R. T., & Markestad, T. (2008). Long-term medical and social consequences of preterm birth. *New England Journal of Medicine, 359,* 262–273.

Moulson, M. C., Fox, N. A., Zeanah, C. H., & Nelson, C. A. (2009). Early adverse experiences and the neurobiology of facial emotion processing. *Developmental Psychology, 45,* 17–30.

MTA Cooperative Group. (2004). National Institute of Mental Health multimodal treatment study of ADHD follow-up: 24-month outcomes of treatment strategies for attention-deficit/hyperactivity disorder. *Pediatrics, 113,* 754–769.

Muhammad, A., & Gagnon, A. (2009). Why should men and women marry and have children? Parenthood, marital status and self-perceived stress among Canadians. *Journal of Health Psychology, 15,* 315–325.

Mulford, C., & Giordano, P. (2008). Teen dating violence: A closer look at adolescent romantic relationships. *National Institute of Justice Journal, 261,* 34–40.

Munakata, Y. (2001). Task-dependency in infant behavior: Toward an understanding of the processes underlying cognitive development. In F. Lacerda, C. von Hofsten, & M. Heimann (Eds.), *Emerging cognitive abilities in early infancy* (pp. 29–52). Hillsdale, NJ: Erlbaum.

Murray, M. L., deVries, C. S., & Wong, I. C. K. (2004). A drug utilisation study of anti-depressants in children and adolescents using the General Practice Research data base. *Archives of the Diseases of Children, 89,* 1098–1102.

Mushquash, C. J., & Bova, D. L. (2007). Cross-cultural assessment and measurement issues. *Journal on Developmental Disabilities, 13,* 53–66.

Mustanski, B. S., DuPree, M. G., Nievergelt, C. M., Bocklandt, S., Schork, N. J., & Hamer, D. H. (2005). A genomewide scan of male sexual orientation. *Human Genetics, 116,* 272–278.

Muter, V., Hulme, C., Snowling, M. J., & Stevenson, J. (2004). Phonemes, rimes, vocabulary, and grammatical skill as foundations of early reading development: Evidence from a longitudinal study. *Developmental Psychology, 40,* 665–681.

Nader, P. R., Bradley, R. H., Houts, R. M., McRitchie, S. L., & O'Brien, M. (2008). Moderate-to-vigorous physical activity from ages 9 to 15 years. *Journal of the American Medical Association, 300,* 295–305.

Nagaraja, J., Menkedick, J., Phelan, K. J., Ashley, P., Zhang, X., & Lanphear, B. P. (2005). Deaths from residential injuries in US children and adolescents, 1985–1997. *Pediatrics, 116,* 454–461.

Najman, J. M., Hayatbakhsh, M. R., Heron, M. A., Bor, W., O'Callaghan, M. J., & Williams, G. M. (2009). The impact of episodic and chronic poverty on child cognitive development. *The Journal of Pediatrics, 154*(2), 284–289.

Nansel, T. R., Overpeck, M., Pilla, R. S., Ruan, W. J., Simons-Morton, B., & Scheidt, P. (2001). Bullying behaviors among U.S. youth: Prevalence and association with psychosocial adjustment. *Journal of the American Medical Association, 285,* 2094–2100.

National Advisory Committee on Immunization. (2006). *Canadian Immunization Guide,* 7th ed. Ottawa, ON: Public Health Agency of Canada, Infectious Disease and Emergency Preparedness Branch, Centre for Infectious Disease Prevention and Control.

National Association for Gifted Children. (n.d.). *Frequently asked questions.* Retrieved April 29, 2010, from http://www.nagc.org/index2.aspx?id=548

National Center for Education Statistics (NCES), United States Department of Education. (2002). Labor market outcomes of noncollege-bound high school graduates: Statistical analysis report. Washington, DC: Author.

National Center for Education Statistics. (2004a). *National assessment of educational progress: The nation's report card. Mathematics highlights 2003* (NCES 2004–451). Washington, DC: U.S. Department of Education.

National Center for Education Statistics. (2006). *Calories in, calories out: Food and exercise in public elementary schools, 2005* (NCES 2006-057). Washington, DC: Author.

National Center for Health Statistics. (2004). *Health, United States, 2004 with chartbook on trends in the health of Americans* (DHHS Publication No. 2004–1232). Hyattsville, MD: Author.

National Center for Health Statistics. (2005). *Health, United States, 2005* (DHHS Publication No. 2005-1232). Hyattsville, MD: Author.

National Center for Health Statistics. (2009). *NCHS Data Brief, 2009.* Hyattsville, MD: Author.

National Center for Injury Prevention and Control. (2004). *Fact sheet: Teen drivers.* Retrieved May 7, 2004, from http://www.cdc.gov/ncipc

National Center for Learning Disabilities. (2004). *Dyslexia: Learning disabilities in reading* [Fact sheet]. Retrieved May 30, 2004, from http:// www.ld.org/LDInfoZone/InfoZone_FactSheet_Dyslexia.cfm

National Clearinghouse on Child Abuse and Neglect Information. (2004). Long-term consequences of child abuse and neglect. Retrieved October, 5, 2004, from http://nccanch.acf.hhs.gov/pubs/factsheets/long term consequences.cfm

National Coalition for the Homeless. (2009). *Why are people homeless?* [NCH fact sheet #1]. Retrieved from http://www.national-homeless.org/factsheets/why.html

National Commission for the Protection of Human Subjects of Biomedical and Behavioral Research. (1978). *Report.* Washington, DC.

National Diabetes Education Program. (2008). *Overview of diabetes in children and adolescents. A fact sheet from the National Diabetes Education Program.* Retrieved from http://ndep.nih.gov/media/diabetes/youth/youth_FS.htm

National High Blood Pressure Education Program Working Group on High Blood Pressure in Children and Adolescents. (2004). The fourth report on the diagnosis, evaluation, and treatment of high blood pressure in children and adolescents. *Pediatrics, 114*(2-Suppl.), 555–576.

National Institute of Child Health and Human Development. (2008). Down syndrome: Overview. Retrieved from http://www.nichd.nih.gov/health/topics/down

National Institute of Child Health and Human Development. (2013). Turner syndrome: Overview. Retrieved from http://www.nichd.nih.gov/health/topics/turner

National Insitute of Drug Abuse. (2008). *Info-Facts 2008: Drugged driving.* Bethesda, MD: Author.

National Institute of Mental Health. (2001). *Teenage brain: A work in progress.* Retrieved March 11, 2004, from http://www.nimh.gov/publicat/teenbrain.cfm

National Institute of Neurological Disorders and Stroke. (2006, January 25). NINDS *Shaken baby syndrome information page.* Retrieved June 20, 2006, from http://www.ninds.nih.gov/disorders/shakenbaby/shaken baby.htm

National Institutes of Health & National Institute of Child Health and Human Development. (2010). Phenylketonuria (PKU). Retrieved February 5, 2012, from http://www.nichd.nih.gov/health/topics/phenylketonuria.cfm

National Library of Medicine. (2003). *Medical encyclopedia: Conduct disorder.* Retrieved April 23, 2005, from http:// www.nlm.nih.gov/medlineplus/ency/article/000919.htm

National Library of Medicine. (2004). *Medical encyclopedia: Oppositional defiant disorder.* Retrieved April 23, 2005, from http://www.nlm.nih.gov/medlineplus/ency/article/001537.htm

National Library of Medicine (n.d.). Triple X syndrome. Retrieved from http://ghr.nlm.nih.gov/condition/triple-x-syndrome

National Reading Panel. (2000). *Report of the National Reading Panel: Teaching children to read: An evidence-based assessment of the scientific research literature on reading and its implications for reading instruction: Reports of the subgroups.* Washington, DC: U.S. Government Printing Office.

National Research Council. (1993b). *Understanding child abuse and neglect.* Washington, DC: National Academy Press.

National Sleep Foundation. (2004). *Sleep in America.* Washington, DC: Author.

National Sleep Foundation. (2006). *2006 sleep in America poll*. Washington, DC: Author.

National Survey on Drug Use and Health. (2008, May 13). Major depressive episode among youths aged 12 to 17 in the U.S.: 2004 to 2006. *The NSDUH Report*. Rockville, MD: Office of Applied Statistics, Substance Abuse and Mental Health Services Administration, U.S. Department of Health and Human Services.

Native Women's Association of Canada. (n.d.). *Healthy babies & children*. Retrieved from http://www.nwac.ca/programs/healthy-babies-children

NDDSIPA [Nipissing District Developmental Screen Intellectual Property Association]. (2000). *Nipissing District Developmental Screen*. North Bay, ON. Retrieved from http://www.ndds.ca/canada/

Neckoway, R., Brownlee, K., & Castellan, B. (2007). Is attachment theory consistent with Aboriginal parenting realities? *First Peoples Child & Family Review, 3*, 65–74.

Neisser, U., Boodoo, G., Bouchard, T. J., Jr., Boykin, A. W., Brody, N., Ceci, S. J., et al. (1996). Intelligence: Knowns and unknowns. *American Psychologist, 51*(2), 77–101.

Neitzel, C., & Stright, A. D. (2003). Relations between parents' scaffolding and children's academic self-regulation: Establishing a foundation of self-regulatory competence. *Journal of Family Psychology, 17*, 147–159.

Nelson, C. A. (2008). A neurobiological perspective on early human deprivation. *Child Development Perspectives, 1*, 13–18.

Nelson, C. A., Monk, C. S., Lin, J., Carver, L. J., Thomas, K. M., & Truwit, C. L. (2000). Functional neuroanatomy of spatial working memory in children. *Developmental Psychology, 36*, 109–116.

Nelson, K. (2005). Evolution and development of human memory systems. In B. J. Ellis & D. F. Bjorklund (Eds.), *Origins of the social mind: Evolutionary psychology and child development* (pp. 319–345). New York: Guilford Press.

Nelson, K., & Fivush, R. (2004). The emergence of autobiographical memory: A social cultural developmental theory. *Psychological Bulletin, 111*, 486–511.

Nelson, M. C., & Gordon-Larsen, P. (2006). Physical activity and sedentary behavior patterns are associated with selected adolescent risk behaviors. *Pediatrics, 117*, 1281–1290.

Neumann, H., McCormick, R. M., Amundson, N. E., & McLean, H. B. (2000). Career counselling First Nations youth: Applying the First Nations Career-Life Planning Model. *Canadian Journal of Counselling, 34*, 172–185.

Newcomb, A. F., & Bagwell, C. L. (1995). Children's friendship relations: A meta-analytic review. *Psychological Bulletin, 117*(2), 306–347.

Newcomb, A. F., Bukowski, W. M., & Pattee, L. (1993). Children's peer relations: A meta-analytic review of popular, rejected, neglected, controversial, and average sociometric status. *Psychological Bulletin, 113*, 99–128.

Newman, R. S. (2005). The cocktail party effect in infants revisited: Listening to one's name in noise. *Developmental Psychology, 41*, 352–362.

Ngo, H., & Schleifer, B. (2005). Immigrant children and youth in focus. *Canadian Issues*, Spring, 29–33.

NICHD Early Child Care Research Network. (2004a). Are child developmental outcomes related to before- and after-school care arrangement? Results from the NICHD Study of Early Child Care. *Child Development, 75*, 280–295.

NICHD Early Child Care Research Network. (2004b). Does class size in first grade relate to children's academic and social performance or observed classroom processes? *Developmental Psychology, 40*, 651–664.

NICHD Early Child Care Research Network. (2005a). Duration and developmental timing of poverty and children's cognitive and social development from birth through third grade. *Child Development, 76*, 795–810.

NICHD Early Child Care Research Network. (2005b). Early child care and children's development in the primary grades: Follow-up results from the NICHD study of early child care. *American Educational Research Journal, 42*(3), 537–570.

NICHD Early Child Care Research Network. (2005c). Predicting individual differences in attention, memory, and planning in first graders from experiences at home, child care, and school. *Developmental Psychology, 41*, 99–114. doi:10.1037/0012-1649.41.1.99

Nilsen, E. S., & Graham, S. A. (2009). The relations between children's communicative perspective-taking and executive functioning. *Cognitive Psychology, 58*, 220–249.

Nirmala, A., Reddy, B. M., & Reddy, P. P. (2008). Genetics of human obesity: An overview. *International Journal of Human Genetics, 8*, 217–226.

Nisbett, R. E. (2005). Heredity, environment, and race differences in IQ: A commentary on Rushton and Jensen (2005). *Psychology, Public Policy, and Law, 11*, 302–310.

Nixon, M. K., Cloutier, P., & Jansson, S. M. (2008). Nonsuicidal self-harm in youth: a population-based survey. *Canadian Medical Association Journal, 178*(3), 306–312. doi: 10.1503/cmaj.061693

Noirot, E., & Algeria, J. (1983). Neonate orientation towards human voice differs with type of feeding. *Behavioral Processes, 8*, 65–71.

Noll, J. G., Trickett, P. K., & Putnam, F. M. (2003). A prospective investigation of the impact of childhood sexual abuse on the development of sexuality. *Journal of Consulting and Clinical Psychology, 71*(3), 575–586.

Nucci, L., Hasebe, Y., & Lins-Dyer, M. T. (2005). Adolescent psychological well-being and parental control. In J. Smetana (Ed.), *Changing boundaries of parental authority during adolescence: New directions for child and adolescent development* (pp. 17–30). San Francisco, CA: Jossey-Bass.

Nugent, J. K., Lester, B. M., Greene, S. M., Wieczorek-Deering, D., & O'Mahony, P. (1996). The effects of maternal alcohol consumption and cigarette smoking during pregnancy on acoustic cry analysis. *Child Development, 67*, 1806–1815.

Ober, C., Tan, Z., Sun, Y., Possick, J. D., Pan, L., Nicolae, R., et al. (2008). Effect of Variation in *CHI3L1* on Serum YKL-40 Level, Risk of Asthma, and Lung Function. *New England Journal of Medicine, 358*, 1682–1691.

O'Brien, C. M., & Jeffery, H. E. (2002). Sleep deprivation, disorganization and fragmentation during opiate withdrawal in newborns. *Pediatric Child Health, 38*, 66–71.

Odenstad, A., Hjern, A., Lindblad, F., Rasmussen, F., Vinnerljun, B., & Dalen, M. (2008, March). Does age at adoption and geographic origin matter? A national cohort study of cognitive test performance in adult intercountry adoptees. *Psychological Medicine, 26*, 1–8

Odgers, C. L., Tach, L. M., Sampson, R. J., Moffitt, T. E., Taylor, A., Matthews, C. L., & Caspi, A. (2009). The protective effects of neighborhood collective efficacy on British children growing up in deprivation: A developmental analysis. *Developmental Psychology, 45*(4), 942–957.

Offer, D., Kaiz, M., Ostrov, E., & Albert, D. B. (2002). Continuity in the family constellation. *Adolescent and Family Health, 3*, 3–8.

Offer, D., Ostrov, E., & Howard, K. I. (1989). Adolescence: What is normal? *American Journal of Diseases of Children, 143*, 731–736.

Office of National Drug Control Policy. (2008). *National drug control strategy 2008 annual report*. Washington, DC: Office of National Drug Control Policy.

Office on Smoking and Health, Centers for Disease Control and Prevention. (2006). *The health consequences of involuntary exposure to tobacco smoke: A report of the surgeon-general* (No. 017-024-01685-3). Washington, DC: U.S. Department of Health and Human Services.

Offit, P. A., Quarles, J., Gerber, M. A., Hackett, C. J., Marcuse, E. K., Kollman, T. R., et al. (2002). Addressing parents' concerns: Do multiple vaccines overwhelm or weaken the infant's immune system? *Pediatrics, 109*, 124–129.

Offord, D. R., Lipman, E. L., & Duku, E. K. (1998). *Sports, the arts and community* programs: Rates and correlates of participation. Working Paper W-98-18E. Ottawa, ON: Applied Research Branch, Strategic Policy, Human Resources Development Canada.

Ofori, B., Oraichi, D., Blais, L., Rey, E., & Berard, A. (2006). Risk of congenital anomalies in pregnant users of nonsteroidal anti-inflammatory drugs: A nested case-control study. *Birth Defects Research. Part B, Developmental and Reproductive Toxicology, 77*(4), 268–279.

Ogden, C. L., Carroll, M. D., Curtin, L. R., McDowell, M. A., Tabak, C. J., & Flegal, K. M. (2006). Prevalence of overweight and obesity in the United States, 1999–2004. *Journal of the American Medical Association, 295,* 1549–1555.

Ohlsson, A., & Shah, P. (2008). *Determinants and prevention of low birth weight: A synopsis of the evidence.* Edmonton, AB: Institute of Health Economics.

Olds, S. W. (2002). *A balcony in Nepal: Glimpses of a Himalayan village.* Lincoln, NE: ASJA Books, an imprint of iUniverse.

O'Leary, C., Nassar, N., Kurinczuk, J., & Bower, C. (2009). Impact of maternal alcohol consumption on fetal growth and preterm birth. *BJOG, 116,* 390–400.

Oliver, L. N., Peters, P. A., & Kohen, D. E. (2012). *Mortality rates among children and teenagers living in Inuit Nunangat, 1994 to 2008* (Component of Statistics Canada Catalogue no. 82-003-X Health Reports). Ottawa, ON: Statistics Canada.

Olson, K., & Shaw, A. (2010). No fair, copycat! What children's response to plagiarism tells us about their understanding of ideas. *Developmental Science, 14,* 431–439. doi:10.1111/j.1467-7687.2010.00993.x

Olson, K. R., & Spelke, E. S. (2008). Foundations of cooperation in young children. *Cognition, 108,* 222–231.

Olson, S. L., Tardif, T. Z., Miller, A., Felt, B., Grabell, A. S., Kessler, D., … & Hirabayashi, H. (2011). Inhibitory control and harsh discipline as predictors of externalizing problems in young children: A comparative study of U.S., Chinese, and Japanese preschoolers. *Journal of Abnormal Child Psychology, 39,* 1163–1175. doi:10.1007/s10802-011-9531-5

Olthof, T., Schouten, A., Kuiper, H., Stegge, H., & Jennekens-Schinkel, A. (2000). Shame and guilt in children: Differential situational antecedents and experiential correlates. *British Journal of Developmental Psychology, 18,* 51–64.

Ontario Federation of Teaching Parents. (n.d.). *Homeschooling frequently asked questions.* Retrieved from http://ontariohomeschool.org/faq.shtml#howmany

Ontario Ministry of Education. (2010). *School food and beverage policy: Quick reference guide.* Toronto, ON. Retrieved from http://

www.dietitians.ca/Dietitians-Views/School-Nutrition-Policy.aspx

Opdal, S. H., & Rognum, T. O. (2004). The sudden infant death syndrome gene: Does it exist? *Pediatrics, 114,* e506–e512.

Organisation for Economic Co-operation and Development. (2004). Education at a glance: OECD indicators—2004. *Education & Skills, 2004*(14), 1–456.

Organisation for Economic Co-operation and Development. (2010). *PISA 2009 results: What students know and can do: Student performance in reading, mathematics and science (volume I).* Paris: OECD Publishing. Retrieved from http://dx.doi.org/10.1787/9789264091450-en

Organisation for Economic Co-operation and Development. (2011). *Lessons from PISA for the United States: Strong performers and successful reformers in education.* Paris: OECD Publishing. Retrieved from http://dx.doi.org/10.1787/9789264096660-en

Orr, D. P., & Ingersoll, G. M. (1995). The contribution of level of cognitive complexity and pubertal timing behavioral risk in young adolescents. *Pediatrics, 95*(4), 528–533.

Oshima-Takane, Y., Goodz, E., & Derevensky, J. L. (1996). Birth order effects on early language development: Do secondborn children learn from overheard speech? *Child Development, 67,* 621–634.

Ossorio, P., & Duster, T. (2005). Race and genetics: Controversies in biomedical, behavioral, and forensic sciences. *American Psychologist, 60,* 115–128.

Ouellette, G. P., & Sénéchal, M. (2008). A window into early literacy: Exploring the cognitive and linguistic underpinnings of invented spelling. *Scientific Studies of Reading, 12*(2), 195–219.

Owens, J., Spirito, A., McGuinn, N., & Nobile, C. (2000). Sleep habits and sleep disturbance in elementary school children. *Developmental and Behavioral Pediatrics, 21,* 27–30.

Owens, R. E. (1996). *Language development* (4th ed.). Boston: Allyn & Bacon.

Oyserman, D., Coon, H. M., & Kemmelmeier M. (2002). Rethinking individualism and collectivism: Evaluation of theoretical assumptions and meta-analyses. *Psychological Bulletin, 128,* 3–72.

Pabayo, R., Spence, J. C., Casey, L., & Storey, K. (2012). Food consumption patterns in preschool children. *Canadian Journal of Dietetic Practice and Research, 73,* 66–71. doi:10.3148/73.2.2012.66

Padilla, A. M., Lindholm, K. J., Chen, A., Duran, R., Hakuta, K., Lambert, W., & Tucker, G. R. (1991). The English-only movement: Myths, reality, and implications for psychology. *American Psychologist, 46*(2), 120–130.

Padilla-Walker, L. M., Coyne, S. M., Fraser, A. M., Dyer, W. J., & Yorgason, J. B. (2012).

Parents and adolescents growing up in the digital age: latent growth curve analysis of proactive media monitoring. *Journal of Adolescence, 35*(5), 1153–1165. doi:10.1016/j.adolescence.2012.03.005

Paglia A., & Adlaf, E. M. (2003). Secular trends in self-reported violent activity among Ontario students, 1983–2001. *Canadian Journal of Public Health, 94,* 212–217.

Paglia-Boak, A., Adlaf, E. M., & Mann, R. E. (2011). *Drug use among Ontario students, 1977–2011: Detailed OSDUHS findings* (CAMH Research Document Series No. 32). Toronto, ON: Centre for Addiction and Mental Health.

Paley, B., & O'Connor, M. H. (2011). Behavioral interventions for children and adolescents with Fetal Alcohol Spectrum disorders. *Alcohol Research & Health, 34*(1), 64–75.

Palkovitz, R. (1985). Fathers' birth attendance, early contact, and extended contact with their newborns: A critical review. *Child Development, 56,* 392–406.

Papadatou-Pastou, M. Martin, M., Munafo, M., & Jones, G. (2008). Sex differences in left-handedness: A meta-analysis of 144 studies. *American Psychological Association Bulletin, 134*(5), 677–699.

Paquette, D., Bolté, C., Turcotte, G., Dubeau, D., & Bouchard, C. (2000). A new typology of fathering: Defining and associated variables. *Infant and Child Development, 9,* 213–230.

Paradis, G., Tremblay, M. S., Janssen, I., Chiolero, A., & Bushnik, T. (2010). Blood pressure in Canadian children and adolescents. *Health Reports, 21*(2), 15–22 (Statistics Canada Catalogue no. 82-003-XPE).

Park, J. M., Metraux, S., & Culhane, D. P. (2010). Behavioral health services use among heads of homeless and housed poor families. *Journal of Health Care for the Poor and Underserved, 21*(2), 582–590.

Parke, R. D. (2004). Development in the family. *Annual Review of Psychology, 55,* 365–399.

Parke, R. D., & Buriel, R. (1998). Socialization in the family: Ethnic and ecological perspectives. In W. Damon (Series Ed.) & N. Eisenberg (Vol. Ed.), *Handbook of child psychology: Vol. 3. Social, emotional, and personality development* (5th ed., pp. 463–552). New York: Wiley.

Parker, J. D., Woodruff, T. J., Basu, R., & Schoendorf, K. C. (2005). Air pollution and birth weight among term infants in Califiornia. *Pediatrics, 115,* 121–128.

Parker, L., Pearce, M. S., Dickinson, H. O., Aitkin, M., & Craft, A. W. (1999). Stillbirths among offspring of male radiation workers at Sellafield Nuclear Reprocessing Plant. *Lancet, 354,* 1407–1414.

Parler, B. D. (2001). Raising a child: The traditional way. In *Aboriginal Head Start (Urban and Northern Communities) National Newsletter.* Spring/summer 2001 (p. 6). Ottawa, ON: Health Canada.

Parr, J. (1982). Introduction. In J. Parr (Ed.), *Childhood and family in Canadian history* (pp. 7–16). Toronto, ON: McClelland and Stewart Limited.

Parten, M. B. (1932). Social play among pre-school children. *Journal of Abnormal and Social Psychology, 27,* 243–269.

Pascal, C. E. (2009). *With our best future in mind: Implementing early learning in Ontario.* Toronto, ON: Government of Ontario. Retrieved from http://www.ontario.ca/en/initiatives/early_learning/ONT06_018865

Pastor, P. N., & Reuben, C. A. (2008). Diagnosed attention deficit hyperactivity disorder and learning disability, United States, 2004–2006. National Center for Health Statistics. *Vital Health Statistics, 10*(237), 1–14.

Patel, H., Feldman, M., & Canadian Paediatric Society, Community Paediatrics Committee. (2011). Universal newborn hearing screening. *Paediatrics and Child Health, 16,* 301–305.

Patrick, H., & Nicklas, T. A. (2005). A review of family and social determinants of children's eating patterns and diet quality. *Journal of the American College of Nutrition, 24*(2), 83–92.

Patrick, K., Norman, G. J., Calfas, K. J., Sallis, J. F., Zabinski, M. F., Rupp, J., & Cella, J. (2004). Diet, physical activity, and sedentary behaviors as risk factors for overweight in adolescence. *Archives of Pediatric Adolescent Medicine, 158,* 385–390.

Patton, G. C., Coffey, C., Carlin, J. B., Sawyer, S. M., Williams, J., Olsson, C. A. & Wake, M. (2011). Overweight and obesity between adolescence and young adulthood: A 10-year prospective cohort study. *Journal of Adolescent Health, 48*(3), 275–280.

Pawelski, J. G., Perrin, E. C., Foy, J. M., Allen, C. E., Crawford, J. E., Del Monte, M., et al. (2006). The effects of marriage, civil union, and domestic partnership laws on the health and well-being of children. *Pediatrics, 118,* 349–364.

Pellegrini, A. D., & Archer, J. (2005). Sex differences in competitive and aggressive behavior: A view from sexual selection theory. In B. J. Ellis & D. F. Bjorklund (Eds.), *Origins of the social mind: Evolutionary psychology and child development* (pp. 219–244). New York: Guilford Press.

Pellegrini, A. D., & Bohn, C. M. (2005). The role of recess in children's cognitive performance and school adjustment. *Educational Researcher, 34*(1), 13–19.

Pellegrini, A. D., Kato, K., Blatchford, P., & Baines, E. (2002). A short-term longitudinal study of children's playground games across the first year of school: Implications for social competence and adjustment to school. *American Educational Research Journal, 39,* 991–1015.

Pellegrini, A. D., & Long, J. D. (2002). A longitudinal study of bullying, dominance, and victimization during the transition from primary school through secondary school. *British Journal of Developmental Psychology, 20,* 259–280.

Pellegrini, A. D., Long, J. D., Roseth, C. J., Bohn, C. M. & Van Ryzin, M. (2007). A short-term longitudinal study of preschoolers' (Homo sapiens) sex segregation: The role of physical activity, sex and time. *Journal of Comparative Psychology, 121,* 282–289.

Pelletier, J. (2012a). *Key findings from Year 1 of Full-Day Early Learning Kindergarten in Peel.* Toronto, ON: Dr. Eric Jackman Institute of Child Study, University of Toronto. Retreived from http://www.oise.utoronto.ca/atkinson/UserFiles/File/Publications/Peel_Year_1_FDELK_Summary_Report.pdf

Pelletier, J. (2012b). *Key findings from Year 2 of Full-Day Early Learning Kindergarten in Peel.* Toronto, ON: Dr. Eric Jackman Institute of Child Study, University of Toronto. Retreived from http://www.researchconnections.org/childcare/resources/24495

Pendlebury, J. D., Wilson, R. J. A., Bano, S., Lumb, K. J., Schneider, J. M., & Hasan, S. U. (2008). Respiratory control in neonatal rats exposed to prenatal cigarette smoke. *American Journal of Respiratory and Critical Care Medicine, 177,* 1255–1261.

Pennington, B. F., Moon, J., Edgin, J., Stedron, J., & Nadel, L. (2003). The neuropsychology of Down syndrome: Evidence for hippocampal dysfunction. *Child Development, 74,* 75–93.

Pepler, D. (2012). The development of dating violence: What doesn't develop, what does develop, how does it develop, and what can we do about it? *Prevention Science, 13,* 402–409. doi:10.1007/s11121-012-0308-z

Pepler, D., Craig, W., O'Connell, P., Atlas, R. & Charach, A. (2004). Making a difference in bullying: Evaluation of a systemic school-based programme in Canada. In P. Smith, D. Pepler & K. Rigby (Eds.) *Bullying in Schools: How Successful Can Interventions Be?* (pp. 125–139). Cambridge, UK: Cambridge University Press.

Pepler, D. J., & Craig, W. M. (2011). Promoting relationships and eliminating violence in Canada. *International Journal of Behavioral Development, 35,* 389–397. doi:10.1177/0165025411407455

Pepler, D. J., German, J., Craig, W., & Yamada, S. (2011). Why worry about bullying? *Healthcare Quarterly, 14,* 72–79.

Pepler, D. J., & Sedighdeilami, F. (1998). *Aggressive girls in Canada.* Report No. W-98-30E. Ottawa, ON: Applied Research Branch, Strategic Policy, Human Resources Development Canada.

Pepper, S. C. (1961). *World hypotheses.* Berkeley, CA: University of California Press.

Perlman, M., Garfinkel, D. A., & Turrell, S. L. (2007). Parent and sibling influences on the quality of children's conflict behaviours across the preschool period. *Social Development, 16,* 619–641. doi: 10.1111/j.1467-9507.2007.00402.x

Perrin, E. M., Finkle, J. P., & Benjamin, J. T. (2007). Obesity prevention and the primary care pediatrician's office. *Current Opinion in Pediatrics, 19*(3), 354–361.

Perry, B. (2002). *How nurture becomes nature: The influence of social structures on brain development.* Retrieved from http://www.ChildTrauma.org

Persad, V. L., Van den Hoff, M. C., Dubé, J. M., & Zimmer, P. (2002). Incidence of open neural tube defects in Nova Scotia after folic acid fortification. *Canadian Medical Association Journal, 167,* 241–245.

Petit, D., Touchette, E., Tremblay, R. E., Boivin, M., & Montplaisir, J. (2007). Dyssomnias and parasomnias in early childhoold. *Pediatrics, 119*(5), e1016–e1025.

Petitto, L. A., Katerelos, M., Levy, B., Gauna, K., Tetault, K., & Ferraro, V. (2001). Bilingual signed and spoken language acquisition from birth: Implications for mechanisms underlying bilingual language acquisition. *Journal of Child Language, 28,* 1–44.

Petitto, L. A., & Kovelman, I. (2003). The bilingual paradox: How signing-speaking bilingual children help us to resolve it and teach us about the brain's mechanisms underlying all language acquisition. *Learning Languages, 8,* 5–18.

Petrill, S. A., Lipton, P. A., Hewitt, J. K., Plomin, R., Cherny, S. S., Corley, R., & DeFries, J. C. (2004). Genetic and environmental contributions to general cognitive ability through the first 16 years of life. *Developmental Psychology, 40,* 805–812.

Pettit, G. S., Bates, J. E., & Dodge, K. A. (1997). Supportive parenting, ecological context, and children's adjustment: A seven-year longitudinal study. *Child Development, 68,* 908–923.

Phillips, L., Norris, S., & Mason, J. (1996). Longitudinal effects of early literacy concepts on reading achievement: A Kindergarten intervention and five-year follow up. *Journal of Literacy Research, 28,* 173–195.

Philp, H., & Kelly, M. (1974). Product and process in cognitive development: Some comparative data on the performance of school age children in different cultures. *British Journal of Educational Psychology, 44,* 248–265.

Phinney, J. S. (1998). Stages of ethnic identity development in minority group adolescents. In R. E. Muuss & H. D. Porton (Eds.), *Adolescent behavior and society: A book of readings* (pp. 271–280). Boston, MA: McGraw-Hill.

Phinney, J. S. (2008). Bridging identities and disciplines: Advances and challenges in understanding multiple identities. In M. Azmitia, M. Syed, & K. Radmacher (Eds.), *The intersections of personal and social identities. New Directions for Child and Adolescent Development, 120,* 97–109.

Phipps, S., & Lethbridge, L. (2006). *Income and the outcomes of children* (Statistics Canada Catalogue no. 11F0019MIE. Ottawa, Ontario. Analytical Studies Branch Research Paper Series, no. 281). Retrieved from http://www.statcan.gc.ca/pub/11f0019m/11f0019m2006281-eng.pdf

Phipps, S. A., Burton, P. S., Osberg, L. S., & Lethbridge, L. N. (2006). Poverty and the extent of child obesity in Canada, Norway and the United States. *The International Association for the Study of Obesity, 7,* 5–12.

Physicians for a Smoke-Free Canada. (1999). *Second hand smoke & children's health.* Ottawa, ON: Author. Retrieved from http://www.smoke-free.ca/factsheets/default.htm

Physicians for a Smoke-Free Canada. (2010). *Exposure to second hand smoke at home - Canada, 2009: Key findings.* Ottawa, ON: Author. Retrieved from http://www.smoke-free.ca/factsheets/default.htm

Piaget, J. (1952). *The origins of intelligence in children.* New York: International Universities Press. (Original work published 1936)

Piaget, J. (1962). *The language and thought of the child* (M. Gabain, Trans.). Cleveland, OH: Meridian. (Original work published 1923)

Piaget, J. (1964). *Six psychological studies.* New York: Vintage.

Piaget, J. (1972). Intellectual evolution from adolescence to adulthood. *Human Development, 15,* 1–12.

Piaget, J., & Inhelder, B. (1967). *The child's conception of space.* New York: Norton.

Picker, J. (2005). The role of genetic and environmental factors in the development of schizophrenia. *Psychiatric Times, 22,* 1–9.

Pickett, W., Streight, S., Simpson, K. & Brison, R. J. (2003). Injuries experienced by infant children: A population-based epidemiological analysis. *Pediatrics, 111,* e365–e370.

Pike, A., Coldwell, J., & Dunn, J. F. (2005). Sibling relationships in early/middle childhood: Children's perspectives and links with individual adjustment. *Journal of Family Psychology, 19,* 523–532.

Pillow, B. H. (2002). Children's and adult's evaluation of the certainty of deductive inferences, inductive inferences and guesses. *Child Development, 73*(3), 779–792.

Pillow, B. H., & Henrichon, A. J. (1996). There's more to the picture than meets the eye: Young children's difficulty understanding biased interpretation. *Child Development, 67,* 803–819.

Plante, J., & Beattie, D. (2004). *Connectivity and ICT integration in Canadian elementary and secondary schools: First results from the Information and Communications Technologies in Schools Survey, 2003–2004* (Catalogue no. 81-595-MIE No. 017). Ottawa, ON: Statistics Canada. Retrieved from http://www5.statcan.gc.ca/bsolc/olc-cel/olc-cel?catno=81-595-MIE2004017&lang=eng

Plomin, R. (1989). Environment and genes: Determinants of behavior. *American Psychologist, 44*(2), 105–111.

Plomin, R. (2004). Genetics and developmental psychology. *Merrill-Palmer Quarterly, 50,* 341–352.

Plomin, R. & Daniels, D. (2011). Why are children in the same family so different from one another? *International Journal of Epidemiology, 40*(3), 563–582.

Plomin, R., & DeFries, J. C. (1999). The genetics of cognitive abilities and disabilities. In S. J. Ceci & W. M. Williams (Eds.), *The nature nurture debate: The essential readings* (pp. 178–195). Malden, MA: Blackwell.

Plomin, R., Owen, M. J., & McGuffin, P. (1994). The genetic bases of behavior. *Science, 264,* 1733–1739.

Plomin, R., & Spinath, F. M. (2004). Intelligence: Genetics, genes, and genomics. *Journal of Personality and Social Psychology, 86,* 112–129.

Plumert, J., & Nichols-Whitehead, P. (1996). Parental scaffolding of young children's spatial communication. *Developmental Psychology, 32,* 523–532.

Pogarsky, G., Thornberry, T. P., & Lizotte, A. J. (2006). Developmental outcomes for children of young mothers. *Journal of Marriage and Family, 68,* 332–344.

Pollitt, E., Gorman, K. S., Engle, P. L., Rivera, J. A. & Martorell, R. (1995). Nutrition in early life and the fulfillment of intellectual potential. *Journal of Nutrition, 125*(suppl), 1111S–1118S.

Pomerantz, E. M., & Saxon, J. L. (2001). Conceptions of ability as stable and self-evaluative processes: A longitudinal examination. *Child Development, 72,* 152–173.

Pomery, E. A., Gibbons, F. X., Gerrard, M., Cleveland, M. J., Brody, G. H., & Wills, T. A. (2005). Families and risk: Prospective analyses of familial and social influences on adolescent substance use. *Journal of Family Psychology, 19,* 560–570.

Pons, F., Harris, P. L., & de Rosnay, M. (2004). Emotion comprehension between 3 and 11 years: Developmental periods and hierar-chical organization. *European Journal of Developmental Psychology, 1*(2), 127–152.

Pope, A. W., Bierman, K. L., & Mumma, G. H. (1991). Aggression, hyperactivity, and inattention-immaturity: Behavior dimensions associated with peer rejection in elementary school boys. *Developmental Psychology, 27,* 663–671.

Posthuma, D., & de Gues, E. J. C. (2006). Progress in the molecular-genetic study of intelligence. *Current Directions in Psychological Science, 36*(1), 1–3.

Public Health Agency of Canada. (2006). *Canadian immunization guide* (7th ed.). Ottawa, ON: Author.

Public Health Agency of Canada. (2008). *Canadian perinatal health report, 2008 edition.* Ottawa, ON: Minister of Health. Retrieved from http://www.publichealth.gc.ca/cphr/

Public Health Agency of Canada. (2008b). *Leading causes of death and hospitalization in Canada.* Ottawa, ON. Retrieved from http://www.phac-aspc.gc.ca/publicat/lcd-pcd97/index-eng.php

Public Health Agency of Canada. (2009). *HIV and AIDS in Canada: Surveillance report to December 31, 2008.* Ottawa, ON: Surveillance and Risk Assessment Division, Centre for Communicable Diseases and Infection Control, Public Health Agency of Canada.

Public Health Agency of Canada (2009b). *Child and youth injury in review, 2009 edition–Spotlight on consumer product safety.* Ottawa, ON: Author. Retrieved from http:// www.publichealth.gc.ca/InjuryReview2009

Public Health Agency of Canada. (2010a). *Canadian incidence study of reported child abuse and neglect—2008: Major findings.* Ottawa, ON: Author.

Public Health Agency of Canada. (2010b). *Summative evaluation of the Community Action Program for Children: 2004–2009.* Ottawa, ON. Retrieved from http://www.phac-aspc.gc.ca/about_apropos/evaluation/·reports-rapports/2009-2010/capc-pace/index-eng.php

Public Health Agency of Canada. (2010c). *Injury surveillance on-line.* Ottawa, ON: Author. Retrieved from http://dsol-smed.phac-aspc.gc.ca/dsol-smed/is-sb/c_ind_matrix-eng.php#matrix

Public Health Agency of Canada. (2010d). *HIV/AIDS among youth in Canada. HIV/AIDS Epi Update.* Ottawa, ON: Author. Retrieved from http://www.phac-aspc.gc.ca/aids-sida/publication/epi/2010/4-eng.php

Public Health Agency of Canada. (2011). *Joint statement on safe sleep: Preventing sudden infant deaths in Canada.* Ottawa, ON: Author. Retrieved from http://www.phac-aspc.gc.ca/hp-ps/dca-dea/stages-etapes/childhood-enfance_0-2/sids/jsss-ecss-eng.php

Public Health Agency of Canada. (2011b). *Children and physical activity scenarios project: Evidence-based visions of the future.* Ottawa, ON: Author. Retrieved from http://www.phac-aspc.gc.ca

Public Health Agency of Canada. (2011c). *Diabetes in Canada: Facts and figures from a public health perspective.* Ottawa, ON: Author. Retrieved from http://www.phac-aspc.gc.ca/cd-mc/publications/diabetes-diabete/facts-figures-faits-chiffres-2011/highlights-saillants-eng.php#chp5

Public Health Agency of Canada. (2012). *A report on mental illnesses in Canada: Chapter 3 Schizophrenia.* Ottawa, ON: Author. Retrieved from http://www.phac-aspc.gc.ca/publicat/miic-mmac/chap_3-eng.php

Public Health Agency of Canada. (2012b). *Evaluation of the Aboriginal Head Start in Urban and Northern Communities Program at the Public Health Agency of Canada.* Ottawa, ON: Author. Retrieved from http://www.phac-aspc.gc.ca/about_apropos/evaluation/reports-rapports/2011-2012/ahsunc-papacun/index-eng.php

Public Health Agency of Canada, Health Surveillance and Epidemiology Division. (2006). *Injuries associated with bicycles: Canadian Hospitals Injury Reporting and Prevention Program (CHIRPP) database.* Ottawa, ON: Author. Retrieved from http://www.phac-aspc.gc.ca/injury-bles/chirpp/injrep-rapbles/index-eng.php

Public Health Agency of Canada, Health Surveillance and Epidemiology Division. (2004–2006). *Injuries Associated with Backyard Trampolines: Canadian Hospitals Injury Reporting and Prevention Program (CHIRPP) database.* Ottawa, ON: Author. Retrieved from http://www.phac-aspc.gc.ca/injury-bles/chirpp/injrep-rapbles/index-eng.php

Puma, M., Bell, S., Cook, R., Heid, C., Broene, P., Jenkins, F., Mashburn, A., & Downer, J. (2012). *Third Grade Follow-up to the Head Start Impact Study Final Report,* OPRE Report # 2012-45. Washington, DC: Office of Planning, Research and Evaluation, Administration for Children and Families, U.S. Department of Health and Human Services. Retrieved from http://www.acf.hhs.gov/programs/opre/research/project/head-start-impact-study-and-follow-up-2000-2012

Putallaz, M., & Bierman, K. L. (Eds.). (2004). *Aggression, antisocial behavior, and violence among girls: A Developmental Perspective.* New York: Guilford Press.

Putnam, F. (2002). Ten-year research update review: Child sexual abuse. *Journal of the American Academy of Child & Adolescent Psychiatry, 42*(3), 269–278.

Quach, J., Hiscock, H., Ukoumunne, O. C., & Wake, M. (2011). A brief sleep intervention improves outcomes in the school entry year: A randomized controlled trial. *Pediatrics, 128,* 692–701. doi:10.1542/peds.2011-0409

Quattrin, T., Liu, E., Shaw, N., Shine, B., & Chiang, E. (2005). Obese children who are referred to the pediatric oncologist: Characteristics and outcome. *Pediatrics, 115,* 348–351.

Quinn, P. C., Eimas, P. D., & Rosenkrantz, S. L. (1993). Evidence for representations of perceptually similar natural categories by 3-month-old and 4-month-old infants. *Perception, 22,* 463–475.

Rabiner, D., & Coie, J. (1989). Effect of expectancy induction on rejected peers' acceptance by unfamiliar peers. *Developmental Psychology, 25,* 450–457.

Rabson, M. (2001, August 30). School system fails aboriginals: Lewis. *Winnipeg Free Press,* A9.

Racine, Y., & Boyle, M. (2002). Family functioning and children's behaviour problems. In J.D. Willms (Ed.), *Vulnerable children: Findings from Canada's National Longitudinal Survey of Children and Youth* (pp. 199–209). Edmonton, AB: The University of Alberta Press.

Raikes, H., Pan, B. A., Luze, G., Tamis-LeMonda, C. S., Brooks-Gunn, J., Constantine, J., et al. (2006). Mother-child book-reading in low-income families: Correlates and outcomes during three years of life. *Child Development, 77,* 924–953.

Raine, A., Mellingen, K., Liu, J., Venables, P., & Mednick, S. (2003). Effects of environmental enrichment at ages 3–5 years in schizotypal personality and antisocial behavior at ages 17 and 23 years. *American Journal of Psychiatry, 160,* 1627–1635.

Rakison, D. H. (2005). Infant perception and cognition. In B. J. Ellis & D. F. Bjorklund (Eds.), *Origins of the social mind* (pp. 317–353). New York: Guilford Press.

Rakoczy, H., Tomasello, M., & Striano, T. (2004). Young children know that trying is not pretending: A test of the "behaving-as-if" construal of children's early concept of pretense. *Developmental Psychology, 40,* 388–399.

Ramani, G. B., & Siegler, R. S. (2008). Promoting broad and stable improvements in low-income children's numerical knowledge through playing number board games. *Child Development, 79,* 375–394.

Ramey, C. T., & Campbell, F. A. (1991). Poverty, early childhood education, and academic competence. In A. Huston (Ed.), *Children reared in poverty* (pp. 190–221). Cambridge, England: Cambridge University Press.

Ramey, C. T., & Ramey, S. L. (1998). Prevention of intellectual disabilities: Early interventions to improve cognitive development. *Preventive Medicine, 21,* 224–232.

Ramey, C. T., & Ramey, S. L. (2003, May). *Preparing America's children for success in school.* Paper prepared for an invited address at the White House Early Childhood Summit on Ready to Read, Ready to Learn, Denver, CO.

Rao, P. A., Beidel, D. C., Turner, S. M., Ammerman, R. T., Crosby, L. E., & Sallee, F. R. (2007). Social anxiety disorder in children and adolescence: Descriptive psychopathology. *Behaviour Research and Therapy, 45*(6), 1181–1191.

Rask-Nissilä, L., Jokinen, E., Terho, P., Tammi, A., Lapinleimu, H., Ronnemaa, T., et al. (2000). Neurological development of 5-year-old children receiving a low-saturated fat, low cholesterol diet since infancy. *Journal of the American Medical Association, 284*(8), 993–1000.

Rathbun, A., West, J., & Germino-Hausken, E. (2004). *From kindergarten through third grade: Children's beginning school experiences* (NCES 2004–007). Washington, DC: National Center for Education Statistics.

Reef, S. E., Strebel, P., Dabbagh, A., Gacic-Dobo, M., & Cochi, S. (2011). Progress toward control of rubella and prevention of congential rubella syndrome—worldwide, 2009. *Journal of Infectious Diseases, 204*(1), 24–27.

Reefhuis, J., Honein, M. A., Schieve, L. A., Correa, A., Hobbs, C. A., Rasmussen, S. A., and the National Birth Defects Prevention Study. (2008). Assisted reproductive technology and major structural birth defects in the United States. *Human Reproduction, 387,* 1–7.

Reese, E. (1995). Predicting children's literacy from mother-child conversations. *Cognitive Development, 10,* 381–405.

Reese, E., & Cox, A. (1999). Quality of adult book reading affects children's emergent literacy. *Developmental Psychology, 35,* 20–28.

Regan L., & Rai, R. (2000). Epidemiology and the medical causes of miscarriage. *Baillière's Clinical Obstetrics and Gynaecology, 14,* 839–854.

Reichenberg, A., Gross, R., Weiser, M., Bresnahan, M., Silverman, J., Harlap, S., et al. (2006). Advancing paternal age and autism. *Archives of General Psychiatry, 63*(9), 1026–1032.

Reiner, W. (2000, May 12). *Cloacal exstrophy: A happenstance model for androgen imprinting.* Presentation at the meeting of the Pediatric Endocrine Society, Boston.

Reiner, W. G., & Gearhart, J. P. (2004). Discordant sexual identity in some genetic males with cloacal exstrophy assigned to female sex at birth. *New England Journal of Medicine, 350*(4), 333–341.

Remafedi, G., French, S., Story, M., Resnick, M. D., & Blum, R. (1998). The relationship between suicide risk and sexual orientation: Results of a population-based study. *American Journal of Public Health, 88,* 57–60.

Remez, L. (2000). Oral sex among adolescents: Is it sex or is it abstinence? *Family Planning Perspectives, 32,* 298–304.

Rende, R., Slomkowski, C., Lloyd-Richardson, E., & Niaura, R. (2005). Sibling effects on substance use in adolescence: Social contagion and genetic relatedness. *Journal of Family Psychology, 19,* 611–618.

Repeal 43 Committee. (n.d.). *The law.* Retrieved from http://www.repeal43.org

Repetti, R. L., Taylor, S. E., & Seeman, T. S. (2002). Risky families: Family social environments and the mental and physical health of the offspring. *Psychological Bulletin, 128*(2), 330–366.

Resnick, L. B. (1989). Developing mathematical knowledge. *American Psychologist, 44,* 162–169.

Rethman, J. (2000). Trends in preventative care: Caries risk assessment and indications for sealants. *The Journal of the American Dental Association, 131*(1), 85–125.

Retschitzki, J. (1989). Evidence of formal thinking in Baule airele players. In D. M. Keats, D. Munro, & L. Mann (Eds.), *Heterogeneity in cross-cultural psychology.* Amsterdam: Swets & Zeitlinger.

Reynolds, A. J., & Temple, J. A. (1998). Extended early childhood intervention and school achievement: Age thirteen findings from the Chicago Longitudinal Study. *Child Development, 69,* 231–246.

Reynolds, A. J., Temple, J. A., Robertson, D. L., & Mann, E. A. (2001). Long-term effects of an early childhood intervention on educational achievement and juvenile arrest. A 15-year follow-up of low-income children in public schools. *Journal of American Medical Association, 285*(18), 2339–2346.

Reynolds, G. (1998). Welcoming place: An urban community of Inuit families. *Canadian Children, 23*(1), 5–11.

Reynolds, J. N., Weinberg, J., Clarren, S., Beaulieu, C., Rasmussen, C., Kobor, M., . . . & Goldowitz, D. (2011). Fetal alcohol spectrum disorders: gene-environment interactions, predictive biomarkers, and the reslationship between structural alterations in the brain and functional outcomes. *Seminars in Pediatric Neurology, 18,* 49–55.

Rhee, S. H. & Waldman, I. D. (2002). Genetic and environmental influences on antisocial behavior: A meta-analysis of twin and adoption studies. *Psychological Bulletin, 128,* 490–529.

Rhoton-Vlasak, A. (2000). Infections and infertility. *Primary Care Update for OB/GYNS, 7*(5), 200–206.

Ricciuti, H. N. (2004). Single parenthood, achievement, and problem behavior in white, black, and Hispanic children. *Journal of Educational Research, 97,* 196–206.

Rice, M. L. (1982). Child language: What children know and how. In T. M. Field, A.

Huston, H. C. Quay, L. Troll, & G. E. Finley (Eds.), *Review of human development research.* New York: Wiley.

Rice, M. L. (1989). Children's language acquisition. *American Psychologist, 44*(2), 149–156.

Rice, M. L., Taylor, C. L., & Zubrick, S. R. (2008). Language outcomes of 7-year-old children with or without a history of late language emergence at 24 months. *Journal of Speech, Language, and Hearing Research, 51,* 394–407.

Richardson, J. (1995). *Achieving gender equality in families: The role of males.* Innocenti Global Seminar, Summary Report. Florence, Italy: UNICEF International Child Development Centre, Spedale degli Innocenti.

Richland, L. E., & Burchinal, M. R. (2013). Early executive function predicts reasoning development. *Psychological Science, 24,* 87–92. doi:10.1177/0956797612450883

Riddell, R. P. (2007). Review of WISC-IV advanced clinical interpretation. *Canadian Psychology, 48,* 51–53.

Rinaldi, C. M., & Howe, N. (2012). Mothers' and fathers' parenting styles and associations with toddlers' externalizing, internalizing, and adaptive behaviors. *Early Childhood Research Quarterly, 27,* 266–273. doi:10.1016/j.ecresq.2011.08.001

Rios-Ellis, B., Bellamy, L., & Shoji, J. (2000). An examination of specific types of *ijime* within Japanese schools. *School Psychology International, 21,* 227–241.

Rivara, F. (1999). Pediatric injury control in 1999: Where do we go from here? *Pediatrics, 103*(4), 883–888.

Rivera, J. A., Sotres-Alvarez, D., Habicht, J.-P., Shamah, T., & Villalpando, S. (2004). Impact of the Mexican Program for Education, Health and Nutrition (Progresa) on rates of growth and anemia in infants and young children. *Journal of the American Medical Association, 291,* 2563–2570.

Roberts, K. C., Shields, M., de Groh, M., Aziz, A., & Gilbert, J.-A. (2012). Overweight and obesity in children and adolescents: Results from the 2009 to 2011 Canadian Health Measures Survey. *Health Reports, 23*(3), 37–41.

Robin, D. J., Berthier, N. E., & Clifton, R. K. (1996). Infants' predictive reaching for moving objects in the dark. *Developmental Psychology, 32,* 824–835.

Rock, A.M., Trainor, L.J., & Addison, T.L. (1999). Distinctive messages in infant-directed lullabies and play songs. *Developmental Psychology, 35,* 527–534.

Rodkin, P. C., Farmer, T. W., Pearl, R., & Van Acker, R. (2000). Heterogeneity of popular boys: Antisocial and prosocial configurations. *Developmental Psychology, 36*(1), 14–24.

Roer-Strier, D., Strier, R., Este, D., Shimoni, R., & Clarke, D. (2005). Fatherhood and

immigration: Challenging the deficit theory. *Child and Family Social Work, 10,* 315–329.

Roessingh, H., & Kover, P. (2003). Variability of ESL learners' acquisition of cognitive academic language proficiency: What can we learn from achievement measures? *TESL Canada Journal/Revue TESL du Canada, 21,* 1–21.

Roessingh, H., Kover, P., & Watt, D. (2005). Developing cognitive academic language proficiency: The journey. *TESL Canada Journal/Revue TESL du Canada, 23,* 1–27.

Rogler, L. H. (2002). Historical generations and psychology: The case of the Great Depression and World War II. *American Psychologist, 57*(12), 1013–1023.

Rogoff, B. (2003). *The cultural nature of human development.* Oxford, UK: Oxford University Press.

Rogoff, B., Mistry, J., Göncü, A., & Mosier, C. (1993). Guided participation in cultural activity by toddlers and caregivers. *Monographs of the Society for Research in Child Development, 58*(8) [Serial No. 236].

Rolls, B. J., Engell, D., & Birch, L. L. (2000). Serving portion size influences 5-year-old but not 3-year-old children's food intake. *Journal of the American Dietetic Association, 100,* 232–234.

Romano, E., Tremblay, R. E., Boulerice, B., & Swisher, R. (2005). Multi-level correlates of childhood physical aggression and prosocial behavior. *Journal of Abnormal Child Psychology, 33*(5), 565–578.

Roopnarine, J. L. (2011). Cultural variations in beliefs about play, parent-child play, and children's play: Meaning for childhood development. In A. D. Pellegrini (ed.), *The Oxford Handbook of the Development of Play* (pp. 19–40). Oxford, UK: Oxford University Press.

Roopnarine, J. L., Hooper, F. H., Ahmeduzzaman, M., & Pollack, B. (1993). Gentle play partners: Mother-child and father-child play in New Delhi, India. In K. MacDonald (Ed.), *Parent-child play* (pp. 287–304). Albany, NY: State University of New York Press.

Roosa, M. W., Deng, S., Ryu, E., Burrell, G. L., Tein, J., Jones, S., . . . & Crowder, S. (2005). Family and child characteristics linking neighborhood context and child externalizing behavior. *Journal of Marriage and Family, 667,* 515–529.

Rose, A. J., & Rudolph, K. D. (2006). A review of sex differences in peer relationship processes: Potential trade-offs for the emotional and behavioral development of girls and boys. *Psychological Bulletin, 132,* 98–131.

Rose, S. A., & Feldman, J. F. (2000). The relation of very low birth weight to basic cognitive skills in infancy and childhood. In C. A. Nelson (Ed.), *The effects of early adversity on neurobehavioral development. The Minnesota Symposia on Child Psychology* (Vol. 31, pp. 31–59). Mahwah, NJ: Erlbaum.

Rose, S. A., Feldman, J. F., & Jankowski, J. J. (2001). Attention and recognition memory in the 1st year of life: A longitudinal study of preterm and full-term infants. *Developmental Psychology, 37*, 135–151.

Rose, S. A., Jankowski, J., & Feldman, J. (2002). Speed of processing and face recognition at 7 and 12 months. *Infancy, 3*(4), 435–455.

Rosen, L. D., Cheever, N. A., & Carrier, L. M. (2008). The association of parenting style and child age with parental limit setting and adolescent MySpace behavior. *Journal of Applied Developmental Psychology, 29*(6), 459–471. doi:10.1016/j.appdev.2008.07.005

Rosenkranz, R. R., Welk, G. J., Hastmann, T. J., & Dzewaltowski, D. A. (2011). Psychosocial and demographic correlates of objectively measured physical activity in structured and unstructured after-school recreation sessions. *Journal of Science and Medicine in Sport, 14*, 306–311. doi:10.1016/j.jsams.2011.01.005

Rossi, R. (1996, August 30). Small schools under microscope. *Chicago Sun-Times*, p. 24.

Rossiter, M. J., & Rossiter, K. R. (2009). Diamonds in the rough: Bridging gaps in supports for at-risk immigrant and refugee youth. *Journal of International Migration and Integration, 10*, 409–429. doi:10.1007/s12134-009-0110-3

Rothbart, M. K., Ahadi, S. A., & Evans, D. E. (2000). Temperament and personality: Origins and outcomes. *Journal of Personality and Social Psychology, 78*, 122–135.

Rothbart, M. K., Ahadi, S. A., Hershey, K. L., & Fisher, P. (2001). Investigations of temperament at three to seven years: The Children's Behavior Questionnaire. *Child Development, 72*, 1394–1408.

Rotermann, M. (2005). Sex, condoms and STDs among young people. *Health Reports, 16*, 39–45 (Statistics Canada Catalogue no. 82-003).

Rotermann, M. (2008). Trends in teen sexual behaviour and condom use. *Health Reports, 19*(3), 1–5 (Statistics Canada Catalogue no. 82-003-XPE).

Roudebush, J. R., Kaufman, J., Johnson, B. H., Abraham, M. R., & Clayton, S. P. (2006). Patient- and family-centered perinatal care: Partnerships with childbearing women and families. *Journal of Perinatal and Neonatal Nursing, 20*, 201–209.

Rouse, C., Brooks-Gunn, J., & McLanahan, S. (2005). Introducing the issue. *The Future of Children, 15*(1), 5–14.

Rovee-Collier, C. (1999). The development of infant memory. *Current Directions in Psychological Science, 8*, 80–85.

Rowe, M. L., Ozcaliskan, S., & Goldin-Meadow, S. (2008). Learning words by hand: Gesture's role in predicting vocabulary development. *First Language, 28*, 182–199.

Rowland, A. S., Umbach, D. M., Stallone, L., Naftel, J., Bohlig, E. M., & Sandler, D. P. (2002). Prevalence of medication treatment for attention-deficit hyperactivity disorder among elementary school children in Johnston County, North Carolina. *American Journal of Public Health, 92*, 231–234.

Royal Commission on New Reproductive Technologies. (1993). *Proceed with care: Final report of the Royal Commission on New Reproductive Technologies*. Ottawa, ON: Canada Government Publishing.

Rubin, K. H., Bukowski, W., & Parker, J. G. (1998). Peer interactions, relationships, and groups. In W. Damon (Series Ed.) & N. Eisenberg (Vol. Ed.), *Handbook of child psychology: Vol. 3. Social, emotional, and personality development* (5th ed., pp. 619–700). New York: Wiley.

Rubin, K. H., Burgess, K. B., Dwyer, K. M., & Hastings, P. D. (2003). Predicting preschoolers' externalizing behavior from toddler temperament, conflict, and maternal negativity. *Developmental Psychology, 39*(1), 164–176.

Rubin, K. H., Burgess, K. B., & Hastings, P. D. (2002). Stability and social-behavioral consequences of toddlers' inhibited temperament and parenting behaviors. *Child Development, 73*(2), 483–495.

Rubin, K. H., Hemphill, S. A., Chen, X., Hastings, P., Sanson, A., Lo Coco, A. … Cui, L. (2006). A cross-cultural study of behavioral inhibition in toddlers: East–west–north–south. *International Journal of Behavioral Development, 30*, 219–226.

Ruble, D. N., & Martin, C. L. (1998). Gender development. In W. Damon (Series ed.) & N. Eisenberg (Vol. Ed.), *Handbook of child psychology: Vol. 3. Social, emotional, and personality development* (5th ed., pp. 933–1016). New York: Wiley.

Ruble, D. N., Martin, C. L., & Berenbaum, S. A. (2006). Gender development. In W. Damon & R. M. Lerner (Series Eds.) & D. Kuhn & R. S. Seigler (Vol. Eds.), *Handbook of child psychology: Vol 2. Cognition, perception, and language* (pp. 858–932). Hoboken, NJ: Wiley.

Rudolph, K. D., Lambert, S. F., Clark, A. G., & Kurlakowsky, K. D. (2001). Negotiating the transition to middle school: The role of self-regulatory processes. *Child Development, 72*(3), 929–946.

Rudy, D., & Grusec, J. (2001). Correlates of authoritarian parenting in individualist and collectivist cultures and implications for understanding the transmission of values. *Journal of Cross-Cultural Psychology, 32*, 202–212.

Rueter, M. A., & Koerner, A. F. (2009). The effect of family communication patterns on adopted adolescent adjustment. *Journal of Marriage and Family, 70*(3), 715–727.

Ruiz, F., & Tanaka, K. (2001). The *ijime* phenomenon and Japan: Overarching consideration for cross-cultural studies. *Psychologia: An International Journal of Psychology in the Orient, 44*, 128–138.

Rushton, J. P., & Jensen, A. R. (2005). Thirty years of research on race differences in cognitive ability. *Psychology, Public Policy, and Law, 11*, 235–294.

Rutter, M. (2002). Nature, nurture, and development: From evangelism through science toward policy and practice. *Child Development, 73*, 1–21.

Rutter, M., & the English and Romanian Adoptees (ERA) Study Team. (1998). Developmental catch-up, and deficit, following adoption after severe global early privation. *Journal of Child Psychology and Psychiatry, 39*, 465–476.

Rutter, M., O'Connor, T. G., & the English and Romanian Adoptees (ERA) Study Team. (2004). Are there biological programming effects for psychological development? Findings from a study of Romanian adoptees. *Developmental Psychology, 40*, 81–94.

Ryan, A. (2001). The peer group as a context for the development of young adolescent motivation and achievement. *Child Development, 72*(4), 1135–1150.

Ryan, A. S. (1997). The resurgence of breast-feeding in the United States. *Pediatrics, 99*. Retrieved from http://www.pediatrics.org/cgi/content/full/99/4/e12

Ryan, A. S. (2000). *Ross Mothers Survey*. Abbott Park, IL: Ross Products Division, Abbott Laboratories.

Ryan, B. A., & Adams, G. R. (1998). *Family relationships and children's school achievement: Data from the National Longitudinal Survey of Children and Youth*. (Catalogue no. W-98-13E). Ottawa, ON: Applied Research Branch, Strategic Policy, Human Resources Development Canada.

Saarni, C., Campos, J. J., Camras, A., & Witherington, D. (2006). Emotional development: Action, communication, and understanding. In N. Eisenberg, W. Damon, & R. Lerner (Eds.), *Handbook of child psychology: Vol. 3. Social, emotional and personality development* (6th ed., pp. 226–299). Hoboken, NJ: Wiley.

Sabbagh, M. A., & Taylor, M. (2000). Neural correlates of theory-of-mind reasoning: An event-related potential study. *Psychological Science, 11*(1), 46–50.

Sack, W. H., Beiser, M., Baker-Brown, G., & Redshirt, R. (1994). Depressive and suicidal symptoms in Indian school children: Findings from the Flower of Two Soils. *American Indian & Alaska Native Mental Health Research, 4*, 81–96.

Sadeh, A., Mindell, J. A., Luedtke, K., Wiegand, B. (2009). Sleep and sleep ecology in the first 3 years: A web-based study. *Journal of Sleep Research, 18,* 60–73. doi: 10.1111/j.1365-2869.2008.00699.x

Sadeh, A., Raviv, A., & Gruber, R. (2000). Sleep patterns and sleep disruptions in school age children. *Developmental Psychology, 36*(3), 291–301.

Safe Kids Canada. (2012). Safety information. Retrieved from http://www.safekidscanada.ca/Parents/Safety-Information/Index.aspx

Saffran, J. R., Pollak, S. D., Seibel, R. L., & Shkolnik, A. (2007). Dog is a dog is a dog: Infant rule learning is not specific to language. *Cognition, 105*(3), 669–680.

Saigal, S., Stoskopf. B., Streiner, D., Boyle, M., Pinelli, J., Paneth, N., & Goddeeris, J. (2006). Transition of extremely low-birth-weight infants from adolescence to young adulthood: Comparison with normal birth-weight controls. *Journal of the American Medical Association, 295,* 667–675.

Saklofske, D. H., Caravan, G., & Schwartz, C. (2000). Concurrent validity of the Wechsler Abbreviated Scale of Intelligence (WASI) with a sample of Canadian children. *Canadian Journal of School Psychology, 16,* 87–94. doi:10.1177/082957350001600106

Saklofske, D. H., & Schwean, V. L. (1995). Psychological and educational assessment of children. In K. Covell (Ed.), *Readings in child development* (pp. 185–208). Toronto, ON: Nelson.

Saklofske, D. H., Zhu, J., Coalson, D. L., Raiford, S. E., & Weiss, L. G. (2010). Cognitive proficiency index for the Canadian edition of the Wechsler Intelligence Scale for Children—Fourth Edition. *Canadian Journal of School Psychology, 25,* 277–286. doi:10.1177/0829573510380539

Saklofske, D. H., Zhu, J., Raiford, S. E., Weiss, L. G., & Coalson, D. (2008). *WISC-IV Technical Report 4.1.2: General Ability Index Canadian Norms (Update version).* Toronto, ON: Harcourt Assessment.

Salkind, N. J. (Ed.). (2005). Smiling. *The encyclopedia of human development.* Thousand Oaks, CA: Sage.

Samara, M., Marlow, N., Wolke, D. for the EPICure Study Group. (2008). Pervasive behavior problems at 6 years of age in a total-population sample of children born at 25 weeks of gestation. *Pediatrics, 122,* 562–573.

Samdal, O., & Dür, W. (2000). The school environment and the health of adolescents. In C. Currie, K. Hurrelmann, W. Settertobulte, R. Smith, & J. Todd (Eds.), *Health and health behaviour among young people: A WHO cross-national study (HBSC) international report* (pp. 49–64). WHO Policy Series: Health Policy for Children and Adolescents, Series No. 1. Copenhagen, Denmark: World Health Organization Regional Office for Europe.

Sampson, H. A. (2004). Update on food allergies. *Journal of Allergy and Clinical Immunology, 113*(5), 805–819.

Samson, L. M., Canadian Paediatric Society (CPS) Adolescent Health Committee, Infectious Diseases and Immunization Committee. (2007). Human papilloma virus vaccine for children and adolescents. *Paediatrics & Child Health, 12,* 599–603.

Sandstrom, M. J., & Coie, J. D. (1999). A developmental perspective on peer rejection: Mechanisms of stability and change. *Child Development 70*(4), 955–966.

Santos, A. (2012). Considerations for education reform in British Columbia. *Canadian Journal of Educational Administration and Policy, 138,* 1–16. Retrieved from http://www.umanitoba.ca/publications/cjeap/pdf_files/santos.pdf

Santos, I. S., Victora, C. G., Huttly, S., & Carvalhal, J. B. (1998). Caffeine intake and low birth weight: A population-based case-control study. *American Journal of Epidemiology, 147,* 620–627.

Santos, R. G., Chartier, M. J., Whalen, J. C., Chateau, D., Boyd, L. (2011). Cluster randomized controlled field trial of the Roots of Empathy program with replication and three-year follow-up. *Healthcare Quarterly, 14,* 80–91.

Sarnecka, B. W., & Carey, S. (2007). How counting represents number: What children must learn and when they learn it. *Cognition, 108*(3), 662–674.

Saswati, S., Chang, J., Flowers, L., Kulkarni, A., Sentelle, G., Jeng, G., et al. (2009). *Assisted reproductive technology surveillance—United States, 2006* (Centers for Disease Control: June, 2009).

Satcher, D. (2001). *Women and smoking: A report of the Surgeon General.* Washington, DC: Department of Health and Human Services.

Saudino, K. J., Wertz, A. E., Gagne, J. R., & Chawla, S. (2004). Night and day: Are siblings as different in temperament as parents say they are? *Journal of Personality and Social Psychology, 87,* 698–706.

Saunders, N. (1997, March). Pregnancy in the 21st century: Back to nature with a little assistance. *Lancet, 349,* s17–s19.

Savage, J. S., Fisher, J. O., & Birch, L. L. (2007). Parental influence on eating behavior: Conception to Adolescence. *Journal of Law, Medicine, and Ethics, 35*(1), 22–34.

Savage, R., Abrami, P. C., Piquette, N., Wood, E., Deleveaux, G., Sanghera-Sidhu, S., & Burgos, G. (2013). A (Pan-Canadian) Cluster Randomized Control Effectiveness Trial of the ABRACADABRA Web-Based Literacy Program. *Journal of Educational Psychology, 105,* 310–328. doi:10.1037/a0031025

Savic, I., Berglund, H., & Lindström, P. (2006). Brain response to putative pheromones.

Proceedings of the National Academy of Sciences, 102(20), 7356–7361.

Savic, I., & Lindström, P. (2008). PET and MRI show differences in cerebral assymetry and functional connectivity between homo- and heterosexual subjects. *Proceedings of the National Academy of Sciences USA, 105*(27), 9403–9408.

Savin-Williams, R. C., & Ream, G. L. (2007). Prevalence and stability of sexual orientation components during adolescence and young adulthood. *Archives of Sexual Behavior, 36,* 385–394 [PubMed].

Savin-Williams, R. C., & Vrangalova, Z. (2013). Mostly heterosexual as a distinct sexual orientation group: A systematic review of the empirical evidence. *Developmental Review, 33*(1), 58–88. doi:10.1016/j.dr.2013.01.001

Saxe, R., & Carey, S. (2006). The perception of causality in infancy. *Acta Psychologica, 123,* 144–165.

Scaldwell, W., Frame, J., & Cookson, D. (1985). Individual assessment of Chippewa, Muncey and Oneida children using the WISC–R. *Canadian Journal of School Psychology, 1,* 15–21.

Scarr, S. (1992). Developmental theories for the 1990s: Development and individual differences. *Child Development, 63,* 1–19.

Scarr, S., & McCartney, K. (1983). How people make their own environments: A theory of genotype-environment effects. *Child Development, 54,* 424–435.

Schack-Nielsen, L., Michaelsen, K. F., Gamborg, M., Mortensen, E. L., & Sørensen, T. I. (2010). Gestational weight gain in relation to offspring body mass index and obesity from infancy through adulthood. *International Journal of Obesity, 34,* 67–74.

Scheers, N. J., Rutherford, G. W., & Kemp, J. S. (2003). Where should infants sleep? A comparison of risk for suffocation of infants sleeping in cribs, adult beds, and other sleeping locations. *Pediatrics, 112,* 883–889.

Scheidt, P., Overpeck, M. D., Whatt, W., & Aszmann, A. (2000). In C. Currie, K. Hurrelmann, W. Settertobulte, R. Smith, & J. Todd (Eds.), *Health and health behaviour among young people: A WHO crossnational study (HBSC) international report* (pp. 24–38). WHO Policy Series: Healthy Policy for Children and Adolescents, Series No. 1. Copenhagen, Denmark: World Health Organization Regional Office for Europe.

Scher, A., Epstein, R., & Tirosh, E. (2004). Stability and changes in sleep regulation: A longitudinal study from 3 months to 3 years. *International Journal of Behavioral Development, 28*(3), 268–274.

Schmitt, S. A., Simpson, A. M., & Friend, M. (2011). A longitudinal assessment of the home literacy environment and early language. *Infant and Child Development, 20*(6), 409–431.

Schmitz, S., Saudino, K. J., Plomin, R., Fulker, D. W., & DeFries, J. C. (1996). Genetic and environmental influences on temperament in middle childhood: Analyses of teacher and tester ratings. *Child Development, 67,* 409–422.

Schneider, M. (2002). *Do school facilities affect academic outcomes?* Washington, DC: National Clearinghouse for Educational Facilities.

Schneider, W. (2010). Memory development in childhood. In U. Goswami (Ed.), *The Wiley-Blackwell Handbook of Childhood Cognitive Development,* 2nd Edition (pp. 347–376). Malden, MA: Blackwell Publishing Ltd.

Schroth, R. J., Harrison, R. L., & Moffatt, M. E. K. (2009). Oral health of indigenous children and the influence of early childhood caries on childhood health and well-being. *Pediatric Clinics of North America, 56,* 1481–1499. doi:10.1016/j.pcl.2009.09.010

Schulenberg, J., O'Malley, P., Backman, J., & Johnston, L. (2005). Early adult transitions and their relation to well-being and substance use. In R. A. Settersten Jr., F. F. Furstenberg Jr., & R. G. Rumbaut (Eds.), *On the frontier of adulthood: Theory, research, and public policy* (pp. 417–453). Chicago: University of Chicago Press.

Schulenberg, J. E., & Zarrett, N. R. (2006). Mental health during emerging adulthood: Continuity and discontinuity in courses, causes, and functions. In J. J. Arnett & J. L. Tanner (Eds.), *Emerging adults in America: Coming of age in the 21st century* (pp. 135–172). Washington DC: American Psychological Association.

Schulting, A. B., Malone, P. S., & Dodge, K. A. (2005). The effect of school-based kindergarten transition policies and practices on child academic outcomes. *Developmental Psychology, 41,* 860–871.

Schulz, M. S., Cowan, C. P., & Cowan, P. A. (2006). Promoting healthy beginnings: A randomized controlled trial of a preventive intervention to preserve marital quality during the transition to parenthood. *Journal of Consulting and Clinical Psychology, 74,* 20–31.

Schwartz, D., Chang, L., & Farver, J. M. (2001). Correlates of victimization in Chinese children's peer groups. *Developmental Psychology, 37*(4), 520–532.

Schwartz, D., Dodge, K. A., Pettit, G. S., Bates, J. E., & the Conduct Problems Prevention Research Group. (2000). Friendship as a moderating factor in the pathway between early harsh home environment and later victimization in the peer group. *Developmental Psychology, 36,* 646–662.

Schwartz, L. L. (2003). A nightmare for King Solomon: The new reproductive technologies. *Journal of Family Psychology, 17,* 292–237.

Schwartzentruber, J., Korshunov, A., Liu, X.-Y., Jones, D. T. W., Pfaff, E., ... Jabado, N. (2012). Driver mutations in histone H3.3 and chromatin remodelling genes in paediatric glioblastoma. *Nature, 482,* 226–231.

Schweinhart, L. J., Barnes, H. V., & Weikart, D. P. (1993). *Significant benefits: The High/Scope Perry Preschool Study through age 27* (Monographs of the High/Scope Educational Research Foundation No. 10). Ypsilanti, MI: High/Scope.

Schweinhart, L .J. (2007). Crime prevention by the High/Scope Perry preschool program. *Victims & Offenders, 2*(2), 141–160.

Schwenck, C., Bjorklund, D. F., & Schneider, W. (2009). Developmental and individual differences in young children's use and maintenance of a selective memory strategy. *Developmental Psychology, 45*(4), 1034–1050.

Searleman, A., & Porac, C. (2003). Lateral preference profiles and right shift attempt histories of consistent and inconsistent left-handers. *Brain & Cognition, 52,* 175–180.

Seifer, R., Schiller, M., Sameroff, A. J., Resnick, S., & Riordan, K. (1996). Attachment, maternal sensitivity, and infant temperament during the first year of life. *Developmental Psychology, 32,* 12–25.

Sell, R. L. (1997). Defining and measuring sexual orientation: A review. *Archives of Sexual Behavior, 26,* 643–658. Retrieved from http://dx.doi.org/10.1007/978-0-387-31334-4_14.

Seltzer, J. A. (2000). Families formed outside of marriage. *Journal of Marriage and the Family, 62,* 1247–1268.

Sénéchal, M., & LeFevre, J. (2002). Parental involvement in the development of children's reading skill: A five-year longitudinal study. *Child Development, 73*(2), 445–460.

Senghas, A., Kita, S., & Ozyürek, A. (2004). Children creating core properties of language: Evidence from an emerging sign language in Nicaragua. *Science, 305,* 1779–1782.

Serbin, L., Poulin-Dubois, D., Colburne, K. A., Sen, M., & Eichstedt, J. A. (2001). Gender stereotyping in infancy: Visual preferences for knowledge of gender-stereotyped toys in the second year. *International Journal of Behavioral Development, 25,* 7–15.

Sethi, A., Mischel, W., Aber, J. L., Shoda, Y., & Rodriguez, M. L. (2000). The role of strategic attention deployment in development of self-regulation: Predicting preschoolers' delay of gratification from mother-toddler interactions. *Developmental Psychology, 36,* 767–777.

The Sex Information and Education Council of Canada. (2004). Adolescent sexual and reproductive health in Canada: A report card in 2004. *The Canadian Journal of Human Sexuality, 13,* 67–81.

Shachar-Dadon, A., Schulkin, J., & Leshem, M. (2009). Adversity before conception will affect adult progeny in rats. *Developmental Psychology, 45*(1), 9–16.

Shanahan, M., Porfeli, E., & Mortimer, J. (2005). Subjective age identity and the transition to adulthood: When do adolescents become adults? In R. A. Settersten Jr., F. F. Furstenberg Jr., & R. G. Rumbaut (Eds.), *On the frontier of adulthood: Theory, research, and public policy* (pp. 225–255). Chicago: University of Chicago Press.

Shankaran, S., Bada, H. S., Smeriglio, V. L., Langer, J. C., Beeghly, M., & Poole, W. K. (2004). The maternal lifestyle study: Cognitive, motor, and behavioral outcomes of cocaine-exposed and opiate-exposed infants through three years of age. *Pediatrics, 113,* 1677–1685.

Shanner, L., & Nisker, J. (2001). Bioethics for clinicians: 26. Assisted reproductive technologies. *Canadian Medical Association Journal, 164,* 1589–1594.

Shannon, J. D., Tamis-LeMonda, C. S., London, K., & Cabrera, N. (2002). Beyond rough and tumble: Low income fathers' interactions and children's cognitive development at 24 months. *Parenting: Science & Practice, 2*(2), 77–104.

Shannon, M. (2000). Ingestion of toxic substances by children. *New England Journal of Medicine, 342,* 186–191.

Shapiro, A. F., & Gottman, J. M. (2003, September). Bringing baby home: Effects on marriage of a psycho-education intervention with couples undergoing the transition to parenthood, evaluation at 1-year post intervention. In A. J. Hawkins (Chair), *Early family interventions.* Symposium conducted at the meeting of the National Council on Family Relations, Vancouver, British Columbia.

Sharma, A. R., McGue, M. K., & Benson, P. L. (1996a). The emotional and behavioral adjustment of United States adopted adolescents, Part I: An overview. *Children and Youth Services Review, 18,* 83–100.

Sharon, T., & DeLoache, J. S. (2003). The role of perseveration in children's symbolic understanding and skill. *Developmental Science, 6*(3), 289–296.

Shaw, B. A., Krause, N., Liang, J., & Bennett, J. (2007). Tracking changes in social relations throughout late life. *Journal of Gerontology: Social Sciences, 62B,* S90–S99.

Shaw, P., Greenstein, D., Lerch, J., Clasen, L., Lenroot, R., Gogtay, N., et al. (2006). Intellectual ability and cortical development in children and adolescents. *Nature, 440,* 676–679.

Shaywitz, S. (2003). *Overcoming dyslexia: A new and complete science-based program for overcoming reading problems at any level.* New York: Knopf.

Shaywitz, S. E. (1998). Current concepts: Dyslexia. *New England Journal of Medicine, 338,* 307–312.

Shaywitz, S. E., Mody, M., & Shaywitz, B. A. (2006). Neural mechanisms in dyslexia. *Current Directions in Psychological Science, 15,* 278–281.

Sheppard, A. J., & Hetherington, R. (2012). A decade of research in Inuit children, youth, and maternal health in Canada: areas of concentrations and scarcities. *International Journal of Circumpolar Health, 71,* 18383.

Shields, M. (2005). Measured obesity: Overweight Canadian children and adolescents. *Nutrition: Findings from the Canadian Community Health Survey,* Issue no. 1 (Catalogue no. 82-620-MWE2005001). Ottawa, ON: Statistics Canada.

Shields, M. (2006). Overweight and obesity among children and youth. *Health Reports, 17*(3), 27–42 (Statistics Canada Catalogue 82-003).

Shiono, P. H., & Behrman, R. E. (1995). Low birth weight: Analysis and recommendations. *The Future of Children, 5*(1), 4–18.

Shulman, S., Scharf, M., Lumer, D., & Maurer, O. (2001). Parental divorce and young adult children's romantic relationships: Resolution of the divorce experience. *American Journal of Orthopsychiatry, 71,* 473–478.

Shwe, H. I., & Markman, E. M. (1997). Young children's appreciation of the mental impact of their communicative signals. *Developmental Psychology, 33*(4), 630–636.

Shweder, R. A., Goodnow, J., Hatano, G., Levine, R. A., Markus, H., & Miller, P. (2006). The cultural psychology of development: One mind, many mentalities. In W. Damon (Ed.), *Handbook of child development* (5th ed., Col. 1., pp. 865–937). New York: Wiley.

Siegler, R. S. (1998). *Children's thinking* (3rd ed.). Upper Saddle River, NJ: Prentice Hall.

Siegler, R. S. (2000). The rebirth of children's learning. *Child Development, 71*(1), 26–35.

Siegler, R. S., & Opfer, J. E. (2003). The development of numerical estimation: Evidence for multiple representations of numerical quantity. *Psychological Science, 14,* 237–243.

Siegler, R. S., & Richards, D. (1982). The development of intelligence. In R. Sternberg (Ed.), *Handbook of human intelligence.* London: Cambridge University Press.

Sieving, R. E., Oliphant, J. A., & Blum, R. W. (2002). Adolescent sexual behavior and sexual health. *Pediatrics in Review, 23,* 407–416.

Simard, V., Moss, E., & Pascuzzo, K. (2011). Early maladaptive schemas and child and adult attachment: A 15-year longitudinal study. *Psychology and Psychotherapy: Theory, Research and Practice, 84,* 349–366. doi:10.1111/j.2044-8341.2010.02009.x

Simen-Kapeu, A., & Veugelers, P. J. (2010). Socio-economic gradients in health behaviours and overweight in children in distinct economic settings. *Canadian Journal of Public Health, 101* (Supplement 3), s32–s36.

Simner, M. L. (1998). The Canadian Psychological Association's stand on beginning reading instruction. *Canadian Journal of Research in Early Childhood Education, 7,* 157–158.

Simon, G. E. (2006). The antidepressant quandary—considering suicide risk when treating adolescent depression. *New England Journal of Medicine, 355,* 2722–2723.

Simon, G. E., Savarino, J., Operskalski, B., & Wang, P. S. (2006). Suicide risk during antidepressant treatment. *American Journal of Psychiatry, 163,* 41–47.

Simonet, F., Wilkins, R., Heaman, M., Smylie, J., Martens, P., Mchugh, N. G. L., … (2010). Urban living is not associated with better birth and infant outcomes among Inuit and First Nations in Quebec. *The Open Women's Health Journal, 4,* 25–31.

Simons, R. L., Chao, W., Conger, R. D., & Elder, G. H. (2001). Quality of parenting as mediator of the effect of childhood defiance on adolescent friendship choices and delinquency: A growth curve analysis. *Journal of Marriage and the Family, 63,* 63–79.

Simpkins, S. D., Fredricks, J. A., & Eccles, J. S. (2012). Charting the Eccles' expectancy-value model from mothers' beliefs in childhood to youths' activities in adolescence. *Developmental Psychology, 48,* 1019–1032. doi:10.1037/a0027468

Simpson, J. E. (2005). Choosing the best prenatal screening protocol. *New England Journal of Medicine, 353,* 2068–2070.

Simpson, K. (2001). The role of testosterone in aggression. *McGill Journal of Medicine, 6,* 32–40.

Sinclair, Judge M., Phillips, D., & Bala, N. (1991). Aboriginal child welfare in Canada. In N. Bala, J. Hornick, & R. Vogl (Eds.), *Canadian child welfare law: Children, families and the state* (pp. 171–194). Toronto, ON: Thompson Educational.

Singer, J. L., & Singer, D. G. (1998). *Barney & Friends* as entertainment and education: Evaluating the quality and effectiveness of a television series for preschool children. In J. K. Asamen & G. L. Berry (Eds.), *Research paradigms, television, and social behavior* (pp. 305–367). Thousand Oaks, CA: Sage.

Singer, L. T., Minnes, S., Short, E., Arendt, K., Farkas, K., Lewis, B., et al. (2004). Cognitive outcomes of preschool children with prenatal cocaine exposure. *Journal of the American Medical Association, 291,* 2448–2456.

Singer-Freeman, K. E., & Goswami, U. (2001). Does half a pizza equal half a box of chocolates? Proportional matching in an analogy task. *Cognitive Development, 16*(3), 811–829.

Singh, S., Wulf, D., Samara, R., & Cuca, Y. P. (2000). Gender differences in the timing of first intercourse: Data from 14 countries. *International Family Planning Perspectives, Part 1, 26,* 21–28.

Skelton, J. A., Cook, S. R., Auinger, P., Klein, J. D., & Barlow, S. E. (2009). Prevalence and trends of severe obesity among US children and adolescents. *Academic Pediatrics, 9,* 322–329.

Skinner, B. F. (1957). *Verbal behavior.* New York: Appleton-Century-Crofts.

Skinner, R., & McFaull, S. (2012). Suicide among children and adolescents in Canada: Trends and sex differences, 1980–2008. *Canadian Medical Association Journal, 184,* 1029–1034. doi:10.1503/cmaj.111867

Skoe, E. E., & Diessner, R. E. (1994). Ethic of care, justice, identity, and gender: An extension and replication. *Merrill-Palmer Quarterly, 40,* 272–289.

Slobin, D. (1970). Universals of grammatical development in children. In W. Levitt & G. Flores d'Arcais (Eds.), *Advances in psycholinguistic research* (pp. 174–186). Amsterdam, The Netherlands: North Holland.

Slobin, D. (1983). Universal and particular in the acquisition of grammar. In E. Wanner & L. Gleitman (Eds.), *Language acquisition: The state of the art* (pp. 128–170). Cambridge, England: Cambridge University Press.

Slobin, D. (1990). The development from child speaker to native speaker. In J. W. Stigler, R.A. Schweder, & G. H. Herdt (Eds.), *Cultural Psychology: Essays on comparative human development* (pp. 233–258). New York: Cambridge University Press.

Slutzky, S., & Simpkins, S. D. (2007). The link between children's sports participation and self-esteem: Exploring the mediating role of sport self-concept. *Psychology of Sport and Exercise, 10*(3), 381–389.

Slyper, A. H. (2006). The pubertal timing controversy in the USA, and a review of possible causative factors for the advance in timing of onset of puberty. *Clinical Endocrinology, 65,* 1–8.

Small, M. Y. (1990). *Cognitive development.* New York: Harcourt Brace.

Smedley, A., & Smedley, B. D. (2005). Race as biology is fiction, racism as a social problem is real: Anthropological and historical perspectives on the social construction of race. *American Psychologist, 60,* 16–26.

Smetana, J., Crean, H., & Campione-Barr, N. (2005). Adolescents' and parents' changing conceptions of parental authority. In J. Smetana (Ed.), *Changing boundaries of parental authority during adolescence: New directions for child and adolescent development, no. 108* (pp. 31–46). San Francisco: Jossey-Bass.

Smetana, J. G., Metzger, A., Gettman, D. C., & Campione-Barr, N. (2006). Disclosure and secrecy in adolescent-parent relationships. *Child Development, 77,* 201–217.

Smilansky, S. (1968). *The effects of sociodramatic play on disadvantaged preschool children.* New York: Wiley.

Smith, A. M., Fried, P. A., Hogan, M. J., & Cameron, I. (2004). Effects of prenatal marijuana on response inhibition: An fMRI study of young adults. *Neurotoxicology and Teratology, 26,* 533–542.

Smith, E., & Jackson, A. (2002). *Does a rising tide lift all boats? The labour market experiences and incomes of recent immigrants, 1995 to 1998.* Ottawa, ON: Canadian Council on Social Development.

Smith, G. C. S., Pell, J. P., Cameron, A. D., & Dobbie, R. (2002). Risk of perinatal death associated with labor after previous cesarean delivery in uncomplicated term pregnancies. *Journal of the American Medical Association, 287,* 2684–2690.

Smith, L. B., & Thelen, E. (2003). Development as a dynamic system. *Trends in Cognitive Sciences, 7,* 343–348.

Smith, L. M., LaGasse, L. L., Derauf, C., Grant, P., Shah, R., Arria, A., et al. (2006). The infant development, environment, and lifestyle study: Effects of prenatal methamphetamine exposure, polydrug exposure, and poverty on intrauterine growth. *Pediatrics, 118,* 1149–1156.

Smith, P. K. (2005a). Play: Types and functions in human development. In A. D. Pellegrini & P. K. Smith (Eds.), *The nature of play* (pp. 271–291). New York: Guilford Press.

Smith, P. K. (2005b). Social and pretend play in children. In A. D. Pellegrini & P. K. Smith (Eds.), *The nature of play* (pp. 173–209). New York: Guilford Press.

Smolak, L., & Murnen, S. K. (2002, February 15). A meta-analytic examination of the relationship between child sexual abuse and eating disorders. *International Journal of Eating Disorders, 31,* 136–150.

Smylie, J., Fell, D., Ohlsson, A., and the Joint Working Group on First Nations, Indian, Inuit, and Métis Infant Mortality of the Canadian Perinatal Surveillance System. (2010). A Review of Aboriginal Infant Mortality Rates in Canada: Striking and Persistent Aboriginal/Non-Aboriginal Inequities. *Canadian Journal of Public Health, 101,* 143–148.

Snider, C. E., Ovens, H., Drummond, A., & Kapur, A. K. (2009). CAEP position statement on gun control. *Canadian Journal of Emergency Medicine, 11,* 64–72.

Snow, M. E., Jacklin, C. N., & Maccoby, E. E. (1983). Sex-of-child differences in father-child interaction at one year of age. *Child Development, 54,* 227–232.

Snyder, E. E., Walts, B., Perusse, L., Chagnon, Y. C., Weisnagel, S. J., Raniken, T., & Bouchard, C. (2004). The human obesity gene map. *Obesity Research, 12,* 369–439.

Snyder, J., Cramer, A., Frank, J., & Patterson, G. R. (2005). The contributions of ineffective discipline and parental hostile attributions of child misbehavior to the development of conduct problems at home and school. *Developmental Psychology, 41,* 30–41.

Sobolewski, J. M., & Amato, P. J. (2005). Economic hardship in the family of origin and children's psychological well-being in adulthood. *Journal of Marriage and Family, 67,* 141–156.

Sobolewski, J. M., & King, V. (2005). The importance of the coparental relationship for nonresident fathers' ties to children. *Journal of Marriage and Family, 67,* 1196–1212.

Society for Neuroscience. (2008). Neural disorders: Advances and challenges. *In Brain facts: A primer on the brain and nervous system* (pp. 36–54). Washington, DC: Author.

Society of Obstetricians and Gynaecologists of Canada. (1998). *Healthy beginnings: Guidelines for care during pregnancy and childbirth.* Policy Statement No. 71. Ottawa, ON: Author.

Society of Obstetricians and Gynaecologists of Canada. (2000). *Healthy beginnings: The complete get-ready-for-baby guide.* Ottawa, ON: Author.

Society of Obstetricians and Gynaecologists of Canada. (2003). Midwifery. *Journal of Obstetrics and Gynaecology Canada, 25,* 239.

Society of Obstetricians and Gynaecologists of Canada. (2005). Guidelines for vaginal birth after previous caesarean birth. *Journal of Obstetrics and Gynaecology Canada, 27,* 164–174.

Soenens, B., Vansteenkiste, M., Luyckx, K., & Goossens, L. (2006). Parenting and adolescent problem behavior: An integrated model with adolescent self-disclosure and perceived parental knowledge as intervening variables. *Developmental Psychology, 42,* 305–318.

Sokol, R. J., Delaney-Black, V., & Nordstrom, B. (2003). Fetal alcohol spectrum disorder. *Journal of the American Medical Association, 209,* 2996–2999.

Sokol, R. Z., Kraft, P., Fowler, I. M., Mamet, R., Kim, E., & Berhane, K. T. (2006). Exposure to environmental ozone alters semen quality. *Environmental Health Perspectives, 114*(3), 360–365.

Soller, L., Ben-Shoshan, M., Harrington, D. W., Fragapane, J., St. Pierre, Y., Godefroy, S. B., La Vielle, S., Elliott, S. J., & Clarke, A. E. (2012). Overall prevalence of self-reported food allergy in Canada. *Journal of Allergy and Clinical Immunology, 130,* 986–988.

Sontag, L. M., Graber, J. A., Brooks-Gunn, J., & Warren, M. (2008). Coping with social stress: Implications for psychopathology in young adolescent girls. *Journal of Abnormal Child Psychology, 36*(8), 1159–1174.

Sontag, L. M., Graber, J. A., & Clemans, K. H. (2011). The role of peer stress and pubertal timing on symptoms of psychopathology during early adolescence. *Journal of Youth and Adolescence, 40*(10), 1371–1382.

Sood, B., Delaney-Black, V., Covington, C., Nordstrom-Klee, B., Ager, J., Templin, T., et al. (2001). Prenatal alcohol exposure and childhood behavior at age 6 to 7 years: I. Dose-response effect. *Pediatrics, 108*(8), e461–e462.

Sorof, J. M., Lai, D., Turner, J., Poffenbarger, T., & Portman, R. J. (2004). Overweight, ethnicity, and the prevalence of hypertension in school-aged children. *Pediatrics, 113,* 475–482.

Spelke, E. S. (1998). Nativism, empiricism, and the origins of knowledge. *Infant Behavior and Development, 21*(2), 181–200.

Spelke, E. S. (2005). Sex differences in intrinsic aptitude for mathematics and science? A critical review. *American Psychologist, 60,* 950–958.

Sperling, M. A. (2004). Prematurity—a window of opportunity? *New England Journal of Medicine, 351,* 2229–2231.

Spinath, F. M., Price, T. S., Dale, P. S., & Plomin, R. (2004). The genetic and environmental origins of language disability and ability. *Child Development, 75,* 445–454.

Spinrad, T. L., Eisenberg, N., Harris, E., Hanish, L., Fabes, R. A., Kupanoff, K., et al. (2004). The relation of children's everyday nonsocial peer play behavior to their emotionality, regulation, and social functioning. *Developmental Psychology, 40,* 67–80.

Sroufe, L. A. (1997). *Emotional development.* Cambridge, England: Cambridge University Press.

Sroufe, L. A., Carlson, E., & Shulman, S. (1993). Individuals in relationships: Development from infancy through adolescence. In D. C. Funder, R. D. Parke, C. Tomlinson-Keasey, & K. Widaman (Eds.), *Studying lives through time: Personality and development* (pp. 315–342). Washington, DC: American Psychological Association.

Staff, J., Mortimer, J. T., & Uggen, C. (2004). Work and leisure in adolescence. In R. M. Lerner & L. Steinberg (Eds.), *Handbook of adolescent development* (2nd ed., pp. 429–450). Hoboken, NJ: Wiley.

Starr, J. M., Deary, I. J., Lemmon, H., & Whalley, L. J. (2000). Mental ability age 11 years and health status age 77 years. *Age and Ageing, 29,* 523–528.

Statistics Canada. (2002). National Longitudinal Survey of Children and Youth: Childhood obesity. *The Daily.* Retrieved from http://www.statcan.gc.ca/daily-quoti-dien/021018/dq021018b-eng.htm

Statistics Canada. (2004). *A portrait of aborigi-nal children living in non-reserve areas: Results from the 2001 aboriginal peoples survey.* Ottawa, ON: Housing, Family and Social Statistics Division.

Statistics Canada. (2007). *Census snapshot of Canada—Families.* Ottawa, ON: Author.

Statistics Canada. (2007b). *Participation and activity limitation survey 2006: Analytical report* (Catalogue no. 89-628-XIE no. 002). Ottawa, ON: Author. Retrieved from http://www5.statcan.gc.ca/bsolc/olc-cel/olc-cel?catno=89-628-X&CHROPG=1&lang=eng

Statistics Canada. (2007c). *Participation and activity limitation survey 2006: Tables.* Ottawa, ON: Author. Retrieved from http://www5.statcan.gc.ca/bsolc/olc-cel/olc-cel?catno= 89-628-X&CHROPG=1&lang=eng

Statistics Canada. (2008). *Canada's ethnocultural mosaic, 2006 census.* Ottawa, ON: Author.

Statistics Canada. (2008a). *Inuit health, educa-tion and country food harvesting* (Catalogue no. 89-637-X 2008004). Ottawa, ON: Author.

Statistics Canada. (2008b). *Aboriginal chil-dren's survey, 2006: Family, community and child care* (Catalogue no. 89-634-X-001). Ottawa, ON: Author.

Statistics Canada. (2008c) *Educational portrait of Canada, Census 2006* (Cat. No. 97-560-X2006001). Ottawa, ON: Author. Retrieved from http://www.statcan.gc.ca/bsolc/english/bsolc?catno=97-560-X2006001

Statistics Canada. (2009a). *School Age LICO: School-age population living in low-income circumstances.* Ottawa, ON: Author.

Statistics Canada. (2009b). *Income in Canada 2007* (Catalogue no.75-202-X). Ottawa, ON: Author.

Statistics Canada. (2009c). *Aboriginal peoples survey, 2006: An overview of the health of the Métis population – Fact sheet* (Cata-logue no. 89-637-X 2009006). Ottawa, ON: Author.

Statistics Canada. (2010). *Study: Projections of the diversity of the Canadian population, 2006 to 2031* (Catalogue no. 91-551-X). Ottawa, ON: Author.

Statistics Canada. (2010b). *Live birth, by birth weight (less than 2,500 grams) and sex, Canada, provinces and territories, annual* (CANSIM Table 102-4005). Ottawa, ON: Author.

Statistics Canada. (2011a). *Income in Canada 2009.* Retrieved from: http://www5.statcan.gc.ca/bsolc/olc-cel/olc-cel?catno=75-202-x&lang=eng

Statistics Canada. (2011b). *Table 102-0562: Leading causes of death, infants, by sex, Canada annual.* Retrieved from http://

www5.statcan.gc.ca/cansim/pick-choisir?lang=geng&p2=33&id=1020562

Statistics Canada. (2011c). *Table 102-4512: Live births, by weeks of gestation and sex, Canada, provinces and territories, annual, CANSIM (database).* Retrieved from http://www5.statcan.gc.ca/cansim/pick-choisir?lang=eng&p2=33&id=1024512

Statistics Canada. (2011d). *Table 102-4516: Live births and fetal deaths (stillbirths), by place of birth (hospital and non-hospital), Canada, provinces and territories, annual, CANSIM (database).* Retrieved from http://www5.statcan.gc.ca/cansim/a26?lang=eng&retrLang=eng&id=1024516&tabMode=dataTable&srchLan=-1&p1=-1&p2=35

Statistics Canada. (2011e). *Breastfeeding 2009.* Ottawa, ON: Author. Retrieved from http://www.statcan.gc.ca/pub/82-625-x/2010002/article/11269-eng.htm

Statistics Canada. (2011f). *Canada Yearbook 2011* (Catalogue no. 11-402-XPE). Ottawa, ON: Author.

Statistics Canada. (2011g). *Divorces and crude divorce rates, Canada, provinces and ter-ritories, annual.* (CANSIM table 101-6501) (in Excel format). Ottawa, ON: Author.

Statistics Canada. (2011h). Leading causes of death. *The Daily.* Ottawa, ON: Author. Retrieved from http://www.statcan.gc.ca/daily-quotidien/111101/dq111101b-eng.htm

Statistics Canada. (2011i). *Doctoral students and university teaching staff* (Catalogue no. 81-599-X Issue no. 006). Ottawa, ON: Author. Retrieved from http://www.statcan.gc.ca/pub/81-599-x/81-599-x2011006-eng.htm

Statistics Canada. (2011j). *Gay pride... by the numbers. 2010 (updated).* Ottawa, ON: Author. Retrieved from http://www42.statcan.gc.ca/smr08/2011/smr08_158_2011-eng.htm

Statistics Canada. (2012a). *Education indica-tors in Canada: Handbook for the Pan-Canadian Education Indicators Program* (Catalogue no. 81-582-G). Ottawa, ON: Author.

Statistics Canada. (2012b). *Portrait of families and living arrangements in Canada: Fami-lies, households and marital status, 2011 Census of Population.* Ottawa, ON: Author. Retrieved from http://www12.statcan.gc.ca/census-recensement/2011/as-sa/98-312-x/98-312-x2011001-eng.cfm

Statistics Canada. (2012c). *Births 2009* (Cata-logue no. 84F0210X. Table 102-4516 - Live births and fetal deaths (stillbirths), by place of birth (hospital and non-hospital), Canada, provinces and territories, annual, CANSIM (database). Ottawa, ON: Minister of Industry.

Statistics Canada. (2012d). *Table 102-0562 - Leading causes of death, infants, by sex, Canada, annual.* CANSIM (database). Retrieved from http://www5.statcan.gc.ca/cansim/a05?lang=eng&id=1020562

Statistics Canada. (2012e). *Persons in low income after tax.* Ottawa, ON: Author. Retrieved from http://www.statcan.gc.ca/tables-tableaux/sum-som/l01/cst01/famil19a-eng.htm

Statistics Canada. (2012f). *Low income lines* (Catalogue no. 75F0002M). Ottawa, ON: Author.

Statistics Canada. (2012g). *Linguistic char-acteristics of Canadians: Language, 2011 census of population* (Catalogue no. 98-314-X2011001). Ottawa, ON: Author. Retrieved from http://www12.statcan.ca/census-recensement/2011/as-sa/98-314-x/98-314-x2011001-eng.cfm

Statistics Canada. (2012h). *Immigrant lan-guages in Canada: Language, 2011 census of population. Census in Brief, 2* (Catalogue no. 98-314-X2011003). Ottawa, ON: Author. Retrieved from http://www12.statcan.gc.ca/census-recensement/2011/as-sa/98-314-x/98-314-x2011003_2-eng.cfm

Statistics Canada. (2012i). *Father's day ... by the numbers. 2012.* Ottawa, ON: Author. Retrieved from http://www42.statcan.gc.ca/smr08/2012/smr08_165_2012-eng.htm

Statistics Canada. (2012j). *Portrait of families and living arrangements in Canada: Fami-lies, households and marital status, 2011 Census of Population.* Ottawa, ON: Author. Retrieved from http://www12.statcan.gc.ca/census-recensement/2011/as-sa/98-312-x/98-312-x2011001-eng.cfm

Statistics Canada. (2012k, September 19). 2011 Census of Population: Families, households, marital status, structural type of dwelling, collectives. *The Daily,* Ottawa, ON: Author. Retrieved from http://www5.statcan.gc.ca

Statistics Canada. (2012l). *Youth crime, 2011.* Ottawa, ON: Author. Retrieved from http://www.statcan.gc.ca/pub/85-005-x/2012001/article/11749-eng.htm

Statistics Canada. (2013a). *Families and house-holds highlight tables, 2011 census.* Ottawa, ON: Author. Retrieved from http://www12.statcan.gc.ca/census-recensement/2011/dp-pd/hlt-fst/fam/index-eng.cfm?Lang=E

Statistics Canada. (2013b). *2011 Census of Canada: Topic-based tabulations. Topic-based tabulation: Conjugal Status (3), Opposite/Same-sex Status (5) and Presence of Children (5) for the Couple Census Fami-lies in Private Households of Canada, Prov-inces, Territories and Census Metropolitan Areas, 2011 Census.* Retrieved from http://www.statscan.ca

Steinberg, L. (2001). We know some things: Parent-adolescent relationships in retrospect and prospect. *Journal of Research on Ado-lescence, 11*(1), 1–19.

Steinberg, L. (2005). Psychological control: Style or substance? In J. Smetana (Ed.), *Changing boundaries of parental authority during adolescence: New directions for child and adolescent development, no. 108* (pp. 71–78). San Francisco: Jossey-Bass.

Steinberg, L. (2008). *Adolescence* (8th ed.). New York: McGraw-Hill.

Steinberg, L., Dornbusch, S. M., & Brown, B. B. (1992). Ethnic differences in adolescent achievement: An ecological perspective. *American Psychologist, 47,* 723–729.

Steinberg, L., Eisengard, B., & Cauffman, E. (2006). Patterns of competence and adjustment among adolescents from authoritative, authoritarian, indulgent, and neglectful homes: A replication in a sample of serious juvenile offenders. *Journal of Research on Adolescence, 16*(1), 47–58.

Steinhausen, H. C. (2002). The outcome of anorexia nervosa in the 20th century. *American Journal of Psychiatry, 159,* 1284–1293.

Stepanikova, I., Nie, N., & He, X. (2010). Time on the Internet at home, loneliness, and life satisfaction: Evidence from panel time-diary data. *Computers in Human Behavior, 26*(3), 329–338. doi:10.1016/j.chb.2009.11.002

Stephen, C., Stevenson, O., & Adley, C. (2013). Young children engaging with technologies at home: The influence of family context. *Journal of Early Childhood Research.* Advance online publication. doi:10.1177/1476718X12466215

Sternberg, R. J. (1985). *Beyond IQ: A triarchic theory of human intelligence.* New York: Cambridge University Press.

Sternberg, R. J. (1987, September 23). The use and misuse of intelligence testing: Misunderstanding meaning, users over-rely on scores. *Education Week,* pp. 22, 28.

Sternberg, R. J. (1997). The concept of intelligence and its role in lifelong learning and success. *American Psychologist, 52,* 1030–1037.

Sternberg, R. J. (2004). Culture and intelligence. *American Psychologist, 59,* 325–338.

Sternberg, R. J. (2005). There are no public policy implications: A reply to Rushton and Jensen (2005). *Psychology, Public Policy, and Law, 11,* 295–301.

Sternberg, R. J., Grigorenko, E. L., & Kidd, K. K. (2005). Intelligence, race, and genetics. *American Psychologist, 60,* 46–59.

Stice, E., Presnell, K., Shaw, H., & Rohde, P. (2005). Psychological and behavioral risk factors for obesity onset in adolescent girls: A prospective study. *Journal of Consulting and Clinical Psychology, 73,* 195–202.

Stipek, D. J., Gralinski, H., & Kopp, C. B. (1990). Self-concept development in the toddler years. *Developmental Psychology, 26,* 972–977.

Stoelhorst, M. S. J., Rijken, M., Martens, S. E., Brand, R., den Ouden, A. L., Wit, J.-M., et al. (2005). Changes in neonatology: Comparison of two cohorts of very preterm infants (gestational age <32 weeks): The Project on Preterm and Small for Gestational Age Infants 1983 and the Leiden Follow-up Project on Prematurity 1996–1997. *Pediatrics, 115,* 396–405.

Stokes, J., & Schmidt, G. (2011). Race, poverty and child protection decision making. *British Journal of Social Work, 41*(6), 1105–1121. doi:10.1093/bjsw/bcr009

Stoll, B. J., Hansen, N. I., Adams-Chapman, I., Fanaroff, A. A., Hintz, S. R., Vohr, B., et al. (2004). Neurodevelopmental and growth impairment among extremely low-birth-weight infants with neonatal infection. *Journal of the American Medical Association, 292,* 2357–2365.

St.-Onge, M., Mercier, P., & De Koninck, J. (2009). Imagery rehearsal therapy for frequent nightmares in children. *Behavioral Sleep Medicine, 7,* 81–98. doi:10.1080/15402000902762360

Stothard, K. J., Tennant, P. W. G., Bell, R., & Rankin, J. (2009). Maternal overweight and obesity and the risk of congenital anomalies: A systematic review and meta-analysis. *Journal of the American Medical Association, 301,* 636–650.

Straus, M. A. (1994). Should the use of corporal punishment by parents be considered child abuse? In M. A. Mason & E. Gambrill (Eds.), *Debating children's lives: Current controversies on children and adolescents* (pp. 196–222). Newbury Park, CA: Sage.

Straus, M. A. (2010). Prevalence, societal causes, and trends in corporal punishment by parents in world perspective. *Law and Contemporary Problems, 73*(1), 1–30.

Straus, M. A., & Stewart, J. H. (1999). Corporal punishment by American parents: National data on prevalence, chronicity, severity, and duration, in relation to child and family characteristics. *Clinical Child and Family Psychology Review, 2*(21), 55–70.

Streissguth, A. P., Bookstein, F. L., Barr, H. M., Sampson, P. D., O'Malley, K., & Young, J. K. (2004). Risk factors for adverse life outcomes in fetal alcohol syndrome and fetal alcohol effects. *Journal of Developmental & Behavioral Pediatrics, 25,* 228–238.

Strenze, T. (2007). Intelligence and socioeconomic success: A meta-analytic review of longitudinal research. *Intelligence, 35*(5), 401–426.

Striegel-Moore, R. H., & Bulik, C. (2007). Risk factors for eating disorders. *American Psychologist, 62,* 181–198.

Stright, A. D., Gallagher, K. C., & Kelley, K. (2008). Infant temperament moderates relations between maternal parenting in early childhood and children's adjustment in first grade. *Child Development, 79,* 186–200.

Strohschein, L. (2005). Parental divorce and child mental health trajectories. *Journal of Marriage and Family, 67,* 1286–1300.

Stroud, L. R., Foster, E., Papandonatos, G. D., Handwerger, K., Granger, D. A., Kivlighan, K. T., & Niaura, R. (2009). Stress response and the adolescent transition: Performance versus peer rejection stressors. *Developmental Psychopathology, 21*(1), 47–68.

Stueve, A., & O'Donnell, L. N. (2005). Early alcohol initiation and subsequent sexual and alcohol risk behaviors among urban youths. *American Journal of Public Health, 95,* 887–893.

Stuttering Foundation. (2006). *Stuttering: Straight talk for teachers* (Pub. No. 0125). Memphis, TN: Author.

Su, C., & Hynie, M. (2011). Effects of life stress, social support, and cultural norms on parenting styles among mainland Chinese, European Canadian, and Chinese Canadian immigrant mothers. *Journal of Cross-Cultural Psychology, 42,* 944–962. doi:10.1177/0022022110381124

Su, T. F., & Costigan, C. L. (2009). The Development of Children's Ethnic Identity in Immigrant Chinese Families in Canada: The Role of Parenting Practices and Children's Perceptions of Parental Family Obligation Expectations. *The Journal of Early Adolescence, 29*(5), 638–663. doi:10.1177/0272431608325418

Substance Abuse and Mental Health Services Administration. (2004, October 22). Alcohol dependence or abuse and age at first use. *The NSDUH Report.* Retrieved December 18, 2004, from http://oas.samhsa.gov/2k4/ageDependence/ageDependence.htm

Substance Abuse and Mental Health Services Administration (SAMHSA), Office of Applied Studies. (2006). Academic performance and substance use among students aged 12 to 17: 2002, 2003, and 2004. *The NSDUH Report* (Issue 18). Rockville, MD: Author.

Sue, S., & Okazaki, S. (2009). Asian-American educational achievements: A phenomenon in search of an explanation. *Asian American Journal of Psychology, S*(1), 45–55.

Sun, Y. (2001). Family environment and adolescents' well-being before and after parents' marital disruption. *Journal of Marriage and the Family, 63,* 697–713.

Surkan, P. J., Stephansson, O., Dickman, P. W., & Cnattingius, S. (2004). Previous preterm and small-for-gestational-age births and the subsequent risk of stillbirth. *New England Journal of Medicine, 350,* 777–785.

Susman, E. J., & Rogol, A. (2004). Puberty and psychological development. In R. M. Lerner & L. Steinberg (Eds.), *Handbook of adolescent psychology* (2nd ed., pp. 15–44). Hoboken, NJ: Wiley.

Sutherland, N. (2000). *Children in English-Canadian society: Framing the twentieth-century consensus.* Waterloo, ON: Wilfrid Laurier University Press.

Swain, I. U., Zelazo, P. R., & Clifton, R. K. (1993). Newborn infants' memory for speech sounds retained over 24 hours. *Developmental Psychology, 29*, 312–323.

Swain, M., & Lapkin, S. (1991). Additive bilingualism and French immersion education: The roles of language proficiency and literacy. In A. G. Reynolds (Ed.), *Bilingualism, multiculturalism, and second language learning: The McGill conference in honour of Wallace E. Lambert* (pp. 203–216). Hillsdale, NJ: Lawrence Erlbaum Associates.

Swallen, K. C., Reither, E. N., Haas, S. A., & Meier, A. M. (2005). Overweight, obesity, and health-related quality of life among adolescents: The National Longitudinal Study of Adolescent Health. *Pediatrics, 115*, 340–347.

Swamy, G. K., Ostbye, T., & Skjaerven, R. (2008). Association of preterm birth with long-term survival, reproduction, and next-generation preterm birth. *Journal of the American Medical Association, 299*, 1429–1436.

Swanston, H. Y., Tebbutt, J. S., O'Toole, B. I., & Oates, R. K. (1997). Sexually abused children 5 years after presentation: A case-control study. *Pediatrics, 100*, 600–608.

Swingley, D., & Fernald, A. (2002). Recognition of words referring to present and absent objects by 24-month-olds. *Journal of Memory and Language, 46*, 39–56.

Szaflarski, J. P., Rajagopal, A., Altaye, M., Byars, A. W., Jacola, L., Schmithorst, V. J., Schapiro, M. B., Plante, E., & Holland, S. K. (2012). Left-handedness and language lateralization in children. *Brain Research, 1433*, 85–97. doi:10.1016/j.brainres.2011.11.026

Tackett, J. L., Krueger, R. F., Iacono, W. G., & McGue, M. (2005). Symptom-based subfactors of DSM-defined conduct disorder: Evidence for etiologic distinctions. *Journal of Abnormal Psychology, 114*, 483–487.

Tamis-LeMonda, C. S., Bornstein, M. H., & Baumwell, L. (2001). Maternal responsiveness and children's achievement of language milestones. *Child Development, 72*(3), 748–767.

Tamis-LeMonda, C. S., Shannon, J. D., Cabrera, N. J., & Lamb, M. E. (2004). Fathers and mothers at play with their 2- and 3-year-olds: Contributions to language and cognitive development. *Child Development, 75*, 1806–1820.

Tarasuk, V., & Eakin, J. M. (2003). Charitable food assistance as symbolic gesture: An ethnographic study of food banks in Ontario. *Social Science & Medicine, 56*, 1505–1515.

Taylor, A. (2010). The contradictory location of high school apprenticeship in Canada. *Journal of Education Policy, 25*, 503–517. doi:10.1080/02680931003735544

Tenenbaum, H., & Leaper, C. (2002). Are parents' gender schemas related to their children's gender-related cognitions? A meta-analysis. *Developmental Psychology, 38*(4), 615–630.

Thanh, T. X. (2010). Drinking alcohol during pregnancy: Evidence from Canadian Community Health Survey 2007/2008. *Journal of Population Therapeutics and Clinical Pharmacology, 17*, e302–e307.

Theakston, A. L. (2012). "The spotty cow tickled the pig with a curly tail": How do sentence position, preferred argument structure, and referential complexity affect children's and adults' choice of referring expression? *Applied Psycholinguistics, 33*, 691–724. doi:10.1017/S0142716411000531

Thelen, E. (1995). Motor development: A new synthesis. *American Psychologist, 50*(2), 79–95.

Thiele, A.T., & Leier, B. (2010). Towards an ethical policy for the prevention of fetal sex selection in Canada. *Journal of Obstetrics and Gynaecology Canada, 32*, 54–57.

Thomas, A., & Chess, S. (1977). *Temperament and development*. New York: Brunner/Mazel.

Thomas, A., & Chess, S. (1984). Genesis and evolution of behavioral disorders: From infancy to early adult life. *American Journal of Psychiatry, 141*(1), 1–9.

Thomas, E. M. (2006). *Readiness to learn at school among five-year-old children in Canada* (Catalogue no. 89-599-MIE, no. 004). Ottawa, ON: Statistics Canada.

Thompson, L. A., Goodman, D. C., Chang, C-H., & Stukel, T. A. (2005). Regional variation in rates of low birth weight. *Pediatrics, 116*, 1114–1121.

Thompson, P. M., Cannon, T. D., Narr, K. L., van Erp, T., Poutanen, V., Huttunen, M., et al. (2001). Genetic influences on brain structure. *Nature Neuroscience, 4*, 1253–1258.

Thompson, P. M., Giedd, J. N., Woods, R. P., MacDonald, D., Evans, A. C., & Toga, A. W. (2000). Growth patterns in the developing brain detected by using continuum mechanical tensor maps. *Nature, 404*, 190–193.

Thompson, R. A. (1990). Vulnerability in research: A developmental perspective on research risk. *Child Development, 61*, 1–16.

Thompson, R. A. (1991). Emotional regulation and emotional development. *Educational Psychology Review, 3*, 269–307.

Thomson, E., & McLanahan, S. S. (2012). Reflections on "Family Structure and Child Well-Being: Economic Resources vs. Parental Socialization." *Social Forces, 91*, 45–53. doi:10.1093/sf/sos119

Thomson, E., Mosley, J., Hanson, T. L., & McLanahan, S. S. (2001). Remarriage, cohabitation, and changes in mothering behavior. *Journal of Marriage and Family, 63*, 370–380.

Timmons, V., Walton, F., O'Keefe, A. R., & Wagner, M. (2008). Families learning together: A family literacy program with Mi'kmaw communities in Atlantic Canada. *Canadian Journal of Native Education, 31*, 94–109.

Tincoff, R., & Jusczyk, P. W. (1999). Some beginnings of word comprehension in 6-month-olds. *Psychological Science, 10*, 172–177.

Tincoff, R., & Jusczyk, P. W. (2011, July 5). Six-month-olds comprehend words that refer to parts of the body. *Infancy*. doi: 10.1111/j.1532-7078.2011.00084.x

Tither, J., & Ellis, B. (2008) Impact of fathers on daughter's age at menarche: A genetically and environmentally controlled sibling study. *Developmental Psychology, 44*(5), 1409–1420.

Tjepkema, M. (2005). Insomnia. *Health Reports, 17*(1), 9–25. Statistics Canada (Catalogue no. 82-003-XPE2005001).

Toga, A., & Thompson, P. M. (2005). Genetics of brain structure and intelligence. *Annual Review of Neurology, 28*, 1–23.

Toga, A. W., Thompson, P. M., & Sowell, E. R. (2006). Mapping brain maturation. *Trends in Neurosciences, 29*(3), 148–159.

Tolan, P. H., Gorman-Smith, D., & Henry, D. B. (2003). The developmental ecology of urban males' youth violence. *Developmental Psychology, 39*, 274–291.

Tomasello, M. (2000a). The item-based nature of children's early syntactic development. *Trends in Cognitive Science, 4*(4), 156–163.

Tomasello, M. (2000b). Do young children have adult syntactic competence? *Cognition, 74*, 209–253. PII: S0010-0277(99)00069-4

Tomasello, M. (2007). Cooperation and communication in the 2nd year of life. *Child Development Perspectives, 1*, 8–12.

Tong, V. T., Jones, J. R., Dietz, P. M., D'Angelo, D., & Bombard, J.M. (2009). Trends in smoking before, during, and after pregnancy; pregnancy risk and monitoring system (PRAMS), United States, 31 sites, 2000–2005. *Morbidity and Mortality Weekly Report, 58*, 1–29.

Toohey, K. and Derwing, T.M. (2008). Hidden losses: How demographics can encourage incorrect assumptions about ESL high school students' success. *Alberta Journal of Educational Research, 54*, 178–193.

Torrance, E. P., & Ball, O. E. (1984). *The Torrance Tests of Creative Thinking Streamlined (revised) manual, Figural A and B*. Bensenville, IL: Scholastic Testing Service, Inc.

Totsika, V., & Sylva, K. (2004). The Home Observation for Measurement of the Environment revisited. *Child and Adolescent Mental Health, 9*, 25–35.

Tough, S., Benzies, K., Fraser-Lee, N., & Newburn-Cook, C. (2007). Factors influencing childbearing decisions and knowledge of perinatal risks among Canadian men and women. *Maternal and Child Health Journal, 11,* 189–98.

Tournier, M., Greenfield, B., Galbaud du Fort, G., Ducruet, T., Magno Zito, J., Cloutier, A.-M., & Moride, Y. (2010). Patterns of antidepressant use in Quebec children and adolescents: Trends and predictors. *Psychiatry Research, 179,* 57–63. doi:10.1016/j.psychres.2010.06.007

Townsend, N. W. (1997). Men, migration, and households in Botswana: An exploration of connections over time and space. *Journal of Southern African Studies, 23,* 405–420.

Transport Canada. (2011). *Road safety in Canada.* Ottawa, ON: Government of Canada. Retrieved from http://www.tc.gc.ca.

Transport Injury Research Foundation. (2011). *The issues—Belt use.* Ottawa, ON: Author. Retrieved from http://yndrc.tirf.ca

Trautner, H. M., Ruble, D. N., Cyphers, L., Kirsten, B., Behrendt, R., & Hartmann, P. (2005). Rigidity and flexibility of gender stereotypes in childhood: Developmental or differential? *Infant and Child Development, 14*(4), 365–381.

Tremblay, L., & Rinaldi, C. M. (2010). The prediction of preschool children's weight from family environment factors: Gender-linked differences. *Eating Behaviors, 11,* 266–275.

Tremblay, M. S., LeBlanc, A. G., Carson, V., Choquette, L., Gorber, S. C., Dillman, C., ... & Canadian Society for Exercise Physiology. (2012). Canadian sedentary behaviour guidelines for the early years (aged 0–4 years). *Applied Physiology Nutrition and Metabolism, 37,* 370–380. doi:10.1139/H2012-019

Tremblay, M. S., LeBlanc, A. G., Kho, M. E., Saunders, T. J., Larouche, R., Colley, R. C., & Connor Gorber, S. (2011b). Systematic review of sedentary behaviour and health indicators in school-aged children and youth. *The International Journal of Behavioral Nutrition and Physical Activity, 8,* 98. doi:10.1186/1479-5868-8-98

Tremblay, M. S., Shields, M., Laviolette, M., Craig, C. L., Janssen, I., & Connor Gorber, S. (2010). Fitness of Canadian children and youth: Results from the 2007–2009 Canadian Health Measures Survey. *Health Reports, 21,* 1–14. Statistics Canada, 82-003-xpe.

Tremblay, M. S., Warburton, D. E., Janssen I., Paterson, D. H., Latimer, A. E., Rhodes, R. E., ... & Duggan, M. (2011). New Canadian physical activity guidelines. *Applied Physiology, Nutrition, and Metabolism, 36,* 36–46. doi:10.1139/H11-009

Tremblay, M. S., & Willms, J. D. (2000). Secular trends in the body mass index of Canadian children. *Canadian Medical Association Journal, 163,* 1429–1433.

Tremblay, R. E. (2008). Development of physical aggression from early childhood to adulthood (rev. ed.). In R. E. Tremblay, R. G. Barr, R. DeV. Peters, & M. Boivin M. (Eds.). *Encyclopedia on Early Childhood Development* (pp. 1–6) [online]. Montreal, QC: Centre of Excellence for Early Childhood Development. Retrieved from http://www.child-encyclopedia.com/documents/TremblayANGxp_rev.pdf.

Tremblay, R. E., Nagin, D. S., Séguin, J. R., Zoccolillo, M., Zelazo, P. D., Boivin, M., ... & Japel, C. (2004). Physical aggression during early childhood: Trajectories and predictors. *Pediatrics, 114*(1), 43–50.

Trionfi, G., & Reese, E. (2009). A good story: Children with imaginary companions create richer narratives. *Child Development, 80*(4), 1301–1313.

Trocmé, N., MacMillan, H., Fallon, B., & DeMarco, R. (2003). Nature and severity of physical harm caused by child abuse and neglect: Results from the Canadian Incidence Study. *Canadian Medical Association Journal, 169*(9), 911–915.

Tronick, E. (1972). Stimulus control and the growth of the infant's visual field. *Perception and Psychophysics, 11,* 373–375.

Tronick, E., Als, H., Adamson, L., Wise, S., & Brazelton, T. B. (1978). The infant's response to entrapment between contradictory messages in face-to-face interaction. *Journal of the American Academy of Child Psychiatry, 17*(1), 1–13.

Tronick, E. Z. (1989). Emotions and emotional communication in infants. *American Psychologist, 44*(2), 112–119.

Tronick, E. Z., Morelli, G. A, & Ivey, P. (1992). The Efe forager infant and toddler's pattern of social relationships: Multiple and simultaneous. *Developmental Psychology, 28,* 568–577.

Trost, S. G., Rosenkranz, R. R., & Dzewaltowski, D. (2008). Physical activity levels among children attending after-school programs. *Medicine and Science in Sports and Exercise, 40,* 622–629.

Tryba, A. K., Peña, F., & Ramirez, J. M. (2006). Gasping activity in vitro: A rhythm dependent on 5-HT2A receptors. *Journal of Neuroscience, 26*(10), 2623–2634.

Tsai, J., & Floyd, R. L. (2004). Alcohol consumption among women who are pregnant or who might become pregnant or who might become pregnant – United States, 2002. *Morbidity and Mortality Weekly Report, 53*(50), 1178–1181.

Tsuchiya, K., Matsumoto, K., Miyachi, T., Tsujii, M., Nakamura, K., Takagai, S., et al. (2008). Paternal age at birth and high-functioning autistic-spectrum disorder in offspring. *British Journal of Psychiatry, 193,* 316–321.

Ttofi, M. M., & Farrington, D. P. (2011). Effectiveness of school-based programs to reduce bullying: A systematic and meta-analytic review. *Journal of Experimental Criminology, 7,* 27–56. doi:10.1007/s11292-010-9109-1

Tucker, P., Irwin, J. D., Bouck, L.M., & Pollet, G. (2006). Preventing paediatric obesity: Recommendations from a community-based qualitative investigation. *Obesity Reviews, 7,* 251–260.

Turati, C., Simion, F., Milani, I., & Umilta, C. (2002). Newborns' preference for faces: What is crucial? *Developmental Psychology, 38,* 875–882.

Turkheimer, E., Haley, A., Waldron, J., D'Onofrio, B., & Gottesman, I. I. (2003). Socioeconomic status modifies heritability of IQ in young children. *Psychological Science, 14,* 623–628.

Turnbull, M., Hart, D., & Lapkin, S. (2003). Grade 6 French immersion students' performance on large-scale reading, writing, and mathematics tests: building explanations. *Alberta Journal of Educational Research, 49,* 6–23.

Turner, P. J., & Gervai, J. (1995). A multi-dimensional study of gender typing in preschool children and their parents: Personality, attitudes, preferences, behavior, and cultural differences. *Developmental Psychology, 31,* 759–772.

Twardosz, S. (2010). "Child maltreatment and the developing brain: A review of neuroscience perspectives." *Aggression and Violent Behavior* (1359–1789), *15*(1), 59.

Twenge, J. M., Campbell, W. K., & Foster, C. A. (2003). Parenthood and marital satsifaction: A meta-analytic review. *Journal of Marriage and Family, 65,* 574–583.

Twigg, R. (2010). Excerpt: Passion for those who care: What foster carers need. *Canada's Children, 17,* 29–32.

Tynes, B. M. (2007). Internet safety gone wild?: Sacrificing the educational and psychosocial benefits of online social environments. *Journal of Adolescent Research, 22*(6), 575–584. doi:10.1177/0743558407303979

Tyson, H. (1991). Outcomes of 1001 midwife-attended home births in Toronto, 1983–1988. *Birth, 18,* 14–19.

Umlauf, M. G., & Chasens, E. R. (2003). Bedwetting—not always what it seems: A sign of sleep-disordered breathing in children. *Journal for Specialists in Pediatric Nursing, 8*(1), 22–31.

UNAIDS. (2006). *Report on the global AIDS epidemic.* Geneva: Author.

United Nations Children's Fund. (2007). *The state of the world's children 2008: Child survival.* New York: Author.

United Nations Children's Fund. (2008a). *State of the world's children: Child survival.* Retrieved from http://www.unicef.org/sowc08/

United Nations Children's Fund. (2008b). *State of the world's children 2009: Maternal and newborn health.* New York: Author.

United Nations Children's Fund. (2008c). *The child care transition, Innocenti Report Card 8, 2008.* Florence: UNICEF Innocenti Research Centre.

United Nations Children's Fund. (2009). *Worldwide deaths of children under five decline, continuing positive trend.* Retrieved from http://www.unicef.org/childsurvival/index_51095.html

United Nations Children's Fund & World Health Organization. (2004). *Low birth weight: Country, regional and global estimates.* New York: UNICEF.

United Nations Demographic Yearbook. (2003). New York: United Nations, Department of Economic and Social Affairs.

University of Virginia Health System. (2004). *How chromosome abnormalities happen: Meiosis, mitosis, maternal age, environment.* Retrieved September 16, 2004, from http://www.healthsystem.virginia.edu/UVA-Health/peds_genetics/happen.cfm

Uppal, S., Kohen, D., & Khan, S. (2007). Educational services and the disabled child. *Education Matters, 3*(5). Retrieved from http://www.statcan.gc.ca/pub/81-004-x/81-004-x2006005-eng.htm

Urquijo, C. R., & Milan, A. (2011). Female population. In Statistics Canada, Social and Aboriginal Statistics Division, *Women in Canada: A Gender-based Statistical Report* (Catalogue no. 89-503-X). Ottawa, ON: Ministry of Industry.

Usalcas, J., & Bowlby, G. (2006). Students in the labour market. *Education Matters, 3*(1) (Statistics Canada Catalogue no. 81-004-XIE). Retrieved from http://www.statcan.gc.ca/pub/81-004-x/2006001/9184-eng.htm

U.S. Department of Health and Human Services. (1999a). *Blending perspectives and building common ground: A report to Congress on substance abuse and child protection.* Washington, DC: U.S. Government Printing Office.

U.S. Department of Health and Human Services. (1999b). *Mental health: A report of the Surgeon General.* Rockville, MD: U.S. Department of Health and Human Services, Substance Abuse and Mental Health Services Administration, National Institutes of Health, National Institute of Mental Health.

U.S. Department of Health and Human Services. (2003a). *State funded pre-kindergarten: What the evidence shows.* Retrieved from http://aspe.hhs.gov/hsp/state-funded-pre-k/index.htm

U.S. Department of Health and Human Services. (2003b). *Strengthening Head Start: What the evidence shows.* Retrieved from http://aspe.hhs.gov/hsp/StrengthenHeadStart03/index.htm

U.S. Department of Health and Human Services (USDHHS), Administration on Children, Youth and Families. (2008). *Child maltreatment 2006.* Washington, DC: U.S. Government Printing Office.

U. S. Preventive Services Task Force. (2006). Screening for speech and language delay in preschool children: Recommendation statement. *Pediatrics, 117,* 497–501.

Vainio, S., Heikkiia, M., Kispert, A., Chin, N., & McMahon, A. P. (1999). Female development in mammals is regulated by Wnt-4 signaling. *Nature, 397,* 405–409.

Valkenburg, P. M., & Peter, J. (2008). Adolescents' identity experiments on the Internet: Consequences for social competence and self-concept unity. *Communication Research, 35*(2), 208–231.

Valkenburg, P. M., & Peter, J. (2009a). The effects of instant messaging n the quality of adolescents' existing friendships: A longitudinal study. *Journal of Communication, 59*(1), 79–97.

Valkenburg, P. M. , & Peter, J. (2009b). Social consequences of the Internet for adolescents: A decade of research. *Current Directions in Psychological Science, 18*(11), 1–5.

Valkenburg, P. M., & Peter, J. (2007). Preadolescents and adolescents' online communication and their closeness to friends. *Developmental Psychology, 43,* 267–277.

Van Allen, M. I., McCourt, C., Lee, N. S. (2002). *Preconception health: folic acid for the primary prevention of neural tube defects. A resource document for health professionals, 2002* (Catalogue no.: H39-607/2002E). Ottawa, ON: Minister of Public Works and Government Services Canada.

van de Beek, C., van Goozen, S. H. M., Buitlaar, J. K., & Cohen-Kettenis, P. T. (2009). Prenatal sex hormones (maternal and amniotic fluid) and gender-related play behavior in 13-month-old infants. *Archives of Sexual Behavior, 38*(1) 6–15.

Van den Boom, D. C. (1994). The influence of temperament and mothering on attachment and exploration: An experimental manipulation of sensitive responsiveness among lower-class mothers with irritable infants. *Child Development, 65,* 1457–1477.

van den Eijnden, R. J. J. M., Meerkerk, G., Vermulst, A. A., Spijkerman, R., & Engels, R. C. M. E. (2008). Online communication, compulsive Internet use, and psychosocial well-being among adolescents: A longitudinal study. *Developmental Psychology, 44*(3), 655–665.

Van de Vijver, F. J. R., & Tanzer, N. K. (2004). Bias and equivalence in cross-cultural assessment: An overview. *Revue Europeene de Psychologie Appliquee, 54,* 119–135.

Vandivere, S., Malm, K., & Radel, L. (2009). Adoption USA: A chartbook based on the 2007 National Survey of Adoptive Parents. Washington, DC: U.S. Department of Health and Human Services, Office of the Assistant Secretary for Planning and Evaluation.

van Goozen, S., Fairchild, G., Snoek, H., & Harold, G. (2007). The evidence for a neurobiological model of childhood antisocial behavior. *Psychological Bulletin, 133,* 149–182.

van IJzendoorn, M. H., & Bakermans-Kranenburg, M. J. (2009). Attachment security and disorganization in maltreating families and orphanages. In: R. E. Tremblay, R. G. Barr, R. DeV. Peters, & M. Boivin (Eds.), *Encyclopedia on early childhood development* [online]. Montreal, QC: Centre of Excellence for Early Childhood Development, 1–7. Retrieved from http://www.child-encyclopedia.com/documents/van_IJzendoorn-Bakermans KranenburgANGxp-Attachment.pdf. Accessed June 6, 2010.

van IJzendoorn, M. H., & Juffer, F. (2005). Adoption is a successful natural intervention enhancing adopted children's IQ and school performance. *Current Directions in Psychological Science, 14,* 326–330.

van IJzendoorn, M. H., Juffer, F., & Poelhuis, C. W. K. (2005). Adoption and cognitive development: A meta-analytic comparison of adopted and nonadopted children's IQ and school performance. *Psychological Bulletin, 131,* 301–316.

van IJzendoorn, M. H., & Sagi, A. (1999). Cross-cultural patterns of attachment: Universal and contextual dimensions. In J. Cassidy & P. R. Shaver (Eds.), *Handbook on attachment theory and research* (pp. 713–734). New York: Guilford Press.

Van Voorhis, B. J. (2007). In vitro fertilization. *New England Journal of Medicine, 356,* 379–386.

Vandell, D. L. (2000). Parents, peer groups, and other socializing influences. *Developmental Psychology, 36,* 699–710.

Vandell, D. L., & Bailey, M. D. (1992). Conflicts between siblings. In C. U. Shantz & W. W. Hartup (Eds.), *Conflict in child and adolescent development* (pp. 242–269). New York: Cambridge University Press.

Vargha-Khadem, F., Gadian, D. G., Watkins, K. E., Connelly, A., Van Paesschen, W., & Mishkin, M. (1997). Differential effects of early hippocampal pathology on episodic and semantic memory. *Science, 277,* 376–380.

Vasiliadis, H.-M., Lesage, A., Adair, C., Wang, P. S., & Kessler, R. C. (2007). Do Canada and the United States differ in prevalence of depression and utilization of services? *Psychiatric Services, 58,* 63–71.

Vaughan Van Hecke, A., Mundy, P., Block, J. J., Delgado, C. E. F., Parlade, M. V., Pomares, Y. B., & Hobson, J. A. (2012). Infant responding to joint attention, executive processes, and self-regulation in preschool children. *Infant Behavior and Development, 35,* 303–311. doi:10.1016/j.infbeh.2011.12.001

Veenstra, R., Lindenberg, S., Oldehinkel, A. J., De Winter, A. F., Verhulst, F. C., & Ormel, J. (2005). Bullying and victimization in elementary schools: A comparison of bullies, victims, bully/victims, and uninvolved preadolescents. *Developmental Psychology, 41,* 672–682.

Ventura, A. K., & Mennella, J. A. (2011). Innate and learned preferences for sweet taste during childhood. *Current Opinion in Clinical Nutrition and Metabolic Care, 14*(4), 379–384.

Vereecken, C., & Maes, L. (2000). Eating habits, dental care and dieting. In C. Currie, K. Hurrelmann, W. Settertobulte, R. Smith, & J. Todd (Eds.), *Health and health behaviour among young people: A WHO cross-national study (HBSC) international report* (pp. 83–96) [WHO Policy Series: Healthy Policy for Children and Adolescents, Series No. 1]. Copenhagen, Denmark: World Health Organization Regional Office for Europe.

Verma, S., & Larson, R. (2003). Editors' notes. In S. Verma & R. Larson (Eds.), Chromosomal congenital anomalies and residence near hazardous waste landfill sites. *Lancet, 359,* 320–322.

Verschueren, K., Marcoen, A., & Schoefs, V. (1996). The internal working model of the self, attachment, and competence in five-year-olds. *Child Development, 67,* 2493–2511.

Vézina, M., & Crompton, S. (2012). *Volunteering in Canada* (Catalogue no. 11-008-X Canadian Social Trends). Ottawa, ON: Statistics Canada.

Vgontzas, A. N., & Kales, A. (1999). Sleep and its disorders. *Annual Review of Medicine, 50,* 387–400.

Viner, R. M., & Cole, T. J. (2005). Television viewing in early childhood predicts adult body mass index. *Journal of Pediatrics, 147,* 429–435.

Vingerhoets, G., Acke, F., Alderweireldt, S., Nys, J., Vandemaele, P., & Achten, E. (2012). Cerebral lateralization of praxis in right- and left-handedness: Same pattern, different strength. *Human Brain Mapping, 33,* 763–777. doi:10.1002/hbm.21247

Vohr, B. R., Wright, L. L., Poole, K., & McDonald, S. A. for the NICHD Neonatal Research Network Follow-up Study. (2005). Neurodevelopmental outcomes of extremely low birth weight infants <30 weeks' gestation between 1993 and 1998. *Pediatrics, 116,* 635–643.

Vondra, J. I., & Barnett, D. (1999). A typical attachment in infancy and early childhood among children at developmental risk. *Monographs of the Society for Research in Child Development, 64*(3) [Serial No. 258].

von Gontard, A., Heron, J., & Joinson, C. (2011). Family history of nocturnal enuresis and urinary incontinence: Results from a large epidemiological study. *The Journal of Urology, 185*(6), 2303–2307.

von Gontard, A., Schmelzer, D., Seifen, S., & Pukrop, R. (2001). Central nervous system involvement in nocturnal enuresis: Evidence of general neuromotor delay and specific brainstem dysfunction. *The Journal of Urology, 166*(6), 2448–2451.

von Hofsten, C. (2004). An action perspective on motor development. *Cognitive Sciences, 8*(1), 266–272.

Votruba-Drzal, E., Li-Grining, C. R., & Maldonado-Carreno, C. (2008). A developmental perspective on full- versus part-day kindergarten and children's academic trajectories through fifth grade. *Child Development, 79,* 957–978.

Vuori, L., Christiansen, N., Clement, J., Mora, J., Wagner, M., & Herrera, M. (1979). Nutritional supplementation and the outcome of pregnancy: 2. Visual habitation at 15 days. *Journal of Clinical Nutrition, 32,* 463–469.

Vygotsky, L. S. (1956). *Selected psychological investigations.* Moscow: Izdstel'sto Akademii Pedagocheskikh Nauk USSR.

Vygotsky, L. S. (1962/1934). *Thought and language.* Cambridge, MA: MIT Press. (Original work published 1934)

Waddell, C., McEwan, K., Shepherd, C. A., Offord, D. R., & Hua, J. M. (2005). A public health strategy to improve the mental health of Canadian children. *Canadian Journal of Psychiatry, 50,* 226–233.

Wade, A., & Beran, T. (2011). Cyberbullying: The new era of bullying. *Canadian Journal of School Psychology, 26,* 44–61. doi:10.1177/0829573510396318

Wadsworth, M. E., Raviv, T., Reinhard, C., Wolff, B., Santiago, C. D., & Einhorn, L. (2008). An indirect effects model of the association between poverty and child functioning: The role of children's poverty-related stress. *The Journal of Loss and Trauma: International Perspectives on Stress and Coping, 13*(2–3), 156–185.

Wadsworth, M. E., & Santiago, C. D. (2008). Risk and resiliency processes in ethnically diverse families in poverty. *Journal of Family Psychology, 22,* 299–410.

Wainright, J. L., Russell, S. T., & Patterson, C. J. (2004). Psychosocial adjustment, school outcomes, and romantic relationships of adolescents with same-sex parents. *Child Development, 75,* 1886–1898.

Waknine, Y. (2006). Highlights from MMWR: Prevalence of U.S. birth defects and more. *Medscape.* Retrieved January 9, 2006, from http://www.medscape.com/viewarticle/ 521056

Wald, N. J. (2004). Folic acid and the prevention of neural-tube defects. *New England Journal of Medicine, 350,* 101–103.

Walk, R. D., & Gibson, E. J. (1961). A comparative and analytical study of visual depth perception. *Psychology Monographs, 75*(15).

Walker, M., & Edmonds, L. (2010). *Measurement of assisted human reproduction outcomes in Canada: A discussion paper prepared for participants of the 2010 Outcomes Roundtable.* Ottawa, ON.

Walker, S. P., Grantham-McGregor, S. M., Powell, C. A., & Chang, S. M. (2000). Effects of growth restriction in early childhood on growth, IQ, and cognition at age 11 to 12 years and the benefits of nutritional supplementation and psychosocial stimulation. *The Journal of Pediatrics, 137*(1), 36–41.

Waller, M. W., Hallfors, D. D., Halpern, C. T., Iritani, B., Ford, C. A., & Guo, G. (2006). Gender differences in associations between depressive symptoms and patterns of substance use and risky sexual behavior among a nationally representative sample of U.S. adolescents. *Archives of Women's Mental Health, 9,* 139–150.

Wang, Q. (2004). The emergence of cultural self-constructs: Autobiographical memory and self-description in European American and Chinese children. *Developmental Psychology, 40,* 3–15.

Wang, Y., & Lobstein, T. (2006). Worldwide trends in childhood overweight and obesity. *International Journal of Obesity, 1*(1), 11–25.

Ward, M. (1998). *The family dynamic: A Canadian perspective* (2nd ed.). Toronto, ON: ITP Nelson.

Ward, M. G. K., & Bennett, S. (2003). Studying child abuse and neglect in Canada: We are just at the beginning. *Canadian Medical Association Journal, 169*(9), 919–920.

Warneken, F. (2013). Young children proactively remedy unnoticed accidents. *Cognition, 126,* 101–108. Retrieved from http://dx.doi.org/10.1016/j.cognition.2012.09.011

Warneken, F., & Tomasello, M. (2006). Altruistic helping in human infants and young chimpanzees. *Science, 311,* 1301–1303.

Warneken, F., & Tomasello, M. (2009). Varieties of altruism in children and chimpanzees. *Trends in Cognitive Sciences, 13,* 397–402. doi:10.1016/j.tics.2009.06.008

Warren, K. R., & Li, T-K. (2005). Genetic polymorphisms: impact on the risk of fetal alcohol spectrum disorders. *Birth Defects Research, 73,* 195–203.

Wasik, B. H., Ramey, C. T., Bryant, D. M., & Sparling, J. J. (1990). A longitudinal study of two early intervention strategies: Project CARE. *Child Development, 61,* 1682–1696.

Wassimi, S., McHugh, N. G. L., Wilkins, R., Heaman, M., Martens, P., Smylie, J., … & Luo, Z.-C. (2010). Community Remoteness, Perinatal Outcomes and Infant Mortality among First Nations in Quebec. *The Open Women's Health Journal, 4,* 32–38.

Watson, J. B., & Rayner, R. (1920). Conditioned emotional reactions. *Journal of Experimental Psychology, 3,* 1–14.

Watt, D., & Roessingh, H. (1994). ESL dropout: the myth of educational equity. *The Alberta Journal of Educational Research, 40,* 283–296.

Watt, D., & Roessingh, H. (2001). The dynamics of ESL dropout: plus ca change…. *Canadian Modern Language Review, 58,* 203–222.

Webster, P. C. (June 9, 2012). Canada curbs Aboriginal health leadership. *The Lancet, 379,* 2137.

Wechsler, D. (2004). *Wechsler Intelligence Scale for Children–Fourth Edition: Canadian Manual.* Toronto, ON: Pearson.

Weinberg, M. K., & Tronick, E. Z. (1996). Infant affective reactions to the resumption of maternal interaction after the still-face. *Child Development, 67*(3), 905–914.

Weinreb, L., Wehler, C., Perloff, J., Scott, R., Hosmer, D., Sagor, L., & Gundersen, C. (2002). Hunger: Its impact on children's health and mental health. *Pediatrics, 110,* 816.

Weinstock, H., Berman, S., & Cates, W., Jr. (2004). Sexually transmitted diseases among American youth: Incidence and prevalence estimates, 2000. *Perspectives on Sexual and Reproductive Health, 36,* 6–10.

Weir, E. (2001). Inhalant use and addiction in Canada. *Canadian Medical Association Journal, 164,* 397.

Weiss, B., Amler, S., & Amler, R. W. (2004). Pesticides. *Pediatrics, 113,* 1030–1036.

Weiss, B., Dodge, K. A., Bates, J. E, & Pettit, G. S. (1992). Some consequences of early harsh discipline: Child aggression and a maladaptive social information processing style. *Child Development, 63,* 1321–1335.

Weiss, L. G., Saklofske, D. H., Prifitera, A., Chen, H.-Y., & Hildebrand, D. (1999). The calculation of the WISC–III general ability index using Canadian norms. *Canadian Journal of School Psychology, 14,* 1–9.

Weisz, J. R., McCarty, C. A., & Valeri, S. M. (2006). Effects of psychotherapy for depression in children and adolescents: A meta-analysis. *Psychological Bulletin, 132,* 132–149.

Wellman, H. M., & Cross, D. (2001). Theory of mind and conceptual change. *Child Development, 72,* 702–707.

Wellman, H. M., & Liu, D. (2004). Scaling theory-of-mind tasks. *Child Development, 75,* 523–541.

Wellman, H. M., Lopez-Duran, S., LaBounty, J., & Hamilton, B. (2008). Infant attention to intentional action predicts preschool theory of mind. *Developmental Psychology, 44,* 618–623.

Wells, K. (2009). Sieccan Newsletter: Research exploring the health, wellness, and safety concerns of sexual minority youth. *The Canadian Journal of Human Sexuality, 18*(4), 221–229.

Wen, S. W., Mery, L. S., Kramer, M. S., Jimenez, V., Trouton, K., Herbert, P., & Chalmers, B. (1999). Attitudes of Canadian women toward birthing centres and midwife care for childbirth. *Canadian Medical Association Journal, 161,* 708–709.

Weng, X., Odouli, R., & Li, D.-K. (2008). Maternal caffeine consumption during pregnancy and the risk of miscarriage: A prospective cohort study. *American Journal of Obstetrics and Gynecology, 198*(3), e279–e287.

Wentworth, N., Benson, J. B., & Haith, M. M. (2000). The development of infants' reaches for stationary and moving targets. *Child Development, 71,* 576–601.

Wentzel, K. R. (2002). Are effective teachers like good parents? Teaching styles and student adjustment in early adolescence. *Child Development, 73,* 287–301.

West, J., Denton, K., & Germino-Hausken, E. (2000, February 17). *America's kindergarteners.* Washington, DC: National Center for Education Statistics, U.S. Department of Education, 70.

Westen, D. (1998). The scientific legacy of Sigmund Freud: Toward a psychodynamically informed psychological science. *Psychological Bulletin, 124,* 333–371.

Westling, E., Andrews, J. A., Hampson, S. E. & Peterson, M. (2008). Pubertal timing and substance use: The effects of gender, parental monitoring, and deviant peers. *Journal of Adolescent Health, 42,* 555–563.

Whalley, L. J., & Deary, I. J. (2001). Longitudinal cohort study of childhood IQ and survival up to age 76. *British Medical Journal, 322,* 819.

White, A. (2001). *Alcohol and adolescent brain development.* Retrieved from http://www.duke.edu/~amwhite/alc_adik_pf.html

White Holman, C., & Goldberg, J. M. (2006). Ethical, Legal, and Psychosocial Issues in Care of Transgender Adolescents. *International Journal of Transgenderism, 9*(3–4), 95–110. doi:10.1300/J485v09n03_05

Whitehurst, G. J., & Lonigan, C. J. (2001). Emergent literacy: Development from prereaders to readers. In S. B. Neuman & D. K. Dickinson (Eds.), *Handbook of Early Literacy Research* (pp. 11–29). New York, NY: Guilford Press.

Whitlock, J., Muehlenkamp, J., Eckenrode, J., Purington, A., Baral Abrams, G., Barreira, P., & Kress, V. (2013). Nonsuicidal self-injury as a gateway to suicide in young adults. *Journal of Adolescent Health, 52*(4), 486–492. doi:10.1016/j.jadohealth.2012.09.010

Whittle, H., Hamilton-Giachritsis, C., Beech, A., & Collings, G. (2013). A review of online grooming: Characteristics and concerns. *Aggression and Violent Behavior, 18*(1), 62–70. doi:10.1016/j.avb.2012.09.003

Widaman, K. F. (2009). Phenylketonuria in children and mothers: Genes, environment, behavior. *Current Directions in Psychological Science, 18*(1), 48–52.

Wilcox, A. J., Dunson, D., & Baird, D. D. (2000). The timing of the "fertile window" in the menstrual cycle: Day specific estimates from a prospective study. *British Medical Journal, 321,* 1259–1262.

Willard, N. E. (2006). *Cyberbullying and cyberthreats.* Eugene, OR: Center for Safe and Responsible Internet Use.

Williams, E. R., & Caliendo, M. A. (1984). *Nutrition: Principles, issues, and applications.* New York: McGraw-Hill.

Williams, S., O'Connor, E., Eder, M., & Whitlock, E. (2009). Screening for child and adolescent depression in primary care settings: A systematic evidence review for the U.S. Preventive Services Task Force. *Pediatrics, 123*(4), 716–735.

Willms, J. D. (1996). Indicators of mathematics achievement in Canadian elementary schools. In Human Resources Development Canada and Statistics Canada, *Growing up in Canada: National Longitudinal Survey of Children and Youth* (pp. 69–82. Catalogue no. 89-550-MPE, no. 1). Ottawa.

Willms, J. D. (2002a). Research findings bearing on Canadian social policy. In J. D. Willms (Ed.), *Vulnerable Children: Findings from Canada's National Longitudinal Survey of Children and Youth* (pp. 331–358). Edmonton, AB: University of Alberta Press.

Willms, J. D. (2002b). Socioeconomic gradients for childhood vulnerability. In J. D. Willms (Ed.), *Vulnerable Children: Findings from Canada's National Longitudinal Survey of Children and Youth* (pp. 71–102). Edmonton, AB: The University of Alberta Press.

Willoughby, M. T., Kupersmidt, J. B., & Voegler-Lee, M. E. (2012). Is preschool executive function causally related to academic achievement? *Child Neuropsychology: A Journal on Normal and Abnormal Development in Childhood and Adolescence, 18*(1), 79–91. Retrieved from http://dx.doi.org/10.1080/09297049.2011.578572

Willows, N. D. (2005). Overweight in Aboriginal children: Prevalence, implications and solutions. *Journal of Aboriginal Health, 2,* 76–85.

Willows, N. D. (2011). Improving the nutritional status of Aboriginal people in Canada. *The Diabetes Communicator.* Retrieved from http://www.diabetes.ca/documents/for-professionals/DC--Spring_2011--N.Willows_.pdf

Willows, N. D., Hanley, A. J. G., & Delormier, T. (2012). A socioecological framework to understand weight-related issues in Aboriginal children in Canada. *Applied Physiology, Nutrition, and Metabolism, 37*(1), 1–13. doi:10.1139/H11-128

Willows, N. D., Iserhoff, R., Napash, L., Leclerc, L., & Verrall, T. (2005). Anxiety about food supply in Cree women with infants in Quebec. *International Journal of Circumpolar Health, 64,* 59–68.

Willows, N. D., Johnson, M. S., & Ball, G. D. C. (2007). Prevalence estimates of overweight and obesity in Cree preschool children in northern Quebec according to international and US reference criteria. *American Journal of Public Health, 97,* 311–316.

Willows, N. D., Veugelers, P., Raine, K., & Kuhle, S. (2009). Prevalence and sociodemographic risk factors related to household food security in Aboriginal peoples in Canada. *Public Health Nutrition, 12,* 1150–1156.

Wilson, B., & Steinman, C. (2000). *Hungercount 2000, a surplus of hunger: Canada's annual survey of emergency food programs.* Toronto, ON: Canadian Association of Food Banks.

Wilson, B., & Tsoa, E. (2001). *Hungercount 2001, food bank lines in insecure times: Canada's annual survey of emergency food programs.* Toronto, ON: Canadian Association of Food Banks.

Wilson, B. J. (2008). Media and children's aggression, fear, and altruism. *Future of Children, 18,* 87–118.

Wilson, B. L., Effken, J. & Butler, R. J. (2010). The relationship between Cesarean section and labor induction. *Journal of Nursing Scholarship, 42*(2), 130–138.

Wilson, E. O. (1975). *Sociobiology: The new synthesis.* Cambridge, MA: Harvard University Press.

Wilson, G. T., Grilo, C. M., & Vitousek, K. M. (2007). Psychological treatment of eating disorders. *American Psychologist, 62,* 199–216.

Wingert, P., & Underwood, A. (1997). Hey–look out world, here I come. *Newsweek* [Special Edition], pp. 12–15.

Winickoff, J. P., Friebely, J., Tanski, S. E., Sherrod, C., Matt, G. E., Hovell, M. F., & McMillen, R. C. (2009). Beliefs about the health effects of "thirdhand" smoke and home smoking bans. *Pediatrics, 123,* e74–e79.

Winner, E. (1997). Exceptionally high intelligence and schooling. *American Psychologist, 52*(10), 1070–1081.

Winner, E. (2000). The origins and ends of giftedness. *American Psychologist, 55,* 159–169.

Winzer, M. (2008). *Children with exceptionalities in Canadian classrooms* (8th ed.). Toronto, ON: Pearson.

Wolak, J., Finkelhor, D., & Mitchell, K. J. (2012). How often are teens arrested for sexting: Data from a national sample of police cases. *Pediatrics, 129*(1), 4–12.

Wolchik, S. A., Sandler, I. N., Millsap, R. E., Plummer, B. A., Greene, S. M., Anderson, E. R., et al. (2002). Six year follow-up of a randomized, controlled trial of preventive interventions for children of divorce. *Journal of the American Medical Association, 288,* 1874–1881.

Wolfe, B. E., Hannon-Engel, S. L., & Mitchell, J. E. (2012). Bulimia nervosa in *DSM-5. Psychiatric Annals, 42,* 406–409. doi:10.3928/00485713-20121105-05

Wolfe, D. A., Crooks, C., Jaffe, P., Chiodo, D., Hughes, R., Ellis, W., . . . & Donner, A. (2009). A school-based program to prevent adolescent dating violence: A cluster randomized trial. *Archives of Pediatrics & Adolescent Medicine, 163,* 692–699.

Wolraich, M. L., Wibbelsman, C. J., Brown, T. E., Evans, S. W., Gotlieb, E. M., Knight, J. R., et al. (2005). Attention-deficit/hyperactivity disorder among adolescents: A review of the diagnosis, treatment, and clinical implications. *Pediatrics, 115,* 1734–1746.

Wong, H., Gottesman, I., & Petronis, A. (2005). Phenotypic differences in genetically identical organisms: The epigenetic perspective. *Human Molecular Genetics, 14*(Review Issue 1), R11–R18.

Wong, M. M., Nigg, J. T., Zucker, R. A., Puttler, L. I., Fitzgerald, H. E., Jester, J. M, . . . & Adams, K. (2006). Behavioral control and resiliency in the onset of alcohol and illicit drug use: A prospective study from preschool to adolescence. *Child Development, 77,* 1016–1033.

Wong, S., Ordean, A., Kahan, M., Gagnon, R., Hudon, L, Basso, M., ...de la Ronde, S. (2011). Substance use in pregnancy. *International Journal of Gynecology & Obstetrics, 114,* 190–202. doi:10.1016/j.ijgo.2011.06.001

Wood, J. J., & Repetti, R. L. (2004). What gets dad involved? A longitudinal study of change in parental child caregiving involvement. *Journal of Family Psychology, 18*(1) 237–249.

Wood, W., & Eagly, A. (2002). A cross-cultural analysis of the behavior of women and men: Implications for the origins of sex differences. *Psychological Bulletin, 128,* 699–727.

Woodruff, T. J., Axelrad, D. A., Kyle, A. D., Nweke, O., Miller, G. G., & Hurley, B. J. (2004). Trends in environmentally related childhood illnesses. *Pediatrics, 113,* 1133–1140.

Woolley, J. D., & Boerger, E. A. (2002). Development of beliefs about the origins and controllability of dreams. *Developmental Psychology, 38*(1), 24–41.

Woolley, J. D., Phelps, K. E., Davis, D. L., & Mandell, D. J. (1999). Where theories of mind meet magic: The development of children's beliefs about wishing. *Child Development, 70,* 571–587.

World Bank. (2006). *Repositioning nutrition as central to development.* Washington, DC: Author.

World Health Organization. (2003). *The world health report—shaping the future.* Retrieved from http://www.who.int/whr/2003/en/

World Health Organization. (2008). *Global burden of disease report: 2004 update.* Retrieved from http://www.who.int/healthinfo/global_burden_disease/2004_report_update/en/index.html

World Health Organization. (2008a). *HIV transmission through breastfeeding: A review of the available evidence 2007 update.* Geneva: WHO Press. Retrieved from whqlibdoc.who.int/publications/2008/9789241596596_eng.pdf

World Health Organization. (2009). *HIV and infant feeding: Revised principles and recommendations rapid advice – November 2009.* Geneva: WHO Press. Retrieved from whqlibdoc.who.int/publications/2009/9789241598873_eng.pdf

World Health Organization. (2010). *Guidelines on HIV and infant feeding 2010: Principles and recommendations for infant feeding in the context of HIVand a summary of evidence.* Geneva: WHO Press. Retrieved from whqlibdoc.who.int/publications/2010/9789241599535_eng.pdf

Worswick, C. (2001). *School performance of the children of immigrants in Canada* (Catalogue no. 11F0019MIE2001178). Ottawa, ON: Statistics Canada.

Worth, K., Gibson, J., Chambers, M. S., Nassau, D., Balvinder, K., Rakhra, A. B., & Sargent, J. (2008). Exposure of U.S. adolescents to extremely violent movies, *Pediatrics, 122*(2), 306–312.

Wright, S. C., Taylor, D. M., & Ruggiero, K. M. (1996). Examining the potential for academic achievement among Inuit children: Comparisons on the Raven Coloured Progressive Matrices. *Journal of Cross-Cultural Psychology, 27,* 733–753.

Wu, Z., Costigan, C. L., Hou, F., Kampen, R., & Schimmele, C. M. (2010). Change and stability in cohabitation and children's educational adjustment. *Journal of Comparative Family Studies, 41*, 557–579.

Wu, Z., Hou, F., & Schimmele. C. M. (2008). Family structure and children's psychosocial outcomes. *Journal of Family Issues, 29*, 1600–1624. doi:10.1177/0192513X08322818

Wynn, K. (1992). Evidence against empiricist accounts of the origins of numerical knowledge. *Mind and Language, 7*, 315–332.

Wyrobek, A. J., Eskenazi, B., Young, S., Arnheim, N., Tiemann-Boege, I., Jabs, E. W., et al. (2006). Advancing age has differential effects on DNA damage, chromatin integrity, gene mutations, and aneuploidies in sperm. *Proceedings of the National Academy of Sciences of the United States of America, 103*(25), 9601–9606.

Xue, Y., Leventhal, T., Brooks-Gunn, J., & Earls, F. (2005). Neighborhood residence and mental health problems of 5- to 11-year-olds. *Archives of General Psychiatry, 62*, 1–10.

Yip, T., Seaton, E. K., & Sellers, R. M. (2006). African American racial identity across the lifespan: Identity status, identity content, and depressive symptoms. *Child Development, 77*, 1504–1517.

Yokota, F., & Thompson, K. M. (2000). Violence in G-rated animated films. *Journal of the American Medical Association, 283*, 2716–2720.

Yoshikawa, H. (1994). Prevention as cumulative protection: Effects of early family support and education on chronic delinquency and its risks. *Psychological Bulletin, 115*(1), 28–54.

Young, K., Holcomb, L., Bonkale, W., Hicks, P., Yazdaini U., & German, D. (2007). 5HTTLPR polymorphism and enlargement of the pulvinar: Unlocking the backdoor to the limbic system. *Biological Psychiatry, 61*(6), 813–818.

Young, M. C., Munoz-Furlong, A., & Sicherer, S. H. (2009). Management of food allergies in school: A perspective for allergists. *Clini-cal Reviews in Allergy and Immunology, 124*(2). 175–182.

Young, T. K., Martens, P. J., Taback, S. P., Sellers, E. A. C., Dean, H. J., Cheang, M., & Flett, B. (2002). Type 2 diabetes mellitus in children: prenatal and early infancy risk factors among native Canadians. *Archives of Pediatric and Adolescent Medicine, 156*, 651–655.

Youngblade, L. M., & Belsky, J. (1992). Parent-child antecedents of 5-year-olds' close friendships: A longitudinal analysis. *Developmental Psychology, 28*, 700–713.

Youngblade, L. M., Theokas, C., Schulenberg, J., Curry, L., Huang, I-C., & Novak, M. (2007). Risk and promotive factors in families, schools, and communities: A contextual model of positive youth development in adolescence. *Pediatrics, 119*(Suppl.), S47–S53.

Yu, S. M., Huang, Z. J., & Singh, G. K. (2004). Health status and health services utilization among U.S. Chinese, Asian Indian, Filipino, and Other Asian/Pacific Islander children. *Pediatrics, 113*(1), 101–107.

Yuki, K., Suzuki, M., & Kurachi, M., (2007, October). Stress sensitization in schizophrenia. *Annals of the New York Academy of Sciences*, 276–290.

Zahn-Waxler, C., Radke-Yarrow, M., Wagner, E., & Chapman, M. (1992). Development of concern for others. *Developmental Psychology, 28*, 126–136.

Zanardo, V., Svegliado, G., Cavallin, F., Giustardi, A., Cosmi, E., Litta, P., & Trevisanuto, D. (2010). Elective cesarean delivery: Does it have a negative effect on breastfeeding? *Birth, 37*(4), 275–279.

Zeiger, J. S., Beaty, T. H., & Liang, K. (2005). Oral clefts, maternal smoking, and TGFA: A meta-analysis of gene-environment interaction. *The Cleft Palate-Craniofacial Journal, 42*(1), 58–63.

Zelazo, P. D., Müller, U., Frye, D., & Marcovitch, S. (2003). The development of executive function in early childhood. *Monographs of the Society for Research in Child Development, 68*(3) [Serial No. 274].

Zeskind, P. S., & Stephens, L. E. (2004). Maternal selective serotonin reuptake inhibitor use during pregnancy and newborn neurobehavior. *Pediatrics, 11*, 368–375.

Zhang, X. (2008). *The post-childbirth employment of Canadian mothers and the earnings trajectories of their continuously employed counterparts, 1983 to 2004.* Ottawa, ON: Statistics Canada. Retrieved from http://www.statcan.gc.ca/pub/11f0019m/11f0019m2008314-eng.pdf

Zhao, D., Zhang, Q., Fu, M., Tang, Y., & Zhao, Y. (2010). Effects of 0physical positions on sleep architectures and post-nap functions among habitual nappers. *Biological Psychology, 83*(3), 207–213. doi:10.1016/j.biopsycho.2009.12.008

Zhu, B.-P., Rolfs, R. T., Nangle, B. E., & Horan, J. M. (1999). Effect of the interval between pregnancies on perinatal outcomes. *New England Journal of Medicine, 340*, 589–594.

Zigler, E., & Styfco, S. J. (1993). Using research and theory to justify and inform Head Start expansion. *Social Policy Report of the Society for Research in Child Development, 7*, 1–21.

Zigler, E., & Styfco, S. J. (1994). Head Start: Criticisms in a constructive context. *American Psychologist, 49*, 127–132.

Zigler, E., & Styfco, S. J. (2001). Extended childhood intervention prepares children for school and beyond. *Journal of the American Medical Association, 285*, 2378–2380.

Zigler, E., Taussig, C., & Black, K. (1992). Early childhood intervention: A promising preventative for juvenile delinquency. *American Psychologist, 47*, 997–1006.

Zwier, S., Araujo, T., Boukes, M., & Willemsen, L. (2011). Boundaries to the articulation of possible selves through social networking sites: The case of Facebook profilers' social connectedness. *CyberPsychology, Behavior, and Social Networking, 14*, 571–576. doi:10.1089/cyber.2010.0612

Zylke, J., & DeAngelis, C. (2007). Pediatric chronic diseases—stealing childhood. *Journal of the American Medical Association, 297*(24), 2765–2766.

BRIEF CONTENTS

p. iii: Rubberball Productions RF; p. v: Fuse/Getty Images RF; p. vi: © Jose Luis Pelaez Inc/Blend Images LLC RF; p. vii (top): © Don Mason/Blend Images LLC RF; p. vii (bottom): Tom Merton/Getty Images RF; p. viii (top): © Bananastock/PictureQuest RF; p. viii (bottom): Design Pics/Don Hammond RF; p. ix: © Don Mason/Blend Images LLC RF; p. x (top): © Ingram Publishing/SuperStock RF; p. (bottom): © John Lund/Sam Diephuis/SuperStock RF; p. xi: Associated Press RF.

CHAPTER 1

Opener: Duane Rieder/Stone/Getty Images; p. 4 (top left): © LOETSCHER CHLAUS / Alamy; p. 4 (top middle): CC Squared Studios/Getty Images RF; p. 4 (top right): Dan Kenyon/Taxi/Getty Images; p. 4 (bottom): Glow Images RF; Table 1.1 (numbered from top down), p. 5: (1) Elke Van de Velde/Getty Images RF; (2) Rubberball Productions RF; (3) Rubberball/Nicole Hill/Getty Images RF; (4) Rubberball/Nicole Hill/Getty Images RF; p. 7: Photo scanned from Karl Pearson, "The Life, Letters, and Labours of Francis Galton" 1860; p. 9: © LOETSCHER CHLAUS / Alamy; p. 11: Debby Wong / Shutterstock.com; p. 12: Copyright © Foodcollection RF; p. 13 (top): Digital Vision RF; p. 13 (bottom left): Bananastock/PictureQuest RF; p. 13 (bottom right): Amos Morgan/Gettty Images RF; p. 14: Nancy Ney/Digital Vision/Getty Images RF; p. 15 (top): The McGraw-Hill Companies, Inc./Charles D. Winters, photographer RF; p. 15 (bottom): © Jose Luis Pelaez Inc/Blend Images LLC RF; p. 16: © Plush Studios/Blend Images LLC RF; p. 20: Digital Vision/PunchStock RF; p. 22: Creatas/PunchStock RF; p. 23: CC Squared Studios/Getty Images RF; p. 25: Dan Kenyon/Taxi/Getty Images; p. 26: Copyright by Oren Jack Turner, Princeton, NJ/Library of Congress Prints and Photographs Division [LC-USZ62-60242] PD.

CHAPTER 2

Opener: Jay P. Morgan/Workbook Stock/Getty Images; p. 34 (top left): MedicalRF.com RF; p. 34 (top middle): © Mark Hunt/Huntstock/CORBIS RF; p. 34 (top right): © Richard Bailey/CORBIS; p. 34: Don W. Fawcett/Photo Researchers, Inc.; p. 35: MedicalRF.com RF; p. 36 (left): MedicalRF.com RF; p. 36 (right): AP Photo/Robin Layton/file; p. 37: © Jose Luis Pelaez Inc/Blend Images LLC RF; p. 38 (left): Adam Gault/OJO Images/Getty Images RF; p. 38 (right): © Oote Boe/Alamy; p. 39 (top): © Allison Rocks! Photography RF; p. 39 (bottom): © ONOKY--Photononstop/Alamy RF; p. 40 (top left): © Plush Studios/Blend Images LLC RF; p. 40 (top right): © Ariel Skelley/Blend Images LLC RF; p. 40 (DD): Glow Images RF; p. 40 (Dd left): © Sean Justice/Corbis RF; p. 40 (Dd right): Glow Images RF; p. 40 (dd): Pixtal/AGE Fotostock RF; p. 40 (bottom left): © Mark Hunt/Huntstock/CORBIS RF; p. 40 (bottom right): OJO Images/ASSOCIATED PRESS RF; p. 43 (mother): Jack Hollingsworth/Getty Images RF; p. 43 (father): Image Source/Getty Images RF; p. 43 (children, all four): Blend Images/Getty Images RF; p. 44 (left): Seide Preis/Photodisc/Getty Images RF; p. 44 (right): © Richard Bailey/CORBIS; p. 45 (top): WurdBendur/Wikipedia Commons; p. 45 (bottom): Purestock/SuperStock; p. 47: RunPhoto/Photodisc/Getty Images RF; p. 48: Image Source/Getty Images RF; p. 49: Digital Vision/Getty Images RF; p. 50: Bradley Mason/Getty Images RF.

CHAPTER 3

Opener: © Gareth Brown/CORBIS; p. 56 (top left): © LookatSciences/Phototake--All rights reserved; p. 56 (top middle): © John Lund/Drew Kelly/Blend Images LLC RF; p. 56 (top right): Saturn Stills/Photo Researchers, Inc.; p. 56 (middle right): © Brian Jackson/Alamy RF; p. 56 (bottom left): Glowimages RM/Alamy; p. 57 (1 month): © Petit Format/Nestle/Science Source/Photo Researchers; p. 57 (3 months): Lennart Nilsson/Albert Bonniers Forlag AB, A CHILD IS BORN, Dell Publishing Company; p. 57 (5 months): James Stevenson/Photo Researchers; p. 58 (top): © Creatas/PunchStock RF; p. 58 (bottom): MedicalRF.com RF; p. 60: © LookatSciences/Phototake--All rights

reserved; p. 61: © liquidlibrary/PictureQuest RF; p. 62 (top): The McGraw-Hill Companies, Inc./Jill Braaten, photographer RF; p. 62 (bottom): Rubberball/Getty Images RF; p. 63 (top): © John Lund/Drew Kelly/Blend Images LLC RF; p. 63 (middle): GK Hart/Vikki Hart/The Image Bank/Getty Images; p. 64: Lawrence Schwartzwald/Splash New/Newscom; p. 65: © BonkersAboutScience/Alamy; p. 66: PhotoLink/Getty Images RF; p. 67 (top): C. Zachariasen / PhotoAlto; p. 67 (bottom): Monkey Business Images Ltd/Photolibrary; p. 70 (top): Blend Images/Alamy RF; p. 70 (bottom): Saturn Stills/Photo Researchers, Inc.

CHAPTER 4

Opener: Frare/Davis Photography/Brand X/CORBIS RF; p. 74 (top left): Elizabeth Crews/The Image Works; p. 74 (top middle): no credit; p. 74 (top right): © Jose Luis Pelaez Inc/Blend Images LLC RF; p. 74 (bottom): © Everett Collection Inc/Alamy; p. 75 (top): Brand X Pictures RF; p. 75 (bottom): © Jose Luis Pelaez Inc/Blend Images LLC RF; p. 76: Zdenek Rosenthaler/Shutterstock; p. 77: © Jose Luis Pelaez Inc/Blend Images LLC RF; p. 78 (top): © Cornstock/Alamy RF; p. 78 (middle): © Jose Luis Pelaez Inc/Blend Images LLC RF; p. 78 (bottom): © Martin Valigursky/Alamy RF; p. 79: © n8n photo / Alamy; p. 80 (top): p. 80 (middle): Cornstock/Jupiter Images RF; p. 80 (rooting): Elizabeth Crews/The Image Works; p. 80 (sucking): Bananastock/PictureQuest RF; p. 80 (grasping): DAL/Getty Images RF; p. 80 (Moro): Elizabeth Crews/The Image Works; p. 82: altrendo images/Getty Images; p. 83: SimplyMui Photography/StockImage/Getty Images; p. 84: Erproductions Ltd/Blend Images LLC RF; p. 85: no credit; p. 86: C Squared Studios/Getty Images RF; p. 91 (top): © Jose Luis Pelaez Inc/Blend Images LLC RF; p. 91 (bottom): Harlow Primate Lab/University of Wisconsin.

CHAPTER 5

Opener: Domino/Taxi/Getty Images; p. 98 (left): Petrenko Andriy/Shutterstock; p. 98 (middle): Pixtal/AGE Fotostock RF; p. 98 (right): © KidStock/Blend Images/CORBIS RF; p. 99: Petrenko Andriy/Shutterstock; p. 100: Adam Crowley/Getty Images RF; p. 102 (top): Brand X Pictures/PunchStock RF; p. 104 (left): Courtesy of Children's Hospital of Michigan; p. 104 (right): Courtesy of Children's Hospital of Michigan; p. 105 (top): © Jose Luis Pelaez Inc/Blend Images LLC RF; p. 105 (middle): Copyright © Foodcollection/StockFood RF; p. 106: CORBIS/PictureQuest RF; p. 107 (Fig. 5.6, numbered left to right): (1) Barbara Penoyar/Getty Images RF; (2) Digital Vision/Getty Images RF; (3) Image Source/Alamy RF; (4) Titus/Getty Images RF; (5) Digital Vision RF; (6) Bananastock/PictureQuest RF; (7) CORBIS/PictureQuest RF; (8) Brand X Pictures/PunchStock RF; p. 107 (bottom): CORBIS/SuperStock RF; p. 108: © Tetra Images/CORBIS RF; p. 109 (top): Pixtal/AGE Fotostock RF; p. 109 (bottom): © Mark Richards/PhotoEdit; p. 110: © KidStock/Blend Images/CORBIS RF; p. 111: Image Source/Veer RF; p. 113: lev radin / Shutterstock.com; p. 114: Ingram Publishing/SuperStock RF.

CHAPTER 6

Opener: © Picture Partners/Alamy; p. 120 (left): Cornstock Images/Getty Images RF; p. 120 (middle): Bananastock/PictureQuest RF; p. 120 (bottom): Dorling Kindersley/Getty Images; p. 121: © Bananastock/PictureQuest RF; p. 123: Teresa De Paul/Blend Images LLC RF; p. 124: Cornstock Images/Getty Images RF; p. 126 (right): Spike Mafford/Getty Images RF; p. 127: Daniel Hurst Photography/Photographer's Choice/Getty Images; p. 128 (top): Realistic Reflections RF; p. 128 (bottom): © Profimedia/CZ a.s./Alamy; p. 129: Bananastock/PictureQuest RF; p. 131: Carey Kikella/Taxi/Getty Images; p. 132: Image Source/Getty Images RF; p. 133: Stockbyte/Getty Images RF; p. 134 (top): Image Source/Veer RF; p. 134 (bottom): © Christina Kennedy/Alamy; p. 135 (top): Glow Images RF; p. 135 (bottom): JGI/Jamie Grill/Blend Images/Getty Images; p. 136 (bottom): © PunchStock/BananaStock RF; p. 137: John Lund/Annabelle Breakey/Getty Images RF; p. 138: Dorling Kindersley/Getty Images.

CHAPTER 7

Opener: La Fée/Flickr/Getty Images RF; p. 144 (left): © Brand X Pictures/PunchStock RF; p. 144 (middle): Kris Hanke/Vetta/Getty Images RF; p. 144 (right): Big Cheese Photo/PunchStock RF; p. 145 (top): With Love Photography/Flickr/Getty Images RF; p. 145 (6 months): Ariel Skelley/Blend Images/Getty Images RF; p. 145 (18–24): © Jose Luis Pelaez Inc/Blend Images LLC RF; p. 145 (2½–3): Design Pics/Kristy-Anne Glubish; p. 146: Ariel Skelley/Blend Images/ASSOCIATED PRESS RF; p. 147: Photodisc/Getty Images RF; p. 148: Dream Pictures/Vanessa Gavalya/Blend Images/ASSOCIATED PRESS RF; p. 149 (left): © Brand X Pictures/PunchStock RF; p. 149 (right): © Ariel Skelley/Blend Images LLC RF; p. 150: Ale Ventura/ASSOCIATED PRESS LLC; p. 151: Hill Street Studios/Blend Images/ASSOCIATED PRESS RF; p. 152: © Jose Luis Pelaez Inc/Blend Images LLC RF; p. 154 (top): Kris Hanke/Vetta/Getty Images RF; p. 154 (bottom): © Life on white/Alamy RF; p. 155: Big Cheese Photo/PunchStock RF; p. 157 (left): ASSOCIATED PRESS RF; p. 157 (right): Jose Luis Pelaez Inc/Blend Images/ASSOCIATED PRESS RF; p. 158: LWA/Sharie Kennedy/Blend Images/ASSOCIATED PRESS RF; p. 159: JGI/Blend Images LLC RF.

CHAPTER 8

Opener: Donald Iain Smith/Flickr/Getty Images RF; p. 164 (left): ASSOCIATED PRESS RF; p. 164 (middle): © moodboard/CORBIS RF; p. 164 (right): Frédéric Cirou/ASSOCIATED PRESS RF; p. 165: © JGI/Blend Images LLC RF; p. 166: ASSOCIATED PRESS RF; p. 168 (top): ASSOCIATED PRESS RF; p. 168 (middle): © Jennie Hart/Alamy; p. 168 (bottom): Jeff Thrower/Shutterstock; p. 170: Purestock/SuperStock; p. 172: © Karin Dreyer/Blend Images LLC; p. 173 (top): © moodboard/CORBIS RF; p. 173 (bottom): Eva Marie Amiya/Photolibrary/Getty Images; p. 174 (top): Michael N. Paras/age footstock; p. 174 (bottom): Image Source/Jackson J. Russel/ASSOCIATED PRESS RF; p. 176: Frédéric Cirou/ASSOCIATED PRESS RF.

CHAPTER 9

Opener: JGI/Blend Images/ASSOCIATED PRESS RF; p. 182 (left): © Ellen B. Senisi/The Image Works; p. 182 (middle): Andy Crawford/Dorling Kindersley/Getty Images; p. 182 (right): © IT Stock Free RF; p. 183: BananaStock/PunchStock; p. 185: © Ellen B. Senisi/The Image Works; p. 186 (top): Jose Luis Pelaez Inc/Blend Images/ASSOCIATED PRESS RF; p. 186 (bottom): © BananaStock RF; p. 187 (top): Paul Burns/Blend Images LLC RF; p. 187 (middle): Terry Vine/Blend Images/Getty Images RF; p. 187 (bottom): Leonard Lessin/Photo Researchers/Getty Images; p. 188 (right): Ned Frisk/Blend Images/ASSOCIATED PRESS RF; p. 188 (left top): © iStockphoto.com; p. 188 (left middle): D. Hurst/Alamy RF; p. 188 (left bottom): The McGraw-Hill Companies/Gary He, photographer; p. 189 (left): Art Vandalay/Getty Images; p. 189 (right): © Robert Mabic/Alamy; p. 191: © CORBIS Cusp/Alamy; p. 194 (top): JGI/Jamie Grill/Getty Images RF; p. 194 (bottom): Andy Crawford/Dorling Kindersley/Getty Images; p. 197: © IT Stock Free RF.

CHAPTER 10

Opener: Image Source/Alamy RF; p. 202 (left): Andrew L/Shutterstock; p. 202 (middle): Peter Zander/Getty Images; p. 202 (right): JGI/Jamie Grill/Blend Images/ASSOCIATED PRESS RF; p. 203 (top): Cornstock/PictureQuest RF; p. 203 (bottom): Steve Skjold/Alamy; p. 204 (left): Design Pics/Leah Warkentin RF; p. 204 (right): KidStock/Blend Images/Getty Images RF; p. 205 (top): Andrew L/Shutterstock; p. 205 (bottom): Robin Lynne Gibson/Photographer's Choice/Getty Images; p. 206 (top): © Andres Paterson/Alamy RF; p. 206 (bottom): Corbis/PictureQuest; p. 207 (portrait): © Jeffrey Blackler/Alamy; p. 207 (book): © Jeffrey Blackler/Alamy; p. 208: Ray Tamara/Getty Images; p. 209: Cavan Images/The Image Bank/Getty Images; p. 210: Peter Zander/Getty Images; p. 212 (right):

The McGraw-Hill Companies/Ken Karp, photographer RF; p. 212 (left): Dave King/Getty Images RF; p. 213: © Life on white/Alamy RF; p. 214: JGI/Jamie Grill/Blend Images/ASSOCIATED PRESS RF; p. 216: Pixtal/AGE Fotostock RF; p. 217: Evgeny Terentev/The Agency Collection/Getty Images RF; p. 218: Image Source/PunchStock RF.

CHAPTER 11

Opener: © Kris Timken/Blend Images LLC RF; p. 224 (top left): © Stockbyte/PunchStock RF; p. 224 (top middle): Jose Luis Pelaez Inc/Blend Images/ASSOCIATED PRESS RF; p. 224 (top right): © Michael Newman/PhotoEdit; p. 224 (bottom): © pierre d'alancaisez/Alamy; p. 225: Richard Hutchings/Digital Light Source RF; p. 226: Eat Well and Be Active Poster. Health Canada, 2011. Reproduced with the permission of the Minister of Health, 2013; p. 227 (left): © Michael Neelon(miscc)/Alamy; p. 227 (right): © BananaStock/PunchStock RF; p. 228: © Stockbyte/PunchStock RF; p. 229: © Jose Luis Pelaez Inc/Blend Images LLC RF; p. 230: Jose Luis Pelaez Inc/Blend Images/ASSOCIATED PRESS RF; p. 231: Ingram Publishing RF; p. 232 (top): © Jose Luis Pelaez Inc/Blend Images LLC RF; p. 232 (bottom): © ZUMA Press Inc./Alamy; p. 234: Brand X Pictures/PunchStock RF; p. 235: Royalty-Free/CORBIS RF; p. 236: © Michael Newman/PhotoEdit.

CHAPTER 12

Opener: © Stockbyte/PunchStock RF; p. 242 (left): Digital Vision/Getty Images RF; p. 242 (middle): © Laura Dwight/PhotoEdit; p. 242 (right): © Erproductions Ltd/Blend Images/CORBIS RF; p. 243: 2007 © Marty Heitner/The Image Works; p. 244: AFP/Getty Images; p. 245: © Dana Neely/Getty Images; p. 246: McGraw-Hill Companies Inc./Janette Beckman, photographer RF; p. 248: Multiple Intelligences figure from p. 164 in Fiore, LifeSmart, 1st Ed. Copyright © 2011 The McGraw-Hill Companies, Inc. Reprinted by permission; p. 248 (numbered clockwise from Naturalistic): (1) Laurence Mouton/Getty Images RF; (2) Barbara Penoyar/Getty Images RF; (3) Mark Andersen/Getty Images RF; (4) © ThinkStock/Masterfile RF; (5) Paul Edmondson/Getty Images RF; (6) © CORBIS RF; (7) Mel Curtis/Getty Images; (8) Halfdark/Getty Images RF; p. 251: B2M Productions/Photographer's Choice/Getty Images; p. 252 (left): SW Productions/Brand X Pictures/Getty Images RF; p. 252 (right): © Siede Preis/Getty Images RF; p. 253 (top): Ben Molyneux/Alamy; p. 253 (bottom): © LWA/Dann Tardif/Blend Images/CORBIS RF; p. 255: Digital Vision/Getty Images RF; p. 258 (top): © Laura Dwight/PhotoEdit; p. 258 (bottom): Pixtal/AGE Fotostock RF; p. 259: Tom Grill/Getty Images RF; p. 260: © Erproductions Ltd/Blend Images/CORBIS RF.

CHAPTER 13

Opener: Drew Myers/CORBIS RF; p. 266 (top left): S. Olsson/PhotoAlto RF; p. 266 (top middle): © Catchlight Visual Services / Alamy; p. 266 (top right): BananaStock/AGE Fotostock RF; p. 266 (bottom): © Maya Barnes Johansen/The Image Works; p. 267 (top): D. Hurst/Alamy RF; p. 267 (right): © Creatas/PunchStock RF; p. 268: © sharpstock/Alamy RF; p. 269 (top): dynamicgraphics/Jupiterimages RF; p. 269 (middle): © PhotoAlto/PictureQuest RF; p. 269 (bottom): Big Cheese Photo/PunchStock RF; p. 271: S. Olsson/PhotoAlto RF; p. 272: © Dave and Les Jacobs/Blend Images LLC RF; p. 274 (right): Eric McCandless/ABC via Getty Images; p. 274 (left): © Catchlight Visual Services / Alamy; p. 277 (numbered clockwise from Rejected): (1) ASSOCIATED PRESS RF; (2) ASSOCIATED PRESS RF; (3) © Leila Cutler/Alamy; (4) Tooga/Getty Images; (5) MBI/Alamy; p. 278: © Stockdisc/PunchStock RF; p. 279: BananaStock/AGE Fotostock RF; p. 280 (top): © Pictorial Press Ltd/Alamy; p. 280 (bottom): Creatas Images/JupiterImages RF; p. 281 (top): THE CANADIAN PRESS/Andrew Vaughan; p. 281 (bottom): Stockbyte/Getty Images RF.

CHAPTER 14

Opener: Design Pics/Kristy-Anne Glubish RF; p. 286 (left): Ron Levine/ Digital Vision/Getty Images RF; p. 286 (middle): S. Olsson/PhotoAlto RF; p. 286 (right): © ZUMA Wire Service/Alamy; p. 288: © CORBIS; p. 289: Leonard McLane/Getty Images RF; p. 290 (top): © Brand X Pictures/PunchStock; p. 290 (bottom): © Brand X Pictures/ PunchStock RF; p. 292: ASSOCIATED PRESS RF; p. 293 (top): © Blend Images/SuperStock RF; p. 293 (bottom): Ron Levine/Digital Vision/Getty Images RF; p. 294 (top): S. Olsson/PhotoAlto RF; p. 294 (bottom): Stock 4B RF; p. 295: ASSOCIATED PRESS RF; p. 296: © Chris Pizzello/Reuters/CORBIS; p. 297: Sanna Lindberg/Getty Images RF; p. 298 (top): Design Pics/Darren Greenwood RF; p. 298 (bottom): © Matti/Alamy RF; p. 299: Design Pics/Nathan Lau RF; p. 300: © ZUMA Wire Service/Alamy.

CHAPTER 15

Opener: © Steve Hix/Somos Images/CORBIS RF; p. 306 (top left): © BananaStock/PunchStock RF; p. 306 (top middle): © Hill Street Studios/Blend Images LLC RF; p. 306 (top right): Andersen/Ross/ Getty Images RF; p. 306 (bottom): Design Pics/Darren Greenwood RF; p. 309 (left): © BananaStock/PunchStock RF; p. 309 (right): Keijiro Komine/amana images/Getty Images; p. 310: Eric Larrayadieu/ Stone/Getty Images; p. 313: Design Pics/Don Hammond RF; p. 314 (top): ASSOCIATED PRESS RF; p. 314 (bottom): Leah Warkentin/ Design Pics/CORBIS RF; p. 315: Mike Kemp/Rubberball/CORBIS RF; p. 316: ASSOCIATED PRESS RF; p. 317 (top): © Hill Street Studios/Blend Images LLC RF; p. 317 (bottom): Thomas Barwick/The Image Bank/Getty Images; p. 319 (top): Pixtal/AGE Fotostock; p. 319 (bottom): Andersen/Ross/Getty Images RF.

CHAPTER 16

Opener: © BananaStock/PunchStock RF; p. 324 (left): PhotoAlto/ PunchStock RF; p. 324 (middle): Daniel Swartz / REVAMP.com; p. 324 (right): Image Source/Getty Images RF; p. 325: Halfdark/ Getty Images RF; p. 327 (top): © Arco Images GmbH/Alamy; p. 327 (bottom): CP PHOTO/Kevin Frayer; p. 328 (top): Fancy Collection/ SuperStock RF; p. 328 (bottom): CommerceandCultureAgency/The Image Bank/Getty Images; p. 330 (left): Burke/Triolo Productions/ Getty Images RF; p. 330 (right): Tony Cordoza/Photographer's Choice RF; p. 331: © Muskopf Photography, LLC / Alamy; p. 333: Design Pics/Don Hammond RF; p. 334: PhotoAlto/PunchStock RF; p. 335: Daniel Swartz / REVAMP.com; p. 336 (right): ASSOCIATED PRESS RF; p. 336 (left): © AKP Photos/Alamy; p. 337: Brand X Pictures/Jupiterimages/Getty Images RF; p. 338 (top): © Hill Street Studios/Blend Images LLC RF; p. 338 (bottom): Image Source/Getty Images RF; p. 339: Oleksiy Maksymenko/Getty Images RF; p. 340: ASSOCIATED PRESS RF.

A

Abbolt, D., 288n
Aber, J.L., 156, 270, 279
Abma, J.C., 329, 330
Abraham, M.R., 76
Abrams, C.L., 271
Abrams, D., 280
Abramson, L.Y., 235
Achter, J.A., 259
Ackerman, D., 197
Adair, C., 299n
Adair, J., 27
Adam, E.K., 152
Adams, G.R., 27, 174, 191
Adamson, L., 152
Adamuti-Trache, M., 319
Addison, T.L., 138
Adesope, O.O., 256
Adlaf, E.M., 286, 297
Adley, C., 255
Adolph, K.E., 107, 108, 109
Agerbo, E., 51
Ahadi, S.A., 147, 148
Ahamad, Y., 229
Ahmed, S., 251
Ahmed, S.F., 39
Ahmeduzzaman, M., 157
Ahnert, L., 151
Ahrons, C.R., 271, 272
Aikens, N., 195
Ainsworth, M.D.S., 150
Aitkin, M., 69
Akitsuki, Y., 267
Aksan, N., 156
Al-Sahab, B., 100, 176
Alaimo, K., 170
Albert, D.B., 332
Albert, T., 173
Alexander, G.R., 88
Alexander, K.L., 253
Algeria, J., 60
Ali, M.M., 329
Aligne, C.A., 67
Allen, A.C., 68
Allen, G.L., 246
Allen, K.R., 275
Allen, M., 88
Allen, S., 92, 137
Alloway, T.P., 246
Almas, A.N., 156
Almeida, D.M., 316
Almli, C.R., 60
Alpern, L., 152
Als, H., 102, 152
Amato, P.R., 271–272, 273, 274, 335
Ambert, A.-M., 271
Ames, E.W., 103
Amit, M., 106
Amler, R.W., 177
Amler, S., 177
Amso, D., 224
Amundson, N., 319
Anastasi, A., 259
Anderson, A.H., 251
Anderson, C.A., 280
Anderson, C.H., 279
Anderson, D., 210

Anderson, E., 274
Anderson, K.D., 100, 169
Anderson, K.J., 157
Anderson, M., 281
Anderson, P., 86
Anderson, R.N., 87, 90, 300
Anderson, S.E., 290
Andres, L., 319
Andrews, J.A., 291
Angold, A., 235
Anisef, P., 317
Annett, M., 168
Anthony, J.C., 338
Antonarakis, E.S., 44
Apgar, V.A., 82n
Aquan-Assee, J., 276
Arai, A.B., 255
Araujo, T., 336
Arbeau, K.A., 64
Arbour, L., 88
Archambault, I., 314
Archer, J., 212, 277, 278
Archer, P., 106
Arden, C.I., 229
Arias, E., 84
Arim, R.G., 288, 290
Armant, D.R., 66
Armer, M., 211
Armson, B.A., 77
Armstrong, M.A., 69
Arner, P., 50
Arnett, J.J., 332, 339, 340
Arshad, 100n
Arterberry, M.E., 105
Asher, M.I., 231
Ashmead, D.H., 108
Askan, N., 268
Astley, S.J., 66
Aszmann, A., 293
Atella, L.D., 64
Atlas, R., 282
Auinger, P., 169
Aumiller, K., 277
Auyeng, B., 207
Awong, T., 156
Aziz, A., 229

B

Bachard, A.M., 64
Bachman, J.G., 297, 339
Baddeley, A.D., 189, 246
Bagwell, C.L., 278
Bailey, L.M., 168
Bailey, M.D., 158
Bailey, N.W., 327
Baillargeon, R., 126n, 129, 130, 155, 157, 218
Baines, E., 228
Baird, D.D., 33, 35
Baker, M., 270
Baker, S.B., 300
Baker-Brown, G., 236
Bakermans-Kranenburg, M.J., 152
Bakersman-Kranenburg, M.J., 276
Bala, N., 9
Balaraman, G., 187

Baldwin, D.A., 153
Ball, G., 169
Ball, H.L., 112, 112n
Ball, J., 196
Ball, O.E., 259
Ball, R.H., 60
Baltes, P.B., 11
Bandura, A., 16t, 19, 30, 205t, 208, 209, 210, 318
Bandy-Hedden, I., 197
Banerji, A., 169
Banks, A., 274
Banks, E., 148
Banta, D., 77
Barbaranelli, C., 318
Barber, B.L., 335
Barkley, R.A., 234
Barlow, S.E., 169
Barnes, H.V., 339
Barnes, J.D., 228, 229
Barnett, D., 150
Barnett, S., 197
Barrington, K.J., 104
Barros, R.M., 228
Barrow, L., 317
Barthel, M., 151
Bartick, M., 100
Bascaramurty, D., 11
Baskett, R., 197
Bassuk, E.L., 175
Basu, R., 64
Bates, E., 133n, 215, 218, 281
Bates, J.E., 211, 214, 338
Batshaw, M.L., 45
Batton, D.G., 104
Bauchner, H., 100
Bauer, 131
Bauer, D., 299
Bauer, P.J., 189
Bauman, L.J., 232
Baumer, E.P., 329
Baumrind, D., 214, 215, 216, 220, 316, 333
Baumwell, L., 137
Bauserman, R., 272
Baxter, C., 276
Baydala, L., 247
Bayley, N., 106, 121
Bayliss, D.M., 246
Beach, J., 256
Bearman, S.K., 295
Beattie, D., 255
Beaty, T.H., 61
Beauchamp, G.K., 60, 105
Beaulieu, A., 229
Beaupré, P., 269, 271, 273
Beckett, C., 102
Beech, A., 280
Beedle, A., 41n
Behrman, R.E., 70, 231
Beintema, 111n
Beirness, D.J., 300
Beiser, M., 10n, 175, 236, 249, 256
Belizzi, M., 169
Bell, D.C., 333
Bell, J.F., 62
Bell, L.G., 333
Bell, R., 61

Bell, T., 215
Bellamy, L., 281
Belsky, J., 152, 290
Bem, S., 205t
Ben-Shoshan, M., 172
Benbow, C.P., 260
Bendersky, M., 68
Benes, F.M., 164
Benjamin, A., 320
Benjamin, J.T., 230
Benjet, C., 215
Bennett, D.S., 68
Bennett, J., 259
Bennett, M., 270
Bennett, S., 113
Benoit, C., 74, 75
Benson, J.B., 108
Benson, P.L., 276
Benzies, K., 64, 196
Beran, T., 280
Berard, A., 66
Berenbaum, S.A., 209
Berenson, A., 63
Bergeman, C.S., 48
Berger, A., 130
Berger, K.S., 280, 281
Berglund, H., 328
Berk, L.E., 194
Berkowitz, L., 279, 280
Berman, S., 331
Berndt, A.E., 157
Berndt, T.J., 336
Bernier, A., 151, 165
Bernier, L., 37
Bernstein, P.S., 75
Berry, R.J., 62
Berthier, N.E., 108
Bertrand, J., 197
Betran, A.P., 78
Beyers, W., 340
Bialystock, E., 187
Biason-Lauber, A., 39
Bierman, K.L., 218, 277
Billow, J.L., 309
Birch, L.L., 60, 169, 288, 295
Birmaher, B., 299
Bisset, S.L., 254
Bittles, A.H., 45
Bjork, J.M., 292
Bjorklund, D.F., 76, 189, 207, 211, 212, 228, 258
Black, 100n
Black, A.E., 215
Black, J.E., 102
Black, K., 339
Black, R.E., 170
Black, T., 114
Blackstock, C., 270
Blair, C., 197
Blair, P.S., 90
Blais, L., 66
Blakemore, C., 60, 292
Blakemore, S., 310
Blasko, D.G., 309
Blatchford, P., 228
Blehar, M.C., 150
Bleske-Rechek, A., 260
Blieszner, R., 275
Blinka, L., 336

Block, R.W., 113
Bloom, B., 172, 233n
Bloom, P., 146
Blum, R., 301
Blum, R.W., 328
Bocskay, K.A., 64
Boden, J.M., 115, 298
Bodrova, E., 212
Boerger, E.A., 186
Boersma, 100n
Bogaert, A.F., 328
Bohn, C.M., 228
Boivin, J.-F., 88
Boivin, M., 165
Bojczyk, K.E., 126
Bojesen, A., 44
Bollinger, M.B., 231
Bolté, C., 6
Bonham, V.L., 8
Boomsma, D.I., 236
Booth, J.L., 244, 246
Bordeleau, S., 165
Borg, D., 217
Borkowski, J.G., 332
Borman, G.D., 254
Bornemann, C., 314
Bornstein, M.H., 48, 125, 135, 137
Borowsky, I.A., 301
Bos, A.F., 168
Bosch, J., 276
Bosch, J.D., 279
Boschi-Pinto, C., 170
Boskovic, R., 66
Boslaugh, S., 84
Bouchard, C., 6
Bouchard, T.J., 50, 191
Bouchey, H.A., 328, 336
Bouck, L.M., 169
Boudreau, J.P., 12, 105, 108
Boudreault, M.A., 300
Boukes, M., 336
Boukydis, C.F.Z., 133
Boulerice, B., 219
Boulton, M.J., 280
Bourguignon, J., 288n
Bova, D.L., 247
Bower, C., 45, 84
Bowlby, G., 318, 320
Bowlby, J., 16t, 150
Boyce, W.F., 280, 281, 293, 329
Boyce, W.T., 174
Boyd, L., 281
Boyd, R., 177
Boyd-Zaharias, J., 254
Boyle, 105
Boyle, M.H., 7, 10, 174, 293
Brabeck, M.M., 313
Bradley, R.H., 92, 122, 230
Brannon, E.M., 183
Branum, A., 172
Brass, G.M., 8
Brass, L.M., 49
Bratton, S.C., 236
Brault, M.-C., 258, 259
Braun, A.R., 132
Braungart-Rieker, J.M., 151
Braver, E.R., 300
Bray, J.H., 271, 274

Brazelton, T.B., 83, 152
Breaux, C., 92
Bredin, S.S.D., 63
Breitkopf, C., 63
Breitkreuz, R., 217
Bremner, D., 247
Brendgen, M., 218
Brennan, P.A., 235
Brent, D.A., 299, 301
Brent, M.R., 134, 137
Brent, R.L., 67
Bresnick, B., 106
Bretherton, I., 152
Brewer, R.D., 297
Bridge, J.A., 237
Bridges, M., 274
Brison, R.J., 90
Broaddus, M., 210
Broadfield, D.C., 132
Broberg, A.G., 215
Brockert, J.F., 64
Brockington, R., 255
Brody, G.H., 158, 270, 276, 277, 339
Brody, L.R., 105
Broekmans, F.J., 35
Broidy, L.M., 218, 234, 279
Bronfenbrenner, U., 16t, 21, 22f, 30
Bronner, E., 254
Bronstein, P., 157, 271
Brooks, J., 154
Brooks, M.G., 175
Brooks, R., 128
Brooks-Gunn, J., 10, 124, 196, 197, 249, 291
Broude, G.J., 111, 112
Brousseau, E., 62
Brown, A.C., 270
Brown, A.S., 297
Brown, B.B., 316, 335, 336
Brown, J., 114
Brown, J.L., 62, 279
Brown, L.M., 325
Brown, S.L., 271, 273, 334
Brownell, C.A., 159
Brownell, M.D., 233n
Brownlee, K., 216, 268
Bruer, J.T., 12
Brunet, M.-L., 245
Bruschi, C.J., 267
Bruton, J.R., 296
Bryan, S.N., 229
Bryant, B.K., 267
Bryant, D.M., 123
Bryant, K., 197
Bryce, 100n
Bryce, J., 170
Bryk, A., 137
Brynelsen, D., 123
Buchanan, A., 273
Büchel, C., 232
Buck Louis, G., 287, 288n
Buckner, J.C., 175
Buehler, C., 338
Buhrmester, D., 278, 335, 336
Buitelaar, J.K., 64, 207
Bukowski, W., 211
Bukowski, W.M., 276, 277

Bulik, C., 295
Bull, R., 189
Bunker, C.H., 78
Burchinal, M., 122
Burchinal, M.R., 189
Burczycka, M., 175
Burgess, K.B., 218
Buriel, R., 268, 269
Burnaby, B., 256
Burns, T.C., 138
Burr, J.F., 63
Burstyn, I., 82
Burton, P.S., 49
Bus, A.G., 195
Bushnell, E.W., 12, 105, 108
Bushnick, 123
Bushnick, T., 231
Bushnik, T., 34, 191
Bussey, K., 208, 209, 210
Butler, R.J., 77
Butler-Jones, D., 328, 330, 331
Byers, M., 63
Byers-Heinlein, K., 138
Byrne, A., 299
Byrne, M., 51, 69
Byrnes, J., 307
Bystron, I., 60

C

Caballero, B., 61
Cabrera, N.J., 92, 137, 273
Cahng, L., 281
Cai, T., 337
Calkins, S.D., 152, 218
Camann, W.R., 79
Camarata, S., 245, 253
Cameron, A.D., 78
Cameron, C., 229
Cameron, I., 68
Cameron, M., 327
Campbell, A., 157, 205
Campbell, F.A., 123
Campbell, W.K., 92
Campbell-Yeo, M., 104
Campione-Barr, N., 334
Campos, J.J., 153, 203
Camras, A., 203
Candy, J., 205
Canham, C.H., 231
Cao, A., 45
Cao, G., 155
Capaldi, D.M., 329
Caplan, M., 159
Caprara, G.V., 252, 318
Capute, A.J., 133n
Caravan, G., 247
Card, N., 278
Carey, S., 129, 183
Carlson, E.A., 150, 151, 152
Carlson, M.J., 334
Carlström, E., 328
Carmody, D.P., 154
Carnethon, M.R., 292
Caro, D.H., 10, 253
Carpenter, M., 134
Carrier, J., 165
Carrier, L.M., 280
Carriger, M.S., 128

Carroll, D., 74, 75
Carryl, E., 269
Carscadden, J., 194
Carskadon, M.A., 293
Carson, G., 66, 67
Carter, R.C., 65n, 66, 67
Carvalhal, J.B., 68
Carver, P.R., 269
Case, R., 20, 247
Casey, B.J., 224
Casey, L., 226
Cashon, C.H., 129
Caspi, A., 10, 148, 236
Cassidy, K.W., 187
Castellan, B., 216, 268
Catalano, R.F., 339
Cates, W.Jr., 331
Cauffman, E., 216, 338
Caughey, A.B., 70
Ceci, S.J., 50, 257
Cen, G., 278
Cernkovich, S.A., 333
Cesario, S.K., 290
Chaffey, G.W., 249
Chahal, H., 227
Chaika, H., 105
Chalmers, B., 77, 87
Chamberlain, L.B., 100
Chambers, C.D., 66
Chambers, R.A., 292
Chan, H.M., 62
Chandler, M.J., 257, 301
Chandler, P., 134
Chandra, A., 328, 329, 330
Chang, C-H., 84
Chang, L., 295
Chang, S., 171
Chao, R.K., 175, 217
Chao, W., 338
Chapman, C., 255, 318
Chapman, M., 146
Chaput, H.H., 129
Charach, A., 282
Charlebois, A., 296
Charles, G., 299
Charlesworth, A., 299
Charlesworth, S., 63
Chartier, M.J., 114, 281
Chase, M., 63
Chasens, E.R., 166
Chassin, L., 298
Chateau, D., 281
Chawala, S., 50
Che, J., 170
Cheever, N.A., 280
Chen, 100n
Chen, C., 316
Chen, E., 174, 233n, 293
Chen, H.-Y., 247
Chen, J., 170
Chen, L., 300
Chen, P.C., 69
Chen, W., 49
Chen, X., 149, 278
Chen, Z., 246
Cheng, S., 275
Cherlin, A.J., 271
Cherry, N.M., 82
Cheruku, S.R., 62

Chervin, R.D., 166, 227
Chesney, J., 237
Chess, S., 50, 146, 147, 147n
Cheung, A.H., 299
Chiang, E., 169
Chin, N., 39
Chiolero, A., 231
Chisholm, K., 103
Chomsky, C.S., 193, 251
Chomsky, N., 132
Chong, C.M., 335
Choudbury, S., 292, 310
Christian, M.S., 67
Christopher, S., 291
Chu, S.Y., 61, 62
Chua, E.F., 246
Chui, T., 7
Chung, H.L., 339
Cicirelli, V.G., 276
Cillessen, A.H.N., 277, 279
Claes, M., 334
Clark, A., 251
Clark, A.G., 236
Clark, M., 176
Clark, P., 197
Clark, S., 329
Clark, W., 229, 230, 293
Clarke, D., 92
Clarren, S., 66
Clarssens, A., 317
Clauson, J., 271
Clayton, E.W., 45
Clayton, S.P., 76
Clemans, K.H., 291
Clements, P., 335
Cleveland, H.H., 298
Clifton, R.K., 105, 108
Cloutier, E., 173, 271
Cloutier, P., 296
Cnattingius, S., 87
Coalson, D.L., 247
Cochi, S., 63
Cohen, B., 151
Cohen, L.B., 129
Cohen, R.A., 172, 278
Cohen-Kettenis, P.T., 207
Coie, J.D., 277, 278, 279, 338
Colak, A., 326
Colbe, H., 280
Colburne, K.A., 157
Colby, A., 313
Coldwell, J., 276
Cole, A., 335
Cole, M., 250
Cole, P.M., 267
Cole, T.J., 169
Coleman, H., 299
Coleman-Phox, K., 90
Coley, R.L., 330, 334
Coll, C.G., 122
Colley, R.C., 228, 229, 293
Collings, G., 280
Collins, F.S., 8
Collins, J., 34, 299
Collins, W.A., 48, 338
Colombo, B., 35
Colombo, J., 62, 128
Compton, S.N., 235
Conboy, B.T., 12

Conger, K., 299, 316
Conger, R.D., 291, 316, 334, 338
Connolly, J., 336
Connor, S., 66, 177
Constant, C., 176
Conway, C.C., 235
Cook, 100n
Cook, C.R., 259
Cook, J.L., 34
Cook, S.R., 169
Cooke, 26
Cookson, D., 247
Coon, H.M., 202
Cooper, W.O., 66
Coplan, R.J., 64, 149, 211, 217
Corbetta, D., 126
Corbin, C., 167
Corrado, R., 218
Correa, A., 63
Corter, C., 269
Corwyn, R.F., 122
Costa, 105
Costello, E.J., 235, 236
Costigan, C.L., 273, 326
Costigan, K.A., 64
Cote, L.R., 135
Cotter, A., 175
Coulombe, J.A., 293
Courage, M.L., 20, 135, 154
Cowan, C.P., 92, 93
Cowan, P.A., 92, 93, 215
Cox, A., 138
Coy, K.C., 156
Coyne, S.M., 280
Craft, A.W., 69
Craig, C.L., 229
Craig, W., 282
Craig, W.M., 279, 281
Cramer, A., 338
Crawford, C., 257
Crawford, H., 296
Crawford, J., 256
Crean, H., 334
Cremo, E., 9, 216
Crick, N., 278, 279
Crockett, L.J., 269
Crompton, S., 327
Crook, C., 157
Cross, D., 186
Crouter, A.C., 209, 269, 277, 335
Crowley, S.L., 275
Cryan, J.R., 197
Cuca, Y.P., 328
Cui, M., 334
Culhane, D.P., 175
Culhane, J.F., 87
Cummins, J., 256, 317
Curenton, S., 186
Currie, C., 281
Curtin, S.C., 87
Cushon, J.A., 10
Cutting, A.L., 187
Cymerman, E., 192

D

Dabbagh, A., 63
Dahinten, V.S., 106, 123, 288
Daiute, C., 252

Dalais, C., 171
Dale, P.S., 194
Dallal, G.E., 290
Daly, K., 6, 92
Daly, R., 237
Daniels, D., 48
Daniels, S.R., 169
Darling, N., 110, 215
Darwin, C., 3, 6, 7, 22, 90, 205t, 207
Datar, A., 170, 230, 252
Davidov, M., 155
Davies, G.A.L., 63
Davis, A.S., 44
Davis, C.C., 159
Davis, D.L., 186
Davis, J., 255, 329
Davis, M., 157
Davison, K.K., 288, 295
Dawson, B.S., 329
Dawson, D.A., 271
Day, J.C., 255
de Castro, B.O., 279
de Groh, M., 229
de Gues, E.J.C., 50
De Koninck, J., 166
De-Kun, L., 90
de Rosnay, M., 204
De Wals, P., 62
De Wolff, M.S., 151
DeAngelis, C., 231
Deardorff, J., 291
Deary, I.J., 247
DeBell, M., 255, 318
DeCasper, A.J., 60
DeCesare, D., 197
Decety, J., 267, 338
DeCicca, P., 252
Deck, A., 274
DeCorby, E., 317
Dee, 100n
DeFranco, E.A., 84
DeFries, J.C., 50
Degan, K.A., 218
DeGuise, J., 279
Delaney, C., 38
Delaney-Black, V., 66
DeLaoche, J.S., 183
Delis, D.C., 297
Dell, C.A., 299
DeLoache, 205
DeLoache, J., 35
Delormier, T., 230
DeMarco, R., 113
DeMaris, A., 333
Deming, D., 196, 252
Denham, S.A., 203, 204
Dennerstein, L., 294
Dennis, T., 203
Dennison, B.A., 169
Denton, K., 197, 252
Deocampo, J., 189
Deptula, D.P., 278
Derevensky, J.L., 138
Derwing, T.M., 317
Deslandes, R., 316
Dessureau, B.K., 133
Deutsch, 209
Devaney, B., 100
Devault, A., 6

DeVos, J., 126n, 129
deVries, C.S., 237
Dewa, C.S., 299
Dewing, P., 207
d'Harcourt, C., 35, 74, 78
Diamond, A., 131
Diamond, L.M., 328
Dibiasi, J., 168
Dick, D.M., 291
Dickens, W.T., 249
Dickinson, H.O., 69
Dickman, P.W., 87
Didow, S., 159
Diego, M., 85
Diehr, P.K., 62
Diessner, R.E., 314
Dietert, R.R., 64
DiFranza, J.R., 67, 176
Dilworth-Bart, J.E., 177
Dingfelder, S., 64
Dion, R., 236, 256
DiPietro, J.A., 60, 64
Dishion, T.J., 216, 277, 338, 339
Dobbie, R., 78
Dodds, J., 106, 107n
Dodge, K.A., 113, 197, 211, 214, 215, 218, 277, 278, 279, 338, 339
Doherty, G., 170
Doherty, M., 329
Dolan, B., 190
Dolan, C.V., 236
Don, A., 67
Donaldson, M.D.C., 44
Donnelly, C., 196
D'Onofrio, B., 249, 272
Dooley, M.D., 7, 174
Dornbusch, S.M., 316
Doucet, A., 157, 273
Dowling, M., 254
Downs, S.M., 230
Doyle, A.B., 287
Doyle, L.W., 86
Drabick, D.A.G., 338
Drewing, T.M., 256
Drey, E.A., 59
Drummond, A., 300
Dryburgh, H., 269, 273
D'Silva, R., 256
Dube, J., 115
Dubé, J.M., 62
Dubeau, D., 6
Dubocovich, M.L., 293
Duckworth, A., 314
Dudenhausen, J.W., 88
Duenwald, M., 36
Duku, E.K., 229
Dunfield, K., 217
Dunger, D.B., 44
Dunham, F., 135
Dunham, P., 135
Dunn, J., 158, 187, 212, 218
Dunn, J.F., 276
Dunning, P., 196
Dunson, D.B., 33, 35
Dür, W., 317
Durbin, A., 176
Durrant, J.E., 114, 215
Duthie, J.K., 309

Dweck, C.S., 203
Dwyer, D.S., 329
Dwyer, K.M., 218
Dyer, W.J., 280
Dynarski, S., 252
Dzakpasu, S., 68, 77
Dzewaltowski, D.A., 277

E

Eagly, A., 207
Eakin, J.M., 170
Earls, F., 10
East, P.L., 335
Eaton, D.K., 286, 293
Eaton, W.W., 51
Eccles, J.S., 267, 307, 310, 314,
    317, 318, 319, 327, 332, 333,
    335
Ecker, J.L., 78
Eckerman, C.O., 159
Eckert, P., 309
Eddleman, K.A., 70
Edelsohn, G., 236
Eden, G.F., 258
Eder, M., 299
Eder, W., 231
Edgin, J., 44
Edmonds, L., 36
Edwards, C.P., 195
Edwards, N., 196
Edwards, N.C., 88
Effken, J., 77
Eftekhary, S., 75
Ege, M.J., 231
Eggebeen, D.J., 273
Eggertson, L., 229
Eiberg, H., 166
Eichstedt, J.A., 157
Eimas, P., 105, 132
Eimas, P.D., 129
Einarson, A., 66
Einspieler, C., 168
Eisenberg, N., 146, 156, 203, 218,
    267, 268, 313–314, 326–327
Eisengart, B., 216
Elder, D.E., 165n, 299
Elder, G.H., 291, 338
Elicker, J., 152, 197
Elkind, D., 308–309, 320
Elliot, J., 246
Elliott, V.S., 259
Ellis, B.J., 290, 291, 329
Ellwood, A.-L., 104
Else-Quest, N., 195
Eltzschig, H.K., 79
Emery, P., 300
Emery, R.E., 271, 272
Emilia, R., 195
Emond, I., 197
Emory, E., 157
Engell, D., 169
England, L., 62
Engle, P.L., 92, 171
Engles, R.C.M.E., 336
Englund, M., 152
Enloe, C.F., 55
Enrom, R., 215
Ensminger, S., 299

Entwisle, D.R., 253
Eppe, S., 219
Eppler, M.A., 108, 109
Epstein, R., 111
Epsy, K.A., 189
Erb, T.A., 169
Erikson, E., 13f, 15, 16–17, 16t,
    30, 149, 154, 160, 204–205,
    266, 282, 324, 341
Espezel, H., 165
Este, D., 92
Estep, K.M., 203
Ettema, J.S., 210
Etzel, R.A., 231
Euling, S., 288n, 290
Evans, A.D., 268
Evans, D.E., 147
Evans, G.W., 253, 270
Ewald, H., 51
Ewart, 100n

F

Fabes, R.A., 203, 210, 212, 218,
    267, 326
Fabricius, W.V., 272
Fagan, J., 91
Fagan, J.F., 127
Fagot, B.I., 151, 209
Fairchild, G., 234
Fallon, B., 113, 114, 270
Fallu, J.-S., 314
Fang, S., 316
Fantino, A.M., 326
Farkas, S.L., 62
Farmer, A.E., 51
Farmer, T.W., 279
Farol, P., 164
Farrie, D., 91
Farrington, D.P., 282, 339
Farver, J.A.M., 212, 219
Farver, J.M., 281
Faught, B., 231
Fauser, B.C., 35
Fawzi, W.W., 84
Fearon, P., 86
Feightner, J.W., 106
Fein, S.B., 112n
Feinberg, A.P., 41
Feldman, J.F., 86, 128, 184n
Feldman, M., 100
Feldman, R.D., 24n, 25n, 26n,
    38n, 43n, 57n, 58n, 188n,
    205n, 228n, 242n
Fell, D.B., 36, 87
Feranil, A.B., 91
Ferber, S,G, 81, 86, 111
Fergusson, D.M., 115, 298
Fernald, A., 133, 135
Fernandes, A., 104
Fernandez, A., 219
Fernandez, C.V., 105
Ferns, C., 256
Ferrao, V., 268
Fewtrell, 100n
Fidler, 100n
Field, A.E., 295
Field, T., 85, 104
Findlay, L.C., 229, 293

Findlay, S., 296
Fingerhut, L.A., 300
Finkelhor, D., 329
Finkle, J.P., 230
Finley, G.A., 104
Finn, J.D., 254, 318
Finn-Stevenson, M., 196
Fiore, E., 84, 245n
Fiore, L., 289n
Fischer, K.W., 130, 313
Fisher, J.O., 60
Fisher, K., 88
Fisher, P., 148
Fivush, R., 189–190
Flavell, J.H., 186, 243, 246, 308
Flaxman, S.M., 22
Flegal, K., 98
Fleming, J.S., 253
Fletcher, J., 214, 215
Fletcher, P., 171
Fleury, D., 269, 270
Flook, L., 253, 316
Flores, G., 88, 175, 233n
Flory, J.D., 217
Flouri, E., 273
Flouris, A.D., 231
Floyd, R.L., 66
Flynn, J.R., 191, 249
Fogel, A., 152
Fomby, P., 271
Fontanel, B., 35, 74, 78
Ford, C.A., 299
Ford, L., 106
Forer, B., 256
Forhan, S.E., 330
Forman, D.R., 156
Fortin, C., 329
Fortune, T.W., 255
Foster, C.A., 92
Foster, G.D., 230
Foulds, H.J.A., 63
Fox, M.K., 100
Fox, N.A., 103, 148, 150, 152,
    211
Fraga, M., 41, 51
Frame, J., 247
François, Y., 297
Franic, S., 236
Frank, J., 338
Frankenburg, W.K., 106, 107n
Franklin, K., 280
Frankman, E.A., 78
Frans, E.M., 69
Franzetta, K., 330
Frappier, Y.J., 300
Fraser, A.M., 64, 280
Fraser-Lee, N., 64
Fredricks, J.A., 267
Freedman, J., 85
Freeman, C., 252
Freeman, J.G., 286, 293, 294,
    295, 297, 298
Freisen, J.W., 326
Frempong, G., 316
French, C.D., 190
French, D.C., 159, 213
French, F., 190
French, R.M., 129
French, S., 301

French, S.A., 230
Freud, S., 13f, 15–16, 16t, 18t,
    30, 205t, 207
Frey, K.S., 281
Frideres, J.S., 256
Fried, P.A., 68
Friend, M., 137
Friendly, M., 9, 195, 196, 256
Friesen, M.D., 115
Frigoletto, F.D.Jr., 78
Frodi, A.M., 157
Frodi, M., 157
Frongillo, E.A., 170
Fryar, C., 09, 224
Fryberg, S.A., 203
Frye, D., 188
Fu, M., 294
Fuentes, E., 88
Fuligni, A.J., 316, 333, 335
Fulker, D.W., 50
Fuller-Thomson, E., 275
Fung, C., 227
Furman, L., 258
Furman, W., 278, 328, 336
Furstenberg, F.F.Jr., 339

G

Gabbard, C.P., 101, 164
Gabhainn, S., 297
Gacic-Dobo, M., 63
Gadow, K.D., 338
Gaffney, 105
Gagne, J.R., 50
Gagné, M.-H., 215
Gagnon, A., 93
Galambos, N.L., 340
Galanello, R., 45
Gallagher, K.C., 148
Galland, B.C., 165n
Gamble, 105
Gamborg, M., 61
Ganger, J., 134
Gannon, P.J., 132
Garber, J., 291
Gardiner, H.W., 74, 88, 106, 307,
    308
Gardner, H., 248, 261
Gardner, M., 335
Garfinkel, D.A., 158
Garner, P.W., 203
Garner, R., 191, 231
Garnett, B., 317
Garriguet, D., 169, 226
Gartrell, N., 274
Garver, K.E., 245
Garvin, R.A., 194
Garwood, M.M., 151
Garzarolli, B., 168
Gates, S., 75
Gathercole, S.E., 246
Gaudet, J., 6
Gault, E.J., 44
Ge, X., 290, 291, 299
Gearhart, J.P., 207
Geary, D.C., 244
Geerts, W.K., 168
Gélis, J., 35
Gelman, S.A., 183

Genesee, F., 137, 255
George, C., 152
Gerber, S.B., 254
Gerlach, A., 7, 268
German, J., 281
Germino-Hausken, E., 197, 252
Gershoff, E., 214
Gershoff, E.T., 270
Gervai, J., 209
Gervais, J., 62
Gettler, L.T., 91
Getzels, J.W., 259
Geva, E., 256
Gibbs, J., 313
Gibson, E.J., 108, 109, 116
Gibson, J.J., 109
Giedd, J.N., 164, 165, 225
Gilbert, J.-A., 229
Gilbert, S., 75
Gilg, 100n
Gilligan, C., 313–314, 325
Gillis, J., 193
Gillman, 166
Gilmore, J., 157, 318
Gilmore, L., 102, 104
Gilstrap, L.L., 50
Ginicola, M., 196
Ginsberg, H., 306
Giordano, P.C., 333, 336, 337
Glantz, S.A., 299
Glaser, D., 102
Glasson, E.J., 45
Glenn, N., 272
Gluckman, P., 41n
Goetz, P., 187
Gogtay, N., 226n
Goh, D.Y.T., 111, 112
Goldberg, J.M., 328
Goldberg, W.A., 112, 112n
Goldenberg, R.L., 85, 87
Goldin-Meadow, S., 134
Goldman, L., 177
Goldsmith, D., 112
Goldstein, M., 137
Goleman, D., 166
Goler, N.C., 69
Golombok, S., 205
Golub, M., 288n, 291
Göncü, E., 131
Gonzales, N.A., 291
Goodman, D.C., 84, 88
Goodnow, J.J., 156, 214, 218
Goodz, E., 138
Goossens, L., 334
Gootman, E., 317
Gordon, M., 146
Gordon-Larsen, P., 292
Gorman, K.S., 171
Gorman-Smith, D., 338
Gornick, J.C., 270
Gosden, R.G., 41
Gosselin, A., 279
Goswami, U., 244
Gotowiec, A., 249
Gottesman, I., 41
Gottesman, I.I., 249
Gottfried, A.E., 253, 259, 269
Gottfried, A.W., 253, 259, 269
Gottlieb, A., 35, 61

Gottlieb, B.H., 340
Gottman, J.M., 92
Goubet, N., 108
Gougeon, P., 268
Graber, J.A., 291
Graham, J.W., 339
Graham, S.A., 184
Gralinski, H., 154
Granholm, E., 297
Grant, A., 9
Grant, H., 203
Grantham-McGregor, S., 171
Gray, J.R., 249
Gray, L., 288n
Gray, M.R., 333
Gray, P.B., 91
Greaves, L., 67
Green, A.P., 157
Green, J., 146
Green-Demers, I., 314
Greene, L., 329
Greene, M.F., 86
Greene, S.M., 66
Greenfield, P., 315–316
Greenland, P., 292
Greer, F.R., 169
Gregorie, D., 37
Grenier, D., 106
Grier, S., 169
Grigorenko, E.L., 8
Grilo, C.M., 295
Groce, N.E., 233n
Gross, G.A., 84
Gross, J.N., 214
Grotpeter, J.K., 279
Gruber, R., 227
Grummer-Strawn, 100n
Grusec, J.E., 155, 156, 214, 216, 218
Grzetich, J., 315
Grzywacz, J.G., 316
Gueldner, B., 281
Guendelman, S., 100
Guilford, J.P., 259
Guilleminault, C., 166
Gulati, M., 292
Gunderson, 166
Gunderson, L., 256, 317
Gunn, D.M., 246
Gunnar, M.R., 151, 152
Gunnoe, M.L., 274
Guo, G., 337
Gutman, L.M., 332, 333
Guttmann, A., 88
Guyer, B., 36, 68, 77, 84

H

Haas, S.A., 294
Habicht, J.-P., 62, 99
Hack, M., 86
Hagenauer, M.H., 293
Haight, W., 137
Haines, S.M.J., 60
Haith, M.M., 104, 105, 108
Halbower, A.C., 227
Haley, A., 249
Hall, W.A., 165
Hallett, D., 257

Hallfors, D.D., 299
Halliwell, G., 249
Halperin, J.M., 217
Halpern, C., 337
Halpern, C.T., 299
Halpern, D.F., 205, 252, 253, 315
Halverson, C.F., 205t
Hamilton, B., 187
Hamilton, L., 275
Hamilton, M.C., 210
Hamilton-Giachritsis, C., 280
Hamish, L.D., 212
Hamlin, J.K., 146
Hamm, B., 275
Hammad, T.A., 237
Hammen, C.L., 235
Hampden-Thompson, G., 316
Hampson, J.G., 207
Hampson, J.L., 207
Hampson, S.E., 291
Handerson, H.A., 211
Handmaker, N.S., 67
Hane, A.A., 148
Hankin, B.L., 235
Hanley, A.J.G., 230
Hanley, W.B., 83
Hanney, L., 236
Hannigan, J.H., 66
Hannon-Engel, S.L., 295
Hansen, D., 64
Hansen, M., 294
Hanson, M., 41n
Hanson, M.D., 293
Hanson, T.L., 274
Hara, H., 281
Harder, T., 88
Hardway, C., 333
Hardy, R., 86
Hardy-Brown, K., 137
Harel, Y., 279
Hargreaves, A., 254
Harnishfeger, K.K., 246
Harold, G., 234
Harris, P.L., 204
Harris, S.J., 76
Harris, S.R., 106
Harrison, R.L., 224
Harrist, A.W., 153, 211
Hart, C., 230
Hart, D., 255
Hart, L., 88
Harter, S., 153, 154, 202, 203, 204, 266, 267
Hartup, W.W., 252, 276, 277, 278, 336
Hasebe, Y., 332
Haslett, S.J., 325
Hastings, P.D., 218
Hastmann, T.J., 277
Hauck, F.R., 112n
Hauser, G., 176
Hawkins, J.D., 339
Hay, D.F., 159
Hayes, A., 45
Haynes, O.M., 125, 151
Haywood, C., 157
He, X., 27
He, Y., 278
Healey, D.M., 217

Heaman, M., 88
Heath, N.L., 296
Hébert, Y.M., 326
Hedges, L.V., 183
Heeren, T., 298
Heffner, L.J., 64
Heikkia, M., 39
Hein, M.M., 210
Heitzler, C., 115
Helms-Erikson, H., 209
Helwig, C.C., 245
Henrich, C., 196
Henrichon, A.J., 186
Henry, D.B., 338
Herald-Brown, S., 277
Herbison, P., 165n
Herdt, G., 288
Hernandez, D., 334
Hernandez-Reif, M., 85
Heron, J., 166
Heron, M.O., 87
Heron, M.P., 169
Herrenkohl, T.I., 339
Herry, Y., 197
Hershey, K., 148
Hertenstein, M.J., 153
Hertzman, C., 175
Hespos, S.J., 129, 130
Hess, S.Y., 62
Hesso, N.A., 88
Hetherington, E.M., 48, 271, 272, 274
Hetherington, R., 88
Hewlett, B.S., 88, 92, 157
Hickling, A.K., 183
Hickman, M., 293
Hildebrand, D., 247
Hill, A.L., 218
Hill, D.A., 45
Hill, J.P., 332
Hill, N.E., 253, 316
Hillier, L., 328
Hillier, T.A., 61
Hinckley, A.F., 64
Hines, A.M., 274
Hines, M., 205
Hingson, R.W., 298
Hiripi, E., 295
Hiscock, H., 227
Hjelmborg, J., 49
Hmphreys, A.P., 228
Hoban, T.F., 111, 165, 166, 227, 293, 294
Hobson, J.A., 166
Hodnett, E.D., 75
Hoedlmoser, K., 227
Hoek, H.W., 295
Hoff, E., 137
Hoff, T., 329
Hofferth, S., 92
Hofferth, S.L., 269
Hofman, P.L., 86
Hofmeyr, G.J., 75
Hogan, M.J., 68
Hojbjerg Gravholt, C., 44
Holder, H., 148
Holland, C.R., 127
Hollos, M., 308
Holloway, R.L., 132

Holm, M., 123
Holstrum, 105
Honberg, L., 231
Hooper, F.H., 157
Hopfer, S., 45
Hopkins, L.M., 70
Horan, J.M., 84
Hornig, M., 110
Horvath, S., 207
Horwitz, B.N., 49
Horwood, J., 115, 298
Hou, F., 175, 273
Houlding, C., 217
Houts, R.M., 230
How, T., 111, 112
Howard, K.I., 332
Howard, K.S., 332
Howe, M.L., 20, 135, 154
Howe, N., 216, 276
Howe, R.B., 11
Howell, R.R., 83
Howes, C., 159
Hoyert, D.L., 36, 67, 87
Hua, J.M., 234, 326
Huang, Z.J., 175
Hudson, J.I., 295
Huesmann, R., 280
Hughes, C., 187, 212, 218
Hughes, I.A., 39
Hughes, L.A., 290
Huhman, M., 115
Huisman, 100n
Huizink, A.C., 64
Hulme, C., 194
Hulsey, T.C., 88
Hungler, K.L., 88
Huot, P.-M., 274
Hussain, R., 45
Huston, A.C., 270
Huttenlocher, J., 137, 183, 192,
    244, 253
Hutty, S., 68
Hwang, C.P., 157
Hwang, S.W., 175
Hyde, J.S., 157, 205, 218, 314, 315
Hyde, M.L., 105
Hyman, H.F., 10n
Hyman, I., 175
Hynie, M., 216

I

Iacono, W.G., 337
Ialongo, N.S., 236
Iasscsohn, J.L., 49
Ibbotson, P., 193
Ichikawa, J., 317
Iervolino, A.C., 205, 210, 338
Iglowstein, I., 165, 293
Ikonomidou, C., 66
Imada, T., 136
Ingersoll, E.W., 111
Ingersoll, G.M., 291
Inhelder, B., 184, 243, 244
Insabella, G.M., 274
Ireland, M., 301
Iruka, I.U., 269
Irwin, J.D., 169
Isaacson, W., 194

Isava, D., 281
Iserhoff, R., 62
Ito, S., 65, 66
Ivey, P., 88
Izard, C.E., 151

J

Jacklin, C.N., 157
Jackson, A., 175
Jackson, B., 296
Jackson, L.A., 313
Jackson, P.W., 259
Jacobson, J.L., 152
Jacobson, K.C., 269
Jaffee, S.R., 67, 113, 214, 314
Jamieson, C.E., 45
Jamieson, J., 217
Jamieson, K., 317
Jankowski, J.J., 86, 128
Jankowski, L., 100
Jankuniene, Z., 269
Janmohamed, Z., 269
Janosz, M., 254, 314
Jansen, P.W., 166
Janssen, I., 231, 280, 281, 293
Janssen, P.A., 75, 76
Janssen, S., 310
Jansson, S.M., 296
Jäntti, M., 270
Janus, A., 255
Janus, M., 197
Janzen, B.L., 10
Janzen, T., 247
Japel, C., 291
Jarrold, C., 246
Jarvi, S., 296
Jarvis, M.J., 298
Jasiobedzka, U., 245
Javaid, M.K., 62
Jean, M., 256
Jefferies, A.L., 66, 86
Jeffrey, H.E., 69
Jeffrey, R.W., 230
Jelalian, E., 230
Jenkins, J., 27
Jenkins, P.L., 169
Jennekens-Schinkel, A., 267
Jenni, O.G., 165
Jensen, A.R., 249
Jeynes, W.H., 251
Ji, B.T., 67
Jipson, J.L., 183
Jodi, K.M., 318
Johnson, B.H., 76
Johnson, D.J., 7, 8
Johnson, J.G., 301
Johnson, M.H., 131
Johnson, M.S., 169
Johnson, N., 9, 216
Johnston, C.C., 104
Johnston, J., 210
Johnston, J.S., 316
Johnston, L.D., 297, 339
Joinson, C., 166
Joly, J., 215
Jones, G., 168
Jones, J., 37, 328
Jones, L.M., 329

Jones, S.E., 297
Jones, S.M., 279
Jordan, N.C., 183, 183n
Joseph, K.S., 36, 68, 86
Joussemet, M., 279
Joy, M.E., 156
Juang, L., 250
Juby, H., 274
Judge, K., 87
Juffer, F., 152, 276
Jung, S., 63
Jusczyk, P., 105
Jusczyk, P.W., 134
Juster, F.T., 228, 229, 268, 333
Juul, S., 44

K

Kacker, H., 315
Kaczorowski, J., 62
Kagan, J., 130, 148, 149
Kahlenberg, S.G., 210
Kahlenberg, S.M., 213
Kaiz, M., 332
Kales, A., 166
Kalil, A., 335
Kampen, R., 273
Kanaya, T., 257
Kanetsuna, T., 281
Kang, C., 232
Kanu, Y., 256
Kaplan, D., 183
Kaplan, N., 152
Kaplow, J.B., 114
Kaplowitz, P.B., 288
Kaprio, J., 291
Kapur, A.K., 300
Kapur, N., 82
Karasik, L.B., 107
Karmous, 100n
Karpinski, A.C., 25, 336
Karremans, J., 337
Kash, K.M., 319
Kassler, R.C., 299n
Kato, K., 228
Katz, A.N., 309
Katz, S.J., 235
Katzman, D.K., 296, 299
Katzmarzyk, P.T., 229
Kaufman, A.S., 247
Kaufman, J., 76, 281
Kaufman, N.L., 247
Kawabata, Y., 278
Kazdin, A.E., 215
Kazmerski, V.A., 309
Keane, S.P., 218
Kearsley, 128
Kearsley, G., 249n
Keating, D., 27
Keel, P.K., 295, 296
Keeler, G., 235
Keenan, K., 155, 157, 205
Kellam, S.G., 236
Keller, M.A., 112, 112n
Kelley, K., 217
Kelley, K., 148
Kelley, M.L., 157
Kellman, P.J., 105
Kelly, J.B., 271, 272

Kelly, M., 308
Kemmelmeier, M., 202
Kemp, J.S., 90
Kere, J., 258
Kerns, K.A., 67, 335
Kerr, D.C.R., 214
Kerrebrock, N., 171
Kessler, R.C., 295
Khan, S., 257
Khan, Y., 164
Kharrazi, M., 67
Khashan, A.S., 51
Khoo, S.T., 335
Kidd, K.K., 8
Kiddoo, D.A., 167
Kilbride, K.M., 317
Killen, J.D., 298
Kim, H., 114
Kim, J., 277, 335
Kim, S., 270
Kim, Y.K., 212
Kim, Y.S., 281
Kim-Cohen, J., 10
Kimball, M.M., 210
Kimmerly, N.L., 150
King, A., 137
King, A.J.C., 293, 294
King, J.C., 62
King, K.M., 298
King, M.A., 293
King, V., 272
King, W.J., 113
Kingdon, C.K., 91
Kins, E., 340
Kinsella, K., 7, 275
Kirby, B., 299
Kirby, D., 330
Kirby, R., 87
Kirk, E., 197
Kirkwood, H., 246
Kirmayer, L.J., 8, 326
Kirmeyer, S., 87
Kirpalani, H.M., 86
Kirscher, P.A., 336
Kirschner, P.A., 25
Kirwil, L., 280
Kisilevsky, B.S., 60, 153
Kispert, A., 39
Kita, S., 136
Klar, A.J.S., 168
Klassen, E.A., 148
Klein, J.D., 169, 329, 331, 332
Klein, M.C., 75, 76
Klein-Velderman, M., 152
Klentrou, P., 231
Klibanoff, R.S., 183
Kloesch, G., 227
Klonsky, E.D., 296
Klump, K.L., 295, 296
Klute, C., 335, 336
Knaack, A., 156, 268
Knafo, A., 217
Knecht, S., 136
Knickmeyer, R.C., 101
Knobloch, H., 106
Knoester, C., 273
Kochanek, K.D., 87
Kochanska, G., 151, 152, 156,
    214, 268

Koerner, A.F., 275
Kogan, M.D., 68, 231
Koh, Y.-J., 281
Kohen, D., 218, 231, 257
Kohen, D.E., 169
Kohlberg, L., 205*t*, 208, 313, 314, 315*n*, 315*t*, 321
Kohler, 330
Kolasa, M., 110
Kolata, G., 45
Konrad, D., 39
Koops, W., 279
Kopack, Klein, A., 195
Kopp, 156
Kopp, C.B., 22*n*, 154
Koren, G., 65
Korner, A., 148
Kosmitzki, C., 88
Kosterman, R., 339
Kovelman, I., 137
Kover, P., 317
Kozlowska, K., 236
Kozmitzki, C., 74, 106, 307, 308
Krakow, J.B., 22*n*
Kral, M.J., 301
Kramer, 100*n*
Kramer, M.S., 68
Krause, N., 259
Krausz, C., 35
Kraut, R., 336
Krebs, N.F., 113
Kreider, R.M., 275
Kridli, A.-O, 233*n*
Kringelbach, M.L., 91
Krishnamoorthy, J.S., 230
Kroger, J., 325
Krueger, R.F., 337
Kruk, R.S., 196, 228*n*, 255
Kruttschnitt, C., 338
Krypianidou, A., 298
Kuczmarski, R.J., 98
Kuh, D., 86, 133*n*
Kuhl, P.K., 12, 133, 134, 135, 136, 137, 138
Kuhle, S., 62, 169, 227, 230
Kuhlmeier, V.A., 217
Kuhn, D., 292, 307, 308, 309, 310
Kuiper, H., 267
Kulig, J.C., 175
Kumwenda, N.I., 100
Kung, H.C., 87
Kunz, A., 278
Kupanoff, K., 267
Kuperman, S., 298
Kupersmidt, J.B., 189
Kupper, L., 337
Kurinczuk, J., 84
Kurlakowsky, K.D., 236
Kurowski, C.O., 133
Kuxhaus, D., 68
Kuzawa, C.W., 91

L

Laberge, L., 166
LaBounty, J., 187
Lack, G., 172
Lacourse, É., 258, 259
Ladd, G., 277

Ladewig, 57*n*
Lafferty, 330
LaFontana, K.M., 277
Lagattuta, K.H., 203, 204
Lagenberg, C., 86
Lagercrantz, H., 78
Lahey, B., 267
Lai, D., 231
Laible, D.J., 156
Laird, G., 175, 176
Laird, J., 318
Laird, R.D., 338
Lalonde, C.E., 133*n*, 257, 301
Lam, K., 88
Lamb, M.E., 88, 92, 137, 151, 157
Lamberg, A., 227
Lambert, S.F., 236
Lambert, W.E., 255
Lamm, C., 245
Lammi-Keefe, C.J., 62
Landon, M.B., 78
Landry, S.H., 192
Landy, S., 216, 217
Lanes, A., 100
Långström, N., 328
Lansford, J.E., 113, 214, 215, 218, 272, 339
Lanting, 100*n*
Lapkin, S., 255, 256
Largo, R.H., 165
Laris, B., 330
Larkina, M., 189
LaRochelle-Côté, S., 268
Larselere, R.E., 214
Larsen, D., 275
Larson, R.W., 286, 288, 314, 315, 332, 333
Larzelere, R.E., 215
Laster, B.M., 133
Laughren, T., 237
Laukys, K., 137
Laursen, B., 336
Lavelli, M., 152
Lavin, T., 256
Lawn, J.E., 87
Lawrence, H.P., 224
Lay, C., 326
Lazar, N.A., 245
Le, H.N., 62
Le Bourdais, C., 274
Leadbeater, B., 281
Leaper, C., 157, 209
LeBlank, C.M.A., 169
Leclerc, D., 316
Leclerc, L., 62
Ledrou, I., 62
Leduc, D., 106
Lee, 100*n*
Lee, A., 66
Lee, J.M., 288, 290
Lee, J.W., 326
Lee, K., 268
Lee, L., 62
Lee, L.S., 106
Lee, N.S., 62
Lee, P., 108
Lee, S.J., 59, 104
Lee, T.M., 293
Lee, Y., 212

Lefebvre, P., 196
Lefever, J.B., 332
LeFevre, J., 138
Legault, L., 314
Legerstee, M., 152
Lehoux, P.M., 276
Leier, B., 46
Leifer, 57*n*
Leigh, E., 246
Leinback, M.D., 209
Leman, P.J., 251
Lemmon, H., 247
Lenhart, A., 329
Lenneberg, E.H., 133*n*
Lennon, M.C., 270
Lenroot, R.K., 164, 165, 225
Leo, A., 226
Leonard, K.A., 300
Leonard, S.A., 267
Leong, D.J., 212
LeRoy, C.J., 103*n*
Lesage, A., 299*n*
Lesch, K.P., 50
Leshem, M., 64
Leslie, A.M., 129
Leslie, L.K., 237
Lester, B.M., 66
Letchford, D., 146
Lethbridge, L., 174
Lethbridge, L.N., 49
Letouneau, N.L., 88
Leung, C., 326
LeVay, S., 328
Leve, L.D., 290
Leventhal, B., 281
Leventhal, T., 10
Levin, B., 254
Levin, I., 195
LeVine, R.A., 88
Levine, S., 192
Levine, S.C., 183, 244, 253
Levitt, C., 77
Levy-Shiff, R., 276
Lew, S., 318
Lewinsohn, P.M., 291
Lewis, M., 68, 145, 145*n*, 146, 151, 154, 156
Lewis, M.D., 245
Lewit, E., 171
Leyerndecker, B., 88
L'Hoir, M.P., 90
Li, 100*n*
Li, D., 278
Li, G., 300
Li, R., 63
Li, T-K., 67
Li, X., 230
Li, Z., 278
Li-Grinning, C.R., 197
Liang, J., 259
Liang, K., 61
Liang, T., 169, 230
Lichtenstein, P., 328
Lie, R.T., 86
Lieberman, E.S., 79
Lieberman, M., 313
Lieven, E., 193
Ligthart, L., 236
Lillard, A., 186, 195

Lin, M.H., 214
Lindström, P., 328
Lins-Dyer, M.T., 332
Liou, T., 295
Liou, Y.M., 295
Lipman, E.L., 7, 10, 174, 175, 229
Lipnowski, S., 169
Lipscomb, S.T., 155
Liszkowski, U., 134
Litivitz, T.L., 173
Littell, S.W., 251
Little, T., 278
Littleton, H., 63
Liu, D., 186
Liu, E., 169
Liu, J., 171
Liu, N., 62
Lizotte, A.J., 332
Lloyd, J.J., 338
Lloyd, M., 189
Lloyd-Richardson, E., 298
Lobstein, T., 229
LoBue, 205
Lock, A., 134
Lock, J., 299
Locunia, M.N., 183
Loeber, R., 339
Loeken, M.R., 63
London, 57*n*
London, K., 92
Loney, S., 11
Long, J.D., 281
Longmore, M.A., 336
Longworth, H.L., 91
Lonigan, C.J., 195
Lopez, N.L., 214
Lopez-Duran, S., 187
Lord, H., 269
Lorenz, F.O., 334
Lorenz, K., 12
Lou, H.C., 64
Lourenco, S.E., 253
Low, S., 268
Lowder, J.L., 78
Lowell, H., 61
Lowery, C.L., 59
Lubinski, D., 259, 260
Lucas, 100*n*
Ludwig, J., 196
Luedkte, K., 112, 165*n*
Lugaila, T.A., 273
Lukas, S.L., 172
Lumer, D., 272
Luna, B., 245, 246, 310
Lundy, B.L., 151, 152
Luo, Z.-C., 84, 88
Lussier, P., 218
Lutke, K., 55
Luttikhuis, H., 230
Luyckx, K., 334
Lynam, D., 278
Lyons, T., 137
Lyons-Ruth, K., 152

M

Maccoby, E.E., 48, 157, 207, 210, 216, 268
MacDermid, S.M., 269

MacDonald, K., 150
MacDorman, M.F., 84, 87, 331
MacKay, M., 113
MacKay, T., 317
MacKinnon, C., 63
MacKinnon, D., 329
Maclean, H., 100
MacLeod, A.A.N., 137
MacMillan, H., 113
MacMillan, H.M., 215
Macmillan, R., 338
Maes, L., 294, 295
Magnabosco, J.L., 170
Maheux, H., 7
Mahoney, J.L., 269
Mahony, T.H., 337
Main, M., 150, 152
Majid, K., 169
Makhoul, I.R., 81, 86, 111
Makino, M., 294
Malanchuk, O., 318
Malaspina, D., 69
Maldonado-Carreno, C., 197
Maletaki, S., 298
Malm, K., 37
Malone, A.F., 106
Malone, F.D., 70
Malone, P.S., 197
Maltais, C., 197
Mandell, D.J., 186
Mandler, J.M., 129
Mang, H., 258
Manhart, 330
Manlove, J., 330
Mann, E.A., 339
Mann, J.J., 301
Mann, R.E., 297
Manning, W.D., 336
Mansfield, C., 45
Mansfield, T.C., 309
Manson, S.M., 236, 256
Marchman, V.A., 133, 135
Marcia, J., 324–325, 341
Marcil-Gratto, N., 274
Marcoen, A., 152
Marcovitch, S., 188
Marcus, G.F., 134
Marcus, M., 288n
Mareschal, D., 129
Markestad, T., 86
Markman, E.M., 135
Markovits, H., 243, 245–246
Marlow, N., 86
Marquardt, E., 272
Marsh, J., 255
Marshall, K., 92, 93, 269, 320
Marshall, P.J., 211
Marteau, T.M., 45
Martin, A.J., 252
Martin, C.L., 157, 205t, 208, 209, 210, 211, 212, 267
Martin, J.A., 36, 56, 61, 64, 67, 69, 74, 78, 82, 84, 86, 216, 331
Martin, M., 168
Martin, S., 337
Martinez, E., 295
Martinez, G.M., 329
Martínez-González, M.A., 295

Martorell, R., 99, 171
Masataka, N., 138
Mason, J., 197
Mâsse, L.C., 257
Mateer, C.A., 67
Matheson, I., 114
Mathews, T.J., 36, 87, 171
Mathur, S., 197
Maticka-Tyndale, E., 330
Matos, M.G., 293
Matsumoto, D., 250
Matthews, K.A., 174
Maurer, O., 272
Maxwell, C.W., 102n
May, K.A., 91
Mayeux, L., 277, 279
Mayhew, D., 300
McAdoo, H.P., 122
McAndrew, M., 256
McCain, M., 102, 123, 197
McCain, M.N., 9, 196
McCall, D.D., 108
McCall, R.B., 128
McCallum, K.E., 296
McCartney, K., 48
McCarty, C.A., 299
McCarty, M.E., 108
McClintock, M., 288
McCluskey, K.W., 249
McConnell, D., 217
McCormick, R.M., 319
McCourt, C., 62
McCuaig, K., 9
McDade, T.W., 91
McDaniel, M., 231
McDonald, D.A., 316
McDonald, J.T., 253
McDonald, S.A., 86
McDorman, M.F., 171
McDowell, M., 09, 224
McDuff, P., 291
McEwan, K., 234
McFaull, S., 301
McGue, M., 191, 337
McGue, M.K., 276
McGuffin, P., 49, 51
McGuinn, N., 227
McHale, S.M., 209, 269, 277, 335
Mcintyre, L., 66, 177
McKay, A., 331
McKeever, W.F., 168
McLanahan, S., 249
McLanahan, S.S., 273, 274
McLean, H.B., 319
McLeod, R., 63
McLoyd, V.C., 214, 215, 270
McMahon, A.P., 39
McMorris, B.J., 338
McMullen, K., 255, 318
Mcneely, C., 329
McQueeny, T., 297
McRitchie, S.L., 230
McTaggart, B., 247
Medland, 168
Mednick, S.A., 171
Meehan, B.T., 298
Meerkerk, G., 336
Meeter, M., 310

Meezan, W., 274
Mehta, S.D., 100
Meier, A.M., 294
Meier, D., 317
Meijer, A.M., 93
Meins, E., 151
Melby, J., 316
Mellingen, K., 171
Meltzoff, A.N., 128
Menacker, F., 36, 331
Mendel, G., 39
Mendelson, C.R., 76
Mendle, J., 290–291
Menke, M.R., 255
Mennella, J.A., 60, 105
Ment, L.R., 86
Mercier, P., 166
Merewood, A., 100
Merikangas, K.R., 49
Mermillod, M., 129
Merrell, K., 281
Merrigan, P., 196
Mertz, J., 315
Mesbah, M., 59
Messinger, D.S., 69
Messinis, L., 298
Metraux, S., 175
Michael, A., 318
Michaelsen, K.F., 61
Michaelson, 100n
Michalaska, K., 267
Middledrop, C.M., 236
Milan, A., 7, 59, 64, 275
Milani, I., 128
Millar, W.J., 36, 100
Miller, A.R., 257
Miller, C.J., 217
Miller, D.C., 61
Miller, E.C., 62
Miller, F., 27
Miller, J.R., 9
Miller, J.W., 297
Miller, M.W., 66
Miller, P.H., 243
Miller, S.A., 243
Miller-Jonson, S., 123
Miller-Loncar, C.L., 192
Millman, R.P., 293
Mills, J.L., 62
Millsap, R.E., 291
Milne, C., 114
Min, M.O., 114
Mindell, J.A., 111, 112, 165n
Miniño, A.M., 300
Minnes, S., 114
Mirza, R., 256
Mischel, W., 156, 209
Misra, D.P., 68
Mistard, J.F., 9
Mistry, J., 131
Mistry, R.S., 270
Mitchell, B., 237
Mitchell, D., 123
Mitchell, E.A., 90
Mitchell, J.E., 295
Mitchell, K.J., 329
Mix, K.S., 244
Mody, M., 258
Moen, K.B., 196

Moffatt, M.E.K., 224
Moffitt, T.E., 10, 204, 332
Mojon, D.S., 278
Mojon-Azzi, S.M., 278
Mojza, E., 314
Molcho, M., 281
Molinari, L., 165
Molnar, Z., 60
Monahan, K.C., 338
Moneta, G., 332
Money, J., 207
Monni, G., 45
Monshouwer, H.J., 279
Montague, D.P.F., 152
Montessori, M., 195
Montgomery-Downs, H.E., 62
Montplaisir, J., 165, 166
Moon, J., 44
Moore, 57n
Moore, C.F., 177
Moore, S.E., 62
Morelli, G.A., 88, 112
Moretti, M.E., 66
Moretti, M.M., 287
Morison, S.J., 103, 104
Morris, 100n
Morris, A.D., 313–314, 326–327
Morris, J.E., 334
Morris, P.A., 21
Morris, P.E., 259
Morrison, J.A., 294
Morrongiello, B.A., 174
Morrow, R.L., 259
Mortensen, 100n
Mortensen, E.L., 61
Mortensen, P.B., 51
Mortimer, J.T., 340
Mortimer, J.T., 320
Moses, L.J., 153
Mosher, W.D., 328, 329
Mosier, C., 131
Mosley, J., 274
Moss, E., 152, 253
Moss, K., 268
Moster, D., 86
Mottola, M.F., 63
Mougeot, C., 197
Moulson, M.C., 103
Muehlenkamp, J.J., 296
Muglia, L.J., 84
Muhajarine, N., 10
Muhammad, A., 93
Mulder, F.J.H., 64
Mulford, C., 337
Müller, U., 188
Mullin, J., 251
Mumma, G.H., 277
Munafo, M., 168
Munakata, Y., 130
Munn, P., 158
Munoz-Furlong, A., 172
Murnen, S.K., 115
Murphy, B.C., 267
Murphy, S.L., 87
Murray, K.T., 156
Murray, M.L., 237
Murre, J., 310
Murry, V.M., 270, 291
Murukulaaratchy, 100n

Mushquash, C.J., 247
Must, A., 290
Mustanski, B.S., 328
Mustard, J.F., 102, 123, 196, 197
Muter, V., 194
Mutter, J.D., 88
Mychasiuk, R., 196

N

Nadel, L., 44
Nader, P.R., 230
Nagaraja, J., 173
Naimark, B., 114
Naimi, T.S., 297
Najman, J.M., 235, 270
Nangle, B.E., 84
Nansel, T.R., 280, 281
Napash, L., 62
Nash, A., 159
Nash, J.M., 103n
Nassar, N., 84
Natsuaki, M.N., 290
Navratil, F., 39
Neckoway, R., 216, 268
Nedecheva, T., 296
Neisser, U., 191
Neitzel, C., 192
Nelson, C.A., 102, 103, 188
Nelson, K., 189–190
Nelson, M.C., 292
Nelson, T., 12
Neumann, H., 319
Newacheck, P.W., 231
Newburn-Cook, C., 64
Newby-Clark, I.R., 340
Newcomb, A.F., 277, 278
Newcombe, N.S., 189, 253
Newman, R.S., 133n, 134
Newman, T.B., 237
Ngo, H., 317
Niaura, R., 298
Nichols, K.E., 214
Nichols-Whitehead, P., 192
Nicklas, T.A., 233n
Nicoladis, E., 137
Nie, N., 27
Nilsen, E.S., 184
Nimrod, C., 36
Nippold, M.A., 309
Nirmala, A., 49
Nisbett, R.E., 249
Nisker, J., 36
Nixon, M.K., 296
Nobile, C., 227
Noirot, E., 60
Noll, J.G., 115
Nordstrom, B., 66
Norris, S., 197
Norton, M.E., 70
Novak, M.F.S.X., 64
Nowgesic, E., 176
Nucci, L., 332, 334
Nugent, J.K., 66, 83

O

Oates, R.K., 115
Ober, C., 231

O'Brien, B.M., 69
O'Brien, M., 230
O'Connell, B., 133n
O'Connell, L., 217
O'Connell, P., 282
O'Connor, E., 299
O'Connor, M.H., 67
Odenstad, A., 276
Odgers, C.L., 339
Odo, D.M., 256
Odoki, 100n
O'Donnell, L.N., 298
Odouli, R., 90
Offer, D., 332
Offit, P.A., 110
Offord, D., 197
Offord, D.R., 7, 174, 229, 234
Ofori, B., 66
Ogbuanu, 100n
Ogden, C., 09
Ogden, C.L., 229
Ohlsson, A., 84, 87
Ojeda, S., 288n
Okamoto, Y., 20
Okazaki, S., 249
O'Keefe, A.R., 193
O'Keefe, C., 135
Oken, 166
Oláh, L.N., 183
Olds, 57n
Olds, S.W., 25n, 26n, 38n, 43n, 57n, 58n, 184n, 205n, 228n, 242n
O'Leary, C., 84
Oliphant, J.A., 328
Oliver, L., 218
Oliver, L.N., 169
Olsen, J., 64
Olson, C.M., 170
Olson, K., 26
Olson, K.R., 217
Olson, L., 88, 175
Olson, L.S., 253
Olson, S.L., 214, 218
Olthof, T., 267
O'Mahony, P., 66
O'Malley, P.M., 339
O.Malley, P.M., 297
Ondracek, P.J., 246
O'Neil, K., 64, 211
Ono, H., 228
Opdal, S.H., 90
Operskalski, B., 237
Opfer, J.E., 244
Oppenhaim, D., 112
Opper, S., 306
Oraichi, D., 66
O'Reilly, A.W., 125
Orr, D.P., 291
Osberg, L.S., 49
Osejo, V.M., 69
Osgood, D.W., 335
Oshima-Takane, Y., 138
Ostbye, T., 86
Ostrov, E., 332
O'Toole, B.I., 115
Ouellette, G.P., 252
Ovens, H., 300
Overpeck, M.D., 293

Owen, 100n
Owen, L.D., 329
Owen, M.J., 49, 51
Owens, E.B., 214
Owens, J.A., 165n, 227
Owens, R.E., 192, 193, 250–251, 309
Oyserman, D., 202
Ozarow, L., 251
Özçaliskan, S., 134
Ozyürek, A., 136

P

Pabayo, R., 226
Pac, S., 100
Padden, D., 12
Padilla, A.M., 256
Padilla-Walker, L.M., 280
Pagani, L.S., 254, 314
Paglia, A., 286
Paglia-Boak, A., 297, 297n, 298
Painter, K., 125
Paley, B., 67
Palkovitz, R., 91
Palmer, F.B., 133n
Palombini, L., 166
Papadatou-Pastou, M., 168
Papalia, D.E., 25n, 26n, 38n, 43n, 57n, 58n, 184n, 205n, 228n, 242n, 299n
Papathanasopoulos, P., 298
Paquette, D., 6
Paquette, G., 279
Paradis, G., 231
Paradis, J., 137
Park, J.M., 175
Parke, R.D., 268, 269
Parker, J.D., 64
Parker, J.G., 211
Parker, L., 69
Parler, B.D., 7
Parr, J., 11
Parten, M.B., 211, 220
Partridge, J.C., 59
Pascal, C.E., 123
Pascuzzo, K., 152
Pastor, P.N., 259
Pastorelli, C., 318
Pastuszak, A., 65
Patel, H., 105
Patrick, H., 233n
Patrick, K., 294
Pattee, L., 277
Patterson, C.J., 274
Patterson, G.R., 338
Patton, G.C., 294
Pavlov, I., 16t, 17
Pawelski, J.G., 274
Paxson, C., 231
Payne, 209
Pearce, M.S., 69
Pearl, R., 279
Pedersen, J., 159
Pelayo, R., 166
Pell, J.P., 78
Pellegrini, A.D., 76, 207, 211, 212, 228, 258, 276, 277, 278, 281

Pelletier, J., 269
Pelletier, L., 314
Pembrey, 40
Peña, F., 90
Pendlebury, J.D., 67
Pennington, B.F., 44
Pepler, D.J., 218, 281, 282, 337
Pepper, S.C., 13
Pérez, C.E., 229
Perfors, A., 133
Perlman, M., 158
Perrin, E.M., 230
Perrin, J.M., 237
Perrin, S.P., 91
Perry, B., 123n
Perry, T.B., 336
Perry-Jenkins, M., 269
Perryman, J.I., 293
Persad, V.L., 62
Persaud, 57n
Pescovitz, O., 288n
Pescovitz, O.H., 290
Peter, J., 336
Peters, P.A., 169
Peterson, L., 329
Peterson, M., 291
Petit, D., 165, 166
Petitto, L.A., 137
Petrill, S.A., 50
Petronis, A., 41
Pettit, G.S., 211, 214, 215, 218, 277, 281, 338
Peyser, H., 274
Phelps, K.E., 186
Philipp, B.L., 100
Phillips, D., 9, 196
Phillips, L., 197
Phillips, P., 7
Philp, H., 308
Phinney, J.S., 326
Phipps, S., 174
Phipps, S.A., 49
Piaget, J., 13f, 18ft, 19–20, 30, 125t, 140, 181, 182, 184, 184f, 194, 198, 211, 241, 242–245, 261, 308, 314, 320
Piccinino, L., 329
Pick, A.D., 109
Picker, J., 51
Pickett, W., 90, 280, 281
Pierre, F., 218
Pike, A., 276
Pillow, B.H., 186, 243
Pinard, D., 268
Pine, D.S., 148
Pinzon, J., 296
Plagemann, A., 88
Plante, J., 255
Plomin, R., 48, 49, 50, 137, 194, 205, 217
Plumert, J., 192
Poelhuis, C.W.K., 276
Poffenbarger, T., 231
Pogarsky, G., 332
Pollack, B., 157
Pollack, S.D., 134
Pollet, G., 169
Pollit, E., 171
Pomerantz, E.M., 203

Pomery, E.A., 335
Pons, F., 204
Poole, K., 86
Pope, A.W., 277
Pope, H.G.Jr., 91, 295
Pope, R.S., 246
Porac, C., 168
Porfeli, E., 340
Porges, S.W., 151
Portman, R.J., 231
Posner, M., 130
Posthuma, D., 50
Potenza, M.N., 292
Potvin, P., 316
Poulin-Dubois, D., 157
Pouliot-Lapointe, J., 215
Powell, B., 275
Powell, C., 171
Powers, B.P., 151
Prabhu, N., 256
Prechtl, 111n
Prentice, S., 9, 195, 196
Presnell, K., 294
Price, T.S., 67, 194
Prifitera, A., 247
Proce, J.M., 277
Pronk, T., 337
Pruitt, J., 12
Pruyne, E., 313
Pukrop, R., 166
Pungello, E., 123
Putallaz, M., 218
Putnam, F., 115

Q

Quach, J., 227
Quattrin, T., 169
Quinn, P.C., 129

R

Rabiner, D., 278
Racine, Y., 10, 293
Racoosin, J., 237
Radel, L., 37
Radke-Yarrow, M., 146
Rahman, Q., 328
Rai, R., 58
Raiford, S.E., 247
Raikes, H., 138
Raine, A., 171
Raine, K., 62
Raju, T.N.K., 112n
Rakic, P., 60
Rakison, D.H., 104, 105, 128
Rakoczy, H., 186
Ralston, H.J.P., 59
Ramani, G.B., 159, 183
Ramey, C.T., 123, 124, 137
Ramey, S.L., 124, 137
Ramirez, J.M., 90
Rand-Giovanetti, E., 246
Rankin, J., 61
Rao, P.A., 235
Rao, S.B., 134
Rask-Nissilä, L., 226
Rathburn, A., 197
Rauch, J., 274

Raver, C.C., 270
Raviv, A., 227
Ray, D., 236
Rayner, R., 17
Ream, G.L., 327
Reddy, B.M., 49
Reddy, P.P., 49
Redshirt, R., 236, 256
Reef, S.E., 63
Reefhuis, J., 36
Rees, E.P., 105
Reese, E., 138, 186, 195
Regan, L., 58
Reichenberg, A., 69
Reid, G.J., 293
Reif, J.S., 64
Reiner, W.G., 207
Reinhold, A., 100
Reinisch, 100n
Reiser, M., 277
Reither, E.N., 294
Reitsma, M., 337
Remafedi, G., 301
Remez, L., 329
Rende, R., 298, 335
Repacholi, B., 152
Repetti, R.L., 92, 253, 270
Resnick, M.D., 301
Resnick, S., 151, 244
Rethman, J., 224
Retschitzki, J., 308
Reuben, C.A., 259
Reusing, S.P., 64
Rey, E., 66
Reynolds, A.J., 339
Reynolds, G., 196
Reynolds, J.N., 67
Reynolds, K.A.A., 255
Rhee, S.H., 337
Rhines, H.M., 156, 268
Rhoads, K., 197
Rhoton-Vlaask, A., 35
Riben, P., 176
Ricciuti, H.N., 334
Rice, M.L., 135, 193, 194
Richards, D., 246
Richards, F.A., 308
Richards, M.H., 332
Richardson, J., 92
Richland, L.E., 189
Rickert, V.I., 299
Riddell, R.P., 190
Rifas-Shiman, 166
Riko, K., 105
Rinaldi, C.M., 100, 216, 276
Riordan, K., 151
Rios-Ellis, B., 281
Rivara, F., 174n
Rivera, J.A., 62, 171
Rivera-Gaxiola, M., 134, 136, 138
Roberto, K.A., 275
Roberts, C., 293
Roberts, K.C., 229
Robertson, D.L., 339
Robin, D.J., 108
Robin, K., 197
Robinette, C.D., 49
Rochat, 154

Rock, A.M., 138
Rodas, C., 274
Rodekamp, E., 88
Rodkin, P.C., 279
Rodriguez, M.L., 156
Roer-Strier, D., 92
Roessingh, H., 317
Roettger, M., 337
Rogan, 100n
Rogers, C.S., 209
Rogers, M.C., 157
Rogler, L.H., 11
Rognum, T.O., 90
Rogoff, B., 112, 131, 193
Rogol, A., 287, 288, 289, 290, 291, 295, 299
Rohde, P., 294
Rolfs, R.T., 84
Rolls, B.J., 169
Romano, E., 215, 219
Roopnarine, J.L., 157, 212
Roosa, M.W., 234, 291
Rosatelli, M.C., 45
Rose, A.J., 228, 277
Rose, R.J., 291
Rose, S.A., 86, 128
Rose, S.P., 130
Rose-Krasnor, L., 215
Rosen, L.D., 280
Rosen, M.A., 59
Rosenkrantz, R.R., 277
Rosenkrantz, S.L., 129
Rosicky, J.G., 153
Ross, H.S., 157
Ross, S., 281, 296
Rossi, R., 317
Rossiter, K.R., 317, 318
Rossiter, M.J., 317, 318
Rotermann, M., 330
Rothbart, M.K., 147, 148, 151
Roudebush, J.R., 76
Rourke, M., 187
Rouse, C., 249, 253
Rouse, D.J., 85
Rovee-Collier, C., 120, 139
Rowe, M.L., 134
Rowland, A.S., 259
Roxborough, L., 257
Roy, K., 91
Rubin, K.H., 149, 211, 218, 278
Ruble, D.N., 157, 208, 209, 210, 212
Rudolph, K.D., 228, 236, 277
Rudy, D., 216
Rueter, M.A., 275
Ruggiero, K.M., 249
Ruiz, F., 281
Rumbaut, R.G., 339
Rundell, L.J., 129
Rushton, J.P., 249
Russell, S.J., 229
Russell, S.T., 274
Rust, J., 205
Rutherford, G.W., 90
Rutherford, P.J., 190
Rutter, M., 46, 47, 49, 104
Rvachew, S., 137
Ryan, A., 99, 316
Ryan, B.A., 27, 174, 191

Ryan, S., 330
Ryncarz, R.A., 313

S

Saarni, C., 203, 267
Sabbagh, M.A., 187
Sack, W., 236, 256
Sacks, D., 300
Sadeh, A., 111, 112, 165n, 227, 293
Saffran, J.R., 134
Sagi, A., 150, 151
Saigal, S., 86
Sakala, C., 75
Saklofske, D.H., 190, 247
Salkind, N.J., 145
Samara, M., 86
Samara, R., 328
Samdal, O., 317
Sameroff, A.J., 151, 214, 318
Sampson, H.A., 171
Samson, L.M., 331
Sanders, 100n
Sanders, P., 157
Sandstrom, M.J., 279
Santiago, C.D., 10
Santos, A., 254
Santos, I.S., 68
Santos, R.G., 281
Saprling, J., 123
Saqib, M., 176
Sarnecka, B.W., 183
Saswati, S., 36
Satcher, D., 330
Saudino, K.J., 50
Saunders, N., 74
Savage, A., 217
Savage, J.S., 60
Savage, R., 255
Savarino, J., 237
Savic, I., 328
Savin-Williams, R.C., 327, 328
Sawalani, G., 278
Saxe, R., 129
Saxon, J.L., 203
Scaldwell, W., 247
Scarr, S., 48
Schabus, M., 227
Schack-Nielsen, L., 61
Schacter, D.L., 246
Schafer, W.D., 150
Schanzenbach, D.W., 317
Scharf, M., 272
Scharfer, C.E., 259
Scheers, N.J., 90
Scheidt, P., 293
Schell, S.L., 174
Schellong, K., 88
Scher, A., 111, 165
Schiariti, V., 257
Schiff, A., 293
Schiller, M., 151
Schimmele, C.M., 273
Schindler, H.S., 330
Schleifer, B., 317
Schmelzer, D., 166
Schmidt, F., 217
Schmidt, G., 270

Schmidt, J., 315
Schmidt, S., 174
Schmitt, S.A., 137
Schmitz, S., 50
Schneider, M., 254
Schneider, W., 189
Schoefs, V., 152
Schoendorf, K.C., 64
Schoenle, E.J., 39
Schölmerich, A., 88
Schouten, A., 267
Schroth, R.J., 224
Schulenberg, J.E., 297, 338, 339
Schulkin, J., 64
Schulting, A.B., 197
Schulz, M.S., 92, 93
Schwartz, C., 247
Schwartz, D., 219, 281
Schwartzentruber, J., 41
Schwean, V.L., 190
Schweinhart, L.J., 196, 339
Schwenck, C., 189
Scott, C., 87
Scullin, M.H., 257
Scwartz, L.L., 36
Searleman, A., 168
Seaton, E.K., 326
Sedighdeilami, F., 218
Seeley, J.R., 291
Seeman, T., 270
Seepersad, S., 333
Seibel, R.L., 134
Seifen, S., 166
Seifer, R., 151
Seleven, S.G., 290
Seligman, M.E.P., 314
Sell, R.L., 327
Sellers, R.M., 326
Seltzer, J.A., 273
Seltzer, M., 137
Sen, M., 157
Senecal, S., 88
Sénéchal, M., 138, 252
Senghas, A., 136
Senman, L., 187
Serbin, L., 157
Service, V., 134
Servis, 209
Sethi, A., 156
Setterstein, R.A.Jr., 339
Seymour, L.C., 76
Shacher-Dadon, A., 64
Shah, P., 84
Shamah, T., 62
Shanahan, M., 340
Shanker, S., 196
Shanner, L., 36
Shannon, D., 88, 137
Shannon, J.D., 92, 273
Shannon, M., 173, 174n
Shapiro, A.F., 92
Shapiro, B.K., 133n
Shapiro, H., 106
Shapka, J.D., 288
Sharma, A.R., 276
Sharon, T., 183
Shaw, A., 26
Shaw, B.A., 259
Shaw, D., 157, 205

Shaw, H., 294
Shaw, N., 169
Shaw, P., 249
Shaywitz, B.A., 258
Shaywitz, S.E., 258
Sheehan, R., 197
Shen, J., 257
Shepard, C.A., 234
Sheppard, A.J., 88
Sherman, P.W., 22
Shi, T., 207
Shibuya, K., 170
Shields, M., 100, 229, 230, 294
Shimoni, R., 92
Shine, B., 169
Shiono, P.H., 70
Shipman, S.A., 88
Shirley, D., 254
Shirley, L., 157, 205
Shkolnik, A., 134
Shoda, Y., 156
Shoji, J., 281
Sholl, W., 252
Shore, C., 133n
Shore, E.L., 313
Shortt, J.W., 268
Shulman, S., 152, 272, 276
Shumow, L., 315
Shwe, H.I., 135
Shweder, R.A., 313
Sicherer, S.H., 172
Siegler, R.S., 183, 188, 244, 246, 252
Sieving, R.E., 328
Signore, C., 112n
Sill, E., 340
Silver, E.J., 228, 233n
Silvestri, L., 166
Simard, V., 152
Simen-Kapeu, A., 230
Simion, F., 128
Simmer, M.L., 251
Simon, G.E., 237
Simonet, F., 88
Simons, R.F., 151
Simons, R.L., 291, 338
Simpkins, S.D., 267
Simpson, A.M., 137
Simpson, H., 300
Simpson, J.E., 70, 207
Simpson, K., 90
Sinclair, J.M., 9
Singal, D., 300
Singer, D.G., 217
Singer, J.L., 217
Singer, L.T., 69, 114
Singer-Freeman, K.E., 244
Singh, G.K., 175
Singh, S., 328
Singhal, 100n
Sippel, W., 288n
Siqueland, E., 105
Sirnick, A., 113
Siskind, J.M., 137
Skajaervan, R., 86
Skakkebaek, N., 288n, 290
Skelton, J.A., 169
Skinner, B.F., 16t, 19, 30, 132
Skinner, R., 301

Skoe, E.E., 314
Slobin, D., 135
Slomkowski, C., 298
Slotkin, T.A., 78
Slutzky, S., 267
Slyper, A.H., 288, 290
Smahal, D., 336
Smedley, A., 7, 8
Smedley, B.D., 7, 8
Smetana, J., 334
Smilansky, S., 211, 220
Smith, A.M., 68
Smith, B.L., 87, 90
Smith, E., 175
Smith, G.C.S., 78
Smith, J., 11, 214, 215, 228
Smith, J.D., 252
Smith, K.E., 192
Smith, L.B., 109
Smith, P.J.S., 63
Smith, P.K., 211, 212, 281
Smith, T.E., 157
Smith, T.S., 157
Smolak, L., 115
Smoot, D.L., 277
Smylie, J., 87, 88
Snider, C.E., 300
Snidman, N., 148, 149
Snodgrass, S.G., 145n
Snoek, H., 234
Snow, M.E., 157
Snowling, M.J., 194
Snyder, E.E., 49
Snyder, J., 268, 338
Sobolewski, J.M., 272, 335
Soenens, B., 334
Sokol, R.J., 66, 67, 69
Soliday, 100n
Soller, L., 172, 172n
Solomon, J., 150
Sommer, M., 232
Sonnentag, S., 314
Sontag, L.M., 291
Sood, B., 66, 67
Soolsma, J., 76
Sorensen, A., 156
Sørensen, T.I., 61
Sorof, J.M., 231
Soto, A., 288n
Sotres-Alvarez, D., 62
Soules, M.R., 35
South, S.J., 329
Sowell, E.R., 101
Sparfkin, J., 338
Sparling, J.J., 123
Spelke, E.S., 130, 205, 217
Spellman, B.A., 129
Spence, J.C., 226
Spence, M.J., 60
Sperling, M.A., 86
Sperling, R.A., 246
Spijkerman, R., 336
Spinard, T.L., 203, 211, 326
Spinath, F.M., 50, 194
Spirito, A., 227
Sroufe, L.A., 144n, 145, 151, 152
St.-Onge, M., 166
St-Deinis, M., 6
St-Laurent, D., 152, 253

Stack, 128
Staff, J., 320
Stafford, F.P., 228
Stamilio, D.M., 84
Stanley-Hagan, M., 274
Starr, J.M., 247
Stedron, J., 44
Stegge, H., 267
Stein, R.E.K., 228, 233n
Steinberg, L., 48, 215, 216, 316, 332, 333, 335, 338, 339
Steinhausen, H.C., 296
Steinman, C., 170
Stepanikova, I., 27
Stephansson, O., 87
Stephen, C., 255
Stephens, L.E., 66
Stern, S.B., 217
Sternberg, R.J., 8, 247–250, 249f, 261, 319
Stevens, F., 106
Stevens, N., 278, 336
Stevenson, H.W., 316
Stevenson, J., 194
Stevenson, O., 255
Stewart, J.H., 214
Stice, E., 294, 295
Stille, S., 256
Stipek, D.J., 154
Stoelhorst, M.S.J., 86
Stokes, J., 270
Stoll, B.J., 85
Stoll, M.F., 271
Stoolmiller, M., 329
Storey, K., 226
Story, M., 230, 301
Stothard, K.J., 61
Straus, M.A., 114, 214, 215
Strebel, P., 63
Streight, S., 90
Streissguth, A.P., 67
Striano, 154
Striano, T., 186
Strickland, B., 231
Striegel-Moore, R.H., 295
Strier, R., 92
Stright, A.D., 148, 192
Strobino, D.M., 36, 84
Strohschein, L., 271
Stroud, L.R., 236
Stucky, B., 278
Stueve, A., 298
Stukel, T.A., 84, 88
Sturm, R., 170, 230
Styfco, S.J., 196
Su, C., 216
Su, T.F., 326
Sue, S., 249
Sukhawathanakul, P., 281
Sun, Y., 278, 334
Surkan, P.J., 87
Susman, E.J., 287, 288, 289, 290, 291, 295, 299
Sutherland, N., 11
Swain, I.U., 105
Swain, M., 255, 256
Swallen, K.C., 294
Swamy, G.K., 86
Swan, S., 288n

Swank, P.R., 192
Swanston, H.Y., 115
Sward, G.D., 155
Sweeney, J.A., 245
Swenson, L., 296
Swingley, D., 135
Swisher, R., 219
Sylva, K., 122, 122n
Szaflarski, J.P., 168
Szkrybalo, J., 157

T

Tackett, J., 156
Tackett, J.L., 337
Taddeo, D., 296
Taillac, C.J., 69
Tait, C.L., 8
Tam, K.K., 216, 217
Tamang, B.L., 267
Tamim, H., 100, 176
Tamis-LeMonda, C.S., 92, 107, 137
Tan, K.W., 44
Tanaka, A., 152
Tanaka, K., 281
Tang, Y., 294
Tanner, J.L., 271, 272
Tanzer, N.K., 190
Tapert, S.F., 297
Tarasuk, V., 170
Tarullo, L., 195
Tastsoglou, E., 326
Taussig, C., 339
Tavares, T., 317
Taveras, 166
Taylor, A., 10, 319
Taylor, B.J., 165n
Taylor, C.L., 194
Taylor, D.M., 249
Taylor, J.R., 292
Taylor, L.C., 253
Taylor, M., 187
Taylor, S.E., 270
Tebbutt, J.S., 115
Temple, J.A., 196, 339
Tenenbaum, H., 209
Tennant, P.W.G., 61
Thacker, S.B., 77
Thanh, T.X., 66
Theakston, A., 193
Thelen, E., 109
Thiele, A.T., 46
Thoman, E.B., 62, 111
Thomas, A., 50, 146, 147, 147n
Thomas, D., 280
Thomas, E.M., 195
Thompson, L.A., 84
Thompson, N.S., 133
Thompson, P.J.L., 289n
Thompson, P.M., 50, 101, 164, 225, 226n, 249
Thompson, R.A., 28, 145, 156
Thompson, R.L., 145n
Thompson, T., 256
Thompson, V., 243, 246
Thomson, E., 273, 274
Thomson, K.M., 279
Thornberry, T.P., 332

Tidball, G., 153
Timmons, V., 193
Tincoff, R., 134
Tipsord, J.M., 277, 338
Tirosh, E., 111
Tisdale, 42n
Tither, J., 290
Tjebkes, T.L., 156
Tjepkema, M., 293
Toga, A., 50, 101, 225
Toga, A.W., 164
Tolan, P.H., 338, 339
Tomany-Korman, S.C., 88, 175
Tomasello, M., 134, 146, 186, 193, 217
Tompkins, M.E., 88
Tong, V.T., 67
Toohey, K., 256
Toppari, J., 288n
Torrance, E.P., 259
Toste, J.R., 296
Totsika, V., 122, 122n
Touchette, E., 165
Tough, S., 34, 64, 196
Tourigny, M., 215
Tournier, M., 237, 299
Tousignant, M., 10n, 175
Touwen, 100n
Townsend, N.W., 92
Trainor, L.J., 138
Trautner, H.M., 208
Travers, J., 289n
Tremblay, L., 100
Tremblay, M.S., 49, 101, 228, 229, 231, 293
Tremblay, R., 291
Tremblay, R.E., 165, 166, 218, 219
Trickett, P.K., 115
Trim, R.S., 298
Trionfi, G., 186
Trocmé, N., 113, 114, 270
Tronick, E.Z., 88, 105, 152, 153
Tryba, A.K., 90
Tsai, J., 66
Tsoa, E., 170
Tsuboi, K., 294
Tsuchiya, K., 69
Ttofi, M.M., 282
Tucker, G.R., 255
Tucker, P., 169
Turati, C., 128
Turcotte, G., 6
Turkheimer, E., 249
Turnbull, M., 255
Turner, J., 231
Turner, P.J., 209
Turrell, S.L., 158
Turtle, M., 164
Twardosz, S., 114
Twenge, J.M., 92
Twigg, R., 114
Tyl, R., 288n
Tynes, B.M., 280
Tyson, D., 316
Tyson, H., 75
Tzoumakis, S., 218
Tzur, G., 130

U

Uggen, C., 320
Ukoumunne, O.C., 227
Ullman, J.B., 253
Umilta, C., 128
Umlauf, M.G., 166
Underwood, A., 101
Ungerleider, C., 256, 317
Updegraff, K.A., 209
Uppal, S., 257
Urban, T.A., 245
Urquijo, C.R., 59
Usalcas, J., 320

V

Vainio, S., 39
Valeri, S.M., 299
Valkenburg, P.M., 336
Van Acker, R., 279
Van Allen, M.I., 62
van de Beek, C., 207
Van de Vijver, F.J.R., 190
Van den Boom, D.C., 151
van den Eijnden, R.J.J.M., 336
Van den Hoff, M.C., 62
van den Wittenboer, G.L.H., 93
van Goozen, S., 207, 234, 337
van IJzendoorn, M.H., 150, 151, 152, 276
Van Ryzin, M., 290
Van Voorhis, B.J., 36
Vandell, D.L., 158
Vandewater, E.A., 270
Vandivere, S., 37
Vansteenkiste, M., 334
Vargha-Khadem, F., 130
Varghese, J., 152
Vasilidis, H.-M., 299n
Vasilyeva, M., 183, 192, 253
Vaspo, J., 159
Vaughan Van Hecke, A., 128
Veenstra, R., 280, 281
Veerman, J.W., 279
Veenstra, V.A., 275
Venables, P.H., 171
Ventura, A.K., 105
Ventura, S.J., 331
Vereecken, C., 294, 295
Verkuyten, M., 326
Verma, S., 333
Vermulst, A.A., 336
Verrall, T., 62
Verschueren, K., 152
Vertraete, M., 196
Verwijmeren, T., 337
Veugelers, P., 62
Veugelers, P.J., 169, 227, 230
Vézina, M., 327
Vgontzas, A.N., 166
Vickerie, J.L., 172
Victoria, C.G., 68
Vigorito, J., 105
Vijayan, S., 134
Viken, R., 291
Vilain, E., 207
Villalpando, S., 62
Viner, R.M., 169

Vingerhoets, G., 168
Vishton, P.M., 134
Vitaro, F., 166
Vitousek, K.M., 295
Voegler-Lee, M.E., 189
Vohr, B.R., 86
von Gontard, A., 166
von Hofsten, C., 108
von Mutius, E., 231
Vondra, J.I., 150
Votruba-Drzal, E., 197, 330
Vrangalova, Z., 327
Vu, L.T.H., 10
Vuori, L., 62
Vygotsky, L., 16t, 19, 20–21, 30, 181, 191, 192, 194, 199, 247, 252

W

Waddell, C., 234, 235
Wade, A., 280
Wadhera, S., 36
Wadsworth, M.E., 10, 86, 270
Wagner, E., 146
Wagner, M., 193
Wainright, J.L., 274
Waknine, Y., 41
Wald, N.J., 62
Waldfogel, J., 231
Waldman, I.D., 337
Waldron, J., 249
Walk, R.D., 108
Walker, J.R., 114
Walker, L.R., 299
Walker, M., 36, 62
Walker, S., 171
Walker-Andrews, A.S., 152
Wall, S., 150
Waller, M., 337
Waller, M.W., 299
Wallman, C., 104
Walston, J., 197
Walton, F., 193
Wang, J.D., 69
Wang, L., 78
Wang, P.S., 237, 299n
Wang, Q., 203
Wang, X., 151
Wang, Y., 229
Ward, M., 7
Ward, M.G.K., 113
Ward, R.H., 64
Warnekan, F., 146
Warneken, F., 217
Warner, M., 300
Warnock, F., 165
Warren, K.R., 67
Warren, M., 291
Warshauer-Baker, E., 8
Wasik, B.H., 123
Wassimi, S., 88
Waters, E., 150
Watitsch, M., 288n
Watson, J.B., 16t, 17–18, 18, 30
Watt, D., 317
Waugh, R.M., 153
Webster, P.C., 88

Wechsler, D., 247
Weeks, M., 149
Wehner, E.A., 336
Weick, M., 280
Weikart, D.P., 339
Weinberg, M.K., 153
Weinreb, L., 176
Weinreb, L.F., 175
Weinstock, H., 331
Weir, E., 299
Weiss, B., 177, 214
Weiss, L.G., 247
Weisz, J.R., 299
Weitzman, M., 67
Welk, G.J., 277
Wellman, H.M., 183, 186, 187
Wells, K., 301
Wen, S.W., 62, 75, 87
Wendt, M., 269, 273
Wentworth, N., 108
Wentzel, K.R., 317
Werker, J.F., 133n, 138
Werner, R.S., 187
Wertz, A.E., 50
West, J., 195, 197, 252
West, M., 137
Westen, D., 16
Westling, E., 291
Whalen, J.C., 281
Whalley, L.J., 247
Whatt, W., 293
Wheeler, K., 127
Wheeler, M.E., 60
Whincup, 100n
White, A., 297
White, W., 197
White Holman, C., 328
Whitehurst, G.J., 195
Whiteman, S., 277
Whitlock, E., 299
Whitlock, J., 296
Whitman, T.L., 332
Whittle, H., 280

Wiater, A., 227
Wickrama, K., 316
Widaman, K.F., 47
Widom, C.S., 114
Wiebe, R.P., 298
Wiebe, S.A., 189
Wiechel, J., 197
Wieczorek-Deering, D., 66
Wiegand, B., 111, 112, 165n
Wigfield, A., 307
Wilcox, A.J., 33
Wilkins, R., 88
Willard, N.E., 336
Wille, D.E., 152
Willemsen, L., 336
Williams, A.M., 175
Williams, S., 299
Willms, J.D., 10, 49, 66, 67, 68,
    84, 175, 191, 217, 253, 288,
    291, 316
Willoughby, M.T., 189
Willows, N.D., 62, 169, 230
Wilson, B., 170
Wilson, B.J., 217
Wilson, B.L., 77
Wilson, E.O., 30
Wilson, G.T., 295, 296
Wilson, M., 245
Wilson, S., 286, 288, 314, 315,
    332
Wims, J.D., 123
Wingert, P., 101
Winickoff, J.P., 67
Winner, E., 259, 260
Winter, M.R., 298
Winzer, M., 259
Wise, S., 152
Witchel, S., 288n
Witherington, D., 203
Wolak, J., 329
Wolfe, B.E., 295
Wolfe, D.A., 337

Wolfe, L.A., 63
Wolff, 111n
Wolke, D., 86
Wolraich, M.L., 259
Wondimu, E.A., 172
Wong, H., 41, 79
Wong, I.C.K., 237
Wong, M.M., 298
Wong, S., 65n
Wood, J.J., 92
Wood, W., 207
Woodcock, R., 245, 253
Woodruff, T.J., 64, 177, 258
Woodward, L.J., 115
Woolley, J.D., 186
Wooten, K.G., 110
Worswick, C., 8
Worth, K., 279
Wrangham, R.W., 213
Wright, L.L., 86
Wright, S.C., 249
Wu, Z., 273
Wulf, D., 328
Wynn, K., 130, 146
Wyrobek, A.J., 69

X

Xu, S.Y., 75
Xu, Y., 219
Xue, Y., 10

Y

Yamada, S., 281
Yang, C.J., 91
Yip, T., 326
Yokota, F., 279
Yorgason, J.B., 280
Yoshikawa, H., 339
Young, A., 134
Young, K., 210, 236
Young, M., 337

Young, M.C., 172
Young, T.K., 62
Youngblade, L.M., 152, 286
Yu, S.M., 175
Yuzpe, A.A., 34

Z

Zahn-Waxler, C., 146
Zaidman-Zait, A., 165
Zain, A.F., 211
Zajac, R., 252
Zanardo, V., 78
Zarrett, N.R., 338
Zeanah, C.H., 103
Zee, P.C., 293
Zeiger, J.S., 61
Zelazo, P.D., 188, 189, 245
Zelazo, P.R., 105, 128
Zerwas, S., 159
Zeskind, P.S., 66
Zhang, Q., 294
Zhang, X., 268
Zhao, D., 294
Zhao, Y., 294
Zheng, S., 149
Zhu, B.-P., 84
Zhu, J., 247
Zibin, T., 299
Zigler, E., 196, 339
Zimmer, P., 62
Zimmerman, F.J., 62
Ziol-Guest, K.M., 335
Zola, I.K., 233n
Zoran, N., 276
Zubernis, L.S., 187
Zubrick, S.R., 194
Zuk, M., 327
Zwier, S., 336
Zylke, J., 231

A

AAP Committee on Drugs, 66
AAP Committee on Public Education, 279
Abecedarian (ABC) Program, 123, 124
Aboriginal children and youth
  access to quality health care, 175
  and career counselling, 319
  child welfare services, 114
  dropping out of school, 318
  education needs of Aboriginal children, 256–257
  housing, 176
  identity formation, 326
  infant mortality, 88–89
  inhalants, 299
  intelligence testing, 190, 249
  midwives, 75
  obesity, 100, 230
  parenting style, 216, 217
  physical activity, 229
  play, and learning, 193
  poverty, 270
  reproductive role, 74
  residential school experience, 9
  safeguarding of heritage, customs and community interests, 28
  suicide, 301
  two-spirited, 327
Aboriginal Head Start Program, 196, 256–257
ABRACADABRA, 255
abuse. See maltreatment
academic achievement. See school
acceleration, 260
accidental injuries, 172–174, 232–234
accommodation, 20
Accutane, 65
achieved identity status, 326
achondroplasia, 43
acquired immune deficiency syndrome (AIDS), 63
active correlations, 48
active development, 13
active sleep, 111
activity levels, 111–112
acute medical conditions, 231
adaptation, 20
ADHD. See attention deficit hyperactivity disorder (ADHD)
adolescence, 286
  anorexia nervosa, 295
  antisocial behaviour, 337–339
  body image, 295–296
  the brain, 291–292
  bulimia nervosa, 295–296
  child-bearing, 331–332
  cognitive development. See cognitive development (adolescence)
  dating violence, 336–337
  death, 300–301

depression, 299
discretionary time, 333
drug use, 296–299
eating disorders, 295–296
educational issues, 314–320
emerging adulthood, 339–340
formal operations, 306–310
friends, 335–336
globalization of, 287
higher education, 318–320
imaginary audience, 309
immature characteristics of adolescent thought, 308–309
individuation, 332–333
information processing, changes in, 309–310
juvenile delinquency, 337–339
language development, 309
moral development, 310–314
nutrition, 294–296
obesity, 294–295
online communication, 336
opportunities, 286
parental monitoring, and self-disclosure, 334
  and parenting styles, 333–334
parents, and adolescents, 332–335
peers, 335–337
personal fable, 309
physical activity, 292–293
physical development, 5
Piagetian approach, 306–310
pregnancy, 64, 331–332
prosocial behaviour, 326–327
psychosocial development. See psychosocial development (adolescence)
puberty, 287–291
risky behaviour, 286
romantic relationships, 336
self-injurious behaviour, 296
sexual behaviour, 328–330
sexuality, 327–332
sexually transmitted infections (STIs), 330–331
sibling relationships, 335
sleep, 293–294
as social construction, 286
students not bound for university or college, 319
suicide, 300–301
vocational issues, 318–320
workplace, 319–320
adolescent growth chart, 289
adolescent growth spurt, 289–290
adolescent rebellion, 332
adoption, 37
adoption studies, 46–47
adoptive families, 275–276
Adult Attachment Interview (AAI), 152
Africa, 171, 287
after-school program director, 269
age, maternal, 64
aggressive behaviour, 218–219
  direct aggression, 218
  gender differences, 218
  hostile aggression, 278

hostile attribution bias, 279
indirect aggression, 218
influences on, 218–219
instrumental aggression, 218, 278
media, influence of, 279–280
middle childhood, 278–282
overt aggression, 218
relational aggression, 218
social aggression, 218
AIDS, 171, 275
air pollution, 177
the Aka of central Africa, 92
alcohol, 65, 66–67, 69, 297
alcohol and drug counsellor, 298
alcohol-related birth defects (ARBD), 66
alcohol-related neurodevelopmental disorder (ARND), 66
alleles, 39
alpha-1 antitrypsin deficiency, 42
alpha thalassemia, 42
alternative educational models, 254
alternative-language learning, 256
altruisitc behaviour, 146, 217–218
altruism, 217
ambivalent attachment, 150
American College of Obstetricians and Gynecologists, 76
American Medical Association, 76
American Sign Language, 136
amniocentesis, 45, 70
amniotic sac, 58
amphetamines, 65
anal stage, 18
ancient beliefs about illness, 233
androgens, 65, 287
anencephaly, 42, 62
anesthesia, 104
anesthesiologist, 78
angiotensin-converting enzyme (ACE) inhibitors, 66
animal research, 65
animism, 183
anorexia nervosa, 295
anoxia, 82
anti-cancer drugs, 65
anticipatory smiling, 145
antisocial behaviour, 337–339
  biological influences, 337–338
  deviancy training, 338
  environment, influence of, 338–339
  family, influence of, 338
  prevention of delinquency, 339
  treatment, 339
anxiety disorders, 234–235
Apgar scale, 82–83
apparent hypocrisy, 309
Arab Americans, 233
Argentina, 333
argumentativeness, 308
Aristotle, 38
art therapist, 333
art therapy, 236

artificial insemination, 35
Asian Americans, 249
Asian parents, 112
assimilation, 20
Assisted Human Reproductive Act, 36
assisted reproductive technology (ART), 35–37
asthma, 231
attachment, 149
  ambivalent attachment, 150
  avoidant attachment, 150
  development of, 149–150
  disorganized-disoriented attachment, 150
  establishment of, 151
  insecure attachment, 150, 152
  long-term effects, 151–152
  mutual regulation, 152–153
  patterns of, 150
  resistant attachment, 150
  secure attachment, 150, 151, 152, 156
  separation anxiety, 151
  Strange Situation, 150
  stranger anxiety, 151
  and temperament, 151
  transmission of attachment patterns, 152
  trust, development of, 149
attention deficit hyperactivity disorder (ADHD), 217, 234, 254, 258–259
audiologist, 105
Austria, 215
authoritarian parenting, 215, 316
authoritative parenting, 215–216, 316, 338
autism, 110
autobiographical memory, 189–190
autonomy versus shame and doubt, 18, 154
autosomes, 38
avoidance of deception, 28
avoidant attachment, 150

B

babbling, 133, 137
Babinski reflex, 81
Babkin reflex, 81
baby talk, 137–138
Bangladesh, 333
barbiturates, 65
bases, 37
basic trust versus mistrust, 18, 149
Baumrind's model, 215–216
Bayley Scales of Infant and Toddler Development, 106, 121, 128
bed-wetting, 166–167
behaviour modification, 236
behaviour therapy, 236
behavioural assessment of newborns, 82–83
behavioural differences, 157
behaviourism, 17–19

behaviourist approach, 120–121
the Beng people, 61
beta thalassemia, 42
bicycling, 174
bilingual children, 187, 254
bilingual education, 256
binge drinkers, 297
binocular vision, 105
bioecological theory, 21, 22
biological approach to gender development, 206, 207
birth. *See* childbirth
birth complications, 84–90
  infant mortality, 87–90
  low-birth-weight babies, 84–85
  postmature, 86
  preterm (premature) infants, 84
  small-for-date (small-for-gestational-age) infants, 84
  stillbirth, 86–87
birth defects
  chromosomal abnormalities, 44–45
  and death in infancy, 85, 87
  dominant inheritance, 43
  genetic abnormalities, 41–46
  genetic counselling, 45–46
  genetic testing, 45–46
  recessive inheritance, 43
  sex-linked inheritance, 43–44
  table of, 42
birth disorders, 41
birth process, 76–79
bisexual, 327
bisexual identity development, 328
bisphenol A (BPA), 290
blastocyst, 57
body image, 295–296
body mass index (BMI), 49
bonding
  and childbirth, 90–91
  father-infant bond, 91
  mother-infant bond, 91
Botswana, 92
the brain
  and adolescence, 291–292
  cerebral cortex, 225, 226
  cerebrum, 101
  early childhood, 165–166
  environmental influences, 292
  extreme environmental deprivation in infancy, 104
  frontal cortex, 291–292
  gestation, development during, 101
  grey matter, 225, 226
  infancy and toddlerhood, 101–103
  intelligence, and brain development, 249
  and language development, 136
  major structures of, 245
  maturation, 154
  middle childhood, development during, 224–225
  neural connections, development of, 103
  plasticity, 102–103

white matter, 225
brain growth spurts, 101
brain scans, 136
Braxton-Hicks contractions, 76
Brazelton Neonatal Behavioral Assessment Scale (NBAS), 82–83
breast-feeding, 67, 78, 99–100
Bronfenbrenner, Urie, 21, 22
Bucharest Early Intervention Project, 102
Bulgaria, 215
bulimia nervosa, 295–296
bullying, 280–282

C

Caesarean delivery, 77–78
caffeine, 67–68
calico cats, 44
calluses, 13
Canada Child Tax Benefit, 175
Canada Health Act, 175
Canada Prenatal Nutrition Program, 87
Canada's Child and Nature Alliance, 229
Canada's Food Guide to Healthy Eating, 226
Canadian certified counsellor (CCC), 216
Canadian Charter of Rights and Freedoms, 11
Canadian Health Measures Survey, 231
Canadian Immunization Guide, 110
Canadian Institutes of Health Research (CIHR), 27
Canadian Medical Association, 215
Canadian Paediatric Society, 104, 172, 230, 280
Canadian Physical Activity Guidelines, 229
Canadian Psychological Association, 27
Canadian Youth Sexual Health and HIV/AIDS Study, 329
canalization, 47
canalized traits, 47
carcinogens, 177
cardinality principle, 183
career counselling, 319
caregiver-infant bond, 90–91
caregivers, 136–137
case study, 24
categorization, 128–129, 183, 242–243
causality, 129, 183
cause-and-effect relationships, 26
cell death, 102
central executive, 189
central nervous system depressants, 65
centration, 184
Centre for Addiction and Mental Health, 297
cephalocaudal principle, 56, 98

cerebral cortex, 225, 226
cerebral palsy, 85
cerebrum, 101
change
  functional change, 310
  nature of, 13
  qualitative change, 13, 14
  quantitative change, 13, 14
  in self-esteem, 203
  structural change, 310
child clinical psychologist, 16, 159
child development, 4
  domains of development, 6
  emerging consensus, 14
  influences on development, 6–12
  issues in development, 12–14
  periods of development, 4, 5
  study of child development, 4–6
  theories. *See* theories of child development
child-directed speech (CDS), 137–138
Child Disability Benefit, 175
child maltreatment. *See* maltreatment
child mortality, 171
child poverty
  in Canada, 9, 10, 11
  effects of, 9–10
  ethnicity, 175
  and the family, 269–270
  higher risk for low-income children, 10
  homelessness, 175–176
  low-income cut-off (LICO), 175
  pour housing, 175–176
  poverty line, 175
  poverty rates, 270
  race, 175
child sexual abuse, 115
child welfare service agencies, 114
childbirth
  birth complications. *See* birth complications
  birth process, 76–79
  and bonding, 90–91
  Caesarean delivery, 77–78
  changes in childbirth, 74–76
  electronic fetal monitoring, 77
  labour and delivery options, 76–79
  Lamaze method, 79
  medicalization of childbirth, 75–76
  medicated *vs.* non-medicated delivery, 78–79
  natural childbirth, 79
  prepared childbirth, 79
  stages of childbirth, 76
  vaginal delivery, 77–78
childhood depression, 235–236
childhood diabetes, 230
childhood hypertension, 231–232
children

in mid-1800s, 11
research with children, 28
rights of, 11
children with disabilities, 257–259
children with special needs, 255–260
  Aboriginal children, needs of, 256–257
  alternative-language learning, 256
  children with disabilities, 257–259
  gifted children, 259–260
  second-language learning, 256
children's books, and gender stereotypes, 210
Chile, 171
chimpanzees, 154, 213
China, 92, 171, 229, 278, 313
Chinese parents, 203
chlamydia, 331
chorionic villi sampling (CVS), 45, 70
chromosomal abnormalities, 44–45
chromosomes, 37
chronic medical conditions, 231–232
circular reactions, 124
class inclusion, 243
class size, 254
classical conditioning, 17–18, 120
classification, 183
classroom influences on academic achievement, 253–255
Club Penguin, 255
co-parenting, 272
co-regulation, 268
co-sleeping, 112
cocaine, 65, 68–69
code emphasis approach, 251
code mixing, 137
code switching, 137
cognitive approaches to gender development, 206, 208
cognitive behavioural therapy, 236
cognitive development, 6
  adolescence. *See* cognitive development (adolescence)
  early childhood. *See* cognitive development (early childhood)
  infancy and toddlerhood. *See* cognitive development (infancy and toddlerhood)
  middle childhood. *See* cognitive development (middle childhood)
  prenatal period, 5
cognitive development (adolescence), 5
  educational issues, 314–320
  formal operations, 306–310
  immature characteristics of adolescent thought, 308–309
  information processing, changes in, 309–310

language development, 309
moral development, 310–314
Piagetian approach, 306–310
vocational issues, 318–320
cognitive development (early childhood), 5
early childhood education, 195–197
information-processing approach, 188–190
language development, 192–195
memory development, 188–190
Piagetian approach, 182–187
preoperational stage, 182–187
psychometric approaches to intelligence, 190–191
Vygotskian approach to measurement and teaching, 191
cognitive development (infancy and toddlerhood), 5
behaviourist approach, 120–121
classical conditioning, 120
cognitive neuroscience approach, 130–131
information-processing approach, 127–130
language development, 132–138
operant conditioning, 120–121
Piagetian approach, 124–127
psychometric approach, 121–124
social-contextual approach, 131
cognitive development (middle childhood), 5
the child in school. See school
concrete operational child, 242–245
information-processing approach, 245–247
language development, 250–252
Piagetian approach, 242–245
psychometric approach, 247–249
cognitive-developmental theory, 206, 208
cognitive levels of play, 211
cognitive neuroscience approach, 130–131
cognitive perspective, 19–21
cognitive-stage theory, 19–20
information-processing approach, 21
socio-cultural theory, 20–21
cognitive-stage theory, 19–20, 20
cognitive stages, 18
cohabiting families, 273–274
cohort, 11
collaborative activities, 146
colostrum, 79
committed compliance, 156
common-law families, 273–274
Community Action Plan for Children (CAPC), 123
Community Action Programme for Children, 87

community development groups, 176
community health nurse, 229
componential element, 248
comprehender, 138
computational estimation, 244
computer games, 280
computer literacy, 255
computer use, 255
conception, 34, 35
conceptual knowledge, 310
concordance rate, 46
concordant, 47
concrete operational child, 242–245
categorization, 242–243
class inclusion, 243
conservation, 243–244
deductive reasoning, 243
inductive reasoning, 243
moral reasoning, 244–245
number and mathematics, 244
spatial relationships, 242
transitive inference, 243
concrete operations stage, 18
condoms, 330
conduct disorder (CD), 234, 338
confidentiality, 28
conflicting emotions, 204
congenital hypothyroidism, 83
congenital malformations, 85
see also birth defects
conscience, 156
conservation, 184–185, 187, 242, 243–244
constructive play, 211
contexts of development, 6–11
culture, 7–8
ethnicity, 7–8
family, 7
historical context, 10–11
race, 7–8
socio-economic status (SES), 8–10
contextual element, 248
contextual perspective, 21
contingent self-esteem, 203
continuous development, 13
continuous positive airway pressure (CPAP), 227
control group, 25
conventional morality, 311, 312
convergent thinking, 259
cooing, 133
Cooley's anemia, 42
cooperative parenting, 272
coordination of secondary schemes, 125
corporal punishment, 214, 215
correlational outcomes, 25
correlational study, 24–25
Costa Rica, 171
counsellor, 319
counting, 183
Criminal Code, 215
critical period, 12
criticalness, 308
Croatia, 215

cross-cultural perspective. *See* diversity
cross-sectional study, 26–27
crying, 133, 145–146
Cuba, 171
cultural differences
see also diversity
fathers and play, 157
guided participation, 131
infant sleep schedules, 111–112
parenting styles, 216
self-definition, 202–203
shyness, 278
cultural scripts, 213
culture, 7
see also cultural differences; diversity
and cognition, 308
conflict in play situations, 213
discretionary time, 333
emotional expression, 267
and gender development, 210
gender differences, and academic achievement, 315
influence on development, 7–8
and IQ, 249, 250
and play, 212–213
and risk factors for victimization, 281
culture-free tests, 250
culture-relevant tests, 250
custody, 272
cyberbullying, 255, 280, 336
Cyprus, 215
cystic fibrosis, 42

D

Darwin, Charles, 3, 22, 90
Darwinian reflex, 81
data collection, 23–24
dating violence, 336–337
deaf children, 135
death
adolescence, 300–301
firearm-related deaths, 300
from injuries, 172–174, 232–234
motor vehicle accidents, 300
suicide, 300–301
surviving the first five years of life, 171
décalage, 244
decentre, 184
deception, 28
declarative knowledge, 310
declarative memory, 130
decoding, 251
deductive reasoning, 242, 243
deferred imitation, 182
dehydroepiandrosterone (DHEA), 287–288
delayed language development, 194
delinquency. *See* antisocial behaviour
delivery options, 76–79
Denmark, 215
dental caries, 172

dentist, 172
Denver Developmental Screening Test, 106
deoxyribonucleic acid (DNA), 37–39
dependent variable, 26
depression
adolescence, 299
childhood depression, 235–236
risk factors, 299
depth perception, 108
describer, 138
developing countries
education, 315
infant mortality, 87
junk food, 169
prenatal care, 68
the developing self
autonomy, development of, 154–155
early childhood, 202–205
emerging sense of self, 153–154
emotions, 203–204, 267
gender, 156–157
infancy and toddlerhood, 153–157
middle childhood, 266–267
representational systems, 266
self-concept, 202–203, 266
self-definition, 202–203
self-esteem, 203, 266–267
socialization, 155–156
developmental psychologist, 15
developmental quotients (DQs), 121–122
developmental research designs, 26–27
deviancy training, 338
diabetes, 63, 230, 231
Diagnostic and Statistical Manual of Mental Disorders-5, 234
diethylstilbestrol (DES), 65, 69
difficult children, 147
diffused identity status, 326
dilation of the cervix, 76
dioxin, 64
direct aggression, 218
discipline, 213
corporal punishment, 214, 215
effectiveness of, 214
forms of discipline, 213–214
inductive reasoning techniques, 214
power assertion, 214
punishment, 213–214
reinforcement, 213–214
withdrawal of love, 214
discontinuous development, 13
dishabituation, 127
disorganized-disoriented attachment, 150
disruptive conduct disorders, 234
divergent thinking, 259
diversity
see also cultural differences
adolescence, globalization of, 287
child mortality, 171

co-sleeping, 112
cognition, 308
corporal punishment, 215
discretionary time, 333
within ethnic groups, 7–8
grandparenting, 275
health care, 233
infant care, 89
IQ, 250
paths to learning, 193
prenatal care, disparities in, 68
sign language, 136
sleep customs, 112
surviving first five years of life,
    171
"terrible twos," 155
divorced parents, 271–272
dizygotic twins, 36, 46, 49
dolphins, 154
domains of development, 6
    see also specific domains of
    development
dominant inheritance, 39, 43
dominant traits, 39
doula, 75
Down syndrome, 44–45, 64, 70
dramatic play, 182, 211
dropping out of school, 317, 318
drowning, 173
drug intake during pregnancy,
    65–69
    alcohol, 66–67
    caffeine, 67–68
    cocaine, 68–69
    marijuana, 68–69
    medical drugs, 65–66
    methamphetamine, 68–69
    nicotine, 67
drug therapy, 236–237
drug use
    adolescence, 296–299
    alcohol, 297
    marijuana, 297–298
    onset of drug use, 298–299
    substance abuse, 296
    tobacco, 298
    trends in, 297
Duchenne muscular dystrophy,
    42
dynamic systems theory (DST),
    109–110
dynamic tests, 247
dyslexia, 257–258

E

early childhood (ages 3 to 6)
    accidental injuries and deaths,
        172–174
    aggressive behaviour, 218–219
    bed-wetting, 166–167
    the brain, 165–166
    cognitive development. *See*
        cognitive development (early
        childhood)
    early childhood education,
        195–197
    environmental influences on
        health, 174–177

food allergies, 171–172
gender, 205–211
health and safety, 169–177
height, 165
information-processing
    approach, 188–190
kindergarten, 197
language development, 192–
    195
motor development, 167–168
night terror, 166
nightmares, 166
obesity, 169–170
oral health, 172
parenting, 213–217
physical development, 5
physical growth, 164–165
Piagetian approach, 182–187
play, 211–213
preoperational stage, 182–187
preschools, 195–196
prosocial behaviour, 217–218
psychometric approaches to
    intelligence, 190–191
psychosocial development. *See*
    psychosocial development
    (early childhood)
sleep, 165–167
sleeptalking, 166
sleepwalking, 166
toilet training, 166–167
undernutrition, 170–171
Vygotskian approach to
    measurement and teaching,
    191
weight, 165
early childhood education,
    195–197
    Aboriginal Head Start Program,
        196
    kindergarten, 197
    Montessori method, 195
    preschools, types of, 195–196
    Project Head Start, 195–196
    Reggio Emilia approach, 195
    universal early childhood
        education and care, 196
early childhood educators
    (ECEs), 4
Early Development Index, 197
early intervention, 122–124
early vocalization, 133
Early Years Report, 123
Early Years Study-2, 196
East Asia, 315
easy children, 147
eating, 174
eating disorders, 295–296
ecological theory of perception,
    108–109
economic stress, 269–270, 334–
    335, 338
    see also child poverty
educational assistant, 258
educational reform, 253–254
egocentrism, 184
Egypt, 169
electronic bullies. *See*
    cyberbullying

electronic fetal monitoring, 77
electronic media, 219
elementary teacher, 253
embryonic disk, 58
embryonic stage, 58–59
embryoscopy, 70
emergent literacy, 194
emerging adulthood, 339–340
emerging sense of self, 153–154
emotion regulation, 203–204
emotional bullying, 281
emotional maltreatment, 112
emotional self-regulation, 267
emotional understanding,
    203–204
emotions, 144
    altruisitc behaviour, 146
    collaborative activities, 146
    conflicting emotions, 204
    crying, 145
    differentiation of emotions, 145
    early emotional responses,
        145–146
    emotional growth, 267
    empathy, 146
    infancy and toddlerhood, 144–
        146
    regulation of, 203–204
    self-conscious emotions, 146
    shared intentionality, 146
    smiling and laughing, 145–146
    social emotions, 204
    understanding, 203–204
empathy, 146, 267
employed mothers, 268–269,
    334–335
encoding, 188
endoderm, 58
English as a second language,
    256
English immersion approach, 256
enrichment, 260
enuresis, 166–167
environment, 13
    antisocial behaviour, influence
        on, 338–339
    and the brain, 292
    characteristics influenced by,
        49–51
    health, environmental
        influences on, 174–177
    and heredity, working together,
        47–49
    influence on development, 6
    influence on gene expression,
        40–41
    intelligence, 50
    physical traits, 49–50
    physiological traits, 49–50
    study of influence of, 46–49
environmental hazards, 64
epidural block, 79
epigenesis, 40–41
episiotomy, 78
episodic memory, 189
equilibration, 20
Erikson, Erik, 16–17, 18
Erikson's psychosocial stages
    autonomy *versus* shame and

doubt, 18, 154
    basic trust *versus* mistrust, 18,
        149
    generativity *versus* stagnation,
        18
    identity *versus* identify
        confusion, 18, 324
    industry *versus* inferiority, 18,
        267
    initiative *versus* guilt, 18,
        204–205
    integrity *versus* despair, 18
    intimacy *versus* isolation, 18
ESL, 256
estrogens, 207, 290
ethanol, 64
ethic of care, 313–314
ethics of research, 27–28
    avoidance of deception, 28
    research with children, 28
    research with diverse
        populations, 28
    right to informed consent, 27
    right to privacy and
        confidentiality, 28
ethnic disparities in infant
    mortality, 88–89
ethnic group, 7
ethnicity
    and child poverty, 175
    and family connectedness, 333
    and identity formation, 325–
        326
    influence on development, 7–8
    and IQ, 249
    and school experiences, 316
ethnographic study, 24
ethology, 22
Europe, 229
European-Americans, 249
European parents, 203
evocative correlations, 48
evolutionary developmental
    approach to gender
    development, 206, 207
evolutionary psychology, 22
evolutionary/sociobiological
    perspective, 22
evolutionary theory, 207
evolved mechanisms, 22
executive function, 188, 245–246
experiential element, 248
experimental group, 25
experiments, 25–26
    field experiments, 26
    groups, 25–26
    laboratory experiments, 26
    natural experiments, 26
    quasi-experiment, 26
    variables, 26
explicit memory, 130
extended family, 7
eye colour, 39

F

Facebook, 336
false beliefs, 186
family, 7

activities, and risky sexual behaviour, 330
and adolescents, 332–335
adoptive families, 275–276
antisocial behaviour, influences on, 338
atmosphere, 268–270, 334
cohabiting families, 273–274
common-law families, 273–274
conflict, 332–333
divorced parents, 271–272
economic stress, 269–270, 334–335, 338
employed mothers, 268–269, 334–335
extended family, 7
gay or lesbian parents, 274–275
and gender development, 209–210
instability, 271
lone-parent families, 272–273
and middle childhood, 268–276
nuclear family, 7
parenting. See parenting
poverty and economic stress, 269–270
sibling relationships. See siblings
skip-generation families, 275
stepfamilies, 274
structure, 270–276, 334
family studies, 46
family therapy, 236
fantasy, 186
fantasy play, 182, 211
fast mapping, 192
fathers
father-infant bond, 91
involvement with children, 273
and play, 157
role of, 92
females
activity of fetuses, 60
maternal factors, 61–69
mothers. See mothers
fertile window, 33
fertility, 35
fertility specialist, 35
fertilization, 34
fetal alcohol effects (FAS/E), 55, 66
fetal alcohol spectrum disorders (FASD), 66
fetal alcohol syndrome (FAS), 55, 66
fetal stage, 59–60
field experiments, 26
fine motor skills, 106, 168
fingerprints, 49
Finland, 215
firearms, 174, 300
fireworks, 174
first ejaculation, 290
first language, 187
First Nations. See Aboriginal children and youth
First Nations Career-Life Planning Model, 319
first sentences, 135

first words, 134–135
Fleury, Theo, 113
fluoride, 172, 173
folic acid, 62
follicle-stimulating hormone (FSH), 287
fontanels, 80
food allergies, 171–172
food banks, 170
foreclosed identity status, 326
foreclosure, 325
forensic psychologist, 272
formal education, 193
formal games with rules, 211
formal operations, 18, 306–310
hypothetical-deductive reasoning, 306–307
reasoning tasks, 307
foster care, 114
fraternal twins. See dizygotic twins
French immersion, 254–255
Freud, Sigmund, 15–16, 18
friendship, 278, 335–336
frontal cortex, 291–292
full-day kindergarten, 197
functional change, 310
functional play, 211

G

Gabon, 171
Gambia, 171
Gardner's theory of multiple intelligences, 248
gay parents, 274–275
gender, 157
and academic achievement, 252–253
and the developing self, 156–157
early childhood, 205–211
gender identity, 205
mental health, and family relations, 333
play, influences on, 212
and school, 315
vs. sex, 157
gender consistency, 208
gender constancy, 208
gender development
biological approach, 206, 207
cognitive approaches, 206, 208
cognitive-developmental theory, 206, 208
evolutionary developmental approach, 206, 207
gender-schema theory, 206, 208
perspectives on, 206–211
psychoanalytic approach, 206, 207
psychosexual theory, 206
social cognitive theory, 206
social learning approach, 206, 208–211
gender differences, 205–206
aggression, 218
biologically based gender differences, 205

cognitive gender differences, 205–206
depression in adolescence, 299
in identity formation, 325
infancy and toddlerhood, 157
parents, effect of, 157
in peer-group relationships, 277
physical differences, 205
gender identity, 205, 208
gender roles, 206
gender-schema theory, 206, 208
gender segregation, 212
gender stability, 208
gender stereotypes, 206
gender-typing, 157, 206
gender-variant identity development, 328
generalized anxiety disorder, 235
generativity versus stagnation, 18
genes, 37, 39
antisocial behaviour, 337–338
and intelligence, 249
genetic abnormalities, 41–46
see also birth defects
genetic code, 37–38
genetic counselling, 45–46
genetic counsellor, 45
genetic testing, 45–46
genetic transmission, patterns of, 39–40
genital herpes, 331
genital stage, 18
genotype, 40
genotype-environment correlation, 48
genotype-environment interaction, 47–49
German measles, 63
Germany, 215
germinal stage, 56–58
Gesell Developmental Schedules, 106
gestation, 56
gestures, 134
Ghana, 171, 328
gifted children, 259–260
Gilligan's theory of moral development, 313–314
globalization of adolescence, 287
gonadotropin-releasing hormone (GnRH), 287
gonorrhea, 331
goodness of fit, 148
grammar, 192–193, 250–251
grandparenting, 275
grasping reflex, 81
Great Britain, 228
grey matter, 225, 226
gross motor skills, 106, 167–168
groups, 25–26
growth. See physical growth
growth chart, 225
guided participation, 131
guilt, 146, 204
the Gusii of Kenya, 112

H

Habitat for Humanity, 176

habituation, 127, 157
half-day kindergarten, 197
hallucinogens, 65
handedness, 168
Happy Meals, 227
haptic perception, 108
Harlow, H., 91
Head Start, 195–196, 219
head trauma, 113
health and safety
accidental injuries, 172–174, 232–234
activity levels, 111–112
adolescence, 294–301
air pollution, 177
ancient beliefs about illness, 233
asthma, 231
chronic medical conditions, 231–232
death, 172–174, 232–234, 300–301
diabetes, 231
early childhood, 169–177
environmental influences on health, 174–177
factors in children's health, 232
food allergies, 171–172
healthy eating habits, 170
hypertension, 231–232
immunizations, 110
infancy and toddlerhood, 110–115
lead, 177
mental health. See mental health
middle childhood, 229–233
obesity, 169–170, 294–295
oral health, 172
overweight, 229–231
pesticide, 177
smoking, 176–177
states of arousal, 111–112
stuttering, 232
undernutrition, 170–171
Health Canada, 99, 226–227
health care, 233
hearing, 105
hearing impairment, 105, 134
height
early childhood, 165
middle childhood, 224
hemophilia, 42
herd immunity, 111
heredity
characteristics influenced by, 49–51
and environment, working together, 47–49
genetic code, 37–38
influence on development, 6
intelligence, 50
mechanisms of heredity, 37–41
nature vs. nurture, 12–13
patterns of genetic transmission, 39–40
physical traits, 49–50
physiological traits, 49–50
psychopathology, 51

sex determination, 38–39
study of influence of, 46–49
temperament, 50
heritability, 46–47
Heritage Language Program, 256
heroin, 65
heterosexuality, 327
heterozygous, 39
higher education, 318–320
hippocampus, 130–131
historical context, 10–11
historical generation, 11
holophrase, 134
home births, 75–76
home environment, 122, 245, 315
Home Observation for
  Measurement of the
  Environment (HOME), 122
home-schooling, 255
homelessness, 175–176
homework, 315
Homo sapiens, 8
homosexual identity
  development, 328
homosexuality, 327–328
homozygous, 39
Hong Kong, 308
horizontal décalage, 244
hormones, 65
  follicle-stimulating hormone
    (FSH), 287
  gonadotropin-releasing
    hormone (GnRH), 287
  luteinizing hormone (LH), 287
  during pregnancy, 207
  and puberty, 287–288
  synthetic growth hormone, 224
hostile aggression, 278
hostile attribution bias, 279
housing, 175–176
HPV, 330–331
human genome, 37
human immunodeficiency virus
  (HIV), 63, 171, 331
human papillomavirus (HPV),
  330–331
Human Resources and Skills
  Development Canada, 319
Hungary, 215
hungry season, 62
Huntington's disease, 43
hypertension, 231–232
hypotheses, 23
hypothetical-deductive reasoning,
  306–307
hypoxia, 82

I

ibuprofen, 66
Iceland, 215
idealism, 308
identical twins. *See* monozygotic
  twins
identification, 207
identities, 183
identity, 324
  crisis and commitment, 324–
    325

ethnic factors in identity
  formation, 325–326
gender differences in identity
  formation, 325
search for, 324–327
status, 324–325
identity achievement, 325
identity diffusion, 325
identity *versus* identify confusion,
  18, 324
the Ifaluk people of Western
  Caroline Islands, 62
imaginary audience, 309
imaginary play, 182
imaginative play, 211
imitation, 133
immigrant children. *See* new
  immigrant children
immunizations, 110
implicit memory, 130
imprinting, 12
in vitro fertilization (IVF), 35–36
inactivity, 230
incomplete dominance, 43
incubator, 85
indecisiveness, 309
independence, 203
independent variable, 26
India, 171, 228, 287, 315, 333
indirect aggression, 218
individual differences, 6, 186–187
individual psychotherapy, 236
individuation, 332–333
Indonesia, 333
inductive reasoning, 243
inductive reasoning techniques,
  214, 242
industry *versus* inferiority, 18,
  267
infancy and toddlerhood (birth to
  three years)
  activity levels, 111–112
  attachment, 149–153
  behaviourist approach, 120–121
  breast-feeding, 67, 78, 99–100
  classical conditioning, 120
  cognitive development. *See*
    cognitive development
    (infancy and toddlerhood)
  cognitive neuroscience
    approach, 130–131
  developing brain, 101–103
  the developing self, 153–157
  early emotional responses,
    145–146
  early growth, 98–101
  early sensory capacities, 104–
    106
  emotions, 144–146
  faces, preference for, 106
  gender differences, 157
  health, 110–115
  hearing, 105
  immunizations, 110
  information-processing
    approach, 127–130
  language development, 132–
    138
  maltreatment, 112–113

motor control, development of,
  107–108
motor development, 106–110
newborn baby. *See* newborn
  baby
non-organic failure to thrive,
  113
nutrition, 99–101
operant conditioning, 120–121
overweight in infancy, 100–101
pain, 104–105
peers, 159
physical development, 5,
  98–101
Piagetian approach, 124–127
picky eaters, 105
psychometric approach, 121–
  124
psychosocial development. *See*
  psychosocial development
  (infancy and toddlerhood)
relationships with other
  children, 158–159
shaken baby syndrome, 113
siblings, 158
sight, 105–106
sleep, 111–112
smell, 105
social attention, 186–187
social-contextual approach, 131
states of arousal, 111–112
taste, 105
temperament, 146–149
"terrible twos," 154–155
touch, 104–105
windy grins, 145
infant mortality, 87–90
  Aboriginal communities, 88–89
  developing countries, 87
  industrialized countries, 88
  infant mortality rate, 87
  injuries, 90
  low birth weights, 88
  racial and ethnic disparities,
    88–89
  sudden infant death syndrome
    (SIDS), 89–90
infant mortality rate, 87
Infant-Toddler HOME Inventory
  (ages 0 to 3), 122
infertility, 34–35
  assisted reproductive
    technology (ART), 35–37
  common causes, 34–35
influences on development
  contexts of development, 6–11
  critical period, 12
  culture, 7–8
  environment, 6
  ethnicity, 7–8
  family, 7
  heredity, 6
  historical context, 10–11
  maturation, 6
  neighbourhoods, 10
  non-normative influences, 11
  normative influences, 11
  race, 7–8
  sensitive periods, 12

socio-economic status (SES),
  8–10
timing of influences, 12
influences on prenatal
  development, 61–69
  drug intake, 65–69
  malnutrition, 62
  maternal age, 64
  maternal anxiety and stress,
    63–64
  maternal factors, 61–69
  maternal illnesses, 63
  nutrition and maternal weight,
    61–62
  outside environmental hazards,
    64
  paternal factors, 69
  physical activity and strenuous
    work, 62–63
information-processing approach,
  21, 127
  adolescence, 309–310
  and development of Piagetian
    abilities, 128–130
  early childhood, 188–190
  executive function, influences
    on development of, 245–246
  habituation, 127
  infancy and toddlerhood, 127–
    130
  intelligence, predictor of, 128
  memory, 246
  middle childhood, 245–247
  and Piagetian tasks, 246–247
  selective attention, 246
  visual processing abilities, 128
informed consent, 27
inhibited, 148
inhibitory control, 246
initiative *versus* guilt, 18,
  204–205
injuries
  accidental injuries, 172–174,
    232–234
  and infant mortality, 90
insecure attachment, 150, 152
instrumental aggression, 218,
  278
insufficiently motile sperm, 34
insurance companies, 25
integrity *versus* despair, 18
intellectual disability, 257
intelligence, 50
  genes and brain development,
    249
  influences on, 249
  information processing as
    predictor, 128
  IQ (intelligence quotient) tests,
    128
  measured intelligence,
    influences on, 190–191
  psychometric approaches,
    190–191
  race and ethnicity, influences
    on IQ, 249
  socio-economic status and IQ,
    191
  testing. *See* intelligence testing

theory of multiple intelligences, 248

triarchic theory of intelligence, 248–249

Vygotskian approach to measurement and teaching, 191

intelligence testing
culture-free tests, 250
culture-relevant tests, 250
dynamic tests, 247
early childhood, 190–191
infants and toddlerhood, 121–122
IQ controversy, 247–248
IQ (intelligence quotient) tests, 121, 190
Kaufman Assessment Battery for Children (K-ABC-II), 247
measurement of intelligence, 247
middle childhood, 247–249
Stanford-Binet Intelligence Scale, 190
traditional psychometric measures, 190
Wechsler Intelligence Scale for Children (WISC-IV), 247
Wechsler Preschool and Primary Scale of Intelligence, Fourth Edition (WPPSI-IV), 190

intelligent behaviour, 121
interdependence, 203
internalization, 156
Internet use, 255, 336
intimacy versus isolation, 18
intimate partner violence, 112
Inuit. See Aboriginal children and youth
invulnerability, 309
IQ (intelligence quotient) tests, 121, 128, 190
irreversibility, 184–185
Islamic countries, 315
Israel, 215
issues in development, 12–14

J

Japan, 333
joint attention, 128
joint custody, 272
junk food, 169
juvenile delinquency, 337–339
biological influences, 337–338
deviancy training, 338
environment, influence of, 338–339
family, influence of, 338
prevention of delinquency, 339
treatment, 339

K

the Kalahari of Africa, 228
kangaroo care, 85–86
Kaufman Assessment Battery for Children (K-ABC-II), 247

kindergarten, 197
Kindergarten to Senior 4 Education Agenda for Student Success, 253–254
Klinefelter syndrome, 44
Kohlberg's cognitive-developmental theory, 208
Kohlberg's theory of moral reasoning, 311–313
Korea, 333
the Kpelle people in North Africa, 250t

L

laboratory experiments, 26
laboratory observation, 24
labour
descent and emergence of the baby, 76
dilation of the cervix, 76
expulsion of the placenta, 76
options, 76–79
stages of, 76
labour and delivery nurse, 77
Lamaze method, 79
language
see also language development
bilingual children, 187, 254
first language, 187
and handedness, 168
language acquisition device (LAD), 132
language development
adolescence, 309
areas of language development, 192–194
brain development, 136
child-directed speech (CDS), 137–138
delayed language development, 194
early childhood, 192–195
early speech, characteristics, 135
early vocalization, 133
first sentences, 135
first words, 134–135
gestures, 134
grammar, 192–193, 250–251
infancy and toddlerhood, 132–138
influences on, 135–138
linguistic speech, 134
literacy, 138, 194–195, 251–252
middle childhood, 250–252
perception of language sounds and structure, 133–134
pragmatics, 193–194, 251
pre-reading skills, 194
prelinguistic speech, 133
private speech, 194
sequence of early language development, 133–135
social interaction, 136–137
social perspective-taking, 309
social speech, 193–194
and symbolic capacities, 126

syntax, 192–193, 250–251
telegraphic speech, 135L
theory of mind, 187
vocabulary, 192, 250–251, 309
lanugo, 80
latency stage, 18
Latin America, 171, 233
Latvia, 215
laughing, 145–146
lawn mowing, 174
laws, 15
lead, 64, 69, 177
learning disabilities (LDs), 257
learning perspective, 17–19
learning to learn, 109
lesbian parents, 274–275
LGBQT (lesbian, gay, bisexual, queer, transgendered, two-spirited), 327
linguistic speech, 134
literacy
in Canada, 254
computer literacy, 255
emergent literacy, 194
middle school, 251–252
preparation for, 138, 194–195
reading, 251–252
writing, 251–252
"Little Albert," 17
locomotor play, 211
lone-parent families, 272–273
long-term memory, 189
longitudinal study, 27
low-birth-weight babies, 84–85
extremely low-birth-weight babies, 86
immediate treatment and outcomes, 85–86
infant mortality, 88
long-term outcomes, 86
protective factors, 86
low sperm count, 34
luteinizing hormone (LH), 287

M

magical thinking, 186
males
activity of fetuses, 60
fathers. See fathers
greater vulnerability, 59
older fathers, 69
paternal factors, 69
Mali, 328
malnutrition, 62
maltreatment
child sexual abuse, 115
contributing factors, 113–114
cultural factors, 113–114
emotional maltreatment, 112
exposure to intimate partner violence, 112
forms of, 112
helping families in trouble, 114
infancy and toddlerhood, 112–113
long-term effects, 114–115
neglect, 112, 113

non-organic failure to thrive, 113
perpetrators, 113
physical abuse, 112
prevention of, 114
sexual abuse, 112
shaken baby syndrome, 113
marijuana, 65, 68–69, 69, 297–298
marital satisfaction, 92–93
maternal age, 64
maternal anxiety, 63–64
maternal factors, 61–69
maternal illnesses, 63
maternal smoking, 67
maternal stress, 63–64
maternal weight, 61–62
mathematics, 242, 244
maturation, 6
of the brain, 154
influence on development, 6
puberty. See puberty
Mauritius, 170
the Mayans, 112, 155
McDonald's, 227
measurement estimation, 244
meconium, 82
media influence on aggression, 279–280
medical assessment of newborns, 82–83
medical drugs, 65–66
medicalization of childbirth, 75–76
medicated delivery, 78–79
meiosis, 37
memory
see also memory development
autobiographical memory, 189–190
in childhood, 189–190
declarative memory, 130
episodic memory, 189
explicit memory, 130
implicit memory, 130
improvements in, 246
long-term memory, 189
metamemory, 246
procedural memory, 130, 189
sensory memory, 188
working memory, 131, 188, 189, 246
memory development
see also memory
basic processes and capacities, 188–189
early childhood, 188–190
encoding, 188
recall, 189
recognition, 189
retrieval, 188
storage, 188
menarche, 290
Mendel, Gregor, 39
menstruation, 290
mental combinations, 125
mental health
anxiety disorders, 234–235
childhood depression, 235–236

depression and adolescence, 299

Diagnostic and Statistical Manual of Mental Disorders-5, 234

disruptive conduct disorders, 234

eating disorders, 295–296

and family relations, 333

middle childhood, 234–237

school phobia, 234–235

treatment techniques, 236–237

mental states, 186

mercury, 64

mesoderm, 58

metacognition, 308

metamemory, 246

methadone, 65

methamphetamine, 68–69

methotrexate, 65

Métis. *See* Aboriginal children and youth

Mexico, 228

the Micronesian Truk, 111

middle childhood (ages 6 to 11)

accidental injuries, 232–234

aggression, 278–282

attention, 245–247

brain development, 224–225

bullying, 280–282

chronic medical conditions, 231–232

co-regulation, 268

cognitive development. *See* cognitive development (middle childhood)

concrete operational child, 242–245

dental care, 224

the family, 268–276

growth chart, 225

health and safety, 229–233

height, 224

information-processing approach, 245–247

intelligence, assessment of, 247–249

language development, 250–252

memory, 245–247

motor development, 228–229

nutrition, 226–227

overweight, 229–231

peers, 276–282

physical development, 5, 224–225

physical play, 228–229

Piagetian approach, 242–245

planning, 245–247

psychometric approach, 247–249

psychosocial development. *See* psychosocial development (middle childhood)

school. *See* school

sleep, 227

tooth development, 224

weight, 224

midwives, 74–75

milestones

motor development milestones, 106, 107

prenatal development, 57

miscarriages, 58

mitosis, 38, 57

Modern Family, 274

monozygotic twins, 36, 47

Montessori method, 195

moral development

adolescence, 310–314

conventional morality, 311, 312

ethic of care, 313–314

Gilligan's theory, 313–314

Kohlberg's theory of moral reasoning, 311–313

postconventional morality, 311, 312

preconventional morality, 311, 312

prosocial behaviour, 326–327

socialization, 155–156

moral reasoning, 244–245

morality of autonomous moral principles, 311

morality of conventional role conformity, 311

moratorium, 325

moratorium identity status, 326

Moro reflex, 81

Morocco, 169, 333

mortality rate, 171, 296

mother-infant bond, 91

motherese, 137

Motherisk program, 66

mothers

employed mothers, 268–269, 334–335

maternal age, 64

maternal anxiety, 63–64

maternal factors, 61–69

maternal illnesses, 63

maternal smoking, 67

maternal stress, 63–64

maternal weight, 61–62

mother-infant bond, 91

motivation, 314–315

motor control, 107–108

motor development

early childhood, 167–168

fine motor skills, 106, 168

gross motor skills, 106, 167–168

handedness, 168

infancy and toddlerhood, 106–110

middle childhood, 228–229

milestones, 106, 107

motor control, development of, 107–108

and perception, 108

theories of, 108–110

motor development theories

dynamic systems theory (DST), 109–110

ecological theory of perception, 108–109

motor vehicle accidents, 173, 300

motor vehicles, 174

movies, 219

multifactorial transmission, 39–40

multiple births, 36

multivitamin supplements, 84

mutations, 39

mutual regulation, 152–153

N

naproxen, 66

National Commission for the Protection of Human Subjects of Biomedical and Behavioral Research, 27

National Longitudinal Survey of Children and Youth (NLSCY), 8, 10, 27, 191, 316

nativism, 132

natural childbirth, 79

natural experiments, 26

Natural Sciences and Engineering Research Council of Canada (NSERC), 27

natural selection, 207

naturalistic observation, 24

nature *vs.* nurture, 12–13, 132

neglect, 112, 113

neglectful parenting, 216

neighbourhoods, 10, 315

neonatal jaundice, 82

neonatal period, 79

neonatal screening for medical conditions, 83

neonate, 79

see also newborn baby

Nepal, 171, 233

neural-tube defects, 42

neurodevelopmental disorders and disabilities, 257

neurons, 60

neuroticism, 50

new immigrant children

access to quality health care, 175

English immersion approach, 256

intelligence testing, 190

school, 316–317

second-language learning, 256

New South Wales, Australia, 308

New York Longitudinal Study (NYLS), 147, 148

newborn baby

Apgar scale, 82–83

body systems, 81–82

Brazelton Neonatal Behavioral Assessment Scale (NBAS), 82–83

caregiver-infant bond, 90–91

colostrum, 79

fathers, role of, 92

fontanels, 80

lanugo, 80

meconium, 82

medical and behavioural assessment, 82–83

neonatal jaundice, 82

neonatal period, 79

neonatal screening for medical conditions, 83

and parents, 90–93

prenatal *vs.* postnatal life, 81

reflex behaviours, 80–81

size, 79–80

vernix caseosa, 80

the Ngoni in East Africa, 74

niche-picking, 48

nicknames, 209

nicotine, 64, 67

Niger, 287

Nigeria, 308

night terror, 166

nightmares, 166

Nipissing District Developmental Screen, 106

nocturnal emission, 290

non-intercourse sexual behaviour, 329

non-medicated delivery, 78–79

non-normative, 11

non-organic failure to thrive, 113

non-shared environmental effects, 49

non-social play, 211, 212

non-steroidal anti-inflammatory drugs (NSAIDs), 66

non-suicidal self-harm, 296

normative, 11

normative age-graded influences, 11

normative history-graded influences, 11

North America, 229

Norway, 215

"Notel," 210

nouns, 135

novelty preference, 128

nuclear family, 7

number, 130, 183, 242, 244

number line estimation, 244

numerosity estimation, 244

nurture *vs.* nature, 12–13, 132

nutrition

adolescence, 294–296

infancy and toddlerhood (birth to age 3), 99–101

and maternal weight, 61–62

middle childhood, 226–227

undernutrition, 170–171

nutritional education, 227

nutritionist, 61

O

obesity, 49, 229

adolescence, 294–295

and bullying, 281

early childhood, 169–170

infancy and toddlerhood, 100–101

object concept, 126

object permanence, 126, 129–130

object play, 211

objects in space, 182–183

observational learning, 19

obsessive-compulsive disorder (OCD), 235
obstructive sleep apnea (OSA), 227
occupational therapist, 107
occupations
    after-school program director, 269
    alcohol and drug counsellor, 298
    anesthesiologist, 78
    art therapist, 333
    audiologist, 105
    behavioural specialist, 218
    Canadian certified counsellor (CCC), 216
    child clinical psychologist, 16, 159
    counsellor, 319
    dentist, 172
    developmental psychologist, 15
    doula, 75
    early childhood educators (ECEs), 4
    educational assistant, 258
    elementary teacher, 253
    fertility specialist, 35
    forensic psychologist, 272
    genetic counsellor, 45
    labour and delivery nurse, 77
    nurse practitioner, 232
    nutritionist, 61
    occupational therapist, 107
    pediatric neurologist, 187
    physical education teacher, 293
    physiotherapist, 108
    public/community health nurse, 229
    resource consultant, 123
    social worker, 37, 152
    social worker in corrections, 338
    sonographer, 70
    speech pathologist, 135
    ultrasound technician, 70
    youth minister, 313
Okinawa, 228
omega-3 fatty acid, 62
online communication, 336
operant conditioning, 18–19, 120–121
opiates, 65
oppositional defiant disorder (ODD), 234
oral health, 172, 224
oral stage, 18
ordinality, 183
organization, 20
organized sports, 229, 267
organogenesis, 61
outside environmental hazards, 64
overregularization, 136
overt aggression, 218
overweight, 229–231
    see also obesity
ovum, 34
ozone levels, 69

P

pain, 78–79, 104–105
Pakistan, 171
palmar reflex, 81
Papua, New Guinea, 308
parental smoking, 176–177
parentese, 137
parenting
    see also fathers; mothers
    and academic achievement, 253, 316
    after divorce, 272
    aggression, influences on, 218
    authoritarian parenting, 316
    caregiver-infant bond, 90–91
    co-regulation, 268
    cooperative parenting, 272
    discipline, forms of, 213–214
    early childhood, 213–217
    emerging control of behaviour, 268
    gender differences, effect on, 157
    grandparenting, 275
    marital satisfaction, 92–93
    and middle childhood, 268
    monitoring, and self-disclosure, 334
    and newborns, 90–93
    parenting styles. See parenting styles
    social interaction, 136–137
parenting styles, 214–217
    Aboriginal parenting style, 216, 217
    and adolescence, 333–334
    authoritarian parenting, 215
    authoritative parenting, 215–216, 316, 338
    Baumrind's model, 215–216
    cultural differences, 216
    neglectful parenting, 216
    permissive parenting, 215
    positive parenting, 216–217
    uninvolved parenting, 216
partial fetal alcohol spectrum disorder (pFASD), 66
participant observation, 24
Partners for Learning, 123–124
parturition, 76
passive correlations, 48
passive development, 13
passive vocabulary, 135, 192
paternal factors, 69
patterns of genetic transmission, 39–40
Pavlov, Ivan, 17
peasant societies, 333
pediatric neurologist, 187
peers, 159
    acceptance by, and academic achievement, 253
    adolescence, 335–336
    aggression, 278–282
    bullying, 280–282
    friendship, 278, 335–336
    and gender development, 210
    gender differences in peer-

group relationships, 277
    middle childhood, 276–282
    negative effects of peer relations, 276–277
    online communication, 336
    popularity, 277–278
    positive effects of peer relations, 276–277
    and prejudice, 277
    romantic relationships, 336
    sexual activity, 329
    unpopular children, 277–278
perception
    depth perception, 108
    ecological theory of perception, 108–109
    haptic perception, 108
    and motor development, 108
    visual cliff, 108
performance measures, 24
performance-oriented, 138
periods of development, 4, 5
permissive parenting, 215
persistent developmental stuttering, 232
personal agency, 154
personal fable, 309
pesticide, 177
pesticides, 69
phallic stage, 18
phenotype, 40, 47
phenylketonuria (PKU), 42, 83
the Philippines, 228
phonemes, 133
phonetic approach, 251
physical abuse, 112
physical activity, 292–293
    during pregnancy, 62–63
physical appearances, 278
physical development, 6
    adolescence, 5
    early childhood (ages 3 to 6), 5
    growth chart, 225
    infancy and toddlerhood (birth to age 3), 5, 98–101
    middle childhood (ages 6 to 11), 5, 224–225
    prenatal period, 5
    puberty. See puberty
physical education teacher, 293
physical growth
    adolescent growth spurt, 289–290
    changes in proportions of the human body, 99
    early childhood, 164–165
    early growth, 98–101
    principles of, 56
physical inactivity, 230
physical play, 228–229
physical traits, 49–50
physiological traits, 49–50
physiotherapist, 108
Piaget, Jean, 18, 19–20
Piagetian approach, 124
    adolescence, 306–310
    early childhood, 182–187
    evaluation, 307–308

infancy and toddlerhood, 124–127
    information processing, 128–130
    object concept, 126
    preoperational stage, 182–187
    sensorimotor stage, 124–127
picky eaters, 105
placenta, 58, 76
plasticity, 12, 102–103
play
    cognitive levels of play, 211
    conflict in play situations, 213
    constructive play, 211
    culture, influences of, 212–213
    dramatic play, 182, 211
    early childhood, 211–213
    early childhood play styles, 212
    fantasy play, 182, 211
    fathers and play, 157
    formal games with rules, 211
    functional play, 211
    gender, influences of, 212
    imaginary play, 182
    imaginative play, 211
    locomotor play, 211
    middle childhood (ages 6 to 11), 228–229
    non-social play, 211, 212
    object play, 211
    organized sports, 229
    physical play, 228–229
    pretend play, 154, 182, 191, 211
    recess, 228
    rough-and-tumble play, 228
    social dimension of play, 211
    social play, 211, 212
    solitary play, 211
play therapy, 236
playgrounds, 174
poison, 174
polycystic kidney disease, 42
polygenic inheritance, 39
popularity, 277–278
positive parenting, 216–217
postconventional morality, 311, 312
postmature, 86
pour housing, 175–176
poverty. See child poverty
power assertion, 214
pragmatics, 193–194, 251
praise, 203
pre-reading skills, 194
preconventional morality, 311, 312
prefrontal cortex, 131
pregnancy
    see also prenatal development
    critical period, 12
    due dates, 76
    epigenetic modification, 40
    hormones, 207
    miscarriages, 58
    older women, and genetic testing, 45
    pregnancy tests, 56
    prevention of, 330

qualitative change, 14
quantitative change, 14
teenage pregnancy, 331–332
prejudice, 277
prelinguistic speech, 133
prenatal development
  brain development during
    gestation, 101
  cognitive development, 5
  developing embryo, 58
  disparities in prenatal care, 68
  drug intake, 65–69
  early development of human
    embryo, 57
  embryonic stage, 58–59
  fetal stage, 59–60
  germinal stage, 56–58
  influences on prenatal
    development, 61–69
  malnutrition, 62
  maternal age, 64
  maternal anxiety and stress,
    63–64
  maternal factors, 61–69
  maternal illnesses, 63
  milestones, 57
  monitoring prenatal
    development, 69–70
  nutrition and maternal weight,
    61–62
  outside environmental hazards,
    64
  paternal factors, 69
  physical activity and strenuous
    work, 62–63
  physical development, 5
  principles of growth, 56
  psychosocial development, 5
  sensitive periods, 59
  stages of prenatal development,
    56–60
preoperational stage, 18, 182
  advances of preoperational
    thought, 182–183
  categorization, 183
  causality, 183
  centration, 184
  conservation, 184–185, 187
  deferred imitation, 182
  egocentrism, 184
  identities, 183
  irreversibility, 184–185
  limits of preoperational
    thought, 184–185
  number, 183
  objects in space, 182–183
  pretend play, 182
  symbolic function, 182
  theory of mind, 185–187
  tranduction, 183
prepared childbirth, 79
preschools, 195–196
prescription drugs, 65–66
pretend play, 154, 182, 191, 211
preterm (premature) infants, 84,
  85
prevention
  accident risks, reducing, 174
  of delinquency, 339

maltreatment, 114
obesity, 169
overweight, 230–231
of pregnancy, 330
sexually transmitted infections
  (STIs), 330
PREVNet (Promoting
  Relationships and Eliminating
  Violence Network), 279, 281
pride, 204
primary circular reaction, 124,
  125, 126
primary sex characteristics, 288
principles of growth, 56
prison inmates, 114
privacy, 28
private speech, 194
procedural knowledge, 310
procedural memory, 130, 189
Project CARE, 123, 124
Project Head Start, 195–196, 219
prosocial behaviour, 217–218,
  267, 326–327
proximodistal principle, 56, 98
psychoanalytic approach to
  gender development, 206, 207
psychoanalytic perspective,
  15–17
  psychosexual development, 15
  psychosocial development,
    16–17
psychometric approach, 121–124
  early intervention, 122–124
  home environment, impact of,
    122
  infants and toddlers, testing,
    121–122
  intelligence, 190–191, 247–249
  traditional psychometric
    measures, 190
psychopathology, 51
psychosexual development, 15
psychosexual stages, 18
psychosexual theory, 206
psychosocial development, 6,
  16–17, 144
  adolescence. See psychosocial
    development (adolescence)
  early childhood. See
    psychosocial development
    (early childhood)
  infancy and toddlerhood. See
    psychosocial development
    (infancy and toddlerhood)
  middle childhood. See
    psychosocial development
    (middle childhood)
  prenatal period, 5
psychosocial development
  (adolescence), 5
  antisocial behaviour, 337–339
  emerging adulthood, 339–340
  family, relationship with,
    332–335
  friends, 335–336
  identity, search for, 324–327
  juvenile delinquency, 337–339
  peers, 335–337
  sexuality, 327–332

psychosocial development (early
    childhood), 5
  aggressive behaviour, 218–219
  gender, 205–211
  parenting, 213–217
  play, 211–213
  prosocial behaviour, 217–218
psychosocial development
    (infancy and toddlerhood), 5
  attachment, 149–153
  the developing self, 153–157
  emotions, 144–146
  highlights of, 144
  relationships with other
    children, 158–159
  temperament, 146–149
psychosocial development
    (middle childhood), 5
  the developing self, 266–267
  the family, 268–276
  peers, 276–282
psychosocial moratorium, 324
psychosocial stages, 18
puberty, 287–291
  adolescent growth spurt, 289–
    290
  early maturation, implications
    of, 291
  epigenetic modification, 40
  hormonal changes, 287–288
  late maturation, implications of,
    291
  regulation of onset and
    progression, 288
  sequence, 288
  signs, 289
  timing, 288–291
pubic hair, 289
public/community health nurse,
  229
punishment, 19, 213–214

Q

qualitative change, 13, 14
quantitative change, 13, 14
quasi-experiment, 26
Quebec, 317

R

race
  and child poverty, 175
  influence on development, 7–8
  and IQ, 249
racial disparities in infant
  mortality, 88–89
radiation, 69
rapid eye movement (REM)
  sleep, 111
Raven's Coloured Progressive
  Matrices, 249
reaction range, 47
reactive correlations, 48
reading, 251–252
reality, 186
recall, 189
receptive vocabulary. See passive
  vocabulary

recess, 228
recessive inheritance, 39, 43
recessive traits, 39
reciprocal determinism, 19
recognition, 189
redshirting, 252
reflex behaviours, 80–81
reflexes, 80–81, 125
Reggio Emilia approach, 195
reinforcement, 19, 213–214
relational aggression, 218
relationships with other children
  infancy and toddlerhood, 158–
    159
  peers, 159
  siblings, 158, 276
replication, 26
representational ability, 125–126
representational systems, 266
research designs
  basic research designs, 24–26
  case study, 24
  correlational study, 24–25
  cross-sectional study, 26–27
  developmental research
    designs, 26–27
  ethnographic study, 24
  experiments, 25–26
  longitudinal study, 27
  participant observation, 24
  sequential design, 26
  sequential study, 27
research methods, 23–28
  basic research designs, 24–26
  developmental research
    designs, 26–27
  ethics of research, 27–28
  forms of data collection, 23–24
  hypotheses, 23
  laboratory observation, 24
  longitudinal study, 27
  naturalistic observation, 24
  performance measures, 24
  self-reports, 23–24
research with children, 28
research with diverse populations,
  28
resilience, 115
resistant attachment, 150
resource consultant, 123
respiratory distress syndrome, 86
retrieval, 188
right to informed consent, 27
right to privacy and
  confidentiality, 28
risk factors, 10
risky behaviour, 286
rollerblading, 174
Romania, 215
Romanian orphanages, 102–104
romantic relationships, 336
rooting reflex, 81
Roots of Empathy, 281
rough-and-tumble play, 228
Royal Commission on New
  Reproductive Technologies,
  37
rubella, 63
Rwanda, 308

S

Safe Schools Act, 281
safety. *See* health and safety
scaffolding, 21, 192
schemes, 20
schizophrenia, 51
school
   adolescence, 314–320
   alternative educational models,
      254
   aspirations, influences on,
      318–319
   CEGEP system of junior
      colleges, 317
   children with special needs,
      255–260
   class size, 254
   classroom influences on
      academic achievement, 253–
      255
   computer use, 255
   dropping out, 317, 318
   educational reform, 253–254
   and ethnicity, 316
   French immersion, 254–255
   and gender, 315
   gender, and academic
      achievement, 252–253
   higher education, 318–320
   home influences on academic
      achievement, 252–253
   home-schooling, 255
   influences on school
      achievement, 314–318
   Internet use, 255
   parenting practices, 253, 316
   peer acceptance, 253
   quality of schooling, 317
   Quebec, 317
   recent immigration, 316–317
   redshirting, 252
   related family characteristics,
      316
   school system influences on
      academic achievement, 253–
      255
   self-efficacy, 314–315
   self-efficacy beliefs, 252,
      318–319
   social influences on academic
      achievement, 252–253
   socio-economic status (SES),
      316
   and socio-economic status
      (SES), 253
   spillover, 316
   student motivation, 314–315
   students not bound for
      university or college, 319
   technology, 315–316
school-age children. *See* middle
   childhood (ages 6 to 11)
school phobia, 234–235
school system influences on
   academic achievement,
   253–255
scientific method, 24
second-hand smoke, 67, 176

second-language learning, 256
secondary circular reactions, 124,
   125, 126
secondary sex characteristics,
   288, 289
secure attachment, 150, 151,
   152, 156
selective attention, 246
selective serotonin reuptake
   inhibitors (SSRIs), 237, 299
self-awareness, 146
self-coherence, 154
self-concept, 153–154, 202–203,
   266
self-conscious emotions, 146
self-consciousness, 309
self-definition, 202–203
self-disclosure, 334
self-efficacy, 19, 314–315
self-efficacy beliefs, 252
self-esteem, 203, 266–267
self-injurious behaviour, 296
self-regulation, 156
self-reports, 23–24
sensitive periods, 12, 59
sensorimotor stage, 18, 124–127
sensory development, 104–106
sensory memory, 188
separation anxiety, 151, 165
separation anxiety disorder, 235
sequential design, 26
sequential study, 27
seriation, 242, 243
sex, 157
sex-category constancy, 208
sex chromosomes, 38
sex determination, 38–39
sex differences, 157
sex education, 330
sex-linked inheritance, 43–44
sexual abuse, 112
sexual behaviour, 328–330
   contraceptives, 330
   early sexual activity and risk
      taking, 328–329
   non-intercourse sexual
      behaviour, 329
   sex education, 330
sexual maturity, 290
   see also puberty
sexual orientation, 327–328
sexuality
   adolescence, 327–332
   bisexual identity development,
      328
   homosexual identity
      development, 328
   sexual behaviour, 328–330
   sexual orientation, 327–328
   sexually transmitted infections
      (STIs), 330–331
   teenage pregnancy and child-
      bearing, 331–332
   transgendered identity
      development, 328
sexually transmitted infections
   (STIs), 330–331
shaken baby syndrome, 113
shame, 146, 204

shared intentionality, 146
shyness, 278
siblings
   adolescents and siblings, 335
   differences between, 48–49
   relationships between, 158, 276
sickle-cell anemia, 42
sight
   infancy and toddlerhood, 105–
      106
   visual processing abilities, 128
sign language, 135, 136
single-parent families, 272–273
situational compliance, 156
skateboarding, 174
Skinner, B.F., 19
skip-generation families, 275
sleep
   active sleep, 111
   adolescence, 293–294
   bed-wetting, 166–167
   co-sleeping, 112
   deprivation, 293
   early childhood, 165–167
   infancy and toddlerhood (birth
      to three years), 111–112
   middle childhood, 227
   night terror, 166
   nightmares, 166
   patterns, changes in, 165
   rapid eye movement (REM)
      sleep, 111
   requirements in childhood, 165
   sleep disturbances, 166
   sleeptalking, 166
   sleepwalking, 166
   snoring, 227
sleep-disordered breathing
   (SDB), 227
sleeptalking, 166
sleepwalking, 166
slow-to-warm-up children, 147
small-for-date (small-for-
   gestational-age) infants, 84
smell, 105
smiling, 145–146
smoking, 67, 176–177, 298
snoring, 227
sociability, 159
social aggression, 218
social anxiety, 235
social attention, 186–187
social cognitive theory, 19, 206,
   209, 210
social competence, 187
social construction, 4
social-contextual approach, 131
   guided participation, 131
   infancy and toddlerhood, 131
social dimension of play, 211
social emotions, 204
social interaction, 136–137,
   194–196
social learning approach to
   gender development, 206,
   208–211
social learning theory, 19
social perspective-taking, 309
social phobia, 235

social play, 211, 212
social referencing, 153
Social Sciences and Humanities
   Research Council of Canada
   (SSHRC), 27
social smiling, 145
social speech, 193–194
social worker, 37, 152
social worker in corrections, 338
socialization, 155–156
   conscience, 156
   factors in success of
      socialization, 156
   and gender development, 209
   self-regulation, 156
Society for Adolescent Medicine,
   299
Society of Obstetricians and
   Gynaecologists of Canada,
   63, 75
socio-cultural theory, 20–21
socio-economic status (SES), 8
   academic achievement, 253
   and academic achievement, 316
   and effective parenting, 270
   environmental influences on
      health, 174–175
   healthy foods, 227, 230
   influence on development, 8–10
   and IQ, 191
   and logical thinking abilities,
      245
   math, 183
   prenatal care, effect on, 68
   school achievement, influence
      on, 27
   underweight babies, 84
sociobiological perspective. *See*
   evolutionary/sociobiological
   perspective
solitary play, 211
sonographer, 70
South America, 229
South Asia, 170
Southeast Asia, 233
spanking law, 215
spatial relationships, 242
spatial thinking, 242
special needs. *See* children with
   special needs
specialness, 309
speech delays, 105, 134
speech pathologist, 135
speech therapy, 232
sperm, 34
spermarche, 290
spina bifida, 42, 62
spontaneous abortion, 58–59
stage theories, 13
stages of childbirth, 76
stages of prenatal development,
   56–60
   embryonic stage, 58–59
   fetal stage, 59–60
   germinal stage, 56–58
   principles of growth, 56
Stanford-Binet Intelligence Scale,
   190
state of arousal, 111–112

stepfamilies, 274
Sternberg's triarchic theory of intelligence, 248–249
still-face paradigm, 152–153
stillbirth, 86–87
stillborn, 59
storage, 188
Strange Situation, 150
stranger anxiety, 151
strenuous work during pregnancy, 62–63
structural change, 310
student motivation, 314–315
Student Success/Learning to 18, 254
study of child development, 4–6
stuttering, 232
sub-Saharan Africa, 170, 275, 315
substance abuse, 296
   see also drug use
substance dependence, 296
sudden infant death syndrome (SIDS), 88, 89–90, 112
suffocation, 112
suicide, 300–301
surfactant, 86
surrogate mother, 36
Sweden, 215
swimming reflex, 81, 174
symbolic function, 182
symbolic gestures, 134
syntax, 192–193, 250–251
synthetic growth hormone, 224

T

tags, 40
taste, 105
Tay-Sachs disease, 42, 45
team sports. *See* organized sports
technology, 315–316
teenagers. *See* adolescence
teething, 98
telegraphic speech, 135, 135L
television, 219, 230, 280
temperament, 50, 146
   and attachment, 151
   biological basis of, 148–149
   categories of, 147
   difficult children, 147
   easy children, 147
   goodness of fit, 148
   infancy and toddlerhood, 146–149
   patterns, 147
   slow-to-warm-up children, 147
   stability of temperament, 148
teratogens, 61
"terrible twos," 154–155
tertiary circular reaction, 125, 126

testosterone, 207
tetracycline, 65
text shortcuts, 308
thalidomide, 65
theories of child development, 16–17
   see also specific theories
   cognitive perspective, 19–21
   contextual perspective, 21
   evolutionary/sociobiological perspective, 22
   learning perspective, 17–19
   psychoanalytic perspective, 15–17
   social learning theory, 19
theory, 14
theory of mind, 185–187
theory of moral reasoning, 311–313
theory of multiple intelligences, 248
theory of sexual selection, 207
thinking
   convergent thinking, 259
   deductive reasoning, 242
   divergent thinking, 259
   hypothetical-deductive reasoning, 306–307
   immature characteristics of adolescent thought, 308–309
   inductive reasoning, 243
   knowledge about thinking, 186
   magical thinking, 186
third-hand smoke, 67
three-mountains task, 184
timing of influences, 12
tobacco, 65, 69, 298
toddlerhood. *See* infancy and toddlerhood (birth to three years)
toilet training, 166–167
tonic neck reflex, 81
tooth development, 224
tooth enamel, 290
Torrance Tests of Creative Thinking, 259–260
touch, 104–105
toxic substances, 174
toxins, 64
toxoplasmosis, 63
tranduction, 183
transforming growth factor alpha, 61
transgendered identity development, 328
transitive inference, 242, 243
transmission of attachment patterns, 152
treatment

delinquency, 339
eating disorders, 296
hypertension, 232
mental health disorders, 236–237
overweight, 230–231
Tri-Council Policy Statement: Ethical Conduct for Research Involving Humans, 27, 28
triarchic theory of intelligence, 248–249
tribal societies, 333
trichomoniasis, 331
Triple P (Positive Parenting Program), 217
Triple X syndrome, 44
trisomy X, 44
trust, 149
Tungasuvvingat Inuit Head Start, 196
Turner's syndrome, 44, 187
twin studies, 47, 49
type 1 diabetes, 231
type 2 diabetes, 231

U

Ukraine, 215
ultrasound, 59
ultrasound technician, 70
umbilical cord, 58
umbilical cord sampling, 70
UN Convention on the Rights of the Child, 11
undernutrition, 170–171
uninhibited, 148
unintentional injury, 173
uninvolved parenting, 216
United States, 228
Universal Child Care Benefit, 175
universal early childhood education and care, 196
unsociability, 149

V

vaccination, 110
vaginal birth after Caesarean (VBAC), 78
vaginal delivery, 77–78
variables, 26
vernix caseosa, 80
video games, 219, 280
Vietnam, 92
violation-of-expectations, 129–130
violence
   dating violence, 336–337
   in the household, 268
   in the media, 279–280

visitation, 272
visual acuity. *See* sight
visual cliff, 108
visual preference, 128
visual processing abilities, 128
visual recognition memory, 128
vocabulary, 192, 250–251, 309
vocational issues, 318–320
the voice, 289
volunteer activity, 326–327
Vygotskian approach, 191
   scaffolding, 21, 192
   zone of proximal development (ZPD), 21, 191–192
Vygotsky, Lev, 20–21

W

Waabinong Head Start Family Resource Centre, 196
walking reflex, 81
the Warlpiri people of Australia, 35
Watson, John B., 17
Wechsler Intelligence Scale for Children (WISC-IV), 247
Wechsler Preschool and Primary Scale of Intelligence, Fourth Edition (WPPSI-IV), 190
weight
   early childhood, 165
   middle childhood, 224
white matter, 225
whole-language approach, 251
witch's milk, 80
withdrawal of love, 214
WITS, 281
working memory, 131, 188, 189, 246
working model, 151
workplace, 319–320
writing, 251–252

X

X-inactivation, 44

Y

Youth Criminal Justice Act, 292
youth minister, 313
Yucatan, 74

Z

Zambia, 169
zone of proximal development (ZPD), 21, 191–192
zygote, 34, 38